The America *Trad*

D0628360

The American Intellectual Tradition

Volume II: 1865 to the Present

SIXTH EDITION

Edited by

DAVID A. HOLLINGER
University of California, Berkeley

and

CHARLES CAPPER
Boston University

New York   *Oxford*
OXFORD UNIVERSITY PRESS
2011

Oxford University Press, Inc., publishes works that further Oxford University's objective of excellence in research, scholarship, and education.

Oxford   New York
Auckland   Cape Town   Dar es Salaam   Hong Kong   Karachi
Kuala Lumpur   Madrid   Melbourne   Mexico City   Nairobi
New Delhi   Shanghai   Taipei   Toronto

With offices in

Argentina   Austria   Brazil   Chile   Czech Republic   France   Greece
Guatemala   Hungary   Italy   Japan   Poland   Portugal   Singapore
South Korea   Switzerland   Thailand   Turkey   Ukraine   Vietnam

Copyright © 2011 by Oxford University Press, Inc.

Published by Oxford University Press, Inc.
198 Madison Avenue, New York, New York 10016
http://www.oup.com

Oxford is a registered trademark of Oxford University Press

All rights reserved. No part of this publication
may be reproduced, stored in a retrieval system, or transmitted,
in any form or by any means, electronic, mechanical,
photocopying, recording, or otherwise, without the prior
permission of Oxford University Press.

Library of Congress Cataloging-in-Publication Data

The American intellectual tradition / edited by David A. Hollinger and
Charles Capper.—6th ed.
     p. cm.
   Includes bibliographical references and index.
     ISBN: 978-0-19-539292-0 (v. 1)—ISBN: 978-0-19-539293-7 (v. 2)
1. United States—Intellectual life—Sources.
I. Hollinger, David A.   II. Capper, Charles.
     E169.1.A47218   2011
     973—dc22   2010024156

Printed in the United States of America
on acid-free paper

For Henry F. May

Contents

Part Four: Reassessing Identities and Solidarities

Preface

If a tradition is a family of disagreements, the American intellectual tradition is a very extended family. Its members include arguments inspired by the interests and ideals of a variety of communities within the United States as well as arguments concerned with the national community itself. The family also embraces arguments responsive to Western, if not universal, issues in philosophy, science, religion, politics, literature, and the arts. Some of the most influential members of this family are intensely aware of their European ancestry, whereas others have married into European families, and still others remain always preoccupied with the family's Americanness. The family currently seems generally content with its extended state; its diverse and contested character is often a source of pride. But not everyone is agreed on just what makes it a family to begin with. And the family is divided, if not confused, over exactly which of its members ought to supervise the education of its young. What disagreements are primary? How should the tradition be structured to ensure its continuation and critical revision? What specific artifacts of discourse have played the greatest role historically in developing the American intellectual tradition?

Answers to these questions are necessarily implied by any sourcebook for the study of American intellectual history. In deciding what to include in this collection, we have been aware of the dynamism and diversity of our subject as well as highly conscious of the differing constructions of it offered by various scholars. We have sought the advice of numerous colleagues and accordingly have designed *The American Intellectual Tradition* to make available to students many of the documents now routinely assigned by teachers of this subject in colleges and universities throughout the United States. Hence these volumes are chiefly practical devices, not outlines of a systematic, comprehensive interpretation of American intellectual history. Yet certain priorities have shaped these volumes, and it is appropriate to make them explicit.

The American Intellectual Tradition is frankly intellectual in orientation. Most of the documents it contains are the result of someone's effort to make an analysis and to persuade others of the correctness of that analysis. Although these documents express "attitudes" and embody "ideas," we have been more sensitive to their status as arguments. Hence most of our selections are of the genres classically associated with purposive discourse: sermon, address, letter, treatise, and essay. We have tried to identify pieces of argumentation that became prominent points of reference for contemporaries or for Americans of later generations. In so doing, we have necessarily been drawn again and again to the work of men and women normally regarded as intellectual leaders: people who were relatively effective at making arguments.

Arguments can be addressed to an infinite number of issues, but the writings in this book respond to issues that have persistently generated extensive intellectual discussion. The bulk of our selections concern the theoretical basis for religious, scientific, artistic, political, social, and economic practice. Because the United States is above all a polity, the American family of disagreements includes a high proportion of arguments concerning the basis of politics. Because the public culture of America has often been caught up in the distinctive ethos of Protestant Christianity, many of our selections—especially in Volume I—are directed to religious issues. Because modern America has been a peculiarly science-preoccupied civilization, many of the selections in Volume II address the character of the scientific enterprise and debate the implications of scientific knowledge. We have also been mindful of categories of race, class, and gender, as well as themes in theology, cultural theory, and American foreign and transnational affairs that have risen to prominence in the humanities and social sciences over the last several decades, and consequently in recent editions we have devoted an increasing amount of space in the sourcebook to these subjects.

In order to give these issues historical shape, we have organized the documents around general themes or movements, which we address briefly in the introduction preceding each main section. Were this a textbook rather than a sourcebook, we would have attempted to indicate the entire structure of discourse surrounding the texts we discuss; here we can do no more than hint at this, leaving it to the instructor to fill in the missing arguments and counterarguments. In framing our selections, we have also tried to avoid what seems to us a failing in many previous anthologies: the packaging of each source as an example of a particular doctrine or movement. Throughout we have emphasized that most intellectual works are dynamic and multifaceted and therefore have meaning in more than one frame of reference. With this in mind, we have written headnotes that highlight the dense internal content of each document as well as the setting in which it was produced.

It is easy to list the names of historically significant American thinkers whose work does not appear in these volumes. Yet, we have resisted the impulse to reduce the length of our selections in order to make room for a greater number of authors. The multiplication of texts by cutting them into mere snippets might have enabled us to more effectively register the social and cultural diversity of American intellectual leadership. Every ideological persuasion and identity group might then find its representative listed in the table of contents. The plural and contested character of the American intellectual tradition might then be acknowledged even more compellingly than is acknowledged by the selections we have decided to include. But the reducing of texts to brief excerpts has a great cost. The rhetorical and discursive power that helped draw attention to a text in the first place can be easily lost. Tensions within a text can be silenced, rendering the authors more univocal than they were. Although we have sometimes printed only a brief selection from a longer work, most of the documents found in *The American Intellectual Tradition* are complete, or nearly complete, essays, addresses, or chapters of books. We hope that what this sourcebook offers in the depth of its selections will compensate for what it lacks in the range of its inclusions.

This sixth edition has been shaped in large part by the advice of colleagues who have used the previous editions in teaching. We have dropped a number of selections and added new ones in an effort to take account of recent scholarship that assigns new historical significance to certain authors and texts. Most of our changes are in the latter parts of Volume II because of greater fluctuations in the consensus of historians about who and what matters in the later twentieth century. We have also updated and in many cases expanded the commentary and citations in the Introductions and headnotes.

The chronologies at the end of each volume list almost as many European textual and sociopolitical events as American ones, reflecting our awareness that American intellectual history is bound up with the larger history of Europe, and indeed that of most of the world. The United States stands intellectually in much the same relation to Europe as Great Britain does: British intellectuals help constitute the discourse of Europe while simultaneously perpetuating and revising their own national tradition. The same can be said of intellectuals in Russia, Spain, Germany, Italy, or France, as well as of those in the United States. Moreover, national cultures are sites of differing international significance at different times. In the seventeenth century, for example, the discourse of an extended Europe went forward without much attention to what was being said in British North America, but in the twentieth century the United States became a major site for this discourse.

Students using this sourcebook can learn more about the authors of these selections, and about the issues being addressed, from the hundreds of thematic and biographical articles in Richard W. Fox and James T. Kloppenberg, eds., *A Companion to American Thought* (Cambridge, Mass., 1995). Students in need of a basic introduction to what is meant by "intellectual history" may be helped by Stefan Collini et al., "What Is Intellectual History" in Juliet Gardiner, ed., *What Is History Today?* (London, 1988), 105–19. Those interested in examples of contemporary scholarship in intellectual history for the period covered by these volumes, as well as current debates about methodological questions in the field, can turn to recent issues of *Modern Intellectual History*, edited for Cambridge University Press by Charles Capper, Anthony La Vopa, Samuel Moyn, and Nicholas Phillipson. Martin Jay, "The Textual Approach to Intellectual History," in Jay's *Force Fields: Between Intellectual History and Cultural Critique* (New York, 1993), 158–66, 220–22, may also be helpful.

For advice regarding this sourcebook, we wish to thank the following individuals: Patrick Allitt of Emory University; Joyce Appleby of the University of California, Los Angeles; Robert C. Bannister of Swarthmore College; Thomas Bender of New York University; Fred Beuttler of the University of Chicago; Casey Nelson Blake of Columbia University; Ruth H. Bloch of the University of California, Los Angeles; Eileen Boris of the University of California, Santa Barbara; Paul Boyer of the University of Wisconsin–Madison; Howard Brick of the University of Michigan; Jennifer Burns of the University of Virginia; Richard Bushman of Columbia University; E. Wayne Carp of Pacific Lutheran University; John Carson of the University of Michigan; Kenneth Cmiel of the University of Iowa; Saul Cornell of Ohio State University; Charles Lloyd Cohen of the University of Wisconsin–Madison; George Cotkin of California State Polytechnic University at San Luis Obispo; David Brion Davis of Yale University; John P. Diggins of the City University of New York; David Engerman of Brandeis University; Elizabeth Faue of Wayne State University; Richard Wightman Fox of the University of Southern California; George M. Fredrickson of Stanford University; Lawrence J. Friedman of Indiana University; Daniel Geary of Trinity College Dublin; James B. Gilbert of the University of Maryland; Nils Gilman of the Monitor Group; Samuel Haber of the University of California, Berkeley; David D. Hall of the Harvard Divinity School; Thomas L. Haskell of Rice University; Hugh Hawkins of Amherst College; David Hoeveler of the University of Wisconsin–Milwaukee; E. Brooks Holifield of Emory University; James Hoopes of Babson College; Daniel Horowitz of Smith College; Daniel Walker Howe of Oxford University; David Johnson of Portland State University; John F. Kasson of the University of North Carolina at Chapel Hill; Linda

K. Kerber of the University of Iowa; Richard King of the University of Nottingham; James T. Kloppenberg of Harvard University; Lloyd S. Kramer of the University of North Carolina at Chapel Hill; Bruce Kuklick of the University of Pennsylvania; Ralph Luker of Antioch College; Kevin Mattson of Ohio State University; Henry F. May of the University of California, Berkeley; Donald B. Meyer of Wesleyan University; Robert Moates Miller of the University of North Carolina at Chapel Hill; Jill Morawski of Wesleyan University; Michael O'Brien of Cambridge University; Lewis Perry of St. Louis University; Mark Pittenger of the University of Colorado; Christopher Phelps of the University of Nottingham; Jon H. Roberts of Boston University; Daniel T. Rodgers of Princeton University; Dorothy Ross of the Johns Hopkins University; Joan Shelly Rubin of the University of Rochester; Ethan Schrum of the University of Pennsylvania; Barbara Sicherman of Trinity University; Daniel Singal of Hobart and William Smith Colleges; Jeffrey Sklansky of Oregon State University; Richard Candida Smith of the University of California, Berkeley; Wilson Smith of the University of California, Davis; John W. Stewart of Princeton Theological Seminary; Justin Suran of the University of California, Berkeley; James Turner of the University of Notre Dame; Robert Westbrook of the University of Rochester; Daniel Wilson of Muhlenberg College; Rosemarie Zagarri of George Mason University; members of the Berkeley Graduate Intellectual History Group and members of the Triangle Intellectual History Seminar. Some of these colleagues would have preferred a somewhat different table of contents, but without their counsel *The American Intellectual Tradition* would be less representative of current teaching practice.

For assistance in preparing this sixth edition of *The American Intellectual Tradition* we wish to thank Andrew J. Ballou and Daniel Immerwahr. We also wish to express our appreciation for the advice and assistance of Brian Wheel, Danniel Schoonebeek, and Claudia Dukeshire of Oxford University Press.

The editors have worked closely at every stage of the preparation of *The American Intellectual Tradition*, but responsibility for Volume I belongs to Charles Capper and for Volume II to David Hollinger.

Berkeley, Calif.   D.A.H.
Boston, Mass.   C.C.
June 2010

Part One

Toward a Secular Culture

Introduction

William James recognized that the life of the mind during his own time was becoming increasingly secular. The Bible, which had for so long been uniquely privileged as a foundation for knowledge and morals, came to be approached more critically, especially in the light of modern science. James did not lament this historic transformation; on the contrary, he welcomed it. Yet he was concerned that the scientific spirit of the age would intimidate people into giving up cherished beliefs about God that might, after all, remain plausible even in the wake of such discoveries as evolution, thermodynamics, and the multiple authorship of various books of the Bible. When James wrote "The Will to Believe" in 1897, he sought to vindicate the individual soul's right to retain aspects of the Protestant heritage not actually proven false by the advancement of secular learning. James himself was an eminent man of science; his defense of religious belief can remind us that many late nineteenth-century American intellectuals were extremely conscious of a tension between religious tradition and scientific innovation.

Not all the documents in Part One manifest this tension as vividly as does James's "The Will to Believe," but these documents do display a tendency, if not a determination, to ground argument in naturalistic and humanistic premises. Even Josiah Royce's overtly biblical "The Problem of Job" did not suggest that scriptural authority enhances an idea's claim to truth. Rather, it was to logical analysis and humane instincts that Royce appealed in arguing for the justness of God's decision to permit the suffering of innocent persons. Charles Augustus Briggs subjected the scriptures to rigorous historical analysis.

Although the persistence of religious concern amid secular initiatives is a vital theme in the intellectual history of the United States during the late nineteenth and early twentieth centuries, these secular initiatives are appropriately central to Part One of this collection. The "culture" more of which Thomas Wentworth Higginson said the nation needed was predominantly secular, and to be housed and promoted largely in the new secular institution of the university. Elizabeth Cady Stanton drew on an individualism she termed Protestant, but when the free-thinking Stanton vindicated the rights of women, she did so largely on the basis of an Enlightenment-inspired tradition of universal human rights. Henry Adams's meditations on "the dynamo and the virgin" culminated not in religious inspiration but in the scientific measurement of its force. Adams's fellow historian, Frederick Jackson Turner, interpreted the whole of American history in terms of the power of a distinctive physical environment. Indeed, the most general and pervasive of the secular initiatives of this era was the effort to install "scientific method" as the chief agency by which culture was to be constituted. This initiative is exemplified best by Charles Peirce's argument for the supremacy of scientific method but is manifest in most of the selections in Part One. "Realism" in literature and the arts was allied with the movement for a more scientific culture, as is made clear by William Dean Howells's plea for a literature that would tell the "truth" about people's actual lives rather than idealize them to suit a parochial moral agenda. More distant yet from the literary culture of idealization and uplift was George Santayana, who called it "genteel" and complained that its overbearingly Protestant sensibility dominated philosophy, as well as literature and the arts.

Gilded Age thinkers often hoped that social science might provide a new, solid foundation for organizing and governing their society. William Graham Sumner partook of the period's interest in explaining social phenomena historically, often with reference to the operation of putative natural laws. This interest is represented in the selection from Charlotte Perkins Gilman, which explains in terms of evolutionary history the subordinate social position of women. But all of these men and women were deeply affected by the Darwinian revolution in natural history, which is the topic of the selection that opens Part One, botanist Asa Gray's careful commentary on Darwin.

Recommendations for Further Reading
Laurence R. Veysey, *The Emergence of the American University* (Chicago, 1965); R. Jackson Wilson, *In Quest of Community: Social Philosophy in the United States, 1860–1920* (New York, 1968); Howard Mumford Jones, *The Age of Energy: Varieties of American Experience, 1865–1915* (New York, 1973); William R. Hutchison, *The Modernist Impulse in American Protestantism* (Cambridge, 1976); Daniel Walker Howe, ed., *Victorian America* (Philadelphia, 1976); Alexandra Oleson and John Voss, eds., *The Organization of Knowledge in America, 1860–1920* (Baltimore, 1979); T. J. Jackson Lears, *No Place of Grace: Antimodernism and the Transformation of American Culture* (New York, 1981); Alan Trachtenberg, *The Incorporation of America: Culture and Society in the Gilded Age* (New York, 1982); Lewis Perry, *Intellectual Life in America: A History* (New York, 1984); James Turner, *Without God, Without Creed: The Origins of Unbelief in America* (Baltimore, 1985); Bruce Kuklick, *Churchmen and Philosophers. From Jonathan Edwards to John Dewey* (New Haven, 1985); Thomas Bender, *New York Intellect: A History of Intellectual Life in New York City from 1750 to the Beginnings of Our Own Time* (New York, 1987); Lawrence W. Levine, *Highbrow/Lowbrow: The Emergence of Cultural Hierarchy* (Cambridge, 1988); Cynthia Eagle Russett, *Sexual Science: The Victorian Construction of Womanhood* (Cambridge, 1989); Samuel Haber, *The Quest for Authority and Honor in the American Professions, 1750–1900* (Chicago, 1991); George Cotkin, *Reluctant Modernism* (Boston, 1992); Mark Pittenger, *American Socialists and Evolutionary Thought, 1870–1920* (Madison, Wis., 1993); James Livingston, *Pragmatism and the Political Economy of Cultural Revolution, 1850–1940* (Chapel Hill, 1994); David E. Shi, *Facing Facts: Realism in American Thought and Culture, 1850–1920* (New York, 1995); Gillis J. Harp, *Positivist Republic: Auguste Comte and the Reconstruction of American Liberalism, 1865–1920* (State College, Pa., 1995); Bruce Kuklick, *Puritans in Babylon: The Ancient Near East and American Intellectual Life 1880–1930* (Princeton, 1996); Rogers M. Smith, *Civic Ideals: Conflicting Visions of Citizenship in U.S. History* (New Haven, 1997); Richard Cándida Smith, *Mallarmé's Children* (Berkeley, 1999); Ronald L. Numbers and John Stenhouse, eds., *Disseminating Darwinism* (New York, 1999); James Turner, *The Liberal Education of Charles Eliot Norton* (Baltimore, Md., 1999); David W. Blight, *Race and Reunion: The Civil War in American Memory* (Cambridge, Mass., 2001); Louis Menand, *The Metaphysical Club* (New York, 2001); Helen Lefkowitz Horowitz, *Reading Sex: Sexual Knowledge and Suppression in Nineteenth-Century America* (New York, 2002); Andrew C. Rieser, *The Chautauqua Moment: Protestants, Progressives, and the Culture of Modern*

Liberalism (New York, 2003); Caroline Winterer, *The Mirror of Antiquity: American Women and the Classical Tradition, 1750–1900* (Ithaca, 2007); Michael Ruse, *The Evolution-Creation Struggle* (Cambridge, Mass., 2005); Leslie Butler, *Critical Americans: Victorian Intellectuals and Transatlantic Liberal Reform* (Chapel Hill, 2007); J. David Hoeveler, *The Evolutionists: American Thinkers Confront Charles Darwin, 1860–1920* (Lanham, Md., 2007)

ASA GRAY

Selection from "Review of Darwin's
On the Origin of Species"
(1860)

No American was more directly involved in the Darwinian revolution in natural history than Asa Gray (1810–88), a botanist of world stature who became the most effective and influential defender of Darwin's ideas in the United States. Gray's review of Darwin's *On the Origin of Species* appeared in 1860, before the chronological beginning point of this volume, but it is included here because it defined the scientific and religious issues addressed for decades thereafter. Many of Gray's contemporaries, even among scientists, resisted Darwin's claim that natural selection was the vital agency of evolution, preferring versions of evolutionary theory that attributed causal force to the environment or to some innate power. The most prominent of these non-Darwinian theories of evolution was that of J. B. Lamarck, a French scientist of the early nineteenth century whose ideas gained great popularity in late nineteenth-century America largely because Lamarck's ideas seemed more easily reconciled with religion. Gray refers to Lamarck in his review. Yet Gray, even though himself a relatively orthodox Protestant, accepted natural selection and tried to explain why it was compatible with faith in God. Darwin himself, who maintained an intimate correspondence with Gray for many years, cautioned Gray that in holding to the idea that the whole evolutionary process was designed by God, Gray was going well beyond the empirical evidence and threatened to make natural selection superfluous. But Gray persisted, and his collection of papers published in 1876, *Darwiniana*, continued his effort to reconcile Darwinian science with his inherited Protestant orthodoxy. The "Mr. Agassiz" Gray mentions was zoologist Louis Agassiz, the leading critic of Darwin among American scientists, and a colleague of Gray's at Harvard University.

The best book on Gray remains A. Hunter Dupree, *Asa Gray: 1810–1888* (Cambridge, Mass., 1959). There are many excellent studies of the Darwinian revolution and the religious controversies it generated. An accessible overview is Michael Ruse, *The Darwinian Revolution: Science Red in Tooth and Claw* (Chicago, 1979). The most rigorously argued and carefully documented of the studies of the religious debate is Jon Roberts, *Darwinism and the Divine in America: Protestant Intellectuals and Organic Evolution, 1859–1900* (Madison, Wis., 1988). A collection of penetrating essays that deal with phases of the Darwinian controversy well into the middle decades of the twentieth century is Ronald L. Numbers, *Darwinism Comes to America* (Cambridge, Mass., 1998). Of the countless works that confront the scientific basis for evolution and address its apparent implications for human life in our own time, one of the finest is Philip Kitcher, *Living with Darwin: Evolution, Design, and the Future of Faith* (New York, 2007).

Who, upon a single perusal, shall pass judgment upon a work like this, to which twenty of the best years of the life of a most able naturalist have been devoted? And who among those naturalists who hold a position that entitles them to pronounce summarily upon the subject, can be expected to divest himself for the nonce of the influence of received and favorite systems? In fact, the controversy now opened is not likely to be settled in an off-hand way, nor is it desirable that it should be. A spirited conflict among opinions of every grade must ensue, which—to borrow an illustration from the doctrine of the book before us—may be likened to the conflict in Nature among races in the struggle for life, which Mr. Darwin describes; through which the views most favored by facts will be developed and tested by "Natural Selection," the weaker ones be destroyed in the process, and the strongest in the long-run alone survive....

The ordinary and generally-received view assumes the independent, specific creation of each kind of plant and animal in a primitive stock, which reproduces its like from generation to generation, and so continues the species. Taking the idea of species from this perennial succession of essentially similar individuals, the chain is logically traceable back to a local origin in a single stock, a single pair, or a single individual, from which all the individuals composing the species have proceeded by natural generation. Although the similarity of progeny to parent is fundamental in the conception of species, yet the likeness is by no means absolute; all species vary more or less, and some vary remarkably— partly from the influence of altered circumstances, and partly (and more really) from unknown constitutional causes which altered conditions favor rather than originate. But these variations are supposed to be mere oscillations from a normal state, and in Nature to be limited if not transitory; so that the primordial differences between species and species at their beginning have not been effaced, nor largely obscured, by blending through variation. Consequently, whenever two reputed species are found to blend in Nature through a series of intermediate forms, community of origin is inferred, and all the forms, however diverse, are held to belong to one species. Moreover, since bisexuality is the rule in Nature (which is practically carried out, in the long-run, far more generally than has been suspected), and the heritable qualities of two distinct individuals are mingled in the off-spring, it is supposed that the general sterility of hybrid progeny interposes an effectual barrier against the blending of the original species by crossing....

Mr. Darwin, on the other hand, holds the orthodox view of the descent of all the individuals of a species not only from a local birthplace, but from a single ancestor or pair; and that each species has extended and established itself, through natural agencies, wherever it could; so that the actual geographical distribution of any species is by no means a primordial arrangement, but a natural result. He goes farther, and this volume is a protracted argument intended to prove that the species we recognize have not been independently created, as such, but have descended, like varieties, from other species. Varieties, on this view, are incipient or possible species: species are varieties of a larger growth and a wider and earlier divergence from the parent stock; the difference is one of degree, not of kind....

The orthodox conception of species is that of lineal descent: all the descendants of a common parent, and no other, constitute a species; they have a certain identity because of their descent, by which they are supposed to be recognizable. So naturalists had a distinct

Source: American Journal of Science, 29 (1860), 153–84. Reprinted by permission of *American Journal of Science*.

idea of what they meant by the term species, and a practical rule, which was hardly the less useful because difficult to apply in many cases, and because its application was indirect: that is, the community of origin had to be inferred from the likeness; such degree of similarity, and such only, being held to be conspecific as could be shown or reasonably inferred to be compatible with a common origin. And the usual concurrence of the whole body of naturalists (having the same data before them) as to what forms are species attests the value of the rule, and also indicates some real foundation for it in Nature. But if species were created in numberless individuals over broad spaces of territory, these individuals are connected only in idea, and species differ from varieties on the one hand, and from genera, tribes, etc., on the other, only in degree; and no obvious natural reason remains for fixing upon this or that degree as specific, at least no natural standard, by which the opinions of different naturalists may be correlated. Species upon this view are enduring, but subjective and ideal. . . .

The gist of Mr. Darwin's work is to show that such varieties are gradually diverged into species and genera through *natural selection*; that natural selection is the inevitable result of the *struggle for existence* which all living things are engaged in; and that this struggle is an unavoidable consequence of several natural causes, but mainly of the high rate at which all organic beings tend to increase.

Curiously enough, Mr. Darwin's theory is grounded upon the doctrine of Malthus and the doctrine of Hobbes. The elder DeCandolle had conceived the idea of the struggle for existence, and, in a passage which would have delighted the cynical philosopher of Malmesbury, had declared that all Nature is at war, one organism with another or with external Nature; and Lyell and Herbert had made considerable use of it. But Hobbes in his theory of society, and Darwin in his theory of natural history, alone have built their systems upon it. However moralists and political economists may regard these doctrines in their original application to human society and the relation of population to subsistence, their thorough applicability to the great society of the organic world in general is now undeniable. And to Mr. Darwin belongs the credit of making this extended application and of working out the immensely diversified results with rare sagacity and untiring patience. He has brought to view *real causes* which have been largely operative in the establishment of the actual association and geographical distribution of plants and animals. In this he must be allowed to have made a very important contribution to an interesting department of science, even if his theory fails in the endeavor to explain the origin or diversity of species. . . .

The interest for the general reader heightens as the author advances on his perilous way and grapples manfully with the most formidable difficulties.

To account, upon these principles, for the gradual elimination and segregation of nearly allied forms—such as varieties, sub-species, and closely-related or representative species—also in a general way for their geographical association and present range, is comparatively easy, is apparently within the bounds of possibility. Could we stop here we should be fairly contented. But, to complete the system, to carry out the principles to their ultimate conclusion, and to explain by them many facts in geographical distribution which would still remain anomalous, Mr. Darwin is equally bound to account for the formation of genera, families, orders, and even classes, by natural selection. He does "not doubt that the theory of descent with modification embraces all the members of the same class," and he concedes that analogy would press the conclusion still further; while he admits that "the more distinct the forms are, the more the arguments fall away in force." To command assent we naturally require decreasing probability to be overbalanced by an increased weight of evidence. An opponent might plausibly, and perhaps quite fairly, urge that the links in the chain of argument are weakest just where the greatest stress falls upon them.

To which Mr. Darwin's answer is, that the best parts of the testimony have been lost. He is confident that intermediate forms must have existed; that in the olden times when the genera, the families, and the orders, diverged from their parent stocks, gradations existed as fine as those which now connect closely related species with varieties. But they have passed and left no sign. The geological record, even if all displayed to view, is a book from which not only many pages, but even whole alternate chapters, have been lost out, or rather which were never printed from the autographs of Nature. The record was actually made in fossil lithography only at certain times and under certain conditions (i.e., at periods of slow subsidence and places of abundant sediment); and of these records all but the last volume is out of print; and of its pages only local glimpses have been obtained. Geologists, except Lyell, will object to this—some of them moderately, others with vehemence. Mr. Darwin himself admits, with a candor rarely displayed on such occasions, that he should have expected more geological evidence of transition than he finds, and that all the most eminent paleontologists maintain the immutability of species.

The general fact, however, that the fossil fauna of each period as a whole is nearly intermediate in character between the preceding and the succeeding faunas, is much relied on. We are brought one step nearer to the desired inference by the similar fact, insisted on by all paleontologists, that fossils from two consecutive formations are far more closely related to each other than are the fossils of two remote formations. Pictet gives a well-known instance—the general resemblance of the organic remains from the several stages of the chalk formation, though the species are distinct at each stage.... What Mr. Darwin now particularly wants to complete his inferential evidence is a proof that the same gradation may be traced in later periods, say in the Tertiary, and between that period and the present; also that the later gradations are finer, so as to leave it doubtful whether the succession is one of species—believed on the one theory to be independent, on the other, derivative—or of varieties, which are confessedly derivative. The proof of the finer gradation appears to be forthcoming. Des Hayes and Lyell have concluded that many of the middle Tertiary and a large proportion of the later Tertiary mollusca are specifically identical with living species; and this is still the almost universally prevalent view. But Mr. Agassiz states that, "in every instance where he had sufficient materials, he had found that the species of the two epochs supposed to be identical by Des Hayes and Lyell were in reality distinct, although closely allied species." Moreover, he is now satisfied, as we understand, that the same gradation is traceable not merely in each great division of the Tertiary, but in particular deposits or successive beds, each answering to a great number of years; where what have passed unquestioned as members of one species, upon closer examination of numerous specimens exhibit differences which in his opinion entitle them to be distinguished into two, three, or more species. It is plain, therefore, that whatever conclusions can be fairly drawn from the present animal and vegetable kingdoms in favor of a gradation of varieties into species, or into what may be regarded as such, the same may be extended to the Tertiary period. In both cases, what some call species others call varieties; and in the later Tertiary shells this difference in judgment affects almost half of the species!...

Mr. Darwin harmonizes and explains [how] adaptation to the conditions of existence is the result of natural selection; unity of type, of unity of descent. Accordingly, as he puts his theory, he is bound to account for the origination of new organs, and for their diversity in each great type, for their specialization, and every adaptation of organ to function and of structure to condition, through natural agencies. Whenever he attempts this he reminds us of Lamarck, and shows us how little light the science of a century devoted to structural investigation has thrown upon the mystery of organization. Here purely natural explanations fail. The organs being given, natural selection may account for some improvement; if given of a variety of sorts or grades, natural selection might determine which should survive and where it should prevail.

On all this ground the only line for the theory to take is to make the most of gradation and adherence to type as suggestive of derivation, and unaccountable upon any other scientific view—deferring all attempts to explain *how* such a metamorphosis was effected, until naturalists have explained *how* the tadpole is metamorphosed into a frog, or one sort of polyp into another. As to *why* it is so, the philosophy of efficient cause, and even the whole argument from design, would stand, upon the admission of such a theory of derivation, precisely where they stand without it. At least there is, or need be, no ground of difference here between Darwin and Agassiz. The latter will admit, with Owen and every morphologist, that hopeless is the attempt to explain the similarity of pattern in members of the same class by utility or the doctrine of final causes. "On the ordinary view of the independent creation of each being, we can only say that so it is, that it has so pleased the Creator to construct each animal and plant." Mr. Darwin, in proposing a theory which suggests a *how* that harmonizes these facts into a system, we trust implies that all was done wisely, in the largest sense designedly, and by an intelligent first cause. The contemplation of the subject on the intellectual side, the amplest exposition of the unity of plan in creation, considered irrespective of natural agencies, leads to no other conclusion.

We are thus, at last, brought to the question, What would happen if the derivation of species were to be substantiated, either as a true physical theory, or as a sufficient hypothesis? What would come of it? The inquiry is a pertinent one, just now. For, of those who agree with us in thinking that Darwin has not established his theory of derivation many will admit with us that he has rendered a theory of derivation much less improbable than before; that such a theory chimes in with the established doctrines of physical science, and is not unlikely to be largely accepted long before it can be proved. Moreover, the various notions that prevail—equally among the most and the least religious—as to the relations between natural agencies or phenomena and efficient cause, are seemingly more crude, obscure, and discordant, than they need be.

It is not surprising that the doctrine of the book should be denounced as atheistical. What does surprise and concern us is, that it should be so denounced by a scientific man, on the broad assumption that a material connection between the members of a series of organized beings is inconsistent with the idea of their being intellectually connected with one another through the Deity, i.e., as products of one mind, as indicating and realizing a preconceived plan. An assumption the rebound of which is somewhat fearful to contemplate, but fortunately one which every natural birth protests against.

It would be more correct to say that the theory in itself is perfectly compatible with an atheistic view of the universe. That is true; but it is equally true of physical theories generally. Indeed, it is more true of the theory of gravitation, and of the nebular hypothesis, than of the hypothesis in question. The latter merely takes up a *particular, proximate cause*, or set of such causes, from which, it is argued, the present diversity of species has or may have contingently resulted. The author does not say *necessarily* resulted; that the actual results in mode and measure, and none other, must have taken place. On the other hand, the theory of gravitation and its extension in the nebular hypothesis assume a *universal and ultimate* physical cause, from which the effects in Nature must *necessarily* have resulted. Now, it is not thought, at least at the present day, that the establishment of the Newtonian theory was a step toward atheism or pantheism. Yet the great achievement of Newton consisted in proving that certain forces (blind forces, so far as the theory is concerned), acting upon matter in certain directions, must *necessarily* produce planetary orbits of the exact measure and form in which observation shows them to exist—a view which is just as consistent with eternal necessity, either in the atheistic or the pantheistic form, as it is with theism....

How the author of this book harmonizes his scientific theory with his philosophy and theology, he has not informed us. Paley in his celebrated analogy with the watch, insists that similar watches, after a manner of generation in animals, the argument from design would be all the stronger. What is to hinder Mr. Darwin from giving Paley's argument a further a-fortiori extension to the supposed case of a watch which sometimes produces better watches, and contrivances adapted to successive conditions, and so at length turns out a chronometer, a town clock, or a series of organisms of the same type? From certain incidental expressions at the close of the volume, taken in connection with the motto adopted from Whewell, we judge it probable that our author regards the whole system of Nature as one which had received at its first formation the impress of the will of its Author, foreseeing the varied yet necessary laws of its action throughout the whole of its existence, ordaining when and how each particular of the stupendous plan should be realized in effect, and—with Him to whom to will is to do—in ordaining doing it. Whether profoundly philosophical or not, a view maintained by eminent philosophical physicists and theologians, such as Babbage on the one hand and Jowett on the other, will hardly be denounced as atheism....

The work is a scientific one, rigidly restricted to its direct object; and by its science it must stand or fall. Its aim is, probably, not to deny creative intervention in Nature—for the admission of the independent origination of certain types does away with all antecedent improbability of as much intervention as may be required—but to maintain that Natural Selection, in explaining the facts, explains also many classes of facts which thousand-fold repeated independent acts of creation do not explain, but leave more mysterious than ever. How far the author has succeeded, the scientific world will in due time be able to pronounce....

THOMAS WENTWORTH HIGGINSON

Selection from "A Plea for Culture"
(1867)

The intellectual style that George Santayana would later patronize as "genteel" was put in place during the era immediately following the Civil War by a formidable cohort of New England writers, prominent among whom was Thomas Wentworth Higginson (1823–1911), whose idealistic account of what "high culture" could do for American society is reprinted here. Higginson was a strong cultural nationalist, viewing the United States as the matrix out of which distinctive and valuable modes of thought and feeling could and should arise. Yet he deeply admired the leading writers and thinkers of Great Britain and to some extent of the rest of Western Europe, and, like so many other American intellectuals of his generation, tried to develop a cultural program that was at once deferential to European accomplishments and robustly patriotic about the democratic ideals of the United States.

Although some intellectuals who shared Higginson's program for culture were politically conservative, Higginson himself was a radical in relation to the rights of women, black Americans, and religious dissenters. He was an influential champion of female writers, especially the reclusive poet Emily Dickinson, whose posthumously published work he edited and promoted. His friendship with her is the subject of Brenda Wineapple, *White Heat: The Friendship of Emily Dickinson and Thomas Wentworth Higginson* (New York, 2008). He believed that the cultural program outlined in this essay flowed from the same basic ethical commitments that had made him an advocate of women throughout his life, an abolitionist before the Civil War, and a reformer in the service of many causes up until the time of his death. Higginson was one of the "secret six" who helped to supply funds for John Brown's raid on Harpers Ferry, Virginia, in 1859. Although Higginson's perspective on black people was heavily patrician, he, unlike many New England whites who shared that perspective, acted in solidarity with blacks in several pivotal moments. During the war, he served as colonel of the First South Carolina Volunteers, composed of ex-slaves, the first all-black fighting unit organized by the federal government. The unit sometimes fought alongside the more famous Fifty-fourth Massachusetts Regiment, composed of free blacks from the North. In *Army Life in a Black Regiment* (Boston, 1870), he described his war experience.

At his funeral, his coffin was draped with the battle flag of the First South Carolina Volunteers. An excellent biography is Tilden G. Edelstein, *Strange Enthusiasm: A Life of Thomas Wentworth Higginson* (New Haven, 1968). The classic account of the development of universities, including their role as engines of the cultural program Higginson outlines here, is Laurence R. Veysey, *The Emergence of the American University* (Chicago, 1965).

Culture is the training and finishing of the whole man, until he sees physical demands to be merely secondary, and pursues science and art as objects of intrinsic worth. It undoubtedly places the fine arts above the useful arts, in a certain sense, and is willingly impoverished in material comforts, if it can thereby obtain nobler living. When this impulse takes the form of a reactionary distrust of the whole spirit of the age, it is unhealthy and morbid. In its healthy form, it simply keeps alive the conviction that the life is more than meat; and so supplies that counterpoise to mere wealth which Europe vainly seeks to secure by aristocracies of birth.

So far as our colleges go, what is needed seems tolerably plain. Our educational system requires a process of addition, not of subtraction; not to save our children from the painful necessity of studying this or that, but to gain for them the opportunity of studying that and more, in their own way. The demand for high culture outruns the supply. This is proved by the palpable fact, that more and more pupils are sent to Europe for instruction, every year; and more from the Western States than from the Eastern. There are more and more young men of fortune whose parents will not stint them in education, at least; more and more poor young men, who will live on bread and water, if need be, to gain knowledge. What we need is the opportunity of high culture somewhere,—that there should be some place in America where a young man may go and study anything that kindles his enthusiasm, and find there instrumentalities to help the flame. As it is now, the maximum range of study in most of our colleges leaves a young man simply with a good preparation for Germany, while the minimum leaves him very ill prepared for America. What we need is a university. Whether this is to be a new creation, or something reared on the foundations now laid at Cambridge, or New Haven, or Ann Arbor, is unimportant. Until we have it somewhere, our means of culture are still provincial.

The essential thing is, that we should recognize, as a nation, the value of all culture, and resolutely organize it into our institutions. As a stimulus to this we must constantly bear in mind, and cheerfully acknowledge, that American literature is not yet copious, American scholarship not profound, American society not highly intellectual, and the American style of execution, in all high arts, yet hasty and superficial. It is not true, as our plain-speaking friend Von Humboldt said, that "the United States are a dead level of mediocrities"; but it is undoubtedly true that our brains as yet lie chiefly in our machine-shops. . . .

What we thus miss in literary culture may be best explained by showing the result of the universal political culture which we possess. It is often noticed that, while the leaders of public affairs in America are usually what are called self-made men, this is not the case with our literary leaders. Among first-class American writers, culture is usually in the second generation; they have usually "tumbled about in a library," as Holmes says, in childhood; at all events, they are usually college-bred men. It has been remarked, for instance, that our eight foremost historians—assuming that this list comprises Prescott, Motley, Bancroft, Hildreth, Sparks, Ticknor, Palfrey, Parkman—were all college graduates, and indeed graduated at a single college. The choice of names may be open to question, but the general fact is undoubted.

Now if it be true that there are fewer among us who rise from the ranks in literature than in politics, it seems not merely to indicate that literature, as being a finer product than statesmanship, implies more elaborate training; but also that our institutions guarantee

Source: "A Plea for Culture," *Atlantic Monthly,* 19, no. 111 (1867), 29–38.

such training in the one case, and not in the other. Every American boy imbibes political knowledge through the pores of his skin; every newspaper, every caucus, contributes to his instruction; and he is expected to have mature convictions before he is fourteen. In the height of the last Presidential contest, a little boy was hung out of a school window by his heels, within my knowledge, because his small comrades disapproved his political sentiments. For higher intellectual pursuits there are not only no such penalties among us, but there are no such opportunities. Yet in Athens—with its twenty thousand statues, with the tragedies of Áschylus enacted for civic prizes, and the histories of Herodotus read at the public games—a boy could no more grow up ignorant of art than he could here remain untrained in politics.

When we are once convinced that this result is desirable, we shall begin to feel the worth of our accumulated wealth. That is true of wealth which Talleyrand said of wisdom,—*everybody* is richer than *anybody*. The richest man in the world cannot afford the parks, the edifices, the galleries, the libraries, which this community can have for itself, whenever it chooses to create them. The Central Park in New York, the Public Library at Boston, the Museum of Comparative Zoölogy at Cambridge,—these are steps towards a more than Athenian culture. These institutions open their vast privileges, free from that sting of selfishness which the private monopolizer feels. Public enthusiasm is roused to sustain them, gifts flow in upon them, and they ennoble the common life around. It was claimed for Athens, that wealth could buy few facilities for culture which poverty did not also share. I take it, we aim at least to secure for the poorest American opportunities such as no wealth could buy in Europe. It may take centuries to accomplish it, but it can be done.

And it will not take so long as one might imagine. Although the great intellectual institutions of Europe are often nominally ancient, yet their effective life has been chiefly in the last few centuries. A hundred years ago, the British Museum and the Bodleian Library had each but about ten thousand volumes. The Imperial Library at Paris had then but fifty thousand, and the present century has added the most valuable half of its seven hundred thousand books. At the time of our Revolution, there were but three public galleries of art in Europe; and the Louvre, "the chief attraction of the most attractive city of the world," is of later origin. One half of the leading German universities are younger than Harvard College. With the immense wealth accumulating in America, and the impulse inherent in democracies to identify one's own name and successes with the common weal, such institutions will rise among us like Aladdin's palace, when public spirit is once thoroughly turned that way....

So long as the sources of art and science are still Transatlantic, we are still a province, not a nation. For these are the highest pursuits of man,—higher than trades or professions, higher than statesmanship, far higher than war. Jean Paul said: "Schiller and Herder were both destined for physicians, but Providence said, No, there are deeper wounds than those of the body,—and so they both became authors." "After all," said Rufus Choate, at the zenith of his professional success, "a book is the only immortality."...

It is observable that in English books and magazines everything seems written for some limited circle,—tales for those who can speak French, essays for those who can understand a Latin quotation. But every American writer must address himself to a vast audience, possessing the greatest quickness and common-sense, with but little culture; and he must command their attention as he may. This has some admirable results: one must put some life into what he writes, or his thirty million auditors will go to sleep; he must write clearly, or they will cease to follow him; must keep clear of pedantry and unknown tongues, or they will turn to some one who can address them in English. On the other hand, these same conditions tempt one to accept a low standard of execution, to substitute artifice for art, and to disregard the more permanent verdict of more select tribunals. The richest thought and the finest literary handling which America has yet produced—as of Emerson, Hawthorne, and Thoreau—reached at first but a small audience, and are but very gradually attaining a wider hold. Rénan has said that every man's work is superficial, until he has learned to content himself with the approbation of a few. This is only one half the truth; but it is the half which Americans find hardest to remember.

But American literature, though its full harvest be postponed for another hundred years, is sure to come to ripeness at last. Our national development in this direction, though slow, is perfectly healthy. There are many influences to retard, but none to distort. Even if the more ideal aims of the artist are treated with indifference, it is a frank indifference; there is no contempt, no jealousy, no call for petty manoeuvres. No man is asked to flatter this vast audience; no man can succeed by flattering; it simply reserves its attention, and lets one obtain its ear if he can. When won, it is worth the winning,—generous in its confidence, noble in its rewards. There is abundant cause for strenuous effort among those who give their lives to the intellectual service of America, but there is no cause for fear. If we can only avoid incorporating superficiality into our institutions, literature will come when all is ready, and when it comes will be of the best. It is not enough to make England or France our standard....

Above all other races and all other times, we should be full of hearty faith. It is but a few years since we heard it said that the age was dull and mean, and inspiration gone. A single gunshot turned meanness to self-sacrifice, mercenary toil to the vigils of the camp and the transports of battle. It linked boyish and girlish life to new opportunities, sweeter self-devotion, more heroic endings; tied and loosed the threads of existence in profounder complications. That is all past now; but its results can never pass. The nation has found its true grandeur by war, but must retain it in peace.

Peace too has its infinite resources, after a nation has once become conscious of itself. It is impossible that human life should ever be utterly impoverished, and all the currents of American civilization now tend to its enrichment. This vast development of rudimentary intellect, this mingling of nationalities, these opportunities of books and travel, educate in this new race a thousand new susceptibilities. Then comes Passion, a hand straying freely through all the chords, and thrilling all with magic. We cannot exclude it, a forbidden guest. It re-creates itself in each generation, and bids art live. *Rouge gagne.* If the romance of life does not assert itself in safe and innocent ways, it finds its outlet with fatal certainty in guilt; as we see colorless Puritanism touched with scarlet glory through the glass of Hawthorne. Every form of human life is romantic; every age may become classic. Lamentations, doubts, discouragements, all are wasted things. Everything is here, between these Atlantic and Pacific shores, save only the perfected utterance that comes with years. Between Shakespeare in his cradle and Shakespeare in Hamlet there was needed but an interval of time, and the same sublime condition is all that lies between the America of toil and the America of art.

CHARLES PEIRCE

"The Fixation of Belief"
(1877)

With this essay of 1877, Charles Peirce (1839–1914) began a series of articles on which much of his fame as a philosopher came to be based. Here he only introduced the topic of this series—"the logic of science"—but in so doing managed to (a) articulate a largely *social* vision of the scientific enterprise, according to which the community rather than the individual knower is the primary agent of cognitive progress; (b) direct the method of science against not only beliefs about nature, but against the entire panorama of inherited beliefs, especially and explicitly *religious* beliefs; (c) assert that open, honest inquiry is decidedly superior *morally* to pious loyalty to an inherited faith; and (d) argue, in what would eventually be recognized as a "pragmatic" mode, that true belief is simply a *habit* that can remain stable, a "fixed opinion."

Peirce's life and work are discussed cogently by R. Jackson Wilson, "Charles Sanders Peirce: The Community of Inquiry," in Wilson's *In Quest of Community: Social Philosophy in the United States, 1860–1920* (New York, 1968), 32–59. An excellent biography is Joseph Brent, *Charles Sanders Peirce: A Life*, 2nd ed. (Bloomington, 1998). For a more technical, philosophically rigorous study, see Murray G. Murphey, *The Development of Peirce's Philosophy* (Cambridge, Mass., 1961). For a lucid account of Peirce's work in relation to his contemporaries in the Harvard milieu, see Bruce Kuklick, *The Rise of American Philosophy: Cambridge, Massachusetts, 1860–1930* (New Haven, 1977), esp. 104–26. Authoritative texts of all of Peirce's major works are being published by the Indiana University Press, *The Writings of Charles S. Peirce. A Chronological Edition* (Bloomington, 1982–). A readable account of Peirce's thought and of his troubled life is that by Josiah Lee Auspitz, "The Greatest Living American Philosopher," *Commentary* (December 1983), 51–64. A critical overview of Peirce scholarship is David Marr, "Signs of C. S. Peirce," *American Literary History* (Winter 1995), 681–99. A readable popular account of Peirce's life in relation to the lives of William James and other contemporaries is Louis Menand, *The Metaphysical Club* (New York, 2001). Detailed studies of Peirce—and of other American philosophers—appear regularly in *The Transactions of the Charles S. Peirce Society.*

Few persons care to study logic, because everybody conceives himself to be proficient enough in the art of reasoning already. But I observe that this satisfaction is limited to one's own ratiocination, and does not extend to that of other men.

We come to the full possession of our power of drawing inferences the last of all our faculties, for it is not so much a natural gift as a long and difficult art. The history of its practice would make a grand subject for a book. The medieval schoolman, following the Romans, made logic the earliest of a boy's studies after grammar, as being very easy. So it was as they understood it. Its fundamental principle, according to them, was, that all knowledge rests on either authority or reason; but that whatever is deduced by reason depends ultimately on a premise derived from authority. Accordingly, as soon as a boy was perfect in the syllogistic procedure, his intellectual kit of tools was held to be complete.

To Roger Bacon, that remarkable mind who in the middle of the thirteenth century was almost a scientific man, the schoolmen's conception of reasoning appeared only an obstacle to truth. He saw that experience alone teaches anything- -a proposition which to us seems easy to understand, because a distinct conception of experience has been handed down to us from former generations; which to him also seemed perfectly clear, because its difficulties had not yet unfolded themselves. Of all kinds of experience, the best, he thought, was interior illumination, which teaches many things about Nature which the external senses could never discover such as the transubstantiation of bread.

Four centuries later, the more celebrated Bacon, in the first book of his "Novum Organum," gave his clear account of experience as something which must be open to verification and re-examination. But, superior as Lord Bacon's conception is to earlier notions, a modern reader who is not in awe of his grandiloquence is chiefly struck by the inadequacy of his view of scientific procedure. That we have only to make some crude experiments, to draw up briefs of the results in certain blank forms, to go through these by rule, checking off everything disproved and setting down the alternatives, and that thus in a few years physical science would be finished up—what an idea! "He wrote on science like a Lord Chancellor," indeed.

The early scientists, Copernicus, Tycho Brahe, Kepler, Galileo, and Gilbert, had methods more like those of their modern brethren. Kepler undertook to draw a curve through the places of Mars; and his greatest service to science was in impressing on men's minds that this was the thing to be done if they wished to improve astronomy; that they were not to content themselves with inquiring whether one system of epicycles was better than another but that they were to sit down by the figures and find out what the curve, in truth, was. He accomplished this by his incomparable energy and courage, blundering along in the most inconceivable way (to us), from one irrational hypothesis to another, until, after trying twenty-two of these, he fell, by the mere exhaustion of his invention, upon the orbit which a mind well furnished with the weapons of modern logic would have tried almost at the outset.

In the same way, every work of science great enough to be remembered for a few generations affords some exemplification of the defective state of the art of reasoning of the time when it was written; and each chief step in science has been a lesson in logic. It was so when Lavoisier and his contemporaries took up the study of Chemistry. The old chemist's maxim had been, "Lege, lege, lege, labora, ora, et relege." Lavoisier's method was not

Source: Popular Science Monthly, 12 (November 1877), 1–15.

to read and pray, not to dream that some long and complicated chemical process would have a certain effect, to put it into practice with dull patience, after its inevitable failure to dream that with some modification it would have another result, and to end by publishing the last dream as a fact: his way was to carry his mind into his laboratory, and to make of his alembics and cucurbits instruments of thought, giving a new conception of reasoning as something which was to be done with one's eyes open, by manipulating real things instead of words and fancies.

The Darwinian controversy is, in large part, a question of logic. Mr. Darwin proposed to apply the statistical method to biology. The same thing has been done in a widely different branch of science, the theory of gases. Though unable to say what the movement of any particular molecule of gas would be on a certain hypothesis regarding the constitution of this class of bodies, Clausius and Maxwell were yet able, by the application of the doctrine of probabilities, to predict that in the long run such and such a proportion of the molecules would, under given circumstances, acquire such and such velocities; that there would take place, every second, such and such a number of collisions, etc.; and from these propositions they were able to deduce certain properties of gases, especially in regard to their heat-relations. In like manner, Darwin, while unable to say what the operation of variation and natural selection in every individual case will be, demonstrates that in the long run they will adapt animals to their circumstances. Whether or not existing animal forms are due to such action, or what position the theory ought to take, forms the subject of a discussion in which questions of fact and questions of logic are curiously interlaced.

The object of reasoning is to find out, from the consideration of what we already know, something else which we do not know. Consequently, reasoning is good if it be such as to give a true conclusion from true premises, and not otherwise. Thus, the question of validity is purely one of fact and not of thinking. A being the premises and B being the conclusion, the question is, whether these facts are really so related that if A is B is. If so, the inference is valid; if not, not. It is not in the least the question whether, when the premises are accepted by the mind, we feel an impulse to accept the conclusion also. It is true that we do generally reason correctly by nature. But that is an accident; the true conclusion would remain true if we had no impulse to accept it; and the false one would remain false, though we could not resist the tendency to believe in it.

We are, doubtless, in the main logical animals, but we are not perfectly so. Most of us, for example, are naturally more sanguine and hopeful than logic would justify. We seem to be so constituted that in the absence of any facts to go upon we are happy and self-satisfied; so that the effect of experience is continually to counteract our hopes and aspirations. Yet a lifetime of the application of this corrective does not usually eradicate our sanguine disposition. Where hope is unchecked by any experience, it is likely that our optimism is extravagant. Logicality in regard to practical matters is the most useful quality an animal can possess, and might, therefore, result from the action of natural selection; but outside of these it is probably of more advantage to the animal to have his mind filled with pleasing and encouraging visions, independently of their truth; and thus, upon unpractical subjects, natural selection might occasion a fallacious tendency of thought.

That which determines us, from given premises, to draw one inference rather than another, is some habit of mind, whether it be constitutional or acquired. The habit is good or otherwise, according as it produces true conclusions from true premises or not; and an inference is regarded as valid or not, without reference to the truth or falsity of its conclusion specially, but according as the habit which determines it is such as to produce true conclusions in general or not. The particular habit of mind which governs this or that inference may be formulated in a proposition whose truth depends on the validity of the inferences which the habit determines; and such a formula is called a *guiding principle* of inference. Suppose, for example, that we observe that a rotating disk of copper quickly comes to rest when placed between the poles of a magnet, and we infer that this will happen with every disk of copper. The guiding principle is, that what is true of one piece of copper is true of another. Such a guiding principle with regard to copper would be much safer than with regard to many other substances—brass, for example.

A book might be written to signalize all the most important of these guiding principles of reasoning. It would probably be, we must confess, of no service to a person whose thought is directed wholly to practical subjects, and whose activity moves along thoroughly beaten paths. The problems which present themselves to such a mind are matters of routine which he has learned once for all to handle in learning his business. But let a man venture into an unfamiliar field, or where his results are not continually checked by experience, and all history shows that the most masculine intellect will ofttimes lose his orientation and waste his efforts in directions which bring him no nearer to his goal, or even carry him entirely astray. He is like a ship on the open sea, with no one on board who understands the rules of navigation. And in such a case some general study of the guiding principles of reasoning would be sure to be found useful.

The subject could hardly be treated, however, without being first limited; since almost any fact may serve as a guiding principle. But it so happens that there exists a division among facts, such that in one class are all those which are absolutely essential as guiding principles, while in the other are all those which have any other interests as object of research. This division is between those which are necessarily taken for granted in asking whether a certain conclusion follows from certain premises, and those which are not implied in that question. A moment's thought will show that a variety of facts are already assumed when the logical question is first asked. It is implied, for instance, that there are such states of mind as doubt and belief—that a passage from one to the other is possible, the object of thought remaining the same, and that this transition is subject to some rules which all minds are alike bound by. As these are facts which we must already know before we can have any clear conception of reasoning at all, it cannot be supposed to be any longer of much interest to inquire into their truth or falsity. On the other hand, it is easy to believe that those rules of reasoning which are deduced from the very idea of the process are the ones which are the most essential; and, indeed, that so long as it conforms to these it will, at least, not lead to false conclusions from true premises. In point of fact, the importance of what may be deduced from the assumptions involved in the logical question turns out to be greater than might be supposed, and this for reasons which it is difficult to exhibit at the outset. The only one which I shall here mention is, that conceptions which are really products of logical reflections, without being readily seen to be so, mingle with our ordinary thoughts, and are frequently the causes of great confusion. This is the case, for example, with the conception of quality. A quality as such is never an object of observation. We can see that a thing is blue or green, but the quality of being blue and the quality of being green are not things which we see; they are products of logical reflections. The truth is, that common-sense, or thought as it first emerges above the level of the narrowly practical, is deeply imbued with that bad logical quality to which the epithet metaphysical is commonly applied; and nothing can clear it up but a severe course of logic.

We generally know when we wish to ask a question and when we wish to pronounce a judgment, for there is a dissimiliarity between the sensation of doubting and that of believing.

But this is not all which distinguishes doubt from belief. There is a practical difference. Our beliefs guide our desires and shape our actions. The Assassins, or followers of the Old Man of the Mountain, used to rush into death at his least command, because they believed that obedience to him would insure everlasting felicity. Had they doubted this, they would not have acted as they did. So it is with every belief, according to its degree. The feeling of believing is a more or less sure indication of there being established in our nature some habit which will determine our actions. Doubt never has such an effect.

Nor must we overlook a third point of difference. Doubt is an uneasy and dissatisfied state from which we struggle to free ourselves and pass into the state of belief; while the latter is a calm and satisfactory state which we do not wish to avoid, or to change to a belief in anything else. On the contrary, we cling tenaciously, not merely to believing, but to believing just what we do believe.

Thus, both doubt and belief have positive effects upon us, though very different ones. Belief does not make us act at once, but puts us into such a condition that we shall behave in a certain way, when the occasion arises. Doubt has not the least effect of this sort, but stimulates us to action until it is destroyed. This reminds us of the irritation of a nerve and the reflex action produced thereby; while for the analogue of belief, in the nervous system, we must look to what are called nervous associations—for example, to that habit of the nerves in consequence of which the smell of a peach will make the mouth water.

The irritation of doubt causes a struggle to attain a state of belief. I shall term this struggle *inquiry*, though it must be admitted that this is sometimes not a very apt designation.

The irritation of doubt is the only immediate motive for the struggle to attain belief. It is certainly best for us that our beliefs should be such as may truly guide our actions so as to satisfy our desires; and this reflection will make us reject any belief which does not seem to have been so formed as to insure this result. But it will only do so by creating a doubt in the place of that belief. With the doubt, therefore, the struggle begins, and with the cessation of doubt it ends. Hence, the sole object of inquiry is the settlement of opinion. We may fancy that this is not enough for us, and that we seek not merely an opinion, but a true opinion. But put this fancy to the test, and it proves groundless; for as soon as a firm belief is reached we are entirely satisfied, whether the belief be false or true. And it is clear that nothing out of the sphere of our knowledge can be our object, for nothing which does not affect the mind can be a motive for a mental effort. The most that can be maintained is, that we seek for a belief that we shall *think* to be true. But we think each one of our beliefs to be true, and, indeed, it is mere tautology to say so.

That the settlement of opinion is the sole end of inquiry is a very important proposition. It sweeps away, at once, various vague and erroneous conceptions of proof. A few of these may be noticed here.

1. Some philosophers have imagined that to start an inquiry it was only necessary to utter or question or set it down on paper, and have even recommended us to begin our studies with questioning everything! But the mere putting of a proposition into the interrogative form does not stimulate the mind to any struggle after belief. There must be a real and living doubt, and without all this discussion is idle.

2. It is a very common idea that a demonstration must rest on some ultimate and absolutely indubitable propositions. These, according to one school, are first principles of a general nature; according to another, are first sensations. But, in point of fact, an inquiry, to have that completely satisfactory result called demonstration, has only to start with propositions perfectly free from all actual doubt. If the premises are not in fact doubted at all, they cannot be more satisfactory that they are.

3. Some people seem to love to argue a point after all the world is fully convinced of it. But no further advance can be made. When doubt ceases, mental action on the subject comes to an end; and, if it did go on, it would be without a purpose.

If the settlement of opinion is the sole object of inquiry, and if belief is of the nature of a habit, why should we not attain the desired end, by taking any answer to a question, which we may fancy, and constantly reiterating it to ourselves, dwelling on all which may conduce to that belief, and learning to turn with contempt and hatred from anything which might disturb it? This simple and direct method is really pursued by many men. I remember once being entreated not to read a certain newspaper lest it might change my opinion upon free-trade. "Lest I might be entrapped by its fallacies and misstatements," was the form of expression. "You are not," my friend said, "a special student of political economy. You might, therefore, easily be deceived by fallacious arguments upon the subject. You might, then, if you read this paper, be led to believe in protection. But you admit that free-trade is the true doctrine; and you do not wish to believe what is not true." I have often known this system to be deliberately adopted. Still oftener, the instinctive dislike of an undecided state of mind, exaggerated into a vague dread of doubt, makes men cling spasmodically to the views they already take. The man feels that, if he only holds to his belief without wavering, it will be entirely satisfactory. Nor can it be denied that a steady and immovable faith yields great peace of mind. It may, indeed, give rise to inconveniences, as if a man should resolutely continue to believe that fire would not burn him, or that he would be eternally damned if he received his *ingesta* otherwise than through a stomach-pump. But then the man who adopts this method will not allow that its inconveniences are greater than its advantages. He will say, "I hold steadfastly to the truth and the truth is always wholesome." And in many cases it may very well be that the pleasure he derives from his calm faith overbalances any inconveniences resulting from its deceptive character. Thus, if it be true that death is annihilation, then the man who believes that he will certainly go straight to heaven when he dies, provided he have fulfilled certain simple observances in this life, has a cheap pleasure which will not be followed by the least disappointment. A similar consideration seems to have weight with many persons in religious topics, for we frequently hear it said, "Oh, I could not believe so-and-so, because I should be wretched if I did." When an ostrich buries its head in the sand as danger approaches, it very likely takes the happiest course. It hides the danger, and then calmly says there is no danger; and, it feels perfectly sure there is none, why should it raise its head to see? A man may go through life, systematically keeping out of view all that might cause a change in his opinions, and if he only succeeds—basing his method, as he does, on two fundamental psychological laws—I do not see what can be said against his doing so. It would be an egotistical impertinence to object that his procedure is irrational, for that only amounts to saying that his method of settling belief is not ours. He does not propose to himself to be rational, and indeed, will often talk with scorn of man's weak and illusive reason. So let him think as he pleases.

But this method of fixing belief, which may be called the method of tenacity, will be unable to hold its ground in practice. The social impulse is against it. The man who adopts it will find that other men think differently from him, and it will be apt to occur to him in some saner moment that their opinions are quite as good as his own, and this will shake his confidence in his belief. This conception, that another man's thought or sentiment may be equivalent to one's own, is a distinctly new step, and a highly important one. It arises from an impulse too strong in man to be suppressed, without danger of destroying the human species. Unless we make ourselves hermits, we shall necessarily influence each other's opinions; so that the problem becomes how to fix belief, not in the individual merely, but in the community.

Let the will of the state act, then, instead of that of the individual. Let an institution be created which shall have for its object to keep correct doctrines before the attention of the people, to reiterate them perpetually, and to teach them to the young; having at the same time power to prevent contrary doctrines from being taught, advocated, or expressed. Let all possible causes of a change of mind be removed from men's apprehensions. Let them be kept ignorant, lest they should learn of some reason to think otherwise than they do. Let their passions be enlisted, so that they may regard private and unusual opinions with hatred and horror. Then, let all men who reject the established belief be terrified into silence. Let the people turn out and tar-and-feather such men, or let inquisitions be made into the manner of thinking of suspected persons, and, when they are found guilty of forbidden beliefs, let them be subjected to some signal punishment. When complete agreement could not otherwise be reached, a general massacre of all who have not thought in a certain way has proved a very effective means of settling opinion in a country. If the power to do this be wanting, let a list of opinions be drawn up, to which no man of the least independence of thought can assent, and let the faithful be required to accept all these propositions, in order to segregate them as radically as possible from the influence of the rest of the world.

This method has, from the earliest times, been one of the chief means of upholding correct theological and political doctrines, and of preserving their universal or catholic character. In Rome, especially, it has been practiced from the days of Numa Pompilius to those of Pius Nonus. This is the most perfect example in history; but wherever there is a priesthood—and no religion has been without one—this method has been more or less made use of. Wherever there is artistocracy, or a guild, or any association of a class of men whose interests depend or are supposed to depend on certain propositions, there will be inevitably found some traces of this natural product of social feeling. Cruelties always accompany this system; and when it is consistently carried out, they become atrocities of the most horrible kind in the eyes of any rational man. Nor should this occasion surprise, for the officer of a society does not feel justified in surrendering the interests of that society for the sake of mercy, as he might his own private interests. It is natural, therefore, that sympathy and fellowship should thus produce a most ruthless power.

In judging this method of fixing belief, which may be called the method of authority, we must, in the first place, allow its immeasurable mental and moral superiority to the method of tenacity. Its success is proportionally greater; and in fact it has over and over again worked the most majestic results. The mere structures of stone which it has caused to be put together—in Siam, for example, in Egypt, and in Europe—have many of them a sublimity hardly more than rivaled by the greatest works of Nature. And, except the geological epochs, there are no periods of time so vast as those which are measured by some of these organized faiths. If we scrutinize the matter closely, we shall find that there has not been one of their creeds which has remained always the same; yet the change is so slow as to be imperceptible during one person's life, so that individual belief remains sensibly fixed. For the mass of mankind, then, there is perhaps no better method than this. If it is their highest impulse to be intellectual slaves, then slaves they ought to remain.

But no institution can undertake to regulate opinions upon every subject. Only the most important ones can be attended to, and on the rest men's minds must be left to the action of natural causes. This imperfection will be no source of weakness so long as men are in such a state of culture that one opinion does not influence another—that is, so long as they cannot put two and two together. But in the most priest-ridden states some individuals will be found who are raised above that condition. These men possess a wider sort of social feeling; they see that men in other countries and in other ages have held to very different doctrines from those which they themselves have been brought up to believe; and they cannot help seeing that it is the mere accident of their having been taught as they have, and of their having been surrounded with the manners and associations they have, that has caused them to believe as they do and not far differently. And their candor cannot resist the reflection that there is no reason to rate their own views at a higher value than those of other nations and other centuries; and this gives rise to doubts in their minds.

They will further perceive that such doubts as these must exist in their minds with reference to every belief which seems to be determined by the caprice either of themselves or of those who originated the popular opinions. The willful adherence to a belief, and the arbitrary forcing of it upon others, must, therefore, both be given up and a new method of settling opinions must be adopted, which shall not only produce an impulse to believe, but shall also decide what proposition it is which is to be believed. Let the action of natural preferences be unimpeded, then, and under their influence let men conversing together and regarding matters in different lights, gradually develop beliefs in harmony with natural causes. This method resembles that by which conceptions of art have been brought to maturity. The most perfect example of it is to be found in the history of metaphysical philosophy. Systems of this sort have not usually rested upon observed facts, at least not in any great degree. They have been chiefly adopted because their fundamental propositions seemed "agreeable to reason." This is an apt expression; it does not mean that which agrees with experience, but that which we find ourselves inclined to believe. Plato, for example, finds it agreeable to reason that the distances of the celestial spheres from one another should be proportional to the different lengths of strings which produce harmonious chords. Many philosophers have been led to their main conclusions by considerations like this; but this is the lowest and least developed form which the method takes, for it is clear that another man might find Kepler's [earlier] theory, that the celestial spheres are proportional to the inscribed and circumscribed spheres of the different regular solids, more agreeable to his reason. But the shock of opinions will soon lead men to rest on preferences of a far more universal nature. Take, for example, the doctrine that man only acts selfishly—that is, from the consideration that acting in one way will afford him more pleasure than acting in another. This rests on no fact in the world, but it has had a wide acceptance as being the only reasonable theory.

This method is far more intellectual and respectable from the point of view of reason than either of the others which we have noticed. But its failure has been the most manifest. It makes of inquiry something similar to the development of taste; but taste, unfortunately, is always more or less a matter of fashion, and accordingly, metaphysicians have never come to any fixed agreement, but the pendulum has swung backward and forward between a more material and a more spiritual philosophy, from the earliest times to the latest. And so from this, which has been called the a priori method, we are driven, in Lord Bacon's phrase, to a true induction. We have examined into this a priori method as something which promised to deliver our opinions from their accidental and capricious element. But development, while it is a process which eliminates the effect of some casual circumstances, only magnifies that of others. This method, therefore, does not differ in a very essential way from that of authority. The government may not have lifted its finger to influence my convictions; I may have been left outwardly quite free to choose, we will say, between monogamy and polygamy, and appealing to my conscience only, I may have concluded that the latter practice is in itself licentious. But when I come to see that the chief obstacle to the spread of Christianity among a people of as high culture as the Hindoos has been a conviction of the immorality of our way of treating women, I cannot help seeing that, though governments do not interfere, sentiments in their development will be very greatly determined by accidental causes. Now, there are some people, among whom I must suppose that my reader is to be found, who, when they see that any belief of theirs is determined by any circumstance extraneous to the facts, will from that moment not merely admit in words that that belief is doubtful, but will experience a real doubt of it, so that it ceases to be a belief.

To satisfy our doubts, therefore, it is necessary that a method should be found by which our beliefs may be caused by nothing human, but by some external permanency—by something upon which our thinking has no effect. Some mystics imagine that they have such a method in a private inspiration from on high. But that is only a form of the method of tenacity, in which the conception of truth as something public is not yet developed. Our external permanency would not be external, in our sense, if it was restricted in its influence to one individual. It must be something which affects, or might affect, every man. And, though these affections are necessarily as various as are individual conditions, yet the method must be such that the ultimate conclusion of every man shall be the same. Such is the method of science. Its fundamental hypothesis, restated in more familiar language, is this: There are real things, whose characters are entirely independent of our opinions about them; whose realities affect our senses according to regular laws, and, though our sensations are as different as our relations to the objects, yet, by taking advantage of the laws of perception, we can ascertain by reasoning how things really are, and any man, if he have sufficient experience and reason enough about it, will be led to the one true conclusion. The new conception here involved is that of reality. It may be asked how I know that there are any realities. If this hypothesis is the sole support of my method of inquiry, my method of inquiry must not be used to support my hypothesis. The reply is this: 1. If investigation cannot be regarded as proving that there are real things, it at least does not lead to a contrary conclusion; but the method and the conception on which it is based remain ever in harmony. No doubts of the method, therefore, necessarily arise from its practice, as is the case with all the others. 2. The feeling which gives rise to any method of fixing belief is a dissatisfaction at two repugnant propositions. But here already is a vague concession that there is some *one* thing to which a proposition should conform. Nobody, therefore, can really doubt that there are realities, or, if he did, doubt would not be a source of dissatisfaction. The hypothesis, therefore, is one which every mind admits. So that the social impulse does not cause me to doubt it. 3. Everybody uses the scientific method about a great many things, and only ceases to use it when he does not know how to apply it. 4. Experience of the method has not led me to doubt it, but, on the contrary, scientific investigation has had the most wonderful triumphs in the way of settling opinion. These afford the explanation of my not doubting the method or the hypothesis which it supposes; and not having any doubt, nor believing that anybody else whom I could influence has, it would be the merest babble for me to say more about it. If there be anybody with a living doubt upon the subject, let him consider it. To describe the method of scientific investigation is the object of this series of papers. At present I have only room to notice some points of contrast between it and other methods of fixing belief.

This is the only one of the four methods which presents any distinction of a right and a wrong way. If I adopt the method of tenacity and shut myself out from all influences, whatever I think necessary to doing this is necessary according to that method. So with the method of authority: the state may try to put down heresy by means which, from a scientific point of view, seems very ill-calculated to accomplish its purposes; but the only test *on that method* is what the state thinks, so that it cannot pursue the method wrongly. So with the a priori method. The very essence of it is to think as one is inclined to think. All metaphysicians will be sure to do that, however they may be inclined to judge each other to be perversely wrong. The Hegelian system recognizes every natural tendency of thought as logical, although it is certain to be abolished by counter-tendencies. Hegel thinks there is a regular system in the succession of these tendencies, in consequence of which, after drifting one way and the other for a long time, opinion will at last go right. And it is true that metaphysicians get the right ideas at last; Hegel's system of Nature represents tolerably the science of that day; and one may be sure that whatever scientific investigation has put out of doubt will presently receive a priori demonstration on the part of the metaphysicians. But with the scientific method the case is different. I may start with known and observed facts to proceed to the unknown; and yet the rules which I follow in doing so may not be such as investigation would approve. The test of whether I am truly following the method is not an immediate appeal to my feelings and purposes, but, on the contrary, itself involves the application of the method. Hence it is that bad reasoning as well as good reasoning is possible; and this fact is the foundation of the practical side of logic.

It is not to be supposed that the first three methods of settling opinion present no advantage whatever over the scientific method. On the contrary, each has some peculiar convenience of its own. The a priori method is distinguished for its comfortable conclusions. It is the nature of the process to adopt whatever belief we are inclined to, and there are certain flatteries to one's vanities which we all believe by nature, until we are awakened from our pleasing dream by rough facts. The method of authority will always govern the mass of mankind; and those who wield the various forms of organized force in the state will never be convinced that dangerous reasoning ought not to be suppressed in some way. If liberty of speech is to be untrammeled from the grosser forms of constraint, then uniformity of opinion will be secured by a moral terrorism to which the respectability of society will give its thorough approval. Following the method of authority is the path of peace. Certain nonconformities are permitted; certain others (considered unsafe) are forbidden. These are different in different countries and in different ages; but, wherever you are let it be known that you seriously hold a tabooed belief, and you may be perfectly sure of being treated with a cruelty no less brutal but more refined than hunting you like a wolf. Thus, the greatest intellectual benefactors of mankind have never dared, and dare not now, to utter the whole of their thought; and thus a shade of prima facie doubt is cast upon every proposition which is considered essential to the security of society. Singularly enough, the persecution does not all come from without; but a man torments himself and is oftentimes most distressed at finding himself believing propositions which he has been brought up to regard with aversion. The peaceful and sympathetic man will, therefore, find it hard to resist the temptation to submit his opinions to authority. But most of all I admire the method of tenacity for its strength, simplicity, and directness. Men who pursue it are distinguished for their decision of character, which becomes very easy with such a mental rule. They do not waste time in trying to make up their minds to what they want, but, fastening like lightning upon whatever alternative comes first, they hold to it to the end, whatever happens, without an instant's irresolution. This is one of the splendid qualities which generally accompany brilliant, unlasting success. It is impossible not to envy the man who can dismiss reason, although we know how it must turn out at last.

Such are the advantages which the other methods of settling opinions have over scientific investigation. A man should consider well of them; and then he should consider that, after all, he wishes his opinions to coincide with the fact, and that there is no reason why the results of these three methods should do so. To bring about this effect is the prerogative of the method of science. Upon such considerations he has to make his choice—a choice which is far more than the adoption of any intellectual opinion, which is one of the ruling decisions of his life, to which when once made he is bound to adhere. The force of habit will sometimes cause a man to hold on to old beliefs, after he is in a condition to see that they have no sound basis. But reflection upon the state of the case will overcome these habits, and he ought to allow reflection full weight. People sometimes shrink from doing this, having an idea that beliefs are wholesome which they cannot help feeling rest on nothing. But let such persons suppose an analogous though different case from their own. Let them ask themselves what they would say to a reformed Mussulman who should hesitate to give up his old notions in regard to the relations of the sexes; or to a reformed Catholic who should still shrink from the Bible. Would they not say that these persons ought to consider the matter fully, and clearly understand the new doctrine, and then ought to embrace it in its entirety? But, above all, let it be considered that what is more wholesome than any particular belief, is integrity of belief; and that to avoid looking into the support of any belief from a fear that it may turn out rotten is quite as immoral as it is disadvantageous. The person who confesses that there is such a thing as truth, which is distinguished from falsehood simply by this, that if acted on it will carry us to the point we aim at and not astray, and then though convinced of this, dares not know the truth and seeks to avoid it, is in a sorry state of mind, indeed.

Yes, the other methods do have their merits: a clear logical conscience does cost something—just as any virtue, just as all that we cherish, costs us dear. But, we should not desire it to be otherwise. The genius of a man's logical method should be loved and reverenced as his bride, whom he has chosen from all the world. He need not condemn the others; on the contrary, he may honor them deeply, and in doing so he only honors her the more. But she is the one that he has chosen, and he knows that he was right in making that choice. And having made it, he will work and fight for her, and will not complain that there are blows to take, hoping that there may be as many and as hard to give, and will strive to be the worthy knight and champion of her from the blaze of whose splendors he draws his inspiration and his courage.

WILLIAM GRAHAM SUMNER

"Sociology"
(1881)

When William Graham Sumner (1840–1910) hailed sociology as a science of nature ready to stand next to physics and biology, he spoke for a host of nineteenth-century intellectuals eager to bring human affairs within the scope of science. But Sumner placed a politically conservative construction on the new science of society; this construction contrasted sharply with the outlook of some other enthusiasts for this new "science," including, for example, Lester Frank Ward, who associated science not with obedience to facts but with the authority of human beings over their own destiny. In this essay of 1881, Sumner interprets as scientific facts the doctrines of Thomas Malthus, David Ricardo, and other economists of the "classical," laissez-faire persuasion. Sumner attacks as scientifically naive the reformers of his own day who proposed to regulate in the public interest the economic activities of individuals. Arguing that "hard work and self-denial" are "the only two things" that really promote human progress, Sumner holds that one's chief mission in life ought to be "to accumulate capital." Sumner acknowledged that this mission involved conflict, while many of his fellow conservatives believed social progress a more harmonious process.

Although Sumner has often been called a social Darwinist, this term exaggerates Sumner's affinities with Darwin and minimizes his ties to the British discipline of political economy that was well developed before Darwin. For a detailed treatment, see Donald C. Bellomy, " 'Social Darwinism' Revisited," *Perspectives in American History,* 1 n.s. (1984), 1–129. Many scholars find the concept of "social Darwinism" misleading. For a helpful discussion of the difficulties with the term and for a judicious review of recent scholarship, see the preface to the second edition of Robert C. Bannister, *Social Darwinism: Science and Myth in Anglo-American Social Thought* (Philadelphia, 1989), xi-xxxi. This book also offers (see pp. 97–113) a valuable account of Sumner's intellectual development.

...Let us...endeavor to define the field of sociology. Life in society is the life of a human society on this earth. Its elementary conditions are set by the nature of human beings and the nature of the earth. We have already become familiar, in biology, with the transcendent importance of the fact that life on earth must be maintained by a struggle against nature, and also by a competition with other forms of life. In the latter fact biology and sociology touch. Sociology is a science which deals with one range of phenomena produced by the struggle for existence, while biology deals with another. The forces are the same, acting on different fields and under different conditions. The sciences are truly cognate. Nature contains certain materials which are capable of satisfying human needs, but those materials must, with rare and mean exceptions, be won by labor, and must be fitted to human use by more labor. As soon as any number of human beings are struggling each to win from nature the material goods necessary to support life, and are carrying on this struggle side by side, certain social forces come into operation. The prime condition of this society will lie in the ratio of its numbers to the supply of materials within its reach. For the supply at any moment attainable is an exact quantity, and the number of persons who can be supplied is arithmetically limited. If the actual number present is very much less than the number who might be supported, the condition of all must be ample and easy. Freedom and facility mark all social relations under such a state of things. If the number is larger than that which can be supplied, the condition of all must be one of want and distress, or else a few must be well provided, the other being proportionately still worse off. Constraint, anxiety, possibly tyranny and repression, mark social relations. It is when the social pressure due to an unfavorable ratio of population to land becomes intense that the social forces develop increased activity. Division of labor, exchange, higher social organization, emigration, advance in the arts, spring from the necessity of contending against the harsher conditions of existence which are continually reproduced as the population surpasses the means of existence on any given status.

The society with which we have to deal does not consist of any number of men. An army is not a society. A man with his wife and his children constitutes a society, for its essential parts are all present, and the number more or less is immaterial. A certain division of labor between the sexes is imposed by nature. The family as a whole maintains itself better under an organization with division of labor than it could if the functions were shared so far as possible. From this germ the development of society goes on by the regular steps of advancement to higher organization, accompanied and sustained by improvements in the arts. The increase of population goes on according to biological laws which are capable of multiplying the species beyond any assignable limits, so that the number to be provided for steadily advances and the status of ease and abundance gives way to a status of want and constraint. Emigration is the first and simplest remedy. By winning more land the ratio of population to land is once more rendered favorable. It is to be noticed, however, that emigration is painful to all men. To the uncivilized man, to emigrate means to abandon a mass of experiences and traditions which have been won by suffering, and to go out to confront new hardships and perils. To the civilized man migration means cutting off old ties of kin and country. The earth has been peopled by man at the cost of this suffering.

On the side of the land also stands the law of the diminishing return as a limitation. More labor gets more from the land, but not proportionately more, hence, if more

Source: William Graham Sumner, Collected Essays in Political and Social Science (New York: Holt, 1885).

men are to be supported, there is need not of a proportionate increase of labor, but of a disproportionate increase of labor. The law of population, therefore, combined with the law of the diminishing returns, constitutes the great underlying condition of society. Emigration, improvements in the arts, in morals, in education, in political organization, are only stages in the struggle of man to meet these conditions, to break their force for a time, and to win room under them for ease and enlargement. Ease and enlargement mean either power to support more men on a given stage of comfort or power to advance the comfort of a given number of men. Progress is a word which has no meaning save in view of the laws of population and the diminishing return, and it is quite natural that anyone who fails to understand those laws should fall into doubt which way progress points, whether towards wealth or poverty. The laws of population and the diminishing return, in their combination, are the iron spur which has driven the race on to all which it has ever achieved, and the fact that population ever advances, yet advances against a barrier which resists more stubbornly at every step of advance, unless it is removed to a new distance by some conquest of man over nature, is the guarantee that the task of civilization will never be ended, but that the need for more energy, more intelligence, and more virtue will never cease while the race lasts. If it were possible for an increasing population to be sustained by proportionate increments of labor, we should all still be living in the original home of the race on the spontaneous products of the earth. Let him, therefore, who desires to study social phenomena first learn the transcendent importance for the whole social organization, industrial, political, and civil, of the ratio of population to land.

We have noticed that the relations involved in the struggle for existence are twofold. There is first the struggle of individuals to win the means of subsistence from nature, and secondly there is the competition of man with man in the effort to win a limited supply. The radical error of the socialists and sentimentalists is that they never distinguish these two relations from each other. They bring forward complaints which are really to be made, if at all, against the author of the universe for the hardships which man has to endure in his struggle with nature. The complaints are addressed, however, to society; that is, to other men under the same hardships. The only social element, however, is the competition of life, and when society is blamed for the ills which belong to the human lot, it is only burdening those who have successfully contended with those ills with the further task of conquering the same ills over again for somebody else. Hence liberty perishes in all socialistic schemes, and the tendency of such schemes is to the deterioration of society by burdening the good members and relieving the bad ones. The law of the survival of the fittest was not made by man and cannot be abrogated by man. We can only, by interfering with it, produce the survival of the unfittest. If a man comes forward with any grievance against the order of society so far as this is shaped by human agency, he must have patient hearing and full redress; but if he addresses a demand to society for relief from the hardships of life, he asks simply that somebody else should get his living for him. In that case he ought to be left to find out his error from hard experience.

The sentimental philosophy starts from the first principle that nothing is true which is disagreeable, and that we must not believe anything which is "shocking," no matter what the evidence may be. There are various stages of this philosophy. It touches on one side the intuitional philosophy which proves that certain things must exist by proving that man needs them, and it touches on the other side the vulgar socialism which affirms that the individual has a right to whatever he needs, and that this right is good against his fellow men. To this philosophy in all its grades the laws of population and the diminishing return have always been very distasteful. The laws which entail upon mankind an inheritance of labor cannot be acceptable to any philosophy which maintains that man comes into the world endowed with natural rights and an inheritor of freedom. It is a death-blow to any intuitional philosophy to find out, as an historical fact, what diverse thoughts, beliefs, and actions man has manifested, and it requires but little actual knowledge of human history to show that the human race has never had any ease which it did not earn, or any freedom which it did not conquer. Sociology, therefore, by the investigations which it pursues, dispels illusions about what society is or may be, and gives instead knowledge of facts which are the basis of intelligent effort by man to make the best of his circumstances on earth. Sociology, therefore, which can never accomplish anything more than to enable us to make the best of our situation, will never be able to reconcile itself with those philosophies which are trying to find out how we may arrange things so as to satisfy any ideal of society.

The competition of life has taken the form, historically, of a struggle for the possession of the soil. In the simpler states of society the possession of the soil is tribal, and the struggles take place between groups, producing the wars and feuds which constitute almost the whole of early history. On the agricultural stage the tribal or communal possession of land exists as a survival, but it gives way to private property in land whenever the community advances and the institutions are free to mold themselves. The agricultural stage breaks up tribal relations and encourages individualization. This is one of the reasons why it is such an immeasurable advance over the lower forms of civilization. It sets free individual energy, and while the social bond gains in scope and variety, it also gains in elasticity, for the solidarity of the group is broken up and the individual may work out his own ends by his own means, subject only to the social ties which lie in the natural conditions of human life. It is only on the agricultural stage that liberty as civilized men understand it exists at all. The poets and sentimentalists, untaught to recognize the grand and world-wide cooperation which is secured by the free play of individual energy under the great laws of the social order, bewail the decay of early communal relations and exalt the liberty of the primitive stages of civilization. These notions all perish at the first touch of actual investigation. The whole retrospect of human history runs downwards towards beast-like misery and slavery to the destructive forces of nature. The whole history has been one series of toilsome, painful, and bloody struggles, first to find out where we were and what were the conditions of greater ease, and then to devise means to get relief. Most of the way the motives of advance have been experience of suffering and instinct. It is only in the most recent years that science has undertaken to teach without and in advance of suffering, and as yet science has to fight so hard against tradition that its authority is only slowly winning recognition. The institutions whose growth constitutes the advance of civilization have their guarantee in the very fact that they grew and became established. They suited man's purpose better than what went before. They are all imperfect, and all carry with them incidental ills, but each came to be because it was better than what went before, and each of which has perished, perished because a better one supplanted it.

It follows once and for all that to turn back to any defunct institution or organization because existing institutions are imperfect is to turn away from advance and is to retrograde. The path of improvement lies forwards. Private property in land, for instance, is an institution which has been developed in the most direct and legitimate manner. It may give way at a future time to some other institution which will grow up by imperceptible stages out of the efforts of men to contend successfully with existing evils, but the grounds for private property in land are easily perceived, and it is safe to say that no a priori scheme of state ownership or other tenure invented en bloc by any philosopher and adopted by legislative act will ever supplant it. To talk of any such thing is to manifest a total misconception of the facts and laws which it is the province of sociology to investigate. The case is less in magnitude but scarcely less out of joint with all correct principle when it is proposed to adopt a unique tax on land, in a country where the rent of land is so low that any important tax on land exceeds it, and therefore becomes indirect, and where also political power is in the hands of small landowners, who hold, without ever having formulated it, a doctrine of absolute property in the soil such as is not held by any other landowners in the world.

Sociology must exert a most important influence on political economy. Political economy is the science which investigates the laws of the material welfare of human societies. It is not its province to teach individuals how to get rich. It is a social science. It was the first branch of sociology which was pursued by man as a science. It is not strange that when the industrial organization of society was studied apart from the organism of which it forms a part it was largely dominated over by arbitrary dogmatism, and that it should have fallen into disrepute as a mere field of opinion, and of endless wrangling about opinions for which no guarantees could be given. The rise of a school of "historical" economists is itself a sign of a struggle towards a positive and scientific study of political economy, in its due relations to other social sciences, and this sign loses none of its significance in spite of the crudeness and extravagance of the opinions of the historical economists, and in spite of their very marked tendency to fall into dogmatism and hobby-riding. Political economy is thrown over-board by all groups and persons whenever it becomes troublesome. When it got in the way of Mr. Gladstone's land-bill he relegated it, by implication, to the planet Saturn, to the great delight of all the fair-traders, protectionists, soft-money men, and others who had found it in the way of their devices. What political economy needs in order to emerge from the tangle in which it is now involved, and to win a dignified and orderly development, is to find its field and its relations to other sciences fairly defined within the wider scope of sociology. Its laws will then take their place not as arbitrary or broken fragments, but in due relation to other laws. Those laws will win proof and establishment from this relation.

For instance, we have plenty of books, some of them by able writers, in which the old-fashioned Malthusian doctrine of population and the Ricardian law of rent are disputed because emigration, advance in the arts, etc., can offset the action of those laws or because those laws are not seen in action in the United States. Obviously no such objections ever could have been raised if the laws in question had been understood or had been put in their proper bearings. The Malthusian law of population and the Ricardian law of rent are cases in which by rare and most admirable acumen powerful thinkers perceived two great laws in particular phases of their action. With wider information it now appears that the law of population breaks the barriers of Malthus' narrower formulae and appears as a great law of biology. The Ricardian law of rent is only a particular application of one of the great conditions of production. We have before us not special dogmas of political economy, but facts of the widest significance for the whole social development of the race. To object that these facts may be set aside by migration or advance in the arts is nothing to the purpose, for this is only altering the constants in the equation, which does not alter the form of the curve, but only its position relatively to some standard line. Furthermore, the laws themselves indicate that they have a maximum point for any society, or any given stage of the arts, and a condition of under-population, or of an extractive industry below its maximum, is just as consistent with the law as a condition of over-population and increasing distress. Hence inferences as to the law of population drawn from the status of an under-populated country are sure to be fallacious. In like manner arguments drawn from American phenomena in regard to rent and wages, when rent and wages are as yet only very imperfectly developed here, lead to erroneous conclusions. It only illustrates the unsatisfactory condition of political economy, and the want of strong criticism in it, that such arguments can find admission to its discussions and disturb its growth.

It is to the pursuit of sociology and the study of the industrial organization in combination with the other organizations of society that we must look for the more fruitful development of political economy. We are already in such a position with sociology that a person who has gained what we now possess of that science will bring to bear upon economic problems a sounder judgment and a more correct conception of all social relations than a person who may have read a library of the existing treatises on political economy. The essential elements of political economy are only corollaries or special cases of sociological principles. One who has command of the law of the conservation of energy as it manifests itself in society is armed at once against socialism, protectionism, paper money, and a score of other economic fallacies. The sociological view of political economy also includes whatever is sound in the dogmas of the "historical school" and furnishes what that school is apparently groping after.

As an illustration of the light which sociology throws on a great number of political and social phenomena which are constantly misconstrued, we may notice the differences in the industrial, political, and civil organizations which are produced all along at different stages of the ratio of population to land.

When a country is under-populated newcomers are not competitors, but assistants. If more come they may produce not only new quotas, but a surplus besides, to be divided between themselves and all who were present before. In such a state of things land is abundant and cheap. The possession of it confers no power or privilege. No one will work for another for wages when he can take up new land and be his own master. Hence it will pay no one to own more land than he can cultivate by his own labor, or with such aid as his own family supplies. Hence, again, land bears little or no rent; there will be no landlords living on rent and no laborers living on wages, but only a middle class of yeoman farmers. All are substantially on an equality, and democracy becomes the political form, because this is the only state of society in which the dogmatic assumption of equality, on which democracy is based, is realized as a fact. The same effects are powerfully reenforced by other facts. In a new and under-populated country the industries which are most profitable are the extractive industries. The characteristic of these, with the exception of some kinds of mining, is that they call for only a low organization of labor and small amount of capital. Hence they allow the workman to become speedily his own master, and they educate him to freedom, independence, and self-reliance. At the same time, the social groups being only vaguely marked off from each other, it is easy to pass from one class of occupations, and consequently from one social grade, to another. Finally, under the same circumstances education, skill, and superior training have but inferior value compared with what they have in densely populated countries. The advantages lie, in an under-populated country, with the coarser, unskilled, manual occupations, and not with the highest developments of science, literature, and art.

If now we turn for comparison to cases of over-population we see that the struggle for existence and the competition of life are intense where the pressure of population is great. This competition draws out the highest achievements. It makes the advantages of capital, education, talent, skill, and training tell to the utmost. It draws out the social scale upwards and downwards to great extremes and produces aristocratic social organizations in spite of all dogmas of equality. Landlords, tenants (i.e., capitalist employers), and laborers are the three primary divisions of any aristocratic order, and they are sure to be developed whenever land bears rent and whenever tillage requires the application of large capital. At the same time liberty has to undergo curtailment. A man who has a square mile to himself can easily do as he likes, but a man who walks Broadway at noon or lives in a tenement-house finds his power to do as he likes limited by scores of considerations for the rights and feelings of his fellowmen. Furthermore, organization with subordination and discipline is essential in order that the society as a whole may win a support from the land. In an over-populated country the extremes of wealth and luxury are presented side by side with the extremes of poverty and distress. They are equally the products of an intense social pressure. The achievements of power are highest, the rewards of prudence, energy, enterprise, foresight, sagacity, and all other industrial virtues is greatest; on the other hand, the penalties of folly, weakness, error, and vice are most terrible. Pauperism, prostitution, and crime are the attendants of a state of society in which science, art, and literature reach their highest developments. Now it is evident that over-population and under-population are only relative terms. Hence as time goes on any under-populated nation is surely moving forward towards the other status, and is speedily losing its natural advantages which are absolute, and also that relative advantage which belongs to it if it is in neighborly relations with nations of dense population and high civilization; viz., the chance to borrow and assimilate from them the products, in arts and science, of high civilization without enduring the penalties of intense social pressure.

We have seen that if we should try by any measures of arbitrary interference and assistance to relieve the victims of social pressure from the calamity of their position we should only offer premiums to folly and vice and extend them further. We have also seen that we must go forward and meet our problems. We cannot escape them by running away. If then it be asked what the wit and effort of man can do to struggle with the problems offered by social pressure, the answer is that he can do only what his instinct has correctly and surely led him to do without any artificial social organization of any kind, and that is, by improvements in the arts, in science, in morals, in political institutions, to widen and strengthen the power of man over nature. The task of dealing with social ills is not a new task. People set about it and discuss it as if the human race had hitherto neglected it, and as if the solution of the problem was to be something new in form and substance, different from the solution of all problems which have hitherto engaged human effort. In truth, the human race has never done anything else but struggle with the problem of social welfare. That struggle constitutes history, or the life of the human race on earth. That struggle embraces all minor problems which occupy attention here, save those of religion, which reaches beyond this world and finds it objects beyond this life. Every successful effort to widen the power of man over nature is a real victory over poverty, vice, and misery, taking things in general and in the long run. It would be hard to find a single instance of a direct assault by positive effort upon poverty, vice, and misery which has not either failed or, if it has not failed directly and entirely, has not entailed other evils greater than the one which it removed. The only two things which really tell on the welfare of man on earth are hard work and self-denial (in technical language, labor and capital), and these tell most when they are brought to bear directly upon the effort to earn an honest living, to accumulate capital, and to bring up a family of children to be industrious and self-denying in their turn. I repeat that this is the way to work for the welfare of man on earth; and what I mean to say is that the common notion that when we are going to work for the social welfare of man we must adopt a great dogma, organize for the realization of some great scheme, have before us an abstract ideal, or otherwise do anything but live honest and industrious lives, is a great mistake. From the standpoint of the sociologist pessimism and optimism are alike impertinent. To be an optimist one must forget the frightful sanctions which are attached to the laws of right living. To be a pessimist one must overlook the education and growth which are the product of effort and self-denial. In either case one is passing judgment on what is inevitably fixed, and on which the approval or condemnation of man can produce no effect. The facts and laws are, once and for all, so, and for us men that is the end of the matter. The only persons for whom there would be any sense in the question whether life is worth living are primarily the yet unborn children, and secondarily the persons who are proposing to found families. For these latter the question would take a somewhat modified form: Will life be worth living for children born of me? This question is, unfortunately, not put to themselves by the appropriate persons as it would be if they had been taught sociology. The sociologist is often asked if he wants to kill off certain classes of troublesome and burdensome persons. No such inference follows from any sound sociological doctrine, but it is allowed to infer, as to a great many persons and classes, that it would have been better for society, and would have involved no pain to them, if they had never been born.

In further illustration of the interpretation which sociology offers of phenomena which are often obscure, we may note the world-wide effects of the advances in the arts and sciences which have been made during the last hundred years. These improvements have especially affected transportation and communication; that is, they have lessened the obstacles of time and space which separate the groups of mankind from each other and have tended to make the whole human race a single unit. The distinction between over-populated and under-populated countries loses its sharpness, and all are brought to an average. Every person who migrates from Europe to America affects the comparative status of the two continents. He lessens the pressure in the country he leaves and increases it in the country to which he goes. If he goes to Minnesota and raises wheat there, which is carried back to the country he left as cheap food for those who have not emigrated, it is evident that the bearing upon social pressure is twofold. It is evident, also, that the problem of social pressure can no longer be correctly studied if the view is confined either to the country of immigration or the country of emigration, but that it must embrace both. It is easy to see, therefore, that the ratio of population to land with which we have to deal is only in peculiar and limited cases that ratio as it exists in England, Germany, or the United States. It is the ratio as it exists in the civilized world, and every year that passes, as our improved arts break down the barriers between different parts of the earth, brings us nearer to the state of things where all the population of Europe, America, Australasia, and South Africa must be considered in relation to all the land of the same territories, for all that territory will be available for all that population, no matter what the proportion may be in which the population is distributed over the various portions of the territory. The British Islands may become one great manufacturing city. Minnesota, Texas, and Australia may not have five persons to the square mile. Yet all will eat the meat of Texas and the wheat of Minnesota and wear the wool of Australia manufactured on the looms of England. That all will enjoy the maximum of food and raiment under that state of things is as clear as anything possibly can be which is not yet an accomplished fact. We are working towards it by all our instincts of profit and improvement. The greatest obstacles are those which come from prejudices, traditions, and dogmas, which are held independently of any observation of facts or any correct reasoning, and which set the right hand working against the left. For instance, the Mississippi Valley was, a century ago, as unavailable to support the population of France and Germany as if it had been in the moon. The Mississippi Valley is now nearer to France and Germany than the British Islands were a century ago, reckoning distance by the only true standard; viz., difficulty of communication. It is a fair way of stating it to say that the improvements in transportation of the last fifty years have added to France and Germany respectively a tract of land of the very highest fertility, equal in area to the territory of those states, and available for the support of their population. The public men of those countries are now declaring that this is a calamity, and are devising means to counteract it.

The social and political effects of the improvements which have been made must be very great. It follows from what we have said about the effects of intense social pressure and high competition that the effect of thus bringing to bear on the great centers of population the new land of outlying countries must be to relieve the pressure in the oldest countries and at the densest centers. Then the extremes of wealth and poverty, culture and brutality, will be contracted and there will follow a general tendency towards an average equality which, however, must be understood only within very broad limits. Such is no doubt the meaning of the general tendency towards equality, the decline of aristocratic institutions, the rise of the proletariat, and the ambitious expansion, in short, which is characteristic of modern civilized society. It would lead me too far to follow out of this line of speculation as to the future, but two things ought to be noticed in passing. (1) There are important offsets to the brilliant promise which there is for mankind in a period during which, for the whole civilized world, there will be a wide margin of ease between the existing population and the supporting power of the available land. These offsets consist in the effects of ignorance, error, and folly—the same forces which have always robbed mankind of half what they might have enjoyed on earth. Extravagant governments, abuses of public credit, wasteful taxation, legislative monopolies and special privileges, juggling with currency, restrictions on trade, wasteful armaments on land and sea, and other follies in economy and statecraft, are capable of wasting and nullifying all the gains of civilization. (2) The old classical civilization fell under an irruption of barbarians from without. It is possible that our new civilization may perish by an explosion from within. The sentimentalists have been preaching for a century notions of rights and equality, of the dignity, wisdom, and power of the proletariat, which have filled the minds of ignorant men with impossible dreams. The thirst for luxurious enjoyment has taken possession of us all. It is the dark side of the power to foresee a possible future good with such distinctness as to make it a motive of energy and persevering industry—a power which is distinctly modern. Now the thirst for luxurious enjoyment, when brought into connection with the notions of rights, of power, and of equality, and dissociated from the notions of industry and economy, produces the notion that a man is robbed of his rights if he has not everything that he wants, and that he is deprived of equality if he sees anyone have more than he has, and that he is a fool if, having the power of the State in his hands, he allows this state of things to last. Then we have socialism, communism, and nihilism; and the fairest conquests of civilization, with all their promise of solid good to man, on the sole conditions of virtue and wisdom, may be scattered to the winds in a war of classes, or trampled underfoot by a mob which can only hate what it cannot enjoy.

It must be confessed that sociology is yet in a tentative and inchoate state. All that we can affirm with certainty is that social phenomena are subject to law, and that the natural laws of the social order are in their entire character like the laws of physics. We can draw in grand outline the field of sociology and foresee the shape that it will take and the relations it will bear to other sciences. We can also already find the standpoint which it will occupy, and, if a figure may be allowed, although we still look over a wide landscape largely enveloped in mist, we can see where the mist lies and define the general features of the landscape, subject to further corrections.... We are face to face with an issue no less grand than this: Shall we, in our general social policy, pursue the effort to realize more completely that constitutional liberty for which we have been struggling throughout modern history, or shall we return to the mediaeval device of functionaries to regulate procedure and to adjust interests? Shall we try to connect with liberty an equal and appropriate responsibility as its essential complement and corrective, so that a man who gets his own way shall accept his own consequences, or shall we yield to the sentimentalism which, after preaching an unlimited liberty, robs those who have been wise out of pity for those who have been foolish? Shall we accept the inequalities which follow upon free competition as the definition of justice, or shall we suppress free competition in the interest of equality and to satisfy a baseless dogma of justice? Shall we try to solve the social entanglements which arise in a society where social ties are constantly becoming more numerous and more subtle, and where contract has only partly superseded custom and status, by returning to the latter, only hastening a more complete development of the former? These certainly are practical questions, and their scope is such that they embrace a great number of minor questions which are before us and which are coming up. It is to the science of society, which will derive true conceptions of society from the facts and laws of the social order, studied without prejudice or bias of any sort, that we must look for the correct answer to these questions. By this observation the field of sociology and the work which it is to do for society are sufficiently defined.

CHARLES AUGUSTUS BRIGGS

Selection from *Biblical Study*
(1883)

If an apparent consequence of the Darwinian revolution in science was to embed human beings more deeply into nature—one of many species that come and go through natural processes—an apparent consequence of the simultaneous revolution in biblical scholarship was to embed the Bible more deeply into culture, making it, in effect, just one of many books created by human beings under particular historical circumstances. Biblical scholars in Germany, especially, but also in France, Britain, and the United States studied the various books of the Bible in their original languages, taking account of archaeological and linguistic discoveries that enabled these scholars to identify more and more precisely just who wrote what segments of which scriptures, when, and why. The scholars who worked in this manner were almost all devout men of faith, who insisted on the reality of the divine inspiration of the ancient canon, but their theology was more liberal than that of most of the average Christians who populated the churches of the United States. Tensions developed between the liberal scholars and their constituents, some of whom found threatening to their faith the idea, for example, that the book of Isaiah had been written by several different men, living generations if not centuries apart from one another.

The Presbyterian scholar Charles Augustus Briggs (1841–1913) of New York City's Union Theological Seminary was the most widely known of these "higher critics." The historical study of the scriptures was commonly called "the higher criticism." Briggs's *Biblical Study*, from which a selection is reprinted here, exemplified both the confident attitude and the methodological orientation of his cohort of seminary professors. His extended discussion of "inerrancy" spoke to the widespread concern that if the scriptures contained factual errors, these writings surely could not be the word of God. Yet for all of Briggs's efforts to show that understanding the real history of something did not diminish its religious value, conservatives were sufficiently troubled to bring Briggs to trial within the Presbyterian Church for heresy in 1891.

The classic study of the liberalization of American Protestantism is William R. Hutchison, *The Modernist Impulse in American Protestantism* (Cambridge, Mass., 1976). A more recent study is Gray Dorrien, *The Making of American Liberal Theology*, vol. 1 (Grand Rapids, Mich., 2003). For a more detailed, account of Briggs's career, see Mark S. Massa, *Charles Augustus Briggs and the Crisis of Historical Criticism* (Minneapolis, 1990). Briggs's approach to the study of Christian scripture can be contrasted to that of Charles Hodge of the Princeton Theological Seminary, a much more conservative scholar, dubious about the utility of historical approaches, whose work and legacy are the subject of John W. Stewart and James H. Moorehead, eds., *Charles Hodge: A Critical Appraisal of His Life and Work* (Grand Rapids, Mich., 2002). The stature of Briggs and Hodge in nineteenth-century America can remind us of the centrality of the theological seminary to American intellectual life prior to the triumph of modern universities in the latter decades of that century.

Recent critical theories arise and work as did their predecessors, in the various departments of exegetical theology. Here is their strength, that they antagonize scholastic dogma
with the Bible itself, and appeal from *school* theology to *biblical* theology. Unless traditional theories of inspiration can vindicate themselves on Bible grounds, meet the critics,
and overcome them in fair conflict, in the sacred fields of the Divine Word, sooner or
later traditional theories will be driven from the field. It will not do to antagonize critical
theories of the Bible with traditional theories of the Bible, for the critic appeals to history
against tradition, to an array of facts against so-called inferences, to the laws of probation
against dogmatic assertion, to the Divine Spirit speaking in the Scriptures against external authority. History, facts, truth, the laws of thought, are all divine products, and most
consistent with the Divine Word, and they will surely prevail.

It is significant that the great majority of professional biblical scholars in the various
universities and theological halls of the world, embracing those of the greatest learning,
industry, and piety, demand a revision of traditional theories of the Bible, on account of
a large induction of new facts from the Bible and history. These critics must be met with
argument and candid reasoning as to these facts and their interpretation, and cannot be
overcome by mere cries of alarm for the Church and the Bible which, in their last analysis,
usually amount to nothing more than peril to certain favorite views. What peril can come
to the Scriptures from a more profound critical study of them? The peril is to scholastic
dogmas and to tradition. But what then are we contending for as evangelical men, for the
faith of the Scriptures, the faith of Wittenberg, of Geneva, and of Westminster, or for the
faith of the Reformed scholastics, and the faith of certain schools of theology and their
chiefs? We must recognize in order to meet this issue, upon which everything depends,
that biblical critics cannot afford to carry the load of the school theology into the conflicts
of the nineteenth century, but must strip to the symbols for a conflict with rationalism
and materialism; and we should not fear as evangelical biblical scholars to accept the challenge of our adversaries and go forth from the breastworks of our symbols to meet them in
fair and honorable warfare in open field with the biblical material itself on the principles
of induction. The sword of the Spirit alone will conquer in this warfare. Are Christian
men afraid to put it to the test? For this is a conflict after all between true criticism and
false criticism; between the criticism which is the product of the evangelical spirit of
the Reformation, and critical principles that are the product of deism and rationalism.
Evangelical criticism has been marching from conquest to conquest, though far too often
at a sad disadvantage, like a storming party who have sallied forth from their breastworks
to attack the trenches of the enemy, finding in the hot encounter that the severest fire
and gravest peril are from the misdirected batteries of their own line. Shall evangelical
criticism in searching the Scriptures be permitted to struggle unhindered with rationalistic criticism, or must it protect itself also from scholastic dogmatism? We do not deny
the right of dogmatism and the a priori method, nor the worth of tradition, within their
proper spheres; but we maintain the equal right of criticism and the inductive method,
and their far greater importance in the acquisition of true and reliable knowledge. If criticism and dogmatism are harnessed together, a span of twin steeds, they will draw the car
of theology rapidly toward its highest ideal; but pulling in opposite directions, especially
in the present crisis, they will tear it to pieces. . . .

Source: Charles Augustus Briggs, *Biblical Study* (New York, 1883), 102–4, 240–47.

That there are errors in the present text of our Bible, and inconsistencies, it seems to us vain to deny. We have come upon some of them in the course of our investigations. There are chronological, geographical, and other circumstantial inconsistencies and errors which we should not hesitate to acknowledge. These errors arise in the department of exegesis more than in higher criticism. It does not follow, however, that circumstantial, incidental errors, such as might arise from the inadvertence or lack of information of an author, are any impeachment of his credibility. If we distinguish between revelation and inspiration, and yet insist upon inerrancy with reference to the latter as well as the former, we virtually do away with the distinction; for no mere man can escape altogether human errors unless divine revelation set even the most familiar things in a new and infallible light, and also so control him that he cannot make a slip of the eye or the hand, a fault in the imagination, in conception, in reasoning, in rhetorical figure, or in grammatical expression; and indeed so raise him above his fellows that he shall see through all their errors in science and philosophy as well as theology, and anticipate the discoveries in all branches of knowledge by thousands of years. Errors of inadvertence in minor details, where the author's position and character are well known, do not destroy his credibility as a witness in any literature or any court of justice. It is not to be presumed that divine inspiration lifted the author above his age any more than was necessary to convey the divine revelation and the divine instruction with infallible certainty to mankind. We have to take into account the extent of the author's human knowledge, his point of view and type of thought, his methods of reasoning and illustration. The question of credibility is to be distinguished from infallibility. The form is credible, the substance alone is infallible. It is claimed by some divines that the *inerrancy* of Scripture is essential to the inspiration of the Scriptures, and that "a proved error in Scripture contradicts not only our doctrine, but the Scripture claims, and therefore its inspiration in making those claims." But *inerrancy* is neither a scriptural nor a symbolical nor a historical term in connection with the subject of Inspiration. These representations of the doctrine of inspiration have no support in the symbols or faith of the Reformation, or in the Westminster Confession, or in the Scriptures. We hold with our revered instructor, the late Henry B. Smith, to *plenary* inspiration rather than verbal. It may be as it is stated. "It (plenary inspiration) is in itself indefinite, and its use contributes nothing, either to the precision or the emphasis of the definition"; but this is as far as the Scriptures or the symbols of faith warrant us in going; it is as far as it is at all safe in the present juncture to advance in definition. *Verbal* inspiration is doubtless a more precise and emphatic definition than *plenary* inspiration; but this very emphasis and precision imperil the doctrine of inspiration itself by bringing it into conflict with a vast array of objections along the whole line of Scripture and history, which must be met and overcome in incessant warfare, where both sides may count on doubtful victories, but where the weak, ignorant, and hesitating, stumble and fall into divers temptations, and may make shipwreck of their faith. From the point of view of biblical criticism, we are not prepared to admit errors in the Scriptures in the original autographs, until they shall be proven. Very many of those alleged have already received sufficient or plausible explanation; others are in dispute between truth-seeking scholars, and satisfactory explanations may hereafter be given. New difficulties are constantly arising and being overcome. It is difficult on the one side to demonstrate an error, as it is on the other side to demonstrate that the Scriptures must be absolutely errorless. It is a question of fact to which all theories and doctrines must yield. It cannot be determined by a priori definitions and statements on either side. Indeed the original autographs have been lost for ages and can never be recovered. How can we determine whether they were absolutely errorless or not? To assume that it must be so, as a deduction from the theory of verbal inspiration, is to beg the whole question.

In the meanwhile we confidently affirm that the doctrine of inspiration as stated in the symbols of faith will maintain its integrity in spite of any circumstantial errors that may be admitted or proved in the Scriptures, so long as these errors do not directly or indirectly disturb the infallibility of its matters of faith or of the historic events and institutions with which they are inseparably united.

Higher criticism comes into conflict with the authority of Scripture when it finds that its statements are not authoritative and its revelations are not credible. If the credibility of a book is impeached, its divine authority and inspiration are also impeached. But to destroy his credibility something more must be presented than trivial matters and minute details that do not affect the author's scope of argument or his religious instructions. We hold that it is an unsafe position to assume, that we must first prove the credibility, inerrancy, and infallibility of a book ere we accept its authority. If inquirers waited until all the supposed errors in our canonical books were satisfactorily explained they would never accept the Bible as a divine revelation. To press the critics to this dilemma, *inerrancy* or *uninspired,* might catch the critics on one of the horns if they were not critical enough to detect the fallacy and escape, but it would be more likely to catch the people, who know nothing of criticism, and so undermine and destroy their faith.

The higher criticism has already strengthened the credibility of Scripture. It has studied the human features of the Bible and learned the wondrous variety of form and color assumed by the divine revelation. Many of the supposed inconsistencies have been found to be different modes of representing the same thing, complementary to one another and combining to give a fuller representation than any one mode could ever have given, as the two sides of the stereoscopic view give a representation superior to that of the ordinary photograph. The unity of statement found in the midst of such wondrous variety of detail in form and color is vastly more convincing than a unity of mere coincidence such as the older harmonists sought to obtain by stretching and straining the Scriptures on the procrustean bed of their hair-splitting scholasticism. Many of the supposed inconsistencies have been found to arise from different stages of divine revelation, in the earlier of which God condescended to the weakness and the ignorance of men, and gave to them the knowledge that they could appropriate, and held up to them ideals that they could understand as to their essence if not in all their details. The earlier are shadows and types, crude and imperfect representations of better things to follow. Many of the supposed inconsistencies result from the popular and unscientific language of the Bible, thus approaching the people of God in different ages in concrete forms and avoiding the abstract. The inconsistencies have resulted from the scholastic abstractions of those who would use the Bible as a text-book, but they do not exist in the concrete of the Bible itself. Many of the supposed inconsistencies arise from a different method of logic and rhetoric in the Oriental writers and the attempt of modern scholars to measure them by Occidental methods. Many of the inconsistencies result from the neglect to appreciate the poetic and imaginative element in the Bible and a lack of æsthetic sense on the part of its interpreters. The higher criticism has already removed a large number of difficulties and will remove many more when it has become a more common study among scholars....

The literary study of the Bible is appropriately called higher criticism to distinguish it from lower criticism which devotes itself to the study of original texts and versions. There are few who have the patience, the persistence, the life-long industry in the examination of the minute details that make up the field of the lower or textual criticism. But the higher criticism is more attractive. It has to do with literary forms and styles and models. It appeals to the imagination and the aesthetic taste as well as to the logical faculty. It kindles the enthusiasm of the young. It will more and more enlist the attention of men of culture and the general public. It is the most inviting and fruitful field of biblical study in our day. Many who are engaged in it are rationalistic and unbelieving, and they are using it with disastrous effect upon the Scriptures and the orthodox faith. There is also a prejudice in some quarters against these studies and an apprehension as to the results. This prejudice is unreasonable. This apprehension is to be deprecated. It is impossible to prevent discussion. The church is challenged to meet the issue. It is a call of Providence to conflict and to the triumph of evangelical truth. The Divine Word will vindicate itself in all its parts. These are not the times for negligent Elis or timorous and presumptuous Uzzahs. Brave Samuels and ardent Davids who fear not to employ new methods and engage in new enterprises and adapt themselves to altered situations, will overcome the Philistines with their own weapons. The higher criticism has rent the crust, with which rabbinical tradition and Christian scholasticism have encased the Old Testament, overlaying the poetic and prophetic elements with the legal and the ritual. Younger biblical scholars have caught glimpses of the beauty and glory of biblical literature. The Old Testament is studied as never before in the Christian church. It is beginning to exert its charming influence upon ministers and people. Christian theology and Christian life will ere long be enriched by it. God's blessing is in it to those who have the Christian wisdom to recognize and the grace to receive and employ it.

LESTER FRANK WARD

"Mind as a Social Factor"
(1884)

Lester Frank Ward (1841–1913) yielded to no one, including his great rival William Graham Sumner, in the degree of his devotion to science in general and to the particular task of developing a science of society. Ward associated such a science not with obedience to facts, but with the authority of human beings over their own destiny. In the essay of 1884 that follows, Ward insisted on the creative powers of the human mind. These powers, Ward declared, were ignored by the conservative laissez-faire versions of social science that warned against meddling with nature. The order of nature is indeed dominated by natural selection, Ward granted, but our own species represents a new stage of evolution. Human beings make progress by protecting the weak rather than by a relentless competition in which only the fit survive; it is perfectly natural for human beings—with their distinctive mental powers—to cooperate, to reduce competition, and to alter through invention the setting in which they live. Let human beings be understood as active, Ward proposed, and the natural world as passive. Ward argued against the treating as "natural" of social arrangements that he—and most twentieth-century social theorists after him—understood to be contingent, changeable products of human action.

A writer of enormous energy, Ward left an imposing shelf of books including *Dynamic Sociology,* 2 vols. (New York, 1883), *Pure Sociology* (New York, 1903), *Applied Sociology* (New York, 1906), and *Glimpses of the Cosmos,* 6 vols. (New York, 1913).

For an analysis of Ward that emphasizes his commitment to secular science, see Robert C. Bannister, *Sociology and Scientism: The American Quest for Objectivity* (Chapel Hill, 1987), 13–14. See also Gillis J. Harp, "Lester Ward: Comtean Whig," *Historical Reflections,* 15 (1988), 523–42. A recent study of his life and career is Edward C. Rafferty, *Apostle of Human Progress: Lester Frank Ward and American Political Thought* (Latham, Md., 2003).

After many centuries of exclusive study of the soul the thinkers of the world turned their attention for some centuries more to the study of the intellect. During all this time, the true influence of mind as a social factor was left quite out of view. At last there rose up the scientific philosophy which essayed to explain the nature of mind. Its dependence upon organisation in general and upon brain in particular was proved by scientific experimentation, and the domain of metaphysics became that of psychology. Mind was shown to be a function of body and psychology became a department of biology. Man has now taken his true position in the animal world as a product of development. Brain, which alone raises him above other animals, has been developed in the same manner as the other anatomical characters. The brain is the organ of the mind, its physical seat and cause. Mind is therefore a natural product of evolution, and its achievements are to be classed and studied along with all other natural phenomena. Such is the scientific conception of mind.

The modern scientist places all objects in the midst of an infinite series of antecedents and consequents. Organic forms as well as inorganic must take their places in this series—the animal no less than the plant, the man no less than the beast. Mind itself is a link of this endless chain. Its activities consist in the transmission of the properties of its antecedents to its consequents. The quantity of force in the universe is constant. No power can increase or diminish it. All attempts on the part of the creatures of this constant and unchangeable force to modify its normal effects are not less vain because such creatures happen to have acquired the faculty of observing the changes going on in nature.

The protracted study of nature's processes leads to admiration of them, and the belief has become prevalent that they are not only unalterable but also in some way necessarily beneficent. Nature has made great progress in developing organised beings and is assumed to be still working in this direction. The natural method is always the true method, and to find it out is the aim of all scientific investigation. Out of this earnest and laudable strife to discover the true method of nature has grown, logically enough, the assumption that when found it must be something of great worth. It is commonly supposed that the highest wisdom of man is to learn and then to follow the ways of nature. Those dissatisfied people who would improve upon the natural course of events are rebuked as meddlers with the unalterable. Their systems are declared Utopian, their laws *bruta fulmina*. All efforts in this direction are held to be trifling and are stigmatised as so many ignorant attempts to nullify the immutable laws of nature.

This general mode of reasoning is carried into all departments of human life.

In government every attempt to improve the condition of the state is condemned and denounced. Curiously enough, here the claim is illogically made that such measures are harmful. In fact, unfortunately for the whole theory, they have often been proved to be so. But this, of course, proves their efficacy. This glaring inconsistency is, however, overlooked, and government is implored, not to adopt wise and successful measures, but to refrain from adopting any, to let society alone, and thus allow the laws of nature to work out their beneficent results.

In commerce and trade absolute freedom is insisted upon. Free trade is the watchword of this entire school. The laws of trade, they maintain, are natural laws. As such they must be better than any human rules. And here again we find them insisting that regulation is injurious to trade, although it is at the same time declared to be nugatory.

Source: Mind, 4 (October 1884), 563–73.

In social affairs these doctrines are carried to their extreme logical outcome. The laws of nature as they manifest themselves in society must be left wholly untouched. The passions of men will neutralise and regulate themselves. Competition can be depended upon to correct abuses. The seller must be allowed to exaggerate and misstate the nature of his wares. This has the effect to sharpen the wits of the buyer, and this develops the brain. To dilute, adulterate, or even poison food and medicine for personal gain is not objectionable, since the destruction thereby of a few unwary consumers only proves their unfitness to survive in society. As in general commerce, so in private business, competition must be free. If a dealer, by selling at a loss, can hold out until all his competitors have been driven from the field, in order then to recover more than his losses by the monopoly he will enjoy, his right to do this must not be questioned. It is under such conditions and by the aid of such discipline that man and society have developed.

Education must be that of experience. Knowledge must be gained by efforts to avoid the consequences of ignorance already felt. The intellectual development of the child must be an epitome of that of the race. It is thus only that nature operates, and surely nature is greater and wiser than man.

All schemes of social reform are unscientific. Public charities tend to bolster up unworthy elements in society that nature has declared unfit to survive. Temperance reforms tend only to abridge individual liberty—for even the liberty to destroy one's self should be respected. Philanthropy is zeal without knowledge, while humanitarianism is fanaticism.

This general class of views antedated by many years the publication by Spencer and Darwin of their formulated doctrines of the "survival of the fittest" and "natural selection." But it cannot be denied that these doctrines, supported as they were by facts fresh from nature, have greatly strengthened this habit of thought. Nature's method is now much better known than formerly, and it is now well understood that an utterly soulless competition constitutes its fundamental characteristic. Surely man cannot go astray in following in the footsteps of nature. Let him learn from the animal world. He has descended from some of the humble stocks which he is now studying. Nature's plan has raised him from the condition of a beast to that of a rational being. It has created and developed society and civilisation. Unless tampered with by "reformers" all the operations of society would be competitive. Competition is the law of nature out of which progress results. Sociology, as its founder insisted, must be based on biology, and the true sociologist must understand this biologic law. Those who propose to apply methods to society which are opposed to the methods of nature are supposed to be ignorant of these fundamental truths are called empiricists, "meddlers," and "tinkers."

Such, I say, is the tenor and tendency of modern scientific thought. I do not say that all scientific men hold these views. I merely maintain that leading ones have formulated and inculcated them as natural deductions from the established facts of science, and that the public mind is rapidly assimilating them, while scarcely any attempts are being made to check their advance.[1]

Is there any way of answering these arguments? Can the *laissez faire* doctrine be successfully met? That all attempts to do this have been timidly made cannot be denied.

---

1.   The social philosophy of Mr. Herbert Spencer possesses this tone throughout, and his disciples, particularly in America, delight in going even farther than their master. The most extreme statement of the *laissez faire* doctrine known to me is that of Prof. W. G. Sumner, in his recent work *Social Classes.*

That these have been few and feeble is equally certain. While there has existed in the minds of many rational persons a vague sense of some hidden fallacy in all this reasoning none have felt competent to formulate their objections with sufficient clearness and force to warrant pitting them against the resistless stream of concurrent science and philosophy of the nineteenth century. There has, however, been developing of late a more or less marked apprehension with regard to the possible consequences of this mode of thought. The feeling is distinct in the best minds, and to a large extent in the public mind that the tendency of modern ideas is nihilistic. It is clear that if they become universally accepted they must work stagnation in society. The *laissez faire* doctrine is a gospel of inaction, the scientific creed is struck with sterility, the policy of resigning all into the hands of Nature is a surrender.

But this recognition is by no means proof that the prevalent opinions are false. At best it can only suggest this on the ground that true doctrines should be progressive. But this would be a *petitio principii*. Nature is not optimistic, still less anthropocentric. For aught we know, the laws of nature are such as make a recognition of strict scientific truth a positive barrier to social advancement. The argument we have been considering must be refuted, if at all, by legitimate counter-argument.

The present attempt to meet some parts of this argument is made in full consciousness of its strength as a factor in modern thought and with due deference to the great names that stand committed to it. The scientific facts which its defenders have brought to its support are, in the main, incontestable. To answer by denying these would be to abjure science and deserve contempt. The method of nature has been correctly interpreted. The doctrines of the survival of the fittest and natural selection are perfectly true doctrines. The law of competition is the fundamental law. It is unquestionably true that progress, not only in primary organic development, but also in society, has resulted from the action of this law.

After conceding all this, the attempt, notwithstanding, to stem the tide of modern scientific thought must, indeed, seem a hopeless one. At the outset it must be frankly acknowledged that if the current views are unsound the fault is not chargeable to science. If there is any defect it must lie in the inferences drawn from the facts and not in the facts themselves. To what extent, then, is the *laissez faire* doctrine, as defined and popularly accepted, an inference? If the method of nature is correctly formulated by that doctrine, wherein lies the fallacy when it is applied to man and to society?

In order to grapple at once with the whole problem let me answer these questions by the open charge that the modern scientific philosophers fail to recognise the true value of the *psychic factor.* Just as the metaphysicians lost their bearings by an empty worship of mind and made philosophy a plaything, so the modern evolutionists have missed their mark by degrading mind to a level with mechanical force. They seem thus about to fling away the grand results that the doctrine of evolution cannot otherwise fail to achieve. Far be it from me to appeal to the prejudices of the enemies of science by casting opprobrium upon scientific deductions, but when I consider the tendencies which are now so unmistakable, and which are so certainly the consequence of the protracted study, on the part of leading scientists, of the unquestionable methods of nature, I think I can, though holding precisely opposite opinions, fully sympathise with Carlyle in characterising the philosophy of evolution as a "gospel of dirt."

But I need not longer dwell upon the blighting influence of this construction of the known laws of nature. Let us approach the kernel of the problem.

The *laissez faire* doctrine fails to recognise that, in the development of mind, a virtually *new power* was introduced into the world. To say that this has been done is no startling announcement. It is no more than has taken place many times in the course of the evolution of living and feeling beings out of the tenuous nebulae of space. For, while it is true that nature makes no leaps, while, so long as we consider their beginning, all the great steps in evolution are due to minute increments repeated through vast periods, still, when we survey the whole field, as we must do to comprehend the scheme, and contrast the extremes, we find that nature has been making a series of enormous strides, and reaching from one plane of development to another. It is these independent achievements of evolution that the true philosopher must study.

Not to mention the great steps in the cosmical history of the solar system and of the earth, we must regard the evolution of protoplasm, the "physical basis of life," as one of those gigantic strides which thenceforth completely revolutionised the surface of our planet. The development of the cell as the unit of organisation was another such stride. The origin of vertebrate life introduced a new element, and the birth of man wrought still another transformation. These are only a few of nature's revolutions. Many more will suggest themselves. And although, in no single one of these cases can it be said at what exact point the new essence commenced to exist, although the development of all these several expressions of Nature's method of concentrating her hitherto diffused forces was accomplished through an unbroken series of minute transitional increments continued through eons of time, still, it is not a whit less true that each of these grand products of evolution, when at length fully formed, constituted a new cosmic energy, and proceeded to stamp all future products and processes with a character hitherto wholly unknown upon the globe.

It is in this sense, and in this only, that I claim the development of mind—of the thinking, reasoning, inventing faculty of the human brain—as another, and one of the best marked, of the great cosmic strides that have characterised the course of evolution and belong to the legitimate methods of nature.

It is, for example, only to a limited extent and in the most general way that we can apply the same canons to the organic as to the inorganic world. It is usually, but falsely, supposed that the student of biology need know nothing of physics, the assumption being that they have nothing in common. While this error is fatal to all fundamental acquaintance with the laws of life, it well illustrates the immensity of the advance from one realm to the other. The same could be said, in varying degrees of obviousness, of every one of the ascending steps to which reference has been made. I freely admit that the theologians and metaphysicians commit the most fatal error in treating the soul, or mind, as independent of the body, but this enormous fallacy is scarcely greater than that of the modern evolutionist, who, finding out their dependence, ignores the *magnitude* of the step by which mind was made a property of body, and proceeds as though no new factor had entered into the world.

But all this may be regarded as mere generality. Let us come to something more specific.

It has always been a marvel to my comprehension that wise men and philosophers, when smitten with the specious logic of the *laissez faire* school, can close their eyes to the most obtrusive fact that civilisation presents. In spite of the influence of philosophy, all forms of which have thus far been negative and nihilistic, the human animal, with his growing intellect, has still ever realised the power that is vouchsafed through mind, and has ever exercised that power. Philosophy would have long since robbed him of it and caused his early extermination from the earth but for the persistence, through heredity, of the impulse to exercise in self-preservation every power in his possession; by which practice alone he first gained his ascendancy ages before philosophy began.

The great fact, then, to which I allude is that, in spite of all philosophy, whether mythologic, metaphysical, or naturalistic, declaring that man must and can do nothing, he *has*, from the very dawn of his intelligence, been transforming the entire surface of planet he inhabits. No other animal performs anything comparable to what man performs. This is solely because no other possesses the developed psychic faculty.

If we analyse mind into its two departments, sense and intellect, we shall see that if is through this latter faculty that these results are accomplished. If we inquire more closely into the mode by which intellect operates, we shall find that it serves as a guiding power to those natural forces with which it is acquainted (and no others), directing them into channels of human advantage. If we seek for a single term by which to characterise with precision the nature of this process, we find this in *Invention*. The essential characteristic of all intellectual action is invention.

Glancing now at the *ensemble* of human achievement, which may be collectively called civilisation, we readily see that it is all the result of this inventive process. All practical art is merely the product of successful invention, and it requires no undue expansion of the term, nor extraordinary power of generalisation, to see in all human institution only modified forms of arts, and true products of the intellectual, or inventive, faculty.

But what is the general result of all this? An entirely new dispensation has been given to the world. All the materials and forces of nature have been thus placed completely under the control of one of the otherwise least powerful of the creatures inhabiting the earth. He has only to know them in order to become their master. Nature has thus been made the servant of man. Thus only has man succeeded in peopling the entire globe while all other animals are restricted to narrow faunal areas. He has also peopled certain portions far more densely than any other species could have done, and he seems destined to continue multiplying his numbers for a long time yet in the future. But this quantitative proof is even less telling than the qualitative. When we confine our attention to the *élite* of mankind we do not need to have the ways specified in detail by which the powers of mind have exalted the intellectual being above all other products of creation. At the present moment the most dense and the most enlightened populations of the globe occupy what are termed temperate latitudes, which means latitudes in which for from three to five months each year vegetation ceases entirely, the waters are locked in ice, and the temperature frequently sinks far below the zero of the Fahrenheit thermometer. Imagine the thin-skinned, furless animal man subsisting in such a climate. Extinguish his fires, banish his clothing, blot out the habitations that deck the civilised landscape. How long would the puny race survive? But these are not products of nature, they are products of *art*, the wages of thought—fruits of the intellect.

When a well-clothed philosopher on a bitter winter's night sits in a warm room well lighted for his purpose and writes on paper with pen and ink in the arbitrary characters of a highly developed language the statement that civilisation is the result of natural laws, and that man's duty is to let nature alone so that untrammeled it may work out a higher civilisation, he simply ignores every circumstance of his existence and deliberately closes his eyes to every fact within the range of his faculties. If man had acted upon his theory there would have been no civilisation, and our philosopher would have remained a troglodyte.

But how shall we distinguish this human, or anthropic, method from the method of nature? Simply by reversing all the definitions. Art is the antithesis of nature. If we call one the natural method we must call the other the artificial method. If nature's process is rightly named natural selection, man's process is artificial selection. The survival of the fittest is simply the survival of the strong, which implies, and might as well be called, the destruction of the weak. And if nature progresses through the destruction of the weak, man progresses through the *protection* of the weak. This is the essential distinction.

In human society the psychic power has operated to secure the protection of the weak in two distinct ways: first, by increasing the supply of the necessities of life, and, secondly, by preventing the destruction of life through the enemies of man. The immediate instrumentality through which the first of these processes is carried on is art, the product of invention. The second process takes place through the establishment of positive institutions.

It is difficult to say which of these agencies has been most effective. Both were always indispensable, and therefore all comparison is unprofitable.

Art operates to protect the weak against adverse surroundings. It is directed against natural forces, chiefly physical. By thus defeating the destructive influences of the elements and hostile forms of life, and by forcing nature to yield an unnatural supply of man's necessities, many who would have succumbed from inability to resist these adverse agencies—the feebler members of society—were able to survive, and population increased and expanded. While no one openly denies this, there is a tendency either to ignore it in politico-economic discussions, or to deny its application to them as an answer to naturalistic arguments.

If, on the other hand, we inquire into the nature of human institutions, we shall perceive that they are of three kinds, tending to protect the weak in three ways, or ascending degrees. These three successively higher means through which this end is attained are, first. Justice, second, Morality, and third, Charity. These forms of action have been reached through the development, respectively, of the three corresponding sentiments: Equity, Beneficence, and Benevolence.

All of these altruistic sentiments are wholly unknown, or known only in the merest embryo, to all animals below man, and therefore no such means of protection exist among them. They are strictly human, or anthropic. Many evolutionists fail to recognise this. Some sociologists refuse to admit it. They look about and see so much injustice, immorality and rapacity that they are led to suppose that only natural methods are in operation in society. This is a great mistake. In point of fact, the keener the sense of justice the more conspicuous the diminishing number of violations of it come to appear, and conversely, the obviousness of injustice proves the general prevalence of justice. It is the same with morality and philanthropy.

If we consider the effect of these three codes of human conduct in the direction of enabling the weaker ones to survive we shall see that it has been immense. Out of the first has arisen government, the chief value and function of which has always been and still is such protection. Great systems of jurisprudence have been elaborated, engrossing the attention of a large portion of the population of enlightened as well as of barbaric states. To say that these have been failures because often weighted with grave defects is to misinterpret history and misunderstand society. No one could probably be found to gainsay that the moral law of society has exerted a salutary influence, yet its aim is strictly altruistic, opposed to the law of the survival of the fittest, and wholly in the direction of enabling those to survive who would not survive without its protection. Finally, the last sentiment to be developed, and doubtless the highest, is so universally recognised as peculiar to man that his very name has been given to it—the sentiment of *humanity*. Yet the mode of protecting the weak arising out of this sentiment is the one that has been most seriously called in question by the naturalistic school. It must be admitted that humanitarian institutions have done far less good than either juridical or ethical institutions. The sentiment itself is of recent origin, the product only of highly developed and greatly refined mental organisation. It exists to an appreciable degree only in a minute fraction of the most enlightened populations. It is rarely directed with judgment; no fixed, self-enforcing code of conduct, as in the other cases, having had time to take shape. The institutions established to enforce it are for the most part poorly supported, badly managed, and often founded on a total misconception of human nature and of the true mode of attaining the end in view. Hence they are specially open to attack. But if ever humanitarian sentiments become diffused throughout the body politic, become the object of deep study, as have those of justice and right, it may be confidently predicted that society will prove itself capable of caring for the most unfortunate of its members in a manner that shall not work demoralisation.

In all these ways man, through his intelligence, has laboured successfully to resist the law of nature. His success is conclusively demonstrated by a comparison of his condition with that of other species of animals. No other cause can be assigned for his superiority. How can the naturalistic philosophers shut their eyes to such obvious facts? Yet, what is their attitude? They condemn all attempts to protect the weak, whether by private or public methods. They claim that it deteriorates the race by enabling the unfit to survive and transmit their inferiority. This is true only in certain cases of hereditary diseases or mental deficiencies, which should be taken account of by man because they are not by nature. Nothing is easier than to show that the unrestricted competition of nature does not secure the survival of the fittest possible, but only of the actually fittest, and in every attempt man makes to obtain something fitter than this actual fittest he succeeds, as witness improved breeds of animals and grafts of fruits. Now, the human method of protecting the weak deals in some such way with men. It not only increases the number but improves the quality.

But "government," at least, must *laissez faire*. It must not "meddle" with natural laws. The laws of trade, business, social intercourse, are natural laws, immutable and indestructible. All interference with them is vain. The fallacy here is a *non sequitur*. It may be readily granted that these laws are immutable and indestructible. Were this not the case it would certainly be hopeless to interfere with their action. But every mechanical invention proves that nothing is easier than to interfere successfully with the operation of these uniform natural forces. They have only to be first thoroughly understood and then they are easily *controlled*. To *destroy* a force is one thing, to control its action is quite another. Those who talk in this way involve themselves in the most palpable inconsistency. They must not be allowed to stop where they do. They must go on and carry their strictures to a logical conclusion. They must deny to government the right to protect its citizens from injustice. This is a clear interference with the natural laws of society. They must deny to society the right to enforce its code of morals. Nothing is more unnatural. They must suppress the healing art which keeps the sick from dying as they do among animals. Nor is this all. They must condemn all interference with physical laws and natural forces. To dam a stream must be characterised as a "vain" attempt to overcome a natural law. The wind must be left free to blow where it will, and not be forced against the fan of a wind-mill. The vapour of heated water must be allowed to float off naturally into the air and not be pent up in a steam-boiler and thence conducted into the cylinder of a steam-engine. All these things and every other device of inventive man are so many attempts to "violate" the laws of nature, which is declared impossible.

What then remains of the *laissez faire* doctrine? Nothing but this: That it is useless, and may be dangerous, to attempt to control natural forces until their character is first well understood. This is a proposition which is true for every department of force, and does not involve the surrender of the whole domain of sociology after it has been demonstrated that society is a theatre of forces.

The truth thus comes forth from a rational study of nature and human society that social progress has been due only in very slight degree to natural evolution as accomplished through the survival of the fittest, and its chief success has resulted from the reduction of competition in the struggle for existence and the protection of the weaker members. Such competition, in so far as it has been permitted to operate, has tended to lower the standard of the fittest and to check advancement. It is not, of course, claimed that the natural method has ever been fully overcome. It has always operated, and still operates, powerfully in many ways. It has been chiefly in the simpler departments of physical and mechanical phenomena that the psychic, or anthropic, method has superseded it. The inventive arts have been the result. Vital forces have yielded to some extent to the influence of mind in bringing about improved stocks of animals and vegetables, and even certain social laws have come under rational control through the establishment of institutions. Still, every step in this progress has been contested. It was not enough that the intellect was feeble and ill-fitted to grapple with such problems. It was not enough that ignorance of nature's laws should cause unnumbered failures. A still stronger barrier was presented by the intellect itself in the form of positive error embodied in philosophy. As already remarked, philosophy has always been negative and nihilistic, and has steadily antagonised the common sense of mankind. It is only quite recently that there has come into existence anything like a truly *positive* philosophy, i.e., a philosophy of *action*....

WILLIAM DEAN HOWELLS

"Pernicious Fiction"
(1887)

Perhaps no single individual was more central to the literary culture of the United States of the late nineteenth and early twentieth centuries than William Dean Howells (1837–1920). Accomplished and supremely influential as novelist, critic, and editor, Howells was at once an old-fashioned moralist—a figure in what came to be patronized as "the genteel tradition"—and a "realist." The piece of 1887 reprinted here expresses both features of Howells's sensibility. Howells displays acute concern for the moral effects of literature on the reader, yet at the same time he insists, in the realist's mode, on "truth" as the ultimate standard for "any work of the imagination." Howells was not prepared to consider the possibility that truth might sometimes conflict with morality or with beauty, but his ideals of morality and beauty were liberal enough to enable him in good conscience to sponsor Mark Twain, Hamlin Garland, Frank Norris, and other writers whose challenge to gentility was deeper than Howells's own.

This responsiveness on Howells's part is the focal point of a chapter ("Literary Hospitality") in Larzer Ziff, *The American 1890s: Life and Times of a Lost Generation* (New York, 1966), 24–49. A solid biography is Kenneth S. Lynn, *William Dean Howells: An American Life* (New York, 1971). For a splendid portrait of the literary culture of which Howells was the center, see Henry F. May, *The End of American Innocence: A Study of the First Years of Our Time, 1912–1917* (New York, 1959); republished with a new afterword by May and with a foreword by David A. Hollinger (New York, 1993), 3–117. For examples of the finest writing to come out of the critics to Howells's cultural "right," the men May calls "custodians of culture," see William Crary Brownell's *French Traits* (New York, 1888) and *British Prose Masters* (1909), and Charles Eliot Norton's *Historical Studies of Church-Building in the Middle Ages: Venice, Siena, Florence* (1880). Two important studies of realism in the arts that address Howells's place in the movement are Amy Kaplan, *The Social Construction of American Realism* (Chicago, 1988); and David E. Shi, *Facing Facts* (New York, 1994). Howells's relationship with Mark Twain is discussed in Henry Nash Smith, *Mark Twain: The Development of a Writer* (Cambridge, Mass., 1962), which remains the most penetrating and sensitive study of the late-Victorian tension between the "gentility" and "reality" felt by both Twain and Howells.

It must have been a passage from Vernon Lee's *Baldwin,* claiming for the novel an indefinitely vast and subtle influence on modern character, which provoked the following suggestive letter from one of our readers:

—,—Co., Md., Sept. 18, 1886.

Dear Sir,—With regard to article IV, in the Editor's Study in the September *Harper,* allow me to say that I have very grave doubts as to the whole list of magnificent things that you seem to think novels have done for the race, and can witness in myself many evil things which they have done for me. Whatever in my mental make-up is wild and visionary, whatever is untrue, whatever is injurious, I can trace to the perusal of some work of fiction. Worse than that, they beget' such high-strung and supersensitive ideas of life that plain industry and plodding perseverance are despised, and matter-of-fact poverty, or everyday, commonplace distress, meets with no sympathy, if indeed noticed at all, by one who has wept over the impossibly accumulated sufferings of some gaudy hero or heroine.

Hoping you will pardon the liberty I have taken in addressing you, I remain,

Most respectfully yours,

———————

We are not sure that we have the controversy with the writer which he seems to suppose, and we should perhaps freely grant the mischievous effects which he says novel-reading has wrought upon him, if we were not afraid that he had possibly reviewed his own experience with something of the inaccuracy we find in his report of our opinions. By his confession he is himself proof that Vernon Lee is right in saying, "The modern human being has been largely fashioned by those who have written about him, and most of all by the novelist," and there is nothing in what he urges to conflict with her claim that "the chief use of the novel" is "to make the shrewd and tolerant a little less shrewd and tolerant, and to make the generous and austere a little more skeptical and easy-going." If he will look more closely at these postulates, we think he will see that in the one she deals with the effect of the novel in the past, and in the other with its duty in the future. We still think that there "is sense if not final wisdom" in what she says, and we are quite willing to acknowledge something of each in our correspondent.

But novels are now so fully accepted by every one pretending to cultivated taste—and they really form the whole intellectual life of such immense numbers of people, without question of their influence, good or bad, upon the mind—that it is refreshing to have them frankly denounced, and to be invited to revise one's ideas and feelings in regard to them. A little honesty, or a great deal of honesty, in this quest will do the novel, as we hope yet to have it, and as we have already begun to have it, no harm; and for our own part we will confess that we believe fiction in the past to have been largely injurious, as we believe the stage play to be still almost wholly injurious, through its falsehood, its folly, its wantonness, and its aimlessness. It may be safely assumed that most of the novel-reading which people fancy is an intellectual pastime is the emptiest dissipation, hardly more related to thought or the wholesome exercise of the mental faculties than opium-eating; in either case the brain is drugged, and left weaker and crazier for the debauch. If this may be called the negative result of the fiction habit, the positive injury that most novels work is by no means so easily to be measured in the case of young men whose character they help so

Source: Harper's Magazine, 74 (April 1887), 824–26.

much to form or deform, and the women of all ages whom they keep so much in ignorance of the world they misrepresent. Grown men have little harm from them, but in the other cases, which are the vast majority, they hurt because they are not true—not because they are malevolent, but because they are idle lies about human nature and the social fabric, which it behooves us to know and to understand, that we may deal justly with ourselves and with one another. One need not go so far as our correspondent, and trace to the fiction habit "whatever is wild and visionary, whatever is untrue, whatever is injurious," in one's life; bad as the fiction habit is, it is probably not responsible for the whole sum of evil in its victims, and we believe that if the reader will use care in choosing from this fungus-growth with which the fields of literature teem every day, he may nourish himself as with the true mushroom, at no risk from the poisonous species.

The tests are very plain and simple, and they are perfectly infallible. If a novel flatters the passions, and exalts them above the principles, it is poisonous; it may not kill, but it will certainly injure; and this test will alone exclude an entire class of fiction, of which eminent examples will occur to all. Then the whole spawn of so-called unmoral romances, which imagine a world where the sins of sense are unvisited by the penalties following, swift or slow, but inexorably sure, in the real world, are deadly poison: these do kill. The novels that merely tickle our prejudices and lull our judgment, or that coddle our sensibilities, or pamper our gross appetite for the marvellous, are not so fatal, but they are innutritious, and clog the soul with un-wholesome vapors of all kinds. No doubt they too help to weaken the mental fibre, and make their readers indifferent to "plodding perseverance and plain industry," and to "matter-of-fact poverty and commonplace distress."

Without taking them too seriously, it still must be owned that the "gaudy hero and heroine" are to blame for a great deal of harm in the world. That heroine long taught by example, if not precept, that Love, or the passion or fancy she mistook for it, was the chief interest of a life which is really concerned with a great many other things; that it was lasting in the way she knew it; that it was worthy of every sacrifice, and was altogether a finer thing than prudence, obedience, reason; that love alone was glorious and beautiful, and these were mean and ugly in comparison with it. More lately she has begun to idolize and illustrate Duty, and she is hardly less mischievous in this new rôle, opposing duty, as she did love, to prudence, obedience, and reason. The stock hero, whom, if we met him, we could not fail to see was a most deplorable person, has undoubtedly imposed himself upon the victims of the fiction habit as admirable. With him, too, love was and is the great affair, whether in its old romantic phase of chivalrous achievement or manifold suffering for love's sake, or its more recent development of the "virile," the bullying, and the brutal, or its still more recent agonies of self-sacrifice, as idle and useless as the moral experiences of the insane asylums. With his vain posturings and his ridiculous splendor he is really a painted barbarian, the prey of his passions, and his delusions, full of obsolete ideals, and the motives and ethics of a savage, which the guilty author of his being does his best—or his worst—in spite of his own light and knowledge, to foist upon the reader as something generous and noble. We are not merely bringing this charge against that sort of fiction which is beneath literature and outside of it, "the shoreless lakes of ditch-water," whose miasms fill the air below the empyrean where the great ones sit; but we are accusing the work of some of the most famous, who have, in this instance or in that, sinned against the truth, which can alone exalt and purify men. We do not say that they have constantly done so, or even commonly done so; but that they have done so at all marks them as of the past, to be read with the due historical allowance for their epoch and their conditions. For we believe that, while inferior writers will and must continue to imitate them in their foibles and their errors, no one hereafter will be able to achieve greatness who is false to humanity, either in its facts or its duties. The light of civilization has already broken even upon the novel, and no conscientious man can now set about painting an image of life without perpetual question of the verity of his work, and without feeling bound to distinguish so clearly that no reader of his may be misled, between what is right and what is wrong, what is noble and what is base, what is health and what is perdition, in the actions and the characters he portrays.

The fiction that aims merely to entertain—the fiction that is to serious fiction as the opéra bouffe, the ballet, and the pantomime are to the true drama—need not feel the burden of this obligation so deeply; but even such fiction will not be gay or trivial to any reader's hurt, and criticism will hold it to account if it passes from painting to teaching folly.

More and more not only the criticism which prints its opinions, but the infinitely vaster and powerfuler criticism which thinks and feels them merely, will make this demand. For our own part we confess that we do not care to judge any work of the imagination without first of all applying this test to it. We must ask ourselves before we ask anything else, Is it true?—true to the motives, the impulses, the principles that shape the life of actual men and women? This truth, which necessarily includes the highest morality and the highest artistry—this truth given, the book *cannot* be wicked and cannot be weak; and without it all graces of style and feats of invention and cunning of construction are so many superfluities of naughtiness. It is well for the truth to have all these, and shine in them, but for falsehood they are merely meretricious, the bedizenment of the wanton; they atone for nothing, they count for nothing. But in fact they come naturally of truth, and grace it without solicitation; they are added unto it. In the whole range of fiction we know of no *true* picture of life—that is, of human nature—which is not also a masterpiece of literature, full of divine and natural beauty. It may have no touch or tint of this special civilization or of that; it had *better* have this local color well ascertained; but the truth is deeper and finer than aspects, and if the book is true to what men and women know of one another's souls it will be true enough, and it will be great and beautiful. It is the conception of literature as something apart from life, superfinely aloof, which makes it really unimportant to the great mass of mankind, without a message or a meaning for them; and it is the notion that a novel may be false in its portrayal of causes and effects that makes literary art contemptible even to those whom it amuses, that forbids them to regard the novelist as a serious or right-minded person. If they do not in some moment of indignation cry out against all novels, as our correspondent does, they remain besotted in the fume of the delusions purveyed to them, with no higher feeling for the author than such maudlin affection as the habitué of an opium-joint perhaps knows for the attendant who fills his pipe with the drug.

ELIZABETH CADY STANTON

"The Solitude of Self"
(1892)

When the seventy-seven-year-old Elizabeth Cady Stanton (1815–1902) stepped down from the presidency of the National American Woman Suffrage Association in 1892, she sought to vindicate the rights of women on the grounds of "the solitude and personal responsibility" of each woman's "individual life." Stanton made other arguments as well—in "The Solitude of Self," reprinted here, and throughout her career—but in treating the political significance and psychological resources of the "Self," she produced one of the most vivid and prophetic testimonials in the entire discourse of modern feminism. Stanton demanded equality for women in the life of the mind as well as the life of politics. She was a distinctively intellectual exemplar for American women and spoke beyond as well as within feminist circles on many issues of her time.

Stanton gained notoriety as a freethinker and was openly critical of Christianity. In *The Woman's Bible* (2 vols., 1895 and 1898), she boldly evaluated sections of scripture in terms of the attitudes toward women promoted by these texts. Stanton's radical views on religious questions and her vocal support for birth control and for revised divorce laws made her an embarrassment to more conservative feminists. During the Progressive Era and the 1920s, American feminist leaders singled out the less controversial Susan B. Anthony as their movement's chief emblem and deliberately de-emphasized Stanton's role in the winning of the vote for women.

A good biography is Lois W. Banner, *Elizabeth Cady Stanton: A Radical for Women's Rights* (Boston, 1980). See also the extensive introductory and editorial comments by Ellen Carol DuBois, ed., *Elizabeth Cady Stanton and Susan B. Anthony: Correspondence, Writings, Speeches* (New York, 1981). The version of "The Solitude of Self," reprinted here, follows DuBois's editing of the text. For an analysis of Stanton's religious ideas and the controversies they generated, see Kathi Kern, *Mrs. Stanton's Bible* (Ithaca, N.Y., 2002).

The point I wish plainly to bring before you on this occasion is the individuality of each human soul; our Protestant idea, the right of individual conscience and judgment; our republican idea, individual citizenship. In discussing the rights of woman, we are to consider, first, what belongs to her as an individual, in a world of her own, the arbiter of her own destiny, an imaginary Robinson Crusoe, with her woman, Friday, on a solitary island. Her rights under such circumstances are to use all her faculties for her own safety and happiness.

Secondly, if we consider her as a citizen, as a member of a great nation, she must have the same rights as all others members, according to the fundamental principles of our Government.

Thirdly, viewed as a woman, an equal factor in civilization, her rights and duties are still the same—individual happiness and development.

Fourthly, it is only the incidental relations of life, such as mother, wife, sister, daughter, which may involve some special duties and training....

The strongest reason for giving woman all the opportunities for higher education, for the full development of her faculties, her forces of mind and body; for giving her the most enlarged freedom of thought and action; a complete emancipation from all forms of bondage, of custom, dependence, superstition; from all the crippling influences of fear—is the solitude and personal responsibility of her own individual life. The strongest reason why we ask for woman a voice in the government under which she lives; in the religion she is asked to believe; equality in social life, where she is the chief factor; a place in the trades and professions, where she may earn her bread, is because of her birthright to self-sovereignty; because, as an individual, she must rely on herself. No matter how much women prefer to lean, to be protected and supported, nor how much men desire to have them do so, they must make the voyage of life alone, and for safety in an emergency, they must know something of the laws of navigation. To guide our own craft, we must be captain, pilot, engineer; with chart and compass to stand at the wheel; to watch the winds and waves, and know when to take in the sail, and to read the signs in the firmament over all. It matters not whether the solitary voyager is man or woman; nature, having endowed them equally, leaves them to their own skill and judgment in the hour of danger, and, if not equal to the occasion, alike they perish.

To appreciate the importance of fitting every human soul for independent action, think for a moment of the immeasurable solitude of self. We come into the world alone, unlike all who have gone before us, we leave it alone, under circumstances peculiar to ourselves. No mortal ever has been, no mortal ever will be like the soul just launched on the sea of life. There can never again be just such a combination of prenatal influences; never again just such environments as make up the infancy, youth and manhood of this one. Nature never repeats herself, and the possibilities of one human soul will never be found in another. No one has ever found two blades of ribbon grass alike, and no one will ever find two human beings alike. Seeing, then, what must be the infinite diversity in human character, we can in a measure appreciate the loss to a nation when any class of the people is uneducated and unrepresented in the government.

We ask for the complete development of every individual, first, for his own benefit and happiness. In fitting out an army, we give each soldier his own knapsack, arms, powder, his blanket, cup, knife, fork and spoon. We provide alike for all their individual necessities; then each man bears his own burden.

Source: Woman's Column, 1892.

Again, we ask complete individual development for the general good; for the consensus of the competent on the whole round of human interests, on all questions of national life; and here each man must bear his share of the general burden. It is sad to see how soon friendless children are left to bear their own burdens, before they can analyze their feelings; before they can even tell their joys and sorrows, they are thrown on their own resources. The great lesson that nature seems to teach us at all ages is self-dependence, self-protection, self-support....

In youth our most bitter disappointments, our brightest hopes and ambitions, are known only to ourselves. Even our friendship and love we never fully share with another; there is something of every passion, in every situation, we conceal. Even so in our triumphs and our defeats....

We ask no sympathy from others in the anxiety and agony of a broken friendship or shattered love. When death sunders our nearest ties, alone we sit in the shadow of our affliction. Alike amid the greatest triumphs and darkest tragedies of life, we walk alone. On the divine heights of human attainment, eulogized and worshipped as a hero or saint, we stand alone. In ignorance, poverty and vice, as a pauper or criminal, alone we starve or steal; alone we suffer the sneers and rebuffs of our fellows; alone we are hunted and hounded through dark courts and alleys, in by-ways and high-ways; alone we stand in the judgment seat; alone in the prison cell we lament our crimes and misfortunes; alone we expiate them on the gallows. In hours like these we realize the awful solitude of individual life, its pains, its penalties, its responsibilities, hours in which the youngest and most helpless are thrown on their own resources for guidance and consolation. Seeing, then, that life must ever be a march and a battle that each soldier must be equipped for his own protection, it is the height of cruelty to rob the individual of a single natural right.

To throw obstacles in the way of a complete education is like putting out the eyes; to deny the rights of property is like cutting off the hands. To refuse political equality is to rob the ostracized of all self-respect; of credit in the market place; of recompense in the world of work, of a voice in choosing those who make and administer the law, a choice in the jury before whom they are tried, and in the judge who decides their punishment. [Think of]...woman's position! Robbed of her natural rights, handicapped by law and custom at every turn, yet compelled to fight her own battles, and in the emergencies of life to fall back on herself for protection....

The young wife and mother, at the head of some establishment, with a kind husband to shield her from the adverse winds of life, with wealth, fortune and position, has a certain harbor of safety, secure against the ordinary ills of life. But to manage a household, have a desirable influence in society, keep her friends and the affections of her husband, train her children and servants well, she must have rare common sense, wisdom, diplomacy, and a knowledge of human nature. To do all this, she needs the cardinal virtues and the strong points of character that the most successful statesman possesses. An uneducated woman trained to dependence, with no resources in herself, must make a failure of any position in life. But society says women do not need a knowledge of the world, the liberal training that experience in public life must give, all the advantages of collegiate education; but when for the lack of all this, the woman's happiness is wrecked, alone she bears her humiliation; and the solitude of the weak and the ignorant is indeed pitiable. In the wild chase for the prizes of life, they are ground to powder.

In age, when the pleasures of youth are passed, children grown up, married and gone, the hurry and bustle of life in a measure over, when the hands are weary of active service, when the old arm chair and the fireside are the chosen resorts, then men and women alike must fall back on their own resources. If they cannot find companionship in books, if they have no interest in the vital questions of the hour, no interest in watching the consummation of reforms with which they might have been identified, they soon pass into their dotage. The more fully the faculties of the mind are developed and kept in use, the longer the period of vigor and active interest in all around us continues. If, from a life-long participation in public affairs, a woman feels responsible for the laws regulating our system of education, the discipline of our jails and prisons, the sanitary condition of our private homes, public buildings and thoroughfares, an interest in commerce, finance, our foreign relations, in any or all these questions, her solitude will at least be respectable, and she will not be driven to gossip or scandal for entertainment.

The chief reason for opening to every soul the doors to the whole round of human duties and pleasures is the individual development thus attained, the resources thus provided under all circumstances to mitigate the solitude that at times must come to everyone....

Inasmuch, then, as woman shares equally the joys and sorrows of time and eternity, is it not the height of presumption in man to propose to represent her at the ballot box and the throne of grace, to do her voting in the state, her praying in the church, and to assume the position of high priest at the family altar?

Nothing strengthens the judgment and quickens the conscience like individual responsibility. Nothing adds such dignity to character as the recognition of one's self-sovereignty; the right to an equal place, everywhere conceded—a place earned by personal merit, not an artificial attainment by inheritance, wealth, family and position. Conceding, then, that the responsibilities of life rest equally on man and woman, that their destiny is the same, they need the same preparation for time and eternity. The talk of sheltering woman from the fierce storms of life is the sheerest mockery, for they beat on her from every point of the compass, just as they do on man, and with more fatal results, for he has been trained to protect himself, to resist, and to conquer. Such are the facts in human experience, the responsibilities of individual sovereignty. Rich and poor, intelligent and ignorant, wise and foolish, virtuous and vicious, man and woman; it is ever the same, each soul must depend wholly on itself.

Whatever the theories may be of woman's dependence on man, in the supreme moments of her life, he cannot bear her burdens. Alone she goes to the gates of death to give life to every man that is born into the world; no one can share her fears, no one can mitigate her pangs; and if her sorrow is greater than she can bear, alone she passes beyond the gates into the vast unknown.

From the mountain-tops of Judea long ago, a heavenly voice bade his disciples, "Bear ye one another's burdens"; but humanity has not yet risen to that point of self-sacrifice; and if ever so willing, how few the burdens are that one soul can bear for another!...

So it ever must be in the conflicting scenes of life, in the long, weary march, each one walks alone. We may have many friends, love, kindness, sympathy and charity, to smooth our pathway in everyday life, but in the tragedies and triumphs of human experience, each mortal stands alone.

But when all artificial trammels are removed, and women are recognized as individuals, responsible for their own environments, thoroughly educated for all positions in life they may be called to fill; with all the resources in themselves that liberal thought and broad culture can give; guided by their own conscience and judgment, trained to self-protection, by a healthy development of the muscular system, and skill in the use of weapons and defence; and stimulated to self-support by a knowledge of the business world and the pleasure that pecuniary independence must ever give; when women are trained in this way, they will in a measure be fitted for those hours of solitude that come alike to all, whether prepared or otherwise. As in our extremity we must depend on ourselves, the dictates of wisdom point to complete individual development.

In talking of education, how shallow the argument that each class must be educated for the special work it proposes to do, and that all those faculties not needed in this special work must lie dormant and utterly wither for want of use, when, perhaps, these will be the very faculties needed in life's greatest emergencies! Some say, "Where is the use of drilling girls in the languages, the sciences, in law, medicine, theology. As wives, mothers, housekeepers, cooks, they need a different curriculum from boys who are to fill all positions. The chief cooks in our great hotels and ocean steamers are men. In our large cities, men run the bakeries; they make our bread, cake and pies. They manage the laundries; they are now considered our best milliners and dressmakers. Because some men fill these departments of usefulness, shall we regulate the curriculum in Harvard and Yale to their present necessities? If not, why this talk in our best colleges of a curriculum for girls who are crowding into the trades and professions, teachers in all our public schools, rapidly filling many lucrative and honorable positions in life?"...

...Women are already the equals of men in the whole realm of thought, in art, science, literature and government.... The poetry and novels of the century are theirs, and they have touched the keynote of reform, in religion, politics and social life. They fill the editor's and professor's chair, plead at the bar of justice, walk the wards of the hospital, speak from the pulpit and the platform. Such is the type of womanhood that an enlightened public sentiment welcomes to-day, and such the triumph of the facts of life over the false theories of the past.

Is it, then, consistent to hold the developed woman of this day within the same narrow political limits as the dame with the spinning wheel and knitting needle occupied in the past? No, no! Machinery has taken the labors of woman as well as man on its tireless shoulders; the loom and the spinning wheel are but dreams of the past; the pen, the brush, the easel, the chisel, have taken their places, while the hopes and ambitions of women are essentially changed.

We see reason sufficient in the outer conditions of human beings for individual liberty and development, but when we consider the self-dependence of every human soul, we see the need of courage, judgment and the exercise of every faculty of mind and body, strengthened and developed by use, in woman as well as man.

Whatever may be said of man's protecting power in ordinary conditions, amid all the terrible disasters by land and sea, in the supreme moments of danger, alone woman must ever meet the horrors of the situation. The Angel of Death even makes no royal pathway for her. Man's love and sympathy enter only into the sunshine of our lives. In that solemn solitude of self, that links us with the immeasurable and the eternal, each soul lives alone forever. A recent writer says: "I remember once, in crossing the Atlantic, to have gone upon the deck of the ship at midnight, when a dense black cloud enveloped the sky, and the great deep was roaring madly under the lashes of demoniac winds. My feeling was not of danger or fear (which is a base surrender of the immortal soul) but of utter desolation and loneliness; a little speck of life shut in by a tremendous darkness...."

And yet, there is a solitude which each and every one of us has always carried with him, more inaccessible than the ice-cold mountains, more profound than the midnight sea; the solitude of self. Our inner being which we call ourself, no eye nor touch of man or angel has ever pierced. It is more hidden than the caves of the gnome; the sacred adytum of the oracle; the hidden chamber of Eleusinian mystery, for to it only omniscience is permitted to enter.

Such is individual life. Who, I ask you, can take, dare take on himself the rights, the duties, the responsibilities of another human soul?

FREDERICK JACKSON TURNER

"The Significance of the Frontier in American History" (1893)

No single essay concerning the history of the United States has ever proved more influential than "The Significance of the Frontier in American History," first presented as a lecture to a group of historians meeting in conjunction with the Chicago World's Fair of 1893. This sweeping account of the whole of the history of the United States and its colonial background was given to the world by a then obscure scholar from the University of Wisconsin, Frederick Jackson Turner (1861–1932). It was the frontier experience itself, Turner insisted, that determined the distinctive course of American society, including its democratic political culture and its individualism. Writing explicitly against a narrative of American history that emphasized the formative power of the eastern seaboard—its institutions, its practices, its relation to the Old World—and against a second narrative that treated the slavery question as central, Turner held that it was "the Great West" that explained the distinctive character of the United States. The immediate occasion for Turner's paper was the finding of the 1890 census that the unoccupied land essential to the frontier experience was no more; hence the frontier had "closed," and the survival of democracy and individualism were implicitly at risk.

Turner wrote relatively little, compared with other historians who achieved the influence Turner achieved. The most important of his writings were collected in a book of essays, *The Frontier in American History* (New York, 1920). Yet his original formulation, and its several later elaborations, swept the field. By the time of his death in 1932, his critics were few and ineffective. In later decades historians found Turner's interpretation much too narrow. Urban environments proved conducive to democratic politics, and a variety of cultural factors—including religion—impressed many historians as having more force in history than Turner had acknowledged. Eventually, Turner was remembered less as a research scholar than as a kind of epic poet: he had used the genre of the historical essay to articulate a particular vision of the world-historical significance of the United States. A common misunderstanding even today about Turner was that he was a specialist in the relatively small subfield of "the American West." In fact, Turner looked at history in national and in global terms; he focused on the West because of his sense of the West's place in the history of democracy, individualism, and indeed of the human spirit.

The best study of Turner's enunciation of the "frontier thesis" is found within Kerwin Lee Klein, *Frontiers of Historical Imagination: Narrating the European Conquest of Native America, 1890–1990* (Berkeley, 1997). See also Allan G. Bogue, *Frederick Jackson Turner: Strange Roads Going Down* (Norman, Okla., 1998). An excellent contemporary discussion of the issues that concerned Turner is François Furstenberg, "The Significance of the Trans-Appalachian Frontier in Atlantic History," *American Historical Review*, 113 (2008), 647–77.

In a recent bulletin of the Superintendent of the Census for 1890 appear these significant words: "Up to and including 1880 the country had a frontier of settlement, but at present the unsettled area has been so broken into by isolated bodies of settlement that there can hardly be said to be a frontier line. In the discussion of its extent, its westward movement, etc., it can not, therefore, any longer have a place in the census reports." This brief official statement marks the closing of a great historic movement. Up to our own day American history has been in a large degree the history of the colonization of the Great West. The existence of an area of free land, its continuous recession, and the advance of American settlement westward, explain American development.

Behind institutions, behind constitutional forms and modifications, lie the vital forces that call these organs into life and shape them to meet changing conditions. The peculiarity of American institutions is, the fact that they have been compelled to adapt themselves to the changes of an expanding people—to the changes involved in crossing a continent, in winning a wilderness, and in developing at each area of this progress out of the primitive economic and political conditions of the frontier into the complexity of city life. Said Calhoun in 1817, "We are great, and rapidly—I was about to say fearfully—growing!" So saying, he touched the distinguishing feature of American life. All peoples show development; the germ theory of politics has been sufficiently emphasized. In the case of most nations, however, the development has occurred in a limited area; and if the nation has expanded, it has met other growing peoples whom it has conquered. But in the case of the United States we have a different phenomenon. Limiting our attention to the Atlantic coast, we have the familiar phenomenon of the evolution of institutions in a limited area, such as the rise of representative government; the differentiation of simple colonial governments into complex organs; the progress from primitive industrial society, without division of labor, up to manufacturing civilization. But we have in addition to this a recurrence of the process of evolution in each western area reached in the process of expansion. Thus American development has exhibited not merely advance along a single line, but a return to primitive conditions on a continually advancing frontier line, and a new development for that area. American social development has been continually beginning over again on the frontier. This perennial rebirth, this fluidity of American life, this expansion westward with its new opportunities, its continuous touch with the simplicity of primitive society, furnish the forces dominating American character. The true point of view in the history of this nation is not the Atlantic coast, it is the Great West. Even the slavery struggle, which is made so exclusive an object of attention by writers like Professor von Holst, occupies its important place in American history because of its relation to westward expansion.

In this advance, the frontier is the outer edge of the wave—the meeting point between savagery and civilization. Much has been written about the frontier from the point of view of border warfare and the chase, but as a field for the serious study of the economist and the historian it has been neglected.

The American frontier is sharply distinguished from the European frontier—a fortified boundary line running through dense populations. The most significant thing about the American frontier is, that it lies at the hither edge of free land. In the census reports

Source: Frederick Jackson Turner, *The Frontier in American History* (New York: Henry Holt & Co., 1920), 1–38.

it is treated as the margin of that settlement which has a density of two or more to the square mile. The term is an elastic one, and for our purposes does not need sharp definition. We shall consider the whole frontier belt, including the Indian country and the outer margin of the "settled area" of the census reports. This paper will make no attempt to treat the subject exhaustively; its aim is simply to call attention to the frontier as a fertile field for investigation, and to suggest some of the problems which arise in connection with it.

In the settlement of America we have to observe how European life entered the continent, and how America modified and developed that life and reacted on Europe. Our early history is the study of European germs developing in an American environment. Too exclusive attention has been paid by institutional students to the Germanic origins, too little to the American factors. The frontier is the line of most rapid and effective Americanization. The wilderness masters the colonist. It finds him a European in dress, industries, tools, modes of travel, and thought. It takes him from the railroad car and puts him in the birch canoe. It strips off the garments of civilization and arrays him in the hunting shirt and the moccasin. It puts him in the log cabin of the Cherokee and Iroquois and runs an Indian palisade around him. Before long he has gone to planting Indian corn and plowing with a sharp stick; he shouts the war cry and takes the scalp in orthodox Indian fashion. In short, at the frontier the environment is at first too strong for the man. He must accept the conditions which it furnishes, or perish, and so he fits himself into the Indian clearings and follows the Indian trails. Little by little he transforms the wilderness, but the outcome is not the old Europe, not simply the development of Germanic germs, any more than the first phenomenon was a case of reversion to the Germanic mark. The fact is, that here is a new product that is American. At first, the frontier was the Atlantic coast. It was the frontier of Europe in a very real sense. Moving westward, the frontier became more and more American. As successive terminal moraines result from successive glaciations, so each frontier leaves its traces behind it, and when it becomes a settled area the region still partakes of the frontier characteristics. Thus the advance of the frontier has meant a steady movement away from the influence of Europe, a steady growth of independence on American lines. And to study this advance, the men who grew up under these conditions, and the political, economic, and social results of it, is to study the really American part of our history....

Loria, the Italian economist, has urged the study of colonial life as an aid in understanding the stages of European development, affirming that colonial settlement is for economic science what the mountain is for geology, bringing to light primitive stratifications. "America," he says, "has the key to the historical enigma which Europe has sought for centuries in vain, and the land which has no history reveals luminously the course of universal history." There is much truth in this. The United States lies like a huge page in the history of society. Line by line as we read this continental page from West to East we find the record of social evolution. It begins with the Indian and the hunter; it goes on to tell of the disintegration of savagery by the entrance of the trader, the pathfinder of civilization; we read the annals of the pastoral stage in ranch life; the exploitation of the soil by the raising of unrotated crops of corn and wheat in sparsely settled farming communities; the intensive culture of the denser farm settlement; and finally the manufacturing organization with city and factory system....

The frontier promoted the formation of a composite nationality for the American people. The coast was preponderantly English, but the later tides of continental immigration flowed across to the free lands. This was the case from the early colonial days. The

Scotch-Irish and the Palatine Germans, or "Pennsylvania Dutch," furnished the dominant element in the stock of the colonial frontier. With these peoples were also the freed indented servants, or redemptioners, who at the expiration of their time of service passed to the frontier. Governor Spotswood of Virginia writes in 1717, "The inhabitants of our frontiers are composed generally of such as have been transported hither as servants, and, being out of their time, settle themselves where land is to be taken up and that will produce the necessarys of life with little labour." Very generally these redemptioners were of non-English stock. In the crucible of the frontier the immigrants were Americanized, liberated, and fused into a mixed race, English in neither nationality nor characteristics. The process has gone on from the early days to our own. Burke and other writers in the middle of the eighteenth century believed that Pennsylvania was "threatened with the danger of being wholly foreign in language, manners, and perhaps even inclinations." The German and Scotch-Irish elements in the frontier of the South were only less great. In the middle of the present century the German element in Wisconsin was already so considerable that leading publicists looked to the creation of a German state out of the commonwealth by concentrating their colonization. Such examples teach us to beware of misinterpreting the fact that there is a common English speech in America into a belief that the stock is also English.

In another way the advance of the frontier decreased our dependence on England. The coast, particularly of the South, lacked diversified industries, and was dependent on England for the bulk of its supplies. In the South there was even a dependence on the Northern colonies for articles of food. Governor Glenn, of South Carolina, writes in the middle of the eighteenth century: "Our trade with New York and Philadelphia was of this sort, draining us of all the little money and bills we could gather from other places for their bread, flour, beer, hams, bacon, and other things of their produce, all which, except beer, our new townships begin to supply us with, which are settled with very industrious and thriving Germans. This no doubt diminishes the number of shipping and the appearance of our trade, but it is far from being a detriment to us." Before long the frontier created a demand for merchants. As it retreated from the coast it became less and less possible for England to bring her supplies directly to the consumer's wharfs, and carry away staple crops, and staple crops began to give way to diversified agriculture for a time. The effect of this phase of the frontier action upon the northern section is perceived when we realize how the advance of the frontier aroused seaboard cities like Boston, New York, and Baltimore, to engage in rivalry for what Washington called "the extensive and valuable trade of a rising empire."

The legislation which most developed the powers of the national government, and played the largest part in its activity, was conditioned on the frontier. Writers have discussed the subjects of tariff, land, and internal improvement, as subsidiary to the slavery question. But when American history comes to be rightly viewed it will be seen that the slavery question is an incident.... The public domain has been a force of profound importance in the nationalization and development of the government. The effects of the struggle of the landed and the landless States, and of the Ordinance of 1787, need no discussion. Administratively the frontier called out some of the highest and most vitalizing activities of the general government. The purchase of Louisiana was perhaps the constitutional turning point in the history of the Republic, inasmuch as it afforded both a new area for national legislation and the occasion of the downfall of the policy of strict construction. But the purchase of Louisiana was called out by frontier needs and demands. As frontier States accrued to the Union the national power grew....

The economic and social characteristics of the frontier worked against sectionalism. The men of the frontier had closer resemblances to the Middle region than to either of the other sections. Pennsylvania had been the seed-plot of frontier emigration, and, although she passed on her settlers along the Great Valley into the west of Virginia and the Carolinas, yet the industrial society of these Southern frontiersmen was always more like that of the Middle region than like that of the tide-water portion of the South, which later came to spread its industrial type throughout the South.

The Middle region, entered by New York harbor, was an open door to all Europe. The tide-water part of the South represented typical Englishmen, modified by a warm climate and servile labor, and living in baronial fashion on great plantations; New England stood for a special English movement—Puritanism. The Middle region was less English than the other sections. It had a wide mixture of nationalities, a varied society, the mixed town and county system of local government, a varied economic life, many religious sects. In short, it was a region mediating between New England and the South, and the East and the West. It represented that composite nationality which the contemporary United States exhibits, that juxtaposition of non-English groups, occupying a valley or a little settlement, and presenting reflections of the map of Europe in their variety. It was democratic and non-sectional, if not national; "easy, tolerant, and contented;" rooted strongly in material prosperity. It was typical of the modern United States. It was least sectional, not only because it lay between North and South, but also because with no barriers to shut out its frontiers from its settled region, and with a system of connecting waterways, the Middle region mediated between East and West as well as between North and South. Thus it became the typically American region. Even the New Englander, who was shut out from the frontier by the Middle region, tarrying in New York or Pennsylvania on his westward march, lost the acuteness of his sectionalism on the way.

The spread of cotton culture into the interior of the South finally broke down the contrast between the "tide-water" region and the rest of the State, and based Southern interests on slavery. Before this process revealed its results the western portion of the South, which was akin to Pennsylvania in stock, society, and industry, showed tendencies to fall away from the faith of the fathers into internal improvement legislation and nationalism. In the Virginia convention of 1829–30, called to revise the constitution, Mr. Leigh, of Chesterfield, one of the tide-water counties, declared:

> One of the main causes of discontent which led to this convention, that which had the strongest influence in overcoming our veneration for the work of our fathers, which taught us to contemn the sentiments of Henry and Mason and Pendleton, which weaned us from our reverence for the constituted authorities of the State, was an overweening passion for internal improvement. I say this with perfect knowledge, for it has been avowed to me by gentlemen from the West over and over again. And let me tell the gentleman from Albemarle (Mr. Gordon) that it has been another principal object of those who set this ball of revolution in motion, to overturn the doctrine of State rights, of which Virginia has been the very pillar, and to remove the barrier she has interposed to the interference of the Federal Government in that same work of internal improvement, by so reorganizing the legislature that Virginia, too, may be hitched to the Federal car.

It was this nationalizing tendency of the West that transformed the democracy of Jefferson into the national republicanism of Monroe and the democracy of Andrew

Jackson. The West of the War of 1812, the West of Clay, and Benton and Harrison, and Andrew Jackson, shut off by the Middle States and the mountains from the coast sections, had a solidarity of its own with national tendencies. On the tide of the Father of Waters, North and South met and mingled into a nation. Interstate migration went steadily on—a process of cross-fertilization of ideas and institutions. The fierce struggle of the sections over slavery on the western frontier does not diminish the truth of this statement; it proves the truth of it. Slavery was a sectional trait that would not down, but in the West it could not remain sectional. It was the greatest of frontiersmen who declared: "I believe this Government can not endure permanently half slave and half free. It will become all of one thing or all of the other." Nothing works for nationalism like intercourse within the nation. Mobility of population is death to localism, and the western frontier worked irresistibly in unsettling population. The effect reached back from the frontier and affected profoundly the Atlantic coast and even the Old World.

But the most important effect of the frontier has been in the promotion of democracy here and in Europe. As has been indicated the frontier is productive of individualism. Complex society is precipitated by the wilderness into a kind of primitive organization based on the family. The tendency is anti-social. It produces antipathy to control, and particularly to any direct control. The tax-gatherer is viewed as a representative of oppression. Prof. Osgood, in an able article, has pointed out that the frontier conditions prevalent in the colonies are important factors in the explanation of the American Revolution, where individual liberty was sometimes confused with absence of all effective government. The same conditions aid in explaining the difficulty of instituting a strong government in the period of the confederacy. The frontier individualism has from the beginning promoted democracy.

The frontier States that came into the Union in the first quarter of a century of its existence came in with democratic suffrage provisions, and had reactive effects of the highest importance upon the older States whose peoples were being attracted there. An extension of the franchise became essential. It was *western* New York that forced an extension of suffrage in the constitutional convention of that State in 1821; and it was *western* Virginia that compelled the tide-water region to put a more liberal suffrage provision in the constitution framed in 1830, and to give to the frontier region a more nearly proportionate representation with the tide-water aristocracy. The rise of democracy as an effective force in the nation came in with western preponderance under Jackson and William Henry Harrison, and it meant the triumph of the frontier—with all of its good and with all of its evil elements. An interesting illustration of the tone of frontier democracy in 1830 comes from the same debates in the Virginia convention already referred to. A representative from western Virginia declared:

> But, sir, it is not the increase of population in the West which this gentleman ought to fear. It is the energy which the mountain breeze and western habits impart to those emigrants. They are regenerated, politically I mean, sir. They soon become *working politicians*; and the difference, sir, between a *talking* and a *working* politician is immense. The Old Dominion has long been celebrated for producing great orators; the ablest metaphysicians in policy; men that can split hairs in all abstruse questions of political economy. But at home, or when they return from Congress, they have negroes to fan them asleep. But a Pennsylvania, a New York, an Ohio, or a western Virginia statesman, though far inferior in logic, metaphysics, and rhetoric to an old Virginia statesman, has this advantage,

that when he returns home he takes off his coat and takes hold of the plow. This gives him bone and muscle, sir, and preserves his republican principles pure and uncontaminated.

So long as free land exists, the opportunity for a competency exists, and economic power secures political power. But the democracy born of free land, strong in selfishness and individualism, intolerant of administrative experience and education, and pressing individual liberty beyond its proper bounds, has its dangers as well as its benefits. Individualism in America has allowed a laxity in regard to governmental affairs which has rendered possible the spoils system and all the manifest evils that follow from the lack of a highly developed civic spirit. In this connection may be noted also the influence of frontier conditions in permitting lax business honor, inflated paper currency and wild-cat banking. The colonial and revolutionary frontier was the region whence emanated many of the worst forms of an evil currency. The West in the War of 1812 repeated the phenomenon on the frontier of that day, while the speculation and wild-cat banking of the period of the crisis of 1837 occurred on the new frontier belt of the next tier of States. Thus each one of the periods of lax financial integrity coincides with periods when a new set of frontier communities had arisen, and coincides in area with these successive frontiers, for the most part. The recent Populist agitation is a case in point. Many a State that now declines any connection with the tenets of the Populists, itself adhered to such ideas in an earlier stage of the development of the State. A primitive society can hardly be expected to show the intelligent appreciation of the complexity of business interests in a developed society. The continual recurrence of these areas of paper-money agitation is another evidence that the frontier can be isolated and studied as a factor in American history of the highest importance.

The East has always feared the result of an unregulated advance of the frontier, and has tried to check and guide it. The English authorities would have checked settlement at the headwaters of the Atlantic tributaries and allowed the "savages to enjoy their deserts in quiet lest the peltry trade should decrease." This called out Burke's splendid protest:

> If you stopped your grants, what would be the consequence? The people would occupy without grants. They have already so occupied in many places. You can not station garrisons in every part of these deserts. If you drive the people from one place, they will carry on their annual tillage and remove with their flocks and herds to another. Many of the people in the back settlements are already little attached to particular situations. Already they have topped the Appalachian Mountains. From thence they behold before them an immense plain, one vast, rich, level meadow; a square of five hundred miles. Over this they would wander without a possibility of restraint; they would change their manners with their habits of life; would soon forget a government by which they were disowned; would become hordes of English Tartars; and, pouring down upon your unfortified frontiers a fierce and irresistible cavalry, become masters of your governors and your counselers, your collectors and comptrollers, and of all the slaves that adhered to them. Such would, and in no long time must, be the effect of attempting to forbid as a crime and to suppress as an evil the command and blessing of Providence, "Increase and multiply." Such would be the happy result of an endeavor to keep as a lair of wild beasts that earth which God, by an express charter, has given to the children of men.

But the English Government was not alone in its desire to limit the advance of the frontier and guide its destinies. Tidewater Virginia and South Carolina gerrymandered those colonies to insure the dominance of the coast in their legislatures. Washington desired to settle a State at a time in the Northwest; Jefferson would reserve from settlement the territory of his Louisiana Purchase north of the thirty-second parallel, in order to offer it to the Indians in exchange for their settlements east of the Mississippi. "When we shall be full on this side," he writes, "we may lay off a range of States on the western bank from the head to the mouth, and so range after range, advancing compactly as we multiply." Madison went so far as to argue to the French minister that the United States had no interest in seeing population extend itself on the right bank of the Mississippi, but should rather fear it. When the Oregon question was under debate, in 1824, Smyth, of Virginia, would draw an unchangeable line for the limits of the United States at the outer limit of two tiers of States beyond the Mississippi, complaining that the seaboard States were being drained of the flower of their population by the bringing of too much land into market. Even Thomas Benton, the man of widest views of the destiny of the West, at this stage of his career declared that along the ridge of the Rocky mountains "the western limits of the Republic should be drawn, and the statue of the fabled god Terminus should be raised upon its highest peak, never to be thrown down." But the attempts to limit the boundaries, to restrict land sales and settlement, and to deprive the West of its share of political power were all in vain. Steadily the frontier of settlement advanced and carried with it individualism, democracy, and nationalism, and powerfully affected the East and the Old World.

The most effective efforts of the East to regulate the frontier came through its educational and religious activity, exerted by interstate migration and by organized societies. Speaking in 1835, Dr. Lyman Beecher declared: "It is equally plain that the religious and political destiny of our nation is to be decided in the West," and he pointed out that the population of the West "is assembled from all the States of the Union and from all the nations of Europe, and is rushing in like the waters of the flood, demanding for its moral preservation the immediate and universal action of those institutions which discipline the mind and arm the conscience and the heart. And so various are the opinions and habits, and so recent and imperfect is the acquaintance, and so sparse are the settlements of the West, that no homogeneous public sentiment can be formed to legislate immediately into being the requisite institutions. And yet they are all needed immediately in their utmost perfection and power. A nation is being 'born in a day.' ... But what will become of the West if her prosperity rushes up to such a majesty of power, while those great institutions linger which are necessary to form the mind and the conscience and the heart of that vast world. It must not be permitted.... Let no man at the East quiet himself and dream of liberty, whatever may become of the West.... Her destiny is our destiny."

With the appeal to the conscience of New England, he adds appeals to her fears lest other religious sects anticipate her own. The New England preacher and school-teacher left their mark on the West. The dread of Western emancipation from New England's political and economic control was paralleled by her fears lest the West cut loose from her religion. Commenting in 1850 on reports that settlement was rapidly extending northward in Wisconsin, the editor of the *Home Missionary* writes: "We scarcely know whether to rejoice or mourn over this extension of our settlements. While we sympathize in whatever tends to increase the physical resources and prosperity of our country, we can not forget that with all these dispersions into remote and still remoter corners of the land the supply of the means of grace is becoming relatively less and less." Acting in accordance with such ideas, home missions were established and Western colleges were erected. As seaboard cities like Philadelphia, New York, and Baltimore strove for the mastery of Western trade, so the various denominations strove for the possession of the West. Thus an intellectual stream from New England sources fertilized the West. Other sections sent their missionaries; but the real struggle was between sects. The contest for power and the expansive tendency furnished to the various sects by the existence of a moving frontier must have had important results on the character of religious organization in the United States. The multiplication of rival churches in the little frontier towns had deep and lasting social effects. The religious aspects of the frontier make a chapter in our history which needs study.

From the conditions of frontier life came intellectual traits of profound importance. The works of travelers along each frontier from colonial days onward describe certain common traits, and these traits have, while softening down, still persisted as survivals in the place of their origin, even when a higher social organization succeeded. The result is that to the frontier the American intellect owes its striking characteristics. That coarseness and strength combined with acuteness and inquisitiveness; that practical, inventive turn of mind, quick to find expedients; that masterful grasp of material things, lacking in the artistic but powerful to effect great ends; that restless, nervous energy; that dominant individualism, working for good and for evil, and withal that buoyancy and exuberance which comes with freedom—these are traits of the frontier, or traits called out elsewhere because of the existence of the frontier. Since the days when the fleet of Columbus sailed into the waters of the New World, America has been another name for opportunity, and the people of the United States have taken their tone from the incessant expansion which has not only been open but has even been forced upon them. He would be a rash prophet who should assert that the expansive character of American life has now entirely ceased. Movement has been its dominant fact, and, unless this training has no effect upon a people, the American energy will continually demand a wider field for its exercise. But never again will such gifts of free land offer themselves. For a moment, at the frontier, the bonds of custom are broken and unrestraint is triumphant. There is not tabula rasa. The stubborn American environment is there with its imperious summons to accept its conditions; the inherited ways of doing things are also there; and yet, in spite of environment, and in spite of custom, each frontier did indeed furnish a new field of opportunity, a gate of escape from the bondage of the past; and freshness, and confidence, and scorn of older society, impatience of its restraints and its ideas, and indifference to its lessons, have accompanied the frontier. What the Mediterranean Sea was to the Greeks, breaking the bond of custom, offering new experiences, calling out new institutions and activities, that, and more, the ever retreating frontier has been to the United States directly, and to the nations of Europe more remotely. And now, four centuries from the discovery of America, at the end of a hundred years of life under the Constitution, the frontier has gone, and with its going has closed the first period of American history.

WILLIAM JAMES

"The Will to Believe"
(1897)

Of the host of late nineteenth-century American intellectuals preoccupied with the relation of religion to science, William James (1842–1910) was uniquely creative and influential. This preoccupation informed his work as a psychologist, philosopher, and popular lecturer and essayist. Although "The Will to Believe" of 1897, which follows, was his most concentrated and widely quoted monument to this preoccupation with the destiny of religion in an age of science, his most probing and detailed exploration of religion was *The Varieties of Religious Experience* (New York, 1902). We also remember James for *The Principles of Psychology* (New York, 1890) and for *Pragmatism* (New York, 1907), a selection from which is found in Part Two.

For an interpretation of James's entire career as a response to the apparent conflict between religion and science, see David A. Hollinger, "William James and the Culture of Inquiry," in Hollinger's *In the American Province: Studies in the History and Historiography of Ideas* (Bloomington, Ind., 1985), 3–22. In "The Will to Believe," James insisted that science had yet to show the falsity of the essentials of religious belief. He argued further that the actual direction taken by science was influenced by the desires and expectations of the inquirers themselves. Many scientists had come to regard religion as a "dead hypothesis," James complained, and were thus not likely to produce evidence to support its validity. "The Will to Believe" is best read in relation to James's foil, an agnostic classic published twenty years before by the British mathematician W. K. Clifford: "The Ethics of Belief," *Contemporary Review*, 29 (1877), 289–309. Clifford was concerned with the social consequences of belief, whereas the more socially complacent James addressed the spiritual anxieties of the individual soul. Clifford told horror stories about frauds, fakers, and dupes and preached the duty of critically scrutinizing all beliefs; James lamented the believer's intimidation by scientific authority and defended the right to resist cognitive tyranny. As James himself later acknowledged, his primary concern in this essay is less with the will than with the legitimacy of relying upon it; a better title might have substituted *right* for "will." A good sampling of the most recent scholarship on James by philosophers, historians, and literary scholars can be found in Ruth Anna Putnam, ed., *The Cambridge Companion to William James* (Cambridge, 1997). The starting point for any study of James's perspective on religion is now Wayne Proudfoot, ed., *William James and a Science of Religions* (New York, 2004). One especially fine monograph is David Lamberth, *William James and the Metaphysics of Experience* (Cambridge, Mass., 1999). For additional comments on James and more bibliographical suggestions, see the headnote to James's "What Pragmatism Means."

In the recently published *Life* by Leslie Stephen of his brother, Fitz-James, there is an account of a school to which the latter went when he was a boy. The teacher, a certain Mr. Guest, used to converse with his pupils in this wise: "Gurney, what is the difference between justification and sanctification?—Stephen, prove the omnipotence of God!" etc. In the midst of our Harvard freethinking and indifference we are prone to imagine that here at your good old orthodox College conversation continues to be somewhat upon this order; and to show you that we at Harvard have not lost all interest in these vital subjects, I have brought with me to-night something like a sermon on justification by faith to read to you,—I mean an essay in justification of faith, a defence of our right to adopt a believing attitude in religious matters, in spite of the fact that our merely logical intellect may not have been coerced. "The Will to Believe," accordingly, is the title of my paper.

I have long defended to my own students the lawfulness of voluntarily adopted faith; but as soon as they have got well imbued with the logical spirit, they have as a rule refused to admit my contention to be lawful philosophically, even though in point of fact they were personally all the time chock-full of some faith or other themselves. I am all the while, however, so profoundly convinced that my own position is correct, that your invitation has seemed to me a good occasion to make my statements more clear. Perhaps your minds will be more open than those with which I have hitherto had to deal. I will be as little technical as I can, though I must begin by setting up some technical distinctions that will help us in the end.

Let us give the name of *hypothesis* to anything that may be proposed to our belief; and just as the electricians speak of live and dead wires, let us speak of any hypothesis as either *live* or *dead*. A live hypothesis is one which appeals as a real possibility to him to whom it is proposed. If I ask you to believe in the Mahdi, the notion makes no electric connection with your nature,—it refuses to scintillate with any credibility at all. As an hypothesis it is completely dead. To an Arab, however (even if he be not one of the Mahdi's followers), the hypothesis is among the mind's possibilities: it is alive. This shows that deadness and liveness in an hypothesis are not intrinsic properties, but relations to the individual thinker. They are measured by his willingness to act. The maximum of liveness in an hypothesis means willingness to act irrevocably. Practically, that means belief; but there is some believing tendency wherever there is willingness to act at all.

Next, let us call the decision between two hypotheses an *option*. Options may be of several kinds. They may be—1, *living* or *dead*; 2, *forced* or *avoidable*; 3, *momentous* or *trivial*; and for our purposes we may call an option a *genuine* option when it is of the forced, living, and momentous kind.

1. A living option is one in which both hypotheses are live ones. If I say to you: "Be a theosophist or be a Mohammedan," it is probably a dead option, because for you neither hypothesis is likely to be alive. But if I say: "Be an agnostic or be a Christian," it is otherwise: trained as you are, each hypothesis makes some appeal, however small, to your belief.

2. Next, if I say to you: "Choose between going out with your umbrella or without it," I do not offer you a genuine option, for it is not forced. You can easily avoid it by not going out at all. Similarly, if I say, "Either love me or hate me," "Either call my theory true or call it false," your option is avoidable. You may remain indifferent to me, neither loving nor hating, and you may decline to offer any judgment as to my theory. But if I say, "Either accept this truth or go without it," I put on you a forced option, for there is no standing place outside of the alternative. Every dilemma

Source: William James, *The Will to Believe* (New York: Longman's, 1897), 1–31.

based on a complete logical disjunction, with no possibility of not choosing, is an option of this forced kind.

3. Finally, if I were Dr. Nansen and proposed to you to join my North Pole expedition, your option would be momentous; for this would probably be your only similar opportunity, and your choice now would either exclude you from the North Pole sort of immortality altogether or put at least the chance of it into your hands. He who refuses to embrace a unique opportunity loses the prize as surely as if he tried and failed. Per contra, the option is trivial when the opportunity is not unique, when the stake is insignificant, or when the decision is reversible if it later prove unwise. Such trivial options abound in the scientific life. A chemist finds an hypothesis live enough to spend a year in its verification: he believes in it to that extent. But if his experiments prove inconclusive either way, he is quit for his loss of time, no vital harm being done.

It will facilitate our discussion if we keep all these distinctions well in mind.

The next matter to consider is the actual psychology of human opinion. When we look at certain facts, it seems as if our passional and volitional nature lay at the root of all our convictions. When we look at others, it seems as if they could know nothing when the intellect had once said its say. Let us take the latter facts up first.

Does it not seem preposterous on the very face of it to talk of our opinions being modifiable at will? Can our will either help or hinder our intellect in its perceptions of truth? Can we, by just willing it, believe that Abraham Lincoln's existence is a myth, and that the portraits of him in *McClure's Magazine* are all of some one else? Can we, by any effort of our will, or by any strength of wish that it were true, believe ourselves well and about when we are roaring with rheumatism in bed, or feel certain that the sum of the two one-dollar bills in our pocket must be a hundred dollars? We can say any of these things, but we are absolutely impotent to believe them, and of just such things is the whole fabric of the truths that we do believe in made up,—matters of fact, immediate or remote, as Hume said, and relations between ideas, which are either there or not there for us if we see them so, and which if not there cannot be put there by any action of our own.

In Pascal's *Thoughts* there is a celebrated passage known in literature as Pascal's wager. In it he tries to force us into Christianity by reasoning as if our concern with truth resembled our concern with the stakes in a game of chance. Translated freely his words are these: You must either believe or not believe what God is—which will you do? Your human reason cannot say. A game is going on between you and the nature of things which at the day of judgment will bring out either heads or tails. Weigh what your gains and your losses would be if you should stake all you have on heads, or God's existence: if you win in such case, you gain eternal beatitude; if you lose, you lose nothing at all. If there were an infinity of chances, and only one for God in this wager, still you ought to stake your all on God; for though you surely risk a finite loss by this procedure, any finite loss is reasonable, even a certain one is reasonable, if there is but the possibility of infinite gain. Go, then, and take holy water, and have masses said; belief will come and stupefy your scruples,—*Cela vous fera croire et vous abêtira*. Why should you not? At bottom, what have you to lose?

You probably feel that when religious faith expresses itself thus, in the language of the gaming-table, it is put to its last trumps. Surely Pascal's own personal belief in masses and holy water had far other springs; and this celebrated page of his is but an argument for others, a last desperate snatch at a weapon against the hardness of the unbelieving heart. We feel that a faith in masses and holy water adopted willfully after such a mechanical calculation would lack the inner soul of faith's reality; and if we were ourselves in the place of the Deity, we would probably take particular pleasure in cutting off believers of this pattern from their infinite reward. It is evident that unless there be some pre-existing tendency to believe in masses and holy water, the option offered to the will by Pascal is not a living option. Certainly no Turk ever took to masses and holy water on its account; and even to us Protestants these means of salvation seem such foregone impossibilities that Pascal's logic, invoked for them specifically, leaves us unmoved. As well might the Mahdi write to us, saying, "I am the Expected One whom God has created in his effulgence. You shall be infinitely happy if you confess me; otherwise you shall be cut off from the light of the sun. Weigh, then, your infinite gain if I am genuine against your finite sacrifice if I am not!" His logic would be that of Pascal; but he would vainly use it on us, for the hypothesis he offers us is dead. No tendency to act on it exists in us to any degree.

The talk of believing by our volition seems, then, from one point of view, simply silly. From another point of view it is worse than silly, it is vile. When one turns to the magnificent edifice of the physical sciences, and sees how it was reared; what thousands of disinterested moral lives of men lie buried in its mere foundations; what patience and postponement, what choking down of preference, what submission to the icy laws of outer fact are wrought into its very stones and mortar; how absolutely impersonal it stands in its vast augustness,—then how besotted and contemptible seems every little sentimentalist who comes blowing his voluntary smoke-wreaths, and pretending to decide things from out of his private dream! Can we wonder if those bred in the rugged and manly school of science should feel like spewing such subjectivism out of their mouths? The whole system of loyalties which grow up in the schools of science go dead against its toleration; so that it is only natural that those who have caught the scientific fever should pass over to the opposite extreme, and write sometimes as if the incorruptibly truthful intellect ought positively to prefer bitterness and unacceptableness to the heart in its cup.

> It fortifies my soul to know
> That, though I perish, Truth is so—

sings Clough, while Huxley exclaims: "My only consolation lies in the reflection that, however bad our posterity may become, so far as they hold by the plain rule of not pretending to believe what they have no reason to believe, because it may be to their advantage so to pretend [the word 'pretend' is surely here redundant], they will not have reached the lowest depth of immorality." And that delicious enfant terrible Clifford writes: "Belief is desecrated when given to unproved and unquestioned statements for the solace and private pleasure of the believer....Whoso would deserve well of his fellows in this matter will guard the purity of his belief with a very fanaticism of jealous care, lest at any time it should rest on an unworthy object, and catch a stain which can never be wiped away.... If [a] belief has been accepted on insufficient evidence [even though the belief be true, as Clifford on the same page explains] the pleasure is a stolen one.... It is sinful because it is stolen in defiance of our duty to mankind. That duty is to guard ourselves from such beliefs as from a pestilence which may shortly master our own body and then spread to the rest of the town.... It is wrong always, everywhere, and for every one, to believe anything upon insufficient evidence."

All this strikes one as healthy, even when expressed, as by Clifford, with somewhat too much of robustious pathos in the voice. Free-will and simple wishing do seem, in the matter of our credences, to be only fifth wheels to the coach. Yet if any one should thereupon assume that intellectual insight is what remains after wish and will and sentimental preference have taken wing, or that pure reason is what then settles our opinions, he would fly quite as directly in the teeth of the facts.

It is only our already dead hypotheses that our willing nature is unable to bring to life again. But what has made them dead for us is for the most part a previous action of our willing nature of an antagonistic kind. When I say "willing nature," I do not mean only such deliberate volitions as may have set up habits of belief that we cannot now escape from,—I mean all such factors of belief as fear and hope, prejudice and passion, imitation and partisanship, the circumpressure of our caste and set. As a matter of fact we find ourselves believing, we hardly know how or why. Mr. Balfour gives the name of "authority" to all those influences, born of the intellectual climate, that make hypotheses possible or impossible for us, alive or dead. Here in this room, we all of us believe in molecules and the conservation of energy, in democracy and necessary progress, in Protestant Christianity and the duty of fighting for "the doctrine of the immortal Monroe," all for no reasons worthy of the name. We see into these matters with no more inner clearness, and probably with much less, than any disbeliever in them might possess. His unconventionality would probably have some grounds to show for its conclusions; but for us, not insight, but the *prestige* of the opinions, is what makes the spark shoot from them and light up our sleeping magazines of faith. Our reason is quite satisfied, in nine hundred and ninety-nine cases out of every thousand of us, if it can find a few arguments that will do to recite in case our credulity is criticised by some one else. Our faith is faith in some one else's faith, and in the greatest matters this is most the case. Our belief in truth itself, for instance, that there is a truth, and that our minds and it are made for each other,—what is it but a passionate affirmation of desire, in which our social system backs us up? We want to have a truth; we want to believe that our experiments and studies and discussions must put us in a continually better and better position towards it; and on this line we agree to fight out our thinking lives. But if a pyrrhonistic sceptic asks us *how we know* all this, can our logic find a reply? No! certainly it cannot. It is just one volition against another,—we willing to go in for life upon a trust or assumption which he, for his part, does not care to make.

As a rule we disbelieve all facts and theories for which we have no use. Clifford's cosmic emotions find no use for Christian feelings. Huxley belabors the bishops because there is no use for sacerdotalism in his scheme of life. Newman, on the contrary, goes over to Romanism, and finds all sorts of reasons good for staying there, because a priestly system is for him an organic need and delight. Why do so few "scientists" even look at the evidence for telepathy, so called? Because they think, as a leading biologist, now dead, once said to me, that even if such a thing were true scientists ought to band together to keep it suppressed and concealed. It would undo the uniformity of Nature and all sorts of other things without which scientists cannot carry on their pursuits. But if this very man had been shown something which as a scientist he might *do* with telepathy, he might not only have examined the evidence, but even have found it good enough. This very law which the logicians would impose upon us—if I may give the name of logicians to those who would rule out our willing nature here—is based on nothing but their own natural wish to exclude all elements for which they, in their professional quality of logicians, can find no use.

Evidently, then, our non-intellectual nature does influence our convictions. There are passional tendencies and volitions which run before and others which come after belief, and it is only the latter that are too late for the fair; and they are not too late when the previous passional work has been already in their own direction. Pascal's argument, instead of being powerless, then seems a regular clincher, and is the last stroke needed to make our faith in masses and holy water complete. The state of things is evidently far from simple; and pure insight and logic, whatever they might do ideally, are not the only things that really do produce our creeds.

Our next duty, having recognized this mixed-up state of affairs, is to ask whether it be simply reprehensible and pathological, or whether, on the contrary, we must treat it as a normal element in making up our minds. The thesis I defend is, briefly stated, this: *Our passional nature not only lawfully may, but must, decide an option between propositions, whenever it is a genuine option that cannot by its nature be decided on intellectual grounds; for to say, under such circumstances, "Do not decide, but leave the question open," is itself a passional decision,—just like deciding yes or no,—and is attended with the same risk of losing the truth.* The thesis thus abstractly expressed will, I trust, soon become quite clear. But I must first indulge in a bit more of preliminary work.

It will be observed that for the purposes of this discussion we are on "dogmatic" ground,—ground, I mean, which leaves systematic philosophical scepticism altogether out of account. The postulate that there is truth, and that it is the destiny of our minds to attain it, we are deliberately resolving to make, though the sceptic will not make it. We part company with him, therefore, absolutely, at this point. But the faith that truth exists, and that our minds can find it, may be held in two ways. We may talk of the *empiricist* way and of the *absolutist* way of believing in truth. The absolutists in this matter say that we not only can attain to knowing truth, but we can *know when* we have attained to knowing it; while the empiricists think that although we may attain it, we cannot infallibly know when. To *know* is one thing, and to know for certain *that* we know is another. One may hold to the first being possible without the second; hence the empiricists and the absolutists, although neither of them is a sceptic in the usual philosophic sense of the term, show very different degrees of dogmatism in their lives.

If we look at the history of opinions, we see that the empiricist tendency has largely prevailed in science, while in philosophy the absolutist tendency has had everything its own way. The characteristic sort of happiness, indeed, which philosophies yield has mainly consisted in the conviction felt by each successive school or system that by it bottom-certitude had been attained. "Other philosophies are collections of opinions, mostly false; *my* philosophy gives standing-ground forever,"—who does not recognize in this the key-note of every system worthy of the name? A system, to be a system at all, must come as a *closed* system, reversible in this or that detail, perchance, but in its essential features never!

Scholastic orthodoxy, to which one must always go when one wishes to find perfectly clear statement, has beautifully elaborated this absolutist conviction in a doctrine which it calls that of "objective evidence." If, for example, I am unable to doubt that I now exist before you, that two is less than three, or that if all men are mortal then I am mortal too, it is because these things illumine my intellect irresistibly. The final ground of this objective evidence possessed by certain propositions is the *adaequatio intellectûs nostri cum rê.* The certitude it brings involves an *aptitudinem ad extorquendum certum assensum* on the part of the truth envisaged, and on the side of the subject a *quietem in cognitione,* when once the object is mentally received, that leaves no possibility of doubt behind; and in the whole transaction nothing operates but the *entitas ipsa* of the object and the *entitas ipsa* of the mind. We slouchy modern thinkers dislike to talk in Latin,—indeed, we dislike to talk in set terms at all; but at bottom our own state of mind is very much like this whenever we uncritically abandon ourselves: You believe in objective evidence, and I do. Of some things we feel that we are certain: we know, and we know that we do know. There is something that gives a click inside of us, a bell that strikes twelve, when the hands of our mental clock have swept the dial and meet over the meridian hour. The greatest empiricists among us are only empiricists on reflection: when left to their instincts, they dogmatize like infallible popes. When the Cliffords tell us how sinful it is to be Christians on such "insufficient evidence," insufficiency is really the last thing they have in mind. For them the evidence is absolutely sufficient, only it makes the other way. They believe so completely in an antichristian order of the universe that there is no living option: Christianity is a dead hypothesis from the start.

But now, since we are all such absolutists by instinct, what in our quality of students of philosophy ought we to do about the fact? Shall we espouse and indorse it? Or shall we treat it as a weakness of our nature from which we must free ourselves, if we can?

I sincerely believe that the latter course is the only one we can follow as reflective men. Objective evidence and certitude are doubtless very fine ideals to play with, but where on this moonlit and dream-visited planet are they found? I am, therefore, myself a complete empiricist so far as my theory of human knowledge goes. I live, to be sure, by the practical faith that we must go on experiencing and thinking over our experience, for only thus can our opinions grow more true; but to hold any one of them—I absolutely do not care which—as if it never could be reinterpretable or corrigible, I believe to be a tremendously mistaken attitude, and I think that the whole history of philosophy will bear me out. There is but one indefectibly certain truth, and that is the truth that pyrrhonistic scepticism itself leaves standing,—the truth that the present phenomenon of consciousness exists. That, however, is the bare starting-point of knowledge, the mere admission of a stuff to be philosophized about. The various philosophies are but so many attempts at expressing what this stuff really is. And if we repair to our libraries what disagreement do we discover! Where is a certainly true answer found? Apart from abstract propositions of comparison (such as two and two are the same as four), propositions which tell us nothing by themselves about concrete reality, we find no proposition ever regarded by any one as evidently certain that has not either been called a falsehood, or at least had its truth sincerely questioned by some one else. The transcending of the axioms of geometry, not in play but in earnest, by certain of our contemporaries (as Zöllner and Charles H. Hinton), and the rejection of the whole Aristotelian logic by the Hegelians, are striking instances in point.

No concrete test of what is really true has ever been agreed upon. Some make the criterion external to the moment of perception, putting it either in revelation, the *consensus gentium*, the instincts of the heart, or the systematized experience of the race. Others make the perceptive moment its own test,—Descartes, for instance, with his clear and distinct ideas guaranteed by the veracity of God; Reid with his "common-sense;" and Kant with his forms of synthetic judgment a priori. The inconceivability of the opposite; the capacity to be verified by sense; the possession of complete organic unity or self-relation, realized when a thing is its own other,—are standards which, in turn, have been used. The much lauded objective evidence is never triumphantly there; it is a mere aspiration or *Grenzbegriff*, marking the infinitely remote ideal of our thinking life. To claim that certain truths now possess it, is simply to say that when you think them true and they *are* true, then their evidence is objective, otherwise it is not. But practically one's conviction that the evidence one goes by is of the real objective brand, is only one more subjective opinion added to the lot. For what a contradictory array of opinions have objective evidence and absolute certitude been claimed! The world is rational through and through,—its existence is an ultimate brute fact; there is a personal God,—a personal God is inconceivable; there is an extra-mental physical world immediately known,—the mind can only know its own ideas; a moral imperative exists,—obligation is only the resultant of desires; a permanent spiritual principle is in every one,—there are only shifting states of mind; there is an endless chain of causes,—there is an absolute first cause; an eternal necessity,—a freedom; a purpose,—no purpose; a primal One,—a primal Many; a universal continuity,—an essential discontinuity in things; an infinity,—no infinity. There is this,—there is that; there is indeed nothing which some one has not thought absolutely true, while his neighbor deemed it absolutely false; and not an absolutist among them seems ever to have considered that the trouble may all the time be essential, and that the intellect, even with truth directly in its grasp, may have no infallible signal for knowing whether it be truth or no. When, indeed, one remembers that the most striking practical application to life of the doctrine of objective certitude has been the conscientious labors of the Holy Office of the Inquisition, one feels less tempted than ever to lend the doctrine a respectful ear.

But please observe, now, that when as empiricists we give up the doctrine of objective certitude, we do not thereby give up the quest or hope of truth itself. We still pin our faith on its existence, and still believe that we gain an ever better position towards it by systematically continuing to roll up experiences and think. Our great difference from the scholastic lies in the way we face. The strength of his system lies in the principles, the origin, the *terminus a quo* of his thought; for us the strength is in the outcome, the upshot, the *terminus ad quem*. Not where it comes from but what it leads to is to decide. It matters not to an empiricist from what quarter an hypothesis may come to him: he may have acquired it by fair means or by foul; passion may have whispered or accident suggested it; but if the total drift of thinking continues to confirm it, that is what he means by its being true.

One more point, small but important, and our preliminaries are done. There are two ways of looking at our duty in the matter of opinion,—ways entirely different, and yet ways about whose difference the theory of knowledge seems hitherto to have shown very little concern. *We must know the truth; and we must avoid error,*—these are our first and great commandments as would-be knowers; but they are not two ways of stating an identical commandment, they are two separable laws. Although it may indeed happen that when we believe the truth *A*, we escape as an incidental consequence from believing the falsehood *B*, it hardly ever happens that by merely disbelieving *B* we necessarily believe *A*. We may in escaping *B* fall into believing other falsehoods, *C* or *D*, just as bad as *B*; or we may escape *B* by not believing anything at all, not even *A*.

Believe truth! Shun error!—these, we see, are two materially different laws; and by choosing between them we may end by coloring differently our whole intellectual life. We may regard the chase for truth as paramount, and the avoidance of error as secondary; or we may, on the other hand, treat the avoidance of error as more imperative, and let truth take its chance. Clifford, in the instructive passage which I have quoted, exhorts us in the latter course. Believe nothing, he tells us, keep your mind in suspense forever, rather than by closing it on insufficient evidence incur the awful risk of believing lies. You, on the other hand, may think that the risk of being in error is a very small matter when compared with the blessings of real knowledge, and be ready to be duped many times in your investigation rather than postpone indefinitely the chance of guessing true. I myself find it impossible to go with Clifford. We must remember that these feelings of our duty about either truth or error are in any case only expressions of our passional life. Biologically considered, our minds are as ready to grind out falsehood as veracity, and he who says, "Better go without belief forever than believe a lie!" merely shows his own preponderant private horror of becoming a dupe. He may be critical of many of his desires and fears, but this fear he slavishly obeys. He cannot imagine any one questioning its binding force. For my own part, I have also a horror of being duped; but I can believe that worse things than being duped may happen to a man in this world: so Clifford's exhortation has to my ears a thoroughly fantastic sound. It is like a general informing his soldiers that it is better to keep out of battle forever than to risk a single wound. Not so are victories either over enemies or over nature gained. Our errors are surely not such awfully solemn things. In a world where we are so certain to incur them in spite of all our caution, a certain lightness of heart seems healthier than this excessive nervousness on their behalf. At any rate, it seems the fittest thing for the empiricist philosopher.

And now, after all this introduction, let us go straight at our question. I have said, and now repeat it, that not only as a matter of fact do we find our passional nature influencing us in our opinions, but that there are some options between opinions in which this influence must be regarded both as an inevitable and as a lawful determinant of our choice.

I fear here that some of you my hearers will begin to scent danger, and lend an inhospitable ear. Two first steps of passion you have indeed had to admit as necessary,—we must think so as to avoid dupery, and we must think so as to gain truth; but the surest path to those ideal consummations, you will probably consider, is from now onwards to take no further passional step.

Well, of course, I agree as far as the facts will allow. Wherever the option between losing truth and gaining it is not momentous, we can throw the chance of *gaining truth* away, and at any rate save ourselves from any chance of *believing falsehood*, by not making up our minds at all till objective evidence has come. In scientific questions, this is almost always the case; and even in human affairs in general, the need of acting is seldom so urgent that a false belief to act on is better than no belief at all. Law courts, indeed, have to decide on the best evidence attainable for the moment, because a judge's duty is to make law as well as to ascertain it, and (as a learned judge once said to me) few cases are worth spending much time over: the great thing is to have them decided on *any* acceptable principle, and got out of the way. But in our dealings with objective nature we obviously are recorders, not makers, of the truth; and decisions for the mere sake of deciding promptly and getting on to the next business would be wholly out of place. Throughout the breadth of physical nature facts are what they are quite independently of us, and seldom is there any such hurry about them that the risks of being duped by believing a premature theory need be faced. The questions here are always trivial options, the hypotheses are hardly living (at any rate not living for us spectators), the choice between believing truth or falsehood is seldom forced. The attitude of sceptical balance is therefore the absolutely wise one if we would escape mistakes. What difference, indeed, does it make to most of us whether we have or have not a theory of the Röntgen rays, whether we believe or not in mind-stuff, or have a conviction about the causality of conscious states? It makes no difference. Such options are not forced on us. On every account it is better not to make them, but still keep weighing reasons *pro et contra* with an indifferent hand.

I speak, of course, here of the purely judging mind. For purposes of discovery such indifference is to be less highly recommended, and science would be far less advanced than she is if the passionate desires of individuals to get their own faiths confirmed had been kept out of the game. See for example the sagacity which Spencer and Weismann now display. On the other hand, if you want an absolute duffer in an investigation, you must, after all, take the man who has no interest whatever in its results: he is the warranted incapable, the positive fool. The most useful investigator, because the most sensitive observer, is always he whose eager interest in one side of the question is balanced by an equally keen nervousness lest he become deceived. Science has organized this nervousness into a regular *technique*, her so-called method of verification; and she has fallen so deeply in love with the method that one may even say she has ceased to care for truth by itself at all. It is only truth as technically verified that interests her. The truth of truths might come in merely affirmative form, and she would decline to touch it. Such truth as that, she might repeat with Clifford, would be stolen in defiance of her duty to mankind. Human passions, however, are stronger than technical rules. "Le coeur a ses raisons," as Pascal says, "que la raison ne connaît pas;" and however indifferent to all but the bare rules of the game the umpire, the abstract intellect, may be, the concrete players who furnish him the materials to judge of are usually, each one of them, in love with some pet "live hypothesis" of his own. Let us agree, however, that wherever there is no forced option, the dispassionately judicial intellect with no pet hypothesis, saving us, as it does, from dupery at any rate, ought to be our ideal.

The question next arises: Are there not somewhere forced options in our speculative questions, and can we (as men who may be interested at least as much in positively gaining truth as in merely escaping dupery) always wait with impunity till the coercive evidence shall have arrived? It seems a priori improbable that the truth should be so nicely adjusted to our needs and powers as that. In the great boarding-house of nature, the cakes and the butter and the syrup seldom come out so even and leave the plates so clean. Indeed, we should view them with scientific suspicion if they did.

Moral questions immediately present themselves as questions whose solution cannot wait for sensible proof. A moral question is a question not of what sensibly exists, but of what is good, or would be good if it did exist. Science can tell us what exists; but to compare the *worths*, both of what exists and of what does not exist, we must consult not science, but what Pascal calls our heart. Science herself consults her heart when she lays it down that the infinite ascertainment of fact and correction of false belief are the supreme goods for man. Challenge the statement, and science can only repeat it oracularly, or else prove it by showing that such ascertainment and correction bring man all sorts of other goods which man's heart in turn declares. The question of having moral beliefs at all or not having them is decided by our will. Are our moral preferences true or false, or are they only odd biological phenomena, making things good or bad for us, but in themselves indifferent? How can your pure intellect decide? If your heart does not *want* a world of moral reality, your head will assuredly never make you believe in one. Mephistophelian scepticism, indeed, will satisfy the head's play-instincts much better than any rigorous idealism can. Some men (even at the student age) are so naturally cool-hearted that the moralistic hypothesis never has for them any pungent life, and in their supercilious presence the hot young moralist always feels strangely ill at ease. The appearance of knowingness is on their side, of naïveté and gullibility on his. Yet, in the inarticulate heart of him, he clings to it that he is not a dupe, and that there is a realm in which (as Emerson says) all their wit and intellectual superiority is no better than the cunning of a fox. Moral scepticism can no more be refuted or proved by logic than intellectual scepticism can. When we stick to it that there is truth (be it of either kind), we do so with our whole nature, and resolve to stand or fall by the results. The sceptic with his whole nature adopts the doubting attitude; but which of us is the wiser. Omniscience only knows.

Turn now from these wide questions of good to a certain class of questions of fact, questions concerning personal relations, states of mind between one man and another. *Do you like me or not?*—for example. Whether you do or not depends, in countless instances, on whether I meet you half-way, am willing to assume that you must like me, and show you trust and expectation. The previous faith on my part in your liking's existence is in such cases what makes your liking come. But if I stand aloof, and refuse to budge an inch until I have objective evidence, until you shall have done something apt, as the absolutists say, *ad extorquendum assensum meum*, ten to one your liking never comes. How many women's hearts are vanquished by the mere sanguine insistence of some man that they *must* love him! he will not consent to the hypothesis that they cannot. The desire for a certain kind of truth here brings about that special truth's existence; and so it is in innumerable cases of other sorts. Who gains promotions, boons, appointments, but the man in whose life they are seen to play the part of live hypotheses, who discounts them, sacrifices other things for their sake before they have come, and takes risks for them in advance? His faith acts on the powers above him as a claim, and creates its own verification. A social organism of any sort whatever, large or small, is what it is because each member proceeds to his own duty with a trust that the other members will simultaneously do theirs. Wherever a desired result is achieved by the co-operation of many independent persons, its existence as a fact is a pure consequence of the precursive faith in one another of those immediately concerned. A government, an army, a commercial system, a ship, a college, an athletic team, all exist on this condition, without which not only is nothing achieved, but nothing is even attempted. A whole train of passengers (individually brave enough) will be looted by a few highwaymen, simply because the latter can count on one another, while each passenger fears that if he makes a movement of resistance, he will be shot before any one else backs him up. If we believed that the whole car-full would rise at once with us, we should each severally rise, and train-robbing would never even be attempted. There are, then, cases where a fact cannot come at all unless a preliminary faith exists in its coming. *And where faith in a fact can help create the fact,* that would be an insane logic which should say that faith running ahead of scientific evidence is the "lowest kind of immorality" into which a thinking being can fall. Yet such is the logic by which our scientific absolutists pretend to regulate our lives!

In truths dependent on our personal action, then, faith based on desire is certainly a lawful and possibly an indispensable thing.

But now, it will be said, these are all childish human cases, and have nothing to do with great cosmical matters, like the question of religious faith. Let us then pass on to that. Religions differ so much in their accidents that in discussing the religious question we must make it very generic and broad. What then do we now mean by the religious hypothesis? Science says things are; morality says some things are better than other things; and religion says essentially two things.

First, she says that the best things are the more eternal things, the overlapping things, the things in the universe that throw the last stone, so to speak, and say the final word. "Perfection is eternal,"—this phrase of Charles Secrétan seems a good way of putting this first affirmation of religion, an affirmation which obviously cannot yet be verified scientifically at all.

The second affirmation of religion is that we are better off even now if we believe her first affirmation to be true.

Now, let us consider what the logical elements of this situation are *in case the religious hypothesis in both its branches be really true*. (Of course, we must admit that possibility at the outset. If we are to discuss the question at all, it must involve a living option. If for any of you religion be a hypothesis that cannot, by any living possibility be true, then you need go no farther. I speak to the "saving remnant" alone.) So proceeding, we see, first, that religion offers itself as a *momentous* option. We are supposed to gain, even now, by our belief, and to lose by our non-belief, a certain vital good. Secondly, religion is a *forced* option, so far as that good goes. We cannot escape the issue by remaining sceptical and waiting for more light, because, although we do avoid error in that way *if religion be untrue*, we lose the good, *if it be true*, just as certainly as if we positively chose to disbelieve. It is as if a man should hesitate indefinitely to ask a certain woman to marry him because he was not perfectly sure that she would prove an angel after he brought her home. Would he not cut himself off from that particular angel-possibility as decisively as if he went and married some one else? Scepticism, then, is not avoidance of option; it is option of a certain particular kind of risk. *Better risk loss of truth than chance of error,*—that is your faith-vetoer's exact position. He is actively playing his stake as much as the believer is; he is backing the field against the religious hypothesis, just as the believer is backing the religious hypothesis against the field. To preach scepticism to us as a duty until "sufficient evidence" for religion be found, is tantamount therefore to telling us, when in presence of the religious hypothesis, that to yield to our fear of its being error is wiser and better than to yield to our hope that it may be true. It is not intellect against all passions, then; it is only intellect with one passion laying down its law. And by what, forsooth, is the supreme wisdom of this passion warranted? Dupery for dupery, what proof is there that dupery through hope is so much worse than dupery through fear? I, for one, can see no proof; and I simply refuse obedience to the scientist's command to imitate his kind of option, in a case where my own stake is important enough to give me the right to choose my own form of risk. If religion be true and the evidence for it be still insufficient, I do not wish, by putting your extinguisher upon my nature (which feels to me as if it had after all some business in this matter), to forfeit my sole chance in life of getting upon the winning side,—that chance depending, of course, on my willingness to run the risk of acting as if my passional need of taking the world religiously might be prophetic and right.

All this is on the supposition that it really may be prophetic and right, and that, even to us who are discussing the matter, religion is a live hypothesis which may be true. Now, to most of us religion comes in a still further way that makes a veto on our active faith even more illogical. The more perfect and more eternal aspect of the universe is represented in our religions as having personal form. The universe is no longer a mere *It* to us, but a *Thou*, if we are religious; and any relation that may be possible from person to person might be possible here. For instance, although in one sense we are passive portions of the universe, in another we show a curious autonomy, as if we were small active centres on our own account. We feel, too, as if the appeal of religion to us *were* made to our own active good-will, as if evidence might be forever withheld from us unless we met the hypothesis half-way. To take a trivial illustration: just as a man who in a company of gentlemen made no advances, asked a warrant for every concession, and believed no one's word without proof, would cut himself off by such churlishness from all the social rewards that a more trusting spirit would earn,—so here, one who should shut himself up in snarling logicality and try to make the gods extort his recognition willy-nilly, or not get it at all, might cut himself off forever from his only opportunity of making the gods' acquaintance. This feeling, forced on us we know not whence, that by obstinately believing that there are gods (although not to do so would be so easy both for our logic and our life) we are doing the universe the deepest service we can, seems part of the living essence of the religious hypothesis. If the hypothesis were true in all its parts, including this one, then pure intellectualism, with its veto on our making willing advances, would be an absurdity; and some participation of our sympathetic nature would be logically required. I, therefore, for one, cannot see my way to accepting the agnostic rules for truth-seeking, or wilfully agree to keep my willing nature out of the game. I cannot do so for this plain reason, that *a rule of thinking which would absolutely prevent me from acknowledging certain kinds of truth if those kinds of truth were really there, would be an irrational rule.* That for me is the long and short of the formal logic of the situation, no matter what the kinds of truth might materially be.

I confess I do not see how this logic can be escaped. But sad experience makes me fear that some of you may still shrink from radically saying with me, *in abstracto*, that we have the right to believe at our own risk any hypothesis that is live enough to tempt our will. I suspect, however, that if this is so, it is because you have got away from the abstract logical point of view altogether, and are thinking (perhaps without realizing it) of some particular religious hypothesis which for you is dead. The freedom to "believe what we will" you apply to the case of some patent superstition; and the faith you think of is the faith defined by the schoolboy when he said, "Faith is when you believe something that you know ain't true." I can only repeat that this is misapprehension. *In concreto*, the freedom to believe can only cover living options which the intellect of the individual cannot by itself resolve; and living options never seem absurdities to him who has them to consider. When I look at the religious question as it really puts itself to concrete men, and when I think of all the possibilities which both practically and theoretically it involves, then this command that we shall put a stopper on our heart, instincts, and courage, and *wait*—acting of course meanwhile more or less as if religion were *not* true[1]—till doomsday, or till such time as our intellect and senses working together may have raked in evidence enough,—this command, I say, seems to me the queerest idol ever manufactured in the philosophic cave. Were we scholastic absolutists, there might be more excuse. If we had an infallible intellect with its objective certitudes, we might feel ourselves disloyal to such a perfect organ of knowledge in not trusting to it exclusively, in not waiting for its releasing word. But if we are empiricists, if we believe that no bell in us tolls to let us know for certain when truth is in our grasp, then it seems a piece of idle fantasticality to preach so solemnly our duty of waiting for the bell. Indeed we *may* wait if we will,—I hope you do not think that I am denying that,—but if we do so, we do so at our peril as much as if we believed. In either case we *act*, taking our life in our hands. No one of us ought to issue vetoes to the other, nor should we bandy words of abuse. We ought, on the contrary, delicately and profoundly to respect one another's mental freedom: then only shall we bring about the intellectual

---

1.   Since belief is measured by action, he who forbids us to believe religion to be true, necessarily also forbids us to act as we should if we did believe it to be true. The whole defence of religious faith hinges upon action. If the action required or inspired by the religious hypothesis is in no way different from that dictated by the naturalistic hypothesis, then religious faith is a pure superfluity, better pruned away, and controversy about its legitimacy is a piece of idle trifling, unworthy of serious minds. I myself believe, of course, that the religious hypothesis gives to the world an expression which specifically determines our reactions, and makes them in a large part unlike what they might be on a purely naturalistic scheme of belief.

republic; then only shall we have that spirit of inner tolerance without which all our outer tolerance is soulless, and which is empiricism's glory; then only shall we live and let live, in speculative as well as in practical things.

I began by a reference to Fitz-James Stephen; let me end by a quotation from him. "What do you think of yourself ? What do you think of the world?...These are questions with which all must deal as it seems good to them. They are riddles of the Sphinx, and in some way or other we must deal with them.... In all important transactions of life we have to take a leap in the dark.... If we decide to leave the riddles unanswered, that is a choice; if we waver in our answer, that, too, is a choice: but whatever choice we make, we make it at our peril. If a man chooses to turn his back altogether on God and the future, no one can prevent him; no one can show beyond reasonable doubt that he is mistaken. If a man thinks otherwise and acts as he thinks, I do not see that any one can prove that he is mistaken. Each must act as he thinks best; and if he is wrong, so much the worse for him. We stand on a mountain pass in the midst of whirling snow and blinding mist, through which we get glimpses now and then of paths which may be deceptive. If we stand still we shall be frozen to death. If we take the wrong road we shall be dashed to pieces. We do not certainly know whether there is any right one. What must we do? 'Be strong and of a good courage.' Act for the best, hope for the best, and take what comes.... If death ends all, we cannot meet death better."

JOSIAH ROYCE

"The Problem of Job"
(1898)

During most of the twentieth century, the Idealist philosopher Josiah Royce (1855–1916) was remembered in the terms proposed by his critics, especially his two great anti-Idealist colleagues at Harvard, William James and George Santayana. To these earthier-than-thou thinkers, Royce was a tender soul, looking always on the bright side, complacently aloof from the strivings and sufferings of real men and women. "The Problem of Job" (1898) lends credibility to this view of Royce, as it justifies the ghastliest of evils as part of God's perfect plan for the universe. But the piece also displays the directness, the relentlessness, and the vigor that led Royce's admirers to compare him to the reigning heavyweight champion of the world: He was the John L. Sullivan of philosophy. And it is the willingness of Job to argue with God, to demand rational answers, that most endears Job to Royce. Although Royce himself does not draw the comparison, his answer to the problem of evil is, in fact, widely at variance with the response provided in the Book of Job. There (Job 42:3–6), God convinces Job that he deserves no answer at all. But Royce, voicing the more rationalist faith characteristic of the liberal Protestantism of his milieu, believes he can give good reasons why a loving and just God allowed Job to suffer and allowed Armenians to be massacred by Turks.

An irony of Royce's reputation is that while he was continually depicted as "soft" by his tougher-than-thou critics, he, rather than they, actually had been born in a California mining camp and had experienced at firsthand the toughness of frontier life often idealized by tenderfeet from the East. Royce wrote a narrative history of early California, and a novel about its violence, *The Feud at Oakfield Creek* (New York, 1887). But Royce's most influential works were systematic works of philosophy, including *The Religious Aspect of Philosophy* (Boston, 1885), *The Spirit of Modern Philosophy* (Boston, 1892), *The Philosophy of Loyalty* (New York, 1908), and *The Problem of Christianity*, 2 vols. (New York, 1913).

Royce's philosophy as a whole is addressed in Bruce Kuklick, *Josiah Royce: An Intellectual Biography* (Indianapolis, 1972). A briefer, more accessible overview can be found in R. Jackson Wilson, *In Quest of Community: Social Philosophy in the United States, 1860–1920* (New York, 1968), 144–70. Two more recent biographies are John Clendenning, *The Life and Thought of Josiah Royce* (Madison, Wis., 1985); and Robert V. Hine, *Josiah Royce: From Grass Valley to Harvard* (Norman, Okla., 1991). The Josiah Royce Society, founded in 2003, promotes the study of Royce's ideas today.

The general problem of evil has received, as is well known, a great deal of attention from the philosophers. Few of them, at least in European thought, have been as fearless in stating the issue as was the original author of Job. The solutions offered have, however, been very numerous. For our purposes they may be reduced to a few.

First, then, one may escape Job's paradox by declining altogether to view the world in teleological terms. Evils, such as death, disease, tempests, enemies, fires, are not, so one may declare, the works of God or of Satan, but are natural phenomena. Natural, too, are the phenomena of our desires, of our pains, sorrows and failures. No divine purpose rules or overrules any of these things. That happens to us, at any time, which must happen, in view of our natural limitations and of our ignorance. The way to better things is to understand nature better than we now do. For this view—a view often maintained in our day—there is no problem of evil, in Job's sense, at all. Evil there indeed is, but the only rational problems are those of natural laws. I need not here further consider this method, not of solving but of abolishing the problem before us, since my intent is, in this paper, to suggest the possibility of some genuinely teleological answer to Job's question. I mention this first view only to recognize, historically, its existence.

In the second place, one may deal with our problem by attempting any one, or a number, of those familiar and popular compromises between the belief in a world of natural law and the belief in a teleological order, which are all, as compromises, reducible to the assertion that the presence of evil in the creation is a relatively insignificant, and an inevitable, incident of a plan that produces sentient creatures subject to law. Writers who expound such compromises have to point out that, since a burnt child dreads the fire, pain is, on the whole, useful as a warning. Evil is a transient discipline whereby finite creatures learn their place in the system of things. Again, a sentient world cannot get on without some experience of suffering, since sentience means tenderness. Take away pain (so one still again often insists), take away pain, and we should not learn our share of natural truth. Pain is the pedagogue to teach us natural science. The contagious diseases, for instance, are useful in so far as they lead us in the end to study Bacteriology, and thus to get an insight into the life of certain beautiful creatures of God whose presence in the world we should otherwise blindly overlook! Moreover (to pass to still another variation of this sort of explanation), created beings obviously grow from less to more. First the lower, then the higher. Otherwise there could be no Evolution. And were there no evolution, how much of edifying natural science we should miss! But if one is evolved, if one grows from less to more, there must be something to make the stages of growth. Now evil is useful to mark the lower stages of evolution. If you are to be, first an infant, then a man, or first a savage, then a civilized being, there must be evils attendant upon the earlier stages of your life—evils that make growth welcome and conscious. Thus, were there no colic and croup, were there no tumbles and crying-spells in infancy, there would be no sufficient incentives to loving parents to hasten the growing robustness of their children, and no motives to impel the children to long to grow big! Just so, cannibalism is valuable as a mark of a lower grade of evolution. Had there been no cannibalism, we should realize less joyously than we do what a respectable thing it is to have become civilized! In brief, evil is, as it were, the dirt of the natural order, whose value is that, when you wash it off, you thereby learn the charm of the bath of evolution.

Source: Josiah Royce, *Studies of Good and Evil* (New York: Appleton, 1898), 1–28.

The foregoing are mere hints of familiar methods of playing about the edges of our problem, as children play barefoot in the shallowest reaches of the foam of the sea. In our poem,...the speeches ascribed to Elihu contain the most hints of some such way of defining evil, as a merely transient incident of the discipline of the individual. With many writers explanations of this sort fill much space. They are even not without their proper place in popular discussion. But they have no interest for whoever has once come into the presence of Job's problem as it is in itself. A moment's thought reminds us of their superficiality. Pain is useful as a warning of danger. If we did not suffer, we should burn our hands off. Yes, but this explanation of one evil presupposes another, and a still unexplained and greater evil, namely, the existence of the danger of which we need to be thus warned. No doubt it is well that the past sufferings of the Armenians should teach the survivors, say the defenseless women and children, to have a wholesome fear in future of Turks. Does that explain, however, the need for the existence, or for the murderous doings of the Turks? If I can only reach a given goal by passing over a given road, say of evolution, it may be well for me to consent to the toilsome journey. Does that explain why I was created so far from my goal? Discipline, toil, penalty, surgery, are all explicable as means to ends, if only it be presupposed that there exists, and that there is quite otherwise explicable, the necessity for the situations which involve such fearful expenses. One justifies the surgery, but not the disease; the toil, but not the existence of the need for the toil; the penalty, but not the situation which has made the penalty necessary, when one points out that evil is in so many cases medicinal or disciplinary or prophylactic—an incident of imperfect stages of evolution, or the price of a distant good attained through misery. All such explanations, I insist, trade upon borrowed capital. But God, by hypothesis, is no borrower. He produces his own capital of ends and means. Every evil is explained on the foregoing plan only by presupposing at least an equal, and often a greater and a preëxistent evil, namely, the very state of things which renders the first evil the only physically possible way of reaching a given goal. But what Job wants his judge to explain is not that evil A is a physical means of warding off some other greater evil B, in this cruel world where the waters wear away even the stones, and where hopes of man are so much frailer than the stones; but why a God who can do whatever he wishes chooses situations where such a heaped-up mass of evil means become what we should call physical necessitites to the ends now physically possible.

No real explanation of the presence of evil can succeed which declares evil to be a merely physical necessity for one who desires, in this present world, to reach a given goal. Job's business is not with physical accidents, but with the God who chose to make this present nature; and an answer to Job must show that evil is not a physical but a logical necessity—something whose non-existence would simply contradict the very essence, the very perfection of God's own nature and power. This talk of medicinal and disciplinary evil, perfectly fair when applied to our poor fate-bound human surgeons, judges, jailors, or teachers, becomes cruelly, even cynically trivial when applied to explain the ways of a God who is to choose, not only the physical means to an end, but the very *Physis* itself in which path and goal are to exist together. I confess, as a layman, that whenever, at a funeral, in the company of mourners who are immediately facing Job's own personal problem, and who are sometimes, to say the least, wide enough awake to desire not to be stayed with relative comforts, but to ask that terrible and uttermost question of God himself, and to require the direct answer—that whenever I say, in such company I have to listen to these half-way answers, to these superficial plashes in the wavelets at the water's edge of sorrow, while the black, unfathomed ocean of finite evil spreads out before our wide-opened eyes—well, at such times this trivial speech about useful burns and salutary medicines makes me, and I fancy others, simply and wearily heartsick. Some words are due to children at school, to peevish patients in the sick-room who need a little temporary quieting. But quite other speech is due to men and women when they are wakened to the higher reason of Job by the fierce anguish of our mortal life's ultimate facts. They deserve either our simple silence, or, if we are ready to speak, the speech of people who ourselves inquire as Job inquired.

A third method of dealing with our problem is in essence identical with the course which, in a very antiquated form, the friends of Job adopt. This method takes its best known expression in the doctrine that the presence of evil in the world is explained by the fact that the value of free will in moral agents logically involves, and so explains and justi- fies, the divine permission of the evil deeds of those finite beings who freely choose to sin, as well as the inevitable fruits of the sins. God creates agents with free will. He does so because the existence of such agents has of itself an infinite worth. Were there no free agents, the highest good could not be. But such agents, because they are free, can offend. The divine justice of necessity pursues such offenses with attendant evils. These evils, the result of sin, must, logically speaking, be permitted to exist, if God once creates the agents who have free will, and himself remains, as he must logically do, a just God. How much ill thus results depends upon the choice of the free agents, not upon God, who wills to have only good chosen, but of necessity must leave his free creatures to their own devices, so far as concerns their power to sin.

This view has the advantage of undertaking to regard evil as a logically necessary part of a perfect moral order, and not as a mere incident of an imperfectly adjusted physical mechanism. So dignified a doctrine, by virtue of its long history and its high theological reputation, needs here no extended exposition. I assume it as familiar, and pass at once to its difficulties. It has its share of truth. There is, I doubt not, moral free will in the universe. But the presence of evil in the world simply cannot be explained by free will alone. This is easy to show. One who maintains this view asserts, in substance, "All real evils are the results of the acts of free and finite moral agents." These agents may be angels or men. If there is evil in the city, the Lord has *not* done it, except in so far as his justice has acted in readjusting wrongs already done. Such ill is due to the deeds of his creatures. But hereupon one asks at once, in presence of any ill, "Who did this?" Job's friends answer: "The sufferer himself; his deed wrought his own undoing. God punishes only the sinner. Every one suf- fers for his own wrongdoing. Your ill is the result of your crime."

But Job, and all his defenders of innocence, must at once reply: "Empirically speaking, this is obviously, in our visible world, simply not true. The sufferer may suffer innocently. The ill is often undeserved. The fathers sin; the child, diseased from birth, degraded, or a born wretch, may pay the penalty. The Turk or the active rebel sins. Armenia's helpless women and babes cry in vain unto God for help."

Hereupon the reply comes, although not indeed from Job's friends: "Alas! it is so. Sin means suffering; but the innocent may suffer *for* the guilty. This, to be sure, is God's way. One cannot help it. It is so." But therewith the whole effort to explain evil as a logically necessary result of free will and of divine justice alone is simply abandoned. The unearned ills are not justly due to the free will that indeed partly caused them, but to God who declines to protect the innocent. God owes the Turk and the rebel their due. He also owes to his innocent creatures, the babes and the women, his shelter. He owes to the sinning father his penalty, but to the son, born in our visible world a lost soul from the womb, God owes the shelter of his almighty wing, and no penalty. Thus Job's cry is once more in place. The ways of God are not thus justified.

But the partisan of free will as the true explanation of ill may reiterate his view in a new form. He may insist that we see but a fragment. Perhaps the soul born here as if lost, or the wretch doomed to pangs now unearned, sinned of old, in some previous state of existence. Perhaps Karma is to blame. You expiate to-day the sins of your own former existences. Thus the Hindoos varied the theme of our familiar doctrine. This is what Hindoo friends might have said to Job. Well, admit even that, if you like; and what then follows? Admit that here or in former ages the free deed of every present sufferer earned as its penalty every ill, physical or moral, that appears as besetting just this sufferer to-day. Admit that, and what logically follows? It follows, so I must insist, that the moral world itself, which this free-will theory of the source of evil, thus abstractly stated, was to save, is destroyed in its very heart and center.

For consider. A suffers ill. B sees A suffering. Can B, the onlooker, help his suffering neighbor, A? Can he comfort him in any true way? No, a miserable comforter must B prove, like Job's friends, so long as B, believing in our present hypothesis, clings strictly to the logic of this abstract free-will explanation of the origin of evil. To A he says: "Well, you suffer for your own ill-doing. I therefore simply cannot relieve you. This is God's world of justice. If I tried to hinder God's justice from working in your case, I should at best only postpone your evil day. It would come, for God is just. You are hungry, thirsty, naked, sick, in prison. What can I do about it? All this is your own deed come back to you. God himself, although justly punishing, is not the author of this evil. You are the sole originator of the ill." "Ah!" so A may cry out, "but can you not give me light, insight, instruction, sympathy? Can you not at least teach me to become good?" "No," B must reply, if he is a logical believer in the sole efficacy of the private free will of each finite agent as the one source, under the divine justice, of that agent's ill: "No, if you deserved light or any other comfort, God, being just, would enlighten you himself, even if I absolutely refused. But if you do not deserve light, I should preach to you in vain, for God's justice would harden your heart against any such good fortune as I could offer you from without, even if I spoke with the tongues of men and of angels. Your free will is yours. No deed of mine could give you a good free will, for what I gave you from without would not be *your* free will at all. Nor can any one but you cause your free will to be this or that. A great gulf is fixed between us. You and I, as sovereign free agents, live in God's holy world in sin-tight compartments and in evil-tight compartments too. I cannot hurt you, nor you me. You are damned for your own sins, while all that I can do is to look out for my own salvation." This, I say, is the logically inevitable result of asserting that every ill, physical or moral, that can happen to any agent, is solely the result of that agent's own free will acting under the government of the divine justice. The only possible consequence would indeed be that we live, every soul of us, in separate, as it were absolutely fire-proof, free-will compartments, so that real coöperation as to good and ill is excluded. What more cynical denial of the reality of any sort of moral world could be imagined than is involved in this horrible thesis, which no sane partisan of the abstract and traditional freewill explanation of the source of evil will to-day maintain, precisely because no such partisan really knows or can know what his doctrine logically means, while still continuing to maintain it. Yet whenever one asserts with pious obscurity that "No harm can come to the righteous," one in fact implies, with logical necessity, just this cynical consequence.

There remains a fourth doctrine as to our problem. This doctrine is in essence the thesis of philosophical idealism, a thesis which I myself feel bound to maintain, and, so far as space here permits, to explain. The theoretical basis of this view, the philosophical reasons for the notion of the divine nature which it implies, I cannot here explain. That is another argument. But I desire to indicate how the view in question deals with Job's problem.

This view first frankly admits that Job's problem is, upon Job's presuppositions, simply and absolutely insoluble. Grant Job's own presupposition that God is a being other than this world, that he is its external creator and ruler, and then all solutions fail. God is then either cruel or helpless, as regards all real finite ill of the sort that Job endures. Job, moreover, is right in demanding a reasonable answer to his question. The only possible answer is, however, one that undertakes to develop what I hold to be the immortal soul of the doctrine of the divine atonement. The answer to Job is: God is not in ultimate essence another being than yourself. He is the Absolute Being. You truly are one with God, part of his life. He is the very soul of your soul. And so, here is the first truth: When you suffer, *your sufferings are God's sufferings*, not his external work, not his external penalty, not the fruit of his neglect, but identically his own personal woe. In you God himself suffers, precisely as you do, and has all your concern in overcoming this grief.

The true question then is: Why does God thus suffer? The sole possible, necessary, and sufficient answer is, Because without suffering, without ill, without woe, evil, tragedy, God's life could not be perfected. This grief is not a physical means to an external end. It is a logically necessary and eternal constituent of the divine life. It is logically necessary that the Captain of your salvation should be perfect through suffering. No outer nature compels him. He chooses this because he chooses his own perfect selfhood. He is perfect. His world is the best possible world. Yet all its finite regions know not only of joy but of defeat and sorrow, for thus alone, in the completeness of his eternity, can God in his wholeness be triumphantly perfect.

This I say, is my thesis. In the absolute oneness of God with the sufferer, in the concept of the suffering and therefore triumphant God, lies the logical solution of the problem of evil. The doctrine of philosophical idealism is, as regards its purely theoretical aspects, a fairly familiar metaphysical theory at the present time. One may, then, presuppose here as known the fact that, for reasons which I have not now to expound, the idealist maintains that there is in the universe but one perfectly real being, namely, the Absolute, that the Absolute is self-conscious, and that his world is essentially in its wholeness the fulfillment *in actu* of an all-perfect ideal. We ourselves exist as fragments of the absolute life, or better, as partial functions in the unity of the absolute and conscious process of the world. On the other hand, our existence and our individuality are not illusory, but are what they are in an organic unity with the whole life of the Absolute Being. This doctrine once presupposed, our present task is to inquire what case idealism can make for the thesis just indicated as its answer to Job's problem.

In endeavoring to grapple with the theoretical problem of the place of evil in a world that, on the whole, is to be conceived, not only as good, but as perfect, there is happily one essentially decisive consideration concerning good and evil which falls directly within the scope of our own human experience, and which concerns matters at once familiar and momentous as well as too much neglected in philosophy. When we use such words as good, evil, perfect, we easily deceive ourselves by the merely abstract meanings which we associate with each of the terms taken apart from the other. We forget the experiences from which the words have been abstracted. To these experiences we must return whenever we want really to comprehend the words. If we take the mere words, in their abstraction, it is easy to say, for instance, that if life has any evil in it at all, it must needs not be so perfect as life would be were there no evil in it whatever. Just so, speaking abstractly, it is easy to say that, in estimating life, one has to set the good over against the evil, and to compare their respective sums. It is easy to declare that, since we hate evil, wherever and just so far as we recognize it, our sole human interest in the world must be furthered by the removal of evil from the world. And thus viewing the case, one readily comes to say that if God views as not only good but perfect a world in which we find so much evil, the divine point of view must be very foreign to ours, so that Job's rebellious pessimism seems well in order, and Prometheus appears to defy the world-ruler in a genuinely humane spirit. Shocked, however, by the apparent impiety of this result, some teachers, considering divine matters, still misled by the same one-sided use of words, have opposed one falsely abstract view by another, and have strangely asserted that the solution must be in proclaiming that since God's world, the real world, in order to be perfect, must be without evil, what we men call evil must be a mere illusion—a mirage of the human point of view—a dark vision which God, who sees all truth, sees not at all. To God, so this view asserts, the eternal world in its wholeness is not only perfect, but has merely the perfection of an utterly transparent crystal, unstained by any color of ill. Only mortal error imagines that there is any evil. There is no evil but only good in the real world, and that is why God finds the world perfect, whatever mortals dream.

Now neither of these abstract views is my view. I consider them both the result of a thoughtless trust in abstract words. I regard evil as a distinctly real fact, a fact just as real as the most helpless and hopeless sufferer finds it to be when he is in pain. Furthermore, I hold that God's point of view is not foreign to ours. I hold that God willingly, freely, and consciously suffers in us when we suffer, and that our grief is his. And despite all this I maintain that the world from God's point of view fulfills the divine ideal and is perfect. And I hold that when we abandon the one-sided abstract ideas which the words good, evil, and perfect suggest, and when we go back to the concrete experiences upon which these very words are founded, we can see, even within the limits of our own experience, facts which make these very paradoxes perfectly intelligible, and even commonplace.

As for that essentially pernicious view, nowadays somewhat current amongst a certain class of gentle but inconsequent people—the view that all evil is *merely* an illusion and that there is no such thing in God's world—I can say of it only in passing that it is often advanced as an idealistic view, but that, in my opinion, it is false idealism. Good idealism it is to regard all finite experience as an appearance, a hint, often a very poor hint, of deeper truth. Good idealism it is to admit that man can err about truth that lies beyond his finite range of experience. And very good idealism it is to assert that all truth, and so all finite experience, exists in and for the mind of God, and nowhere outside of or apart from God. But it is not good idealism to assert that any facts which fall within the range of finite experience are, even while they are experienced, mere illusions. God's truth is inclusive, not exclusive. What you experience God experiences. The difference lies only in this, that God sees in unity what you see in fragments. For the rest, if one said, "The source and seat of evil is only the error of mortal mind," one would but have changed the name of one's problem. If the evil were but the error, the error would still be the evil, and altering the name would not have diminished the horror of the evil of this finite world.

But I hasten from the false idealism to the true; from the abstractions to the enlightening insights of our life. As a fact, idealism does not say: The finite world is, as such, a mere illusion. A sound idealism says, whatever we experience is a fragment, and, as far as it goes, a genuine fragment of the truth of the divine mind. With this principle before us, let us consider directly our own experiences of good and of evil, to see whether they are as abstractly opposed to each other as the mere words often suggest. We must begin with the elementary and even trivial facts. We shall soon come to something deeper.

By good, as we mortals experience it, we mean something that, when it comes or is expected, we actively welcome, try to attain or keep, and regard with content. By evil in general, as it is in our experience, we mean whatever we find in any sense repugnant and intolerable. I use the words repugnant and intolerable because I wish to indicate that words for evil frequently, like the words for good, directly refer to our actions as such. Commonly and rightly, when we speak of evil, we make reference to acts of resistance, of struggle, of shrinking, of flight, of removal of ourselves from a source of mischief—acts which not only follow upon the experience of evil, but which serve to define in a useful fashion what we mean by evil. The opposing acts of pursuit and of welcome define what we mean by good. By the evil which we experience we mean precisely whatever we regard as something to be gotten rid of, shrunken from, put out of sight, of hearing, or of memory, eschewed, expelled, assailed, or otherwise directly or indirectly resisted. By good we mean whatever we regard as something to be welcomed, pursued, won, grasped, held, persisted in, preserved. And we show all this in our acts in presence of any grade of good or evil, sensuous, aesthetic, ideal, moral. To shun, to flee, to resist, to destroy, these are our primary attitudes towards ill; the opposing acts are our primary attitudes towards the good; and whether you regard us as animals or as moralists, whether it is a sweet taste, a poem, a virtue, or God that we look to as good, and whether it is a burn or a temptation, an outward physical fore, or a stealthy, inward, ideal enemy, that we regard as evil. In all our organs of voluntary movement, in all our deeds, in a turn of the eye, in a sigh, a groan, in a hostile gesture, in an act of silent contempt, we can show in endlessly varied ways the same general attitude of repugnance.

But man is a very complex creature. He has many organs. He performs many acts at once, and he experiences his performance of these acts in one highly complex life of consciousness. As the next feature of his life we all observe that he can at the same time shun one object and grasp at another. In this way he can have at once present to him a consciousness of good and a consciousness of ill. But so far in our account these sorts of experience appear merely as facts side by side. Man loves, and he *also* hates, loves this, and hates that, assumes an attitude of repugnance towards one object, while he welcomes another. So far the usual theory follows man's life, and calls it an experience of good and ill as mingled but exclusively and abstractly opposed facts. For such a view the final question as to the worth of a man's life is merely the question whether there are more intense acts of satisfaction and of welcome than of repugnance and disdain in his conscious life.

But this is by no means an adequate notion of the complexity of man's life, even as an animal. If every conscious act of hindrance, of thwarting, of repugnance, means just in so far an awareness of some evil, it is noteworthy that men can have and can show just such tendencies, not only towards external experiences, but towards their own acts. That is, men can be seen trying to thwart and to hinder even their own acts themselves, at the very moment when they note the occurrence of these acts. One can consciously have an impulse to do something, and at that very moment a conscious disposition to hinder or to thwart as an evil that very impulse. If, on the other hand, every conscious act of attainment, of pursuit, of reinforcement, involves the awareness of some good, it is equally obvious that one can show by one's acts a disposition to reinforce or to emphasize or to increase, not only the externally present gifts of fortune, but also one's own deeds, in so far as one observes them. And in our complex lives it is common enough to find ourselves actually trying to reinforce and to insist upon a situation which involves for us, even at the moment of its occurrence, a great deal of repugnance. In such cases we often act as if we felt the very thwarting of our own primary impulses to be so much of a conscious good that we persist in pursuing and reinforcing the very situation in which this thwarting and hindering of our own impulses is sure to arise.

In brief, as phenomena of this kind show, man is a being who can to a very great extent find a sort of secondary satisfaction in the very act of thwarting his own desires, and thus of assuring for the time his own dissatisfactions. On the other hand, man can to an indefinite degree find himself dissatisfied with his satisfaction and disposed to thwart, not merely his external enemies, but his own inmost impulses themselves. But I now affirm that in all such cases you cannot simply say that man is preferring the less of two evils, or the greater of two goods, as if the good and evil stood merely side by side in his experience. On the contrary, in such cases, man is not merely setting his acts or his estimates of good and evil side by side and taking the sum of each; but he is making his own relatively primary acts, impulses, desires, the objects of all sorts of secondary impulses, desires, and reflective observations. His whole inner state is one of tension: and he is either making a secondary experience of evil out of his estimate of a primary experience of good, as is the case when he at once finds himself disposed to pursue a given good and to thwart this pursuit as being an evil pursuit; or else he is making a secondary experience of good out of his primary experience of evil, as when he is primarily dissatisfied with his situation, but yet secondarily regards this very dissatisfaction as itself a desirable state. In this way man comes not only to love some things and also to hate other things, he comes to love his own hates and to hate his own loves in an endlessly complex hierarchy of superposed interests in his own interests.

Now it is easy to say that such states of inner tension, where our conscious lives are full of a warfare of the self with itself, are contradictory or absurd states. But it is easy to say this only when you dwell on the words and fail to observe the facts of experience. As a fact, not only our lowest but our highest states of activity are the ones which are fullest of this crossing, conflict, and complex interrelation of loves and hates, of attractions and repugnances. As a merely physiological fact, we begin no muscular act without at the same time initiating acts which involve the innervation of opposing sets of muscles, and these opposing sets of muscles hinder each other's freedom. Every sort of control of movement means the conflicting play of opposed muscular impulses. We do nothing simple, and we will no complex act without willing what involves a certain measure of opposition between the impulses or partial acts which go to make up the whole act. If one passes from single acts to long series of acts, one finds only the more obviously this interweaving of repugnance and of acceptance, of pursuit and of flight upon which every complex type of conduct depends.

One could easily at this point spend time by dwelling upon numerous and relatively trivial instances of this interweaving of conflicting motives as it appears in all our life. I prefer to pass such instances over with a mere mention. There is, for instance, the whole marvelous consciousness of play, in its benign and in its evil forms. In any game that fascinates, one loves victory and shuns defeat, and yet as a loyal supporter of the game scorns anything that makes victory certain in advance; thus as a lover of fair play preferring to risk the defeat that he all the while shuns, and partly thwarting the very love of victory that from moment to moment fires his hopes. There are, again, the numerous cases in which we prefer to go to places where we are sure to be in a considerable measure dissatisfied;

to engage, for instance, in social functions that absorbingly fascinate us despite or even in view of the very fact that, as long as they continue, they keep us in a state of tension which makes us, amongst other things, long to have the whole occasion over. Taking a wider view, one may observe that the greater part of the freest products of the activity of civilization, in ceremonies, in formalities, in the long social drama of flight, of pursuit, of repartee, of contest and of courtesy, involve an elaborate and systematic delaying and hindering of elemental human desires, which we continually outwit, postpone and thwart, even while we nourish them. When students of human nature assert that hunger and love rule the social world, they recognize that the elemental in human nature is trained by civilization into the service of the highest demands of the Spirit. But such students have to recognize that the elemental rules the higher world only in so far as the elemental is not only cultivated, but endlessly thwarted, delayed, outwitted, like a constitutional monarch, who is said to be a sovereign, but who, while he rules, must not govern.

But I pass from such instances, which in all their universality are still, I admit, philosophically speaking trivial, because they depend upon the accidents of human nature. I pass from these instances to point out what must be the law, not only of human nature, but of every broader form of life as well. I maintain that this organization of life by virtue of the tension of manifold impulses and interests is not a mere accident of our imperfect human nature, but must be a type of the organization of every rational life. There are good and bad states of tension, there are conflicts that can only be justified when resolved into some higher form of harmony. But I insist that, in general, the only harmony that can exist in the realm of the spirit is the harmony that we possess when we thwart the present but more elemental impulse for the sake of the higher unity of experience; as when we rejoice in the endurance of the tragedies of life, because they show us the depth of life, or when we know that it is better to have loved and lost than never to have loved at all, or when we possess a virtue in the moment of victory over the tempter. And the reason why this is true lies in the fact that the more one's experience fulfills ideals, the more that experience presents to one, not of ignorance, but of triumphantly wealthy acquaintance with the facts of manifold, varied and tragic life, full of tension and thereby of unity. Now this is an universal and not merely human law. It is not those innocent of evil who are fullest of the life of God, but those who in their own case have experienced the triumph over evil. It is not those naturally ignorant of fear, or those who, like Siegfried, have never shivered, who possess the genuine experience of courage; but the brave are those who have fears, but control their fears.

Such know the genuine virtues of the hero. Were it otherwise, only the stupid could be perfect heroes.

To be sure it is quite false to say, as the foolish do, that the object of life is merely that we may "know life" as an irrational chaos of experiences of good and evil. But knowing the good in life is a matter which concerns the form, rather than the mere content of life. One who knows life wisely knows indeed much of the content of life; but he knows the good of life in so far as, in the unity of his experience, he finds the evil of his experience not abolished, but subordinated, and in so far relatively thwarted by a control which annuls its triumph even while experiencing its existence.

Generalizing the lesson of experience we may then say: It is logically impossible that a complete knower of truth should fail to know, to experience, to have present to his insight, the fact of actually existing evil. On the other hand, it is equally impossible for one to know a higher good than comes from the subordination of evil to good in a total experience. When one first loving, in an elemental way, whatever you please, himself hinders, delays, thwarts his elemental interest in the interest of some larger whole of experience, he not only knows more fact, but he possesses a higher good than would or could be present to one who was aware neither of the elemental impulse, nor of the thwarting of it in the tension of a richer life. The knowing of the good, in the higher sense, depends upon contemplating the overcoming and subordination of a less significant impulse, which survives even in order that it should be subordinated. Now this law, this form of the knowledge of the good, applies as well to the existence of moral as to that of sensuous ill. If moral evil were simply destroyed and wiped away from the external world, the knowledge of moral goodness would also be destroyed. For the love of moral good is the thwarting of lower loves for the sake of the higher organization. What is needed, then, for the definition of the divine knowledge of a world that in its wholeness is perfect, is not divine knowledge that shall ignore, wipe out and utterly make naught the existence of any ill, whether physical or moral, but a divine knowledge to which shall be present that love of the world as a whole which is fulfilled in the endurance of physical ill, in the subordination of moral ill, in the thwarting of impulses which survive even when subordinated, in the acceptance of repugnances which are still eternal, in the triumph over an enemy that endures even through its eternal defeat, and in the discovery that the endless tension of the finite world is included in the contemplative consciousness of the repose and harmony of eternity. To view God's nature thus is to view his nature as the whole idealistic theory views him, not as the Infinite One beyond the finite imperfections, but as the being whose unity determines the very constitution, the lack, the tension, and relative disharmony of the finite world.

The existence of evil, then, is not only consistent with the perfection of the universe, but is necessary for the very existence of that perfection. This is what we see when we no longer permit ourselves to be deceived by the abstract meanings of the words good and evil into thinking that these two opponents exist merely as mutually exclusive facts side by side in experience, but when we go back to the facts of life and perceive that all relatively higher good, in the trivial as in the more truly spiritual realm, is known only in so far as, from some higher reflective point of view, we accept as good the thwarting of an existent interest that is even thereby declared to be a relative ill, and love a tension of various impulses which even thereby involves, as the object of our love, the existence of what gives us aversion or grief. Now if the love of God is more inclusive than the love of man, even as the divine world of experience is richer than the human world, we can simply set no human limit to the intensity of conflict, to the tragedies of existence, to the pangs of finitude, to the degree of moral ill, which in the end is included in the life that God not only loves, but finds the fulfillment of the perfect ideal. If peace means satisfaction, acceptance of the whole of an experience as good, and if even we, in our weakness, can frequently find rest in the very presence of conflict and of tension, in the very endurance of ill in a good cause, in the hero's triumph over temptation, or in the mourner's tearless refusal to accept the lower comforts of forgetfulness, or to wish that the lost one's preciousness had been less painfully revealed by death—well, if even we know our little share of this harmony in the midst of the wrecks and disorders of life, what limit shall we set to the divine power to face this world of his own sorrows, and to find peace in the victory over all its ills.

But in the last expression I have pronounced the word that serves to link this theory as to the place of evil in a good world with the practical problem of every sufferer. Job's rebellion came from the thought that God, as a sovereign, is far off, and that, for his pleasure, his creature suffers. Our own theory comes to the mourner with the assurance: "Your suffering, just as it is in you, is God's suffering. No chasm divides you from God.

He is not remote from you even in his eternity. He is here. His eternity means merely the completeness of his experience. But that completeness is inclusive. Your sorrow is one of the included facts." I do not say: "God sympathizes with you from without, would spare you if he could, pities you with helpless external pity merely as a father pities his children." I say: "God here sorrows, not *with* but *in* your sorrow. Your grief is identically his grief, and what you know as your loss, God knows as his loss, just in and through the very moment when you grieve."

But hereupon the sufferer perchance responds: "If this is God's loss, could he not have prevented it? To him are present in unity all the worlds; and yet he must lack just this for which I grieve." I respond: "He suffers here that he may triumph. For the triumph of the wise is no easy thing. Their lives are not light, but sorrowful. Yet they rejoice in their sorrow, not, to be sure, because it is mere experience, but because, for them, it becomes part of a strenuous whole of life. They wander and find their home even in wandering. They long, and attain through their very love of longing. Peace they find in triumphant warfare. Contentment they have most of all in endurance. Sovereignty they win in endless service. The eternal world contains Gethsemane."

Yet the mourners may still insist: "If my sorrow is God's, his triumph is not mine. Mine is the woe. His is the peace." But my theory is a philosophy. It proposes to be coherent. I must persist: "It is your fault that you are thus sundered from God's triumph. His experience in its wholeness cannot now be yours, for you just as you—this individual—are now but a fragment, and see his truth as through a glass darkly. But if you see his truth at all, through even the dimmest light of a glimmering reason, remember, that truth is in fact your own truth, your own fulfillment, the whole from which your life cannot be divorced, the reality that you mean even when you most doubt, the desire of your heart even when you are most blind, the perfection that you unconsciously strove for even when you were an infant, the complete Self apart from whom you mean nothing, the very life that gives your life the only value which it can have. In thought, if not in the fulfillment of thought, in aim if not in attainment of aim, in aspiration if not in the presence of the revealed fact, you can view God's triumph and peace as your triumph and peace. Your defeat will be no less real than it is, nor will you falsely call your evil a mere illusion. But you will see not only the grief but the truth, your truth, your rescue, your triumph."

Well, to what ill-fortune does not just such reasoning apply? I insist: our conclusion is essentially universal. It discounts any evil that experience may contain. All the horrors of the natural order, all the concealments of the divine plan by our natural ignorance, find their general relation to the unity of the divine experience indicated in advance by this account of the problem of evil.

"Yes," one may continue, "ill-fortune you have discovered, but how about moral evil? What if the sinner now triumphantly retorts: 'Aha! So my will is God's will. All then is well with me.'" I reply: What I have said disposes of moral ill precisely as definitely as of physical ill. What the evil will is to the good man, whose goodness depends upon its existence, but also upon the thwarting and the condemnation of its aim, just such is the sinner's will to the divine plan. God's will, we say to the sinner, is your will. Yes, but it is your will thwarted, scorned, over-come, defeated. In the eternal world you are seen, possessed, present, but your damnation is also seen including and thwarting you. Your apparent victory in this world stands simply for the vigor of your impulses. God will you not to triumph. And that is the use of you in the world—the use of evil generally—to be hated but endured, to be triumphed over through the very fact of your presence, to be willed down even in the very life of which you are a part.

But to the serious moral agent we say: What you mean when you say that evil in this temporal world ought not to exist, and ought to be suppressed, is simply what God means by seeing that evil ought to be and is endlessly thwarted, endured, but subordinated. In the natural world you are the minister of God's triumph. Your deed is his. You can never clean the world of evil: but you can subordinate evil. The justification of the presence in the world of the morally evil becomes apparent to us mortals only in so far as this evil is overcome and condemned. It exists only that it may be cast down. Courage, then, for God works in you. In the order of time you embody in outer acts what is for him the truth of his eternity.

CHARLOTTE PERKINS GILMAN

Selection from *Women and Economics*
(1898)

So prominent in the history of feminist theory in America are the works of Charlotte Perkins Gilman (1860–1935) that she is often called the Marx and the Veblen of American feminism. The selection herein—from *Women and Economics,* 1898—displays the sweep and the conviction with which she addressed the evolutionary-historical matrix of women's condition. Gilman argues that women, once forced into relations of dependency by men, were "cut off from the direct action of natural selection, that mighty force which heretofore had acted on male and female alike with inexorable and beneficial effect," developing the strength, skill, endurance and courage that made the human species what it was to become. In her conception of the evolutionary process, Gilman was much influenced by Lester Frank Ward. Gilman was an economist and an evolutionary theorist and also an accomplished writer of fiction and verse. Her utopian novel *Herland* (New York, 1979) was first published serially in 1915. Her short story of 1892, "The Yellow Wallpaper," has inspired extensive critical attention. For an interpretation of this story in relation to *Women and Economics,* see Walter Benn Michaels, *The Gold Standard and the Logic of Naturalism* (Berkeley, 1987), 3–28.

For a biography, see Ann J. Lane, *To Herland and Beyond* (New York, 1990). Gilman's early years are the subject of a more detailed study, Mary A. Hill, *Charlotte Perkins Gilman: The Making of a Radical Feminist* (Philadelphia, 1980). The most recent scholarly study in Judith A. Allen, *The Feminism of Charlotte Perkins Gilman: Sexualities, Histories, Progressivism* (Chicago, 2009). Gilman's participation in the Populist movement is clarified in Charles Postel, *The Populist Vision* (New York, 2007). Two important histories of early twentieth-century American feminist intellectuals are Rosalind Rosenberg, *Beyond Separate Spheres: Intellectual Roots of Modern Feminism* (New Haven, 1982); and Nancy F. Cott, *The Grounding of Modern Feminism* (New Haven, 1987).

Having seen the disproportionate degree of sex-distinction in humanity and its greater manifestation in the female than in the male, and having seen also the unique position of the human female as an economic dependant on the male of her species, it is not difficult to establish a relation between these two facts. The general law acting to produce this condition of exaggerated sex-development... is as follows: the natural tendency of any function to increase in power by use causes sex-activity to increase under the action of sexual selection. This tendency is checked in most species by the force of natural selection, which diverts the energies into other channels and developes race-activities. Where the female finds her economic environment in the male, and her economic advantage is directly conditioned upon the sex-relation, the force of natural selection is added to the force of sexual selection, and both together operate to develop sex-activity. In any animal species, free from any other condition, such a relation would have inevitably developed sex to an inordinate degree, as may be readily seen in the comparatively similar cases of those insects where the female, losing economic activity and modified entirely to sex, becomes a mere egg-sac, an organism with no powers of self-preservation, only those of race-preservation. With these insects the only race-problem is to maintain and reproduce the species, and such a condition is not necessarily evil; but with a race like ours, whose development as human creatures is but comparatively begun, it is evil because of its check to individual and racial progress. There are other purposes before us besides mere maintenance and reproduction.

It should be clear to any one accustomed to the working of biological laws that all the tendencies of a living organism are progressive in their development, and are held in check by the interaction of their several forces. Each living form, with its dominant characteristics, represents a balance of power, a sort of compromise. The size of earth's primeval monsters was limited by the tensile strength of their material. Sea monsters can be bigger, because the medium in which they move offers more support. Birds must be smaller for the opposite reason. The cow requires many stomachs of a liberal size, because her food is of low nutritive value; and she must eat large quantities to keep her machine going. The size of arboreal animals, such as monkeys or squirrels, is limited by the nature of their habitat: creatures that live in trees cannot be so big as creatures that live on the ground. Every quality of every creature is relative to its condition, and tends to increase or decrease accordingly; and each quality tends to increase in proportion to its use, and to decrease in proportion to its disuse. Primitive man and his female were animals, like other animals. They were strong, fierce, lively beasts; and she was as nimble and ferocious as he, save for the added belligerence of the males in their sex-competition. In this competition, he, like the other male creatures, fought savagely with his hairy rivals; and she, like the other female creatures, complacently viewed their struggles, and mated with the victor. At other times she ran about in the forest, and helped herself to what there was to eat as freely as he did.

There seems to have come a time when it occurred to the dawning intelligence of this amiable savage that it was cheaper and easier to fight a little female, and have it done with, than to fight a big male every time. So he instituted the custom of enslaving the female; and she, losing freedom, could no longer get her own food nor that of her young. The mother ape, with her maternal function well fulfilled, flees leaping through the forest,— plucks her fruits and nuts, keeps up with the movement of the tribe, her young one on her

Source: Charlotte Perkins Gilman, *Women and Economics* (Boston: Small, Maynard & Co., 1898), 58–75.

back or held in one strong arm. But the mother woman, enslaved, could not do this. Then man, the father, found that slavery had its obligations: he must care for what he forbade to care for itself, else it died on his hands. So he slowly and reluctantly shouldered the duties of his new position. He began to feed her, and not only that, but to express in his own person the thwarted uses of maternity: he had to feed the children, too. It seems a simple arrangement. When we have thought of it at all, we have thought of it with admiration. The naturalist defends it on the ground of advantage to the species through the freeing of the mother from all other cares and confining her unreservedly to the duties of maternity. The poet and novelist, the painter and sculptor, the priest and teacher, have all extolled this lovely relation. It remains for the sociologist, from a biological point of view, to note its effects on the constitution of the human race, both in the individual and in society.

When man began to feed and defend woman, she ceased proportionately to feed and defend herself. When he stood between her and her physical environment, she ceased proportionately to feel the influence of that environment and respond to it. When he became her immediate and all-important environment, she began proportionately to respond to this new influence, and to be modified accordingly. In a free state, speed was of as great advantage to the female as to the male, both in enabling her to catch prey and in preventing her from being caught by enemies; but, in her new condition, speed was a disadvantage. She was not allowed to do the catching, and it profited her to be caught by her new master. Free creatures, getting their own food and maintaining their own lives, develop an active capacity for attaining their ends. Parasitic creatures, whose living is obtained by the exertions of others, develop powers of absorption and of tenacity,—the powers by which they profit most. The human female was cut off from the direct action of natural selection, that mighty force which heretofore had acted on male and female alike with inexorable and beneficial effect, developing strength, developing skill, developing endurance, developing courage,—in a word, developing species. She now met the influence of natural selection acting indirectly through the male, and developing, of course, the faculties required to secure and obtain a hold on him. Needless to state that these faculties were those of sex-attraction, the one power that has made him cheerfully maintain, in what luxury he could, the being in whom he delighted. For many, many centuries she had no other hold, no other assurance of being fed. The young girl had a prospective value, and was maintained for what should follow; but the old woman, in more primitive times, had but a poor hold on life. She who could best please her lord was the favorite slave or favorite wife, and she obtained the best economic conditions.

With the growth of civilization, we have gradually crystallized into law the visible necessity for feeding the helpless female; and even old women are maintained by their male relatives with a comfortable assurance. But to this day—save, indeed, for the increasing army of women wage-earners, who are changing the face of the world by their steady advance toward economic independence—the personal profit of women bears but too close a relation to their power to win and hold the other sex. From the odalisque with the most bracelets to the débutante with the most bouquets, the relation still holds good,— woman's economic profit comes through the power of sex-attraction.

When we confront this fact boldly and plainly in the open market of vice, we are sick with horror. When we see the same economic relation made permanent, established by law, sanctioned and sanctified by religion, covered with flowers and incense and all accumulated sentiment, we think it innocent, lovely, and right. The transient trade we think evil. The bargain for life we think good. But the biological effect remains the same. In both cases the female gets her food from the male by virtue of her sex-relationship to him. In both cases, perhaps even more in marriage because of its perfect acceptance of the situation, the female of genus homo, still living under natural law, is inexorably modified to sex in an increasing degree.

Followed in specific detail, the action of the changed environment upon women has been in given instances as follows: in the matter of mere passive surroundings she has been immediately restricted in her range. This one factor has an immense effect on man and animal alike. An absolutely uniform environment, one shape, one size, one color, one sound, would render life, if any life could be, one helpless, changeless thing. As the environment increases and varies, the development of the creature must increase and vary with it; for he acquires knowledge and power, as the material for knowledge and the need for power appear. In migratory species the female is free to acquire the same knowledge as the male by the same means, the same development by the same experiences. The human female has been restricted in range from the earliest beginning. Even among savages, she has a much more restricted knowledge of the land she lives in. She moves with the camp, of course, and follows her primitive industries in its vicinity; but the war-path and the hunt are the man's. He has a far larger habitat. The life of the female savage is freedom itself, however, compared with the increasing constriction of custom closing in upon the woman, as civilization advanced, like the iron torture chamber of romance. Its culmination is expressed in the proverb: "A woman should leave her home but three times,—when she is christened, when she is married, and when she is buried." Or this: "The woman, the cat, and the chimney should never leave the house." The absolutely stationary female and the wide-ranging male are distinctly human institutions, after we leave behind us such low forms of life as the gypsy moth, whose female seldom moves more than a few feet from the pupa moth. She has aborted wings, and cannot fly. She waits humbly for the winged male, lays her myriad eggs, and dies,—a fine instance of modification to sex.

To reduce so largely the mere area of environment is a great check to race-development; but it is not to be compared in its effects with the reduction in voluntary activity to which the human female has been subjected. Her restricted impression, her confinement to the four walls of the home, have done great execution, of course, in limiting her ideas, her information, her thought-processes, and power of judgment; and in giving a disproportionate prominence and intensity to the few things she knows about; but this is innocent in action compared with her restricted expression, the denial of freedom to act. A living organism is modified far less through the action of external circumstances upon it and its reaction thereto, than through the effect of its own exertions. Skin may be thickened gradually by exposure to the weather; but it is thickened far more quickly by being rubbed against something, as the handle of an oar or of a broom. To be surrounded by beautiful things has much influence upon the human creature: to make beautiful things has more. To live among beautiful surroundings and make ugly things is more directly lowering than to live among ugly surroundings and make beautiful things. What we do modifies us more than what is done to us. The freedom of expression has been more restricted in women than the freedom of impression, if that be possible. Something of the world she lived in she has seen from her barred windows. Some air has come through the purdah's folds, some knowledge has filtered to her eager ears from the talk of men. Desdemona learned somewhat of Othello. Had she known more, she might have lived longer. But in the ever-growing human impulse to create, the power and will to make, to do, to express one's new spirit in new forms,—here she has been utterly debarred. She might work as she had worked from the beginning,—at the primitive labors of the household; but in the inevitable expansion of even those industries to professional levels we have striven to hold her back. To work with her own hands, for nothing, in direct body-service to her own family,—this has been permitted,—yes, compelled. But to be and do anything further from this she has been forbidden. Her labor has not only been limited in kind, but in degree. Whatever she has been allowed to do must be done in private and alone, the first-hand industries of savage times.

Our growth in industry has been not only in kind, but in class. The baker is not in the same industrial grade with the house-cook, though both make bread. To specialize any form of labor is a step up: to organize it is another step. Specialization and organization are the basis of human progress, the organic methods of social life. They have been forbidden to women almost absolutely. The greatest and most beneficent change of this century is the progress of women in these two lines of advance. The effect of this check in industrial development, accompanied as it was by the constant inheritance of increased racial power, has been to intensify the sensations and emotions of women, and to develop great activity in the lines allowed. The nervous energy that up to present memory has impelled women to labor incessantly at something, be it the veriest folly of fancy work, is one mark of this effect.

In religious development the same dead-line has held back the growth of women through all the races and ages. In dim early times she was sharer in the mysteries and rites; but, as religion developed, her place receded, until Paul commanded her to be silent in the churches. And she had been silent until to-day. Even now, with all the ground gained, we have but the beginnings—the slowly forced and disapproved beginnings—of religious equality for the sexes. In some nations, religion is held to be a masculine attribute exclusively, it being even questioned whether women have souls. An early Christian council settled that important question by vote, fortunately deciding that they had. In a church whose main strength has always been derived from the adherence of women, it would have been an uncomfortable reflection not to have allowed them souls. Ancient family worship ran in the male line. It was the son who kept the sacred grandfathers in due respect, and poured libations to their shades. When the woman married, she changed her ancestors, and had to worship her husband's progenitors, instead of her own. This is why the Hindu and the Chinaman and many others of like stamp must have a son to keep them in countenance,—a deep-seated sex-prejudice, coming to slow extinction as women rise in economic importance.

It is painfully interesting to trace the gradual cumulative effect of these conditions upon women: first, the action of large natural laws, acting on her as they would act on any other animal; then the evolution of social customs and laws (with her position as the active cause), following the direction of mere physical forces, and adding heavily to them; then, with increasing civilization, the unbroken accumulation of precedent, burnt into each generation by the growing force of education, made lovely by art, holy by religion, desirable by habit; and, steadily acting from beneath, the unswerving pressure of economic necessity upon which the whole structure rested. These are strong modifying conditions, indeed.

The process would have been even more effective and far less painful but for one important circumstance. Heredity has no Salic law. Each girl child inherits from her father a certain increasing percentage of human development, human power, human tendency; and each boy as well inherits from his mother the increasing percentage of sex-development, sexpower, sex-tendency. The action of heredity has been to equalize what every tendency of environment and education made to differ. This has saved us from such a female as the gypsy moth. It has held up the woman, and held down the man. It has set iron bounds to our absurd effort to make a race with one sex a million years behind the other. But it has added terribly to the pain and difficulty of human life,—a difficulty and a pain that should have taught us long since that we were living on wrong lines. Each woman born, re-humanized by the current of race activity carried on by her father and re-womanized by her traditional position, has had to live over again in her own person the same process of restriction, repression, denial; the smothering "no" which crushed down all her human desires to create, to discover, to learn, to express, to advance. Each woman has had, on the other hand, the same single avenue of expression and attainment; the same one way in which alone she might do what she could, get what she might. All other doors were shut, and this one always open; and the whole pressure of advancing humanity was upon her. No wonder that young Daniel in the apocryphal tale proclaimed: "The king is strong! Wine is strong! But women are stronger!"

To the young man confronting life the world lies wide. Such powers as he has he may use, must use. If he chooses wrong at first, he may choose again, and yet again. Not effective or successful in one channel, he may do better in another. The growing, varied needs of all mankind call on him for the varied service in which he finds his growth. What he wants to be, he may strive to be. What he wants to get, he may strive to get. Wealth, power, social distinction, fame,—what he wants he can try for.

To the young woman confronting life there is the same world beyond, there are the same human energies and human desires and ambition within. But all that she may wish to have, all that she may wish to do, must come through a single channel and a single choice. Wealth, power, social distinction, fame,—not only these, but home and happiness, reputation, ease and pleasure, her bread and butter,—all, must come to her through a small gold ring. This is a heavy pressure. It has accumulated behind her through heredity, and continued about her through environment. It has been subtly trained into her through education, till she herself has come to think it a right condition, and pours its influence upon her daughter with increasing impetus. Is it any wonder that women are over-sexed? But for the constant inheritance from the more human male, we should have been queen bees, indeed, long before this. But the daughter of the soldier and the sailor, of the artist, the inventor, the great merchant, has inherited in body and brain her share of his development in each generation, and so stayed somewhat human for all her femininity.

All morbid conditions tend to extinction. One check has always existed to our inordinate sex-development,—nature's ready relief, death. Carried to its furthest excess, the individual has died, the family has become extinct, the nation itself has perished, like Sodom and Gomorrah. Where one function is carried to unnatural excess, others are weakened, and the organism perishes. We are familiar with this in individual cases,—at least, the physician is. We can see it somewhat in the history of nations. From younger races, nearer savagery, nearer the healthful equality of pre-human creatures, has come each new start in history. Persia was older than Greece, and its highly differentiated sexuality had produced the inevitable result of enfeebling the racial qualities. The Greek commander stripped the rich robes and jewels from his Persian captives, and showed their unmanly feebleness to his men. "You have such bodies as these to fight for such plunder as this," he said. In the country, among peasant classes, there is much less sex-distinction than in cities, where wealth enables the women to live in absolute idleness; and even the men manifest the same characteristics. It is from the country and the lower classes that the fresh blood pours into the cities, to be weakened in its turn by the influence of this unnatural distinction until there is none left to replenish the nation.

The inevitable trend of human life is toward higher civilization; but, while that civilization is confined to one sex, it inevitably exaggerates sex-distinction, until the increasing evil of this condition is stronger than all the good of the civilization attained, and the nation falls. Civilization, be it understood, does not consist in the acquisition of luxuries. Social development is an organic development. A civilized State is one in which the citizens live in organic industrial relation. The more full, free, subtle, and easy that relation; the more perfect the differentiation of labor and exchange of product, with their correlative institutions,—the more perfect is that civilization. To eat, drink, sleep, and keep warm,—these are common to all animals, whether the animal couches in a bed of leaves or one of eiderdown, sleeps in the sun to avoid the wind or builds a furnace-heated house, lies in wait for game or orders a dinner at a hotel. These are but individual animal processes. Whether one lays an egg or a million eggs, whether one bears a cub, a kitten, or a baby, whether one broods its chickens, guards its litter, or tends a nursery full of children, these are but individual animal processes. But to serve each other more and more widely; to live only by such service; to develop special functions, so that we depend for our living on society's return for services that can be of no direct use to ourselves,—this is civilization, our human glory and race-distinction.

All this human progress has been accomplished by men. Women have been left behind, outside, below, having no social relation whatever, merely the sex-relation, whereby they lived. Let us bear in mind that all the tender ties of family are ties of blood, of sex-relationship. A friend, a comrade, a partner,—this is a human relative. Father, mother, son, daughter, sister, brother, husband, wife,—these are sex-relatives. Blood is thicker than water, we say. True. But ties of blood are not those that ring the world with the succeeding waves of progressive religion, art, science, commerce, education, all that makes us human. Man is the human creature. Woman has been checked, starved, aborted in human growth; and the swelling forces of race-development have been driven back in each generation to work in her through sex-functions alone.

This is the way in which the sexuo-economic relation has operated in our species, checking race-development in half of us, and stimulating sex-development in both.

HENRY ADAMS

"The Dynamo and the Virgin"
(1907)

Henry Adams (1838–1918), grandson of President John Quincy Adams and great-grandson of President John Adams, wrote his autobiography in the third person and attributed to himself the humble role of seeker of education. In the chapter from *The Education of Henry Adams* (Boston, 1918; limited edition, 1907) reprinted here, Adams presents himself with characteristic artifice: He is a "pupil," instructed by scientists and by experience, here viewing a dynamo in an exhibition hall in 1900. He contemplates the virtually infinite power of the dynamo and meditates on its historical significance. The "Langley" to which Adams refers is an astronomer friend, Samuel Langley, who accompanied Adams to the Paris Exhibition of 1900, the setting for this scene of the *Education*. Adams's references to 1893 and to Chicago invoke exhibits at the Chicago World's Fair, where Adams's interest in "force" had been stimulated as reported in an earlier chapter of the *Education*.

Adams's fascination with the culture of medieval Europe—as seen in his comments on "the Virgin"—was the impetus behind another of his great works, *Mont-Saint Michel and Chartres* (New York, 1913). His fascination with the culture of the United States, also seen in his musings about American obliviousness to Venus as well as to the Virgin, was expressed in many of his works, including his formidable *History of the United States of America During the Administrations of Thomas Jefferson and James Madison*, 9 vols. (New York, 1889–91).

One of the most studied of all American intellectuals, Adams is the subject of countless books, of which one of the most helpful remains J. C. Levenson, *The Mind and Art of Henry Adams* (Stanford, 1957). A one-volume abridgment of a standard, three-volume biography is Ernest Samuels, *Henry Adams* (Cambridge, Mass., 1989). An even more accessible introduction to Adams's work is David R. Contosta, *Henry Adams and the American Experiment* (Boston, 1980). For a discussion of Adams in relation to the medievalist, antimodern enthusiasms of the turn of the century, see T. J. Jackson Lears, *No Place of Grace: Antimodernism and the Transformation of American Culture, 1880–1920* (New York, 1982), 262–97. For developments in scholarship on Adams, see John Carlos Rowe, ed., *New Essays on the Education of Henry Adams* (New York, 1996). A recent biography by one of the best writers of our time is Garry Wills, *Henry Adams and the Making of America* (New York, 2005).

UNTIL THE GREAT EXPOSITION of 1900 closed its doors in November, Adams haunted it, aching to absorb knowledge, and helpless to find it. He would have liked to know how much of it could have been grasped by the best informed man in the world. While he was thus meditating chaos, Langley came by, and showed it to him. At Langley's behest, the Exhibition dropped its superfluous rags and stripped itself to the skin, for Langley knew what to study, and why, and how; while Adams might as well have stood outside in the night, staring at the Milky Way. Yet Langley said nothing new, and taught nothing that one might not have learned from Lord Bacon, three hundred years before; but though one should have known the Advancement of Science as well as one knew the Comedy of Errors, the literary knowledge counted for nothing until some teacher should show how to apply it. Bacon took a vast deal of trouble in teaching King James I and his subjects, American or other, towards the years 1620, that true science was the development or economy of forces; yet an elderly American in 1900 knew neither the formula nor the forces; or even so much as to say to himself that his historical business in the Exposition concerned only the economics or developments of force since 1893, when he began the study at Chicago.

Nothing in education is so astonishing as the amount of ignorance it accumulates in the form of inert facts. Adams had looked at most of the accumulations of art in the storehouses called Art Museums; yet he did not know how to look at the art-exhibits of 1900. He had studied Karl Marx and his doctrines of history with profound attention, yet he could not apply them at Paris. Langley, with the ease of a great master of experiment, threw out of the field every exhibit that did not reveal a new application of force, and naturally threw out, to begin with, almost the whole art-exhibit. Equally, he ignored almost the whole industrial exhibit. He led his pupil directly to the forces. His chief interest was in new motors to make his air-ship feasible, and he taught Adams the astonishing complexities of the new Daimler motor, and of the automobile, which, since 1893, had become a nightmare at a hundred kilometers an hour, almost as destructive as the electric tram which was only ten years older; and threatening to become as terrible as the locomotive steam-engine itself, which was almost exactly Adams's own age.

Then he showed his scholar the great hall of dynamos, and explained how little he knew about electricity or force of any kind, even of his own special sun, which spouted heat in inconceivable volume, but which, as far as he knew, might spout less or more, at any time, for all the certainty he felt in it. To him, the dynamo itself was but an ingenious channel for conveying somewhere the heat latent in a few tons of poor coal hidden in a dirty engine-house carefully kept out of sight; but to Adams the dynamo became a symbol of infinity. As he grew accustomed to the great gallery of machines, he began to feel the forty-foot dynamos as a moral force, much as the early Christians felt the Cross. The planet itself seemed less impressive, in its old-fashioned, deliberate, annual or daily revolution, than this huge wheel, revolving within arm's-length at some vertiginous speed, and barely murmuring,—scarcely humming an audible warning to stand a hair's-breadth further for respect of power,—while it would not wake the baby lying close against its frame. Before the end, one began to pray to it; inherited instinct taught the natural expression of man before silent and infinite force. Among the thousand symbols of ultimate energy, the dynamo was not so human as some, but it was the most expressive.

Yet the dynamo, next to the steam-engine, was the most familiar of exhibits. For Adams's objects its values lay chiefly in its occult mechanism. Between the dynamo in

Source: Henry Adams, *The Education of Henry Adams: An Autobiography* (Boston: Houghton-Mifflin, 1918).

the gallery of machines and the engine-house outside, the break of continuity amounted to abysmal fracture for a historian's objects. No more relation could he discover between the steam and the electric current than between the Cross and the cathedral. The forces were interchangeable if not reversible, but he could see only an absolute *fiat* in electricity as in faith. Langley could not help him. Indeed, Langley seemed to be worried by the same trouble, for he constantly repeated that the new forces were anarchical, and especially that he was not responsible for the new rays, that were little short of parricidal in their wicked spirit towards science. His own rays, with which he had doubled the solar spectrum, were altogether harmless and beneficient; but Radium denied its God—or, what was to Langley the same thing, denied the truths of his Science. The force was wholly new.

A historian who asked only to learn enough to be as futile as Langley or Kelvin, made rapid progress under this teaching, and mixed himself up in the tangle of ideas until he achieved a sort of Paradise of ignorance vastly consoling to his fatigued senses. He wrapped himself in vibrations and rays which were new, and he would have hugged Marconi and Branly had he met them, as he hugged the dynamo; while he lost his arithmetic in trying to figure out the equation between the discoveries and the economies of force. The economies, like the discoveries, were absolute, supersensual, occult; incapable of expression in horsepower. What mathematical equivalent could he suggest as the value of a Branly coherer? Frozen air, or the electric furnace had some scale of measurement, no doubt, if somebody could invent a thermometer adequate to the purpose; but X-rays had played no part whatever in man's consciousness, and the atom itself had figured only as a fiction of thought. In these seven years man had translated himself into a new universe which had no common scale of measurement with the old. He had entered a supersensual world, in which he could measure nothing except by chance collisions of movements imperceptible to his senses, perhaps even imperceptible to his instruments, but perceptible to each other, and so to some known ray at the end of the scale. Langley seemed prepared for anything, even for an indeterminable number of universes interfused,—physics stark mad in metaphysics.

Historians undertake to arrange sequences,—called stories, or histories—assuming in silence a relation of cause and effect. These assumptions, hidden in the depths of dusty libraries, have been astounding, but commonly unconscious and childlike; so much so, that if any captious critic were to drag them to light, historians would probably reply, with one voice, that they had never supposed themselves required to know what they were talking about. Adams, for one, had toiled in vain to find out what he meant. He had even published a dozen volumes of American history for no other purpose than to satisfy himself whether, by the severest process of stating, with the least possible comment, such facts as seemed sure, in such order as seemed rigorously consequent, he could fix for a familiar moment a necessary sequence of human movement. The result had satisfied him as little as at Harvard College. Where he saw sequence, other men saw something quite different, and no one saw the same unit of measure. He cared little about his experiments and less about his statesmen, who seemed to him quite as ignorant as himself and, as a rule, no more honest; but he insisted on a relation of sequence, and if he could not reach it by one method, he would try as many methods as science knew. Satisfied that the sequence of men led to nothing and that the sequence of their society could lead no further, while the mere sequence of time was artificial, and the sequence of thought was chaos, he turned at last to the sequence of force; and thus it happened that, after ten years' pursuit, he found himself lying in the Gallery of Machines at the Great Exposition of 1900, with his historical neck broken by the sudden irruption of force totally new.

Since no one else showed much concern, an elderly person without other cares, had no need to betray alarm. The year 1900 was not the first to upset schoolmasters. Copernicus and Galileo had broken many professional necks about 1600; Columbus had stood the world on its head towards 1500; but the nearest approach to the revolution of 1900 was that of 310, when Constantine set up the Cross. The rays that Langley disowned, as well as those which he fathered, were occult, supersensual, irrational; they were a revelation of mysterious energy like that of the Cross; they were what, in terms of mediæval science, were called immediate modes of the divine substance.

The historian was thus reduced to his last resources. Clearly if he was bound to reduce all these forces to a common value, this common value could have no measure but that of their attraction on his own mind. He must treat them as they had been felt; as convertible, reversible, interchangeable attractions on thought. He made up his mind to venture it; he would risk translating rays into faith. Such a reversible process would vastly amuse a chemist, but the chemist could not deny that he, or some of his fellow physicists, could feel the force of both. When Adams was a boy in Boston, the best chemist in the place had probably never heard of Venus except by way of scandal, or of the Virgin except as idolatry; neither had he heard of dynamos or automobiles or radium; yet his mind was ready to feel the force of all, though the rays were unborn and the women were dead.

Here opened another totally new education, which promised to be by far the most hazardous of all. The knife-edge along which he must crawl, like Sir Lancelot in the twelfth century, divided two kingdoms of force which had nothing in common but attraction. They were as different as a magnet is from gravitation, supposing one knew what a magnet was, or gravitation, or love. The force of the Virgin was still felt at Lourdes, and seemed to be as potent as X-rays; but in America neither Venus nor Virgin ever had value as force;—at most as sentiment. No American had ever been truly afraid of either.

This problem in dynamics gravely perplexed an American historian. The Woman had once been supreme; in France she still seemed potent, not merely as a sentiment but as a force; why was she unknown in America? for evidently America was ashamed of her, and she was ashamed of herself, otherwise they would not have strewn fig-leaves so profusely all over her. When she was a true force, she was ignorant of fig-leaves, but the monthly-magazine-made American female had not a feature that would have been recognised by Adam. The trait was notorious, and often humorous, but anyone brought up among Puritans knew that sex was sin. In any previous age, sex was strength. Neither art nor beauty was needed. Everyone, even among Puritans, knew that neither Diana of the Ephesians nor any of the oriental Goddesses was worshipped for her beauty. She was Goddess because of her force; she was the animated dynamo; she was reproduction—the greatest and most mysterious of all energies; all she needed was to be fecund. Singularly enough, not one of Adams's many schools of education had ever drawn his attention to the opening lines of Lucretius, though they were perhaps the finest in all Latin literature, where the poet invoked Venus exactly as Dante invoked the Virgin:

> "Quaequoniam rerum naturam *sola* gubernas."

The Venus of Epicurean philosophy survived in the Virgin of the Schools:—

> "Donna, sei tanto grande, e tanto vali,
> Che qual vuol grazia, e a te non ricorre,
> Sua disianza vuol volar senz' ali."

All this was to American thought as though it had never existed. The true American knew something of the facts, but nothing of the feelings; he read the letter but he never felt the law. Before this historical chasm, a mind like that of Adams felt itself helpless; he turned from the Virgin to the Dynamo as though he were a Branly coherer. On one side, at the Louvre and at Chartres, as he knew by the record of work actually done and still before his eyes, was the highest energy ever known to man, the creator of four-fifths of his noblest art, exercising vastly more attraction over the human mind than all the steam-engines and dynamos ever dreamed of; and yet this energy was unknown to the American mind. An American Virgin would never dare command; an American Venus would never dare exist.

The question, which to any plain American of the nineteenth century seemed as remote as it did to Adams, drew him almost violently to study, once it was posed; and on this point Langleys were as useless as though they were Herbert Spencers or dynamos. The idea survived only as art. There one turned as naturally as though the artist were himself a woman. Adams began to ponder, asking himself whether he knew of any American artist who had ever insisted on the power of sex, as every classic had always done; but he could think only of Walt Whitman; Bret Harte, as far as the magazines would let him venture; and one or two painters, for the flesh-tones. All the rest had used sex for sentiment, never for force; to them, Eve was a tender flower, and Herodias an unfeminine horror. American art, like the American language and American education was as far as possible sexless. Society regarded this victory over sex as its greatest triumph, and the historian readily admitted it, since the moral issue, for the moment, did not concern one who was studying the relations of unmoral force. He cared nothing for the sex of the dynamo until he could measure its energy....

GEORGE SANTAYANA

"The Genteel Tradition in American Philosophy" (1913)

One of the most incisive and influential constructions of American intellectual history ever written was contributed by a cosmopolitan philosopher who was born in Spain, died in Italy, and maintained a sardonic aloofness from American life even during his time in the United States. George Santayana (1863–1952) returned to his native Europe shortly after his legendary lecture at Berkeley, which is reprinted here. "The Genteel Tradition in American Philosophy" was at once a grand narrative, in which were charted the destinies of Calvinism and Transcendentalism, and a critical portrait of a single academic department, the Department of Philosophy at Harvard, where Santayana taught from 1889 to 1912. Santayana associated the genteel tradition with his colleague Josiah Royce and linked the turn against it with another colleague, William James. Santayana's image of a country with two mentalities—one an inherited, feminine "Intellect" inhabiting a "colonial mansion" and the other a practical, masculine "Will" inhabiting a "sky-scraper"—was discussed by both popular and academic commentators on America throughout the twentieth century.

Santayana was influential not only as a commentator on American culture but also as a metaphysician and an aesthetic theorist. *The Sense of Beauty* (New York, 1896) and *The Life of Reason*, 5 vols. (New York, 1905–6) were among the major works he completed while in the United States, but he retained a large American following attentive to *Scepticism and Animal Faith* (New York, 1923) and *Realms of Being*, 4 vols. (New York, 1927–40). A new, comprehensive edition of Santayana's works is being published by the MIT press. Eight volumes of letters and four volumes of philosophical essays, have now appeared.

In recent years Santayana has generated less attention from philosophers than from scholars in other disciplines. The two leading books on Santayana of recent date have been written by professors of literature and religion, respectively: John McCormick, *George Santayana: A Biography* (New York, 1987); and Henry Samuel Levinson, *Santayana, Pragmatism, and the Spiritual Life* (Chapel Hill, 1992). See also Irving Singer, *George Santayana: Literary Philosophy* (New Haven, 2000). For a concise overview of Santayana's philosophical work, see Timothy L. S. Sprigg, *Santayana: An Examination of His Philosophy* (New York, 1995).

LADIES AND GENTLEMEN,—The privilege of addressing you to-day is very welcome to me, not merely for the honour of it, which is great, nor for the pleasures of travel, which are many, when it is California that one is visiting for the first time, but also because there is something I have long wanted to say which this occasion seems particularly favourable for saying. America is still a young country, and this part of it is especially so; and it would have been nothing extraordinary if, in this young country, material preoccupations had altogether absorbed people's minds, and they had been too much engrossed in living to reflect upon life, or to have any philosophy. The opposite, however, is the case. Not only have you already found time to philosophise in California, as your society proves, but the eastern colonists from the very beginning were a sophisticated race. As much as in clearing the land and fighting the Indians they were occupied, as they expressed it, in wrestling with the Lord. The country was new, but the race was tried, chastened, and full of solemn memories. It was an old wine in new bottles; and America did not have to wait for its present universities, with their departments of academic philosophy, in order to possess a living philosophy—to have a distinct vision of the universe and definite convictions about human destiny.

Now this situation is a singular and remarkable one, and has many consequences, not all of which are equally fortunate. America is a young country with an old mentality: it has enjoyed the advantages of a child carefully brought up and thoroughly indoctrinated; it has been a wise child. But a wise child, an old head on young shoulders, always has a comic and an unpromising side. The wisdom is a little thin and verbal, not aware of its full meaning and grounds; and physical and emotional growth may be stunted by it, or even deranged. Or when the child is too vigorous for that, he will develop a fresh mentality of his own, out of his observations and actual instincts; and this fresh mentality will interfere with the traditional mentality, and tend to reduce it to something perfunctory, conventional, and perhaps secretly despised. A philosophy is not genuine unless it inspires and expresses the life of those who cherish it. I do not think the hereditary philosophy of America has done much to atrophy the natural activities of the inhabitants; the wise child has not missed the joys of youth or of manhood; but what has happened is that the hereditary philosophy has grown stale, and that the academic philosophy afterwards developed has caught the stale odour from it. America is not simply, as I said a moment ago, a young country with an old mentality: it is a country with two mentalities, one a survival of the beliefs and standards of the fathers, the other an expression of the instincts, practice, and discoveries of the younger generation. In all the higher things of the mind—in religion, in literature, in the moral emotions—it is the hereditary spirit that still prevails, so much so that Mr. Bernard Shaw finds that America is a hundred years behind the times. The truth is that one-half of the American mind, that not occupied intensely in practical affairs, has remained, I will not say high-and-dry, but slightly becalmed; it has floated gently in the back-water, while, alongside, in invention and industry and social organisation, the other half of the mind was leaping down a sort of Niagara Rapids. This division may be found symbolised in American architecture: a neat reproduction of the colonial mansion—with some modern comforts introduced surreptitiously—stands beside the sky-scraper. The American Will inhabits the sky-scraper; the American Intellect inhabits the colonial mansion. The one is the sphere of the American man; the other, at least predominantly, of the American woman. The one is all aggressive enterprise; the other is all genteel tradition.

Source: George Santayana, *Winds of Doctrine* (London: J. M. Dent & Co., 1913), 186–215.

Now, with your permission, I should like to analyse more fully how this interesting situation has arisen, how it is qualified, and whither it tends. And in the first place we should remember what, precisely, that philosophy was which the first settlers brought with them into the country. In strictness there was more than one; but we may confine our attention to what I will call Calvinism, since it is on this that the current academic philosophy has been grafted. I do not mean exactly the Calvinism of Calvin, or even of Jonathan Edwards; for in their systems there was much that was not pure philosophy, but rather faith in the externals and history of revelation. Jewish and Christian revelation was interpreted by these men, however, in the spirit of a particular philosophy, which might have arisen under any sky, and been associated with any other religion as well as with Protestant Christianity. In fact, the philosophical principle of Calvinism appears also in the Koran, in Spinoza, and in Cardinal Newman; and persons with no very distinctive Christian belief, like Carlyle or like Professor Royce, may be nevertheless, philosophically, perfect Calvinists. Calvinism, taken in this sense, is an expression of the agonised conscience. It is a view of the world which an agonised conscience readily embraces, if it takes itself seriously, as, being agonised, of course it must. Calvinism, essentially, asserts three things: that sin exists, that sin is punished, and that it is beautiful that sin should exist to be punished. The heart of the Calvinist is therefore divided between tragic concern at his own miserable condition, and tragic exultation about the universe at large. He oscillates between a profound abasement and a paradoxical elation of the spirit. To be a Calvinist philosophically is to feel a fierce pleasure in the existence of misery, especially of one's own, in that this misery seems to manifest the fact that the Absolute is irresponsible or infinite or holy. Human nature, it feels, is totally depraved: to have the instincts and motives that we necessarily have is a great scandal, and we must suffer for it; but that scandal is requisite, since otherwise the serious importance of being as we ought to be would not have been vindicated.

To those of us who have not an agonised conscience this system may seem fantastic and even unintelligible; yet it is logically and intently thought out from its emotional premises. It can take permanent possession of a deep mind here and there, and under certain conditions it can become epidemic. Imagine, for instance, a small nation with an intense vitality, but on the verge of ruin, ecstatic and distressful, having a strict and minute code of laws, that paints life in sharp and violent chiaroscuro, all pure righteousness and black abominations, and exaggerating the consequences of both perhaps to infinity. Such a people were the Jews after the exile, and again the early Protestants. If such a people is philosophical at all, it will not improbably be Calvinistic. Even in the early American communities many of these conditions were fulfilled. The nation was small and isolated; it lived under pressure and constant trial; it was acquainted with but a small range of goods and evils. Vigilance over conduct and an absolute demand for personal integrity were not merely traditional things, but things that practical sages, like Franklin and Washington, recommended to their countrymen, because they were virtues that justified themselves visibly by their fruits. But soon these happy results themselves helped to relax the pressure of external circumstances, and indirectly the pressure of the agonised conscience within. The nation became numerous; it ceased to be either ecstatic or distressful; the high social morality which on the whole it preserved took another colour; people remained honest and helpful out of good sense and good will rather than out of scrupulous adherence to any fixed principles. They retained their instinct for order, and often created order with surprising quickness; but the sanctity of law, to be obeyed for its own sake, began to escape them; it seemed too unpractical a notion, and not quite serious. In fact, the second and native-born American mentality began to take shape. The sense of sin totally evaporated. Nature, in the words of Emerson, was all beauty and commodity; and while operating on it laboriously, and drawing quick returns, the American began to drink in inspiration from it æsthetically. At the same time, in so broad a continent, he had elbow-room. His neighbours helped more than they hindered him; he wished their number to increase. Good will became the great American virtue; and a passion arose for counting heads, and square miles, and cubic feet, and minutes saved—as if there had been anything to save them for. How strange to the American now that saying of Jonathan Edwards, that men are naturally God's enemies! Yet that is an axiom to any intelligent Calvinist, though the words he uses may be different. If you told the modern American that he is totally depraved, he would think you were joking, as he himself usually is. He is convinced that he always has been, and always will be, victorious and blameless.

Calvinism thus lost its basis in American life. Some emotional natures, indeed, reverted in their religious revivals or private searchings of heart to the sources of the tradition; for any of the radical points of view in philosophy may cease to be prevalent, but none can cease to be possible. Other natures, more sensitive to the moral and literary influences of the world, preferred to abandon parts of their philosophy, hoping thus to reduce the distance which should separate the remainder from real life.

Meantime, if anybody arose with a special sensibility or a technical genius, he was in great straits; not being fed sufficiently by the world, he was driven in upon his own resources. The three American writers whose personal endowment was perhaps the finest—Poe, Hawthorne, and Emerson—had all a certain starved and abstract quality. They could not retail the genteel tradition; they were too keen, too perceptive, and too independent for that. But life offered them little digestible material, nor were they naturally voracious. They were fastidious, and under the circumstances they were starved. Emerson, to be sure, fed on books. There was a great catholicity in his reading; and he showed a fine tact in his comments, and in his way of appropriating what he read. But he read transcendentally, not historically, to learn what he himself felt, not what others might have felt before him. And to feed on books, for a philosopher or a poet, is still to starve. Books can help him to acquire form, or to avoid pitfalls; they cannot supply him with substance, if he is to have any. Therefore the genius of Poe and Hawthorne, and even of Emerson, was employed on a sort of inner play, or digestion of vacancy. It was a refined labour, but it was in danger of being morbid, or tinkling, or self-indulgent. It was a play of intra-mental rhymes. Their mind was like an old music-box, full of tender echoes and quaint fancies. These fancies expressed their personal genius sincerely, as dreams may; but they were arbitrary fancies in comparison with what a real observer would have said in the premises. Their manner, in a word, was subjective. In their own persons they escaped the mediocrity of the genteel tradition, but they supplied nothing to supplant it in other minds.

The churches, likewise, although they modified their spirit, had no philosophy to offer save a new emphasis on parts of what Calvinism contained. The theology of Calvin, we must remember, had much in it besides philosophical Calvinism. A Christian tenderness, and a hope of grace for the individual, came to mitigate its sardonic optimism; and it was these evangelical elements that the Calvinistic churches now emphasised, seldom and with blushes referring to hell-fire or infant damnation. Yet philosophic Calvinism, with a theory of life that would perfectly justify hell-fire and infant damnation if they happened to exist, still dominates the traditional metaphysics. It is an ingredient, and the decisive ingredient, in what calls itself idealism. But in order to see just what part Calvinism plays in current idealism, it will be necessary to distinguish the other chief element in that complex system, namely, transcendentalism.

Transcendentalism is the philosophy which the romantic era produced in Germany, and independently, I believe, in America also. Transcendentalism proper, like romanticism, is not any particular set of dogmas about what things exist; it is not a system of the universe regarded as a fact, or as a collection of facts. It is a method, a point of view, from which any world, no matter what it might contain, could be approached by a self-conscious observer. Transcendentalism is systematic subjectivism. It studies the perspectives of knowledge as they radiate from the self; it is a plan of those avenues of interference by which our ideas of things must be reached, if they are to afford any systematic or distant vistas. In other words, transcendentalism is the critical logic of science. Knowledge, it says, has a station, as in a watchtower, it is always seated here and now, in the self of the moment. The past and the future, things inferred and things conceived, lie around it, painted as upon a panorama. They cannot be lighted up save by some centrifugal ray of attention and present interest, by some active operation of the mind.

This is hardly the occasion for developing or explaining this delicate insight; suffice it to say, lest you should think later that I disparage transcendentalism, that as a method I regard it as correct and, when once suggested, unforgettable. I regard it as the chief contribution made in modern times to speculation. But it is a method only, an attitude we may always assume if we like and that will always be legitimate. It is no answer, and involves no particular answer, to the question: What exists; in what order is what exists produced; what is to exist in the future? This question must be answered by observing the object, and tracing humbly the movement of the object. It cannot be answered at all by harping on the fact that this object, if discovered, must be discovered by somebody, and by somebody who has an interest in discovering it. Yet the Germans who first gained the full transcendental insight were romantic people; they were more or less frankly poets; they were colossal egotists, and wished to make not only their own knowledge but the whole universe centre about themselves. And full as they were of their romantic isolation and romantic liberty, it occurred to them to imagine that all reality might be a transcendental self and a romantic dreamer like themselves; nay, that it might be just their own transcendental self and their own romantic dreams extended indefinitely. Transcendental logic, the method of discovery for the mind, was to become also the method of evolution in nature and history. Transcendental method, so abused, produced transcendental myth. A conscientious critique of knowledge was turned into a sham system of nature. We must therefore distinguish sharply the transcendental grammar of the intellect, which is significant and potentially correct, from the various transcendental systems of the universe, which are chimeras.

In both its parts, however, transcendentalism had much to recommend it to American philosophers, for the transcendental method appealed to the individualistic and revolutionary temper of their youth, while transcendental myths enabled them to find a new status for their inherited theology, and to give what parts of it they cared to preserve some semblance of philosophical backing. This last was the use to which the transcendental method was put by Kant himself, who first brought it into vogue, before the terrible weapon had got out of hand, and become the instrument of pure romanticism. Kant came, he himself said, to remove knowledge in order to make room for faith, which in his case meant faith in Calvinism. In other words, he applied the transcendental method to matters of fact, reducing them thereby to human ideas, in order to give to the Calvinistic postulates of conscience a metaphysical validity. For Kant had a genteel tradition of his own, which he wished to remove to a place of safety, feeling that the empirical world had become too hot for it; and this play of safety was the region of transcendental myth. I need hardly say how perfectly this expedient suited the needs of philosophers in America, and it is no accident if the influence of Kant soon became dominant here. To embrace this philosophy was regarded as a sign of profound metaphysical insight, although the most mediocre minds found no difficulty in embracing it. In truth it was a sign of having been brought up in the genteel tradition, of feeling it weak, and of wishing to save it.

But the transcendental method, in its way, was also sympathetic to the American mind. It embodied, in a radical form, the spirit of Protestantism as distinguished from its inherited doctrines; it was autonomous, undismayed, calmly revolutionary; it felt that Will was deeper than Intellect; it focussed everything here and now, and asked all things to show their credentials at the bar of the young self, and to prove their value for this latest born moment. These things are truly American; they would be characteristic of any young society with a keen and discursive intelligence, and they are strikingly exemplified in the thought and in the person of Emerson. They constitute what he called self-trust. Self-trust, like other transcendental attitudes, may be expressed in metaphysical fables. The romantic spirit may imagine itself to be an absolute force, evoking and moulding the plastic world to express its varying moods. But for a pioneer who is actually a world-builder this metaphysical illusion has a partial warrant in historical fact; far more warrant than it could boast of in the fixed and articulated society of Europe, among the moonstruck rebels and sulking poets of the romantic era. Emerson was a shrewd Yankee, by instinct on the winning side; he was a cheery, child-like soul, impervious to the evidence of evil, as of everything that it did not suit his transcendental individuality to appreciate or to notice. More, perhaps, than anybody that has ever lived, he practised the transcendental method in all its purity. He had no system. He opened his eyes on the world every morning with a fresh sincerity, marking how things seemed to him then, or what they suggested to his spontaneous fancy. This fancy, for being spontaneous, was not always novel; it was guided by the habits and training of his mind, which were those of a preacher. Yet he never insisted on his notions so as to turn them into settled dogmas; he felt in his bones that they were myths. Sometimes, indeed, the bad example of other transcendentalists, less true than he to their method, or the pressing questions of unintelligent people, or the instinct we all have to think our ideas final, led him to the very verge of system-making; but he stopped short. Had he made a system out of his notion of compensation, or the over-soul, or spiritual laws, the result would have been as thin and forced as it is in other transcendental systems. But he coveted truth; and he returned to experience, to history, to poetry, to the natural science of his day, for new starting-points and hints toward fresh transcendental musings.

To covet truth is a very distinguished passion. Every philosopher says he is pursuing the truth, but this is seldom the case. As Mr. Bertrand Russell has observed, one reason why philosophers often fail to reach the truth is that often they do not desire to reach it. Those who are genuinely concerned in discovering what happens to be true are rather the men of science, the naturalists, the historians; and ordinarily they discover it, according to their lights. The truths they find are never complete, and are not always important; but they are integral parts of the truth, facts and circumstances that help to fill in the picture, and that no later interpretation can invalidate or afford to contradict. But professional philosophers are usually only apologists: that is, they are absorbed in defending some vested illusion or some eloquent idea. Like lawyers or detectives, they study the case for which they are retained, to see how much evidence or semblance of evidence they can gather for the defence, and how much prejudice they can raise against the witnesses for the prosecution; for they know they are defending prisoners suspected by the world, and perhaps by their own good sense, of falsification. They do not covet truth, but victory and the dispelling of their own doubts. What they defend is some system, that is, some view about the totality of things, of which men are actually ignorant. No system would have ever been framed if people had been simply interested in knowing what is true, whatever it may be. What produces systems is the interest in maintaining against all comers that some favourite or inherited idea of ours is sufficient and right. A system may contain an account of many things which, in detail, are true enough; but as a system, covering infinite possibilities that neither our experience nor our logic can prejudge, it must be a work of imagination and a piece of human soliloquy. It may be expressive of human experience, it may be poetical; but how should any one who really coveted truth suppose that it was true?

Emerson had no system; and his coveting truth had another exceptional consequence: he was detached, unworldly, contemplative. When he came out of the conventicle or the reform meeting, or out of the rapturous close atmosphere of the lecture-room, he heard Nature whispering to him: "Why so hot, little sir?" No doubt the spirit or energy of the world is what is acting in us, as the sea is what rises in every little wave; but it passes through us, and cry out as we may, it will move on. Our privilege is to have perceived it as it moves. Our dignity is not in what we do, but in what we understand. The whole world is doing things. We are turning in that vortex; yet within us is silent observation, the speculative eye before which all passes, which bridges the distances and compares the combatants. On this side of his genius Emerson broke away from all conditions of age or country and represented nothing except intelligence itself.

There was another element in Emerson, curiously combined with transcendentalism, namely, his love and respect for Nature. Nature, for the transcendentalist, is precious because it is his own work, a mirror in which he looks at himself and says (like a poet relishing his own verses), "What a genius I am! Who would have thought there was such stuff in me?" And the philosophical egotist finds in his doctrine a ready explanation of whatever beauty and commodity nature actually has. No wonder, he says to himself, that nature is sympathetic, since I made it. And such a view, one-sided and even fatuous as it may be, undoubtedly sharpens the vision of a poet and a moralist to all that is inspiriting and symbolic in the natural world. Emerson was particularly ingenious and clear-sighted in feeling the spiritual uses of fellowship with the elements. This is something in which all Teutonic poetry is rich and which forms, I think, the most genuine and spontaneous part of modern taste, and especially of American taste. Just as some people are naturally enthralled and refreshed by music, so others are by landscape. Music and landscape make up the spiritual resources of those who cannot or dare not express their unfulfilled ideals in words. Serious poetry, profound religion (Calvinism, for instance), are the joys of an unhappiness that confesses itself; but when a genteel tradition forbids people to confess that they are unhappy, serious poetry and profound religion are closed to them by that; and since human life, in its depths, cannot then express itself openly, imagination is driven for comfort into abstract arts, where human circumstances are lost sight of, and human problems dissolve in a purer medium. The pressure of care is thus relieved, without its quietus being found in intelligence. To understand oneself is the classic form of consolation; to elude oneself is the romantic. In the presence of music or landscape human experience eludes itself; and thus romanticism is the bond between transcendental and naturalistic sentiment. The winds and clouds come to minister to the solitary ego.

Have there been, we may ask, any successful efforts to escape from the genteel tradition, and to express something worth expressing behind its back? This might well not have occurred as yet; but America is so precocious, it has been trained by the genteel tradition to be so wise for its years, that some indications of a truly native philosophy and poetry are already to be found. I might mention the humorists, of whom you here in California have had your share. The humorists, however, only half escape the genteel tradition; their humour would lose its savour if they had wholly escaped it. They point to what contradicts it in the facts; but not in order to abandon the genteel tradition, for they have nothing solid to put in its place. When they point out how ill many facts fit into it, they do not clearly conceive that this militates against the standard, but think it a funny perversity in the facts. Of course, did they earnestly respect the genteel tradition, such an incongruity would seem to them sad, rather than ludicrous. Perhaps the prevalence of humour in America, in and out of season, may be taken as one more evidence that the genteel tradition is present pervasively, but everywhere weak. Similarly in Italy, during the Renaissance, the Catholic tradition could not be banished from the intellect, since there was nothing articulate to take its place; yet its hold on the heart was singularly relaxed. The consequence was that humorists could regale themselves with the foibles of monks and of cardinals, with the credulity of fools, and the bogus miracles of the saints; not intending to deny the theory of the church, but caring for it so little at heart that they could find it infinitely amusing that it should be contradicted in men's lives and that no harm should come of it. So when Mark Twain says, "I was born of poor but dishonest parents," the humor depends on the parody of the genteel Anglo-Saxon convention that it is disreputable to be poor; but to hint at the hollowness of it would not be amusing if it did not remain at bottom one's habitual conviction.

The one American writer who has left the genteel tradition entirely behind is perhaps Walt Whitman. For this reason educated Americans find him rather an unpalatable person, who they sincerely protest ought not to be taken for a representative of their culture; and he certainly should not, because their culture is so genteel and traditional. But the foreigner may sometimes think otherwise, since he is looking for what may have arisen in America to express, not the polite and conventional American mind, but the spirit and the inarticulate principles that animate the community, on which its own genteel mentality seems to sit rather lightly. When the foreigner opens the pages of Walt Whitman, he thinks that he has come at last upon something representative and original. In Walt Whitman democracy is carried into psychology and morals. The various sights, moods, and emotions are given each one vote; they are declared to be all free and equal, and the innumerable commonplace moments of life are suffered to speak like the others. Those moments formerly reputed great are not excluded, but they are made to march in the ranks with their companions—plain foot-soldiers and servants of the hour. Nor does the refusal to discriminate stop there; we must carry our principle further down, to the animals, to inanimate nature, to the cosmos as a whole. Whitman became a pantheist; but his pantheism, unlike that of the Stoics and of Spinoza, was unintellectual, lazy, and self-indulgent; for he simply felt jovially that everything real was good enough, and that he was good enough himself. In him Bohemia rebelled against the genteel tradition; but the reconstruction that alone can justify revolution did not ensue. His attitude, in principle, was utterly disintegrating; his poetic genius fell back to the lowest level, perhaps, to which it is possible for poetic genius to fall. He reduced his imagination to a passive sensorium for the registering of impressions. No element of construction remained in it, and therefore no element of penetration. But his scope was wide; and his lazy, desultory apprehension was poetical. His work, for the very reason that it is so rudimentary, contains a beginning, or rather many beginnings, that might possibly grow into a noble moral imagination, a worthy filling for the human mind. An American in the nineteenth century who completely disregarded the genteel tradition could hardly have done more.

But there is another distinguished man, lately lost to this country, who has given some rude shocks to this tradition and who, as much as Whitman, may be regarded as representing the genuine, the long silent American mind—I mean William James. He and his brother Henry were as tightly swaddled in the genteel tradition as any infant geniuses could be, for they were born before 1850, and in a Swedenborgian household. Yet they burst those bands almost entirely. The ways in which the two brothers freed themselves, however, are interestingly different. Mr. Henry James has done it by adopting the point of view of the outer world, and by turning the genteel American tradition, as he turns everything else, into a subject-matter for analysis. For him it is a curious habit of mind, intimately comprehended, to be compared with other habits of mind, also well known to him. Thus he has overcome the genteel tradition in the classic way, by understanding it. With William James too this infusion of worldly insight and European sympathies was a potent influence, especially in his earlier days; but the chief source of his liberty was another. It was his personal spontaneity, similar to that of Emerson, and his personal vitality, similar to that of nobody else. Convictions and ideas came to him, so to speak, from the subsoil. He had a prophetic sympathy with the dawning sentiments of the age, with the moods of the dumb majority. His scattered words caught fire in many parts of the world. His way of thinking and feeling represented the true America, and represented in a measure the whole ultra-modern, radical world. Thus he eluded the genteel tradition in the romantic way, by continuing it into its opposite. The romantic mind, glorified in Hegel's dialectic (which is not dialectic at all, but a sort of tragic-comic history of experience), is always rendering its thoughts unrecognisable through the infusion of new insights, and through the insensible transformation of the moral feeling that accompanies them, till at last it has completely reversed its old judgments under cover of expanding them. Thus the genteel tradition was led a merry dance when it fell again into the hands of a genuine and vigorous romanticist like William James. He restored their revolutionary force to its neutralised elements, by picking them out afresh, and emphasising them separately, according to his personal predilections.

For one thing, William James kept his mind and heart wide open to all that might seem, to polite minds, odd, personal, or visionary in religion and philosophy. He gave a sincerely respectful hearing to sentimentalists, mystics, spiritualists, wizards, cranks, quacks, and impostors—for it is hard to draw the line, and James was not willing to draw it prematurely. He thought, with his usual modesty, that any of these might have something to teach him. The lame, the halt, the blind, and those speaking with tongues could come to him with the certainty of finding sympathy; and if they were not healed, at least they were comforted, that a famous professor should take them so seriously; and they began to feel that after all to have only one leg, or one hand, or one eye, or to have three, might be in itself no less beauteous than to have just two, like the stolid majority. Thus William James became the friend and helper of those groping, nervous, half-educated, spiritually disinherited, passionately hungry individuals of which America is full. He became, at the same time, their spokesman and representative before the learned world; and he made it a chief part of his vocation to recast what the learned world has to offer, so that as far as possible it might serve the needs and interests of these people.

Yet the normal practical masculine American, too, had a friend in William James. There is a feeling abroad now, to which biology and Darwinism lend some colour, that theory is simply an instrument for practice, and intelligence merely a help toward material survival. Bears, it is said, have fur and claws, but poor naked man is condemned to be intelligent, or he will perish. This feeling William James embodied in that theory of thought and of truth which he called pragmatism. Intelligence, he thought, is no miraculous, idle faculty, by which we mirror passively any or everything that happens to be true, reduplicating the real world to no purpose. Intelligence has its roots and its issue in the context of events; it is one kind of practical adjustment, an experimental act, a form of vital tension. It does not essentially serve to picture other parts of reality, but to connect them. This view was not worked out by William James in its psychological and historical details; unfortunately he developed it chiefly in controversy against its opposite, which he called intellectualism, and which he hated with all the hatred of which his kind heart was capable. Intellectualism, as he conceived it, was pure pedantry; it impoverished and verbalised everthing, and tied up nature in red tape. Ideas and rules that may have been occasionally useful if put in the place of the full-blooded irrational movement of life which had called them into being; and these abstractions, so soon obsolete, it strove to fix and to worship for ever. Thus all creeds and theories and all formal precepts sink in the estimation of the pragmatist to a local and temporary grammar of action; a grammar that must be changed slowly by time, and may be changed quickly by genius. To know things as a whole, or as they are eternally, if there is anything eternal in them, is not only beyond our powers, but would prove worthless, and perhaps even fatal to our lives. Ideas are not mirrors, they are weapons; their function is to prepare us to meet events, as future experience may unroll them. Those ideas that disappoint us are false ideas; those to which events are true are true themselves.

This may seem a very utilitarian view of the mind; and I confess I think it a partial one, since the logical force of beliefs and ideas, their truth or falsehood as assertions, has been overlooked altogether, or confused with the vital force of the material processes which these ideas express. It is an external view only, which marks the place and conditions of the mind in nature, but neglects its specific essence; as if a jewel were defined as a round hole in a ring. Nevertheless, the more materialistic the pragmatist's theory of the mind is, the more vitalistic his theory of nature will have to become. If the intellect is a device produced in organic bodies to expedite their processes, these organic bodies must have interests and a chosen direction in their life; otherwise their life could not be expedited, nor could anything be useful to it. In other words—and this is a third point at which the philosophy of William James has played havoc with the genteel tradition, while ostensibly defending it—nature must be conceived anthropomorphically and in psychological terms. Its purposes are not to be static harmonies, self-unfolding destinies, the logic of spirit, the spirit of logic, or any other formal method and abstract law; its purposes are to be concrete endeavours, finite efforts of souls living in an environment which they transform and by which they, too, are affected. A spirit, the divine spirit as much as the human, as this new animism conceives it, is a romantic adventurer. Its future is undetermined. Its scope, its duration, and the quality of its life are all contingent. This spirit grows; it buds and sends forth feelers, sounding the depths around for such other centres of force or life as may exist there. It has a vital momentum, but no predetermined goal. It uses its past as a stepping-stone, or rather as a diving-board, but has an absolutely fresh will at each moment to plunge this way or that into the unknown. The universe is an experiment; it is unfinished. It has no ultimate or total nature, because it has no end. It embodies no formula or statable law; any formula is at best a poor abstraction, describing what, in some region and for some time, may be the most striking characteristic of existence; the law is a description *a posteriori* of the habit things have chosen to acquire, and which they may possibly throw off altogether. What a day may bring forth is uncertain; uncertain even to God. Omniscience is impossible; time is real; what had been omniscience hitherto might discover something more to-day. "There shall be news," William James was fond of saying with rapture, quoting from the unpublished poem of an obscure friend, "there shall be news in heaven!" There is almost certainly, he thought, a God now; there may be several gods, who might exist together, or one after the other. We might, by our conspiring sympathies, help to make a new one. Much in us is doubtless immortal; we survive death for some time in a recognisable form; but what our career and transformations may be in the sequel we cannot tell, although we may help to determine them by our daily choices. Observation must be continual if our ideas are to remain true. Eternal vigilance is the price of knowledge; perpetual hazard, perpetual experiment keep quick the edge of life.

This is, so far as I know, a new philosophical vista; it is a conception never before presented, although implied, perhaps, in various quarters, as in Norse and even Greek mythology. It is a vision radically empirical and radically romantic; and as William James himself used to say, the visions and not the arguments of a philosopher are the interesting and influential things about him. William James, rather too generously, attributed this vision to M. Bergson, and regarded him in consequence as a philosopher of the first rank, whose thought was to be one of the turning-points in history. M. Bergson had killed intellectualism. It was his book on creative evolution, said James with humorous emphasis, that had come at last to *"écraser l'infâme."* We may suspect, notwithstanding, that intellectualism, infamous and crushed, will survive the blow; and if the author of the Book of Ecclesiastes were now alive, and heard that there shall be news in heaven, he would doubtless say that there may possibly be news there, but that under the sun there is nothing new—not even radical empiricism or radical romanticism, which from the beginning of the world has been the philosophy of those who as yet had had little experience; for to the blinking little child it is not merely something in the world that is new daily, but everything is new all day.

I am not concerned with the rights and wrongs of that controversy; my point is only that William James, in this genial evolutionary view of the world, has given a rude shock to the genteel tradition. What! The world a gradual improvisation? Creation unpremeditated? God a sort of young poet or struggling artist? William James is an advocate of theism; pragmatism adds one to the evidences of religion; that is excellent. But is not the cool abstract piety of the genteel getting more than it asks for? This empirical naturalistic God is too crude and positive a force; he will work miracles, he will answer prayers, he may inhabit distinct places, and have distinct conditions under which alone he can operate; he is a neighbouring being, whom we can act upon, and rely upon for specific aids, as upon a personal friend, or a physician, or an insurance company. How disconcerting! Is not this new theology a little like superstition? And yet how interesting, how exciting, if it should happen to be true! I am far from wishing to suggest that such a view seems to me more probable than conventional idealism or than Christian orthodoxy. All three are in the region of dramatic system-making and myth to which probabilities are irrelevant. If one man says the moon is sister to the sun, and another that she is his daughter, the question is not which notion is more probable, but whether either of them is at all expressive. The so-called evidences are devised afterwards, when faith and imagination have prejudged the issue. The force of William James's new theology, or romantic cosmology, lies only in this: that it has broken the spell of the genteel tradition, and enticed faith in a new direction, which on second thoughts may prove no less alluring than the old. The important fact is not that the new fancy might possibly be true—who shall know that?—but that it has entered the heart of a leading American to conceive and to cherish it. The genteel tradition cannot be dislodged by these insurrections; there are circles to which it is still congenial, and where it will be preserved. But it has been challenged and (what is perhaps more insidious) it has been discovered. No one need be browbeaten any longer into accepting it. No one need be afraid, for instance, that his fate is sealed because some young prig may call him a dualist; the pint would call the quart a dualist, if you tried to pour the quart into him. We need not be afraid of being less profound, for being direct and sincere. The intellectual world may be traversed in many directions; the whole has not been surveyed; there is a great career in it open to talent. That is a sort of knell, that tolls the passing of the genteel tradition. Something else is now in the field; something else can appeal to the imagination, and be a thousand times more idealistic than academic idealism, which is often simply a way of white-washing and adoring things as they are. The illegitimate monopoly which the genteel tradition had established over what ought to be assumed and what ought to be hoped for has been broken down by the first-born of the family, by the genius of the race. Henceforth there can hardly be the same peace and the same pleasure in hugging the old properties. Hegel will be to the next generation what Sir William Hamilton was to the last. Nothing will have been disproved, but everything will have been abandoned. An honest man has spoken, and the cant of the genteel tradition has become harder for young lips to repeat.

With this I have finished such a sketch as I am here able to offer you of the genteel tradition in American philosophy. The subject is complex, and calls for many an excursus and qualifying footnote; yet I think the main outlines are clear enough. The chief fountains of this tradition were Calvinism and transcendentalism. Both were living fountains; but to keep them alive they required, one an agonised conscience, and the other a radical subjective criticism of knowledge. When these rare metaphysical preoccupations disappeared—and the American atmosphere is not favourable to either of them—the two systems ceased to be inwardly understood; they subsisted as sacred mysteries only; and the combination of the two in some transcendental system of the universe (a contradiction in principle) was doubly artificial. Besides, it could hardly be held with a single mind. Natural science, history, the beliefs implied in labour and invention, could not be disregarded altogether; so that the transcendental philosopher was condemned to a double allegiance, and to not letting his left hand know the bluff that his right hand was making. Nevertheless, the difficulty in bringing practical inarticulate convictions to expression is very great, and the genteel tradition has subsisted in the academic mind for want of anything equally academic to take its place.

The academic mind, however, has had its flanks turned. On the one side came the revolt of the Bohemian temperament, with its poetry of crude naturalism; on the other side came an impassioned empiricism, welcoming popular religious witnesses to the unseen, reducing science to an instrument of success in action, and declaring the universe to be wild and young, and not to be harnessed by the logic of any school.

This revolution, I should think, might well find an echo among you, who live in a thriving society, and in the presence of a virgin and prodigious world. When you transform nature to your uses, when you experiment with her forces, and reduce them to industrial agents, you cannot feel that nature was made by you or for you, for then these adjustments would have been pre-established. Much less can you feel it when she destroys your labour of years in a momentary spasm. You must feel, rather, that you are an offshoot of her life; one brave little force among her immense forces. When you escape, as you love to do, to your forests and your sierras, I am sure again that you do not feel you made them, or that they were made for you. They have grown, as you have grown, only more massively and more slowly. In their non-human beauty and peace they stir the sub-human depths and the superhuman possibilities of your own spirit. It is no transcendental logic that they teach; and they give no sign of any deliberate morality seated in the world. It is rather the vanity and superficiality of all logic, the needlessness of argument, the relativity of morals, the strength of time, the fertility of matter, the variety, the unspeakable variety, of possible life. Everything is measurable and conditioned, indefinitely repeated, yet, in repetition, twisted somewhat from its old form. Everywhere is beauty and nowhere permanence, everywhere an incipient harmony, nowhere an intention, nor a responsibility, nor a plan. It is the irresistible suasion of this daily spectacle, it is the daily discipline of contact with things, so different from the verbal discipline of the schools, that will, I trust, inspire the philosophy of your children. A Californian whom I had recently the pleasure of meeting observed that, if the philosophers had lived among your mountains their systems would have been different from what they are. Certainly, I should say, very different from what those systems are which the European genteel tradition has handed down since Socrates; for these systems are egotistical; directly or indirectly they are anthropocentric, and inspired by the conceited notion that man, or human reason, or the human distinction between good and evil, is the centre and pivot of the universe. That is what the mountains and the woods should make you at last ashamed to assert. From what, indeed, does the society of nature liberate you, that you find it so sweet? It is hardly (is it?) that you wish to forget your past, or your friends, or that you have any secret contempt for your present ambitions. You respect these, you respect them perhaps too much; you are not suffered by the genteel tradition to criticise or to reform them at all radically. No; it is the yoke of this genteel tradition itself that these primeval solitudes lift from your shoulders. They suspend your forced sense of your own importance not merely as individuals, but even as men. They allow you, in one happy moment, at once to play and to worship, to take yourselves simply, humbly, for what you are, and to salute the wild, indifferent, noncensorious infinity of nature. You are admonished that what you can do avails little materially, and in the end nothing. At the same time, through wonder and pleasure, you are taught speculation. You learn what you are really fitted to do, and where lie your natural dignity and joy, namely, in representing many things, without being them, and in letting your imagination, through sympathy, celebrate and echo their life. Because the peculiarity of man is that his machinery for reaction on external things has involved an imaginative transcript of these things, which is preserved and suspended in his fancy; and the interest and beauty of this inward landscape, rather than any fortunes that may await his body in the outer world, constitute his proper happiness. By their mind, its scope, quality, and temper, we estimate men, for by the mind only do we exist as men, and are more than so many storage-batteries for material energy. Let us therefore be frankly human. Let us be content to live in the mind.

Part Two

*Social Progress
and the Power
of Intellect*

Introduction

In an essay of 1917 reprinted herein, the young journalist Randolph Bourne denounced John Dewey for supporting American involvement in the Great War. The eminent philosopher had led contemporary American intellectuals to relinquish their independent critical voice, Bourne complained; no longer could these now-compromised intellectuals hope to be more than servants of the war administration of President Woodrow Wilson. This disagreement between Bourne and Dewey is one of the most famous episodes in the intellectual history of the first third of the twentieth century. This period—to which Part Two is devoted—is appropriately remembered for the fierceness of its conflicts over the proper responsibilities of intellectuals. And no one had done more than Dewey himself—one of whose contributions appears here—to convince men and women with intelligence and learning that the destiny of their society depended in large part on *them*. The systematic use of human intelligence and the proper education of the public could create, according to Dewey, a modern social order more responsive than any previous one to the vital needs of every individual. No single writer expressed the Progressive Era version of this faith in intellect than Walter Lippmann.

Bourne himself was something of a disciple of Dewey's and hence all the more troubled when Dewey himself interpreted differently than Bourne did the implications of ideals the two men shared. In a 1916 essay we find Bourne calling explicitly for the formation of a new "intelligentsia" within American society. Another follower of Dewey, the philosopher Sidney Hook, emerged in the 1930s as a champion among Marxists of intellectual and political independence from the Soviet Union and the Communist Party of the United States. Part Two also includes a selection from Wilson himself, the American president who put the most faith in theoretical argumentation.

Wilson's now notorious tendency to see Anglo-Saxons as the carrier of the world's progress contrasts vividly with the outlook of his contemporary, W. E. B. Du Bois. This black polymath argued that black Americans, as a result of their being kept at the margins of society, had developed a "second sight," a capacity to see things that the empowered white majority missed. In the meantime, the journalist and critic H. L. Mencken lacerated the majority culture of the United States—the culture for which the strict Presbyterian Wilson was in many ways an emblem—for its "Puritanism."

An overly puritanical moral heritage was also a target of anthropologist Margaret Mead, for whom the life of South Pacific islanders was a heuristic countermodel to the life of early twentieth-century America. Mead was highly self-conscious about the role that social scientists like herself could play in improving society. Mead's fellow social scientist Thorstein Veblen had performed this role through an ironic and sarcastic description of the American leisure class, but Mead herself, speaking in a more moralistic voice, contrasted the failings of her own modern American culture with the apparent successes of some primitive societies studied by anthropologists.

The enlargement of social science's space in American intellectual life is a noteworthy feature of this period.

Mead and Veblen represent also a relativistic perspective on social norms that became popular among educated Americans throughout the period covered in Part Two. This perspective is also evident in Dewey's work and in the strictures against natural law offered by U.S. Supreme Court Justice Oliver Wendell Holmes, Jr. But perhaps the most powerful critic of absolute rules was William James.

James is no less pertinent to the theme of "Social Progress and the Power of Intellect" than was Dewey because he was both a social meliorist and an intellectual voluntarist. As a meliorist, he looked to the gradual improvement of the lives of human beings; as a voluntarist, he believed that truth was partly made by inquiring minds rather than merely uncovered when veils of illusion were removed. Both dispositions were manifest in James's pragmatism. James's specific philosophical doctrines were controversial, but in his devotion to active intellectual inquiry in the interests of human welfare, he was both an influence on and an emblem for the culture of many educated Americans during the early decades of the twentieth century.

But not all contributors to Part Two connected social progress and intellect. Reformer Jane Addams placed more emphasis on moral conviction. Avowed reactionary John Crowe Ransom repudiated the very idea of progress. Literary crtic Joseph Wood Krutch despaired over the direction of modern life.

Recommendations for Further Reading
Frederick J. Hoffman, *The 20s* (New York, 1955); Henry F. May, *The End of American Innocence: A Study of the First Years of Our Time* (New York, 1959); Daniel Aaron, *Writers on the Left* (New York, 1961); Christopher Lasch, *The New Radicalism in America: The Emergence of the Intellectual as a Social Type, 1889–1963* (New York, 1965); Jean B. Quandt, *From the Small Town to the Great Community: The Social Thought of Progressive Intellectuals* (New Brunswick, N.J., 1970); Edward A. Purcell, Jr., *The Crisis of Democratic Theory: Scientific Naturalism and the Problem of Value* (Lexington, Ky., 1973); Richard Pells, *Radical Visions and American Dreams: Culture and Social Thought in the Depression Years* (New York, 1973); Morton G. White, *Social Thought in America: The Revolt Against Formalism,* 3rd ed. (New York, 1976); Bruce Kuklick, *The Rise of American Philosophy: Cambridge, Massachusetts, 1860–1930* (New Haven, 1977); J. David Hoeveler, *The New Humanism: A Critique of Modern America, 1900–1940* (Charlottesville, Va., 1977); Fred H. Matthews, *Quest for an American Sociology: Robert E. Park and the Chicago School* (Montreal, 1977); Rosalind Rosenberg, *Beyond Separate Spheres: Intellectual Roots of Modern Feminism* (New Haven, 1982); Daniel J. Kevles, *In the Name of Eugenics: Genetics and the Uses of Human Heredity* (New York, 1985); James T. Kloppenberg, *Uncertain Victory: Social Democracy and Progressivism in European and American Thought, 1870–1920* (New York, 1986); William R. Hutchison, *Errand to the World: American Protestant Thought and Foreign Missions* (Chicago, 1987); Peter Novick, *That Noble Dream: The "Objectivity Question" and the American Historical Profession* (New York, 1988); Miles Orvell, *The Real Thing: Imitation and Authenticity in American Culture, 1880–1940* (Chapel Hill, 1989); Casey Nelson Blake, *The Beloved Community: The Cultural Criticism of Randolph Bourne, Van Wyck Brooks, Waldo Frank, and Lewis Mumford* (Chapel Hill, 1990); Daniel J. Wilson, *Science, Community, and the Transformation of American Philosophy, 1860–1930* (Chicago, 1990); Dorothy Ross, *The Origins of American Social Science* (New York, 1991); Susanne Klingenstein, *Jews in the American Academy, 1900–1940: The Dynamics of Intellectual Assimilation* (New Haven, 1991); Andrew Feffer, *The Chicago Pragmatists and American Progressivism* (Chicago, 1993); Thomas Bender, *Intellect and Public Life: Essays on the Social*

History of Academic Intellectuals in the United States (Baltimore, 1993); Dorothy Ross, ed., *The Modernist Impulse in the Human Sciences, 1870–1930* (Baltimore, 1994); Mark C. Smith, *Social Science in the Crucible: The American Debate Over Objectivity and Purpose, 1918–1941* (Durham, 1994); Elizabeth Lunbeck, *The Psychiatric Persuasion: Knowledge, Gender, and Power in Modern America* (Princeton, 1994); John M. Jordan, *Machine-Age Ideology: Social Engineering and American Liberalism, 1911–1939* (Chapel Hill, 1994); Ann Douglas, *Terrible Honesty: Mongrel Manhattan in the 1920s* (New York, 1995); Leon Fink, *Progressive Intellectuals and the Dilemmas of Democratic Commitment* (Cambridge, 1997); Daniel Rodgers, *Atlantic Crossings: Social Politics in a Progressive Age* (Cambridge, Mass., 1998); Brian Lloyd, *Left Out: Pragmatism, Exceptionalism, and the Poverty of American Marxism, 1890–1922* (Baltimore, 1997); Eric Caplan, *Mind Games: American Culture and the Birth of Psychotherapy* (Berkeley, 1998); Julie A. Reuben, *The Making of the Modern University: Intellectual Transformation and the Marginalization of Morality* (Chicago, 1996); Alex Zwerdling, *Improvised Europeans: American Literary Expatriates and the Siege of London* (New York, 1998); James T. Kloppenberg, *The Virtues of Liberalism* (New York, 1998); Henry Yu, *Thinking Orientals* (New York, 2001); Jonathan Hansen, *The Lost Promise of Patriotism* (Chicago, 2003); Andrew Heinze, *Jews and the American Soul* (Princeton, 2004); Jonathan Spiro, *Defending the Master Race: Conservation, Eugenics, and the Legacy of Madison Grant* (Hanover, N.H., 2008); Susan Nance, *How the Arabian Nights Inspired the American Dream, 1790–1935* (Chapel Hill, 2009); Leonard Harris and Charles Molesworth, *Alain L. Locke: The Biography of a Philosopher* (Chicago, 2008); Sarah Igo, *The Averaged American: Surveys, Citizens, and the Making of a Mass Public* (Cambridge, Mass., 2007); Diana Selig, *Americans All: The Cultural Gifts Movement* (Cambridge, Mass., 2008). Jonathan Spiro, *Defending the Master Race: Conservation, Eugenics, and the Legacy of Madison Grant* (Hanover, N.H., 2008); Leonard Harris and Charles Molesworth, *Alain L. Locke: The Biography of a Philosopher* (Chicago, 2008); Susan Nance, *How the Arabian Nights Inspired the American Dream, 1790–1955* (Chapel Hill, 2009).

JANE ADDAMS

"The Subjective Necessity of Social Settlements" (1892)

Jane Addams (1860–1935) was one of the most influential and indefatigable social reformers in all American history. Although based in Chicago at Hull House—the settlement house she created to serve the needs of a poor, largely immigrant neighborhood—she helped to lead a host of national movements, including the 1912 presidential campaign of Theodore Roosevelt. Addams was the founding president of the Woman's International League for Peace and Freedom and in 1931 shared the Nobel Peace Prize. Addams wrote widely on the theory and practice of social reform and international reconciliation. In the selection that follows, she scrutinizes in a social and religious context the motives of men and women who, like herself, had devoted themselves to the improvement of society. "The Subjective Necessity of Social Settlements" was first delivered as an address to a conference of social workers in 1892, but it gained fame as a classic statement of reform commitment after 1910 when it appeared in Addams's most widely appreciated book, *Twenty Years at Hull-House*.

"The Subjective Necessity of Social Settlements" is also a strong statement of the "social gospel," a movement in American Protestantism devoted to the vigorous application of Christian ethics to the contemporary social and economic world. For a more extensive expression of this outlook, see two books by the theologian Walter Rauschenbusch, *Christianity and the Social Crisis* (New York, 1908) and *A Theology for the Social Gospel* (New York, 1917). For differing historical perspectives on the social gospel, see Henry F. May, *Protestant Churches and Industrial America* (New York, 1949); and Susan Curtis, *A Consuming Faith: The Social Gospel and Modern American Culture* (Baltimore, 1991).

For Addams's life and work, see Victoria Bissell Brown, *The Education of Jane Addams* (Philadelphia, 2003); and Louise W. Knight, *Citizen Jane Addams and the Struggle for Democracy* (Chicago, 2005). For a detailed study of Jane Addams's work with immigrants and of the ideology Addams and her coworkers shared, see Rivka Shpak Lissak, *Pluralism and Progressives: Hull House and the New Immigrants, 1890–1919* (Chicago, 1989). But some of the best insights into Addams are developed by Kathryn Kish Sklar in a book focused on Addams's contemporary, Florence Kelley; see Sklar, *Florence Kelley and the Nation's Work* (New Haven, 1995). An excellent starting point for the study of Addams in Marilyn Fischer et al., eds., *Jane Addams and the Practice of Democracy* (Urbana, 2009).

...This paper is an attempt to analyze the motives which underlie a movement based, not only upon conviction, but upon genuine emotion, wherever educated young people are seeking an outlet for that sentiment of universal brotherhood, which the best spirit of our times is forcing from an emotion into a motive. These young people accomplish little toward the solution of this social problem, and bear the brunt of being cultivated into unnourished, oversensitive lives. They have been shut off from the common labor by which they live which is a great source of moral and physical health. They feel a fatal want of harmony between their theory and their lives, a lack of coördination between thought and action. I think it is hard for us to realize how seriously many of them are taking to the notion of human brotherhood, how eagerly they long to give tangible expression to the democratic ideal. These young men and women, longing to socialize their democracy, are animated by certain hopes which may be thus loosely formulated; that if in a democratic country nothing can be permanently achieved save through the masses of the people, it will be impossible to establish a higher political life than the people themselves crave; that it is difficult to see how the notion of a higher civic life can be fostered save through common intercourse; that the blessings which we associate with a life of refinement and cultivation can be made universal and must be made universal if they are to be permanent; that the good we secure for ourselves is precarious and uncertain, is floating in mid-air, until it is secured for all of us and incorporated into our common life. It is easier to state these hopes than to formulate the line of motives, which I believe to constitute the trend of the subjective pressure toward the Settlement. There is something primordial about these motives, but I am perhaps overbold in designating them as a great desire to share the race life. We all bear traces of the starvation struggle which for so long made up the life of the race. Our very organism holds memories and glimpses of that long life of our ancestors which still goes on among so many of our contemporaries. Nothing so deadens the sympathies and shrivels the power of enjoyment as the persistent keeping away from the great opportunities for helpfulness and a continual ignoring of the starvation struggle which makes up the life of at least half the race. To shut one's self away from that half of the race life is to shut one's self away from the most vital part of it; it is to live out but half the humanity to which we have been born heir and to use but half our faculties. We have all had longings for a fuller life which should include the use of these faculties. These longings are the physical complement of the "Intimations of Immortality," on which no ode has yet been written. To portray these would be the work of a poet, and it is hazardous for any but a poet to attempt it.

You may remember the forlorn feeling which occasionally seizes you when you arrive early in the morning a stranger in a great city: the stream of laboring people goes past you as you gaze through the plate-glass window of your hotel; you see hard workingmen lifting great burdens; you hear the driving and jostling of huge carts and your heart sinks with a sudden sense of futility. The door opens behind you and you turn to the man who brings you in your breakfast with a quick sense of human fellowship. You find yourself praying that you may never lose your hold on it all. A more poetic prayer would be that the great mother breasts of our common humanity, with its labor and suffering and its homely comforts, may never be withheld from you. You turn helplessly to the waiter and feel that it would be almost grotesque to claim from him the sympathy you crave because civilization has placed you apart, but you resent your position with a sudden sense of snobbery.

Source: Jane Addams, *Twenty Years at Hull-House* (New York: Macmillan, 1910), 91–100.

Literature is full of portrayals of these glimpses: they come to shipwrecked men on rafts; they overcome the differences of an incongruous multitude when in the presence of a great danger or when moved by a common enthusiasm. They are not, however, confined to such moments, and if we were in the habit of telling them to each other, the recital would be as long as the tales of children are, when they sit down on the green grass and confide to each other how many times they have remembered that they lived once before. If these childish tales are the stirring of inherited impressions, just so surely is the other the striving of inherited powers.

"It is true that there is nothing after disease, indigence and a sense of guilt, so fatal to health and to life itself as the want of a proper outlet for active faculties." I have seen young girls suffer and grow sensibly lowered in vitality in the first years after they leave school. In our attempt then to give a girl pleasure and freedom from care we succeed, for the most part, in making her pitifully miserable. She finds "life" so different from what she expected it to be. She is besotted with innocent little ambitions, and does not understand this apparent waste of herself, this elaborate preparation, if no work is provided for her. There is a heritage of noble obligation which young people accept and long to perpetuate. The desire for action, the wish to right wrong and alleviate suffering haunts them daily. Society smiles at it indulgently instead of making it of value to itself. The wrong to them begins even farther back, when we restrain the first childish desires for "doing good" and tell them that they must wait until they are older and better fitted. We intimate that social obligation begins at a fixed date, forgetting that it begins with birth itself. We treat them as children who, with strong-growing limbs, are allowed to use their legs but not their arms, or whose legs are daily carefully exercised that after a while their arms may be put to high use. We do this in spite of the protest of the best educators, Locke and Pestalozzi. We are fortunate in the meantime if their unused members do not weaken and disappear. They do sometimes. There are a few girls who, by the time they are "educated," forget their old childish desires to help the world and to play with poor little girls "who haven't play things." Parents are often inconsistent: they deliberately expose their daughters to knowledge of the distress in the world; they send them to hear missionary addresses on famines in India and China; they accompany them to lectures on the suffering in Siberia; they agitate together over the forgotten region of East London. In addition to this, from babyhood the altruistic tendencies of these daughters are persistently cultivated. They are taught to be self-forgetting and self-sacrificing, to consider the good of the whole before the good of the ego. But when all this information and culture show results, when the daughter comes back from college and begins to recognize her social claim to the "submerged tenth," and to evince a disposition to fulfill it, the family claim is strenuously asserted; she is told that she is unjustified, ill-advised in her efforts. If she persists, the family too often are injured and unhappy unless the efforts are called missionary and the religious zeal of the family carry them over their sense of abuse. When this zeal does not exist, the result is perplexing. It is a curious violation of what we would fain believe a fundamental law—that the final return of the deed is upon the head of the doer. The deed is that of exclusiveness and caution, but the return, instead of falling upon the head of the exclusive and cautious, falls upon a young head full of generous and unselfish plans. The girl loses something vital out of her life to which she is entitled. She is restricted and unhappy; her elders, meanwhile, are unconscious of the situation and we have all the elements of a tragedy.

We have in America a fast-growing number of cultivated young people who have no recognized outlet for their active faculties. They hear constantly of the great social maladjustment, but no way is provided for them to change it, and their uselessness hangs about them heavily. Huxley declares that the sense of uselessness is the severest shock which the human system can sustain, and that if persistently sustained, it results in atrophy of function. These young people have had advantages of college, of European travel, and of economic study, but they are sustaining this shock of inaction. They have pet phrases, and they tell you that the things that make us all alike are stronger than the things that make us different. They say that all men are united by needs and sympathies far more permanent and radical than anything that temporarily divides them and sets them in opposition to each other. If they affect art, they say that the decay in artistic expression is due to the decay in ethics, that art when shut away from the human interests and from the great mass of humanity is self-destructive. They tell their elders with all the bitterness of youth that if they expect success from them in business or politics or in whatever lines their ambition for them has run, they must let them consult all of humanity; that they must let them find out what the people want and how they want it. It is only the stronger young people, however, who formulate this. Many of them dissipate their energies in so-called enjoyment. Others not content with that, go on studying and go back to college for their second degrees; not that they are especially fond of study, but because they want something definite to do, and their powers have been trained in the direction of mental accumulation. Many are buried beneath this mental accumulation which lowered vitality and discontent. Walter Besant says they have had the vision that Peter had when he saw the great sheet let down from heaven, wherein was neither clean nor unclean. He calls it the sense of humanity. It is not philanthropy nor benevolence, but a thing fuller and wider than either of these.

This young life, so sincere in its emotion and good phrase and yet so undirected, seems to me as pitiful as the other great mass of destitute lives. One is supplementary to the other, and some method of communication can surely be devised. Mr. Barnett, who urged the first Settlement—Toynbee Hall, in East London—recognized this need of outlet for the young men of Oxford and Cambridge, and hoped that the Settlement would supply the communication. It is easy to see why the Settlement movement originated in England, where the years of education are more constrained and definite than they are here, where class distinctions are more rigid. The necessity of it was greater there, but we are fast feeling the pressure of the need and meeting the necessity for Settlements in America. Our young people feel nervously the need of putting theory into action, and respond quickly to the Settlement form of activity.

Other motives which I believe make toward the Settlement are the result of a certain renaissance going forward in Christianity. The impulse to share the lives of the poor, the desire to make social service, irrespective of propaganda, express the spirit of Christ, is as old as Christianity itself. We have no proof from the records themselves that the early Roman Christians, who strained their simple art to the point of grotesqueness in their eagerness to record a "good news" on the walls of the catacombs, considered this good news a religion. Jesus had no set of truths labeled Religious. On the contrary, his doctrine was that all truth is one, that the appropriation of it is freedom. His teaching had no dogma to mark it off from truth and action in general. He himself called it a revelation—a life. These early Roman Christians received the Gospel message, a command to love all men, with a certain joyous simplicity. The image of the Good Shepherd is blithe and gay beyond the gentlest shepherd of Greek mythology; the hart no longer pants, but rushes to the water brooks. The Christians looked for the continuous revelation, but believed what Jesus said, that this revelation, to be retained and made manifest, must be put into terms of action; that action is the only medium man has for receiving and appropriating truth; that the doctrine must be known through the will.

That Christianity has to be revealed and embodied in the line of social progress is a corollary to the simple proposition that man's action is found in his social relationships in the way in which he connects with his fellows; that his motives for action are the zeal and affection with which he regards his fellows. By this simple process was created a deep enthusiasm for humanity, which regarded man as at once the organ and the object of revelation; and by this process came about the wonderful fellowship, the true democracy of the early Church, that so captivates the imagination. The early Christians were pre-eminently non-resistant. They believed in love as a cosmic force. There was no iconoclasm during the minor peace of the Church. They did not yet denounce nor tear down temples, nor preach the end of the world. They grew to a mighty number but it never occurred to them, either in their weakness or in their strength, to regard other men for an instant as their foes or as aliens. The spectacle of the Christians loving all men was the most astounding Rome had ever seen. They were eager to sacrifice themselves for the weak, for children, and for the aged; they identified themselves with slaves and did not avoid the plague; they longed to share the common lot that they might receive the constant revelation. It was a new treasure which the early Christians added to the sum of all treasures, a joy hitherto unknown in the world—the joy of finding the Christ which lieth in each man, but which no man can unfold save in fellowship. A happiness ranging from the heroic to the pastoral enveloped them. They were to possess a revelation as long as life had new meaning to unfold, new action to propose.

I believe that there is a distinct turning among many young men and women toward this simple acceptance of Christ's message. They resent the assumption that Christianity is a set of ideas which belong to the religious consciousness, whatever that may be. They insist that it cannot be proclaimed and instituted apart from the social life of the community and that it must seek a simple and natural expression in the social organism itself. The Settlement movement is only one manifestation of that wider humanitarian movement which throughout Christendom, but pre-eminently in England, is endeavoring to embody itself, not in a sect, but in society itself.

I believe that this turning, this renaissance of the early Christian humanitarianism, is going on in America, in Chicago, if you please, without leaders who write or philosophize, without much speaking, but with a bent to express in social service and in terms of action the spirit of Christ. Certain it is that spiritual force is found in the Settlement movement, and it is also true that this force must be evoked and must be called into play before the success of any Settlement is assured. There must be the overmastering belief that all that is noblest in life is common to men as men, in order to accentuate the likenesses and ignore the differences which are found among the people whom the Settlement constantly brings into juxtaposition. It may be true, as the Positivists insist, that the very religious fervor of man can be turned into love for his race, and his desire for a future life into content to live in the echo of his deeds; Paul's formula of seeking for the Christ which lieth in each man and founding our likenesses on him, seems a simpler formula to many of us.

In a thousand voices singing the Hallelujah Chorus in Handel's "Messiah," it is possible to distinguish the leading voices, but the differences of training and cultivation between them and the voices of the chorus, are lost in the unity of purpose and in the fact that they are all human voices lifted by a high motive. This is a weak illustration of what a Settlement attempts to do. It aims, in a measure, to develop whatever of social life its neighborhood may afford, to focus and give form to that life, to bring to bear upon it the results of cultivation and training; but it receives in exchange for the music of isolated voices the volume and strength of the chorus. It is quite impossible for me to say in what proportion or degree the subjective necessity which led to the opening of Hull-House combined the three trends: first, the desire to interpret democracy in social terms; secondly, the impulse beating at the very source of our lives, urging us to aid in the race progress; and, thirdly, the Christian movement toward humanitarianism. It is difficult to analyze a living thing; the analysis is at best imperfect. Many more motives may blend with the three trends; possibly the desire for a new form of social success due to the nicety of imagination, which refuses worldly pleasures unmixed with the joys of self-sacrifice; possibly a love of approbation, so vast that it is not content with the treble clapping of delicate hands, but wishes also to hear the brass notes from toughened palms, may mingle with these.

The Settlement, then, is an experimental effort to aid in the solution of the social and industrial problems which are engendered by the modern conditions of life in a great city. It insists that these problems are not confined to any one portion of a city. It is an attempt to relieve, at the same time, the overaccumulation at one end of society and the destitution at the other; but it assumes that this overaccumulation and destitution is most sorely felt in the things that pertain to social and educational privileges. From its very nature it can stand for no political or social propaganda. It must, in a sense, give the warm welcome of an inn to all such propaganda, if perchance one of them be found an angel. The one thing to be dreaded in the Settlement is that it lose its flexibility, its power of quick adaptation, its readiness to change its methods as its environment may demand. It must be open to conviction and must have a deep and abiding sense of tolerance. It must be hospitable and ready for experiment. It should demand from its residents a scientific patience in the accumulation of facts and the steady holding of their sympathies as one of the best instruments for that accumulation. It must be grounded in a philosophy whose foundation is on the solidarity of the human race, a philosophy which will not waver when the race happens to be represented by a drunken woman or an idiot boy. Its residents must be emptied of all conceit of opinion and all self-assertion, and ready to arouse and interpret the public opinion of their neighborhood. They must be content to live quietly side by side with their neighbors, until they grow into a sense of relationship and mutual interests. Their neighbors are held apart by differences of race and language which the residents can more easily overcome. They are bound to see the needs of their neighborhood as a whole, to furnish data for legislation, and to use their influence to secure it. In short, residents are pledged to devote themselves to the duties of good citizenship and to the arousing of the social energies which too largely lie dormant in every neighborhood given over to industrialism. They are bound to regard the entire life of their city as organic, to make an effort to unify it, and to protest against its overdifferentiation....

THORSTEIN VEBLEN

Selection from *The Theory of the Leisure Class* (1899)

No evolutionary social theorist put Darwinian formulations to more critical uses than Thorstein Veblen (1857–1929). At once playful, angry, mordant, and ironic, Veblen sketched in *The Theory of the Leisure Class: An Economic Study of Institutions* (New York, 1899) a picture of the turn-of-the-century "new rich" that endures in American literature and political economy. In our selections from this book reprinted here, Veblen depicts people of this class as social parasites who only "retard the adaptation of human nature to the exigencies of modern industrial life." Veblen went on to write a number of other influential books, including *The Theory of Business Enterprise* (New York, 1904), *The Higher Learning in America* (New York, 1918), *The Place of Science in Modern Civilization* (New York, 1919), *The Engineers and the Price System* (New York, 1921), and *Absentee Ownership* (New York, 1923). Eager as he was to see intellectual men and women lead society, Veblen remained alienated from the prevailing academic culture of his own time. He bounced from faculty to faculty and died in a cabin in the wooded hills above Stanford University.

The most comprehensive study of his life and thought was written shortly after his death: Joseph Dorfmann, *Thorstein Veblen and His America* (New York, 1934). A recent biographical volume is Rick Tilman, *Thorstein Veblen and the Enrichment of Evolutionary Naturalism* (Columbia, Mo., 2007). Perhaps the most succinct and penetrating introduction to Veblen's ideas is C. Wright Mills's introduction to the Mentor edition of *The Theory of the Leisure Class* (New York, 1953), vi–xix. See also the discussion of Veblen in relation to the development of the social sciences in the United States, in Dorothy Ross, *The Origins of American Social Science* (New York, 1991), 204–16. Among the most important of recent studies is Nils Gilman, "Thorstein Veblen's Neglected Feminism," *Journal of Economic Issues*, 33 (1999), 689–99. A provocative analysis of Veblen's writing in relation to that of his contemporary, the novelist Theodore Dreiser, is Clare Virginia Eby, *Dreiser and Veblen: Saboteurs of the Status Quo* (Columbia, Mo., 1999).

The life of man in society, just like the life of other species, is a struggle for existence, and therefore it is a process of selective adaptation. The evolution of social structure has been a process of natural selection of institutions. The progress which has been and is being made in human institutions and in human character may be set down, broadly, to a natural selection of the fittest habits of thought and to a process of enforced adaptation of individuals to an environment which has progressively changed with the growth of the community and with the changing institutions under which men have lived. Institutions are not only themselves the result of a selective and adaptive process which shapes the prevailing or dominant types of spiritual attitude and aptitudes; they are at the same time special methods of life and of human relations, and are therefore in their turn efficient factors of selection. So that the changing institutions in their turn make for a further selection of individuals endowed with the fittest temperament, and a further adaptation of individual temperament and habits to the changing environment through the formation of new institutions.

The forces which have shaped the development of human life and of social structure are no doubt ultimately reducible to terms of living tissue and material environment; but proximately, for the purpose in hand, these forces may best be stated in terms of an environment, partly human, partly non-human, and a human subject with a more or less definite physical and intellectual constitution. Taken in the aggregate or average, this human subject is more or less variable; chiefly, no doubt, under a rule of selective conservation of favourable variations. The selection of favourable variations is perhaps in great measure a selective conservation of ethnic types. In the life history of any community whose population is made up of a mixture of divers ethnic elements, one or another of several persistent and relatively stable types of body and of temperament rises into dominance at any given point. The situation, including the institutions in force at any given time, will favour the survival and dominance of one type of character in preference to another; and the type of man so selected to continue and to further elaborate the institutions handed down from the past will in some considerable measure shape these institutions in his own likeness. But apart from selection as between relatively stable types of character and habits of mind, there is no doubt simultaneously going on a process of selective adaptation of habits of thought within the general range of aptitudes which is characteristic of the dominant ethnic type or types. There may be a variation in the fundamental character of any population by selection between relatively stable types; but there is also a variation due to adaptation in detail within the range of the type, and to selection between specific habitual views regarding any given social relation or group of relations.

For the present purpose, however, the question as to the nature of the adaptive process— whether it is chiefly a selection between stable types of temperament and character, or chiefly an adaptation of men's habits of thought to changing circumstances—is of less importance than the fact that, by one method or another, institutions change and develop. Institutions must change with changing circumstances, since they are of the nature of an habitual method of responding to the stimuli which these changing circumstances afford. The development of these institutions is the development of society. The institutions are, in substance, prevalent habits of thought with respect to particular relations and particular functions of the individual and of the community; and the scheme of

Source: Thorstein Veblen, *The Theory of the Leisure Class: An Economic Study of Institutions* (New York: Macmillan, 1899), 188–213, 233–44.

life, which is made up of the aggregate of institutions in force at a given time or at a given point in the development of any society, may, on the psychological side, be broadly characterised as a prevalent spiritual attitude or a prevalent theory of life. As regards its generic features, this spiritual attitude or theory of life is in the last analysis reducible to terms of a prevalent type of character.

The situation of to-day shapes the institutions of to-morrow through a selective, coercive process, by acting upon men's habitual view of things, and so altering or fortifying a point of view or a mental attitude handed down from the past. The institutions—that is to say the habits of thought—under the guidance of which men live are in this way received from an earlier time; more or less remotely earlier, but in any event they have been elaborated in and received from the past. Institutions are products of the past process, are adapted to past circumstances, and are therefore never in full accord with the requirements of the present. In the nature of the case, this process of selective adaptation can never catch up with the progressively changing situation in which the community finds itself at any given time; for the environment, the situation, the exigencies of life which enforce the adaptation and exercise the selection, change from day to day; and each successive situation of the community in its turn tends to obsolescence as soon as it has been established. When a step in the development has been taken, this step itself constitutes a change of situation which requires a new adaptation; it becomes the point of departure for a new step in the adjustment, and so on interminably.

It is to be noted then, although it may be a tedious truism, that the institutions of to-day—the present accepted scheme of life—do not entirely fit the situation of to-day. At the same time, men's present habits of thought tend to persist indefinitely, except as circumstances enforce a change. These institutions which have so been handed down, these habits of thought, points of view, mental attitudes and aptitudes, or what not, are therefore themselves a conservative factor. This is the factor of social inertia, psychological inertia, conservatism.

Social structure changes, develops, adapts itself to an altered situation, only through a change in the habits of thought of the several classes of the community; or in the last analysis, through a change in the habits of thought of the individuals which make up the community. The evolution of society is substantially a process of mental adaptation on the part of individuals under the stress of circumstances which will no longer tolerate habits of thought formed under and conforming to a different set of circumstances in the past. For the immediate purpose it need not be a question of serious importance whether this adaptive process is a process of selection and survival of persistent ethnic types or a process of individual adaptation and an inheritance of acquired traits.

Social advance, especially as seen from the point of view of economic theory, consists in a continued progressive approach to an approximately exact "adjustment of inner relations to outer relations"; but this adjustment is never definitively established, since the "outer relations" are subject to constant change as a consequence of the progressive change going on in the "inner relations." But the degree of approximation may be greater or less, depending on the facility with which an adjustment is made. A readjustment of men's habits of thought to conform with the exigencies of an altered situation is in any case made only tardily and reluctantly, and only under the coercion exercised by a situation which has made the accredited views untenable. The readjustment of institutions and habitual views to an altered environment is made in response to pressure from without; it is of the nature of a response to stimulus. Freedom and facility of readjustment, that is to say capacity for growth in social structure, therefore depends in great measure on the degree of freedom with which the situation at any given time acts on the individual members of the community—the degree of exposure of the individual members to the constraining forces of the environment. If any portion or class of society is sheltered from the action of the environment in any essential respect, that portion of the community, or that class, will adapt its views and its scheme of life more tardily to the altered general situation; it will in so far tend to retard the process of social transformation. The wealthy leisure class is in such a sheltered position with respect to the economic forces that make for change and readjustment. And it may be said that the forces which make for a readjustment of institutions, especially in the case of a modern industrial community, are, in the last analysis, almost entirely of an economic nature.

Any community may be viewed as an industrial or economic mechanism, the structure of which is made up of what is called its economic institutions. These institutions are habitual methods of carrying on the life process of the community in contact with the material environment in which it lives. When given methods of unfolding human activity in this given environment have been elaborated in this way, the life of the community will express itself with some facility in these habitual directions. The community will make use of the forces of the environment for the purposes of its life according to methods learned in the past and embodied in these institutions. But as population increases, and as men's knowledge and skill in directing the forces of nature widen, the habitual methods of relation between the members of the group, and the habitual method of carrying on the life process of the group as a whole no longer give the same result as before; nor are the resulting conditions of life distributed and apportioned in the same manner or with the same effect among the various members as before. If the scheme according to which the life process of the group was carried on under the earlier conditions gave approximately the highest attainable result—under the circumstances— in the way of efficiency or facility of the life process of the group; then the same scheme of life unaltered will not yield the highest result attainable in this respect under the altered conditions. Under the altered conditions of population, skill, and knowledge, the facility of life as carried on according to the traditional scheme may not be lower than under the earlier conditions; but the chances are always that it is less than might be if the scheme were altered to suit the altered conditions.

The group is made up of individuals, and the group's life is the life of individuals carried on in at least ostensible severalty. The group's accepted scheme of life is the consensus of views held by the body of these individuals as to what is right, good, expedient, and beautiful in the way of human life. In the redistribution of the conditions of life that comes of the altered method of dealing with the environment, the outcome is not an equable change in the facility of life throughout the group. The altered conditions may increase the facility of life for the group as a whole, but the redistribution will usually result in a decrease of facility or fulness of life for some members of the group. An advance in technical methods, in population, or in industrial organisation will require at least some of the members of the community to change their habits of life, if they are to enter with facility and effect into the altered industrial methods; and in doing so they will be unable to live up to the received notions as to what are the right and beautiful habits of life.

Any one who is required to change his habits of life and his habitual relations to his fellow-men will feel the discrepancy between the method of life required of him by the newly arisen exigencies, and the traditional scheme of life to which he is accustomed. It is the individuals placed in this position who have the liveliest incentive to reconstruct the received scheme of life and are most readily persuaded to accept new standards; and it is through the need of the means of livelihood that men are placed in such a position. The pressure exerted by the environment upon the group, and making for a readjustment of the group's scheme of life, impinges upon the members of the group in the form of pecuniary exigencies; and it is owing to this fact—that external forces are in great part translated into the form of pecuniary or economic exigencies—it is owing to this fact that we can say that the forces which count toward a readjustment of institutions in any modern industrial community are chiefly economic forces; or more specifically, these forces take the form of pecuniary pressure. Such a readjustment as is here contemplated is substantially a change in men's views as to what is good and right, and the means through which a change is wrought in men's apprehension of what is good and right is in large part the pressure of pecuniary exigencies.

Any change in men's views as to what is good and right in human life makes its way but tardily at the best. Especially is this true of any change in the direction of what is called progress; that is to say, in the direction of divergence from the archaic position—from the position which may be accounted the point of departure at any step in the social evolution of the community. Retrogression, reapproach to a standpoint to which the race has been long habituated in the past, is easier. This is especially true in case the development away from this past standpoint has not been due chiefly to a substitution of an ethnic type whose temperament is alien to the earlier standpoint.

The cultural stage which lies immediately back of the present in the life history of Western civilisation is what has here been called the quasi-peaceable stage. At this quasi-peaceable stage the law of status is the dominant feature in the scheme of life. There is no need of pointing out how prone the men of to-day are to revert to the spiritual attitude of mastery and of personal subservience which characterises that stage. It may rather be said to be held in an uncertain abeyance by the economic exigencies of today, than to have been definitively supplanted by a habit of mind that is in full accord with these later-developed exigencies. The predatory and quasi-peaceable stages of economic evolution seem to have been of long duration in the life history of all the chief ethnic elements which go to make up the populations of the Western culture. The temperament and the propensities proper to those cultural stages have, therefore, attained such a persistence as to make a speedy reversion to the broad features of the corresponding psychological constitution inevitable in the case of any class or community which is removed from the action of those forces that make for a maintenance of the later-developed habits of thought.

It is a matter of common notoriety that when individuals, or even considerable groups of men, are segregated from a higher industrial culture and exposed to a lower cultural environment, or to an economic situation of a more primitive character, they quickly show evidence of reversion toward the spiritual features which characterise the predatory type; and it seems probable that the dolicho-blond type of European man is possessed of a greater facility for such reversion to barbarism than the other ethnic elements with which that type is associated in the Western culture. Examples of such a reversion on a small scale abound in the later history of migration and colonisation. Except for the fear of offending that chauvinistic patriotism which is so characteristic a feature of the predatory culture, and the presence of which is frequently the most striking mark of reversion in modern communities, the case of the American colonies might be cited as an example of such a reversion on an unusually large scale, though it was not a reversion of very large scope.

The leisure class is in great measure sheltered from the stress of those economic exigencies which prevail in any modern, highly organised industrial community. The exigencies of the struggle for the means of life are less exacting for this class than for any other; and as a consequence of this privileged position we should expect to find it one of the least responsive of the classes of society to the demands which the situation makes for a further growth of institutions and a readjustment to an altered industrial situation. The leisure class is the conservative class. The exigencies of the general economic situation of the community do not freely or directly impinge upon the members of this class. They are not required under penalty of forfeiture to change their habits of life and their theoretical views of the external world to suit the demands of an altered industrial technique, since they are not in the full sense an organic part of the industrial community. Therefore these exigencies do not readily produce, in the members of this class, that degree of uneasiness with the existing order which alone can lead any body of men to give up views and methods of life that have become habitual to them. The office of the leisure class in social evolution is to retard the movement and to conserve what is obsolescent. This proposition is by no means novel; it has long been one of the commonplaces of popular opinion.

The prevalent conviction that the wealthy class is by nature conservative has been popularly accepted without much aid from any theoretical view as to the place and relation of that class in the cultural development. When an explanation of this class conservatism is offered, it is commonly the invidious one that the wealthy class opposes innovation because it has a vested interest, of an unworthy sort, in maintaining the present conditions. The explanation here put forward imputes no unworthy motive. The opposition of the class to changes in the cultural scheme is instinctive, and does not rest primarily on an interested calculation of material advantages; it is an instinctive revulsion at any departure from the accepted way of doing and of looking at things—a revulsion common to all men and only to be overcome by stress of circumstances. All change in habits of life and of thought is irksome. The difference in this respect between the wealthy and the common run of mankind lies not so much in the motive which prompts to conservatism as in the degree of exposure to the economic forces that urge a change. The members of the wealthy class do not yield to the demand for innovation as readily as other men because they are not constrained to do so.

This conservatism of the wealthy class is so obvious a feature that it has even come to be recognised as a mark of respectability. Since conservatism is a characteristic of the wealthier and therefore more reputable portion of the community, it has acquired a certain honorific or decorative value. It has become prescriptive to such an extent that an adherence to conservative views is comprised as a matter of course in our notions of respectability; and it is imperatively incumbent on all who would lead a blameless life in point of social repute. Conservatism, being an upper-class characteristic, is decorous; and conversely, innovation, being a lower-class phenomenon, is vulgar. The first and most unreflected element in that instinctive revulsion and reprobation with which we turn from all social innovators is this sense of the essential vulgarity of the thing. So that even in cases where one recognises the substantial merits of the case for which the innovator is spokesman—as may easily happen if the evils which he seeks to remedy are sufficiently remote in point of time or space or personal contact—still one cannot but be sensible of the fact that the innovator is a person with whom it is at least distasteful to be associated, and from whose social contact one must shrink. Innovation is bad form.

The fact that the usages, actions, and views of the well-to-do leisure class acquire the character of a prescriptive canon of conduct for the rest of society, gives added weight and reach to the conservative influence of that class. It makes it incumbent upon all reputable people to follow their lead. So that, by virtue of its high position as the avatar of good form, the wealthier class comes to exert a retarding influence upon social development far in excess of that which the simple numerical strength of the class would assign it. Its prescriptive example acts to greatly stiffen the resistance of all other classes against any innovation, and to fix men's affections upon the good institutions handed down from an earlier generation.

There is a second way in which the influence of the leisure class acts in the same direction, so far as concerns hindrance to the adoption of a conventional scheme of life more in accord with the exigencies of the time. This second method of upper-class guidance is not in strict consistency to be brought under the same category as the instinctive conservatism and aversion to new modes of thought just spoken of; but it may as well be dealt with here, since it has at least this much in common with the conservative habit of mind that it acts to retard innovation and the growth of social structure. The code of proprieties, conventionalities, and usages in vogue at any given time and among any given people has more or less of the character of an organic whole; so that any appreciable change in one point of the scheme involves something of a change or readjustment at other points also, if not a reorganisation all along the line. When a change is made which immediately touches only a minor point in the scheme, the consequent derangement of the structure of conventionalities may be inconspicuous; but even in such a case it is safe to say that some derangement of the general scheme, more or less far-reaching, will follow. On the other hand, when an attempted reform involves the suppression or thorough-going remodelling of an institution of first-rate importance in the conventional scheme, it is immediately felt that a serious derangement of the entire scheme would result; it is felt that a readjustment of the structure to the new form taken on by one of its chief elements would be a painful and tedious, if not a doubtful process.

In order to realise the difficulty which such a radical change in any one feature of the conventional scheme of life would involve, it is only necessary to suggest the suppression of the monogamic family, or of the agnatic system of consanguinity, or of private property, or of the theistic faith, in any country of the Western civilisation; or suppose the suppression of ancestor worship in China, or of the caste system in India, or of slavery in Africa, or the establishment of equality of the sexes in Mohammedan countries. It needs no argument to show that the derangement of the general structure of conventionalities in any of these cases would be very considerable. In order to effect such an innovation a very far-reaching alteration of men's habits of thought would be involved also at other points of the scheme than the one immediately in question. The aversion to any such innovation amounts to a shrinking from an essentially alien scheme of life.

The revulsion felt by good people at any proposed departure from the accepted methods of life is a familiar fact of everyday experience. It is not unusual to hear those persons who dispense salutary advice and admonition to the community express themselves forcibly upon the far-reaching pernicious effects which the community would suffer from such relatively slight changes as the disestablishment of the Anglican Church, an increased facility of divorce, adoption of female suffrage, prohibition of the manufacture and sale of intoxicating beverages, abolition or restriction of inheritance, etc. Any one of these innovations would, we are told, "shake the social structure to its base," "reduce society to chaos," "subvert the foundations of morality," "make life intolerable," "confound the order of nature," etc. These various locutions are, no doubt, of the nature of hyperbole; but, at the same time, like all overstatement, they are evidence of a lively sense of the gravity of the consequences which they are intended to describe. The effect of these and like innovations in deranging the accepted scheme of life is felt to be of much graver consequence than the simple alteration of an isolated item in a series of contrivances for the convenience of men in society. What is true in so obvious a degree of innovations of first-rate importance is true in a less degree of changes of a smaller immediate importance. The aversion to change is in large part an aversion to the bother of making the readjustment which any given change will necessitate; and this solidarity of the system of institutions of any given culture or of any given people strengthens the instinctive resistance offered to any change in men's habits of thought, even in matters which, taken by themselves, are of minor importance.

A consequence of this increased reluctance, due to the solidarity of human institutions, is that any innovation calls for a greater expenditure of nervous energy in making the necessary readjustment than would otherwise be the case. It is not only that a change in established habits of thought is distasteful. The process of readjustment of the accepted theory of life involves a degree of mental effort—a more or less protracted and laborious effort to find and to keep one's bearings under the altered circumstances. This process requires a certain expenditure of energy, and so presumes, for its successful accomplishment, some surplus of energy beyond that absorbed in the daily struggle for subsistence. Consequently it follows that progress is hindered by underfeeding and excessive physical hardship, no less effectually than by such a luxurious life as will shut out discontent by cutting off the occasion for it. The abjectly poor, and all those persons whose energies are entirely absorbed by the struggle for daily sustenance, are conservative because they cannot afford the effort of taking thought for the day after to-morrow; just as the highly prosperous are conservative because they have small occasion to be discontented with the situation as it stands to-day.

From this proposition it follows that the institution of a leisure class acts to make the lower classes conservative by withdrawing from them as much as it may of the means of sustenance, and so reducing their consumption, and consequently their available energy, to such a point as to make them incapable of the effort required for the learning and adoption of new habits of thought. The accumulation of wealth at the upper end of the pecuniary scale implies privation at the lower end of the scale. It is a commonplace that, wherever it occurs, a considerable degree of privation among the body of the people is a serious obstacle to any innovation.

This direct inhibitory effect of the unequal distribution of wealth is seconded by an indirect effect tending to the same result. As has already been seen, the imperative example set by the upper class in fixing the canons of reputability fosters the practice of conspicuous consumption. The prevalence of conspicuous consumption as one of the main elements in the standard of decency among all classes is of course not traceable wholly to the example of the wealthy leisure class, but the practice and the insistence on it are no doubt strengthened by the example of the leisure class. The requirements of decency in this matter are very considerable and very imperative; so that even among classes whose pecuniary position is sufficiently strong to admit a consumption of goods considerably in excess of the subsistence minimum, the disposable surplus left over after the more imperative physical needs are satisfied is not infrequently diverted to the purpose of a conspicuous decency, rather than to added physical comfort and fulness of life. Moreover, such surplus energy as is available is also likely to be expended in the acquisition of goods for conspicuous consumption or conspicuous hoarding. The result is that the requirements of pecuniary reputability tend (1) to leave but a scanty subsistence minimum available for other than conspicuous consumption, and (2) to absorb any surplus energy which may be available after the bare physical necessities of life have been provided for. The outcome of the whole is a strengthening of the general conservative attitude of the community. The institution of a leisure class hinders cultural development immediately (1) by the inertia proper to the class itself, (2) through its prescriptive example of conspicuous waste and of conservatism, and (3) indirectly through that system of unequal distribution of wealth and sustenance on which the institution itself rests.

To this is to be added that the leisure class has also a material interest in leaving things as they are. Under the circumstances prevailing at any given time this class is in a privileged position, and any departure from the existing order may be expected to work to the detriment of the class rather than the reverse. The attitude of the class, simply as influenced by its class interest, should therefore be to let well-enough alone. This interested motive comes in to supplement the strong instinctive bias of the class, and so to render it even more consistently conservative than it otherwise would be.

All this, of course, has nothing to say in the way of eulogy or deprecation of the office of the leisure class as an exponent and vehicle of conservatism or reversion in social structure. The inhibition which it exercises may be salutary or the reverse. Whether it is the one or the other in any given case is a question of casuistry rather than of general theory. There may be truth in the view (as a question of policy) so often expressed by the spokesmen of the conservative element, that without some such substantial and consistent resistance to innovation as is offered by the conservative well-to-do classes, social innovation and experiment would hurry the community into untenable and intolerable situations; the only possible result of which would be discontent and disastrous reaction. All this, however, is beside the present argument.

But apart from all deprecation, and aside from all question as to the indispensability of some such check on headlong innovation, the leisure class, in the nature of things, consistently acts to retard that adjustment to the environment which is called social advance or development. The characteristic attitude of the class may be summed up in the maxim: "Whatever is, is right"; whereas the law of natural selection, as applied to human institutions, gives the axiom: "Whatever is, is wrong." Not that the institutions of to-day are wholly wrong for the purposes of the life of to-day, but they are, always and in the nature of things, wrong to some extent. They are the result of a more or less inadequate adjustment of the methods of living to a situation which prevailed at some point in the past development; and they are therefore wrong by something more than the interval which separates the present situation from that of the past. "Right" and "wrong" are of course here used without conveying any reflection as to what ought or ought not to be. They are applied simply from the (morally colourless) evolutionary standpoint and are intended to designate compatibility or incompatibility with the effective evolutionary process. The institution of a leisure class, by force of class interest and instinct, and by precept and prescriptive example, makes for the perpetuation of the existing maladjustment of institutions, and even favours a reversion to a somewhat more archaic scheme of life; a scheme which would be still farther out of adjustment with the exigencies of life under the existing situation even than the accredited, obsolescent scheme that has come down from the immediate past.

But after all has been said on the head of conservation of the good old ways, it remains true that institutions change and develop. There is a cumulative growth of customs and habits of thought; a selective adaptation of conventions and methods of life. Something is to be said of the office of the leisure class in guiding this growth as well as in retarding it; but little can be said here of its relation to institutional growth except as it touches the institutions that are primarily and immediately of an economic character.

These institutions—the economic structure—may be roughly distinguished into two classes or categories, according as they serve one or the other of two divergent purposes of economic life.

To adapt the classical terminology, they are institutions of acquisition or of production; or to revert to terms already employed in a different connection in earlier chapters, they are pecuniary or industrial institutions; or in still other terms, they are institutions serving either the invidious or the non-invidious economic interest. The former category have to do with "business," the latter with industry, taking the latter word in the mechanical sense. The latter class are not often recognised as institutions, in great part because they do not immediately concern the ruling class, and are, therefore, seldom the subject of legislation or of deliberate convention. When they do receive attention they are commonly approached from the pecuniary or business side; that being the side or phase of economic life that chiefly occupies men's deliberations in our time, especially the deliberations of the upper classes. These classes have little else than a business interest in things economic, and on them at the same time it is chiefly incumbent to deliberate upon the community's affairs.

The relation of the leisure (that is, propertied non-industrial) class to the economic process is a pecuniary relation—a relation of acquisition, not of production; of exploitation, not of serviceability. Indirectly their economic office may, of course, be of the utmost importance to the economic life process; and it is by no means here intended to depreciate the economic function of the propertied class or of the captains of industry. The purpose is simply to point out what is the nature of the relation of these classes to the industrial process and to economic institutions. Their office is of a parasitic character, and their interest is to divert what substance they may to their own use, and to retain whatever is under their hand. The conventions of the business world have grown up under the selective surveillance of this principle of predation or parasitism. They are conventions of ownership; derivatives, more or less remote, of the ancient predatory culture. But these pecuniary institutions do not entirely fit the situation of to-day, for they have grown up under a past situation differing somewhat from the present. Even for effectiveness in the pecuniary way, therefore, they are not as apt as might be. The changed industrial life requires changed methods of acquisition; and the pecuniary classes have some interest in so adapting the pecuniary institutions as to give them the best effect for acquisition of private gain that is compatible with the continuance of the industrial process out of which this gain arises. Hence there is a more or less consistent trend in the leisure-class guidance of institutional growth, answering to the pecuniary ends which shape leisure-class economic life.

The effect of the pecuniary interest and the pecuniary habit of mind upon the growth of institutions is seen in those enactments and conventions that make for security of property, enforcement of contracts, facility of pecuniary transactions, vested interests. Of such bearing are changes affecting bankruptcy and receiverships, limited liability, banking and currency, coalitions of labourers or employers, trusts and pools. The community's institutional furniture of this kind is of immediate consequence only to the propertied classes, and in proportion as they are propertied; that is to say, in proportion as they are to be ranked with the leisure class. But indirectly these conventions of business life are of the gravest consequence for the industrial process and for the life of the community. And in guiding the institutional growth in this respect, the pecuniary classes, therefore, serve a purpose of the most serious importance to the community, not only in the conservation of the accepted social scheme, but also in shaping the industrial process proper.

The immediate end of this pecuniary institutional structure and of its amelioration is the greater facility of peaceable and orderly exploitation; but its remoter effects far outrun this immediate object. Not only does the more facile conduct of business permit industry and extra-industrial life to go on with less perturbation; but the resulting elimination of disturbances and complications calling for an exercise of astute discrimination in everyday affairs acts to make the pecuniary class itself superfluous. As fast as pecuniary transactions are reduced to routine, the captain of industry can be dispensed with. This consummation, it is needless to say, lies yet in the indefinite future. The ameliorations wrought in favour of the pecuniary interest in modern institutions tend, in another field, to substitute the "soulless" joint-stock corporation for the captain, and so they make also for the dispensability of the great leisure-class function of ownership. Indirectly, therefore, the bent given to the growth of economic institutions by the leisure-class influence is of very considerable industrial consequence....

The institution of a leisure class has an effect not only upon social structure but also upon the individual character of the members of society. So soon as a given proclivity or a given point of view has won acceptance as an authoritative standard or norm of life it will react upon the character of the members of the society which has accepted it as a norm. It will to some extent shape their habits of thought and will exercise a selective surveillance over the development of men's aptitudes and inclinations. This effect is wrought partly by a coercive, educational adaptation of the habits of all individuals, partly by a selective elimination of the unfit individuals and lines of descent. Such human material as does not lend itself to the methods of life imposed by the accepted scheme suffers more or less elimination as well as repression. The principles of pecuniary emulation and of industrial exemption have in this way been erected into canons of life, and have become coercive factors of some importance in the situation to which men have to adapt themselves.

These two broad principles of conspicuous waste and industrial exemption affect the cultural development both by guiding men's habits of thought, and so controlling the growth of institutions, and by selectively conserving certain traits of human nature that conduce to facility of life under the leisure-class scheme, and so controlling the effective temper of the community. The proximate tendency of the institution of a leisure class in shaping human character runs in the direction of spiritual survival and reversion. Its effect upon the temper of a community is of the nature of an arrested spiritual development....

The constituency of the leisure class is kept up by a continual selective process, whereby the individuals and lines of descent that are eminently fitted for an aggressive pecuniary competition are withdrawn from the lower classes. In order to reach the upper levels the aspirant must have, not only a fair average complement of the pecuniary aptitudes, but he must have these gifts in such an eminent degree as to overcome very material difficulties that stand in the way of his ascent. Barring accidents, the *nouveaux arrivés* are a picked body.

This process of selective admission has, of course, always been going on; ever since the fashion of pecuniary emulation set in,—which is much the same as saying, ever since the institution of a leisure class was first installed. But the precise ground of selection has not always been the same, and the selective process has therefore not always given the same results. In the early barbarian, or predatory stage proper, the test of fitness was prowess, in the naïve sense of the word. To gain entrance to the class, the candidate must be gifted with clannishness, massiveness, ferocity, unscrupulousness, and tenacity of purpose. These were the qualities that counted toward the accumulation and continued tenure of wealth. The economic basis of the leisure class, then as later, was the possession of wealth; but the methods of accumulating wealth, and the gifts required for holding it, have changed in some degree since the early days of the predatory culture. In consequence of the selective process the dominant traits of the early barbarian leisure class were bold aggression, an alert sense of status, and a free resort to fraud. The members of the class held their place by tenure of prowess. In the later barbarian culture society attained settled methods of acquisition and possession under the quasi-peaceable régime of status. Simple aggression and unrestrained violence in great measure gave place to shrewd practise and chicanery, as the best approved method of accumulating wealth. A different range of aptitudes and propensities would then be conserved in the leisure class. Masterful aggression, and the correlative massiveness, together with a ruthlessly consistent sense of status, would still count among the most splendid traits of the class. These have remained in our traditions as the typical "aristocratic virtues." But with these were associated an increasing complement of the less obtrusive pecuniary virtues; such as providence, prudence, and chicane. As time has gone on, and the modern peaceable stage of pecuniary culture has been approached, the last-named range of aptitudes and habits has gained in relative effectiveness for pecuniary ends, and they have counted for relatively more in the selective process under which admission is gained and place is held in the leisure class.

The ground of selection has changed, until the aptitudes which now qualify for admission to the class are the pecuniary aptitudes only. What remains of the predatory barbarian traits is the tenacity of purpose or consistency of aim which distinguished the successful predatory barbarian from the peaceable savage whom he supplanted. But this trait can not be said characteristically to distinguish the pecuniarily successful upper-class man from the rank and file of the industrial classes. The training and the selection to which the latter are exposed in modern industrial life give a similarly decisive weight to this trait. Tenacity of purpose may rather be said to distinguish both these classes from two others: the shiftless ne'er-do-well and the lower-class delinquent. In point of natural endowment the pecuniary man compares with the delinquent in much the same way as the industrial man compares with the good-natured shiftless dependent. The ideal pecuniary man is like the ideal delinquent in his unscrupulous conversion of goods and persons to his own ends, and in a callous disregard of the feelings and wishes of others and of the remoter effects of his actions; but he is unlike him in possessing a keener sense of status, and in working more consistently and farsightedly to a remoter end. The kinship of the two types of temperament is further shown in a proclivity to "sport" and gambling, and a relish of aimless emulation. The ideal pecuniary man also shows a curious kinship with the delinquent in one of the concomitant variations of the predatory human nature. The delinquent is very commonly of a superstitious habit of mind; he is a great believer in luck, spells, divination and destiny, and in omens and shamanistic ceremony. Where circumstances are favourable, this proclivity is apt to express itself in a certain servile devotional fervour and a punctilious attention to devout observances; it may perhaps be better characterised as devoutness than as religion. At this point the temperament of the delinquent has more in common with the pecuniary and leisure classes than with the industrial man or with the class of shiftless dependents.

Life in a modern industrial community, or in other words life under the pecuniary culture, acts by a process of selection to develop and conserve a certain range of aptitudes and propensities. The present tendency of this selective process is not simply a reversion to a given, immutable ethnic type. It tends rather to a modification of human nature differing in some respects from any of the types or variants transmitted out of the past. The objective point of the evolution is not a single one. The temperament which the evolution acts to establish as normal differs from any one of the archaic variants of human nature in its greater stability of aim—greater singleness of purpose and greater persistence in effort. So far as concerns economic theory, the objective point of the selective process is on the whole single to this extent; although there are minor tendencies of considerable importance diverging from this line of development. But apart from this general trend the line of development is not single. As concerns economic theory, the development in other respects runs on two divergent lines. So far as regards the selective conservation of capacities or aptitudes in individuals, these two lines may be called the pecuniary and the industrial. As regards the conservation of propensities, spiritual attitude, or animus, the two may be called the invidious or self-regarding and the non-invidious or economical. As regards the intellectual or cognitive bent of the two directions of growth, the former may be characterised as the personal standpoint, of conation, qualitative relation, status, or worth; the latter as the impersonal standpoint, of sequence, quantitative relation, mechanical efficiency, or use.

The pecuniary employments call into action chiefly the former of these two ranges of aptitudes and propensities, and act selectively to conserve them in the population. The industrial employments, on the other hand, chiefly exercise the latter range, and act to conserve them. An exhaustive psychological analysis will show that each of these two ranges of aptitudes and propensities is but the multiform expression of a given temperamental bent. By force of the unity or singleness of the individual, the aptitudes, animus, and interests comprised in the first-named range belong together as expressions of a given variant of human nature. The like is true of the latter range. The two may be conceived as alternative directions of human life, in such a way that a given individual inclines more or less consistently to the one or the other. The tendency of the pecuniary life is, in a general way, to conserve the barbarian temperament, but with the substitution of fraud and prudence, or administrative ability, in place of that predilection for physical damage that characterises the early barbarian. This substitution of chicane in place of devastation takes place only in an uncertain degree. Within the pecuniary employments the selective action runs pretty consistently in this direction, but the discipline of pecuniary life, outside the competition for gain, does not work consistently to the same effect. The discipline of modern life in the consumption of time and goods does not act unequivocally to eliminate the aristocratic virtues or to foster the bourgeois virtues. The conventional scheme of decent living calls for a considerable exercise of the earlier barbarian traits....

From what has been said, it appears that the leisure-class life and the leisure-class scheme of life should further the conservation of the barbarian temperament; chiefly of the quasi-peaceable, or bourgeois, variant, but also in some measure of the predatory variant. In the absence of disturbing factors, therefore, it should be possible to trace a difference of temperament between the classes of society. The aristocratic and the bourgeois virtues—that is to say the destructive and pecuniary traits—should be found chiefly among the upper classes, and the industrial virtues—that is to say the peaceable traits— chiefly among the classes given to mechanical industry.

In a general and uncertain way this holds true, but the test is not so readily applied nor so conclusive as might be wished. There are several assignable reasons for its partial failure. All classes are in a measure engaged in the pecuniary struggle, and in all classes the possession of the pecuniary traits counts towards the success and survival of the individual. Wherever the pecuniary culture prevails, the selective process by which men's habits of thought are shaped, and by which the survival of rival lines of descent is decided, proceeds proximately on the basis of fitness for acquisition. Consequently, if it were not for the fact that pecuniary efficiency is on the whole incompatible with industrial efficiency, the selective action of all occupations would tend to the unmitigated dominance of the pecuniary temperament. The result would be the installation of what has been known as the "economic man," as the normal and definitive type of human nature. But the "economic man," whose only interest is the self-regarding one and whose only human trait is prudence, is useless for the purposes of modern industry.

The modern industry requires an impersonal, non-invidious interest in the work in hand. Without this the elaborate processes of industry would be impossible, and would, indeed, never have been conceived. This interest in work differentiates the workman from the criminal on the one hand, and from the captain of industry on the other. Since work must be done in order to the continued life of the community, there results a qualified selection favouring the spiritual aptitude for work, within a certain range of occupations. This much, however, is to be conceded, that even within the industrial occupations the selective elimination of the pecuniary traits is an uncertain process, and that there is consequently an appreciable survival of the barbarian temperament even within these occupations. On this account there is at present no broad distinction in this respect between the leisure-class character and the character of the common run of the population.

The whole question as to a class distinction in respect of spiritual make-up is also obscured by the presence, in all classes of society, of acquired habits of life that closely simulate inherited traits and at the same time act to develop in the entire body of the population the traits which they simulate. These acquired habits, or assumed traits of character, are not commonly of an aristocratic cast. The prescriptive position of the leisure class as the exemplar of reputability has imposed many features of the leisure-class theory of life upon the lower classes; with the result that there goes on, always and throughout society, a more or less persistent cultivation of these aristocratic traits. On this ground also these traits have a better chance of survival among the body of the people than would be the case if it were not for the precept and example of the leisure class. As one channel, and an important one, through which this transfusion of aristocratic views of life, and consequently more or less archaic traits of character, goes on, may be mentioned the class of domestic servants. These have their notions of what is good and beautiful shaped by contact with the master class and carry the preconceptions so acquired back among their low-born equals, and so disseminate the higher ideals abroad through the community without the loss of time which this dissemination might otherwise suffer. The saying, "Like master, like man," has a greater significance than is commonly appreciated for the rapid popular acceptance of many elements of upper-class culture.

There is also a further range of facts that go to lessen class differences as regards the survival of the pecuniary virtues. The pecuniary struggle produces an underfed class, of large proportions. This underfeeding consists in a deficiency of the necessaries of life or of the necessaries of a decent expenditure. In either case the result is a closely enforced struggle for the means with which to meet the daily needs; whether it be the physical or the higher needs. The strain of self-assertion against odds takes up the whole energy of the individual; he bends his efforts to compass his own invidious ends alone, and becomes continually more narrowly self-seeking. The industrial traits in this way tend to obsolescence through disuse. Indirectly, therefore, by imposing a scheme of pecuniary decency and by withdrawing as much as may be of the means of life from the lower classes, the institution of a leisure class acts to conserve the pecuniary traits in the body of the population. The result is an assimilation of the lower classes to the type of human nature that belongs primarily to the upper classes only.

It appears, therefore, that there is no wide difference in temperament between the upper and the lower classes; but it appears also that the absence of such a difference is in good part due to the prescriptive example of the leisure class and to the popular acceptance of those broad principles of conspicuous waste and pecuniary emulation on which the institution of a leisure class rests. The institution acts to lower the industrial efficiency of the community and retard the adaptation of human nature to the exigencies of modern industrial life....

WOODROW WILSON

"The Ideals of America"
(1902)

Among the many claims to fame of Woodrow Wilson (1856–1924) was the eloquence and conviction with which he articulated a vision of the role of the United States in world affairs. No words of this scholar-president—perhaps the most theoretically engaged figure to occupy the American presidency since Thomas Jefferson—have been more widely quoted than his call to Americans in 1917 to "make the world safe for democracy" by entering World War I. Long before he became the president, Wilson was a formidable theorist of American democracy's place in world history. In the essay reprinted here, written a decade before his election, Wilson takes stock of the Spanish-American War and meditates on the responsibility the United States has accepted for the welfare of the population of the Philippines. A striking feature of this essay is the effort Wilson makes to vindicate democratic values while defending the American role in the Philippines. Although Wilson does not declare himself to be an "imperialist," his utterances about "subject" peoples as virtually children in relation to Americans partake of a perspective most historians today would call imperialist, as do some of his sweeping formulations about the United States as a world power. Another striking feature is the overwhelmingly English frame of reference in which Wilson understands democracy and the political culture of the United States.

Wilson wrote this essay shortly after he took office as president of Princeton University. Eight years later, in 1910, he was elected governor of New Jersey, then served as president of the United States from 1913 to 1921. Prior to taking the presidency of Princeton, Wilson had been a political scientist, best known for *Congressional Government* (Baltimore, 1885). His political ideology as a "progressive" was expressed in *The New Freedom* (New York, 1913).

Wilson is the subject of hundreds of books and articles dealing with every aspect of his life and thought. The most reliable biography is John Milton Cooper, Jr., *Woodrow Wilson: A Biography* (New York, 2009). See also Thomas J. Knock, *To End All Wars: Woodrow Wilson and the Quest for a New World Order* (New York, 1992).

We do not think or speak of the War for Independence as if we were aged men who, amidst alien scenes of change, comfort themselves with talk of great things done in days long gone by, the like of which they may never hope to see again. The spirit of the old days is not dead. If it were, who amongst us would care for its memory and distant, ghostly voice? It is the distinguishing mark, nay the very principle of life in a nation alive and quick in every fibre, as ours is, that all its days are great days,—are to its thought single and of a piece. Its past it feels to have been but the prelude and earnest of its present. It is from its memories of days old and new that it gets its sense of identity, takes its spirit of action, assures itself of its power and its capacity, and knows its place in the world. Old colony days, and those sudden days of revolution when debate turned to action and heady winds as if of destiny blew with mighty breath the long continent through, were our own days, the days of our childhood and our headstrong youth. We have not forgotten. Our memories make no effort to recall the time. The battle of Trenton is as real to us as the battle of San Juan hill. . . .

No war ever transformed us quite as the war with Spain transformed us. No previous years ever ran with so swift a change as the years since 1898. We have witnessed a new revolution. We have seen the transformation of America completed. That little group of states, which one hundred and twenty-five years ago cast the sovereignty of Britain off, is now grown into a mighty power. That little confederation has now massed and organized its energies. A confederacy is transformed into a nation. The battle of Trenton was not more significant than the battle of Manila. The nation that was one hundred and twenty-five years in the making has now stepped forth into the open arena of the world.

I ask you to stand with me at this new turning-point of our life, that we may look before and after, and judge ourselves alike in the light of that old battle fought here in these streets, and in the light of all the mighty processes of our history that have followed. We cannot too often give ourselves such challenge of self-examination. It will hearten, it will steady, it will moralize us to reassess our hopes, restate our ideals, and make manifest to ourselves again the principles and the purposes upon which we act. We are else without chart upon a novel voyage.

What are our thoughts now, as we look back from this altered age to the Revolution which to-day we celebrate? How do we think of its principles and of its example? Do they seem remote and of a time not our own, or do they still seem stuff of our thinking, principles near and intimate, and woven into the very texture of our institutions? What say we now of liberty and of self-government, its embodiment? What lessons have we read of it on our journey hither to this high point of outlook at the beginning of a new century? Do those old conceptions seem to us now an ideal modified, of altered face, and of a mien not shown in the simple days when the government was formed?

Of course forms have changed. The form of the Union itself is altered, to the model that was in Hamilton's thought rather than to that which Jefferson once held before us, adorned, transfigured, in words that led the mind captive. Our ways of life are profoundly changed since that dawn. The balance of the states against the Federal government, however it may strike us now as of capital convenience in the distribution of powers and the quick and various exercise of the energies of the people, no longer seems central to our conceptions of governmental structure, no longer seems of the essence of the people's liberty. We are no longer strenuous about the niceties of constitutional law; no longer dream

Source: Woodrow Wilson, "The Ideals of America," *Atlantic Monthly* (December 1902), 721, 726–34.

that a written law shall save us, or that by ceremonial cleanliness we may lift our lives above corruption. But has the substance of things changed with us, also? Wherein now do we deem the life and very vital principle of self-government to lie? Where is that point of principle at which we should wish to make our stand and take again the final risk of revolution? What other crisis do we dream of that might bring in its train another battle of Trenton?

These are intensely practical questions. We fought but the other day to give Cuba self-government. It is a point of conscience with us that the Philippines shall have it, too, when our work there is done and they are ready. But when will our work there be done, and how shall we know when they are ready? How, when our hand is withdrawn from her capitals and she plays her game of destiny apart and for herself, shall we be sure that Cuba has this blessing of liberty and self-government, for which battles are justly fought and revolutions righteously set afoot? If we be apostles of liberty and of self-government, surely we know what they are, in their essence and without disguise of form, and shall not be deceived in the principles of their application by mere differences between this race and that. We have given pledges to the world and must redeem them as we can.

Some nice tests of theory are before us,—are even now at hand. There are those amongst us who have spoken of the Filipinos as standing where we stood when we were in the throes of that great war which was turned from fear to hope again in that battle here in the streets of Trenton which we are met to speak of, and who have called Aguinaldo, the winning, subtile youth now a prisoner in our hands at Manila, a second Washington. Have they, then, forgot that tragic contrast upon which the world gazed in the days when our Washington was President: on the one side of the sea, in America, peace, an ordered government, a people busy with the tasks of mart and home, a group of commonwealths bound together by strong cords of their own weaving, institutions sealed and confirmed by debate and the suffrages of free men, but not by the pouring out of blood in civil strife,—on the other, in France, a nation frenzied, distempered, seeking it knew not what,—a nation which poured its best blood out in a vain sacrifice, which cried of liberty and self-government until the heavens rang and yet ran straight and swift to anarchy, to give itself at last, with an almost glad relief, to the masterful tyranny of a soldier? "I should suspend my congratulations on the new liberty of France," said Burke, the master who had known our liberty for what it was, and knew this set up in France to be spurious,—"I should suspend my congratulations on the new liberty of France until I was informed how it had been combined with government; with public force; with the discipline and obedience of armies; with the collection of an effective and well-distributed revenue; with morality and religion; with the solidity of property; with peace and order; with social and civil manners." Has it not taken France a century to effect the combination; and are all men sure that she has found it even now? And yet were not these things combined with liberty amongst us from the very first?

How interesting a light shines upon the matter of our thought out of that sentence of Burke's! How liberty had been combined with government! Is there here a difficulty, then? Are the two things not kindly disposed toward one another? Does it require any nice art and adjustment to unite and reconcile them? Is there here some cardinal test which those amiable persons have overlooked, who have dared to cheer the Filipino rebels on in their stubborn resistance to the very government they themselves live under and owe fealty to? Think of Washington's passion for order, for authority, for some righteous public force which should teach individuals their place under government, for the solidity of property, for morality and sober counsel. It was plain that he cared not a whit for liberty without these things to sustain and give it dignity. "You talk, my good sir," he exclaimed, writing to Henry Lee in Congress, "you talk of employing influence to appease the present tumults in Massachusetts. I know not where that influence is to be found, or, if attainable, that it would be a proper remedy for the disorders. *Influence* is no *government*. Let us have one by which our lives, liberties, and properties will be secured, or let us know the worst at once." In brief, the fact is this, that liberty is the privilege of maturity, of self-control, of self-mastery and a thoughtful care for righteous dealings,—that some peoples may have it, therefore, and others may not.

We look back to the great men who made our government as to a generation, not of revolutionists, but of statesmen. They fought, not to pull down, but to preserve,—not for some fair and far-off thing they wished for, but for a familiar thing they had and meant to keep. Ask any candid student of the history of English liberty, and he will tell you that these men were of the lineage of Pym and Hampden, of Pitt and Fox; that they were men who consecrated their lives to the preservation intact of what had been wrought out in blood and sweat by the countless generations of sturdy freemen who had gone before them.…

It is plain enough that the reason why the English in America got self-government and knew how to use it, and the French in America did not, was, that the English had had a training under the kings of England and the French under the kings of France. In the one country men did all things at the bidding of officers of the crown; in the other, officers of the crown listened, were constrained to listen, to the counsels of laymen drawn out of the general body of the nation. And yet the kings of England were no less kings than the kings of France. Obedience is everywhere the basis of government, and the English were not ready either in their life or in their thought for a free régime under which they should choose their kings by ballot. For that régime they could be made ready only by the long drill which should make them respect above all things the law and the authority of governors. Discipline—discipline generations deep—had first to give them an ineradicable love of order, the poise of men self-commanded, the spirit of men who obey and yet speak their minds and are free, before they could be Americans.

No doubt a king did hold us together until we learned how to hold together of ourselves. No doubt our unity as a nation does come from the fact that we once obeyed a king. No one can look at the processes of English history and doubt that the throne has been its centre of poise, though not in our days its centre of force. Steadied by the throne, the effective part of the nation has, at every stage of its development, dealt with and controlled the government in the name of the whole. The king and his subjects have been partners in the great undertaking. At last, in our country, in this best trained portion of the nation, set off by itself, the whole became fit to act for itself, by veritable popular representation, without the make-weight of a throne. That is the history of our liberty. You have the spirit of English history, and of English royalty, from King Harry's mouth upon the field of Agincourt:—

> "We few, we happy few, we band of brothers;
> For he to-day that sheds his blood with me
> Shall be my brother; be he ne'er so vile,
> This day shall gentle his condition:
> And gentlemen in England now a-bed
> Shall think themselves accursed they were not here,
> And hold their manhoods cheap whiles any speaks
> That fought with us upon Saint Crispin's day."

It is thus the spirit of English life has made comrades of us all to be a nation.

This is what Burke meant by combining government with liberty,—the spirit of obedience with the spirit of free action. Liberty is not itself government. In the wrong hands,—in hands unpracticed, undisciplined,—it is incompatible with government. Discipline must precede it,—if necessary, the discipline of being under masters. Then will self-control make it a thing of life and not a thing of tumult, a tonic, not an insurgent madness in the blood. Shall we doubt, then, what the conditions precedent to liberty and self-government are, and what their invariable support and accompaniment must be, in the countries whose administration we have taken over in trust, and particularly in those far Philippine Islands whose government is our chief anxiety? We cannot give them any quittance of the debt ourselves have paid. They can have liberty no cheaper than we got it. They must first take the discipline of law, must first love order and instinctively yield to it. It is the heathen, not the free citizen of a self-governed country, who "in his blindness bows down to wood and stone, and don't obey no orders unless they is his own." We are old in this learning and must be their tutors.

But we may set them upon the way with an advantage we did not have until our hard journey was more than half made. We can see to it that the law which teaches them obedience is just law and even-handed. We can see to it that justice be free and unpurchasable among them. We can make order lovely by making it the friend of every man and not merely the shield of some. We can teach them by our fairness in administration that there may be a power in government which, though imperative and irresistible by those who would cross or thwart it, does not act for its own aggrandizement, but is the guarantee that all shall fare alike. That will infinitely shorten their painful tutelage. Our pride, our conscience will not suffer us to give them less.

And, if we are indeed bent upon service and not mastery, we shall give them more. We shall take them into our confidence and suffer them to teach us, as our critics. No man can deem himself free from whom the government hides its action, or who is forbidden to speak his mind about affairs, as if government were a private thing which concerned the governors alone. Whatever the power of government, if it is just, there may be publicity of governmental action and freedom of opinion; and public opinion gathers head effectively only by concerted public agitation. These are the things—knowledge of what the government is doing and liberty to speak of it—that have made Englishmen feel like free men, whether they liked their governors or not: the right to know and the right to speak out,—to speak out in plain words and in open counsel. Privacy, official reticence, governors hedged about and inaccessible,—these are the marks of arbitrary government, under which spirited men grow restive and resentful. The mere right to criticise and to have matters explained to them cools men's tempers and gives them understanding in affairs. This is what we seek among our new subjects: that they shall understand us, and after free conference shall trust us: that they shall perceive that we are not afraid of criticism, and that we are ready to explain and to take suggestions from all who are ready, when the conference is over, to obey.

There will be a wrong done, not if we govern and govern as we will, govern with a strong hand that will brook no resistance, and according to principles of right gathered from our own experience, not from theirs, which has never yet touched the vital matter we are concerned with; but only if we govern in the spirit of autocrats and of those who serve themselves, not their subjects. The whole solution lies less in our methods than in our temper. We must govern as those who learn; and they must obey as those who are in tutelage. They are children and we are men in these deep matters of government and justice.

If we have not learned the substance of these things no nation is ever likely to learn it, for it is taken from life, and not from books. But though children must be foolish, impulsive, headstrong, unreasonable, men may be arbitrary, self-opinionated, impervious, impossible, as the English were in their Oriental colonies until they learned. We should be inexcusable to repeat their blunders and wait as long as they waited to learn how to serve the peoples whom we govern. It is plain we shall have a great deal to learn; it is to be hoped we shall learn it fast.

There are, unhappily, some indications that we have ourselves yet to learn the things we would teach. You have but to think of the large number of persons of your own kith and acquaintance who have for the past two years been demanding, in print and out of it, with moderation and the air of reason and without it, that we give the Philippines independence and self-government now, at once, out of hand. It were easy enough to give them independence, if by independence you mean only disconnection with any government outside the islands, the independence of a rudderless boat adrift. But self-government? How is that "given"? *Can* it be given? Is it not gained, earned, graduated into from the hard school of life?....

You cannot call a miscellaneous people, unknit, scattered, diverse of race and speech and habit, a nation, a community. That, at least, we got by serving under kings: we got the feeling and the organic structure of a community. No people can form a community or be wisely subjected to common forms of government who are as diverse and as heterogeneous as the people of the Philippine Islands. They are in no wise knit together. They are of many races, of many stages of development, economically, socially, politically disintegrate, without community of feeling because without community of life, contrasted alike in experience and in habit, having nothing in common except that they have lived for hundreds of years together under a government which held them always where they were when it first arrested their development. You may imagine the problem of self-government and of growth for such a people,—if so be you have an imagination and are no doctrinaire. If there is difficulty in our own government here at home because the several sections of our own country are disparate and at different stages of development, what shall we expect, and what patience shall we not demand of ourselves, with regard to our belated wards beyond the Pacific? We have here among ourselves hardly sufficient equality of social and economic conditions to breed full community of feeling. We have learned of our own experience what the problem of self-government is in such a case.

That liberty and self-government are things of infinite difficulty and nice accommodation we above all other peoples ought to know who have had every adventure in their practice. Our very discontent with the means we have taken to keep our people clear-eyed and steady in the use of their institutions is evidence of our appreciation of what is required to sustain them. We have set up an elaborate system of popular education, and have made the maintenance of that system a function of government, upon the theory that only systematic training can give the quick intelligence, the "variety of information and excellence of discretion" needed by a self-governed people. We expect as much from school teachers as from governors in the Philippines and in Porto Rico: we expect from them the *morale* that is to sustain our work there. And yet, when teachers have done their utmost and the school bills are paid, we doubt, and know that we have reason to doubt, the efficacy of what we have done. Books can but set the mind free, can but give it the freedom of the world of thought. The world of affairs has yet to be attempted, and the schooling of action must supplement the schooling of the written page. Men who have an actual hand in government, men who vote and sustain by their thoughts the whole movement of affairs, men who have the making or the confirming of policies, must have reasonable hopes, must act within the reasonable bounds set by hard experience.

By education, no doubt, you acquaint men, while they are yet young and quick to take impressions, with the character and spirit of the polity they live under; give them some sentiment of respect for it, put them in the air that has always lain about it, and prepare them to take the experience that awaits them. But it is from the polity itself and their own contact with it that they must get their actual usefulness in affairs, and only that contact, intelligently made use of, makes good citizens. We would not have them remain children always and act always on the preconceptions taken out of the books they have studied. Life is their real master and tutor in affairs.

And so the character of the polity men live under has always had a deep significance in our thoughts. Our greater statesmen have been men steeped in a thoughtful philosophy of politics, men who pondered the effect of this institution and that upon morals and the life of society, and thought of character when they spoke of affairs. They have taught us that the best polity is that which most certainly produces the habit and the spirit of civic duty, and which calls with the most stirring and persuasive voice to the leading characters of the nation to come forth and give it direction. It must be a polity which shall stimulate, which shall breed emulation, which shall make men seek honor by seeking service. These are the ideals which have formed our institutions, and which shall mend them when they need reform. We need good leaders more than an excellent mechanism of action in characters and constitutions. We need men of devotion as much as we need good laws. The two cannot be divorced and self-government survive.

It is this thought that distresses us when we look upon our cities and our states and see them ruled by bosses. Our methods of party organization have produced bosses, and they are as natural and inevitable a product of our politics, no doubt, at any rate for the time being and until we can see our way to better things, as the walking delegate and the union president are of the contest between capital and federated labor. Both the masters of strikes and the masters of caucuses are able men, too, with whom we must needs deal with our best wits about us. But they are not, if they will pardon me for saying so, the leading characters I had in mind when I said that the excellence of a polity might be judged by the success with which it calls the leading characters of a nation forth to its posts of command. The polity which breeds bosses breeds managing talents rather than leading characters,— very excellent things in themselves, but not the highest flower of politics. The power to govern and direct primaries, combine primaries for the control of conventions, and use conventions for the nomination of candidates and the formulation of platforms agreed upon beforehand is an eminently useful thing in itself, and cannot be dispensed with, it may be, in democratic countries, where men must act, not helter skelter, but in parties, and with a certain party discipline, not easily thrown off; but it is not the first product of our politics we should wish to export to Porto Rico and the Philippines.

No doubt our study of these things which lie at the front of our own lives, and which must be handled in our own progress, will teach us how to be better masters and tutors to those whom we govern. We have come to full maturity with this new century of our national existence and to full self-consciousness as a nation. And the day of our isolation is past. We shall learn much ourselves now that we stand closer to other nations and compare ourselves first with one and again with another. Moreover, the centre of gravity has shifted in the action of our Federal government. It has shifted back to where it was at the opening of the last century, in that early day when we were passing from the gristle to the bone of our growth. For the first twenty-six years that we lived under our

Federal constitution foreign affairs, the sentiment and policy of nations over sea, dominated our politics, and our Presidents were our leaders. And now the same thing has come about again. Once more it is our place among the nations that we think of; once more our Presidents are our leaders.

The centre of our party management shifts accordingly. We no longer stop upon questions of what this state wants or that, what this section will demand or the other, what this boss or that may do to attach his machine to the government. The scale of our thought is national again. We are sensitive to airs that come to us from off the seas. The President and his advisers stand upon our chief coign of observation, and we mark their words as we did not till this change came. And this centring of our thoughts, this looking for guidance in things which mere managing talents cannot handle, this union of our hopes, will not leave us what we were when first it came. Here is a new world for us. Here is a new life to which to adjust our ideals.

It is by the widening of vision that nations, as men, grow and are made great. We need not fear the expanding scene. It was plain destiny that we should come to this, and if we have kept our ideals clear, unmarred, commanding through the great century and the moving scenes that made us a nation, we may keep them also through the century that shall see us a great power in the world. Let us put our leading characters at the front; let us pray that vision may come with power; let us ponder our duties like men of conscience and temper our ambitions like men who seek to serve, not to subdue, the world; let us lift our thoughts to the level of the great tasks that await us, and bring a great age in with the coming of our day of strength.

W. E. B. DU BOIS

Selection from *The Souls of Black Folk* (1903)

W. E. B. Du Bois (1868–1963) died in Africa, an expatriate, at almost the same moment that Martin Luther King, Jr., was delivering his "I Have a Dream" speech in front of the Lincoln Memorial, bringing to a climax one of the greatest civil rights demonstrations in American history. By 1963 Du Bois had largely been forgotten in the United States, although he had once been a prominent figure in the National Association for the Advancement of Colored People and had etched a formidable record as a historian, literary essayist, social critic, and editor. Even before the turn of the century, Du Bois had written two important books, one a history of the suppression of the African slave trade and the other a sociological study of the black population of Philadelphia. A fine anthology of work from all stages of Du Bois's career is Eric Sundquist, ed., *The Oxford W. E. B. Du Bois Reader* (New York, 1996). Since Du Bois's death, his stature has grown steadily, and he is now one of the most widely appreciated and carefully studied of all American intellectuals.

The selection that follows is the opening chapter of Du Bois's most enduring book, *The Souls of Black Folk* (Chicago, 1903). This chapter includes some of the most-quoted of Du Bois's formulations, including his description of the "double-consciousness" and "second sight" he attributed to black people. In another, almost as legendary chapter of *The Souls of Black Folk*—"On Mr. Booker T. Washington and Others"—Du Bois criticized the program of the most influential African-American of that period. Du Bois found fault with Washington's willingness to subordinate political equality to the limited economic progress that could be made in partnership with the white business establishment. But Washington's ideas are best approached through his own writings, especially his autobiography, *Up From Slavery* (New York, 1901). Du Bois's thought can also be usefully examined in comparison to Alexander Crummell, especially as available in Wilson J. Moses, ed., *Destiny and Race* (Amherst, Mass., 1992).

Prominent among scholarly studies of Du Bois are the following: David Levering Lewis, *W. E. B. Du Bois: Biography of a Race, 1868–1919* (New York, 1993); Lewis's second volume, *W. E. B. Du Bois, 1919–1963: The Fight for Equality and the American Century* (New York, 2000); and Adolph Reed, Jr., *W. E. B. Du Bois and American Political Thought* (New York, 1997). Du Bois figures large in an important, recent reinterpretation of the African-American intellectual tradition: Ross Posnock, *Color and Culture: Black Writers and the Making of the Modern Intellectual* (Cambridge, Mass., 1998). But the most succinct starting point for the study of Du Bois is the introduction to the edition of *The Souls of Black Folk* edited by David W. Blight and Robert Gooding-Williams (Boston, 1997), 1–30.

O water, voice of my heart, crying in the sand,
  All night long crying with a mournful cry,
As I lie and listen, and cannot understand
  The voice of my heart in my side or the voice of the sea,
O water, crying for rest, is it I, is it I?
  All night long the water is crying to me.

Unresting water, there shall never be rest
  Till the last moon droop and the last tide fail,
And the fire of the end begin to burn in the west;
  And the heart shall be weary and wonder and cry like the sea,
All life long crying without avail,
  As the water all night long is crying to me.

ARTHUR SYMONS

Between me and the other world there is ever an unasked question: unasked by some through feelings of delicacy; by others through the difficulty of rightly framing it. All, nevertheless, flutter round it. They approach me in a half-hesitant sort of way, eye me curiously or compassionately, and then, instead of saying directly, How does it feel to be a problem? they say, I know an excellent colored man in my town; or, I fought at Mechanicsville; or, Do not these Southern outrages make your blood boil? At these I smile, or am interested, or reduce the boiling to a simmer, as the occasion may require. To the real question, How does it feel to be a problem? I answer seldom a word.

And yet, being a problem is a strange experience,—peculiar even for one who has never been anything else, save perhaps in babyhood and in Europe. It is in the early days of rollicking boyhood that the revelation first bursts upon one, all in a day, as it were. I remember well when the shadow swept across me. I was a little thing, away up in the hills of New England, where the dark Housatonic winds between Hoosac and Taghkanic to the sea. In a wee wooden schoolhouse, something put it into the boys' and girls' heads to buy gorgeous visiting-cards—ten cents a package—and exchange. The exchange was merry, till one girl, a tall newcomer, refused my card,—refused it peremptorily, with a glance. Then it dawned upon me with a certain suddenness that I was different from the others; or like, mayhap, in heart and life and longing, but shut out from their world by a vast veil. I had thereafter no desire to tear down that veil, to creep through; I held all beyond it in common contempt, and lived above it in a region of blue sky and great wandering shadows. That sky was bluest when I could beat my mates at examination-time, or beat them at a foot-race, or even beat their stringy heads. Alas, with the years all this fine contempt began to fade; for the worlds I longed for, and all their dazzling opportunities, were theirs, not mine. But they should not keep these prizes, I said; some, all, I would wrest from them. Just how I would do it I could never decide: by reading law, by healing the sick, by telling the wonderful tales that swam in my head,—some way. With other black boys the strife was not so fiercely sunny: their youth shrunk into tasteless sycophancy, or into silent hatred of the pale world about them and mocking distrust of everything white; or wasted itself in a bitter cry, Why did God make me an outcast and a stranger in mine own house? The shades of the prison-house closed round about us all: walls strait and stubborn to the whitest, but relentlessly narrow, tall, and unscalable to sons of night who must plod darkly on in resignation, or beat unavailing palms against the stone, or steadily, half hopelessly, watch the streak of blue above.

After the Egyptian and Indian, the Greek and Roman, the Teuton and Mongolian, the Negro is a sort of seventh son, born with a veil, and gifted with second-sight in this American world,—a world which yields him no true self-consciousness, but only lets him see himself through the revelation of the other world. It is a peculiar sensation, this double-consciousness, this sense of always looking at one's self through the eyes of others, of measuring one's soul by the tape of a world that looks on in amused contempt and pity. One ever feels his two-ness,—an American, a Negro; two souls, two thoughts, two unreconciled strivings; two warring ideals in one dark body, whose dogged strength alone keeps it from being torn asunder.

The history of the American Negro is the history of this strife,—this longing to attain self-conscious manhood, to merge his double self into a better and truer self. In this merging he wishes neither of the older selves to be lost. He would not Africanize America, for America has too much to teach the world and Africa. He would not bleach his Negro soul in a flood of white Americanism, for he knows that Negro blood has a message for the world. He simply wishes to make it possible for a man to be both a Negro and an American, without being cursed and spit upon by his fellows, without having the doors of Opportunity closed roughly in his face.

This, then, is the end of his striving: to be a co-worker in the kingdom of culture, to escape both death and isolation, to husband and use his best powers and his latent genius. These powers of body and mind have in the past been strangely wasted, dispersed, or forgotten. The shadow of a mighty Negro past flits through the tale of Ethiopia the Shadowy and of Egypt the Sphinx. Throughout history, the powers of single black men flash here and there like falling stars, and die sometimes before the world has rightly gauged their brightness. Here in America, in the few days since Emancipation, the black man's turning hither and thither in hesitant and doubtful striving has often made his very strength to lose effectiveness, to seem like absence of power, like weakness. And yet it is not weakness,—it is the contradiction of double aims. The double-aimed struggle of the black artisan—on the one hand to escape white contempt for a nation of mere hewers of wood and drawers of water, and on the other hand to plough and nail and dig for a poverty-stricken horde—could only result in making him a poor craftsman, for he had but half a heart in either cause. By the poverty and ignorance of his people, the Negro minister or doctor was tempted toward quackery and demagogy; and by the criticism of the other world, toward ideals that made him ashamed of his lowly tasks. The would-be black savant was confronted by the paradox that the knowledge his people needed was a twice-told tale to his white neighbors, while the knowledge which would teach the white world was Greek to his own flesh and blood. The innate love of harmony and beauty that set the ruder souls of his people a-dancing and a-singing raised but confusion and doubt in the soul of the black artist; for the beauty revealed to him was the soul-beauty of a race which his larger audience despised, and he could not articulate the message of another people. This waste of double aims, this seeking to satisfy two unreconciled ideals, has wrought sad havoc with the courage and faith and deeds of ten thousand thousand people,—has sent them often wooing false gods and invoking false means of salvation, and at times has even seemed about to make them ashamed of themselves.

Away back in the days of bondage they thought to see in one divine event the end of all doubt and disappointment; few men ever worshipped Freedom with half such unquestioning faith as did the American Negro for two centuries. To him, so far as he thought and dreamed, slavery was indeed the sum of all villainies, the cause of all sorrow, the root of all prejudice; Emancipation was the key to a promised land of sweeter beauty than ever stretched before the eyes of wearied Israelites. In song and exhortation swelled one refrain—Liberty; in his tears and curses the God he implored had Freedom in his right hand. At last it came,—suddenly, fearfully, like a dream. With one wild carnival of blood and passion came the message in his own plaintive cadences:—

> "Shout, O children!
> Shout, you're free!
> For God has bought your liberty!"

Years have passed away since then,—ten, twenty, forty; forty years of national life, forty years of renewal and development, and yet the swarthy spectre sits in its accustomed seat at the Nation's feast. In vain do we cry to this our vastest social problem:—

> "Take any shape but that, and my firm nerves
> Shall never tremble!"

The Nation has not yet found peace from its sins; the freedman has not yet found in freedom his promised land. Whatever of good may have come in these years of change, the shadow of a deep disappointment rests upon the Negro people,—a disappointment all the more bitter because the unattained ideal was unbounded save by the simple ignorance of a lowly people.

The first decade was merely a prolongation of the vain search for freedom, the boon that seemed ever barely to elude their grasp,—like a tantalizing will-o'-the-wisp, maddening and misleading the headless host. The holocaust of war, the terrors of the Ku-Klux Klan, the lies of carpetbaggers, the disorganization of industry, and the contradictory advice of friends and foes, left the bewildered serf with no new watchword beyond the old cry for freedom. As the time flew, however, he began to grasp a new idea. The ideal of liberty demanded for its attainment powerful means, and these the Fifteenth Amendment gave him. The ballot, which before he had looked upon as a visible sign of freedom, he now regarded as the chief means of gaining and perfecting the liberty with which war had partially endowed him. And why not? Had not votes made war and emancipated millions? Had not votes enfranchised the freedmen? Was anything impossible to a power that had done all this? A million black men started with renewed zeal to vote themselves the kingdom. So the decade flew away, the revolution of 1876 came, and left the half-free serf weary, wondering, but still inspired. Slowly but steadily, in the following years, a new vision began gradually to replace the dream of political power,—a powerful movement, the rise of another ideal to guide the unguided, another pillar of fire by night after a clouded day. It was the ideal of "book-learning"; the curiosity, born of compulsory ignorance, to know and test the power of the cabalistic letters of the white man, the longing to know. Here at last seemed to have been discovered the mountain path to Canaan; longer than the highway of Emancipation and law, steep and rugged, but straight, leading to heights high enough to overlook life.

Up the new path the advance guard toiled, slowly, heavily, doggedly; only those who have watched and guided the faltering feet, the misty minds, the dull understandings, of the dark pupils of these schools know how faithfully, how piteously, this people strove to learn. It was weary work. The cold statistician wrote down the inches of progress here and there, noted also where here and there a foot had slipped or some one had fallen. To the tired climbers, the horizon was ever dark, the mists were often cold, the Canaan was always dim and far away. If, however, the vistas disclosed as yet no goal, no resting-place, little but flattery and criticism, the journey at least gave leisure for reflection and self-examination; it changed the child of Emancipation to the youth with dawning self-consciousness, self-realization, self-respect. In those sombre forests of his striving his own soul rose before him, and he saw himself,—darkly as through a veil, and yet he saw in himself some faint revelation of his power, of his mission. He began to have a dim feeling that, to attain his place in the world, he must be himself, and not another. For the first time he sought to analyze the burden he bore upon his back, that dead-weight of social degradation partially masked behind a half-named Negro problem. He felt his poverty; without a cent, without a home, without land, tools, or savings, he had entered into competition with rich, landed, skilled neighbors. To be a poor man is hard, but to be a poor race in a land of dollars is the very bottom of hardships. He felt the weight of his ignorance,—not simply of letters, but of life, of business, of the humanities; the accumulated sloth and shirking and awkwardness of decades and centuries shackled his hands and feet. Nor was his burden all poverty and ignorance. The red stain of bastardy, which two centuries of systematic legal defilement of Negro women had stamped upon his race, meant not only the loss of ancient African chastity, but also the hereditary weight of a mass of corruption from white adulterers, threatening almost the obliteration of the Negro home.

A people thus handicapped ought not to be asked to race with the world, but rather allowed to give all its time and thought to its own social problems. But alas! while sociologists gleefully count his bastards and his prostitutes, the very soul of the toiling, sweating black man is darkened by the shadow of a vast despair. Men call the shadow prejudice, and learnedly explain it as the natural defence of culture against barbarism, learning against ignorance, purity against crime, the "higher" against the "lower" races. To which the Negro cries Amen! and swears that to so much of this strange prejudice as is founded on just homage to civilization, culture, righteousness, and progress, he humbly bows and meekly does obeisance. But before that nameless prejudice that leaps beyond all this he stands helpless, dismayed, and well-nigh speechless; before that personal disrespect and mockery, the ridicule and systematic humiliation, the distortion of fact and wanton license of fancy, the cynical ignoring of the better and the boisterous welcoming of the worse, the all-pervading desire to inculcate disdain for everything black, from Toussaint to the devil,—before this there rises a sickening despair that would disarm and discourage any nation save that black host to whom "discouragement" is an unwritten word.

But the facing of so vast a prejudice could not but bring the inevitable self-questioning, self-disparagement, and lowering of ideals which ever accompany repression and breed in an atmosphere of contempt and hate. Whisperings and portents came borne upon the four winds: Lo! we are diseased and dying, cried the dark hosts; we cannot write, our voting is vain; what need of education, since we must always cook and serve? And the Nation echoed and enforced this self-criticism, saying. Be content to be servants, and nothing more; what need of higher culture for half-men? Away with the black man's ballot, by force or fraud,—and behold the suicide of a race! Nevertheless, out of the evil came something of good,—the more careful adjustment of education to real life, the clearer perception of the Negroes' social responsibilities, and the sobering realization of the meaning of progress.

So dawned the time of Sturm und Drang: storm and stress to-day rocks our little boat on the mad waters of the world-sea; there is within and without the sound of conflict, the burning of body and rending of soul; inspiration strives with doubt, and faith with vain questionings. The bright ideals of the past,—physical freedom, political power, the training of brains and the training of hands,—all these in turn have waxed and waned, until even the last grows dim and overcast. Are they all wrong,—all false? No, not that, but each alone was over-simple and incomplete,—the dreams of a credulous race-childhood, or the fond imaginings, of the other world which does not know and does not want to know our power. To be really true, all these ideals must be melted and welded into one. To be training of the schools we need to-day more than ever,—the training of deft hands, quick eyes and ears, and above all the broader, deeper, higher culture of gifted minds and pure hearts. The power of the ballot we need in sheer self-defence,—else what shall save us from a second slavery? Freedom, too, the long-sought, we still seek,—the freedom of life and limb, the freedom to work and think, the freedom to love and aspire. Work, culture, liberty,—all these we need, not singly but together, not successively but together, each growing and aiding each, and all striving toward that vaster ideal that swims before the Negro people, the ideal of human brotherhood, gained through the unifying ideal of Race; the ideal of fostering and developing the traits and talents of the Negro, not in opposition to or contempt for other races, but rather in large conformity to the greater ideals of the American Republic, in order that some day on American soil two world-races may give each to each those characteristics both so sadly lack. We the darker ones come even now not altogether empty-handed: there are to-day no truer exponents of the pure human spirit of the Declaration of Independence than the American Negroes; there is no true American music but the wild sweet melodies of the Negro slave; the American fairy tales and folk-lore are Indian and African; and, all in all, we black men seem the sole oasis of simple faith and reverence in a dusty desert of dollars and smartness. Will America be poorer if she replace her brutal dyspeptic blundering with light-hearted but determined Negro humility? or her coarse and cruel wit with loving jovial good-humor? or her vulgar music with the soul of the Sorrow Songs?

Merely a concrete test of the underlying principles of the great republic is the Negro Problem, and the spiritual striving of the freedmen's sons is the travail of souls whose burden is almost beyond the measure of their strength, but who bear it in the name of an historic race, in the name of this the land of their fathers' fathers, and in the name of human opportunity.

WILLIAM JAMES

"What Pragmatism Means"
(1907)

William James (1842–1910) opened *Pragmatism* (New York, 1907) with an account of the "present dilemma of philosophy," according to which individuals were asked to choose between two obviously deficient alternatives: a "tender-minded" religious idealism and a "tough-minded" scientific materialism:

The Tender-Minded	*The Tough-Minded*
Rationalistic (going by "principles")	Empiricist (going by "facts")
Intellectualistic	Sensationalistic
Idealistic	Materialistic
Optimistic	Pessimistic
Religious	Irreligious
Free willist	Fatalistic
Monistic	Pluralistic
Dogmatical	Skeptical

James offered pragmatism as a viable middle way. "What Pragmatism Means," which follows, is the second chapter of *Pragmatism*, directly following James's characterization of philosophy's dilemma. Here James projects his vision of an open, contingent universe within which people continually test and revise their store of "truths" against new experiences. Although James's arguments were used by readers in many different secular contexts, James himself reminds readers of the religious preoccupations that render philosophy's dilemma so troubling to him. He returns to religion near the end of the essay and defends pragmatism as a means of widening the search for God.

The most comprehensive work on James is Gerald Myers, *William James* (New Haven, 1986). A more historical study, and one that takes account of the professional and institutional matrix of James's work, is Bruce Kuklick, *The Rise of American Philosophy: Cambridge, Massachusetts, 1860–1930* (New Haven, 1977). The most valuable resource for studying James remains Ralph Barton Perry, *The Thought and Character of William James*, 2 vols. (Boston, 1935), in which an extensive selection from James's correspondence appears along with Perry's interpretive narrative of James's development as a thinker. An account of James as a public intellectual is George Cotkin, *William James: Public Philosopher* (Baltimore, 1990). For a critical assessment of scholarship on pragmatism, see James T. Kloppenberg, "Pragmatism: An Old Name for Some New Ways of Thinking?" *Journal of American History*, 83 (1996), 100–138. A recent, provocative contribution is Colin Koopman, *Pragmatism as Transition Historicity and Hope in James, Dewey, and Rorty* (New York, 2009). For additional comments on James, see the headnote to "The Will to Believe."

Some years ago, being with a camping party in the mountains, I returned from a solitary ramble to find every one engaged in a ferocious metaphysical dispute. The corpus of the dispute was a squirrel—a live squirrel supposed to be clinging to one side of a tree-trunk; while over against the tree's opposite side a human being was imagined to stand. This human witness tries to get sight of the squirrel by moving rapidly round the tree, but no matter how fast he goes, the squirrel moves as fast in the opposite direction, and always keeps the tree between himself and the man, so that never a glimpse of him is caught. The resultant metaphysical problem is this: *Does the man go round the squirrel or not?* He goes round the tree, sure enough, and the squirrel is on the tree; but does he go round the squirrel? In the unlimited leisure of the wilderness, discussion had been worn threadbare. Every one had taken sides, and was obstinate; and the numbers on both sides were even. Each side, when I appeared, therefore appealed to me to make it a majority. Mindful of the scholastic adage that whenever you meet a contradiction you must make a distinction, I immediately sought and found one, as follows: "Which party is right," I said, "depends on what you *practically mean* by 'going round' the squirrel. If you mean passing from the north of him to the east, then to the south, and then to the west, and then to the north of him again, obviously the man does go round him, for he occupies these successive positions. But if on the contrary you mean being first in front of him, then on the right of him, then behind him, then on his left, and finally in front again, it is quite as obvious that the man fails to go round him, for by the compensating movements the squirrel makes, he keeps his belly turned towards the man all the time, and his back turned away. Make the distinction, and there is no occasion for any further dispute. You are both right and both wrong according as you conceive the verb 'to go round' in one practical fashion or the other."

Although one or two of the hotter disputants called my speech a shuffling evasion, saying they wanted no quibbling or scholastic hair-splitting, but meant just plain honest English "round," the majority seemed to think that the distinction had assuaged the dispute.

I tell this trivial anecdote because it is a peculiarly simple example of what I wish now to speak of as the *pragmatic method.* The pragmatic method is primarily a method of settling metaphysical disputes that otherwise might be interminable. Is the world one or many?—fated or free?—material or spiritual?—here are notions either of which may or may not hold good of the world; and disputes over such notions are unending. The pragmatic method in such cases is to try to interpret each notion by tracing its respective practical consequences. What difference would it practically make to any one if this notion rather than that notion were true? If no practical difference whatever can be traced, then the alternatives mean practically the same thing, and all dispute is idle. Whenever a dispute is serious, we ought to be able to show some practical difference that must follow from one side or the other's being right.

A glance at the history of the idea will show you still better what pragmatism means. The term is derived from the same Greek word πράγμα, meaning action, from which our words "practice" and "practical" come. It was first introduced into philosophy by Mr. Charles Peirce in 1878. In an article entitled "How to Make Our Ideas Clear," in the *Popular Science Monthly* for January of that year Mr. Peirce, after pointing out that our beliefs are really rules for action, said that, to develop a thought's meaning, we need only

Source: William James, *Pragmatism* (New York: Longman's, 1907), 48–81.

determine what conduct it is fitted to produce: that conduct is for us its sole significance. And the tangible fact at the root of all our thought-distinctions, however subtle, is that there is no one of them so fine as to consist in anything but a possible difference of practice. To attain perfect clearness in our thoughts of an object, then, we need only consider what conceivable effects of a practical kind the object may involve—what sensations we are to expect from it, and what reactions we must prepare. Our conception of these effects, whether immediate or remote, is then for us the whole of our conception of the object, so far as that conception has positive significance at all.

This is the principle of Peirce, the principle of pragmatism. It lay entirely unnoticed by any one for twenty years, until I, in an address before Professor Howison's Philosophical Union at the University of California, brought it forward again and made a special application of it to religion. By that date (1898) the times seemed ripe for its reception. The word "pragmatism" spread, and at present it fairly spots the pages of the philosophic journals. On all hands we find the "pragmatic movement" spoken of, sometimes with respect, sometimes with contumely, seldom with clear understanding. It is evident that the term applies itself conveniently to a number of tendencies that hitherto have lacked a collective name, and that it has "come to stay."

To take in the importance of Peirce's principle, one must get accustomed to applying it to concrete cases. I found a few years ago that Ostwald, the illustrious Leipzig chemist, had been making perfectly distinct use of the principle of pragmatism in his lectures on the philosophy of science, though he had not called it by that name.

"All realities influence our practice," he wrote me, "and that influence is their meaning for us. I am accustomed to put questions to my classes in this way: In what respects would the world be different if this alternative or that were true? If I can find nothing that would become different, then the alternative has no sense."

That is, the rival views mean practically the same thing, and meaning, other than practical, there is for us none. Ostwald in a published lecture gives this example of what he means. Chemists have long wrangled over the inner constitution of certain bodies called "tautomerous." Their properties seemed equally consistent with the notion that an instable hydrogen atom oscillates inside of them, or that they are instable mixtures of two bodies. Controversy raged, but never was decided. "It would never have begun," says Ostwald, "if the combatants had asked themselves what particular experimental fact could have been made different by one or the other view being correct. For it would then have appeared that no difference of fact could possibly ensue; and the quarrel was as unreal as if, theorizing in primitive times about the raising of dough by yeast, one party should have invoked a 'brownie,' while another insisted on an 'elf' as the true cause of the phenomenon."

It is astonishing to see how many philosophical disputes collapse into insignificance the moment you subject them to this simple test of tracing a concrete consequence. There can *be* no difference anywhere that doesn't *make* a difference elsewhere—no difference in abstract truth that doesn't express itself in a difference in concrete fact and in conduct consequent upon that fact, imposed on somebody, somehow, somewhere, and somewhen. The whole function of philosophy ought to be to find out what definite difference it will make to you and me, at definite instants of our life, if this world-formula or that world-formula be the true one.

There is absolutely nothing new in the pragmatic method. Socrates was an adept at it. Aristotle used it methodically. Locke, Berkeley, and Hume made momentous contributions to truth by its means. Shadworth Hodgson keeps insisting that realities are only what they are "known as." But these forerunners of pragmatism used it in fragments: they were preluders only. Not until in our time has it generalized itself, become conscious of a universal mission, pretended to a conquering destiny. I believe in that destiny, and I hope I may end by inspiring you with my belief.

Pragmatism represents a perfectly familiar attitude in philosophy, the empiricist attitude, but it represents it, as it seems to me, both in a more radical and in a less objectionable form that it has ever yet assumed. A pragmatist turns his back resolutely and once for all upon a lot of inveterate habits dear to professional philosophers. He turns away from abstraction and insufficiency, from verbal solutions, from bad a priori reasons, from fixed principles, closed systems, and pretended absolutes and origins. He turns towards concreteness and adequacy, towards facts, towards action and towards power. That means the empiricist temper regnant and the rationalist temper sincerely given up. It means the open air and possibilities of nature, as against dogma, artificiality, and the pretence of finality in truth.

At the same time it does not stand for any special results. It is a method only. But the general triumph of that method would mean an enormous change in what I called in my last lecture the "temperament" of philosophy. Teachers of the ultra-rationalistic type would be frozen out, much as the courtier type is frozen out in republics, as the ultramontane type of priest is frozen out in Protestant lands. Science and metaphysics would come much nearer together, would in fact work absolutely hand in hand.

Metaphysics has usually followed a very primitive kind of quest. You know how men have always hankered after unlawful magic, and you know what a great part in magic words have always played. If you have his name, or the formula of incantation that binds him, you can control the spirit, genie, afrite, or whatever the power may be. Solomon knew the names of all the spirits, and having their names, he held them subject to his will. So the universe has always appeared to the natural mind as a kind of enigma, of which the key must be sought in the shape of some illuminating or power-bringing word or name. That word names the universe's *principle*, and to possess it is after a fashion to possess the universe itself. "God," "Matter," "Reason," "the Absolute," "Energy," are so many solving names. You can rest when you have them. You are at the end of your metaphysical quest.

But if you follow the pragmatic method, you cannot look on any such word as closing your quest. You must bring out of each word its practical cash-value, set it at work within the stream of your experience. It appears less as a solution, then, than as a program for more work, and more particularly as an indication of the ways in which existing realities may be *changed*.

Theories thus become instruments, not answers to enigmas, in which we can rest. We don't lie back upon them, we move forward, and, on occasion, make nature over again by their aid. Pragmatism unstiffens all our theories, limbers them up and sets each one at work. Being nothing essentially new, it harmonizes with many ancient philosophic tendencies. It agrees with nominalism, for instance, in always appealing to particulars; with utilitarianism in emphasizing practical aspects; with positivism in its disdain for verbal solutions, useless questions and metaphysical abstractions.

All these, you see, are *anti-intellectualist* tendencies. Against rationalism as a pretension and a method pragmatism is fully armed and militant. But, at the outset, at least, it stands for no particular results. It has no dogmas, and no doctrines save its method. As the young Italian pragmatist Papini has well said, it lies in the midst of our theories, like a corridor in a hotel. Innumerable chambers open out of it. In one you may find a man writing an atheistic volume; in the next some one on his knees praying for faith and strength; in a third a chemist investigating a body's properties. In a fourth a system of idealistic metaphysics is being excogitated; in a fifth the impossibility of metaphysics is being shown. But they all own the corridor, and all must pass through it if they want a practicable way of getting into or out of their respective rooms.

No particular results then, so far, but only an attitude of orientation, is what the pragmatic method means. *The attitude of looking away from first things, principles, "categories," supposed necessities; and of looking towards last things, fruits, consequences, facts.*

So much for the pragmatic method! You may say that I have been praising it rather than explaining it to you, but I shall presently explain it abundantly enough by showing how it works on some familiar problems. Meanwhile the word pragmatism has come to be used in a still wider sense, as meaning also a certain *theory of truth....*

One of the most successfully cultivated branches of philosophy in our time is what is called inductive logic, the study of the conditions under which our sciences have evolved. Writers on this subject have begun to show a singular unanimity as to what the laws of nature and elements of fact mean, when formulated by mathematicians, physicists and chemists. When the first mathematical, logical, and natural uniformities, the first *laws*, were discovered, men were so carried away by the clearness, beauty and simplification that resulted, that they believed themselves to have deciphered authentically the eternal thoughts of the Almighty. His mind also thundered and reverberated in syllogisms. He also thought in comic sections, squares and roots and ratios, and geometrized like Euclid. He made Kepler's laws for the planets to follow; he made velocity increase proportionally to the time in falling bodies; he made the law of the sines for light to obey when refracted; he established the classes, orders, families and genera of plants and animals, and fixed the distances between them. He thought the archetypes of all things, and devised their variations; and when we rediscover any one of these his wondrous institutions, we seize his mind in its very literal intention.

But as the sciences have developed further, the notion has gained ground that most, perhaps all, of our laws are only approximations. The laws themselves, moreover, have grown so numerous that there is no counting them; and so many rival formulations are proposed in all the branches of science that investigators have become accustomed to the notion that no theory is absolutely a transcript of reality, but that any one of them may from some point of view be useful. Their great use is to summarize old facts and to lead to new ones. They are only a man-made language, a conceptual shorthand, as some one calls them, in which we write our reports of nature; and languages, as is well known, tolerate much choice of expression and many dialects.

Thus human arbitrariness has driven divine necessity from scientific logic. If I mention the names of Sigwart, Mach, Ostwald, Pearson, Milhaud, Poincaré, Duhem, Ruyssen, those of you who are students will easily identify the tendency I speak of, and will think of additional names.

Riding now on the front of this wave of scientific logic Messrs. Schiller and Dewey appear with the pragmatistic account of what truth everywhere signifies. Everywhere, these teachers say, "truth" in our ideas and beliefs means the same thing that it means in science. It means, they say, nothing but this, *that ideas (which themselves are but parts of our experience) become true just in so far as they help us to get into satisfactory relation with other parts of our experience,* to summarize them and get about among them by conceptual short-cuts instead of following the interminable succession of particular phenomena. Any idea upon which we can ride, so to speak; any idea that will carry us prosperously from any one part of our experience to any other part, linking things satisfactorily, working securely, simplifying, saving labor; is true for just so much, true in so far forth, true *instrumentally.* This is the "instrumental" view of truth taught so successfully at Chicago, the view that truth in our ideas means their power to "work," promulgated so brilliantly at Oxford.

Messrs. Dewey, Schiller, and their allies, in reaching this general conception of all truth, have only followed the example of geologists, biologists and philologists. In the establishment of these other sciences, the successful stroke was always to take some simple process actually observable in operation—as denudation by weather, say, or variation from parental type, or change of dialect by incorporation of new words and pronunciations—and then to generalize it, making it apply to all times, and produce great results by summating its effects through the ages.

The observable process which Schiller and Dewey particularly singled out for generalization is the familiar one by which any individual settles into *new opinions.* The process here is always the same. The individual has a stock of old opinions already, but he meets a new experience that puts them to a strain. Somebody contradicts them; or in a reflective moment he discovers that they contradict each other; or he hears of facts with which they are incompatible; or desires arise in him which they cease to satisfy. The result is an inward trouble to which his mind till then had been a stranger, and from which he seeks to escape by modifying his previous mass of opinions. He saves as much of it as he can, for in this matter of belief we are all extreme conservatives. So he tries to change first this opinion, and then that (for they resist change very variously), until at last some new idea comes up which he can graft upon the ancient stock with a minimum of disturbance of the latter, some idea that mediates between the stock and the new experience and runs them into one another most felicitously and expediently.

This new idea is then adopted as the true one. It preserves the older stock of truths with a minimum of modification, stretching them just enough to make them admit the novelty, but conceiving that in ways as familiar as the case leaves possible. An *outrée* explanation, violating all our preconceptions, would never pass for a true account of a novelty. We should scratch round industriously till we found something less excentric. The most violent revolutions in an individual's beliefs leave most of his old order standing. Time and space, cause and effect, nature and history, and one's own biography remain untouched. New truth is always a go-between, a smoother-over of transitions. It marries old opinion to new fact so as ever to show a minimum of jolt, a maximum of continuity. We hold a theory true just in proportion to its success in solving this "problem of maxima and minima." But success in solving this problem is eminently a matter of approximation. We say this theory solves it on the whole more satisfactorily than that theory; but that means more satisfactorily to ourselves, and individuals will emphasize their points of satisfaction differently. To a certain degree, therefore, everything here is plastic.

The point I now urge you to observe particularly is the part played by the older truths. Failure to take account of it is the source of much of the unjust criticism levelled against pragmatism. Their influence is absolutely controlling. Loyalty to them is the first principle—in most cases it is the only principle; for by far the most usual way of handling phenomena so novel that they would make for a serious rearrangement of our preconception is to ignore them altogether, or to abuse those who bear witness for them.

You doubtless wish examples of this process of truth's growth, and the only trouble is their superabundance. The simplest case of new truth is of course the mere numerical addition of new kinds of facts, or of new single facts of old kinds, to our experience—an addition that involves no alteration in the old beliefs. Day follows day, and contents are simply added. The new contents themselves are not true, they simply *come* and *are.* Truth is *what we say about* them, and when we say that they have come, truth is satisfied by the plain additive formula.

But often the day's contents oblige a rearrangement. If I should now utter piercing shrieks and act like a maniac on this platform, it would make many of you revise your ideas as to the probable worth of my philosophy. "Radium" came the other day as part of the day's content, and seemed for a moment to contradict our ideas of the whole order of nature, that order having come to be identified with what is called the conservation of energy. The mere sight of radium paying heat away indefinitely out of its own pocket seemed to violate that conservation. What to think? If the radiations from it were nothing but an escape of unsuspected "potential" energy, pre-existent inside of the atoms, the principle of conservation would be saved. The discovery of "helium" as the radiation's outcome, opened a way to this belief. So Ramsay's view is generally held to be true, because, although it extends our old ideas of energy, it causes a minimum of alteration in their nature.

I need not multiply instances. A new opinion counts as "true" just in proportion as it gratifies the individual's desire to assimilate the novel in his experience to his beliefs in stock. It must both lean on old truth and grasp new fact; and its success (as I said a moment ago) in doing this, is a matter for the individual's appreciation. When old truth grows, then, by new truth's addition, it is for subjective reasons. We are in the process and obey the reasons. That new idea is truest which performs most felicitously its function of satisfying our double urgency. It makes itself true, gets itself classed as true, by the way it works; grafting itself then upon the ancient body of truth, which thus grows much as a tree grows by the activity of a new layer of cambium.

Now Dewey and Schiller proceed to generalize this observation and to apply it to the most ancient parts of truth. They also once were plastic. They also were called true for human reasons. They also mediated between still earlier truths and what in those days were novel observations. Purely objective truth, truth in whose establishment the function of giving human satisfaction in marrying previous parts of experience with newer parts play no rôle whatever, is nowhere to be found. The reasons why we call things true is the reason why they *are* true, for "to be true" *means* only to perform this marriage-function.

The trail of the human serpent is thus over everything. Truth independent; truth that we *find* merely; truth no longer malleable to human need; truth incorrigible, in a word; such truth exists indeed superabundantly—or is supposed to exist by rationalistically minded thinkers; but then it means only the dead heart of the living tree, and its being there means only that truth also has its paleontology, and its "prescription," and may grow stiff with years of veteran service and petrified in men's regard by sheer antiquity. But how plastic even the oldest truths nevertheless really are has been vividly shown in our day by the transformation of logical and mathematical ideas, a transformation which seems even to be invading physics. The ancient formulas are reinterpreted as special expressions of much wider principles, principles that our ancestors never got a glimpse of in their present shape and formulation.

Mr. Schiller still gives to all this view of truth the name of "Humanism," but, for this doctrine too, the name of pragmatism seems fairly to be in the ascendant, so I will treat it under the name of pragmatism in these lectures.

Such then would be the scope of pragmatism—first, a method and second, a genetic theory of what is meant by truth....

You will probably be surprised to learn...that Messrs. Schiller's and Dewey's theories have suffered a hailstorm of contempt and ridicule. All rationalism has risen against them. In influential quarters Mr. Schiller, in particular, has been treated like an impudent schoolboy who deserves a spanking. I should not mention this but for the fact that it throws so much sidelight upon that rationalistic temper to which I have opposed the temper of pragmatism. Pragmatism is uncomfortable away from facts. Rationalism is comfortable only in the presence of abstractions. This pragmatist talk about truths in the plural, about their utility and satisfactoriness, about the success with which they "work," etc., suggests to the typical intellectualist mind a sort of coarse lame second-rate makeshift article of truth. Such truths are not real truth. Such tests are merely subjective. As against this, objective truth must be something non-utilitarian, haughty, refined, remote, august, exalted. It must be an absolute reality. It must be what we *ought* to think unconditionally. The conditioned ways in which we *do* think are so much irrelevance and matter for psychology. Down with psychology, up with logic, in all this question!

See the exquisite contrast of the types of mind! The pragmatist clings to facts and concreteness, observes truth at its work in particular cases, and generalizes. Truth, for him, becomes a class-name for all sorts of definite working-values in experience. For the rationalist it remains a pure abstraction, to the bare name of which we must defer. When the pragmatist undertakes to show in detail just *why* we must defer, the rationalist is unable to recognize the concretes from which his own abstraction is taken. He accuses us of *denying* truth; whereas we have only sought to trace exactly why people follow it and always ought to follow it. Your typical ultra-abstractionist fairly shudders at concreteness: other things equal, he positively prefers the pale and spectral. If the two universes were offered, he would always choose the skinny outline rather than the rich thicket of reality. It is so much purer, clearer, nobler.

I hope that as these lectures go on, the concreteness and closeness to facts of the pragmatism which they advocate may be what approves itself to you as its most satisfactory peculiarity. It only follows here the example of the sister-sciences, interpreting the unobserved by the observed. It brings old and new harmoniously together. It converts the absolutely empty notion of a static relation of "correspondence" (what that may mean we must ask later) between our minds and reality, into that of a rich and active commerce (that any one may follow in detail and understand) between particular thoughts of ours, and the great universe of other experiences in which they play their parts and have their uses.

But enough of this at present. The justification of what I say must be postponed. I wish now to add a word in further explanation of the claim I made at our last meeting, that pragmatism may be a happy harmonizer of empiricist ways of thinking with the more religious demands of human beings.

Men who are strongly of the fact-loving temperament, you may remember me to have said, are liable to be kept at a distance by the small sympathy with facts which that philosophy from the present-day fashion of idealism offers them. It is far too intellectualistic. Old fashioned theism was bad enough, with its notion of God as an exalted monarch, made up of a lot of unintelligible or preposterous "attributes"; but, so long as it held strongly by the argument from design, it kept some touch with concrete realities. Since, however, Darwinism has once for all displaced design from the minds of the "scientific," theism has lost that foothold; and some kind of an immanent or pantheistic deity working in things rather than above them is, if any, the kind recommended to our contemporary imagination. Aspirants to a philosophic religion turn, as a rule, more hopefully nowadays towards idealistic pantheism than towards the older dualistic theism, in spite of the fact that the latter still counts able defenders.

But, as I said in my first lecture, the brand of pantheism offered is hard for them to assimilate if they are lovers of facts, or empirically minded. It is the absolutistic brand, spurning the dust and reared upon pure logic. It keeps no connexion whatever with concreteness. Affirming the Absolute Mind, which is its substitute for God, to be the rational presupposition of all particulars of fact, whatever they may be, it remains supremely indifferent to what the particular facts in our world actually are. Be they what they may, the Absolute will father them. Like the sick lion in Esop's fable, all footprints lead into his den, but *nulla vestigia retrorsum*. You cannot redescend into the world of particulars by the Absolute's aid, or deduce any necessary consequences of detail important for your life from your idea of his nature. He gives you indeed the assurance that all is well with *Him*, and for his eternal way of thinking; but thereupon he leaves you to be finitely saved by your own temporal devices.

Far be it from me to deny the majesty of this conception, or its capacity to yield religious comfort to a most respectable class of minds. But from the human point of view, no one can pretend that it doesn't suffer from the faults of remoteness and abstractness. It is eminently a product of what I have ventured to call the rationalistic temper. It disdains empiricism's needs. It substitutes a pallid outline for the real world's richness. It is dapper, it is noble in the bad sense, in the sense in which to be noble is to be inapt for humble service. In this real world of sweat and dirt, it seems to me that when a view of things is "noble," that ought to count as a presumption against its truth, and as a philosophic disqualification. The prince of darkness may be a gentleman, as we are told he is, but whatever the God of earth and heaven is, he can surely be no gentleman. His menial services are needed in the dust of our human trials, even more than his dignity is needed in the empyrean.

Now pragmatism, devoted though she be to facts, has no such materialistic bias as ordinary empiricism labors under. Moreover, she has no objection whatever to the realizing of abstractions, so long as you get about among particulars with their aid and they actually carry you somewhere. Interested in no conclusions but those which our minds and our experiences work out together, she has no a priori prejudices against theology. *If theological ideas prove to have a value for concrete life, they will be true, for pragmatism, in the sense of being good for so much. For how much more they are true, will depend entirely on their relations to the other truths that also have to be acknowledged.*

What I said just now about the Absolute, of transcendental idealism, is a case in point. First, I called it majestic and said it yielded religious comfort to a class of minds, and then I accused it of remoteness and sterility. But so far as it affords such comfort, it surely is not sterile; it has that amount of value; it performs a concrete function. As a good pragmatist, I myself ought to call the Absolute true "in so far forth," then; and I unhesitatingly now do so.

But what does *true in so far forth* mean in this case? To answer, we need only apply the pragmatic method. What do believers in the Absolute mean by saying that their belief affords them comfort? They mean that since, in the Absolute finite evil is "overruled" already, we may, therefore, whenever we wish, treat the temporal as if it were potentially the eternal, be sure that we can trust its outcome, and, without sin, dismiss our fear and drop the worry of our finite responsibility. In short, they mean that we have a right ever and anon to take a moral holiday, to let the world wag in its own way, feeling that its issues are in better hands than ours and are none of our business.

The universe is a system of which the individual members may relax their anxieties occasionally, in which the don't-care mood is also right for men, and moral holidays in order—that, if I mistake not, is part, at least, of what the Absolute is "known-as," that is the great difference in our particular experiences which his being true makes, for us, that is his cash-value when he is pragmatically interpreted. Farther than that the ordinary lay-reader in philosophy who thinks favorably of absolute idealism does not venture to sharpen his conceptions. He can use the Absolute for so much, and so much is very precious. He is pained at hearing you speak incredulously of the Absolute, therefore, and disregards your criticism because they deal with aspects of the conception that he fails to follow.

If the Absolute means this, and means no more than this, who can possibly deny the truth of it? To deny it would be to insist that men should never relax, and that holidays are never in order.

I am well aware how odd it must seem to some of you to hear me say that an idea is "true" so long as to believe it is profitable to our lives. That it is *good*, for as much as it profits, you will gladly admit. If what we do by its aid is good, you will allow the idea itself to be good in so far forth, for we are the better for possessing it. But is it not a strange misuse of the word "truth," you will say, to call ideas also "true" for this reason?

To answer this difficulty fully is impossible at this stage of my account. You touch here upon the very central point of Messrs. Schiller's, Dewey's, and my own doctrine of truth, which I cannot discuss with detail until my sixth lecture. Let me now say only this, the truth is *one species of good*, and not, as is usually supposed, a category distinct from good, and coordinate with it. *The true is the name of whatever proves itself to be good in the way of belief, and good, too, for definite, assignable reasons.* Surely you must admit this, that if there were *no good* for life in true ideas, or if the knowledge of them were positively disadvantageous and false ideas the only useful ones, then the current notion that truth is divine and precious, and its pursuit a duty, could never have grown up or become a dogma. In a world like that, our duty would be to *shun* truth, rather. But in this world, just as certain foods are not only agreeable to our taste, but good for our teeth, our stomach, and our tissues; so certain ideas are not only agreeable to think about, or agreeable as supporting other ideas that we are fond of, but they are also helpful in life's practical struggles. If there be any life that it is really better we should lead, and if there be any idea which, if believed in, would help us to lead that life, then it would be really better for us to believe in that idea, *unless, indeed, belief in it incidentally clashed with other greater vital benefits.*

"What would be better for us to believe!" This sounds very like a definition of truth. It comes very near to saying "what we *ought* to believe"; and in *that* definition none of you would find any oddity. Ought we ever not to believe what it is *better* for us to believe? And can we then keep the notion of what is better for us, and what is true for us, permanently apart?

Pragmatism says no, and I fully agree with her. Probably you also agree, so far as the abstract statement goes, but with a suspicion that if we practically did believe everything that made for good in our own personal lives, we should be found indulging all kinds of fancies about this world's affairs, and all kinds of sentimental superstitions about a world hereafter. Your suspicion here is undoubtedly well founded, and it is evident that something happens when you pass from the abstract to the concrete that complicates the situation.

I said just now that what is better for us to believe is true *unless the belief incidentally clashes with some other vital benefit.* Now in real life what vital benefits is any particular belief of ours most liable to clash with? What indeed except the vital benefits yielded by *other beliefs* when these prove incompatible with the first ones? In other words, the greatest enemy of any one of our truths may be the rest of our truths. Truths have once for all this desperate instinct of self-preservation and of desire to extinguish whatever contradicts them. My belief in the Absolute, based on the good it does me, must run the gauntlet of all my other beliefs. Grant that it may be true in giving me a moral holiday. Nevertheless, as I conceive it—and let me speak now confidentially, as it were, and merely in my own private person—it clashes with other truths of mine whose benefits I hate to give up on its account. It happens to be associated with a kind of logic of which I am the enemy, I find that it entangles me in metaphysical paradoxes that are inacceptable, etc., etc. But as I have enough trouble in life already without adding the trouble of carrying these intellectual inconsistencies, I personally just give up the Absolute. I just *take* my moral holidays; or else as a professional philosopher, I try to justify them by some other principle.

If I could restrict my notion of the Absolute to its bare holiday-giving value, it wouldn't clash with my other truths. But we cannot easily thus restrict our hypotheses. They carry supernumerary features, and these it is that clash so. My disbelief in the Absolute means then disbelief in those other supernumerary features, for I fully believe in the legitimacy of taking moral holidays.

You see by this what I meant when I called pragmatism a mediator and reconciler and said, borrowing the word from Papini, that she "unstiffens" our theories. She has in fact no prejudices whatever, no obstructive dogmas, no rigid canons of what shall count as proof. She is completely genial. She will entertain any hypothesis, she will consider any evidence. It follows that in the religious field she is at a great advantage both over positivistic empiricism, with its anti-theological bias, and over religious rationalism, with its exclusive interest in the remote, the noble, the simple, and the abstract in the way of conception.

In short, she widens the field of search for God. Rationalism sticks to logic and the empyrean. Empiricism sticks to the external senses. Pragmatism is willing to take anything, to follow either logic or the senses and to count the humblest and most personal experiences. She will count mystical experiences if they have practical consequences. She will take a God who lives in the very dirt of private fact—if that should seem a likely place to find him.

Her only test of probable truth is what works best in the way of leading us, what fits every part of life best and combines with the collectivity of experiences demands, nothing being omitted. If theological ideas should do this, if the notion of God, in particular, should prove to do it, how could pragmatism possibly deny God's existence? She could see no meaning in treating as "not true" a notion that was pragmatically so successful. What other kind of truth could there be, for her, than all this agreement with concrete reality?

WALTER LIPPMANN

Selection from *Drift and Mastery*
(1914)

The intellectuals who called themselves "progressive" in the first two decades of the twentieth century, and whose self-definition has generally been flattered by historians, believed that human beings could bring their own destiny under more of their own power if only they applied their minds to the task more vigorously and more rigorously than their predecessors. "Progressives" ended up going off in a number of different directions, in terms of specific policy initiatives, but their common "can-do" spirit was expressed with rare cogency in 1914 by a young journalist only a few years out of college. *In Drift and Mastery*, Walter Lippmann (1889–1974) created what is now remembered as one of the great classics of American social criticism. In the selection reprinted here, Lippmann developed his central idea: that science, broadly construed as the systematic use of evidence-based reasoning, was "the discipline of democracy," and could, if men and women were courageous enough to use it unflinchingly, bring the chaos of modern life under greater control than had been exercised by the various interest and inertias that dominated the life of the society.

Lippmann went on to become one of the most prolific and respected political commentators of the twentieth century. The most famous of his books included *Public Opinion* (New York, 1922), *A Preface to Morals* (New York, 1929), and *The Public Philosophy* (New York, 1955), all of which were more reserved than *Drift and Mastery* concerning the capacity of reform to put the national house in good order, but all of which displayed the judicious, rational temper for which Lippmann was always known. The same sensibility marked "Today and Tomorrow," Lippmann's daily newspaper column published in up to two hundred American newspapers from 1931 to 1967. This reputation for deliberation and probity gave special weight to Lippmann's voice in the mid- and late 1960s when he voiced sharp and persistent opposition to the Vietnam War, accusing President Lyndon Johnson of betraying the promise of the nation. But it was as a progressive, especially as the author of *Drift and Mastery*, that Lippmann made his deepest mark on his times. For a close study of that book and the immediate context in which it was written and received, see David A. Hollinger, *In the American Province: Studies in Mid-Twentieth Century American Intellectual History* (Bloomington, 1985), 44–55.

The most comprehensive and thoroughly documented study of Lippmann is Ronald Steel, *Walter Lippmann and the American Century* (Boston, 1980). Another valuable study, focusing more than Steel does on Lippmann's writings, is Stephen Blum, *Walter Lippmann: Cosmopolitan in the Century of Total War* (Ithaca, 1984).

....Tradition will not work in the complexity of modern life. For if you ask Americans to remain true to the traditions of all their Fathers, there would be a pretty confusion if they followed your advice. There is great confusion, as it is, due in large measure to the persistency with which men follow tradition in a world unsuited to it. They modify a bit, however, they apply "the rule of reason" to their old loyalties, and so a little adjustment is possible. But there can be no real cohesion for America in following scrupulously the inherited ideals of our people. Between the Sons of the Revolution, the Ancient Order of Hibernians, the Orangemen, the plantation life of the South, the refugees from Russia, the Balkan Slavs, there is in their traditions a conflict of prejudice and custom that would make all America as clamorous as the Stock Exchange on a busy day. Nor is there going to be lasting inspiration for Bulgarian immigrants in the legend of the Mayflower.

The only possible cohesion now is a loyalty that looks forward. America is preëminently the country where there is practical substance in Nietzsche's advice that we should live not for our fatherland but for our children's land.

To do this men have to substitute purpose for tradition: and that is, I believe, the profoundest change that has ever taken place in human history. We can no longer treat life as something that has trickled down to us. We have to deal with it deliberately, devise its social organization, alter its tools, formulate its method, educate and control it. In endless ways we put intention where custom has reigned. We break up routines, make decisions, choose our ends, select means.

The massive part of man's life has always been, and still is, subconscious. The influence of his intelligence seems insignificant in comparison with attachments and desires, brute forces, and natural catastrophes. Our life is managed from behind the scenes: we are actors in dramas that we cannot interpret. Of almost no decisive event can we say: this was our own choosing. We happen upon careers, necessity pushing, blind inclination pulling. If we stop to think we are amazed that we should be what we are. And so we have come to call mysterious everything that counts, and the more mysterious the better some of us pretend to think it is. We drift into our work, we fall in love, and our lives seem like the intermittent flicker of an obstinate lamp. War panics, and financial panics, revivals, fads sweep us before them. Men go to war not knowing why, hurl themselves at cannon as if they were bags of flour, seek impossible goals, submit to senseless wrongs, for mankind lives to-day only in the intervals of a fitful sleep.

There is indeed a dreaming quality in life: moved as it is from within by unconscious desires and habits, and from without by the brute forces of climate and soil and wind and tide. There are stretches in every day when we have no sense of ourselves at all, and men often wake up with a start: "Have I lived as long as I'm supposed to have lived?...Here I am, this kind of person who has passed through these experiences—well, I didn't quite know it."

That, I think, is the beginning of what we call reflection: a desire to realize the drama in which we are acting, to be awake during our own lifetime. When we cultivate reflection by watching ourselves and the world outside, the thing we call science begins. We draw the hidden into the light of consciousness, record it, compare phases of it, note its history, experiment, reflect on error, and we find that our conscious life is no longer a trivial iridescence, but a progressively powerful way of domesticating the brute.

This is what mastery means: the substitution of conscious intention for unconscious striving. Civilization, it seems to me, is just this constant effort to introduce plan where there has been clash, and purpose into the jungles of disordered growth. But to shape the

Source: Walter Lippmann, *Drift and Mastery* (New York, 1914), 146–55.

world nearer to the heart's desire requires a knowledge of the heart's desire and of the world. You cannot throw yourself blindly against unknown facts and trust to luck that the result will be satisfactory.

Yet from the way many business men, minor artists, and modern philosophers talk you would think that the best world can be created by the mere conflict of economic egotisms, the mere eruption of fantasy, and the mere surge of blind instinct. There is to-day a widespread attempt to show the futility of ideas. Now in so far as this movement represents a critical insight into the emotional basis of ideas, it is a fundamental contribution to human power. But when it seeks to fall back upon the unconscious, when the return to nature is the ideal of a deliberate vegetable, this movement is like the effort of the animal that tried to eat itself: the tail could be managed and the hind legs, but the head was an insurmountable difficulty. You can have misleading ideas, but you cannot escape ideas. To give up theory, to cease formulating your desire is not to reach back, as some people imagine, to profounder sources of inspiration. It is to put yourself at the mercy of stray ideas, of ancient impositions or trumped-up fads. Accident becomes the master, the accident largely of your own training, and you become the plaything of whatever happens to have accumulated at the bottom of your mind, or to find itself sanctified in the newspaper you read and the suburb that suited your income.

There have been fine things produced in the world without intention. Most of our happiness has come to us, I imagine, by the fortunate meeting of events. But happiness has always been a precarious incident, elusive and shifting in an unaccountable world. In love, especially, men rejoice and suffer through what are to them mysterious ways. Yet when it is suggested that the intelligence must invade our unconscious life, men shrink from it as from dangerous and clumsy meddling. It is dangerous and clumsy now, but it is the path we shall have to follow. We have to penetrate the dreaming brute in ourselves, and make him answerable to our waking life.

It is a long and difficult process, one for which we are just beginning to find a method. But there is no other way that offers any hope. To shove our impulses underground by the taboo is to force them to virulent and uncontrolled expression. To follow impulse wherever it leads means the satisfaction of one impulse at the expense of all the others. The glutton and the rake can satisfy only their gluttonous and rakish impulses, and that isn't enough for happiness. What civilized men aim at is neither whim nor taboo, but a frank recognition of desire, disciplined by a knowledge of what is possible, and ordered by the conscious purpose of their lives....

If the scientific temper were as much a part of us as the faltering ethics we now absorb in our childhood, then we might hope to face our problems with something like assurance. A mere emotion of futurity, that sense of "vital urge" which is so common to-day, will fritter itself away unless it comes under the scientific discipline, where men use language accurately, know fact from fancy, search out their own prejudice, are willing to learn from failures, and do not shrink from the long process of close observation. Then only shall we have a substitute for authority. Rightly understood science is the culture under which people can live forward in the midst of complexity, and treat life not as something given but as something to be shaped. Custom and authority will work in a simple and unchanging civilization, but in our world only those will conquer who can understand.

There is nothing accidental then in the fact that democracy in politics is the twin-brother of scientific thinking. They had to come together. As absolutism falls, science arises. It *is* self-government. For when the impulse which overthrows kings and priests and unquestioned creeds becomes self-conscious we call it science.

Inventions and laboratories, Greek words, mathematical formulae, fat books, are only the outward sign of an attitude toward life, an attitude which is self-governing, and most adequately named humanistic. Science is the irreconcilable foe of bogeys, and therefore, a method of laying the conflicts of the soul. It is the unfrightened, masterful and humble approach to reality—the needs of our natures and the possibilities of the world. The scientific spirit is the discipline of democracy, the escape from drift, the outlook of a free man. Its direction is to distinguish fact from fancy; its "enthusiasm is for the possible"; its promise is the shaping of fact to a chastened and honest dream.

But, you will say, granted that the breakdown of authority in a complicated world has left men spiritually homeless, and made their souls uneasy; granted that it may be possible to exorcise many of the bogeys which haunt them, and to cultivate a natural worldliness in which economic and sexual terror will have been reduced; granted that women are tending to create a new environment for the child in which the property sense will not be stimulated morbidly, and where coöperation will become as obvious as obedience and isolation were in the past; suppose too, that an expanding civilization gives such varied resources that man will live more fully, and rely less on the compensations of thwarted desire; suppose that the spirit of science pervades his daily work, not as a mutilated specialty, but as a rich interest in the world with a vivid desire to shape it,—suppose all that, would there not be lacking the one supreme virtue of the older creeds, their capacity for binding the world together?

There would be justice in such a criticism. There is a terrible loneliness that comes to men when they realize their feebleness before a brutally uninterested universe. In his own life-work, say as a teacher, a person may be making some one class-room more serviceable to a few children. But he will feel, as the more imaginative teachers do, that his work is like that of Sisyphus, he no sooner achieves a thing than it is undone. How can he educate a child for a few hours a day, when the home, the streets, the newspapers, the movies, the shop, are all busy miseducating? Wherever there is a constructive man at work you are likely to find this same complaint, that he is working alone. He may be heartwhole and eager, without bogeys or unnecessary fears. He may be free of the weaknesses that have reared so many faiths, and yet he seeks assurance in a communion with something outside himself, at the most perhaps, in a common purpose, at least, in a fellowship effort.

Religions have placed human action in a large and friendly setting. They have enabled men to play their little rôle by making it essential to the drama of eternity. "God needs me, Christ died for me, after all I may be a poor creature, but I'm indispensable." And, as if by feeling themselves part of greatness, men have added to their stature. So even the meekest freshman in a grandstand is a more exalted person because his college team has captured the front page of the newspapers. He may be merely one in thousands who cheered for the eleven heroes, yet somehow he has partaken of their heroism. He is like the cockney who talks of "our Empire," like the Irish immigrants who tell how we licked the British at Yorktown, like the crank whose society of eight people is entitled "Association for Advancing the Human Race." It is well known that in a strike it matters enormously whether the men are fighting for a "fair day's wage" or for "the emancipation of labor."

The history of martyrs is the history of people who expanded to their faith. Indeed, men have shaken destiny because they felt they embodied it. Patriotism, the Cause, Humanity, Perfection, Righteousness, Liberty,—all of them large and windy abstractions to outsiders, are more powerful than dynamite to those who feel them. "My country is the world," said Garrison, while Boston hated him. "I fight for women," says Mrs. Pankhurst.

"I am a fate," said Nietzsche. "This is the true joy in life," says Bernard Shaw, "the being used for a purpose recognized by yourself as a mighty one."

It is no idle question then to ask what there is in the outlook of a modern man to bind his world together. Well, if he is looking for absolute assurance, an infallible refuge in weakness and terror, we have to answer that there is no such certainty. He may learn that while there is no promise of ultimate salvation, there is at least no fear of ultimate damnation; that in the modern world things are not so irremediable, and he may meet a large charity in its endless variety. He can find some understanding, an assurance perhaps of life's resiliency, he may come to know that nothing is so final as he thought it was, that the future is not staked on one enterprise, that life rises out of its own ashes, and renews its own opportunities. But if he demands personal guarantees, he may have to lie in order to get them.

Almost all men do require something to focus their interest in order to sustain it. A great idea like Socialism has done that for millions. But Socialism simply as a great passion can easily produce its superstitions and its barbarisms. What men need in their specialties in order to enable them to coöperate is not alone a binding passion, but a common discipline. Science, I believe, implies such a discipline. It is the fact that scientists approach the world with an understood method that enables them to give and take from each other whether they live in Calcutta or in San Francisco. The scientific world is the best example we have to-day of how specialists can coöperate. Of course there are profound disagreements, intrigues, racial and national prejudices, even among scientific men, for a common method will not wipe out the older cleavages, and it is not a perfectly cohesive force. But for the kind of civilization we are entering it is as yet the best we know.

There are undoubtedly beginnings of such a common method in public affairs. We read English books for help in dealing with American conditions. Social legislation is to-day a world-wide interest, so that reformers in Oregon may draw upon Australasian experiment.[1] The labor movement has international organization with the result that its experience becomes available for use. There is no need to multiply examples. Instruments of a coöperative mind are being forged, be it the world-wide moving picture or some immense generalization of natural science.

This work has aroused in many men the old sense of cosmic wonder, and called forth devotion to impersonal ends. Nor can it be denied that in the study of institutions, in laboratories of research, there have appeared the same loyalty and courage to which the old religions could point as to their finest flower. Moreover, these devotions which science can show, come in the main redeemed from barbarism and pointed to civilized use. There is, to be sure, a certain raw novelty in modern forms of devotion, as there is in uninhabited houses, in new clothes and in new wine—they have hardly felt the mellowing of human contact, that saturation of brute things with the qualities of their users, which makes men love the old, the inadequate, the foolish, as against what is sane and clean, but unfamiliar. Science, too, is a concrete and essentially humble enterprise; spiritually sufficient it may be, to-day, only for the more robust. But the release from economic want, the emancipation from manufactured bogeys, the franker acceptance of normal desire, should tend to make men surer of themselves. And so most of them may not find it necessary to believe the impossible, but will reach their satisfaction in contemplating reality, in decorating it, shaping it, and conquering it....

1.   Oregon was the state in which "direct legislation" was most enthusiastically adopted. Oregon and other states drew on Australia's development of the secret or "*Australian*" ballot. New Zealand early adopted the referendum, taxation of land monopoly, and various kinds of public ownership.

RANDOLPH BOURNE

"Trans-National America" (1916)
"Twilight of Idols" (1917)

In "Trans-National America" (1916), Randolph Bourne (1886–1918) condemned the Anglo-conformist ideology often associated with the figure of the melting pot and called instead for the dynamic mixing and mingling of diverse peoples in the interests of new cultural combinations. Bourne was the most influential of the handful of intellectuals who opposed the nativism dominant among Americans of Protestant Anglo-Saxon stock during the era of World War I. The ideal of cosmopolitanism to which Bourne gave voice was destined during the next several decades to serve as a rallying point for immigrant intellectuals as well as for antiprovincial Anglo-Protestants like Bourne himself. This function of the cosmopolitan ideal is addressed in David A. Hollinger, "Ethnic Diversity, Cosmopolitanism, and the Emergence of the American Liberal Intelligentsia," in Hollinger's *In the American Province: Studies in the History and Historiography of Ideas* (Bloomington, Ind., 1985), 56–73.

Bourne's vision for America was slightly different from that of Horace Kallen, whose criticism of the "melting pot" helped to inspire Bourne's defense of cultural diversity. Kallen's "Democracy vs the Melting Pot," *Nation* (February 18 and 25, 1915), looked to the United States as a broad canopy providing protection for immigrant groups expected to remain enduring, relatively autonomous presences in American life. But Bourne accepted a greater measure of cross-fertilization, and anticipated the development of a new, distinctive culture.

Bourne is also remembered for his vindication, during World War I, of the vocation of the intellectual as an independent critic of prevailing authorities. The most influential of Bourne's writings on this theme was "Twilight of Idols" (1917), the second Bourne essay reprinted here. This attack on John Dewey and other "pragmatic" and "instrumentalist" intellectuals for their support of the war opens and closes with invocations of another great pragmatist, William James. James offered some of the "poetic vision" that Bourne believed Dewey lacked. For a fair-minded account of the Dewey-Bourne disagreement that emphasizes Bourne's continued indebtedness to Dewey, see Robert B. Westbrook, *John Dewey and American Democracy* (Ithaca, 1991), esp. 202–12. For a careful study of Bourne and the other "Young America" critics of his generation, see Casey Nelson Blake, *Beloved Community: The Cultural Criticism of Randolph Bourne, Van Wyck Brooks, Waldo Frank, and Lewis Mumford* (Chapel Hill, 1991). The best study of the debates over American nationalism carried on during Bourne's generation is Jonathan Hansen, *The Lost Promise of Patriotism* (Chicago, 2003).

"Trans-National America"
(1916)

No reverberatory effect of the great war has caused American public opinion more solicitude than the failure of the "melting-pot." The discovery of diverse nationalistic feelings among our great alien population has come to most people as an intense shock. It has brought out the unpleasant inconsistencies of our traditional beliefs. We have had to watch hard-hearted old Brahmins virtuously indignant at the spectacle of the immigrant refusing to be melted, while they jeer at patriots like Mary Antin who write about "our forefathers." We have had to listen to publicists who express themselves as stunned by the evidence of vigorous nationalistic and cultural movements in this country among Germans, Scandinavians, Bohemians, and Poles, while in the same breath they insist that the alien shall be forcibly assimilated to that Anglo-Saxon tradition which they unquestioningly label "American."

As the unpleasant truth has come upon us that assimilation in this country was proceeding on lines very different from those we had marked out for it, we found ourselves inclined to blame those who were thwarting our prophecies. The truth became culpable. We blamed the war, we blamed the Germans. And then we discovered with a moral shock that these movements had been making great headway before the war even began. We found that the tendency, reprehensible and paradoxical as it might be, has been for the national clusters of immigrants, as they became more and more firmly established and more and more prosperous, to cultivate more and more assiduously the literatures and cultural traditions of their homelands. Assimilation, in other words, instead of washing out the memories of Europe, made them more and more intensely real. Just as these clusters became more and more objectively American, did they become more and more German or Scandinavian or Bohemian or Polish.

To face the fact that our aliens are already strong enough to take a share in the direction of their own destiny, and that the strong cultural movements represented by the foreign press, schools, and colonies are a challenge to our facile attempts, is not, however, to admit the failure of Americanization. It is not to fear the failure of democracy. It is rather to urge us to an investigation of what Americanism may rightly mean. It is to ask ourselves whether our ideal has been broad or narrow—whether perhaps the time has not come to assert a higher ideal than the "melting-pot." Surely we cannot be certain of our spiritual democracy when, claiming to melt the nations within us to a comprehension of our free and democratic institutions, we fly into panic at the first sign of their own will and tendency. We act as if we wanted Americanization to take place only on our own terms, and not by the consent of the governed. All our elaborate machinery of settlement and school and union, of social and political naturalization, however, will move with friction just in so far as it neglects to take into account this strong and virile insistence that America shall be what the immigrant will have a hand in making it, and not what a ruling class, descendant of those British stocks which were the first permanent immigrants, decide that

Source: Atlantic Monthly, 118 (July 1916), 86–97.

America shall be made. This is the condition which confronts us, and which demands a clear and general readjustment of our attitude and our ideal.

Mary Antin is right when she looks upon our foreign-born as the people who missed the Mayflower and came over on the first boat they could find. But she forgets that when they did come it was not upon other Mayflowers, but upon a "Maiblume," a "Fleur de Mai," a "Fior di Maggio," a "Majblomst." These people were not mere arrivals from the same family, to be welcomed as understood and long-loved, but strangers to the neighborhood, with whom a long process of settling down had to take place. For they brought with them their national and racial characters, and each new national quota had to wear slowly away the contempt with which its mere alienness got itself greeted. Each had to make its way slowly from the lowest strata of unskilled labor up to a level where it satisfied the accredited norms of social success.

We are all foreign-born or the descendants of foreign-born, and if distinctions are to be made between us they should rightly be on some other ground than indigenousness. The early colonists came over with motives no less colonial than the later. They did not come to be assimilated in an American melting-pot. They did not come to adopt the culture of the American Indian. They had not the smallest intention of "giving themselves without reservation" to the new country. They came to get freedom to live as they wanted to. They came to escape from the stifling air and chaos of the old world; they came to make their fortune in a new land. They invented no new social framework. Rather they brought over bodily the old ways to which they had been accustomed. Tightly concentrated on a hostile frontier, they were conservative beyond belief. Their pioneer daring was reserved for the objective conquest of material resources. In their folkways, in their social and political institutions, they were, like every colonial people, slavishly imitative of the mother-country. So that, in spite of the "Revolution," our whole legal and political system remained more English than the English, petrified and unchanging, while in England law developed to meet the needs of the changing times.

It is just this English-American conservatism that has been our chief obstacle to social advance. We have needed the new peoples—the order of the German and Scandinavian, the turbulence of the Slav and Hun—to save us from our own stagnation. I do not mean that the illiterate Slav is now the equal of the New Englander of pure descent. He is raw material to be educated, not into a New Englander, but into a socialized American.... Let us cease to think of ideals like democracy as magical qualities inherent in certain peoples. Let us speak, not of inferior races, but of inferior civilizations. We are all to educate and to be educated. These peoples in America are in a common enterprise. It is not what we are now that concerns us, but what this plastic next generation may become in the light of a new cosmopolitan ideal.

We are not dealing with static factors, but with fluid and dynamic generations. To contrast the older and the newer immigrants and see the one class as democratically motivated by love of liberty, and the other by mere money-getting, is not to illuminate the future. To think of earlier nationalities as culturally assimilated to America, while we picture the later as a sodden and resistive mass, makes only for bitterness and misunderstanding. There may be a difference between these earlier and these later stocks, but it lies neither in motive for coming nor in strength of cultural allegiance to the homeland. The truth is that no more tenacious cultural allegiance to the mother country has been shown by any alien nation than by the ruling class of Anglo-Saxon descendants in these American States. English snobberies, English religion, English literary styles, English literary reverences and canons, English ethics, English superiorities, have been the cultural food that we have drunk in from our mothers' breasts. The distinctively American spirit—pioneer, as distinguished from the reminiscently English—that appears in Whitman and Emerson and James, has had to exist on sufferance alongside of this other cult, unconsciously belittled by our cultural makers of opinion. No country has perhaps had so great indigenous genius which had so little influence on the country's traditions and expressions. The unpopular and dreaded German-American of the present day is a beginning amateur in comparison with those foolish Anglophiles of Boston and New York and Philadelphia whose reversion to cultural type sees uncritically in England's cause the cause of Civilization, and, under the guise of ethical independence of thought, carries along European traditions which are no more "American" than the German categories themselves....

The non-English American can scarcely be blamed if he sometimes thinks of the Anglo-Saxon predominance in America as little more than a predominance of priority. The Anglo-Saxon was merely the first immigrant, the first to found a colony. He has never really ceased to be the descendant of immigrants, nor has he ever succeeded in transforming that colony into a real nation, with a tenacious, richly woven fabric of native culture. Colonials from the other nations have come and settled down beside him. They found no definite native culture which should startle them out of their colonialism, and consequently they looked back to their mother-country, as the earlier Anglo-Saxon immigrant was looking back to his. What has been offered the newcomer has been the chance to learn English, to become a citizen, to salute the flag. And those elements of our ruling classes who are responsible for the public schools, the settlements, all the organizations for amelioration in the cities, have every reason to be proud of the care and labor which they have devoted to absorbing the immigrant. His opportunities the immigrant has taken to gladly, with almost a pathetic eagerness to make his way in the new land without friction or disturbance. The common language has made not only for the necessary communication, but for all the amenities of life.

If freedom means the right to do pretty much as one pleases, so long as one does not interfere with others, the immigrant has found freedom, and the ruling element has been singularly liberal in its treatment of the invading hordes. But if freedom means a democratic coöperation in determining the ideals and purposes and industrial and social institutions of a country, then the immigrant has not been free, and the Anglo-Saxon element is guilty of just what every dominant race is guilty of in every European country: the imposition of its own culture upon the minority peoples. The fact that this imposition has been so mild and, indeed, semi-conscious does not alter its quality. And the war has brought out just the degree to which that purpose of "Americanizing," that is, "Anglo-Saxonizing," the immigrant has failed.

For the Anglo-Saxon now in his bitterness to turn upon the other peoples, talk about their "arrogance," scold them for not being melted in a pot which never existed, is to betray the unconscious purpose which lay at the bottom of his heart. It betrays too the possession of a racial jealousy similar to that of which he is now accusing the so-called "hyphenates." Let the Anglo-Saxon be proud enough of the heroic toil and heroic sacrifices which moulded the nation. But let him ask himself, if he had had to depend on the English descendants, where he would have been living to-day. To those of us who see in the exploitation of unskilled labor the strident red leit-motif of our civilization, the settling of the country presents a great social drama as the waves of immigration broke over it.

Let the Anglo-Saxon ask himself where he would have been if these races had not come? Let those who feel the inferiority of the non-Anglo-Saxon immigrant contemplate that region of the States which has remained the most distinctively "American," the South. Let him ask himself whether he would really like to see the foreign hordes Americanized into such an Americanization. Let him ask himself how superior this native civilization is to the great "alien" states of Wisconsin and Minnesota, where Scandinavians, Poles, and Germans have self-consciously labored to preserve their traditional culture, while being outwardly and satisfactorily American. Let him ask himself how much more wisdom, intelligence, industry and social leadership has come out of these alien states than out of all the truly American ones. The South, in fact, while this vast Northern development has gone on, still remains an English colony, stagnant and complacent, having progressed culturally scarcely beyond the early Victorian era. It is culturally sterile because it has had no advantage of cross-fertilization like the Northern states. What has happened in states such as Wisconsin and Minnesota is that strong foreign cultures have struck root in a new and fertile soil. America has meant liberation, and German and Scandinavian political ideas and social energies have expanded to a new potency. The process has not been at all the fancied "assimilation" of the Scandinavian or Teuton. Rather has it been a process of their assimilation of us—I speak as an Anglo-Saxon. The foreign cultures have not been melted down or run together, made into some homogeneous Americanism, but have remained distinct but coöperating to the greater glory and benefit, not only of themselves but of all the native "Americanism" around them.

What we emphatically do not want is that these distinctive qualities should be washed out into a tasteless, colorless fluid of uniformity. Already we have far too much of this insipidity,—masses of people who are cultural half-breeds, neither assimilated Anglo-Saxons nor nationals of another culture. Each national colony in this country seems to retain in its foreign press, its vernacular literature, its schools, its intellectual and patriotic leaders, a central cultural nucleus. From this nucleus the colony extends out by imperceptible gradations to a fringe where national characteristics are all but lost. Our cities are filled with these half-breeds who retain their foreign names but have lost the foreign savor. This does not mean that they have actually been changed into New Englanders or Middle Westerners. It does not mean that they have been really Americanized. It means that, letting slip from them whatever native culture they had, they have substituted for it only the most rudimentary American—the American culture of the cheap newspaper, the "movies," the popular song, the ubiquitous automobile. The unthinking who survey this class call them assimilated, Americanized. The great American public school has done its work. With these people our institutions are safe. We may thrill with dread at the aggressive hyphenate, but this tame flabbiness is accepted as Americanization. The same moulders of opinion whose ideal is to melt the different races into Anglo-Saxon gold hail this poor product as the satisfying result of their alchemy.

Yet a truer cultural sense would have told us that it is not the self-conscious cultural nuclei that sap at our American life, but these fringes. It is not the Jew who sticks proudly to the faith of his fathers and boasts of that venerable culture of his who is dangerous to America, but the Jew who has lost the Jewish fire and become a mere elementary, grasping animal. It is not the Bohemian who supports the Bohemian schools in Chicago whose influence is sinister, but the Bohemian who has made money and has got into ward politics. Just so surely as we tend to disintegrate these nuclei of nationalistic culture do we tend to create hordes of men and women without a spiritual country, cultural outlaws, without taste, without standards but those of the mob. We sentence them to live on the most rudimentary planes of American life. The influences at the centre of the nuclei are centripetal. They make for the intelligence and the social values which mean an enhancement of life.

And just because the foreign-born retains this expressiveness is he likely to be a better citizen of the American community. The influences at the fringe, however, are centrifugal, anarchical. They make for detached fragments of peoples. Those who came to find liberty achieve only license. They become the flotsam and jetsam of American life, the downward undertow of our civilization with its leering cheapness and falseness of taste and spiritual outlook, the absence of mind and sincere feeling which we see in our slovenly towns, our vapid moving pictures, our popular novels, and in the vacuous faces of the crowds on the city street. This is the cultural wreckage of our time, and it is from the fringes of the Anglo-Saxon as well as the other stocks that it falls. America has as yet no impelling integrating force. It makes too easily for this detritus of cultures. In our loose, free country, no constraining national purpose, no tenacious folk-tradition and folk-style hold the people to a line.

The war has shown us that not in any magical formula will this purpose be found. No intense nationalism of the European plan can be ours. But do we not begin to see a new and more adventurous ideal? Do we not see how the national colonies in America, deriving power from the deep cultural heart of Europe and yet living here in mutual toleration, freed from the age-long tangles of races, creeds, and dynasties, may work out a federated ideal? America is transplanted Europe, but a Europe that has not been disintegrated and scattered in the transplanting as in some Dispersion. Its colonies live here inextricably mingled, yet not homogeneous. They merge but they do not fuse.

America is a unique sociological fabric, and it bespeaks poverty of imagination not to be thrilled at the incalculable potentialities of so novel a union of men. To seek no other goal than the weary old nationalism,—belligerent, exclusive, inbreeding, the poison of which we are witnessing now in Europe,—is to make patriotism a hollow sham, and to declare that, in spite of our boastings, America must ever be a follower and not a leader of nations.

If we come to find this point of view plausible, we shall have to give up the search for our native "American" culture. With the exception of the South and that New England which, like the Red Indian, seems to be passing into solemn oblivion, there is no distinctively American culture. It is apparently our lot rather to be a federation of cultures. This we have been for half a century, and the war has made it ever more evident that this is what we are destined to remain. This will not mean, however, that there are not expressions of indigenous genius that could not have sprung from any other soil. Music, poetry, philosophy, have been singularly fertile and new. Strangely enough, American genius has flared forth just in those directions which are least understood of the people. If the American note is bigness, action, the objective as contrasted with the reflective life, where is the epic expression of this spirit? Our drama and our fiction, the peculiar fields for the expression of action and objectivity, are somehow exactly the fields of the spirit which remain poor and mediocre. American materialism is in some way inhibited from getting into impressive artistic form its own energy with which it bursts. Nor is it any better in architecture, the least romantic and subjective of all the arts. We are inarticulate of the very values which we profess to idealize. But in the finer forms—music, verse, the essay, philosophy— the American genius puts forth work equal to any of its contemporaries. Just in so far as our American genius has expressed the pioneer spirit, the adventurous, forward-looking drive of a colonial empire, is it representative of that whole America of the many races and peoples, and not of any partial or traditional enthusiasm. And only as that pioneer note is sounded can we really speak of the American culture. As long as we thought of

Americanism in terms of the "melting-pot," our American cultural tradition lay in the past. It was something to which the new Americans were to be moulded. In the light of our changing ideal of Americanism, we must perpetrate the paradox that our American cultural tradition lies in the future. It will be what we all together make out of this incomparable opportunity of attacking the future with a new key.

Whatever American nationalism turns out to be, it is certain to become something utterly different from the nationalisms of twentieth-century Europe. This wave of reactionary enthusiasm to play the orthodox nationalistic game which is passing over the country is scarcely vital enough to last. We cannot swagger and thrill to the same national selffeeling. We must give new edges to our pride. We must be content to avoid the unnumbered woes that national patriotism has brought in Europe, and that fiercely heightened pride and self-consciousness. Alluring as this is, we must allow our imaginations to transcend this scarcely veiled belligerency. We can be serenely too proud to fight if our pride embraces the creative forces of civilization which armed contest nullifies. We can be too proud to fight if our code of honor transcends that of the schoolboy on the playground surrounded by his jeering mates. Our honor must be positive and creative, and not the mere jealous and negative protectiveness against metaphysical violations of our technical rights. When the doctrine is put forth that in one American flows the mystic blood of all our country's sacred honor, freedom, and prosperity, so that an injury to him is to be the signal for turning our whole nation into that clan-feud of horror and reprisal which would be war, then we find ourselves back among the musty schoolmen of the Middle Ages, and not in any pragmatic and realistic America of the twentieth century.

We should hold our gaze to what America has done, not what mediaeval codes of dueling she has failed to observe. We have transplanted European modernity to our soil, without the spirit that inflames it and turns all its energy into mutual destruction. Out of these foreign peoples there has somehow been squeezed the poison. An America, "hyphenated" to bitterness, is somehow non-explosive. For, even if we all hark back in sympathy to a European nation, even if the war has set every one vibrating to some emotional string twanged on the other side of the Atlantic, the effect has been one of almost dramatic harmlessness....

The failure of the melting-pot, far from closing the great American democratic experiment, means that it has only just begun. Whatever American nationalism turns out to be, we see already that it will have a color richer and more exciting than our ideal has hitherto encompassed. In a world which has dreamed of internationalism, we find that we have all unawares been building up the first international nation. The voices which have cried for a tight and jealous nationalism of the European pattern are failing. From that ideal, however valiantly and disinterestedly it has been set for us, time and tendency have moved us further and further away. What we have achieved has been rather a cosmopolitan federation of national colonies, of foreign cultures, from whom the sting of devastating competition has been removed. America is already the world-federation in miniature, the continent where for the first time in history has been achieved that miracle of hope, the peaceful living side by side, with character substantially preserved, of the most heterogeneous peoples under the sun. Nowhere else has such contiguity been anything but the breeder of misery. Here, notwithstanding our tragic failures of adjustment, the outlines are already too clear not to give us a new vision and a new orientation of the American mind in the world.

It is for the American of the younger generation to accept this cosmopolitanism, and carry it along with self-conscious and fruitful purpose. In his colleges, he is already getting, with the study of modern history and politics, the modern literatures, economic geography, the privilege of a cosmopolitan outlook such as the people of no other nation of to-day in Europe can possibly secure. If he is still a colonial, he is no longer the colonial of one partial culture, but of many. He is a colonial of the world. Colonialism has grown into cosmopolitanism, and his mother-land is no one nation, but all who have anything life-enhancing to offer to the spirit. That vague sympathy which the France of ten years ago was feeling for the world—a sympathy which was drowned in the terrible reality of war—may be the modern American's, and that in a positive and aggressive sense. If the American is parochial, it is in sheer wantonness or cowardice. His provincialism is the measure of his fear of bogies or the defect of his imagination.

Indeed, it is not uncommon for the eager Anglo-Saxon who goes to a vivid American university to-day to find his true friends not among his own race but among the acclimatized German or Austrian, the acclimatized Jew, the acclimatized Scandinavian or Italian. In them he finds the cosmopolitan note. In these youths, foreign-born or the children of foreign-born parents, he is likely to find many of his old inbred morbid problems washed away. These friends are oblivious to the repressions of that tight little society in which he so provincially grew up. He has a pleasurable sense of liberation from the stale and familiar attitudes of those whose ingrowing culture has scarcely created anything vital for his America of to-day. He breathes a larger air. In his new enthusiasms for continental literature, for unplumbed Russian depths, for French clarity of thought, for Teuton philosophies of power, he feels himself citizen of a larger world. He may be absurdly superficial, his outward-reaching wonder may ignore all the stiller and homelier virtues of his Anglo-Saxon home, but he has at least found the clue to that international mind which will be essential to all men and women of good-will if they are ever to save this Western world of ours from suicide. His new friends have gone through a similar evolution. America has burned most of the baser metal also from them. Meeting now with this common American background, all of them may yet retain that distinctiveness of their native cultures and their national spiritual slants. They are more valuable and interesting to each other for being different, yet that difference could not be creative were it not for this new cosmopolitan outlook which America has given them and which they all equally possess.

A college where such a spirit is possible even to the smallest degree, has within itself already the seeds of this international intellectual world of the future. It suggests that the contribution of America will be an intellectual internationalism which goes far beyond the mere exchange of scientific ideas and discoveries and the cold recording of facts. It will be an intellectual sympathy which is not satisfied until it has got at the heart of the different cultural expressions, and felt as they feel. It may have immense preferences, but it will make understanding and not indignation its end. Such a sympathy will unite and not divide.

Against the thinly disguised panic which calls itself "patriotism" and the thinly disguised militarism which calls itself "preparedness" the cosmopolitan ideal is set. This does not mean that those who hold it are for a policy of drift. They, too, long passionately for an integrated and disciplined America. But they do not want one which is integrated only for domestic economic exploitation of the workers or for predatory economic imperialism among the weaker peoples. They do not want one that is integrated by coercion or militarism, or for the truculent assertion of a mediaeval code of honor and of doubtful rights. They believe that the most effective integration will be one which coördinates the diverse elements and turns them consciously toward working out together the place of America in the world-situation. They demand for integration a genuine integrity, a wholeness and soundness of enthusiasm and purpose which can only come when no national colony within our America feels that it is being discriminated against or that its cultural case is being prejudged. This strength of coöperation, this feeling that all who are here may have a hand in the destiny of America, will make for a finer spirit of integration than any narrow "Americanism" or forced chauvinism.

In this effort we may have to accept some form of that dual citizenship which meets with so much articulate horror among us. Dual citizenship we may have to recognize as the rudimentary form of that international citizenship to which, if our words mean anything, we aspire. We have assumed unquestioningly that mere participation in the political life of the United States must cut the new citizen off from all sympathy with his old allegiance. Anything but a bodily transfer of devotion from one sovereignty to another has been viewed as a sort of moral treason against the Republic. We have insisted that the immigrant whom we welcomed escaping from the very exclusive nationalism of his European home shall forthwith adopt a nationalism just as exclusive, just as narrow, and even less legitimate because it is founded on no warm traditions of his own. Yet a nation like France is said to permit a formal and legal dual citizenship even at the present time. Though a citizen of hers may pretend to cast off his allegiance in favor of some other sovereignty, he is still subject to her laws when he returns. Once a citizen, always a citizen, no matter how many new citizenships he may embrace. And such a dual citizenship seems to us sound and right. For it recognizes that, although the Frenchman may accept the formal institutional framework of his new country and indeed become intensely loyal to it, yet his Frenchness he will never lose. What makes up the fabric of his soul will always be of this Frenchness, so that unless he becomes utterly degenerate he will always to some degree dwell still in his native environment.

Indeed, does not the cultivated American who goes to Europe practice a dual citizenship, which, if not formal, is no less real? The American who lives abroad may be the least expatriate of men. If he falls in love with French ways and French thinking and French democracy and seeks to saturate himself with the new spirit, he is guilty of at least a dual spiritual citizenship. He may be still American, yet he feels himself through sympathy also a Frenchman. And he finds that this expansion involves no shameful conflict within him, no surrender of his native attitude. He has rather for the first time caught a glimpse of the cosmopolitan spirit. And after wandering about through many races and civilizations he may return to America to find them all here living vividly and crudely, seeking the same adjustment that he made. He sees the new peoples here with a new vision. They are no longer masses of aliens, waiting to be "assimilated," waiting to be melted down into the indistinguishable dough of Anglo-Saxonism. They are rather threads of living and potent cultures, blindly striving to weave themselves into a novel international nation, the first the world has seen. In an Austria-Hungary or a Prussia the stronger of these cultures would be moving almost instinctively to subjugate the weaker. But in America those wills-to-power are turned in a different direction into learning how to live together.

Along with dual citizenship we shall have to accept, I think, that free and mobile passage of the immigrant between America and his native land again which now arouses so much prejudice among us. We shall have to accept the immigrant's return for the same reason that we consider justified our own flitting about the earth. To stigmatize the alien who works in America for a few years and returns to his own land, only perhaps to seek American fortune again, is to think in narrow nationalistic terms. It is to ignore the cosmopolitan significance of this migration. It is to ignore the fact that the returning immigrant is often a missionary to an inferior civilization.

This migratory habit has been especially common with the unskilled laborers who have been pouring into the United States in the last dozen years from every country in southeastern Europe. Many of them return to spend their earnings in their own country or to serve their country in war. But they return with an entirely new critical outlook, and a sense of the superiority of American organization to the primitive living around them. This continued passage to and fro has already raised the material standard of living in many regions of these backward countries. For these regions are thus endowed with exactly what they need, the capital for the exploitation of their natural resources, and the spirit of enterprise. America is thus educating these laggard peoples from the very bottom of society up, awaking vast masses to a new-born hope for the future. In the migratory Greek, therefore, we have not the parasitic alien, the doubtful American asset, but a symbol of that cosmopolitan interchange which is coming, in spite of all war and national exclusiveness.

Only America, by reason of the unique liberty of opportunity and traditional isolation for which she seems to stand, can lead in this cosmopolitan enterprise. Only the American—and in this category I include the migratory alien who has lived with us and caught the pioneer spirit and a sense of new social vistas—has the chance to become that citizen of the world. America is coming to be, not a nationality but a trans-nationality, a weaving back and forth, with the other lands, of many threads of all sizes and colors. Any movement which attempts to thwart this weaving, or to dye the fabric any one color, or disentangle the threads of the strands, is false to this cosmopolitan vision. I do not mean that we shall necessarily glut ourselves with the raw product of humanity. It would be folly to absorb the nations faster than we could weave them. We have no duty either to admit or reject. It is purely a question of expediency. What concerns us is the fact that the strands are here. We must have a policy and an ideal for an actual situation. Our question is, What shall we do with our America? How are you likely to get the more creative America—by confining our imaginations to the ideal of the melting-pot, or broadening them to some such cosmopolitan conception as I have been vaguely sketching?

The war has shown America to be unable, though isolated geographically and politically from a European world-situation, to remain aloof and irresponsible. She is a wandering star in a sky dominated by two colossal constellations of states. Can she not work out some position of her own, some life of being in, yet not quite of, this seething and embroiled European world? This is her only hope and promise....

Is it a wild hope that the undertow of opposition to metaphysics in international relations, opposition to militarism, is less a cowardly provincialism than a groping for this higher cosmopolitan ideal? One can understand the irritated restlessness with which our proud pro-British colonists contemplate a heroic conflict across the seas in which they have no part. It was inevitable that our necessary inaction should evolve in their minds into the bogey of national shame and dishonor. But let us be careful about accepting their sensitiveness as final arbiter. Let us took at our reluctance rather as the first crude beginnings of assertion on the part of certain strands in our nationality that they have a right to a voice in the construction of the American ideal. Let us face realistically the America we have around us. Let us work with the forces that are at work. Let us make something of this transnational spirit instead of outlawing it. Already we are living this cosmopolitan America. What we need is everywhere a vivid consciousness of the new ideal. Deliberate headway must be made against the survivals of the melting-pot ideal for the promise of American life.

We cannot Americanize America worthily by sentimentalizing and moralizing history. When the best schools are expressly renouncing the questionable duty of teaching patriotism by means of history, it is not the time to force shibboleth upon the immigrant. This form of Americanization has been heard because it appealed to the vestiges of our old sentimentalized and moralized patriotism. This has so far held the field as the expression of the new American's new devotion. The inflections of other voices have been drowned. They must be heard. We must see if the lesson of the war has not been for hundreds of these later Americans a vivid realization of their trans-nationality, a new consciousness of what America meant to them as a citizenship in the world. It is the vague historic idealisms which have provided the fuel for the European flame. Our American ideal can make no progress until we do away with this romantic gilding of the past.

All our idealisms must be those of future social goals in which all can participate, the good life of personality lived in the environment of the Beloved Community. No mere doubtful triumphs of the past, which redound to the glory of only one of our trans-nationalities, can satisfy us. It must be a future America, on which all can unite, which pulls us irresistibly toward it, as we understand each other more warmly.

To make real this striving amid dangers and apathies is work for a younger *intelligentsia* of America. Here is an enterprise of integration into which we can all pour ourselves, of a spiritual welding which should make us, if the final menace ever came, not weaker, but infinitely strong.

"Twilight of Idols"
(1917)

Where are the seeds of American promise? Man cannot live by politics alone, and it is small cheer that our best intellects are caught in the political current and see only the hope that America will find her soul in the remaking of the world. If William James were alive would he be accepting the war-situation so easily and complacently? Would he be chiding the over-stimulated intelligence of peace-loving idealists, and excommunicating from the ranks of liberal progress the pitiful remnant of those who struggle "above the battle?" I like to think that his gallant spirit would have called for a war to be gallantly played, with insistent care for democratic values at home, and unequivocal alliance with democratic elements abroad for a peace that should promise more than a mere union of benevolent imperialisms. I think of James now because the recent articles of John Dewey's on the war suggest a slackening in his thought for our guidance and stir, and the inadequacy of his pragmatism as a philosophy of life in this emergency. Whether James would have given us just that note of spiritual adventure which would make the national enterprise seem creative for an American future,—this; we can never know. But surely that philosophy of Dewey's which we had been following so uncritically for so long, breaks down almost noisily when it is used to grind out interpretation for the present crisis. These articles on "Conscience and Compulsion," "The Future of Pacifism," "What America Will Fight For," "Conscription of Thought," which *The New Republic* has been printing, seem to me to be a little off-color. A philosopher who senses so little the sinister forces of war, who is so much more concerned over the excesses of the pacifists than over the excesses of military policy, who can feel only amusement at the idea that any one should try to conscript thought, who assumes that the war-technique can be used without trailing along with it the mob-fanaticism, the injustices and hatreds, that are organically bound up with it, is speaking to another element of the younger intelligentsia than that to which I belong. Evidently the attitudes which war calls out are fiercer and more incalculable than Professor Dewey is accustomed to take into his hopeful and intelligent imagination, and the pragmatist mind, in trying to adjust itself to them, gives the air of grappling, like the pioneer who challenges the arid plains, with a power too big for it. It is not an arena of creative intelligence our country's mind is now, but of mob-psychology. The soldiers who tried to lynch Max Eastman showed that current patriotism is not a product of the will to remake the world. The luxuriant releases of explosive hatred for which peace apparently gives far too little scope cannot be wooed by sweet reasonableness, nor can they be the raw material for the creation of rare liberal political structures. All that can be done is to try to keep your country out of situations where such expressive releases occur. If you have willed the situation, however, or accepted it as inevitable, it is fatuous to protest against the gay debauch of hatred and fear and swagger that must mount and mount, until the heady and virulent poison of war shall have created its own anti-toxin of ruin and disillusionment. To talk as if war were anything else than such a poison is to show that your philosophy has

Source: Randolph Bourne, "Twilight of Idols," *The Seven Arts*, 11 (October 1917), 688–702.

never been confronted with the pathless and the inexorable, and that, only dimly feeling the change, it goes ahead acting as if it had not got out of its depth. Only a lack of practice with a world of human nature so raw-nerved, irrational, uncreative, as an America at war was bound to show itself to be, can account for the singular unsatisfactoriness of these latter utterances of Dewey. He did have one moment of hesitation just before the war began, when the war and its external purposes and unifying power seemed the small thing beside that internal adventure which should find our American promise. But that perspective has now disappeared, and one finds Dewey now untainted by skepticism as to our being about a business to which all our idealism should rally. That failure to get guaranties that this country's efforts would obligate the Allies to a democratic world-order Dewey blames on the defection of the pacifists, and then somehow manages to get himself into a "we" who "romantically," as he says, forewent this crucial link of our strategy. Does this easy identification of himself with undemocratically-controlled foreign policy mean that a country is democratic when it accepts what its government does, or that war has a narcotic effect on the pragmatic mind? For Dewey somehow retains his sense of being in the controlling class, and ignores those anxious questions of democrats who have been his disciples but are now resenters of the war.

What I come to is a sense of suddenly being left in the lurch, of suddenly finding that a philosophy upon which I had relied to carry us through no longer works. I find the contrast between the idea that creative intelligence has free functioning in wartime, and the facts of the inexorable situation, too glaring. The contrast between what liberals ought to be doing and saying if democratic values are to be conserved, and what the real forces are imposing upon them, strikes too sternly on my intellectual senses. I should prefer some philosophy of War as the grim and terrible cleanser to this optimism-haunted mood that continues unweariedly to suggest that all can yet be made to work for good in a mad and half-destroyed world. I wonder if James, in the face of such disaster, would not have abandoned his "moral equivalent of war" for an "immoral equivalent" which, in swift and periodic saturnalia, would have acted as vaccination against the sure pestilence of war.

Dewey's philosophy is inspiring enough for a society at peace, prosperous and with a fund of progressive good-will. It is a philosophy of hope, of clear-sighted comprehension of materials and means. Where institutions are at all malleable, it is the only clue for improvement. It is scientific method applied to "uplift." But this careful adaptation of means to desired ends, this experimental working out of control over brute forces and dead matter in the interests of communal life, depends on a store of rationality, and is effective only where there is strong desire for progress. It is precisely the school, the institution to which Dewey's philosophy was first applied, that is of all our institutions the most malleable. And it is the will to educate that has seemed, in these days, among all our social attitudes the most rationally motivated. It was education, and almost education alone, that seemed susceptible to the steady pressure of an "instrumental" philosophy. Intelligence really seemed about to come into conscious control of an institution, and that one the most potent in moulding the attitudes needed for a civilized society and the aptitudes needed for the happiness of the individual.

For both our revolutionary conceptions of what education means, and for the intellectual strategy of its approach, this country is immeasurably indebted to the influence of Professor Dewey's philosophy. With these ideas sincerely felt, a rational nation would have chosen education as its national enterprise. Into this it would have thrown its energy though the heavens fell and the earth rocked around it. But the nation did not use its isolation from the conflict to educate itself. It fretted for three years and then let war, not education, be chosen, at the almost unanimous behest of our intellectual class, from motives alien to our cultural needs, and for political ends alien to the happiness of the individual. But nations, of course, are not rational entities, and they act within their most irrational rights when they accept war as the most important thing the nation can do in the face of metaphysical menaces of imperial prestige. What concerns us here is the relative ease with which the pragmatist intellectuals, with Professor Dewey at the head, have moved out their philosophy, bag and baggage, from education to war. So abrupt a change in the direction of the national enterprise, one would have expected to cause more emotion, to demand more apologetics. His optimism may have told Professor Dewey that war would not materially demoralize our growth—would, perhaps, after all, be but an incident in the nation's life—but it is not easy to see how, as we skate toward the bankruptcy of war-billions, there will be resources available for educational enterprise that does not contribute directly to the war-technique. Neither is any passion for growth, for creative mastery, going to flourish among the host of militaristic values and new tastes for power that are springing up like poisonous mushrooms on every hand.

How could the pragmatist mind accept war without more violent protest, without a greater wrench? Either Professor Dewey and his friends felt that the forces were too strong for them, that the war had to be, and it was better to take it up intelligently than to drift blindly in; or else they really expected a gallant war, conducted with jealous regard for democratic values at home and a captivating vision of international democracy as the end of all the toil and pain. If their motive was the first, they would seem to have reduced the scope of possible control of events to the vanishing point. If the war is too strong for you to prevent, how is it going to be weak enough for you to control and mould to your liberal purposes? And if their motive was to shape the war firmly for good, they seem to have seriously miscalculated the fierce urgencies of it. Are they to be content, as the materialization of their hopes, with a doubtful League of Nations and the suppression of the I. W. W.? Yet the numbing power of the war-situation seems to have kept them from realizing what has happened to their philosophy. The betrayal of their first hopes has certainly not discouraged them. But neither has it roused them to a more energetic expression of the forces through which they intend to realize them. I search Professor Dewey's articles in vain for clues as to the specific working-out of our democratic desires, either nationally or internationally, either in the present or in the reconstruction after the war. No programme is suggested, nor is there feeling for present vague popular movements and revolts. Rather are the latter chided, for their own vagueness and impracticalities. Similarly, with the other prophets of instrumentalism who accompany Dewey into the war, democracy remains an unanalyzed term, useful as a call to battle, but not an intellectual tool, turning up fresh sod for the changing future. Is it the political democracy of a plutocratic America that we are fighting for, or is it the social democracy of the new Russia? Which do our rulers really fear more, the menace of Imperial Germany, or the liberating influence of a socialist Russia? In the application of their philosophy to politics, our pragmatists are sliding over this crucial question of ends. Dewey says our ends must be intelligently international rather than chauvinistic. But this gets us little distance along our way.

In this difficult time the light that has been in liberals and radicals has become darkness. If radicals spend their time holding conventions to attest their loyalty and stamp out the "enemies within," they do not spend it in breaking intellectual paths, or giving us shining ideas to which we can attach our faith and conscience. The spiritual apathy from which the more naive of us suffer, and which the others are so busy fighting, arises largely from sheer default of a clear vision that would melt it away. Let the motley crew of ex-socialists, and labor radicals, and liberals, and pragmatist philosophers, who have united for the prosecution of the war, present a coherent and convincing democratic programme, and they will no longer be confronted with the skepticism of the conscientious and the impossibilist. But when the emphasis is on technical organization, rather than organization of ideas, on strategy rather than desires, one begins to suspect that no programme is presented because they have none to present. This burrowing into war-technique hides the void where a democratic philosophy should be. Our intellectuals consort with war-boards in order to keep their minds off the question what the slow masses of the people are really desiring, or toward what the best hope of the country really drives. Similarly the blaze of patriotism on the part of the radicals serves the purpose of concealing the feebleness of their intellectual light.

Is the answer that clear formulation of democratic ends must be postponed until victory in the war is attained? But to make this answer is to surrender the entire case. For the support of the war by radicals, realists, pragmatists, is due —or so they say—to the fact that the war is not only saving the cause of democracy, but is immensely accelerating its progress. Well, what are those gains? How are they to be conserved? What do they lead to? How can we further them? Into what large idea of society do they group? To ignore these questions, and think only of the war-technique and its accompanying devotions, is to undermine the foundations of these people's own faith.

A policy of "win the war first" must be, for the radical, a policy of intellectual suicide. Their support of the war throws upon them the responsibility of showing inch by inch the democratic gains, and of laying out a charter of specific hopes. Otherwise they confess that they are impotent and that the war is submerging their expectations, or that they are not genuinely imaginative and offer little promise for future leadership.

It may seem unfair to group Professor Dewey with Mr. Spargo and Mr. Gompers, Mr. A. M. Simons, and the Vigilantes. I do so only because in their acceptance of the war, they are all living that popular American "instrumental" philosophy which Professor Dewey has formulated in such convincing and fascinating terms. On an infinitely more intelligent plane, he is yet one with them in his confidence that the war is motivated by democratic ends and is being made to serve them. A high mood of confidence and self-righteousness moves them all, a keen sense of control over events that makes them eligible to discipleship under Professor Dewey's philosophy. They are all hostile to impossibilism, to apathy, to any attitude that is not a cheerful and brisk setting to work to use the emergency to consolidate the gains of democracy. Not, Is it being used? but, Let us make a flutter about using it! This unanimity of mood puts the resenter of war out of the arena. But he can still seek to explain why this philosophy which has no place for the inexorable should have adjusted itself so easily to the inexorable of war, and why, although a philosophy of the creative intelligence in using means toward ends, it should show itself so singularly impoverished in its present supply of democratic values.

What is the matter with the philosophy? One has a sense of having come to a sudden, short stop at the end of an intellectual era. In the crisis, this philosophy of intelligent control just does not measure up to our needs. What is the root of this inadequacy that is felt so keenly by our restless minds? Van Wyck Brooks has pointed out searchingly the lack of poetic vision in our pragmatist "awakeners." Is there something in these realistic attitudes that works actually against poetic vision, against concern for the quality of life as above machinery of life? Apparently there is. The war has revealed a younger intelligentsia, trained up in the pragmatic dispensation, immensely ready for the executive ordering of events, pitifully unprepared for the intellectual interpretation or the idealistic focussing of ends. The young men in Belgium, the officers' training corps, the young men being sucked into the councils at Washington and into war-organization everywhere, have among them a definite element, upon whom Dewey, as veteran philosopher, might well bestow a papal blessing. They have absorbed the secret of scientific method as applied to political administration. They are liberal, enlightened, aware. They are touched with creative intelligence toward the solution of political and industrial problems. They are a wholly new force in American life, the product of the swing in the colleges from a training that emphasized classical studies to one that emphasized political and economic values. Practically all this element, one would say, is lined up in service of the war-technique. There seems to have been a peculiar congeniality between the war and these men. It is as if the war and they have been waiting for each other. One wonders what scope they would have had for their intelligence without it. Probably most of them would have gone into industry and devoted themselves to sane reorganization schemes. What is significant is that it is the technical side of the war that appeals to them, not the interpretative or political side. The formulation of values and ideals; the production of articulate and suggestive thinking, had not, in their education, kept pace, to any extent whatever, with their technical aptitude. The result is that the field of intellectual formulation is very poorly manned by this younger intelligentsia. While they organize the war, formulation of opinion is left largely in the hands of professional patriots, sensational editors, archaic radicals. The intellectual work of this younger intelligentsia is done by the sedition-hunting Vigilantes, and by the saving remnant of older liberals. It is true, Dewey calls for a more attentive formulation of war-purposes and ideas, but he calls largely to deaf ears. His disciples have learned all too literally the instrumental attitude toward life, and, being immensely intelligent and energetic, they are making themselves efficient instruments of the war-technique, accepting with little question the ends as announced from above. That those ends are largely negative does not concern them, because they have never learned not to subordinate idea to technique. Their education has not given them a coherent system of large ideas, or a feeling for democratic goals. They have, in short, no clear philosophy of life except that of intelligent service, the admirable adaptation of means to ends. They are vague as to what kind of a society they want, or what kind of society America needs, but they are equipped with all the administrative attitudes and talents necessary to attain it.

To those of us who have taken Dewey's philosophy almost as our American religion, it never occurred that values could be subordinated to technique. We were instrumentalists, but we had our private utopias so clearly before our minds that the means fell always into its place as contributory. And Dewey, of course, always meant his philosophy, when taken as a philosophy of life, to start with values. But there was always that unhappy ambiguity in his doctrine as to just how values were created, and it became easier and easier to assume that just any growth was justified and almost any activity valuable so long as it achieved ends. The American, in living out this philosophy, has habitually confused results with product, and been content with getting somewhere without asking too closely whether it was the desirable place to get. It is now becoming plain that unless you start with the vividest kind of poetic vision, your instrumentalism is likely to land you just where it has landed this younger intelligentsia which is so happily and busily engaged in the national enterprise of war. You must have your vision and you must have your technique. The practical effect of Dewey's philosophy has evidently been to develop the sense of the latter at the expense of the former. Though he himself would develop them together, even in him there seems to be a flagging of values, under the influence of war. *The New Republic* honorably clamors for the Allies to subordinate military strategy to political ends, technique to democratic values. But war always undermines values. It is the outstanding lesson of the whole war that statesmen cannot be trusted to get this perspective right, that their only motto is, first to win and then grab what they can. The struggle against this statesman-like animus must be a losing one as long as we have not very clear and very determined and very revolutionary democratic ideas and programmes to challenge them with. The trouble with our situation is not only that values have been generally ignored in favor of technique, but that those who have struggled to keep values foremost, have been too bloodless and too nearsighted in their vision. The defect of any philosophy of "adaptation" or "adjustment," even when it means adjustment to changing, living experience, is that there is no provision for thought or experience getting beyond itself. If your ideal is to be adjustment to your situation, in radiant co-operation with reality, then your success is likely to be just that and no more. You never transcend anything. You grow, but your spirit never jumps out of your skin to go on wild adventures. If your policy as a publicist reformer is to take what you can get, you are likely to find that you get something less than you should be willing to take. Italy in the settlement is said to be demanding one hundred in order to get twenty, and this machiavellian principle might well be adopted by the radical. Vision must constantly outshoot technique, opportunist efforts usually achieve less even than what seemed obviously possible. An impossibilist élan that appeals to desire will often carry further. A philosophy of adjustment will not even make for adjustment. If you try merely to "meet" situations as they come, you will not even meet them. Instead you will only pile up behind you deficits and arrears that will some day bankrupt you.

We are in the war because an American Government practised a philosophy of adjustment, and an instrumentalism for minor ends, instead of creating new values and setting at once a large standard to which the nations might repair. An intellectual attitude of mere adjustment, of mere use of the creative intelligence to make your progress, must end in caution, regression, and a virtual failure to effect even that change which you so clear-sightedly and desirously see. This is the root of our dissatisfaction with much of the current political and social realism that is preached to us. It has everything good and wise except the obstreperous vision that would drive and draw all men into it.

The working-out of this American philosophy in our intellectual life then has meant an exaggerated emphasis on the mechanics of life at the expense of the quality of living. We suffer from a real shortage of spiritual values. A philosophy that worked when we were trying to get that material foundation for American life in which more impassioned living could flourish no longer works when we are faced with inexorable disaster and the hysterias of the mob. The note of complacency which we detect in the current expressions of this philosophy has a bad taste. The congruous note for the situation would seem to be, on the contrary, that of robust desperation,—a desperation that shall rage and struggle until new values come out of the travail, and we see some glimmering of our democratic way. In the creation of these new values, we may expect the old philosophy, the old radicalism, to be helpless. It has found a perfectly definite level, and there is no reason to think that it will not remain there. Its flowering appears in the technical organization of the war by an earnest group of young liberals, who direct their course by an opportunist programme of State-socialism at home and a league of benevolently-imperialistic nations abroad. At their best they can give us a government by prudent, enlightened college men instead of by politicians. At their best, they can abolish war by making everybody a partner in the booty of exploitation. That is all, and it is technically admirable. Only there is nothing in the outlook that touches in any way the happiness of the individual, the vivifying of the personality, the comprehension of social forces, the flair of art,—in other words, the quality of life. Our intellectuals have failed us as value-creators, even as value-emphasizers. The allure of the martial in war has passed only to be succeeded by the allure of the technical. The allure of fresh and true ideas, of free speculation, of artistic vigor, of cultural styles, of intelligence suffused by feeling, and feeling given fibre and outline by intelligence, has not come, and can hardly come, we see now, while our reigning philosophy is an instrumental one.

Whence can come this allure? Only from those who are thorough malcontents. Irritation at things as they are, disgust at the continual frustrations and aridities of American life, deep dissatisfaction with self and with the groups that give themselves forth as hopeful—out of such moods there might be hammered new values. The malcontents would be men and women who could not stomach the war, or the reactionary idealism that has followed in its train. They are quite through with the professional critics and classicists who have let cultural values die through their own personal ineptitude. Yet these malcontents have no intention of being cultural vandals, only to slay. They are not barbarians, but seek the vital and the sincere everywhere. All they want is a new orientation of the spirit that shall be modern, an orientation to accompany that technical orientation which is fast coming, and which the war accelerates. They will be harsh and often bad-tempered, and they will feel that the break-up of things is no time for mellowness. They will have a taste for spiritual adventure, and for sinister imaginative excursions. It will not be Puritanism so much as complacency that they will fight. A tang, a bitterness, an intellectual fibre, a verve, they will look for in literature, and their most virulent enemies will be those unaccountable radicals who are still morally servile, and are now trying to suppress all free speculation in the interests of nationalism. Something more mocking, more irreverent, they will constantly want. They will take institutions very lightly, indeed will never fail to be surprised at the seriousness with which good radicals take the stated offices and systems. Their own contempt will be scarcely veiled, and they will be glad if they can tease, provoke, irritate thought on any subject. These malcontents will be more or less of the American tribe of talent who used either to go immediately to Europe, or starved submissively at home. But these people will neither go to Europe, nor starve submissively. They are too much entangled emotionally in the possibilities of American life to leave it, and they have no desire whatever to starve. So they are likely to go ahead beating their heads at the wall until they are either bloody or light appears. They will give offense to their elders who cannot see what all the concern is about, and they will hurt the more middle-aged sense of adventure upon which the better integrated minds of the younger generation will have compromised. Optimism is often compensatory, and the optimistic mood in American thought may mean merely that American life is too terrible to face. A more skeptical, malicious, desperate, ironical mood may actually be the sign of more vivid and more stirring life fermenting in America today. It may be a sign of hope. That thirst for more of the intellectual "war and laughter" that we find Nietzsche calling us to may bring us satisfactions that optimism-haunted philosophies could never bring. Malcontentedness may be the beginning of the promise. That is why I evoked the spirit of William James, with its gay passion for ideas, and its freedom of speculation, when I felt the slightly pedestrian gait into which the war had brought pragmatism. It is the creative desire more than the creative intelligence that we shall need if we are ever to fly.

H. L. MENCKEN

"Puritanism as a Literary Force"
(1917)

Irascible, iconoclastic, playful, brooding, H. L. Mencken (1880–1956) was one of the greatest journalists in the history of the United States, and one of the most widely quoted critics of American civilization. Mencken enjoyed lambasting "the Booboisie," as he characterized the American middle class. Mencken's name became an emblem for the 1920s revolt against Victorianism, which Mencken associated with the older heritage of Puritanism. It was during the 1920s that Mencken achieved his greatest popularity, especially as a newspaper columnist and as a regular essayist for *American Mercury*. The selection reprinted here dates from 1917, but in this, his most famous attack on the prevailing literary culture of the United States, Mencken displayed most vividly the style and the themes that were to mark his work for the next thirty years.

Most of "Puritanism as a Literary Force" interprets American literature in relation to the New England Puritans of old, but toward the end of this essay, Mencken turns to what he calls the "new" Puritanism of his own time. Here, what he is most concerned to criticize is the use of state power to regulate private life, including the publication and circulation of what some called "immoral" literature. His references to "Comstock" are to Anthony Comstock, Victorian America's most famous and energetic advocate of censorship. The Leon Kellner to whom Mencken refers was the author of a book on American literature that provided the immediate stimulus for this essay of Mencken's.

Mencken was also an energetic amateur scholar, whose *The American Language* (New York, 1919) was his most respected and enduring inquiry into the cultural life of the United States. Mencken revised this study of the development of English in America through many editions and a number of supplements, bearing witness to his extraordinary fascination with both language and America, until a stroke diminished his capabilities in 1948.

Mencken has inspired dozens of biographical and critical studies; one lively and informative account is William Manchester, *Disturber of the Peace: The Life of H. L. Mencken*, 2nd ed. (Amherst, Mass., 1986). Another biography is Fred C. Hobson, *H. L. Mencken: A Life* (New York, 1993). Yet another is Marion Elizabeth Rodgers, *Mencken: The American Iconoclast* (New York, 2005).

"Calvinism," says Dr. Leon Kellner, in his excellent little history of American literature, "is the natural theology of the disinherited; it never flourished, therefore, anywhere as it did in the barren hills of Scotland and in the wilds of North America." The learned doctor is here speaking of theology in what may be called its narrow technical sense—that is, as a theory of God. Under Calvinism, in the New World as well as in the Old, it became no more than a luxuriant demonology; even God himself was transformed into a superior sort of devil, ever wary and wholly merciless. That primitive demonology still survives in the barbaric doctrines of the Methodists and Baptists, particularly in the South; but it has been ameliorated, even there, by a growing sense of the divine grace, and so the old God of Plymouth Rock, as practically conceived, is now scarcely worse than the average jail warden or Italian padrone. On the ethical side, however, Calvinism is dying a much harder death, and we are still a long way from the enlightenment. Save where Continental influences have measurably corrupted the Puritan idea—e.g., in such cities as New York, St. Louis and New Orleans, the prevailing American view of the world and its mysteries is still a purely moral one, and no other human concern gets half the attention that is endlessly lavished upon the problem of conduct, particularly of the other fellow. It needed no announcement of a President of the United States to define the republic's destiny as that of an international expert in morals, and the mentor and exemplar of the less righteous nations. Within, as well as without, the eternal rapping of knuckles and proclaiming of new austerities goes on. The American, save in moments of conscious and swiftly lamented deviltry, casts up all ponderable values, including even the values of beauty, in terms of right and wrong. He is beyond all things else, a judge and a policeman; he believes firmly that there is a mysterious power in law; he supports and embellishes its operation with a fanatical vigilance.

Naturally enough, this moral obsession has given a strong colour to American literature. In truth, it has coloured it so brilliantly that American literature is set off sharply from all other literatures. In none other will you find so wholesale and ecstatic a sacrifice of aesthetic ideas, of all the fine gusto of passion and beauty, to notions of what is meet, proper and nice. From the books of grisly sermons that were the first American contribution to letters down to that amazing literature of "inspiration" which now flowers so prodigiously, with two literary Presidents among its chief virtuosi, one observes no relaxation of the moral pressure. In the history of every other literature there have been periods of what might be called moral innocence—periods in which a naif joie de vivre has broken through all concepts of duty and responsibility, and the wonder and glory of the universe have been hymned with unashamed zest. The age of Shakespeare comes to mind at once: the violence of the Puritan reaction offers a measure of the pendulum's wild swing. But in America no such general rising of the blood has ever been seen. The literature of the nation, even the literature of the enlightened minority, has been under harsh Puritan restraints from the beginning, and despite a few stealthy efforts at revolt—usually quite without artistic value or even common honesty, as in the case of the cheap fiction magazines and that of smutty plays on Broadway, and always very shortlived—it shows not the slightest sign of emancipating itself today. The American, try as he will, can never imagine any work of the imagination as wholly devoid of moral content. It must either tend toward the promotion of virtue, or be suspect and abominable.

Source: H. L. Mencken, *A Book of Prefaces* (New York, 1917), 197–202, 209–19, 231–42.

If any doubt of this is in your mind, turn to the critical articles in the newspapers and literary weeklies; you will encounter enough proofs in a month's explorations to convince you forever. A novel or a play is judged among us, not by its dignity of conception, its artistic honesty, its perfection of workmanship, but almost entirely by its orthodoxy of doctrine, its platitudinousness, its usefulness as a moral tract. A digest of the reviews of such a book as David Graham Phillips' "Susan Lenox" or of such a play as Ibsen's "Hedda Gabler" would make astounding reading for a Continental European. Not only the childish incompetents who write for the daily press, but also most of our critics of experience and reputation, seem quite unable to estimate a piece of writing as a piece of writing, a work of art as a work of art; they almost inevitably drag in irrelevant gabble as to whether this or that personage in it is respectable, or this or that situation in accordance with the national notions of what is edifying and nice. Fully nine-tenths of the reviews of Dreiser's "The Titan," without question the best American novel of its year, were devoted chiefly to indigent denunciations of the morals of Frank Cowperwood, its central character. That the man was superbly imagined and magnificently depicted, that he stood out from the book in all the flashing vigour of life, that his creation was an artistic achievement of a very high and difficult order—these facts seem to have made no impression upon the reviewers whatever. They were Puritans writing for Puritans, and all they could see in Cowperwood was an anti-Puritan, and in his creator another. It will remain for Europeans, I daresay, to discover the true stature of "The Titan," as it remained for Europeans to discover the true stature of "Sister Carrie."

Just how deeply this corrective knife has cut you may find plainly displayed in Dr. Kellner's little book. He sees the throttling influence of an ever alert and bellicose Puritanism, not only in our grand literature, but also in our petit literature, our minor poetry, even in our humour. The Puritan's utter lack of aesthetic sense, his distrust of all romantic emotion, his unmatchable intolerance of opposition, his unbreakable belief in his own bleak and narrow views, his savage cruelty of attack, his lust for relentless and barbarous persecution—these things have put an almost unbearable burden upon the exchange of ideas in the United States, and particularly upon that form of it which involves playing with them for the mere game's sake....

This Puritan bedevilment by the idea of personal sin, this reign of the God-crazy, gave way in later years, as we shall see, to other and somewhat milder forms of pious enthusiasm. At the time of the Revolution, indeed, the importation of French political ideas was accompanied by an importation of French theological ideas, and such men as Franklin and Jefferson dallied with what, in those days at least, was regarded as downright atheism. Even in New England this influence made itself felt; there was a gradual letting down of Calvinism to the softness of Unitarianism, and that change was presently to flower in the vague temporizing of Transcendentalism. But as Puritanism, in the strict sense, declined in virulence and took deceptive new forms, there was a compensating growth of its brother, Philistinism, and by the first quarter of the nineteenth century, the distrust of beauty, and of the joy that is its object, was as firmly established throughout the land as it had ever been in New England. The original Puritans had at least been men of a certain education, and even of a certain austere culture. They were inordinately hostile to beauty in all its forms, but one somehow suspects that much of their hostility was due to a sense of their weakness before it, a realization of its disarming psychical pull. But the American of the new republic was of a different kidney. He was not so much hostile to beauty as devoid of any consciousness of it; he stood as unmoved before its phenomena as a savage before a table of logarithms. What he had set up on this continent, in brief, was a commonwealth of peasants and small traders, a paradise of the third rate, and its national philosophy, almost wholly unchecked by the more sophisticated and civilized ideas of an aristocracy, was precisely the philosophy that one finds among peasants and small traders at all times and everywhere. The difference between the United States and any other nation did not lie in any essential difference between American peasants and other peasants, but simply in the fact that here, alone, the voice of the peasant was the single voice of the nation—that here, alone, the only way to eminence and public influence was the way of acquiescence in the opinions and prejudices of the stupid and Philistine mob. Jackson was the *Stammvater* of the new statesmen and philosophers; he carried the mob's distrust of good taste even into the field of conduct; he was the first to put the rewards of conformity above the dictates of common decency; he founded a whole hierarchy of Philistine messiahs, the roaring of which still belabours the ear.

Once established, this culture of the intellectually disinherited tended to defend and perpetuate itself. On the one hand, there was no appearance of a challenge from within, for the exigeant problems of existence in a country that was yet but half settled and organized left its people with no energy for questioning what at least met their grosser needs, and so met the pragmatic test. And on the other hand, there was no critical pressure from with-out, for the English culture which alone reached over the sea was itself entering upon its Victorian decline, and the influence of the native aristocracy—the degenerating *Junkers* of the great estates and the boorish magnates of the city bourgeoisie—was quite without any cultural direction at all. The chief concern of the American people, even above the bread-and-butter question, was politics. They were incessantly hag-ridden by political difficul-ties, both internal and external, of an inordinate complexity, and these occupied all the leisure they could steal from the sordid work of everyday. More, their new and troubled political ideas tended to absorb all the rancorous certainty of their fading religious ideas, so that devotion to a theory or a candidate became translated into devotion to a revelation, and the game of politics turned itself into a holy war. The custom of connecting purely political doctrines with pietistic concepts of an inflammable nature, then firmly set up by skilful persuaders of the mob, has never quite died out in the United States. There has not been a presidential contest since Jackson's day without its Armageddons, its marching of Christian soldiers, its crosses of gold, its crowns of thorns. The most successful American politicians, beginning with the anti-slavery agitators, have been those most adept at twist-ing the ancient gauds and shibboleths of Puritanism to partisan uses. Every campaign that we have seen for eighty years has been, on each side, a pursuit of bugaboos, a denunciation of heresies, a snouting up of immoralities.

But it was during the long contest against slavery, beginning with the appearance of William Lloyd Garrison's *Liberator* in 1831 and ending at Appomattox, that this gigantic supernaturalization of politics reached its most astounding heights. In those days, indeed, politics and religion coalesced in a manner not seen in the world since the Middle Ages, and the combined pull of the two was so powerful that none could quite resist it. All men of any ability and ambition turned to political activity for self-expression. It engaged the press to the exclusion of everything else; it conquered the pulpit; it even laid its hand upon industry and trade. Drawing the best imaginative talent into its service—Jefferson and Lincoln may well stand as examples—it left the cultivation of belles lettres, and of all the other arts no less, to women and admittedly second-rate men. And when, break-ing through this taboo, some chance first-rate man gave himself over to purely aesthetic expression, his reward was not only neglect, but even a sort of ignominy, as if such enter-prises were not fitting for males with hair on their chests. I need not point to Poe and

Whitman, both disdained as dreamers and wasters, and both proceeded against with the utmost rigours of outraged Philistinism.

In brief, the literature of that whole period, as Algernon Tassin shows in "The Magazine in America," was almost completely disassociated from life as men were then living it. Save one counts in such crude politico-puritan tracts as "Uncle Tom's Cabin," it is difficult to find a single contemporaneous work that interprets the culture of the time, or even accurately represents it. Later on, it found historians and anatomists, and in one work, at least, to wit, "Huckleberry Finn," it was studied and projected with the highest art, but no such impulse to make imaginative use of it showed itself contemporaneously, and there was not even the crude sentimentalization of here and now that one finds in the popular novels of today. Fenimore Cooper filled his romances, not with the people about him, but with the Indians beyond the sky-line, and made them half-fabulous to boot. Irving told fairy tales about the forgotten Knickerbockers; Hawthorne turned backward to the Puritans of Plymouth Rock; Longfellow to the Acadians and the prehistoric Indians; Emerson took flight from earth altogether; even Poe sought refuge in a land of fantasy. It was only the frank second-raters— e.g., Whittier and Lowell—who ventured to turn to the life around them, and the banality of the result is a sufficient indication of the crudeness of the current taste, and the mean position assigned to the art of letters. This was pre-eminently the era of the moral tale, the Sunday-school book. Literature was conceived, not as a thing in itself, but merely as a hand-maiden to politics or religion. The great celebrity of Emerson in New England was not the celebrity of a literary artist, but that of a theologian and metaphysician; he was esteemed in much the same way that Jonathan Edwards had been esteemed. Even down to our own time, indeed, his vague and empty philosophizing has been put above his undeniable capacity for graceful utterance, and it remained for Dr. Kellner to consider him purely as a literary artist, and to give him due praise for his skill.

The Civil War brought that era of sterility to an end. As I shall show later on, the shock of it completely reorganized the American scheme of things, and even made certain important changes in the national Puritanism, or, at all events, in its machinery. Whitman, whose career straddled, so to speak, the four years of the war, was the leader—and for a long while, the only trooper—of a double revolt. On the one hand he offered a courageous challenge to the intolerable prudishness and dirty-mindedness of Puritanism, and on the other hand he boldly sought the themes and even the modes of expression of his poetry in the arduous, contentious and highly melodramatic life that lay all about him. Whitman, however, was clearly before his time. His countrymen could see him only as immoralist; save for a pitiful few of them, they were dead to any understanding of his stature as artist, and even unaware that such a category of men existed. He was put down as an invader of the public decencies, a disturber of the public peace; even his eloquent war poems, surely the best of all his work, were insufficient to get him a hearing; the sentimental rubbish of "The Blue and the Gray" and the ecstatic super-naturalism of "The Battle Hymn of the Republic" were far more to the public taste. Where Whitman failed, indeed, all subsequent explorers of the same field have failed with him, and the great war has left no more mark upon American letters than if it had never been fought. Nothing remotely approaching the bulk and beam of Tolstoi's "War and Peace," or, to descend to a smaller scale, Zola's "The Attack on the Mill," has come out of it. Its appeal to the national imagination was undoubtedly of the most profound character; it coloured politics for fifty years, and is today a dominating influence in the thought of whole sections of the American people. But in all that stirring up there was no upheaval of artistic consciousness, for the plain reason that there was no artistic consciousness there to heave up, and all we have in the way of Civil War literature is a few conventional melodramas, a few half-forgotten short stories by Ambrose Bierce and Stephen Crane, and a half dozen idiotic popular songs in the manner of Randall's "Maryland, My Maryland."

In the seventies and eighties, with the appearance of such men as Henry James, William Dean Howells, Mark Twain and Bret Harte, a better day seemed to be dawning. Here, after a full century of infantile romanticizing, were four writers who at least deserved respectful consideration as literary artists, and what is more, three of them turned from the conventionalized themes of the past to the teeming and colourful life that lay under their noses. But this promise of better things was soon found to be no more than a promise. Mark Twain, after "The Gilded Age," slipped back into romanticism tempered by Philistinism, and was presently in the era before the Civil War, and finally in the Middle Ages, and even beyond. Harte, a brilliant technician, had displayed his whole stock when he had displayed his technique: his stories were not even superficially true to the life they presumed to depict; one searched them in vain for an interpretation of it; they were simply idle tales. As for Howells and James, both quickly showed that timorousness and reticence which are the distinguishing marks of the Puritan, even in his most intellectual incarnations. The American scene that they depicted with such meticulous care was chiefly peopled with marionettes. They shrunk, characteristically, from those larger, harsher clashes of will and purpose which one finds in all truly first-rate literature. In particular, they shrunk from any interpretation of life which grounded itself upon an acknowledgment of its inexorable and inexplicable tragedy. In the vast combat of instincts and aspirations about them they saw only a feeble jousting of comedians, unserious and insignificant. Of the great questions that have agitated the minds of men in Howells' time one gets no more than a faint and far-away echo in his novels. His investigations, one may say, are carried on *in vacuo;* his discoveries are not expressed in terms of passion, but in terms of giggles.

In the followers of Howells and James one finds little save an empty imitation of their emptiness, a somewhat puerile parodying of their highly artful but essentially personal technique. To wade through the books of such characteristic American fictioneers as Frances Hodgson Burnett, Mary E. Wilkins Freeman, F. Hopkinson Smith, Alice Brown, James Lane Allen, Winston Churchill, Ellen Glasgow, Gertrude Atherton and Sarah Orne Jewett is to undergo an experience that is almost terrible. The flow of words is completely purged of ideas; in place of them one finds no more than a romantic restatement of all the old platitudes and formulae. To call such an emission of graceful poppycock a literature, of course, is to mouth an absurdity, and yet, if the college professors who write treatises on letters are to be believed, it is the best we have to show....

The distinguishing mark of the elder Puritanism, at least after it had attained to the stature of a national philosophy, was its appeal to the individual conscience, its exclusive concern with the elect, its strong flavour of self-accusing. Even the rage against slavery was, in large measure, an emotion of the mourners' bench. The thing that worried the more ecstatic Abolitionists was their sneaking sense of responsibility, the fear that they themselves were flouting the fire by letting slavery go on. The thirst to punish the concrete slave-owner, as an end in itself, did not appear until opposition had added exasperation to fervour. In most of the earlier harangues against his practice, indeed, you will find a perfect willingness to grant that slave-owner's good faith, and even to compensate him for his property. But the new Puritanism—or, perhaps more accurately, considering the shades of prefixes, the neo-Puritanism—is a frank harking back to the primitive spirit. The original Puritan of the bleak New England coast was not content to flay his own wayward carcass:

full satisfaction did not sit upon him until he had jailed a Quaker. That is to say, the sinner who excited his highest zeal and passion was not so much himself as his neighbour; to borrow a term from psychopathology, he was less the masochist than the sadist. And it is that very peculiarity which sets off his descendant of today from the ameliorated Puritan of the era between the Revolution and the Civil War. The new Puritanism is not ascetic, but militant. Its aim is not to lift up saints but to knock down sinners. Its supreme manifestation is the vice-crusade, an armed pursuit of helpless outcasts by the whole military and naval forces of the Republic. Its supreme hero is Comstock Himself, with his pious boast that the sinners he jailed during his astounding career, if gathered into one penitential party, would have filled a train of sixty-one coaches, allowing sixty to the coach....

In brief, Puritanism has become bellicose and tyrannical by becoming rich. The will to power has been aroused to a high flame by an increase in the available draught and fuel, as militarism is engendered and nourished by the presence of men and materials. Wealth, discovering its power, has reached out its long arms to grab the distant and innumerable sinner; it has gone down into its deep pockets to pay for his costly pursuit and flaying; it has created the Puritan entrepreneur, the daring and imaginative organizer of Puritanism, the baron of moral endeavour, the invincible prophet of new austerities. And, by the same token, it has issued its letters of marque to the Puritan mercenary, the professional hound of heaven, the moral *Junker*, the Comstock, and out of his skill at his trade there has arisen the whole machinery, so complicated and so effective, of the new Holy Office.

Poverty is a soft pedal upon all branches of human activity, not excepting the spiritual, and even the original Puritans, for all their fire, felt its throttling caress....

Poverty, of course, is no discredit, but at all events, it is a subtle criticism. The man oppressed by material wants is not in the best of moods for the more ambitious forms of moral adventure. He not only lacks the means; he is also deficient in the self-assurance, the sense of superiority, the secure and lofty point of departure. If he is haunted by notions of the sinfulness of his neighbours, he is apt to see some of its worst manifestations within himself, and that disquieting discovery will tend to take his thoughts from the other fellow. It is by no arbitrary fiat, indeed, that the brothers of all the expiatory orders are vowed to poverty. History teaches us that wealth, whenever it has come to them by chance, has put an end to their soul-searching. The Puritans of the elder generations, with few exceptions, were poor. Nearly all Americans, down to the Civil War, were poor. And being poor, they subscribed to a *Sklavmoral*. That is to say, they were spiritually humble. Their eyes were fixed, not upon the abyss below them, but upon the long and rocky road ahead of them. Their moral passion spent most of its force in self-accusing, self-denial and self-scourging. They began by howling their sins from the mourners' bench; they came to their end, many of them, in the supreme immolation of battle.

But out of the War came prosperity, and out of prosperity came a new morality, to wit, the *Herrenmoral*. Many great fortunes were made in the War itself; an uncountable number got started during the two decades following. What is more, this material prosperity was generally dispersed through all classes: it affected the common workman and the remote farmer quite as much as the actual merchant and manufacturer. Its first effect, as we all know, was a universal cockiness, a rise in pretensions, a comforting feeling that the Republic was a success, and with it, its every citizen. This change made itself quickly obvious, and even odious, in all the secular relations of life. The American became a sort of braggart playboy of the western world, enormously sure of himself and ludicrously contemptuous of all other men. And on the ghostly side there appeared the same accession of confidence, the same sure assumption of authority, though at first less self-evidently and offensively. The religion of the American thus began to lose its inward direction; it became less and less a scheme of personal salvation and more and more a scheme of pious derring-do. The revivals of the 70's had all the bounce and fervour of those of half a century before, but the mourners' bench began to lose its standing as their symbol, and in its place appeared the collection basket. Instead of accusing himself, the convert volunteered to track down and bring in the other fellow. His enthusiasm was not for repentance, but for what he began to call service. In brief, the national sense of energy and fitness gradually superimposed itself upon the national Puritanism, and from that marriage sprung a keen *Wille zur Macht*, a lusty will to power. The American Puritan, by now, was not content with the rescue of his own soul; he felt an irresistible impulse to hand salvation on, to disperse and multiply it, to ram it down reluctant throats, to make it free, universal and compulsory. He had the men, he had the guns and he had the money too. All that was needed was organization. The rescue of the unsaved could be converted into a wholesale business, unsentimentally and economically conducted, and with all the usual aids to efficiency, from skilful sales management to seductive advertising, and from rigorous accounting to the diligent shutting off of competition.

Out of that new will to power came many enterprises more or less futile and harmless, with the "institutional" church at their head. Piety was cunningly disguised as basketball, billiards and squash; the sinner was lured to grace with Turkish baths, lectures on foreign travel, and free instructions in stenography, rhetoric and double-entry book-keeping. Religion lost all its old contemplative and esoteric character, and became a frankly worldly enterprise, a thing of balance-sheets and ponderable profits, heavily capitalized and astutely manned. There was no longer any room for the spiritual type of leader, with his white choker and his interminable fourthlies. He was displaced by a brisk gentleman in a "business suit" who looked, talked and thought like a seller of Mexican mine stock. Scheme after scheme for the swift evangelization of the nation was launched, some of them of truly astonishing sweep and daring. They kept pace, step by step, with the mushroom growth of enterprise in the commercial field. The Y. M. C. A. swelled to the proportions of a Standard Oil Company, a United States Steel Corporation. Its huge buildings began to rise in every city; it developed a swarm of specialists in new and fantastic moral and social sciences; it enlisted the same gargantuan talent which managed the railroads, the big banks and the larger national industries. And beside it rose the Young People's Society of Christian Endeavour, the Sunday-school associations and a score of other such grandiose organizations, each with its seductive baits for recruits and money. Even the enterprises that had come down from an elder and less expansive day were pumped up and put on a Wall Street basis: the American Bible Society, for example, began to give away Bibles by the million instead of by the thousand, and the venerable Tract Society took on the feverish ardour of a daily newspaper, even of a yellow journal. Down into our own day this trustification of pious endeavour has gone on. The Men and Religion Forward Movement proposed to convert the whole country by 12 o'clock noon of such and such a day; the Order of Gideons plans to make every traveller read the Bible (American Revised Version!) whether he will or not; in a score of cities there are committees of opulent devotees who take half-pages in the newspapers, and advertise the Decalogue and the Beatitudes as if they were commodities of trade.

Thus the national energy which created the Beef Trust and the Oil Trust achieved equal marvels in the field of religious organization and by exactly the same methods. One needs be no psychologist to perceive in all this a good deal less actual religious zeal than mere lust for staggering accomplishment, for empty bigness, for the unprecedented and the prodigious. Many of these great religious enterprises, indeed, soon lost all save the faintest flavour of devotion—for example, the Y. M. C. A., which is now no more than a sort of national club system, with its doors open to any one not palpably felonious. (I have drunk cocktails in Y. M. C. A. lamaseries, and helped fallen lamas to bed.) But while the war upon godlessness thus degenerated into a secular sport in one direction, it maintained all its pristine quality, and even took on a new ferocity in another direction. Here it was that the lamp of American Puritanism kept on burning; here, it was, indeed, that the lamp became converted into a huge bonfire, or rather a blast-furnace, with flames mounting to the very heavens, and sinners stacked like cordwood at the hand of an eager black gang. In brief, the new will to power, working in the true Puritan as in the mere religious sportsman, stimulated him to a campaign of repression and punishment perhaps unequalled in the history of the world, and developed an art of militant morality as complex in technique and as rich in professors as the elder art of iniquity.

If we take the passage of the Comstock Postal Act, on March 3, 1873, as a starting point, the legislative stakes of this new Puritan movement sweep upward in a grand curve to the passage of the Mann and Webb Acts, in 1910 and 1913, the first of which ratifies the Seventh Commandment with a salvo of artillery, and the second of which puts the overwhelming power of the Federal Government behind the enforcement of the prohibition laws in the so-called "dry" States. The mind at once recalls the salient campaigns of this war of a generation: first the attack upon "vicious" literature, begun by Comstock and the New York Society for the Suppression of Vice, but quickly extending to every city in the land; then the long fight upon the open gambling house, culminating in its practical disappearance; then the recrudescence of prohibition, abandoned at the outbreak of the Civil War, and the attempt to enforce it in a rapidly growing list of States; then the successful onslaught upon the Louisiana lottery, and upon its swarm of rivals and successors; then the gradual stamping-out of horse-racing, until finally but two or three States permitted it, and the consequent attack upon the pool-room; then the rise of a theatre-censorship in most of the large cities, and of a moving picture censorship following it; then the revival of Sabbatarianism, with the Lord's Day Alliance, a Canadian invention, in the van; then the gradual tightening of the laws against sexual irregularity, with the unenforceable New York Adultery Act as a typical product; and lastly, the general ploughing up and emotional discussion of sexual matters, with compulsory instruction in "sex hygiene" as its mildest manifestation and the medieval fury of the vice crusade as its worst. Differing widely in their targets, these various Puritan enterprises had one character in common: they were all efforts to combat immorality with the weapons designed for crime. In each of them there was a visible effort to erect the individual's offence against himself into an offence against society. Beneath all of them there was the dubious principle—the very determining principle, indeed, of Puritanism—that it is competent for the community to limit and condition the private acts of its members, and with it the inevitable corollary that there are some members of the community who have a special talent for such legislation, and that their arbitrary fiats are, and of a right ought to be, binding upon all....

OLIVER WENDELL HOLMES, JR.

"Natural Law"
(1918)

Oliver Wendell Holmes, Jr., (1841–1935) did more than any other American thinker to develop and popularize the insight that law is a living, changing part of culture, responsive to the shifting circumstances with which societies must cope. He argued along these lines as early as 1881, when he published his greatest work, *The Common Law,* but Holmes achieved broader influence during the Progressive Era and the 1920s while serving as a justice of the U.S. Supreme Court. Although Holmes was aloof from the reform movements of this era, his refusal to defend the vested interests of his upper-class milieu endeared him to younger, liberal intellectuals, who tended to exaggerate his "progressive" tendencies.

Holmes inspired many "legal realists" of the 1930s and was appreciated even by some of the "critical legal studies" scholars of the 1980s. For introductions to these movements, see Laura Kalman, *Legal Realism at Yale, 1927–1960* (Chapel Hill, 1986); and Roberto Unger, *The Critical Legal Studies Movement* (Cambridge, Mass., 1986). Holmes's most important theoretical essays, "Privilege, Malice, and Intent" (1894) and "The Path of the Law" (1896), are available in Holmes's *Collected Legal Papers* (Boston, 1920), from which is reprinted here the essay of 1918, "Natural Law." This brief piece expresses the historicist bent of Holmes's jurisprudence and displays the aphoristic style in which he often dealt with theoretical issues.

The most important study of Holmes's legal philosophy is Thomas C. Grey, "Holmes and Legal Pragmatism," *Stanford Law Review,* 41 (1989), 787–870, although Grey is more concerned with extracting from Holmes the rudiments of a legal pragmatism suitable to our own time than he is clarifying Holmes's relationship with James, Dewey, and other pragmatists of Holmes's own generation. An earlier study that emphasizes Holmes's aristocratic biases, his distance from the more democratic Dewey, and his unwillingness to make commitments is Yosal Rogat, "The Judge as Spectator," *University of Chicago Law Review,* 31 (1964), 213–56. The most reliable and comprehensive of the many biographies is G. Edward White, *Justice Oliver Wendell Holmes: Law and the Inner Self* (New York, 1994). A sound starting point for the study of Holmes is the collection of essays edited by Robert W. Gordon, *The Legacy of Oliver Wendell Holmes, Jr.* (Stanford, 1992). An engaging interpretation of Holmes's life and thought focused on the impact of the Civil War on Holmes is found within Louis Menand, *The Metaphysical Club* (New York, 2001). See also the classic account of Holmes's relation to the Civil War, Edmund Wilson, *Patriotic Gore* (New York, 1962), 743–96.

It is not enough for the knight of romance that you agree that his lady is a very nice girl—if you do not admit that she is the best that God ever made or will make, you must fight. There is in all men a demand for the superlative, so much so that the poor devil who has no other way of reaching it attains it by getting drunk. It seems to me that this demand is at the bottom of the philosopher's effort to prove that truth is absolute and of the jurist's search for criteria of universal validity which he collects under the head of natural law.

I used to say, when I was young, that truth was the majority vote of that nation that could lick all others. Certainly we may expect that the received opinion about the present war will depend a good deal upon which side wins (I hope with all my soul it will be mine), and I think that the statement was correct in so far as it implied that our test of truth is a reference to either a present or an imagined future majority in favor of our view. If, as I have suggested elsewhere, the truth may be defined as the system of my (intellectual) limitations, what gives it objectivity is the fact that I find my fellow man to a greater or less extent (never wholly) subject to the same *Can't Helps*. If I think that I am sitting at a table I find that the other persons present agree with me; so if I say that the sum of the angles of a triangle is equal to two right angles. If I am in a minority of one they send for a doctor or lock me up; and I am so far able to transcend the to me convincing testimony of my senses or my reason as to recognize that if I am alone probably something is wrong with my works.

Certitude is not the test of certainty. We have been cock-sure of many things that were not so. If I may quote myself again, property, friendship, and truth have a common root in time. One can not be wrenched from the rocky crevices into which one has grown for many years without feeling that one is attacked in one's life. What we most love and revere generally is determined by early associations. I love granite rocks and barberry bushes, no doubt because with them were my earliest joys that reach back through the past eternity of my life. But while one's experience thus makes certain preferences dogmatic for oneself, recognition of how they came to be so leaves one able to see that others, poor souls, may be equally dogmatic about something else. And this again means scepticism. Not that one's belief or love does not remain. Not that we would not fight and die for it if important—we all, whether we know it or not—are fighting to make the kind of a world that we should like—but that we have learned to recognize that others will fight and die to make a different world, with equal sincerity or belief. Deep-seated preferences can not be argued about—you can not argue a man into liking a glass of beer—and therefore, when differences are sufficiently far reaching we try to kill the other man rather than let him have his way. But that is perfectly consistent with admitting that, so far as appears, his grounds are just as good as ours.

The jurists who believe in natural law seem to me to be in that naïve state of mind that accepts what has been familiar and accepted by them and their neighbors as something that must be accepted by all men everywhere. No doubt it is true that, so far as we can see ahead, some arrangements and the rudiments of familiar institutions seem to be necessary elements in any society that may spring from our own and that would seem to us to be civilized—some form of permanent association between the sexes—some residue of property individually owned—some mode of binding oneself to specified future conduct—at the bottom of all, some protection for the person. But without speculating

Source: Oliver Wendell Holmes, Jr., *Natural Law,* 32 (Cambridge, Mass.: Harvard Law Review, 1918). Copyright © 2005 by the Harvard Law Review Association.

whether a group is imaginable in which all but the last of these might disappear and the last be subject to qualifications that most of us would abhor, the question remains as to the *Ought* of natural law.

It is true that beliefs and wishes have a transcendental basis in the sense that their foundation is arbitrary. You can not help entertaining and feeling them, and there is an end of it. As an arbitrary fact people wish to live, and we say with various degrees of certainty that they can do so only on certain conditions. To do it they must eat and drink. That necessity is absolute. It is a necessity of less degree but practically general that they should live in society. If they live in society, so far as we can see, there are further conditions. Reason working on experience does tell us, no doubt, that if our wish to live continues, we can do it only on those terms. But that seems to me the whole of the matter. I see no a priori duty to live with others and in that way, but simply a statement of what I must do if I wish to remain alive. If I do live with others they tell me that I must do and abstain from doing various things or they will put the screws on to me. I believe that they will, and being of the same mind as to their conduct I not only accept the rules but come in time to accept them with sympathy and emotional affirmation and begin to talk about duties and rights. But for legal purposes a right is only the hypostasis of a prophecy—the imagination of a substance supporting the fact that the public force will be brought to bear upon those who do things said to contravene it—just as we talk of the force of gravitation accounting for the conduct of bodies in space. One phrase adds no more than the other to what we know without it. No doubt behind these legal rights is the fighting will of the subject to maintain them, and the spread of his emotions to the general rules by which they are maintained; but that does not seem to me the same thing as the supposed a priori discernment of a duty or the assertion of a preëxisting right. A dog will fight for his bone.

The most fundamental of the supposed preëxisting rights—the right to life—is sacrificed without a scruple not only in war, but whenever the interest of society, that is, of the predominant power in the community, is thought to demand it. Whether that interest is the interest of mankind in the long run no one can tell, and as, in any event, to those who do not think with Kant and Hegel it is only an interest, the sanctity disappears. I remember a very tenderhearted judge being of opinion that closing a hatch to stop a fire and the destruction of a cargo was justified even if it was known that doing so would stifle a man below. It is idle to illustrate further, because to those who agree with me I am uttering commonplaces and to those who disagree I am ignoring the necessary foundations of thought. The a priori men generally call the dissentients superficial. But I do agree with them in believing that one's attitude on these matters is closely connected with one's general attitude toward the universe. Proximately, as has been suggested, it is determined largely by early associations and temperament, coupled with the desire to have an absolute guide. Men to a great extent believe what they want to—although I see in that no basis for a philosophy that tells us what we should want to want.

Now when we come to our attitude toward the universe I do not see any rational ground for demanding the superlative—for being dissatisfied unless we are assured that our truth is cosmic truth, if there is such a thing—that the ultimates of a little creature on this earth are the last word of the unimaginable whole. If a man sees no reason for believing that significance, consciousness and ideals are more than marks of the finite, that does not justify what has been familiar in French sceptics: getting upon a pedestal and professing to look with haughty scorn upon a world in ruins. The real conclusion is that the part can not swallow the whole—that our categories are not, or may not be, adequate to formulate what we cannot know. If we believe that we come out of the universe, not it out of us, we must admit that we do not know what we are talking about when we speak of brute matter. We do know that a certain complex of energies can wag its tail and another can make syllogisms. These are among the powers of the unknown, and if, as may be, it has still greater powers that we can not understand, as Fabre in his studies of instinct would have us believe, studies that gave Bergson one of the strongest strands for his philosophy and enabled Maeterlinck to make us fancy for a moment that we heard a clang from behind phenomena—if this be true, why should we not be content? Why should we employ the energy that is furnished to us by the cosmos to defy it and shake our fist at the sky? It seems to me silly.

That the universe has in it more than we understand, that the private soldiers have not been told the plan of the campaign, or even that there is one, rather than some vaster unthinkable to which every predicate is an impertinence, has no bearing upon our conduct. We still shall fight—all of us because we want to live, some, at least, because we want to realize our spontaneity and prove our powers, for the joy of it, and we may leave to the unknown the supposed final valuation of that which in any event has value to us. It is enough for us that the universe has produced us and has within it, as less than it, all that we believe and love. If we think of our existence not as that of a little god outside, but as that of a ganglion within, we have the infinite behind us. It gives us our only but our adequate significance. A grain of sand has the same, but what competent person supposes that he understands a grain of sand? That is as much beyond our grasp as man. If our imagination is strong enough to accept the vision of ourselves as parts inseverable from the rest, and to extend our final interest beyond the boundary of our skins, it justifies the sacrifice even of our lives for ends outside of ourselves. The motive, to be sure, is the common wants and ideals that we find in man. Philosophy does not furnish motives, but it shows men that they are not fools for doing what they already want to do. It opens to the forlorn hopes on which we throw ourselves away, the vista of the farthest stretch of human thought, the chords of a harmony that breathes from the unknown.

JOHN DEWEY

"Philosophy and Democracy"
(1918)

The name of John Dewey (1859–1952) is appropriately remembered in relation to so many ideas and movements that his role in the history of American thought is less easily indicated in a sourcebook of this kind than is the role of perhaps any other thinker represented within these two covers. Dewey did creative work in philosophy and psychology as early as the mid-1880s, rose to national prominence in the Progressive Era as a theorist of educational and political reform, and went on during the 1920s and 1930s to publish almost a dozen influential books that renewed his standing as the preeminent liberal intellectual in the United States. In his ninetieth year he coauthored a treatise on epistemology, on which he worked while helping his new, young wife look after two Belgian orphans the Deweys had adopted at the end of World War II.

Dewey's prose was oblique, but he managed to convey an earnest and almost messianic faith in the powers of human intelligence. His contemporary, Justice Oliver Wendell Holmes, Jr., caught this quality when he observed that Dewey spoke as God would have spoken "had He been inarticulate but keenly desirous to tell you how it was."

The paper reprinted here is one of Dewey's most lucid and ambitious essays, in which he sets forth his vision of philosophy as a democratic, reforming practice. "Philosophy and Democracy" was delivered at the University of California at Berkeley in the same lecture series in which William James first introduced the concept of pragmatism and in which George Santayana criticized "the genteel tradition."

The most comprehensive and discerning book on Dewey is Robert Westbrook, *John Dewey and American Democracy* (Ithaca, 1991). Two highly valuable studies are Steven C. Rockefeller, *John Dewey: Religious Faith and Democratic Humanism* (New York, 1991); and Alan Ryan, *John Dewey and the High Tide of American Liberalism* (New York, 1995). The extent to which Dewey departed from his "pragmatic" forebears, Peirce and James, is emphasized in R. W. Sleeper, *The Necessity of Pragmatism: John Dewey's Conception of Philosophy* (New Haven, 1986). Dewey's perpetuation in a secular context of the sensibility of liberal Protestantism is traced in Bruce Kuklick, *Churchmen and Philosophers: From Jonathan Edwards to John Dewey* (New Haven, 1985). Dewey's contributions as a theorist of liberalism are clarified in James T. Kloppenberg, *Uncertain Victory: Social Democracy and Progressivism in European and American Social Thought, 1870–1920* (New York, 1986).

Why such a title as Philosophy and Democracy? Why Philosophy and Democracy, any more than Chemistry and Oligarchy, Mathematics and Aristocracy, Astronomy and Monarchy? Is not the concern of philosophy with truth, and can truth vary with political and social institutions any more than with degrees of latitude and meridians of longitude? Is there one ultimate reality for men who live where suffrage is universal and another and different reality where limited suffrage prevails? If we should become a socialistic republic next week would that modify the nature of the ultimates and absolutes with which philosophy deals any more than it would affect the principles of arithmetic or the laws of physics?

Such questions, I fancy, lurk in your minds when they are confronted by a title like that which is chosen. It is well that these questions should not be allowed to lurk in subconscious recesses, but should be brought out into the open. For they have to do with what is the first and last problem for a student of philosophy: The problem of what after all is the business and province of philosophy itself. What is it about? What is it after? What would it have to be possessed of in order to be satisfied? To such questions as these must the remarks be chiefly addressed, leaving the nominal and explicit subject of the relation of democracy to philosophy to figure for the most part as a corollary or even as a postscript.

If then we return to the imaginary interrogations with which we set out we shall find that a certain assumption underlies them—or rather two assumptions. One is that philosophy ranks as a science, that its business is with a certain body of fixed and finished facts and principles. Philosophy is viewed not as its etymology would lead us to expect as a form of love or desire, but as a form of knowledge, of apprehension and acknowledgment of a system of truths comparable in its independence of human wish and effort with the truths of physics. Such, I take it, is the first assumption. The second is that since the realities or truths to be known must be marked off from those of physics and mathematics in order that philosophy may be itself a distinctive form of knowledge, philosophy somehow knows reality more *ultimately* than do the other sciences. It approaches truth with an effort at a more comprehensive, a more completely total vision, and takes reality at a deeper and more fundamental level than do those subjects which orthodox philosophers have loved to call the *special* sciences. What they take piecemeal and therefore more or less erroneously (since a fragment arbitrarily torn from the organic whole is not truly a truth) philosophy takes *teres et rotundus*. What they take superficially, in, so to say, its appearance, philosophy takes at that deeper level where connections and relations within the whole are found.

Some such suppositions as these have, I think, been fostered by many philosophers. They are in the back of the minds of many students when they come to the study of philosophy. They are equally in the minds of many foes of philosophy who also compare philosophy with science, but only to contrast them—at the expense of philosophy. Philosophy, they say, is circular and disputatious; it settles nothing, for its schools are still divided much as they were in the times of the Greeks, engaged in arguing the same questions. Science is progressive; it settles some things and moves on to others. Philosophy moreover is sterile. Where are its works? Where are its concrete applications and living fruits? Hence they conclude that while philosophy is a form of knowledge or science, it is a pretentious

Source: The Collected Works of John Dewey, Middle Works: vol. 11, *1918–1919*. Reprinted by permission of Southern Illinois University Press. Copyright © 1982.

and pseudo-form, an effort at a kind of knowledge which is impossible—impossible at all events to human minds.

Yet every generation, no matter how great the advance of positive knowledge, nor how great the triumphs of the special sciences, shows in its day discontent with all these proved and ascertained results and turns afresh and with infinite hope to philosophy, as to a deeper, more complete and more final revelation. Something is lacking in even the most demonstrated of scientific truths which breeds dissatisfaction, and a yearning for something more conclusive and more mind-filling.

In the face of such perplexities as these there is, I think, another alternative, another way out. Put baldly, it is to deny that philosophy is in any sense whatever a form of knowledge. It is to say that we should return to the original and etymological sense of the word, and recognize that philosophy is a form of desire, of effort at action—a love, namely, of wisdom; but with the thorough proviso, not attached to the Platonic use of the word, that wisdom, whatever it is, is not a mode of science or knowledge. A philosophy which was conscious of its own business and province would then perceive that it is an intellectualized wish, an aspiration subjected to rational discriminations and tests, a social hope reduced to a working program of action, a prophecy of the future, but one disciplined by serious thought and knowledge.

These are statements at once sweeping and vague. Let us recur to the question of whether there is such a thing as a philosophy which is distinctively that of a social order, a distinctive type appropriate to a democracy or to a feudalism. Let us consider the matter not theoretically but historically. In point of fact, nobody would deny that there has been a German, a French, an English philosophy in a sense in which there have not been national chemistries or astronomies. Even in science there is not the complete impersonal detachment which some views of it would lead us to expect. There is difference in color and temper, in emphasis and preferred method characteristic of each people. But these differences are inconsiderable in comparison with those which we find in philosophy. There the differences have been differences in standpoint, outlook and ideal. They manifest not diversities of intellectual emphasis so much as incompatabilities of temperament and expectation. They are different ways of construing life. They indicate different practical ethics of life, not mere variations of intellectual assent. In reading Bacon, Locke, Descartes, Comte, Hegel, Schopenhauer, one says to oneself this could have proceeded only from England, or France, or Germany, as the case may be. The parallelisms with political history and social needs are obvious and explicit.

Take the larger divisions of thought. The conventional main division of philosophy is into ancient, medieval and modern. We may make a similar division in the history of science. But there the meaning is very different. We either mean merely to refer to the stage of ignorance and of knowledge found in certain periods, or we mean not science at all but certain phases of philosophy. When we take science proper, astronomy or geometry, we do not find Euclid especially Greek in his demonstrations. No, ancient, medieval, modern, express in philosophy differences of interest and of purpose characteristic of great civilizations, great social epochs, differences of religious and social desire and belief. They are applicable to philosophy only because economic, political and religious differences manifest themselves in philosophy in fundamentally the same ways that they are shown in other institutions. The philosophies embodied not colorless intellectual readings of reality, but men's most passionate desires and hopes, their basic beliefs about the sort of life to be lived. They started not from science, not from ascertained knowledge, but from moral convictions, and then resorted to the best knowledge and the best intellectual methods available in their day to give the form of demonstration to what was essentially an attitude of will, or a moral resolution to prize one mode of life more highly than another, and the wish to persuade other men that this was the wise way of living.

And this explains what is meant by saying that love of wisdom is not after all the same thing as eagerness for scientific knowledge. By wisdom we mean not systematic and proved knowledge of fact and truth, but a conviction about moral values, a sense for the better kind of life to be led. Wisdom is a moral term, and like every moral term refers not to the constitution of things already in existence, not even if that constitution be magnified into eternity and absoluteness. As a moral term it refers to a choice about something to be done, a preference for living this sort of life rather than that. It refers not to accomplished reality but to a desired future which our desires, when translated into articulate conviction, may help bring into existence.

There are those who think that such statements give away the whole case for philosophy. Many critics and foes of philosophy coming from the camp of science would doubtless claim they were admissions of the claims that philosophy has always been a false light, a pretentious ambition; and that the lesson is that philosophers should sit down in humility and accept the ascertainments of the special sciences, and not go beyond the task of weaving these statements into a more coherent fabric of expression. Others would go further and find in such statements a virtual confession of the futility of all philosophizing.

But there is another way of taking the matter. One might rather say that the fact that the collective purpose and desire of a given generation and people dominates its philosophy is evidence of the sincerity and vitality of that philosophy; that failure to employ the known facts of the period in support of a certain estimate of the proper life to lead would show lack of any holding and directing force in the current social ideal. Even wresting facts to a purpose, obnoxious as it is, testifies to a certain ardency in the vigor with which a belief about the right life to be led is held. It argues moral debility if the slave Epictetus and the Emperor Aurelius entertain just the same philosophy of life, even though both belong to the same Stoic school. "A community devoted to industrial pursuits, active in business and commerce, is not likely to see the needs and possibilities of life in the same way as a country with high esthetic culture and little enterprise in turning the energies of nature to mechanical account. A social group with a fairly continuous history will respond mentally to a crisis in a very different way from one which has felt the shock of distinct breaks." Different hues of philosophic thought are bound to result. Women have as yet made little contribution to philosophy. But when women who are not mere students of other persons' philosophy set out to write it, we cannot conceive that it will be the same in viewpoint or tenor as that composed from the standpoint of the different masculine experience of things. Institutions, customs of life, breed certain systematized predilections and aversions. The wise man reads historic philosophies to detect in them intellectual formulations of men's habitual purposes and cultivated wants, not to gain insight into the ultimate nature of things or information about the make-up of reality. As far as what is loosely called reality figures in philosophies, we may be sure that it signifies those selected aspects of the world which are chosen because they lend themselves to the support of men's judgment of the worthwhile life, and hence are most highly prized. In philosophy, "reality" is a term of value or choice.

To deny however that philosophy is in any essential sense a form of science or of knowledge, is not to say that philosophy is a mere arbitrary expression of wish or feeling or a vague suspiration after something, nobody knows what. All philosophy bears an intellectual impress because it is an effort to convince some one, perhaps the writer himself, of the reasonableness of some course of life which has been adopted from custom or instinct. Since it is addressed to man's intelligence, it must employ knowledge and established beliefs, and it must proceed in an orderly way, logically. The art of literature catches men unaware and employs a charm to bring them to a spot whence they see vividly and intimately some picture which embodies life in a meaning. But magic and immediate vision are denied the philosopher. He proceeds prosaically along the highway, pointing out recognizable landmarks, mapping the course, and labeling with explicit logic the stations reached. This means of course that philosophy must depend upon the best science of its day. It can intellectually recommend its judgments of value only as it can select relevant material from that which is recognized to be established truth, and can persuasively use current knowledge to drive home the reasonableness of its conception of life. It is this dependence upon the method of logical presentation and upon scientific subject matter which confers upon philosophy the garb, though not the form, of knowledge.

Scientific form is a vehicle for conveying a non-scientific conviction, but the carriage is necessary, for philosophy is not mere passion but a passion that would exhibit itself as a reasonable persuasion. Philosophy is therefore always in a delicate position, and gives the heathen and Philistine an opportunity to rage. It is always balancing between sophistry, or pretended and illegitimate knowledge, and vague, incoherent mysticism—not of necessity mysticism in its technical definition, but in that sense of the mysterious and misty which affects the popular meaning of the word. When the stress is too much on intellectual form, when the original moral purpose has lost its vitality, philosophy becomes learned and dialectical. When there is cloudy desire, unclarified and unsustained by the logical exhibition of attained science, philosophy becomes hortatory, edifying, sentimental, or fantastic and semi-magical. The perfect balance may hardly be attained by man, and there are few indeed who can, like Plato, even rhythmically alternate with artistic grace from one emphasis to the other. But what makes philosophy hard work and also makes its cultivation worth while, is precisely the fact that it assumes the responsibility for setting forth some ideal of a collective good life by the methods which the best science of the day employs in its quite different task, and with the use of the characteristic knowledge of its day. The philosopher fails when he avoids sophistry, or the conceit of knowledge, only to pose as a prophet of miraculous intuition or mystic revelation or a preacher of pious nobilities of sentiment.

Perhaps we can now see why it is that philosophers have so often been led astray into making claims for philosophy which when taken literally are practically insane in their inordinate scope, such as the claim that philosophy deals with some supreme and total reality beyond that with which the special sciences and arts have to do. Stated sincerely and moderately, the claim would take the form of pointing out that no knowledge as long as it remains just knowledge, just apprehension of fact and truth, is complete or satisfying. Human nature is such that it is impossible that merely finding out that things are thus and so can long content it. There is an instinctive uneasiness which forces men to go beyond any intellectual grasp or recognition, no matter how extensive. Even if a man had seen the whole existent world and gained insight into its hidden and complicated structure, he would after a few moments of ecstasy at the marvel thus revealed to him become dissatisfied to remain at that point. He would begin to ask himself what of it? What is it all about? What does it all mean? And by these questions he would not signify the absurd search for a knowledge greater than all knowledge, but would indicate the need for projecting even the completest knowledge upon a realm of another dimension—namely, the dimension of action. He would mean: What am I to do about it? What course of activity does this state of things require of me? What possibilities to be achieved by my own thought turned over into deed does it open up to me? What new responsibilities does this knowledge impose? To what new adventures does it invite? All knowledge in short makes a difference. It opens new perspectives and releases energy to new tasks. This happens anyway and continuously, philosophy or no philosophy. But philosophy tries to gather up the threads into a central stream of tendency, to inquire what more fundamental and general attitudes of response the trend of knowledge exacts of us, to what new fields of action it calls us. It is in this sense, a practical and moral sense, that philosophy can lay claim to the epithets of universal, basic and superior. Knowledge is partial and incomplete, any and all knowledge, till we have placed it in the context of a future which cannot be known, but only speculated about and resolved upon. It is, to use in another sense a favorite philosophical term, a matter of *appearance,* for it is not self-enclosed, but an indication of something to be done.

As was intimated at the outset, considerable has been said about philosophy, but nothing as yet about democracy. Yet, I hope, certain implications are fairly obvious. There has been, roughly speaking, a coincidence in the development of modern experimental science and of democracy. Philosophy has no more important question than a consideration of how far this may be mere coincidence, and how far it marks a genuine correspondence. Is democracy a comparatively superficial human expedient, a device of petty manipulation, or does nature itself, as that is uncovered and understood by our best contemporaneous knowledge, sustain and support our democratic hopes and aspirations? Or, if we choose to begin arbitrarily at the other end, if to construct democratic institutions is our aim, how then shall we construe and interpret the natural environment and natural history of humanity in order to get an intellectual warrant for our endeavors, a reasonable persuasion that our undertaking is not contradicted by what science authorizes us to say about the structure of the world? How shall we read what we call reality (that is to say the world of existence accessible to verifiable inquiry) so that we may essay our deepest political and social problems with a conviction that they are to a reasonable extent sanctioned and sustained by the nature of things? Is the world as an object of knowledge at odds with our purposes and efforts? Is it merely neutral and indifferent? Does it lend itself equally to all our social ideals, which means that it gives itself to none, but stays aloof, ridiculing as it were the ardor and earnestness with which we take our trivial and transitory hopes and plans? Or is its nature such that it is at least willing to coöperate, that it not only does not say us nay, but gives us an encouraging nod?

Is not this, you may ask, taking democracy too seriously? Why not ask the question about say presbyterianism or free verse? Well, I would not wholly deny the pertinency of similar questions about such movements. All deliberate action of mind is in a way an experiment with the world to see what it will stand for, what it will promote and what frustrate. The world is tolerant and fairly hospitable. It permits and even encourages all sorts of experiments. But in the long run some are more welcomed and assimilated than others. Hence there can be no difference save one of depth and scope between the questions of the relation of the world to a scheme of conduct in the form of church government or a form of art and that of its relation to democracy. If there be a difference, it is only because democracy is a form of desire and endeavor which reaches further and condenses into itself more issues.

This statement implies a matter of definition. What is meant by democracy? It can certainly be defined in a way which limits the issue to matters which if they bear upon philosophy at all affect it only in limited and technical aspects. Anything that can be said in the way of definition in the remaining space must be, and confessedly is, arbitrary. The arbitrariness may however, be mitigated by linking up the conception with the historic formula of the greatest liberal movement of history—the formula of liberty, equality and fraternity. In referring to this, we only exchange arbitrariness for vagueness. It would be hard indeed to arrive at any consensus of judgment about the meaning of any one of the three terms inscribed on the democratic banner. Men did not agree in the eighteenth century and subsequent events have done much to accentuate their differences. Do they apply purely politically, or do they have an economic meaning?—to refer to one great cleavage which in the nineteenth century broke the liberal movement into two factions, now opposed to one another as liberal and conservative were once opposed.

Let us then take frank advantage of the vagueness and employ the terms with a certain generosity and breadth. What does the demand for liberty imply for philosophy, when we take the idea of liberty as conveying something of decided moral significance? Roughly speaking, there are two typical ideas of liberty. One of them says that freedom is action in accord with the consciousness of fixed law; that men are free when they are rational, and they are rational when they recognize and consciously conform to the necessities which the universe exemplified. As Tolstoi says, even the ox would be free if it recognized the yoke about its neck and took the yoke for the law of its own action instead of engaging in a vain task of revolt which escapes no necessity but only turns it in the direction of misery and destruction. This is a noble idea of freedom embodied, both openly and disguisedly, in classic philosophies. It is the only view consistent with any form of absolutism whether materialistic or idealistic, whether it considers the necessary relations which form the universe to be physical in character or spiritual. It holds of any view which says that reality exists under the form of eternity, that it is, to use a technical term, a *simul totum,* an all at once and forever affair, no matter whether the all at once be of mathematical-physical laws and structures, or a comprehensive and exhaustive divine consciousness. Of such a conception one can only say that however noble, it is not one which is spontaneously congenial to the idea of liberty in a society which has set its heart on democracy.

A philosophy animated, be it unconsciously or consciously, by the strivings of men to achieve democracy will construe liberty as meaning a universe in which there is real uncertainty and contingency, a world which is not all in, and never will be, a world which in some respect is incomplete and in the making, and which in these respects may be made this way or that according as men judge, prize, love and labor. To such a philosophy any notion of a perfect or complete reality, finished, existing always the same without regard to the vicissitudes of time, will be abhorrent. It will think of time not as that part of reality which for some strange reason has not yet been traversed, but as a genuine field of novelty, of real and unpredictable increments to existence, a field for experimentation and invention. It will indeed recognize that there is in things a grain against which we cannot successfully go, but it will also insist that we cannot even discover what that grain is except as we make this new experiment and that fresh effort, and that consequently the mistake, the effort which is frustrated in direct execution, is as true a constituent of the world as is the act which most carefully observes law. For it is the grain which is rubbed the wrong way which more clearly stands out. It will recognize that in a world where discovery is genuine, error is an inevitable ingredient of reality, and that man's business is not to avoid it—or to cultivate the illusion that it is mere appearance—but to turn it to account, to make it fruitful. Nor will such a philosophy be mealy-mouthed in admitting that where contingency is real and experiment is required, good fortune and bad fortune are facts. It will not construe all accomplishment in terms of merit and virtue, and all loss and frustration in terms of demerit and just punishment. Because it recognizes that contingency coöperates with intelligence in the realization of every plan, even the one most carefully and wisely thought out, it will avoid conceit and intellectual arrogance. It will not fall into the delusion that consciousness is or can be everything as a determiner of events. Hence it will be humbly grateful that a world in which the most extensive and accurate thought and reason can only take advantage of events is also a world which gives room to move about in, and which offers the delights of consummations that are new revelations, as well as those defeats that are admonishments to conceit.

The evident contrast of equality is inequality. Perhaps it is not so evident that inequality means practically inferiority and superiority. And that this relation works out practically in support of a régime of authority or feudal hierarchy in which each lower or inferior element depends upon, holds from, one superior from which it gets direction and to which it is responsible. Let one bear this idea fully in mind and he will see how largely philosophy has been committed to a metaphysics of feudalism. By this I mean it has thought of things in the world as occupying certain grades of value, or as having fixed degrees of truth, ranks of reality.

The traditional conception of philosophy to which I referred at the outset, which identifies it with insight into supreme reality or ultimate and comprehensive truth, shows how thoroughly philosophy has been committed to a notion that inherently some realities are superior to others, are better than others. Now any such philosophy inevitably works in behalf of a régime of authority, for it is only right that the superior should lord it over the inferior. The result is that much of philosophy has gone to justifying the particular scheme of authority in religion or social order which happened to exist at a given time. It has become unconsciously an apologetic for the established order, because it has tried to show the rationality of this or that existent hierarchical grading of values and schemes of life. Or when it has questioned the established order it has been a revolutionary search for some rival principle of authority.

How largely indeed has historic philosophy been a search for an indefeasible seat of authority! Greek philosophy began when men doubted the authority of custom as a regulator of life; it sought in universal reason or in the immediate particular, in being or in flux, a rival source of authority, but one which as a rival was to be as certain and definite as ever custom had been. Medieval philosophy was frankly an attempt to reconcile authority with reason, and modern philosophy began when man doubting the authority of revelation began a search for some authority which should have all the weight, certainty and inerrancy previously ascribed to the will of God embodied in the divinely instituted church.

Thus for the most part the democratic practice of life has been at an immense intellectual disadvantage. Prevailing philosophies have unconsciously discountenanced it. They have failed to furnish it with articulation, with reasonableness, for they have at bottom been committed to the principle of a single, final and unalterable authority from which all lesser authorities are derived. The men who questioned the divine right of kings did so in the name of another absolute. The voice of the people was mythologized into the voice of God. Now a halo may be preserved about the monarch. Because of his distance, he can be rendered transcendentally without easy detection. But the people are too close at hand, too obviously empirical, to be lent to deification. Hence democracy has ranked for the most part as an intellectual anomaly, lacking philosophical basis and logical coherency, but upon the whole to be accepted because somehow or other it works better than other schemes and seems to develop a more kindly and humane set of social institutions. For when it has tried to achieve a philosophy it has clothed itself in an atomistic individualism, as full of defects and inconsistencies in theory as it was charged with obnoxious conse-quences when an attempt was made to act upon it.

Now whatever the idea of equality means for democracy, it means, I take it, that the world is not to be construed as a fixed order of species, grades or degrees. It means that every existence deserving the name of existence has something unique and irreplaceable about it, that it does not exist to illustrate a principle, to realize a universal or to embody a kind or class. As philosophy it denies the basic principle of atomistic individualism as truly as that of rigid feudalism. For the individualism traditionally associated with democracy makes equality quantitative, and hence individuality something external and mechanical rather than qualitative and unique.

In social and moral matters, equality does not mean mathematical equivalence. It means rather the inapplicability of considerations of greater and less, superior and infe-rior. It means that no matter how great the quantitative differences of ability, strength, position, wealth, such differences are negligible in comparison with something else—the fact of individuality, the manifestation of something irreplaceable. It means, in short, a world in which an existence must be reckoned with on its own account, not as something capable of equation with and transformation into something else. It implies, so to speak, a metaphysical mathematics of the incommensurable in which each speaks for itself and demands consideration on its own behalf.

If democratic equality may be construed as individuality, there is nothing forced in understanding fraternity as continuity, that is to say, as association and interaction with-out limit. Equality, individuality, tends to isolation and independence. It is centrifugal. To say that what is specific and unique can be exhibited and become forceful or actual only in relationship with other like beings is merely, I take it, to give a metaphysical version to the fact that democracy is concerned not with freaks or geniuses or heroes or divine leaders but with associated individuals in which each by intercourse with others somehow makes the life of each more distinctive.

All this, of course, is but by way of intimation. In spite of its form it is not really a plea for a certain kind of philosophizing. For if democracy be a serious, important choice and predilection it must in time justify itself by generating its own child of wisdom, to be justified in turn by its children, better institutions of life. It is not so much a ques-tion as to whether there will be a philosophy of this kind as it is of just who will be the philosophers associated with it. And I cannot conclude without mentioning the name of one through whom this vision of a new mode of life has already spoken with beauty and power—William James.

MARGARET MEAD

Selection from *Coming of Age in Samoa* (1928)

The most obvious function performed by social scientists in modern America has been a cognitive one: the advancement of knowledge about society. Another, more subtle function has been a moral one: the articulation and criticism of standards for conduct. The role of the public moralist had long been performed by the clergy and by men and women of letters, but in the twentieth century this role increasingly came to be filled by psychologists, anthropologists, sociologists, and other practitioners of social science. The anthropologist Margaret Mead (1901–78) was perhaps the most influential single example of "the social scientist as public moralist." Mead wrote thirty-four books on a multitude of topics, many of which were only remotely anthropological. She was a formidable presence in American intellectual life for half a century, beginning with her *Coming of Age in Samoa* (1928), from which the selection that follows is taken.

Mead's study of adolescent girls in Samoa was offered frankly as a means of fostering a critical perspective on the growing-up experiences of young people in Mead's own society. In our excerpt she sums up the lessons she wishes readers to derive from her study. Mead was an inveterate enemy of American middle-class provincialism and invited her readers to develop a diverse culture in which individuals could choose between a great variety of ways of life. Although she expressed much sympathy for the homogeneous, easygoing culture she attributed to the people of Samoa, she defended the heterogeneous, complex culture of modern America and sought to foster the knowledge and attitudes that would better equip Americans to take advantage of their opportunities.

Along with her close friend, Ruth Benedict, whose *Patterns of Culture* (New York, 1934) was an academic best-seller for more than thirty years, Mead led in the popularization of "cultural relativism." For a history of this persuasion, see David A. Hollinger, "Cultural Relativism," in *The Cambridge History of Science*, vol. 7 (New York, 2002), 708–20.

The place to begin the study of Mead is Lois Banner, *Intertwined Lives: Margaret Mead, Ruth Benedict, and Their Circle* (New York, 2003). A recent study of Mead's popular appeal is Nancy Lutkehaus, *Margaret Mead: The Making of an American Icon* (Princeton, 2008). A discerning inquiry into Mead's relation to the Cold War is Peter Mandler, "One World, Many Cultures: Margaret Mead and the Limits to Cold War Anthropology," *History Workshop Journal*, 68 (2009), 149–72. See also John Gilkeson, *Anthropologists and the Rediscovery of America, 1886–1965* (Chicago, 2010).

For many chapters we have followed the lives of Samoan girls, watched them change from babies to baby tenders, learn to make the oven and weave fine mats, forsake the life of the gang to become more active members of the household, defer marriage through as many years of casual love-making as possible, finally marry and settle down to rearing children who will repeat the same cycle. As far as our material permitted, an experiment has been conducted to discover what the process of development was like in a society very different from our own. Because the length of human life and the complexity of our society did not permit us to make our experiment here, to choose a group of baby girls and bring them to maturity under conditions created for the experiment, it was necessary to go instead to another country where history had set the stage for us. There we found girl children pass-ing through the same process of physical development through which our girls go, cutting their first teeth and losing them, cutting their second teeth, growing tall and ungainly, reaching puberty with their first menstruation, gradually reaching physical maturity, and becoming ready to produce the next generation. It was possible to say: Here are the proper conditions for an experiment; the developing girl is a constant factor in America and in Samoa; the civilisation of America and the civilisation of Samoa are different. In the course of development, the process of growth by which the girl baby becomes a grown woman, are the sudden and conspicuous bodily changes which take place at puberty accompa-nied by a development which is spasmodic, emotionally charged, and accompanied by an awakened religious sense, a flowering of idealism, a great desire for assertion of self against authority—or not? Is adolescence a period of mental and emotional distress for the grow-ing girl as inevitably as teething is a period of misery for the small baby? Can we think of adolescence as a time in the life history of every girl child which carries with it symptoms of conflict and stress as surely as it implies a change in the girl's body?

Following the Samoan girls through every aspect of their lives we have tried to answer this question, and we found throughout that we had to answer it in the negative. The ado-lescent girl in Samoa differed from her sister who had not reached puberty in one chief respect, that in the older girl certain bodily changes were present which were absent in the younger girl. There were no other great differences to set off the group passing through adolescence from the group which would become adolescent in two years or the group which had become adolescent two years before.

And if one girl past puberty is undersized while her cousin is tall and able to do heavier work, there will be a difference between them, due to their different physical endowment, which will be far greater than that which is due to puberty. The tall, husky girl will be isolated from her companions, forced to do longer, more adult tasks, rendered shy by a change of clothing, while her cousin, slower to attain her growth, will still be treated as a child and will have to solve only the slightly fewer problems of childhood. The precedent of educators here who recommend special tactics in the treatment of adolescent girls translated into Samoan terms would read: Tall girls are different from short girls of the same age, we must adopt a different method of educating them.

But when we have answered the question we set out to answer we have not finished with the problem. A further question presents itself. If it is proved that adolescence is not necessarily a specially difficult period in a girl's life—and proved it is if we can find any society in which that is so—then what accounts for the presence of storm and stress in

Source: Margaret Mead, *Coming of Age in Samoa* (New York: Morrow, 1955), 195–206, 234–35, 244–48. Reprinted by permission of HarperCollins Publishers, Inc. Copyright ©1928, 1949, 1955, 1961, 1973 by Margaret Mead.

American adolescents? First, we may say quite simply, that there must be something in the two civilisations to account for the difference. If the same process takes a different form in two different environments, we cannot make any explanations in terms of the process, for that is the same in both cases. But the social environment is very different and it is to it that we must look for an explanation. What is there in Samoa which is absent in America, what is there in America which is absent in Samoa, which will account for this difference?

Such a question has enormous implications and any attempt to answer it will be subject to many possibilities of error. But if we narrow our question to the way in which aspects of Samoan life which irremediably affect the life of the adolescent girl differ from the forces which influence our growing girls, it is possible to try to answer it.

The background of these differences is a broad one, with two important components; one is due to characteristics which are Samoan, the other to characteristics which are primitive.

The Samoan background which makes growing up so easy, so simple a matter, is the general casualness of the whole society. For Samoa is a place where no one plays for very high stakes, no one pays very heavy prices, no one suffers for his convictions or fights to the death for special ends. Disagreements between parent and child are settled by the child's moving across the street, between a man and his village by the man's removal to the next village, between a husband and his wife's seducer by a few fine mats. Neither poverty nor great disasters threaten the people to make them hold their lives dearly and tremble for continued existence. No implacable gods, swift to anger and strong to punish, disturb the even tenor of their days. Wars and cannibalism are long since passed away and now the greatest cause for tears, short of death itself, is a journey of a relative to another island. No one is hurried along in life or punished harshly for slowness of development. Instead the gifted, the precocious, are held back, until the slowest among them have caught the pace. And in personal relations, caring is as slight. Love and hate, jealousy and revenge, sorrow and bereavement, are all matters of weeks. From the first months of its life, when the child is handed carelessly from one woman's hands to another's, the lesson is learned of not caring for one person greatly, not setting high hopes on any one relationship.

And just as we may feel that the Occident penalises those unfortunates who are born into Western civilisation with a taste for meditation and a complete distaste for activity, so we may say that Samoa is kind to those who have learned the lesson of not caring, and hard upon those few individuals who have failed to learn it. Lola and Mala and little Siva, Lola's sister, all were girls with a capacity for emotion greater than their fellows. And Lola and Mala, passionately desiring affection and too violently venting upon the community their disappointment over their lack of it, were both delinquent, unhappy misfits in a society which gave all the rewards to those who took defeat lightly and turned to some other goal with a smile.

In this casual attitude towards life, in this avoidance of conflict, of poignant situations, Samoa contrasts strongly not only with America but also with most primitive civilisations. And however much we may deplore such an attitude and feel that important personalities and great art are not born in so shallow a society, we must recognise that here is a strong factor in the painless development from childhood to womanhood. For where no one feels very strongly, the adolescent will not be tortured by poignant situations. There are no such disastrous choices as those which confronted young people who felt that the service of God demanded forswearing the world forever, as in the Middle Ages, or cutting off one's finger as a religious offering, as among the Plains Indians. So, high up in our list of explanations we must place the lack of deep feeling which the Samoans have conventionalised until it is the very framework of all their attitudes toward life.

And next there is the most striking way in which all isolated primitive civilisation and many modern ones differ from our own, in the number of choices which are permitted to each individual. Our children grow up to find a world of choices dazzling their unaccustomed eyes. In religion they may be Catholics, Protestants, Christian Scientists, Spiritualists, Agnostics, Atheists, or even pay no attention at all to religion. This is an unthinkable situation in any primitive society not exposed to foreign influence. There is one set of gods, one accepted religious practice, and if a man does not believe, his only recourse is to believe less than his fellows; he may scoff but there is no new faith to which he may turn. Present-day Manu'a approximates this condition; all are Christians of the same sect. There is no conflict in matters of belief although there is a difference in practice between Church-members and non-Church-members. And it was remarked that in the case of several of the growing girls the need for choice between these two practices may some day produce a conflict. But at present the Church makes too slight a bid for young unmarried members to force the adolescent to make any decision.

Similarly, our children are faced with half a dozen standards of morality: a double sex standard for men and women, a single standard for men and women, and groups which advocate that the single standard should be freedom while others argue that the single standard should be absolute monogamy. Trial marriage, companionate marriage, contract marriage—all these possible solutions of a social impasse are paraded before the growing children while the actual conditions in their own communities and the moving pictures and magazines inform them of mass violations of every code, violations which march under no banners of social reform.

The Samoan child faces no such dilemma. Sex is a natural, pleasurable thing; the freedom with which it may be indulged in is limited by just one consideration, social status. Chiefs' daughters and chiefs' wives should indulge in no extra-marital experiments. Responsible adults, heads of households and mothers of families should have too many important matters on hand to leave them much time for casual amorous adventures. Every one in the community agrees about the matter, the only dissenters are the missionaries who dissent so vainly that their protests are unimportant. But as soon as a sufficient sentiment gathers about the missionary attitude with its European standard of sex behaviour, the need for choice, the forerunner of conflict, will enter into Samoan society.

Our young people are faced by a series of different groups which believe different things and advocate different practices, and to each of which some trusted friend or relative may belong. So a girl's father may be a Presbyterian, an imperialist, a vegetarian, a teetotaler, with a strong literary preference for Edmund Burke, a believer in the open shop and a high tariff, who believes that woman's place is in the home, that young girls should wear corsets, not roll their stockings, not smoke, nor go riding with young men in the evening. But her mother's father may be a Low Episcopalian, a believer in high living, a strong advocate of States' Rights and the Monroe Doctrine, who reads Rabelais, likes to go to musical shows and horse races. Her aunt is an agnostic, an ardent advocate of woman's rights, an internationalist who rests all her hopes on Esperanto, is devoted to Bernard Shaw, and spends her spare time in campaigns of anti-vivisection. Her elder brother, whom she admires exceedingly, has just spent two years at Oxford. He is an Anglo-Catholic, an enthusiast concerning all things mediaeval, writes mystical poetry, reads Chesterton, and means to devote his life to seeking for the lost secret of mediaeval stained glass. Her mother's younger brother is an engineer, a strict materialist, who never recovered from reading Haeckel in his youth; he scorns art, believes that science will save the world, scoffs at everything that was said and thought before the nineteenth century, and ruins his health by experiments in the scientific elimination of sleep. Her mother is of a quietistic frame of mind, very much interested in Indian philosophy, a pacifist, a strict non-participator in life, who in spite of her daughter's devotion to her will not make any move to enlist her enthusiasms. And this may be within the girl's own household. Add to it the groups represented, defended, advocated by her friends, her teachers, and the books which she reads by accident, and the list of possible enthusiasms, of suggested allegiances, incompatible with one another, becomes appalling.

The Samoan girl's choices are far otherwise. Her father is a member of the Church and so is her uncle. Her father lives in a village where there is good fishing, her uncle in a village where there are plenty of cocoanut crabs. Her father is a good fisherman and in his house there is plenty to eat; her uncle is a talking chief and his frequent presents of bark cloth provide excellent dance dresses. Her paternal grandmother, who lives with her uncle, can teach her many secrets of healing; her maternal grandmother, who lives with her mother, is an expert weaver of fans. The boys in her uncle's village are admitted younger into the *Aumaga* and are not much fun when they come to call; but there are three boys in her own village whom she likes very much. And her great dilemma is whether to live with her father or her uncle, a frank, straightforward problem which introduces no ethical perplexities, no question of impersonal logic. Nor will her choice be taken as a personal matter, as the American girl's allegiance to the views of one relative might be interpreted by her other relatives. The Samoans will be sure she chose one residence rather than the other for perfectly good reasons, the food was better, she had a lover in one village, or she had quarrelled with a lover in the other village. In each case she was making concrete choices within one recognised pattern of behaviour. She was never called upon to make choices involving an actual rejection of the standards of her social group, such as the daughter of Puritan parents, who permits indiscriminate caresses, must make in our society.

And not only are our developing children faced by a series of groups advocating different and mutually exclusive standards, but a more perplexing problem presents itself to them. Because our civilisation is woven of so many diverse strands, the ideas which any one group accepts will be found to contain numerous contradictions. So if the girl has given her allegiance whole-heartedly to some one group and has accepted in good faith their asseverations that they alone are right and all other philosophies of life are Antichrist and anathema, her troubles are still not over. While the less thoughtful receives her worst blows in the discovery that what father thinks is good, grandfather thinks is bad, and that things which are permitted at home are banned at school, the more thoughtful child has subtler difficulties in store for her. If she has philosophically accepted the fact that there are several standards among which she must choose, she may still preserve a childlike faith in the coherence of her chosen philosophy. Beyond the immediate choice which was so puzzling and hard to make, which perhaps involved hurting her parents or alienating her friends, she expects peace. But she has not reckoned with the fact that each of the philosophies with which she is confronted is itself but the half-ripened fruit of compromise. If she accepts Christianity, she is immediately confused between the Gospel teachings concerning peace and the value of human life and the Church's whole-hearted acceptance of war. The compromise made seventeen centuries ago between the Roman philosophy of war and domination, and the early Church doctrine of peace and humility, is still present to confuse the modern child. If she accepts the philosophic premises upon which the Declaration of Independence of the United States was founded, she finds herself faced with the necessity of reconciling the belief in the equality of man and our institutional pledges of equality and opportunity with our treatment of the Negro and the Oriental. The diversity of standards in present-day society is so striking that the dullest, the most incurious, cannot fail to notice it. And this diversity is so old, so embodied in semi-solutions, in those compromises between different philosophies which we call Christianity, or democracy, or humanitarianism, that it baffles the most intelligent, the most curious, the most analytical.

So for the explanation of the lack of poignancy in the choices of growing girls in Samoa, we must look to the temperament of the Samoan civilisation which discounts strong feeling. But for the explanation of the lack of conflict we must look principally to the difference between a simple, homogeneous primitive civilisation, a civilisation which changes so slowly that to each generation it appears static, and a motley, diverse, heterogeneous modern civilisation. . . .

We have been comparing point for point, our civilisation and the simpler civilisation of Samoa, in order to illuminate our own methods of education. If now we turn from the Samoan picture and take away only the main lesson which we learned there, that adolescence is not necessarily a time of stress and strain, but that cultural conditions make it so, can we draw any conclusions which might bear fruit in the training of our adolescents?

At first blush the answer seems simple enough. If adolescents are only plunged into difficulties and distress because of conditions in their social environment, then by all means let us so modify that environment as to reduce this stress and eliminate this strain and anguish of adjustment. But, unfortunately, the conditions which vex our adolescents are the flesh and bone of our society, no more subject to straightforward manipulation upon our part than is the language which we speak. We can alter a syllable here, a construction there; but the great and far-reaching changes in linguistic structure (as in all parts of culture) are the work of time, a work in which each individual plays an unconscious and inconsiderable part. The principal causes of our adolescents' difficulty are the presence of conflicting standards and the belief that every individual should make his or her own choices, coupled with a feeling that choice is an important matter. Given these cultural attitudes, adolescence, regarded now not as a period of physiological change, for we know that physiological puberty need not produce conflict, but as the beginning of mental and emotional maturity, is bound to be filled with conflicts and difficulties. A society which is clamouring for choice, which is filled with many articulate groups, each urging its own brand of salvation, its own variety of economic philosophy, will give each new generation no peace until all have chosen or gone under, unable to bear the conditions of choice. The stress is in our civilisation, not in the physical changes through which our children pass, but it is none the less real nor the less inevitable in twentieth-century America. . . .

Granting that society presents too many problems to her adolescents, demands too many momentous decisions on a few months' notice, what is to be done about it? One panacea suggested would be to postpone at least some of the decisions, keep the child economically dependent, or segregate her from all contact with the other sex, present her with only one set of religious ideas until she is older, more poised, better able to deal critically with the problems which will confront her. In a less articulate fashion, such an idea is back of various schemes for the prolongation of youth, through raising the working age, raising the school age, shielding school children from a knowledge of controversies like evolution versus fundamentalism, or any knowledge of sex hygiene or birth control. Even if such measures, specially initiated and legislatively enforced, could accomplish the end which they seek and postpone the period of choice, it is doubtful whether such a development would be desirable. It is unfair that very young children should be the battleground for conflicting standards, that their development should be hampered by propagandist attempts to enlist and condition them too young. It is probably equally unfair to culturally defer the decisions too late. Loss of one's fundamental religious faith is more of a wrench at thirty than at fifteen simply in terms of the number of years of acceptance which have accompanied the belief. A sudden knowledge of hitherto unsuspected aspects of sex, or a shattering of all the old conventions concerning sex behaviour, is more difficult just in terms of the strength of the old attitudes. Furthermore, in practical terms, such schemes would be as they are now, merely local, one state legislating against evolution, another against birth control, or one religious group segregating its unmarried girls. And these special local movements would simply unfit groups of young people for competing happily with children who had been permitted to make their choices earlier. Such an educational scheme, in addition to being almost impossible of execution, would be a step backward and would only beg the question.

Instead, we must turn all of our educational efforts to training our children for the choices which will confront them. Education, in the home even more than at school, instead of being a special pleading for one régime, a desperate attempt to form one particular habit of mind which will withstand all outside influences, must be a preparation for those very influences. Such an education must give far more attention to mental and physical hygiene than it has given hitherto. The child who is to choose wisely must be healthy in mind and body, handicapped in no preventable fashion. And even more importantly, this child of the future must have an open mind. The home must cease to plead an ethical cause or a religious belief with smiles or frowns, caresses or threats. The children must be taught how to think, not what to think. And because old errors die slowly, they must be taught tolerance, just as to-day they are taught intolerance. They must be taught that many ways are open to them, no one sanctioned above its alternative, and that upon them and upon them alone lies the burden of choice. Unhampered by prejudices, unvexed by too early conditioning to any one standard, they must come clear-eyed to the choices which lie before them.

For it must be realised by any student of civilisation that we pay heavily for our heterogeneous, rapidly changing civilisation; we pay in high proportions of crime and delinquency, we pay in the conflicts of youth, we pay in an ever-increasing number of neuroses, we pay in the lack of a coherent tradition without which the development of art is sadly handicapped. In such a list of prices, we must count our gains carefully, not to be discouraged. And chief among our gains must be reckoned this possibility of choice, the recognition of many possible ways of life, where other civilisations have recognised only one. Where other civilisations give a satisfactory outlet to only one temperamental type, be he mystic or soldier, business man or artist, a civilisation in which there are many standards offers a possibility of satisfactory adjustment to individuals of many different temperamental types, of diverse gifts and varying interests.

At the present time we live in a period of transition. We have many standards but we still believe that only one standard can be the right one. We present to our children the picture of a battle-field where each group is fully armoured in a conviction of the righteousness of its cause. And each of these groups make forays among the next generation. But it is unthinkable that a final recognition of the great number of ways in which man, during the course of history and at the present time, is solving the problems of life, should not bring with it in turn the downfall of our belief in a single standard. And when no one group claims ethical sanction for its customs, and each group welcomes to its midst only those who are temperamentally fitted for membership, then we shall have realised the high point of individual choice and universal toleration which a heterogeneous culture and a heterogeneous culture alone can attain. Samoa knows but one way of life and teaches it to her children. Will we, who have the knowledge of many ways, leave our children free to choose among them?

JOSEPH WOOD KRUTCH

Selection from *The Modern Temper*
(1929)

Intellectuals of many different generations become convinced that their own time is one of especially profound transition. Many American thinkers of the 1920s believed that almost everything was up for grabs, and that old certainties in one domain after another were rendered anachronistic by world-historical events, above all the advancement of scientific knowledge. An enduring monument of this mood is *The Modern Temper*, a searching, somewhat misanthropic essay of 1929 by the literary critic Joseph Wood Krutch (1893–1970). Reprinted here is the opening chapter, commonly regarded as the classical expression of "disillusionment" as that feeling is associated with the 1920s. Krutch, who counterintuitively pronounced his last name "krootch," not "crutch" as in a pair of crutches, insisted that "the human spirit" itself must either perish or make a "readjustment more stupendous than any made before."

Not all 1920s intellectuals were disillusioned, of course. Within the ranks of the writers whom we remember for having expressed prominent sensibilities of the period, Krutch's gloomy reflections can be contrasted with the more upbeat acceptance of "modernity" by John Dewey and the ferocious iconoclasm of H. L. Mencken. Krutch is often seen as a "lost generation" writer, who rendered in prose some of the preoccupations associated with Ernest Hemingway and other contemporary novelists and poets. Born and raised in Tennessee, Krutch moved to New York in his early twenties and was immediately caught up in the bohemian life of Greenwich Village.

Krutch went on to an illustrous career as a drama critic for the *Nation* magazine, taught for many years at Columbia University, and in his later life moved to Arizona and developed a new, equally distinguished career as a nature writer and commentator on ecological issues. His *Voice of the Desert* (New York, 1954) was an early representative of these much more affirmative engagements, which have little in common with the angst-ridden *Modern Temper*. The most important of Krutch's later works are conveniently available in the edited volume *The Best Nature Writings of Joseph Wood Krutch* (New York, 1970). But Krutch's greatest legacy was the remarkable cogency with which he summed up a set of anxieties common to writers of the 1920s.

For a biographical study, see John D. Margolis, *A Writer's Life: Joseph Wood Krutch* (Knoxville, Tenn., 1980). The best single study of *The Modern Temper* is Peter Gregg Slater, "The Negative Secularism of the Modern Temper," *American Quarterly*, 33 (1981), 185–205.

It is one of Freud's quaint conceits that the child in its mother's womb is the happiest of living creatures. Into his consciousness no conflict has yet entered, for he knows no limitations to his desires and the universe is exactly as he wishes it to be. All his needs are satisfied before even he becomes aware of them, and if his awareness is dim, that is but the natural result of a complete harmony between the self and the environment, since, as Spencer pointed out in a remote age, to be omniscient and omnipotent would be to be without any consciousness whatsoever. The discomfort of being born is the first warning which he receives that any event can be thrust upon him; it is the first limitation of his omnipotence which he perceives, and he is cast upon the shores of the world wailing his protest against the indignity to which he has been subjected. Years pass before he learns to control the expression of enraged surprise which arises within him at every unpleasant fact with which he is confronted, and his parents conspire so to protect him that he will learn only by very slow stages how far is the world from his heart's desire.

The cradle is made to imitate as closely as may be the conditions, both physical and spiritual, of the womb. Of its occupant no effort is demanded, and every precaution is taken to anticipate each need before it can arise. If, as the result of any unforeseen circumstance, any unsatisfied desire is born, he need only raise his voice in protest to cause the entire world in so far as he knows it—his nurse or his parents—to rush to his aid. The whole of his physical universe is obedient to his will and he is justified by his experience in believing that his mere volition controls his destiny. Only as he grows older does he become aware that there are wills other than his own or that there are physical circumstances rebellious to any human will. And only after the passage of many years does he become aware of the full extent of his predicament in the midst of a world which is in very few respects what he would wish it to be.

As a child he is treated as a child, and such treatment implies much more than the physical coddling of which Freud speaks. Not only do those who surround him coöperate more completely than they ever will again to satisfy his wishes in material things, but they encourage him to live in a spiritual world far more satisfactory than their own. He is carefully protected from any knowledge of the cruelties and complexities of life; he is led to suppose that the moral order is simple and clear, that virtue triumphs, and that the world is, as the desires of whole generations of mankind have led them to try to pretend that it is, arranged according to a pattern which would seem reasonable and satisfactory to human sensibilities. He is prevented from realizing how inextricably what men call good and evil are intertwined, how careless is Nature of those values called mercy and justice and righteousness which men have come, in her despite, to value; and he is, besides, encouraged to believe in a vast mythology peopled with figments which range all the way from the Saints to Santa Claus and which represent projections of human wishes which the adult has come to recognize as no more than projections, but which he is willing that the child, for the sake of his own happiness, should believe real. Aware how different is the world which experience reveals from the world which the spirit desires, the mature, as though afraid that reality could not be endured unless the mind had been gradually inured to it, allow the child to become aware of it only by slow stages, and little by little he learns, not only the limitations of his will, but the moral discord of the world. Thus it is, in a very important sense, true that the infant does come trailing clouds of glory from that heaven

Source: Joseph Wood Krutch, *The Modern Temper* (New York: Harcourt, 1929), 3–26.

which his imagination creates, and that as his experience accumulates he sees it fade away into the light of common day.

Now races as well as individuals have their infancy, their adolescence, and their maturity. Experience accumulates not only from year to year but from generation to generation, and in the life of each person it plays a little larger part than it did in the life of his father. As civilization grows older it too has more and more facts thrust upon its consciousness and is compelled to abandon one after another, quite as the child does, certain illusions which have been dear to it. Like the child, it has instinctively assumed that what it would like to be true is true, and it never gives up any such belief until experience in some form compels it to do so. Being, for example, extremely important to itself, it assumes that it is extremely important to the universe also. The earth is the center of all existing things, man is the child and the protégé of those gods who transcend and who will ultimately enable him to transcend all the evils which he has been compelled to recognize. The world and all that it contains were designed for him, and even those things which seem noxious have their usefulness only temporarily hid. Since he knows but little he is free to imagine, and imagination is always the creature of desire.

The world which any consciousness inhabits is a world made up in part of experience and in part of fancy. No experience, and hence no knowledge, is complete, but the gaps which lie between the solid fragments are filled in with shadows. Connections, explanations, and reasons are supplied by the imagination, and thus the world gets its patterned completeness from material which is spun out of the desires. But as time goes on and experience accumulates there remains less and less scope for the fancy. The universe becomes more and more what experience has revealed, less and less what imagination has created, and hence, since it was not designed to suit man's needs, less and less what he would have it be. With increasing knowledge his power to manipulate his physical environment increases, but in gaining the knowledge which enables him to do so he surrenders insensibly the power which in his ignorance he had to mold the universe. The forces of nature obey him, but in learning to master them he has in another sense allowed them to master him. He has exchanged the universe which his desires created, the universe made for man, for the universe of nature of which he is only a part. Like the child growing into manhood, he passes from a world which is fitted to him into a world for which he must fit himself.

If, then, the world of poetry, mythology, and religion represents the world as a man would like to have it, while science represents the world as he gradually comes to discover it, we need only compare the two to realize how irreconcilable they appear. For the cozy bowl of the sky arched in a protecting curve above him he must exchange the cold immensities of space, and, for the spiritual order which he has designed, the chaos of nature. God he had loved *because* God was anthropomorphic, because He was made in man's own image, with purposes and desires which were human and hence understandable. But Nature's purpose, if purpose she can be said to have, is no purpose of his and is not understandable in his terms. Her desire merely to live and to propagate in innumerable forms, her ruthless indifference to his values, and the blindness of her irresistible will strike terror to his soul, and he comes in the fullness of his experience to realize that the ends which he proposes to himself—happiness and order and reason—are ends which he must achieve, if he achieve them at all, in her despite. Formerly he had believed in even his darkest moments that the universe was rational if he could only grasp its rationality, but gradually he comes to suspect that rationality is an attribute of himself alone and that there is no reason to suppose that his own life has any more meaning than the life of the humblest insect that crawls from one annihilation to another. Nature, in her blind thirst for life, has filled every possible cranny of the rotting earth with some sort of fantastic creature, and among them man is but one—perhaps the most miserable of all, because he is the only one in whom the instinct of life falters long enough to enable it to ask the question "Why?" As long as life is regarded as having been created, creating may be held to imply a purpose, but merely to have come into being is, in all likelihood, merely to go out of it also.

Fortunately, perhaps, man, like the individual child, was spared in his cradle the knowledge which he could not bear. Illusions have been lost one by one. God, instead of disappearing in an instant, has retreated step by step and surrendered gradually his control of the universe. Once he decreed the fall of every sparrow and counted the hairs upon every head; a little later he became merely the original source of the laws of nature, and even today there are thousands who, unable to bear the thought of losing him completely, still fancy that they can distinguish the uncertain outlines of a misty figure. But the rôle which he plays grows less and less, and man is left more and more alone in a universe to which he is completely alien. His world was once, like the child's world, three-quarters myth and poetry. His teleological concepts molded it into a form which he could appreciate and he gave to it moral laws which would make it meaningful, but step by step the outlines of nature have thrust themselves upon him, and for the dream which he made is substituted a reality devoid of any pattern which he can understand.

In the course of this process innumerable readjustments have been made, and always with the effort to disturb as little as possible the myth which is so much more full of human values than the fact which comes in some measure to replace it. Thus, for example, the Copernican theory of astronomy, removing the earth from the center of the universe and assigning it a very insignificant place among an infinitude of whirling motes, was not merely resisted as a fact, but was, when finally accepted, accepted as far as possible without its implications. Even if taken entirely by itself and without the whole system of facts of which it is a part, it renders extremely improbable the assumption, fundamental in most human thought, that the universe has man as its center and is hence understandable in his terms, but this implication was disregarded just as, a little later, the implications of the theory of evolution were similarly disregarded. It is not likely that if man had been aware from the very beginning that his world was a mere detail in the universe, and himself merely one of the innumerable species of living things, he would ever have come to think of himself, as he even now tends to do, as a being whose desires must be somehow satisfiable and whose reason must be matched by some similar reason in nature. But the myth, having been once established, persists long after the assumptions upon which it was made have been destroyed, because, being born of desire, it is far more satisfactory than any fact.

Unfortunately, perhaps, experience does not grow at a constant, but at an accelerated, rate. The Greeks who sought knowledge, not through the study of nature, but through the examination of their own minds, developed a philosophy which was really analogous to myth, because the laws which determined its growth were dictated by human desires, and they discovered few facts capable of disturbing the pattern which they devised. The Middle Ages retreated still further into themselves, but with the Renaissance man began to surrender himself to nature, and the sciences, each nourishing the other, began their iconoclastic march. Three centuries lay between the promulgation of the Copernican theory and the publication of the *Origin of Species,* but in sixty-odd years which have elapsed since that latter event the blows have fallen with a rapidity which left no interval for recovery. The structures which are variously known as mythology, religion, and philosophy, and which are alike in that each has as its function the interpretation of experience in terms which have human values, have collapsed under the force of successive attacks and shown themselves utterly incapable of assimilating the new stores of experience which have been dumped upon the world. With increasing completeness science maps out the pattern of nature, but the latter has no relation to the pattern of human needs and feelings.

Consider, for example, the plight of ethics. Historical criticism having destroyed what used to be called by people of learning and intelligence "Christian Evidences," and biology having shown how unlikely it is that man is the recipient of any transcendental knowledge, there remains no foundation in authority for ideas of right and wrong; and if, on the other hand, we turn to the traditions of the human race, anthropology is ready to prove that no consistent human tradition has ever existed. Custom has furnished the only basis which ethics have ever had, and there is no conceivable human action which custom has not at one time justified and at another condemned. Standards are imaginary things, and yet it is extremely doubtful if man can live well, either spiritually or physically, without the belief that they are somehow real. Without them society lapses into anarchy and the individual becomes aware of an intolerable disharmony between himself and the universe. Instinctively and emotionally he is an ethical animal. No known race is so low in the scale of civilization that it has not attributed a moral order to the world, because no known race is so little human as not to suppose a moral order so innately desirable as to have an inevitable existence. It is man's most fundamental myth, and life seems meaningless to him without it. Yet, as that systematized and cumulative experience which is called science displaces one after another the myths which have been generated by need, it grows more and more likely that he must remain an ethical animal in a universe which contains no ethical element.

Mystical philosophers have sometimes said that they "accepted the universe." They have, that is to say, formed of it some conception which answered the emotional needs of their spirit and which brought them a sense of being in harmony with its aims and processes. They have been aware of no needs which nature did not seem to supply and of no ideals which she too did not seem to recognize. They have felt themselves one with her because they have had the strength of imagination to make her over in their own image, and it is doubtful if any man can live at peace who does not thus feel himself at home. But as the world assumes the shape which science gives it, it becomes more and more difficult to find such emotional correspondences. Whole realms of human feeling, like the realm of ethics, find no place for themselves in the pattern of nature and generate needs for which no satisfaction is supplied. What man knows is everywhere at war with what he wants.

In the course of a few centuries his knowledge, and hence the universe of which he finds himself an inhabitant, has been completely revolutionized, but his instincts and his emotions have remained, relatively at least, unchanged. He is still, as he always was, adjusted to the orderly, purposeful, humanized world which all peoples unburdened by experience have figured to themselves, but that world no longer exists. He has the same sense of dignity to which the myth of his descent from the gods was designed to minister, and the same innate purposefulness which led him to attribute a purpose to nature, but he can no longer think in terms appropriate to either. The world which his reason and his investigation reveal is a world which his emotions cannot comprehend.

Casually he accepts the spiritual iconoclasm of science, and in the detachment of everyday life he learns to play with the cynical wisdom of biology and psychology, which explain away the awe of emotional experience just as earlier science explained away the awe of conventional piety. Yet, under the stress of emotional crises, knowledge is quite incapable of controlling his emotions or of justifying them to himself. In love, he calls upon the illusions of man's grandeur and dignity to help him accept his emotions, and faced with tragedy he calls upon illusion to dignify his suffering; but lyric flight is checked by the rationality which he has cultivated, and in the world of metabolism and hormones, repressions and complexes, he finds no answer for his needs. He is feeling about love, for example, much as the troubadour felt, but he thinks about it in a very different way. Try as he may, the two halves of his soul can hardly be made to coalesce, and he cannot either feel as his intelligence tells him that he should feel or think as his emotions would have him think, and thus he is reduced to mocking his torn and divided soul. In the grip of passion he cannot, as some romanticist might have done, accept it with a religious trust in the mystery of love, nor yet can he regard it as a psychiatrist, himself quite free from emotion, might suggest—merely as an interesting specimen of psychical botany. Man *qua* thinker may delight in the intricacies of psychology, but man *qua* lover has not learned to feel in its terms; so that, though complexes and ductless glands may serve to explain the feelings of another, one's own still demand all these symbols of the ineffable in which one has long ceased to believe.

Time was when the scientist, the poet, and the philosopher walked hand in hand. In the universe which the one perceived the other found himself comfortably at home. But the world of modern science is one in which the intellect alone can rejoice. The mind leaps, and leaps perhaps with a sort of elation, through the immensities of space, but the spirit, frightened and cold, longs to have once more above its head the inverted bowl beyond which may lie whatever paradise its desires may create. The lover who surrendered himself to the Implacable Aphrodite or who fancied his foot upon the lowest rung of the Platonic ladder of love might retain his self-respect, but one can neither resist nor yield gracefully to a carefully catalogued psychosis. A happy life is a sort of poem, with a poem's elevation and dignity, but emotions cannot be dignified unless they are first respected. They must seem to correspond with, to be justified by, something in the structure of the universe itself; but though it was the function of religion and philosophy to hypostatize some such correspondence, to project a humanity upon nature, or at least to conceive of a humane force above and beyond her, science finds no justification for such a process and is content instead to show how illusions were born.

The most ardent love of truth, the most resolute determination to follow nature no matter to what black abyss she may lead, need not blind one to the fact that many of the lost illusions had, to speak the language of science, a survival value. Either individuals or societies whose life is imbued with a cheerful certitude, whose aims are clear, and whose sense of the essential rightness of life is strong, live and struggle with an energy unknown to the skeptical and the pessimistic. Whatever the limitations of their intellects as instruments of criticism, they possess the physical and emotional vigor which is, unlike critical intelligence, analogous to the processes of nature. They found empires and conquer wildernesses, and they pour the excess of their energy into works of art which the intelligence of more sophisticated peoples continue to admire even though it has lost the faith in life which is requisite for the building of a Chartres or the carving of a Venus de Milo. The one was not erected to a law of nature or the other designed to celebrate the libido, for each presupposed a sense of human dignity which science nowhere supports.

Thus man seems caught in a dilemma which his intellect has devised. Any deliberately managed return to a state of relative ignorance, however desirable it might be argued to be, is obviously out of the question. We cannot, as the naïve proponents of the various religions, new and old, seem to assume, believe one thing and forget another merely because we happen to be convinced that it would be desirable to do so; and it is worth observing that the new psychology, with its penetrating analysis of the influence of desire upon belief, has so adequately warned the reason of the tricks which the will can play upon it that it has greatly decreased the possibility of beneficent delusion and serves to hold the mind in a steady contemplation of that from which it would fain escape. Weak and uninstructed intelligences take refuge in the monotonous repetition of once living creeds, or are even reduced to the desperate expedient of going to sleep amid the formulae of the flabby pseudo-religions in which the modern world is so prolific. But neither of these classes affords any aid to the robust but serious mind which is searching for some terms upon which it may live.

And if we are, as by this time we should be, free from any teleological delusion, if we no longer make the unwarranted assumption that every human problem is somehow of necessity solvable, we must confess it may be that for the sort of being whom we have described no survival is possible in any form like that which his soul has now taken. He is a fantastic thing that has developed sensibilities and established values beyond the nature which gave him birth. He is of all living creatures the one to whom the earth is the least satisfactory. He has arrived at a point where he can no longer delude himself as to the extent of his predicament, and should he either become modified or disappear the earth would continue to spin and the grass to grow as it has always done. Of the thousands of living species the vast majority would be as unaware of his passing as they are unaware now of his presence, and he would go as a shadow goes. His arts, his religions, and his civilizations—these are fair and wonderful things, but they are fair and wonderful to him alone. With the extinction of his poetry would be extinguished also the only sensibility for which it has any meaning, and there would remain nothing capable of feeling a loss. Nothing would be left to label the memory of his discontent "divine," and those creatures who find in nature no lack would resume their undisputed possession of the earth.

Anthropoid in form some of them might continue to be, and possessed as well of all of the human brain that makes possible a cunning adaption to the conditions of physical life. To them nature might yield up subtler secrets than any yet penetrated; their machines might be more wonderful and their bodies more healthy than any yet known—even though there had passed away, not merely all myth and poetry, but the need for them as well. Cured of his transcendental cravings, content with things as they are, accepting the universe as experience had shown it to be, man would be freed of his soul and, like the other animals, either content or at least desirous of nothing which he might not hope ultimately to obtain.

Nor can it be denied that certain adumbrations of this type have before now come into being. Among those of keener intellect there are scientists to whom the test tube and its contents are all-sufficient, and among those of coarser grain, captains of finance and builders of mills, there are those to whom the acquirement of wealth and power seems to constitute a life in which no lack can be perceived. Doubtless they are not new types; doubtless they have always existed; but may they not be the strain from which Nature will select the coming race? Is not their creed the creed of Nature, and are they not bound to triumph over those whose illusions are no longer potent because they are no longer really believed? Certain philosophers, clinging desperately to the ideal of a humanized world, have proposed a retreat into the imagination. Bertrand Russell in his popular essay, *A Free Man's Worship*, Unamuno and Santayana *passim* throughout their works, have argued that the way of salvation lay in a sort of ironic belief, in a determination to act as though one still believed the things which once were really held true. But is not this a desperate expedient, a last refuge likely to appeal only to the leaders of a lost cause? Does it not represent the last, least substantial, phase of fading faith, something which borrows what little substance it seems to have from a reality of the past? If it seems half real to the sons of those who lived in the spiritual world of which it is a shadow, will it not seem, a little further removed, only a faint futility? Surely it has but little to oppose to those who come armed with the certitudes of science and united with, not fleeing from, the nature amid which they live.

And if the dilemma here described is itself a delusion it is at least as vividly present and as terribly potent as those other delusions which have shaped or deformed the human spirit. There is no significant contemporary writer upon philosophy, ethics, or esthetics whose speculations do not lead him to it in one form or another, and even the less reflective are aware of it in their own way. Both our practical morality and our emotional lives are adjusted to a world which no longer exists. In so far as we adhere to a code of conduct, we do so largely because certain habits still persist, not because we can give any logical reason for preferring them, and in so far as we indulge ourselves in the primitive emotional satisfactions—romantic love, patriotism, zeal for justice, and so forth—our satisfaction is the result merely of the temporary suspension of our disbelief in the mythology upon which they are founded. Traditionalists in religion are fond of asserting that our moral codes are flimsy because they are rootless; but, true as this is, it is perhaps not so important as the fact that our emotional lives are rootless too.

If the gloomy vision of a dehumanized world which has just been evoked is not to become a reality, some complete readjustment must be made, and at least two generations have found themselves unequal to the task. The generation of Thomas Henry Huxley, so busy with destruction as never adequately to realize how much it was destroying, fought with such zeal against frightened conservatives that it never took time to do more than assert with some vehemence that all would be well, and the generation that followed either danced amid the ruins or sought by various compromises to save the remains of a few tottering structures. But neither patches nor evasions will serve. It is not a changed world but a new one in which man must henceforth live if he lives at all, for all his premises have been destroyed and he must proceed to new conclusions. The values which he thought established have been swept away along with the rules by which he thought they might be attained.

To this fact many are not yet awake, but our novels, our poems, and our pictures are enough to reveal that a generation aware of its predicament is at hand. It has awakened to the fact that both the ends which its fathers proposed to themselves and the emotions from which they drew their strength seem irrelevant and remote. With a smile, sad or mocking, according to individual temperament, it regards those works of the past in which were summed up the values of life. The romantic ideal of a world well lost for love and the classic ideal of austere dignity seem equally ridiculous, equally meaningless when referred, not to the temper of the past, but to the temper of the present. The passions which swept through the once major poets no longer awaken any profound response, and only in the bleak, torturous complexities of a T. S. Eliot does it find its moods given adequate expression. Here disgust speaks with a robust voice and denunciation is confident, but ecstasy, flickering and uncertain, leaps fitfully up only to sink back among the cinders. And if the poet, with his gift of keen perceptions and his power of organization, can achieve only the most momentary and unstable adjustments, what hope can there be for those whose spirit is a less powerful instrument?

And yet it is with such as he, baffled, but content with nothing which plays only upon the surface, that the hope for a still humanized future must rest. No one can tell how many of the old values must go or how new the new will be. Thus, while under the influence of the old mythology the sexual instinct was transformed into romantic love and tribal solidarity into the religion of patriotism, there is nothing in the modern consciousness capable of effecting these transmutations. Neither the one nor the other is capable of being, as it once was, the raison d'être of a life or the motif of a poem which is not, strictly speaking, derivative and anachronistic. Each is fading, each becoming as much a shadow as devotion to the cult of purification through self-torture. Either the instincts upon which they are founded will achieve new transformations or they will remain merely instincts, regarded as having no particular emotional significance in a spiritual world which, if it exists at all, will be as different from the spiritual world of, let us say, Robert Browning as that world is different from the world of Cato the Censor.

As for this present unhappy time, haunted by ghosts from a dead world and not yet at home in its own, its predicament is not, to return to the comparison with which we began, unlike the predicament of the adolescent who has not yet learned to orient himself without reference to the mythology amid which his childhood was passed. He still seeks in the world of his experience for the values which he had found there, and he is aware only of a vast disharmony. But boys—most of them, at least—grow up, and the world of adult consciousness has always held a relation to myth intimate enough to make readjustment possible. The finest spirits have bridged the gulf, have carried over with them something of a child's faith, and only the coarsest have grown into something which was no more than finished animality. Today the gulf is broader, the adjustment more difficult, than ever it was before, and even the possibility of an actual human maturity is problematic. There impends for the human spirit either extinction or a readjustment more stupendous than any made before.

JOHN CROWE RANSOM

"Reconstructed but Unregenerate"
(1930)

"I'll take my stand in Dixie," runs the key refrain in a song long popular with Southerners nostalgic for the antebellum South and the Confederacy. In 1930, these words were used by the dozen Southern writers who contributed to *I'll Take My Stand: The South and the Agrarian Tradition* (New York, 1930). This manifesto against industrial civilization, science, and liberalism attracted a great deal of attention in the context of the Depression, when even non-Southerners were ready to listen to its skeptical response to the prevailing order. The deliberately reactionary men who wrote this book appeared, in the political spectrum of the early Depression years, as extreme right-wing counterpoints to the communists on the far left. The authors became known as the "Nashville Agrarians" because several of them were affiliated with Vanderbilt University, in Nashville, Tennessee. Among these were the poet and critic John Crowe Ransom (1888–1974), who edited *I'll Take My Stand*. "Reconstructed but Unregenerate," which follows, was Ransom's contribution to the collection. He soon lost interest in agrarianism as an economic program, turned his attention to literary criticism, and became one of the most respected scholars in the movement for rigorous textual analysis that came to be called the New Criticism. Ransom also lost interest in the South and, despite the exceedingly romantic description of the Old South he offered in "Reconstructed but Unregenerate," left Nashville in 1939 to live and teach in Ohio. The other contributors to *I'll Take My Stand* also went their separate ways. The best known of the other agrarians were the poets Alan Tate and Donald Davidson, and Robert Penn Warren, who later wrote one of the most acclaimed novels of the midcentury, *All the King's Men* (New York, 1946). Warren's contribution to *I'll Take My Stand*, "The Briar Patch," was a defense of racial segregation, although so mild in spirit for the times that some of the other agrarians were uncomfortable with its relative liberalism.

For an informative account of the agrarian movement and Ransom's role in it, see Daniel J. Singal, *The War Within: From Victorian to Modernist Thought in the South, 1919–1945* (Chapel Hill, 1982), 198–231. See also the studies of the careers of several of the agrarians in Michael O'Brien, *The Idea of the American South, 1920–1941* (Baltimore, 1979). A generous attitude toward Ransom is displayed in Mark G. Malvasi, *The Unregenerate South: The Agrarian Thought of John Crowe Ransom, Allen Tate, and Donald Davidson* (Baton Rouge, 1997). See also Eugene Genovese, *The Southern Tradition: The Achievement and Limitations of an American Conservatism* (Cambridge, Mass., 1994).

It is out of fashion in these days to look backward rather than forward. About the only American given to it is some unreconstructed Southerner, who persists in his regard for a certain terrain, a certain history, and a certain inherited way of living. He is punished as his crime deserves. He feels himself in the American scene as an anachronism, and knows he is felt by his neighbors as a reproach.

Of course he is a tolerably harmless reproach. He is like some quaint local character of eccentric but fixed principles who is thoroughly and almost pridefully accepted by the village as a rare exhibit in the antique kind. His position is secure from the interference of the police, but it is of a rather ambiguous dignity.

I wish now that he were not so entirely taken for granted, and that as a reproach he might bear a barb and inflict a sting. I wish that the whole force of my own generation in the South would get behind his principles and make them an ideal which the nation at large would have to reckon with. But first I will describe him in the light of the position he seems now to occupy actually before the public.

His fierce devotion is to a lost cause—though it grieves me that his contemporaries are so sure it is lost. They are so far from fearing him and his example that they even in the excess of confidence offer him a little honor, a little petting. As a Southerner I have observed this indulgence and I try to be grateful. Obviously it does not constitute a danger to the Republic; distinctly it is not treasonable. They are good enough to attribute a sort of glamour to the Southern life as it is defined for them in a popular tradition. They like to use the South as the nearest available locus for the scenes of their sentimental songs, and sometimes they send their daughters to the Southern seminaries. Not too much, of course, is to be made of this last gesture, for they do not expose to this hazard their sons, who in our still very masculine order will have to discharge the functions of citizenship, and who must accordingly be sternly educated in the principles of progress at progressive institutions of learning. But it does not seem to make so much difference what principles of a general character the young women acquire, since they are not likely to be impaired by principles in their peculiar functions, such as virtue and the domestic duties. And so, at suitable seasons, and on the main-line trains, one may see them in some numbers, flying south or flying north like migratory birds; and one may wonder to what extent their philosophy of life will be affected by two or three years in the South. One must remember that probably their parents have already made this calculation and are prepared to answer, Not much.

The Southerner must know, and in fact he does very well know, that his antique conservatism does not exert a great influence against the American progressivist doctrine. The Southern idea today is down, and the progressive or American idea is up. But the historian and the philosopher, who take views that are thought to be respectively longer and deeper than most, may very well reverse this order and find that the Southern idea rather than the American has in its favor the authority of example and the approval of theory. And some prophet may even find it possible to expect that it will yet rise again.

I will propose a thesis which seems to have about as much cogency as generalizations usually have: The South is unique on this continent for having founded and defended a

Source: Twelve Southerners, *I'll Take My Stand: The South and the Agrarian Tradition.* Reprinted by permission of Louisiana State University Press. Copyright © 1930 by Harper & Brothers. Copyright renewed © 1958 by Donald Davidson. Introduction copyright © 1962, 1977 by Louis D. Rubin, Jr. Biographical essays copyright © 1962, 1977 by Virginia Rock.

culture which was according to the European principles of culture; and the European principles had better look to the South if they are to be perpetuated in this country.

The nearest of the European cultures which we could examine is that of England; and this is of course the right one in the case, quite aside from our convenience. England was actually the model employed by the South, in so far as Southern culture was not quite indigenous. And there is in the South even today an Anglophile sentiment quite anomalous in the American scene.

England differs from America doubtless in several respects, but most notably in the fact that England did her pioneering an indefinite number of centuries ago, did it well enough, and has been living pretty tranquilly on her establishment ever since, with infrequent upheavals and replacements. The customs and institutions of England seem to the American observer very fixed and ancient. There is no doubt that the English tradition expresses itself in many more or less intangible ways, but it expresses itself most importantly in a material establishment; and by this I mean the stable economic system by which Englishmen are content to take their livelihood from the physical environment. The chief concern of England's half-mythical pioneers, as with pioneers anywhere, was with finding the way to make a living. Evidently they found it. But fortunately the methods they worked out proved transmissible, proved, in fact, the main reliance of the succeeding generations. The pioneers explored the soil, determined what concessions it might reasonably be expected to make of them, housed themselves, developed all their necessary trades, and arrived by painful experiment at a thousand satisfactory recipes by which they might secure their material necessities. Their descendants have had the good sense to consider that this establishment was good enough for them. They have elected to live their comparatively easy and routine lives in accordance with the tradition which they inherited, and they have consequently enjoyed a leisure, a security, and an intellectual freedom that were never the portion of pioneers.

The pioneering life is not the normal life, whatever some Americans may suppose. It is not, if we look for the meaning of European history. The lesson of each of the European cultures now extant is in this—that European opinion does not make too much of the intense practical enterprises, but is at pains to define rather narrowly the practical effort which is prerequisite to the reflective and aesthetic life. Boys are very well pleased to employ their muscles almost exclusively, but men prefer to exercise their minds. It is the European intention to live materially along the inherited line of least resistance, in order to put the surplus of energy into the free life of the mind. Thus is engendered that famous, or infamous, European conservatism, which will appear stupid, necessarily, to men still fascinated by materialistic projects, men in a state of arrested adolescence; for instance, to some very large if indefinite fraction of the population of these United States.

I have in mind here the core of unadulterated Europeanism, with its self-sufficient, backward-looking, intensely provincial communities. The human life of English provinces long ago came to terms with nature, fixed its roots somewhere in the spaces between the rocks and in the shade of the trees, founded its comfortable institutions, secured its modest prosperity—and then willed the whole in perpetuity to the generations which should come after, in the ingenuous confidence that it would afford them all the essential human satisfactions. For it is the character of a seasoned provincial life that it is realistic, or successfully adapted to its natural environment, and that as a consequence it is stable, or hereditable. But it is the character of our urbanized, anti-provincial, progressive, and mobile American life that it is in a condition of eternal flux. Affections, and long memories, attach to the ancient bowers of life in the provinces; but they will not attach to what is always changing. Americans, however, are peculiar in being somewhat averse to these affections for natural objects, and to these memories.

Memories of the past are attended with a certain pain called nostalgia. It is hardly a technical term in our sociology or our psychiatry, but it might well be. Nostalgia is a kind of growing-pain, psychically speaking. It occurs to our sorrow when we have decided that it is time for us, marching to some magnificent destiny, to abandon an old home, an old provincial setting, or an old way of living to which we had become habituated. It is the complaint of human nature in its vegetative aspect, when it is plucked up by the roots from the place of its origin and transplanted in foreign soil, or even left dangling in the air. And it must be nothing else but nostalgia, the instinctive objection to being transplanted, that chiefly prevents the deracination of human communities and their complete geographical dispersion as the casualties of an insatiable wanderlust.

Deracination in our Western life is the strange discipline which individuals turn upon themselves, enticed by the blandishments of such fine words as Progressive, Liberal, and Forward-looking. The progressivist says in effect: Do not allow yourself to feel home-sick; form no such powerful attachments that you will feel a pain in cutting them loose; prepare your spirit to be always on the move. According to this gospel, there is no rest for the weary, not even in heaven. The poet Browning expresses an ungrateful intention, the moment he shall enter into his reward, to "fight onward, there as here." The progressivist H. G. Wells has outlined very neatly his scheme of progress, the only disheartening feature being that he has had to revise it a good many times, and that the state to which he wants us to progress never has any finality or definition. Browning and Wells would have made very good Americans, and I am sure they have got the most of their disciples on this side of the Atlantic; they have not been good Europeans. But all the true progressivists intend to have a program so elastic that they can always propose new worlds to conquer. If his Utopia were practicable really, and if the progressivist should secure it, he would then have to defend it from further progress, which would mean his transformation from a progressivist into a conservative. Which is unthinkable.

The gospel of Progress is a curious development, which does not reflect great credit on the supposed capacity of our species for formulating its own behavior. Evidently the formula may involve its practitioners in self-torture and suicide just as readily as in the enjoyment of life. In most societies man has adapted himself to environment with plenty of intelligence to secure easily his material necessities from the graceful bounty of nature. And then, ordinarily, he concludes a truce with nature, and he and nature seem to live on terms of mutual respect and amity, and his loving arts, religions, and philosophies come spontaneously into being: these are the blessings of peace. But the latter-day societies have been seized—none quite so violently as our American one—with the strange idea that the human destiny is not to secure an honorable peace with nature, but to wage an unrelenting war on nature. Men, therefore, determine to conquer nature to a degree which is quite beyond reason so far as specific human advantage is concerned, and which enslaves them to toil and turnover. Man is boastfully declared to be a natural scientist essentially, whose strength is capable of crushing and making over to his own desires the brute materiality which is nature; but in his infinite contention with this materiality he is really capitulating to it. His engines transform the face of nature—a little—but when they have been perfected, he must invent new engines that will perform even more heroically. And always the next engine of his invention, even though it be that engine which is to invade the material atom and exploit the most secret treasury of nature's wealth, will be a physical engine; and the man who uses it will be engaged in substantially the same struggle as was the primitive Man with the Hoe.

This is simply to say that Progress never defines its ultimate objective, but thrusts its victims at once into an infinite series. Our vast industrial machine, with its laboratory centers of experimentation, and its far-flung organs of mass production, is like a Prussianized state which is organized strictly for war and can never consent to peace. Or, returning to the original figure, our progressivists are the latest version of those pioneers who conquered the wilderness, except that they are pioneering on principle, or from force of habit, and without any recollection of what pioneering was for.

Along with the gospel of Progress goes the gospel of Service. They work beautifully as a team.

Americans are still dreaming the materialistic dreams of their youth. The stuff these dreams were made on was the illusion of preeminent personal success over a material opposition. Their tone was belligerence, and the euphemism under which it masqueraded was ambition. But men are not lovely, and men are not happy, for being too ambitious. Let us distinguish two forms under which ambition drives men on their materialistic projects; a masculine and a feminine.

Ambitious men fight, first of all, against nature; they propose to put nature under their heel; this is the dream of scientists burrowing in their cells, and then of the industrial men who beg of their secret knowledge and go out to trouble the earth. But after a certain point this struggle is vain, and we only use ourselves up if we prolong it. Nature wears out man before man can wear out nature; only a city man, a laboratory man, a man cloistered from the normal contacts with the soil, will deny that. It seems wiser to be moderate in our expectations of nature, and respectful; and out of so simple a thing as respect for the physical earth and its teeming life comes a primary joy, which is an inexhaustible source of arts and religions and philosophies.

Ambitious men are belligerent also in the way they look narrowly and enviously upon one another; and I do not refer to such obvious disasters as wars and the rumors of wars. Ambition of the first form was primary and masculine, but there is a secondary form which is typically feminine, though the distribution between the sexes may not be without the usual exceptions. If it is Adam's curse to will perpetually to work his mastery upon nature, it is Eve's curse to prompt Adam every morning to keep up with the best people in the neighborhood in taking the measure of his success. There can never be stability and establishment in a community whose every lady member is sworn to see that her mate is not eclipsed in the competition for material advantages; that community will fume and ferment, and every constituent part will be in perpetual physical motion. The good life depends on leisure, but leisure depends on an establishment, and the establishment depends on a prevailing magnanimity which scorns personal advancement at the expense of the free activity of the mind.

The masculine form is hallowed by Americans, as I have said, under the name of Progress. The concept of Progress is the concept of man's increasing command, and eventually perfect command, over the forces of nature; a concept which enhances too readily our conceit, and brutalizes our life. I believe there is possible no deep sense of beauty, no heroism of conduct, and no sublimity of religion, which is not informed by the humble sense of man's precarious position in the universe. The feminine form is likewise hallowed among us under the name of Service. The term has many meanings, but we come finally to the one which is critical for the moderns; service means the function of Eve, it means the seducing of laggard men into fresh struggles with nature. It has special application to the apparently stagnant sections of mankind, it busies itself with the heathen Chinee, with the Roman Catholic Mexican, with the "lower" classes in our own society. Its motive is missionary. Its watchwords are such as Protestantism, individualism, Democracy, and the point of its appeal is a discontent, generally labeled "divine."

Progress and Service are not European slogans, they are Americanisms. We alone have devoted our lives to ideals which are admirable within their proper limits, but which expose us to slavery when pursued without critical intelligence. Some Europeans are taken in by these ideals, but hardly the American communities on the whole. Herr Spengler, with a gesture of defeat, glorifies the modern American captain of industry when he compares his positive achievements with the futilities of modern poets and artists. Whereupon we may well wish to save Europe from even so formidable a European as Spengler, hoping that he may not convert Europe to his view. And it is hardly likely; Europe is founded on a principle of conservatism, and is deeply scornful of the American and pioneer doctrine of the strenuous life. In 1918 there was danger that Europe might ask to be Americanized, and American missionaries were quite prepared to answer the call. But since then there has been a revulsion in European opinion, and this particular missionary enterprise confronts now an almost solid barrier of hostility. Europe is not going to be Americanized through falling suddenly in love with strenuousness. It only remains to be seen whether Europe may not be Americanized after all through envy, and through being reminded ceaselessly of our superior prosperity. That is an event to be determined by the force of European magnanimity; Europe's problem, not ours.

The Southern states were settled, of course, by miscellaneous strains. But evidently the one which determined the peculiar tradition of the South was the one which came out of Europe most convinced of the virtues of establishment, contrasting with those strains which seem for the most part to have dominated the other sections, and which came out of Europe feeling rebellious toward all establishments. There are a good many faults to be found with the old South, but hardly the fault of being intemperately addicted to work and to gross material prosperity. The South never conceded that the whole duty of man was to increase material production, or that the index to the degree of his culture was the volume of his material production. His business seemed to be rather to envelop both his work and his play with a leisure which permitted the activity of intelligence. On this assumption the South pioneered her way to a sufficiently comfortable and rural sort of establishment, considered that an establishment was something stable, and proceeded to enjoy the fruits thereof. The arts of the section, such as they were, were not immensely passionate, creative, and romantic; they were the eighteenth-century social arts of dress, conversation, manners, the table, the hunt, politics, oratory, the pulpit. These were arts of living and not arts of escape; they were also community arts, in which every class of society could participate after its kind. The South took life easy, which is itself a tolerably comprehensive art.

But so did other communities in 1850, I believe. And doubtless some others do so yet; in part of New England, for example. If there are such communities, this is their token, that they are settled. Their citizens are comparatively satisfied with the life they have inherited, and are careful to look backward quite as much as they look forward. Before the Civil War there must have been many such communities this side of the frontier. The difference between the North and the South was that the South was constituted by such communities and made solid. But solid is only a comparative term here. The South as a culture had more solidity than another section, but there were plenty of gaps in it. The most we can say is that the Southern establishment was completed in a good many of the Southern communities, and that this establishment was an active formative influence on the spaces between, and on the frontier spaces outlying, which had not yet perfected their organization of the economic life.

The old Southern life was of course not so fine as some of the traditionalists like to believe. It did not offer serious competition against the glory that was Greece or the grandeur that was Rome. It hardly began to match the finish of the English, or any other important European civilization. It is quite enough to say that it was a way of life which had been considered and authorized. The establishment had a sufficient economic base, it was meant to be stable rather than provisional, it had got beyond the pioneering stage, it provided leisure, and its benefits were already being enjoyed. It may as well be admitted that Southern society was not an institution of very showy elegance, for the so-called aristocrats were mostly home-made and countrified. Aristocracy is not the word which defines this social organization so well as squirearchy, which I borrow from a recent article by Mr. William Frierson in the *Sewanee Review*. And even the squires, and the other classes, too, did not define themselves very strictly. They were loosely graduated social orders, not fixed as in Europe. Their relations were personal and friendly. It was a kindly society, yet a realistic one; for it was a failure if it could not be said that people were for the most part in their right places. Slavery was a feature monstrous enough in theory, but, more often than not, humane in practice; and it is impossible to believe that its abolition alone could have effected any great revolution in society.

The fullness of life as it was lived in the ante-bellum South by the different social orders can be estimated today only by the application of some difficult sociological technique. It is my thesis that all were committed to a form of leisure, and that their labor itself was leisurely. The only Southerners who went abroad to Washington and elsewhere, and put themselves into the record, were those from the top of the pyramid. They held their own with their American contemporaries. They were not intellectually as seasoned as good Europeans, but then the Southern culture had had no very long time to grow, as time is reckoned in these matters: it would have borne a better fruit eventually. They had a certain amount of learning, which was not as formidable as it might have been: but at least it was classical and humanistic learning, not highly scientific, and not wildly scattered about over a variety of special studies.

Then the North and the South fought, and the consequences were disastrous to both. The Northern temper was one of jubilation and expansiveness, and now it was no longer shackled by the weight of the conservative Southern tradition. Industrialism, the latest form of pioneering and the worst, presently overtook the North, and in due time has now produced our present American civilization. Poverty and pride overtook the South; poverty to bring her institutions into disrepute and to sap continually at her courage; and a false pride to inspire a distaste for the thought of fresh pioneering projects, and to doom her to an increasing physical enfeeblement.

It is only too easy to define the malignant meaning of industrialism. It is the contemporary form of pioneering; yet since it never consents to define its goal, it is a pioneering on principle, and with an accelerating speed. Industrialism is a program under which men, using the latest scientific paraphernalia, sacrifice comfort, leisure, and the enjoyment of life to win Pyrrhic victories from nature at points of no strategic importance. Ruskin and Carlyle feared it nearly a hundred years ago, and now it may be said that their fears have been realized partly in England, and with almost fatal completeness in America.

Industrialism is an insidious spirit, full of false promises and generally fatal to establishments since, when it once gets into them for a little renovation, it proposes never again to leave them in peace. Industrialism is rightfully a menial, of almost miraculous cunning but no intelligence; it needs to be strongly governed or it will destroy the economy of the household. Only a community of tough conservative habit can master it.

The South did not become industrialized; she did not repair the damage to her old establishment, either, and it was in part because she did not try hard enough. Hers is the case to cite when we would show how the good life depends on an adequate pioneering, and how the pioneering energy must be kept ready for call when the establishment needs overhauling. The Southern tradition came to look rather pitiable in its persistence when the twentieth century had arrived, for the establishment was quite depreciated. Unregenerate Southerners were trying to live the good life on a shabby equipment, and they were grotesque in their effort to make an art out of living when they were not decently making the living. In the country districts great numbers of these broken-down Southerners are still to be seen in patched blue-jeans, sitting on ancestral fences, shotguns across their laps and hound-dogs at their feet, surveying their unkempt acres while they comment shrewdly on the ways of God. It is their defect that they have driven a too easy, an unmanly bargain with nature, and that their æstheticism is based on insufficient labor.

But there is something heroic, and there may prove to be yet something very valuable to the Union, in their extreme attachment to a certain theory of life. They have kept up a faith which was on the point of perishing from this continent.

Of course it was only after the Civil War that the North and the South came to stand in polar opposition to each other. Immediately after Appomattox it was impossible for the South to resume even that give-and-take of ideas which had marked her antebellum relations with the North. She was offered such terms that acquiescence would have been abject. She retired within her borders in rage and held the minimum of commerce with the enemy. Persecution intensified her tradition, and made the South more solid and more Southern in the year 1875, or thereabouts, than ever before. When the oppression was left off, naturally her guard relaxed. But though the period of persecution had not been long, nevertheless the Southern tradition found itself then the less capable of uniting gracefully with the life of the Union; for that life in the meantime had been moving on in an opposite direction. The American progressive principle was like a ball rolling down the hill with an increasing momentum, and by 1890 or 1900 it was clear to any intelligent Southerner that it was a principle of boundless aggression against nature which could hardly offer much to a society devoted to the arts of peace.

But to keep on living shabbily on an insufficient patrimony is to decline, both physically and spiritually. The South declined.

And now the crisis in the South's decline has been reached.

Industrialism has arrived in the South. Already the local chambers of commerce exhibit the formidable data of Southern progress. A considerable party of Southern opinion, which might be called the New South party, is well pleased with the recent industrial accomplishments of the South and anxious for many more. Southerners of another school, who might be said to compose an Old South party, are apprehensive lest the section become completely and uncritically devoted to the industrial ideal precisely as the other sections of the Union are. But reconstruction is actually under way. Tied politically and economically to the Union, her borders wholly violable, the South now sees very well that she can restore her prosperity only within the competition of an industrial system.

After the war the Southern plantations were often broken up into small farms. These have yielded less and less of a living, and it said that they will never yield a good living until once more they are integrated into large units. But these units will be industrial units, controlled by a board of directors or an executive rather than a squire, worked with machinery, and manned not by farmers living at home, but by "labor." Even so they will not, according to Mr. Henry Ford, support the population that wants to live on them. In the off seasons the laborers will have to work in factories, which henceforth are to be counted on as among the charming features of Southern landscape. The Southern problem is complicated, but at its center is the farmer's problem, and this problem is simply the most acute version of that general agrarian problem which inspires the despair of many thoughtful Americans today.

The agrarian discontent in America is deeply grounded in the love of the tiller for the soil, which is probably, it must be confessed, not peculiar to the Southern specimen, but one of the more ineradicable human attachments, be the tiller as progressive as he may. In proposing to wean men from this foolish attachment, industrialism sets itself against the most ancient and the most humane of all the modes of human livelihood. Do Mr. Hoover and the distinguished thinkers at Washington see how essential is the mutual hatred between the industrialists and the farmers, and how mortal is their conflict? The gentlemen at Washington are mostly preaching and legislating to secure the fabulous "blessings" of industrial progress; they are on the industrial side. The industrialists have a doctrine which is monstrous, but they are not monsters personally; they are forward-lookers with nice manners, and no American progressivist is against them. The farmers are boorish and inarticulate by comparison. Progressivism is against them in their fight, though their traditional status is still so strong that soft words are still spoken to them. All the solutions recommended for their difficulties are really enticements held out to them to become a little more cooperative, more mechanical, more mobile— in short, a little more industrialized. But the farmer who is not a mere laborer, even the farmer of the comparatively new places like Iowa and Nebraska, is necessarily among the more stable and less progressive elements of society. He refuses to mobilize himself and become a unit in the industrial army, because he does not approve of army life.

I will use some terms which are hardly in his vernacular. He identifies himself with a spot of ground, and this ground carries a good deal of meaning; it defines itself for him as nature. He would till it not too hurriedly and not too mechanically to observe in it the contingency and the infinitude of nature; and so his life acquires its philosophical and even its cosmic consciousness. A man can contemplate and explore, respect and love, an object as substantial as a farm or a native province. But he cannot contemplate nor explore, respect nor love, a mere turnover, such as an assemblage of "natural resources," a pile of money, a volume of produce, a market, or a credit system. It is into precisely these intangibles that industrialism would translate the farmer's farm. It means the dehumanization of his life.

However that may be, the South at last, looking defensively about her in all directions upon an industrial world, fingers the weapons of industrialism. There is one powerful voice in the South which, tired of a long status of disrepute, would see the South made at once into a section second to none in wealth, as that is statistically reckoned, and in progressiveness, as that might be estimated by the rapidity of the industrial turnover. This desire offends those who would still like to regard the South as, in the old sense, a home;

but its expression is loud and insistent. The urban South, with its heavy importation of regular American ways and regular American citizens, has nearly capitulated to these novelties. It is the village South and the rural South which supply the resistance, and it is lucky for them that they represent a vast quantity of inertia.

Will the Southern establishment, the most substantial exhibit on this continent of a society of the European and historic order, be completely crumbled by the powerful acid of the Great Progressive Principle? Will there be no more looking backward but only looking forward? Is our New World to be dedicated forever to the doctrine of newness?

It is in the interest of America as a whole, as well as in the interest of the South, that these questions press for an answer. I will enter here the most important items of the situation as well as I can; doubtless they will appear a little over-sharpened for the sake of exhibition.

(1) The intention of Americans at large appears now to be what it was always in danger of becoming: an intention of being infinitely progressive. But this intention cannot permit of an established order of human existence, and of that leisure which conditions the life of intelligence and the arts.

(2) The old South, if it must be defined in a word, practiced the contrary and European philosophy of establishment as the foundation of the life of the spirit. The antebellum Union possessed, to say the least, a wholesome variety of doctrine.

(3) But the South was defeated by the Union on the battlefield with remarkable decisiveness, and the two consequences have been dire: the Southern tradition was physically impaired, and has ever since been unable to offer an attractive example of its philosophy in action; and the American progressive principle has developed into a pure industrialism without any check from a Southern minority whose voice ceased to make itself heard.

(4) The further survival of the Southern tradition as a detached local remnant is now unlikely. It is agreed that the South must make contact again with the Union. And in adapting itself to the actual state of the Union, the Southern tradition will have to consent to a certain industrialization of its own.

(5) The question at issue is whether the South will permit herself to be so industrialized as to lose entirely her historic identity, and to remove the last substantial barrier that has stood in the way of American progressivism; or will accept industrialism, but with a very bad grace, and will manage to maintain a good deal of her traditional philosophy.

The hope which is inherent in the situation is evident from the terms in which it is stated. The South must be industrialized—but to a certain extent only, in moderation. The program which now engages the Southern leaders is to see how the South may handle this fire without being burnt badly. The South at last is to be physically reconstructed; but it will be fatal if the South should conceive it as her duty to be regenerated and get her spirit reborn with a totally different orientation toward life.

Fortunately, the Southern program does not have to be perfectly vague. There are at least two definite lines, along either of which an intelligent Southern policy may move in the right general direction; it may even move back and forth between them and still advance.

The first course would be for the Southern leaders to arouse the sectional feeling of the South to its highest pitch of excitement in defense of all the old ways that are threatened. It might seem ungrateful to the kind industrialists to accept their handsome services in such a churlish spirit. But if one thing is more certain than another, it is that these gentlemen will not pine away in their discouragement; they have an inextinguishable enthusiasm for their rôle. The attitude that needs artificial respiration is the attitude of resistance on the part of the natives to the salesmen of industrialism. It will be fiercest and most effective if industrialism is represented to the Southern people as—what it undoubtedly is for the most part—a foreign invasion of Southern soil, which is capable of doing more devastation than was wrought when Sherman marched to the sea. From this point of view it will be a great gain if the usually-peaceful invasion forgets itself now and then, is less peaceful, and commits indiscretions. The native and the invader will be sure to come to an occasional clash, and that will offer the chance to revive ancient and almost forgotten animosities. It will be in order to proclaim to Southerners that the carpet-baggers are again in their midst. And it will be well to seize upon and advertise certain Northern industrial communities as horrible examples of a way of life we detest—not failing to point out the human catastrophe which occurs when a Southern village or rural community becomes the cheap labor of a miserable factory system. It will be a little bit harder to impress the people with the fact that the new so-called industrial "slavery" fastens not only upon the poor, but upon the middle and better classes of society, too. To make this point it may be necessary to revive such an antiquity as the old Southern gentleman and his lady, and their scorn for the dollar-chasers.

Such a policy as this would show decidedly a sense of what the Germans call Realpolitik. It could be nasty and it could be effective.

Its net result might be to give to the South eventually a position in the Union analogous more or less to the position of Scotland under the British crown—a section with a very local and peculiar culture that would, nevertheless, be secure and respected. And Southern traditionalists may take courage from the fact that it was Scottish stubbornness which obtained this position for Scotland; it did not come gratuitously, it was the consequence of an intense sectionalism that fought for a good many years before its fight was won.

That is one policy. Though it is not the only one, it may be necessary to employ it, with discretion, and to bear in mind its Scottish analogue. But it is hardly handsome enough for the best Southerners. Its methods are too easily abused; it offers too much room for the professional demagogue; and one would only as a last resort like to have the South stake upon it her whole chance of survival. After all, the reconstruction may be undertaken with some imagination, and not necessarily under the formula of a literal restoration. It does not greatly matter to what extent the identical features of the old Southern establishment are restored; the important consideration is that there be an establishment for the sake of stability.

The other course may not be so easily practicable, but it is certainly more statesmanlike. That course is for the South to reënter the American political field with a determination and an address quite beyond anything she has exhibited during her half-hearted national life of the last half a century. And this means specifically that she may pool her own stakes with the stakes of other minority groups in the Union which are circumstanced similarly. There is in active American politics already, to start with, a very belligerent if somewhat uninformed Western agrarian party. Between this party and the South there is much community of interest; both desire to defend home, stability of life, the practice of leisure, and the natural enemy of both is the insidious industrial system. There are also, scattered here and there, numerous elements with the same general attitude which would have some power if united: the persons and even communities who are thoroughly tired of progressivism and its spurious benefits, and those who have recently acquired, or miraculously through the generations preserved, a European point of view—sociologists, educators, artists, religionists, and ancient New England townships. The combination of these elements with the Western farmers and the old-fashioned South would make a formidable bloc. The South is numerically much the most substantial of these three groups, but has done next to nothing to make the cause prevail by working inside the American political system.

The unifying effective bond between these geographically diverse elements of public opinion will be the clean-cut policy that the rural life of America must be defended, and the world made safe for the farmers. My friends are often quick to tell me that against the power of the industrial spirit no such hope can be entertained. But there are some protests in these days rising against the industrial ideal, even from the centers where its grip is the stoutest; and this would indicate that our human intelligence is beginning again to assert itself. Of course this is all the truer of the European countries, which have required less of the bitter schooling of experience. Thus Dean Inge declares himself in his Romanes Lecture on "The Idea of Progress":

> I believe that the dissatisfaction with things as they are is caused not only by the failure of nineteenth-century civilization, but partly also by its success. We no longer wish to progress on those lines if we could. Our apocalyptic dream is vanishing into thin air. It may be that the industrial revolution which began in the reign of George the Third has produced most of its fruits, and has had its day. We may have to look forward to such a change as is imagined by Anatole France at the end of his *Isle of Penguins,* when, after an orgy of revolution and destruction, we shall slide back into the quiet rural life of the early modern period. If so, the authors of the revolution will have cut their own throats, for there can be no great manufacturing towns in such a society. Their disappearance will be no great loss. The race will have tried a great experiment, and will have rejected it as unsatisfying.

The South has an important part to play, if she will, in such a counter-revolution. But what pitiful service have the inept Southern politicians for many years been rendering to the cause! Their Southern loyalty at Washington has rarely had any more imaginative manifestation than to scramble vigorously for a Southern share in the federal pie. They will have to be miraculously enlightened.

I get quickly beyond my depth in sounding these political possibilities. I will utter one last fantastic thought.

No Southerner ever dreams of heaven, or pictures his Utopia on earth, without providing room for the Democratic party. Is it really possible that the Democratic party can be held to a principle, and that the principle can now be defined as agrarian, conservative, anti-industrial? It may not be impossible, after all. If it proves possible, then the South may yet be rewarded for a sentimental affection that has persisted in the face of many betrayals.

SIDNEY HOOK

"Communism without Dogmas"
(1934)

The most systematic and resourceful student of Marxist thought in the United States during the 1930s was Sidney Hook (1901–89), a philosopher who had studied with John Dewey. Parts of Hook's essay, "Communism without Dogmas," were designed as an answer to Dewey, and to two other liberal philosophers, Morris R. Cohen and Bertrand Russell, who rejected Hook's revolutionary, communist program. But the core of the essay—the part reprinted here—went beyond specific responses to Dewey, Cohen, and Russell. Hook subjected to withering and often sarcastic criticism the specific interpretations of Marxism then being advanced by the Communist Party. Hook professed to be a "communist" but found the Communist Party itself to be in the thrall of a series of religious-like "dogmas" that obscured the more scientific perspective that, according to Hook, Marx himself had represented. Hook called for a new Communist movement that would be independent from the international network of parties directed by Soviet leader Joseph Stalin. Hook's references to "NRA" are to the National Recovery Administration, an agency of the New Deal.

Later in life, Hook found Marx's teaching less persuasive, even as he continued and sharpened the critique of orthodox, Soviet-directed communism he had begun in the early 1930s. In the 1950s, Hook became one of the nation's most vociferous critics of communism, and gained notoriety for his treatment in *Heresy Yes, Conspiracy No!* (New York, 1952), of the issue of the suitability of members of the Communist Party for teaching appointments in American colleges and universities. Hook was widely understood to deny that members of the Communist Party deserved the protections of academic freedom, but he vigorously contested many constructions of his argument. For Hook's own review of the debates over his stance in the McCarthy Era, see his autobiography, *Out of Step: An Unquiet Life in the 20th Century* (New York, 1987), esp. 498–508. Many of the writings of Hook's later career were collected in *The Quest for Being* (New York, 1961) and *Pragmatism and the Tragic Sense of Life* (New York, 1974).

Yet historians now agree that Hook did his most creative and distinctive work in the 1930s. He produced a series of trenchant, critical commentaries on Marxism and on contemporary leftist politics. Chief among these were *Toward an Understanding of Karl Marx* (New York, 1933), *From Hegel to Marx: Studies in the Intellectual Development of Marx* (New York, 1936; Morningside edition with an introduction by Christopher Phelps, New York, 1994), and *Reason, Social Myths, and Democracy* (New York, 1940).

The best study of Hook's thought is restricted to its early years, and sheds helpful light on "Communism without Dogmas": Christopher Phelps, *Young Sidney Hook: Marxist and Pragmatist* (Ithaca, 1997). This supersedes all earlier treatments, but one classic work on Hook's generation of American intellectuals engaged with communism still merits attention: Daniel Aaron, *Writers on the Left* (New York, 1961). The entirety of Hook's "Communism without Dogmas," and of the essays Dewey, Cohen, and Russell wrote under the common title "Why I Am Not a Communist" are available in a volume edited by Hook, *The Meaning of Marx* (New York, 1934).

To begin with I wish to make it perfectly clear that if by communism one means an acceptance of the present principles and tactics of the Third International, or any of its affiliated organizations, I am not a communist. But to define communism in terms of membership in a specific organization is as inadequate as to define Christianity in terms of membership in any particular church. I believe that communist principles are more important than communist organizations, for they enable us to judge the theory and practice of existing communist organizations in their light. It is these principles I wish to make the basis of discussion—principles to be found in the writings of Marx and Engels, and in the economic and political works of Lenin and Trotsky. Here, again, some further distinctions are necessary. If by communism one means a form of social organization in which the associated producers democratically control the production and distribution of goods, then it is possible to be a communist without being a Marxist, although every Marxist must be a communist. Marxism, then, can only be significantly defined as *the theory and practice of achieving communism or a class-less society*. When I speak of *Marxian* communism, again I do not mean the communism preached and practised today by "official" and "orthodox" Communist parties in Europe and America. In fact it seems to me that just as Marx and Engels in 1848 called themselves communists to set themselves off from bourgeois socialists who had debased the term socialism, so it may soon become necessary to find another name for communism to differentiate it from the Communist Party which has succeeded in corrupting the meaning of the term by its mistaken theories and tragically sectarian tactics....

My own position is briefly that the fundamental doctrine of communism is sound but it has been so wrapped up in certain dogmas that its logic and force has been obscured. What I desire to do is to enumerate some of the more important dogmas of official communism, show that they are false, trace their baleful influence upon the existing theory and practice of communists and point to the necessity of reformulating the communist position in such a way—that without surrendering in the slightest its revolutionary character—its appeal can be made both more widespread and effective than it has yet been in America.

1. The first dogma I wish to discuss is the view that communism is inevitable. Although in some of the practical analyses which communists make of daily affairs, the plain implication of their statements is that communism is not inevitable, yet the canonic doctrine of official communism as well as of old line orthodox socialism, leaves little doubt that this view is not merely an expression of an emotional faith or a devout hope, but a fixed article of belief. It requires very little analysis to show that no proof can be offered of the inevitability of the victory of a proletarian revolution; and indeed all that Marx established was that the functioning of an economic order which fulfilled certain ideal conditions would in the course of time (1) lead to a progressive inability to dispose of commodities produced, to provide employment and to make a profitable return upon invested capital, and (2) result, in virtue of the processes of concentration and centralization, in the generation of the objective conditions for a new social order. Where he speaks of the expropriation of the expropriators in the "future present" tense, it is either dramatic, revolutionary prophecy or a prediction on the basis of certain psychological assumptions

Source: Sidney Hook, "Communism Without Dogmas," *Modern Monthly* (April 1934): 146, 152–55, 158–63. Reprinted by permission of Ernest B. Hook.

whose truth and invariance are by no means self-evident. The spatial metaphor of the collapse and breakdown of capitalism has been taken too literally. Capitalism may break down in the sense that the mechanisms of production, circulation and credit no longer function in a way to keep the majority of the population adequately fed or housed. But the social order which is ultimately based on human activities never breaks down. Human beings never cease their functioning; they go on from one act to another—either to a defense of what has broken down, in the sense considered before, or to attack.

To deny that communism is inevitable is not to deny the existence of social determinism any more than the scientist's denial of inevitability in nature implies the denial of causality. No. What is denied is that the conjunction of all the different factors (objective and subjective) which are necessary for social revolution can be deduced from an analysis of any unique set of economic data. Stated concretely, a Marxist examining the structure of the NRA can predict that in all likelihood the NRA will fail to accomplish its purposes. He cannot say on the basis of the economic analysis alone whether this failure of the NRA will produce a psychological reaction towards Fascism or Communism. *That, in part, depends upon his own activities.* Nor can he say whether, if the class-conscious masses do rise up to seize power, they will win the victory. *That, in part, depends upon the intelligence and courage of those who lead them.* All the factors are determined, but there is no one independent variable of which all the others are necessary functions. And one of the factors which determines or fails to determine the conjunction of all the necessary conditions into one complex sufficient condition is the activity which we undertake *now* after reflection.

The theoretical and practical consequences of this false theory of inevitability are more momentous than the question of its intrinsic validity. The first of them is that it makes unintelligible any activity in behalf of communism. I am not saying that belief in inevitability paralyzes activity in behalf of communism. On the contrary. It has often been pointed out that men are more ready to fight, and will fight more vigorously, in a battle in which they are sure they will win. What I am saying is that the belief in inevitability makes that activity unintelligible and unintelligent. In assuming that the consequences of one action or another are the same as far as the coming of communism is concerned, it denies that there are *genuine* alternatives of action—something which its propaganda assumes. It denies that moral judgments and evaluations of social activity are meaningful—something without which its agitation could not be successful. It denies that thinking makes any difference to the ultimate outcome, yet it propagates a theory according to which theory and practice go hand in hand. It denies that mistakes are possible, or if possible that they are important, or if important, that they could have been avoided. If the Panglosses believe (after Bradley) that "the world is the best of all possible worlds and everything in it is a necessary evil"; orthodox communists believe that communism is the only form of society possible after capitalism and every mistake they make is a necessary means of achieving it.

The second consequence of the dogma of inevitability is that it strengthens the belief in the doctrine of "spontaneity," which teaches that the daily experiences of the working class spontaneously generates political class consciousness. If the economic consequences of capitalism lead inevitably to communism, then, since it is admitted that the revolution—like all history—is made by men, it must be held that the economic consequences of capitalism inevitably give rise to revolutionary class consciousness. In fact, this is the belief both of orthodox social-democracy and present-day official communism, Lenin's *What's To Be Done?* to the contrary notwithstanding. When it is believed that revolutionary consciousness develops spontaneously in the masses; there takes place a systematic and wholesale over-estimation of the readiness for revolutionary activity upon the part of tradeunions, unemployed organizations, co-operatives, etc., a mistaking of restiveness for radicalism, a tendency to read into the masses the perfervid psychological intensity of an isolated, political group which thinks that because it *calls* itself a vanguard it has thereby created a mass army behind it. Worst of all the doctrine of spontaneity is used as a justification for the policy of split and schismatic fission. What difference does it make that the ranks are thinned or if doctrinal content is watered down, when there is an unlimited reservoir of revolutionary energy which is sure to boil over as the heat of the class struggle increases? The doctrine of spontaneity makes it easy to mistake the wish for the deed, to rely upon the magic incantation of slogan and resolutions, and to take comfort in the "voice," the "logic," the "dictates" of historic destiny or whatever other pious formula may be found. These tend to become substitutes for the patient accumulation of organizational power, and for the development of realistic techniques of actually reaching the working masses, winning those who are reached and holding those who are won.

A further consequence of the dogma of inevitability is that it makes for an uncritical acceptance and imitation of the strategy and tactics employed by the first working-class group which comes to power. If communism is inevitable then everything leading up to it is regarded as inevitable. Precedents of tactics which originally flowed from a special historical situation are converted into precedents of principle. The Russification of the strategy, tactics and very terminology of communist parties of the world is a case in point. A theory which is avowedly scientific must approach the problem of the conquest of power with the same care and regard for the national economic, cultural and psychological terrain as an army campaigning against another must consider the physical terrain....

2. The second dogma which I wish to question is the view that all communists *must be* dialectical materialists and that all dialectical materialists *must be* communists. It is this proposition which is the source of that peculiar hodge-podge of politics, antiquated science, proletarian culture, idealistic philosophy, and mystical nonsense which goes by the name of the present-day party-attitude-in-philosophy. That it is not Marxian does not have to be argued except against those who assume that Marx developed a philosophical attitude in violation of common sense, the laws of logic, elementary notions of scientific method and the proposition that twice two is four....

What is the genuine Marxian view of the relation between communism and other fields and branches of science and philosophy? Surely there are some views which are necessarily implied, and others which are denied, by the communist position. What is the method by which this is determined? I wish to sketch briefly what I believe to be the true answer to these questions.

To begin with we must ask what is the fundamental view which distinguishes Marxism from all species of liberalism and socialism. It is clear that the key proposition of Marxism, insofar as it is a touchstone of differentiation from other social philosophies, is the theory of the state. For from the proposition that the state is the coercive instrument of the ruling class there follow all the other essential propositions: which deal with the manner in which it must be overthrown, what must take its place, etc. But now the Marxian theory of the state presupposes other views. It is not presented as something self-evidently true but as a consequence of the application of the theory of historical materialism to social life. A Marxist, then, must be an historical materialist and cannot consistently adhere to any contrary or contradictory philosophy of history. But historical materialism is the belief that "the mode of production in material life conditions the general character of the social, political and spiritual processes of life." (Marx). Now the extent to which this conditioning goes on is an empirical matter; different historical materialists have different theories which stress the influence of the mode of economic production in varying ways. Some admit an element of invariance in form in different material cultures; some deny it. Some exempt certain periods of music and fine arts from the scope of explanation; others include it. Some underscore reciprocal influences between different factors; others do not. *But it is interesting to observe that all species of historical materialism whether it be that of Bukharin or Trotsky, Bogdanov or Gorter, Lukac's or Korsch are compatible with the view that the state is the coercive arm of the ruling class.* Consequently the acceptance of this last proposition does not necessarily imply *any particular one* of the different theories of historical materialism. I am not saying that all of these different theories of historical materialism are true. Only one can be true. But which one is true can only be determined by further historical research and analysis and not by a logical deduction from the Marxian theory of the state.

But now every historical materialist, no matter what his differences with others of his school, is committed to the propositions which are presupposed by the theory of historical materialism. For example he must subscribe to a realistic theory of knowledge, for he holds that the social relations into which men enter are indispensable to their existence and independent of their individual wills and consciousness. All subjectivist epistemologies are therefore ruled out. But there are at least 27 different realistic epistemologies which acknowledge the objective existence of the external world and recognize the dependence of consciousness upon the structure of the nervous system. *All of them are compatible with the theory of historical materialism.* Not all of these realistic epistemologies can be true. Some realists believe that ideas are reflex images of things, others that they are signs, still others that they are outgrowths of things. Only one of these theories can be true. But which one is true can only be determined by further philosophical and psychological analysis and not by a logical deduction from the theory of historical materialism.

A realistic theory of epistemology in the light of the development of the nervous system presupposes an evolutionary biology. But whether this evolutionary biology must be of a Lamarckian or Darwinian type it leaves undetermined, *for both are compatible with it even though only one can be true.* And the best proof of this that any Marxist can desire is the fact that Marx sketched his realistic activistic theory of perception and his theory of historical materialism fully fourteen years before Darwin published his *Origin of Species.* How then can one claim that all of these theories logically involve each other? An acceptance of a realistic evolutionary biology in turn presupposes a belief in the existence of a physical world with a definite structure. But whether the structure of the world be Newtonian or Einsteinian is irrelevant to biology, for both are compatible with its findings, even if only one can be true. None of Marx's historical, economic and political doctrines had anything to do with the physics of his times.

It should be carefully noted that the combined implications of an evolutionary biology and psychology with their naturalistic, functional interpretation of purpose, are incompatible with any religious belief or any doctrine of cosmic design. A Marxist, then, cannot consistently subscribe to any religion, and the essence of any religion, as creed if not ritual, is belief in supernatural purpose.

In addition to the argument above there is one simple fact which is fatal to the conception that dialectical materialism is a monistic theory which synthesizes all available knowledge from physics to the dictatorship of the proletariat into one organic whole. Marx's theories of historical materialism, surplus value, class struggle, state and proletarian dictatorship were developed at a time when the physics, chemistry, biology, geology, and anthropology of his day, and in which he naturally believed, had reached a certain stage. How can we hold that the first set of theories are still true to-day while the second set of beliefs (physics, etc.) are quite definitely false unless we admit that there is no *logical* connection between them? And if we admit this, why cannot a man be a communist who accepts all the distinctive propositions of Marx and yet disregards the pronouncements of the pundits of dialectical materialism on such questions as to whether light travels in waves, particles or wavicules, or whether the geometry of space is describable in Euclidean, Lobochevskian or Reimannian terms, or whether electrons take time in jumping from one orbit to another—questions which orthodox dialectical materialists have sought to answer with great courage but little knowledge?

To conclude this phase of the argument, then, a communist *must* be a dialectical materialist only in the sense that he is committed to all the necessary conditions which the affirmation of the communist position implies; but there is no intelligible sense, except by arbitrary definition, in which a dialectical materialist must be a communist.

The full significance of the dogma that dialectical materialism and the social philosophy of communism mutually imply each other can only be grasped when it is taken together with the previous dogma, already discussed, that communism is inevitable. For it now follows that dialectical materialism, as a synthesis of the material and methods of the sciences, necessarily implies the victory of the communist revolution. It not only gathers the relevant material on the basis of which valid social ideals may be formulated; it teaches that in the nature of things these social ideals *must* arise and *must* triumph....

Even if life on this planet were destroyed, this philosophy offers the assurance that it would arise somewhere else and begin its pilgrimage to that one far-off event—or succession of events—towards which the cosmos is striving. Communism, it is admitted, will disappear but the same natural processes which insure its disappearance *necessitate* its coming—the Lord be praised!

> *"But what passes away at one point of the universe, develops anew at another.* One solar system passes away, new ones develop. Life passes away from the earth, it arises elsewhere anew. *In this sense,* dialectical materialism asserts an eternal development; what exists evolves. It evolves because the dialectical self-movement of every thing which exists is a driving force towards development. *Decay holds in general for special cases, the endlessness of development holds only for the infinite universe sub specie aeternitalis."* (Rudas, *Labour Monthly,* Sept. 1933.—Italics in the original.)

This not only suggests the familiar consolations of religion; it is an outright expression of the theology of absolute idealism with all its attendant logical difficulties. What an ironic illustration of the alleged dialectic law of the transformation of a thesis into its opposite! Marxism which is militant atheism presented as sentimental theology! The indignant repudiation of this charge by Rudas and other orthodox dialectical materialists is only a measure of their inconsistency and of their failure to grasp the essence of the religious attitude. Because they eschew the use of the word *God* or *Absolute Spirit* and insist that there is no external source of movement but that every movement is *self-movement,* they feel that they have escaped religion when all they have done is to replace a transcendant theology with an immanent theology. For what is essential to religion is not the use of the term God but the belief that the universe is somehow friendly to man and human purpose, that natural processes are such that they must realize the highest human ideals (e.g., communism, if one believes in it), that these processes cannot be adequately understood without such reference, and that despite momentary defeats and set-backs the victory of the highest human ideals (i.e., the proletarian revolution) is guaranteed by the mechanisms of nature and society. To inspire this belief in the minds and hearts of its adherents is the precise function of the theology of orthodox dialectical materialism. It is as far removed from the philosophy of Marx as the philosophy of Marx is removed from the absolute idealism of Hegel which Marx criticized for its supernaturalism, mysticism and logical inconsistency. This must be stressed not only against orthodox dialectical materialists but also against critics of Marx, like Max Eastman, who attribute to Marx the silly views of the present day orthodox brood whom he would have been the first to disown.

3. The third dogma I wish to consider flows out of the confusion among official party communists on the nature of dictatorship and democracy. I have already argued that truly understood communism does not involve the negation of democracy but its fulfillment, and that one of the criteria by which a communist evaluates the culture of a civilization is by the character of its democratic processes and the possibility of their expansion. Such a statement, however, in its abstract form can be easily misunderstood. To non-communists it will appear as a deliberate evasion of the true communist position; to communists as an inadmissable concession to bourgeois democracy.

Now the dogma I wish to challenge is that the state will necessarily wither away and that any automatic guarantees can be provided against the abuse of power by those who constitute the leadership of the Communist Party during this transitional period. I am particularly anxious to do this because there are some official communists who think that "the dictatorship of the proletariat" justifies the denial of democratic rights to dissenting proletarian groups which, although they accept the class basis of the state, may differ with certain policies of the Communist Party. Some go even further and justify the ruthless suppression of dissenting factions in the Communist Party and the abrogation of all party democracy except for those who agree with the leadership. In this way the political processes of the workers' state are corrupted and become the means by which a bureaucracy keeps itself in power. The only possible instrumentality by which the "withering away of the state" can be assured is discarded. The result is a degenerate workers' state in which the most important decisions are made by an uncontrollable bureaucracy. In such a state, the workers may be kept well-fed and housed because the social nature of production makes it impossible for the bureaucrats to accumulate capital although they can squander social wealth and human energy by costly mistakes. In such a state, however, the workers can never be free to criticize and control the bureaucracy nor individually free from the bureaucratic terror which can imprison or exile them at will. Let us remember that it was the materialist, Marx, who said that "the proletariat regards its courage, self-confidence, independence and sense of personal dignity as more necessary than its daily bread."

According to communist theory, the Communist Party is the vanguard of the proletariat not only in the struggle to overthrow capitalism but in the transitional period as well. This means that the function of the Communist Party is not to exercise a dictatorship over the proletariat but to educate the proletariat to a consciousness of its class interest and to lead in the execution of the class will. In the transition period the necessity of preserving the Workers' State against counter-revolution is so great that the Communist Party contests with some justification the right of other working class-parties to exist as political parties. *All the more imperative does it therefore become to permit the workers' councils or Soviets, the trade-unions and other working class associations the fullest freedom of discussion and criticism* so that the policies of the Communist Party may be checked by the experience of the class whose vanguard it proclaims itself to be. The

Communist Party itself must be subject to some system of democratic controls otherwise with what authority, aside from force, can it promulgate its own laws as the laws of the Workers' State? Where the vital life of the Workers' Councils is throttled by the imposition of controls from the Communist Party, where the accounting for responsibilities in social production is made to the Party and not to the executive organs of the Councils themselves, where foreign politicies are determined by the Party—in short, *where the Councils reign but the Party rules*—there we may have a workers' state but not a workers' democracy.

Where the Communist Party preempts all the functions of the government, the social problems which arise receive articulate discussion not in the Workers' Councils but in the Party circles. The same logic, however, which removes the power to make the important decisions from the hands of the representatives of the Workers' Councils, which reveals its distrust of the considered opinions and desires of the rank and file producers, leads to the abrogation of party democracy. Control is from "the leader" down who in the intervals between party Congresses can always insure, by virtue of the bureaucratic administration of the party apparatus and press, a chorus of *Vivas!* sufficient to drown out whatever muttered opposition there is.

From whence, then, the certainty that the state and, therefore, the political party will "wither away" unless the democratic institutions of the workers' state are permitted to function and expand? The existence of a bureaucracy means the existence, to be sure, not of an independent class but of a social group capable of abusing power. That the possibilities of the abuse of power in *economic* matters will be limited by the progressive development of productive forces, which in time will provide material necessities for all, is beside the point. There are abuses of power other than economic—abuses to which the increasing complexity of personality in a socialized society may make men peculiarly sensitive. Theoretically it is not inconceivable that a bureaucracy may begin to restrict privileges of higher education to its partisans, to develop a mythology which tends to perpetuate its own rule, and to attempt to initiate government by experts. There are no guaranteed safeguards against this eventuality except untiring activity to make the proletarian dictatorship not only in its *property form* but in its *political functioning,* a proletarian democracy.

It is for this reason that it seems to me desirable to counterpose "a workers' democracy" to "bourgeois dictatorship." At certain times even lexicography has political implications—and at no time more than to-day. The slogan "a workers' democracy," on the one hand, marks off the true communist from the official communist who uses the phrase "dictatorship of the proletariat" as a euphemism for the dictatorship of the Communist Party bureaucracy over its own members and over the working class; and, on the other hand, the slogan "a workers' democracy" prevents the too easy identification on the part of the unpolitical worker of the proletarian dictatorship with the Fascist dictatorships. The dictatorship of the Fascist party is an essential part of the political system of Fascism and is the only way by which capitalism can preserve itself against disintegration; the dictatorship of the Communist Party bureaucracy is a foreign excrescense upon the structure of the Workers' State, as well as upon the true communist party.

4. The fourth dogma I wish to discuss represents not so much a part of the creed of orthodox communism but a tendency observable in its cultural philosophy and practice. This is the dogma of "the collective man." The communist party claims to have no official line for creative artists to follow but the fact that, by its own theories, art is an expression of social conditions, and therefore of politics, and the further fact that its politics leaves

no room for any critical dissent, give a characteristic stamp to the literature, art and very patterns of life which the official press approves.

From the premise that history can be most adequately understood, and made, by the guiding principles of the class-struggle, some communists have inferred that the only valid ideals for life and letters are those that celebrate the achievements of the mass and the class. The "collectivity" as the hero of the novel, the objective political needs of the moment as the theme of poetry, the selected historical event as the subject matter of the play—all this of course is nothing new. It may be found in some of the great artistic treasures of earlier times. Nor is this emphasis peculiarly characteristic of what has been called "proletarian culture." The fascization of culture in Italy and Germany similarly attacks (from different ideological premises) individualistic and personal artistic forms as decadent, liberal and smacking of petty-bourgeois anarchy. It, too, seeks to convert the politically exigent into the aesthetically relevant. In fact it carries matters to absurdity by making political implications the sole consideration. But for historical reasons the cultural ideals of communism—even in "the transitional period"—have been interpreted as involving the glorification of the mass and the disparagement of the individual. Hostile critics who desire to lump fascism and communism together have not hesitated to say that the only difference between the cultural philosophy of fascism and communism is that where the latter says "proletariat," the former says "the state," and that what they both mean is, "the political party."

It cannot be too much stressed, therefore, that communism is hostile to individualism, as a social theory, and not to individuality, as a social value. It seeks to provide the material guarantee of security without which the free development of individuality or personality is an empty or impossible ideal. But the *free development of personality remains its ideal*; difference, uniqueness, independence, and creative originality are intrinsic values to be fostered and strengthened; and indeed one of the strongest arguments against capitalism is that it prevents these values from flourishing for all but a few. Communists recognize, however, that the social content of these values, the forms and conditions of their expression, are historical variables. They therefore repudiate the notion that because the social content and patterns of personality in a communist culture will be different from those of the 18th century country squire, the 19th century industrial free-booter or the 20th century captain of industry—they are any less genuine and valuable. But they grant—as everyone must—that in any society where mechanical impositions of external constraints upon conduct or thought exist, where material deprivation and psychic lynching are the automatic consequences of cultural criticism, a premium is placed upon social conformity and upon that type of virtue which is made up of two parts inconspicuity, one part silence and one part diplomatic assent.

Where the free development of personality remains the ideal, there can be no abridgement—even in the transitional period, only *one* of whose limits, let it be remembered, is determined—of the right to believe and actively hold independent or unpopular views in all cultural and scientific fields. That this right may sometimes lead to an expression of views which border on the *politically dangerous* is no more a justification for censoring critical and independent cultural thought than the fact that sometimes anecdotes circulate which undermine the prestige of the political leader constitutes a reason for declaring a political taboo against humor. One of the reasons why official communists do not see this can be traced to their uncritical assumption that the whole of culture is involved in, and relevant to, a criticism of any part of it. Consequently, to challenge the ruling dogma in philosophy or art is also to strike a blow at the foundations of the workers' state. This belief in a cultural monism will no more stand analysis than the belief in a metaphysical monism. It can flourish only when the fear of having to answer critical questions about the validity of the political line of the party is so great that all forms of criticism are discouraged, lest the habit of criticism spread. But where there is no criticism, intellectual life perishes.

One more word in conclusion. No matter what the cultural and moral philosophy of communists be, I do not think it is an exaggeration to say that communism, as a social system, will be an immense improvement over capitalism as far as the distribution of material goods and comforts is concerned. But the extent to which communism as a social system makes possible the development of a free culture for free and creative personalities,—that does not depend upon the system of economic production but primarily upon the living communist men and women themselves, upon the type of leadership which arises and the type of membership which permits that leadership to develop. It seems to me that only communism can save the world from its social evils; it seems to me to be just as evident that the official Communist Party or any of its subsidiary organizations cannot be regarded as a Marxist, critical or revolutionary party today. The conclusion is, therefore, clear: *the time has now come to build a new communist party and a new communist international.*

Part Three

To Extend Democracy and to Formulate the Modern

Introduction

What does it mean to be "modern"? How much "democracy" do we really have in the United States, and what are the prospects for its expansion within our society and beyond? These two questions were among those attracting the most persistent attention from American intellectuals between the late 1930s and the very early 1960s, the period to which Part Three is devoted. Clement Greenberg's vindication of avant-garde art and David Lilienthal's defense of the New Deal introduce themes that reappear in many different contexts in later selections.

One complexity that has confused some students of the period is that what counts as "modern" for literary and cultural commentators like Lionel Trilling is very different from what counts as modern for social scientists like W. W. Rostow. For Trilling, the modern is a distinctive sensibility somewhat distant from the Enlightenment and associated with the sympathetic exploration of the irrational, even to the point of a certain willingness to "look into the abyss." Yet for Rostow and other "modernization theorists," the modern is a highly rational social order, predicated on industrialization and technological progress, fulfilling rather than repudiating the Enlightenment. Many of the writers Trilling surveys in his discussion of cultural modernism are indeed quite alienated from the social order that Rostow celebrates as modern.

Intellectuals during this period were more concerned with foreign policy than in any earlier time. George Kennan's classic formulation of "realist" diplomatic doctrine illustrates this engagement. The period also featured the new importance of scientists as public intellectuals. There can be no better example of this than J. Robert Oppenheimer.

The limits of democracy within the United States are the preoccupation of Gunnar Myrdal, who wrote about the failure of the nation to respect the humanity and indeed the basic civil rights of black citizens. James Baldwin's commentary on black life in the United States and its representation in the arts partakes of the same concern. John Courtney Murray's discussion in 1960 of the relation of American democracy to Catholic theology sketched a framework within which many Catholics felt more comfortable with American political life, and in which many Protestants diminished their long-standing anti-Catholic feelings. Murray built on the perspective developed by the Protestant theologian Reinhold Niebuhr in 1944, according to which religious rather than secular foundations for democracy were ultimately the most substantial.

What role "ideology" could play in democracy was a matter of considerable controversy for a generation that witnessed Nazism and Stalinism. The function of ideology in totalitarian regimes was analyzed by émigré philosopher Hannah Arendt in 1953, and, by 1960, Daniel Bell registered the common feeling that whatever was good about "ideology" had been exhausted. Ideology by most definitions figures in Whittaker Chambers's classic anti-communist manifesto of 1952. Reference to

Chambers can remind us that virtually all of the intellectuals who discussed democracy during the twenty years after World War II did so in the context of the Cold War. This was certainly true of Milton Friedman, the most widely appreciated American economist of the second half of the twentieth century. Friedman is often considered a "conservative," but Part Three also includes conservatives of two very different kinds: the corporate theorist Peter F. Drucker and the extreme libertarian Ayn Rand.

Sigmund Freud was one of the great "moderns" addressed by Trilling. Twentieth-century American intellectuals took Freud's ideas in a great variety of directions. Part Three includes one of the most popular revisions of Freud to flourish in the United States, that developed by émigré Erik H. Erikson in 1950. The presence of Erikson and Arendt in Part Three can serve as reminders that a prominent feature of the intellectual history of this period was the impact of a cohort of creative and independently minded intellectuals driven out of Europe by Hitler.

Recommendations for Further Reading
H. Stuart Hughes, *The Sea Change: The Migration of Social Thought, 1930–1965* (New York, 1975); Daniel Joseph Singal, *The War Within: From Victorian to Modernist Thought in the South, 1919–1945* (Chapel Hill, 1982); James Sloan Allen, *The Romance of Commerce and Culture: Capitalism, Modernism, and the Chicago-Aspen Crusade for Cultural Reform* (Chicago, 1983); Richard Pells, *The Liberal Mind in a Conservative Age* (New York, 1985); Martin Jay, *Permanent Exiles: Essays on the Intellectual Migration from Germany to America* (New York, 1986); Terry A. Cooney, *The Rise of the New York Intellectuals: Partisan Review and Its Circle, 1934–1945* (Madison, Wis., 1986); Paul S. Boyer, *By the Bomb's Early Light: American Thought and Culture at the Dawn of the Atomic Age* (New York, 1986); Ellen W. Schrecker, *No Ivory Tower: McCarthyism and the Universities* (New York, 1986); Spencer Weart, *Nuclear Fear: A History of Images* (Cambridge, Mass., 1988); Lary May, ed., *Recasting America: Culture and Politics in the Age of Cold War* (Chicago, 1989); Stephen J. Whitfield, *Cold War Culture* (Baltimore, 1990); Daniel J. Singal, ed., *Modernist Culture in America* (Belmont, Calif., 1991); Thomas Hill Schaub, *American Fiction in the Cold War* (Madison, Wis., 1991); Greg Mitman, *The State of Nature: Ecology, Community, and American Social Thought, 1900–1950* (Chicago, 1992); Ronald Numbers, *The Creationists* (New York, 1992); Joan Shelly Rubin, *The Making of Middlebrow Culture* (Chapel Hill, 1992); Wilfred M. McClay, *The Masterless: Self and Society in Modern America* (Chapel Hill, 1994); George Marsden, *The Soul of the American University* (New York, 1994); Ron Robin, *The Barbed-Wire College: Reeducating German POWs in the United States During World War II* (Princeton, 1995); Richard Cándida Smith, *Utopia and Dissent: Art, Poetry, and Politics in California* (Berkeley, 1995); Ellen Herman, *The Romance of American Psychology: Political Culture in the Age of Experts* (Berkeley, 1995); David A. Hollinger, *Science, Jews, and Secular Culture: Studies in Mid-Twentieth Century American Intellectual History* (Princeton, 1996); Peter J. Conn, *Pearl S. Buck: A Cultural Biography* (New York, 1996); Michael Denning, *The Cultural Front: The Laboring of American Culture in the Twentieth Century* (New York, 1997); Katherine Pandora, *Rebels Within the Ranks: Psychologists' Critique of Scientific Authority and Democratic Realities in New Deal America* (New York, 1997); Christopher Simpson, *The Science of Coercion* (New York, 1997); Christopher Simpson, ed., *Universities and Empire: Money and Politics in the Social Sciences During the Cold War* (New York, 1998); Mary S. Morgan and Malcolm Rutherford, eds., *From Interwar Pluralism to Postwar Neoclassicism* (Durham, N.C., 1998); Jessica Wang, *American Science in an Age of Anxiety: Scientists, Anticommunism, and the Cold War* (Chapel Hill, 1999); John McGreevy, *Catholicism and American Freedom* (New York, 2003); Daniel Horowitz, *The Anxieties of Affluence: Critiques of American Consumer Culture, 1939–1979* (Amherst, Mass., 2004); George Cotkin, *Existentialism in America* (Chicago, 2003); S. M. Amadae, *Rationalizing*

Capitalist Democracy: The Cold War and the Origins of Rational Choice Liberalism (Chicago, 2003); Martin J. Sherwin and Kai Bird, *American Prometheus: J. Robert Oppenheimer* (New York, 2005); Howard Brick, *Transcending Capitalism* (Ithaca, 2006); Elizabeth Borgwardt, *New Deal for the World* (Cambridge, Mass., 2005); David Engerman, *Know Your Enemy* (New York, 2009); Rebecca Lemov, *World as Laboratory: Experiments with Mice, Mazes, and Men* (New York, 2005); Karen J. Leong, *The China Mystique: Pearl Buck, Anna May Wong, Mayling Soong, and the Transformation of American Orientalism* (Berkeley, 2005); T. Jeremy Gunn, *Spiritual Weapons: The Cold War and the Forging of an American National Religion* (Westport, Conn., 2009); Andrew Hartman, *Education and the Cold War: The Battle for the American School* (New York, 2008).

CLEMENT GREENBERG

"Avant-Garde and Kitsch"
(1939)

The "high" culture produced by an avant-garde of critical artists true to the formal imperatives of their art will resist the manipulations of totalitarian politics, Clement Greenberg (1909–94) argued in 1939. But such "lower" arts as "magazine covers, illustrations, ads, slick and pulp fiction, comics, Tin Pan Alley music, tap dancing, Hollywood movies, etc." can easily serve the nefarious political purposes of the worst of contemporary political regimes. This association of modernist culture with lofty moral and political purpose proved an inspiration to many artists and critics during the midcentury decades. But in later years it was much resented; Greenberg became a favorite target for antielitists eager to defend "popular culture" against what they saw as the patronizing, arrogant dismissal encouraged by Greenberg.

A suspicion of mass culture on the part of Greenberg and many of his contemporaries was driven, in part, by political experiences of the 1930s involving the communist movement. Leaders of this movement had often defended the use of art as a form of propaganda and had condemned critics who, out of an apparent excess of aesthetic scruple, withheld approval of politically functional art. The *Partisan Review* established its reputation by proclaiming both socialist politics and the autonomy of artists and intellectuals. This combination of commitments informs Greenberg's "Avant-Garde and Kitsch," Harold Rosenberg's "The Fall of Paris" (1940), and a number of other classic *Partisan Review* contributions of the late 1930s and early 1940s. For a study of this magazine and the writers who made it, see Terry A. Cooney, *The Rise of the New York Intellectuals: Partisan Review and Its Circle, 1934–1945* (Madison, Wis., 1986). Although socialist politics had dropped out of the work of virtually all of the *Partisan Review* intellectuals by the mid-1940s, the faith in the political and moral efficacy of the independent artist-hero remained a prominent feature of the cultural politics of the Cold War era.

Greenberg was an obscure customshouse clerk when he produced this vindication of modernist high culture. But he soon became one of the most influential art critics of his time, especially in his capacity as a columnist for the *Nation*. The most important of his essays were published in a collection edited by John O'Brien, *Clement Greenberg* (Chicago, 1986). Greenberg's career is the subject of Donald B. Kuspit, *Clement Greenberg: Art Critic* (Madison, Wis., 1979). One biography is Florence Rubenfeld, *Clement Greenberg: A Life* (New York, 1997). See also Alice Goldfarb Marquis, *Art Czar: The Rise and Fall of Clement Greenberg* (Boston, 2006).

One and the same civilization produces simultaneously two such different things as a poem by T. S. Eliot and a Tin Pan Alley song, or a painting by Braque and a *Saturday Evening Post* cover. All four are on the order of culture, and ostensibly, parts of the same culture and products of the same society. Here, however, their connection seems to end. A poem by Eliot and a poem by Eddie Guest—what perspective of culture is large enough to enable us to situate them in an enlightening relation to each other? Does the fact that a disparity such as this within the frame of a single cultural tradition, is and has been taken for granted—does this fact indicate that the disparity is a part of the natural order of things? Or is it something entirely new, and particular to our age?

The answer involves more than an investigation in aesthetics. It appears to me that it is necessary to examine more closely and with more originality than hitherto the relationship between aesthetic experience as met by the specific—not generalized—individual, and the social and historical contexts in which that experience takes place. What is brought to light will answer, in addition to the question posed above, other and perhaps more important ones.

A society, as it becomes less and less able, in the course of its development, to justify the inevitability of its particular forms, breaks up the accepted notions upon which artists and writers must depend in large part for communication with their audiences. It becomes difficult to assume anything. All the verities involved by religion, authority, tradition, style, are thrown into question, and the writer or artist is no longer able to estimate the response of his audience to the symbols and references with which he works. In the past such a state of affairs has usually resolved itself into a motionless Alexandrianism, an academicism in which the really important issues are left untouched because they involve controversy, and in which creative activity dwindles to virtuosity in the small details of form, all larger questions being decided by the precedent of the old masters. The same themes are mechanically varied in a hundred different works, and yet nothing new is produced: Statius, mandarin verse, Roman sculpture, Beaux Arts painting, neo-republican architecture.

It is among the hopeful signs in the midst of the decay of our present society that we—some of us—have been unwilling to accept this last phase for our own culture. In seeking to go beyond Alexandrianism, a part of Western bourgeois society has produced something unheard of heretofore: avant-garde culture. A superior consciousness of history—more precisely, the appearance of a new kind of criticism of society, an historical criticism—made this possible. This criticism has not confronted our present society with timeless utopias, but has soberly examined in the terms of history and of cause and effect the antecedents, justifications and functions of the forms that lie at the heart of every society. Thus our present bourgeois social order was shown to be, not an eternal, "natural" condition of life, but simply the latest term in a succession of social orders. New perspectives of this kind, becoming a part of the advanced intellectual conscience of the fifth and sixth decades of the nineteenth century, soon were absorbed by artists and poets, even if unconsciously for the most part. It was no accident, therefore, that the birth of the avant-garde coincided chronologically—and geographically too—with the first bold development of scientific revolutionary thought in Europe.

True, the first settlers of Bohemia—which was then identical with the avant-garde—turned out soon to be demonstratively uninterested in politics. Nevertheless, without the

Source: Partisan Review (Fall 1939), 34–49. Reprinted by permission of the University of Chicago Press.

circulation of revolutionary ideas in the air about them, they would never have been able to isolate their concept of the "bourgeois" in order to define what they were *not*. Nor, without the moral aid of revolutionary political attitudes would they have had the courage to assert themselves as aggressively as they did against the prevailing standards of society. Courage indeed was needed for this, because the avant-garde's emigration from bourgeois society to Bohemia meant also an emigration from the markets of capitalism, upon which artists and writers had been thrown by the falling away of aristocratic patronage. (Ostensibly, at least, it meant this—meant starving in a garret—although, as will be shown later, the avant-garde remained attached to bourgeois society precisely because it needed its money.)

Yet it is true that once the avant-garde had succeeded in "detaching" itself from society, it proceeded to turn around and repudiate revolutionary politics as well as bourgeois. The revolution was left inside society, a part of that welter of ideological struggle which art and poetry find so unpropitious as soon as it begins to involve those "precious," axiomatic beliefs upon which culture thus far has had to rest. Hence it was developed that the true and most important function of the avant-garde was not to "experiment," but to find a path along which it would be possible to keep culture *moving* in the midst of ideological confusion and violence. Retiring from public altogether, the avant-garde poet or artist sought to maintain the high level of his art by both narrowing and raising it to the expression of an absolute in which all relativities and contradictions would be either resolved or beside the point. "Art for art's sake" and "pure poetry" appear, and subject-matter or content becomes something to be avoided like a plague.

It has been in search of the absolute that the avant-garde has arrived at "abstract" or "non-objective" art—and poetry, too. The avant-garde poet or artist tries in effect to imitate God by creating something valid solely on its own terms in the way nature itself is valid, in the way a landscape—not its picture—is aesthetically valid; something *given*, increate, independent of meanings, similars, or originals. Content is to be dissolved so completely into form that the work of art or literature cannot be reduced in whole or in part to anything not itself.

But the absolute is absolute, and the poet or artist, being what he is, cherishes certain relative values more than others. The very values in the name of which he invokes the absolute are relative values, the values of aesthetics. And so he turns out to be imitating, not God—and here I use "imitate" in its Aristotelian sense—but the disciplines and processes of art and literature themselves. This is the genesis of the "abstract." In turning his attention away from subject-matter or common experience, the poet or artist turns it in upon the medium of his own craft. The non-representational or "abstract," if it is to have aesthetic validity, cannot be arbitrary and accidental, but must stem from obedience to some worthy constraint or original. This constraint, once the world of common, extraverted experience has been renounced, can only be found in the very processes or disciplines by which art and literature have already imitated the former. These themselves become the subject matter of art and literature. If, to continue with Aristotle, all art and literature are imitation, then what we have here is the imitation of imitating. To quote Yeats:

> "Nor is there singing school but studying
> Monuments of its own magnificence."

Picasso, Braque, Mondrian, Miro, Kandinsky, Brancusi, even Klee, Matisse and Cezanne, derive their chief inspiration from the medium they work in. The excitement of their art seems to lie most of all in its pure preoccupation with the invention and arrangement of spaces, surfaces, shapes, colors, etc., to the exclusion of whatever is not necessarily implicated in these factors. The attention of poets like Rimbaud, Mallarmé, Valéry, Eluard, Pound, Hart Crane, Stevens, even Rilke and Yeats, appears to be centered on the effort to create poetry and on the "moments" themselves of poetic conversion rather than on experience to be converted into poetry. Of course, this cannot exclude other preoccupations in their work, for poetry must deal with words, and words must communicate. Certain poets, such as Mallarmé and Valéry, are more radical in this respect than others—leaving aside those poets who have tried to compose poetry in pure sound alone. However, if it were easier to define poetry, modern poetry would be much more "pure" and "abstract." ... As for the other fields of literature—the definition of avant-garde aesthetics advanced here is no Procrustean bed. But aside from the fact that most of our best contemporary novelists have gone to school with the avant-garde, it is significant that Gide's most ambitious book is a novel about the writing of a novel, and that Joyce's *Ulysses* and *Finnegan's Wake* seem to be above all, as one French critic says, the reduction of experience to expression for the sake of expression, the expression mattering more than what is being expressed.

That avant-garde culture is the imitation of imitating—the fact itself—calls for neither approval nor disapproval. It is true that this culture contains within itself some of the very Alexandrianism it seeks to overcome. The lines quoted from Yeats above referred to Byzantium, which is very close to Alexandria; and in a sense this imitation of imitating is a superior sort of Alexandrianism. But there is one most important difference: the avant-garde moves, while Alexandrianism stands still. And this, precisely, is what justifies the avant-garde's methods and makes them necessary. The necessity lies in the fact that by no other means is it possible today to create art and literature of a high order. To quarrel with necessity by throwing about terms like "formalism," "purism," "ivory tower" and so forth is either dull or dishonest. This is not to say, however, that it is to the social advantage of the avant-garde that it is what it is. Quite the opposite.

The avant-garde's specialization of itself, the fact that its best artists are artists' artists, its best poets, poets' poets, has estranged a great many of those who were capable formerly of enjoying and appreciating ambitious art and literature, but who are now unwilling or unable to acquire an initiation into their craft secrets. The masses have always remained more or less indifferent to culture in the process of development. But today such culture is being abandoned by those to whom it actually belongs—our ruling class. For it is to the latter that the avant-garde belongs. No culture can develop without a social basis, without a source of stable income. And in the case of the avant-garde this was provided by an elite among the ruling class of that society from which it assumed itself to be cut off, but to which it has always remained attached by an umbilical cord of gold. The paradox is real. And now this elite is rapidly shrinking. Since the avant-garde forms the only living culture we now have, the survival in the near future of culture in general is thus threatened.

We must not be deceived by superficial phenomena and local successes. Picasso's shows still draw crowds, and T. S. Eliot is taught in the universities; the dealers in modernist art are still in business, and the publishers still publish some "difficult" poetry. But the avant-garde itself, already sensing the danger, is becoming more and more timid every day that passes. Academicism and commercialism are appearing in the strangest places. This can mean only one thing: that the avant-garde is becoming unsure of the audience it depends on—the rich and the cultivated.

Is it the nature of avant-garde culture that is alone responsible for the danger it finds itself in? Or is that only a dangerous liability? Are there other, and perhaps more important, factors involved?

Where there is an avant-garde, generally we also find a rear-guard. True enough—simultaneously with the entrance of the avant-garde, a second new cultural phenomenon appeared in the industrial West: that thing to which the Germans give the wonderful name of *Kitsch:* popular, commercial art and literature with their chromeotypes, magazine covers, illustrations, ads, slick and pulp fiction, comics, Tin Pan Alley music, tap dancing, Hollywood movies, etc., etc. For some reason this gigantic apparition has always been taken for granted. It is time we looked into its whys and wherefores.

Kitsch is a product of the industrial revolution which urbanized the masses of Western Europe and America and established what is called universal literacy.

Previous to this the only market for formal culture, as distinguished from folk culture, had been among those who in addition to being able to read and write could command the leisure and comfort that always goes hand in hand with cultivation of some sort. This until then had been inextricably associated with literacy. But with the introduction of universal literacy, the ability to read and write became almost a minor skill like driving a car, and it no longer served to distinguish an individual's cultural inclinations, since it was no longer the exclusive concomitant of refined tastes. The peasants who settled in the cities as proletariat and petty bourgeois learned to read and write for the sake of efficiency, but they did not win the leisure and comfort necessary for the enjoyment of the city's traditional culture. Losing, nevertheless, their taste for the folk culture whose background was the countryside, and discovering a new capacity for boredom at the same time, the new urban masses set up a pressure on society to provide them with a kind of culture fit for their own consumption. To fill the demand of the new market a new commodity was devised: ersatz culture, kitsch, destined for those who, insensible to the values of genuine culture, are hungry nevertheless for the diversion that only culture of some sort can provide.

Kitsch, using for raw material the debased and academicized simulacra of genuine culture, welcomes and cultivates this insensibility. It is the source of its profits. Kitsch is mechanical and operates by formulas. Kitsch is vicarious experience and faked sensations. Kitsch changes according to style, but remains always the same. Kitsch is the epitome of all that is spurious in the life of our times. Kitsch pretends to demand nothing of its customers except their money—not even their time.

The pre-condition for kitsch, a condition without which kitsch would be impossible, is the availability close at hand of a fully matured cultural tradition, whose discoveries, acquisitions and perfected self-consciousness kitsch can take advantage of for its own ends. It borrows from it devices, tricks, strategems, rules of thumb, themes, converts them into a system and discards the rest. It draws its life blood, so to speak, from this reservoir of accumulated experience. This is what is really meant when it is said that the popular art and literature of today were once the daring, esoteric art and literature of yesterday. Of course, no such thing is true. What is meant is that when enough time has elapsed the new is looted for new "twists," which are then watered down and served up as kitsch. Self-evidently, all kitsch is academic, and conversely, all that's academic is kitsch. For what is called the academic as such no longer has an independent existence, but has become the stuffed-shirt "front" for kitsch. The methods of industrialism displace the handicrafts.

Because it can be turned out mechanically, kitsch has become an integral part of our productive system in a way in which true culture could never be except accidentally. It has been capitalized at a tremendous investment which must show commensurate returns; it is compelled to extend as well as to keep its markets. While it is essentially its own salesman, a great sales apparatus has nevertheless been created for it, which brings pressure to bear on every member of society. Traps are laid even in those areas, so to speak, that are the preserves of genuine culture. It is not enough today, in a country like ours, to have an inclination towards the latter; one must have a true passion for it that will give him the power to resist the faked article that surrounds and presses in on him from the moment he is old enough to look at the funny papers. Kitsch is deceptive. It has many different levels, and some of them are high enough to be dangerous to the naive seeker of true light. A magazine like the *New Yorker,* which is fundamentally high-class kitsch for the luxury trade, converts and waters down a great deal of avant-garde material for its own uses. Nor is every single item of kitsch altogether worthless. Now and then it produces something of merit, something that has an authentic folk flavor; and these accidental and isolated instances have fooled people who should know better.

Kitsch's enormous profits are a source of temptation to the avant-garde itself, and its members have not always resisted this temptation. Ambitious writers and artists will modify their work under the pressure of kitsch, if they do not succumb to it entirely. And then those puzzling border-line cases appear, such as the popular novelist, Simenon, in France, and Steinbeck in this country. The net result is always to the detriment of true culture, in any case.

Kitsch has not been confined to the cities in which it was born, but has flowed out over the countryside, wiping out folk culture. Nor has it shown any regard for geographical and national-cultural boundaries. Another mass product of Western industrialism, it has gone on a triumphal tour of the world, crowding out and defacing native cultures in one colonial country after another, so that it is now by way of becoming a universal culture, the first universal culture ever beheld. Today the Chinaman, no less than the South American Indian, the Hindu, no less than the Polynesian, have come to prefer to the products of their native art magazine covers, rotogravure sections and calendar girls. How is this virulence of kitsch, this irresistible attractiveness, to be explained? Naturally, machine-made kitsch can undersell the native handmade article, and the prestige of the West also helps, but why is kitsch a so much more profitable export article than Rembrandt? One, after all, can be reproduced as cheaply as the other.

In his last article on the Soviet cinema in the *Partisan Review,* Dwight Macdonald points out that kitsch has in the last ten years become the dominant culture in Soviet Russia. For this he blames the political regime—not only for the fact that kitsch is the official culture, but also that it is actually the dominant, most popular culture; and he quotes the following from Kurt London's *The Seven Soviet Arts:* "...the attitude of the masses both to the old and new art styles probably remains essentially dependent on the nature of the education afforded them by their respective states." Macdonald goes on to say: "Why after all should ignorant peasants prefer Repin (a leading exponent of Russian academic kitsch in painting) to Picasso, whose abstract technique is at least as relevant to their own primitive folk art as is the former's realistic style? No, if the masses crowd into the Tretyakov (Moscow's museum of contemporary Russian art: kitsch) it is largely because they have been conditioned to shun 'formalism' and to admire 'socialist realism.'"

In the first place it is not a question of a choice between merely the old and merely the new, as London seems to think—but of a choice between the bad, up-to-date old and the genuinely new. The alternative to Picasso is not Michelangelo, but kitsch. In the second place, neither in backward Russia nor in the advanced West do the masses prefer kitsch simply because their governments condition them towards it. Where state educational systems take the trouble to mention art, we are told to respect the old masters, not kitsch; and yet we go and hang Maxfield Parrish or his equivalent on our walls, instead of Rembrandt and Michelangelo. Moreover, as Macdonald himself points out, around 1925 when the Soviet regime was encouraging avant-garde cinema, the Russian masses continued to prefer Hollywood movies. No, "conditioning" does not explain the potency of kitsch....

All values are human values, relative values, in art as well as elsewhere. Yet there does seem to have been more or less of a general agreement among the cultivated of mankind over the ages as to what is good art and what bad. Taste has varied, but not beyond certain limits: contemporary connoisseurs agree with eighteenth century Japanese that Hokusai was one of the greatest artists of his time; we even agree with the ancient Egyptians that Third and Fourth Dynasty art was the most worthy of being selected as their paragon by those who came after. We may have come to prefer Giotto to Raphael, but we still do not deny that Raphael was one of the best painters of his *time*. There has been an agreement then, and this agreement rests, I believe, on a fairly constant distinction made between those values only to be found in art and the values which can be found elsewhere. Kitsch, by virtue of rationalized technique that draws on science and industry, has erased this distinction in practice.

Let us see for example what happens when an ignorant Russian peasant such as Macdonald mentions stands with hypothetical freedom of choice before two paintings, one by Picasso, the other by Repin. In the first he sees, let us say, a play of lines, colors and spaces that represent a woman. The abstract technique—to accept Macdonald's supposition, which I am inclined to doubt—reminds him somewhat of the icons he has left behind him in the village, and he feels the attraction of the familiar. We will even suppose that he faintly surmises some of the great art values the cultivated find in Picasso. He turns next to Repin's picture and sees a battle scene. The technique is not so familiar—as technique. But that weighs very little with the peasant; for he suddenly discovers values in Repin's picture which seem far superior to the values he has been accustomed to finding in icon art; and the unfamiliar technique itself is one of the sources of those values: the values of the vividly recognizable, the miraculous and the sympathetic. In Repin's picture the peasant recognizes and sees things in the way in which he recognizes and sees things outside of pictures—there is no discontinuity between art and life, no need to accept a convention and say to oneself, that icon represents Jesus because it intends to represent Jesus, even if it does not remind me very much of a man. That Repin can paint so realistically that identifications are self-evident immediately and without any effort on the part of the spectator— that is miraculous. The peasant is also pleased by the wealth of self-evident meanings which he finds in the picture: "it tells a story." Picasso and the icons are so austere and barren in comparison. What is more, Repin heightens reality and makes it dramatic: sunset, exploding shells, running and falling men. There is no longer any question of Picasso or icons. Repin is what the peasant wants, and nothing else but Repin. It is lucky, however, for Repin that the peasant is protected from the products of American capitalism, for he would not stand a chance next to a *Saturday Evening Post* cover by Norman Rockwell.

Ultimately, it can be said that the cultivated spectator derives the same values from Picasso that the peasant gets from Repin, since what the latter enjoys in Repin is somehow art too, on however low a scale, and he is sent to look at pictures by the same instincts that send the cultivated spectator. But the ultimate values which the cultivated spectator derives from Picasso are derived at a second remove, as the result of reflection upon the immediate impression left by the plastic values. It is only then that the recognizable, the miraculous and the sympathetic enter. They are not immediately or externally present in Picasso's painting, but must be projected into it by the spectator sensitive enough to react sufficiently to plastic qualities. They belong to the "reflected" effect. In Repin, on the other hand, the "reflected" effect has already been included in the picture, ready for the spectator's unreflective enjoyment. Where Picasso paints *cause*, Repin paints *effect*. Repin predigests art for the spectator and spares him effort, provides him with a short cut to the pleasure of art that detours what is necessarily difficult in genuine art. Repin, or kitsch, is synthetic art.

The same point can be made with respect to kitsch literature: it provides vicarious experience for the insensitive with far greater immediacy than serious fiction can hope to do. And Eddie Guest and the *Indian Love Lyrics* are more poetic than T. S. Eliot and Shakespeare.

If the avant-garde imitates the processes of art, kitsch, we now see, imitates its effects. The neatness of this antithesis is more then contrived; it corresponds to and defines the tremendous interval that separates from each other two such simultaneous cultural phenomena as the avant-garde and kitsch. This interval, too great to be closed by all the infinite gradations of popularized "modernism" and "modernistic" kitsch, corresponds in turn to a social interval, a social interval that has always existed in formal culture as elsewhere in civilized society, and whose two termini converge and diverge in fixed relation to the increasing or decreasing stability of the given society. There has always been on one side the minority of the powerful—and therefore the cultivated—and on the other the great mass of the exploited and poor—and therefore the ignorant. Formal culture has always belonged to the first, while the last have had to content themselves with folk or rudimentary culture, or kitsch.

In a stable society which functions well enough to hold in solution the contradictions between its classes the cultural dichotomy becomes somewhat blurred. The axioms of the few are shared by the many; the latter believe superstitiously what the former believe soberly. And at such moments in history the masses are able to feel wonder and admiration for the culture, on no matter how high a plane, of its masters. This applies at least to plastic culture, which is accessible to all.

In the Middle Ages the plastic artist paid lip service at least to the lowest common denominators of experience. This even remained true to some extent until the seventeenth century. There was available for imitation a universally valid conceptual reality, whose order the artist could not tamper with. The subject matter of art was prescribed by those who commissioned works of art, which were not created, as in bourgeois society, on speculation. Precisely because his content was determined in advance, the artist was free to concentrate on his medium. He needed not to be philosopher or visionary, but simply artificer. As long as there was general agreement as to what were the worthiest subjects for art, the artist was relieved of the necessity to be original and inventive in his "matter" and could devote all his energy to formal problems. For him the medium became, privately, professionally, the content of his art, even as today his medium is the public content of the abstract painter's art—with that difference, however, that the medieval artist had to suppress his professional preoccupation in public—had always to suppress and subordinate the personal and professional in the finished, official work of art. If, as an ordinary member of the Christian community, he felt some personal emotion about his subject matter, this only contributed to the enrichment of the work's public meaning. Only with the Renaissance do the inflections of the personal become legitimate, still to be kept, however, within the limits of the simply and universally recognizable. And only with Rembrandt do "lonely" artists begin to appear, lonely in their art.

But even during the Renaissance, and as long as Western art was endeavoring to perfect its technique, victories in this realm could only be signalized by success in realistic imitation, since there was no other objective criterion at hand. Thus the masses could still find in the art of their masters objects of admiration and wonder. Even the bird who pecked at the fruit in Zeuxes' picture could applaud.

It is a platitude that art becomes caviar to the general when the reality it imitates no longer corresponds even roughly to the reality recognized by the general. Even then, however, the resentment the common man may feel is silenced by the awe in which he stands of the patrons of this art. Only when he becomes dissatisfied with the social order they administer does he begin to criticize their culture. Then the plebeian finds courage for the first time to voice his opinions openly. Every man, from Tammany aldermen to Austrian house-painters, finds that he is entitled to his opinion. Most often this resentment towards culture is to be found where the dissatisfaction with society is a reactionary dissatisfaction which expresses itself in revivalism and puritanism, and latest of all, in fascism. Here revolvers and torches begin to be mentioned in the same breath as culture. In the name of godliness or the blood's health, in the name of simple ways and solid virtues, the statue-smashing commences.

Returning to our Russian peasant for the moment, let us suppose that after he has chosen Repin in preference to Picasso, the state's educational apparatus comes along and tells him that he is wrong, that he should have chosen Picasso—and shows him why. It is quite possible for the Soviet state to do this. But things being as they are in Russia—and everywhere else—the peasant soon finds that the necessity of working hard all day for his living and the rude, uncomfortable circumstances in which he lives do not allow him enough leisure, energy and comfort to train for the enjoyment of Picasso. This needs, after all, a considerable amount of "conditioning." Superior culture is one of the most artificial of all human creations, and the peasant finds no "natural" urgency within himself that will drive him towards Picasso in spite of all difficulties. In the end the peasant will go back to kitsch when he feels like looking at pictures, for he can enjoy kitsch without effort. The state is helpless in this matter and remains so as long as the problems of production have not been solved in a socialist sense. The same holds true, of course, for capitalist countries and makes all talk of art for the masses there nothing but demagogy.

Where today a political regime establishes an official cultural policy, it is for the sake of demagogy. If kitsch is the official tendency of culture in Germany, Italy and Russia, it is not because their respective governments are controlled by philistines, but because kitsch is the culture of the masses in these countries, as it is everywhere else. The encouragement of kitsch is merely another of the inexpensive ways in which totalitarian regimes seek to ingratiate themselves with their subjects. Since these regimes cannot raise the cultural level of the masses—even if they wanted to—by anything short of a surrender to international socialism, they will flatter the masses by bringing all culture down to their level. It is for this reason that the avant-garde is outlawed, and not so much because a superior culture is inherently a more critical culture. (Whether or not the avant-garde could possibly flourish under a totalitarian regime is not pertinent to the question at this point.) As matter of fact, the main trouble with avant-garde art and literature, from the point of view of Fascists and Stalinists, is not that they are too critical, but that they are too "innocent," that it is too difficult to inject effective propaganda into them, that kisch is more pliable to this end. Kitsch keeps a dictator in closer contact with the "soul" of the people. Should the official culture be one superior to the general mass-level, there would be a danger of isolation.

Nevertheless, if the masses were conceivably to ask for avant-garde art and literature, Hitler, Mussolini and Stalin would not hesitate long in attempting to satisfy such a demand. Hitler is a bitter enemy of the avant-garde, both on doctrinal and personal grounds, yet this did not prevent Goebbels in 1932–33 from strenuously courting avant-garde artists and writers. When Gottfried Benn, an Expressionist poet, came over to the Nazis he was welcomed with a great fanfare, although at that very moment Hitler was denouncing Expressionism as *Kulturbolschewismus*. This was at a time when the Nazis felt that the prestige which the avant-garde enjoyed among the cultivated German public could be of advantage to them, and practical considerations of this nature, the Nazis being the skilful politicians they are, have always taken precedence over Hitler's personal inclinations. Later the Nazis realized that it was more practical to accede to the wishes of the masses in matters of culture than to those of their paymasters; the latter, when it came to a question of preserving power, were as willing to sacrifice their culture as they were their moral principles, while the former, precisely because power was being withheld from them, had to be cozened in every other way possible. It was necessary to promote on a much more grandiose style than in the democracies the illusion that the masses actually rule. The literature and art they enjoy and understand were to be proclaimed the only true art and literature and any other kind was to be suppressed. Under these circumstances people like Gottfried Benn, no matter how ardently they support Hitler, become a liability; and we hear no more of them in Nazi Germany.

We can see then that although from one point of view the personal philistinism of Hitler and Stalin is not accidental to the political roles they play, from another point of view it is only an incidentally contributory factor in determining the cultural policies of their respective regimes. Their personal philistinism simply adds brutality and double-darkness to policies they would be forced to support anyhow by the pressure of all their other policies—even were they, personally, devotees of avant-garde culture. What the acceptance of the isolation of the Russian Revolution forces Stalin to do, Hitler is compelled to do by his acceptance of the contradictions of capitalism and his efforts to freeze them. As for Mussolini—his case is a perfect example of the *disponibilité* of a realist in these matters. For years he bent a benevolent eye on the Futurists and built modernistic railroad stations and government-owned apartment houses. One can still see in the suburbs of Rome more modernistic apartments than almost anywhere else in the world. Perhaps Fascism wanted to show its up-to-datedness, to conceal the fact that it was a retrogression; perhaps it wanted to conform to the tastes of the wealthy élite it served. At any rate Mussolini seems to have realized lately that it would be more useful to him to please the cultural tastes of the Italian masses than those of their masters. The masses must be provided with objects of admiration and wonder; the latter can dispense with them. And so we find Mussolini announcing a "new Imperial style." Marinetti, Chirico, et al. are sent into the outer darkness, and the new railroad station in Rome will not be modernistic. That Mussolini was late in coming to this only illustrates again the relative hesitancy with which Italian fascism has drawn the necessary implications of its role....

Capitalism in decline finds that whatever of quality it is still capable of producing becomes almost invariably a threat to its own existence. Advances in culture no less than advances in science and industry corrode the very society under whose aegis they are made possible. Here, as in every other question today, it becomes necessary to quote Marx word for word. Today we no longer look towards socialism for a new culture—as inevitably as one will appear, once we do have socialism. Today we look to socialism *simply* for the preservation of whatever living culture we have right now.

DAVID E. LILIENTHAL

Selection from *TVA: Democracy on the March* (1944)

One of the most robust and persistently hopeful voices of the New Deal was a son of Czech immigrants who became a prominent Wisconsin attorney, David Lilienthal (1899–1981). He was the central figure in the New Deal's most extensive project in social reconstruction, the Tennessee Valley Authority, of which he was chairman from 1941 to 1946. The following selection is the concluding chapter of *TVA: Democracy on the March*, Lilienthal's 1944 book recounting the history of the project and defending the use of public authority to better the lives of American citizens. Lilienthal entitled this chapter "It Can be Done: Dreamers with Shovels," which captures the can-do spirit Lilienthal continued to embrace even at a time when the more sober and chastened voice of Reinhold Niebuhr had come into prominence. Although Lilienthal is here addressing one river valley in one country, his reflections are about human striving in general, and his ultimate arena is the globe. *TVA: Democracy on the March* opens with the thought that what happened in the Tennessee River Valley might well have happened in a thousand valleys throughout the world: "In Missouri and in Arkansas, in Brazil and in the Argentine, in China and in India" there are rivers "waiting to be controlled" and a better life for humankind waiting to be created. Lilienthal's vision of the New Deal expanded across the earth under the aegis of a spreading but contested democracy prefigured important themes in American thought during the Cold War, when the "modernization" of the "underdeveloped" parts of the world became a preoccupation of many American policy makers and social scientific intellectuals. Lilienthal's pronouncement was one of a number of differing statements about the direction of the world and of America's role in it enunciated during World War II, and can be instructively read alongside two other, vividly contrasting declarations. Somewhat to Lilienthal's left was Vice President Henry Wallace's "The Century of the Common Man" (*New Republic*, May 25, 1942). *Time-Life* publisher Henry Luce sketched a more conservative future in "The American Century" *(Life*, February 17, 1941).

Lilienthal himself was asked by President Harry Truman in 1946 to become chairman of the Atomic Energy Commission, the new government agency charged with supervising the development of atomic energy in the wake of the use of atomic bombs on the Japanese in 1945. Lilienthal served in this capacity until 1955, and has left in diaries what historians now regard as an indispensable private record of some of the most fast-moving events in the history of technology's relation to politics: *The Journals of David E. Lilienthal*, 7 vols. (New York, 1964–83). Although Lilienthal was never a communist, he was often accused by conservative Republican politicians of holding inappropriately left-wing views. He defended himself in public congressional testimony and in a book, *This I Do Believe!* (New York, 1955). A study of Lilienthal's career by a political scientist is S. M. Neuse, *David E. Lilienthal: The Journey of an American Liberal* (Knoxville, Tenn., 1996). On the global spread of Lilienthal's ideas, see David Ekbadh, *The Great American Mission: Modernization and the Construction of an American World Order* (Princeton, 2009).

In this one of the thousand valleys of the earth the physical setting of men's living has improved. Each day the change becomes more pronounced. The river is productive, the land more secure and fruitful, the forests are returning, factories and workshops and new houses and electric lines have put a different face upon the Tennessee Valley.

Is this really genuine improvement? Has it enhanced the quality of human existence? Are men's lives richer, fuller, more "human" as a result of such changes in our physical surroundings? To most people, I am sure, the answer is in the clear affirmative. But, in appraising the meaning of this valley's experience, the doubts on this score can by no means be ignored, nor dealt with out of hand; people not only raise such questions but answer them differently from the way most of us would answer them.

There are those who believe that material progress does not and cannot produce good, and may indeed stand as a barrier to it. To those, and there are many who hold such belief, mechanical progress, technology, the machine, far from improving the lot of men are actually seen as a source of debasement and condemned as "materialism."

The whole theme and thesis of this book challenges these ideas and the philosophy upon which they rest. I do not, of course, believe that when men change their physical environment they are inevitably happier or better. The machine that frees a man's back of drudgery does not thereby make his spirit free. Technology has made us more productive, but it does not necessarily enrich our lives. Engineers can build us great dams but only great people make a valley great. There is no technology of goodness. Men must make themselves spiritually free.

But because these changes in our physical environment in the valley do not in and of themselves make us happier, more generous, kinder, it does not follow that they have no relation to our spiritual life.

We have a choice. There is the important fact. Men are not powerless, they have it in their hands to use the machine to augment the dignity of human existence. True, they may have so long denied themselves the use of that power to decide, which is theirs, may so long have meekly accepted the dictation of bosses of one stripe or another or the ministrations of benevolent nursemaids, that the muscles of democratic choice have atrophied. But that strength is always latent; history has shown how quickly it revives. How we shall *use* physical betterment—that decision is ours to make. We are not carried irresistibly by forces beyond our control, whether they are given some mystic term or described as the "laws of economics." We are not inert objects on a wave of the future.

Except for saints and great ascetics, I suppose most people would agree that poverty and physical wretchedness are evils, in and of themselves. But because extreme poverty is an evil it does not follow that a comfortable or a high material standard of living is good. A Tennessee Valley farm wife who now has an electric pump that brings water into her kitchen may or may not be more generous of spirit, less selfish, than when she was forced to carry her water from the spring day after day. A once destitute sharecropper who now has an interesting factory job at good wages and lives in a comfortable house in town may or may not be more tolerant, more rational, more thoughtful of others, more active in community concerns. We all know that some of the least admirable men are found among those who have come up from poverty to a "high standard of living."

Whether happiness or unhappiness, freedom or slaver, in short whether good or evil results from an improved environment depends largely upon how the change has been

Source: David Lilienthal, *TVA: Democracy on the March* (New York: Harper & Row, 1944), 217–25.

brought about, upon the methods by which the physical results have been reached, and in what spirit and for what purpose the fruits of that change are used. Because a higher standard of living, a greater productiveness and a command over nature are not good in and of themselves does not mean that we cannot make good of them, that they cannot be a source of inner strength.

The basic objection to all efforts to use the machine—human betterment lies in an attitude of absolute pessimism: that life is an evil in itself; that therefore anything, which seeks to mitigate its inescapable pain and utter dullness is misdirected and futile. To men who in sincerity and passion hold to this faith, there is no answer that will satisfy them. Although there are few people in America who would admit that they hold such sweepingly negative views, they are nevertheless important; for such a faith (or lack of faith) colors and affects far less drastic but far more widely held objections to material changes. Many people, for example, although not denying the worth of life itself, are committed to the closely related belief that mankind is essentially wicked and naturally and irretrievably inclined to evil. This "prodigious malignity of the human heart," they assert, marks down as folly and misguided any efforts to improve men's physical surroundings.

That there are evil tendencies in mankind few who have lived through the last quarter century would care to deny. But of this I am sure and confident: the *balance*, the overwhelming balance, is on the side of good. This is a matter of faith, for where is the statistician or logician who can prove or disprove on which side the balance stands? But by the very act of faith in the essential goodness of men we further that goodness, just as the Nazi faith in the wickedness of men has nourished human animality and depravity by the very act of believing in it.

Democracy is a literal impossibility without faith that on balance the good in men far outweighs the evil. Every effort to cherish the overtones of human imagination in music, painting, or poetry rests upon that same faith, makes that same assumption. And so it is with what we have been seeking to do in this valley. To call it "materialistic" answers nothing. The rock upon which all these efforts rest is a faith in human beings.

I recognize that I am dealing with a broad issue of religious and philosophical thought upon which a great debate has raged for centuries and still continues. But it cannot be ignored, even if it cannot here be adequately discussed. I must let the matter rest, for present purposes, by quoting the statements of two modern thinkers upon this matter, whose words state the essentials of my own conviction.

The first is that of the great contemporary philosopher of China, Dr. Hu Shih, until recently Ambassador to the United States. He refers to the argument embraced as truth by countless millions in the Orient, and by not a few among our own people, that improvements in physical surroundings are no aid to the spirit, and that those civilizations which regard such advances as important are "materialistic." Then he says:

> For to me that civilization is materialistic which is limited by matter and incapable of transcending it; which feels itself powerless against its material environment and fails to make the full use of human intelligence for the conquest of nature and for the improvement of the conditions of man. Its sages and saints may do all they can to glorify contentment and hypnotize the people into a willingness to praise their gods and abide by their fate. But that very self-hypnotizing philosophy is more materialistic than the dirty houses they live in, the scanty food they eat, and the clay and wood with which they make the images of their gods.

On the other hand, that civilization which makes the fullest possible use of human ingenuity and intelligence in search of truth in order to control nature and transform matter for the service of mankind, to liberate the human spirit from ignorance, superstition, and slavery to the forces of nature, and to reform social and political institutions for the benefit of the greatest number—such a civilization is highly idealistic and spiritual.

The words of Pope Pius XI, in his famous encyclical *Quadragesimo Anno,* are equally simple, and the conclusion he draws convincing:

Then only will the economic and social organism be soundly established and attain its end, when it secures for all and each those goods which the wealth and resources of nature, technical achievement and the social organization of economic affairs can give. These goods should be sufficient to supply all needs and an honest livelihood, and to uplift men to that higher level of prosperity and culture which, provided it be used with prudence, is not only no hindrance but is of singular help to virtue.

But in addition to the philosophical protests there is a further and more widely held objection to such an enterprise as we have seen in this valley. The hideous belief has been spread over the earth that the price of material progress and freedom from want must be the complete surrender of individual freedom. The acceptance of this doctrine has been indeed the principal event of our lifetime. And it remains the faith of the people of Germany and Japan, the most advanced technical nations on the continent of Europe and in all the Orient.

Here in the United States, too, there are people of great influence who have essentially that conviction. They seek to persuade America, chiefly by subtle indirection, that modern technology demands that ordinary people (they do not, of course, think of themselves as such) abandon the ideal of individual freedom and the right to a voice in then own destiny, that only by yielding up such mistaken ideas is it possible for modern industry to raise their "standard of living." There is irony and yet an awful fitness in the fact that arch-conservatives and ultra-radicals are joined in agreement at this point. This spirit of defeatism about the individual in modern life and therefore about democracy is far too widespread to be ignored, and the support it receives in our own country too great to be dismissed lightly.

The technical results in the Tennessee Valley, the achievements of many kinds of experts, are of course matters of no little importance. But, speaking as an administrator and a citizen, unless these technical products strengthen the conviction that machines and science can be used by men for their greater individual and spiritual growth, then so far as I am concerned the physical accomplishments and the material benefits would be of dubious value indeed.

There are few who fail to see that modern applied science and the machine are threats to the development of the individual personality, the very purpose of democratic institutions. It is for this reason that the experience of the last ten years in the valley of the Tennessee is heartening. In this one valley (in some ways the world in microcosm) it has been demonstrated that methods can be developed—methods I have described as grassroots democracy—which do create an opportunity for greater happiness and deeper experience, for freedom, in the very course of technical progress. Indeed this valley, even in the brief span of a decade, supports a conviction that when the use of technology has a moral purpose and when its methods are thoroughly democratic, far from forcing the surrender of individual freedom and the things of the spirit to the machine, the machine can be made to promote those very ends.

It is enormously important that we have that conviction, that we have evidence which clearly supports that conviction. For here is the reality: This job must be done, this task of changing our physical environment through science and the machine. It ought to be done by democrats, by those who believe that people come first, by those who have faith in the capacities of many men and not of only a few. It cannot be done by defeatists. And it ought not be done by those who believe that human beings are inherently wicked. But it is a job that must be done. And it will be done—*by someone*. The only questions open are: How will it be done? Who will benefit? The answers will largely be provided by that intangible known as faith.

Faith is the greatest power in the world of men, the most "practical" force of all. How is faith sustained and built ever stronger? By the redemption of faith through works. Take the simple case of a farmer on one of these demonstration farms. When you talk with him you can sense at once that his faith has been stirred. He has actually seen something happen on his own homestead that he never believed could come true for him. He has seen what science can do for his land, what it can do under his own rooftree, what it can do in his community among his neighbors. What he and his wife have seen with their eyes gives them added faith that other equally impossible things can happen, too, on their farm, in their community, in the nation. They come to feel—"It *can* be done."

Faith that individual personality can flourish side by side with the machine and with science is vital in this: that men have only to have a faith that is deep enough, a belief sufficiently firm, in their daily work and living, that these things can be done—and then they will be done. For no insoluble physical problems stand in the way. There is no insuperable material barrier. The only serious obstacles are in the minds of men. These are not inconsiderable, it is true, but thinking put them there; a new kind of thinking can remove them. The great thing that has transpired in the Tennessee Valley is this growing faith not only that the scientific progress of our time can be used as a tool to create higher income and more comfortable living, but that technology can give men a choice, a genuine choice of alternatives, and that it can be used to make men free as they have never been before.

But there must be more than a conviction, a sure confidence, that it can be done. There must be a *sense of urgency*, a sense that this is the day on which to turn the first shovel. There are some who dream great dreams but never feel this urgency "to do something about it." This is in character for the intellectual gone to seed, the perfectionist, the "cooler head," the defeatist, the nostalgic liberal, the cynic about human possibilities. They are preoccupied in conjuring up all the possible difficulties and multiplying them. But the dreamers with shovels in their hands know that to start is important. The dreamers with shovels want only a job that is magnificent enough, room enough to stand in, and a chance to make a start.

They see a start as only that. For this is a continuing process, this improving the physical environment of men. It is never finished. There is no end, no blueprint of a finished product.

I share with many of my neighbors in the Tennessee Valley a deep conviction that it can be done, the modern job of building our resources and making the machine work for all men. And because of our experience together we believe that it can be done by such methods and with such purposes as will enrich the things of the spirit. This experience convinces me that science and invention can be consciously and deliberately directed to achieving the kind of world that people want. If it is decentralized industry men want, "family farming," or pleasant cities not too large, an end to smoke and congestion and filth—there are modern tools which can be turned to just such ends. The people, working through their private enterprises and public institutions which are democratic in spirit, can get substantially the kind of community and country they want.

The physical job will be done. If not democratically, it will be done in an antidemocratic way. It will be done perhaps by a small group of huge private corporations, controlling the country's resources; or by a tight clique of politicians; or by some other group or alliance of groups that is ready to take this responsibility which the people themselves decline to take. The smooth-talking centralizers, the managerial elite, cynical politicians, everyone without faith in the capacities of the people themselves to find a way will be hard at work seeking to draw off the benefits and control the development of the resources by which in turn they will control the lives of men. These are the gravest of dangers. No one can minimize the hazards of the gathering storm, or fail to see that troubled days lie ahead for democracy in our country. But catastrophe need not befall us. If as a people, in our daily living, we will only use the strength our democratic inheritance gives us, these attacks from within can be turned back and decisively defeated. Democracy can emerge revitalized by the test and conflict.

Here in the valley where I have been writing this statement of faith, the people know the job of our time can be done, for they have read the signs and reaped the first token harvest. They know it can be done, not only *for* the people but *by* the people.

GUNNAR MYRDAL

Selection from *An American Dilemma* (1944)

One of the twentieth century's most forthright and influential formulations of traditional American ideals was written by an "outsider," the Swedish economist Gunnar Myrdal (1898–1987). The occasion was the publication in 1944 of a 1,483-page analysis of the place of black people in the United States. *An American Dilemma: The Negro Problem and American Democracy* was the product of a six-year effort by a team of researchers assembled by Myrdal in response to a commission from a private foundation, the Carnegie Corporation. Although the bulk of this study consisted of social scientific data and analysis, Myrdal framed the whole report in terms of a gap between American ideals and the reality of how black people lived in the United States. Hence his articulation of "the American Creed" in the opening pages served to cast into bold relief the facts that were to follow: The prejudicial treatment of Negroes was an anomaly, a striking case in which Americans had failed to live up to their ideals.

In trying to reinforce what he took to be the American moral conscience in specific relation to "the Negro Problem," Myrdal exaggerated the extent to which the "Creed" had been accepted, and had been acted upon in other areas of American life. But his formulation of American democratic ideology resonated well beyond the specific policy dilemma that inspired it. It appeared while the United States was engaged in a war against powers who offered not even lip service to the ideology Myrdal attributed to Americans, and was widely read during the subsequent Cold War era when Americans were preoccupied with distinguishing themselves ideologically from the Soviet Union.

The most comprehensive study of Myrdal's project is Walter A. Jackson, *Gunnar Myrdal and America's Conscience: Social Engineering and Racial Liberalism, 1938–1987* (Chapel Hill, 1990). A valuable account of the reception of *An American Dilemma* is David W. Southern, *Gunnar Myrdal and Black-White Relations: The Use and Abuse of "An American Dilemma," 1944–1969* (Baton Rouge, 1987). A critique influential during the 1960s can be found in Ralph W. Ellison, *Shadow and Act* (New York, 1964), 303–17. For perspectives of the 1990s, see the special issue of *Daedalus* (Winter 1995), "*An American Dilemma* Revisited."

It is a commonplace to point out the heterogeneity of the American nation and the swift succession of all sorts of changes in all its component parts and, as it often seems, in every conceivable direction. America is truly a shock to the stranger. The bewildering impression it gives of dissimilarity throughout and of chaotic unrest is indicated by the fact that few outside observers—and, indeed, few native Americans—have been able to avoid the intellectual escape of speaking about America as "paradoxical."

Still there is evidently a strong unity in this nation and a basic homogeneity and stability in its valuations. Americans of all national origins, classes, regions, creeds, and colors, have something in common: a social *ethos*, a political creed. It is difficult to avoid the judgment that this "American Creed" is the cement in the structure of this great and disparate nation.

When the American Creed is once detected, the cacophony becomes a melody. The further observation then becomes apparent: that America, compared to every other country in Western civilization, large or small, has the *most explicitly expressed* system of general ideals in reference to human interrelations. This body of ideals is more widely understood and appreciated than similar ideals are anywhere else. The American Creed is not merely—as in some other countries—the implicit background of the nation's political and judicial order as it functions. To be sure, the political creed of America is not very satisfactorily effectuated in actual social life. But as principles which ought to rule, the Creed has been made conscious to everyone in American society.

Sometimes one even gets the impression that there is a relation between the intense apprehension of high and uncompromising ideals and the spotty reality. One feels that it is, perhaps, the difficulty of giving reality to the ethos in this young and still somewhat unorganized nation—that it is the prevalence of "wrongs" in America, "wrongs" judged by the high standards of the national Creed—which helps make the ideals stand out so clearly. America is continuously struggling for its soul. These principles of social ethics have been hammered into easily remembered formulas. All means of intellectual communication are utilized to stamp them into everybody's mind. The schools teach them, the churches preach them. The courts pronounce their judicial decisions in their terms. They permeate editorials with a pattern of idealism so ingrained that the writers could scarcely free themselves from it even if they tried. They have fixed a custom of indulging in high-sounding generalities in all written or spoken addresses to the American public, otherwise so splendidly gifted for the matter-of-fact approach to things and problems. Even the stranger, when he has to appear before an American audience, feels this, if he is sensitive at all, and finds himself espousing the national Creed, as this is the only means by which a speaker can obtain human response from the people to whom he talks.

The Negro people in America are no exception to the national pattern. "It was a revelation to me to hear Negroes sometimes indulge in a glorification of American democracy in the same uncritical way as unsophisticated whites often do," relates the Dutch observer, Bertram Schrieke. A Negro political scientist, Ralph Bunche, observes:

> Every man in the street, white, black, red or yellow, knows that this is "the land of the free," the "land of opportunity," the "cradle of liberty," the "home of democracy," that the American flag symbolizes the "equality of all men" and

Source: Gunnar Myrdal, *An American Dilemma* (New York: Harper & Row, 1944), 3–12, 24–25. Reprinted by permission of HarperCollins Publishers, Inc.

guarantees to us all "the protection of life, liberty and property," freedom of speech, freedom of religion and racial tolerance.

The present writer has made the same observation. The American Negroes know that they are a subordinated group experiencing, more than anybody else in the nation, the consequences of the fact that the Creed is not lived up to in America. Yet their faith in the Creed is not simply a means of pleading their unfulfilled rights. They, like the whites, are under the spell of the great national suggestion. With one part of themselves they actually believe, as do the whites, that the Creed is ruling America.

These ideals of the essential dignity of the individual human being, of the fundamental equality of all men, and of certain inalienable rights to freedom, justice, and a fair opportunity represent to the American people the essential meaning of the nation's early struggle for independence. In the clarity and intellectual boldness of the Enlightenment period these tenets were written into the Declaration of Independence, the Preamble of the Constitution, the Bill of Rights and into the constitutions of the several states. The ideals of the American Creed have thus become the highest law of the land. The Supreme Court pays its reverence to these general principles when it declares what is constitutional and what is not. They have been elaborated upon by all national leaders, thinkers and statesmen. America has had, throughout its history, a continuous discussion of the principles and implications of democracy, a discussion which, in every epoch, measured by any standard, remained high, not only quantitatively but also qualitatively. The flow of learned treatises and popular tracts on the subject has not ebbed, nor is it likely to do so. In all wars, including the present one, the American Creed has been the ideological foundation of national morale.

The American Creed is identified with America's peculiar brand of nationalism, and it gives the common American his feeling of the historical mission of America in the world—a fact which just now becomes of global importance but which is also of highest significance for the particular problem studied in this book. The great national historian of the middle nineteenth century, George Bancroft, expressed this national feeling of pride and responsibility:

> In the fulness of time a republic rose in the wilderness of America. Thousands of years had passed away before this child of the ages could be born. From whatever there was of good in the systems of the former centuries she drew her nourishment; the wrecks of the past were her warnings... The fame of this only daughter of freedom went out into all the lands of the earth; from her the human race drew hope.

And Frederick J. Turner, who injected the naturalistic explanation into history that American democracy was a native-born product of the Western frontier, early in this century wrote in a similar vein:

> Other nations have been rich and prosperous and powerful. But the United States has believed that it had an original contribution to make to the history of society by the production of a self-determining, self-restrained, intelligent democracy.

Wilson's fourteen points and Roosevelt's four freedoms have more recently expressed to the world the boundless idealistic aspirations of this American Creed. For a century and more before the present epoch, when the oceans gave reality to the Monroe Doctrine,

America at least applauded heartily every uprising of the people in any corner of the world. This was a tradition from America's own Revolution. The political revolutionaries of foreign countries were approved even by the conservatives in America. And America wanted generously to share its precious ideals and its happiness in enjoying a society ruled by its own people with all who would come here. James Truslow Adams tells us:

> The American dream that has lured tens of millions of all nations to our shores in the past century has not been a dream of merely material plenty, though that has doubtless counted heavily. It has been much more than that. It has been a dream of being able to grow to fullest development as man and woman, unhampered by the barriers which had slowly been erected in older civilizations, unrepressed by social orders which had developed for the benefit of classes rather than for the simple human being of any and every class. And that dream has been realized more fully in actual life here than anywhere else, though very imperfectly even among ourselves.

This is what the Western frontier country could say to the "East." And even the skeptic cannot help feeling that, perhaps, this youthful exuberant America has the destiny to do for the whole Old World what the frontier did to the old colonies. *American nationalism is permeated by the American Creed,* and therefore becomes international in its essence.

It is remarkable that a vast democracy with so many cultural disparities has been able to reach this unanimity of ideals and to elevate them supremely over the threshold of popular perception. Totalitarian fascism and nazism have not in their own countries —at least not in the short range of their present rule—succeeded in accomplishing a similar result, in spite of the fact that those governments, after having subdued the principal precepts most akin to the American Creed, have attempted to coerce the minds of their people by means of a centrally controlled, ruthless, and scientifically contrived apparatus of propaganda and violence.

There are more things to be wondered about. The disparity of national origin, language, religion, and culture, during the long era of mass immigration into the United States, has been closely correlated with income differences and social class distinctions. Successive vintages of "Old Americans" have owned the country and held the dominant political power; they have often despised and exploited "the foreigners." To this extent conditions in America must be said to have been particularly favorable to the stratification of a rigid class society.

But it has not come to be. On the question of why the trend took the other course, the historians, from Turner on, point to the free land and the boundless resources. The persistent drive from the Western frontier—now and then swelling into great tides as in the Jeffersonian movement around 1800, the Jacksonian movement a generation later, and the successive third-party movements and breaks in the traditional parties—could, however, reach its historical potency only because of the fact that America, from the Revolution onward, had an equalitarian creed as a going national *ethos.* The economic determinants and the force of the ideals can be shown to be interrelated. But the latter should not be relegated to merely a dependent variable. Vernon L. Parrington, the great historian of the development of the American mind, writes thus:

> The humanitarian idealism of the Declaration [of Independence] has always echoed as a battle-cry in the hearts of those who dream of an America dedicated to democratic ends. It cannot be long ignored or repudiated, for sooner or later

it returns to plague the council of practical politics. It is constantly breaking out in fresh revolt.... Without its freshening influence our political history would have been much more sordid and materialistic.

Indeed, the new republic began its career with a reaction. Charles Beard, in *An Economic Interpretation of the Constitution of the United States,* and a group of modern historians, throwing aside the much cherished national mythology which had blurred the difference in spirit between the Declaration of Independence and the Constitution, have shown that the latter was conceived in considerable suspicion against democracy and fear of "the people." It was dominated by property consciousness and designed as a defense against the democratic spirit let loose during the Revolution.

But, admitting all this, the Constitution which actually emerged out of the compromises in the drafting convention provided for the most democratic state structure in existence anywhere in the world at that time. And many of the safeguards so skillfully thought out by the conservatives to protect "the rich, the wellborn, and the capable" against majority rule melted when the new order began to function. Other conservative safeguards have fastened themselves into the political pattern. And "in the ceaseless conflict between the man and the dollar, between democracy and property"—again to quote Parrington—property has for long periods triumphed and blocked the will of the people. And there are today large geographical regions and fields of human life which, particularly when measured by the high goals of the American Creed, are conspicuously lagging. But taking the broad historical view, the American Creed has triumphed. It has given the main direction to change in this country. America has had gifted conservative statesmen and national leaders, and they have often determined the course of public affairs. But with few exceptions, only the liberals have gone down in history as national heroes. America is, as we shall point out, conservative in fundamental principles, and in much more than that, though hopefully experimentalistic in regard to much of the practical arrangements in society. But *the principles conserved are liberal* and some, indeed, are radical.

America got this dynamic Creed much as a political convenience and a device of strategy during the long struggle with the English Crown, the London Parliament and the various British powerholders in the colonies. It served as the rallying center for the growing national unity that was needed. Later it was a necessary device for building up a national morale in order to enlist and sustain the people in the Revolutionary War. In this spirit the famous declarations were resolved, the glorious speeches made, the inciting pamphlets written and spread. "The appeal to arms would seem to have been brought about by a minority of the American people, directed by a small group of skillful leaders, who, like Indian scouts, covered their tracks so cleverly, that only the keenest trailers can now follow their course and understand their strategy."

But the Creed, once set forth and disseminated among the American people, became so strongly entrenched in their hearts, and the circumstances have since then been so relatively favorable, that it has succeeded in keeping itself very much alive for more than a century and a half.

The American Creed is a humanistic liberalism developing out of the epoch of Enlightenment when America received its national consciousness and its political structure. The Revolution did not stop short of anything less than the heroic desire for the "emancipation of human nature." The enticing flavor of the eighteenth century, so dear to every intellectual and rationalist, has not been lost on the long journey up to the present time. Let us quote a contemporary exegesis:

> Democracy is a form of political association in which the general control and direction of the commonwealth is habitually determined by the bulk of the community in accordance with understandings and procedures providing for popular participation and consent. Its postulates are:
>
> 1. The essential dignity of man, the importance of protecting and cultivating his personality of the personality within the frame-work of the common good in a formula of liberty, justice, welfare.
> 2. The perfectibility of man; confidence in the possibilities of the human personality, as over against the doctrines of caste, class, and slavery.
> 3. That the gains of commonwealths are essentially mass gains rather than the efforts of the few and should be diffused as promptly as possible throughout the community without too great delay or too wide a spread in differentials.
> 4. Confidence in the value of the consent of the governed expressed in institutions, understandings and practices as a basis of order, liberty, justice.
> 5. The value of decisions arrived at by common counsel rather than by violence and brutality.
>
> These postulates rest upon (1) reason in regarding the essential nature of the political man, upon (2) observation, experience and inference, and (3) the fulfillment of the democratic ideal is strengthened by a faith in the final triumph of ideals of human behavior in general and of political behavior in particular.

For practical purposes the main norms of the American Creed as usually pronounced are centered in the belief in equality and in the rights to liberty. In the Declaration of Independence—as in the earlier Virginia Bill of Rights—equality was given the supreme rank and the rights to liberty are posited as derived from equality. This logic was even more clearly expressed in Jefferson's original formulation of the first of the "self-evident truths": "All men are created equal *and from that equal creation* they derive rights inherent and unalienable, among which are the preservation of life and liberty and the pursuit of happiness."

Liberty, in a sense, was easiest to reach. It is a vague ideal: everything turns around *whose* liberty is preserved, to *what extent* and *in what direction*. In society liberty for one may mean the suppression of liberty for others. The result of competition will be determined by who got a head start and who is handicapped. In America as everywhere else—and sometimes, perhaps, on the average, a little more ruthlessly—liberty often provided an opportunity for the stronger to rob the weaker. Against this, the equalitarianism in the Creed has been persistently revolting. The struggle is far from ended. The reason why American liberty was not more dangerous to equality was, of course, the open frontier and the free land. When opportunity became bounded in the last generation, the inherent conflict between equality and liberty flared up. Equality is slowly winning. The New Deal during the 'thirties was a landslide.

If the European philosophy of Enlightenment was one of the ideological roots of the American Creed, another equally important one was Christianity, particularly as it took the form in the colonies of various lower class Protestant sects, split off from the Anglican Church. "Democracy was envisaged in religious terms long before it assumed a political terminology."

It is true that modern history has relegated to the category of the pious patriotic myths the popular belief that all the colonies had been founded to get religious liberty, which could not be had in the Old World. Some of the colonies were commercial adventures and the settlers came to them, and even to the religious colonies later, to improve their economic status. It is also true that the churches in the early colonial times did not always exactly represent the idea of democratic government in America but most often a harsher tyranny over people's souls and behavior than either King or Parliament ever cared to wield.

But the myth itself is a social reality with important effects. It was strong already in the period of the Revolution and continued to grow. A small proportion of new immigrants throughout the nineteenth century came for religious reasons, or partly so, and a great many more wanted to rationalize their uprooting and transplantation in such terms. So religion itself in America took on a spirit of fight for liberty. The Bible is full of support for such a spirit. It consists to a large extent of the tales of oppression and redemption from oppression: in the Old Testament of the Jewish people and in the New Testament of the early Christians. The rich and mighty are most often the wrongdoers, while the poor and lowly are the followers of God and Christ.

The basic teaching of Protestant Christianity is democratic. We are all poor sinners and have the same heavenly father. The concept of natural rights in the philosophy of Enlightenment corresponded rather closely with the idea of moral law in the Christian faith:

> The doctrine of the free individual, postulating the gradual escape of men from external political control, as they learned to obey the moral law, had its counterpart in the emphasis of evangelicism upon the freedom of the regenerated man from the terrors of the Old Testament code framed for the curbing of unruly and sinful generations. The philosophy of progress was similar to the Utopian hopes of the millennarians. The mission of American democracy to save the world from the oppression of autocrats was a secular version of the destiny of Christianity to save the world from the governance of Satan.

But apart from the historical problem of the extent to which church and religion in America actually inspired the American Creed, they became a powerful container and preserver of the Creed when it was once in existence. This was true from the beginning. While in Europe after the Napoleonic Wars the increasing power of the churches everywhere spelled a period of reaction, the great revivals beginning around 1800 in America were a sort of religious continuation of the Revolution.

> In this way great numbers whom the more-or-less involved theory of natural rights had escaped came under the leveling influence of a religious doctrine which held that all men were equal in the sight of God. Throughout the Revival period the upper classes looked upon the movement as "a religious distemper" which spread like a contagious disease, and they pointed out that it made its greatest appeal to "those of weak intellect and unstable emotions, women, adolescents, and Negroes." But to the poor farmer who had helped to win the Revolution only to find himself oppressed as much by the American ruling classes as he had ever been by Crown officials, the movement was "the greatest stir of Religion since the day of Pentecost."

Religion is still a potent force in American life. "They are a religious people," observed Lord Bryce about Americans a half a century ago, with great understanding for the importance of this fact for their national ideology. American scientific observers are likely to get their attentions fixed upon the process of progressive secularization to the extent that they do not see this main fact, that America probably is still the most religious country in the Western world. Political leaders are continuously deducing the American Creed out of the Bible. Vice-President Henry Wallace, in his historic speech of May 8, 1942, to the Free World Association, where he declared the present war to be "a fight between a slave world and a free world" and declared himself for "a people's peace" to inaugurate "the century of the common man," spoke thus:

> The idea of freedom—the freedom that we in the United States know and love so well—is derived from the Bible with its extraordinary emphasis on the dignity of the individual. Democracy is the only true political expression of Christianity.
>
> The prophets of the Old Testament were the first to preach social justice. But that which was sensed by the prophets many centuries before Christ was not given complete and powerful political expression until our Nation was formed as a Federal Union a century and a half ago.

Ministers have often been reactionaries in America. They have often tried to stifle free speech; they have organized persecution of unpopular dissenters and have even, in some regions, been active as the organizers of the Ku Klux Klan and similar "un- American" (in terms of the American Creed) movements. But, on the whole, church and religion in America are a force strengthening the American Creed. The fundamental tenets of Christianity press for expression even in the most bigoted setting. And, again on the whole, American religion is not particularly bigoted, but on the contrary, rather open-minded. The mere fact that there are many denominations, and that there is competition between them, forces American churches to a greater tolerance and ecumenical understanding and to a greater humanism and interest in social problems than the people in the churches would otherwise call for.

I also believe that American churches and their teachings have contributed something essential to the emotional temper of the Creed and, indeed, of the American people. Competent and sympathetic foreign observers have always noted the generosity and helpfulness of Americans. This and the equally conspicuous formal democracy in human contacts have undoubtedly had much to do with the predominantly lower class origin of the American people, and even more perhaps, with the mobility and the opportunities— what de Tocqueville called the "equality of condition"—in the nation when it was in its formative stage. But I cannot help feeling that the Christian neighborliness of the common American reflects, also, an influence from the churches. Apart from its origin, this temper of the Americans is part and parcel of the American Creed. It shows up in the Americans' readiness to make financial sacrifices for charitable purposes. No country has so many cheerful givers as America. It was not only "rugged individualism," nor a relatively continuous prosperity, that made it possible for America to get along without a publicly organized welfare policy almost up to the Great Depression in the 'thirties but it was also the world's most generous private charity.

The third main ideological influence behind the American Creed is English law. The indebtedness of American civilization to the culture of the mother country is nowhere else as great as in respect to the democratic concept of law and order, which it inherited almost without noticing it. It is the glory of England that, after many generations of hard struggle, it established the principles of justice, equity, and equality before the law even in an age when the rest of Europe (except for the cultural islands of Switzerland, Iceland, and Scandinavia) based personal security on the arbitrary police and on *lettres de cachet*.

This concept of a government "of laws and not of men" contained certain fundamentals of both equality and liberty. It will be a part of our task to study how these elemental demands are not nearly realized even in present-day America. But in the American Creed they have never been questioned. And it is no exaggeration to state that the philosophical ideas of human equality and the inalienable rights to life, liberty, and property, hastily sowed on American ground in a period of revolution when they were opportune—even allowing ever so much credit to the influences from the free life on the Western frontier—would not have struck root as they did if the soil had not already been cultivated by English law....

From the point of view of the American Creed the status accorded the Negro in America represents nothing more and nothing less than a century-long lag of public morals. In principle the Negro problem was settled long ago; in practice the solution is not effectuated. The Negro in America has not yet been given the elemental civil and political rights of formal democracy, including a fair opportunity to earn his living, upon which a general accord was already won when the American Creed was first taking form. And this anachronism constitutes the contemporary "problem" both to Negroes and to whites.

If those rights were respected, many other pressing social problems would, of course, still remain. Many Negroes would, together with many whites, belong to groups which would invoke the old ideals of equality and liberty in demanding more effective protection for their social and economic opportunities. But there would no longer be a Negro problem. This does not mean that the Negro problem is an easy problem to solve. It is a tremendous task for theoretical research to find out why the Negro's status is what it is. In its unsolved form it further intertwines with all other social problems. It is simple only in the technical sense that in America the value premises—if they are conceived to be the ideals of the American Creed—are extraordinarily specific and definite.

Finally, in order to avoid possible misunderstandings, it should be explained that we have called this Creed "American" in the sense that it is adhered to by the Americans. This is the only matter which interests us in this book, which is focused upon the Negro problem as part of American life and American politics. But this Creed is, of course, no American monopoly. With minor variations, some of which, however, are not without importance, the American Creed is the common democratic creed. "American ideals" are just humane ideals as they have matured in our common Western civilization upon the foundation of Christianity and pre-Christian legalism and under the influence of the economic, scientific, and political development over a number of centuries. The American Creed is older and wider than America itself.

REINHOLD NIEBUHR

Selection from *The Children of Light and the Children of Darkness* (1944)

Reinhold Niebuhr (1892–1971) was for several decades the nation's most quoted and respected critic of modern thought's drift away from explicitly Christian foundations. Niebuhr owed much of his influence to the skill with which he—a Protestant preacher and seminary professor—brought the perspectives of liberal theology to bear on the political, social, and cultural issues of the middle third of the twentieth century. An effective polemicist against pacifism, communism, and other utopian projects under attack in the 1940s and 1950s, Niebuhr won a large following among secular intellectuals ("atheists for Niebuhr," such men and women were sometimes called). Although Niebuhr was sometimes associated in the public mind with the neoorthodox movement led by the Swiss theologian Karl Barth, his most vital engagements were decidedly more worldly and contemporary than Barth's. This was especially true of *Moral Man and Immoral Society* (New York, 1932), which first made Niebuhr famous. This work of political criticism supported collective action by workers against their capitalist oppressors, and it included a critique of Christian pacifism so vehement as to lead some of Niebuhr's ministerial colleagues to accuse him of abandoning the ethics of Jesus for the "tough-minded" views of Pontius Pilate. Niebuhr pulled back from this extremity in *An Interpretation of Christian Ethics* (New York, 1935), but the affairs of civil society always remained at the center of his gaze, and he continued to project a "tougher-than-thou" persona.

In *The Children of Light and the Children of Darkness* (New York, 1944), a selection from which follows, Niebuhr criticized the intellectual tradition of the Enlightenment for what he insisted was its prevailing optimism regarding human character. Niebuhr's most theologically ambitious work was *The Nature and Destiny of Man,* 2 vols. (New York, 1943). The most important book of his later career was an interpretation of the history of the United States in world-historical perspective, *The Irony of American History* (1952). During the 1950s and much of the 1960s, Niebuhr exercised great influence through his contributions to magazines, especially *Christianity and Crisis*.

The best historical study of Niebuhr's early career is Richard Wightman Fox, *Reinhold Niebuhr: A Biography* (New York, 1986), although many of Niebuhr's disciples and surviving friends found this book insufficiently warm in its appreciation for Niebuhr's personality and intellectual contributions. The widespread desire for a more consistently enthusiastic account is well satisfied by Charles C. Brown, *Niebuhr and His Age: Reinhold Niebuhr's Prophetic Role in the Twentieth Century* (Philadelphia, 1992). A second, revised edition of Fox's biography (Ithaca, 1996) contains a judicious and humane discussion of recent writings on Niebuhr, including those critical of Fox's own interpretation. The most compelling interpretation of Niebuhr's thought in the context of the history of theology is in Gary Dorrien, *The Making of American Liberal Theology,* vol. 2 (Grand Rapids, Mich., 2004) 435–64.

We may well designate the moral cynics, who know no law beyond their will and interest, with a scriptural designation of "children of this world" or "children of darkness." Those who believe that self-interest should be brought under the discipline of a higher law could then be termed "the children of light." This is no mere arbitrary device; for evil is always the assertion of some self-interest without regard to the whole, whether the whole be conceived as the immediate community, or the total community of mankind, or the total order of the world. The good is, on the other hand, always the harmony of the whole on various levels. Devotion to a subordinate and premature "whole" such as the nation, may of course become evil, viewed from the perspective of a larger whole, such as the community of mankind. The "children of light" may thus be defined as those who seek to bring self-interest under the discipline of a more universal law and in harmony with a more universal good.

According to the scripture "the children of this world are in their generation wiser than the children of light." This observation fits the modern situation. Our democratic civilization has been built, not by children of darkness but by foolish children of light. It has been under attack by the children of darkness, by the moral cynics, who declare that a strong nation need acknowledge no law beyond its strength. It has come close to complete disaster under this attack, not because it accepted the same creed as the cynics; but because it underestimated the power of self-interest, both individual and collective, in modern society. The children of light have not been as wise as the children of darkness.

The children of darkness are evil because they know no law beyond the self. They are wise, though evil, because they understand the power of self-interest. The children of light are virtuous because they have some conception of a higher law than their own will. They are usually foolish because they do not know the power of self-will. They underestimate the peril of anarchy in both the national and the international community. Modern democratic civilization is, in short, sentimental rather than cynical. It has an easy solution for the problem of anarchy and chaos on both the national and international level of community, because of its fatuous and superficial view of man. It does not know that the same man who is ostensibly devoted to the "common good" may have desires and ambitions, hopes and fears, which set him at variance with his neighbor.

It must be understood that the children of light are foolish not merely because they underestimate the power of self-interest among the children of darkness. They underestimate this power among themselves. The democratic world came so close to disaster not merely because it never believed that Nazism possessed the demonic fury which it avowed. Civilization refused to recognize the power of class interest in its own communities. It also spoke glibly of an international conscience; but the children of darkness meanwhile skilfully set nation against nation. They were thereby enabled to despoil one nation after another, without every civilized nation coming to the defence of each. Moral cynicism had a provisional advantage over moral sentimentality. Its advantage lay not merely in its own lack of moral scruple but also in its shrewd assessment of the power of self-interest, individual and national, among the children of light, despite their moral protestations.

While our modern children of light, the secularized idealists, were particularly foolish and blind, the more "Christian" children of light have been almost equally guilty of this error. Modern liberal Protestantism was probably even more sentimental in its appraisal of the moral realities in our political life than secular idealism, and Catholicism could see

Source: Reinhold Niebuhr, *The Children of Light and the Children of Darkness* (New York: Scribner's, 1944), 10–22, 31–38. Reprinted by permission of Prentice-Hall, Inc. Copyright renewed 1972 by Ursula Keppel-Compton Niebuhr.

nothing but cynical rebellion in the modern secular revolt against Catholic universalism and a Catholic "Christian" civilization. In Catholic thought medieval political universalism is always accepted at face value. Rebellion against medieval culture is therefore invariably regarded as the fruit of moral cynicism. Actually the middle-class revolt against the feudal order was partially prompted by a generous idealism, not unmixed of course with peculiar middle-class interests. The feudal order was not so simply a Christian civilization as Catholic defenders of it aver. It compounded its devotion to a universal order with the special interests of the priestly and aristocratic bearers of effective social power. The rationalization of their unique position in the feudal order may not have been more marked than the subsequent rationalization of bourgeois interests in the liberal world. But it is idle to deny this "ideological taint" in the feudal order and to pretend that rebels against the order were merely rebels against order as such. They were rebels against a particular order which gave an undue advantage to the aristocratic opponents of the middle classes. The blindness of Catholicism to its own ideological taint is typical of the blindness of the children of light.

Our modern civilization, as a middle-class revolt against an aristocratic and clerical order, was irreligious partly because a Catholic civilization had so compounded the eternal sanctities with the contingent and relative justice and injustice of an agrarian-feudal order, that the new and dynamic bourgeois social force was compelled to challenge not only the political-economic arrangements of the order but also the eternal sanctities which hallowed it.

If modern civilization represents a bourgeois revolt against feudalism, modern culture represents the revolt of new thought, informed by modern science, against a culture in which religious authority had fixed premature and too narrow limits for the expansion of science and had sought to restrain the curiosity of the human mind from inquiring into "secondary causes." The culture which venerated science in place of religion, worshipped natural causation in place of God, and which regarded the cool prudence of bourgeois man as morally more normative than Christian love, has proved itself to be less profound than it appeared to be in the seventeenth and eighteenth centuries. But these inadequacies, which must be further examined as typical of the foolishness of modern children of light, do not validate the judgment that these modern rebels were really children of darkness, intent upon defying the truth or destroying universal order.

The modern revolt against the feudal order and the medieval culture was occasioned by the assertion of new vitalities in the social order and the discovery of new dimensions in the cultural enterprise of mankind. It was truly democratic in so far as it challenged the premature and tentative unity of a society and the stabilization of a culture, and in so far as it developed new social and cultural possibilities. The conflict between the middle classes and the aristocrats, between the scientists and the priests, was not a conflict between children of darkness and children of light. It was a conflict between pious and less pious children of light, both of whom were unconscious of the corruption of self-interest in all ideal achievements and pretensions of human culture.

In this conflict the devotees of medieval religion were largely unconscious of the corruption of self-interest in their own position; but it must be admitted that they were not as foolish as their secular successors in their estimate of the force of self-interest in human society. Catholicism did strive for an inner and religious discipline upon inordinate desire; and it had a statesmanlike conception of the necessity of legal and political restraint upon the power of egotism, both individual and collective, in the national and the more universal human community.

Our modern civilization, on the other hand, was ushered in on a wave of boundless social optimism. Modern secularism is divided into many schools. But all the various schools agreed in rejecting the Christian doctrine of original sin. It is not possible to explain the subtleties or to measure the profundity of this doctrine in this connection. But it is necessary to point out that the doctrine makes an important contribution to any adequate social and political theory the lack of which has robbed bourgeois theory of real wisdom; for it emphasizes a fact which every page of human history attests. Through it one may understand that no matter how wide the perspectives which the human mind may reach, how broad the loyalties which the human imagination may conceive, how universal the community which human statecraft may organize, or how pure the aspirations of the saintliest idealists may be, there is no level of human moral or social achievement in which there is not some corruption of inordinate self-love.

This sober and true view of the human situation was neatly rejected by modern culture. That is why it conceived so many fatuous and futile plans for resolving the conflict between the self and the community; and between the national and the world community. Whenever modern idealists are confronted with the divisive and corrosive effects of man's self-love, they look for some immediate cause of this perennial tendency, usually in some specific form of social organization. One school holds that men would be good if only political institutions would not corrupt them; another believes that they would be good if the prior evil of a faulty economic organization could be eliminated. Or another school thinks of this evil as no more than ignorance, and therefore waits for a more perfect educational process to redeem man from his partial and particular loyalties. But no school asks how it is that an essentially good man could have produced corrupting and tyrannical political organizations or exploiting economic organizations, or fanatical and superstitious religious organizations.

The result of this persistent blindness to the obvious and tragic facts of man's social history is that democracy has had to maintain itself precariously against the guile and the malice of the children of darkness, while its statesmen and guides conjured up all sorts of abstract and abortive plans for the creation of perfect national and international communities.

The confidence of modern secular idealism in the possibility of an easy resolution of the tension between individual and community, or between classes, races and nations is derived from a too optimistic view of human nature. This too generous estimate of human virtue is intimately related to an erroneous estimate of the dimensions of the human stature. The conception of human nature which underlies the social and political attitudes of a liberal democratic culture is that of an essentially harmless individual. The survival impulse, which man shares with the animals, is regarded as the normative form of his egoistic drive. If this were a true picture of the human situation man might be, or might become, as harmless as seventeenth- and eighteenth-century thought assumed. Unfortunately for the validity of this picture of man, the most significant distinction between the human and the animal world is that the impulses of the former are "spiritualized" in the human world. Human capacities for evil as well as for good are derived from this spiritualization. There is of course always a natural survival impulse at the core of all human ambition. But this survival impulse cannot be neatly disentangled from two forms of its spiritualization. The one form is the desire to fulfill the potentialities of life and not merely to maintain its existence. Man is the kind of animal who cannot merely live. If he lives at all he is bound to seek the realization of his true nature; and to his true nature belongs his fulfillment in the lives of others. The will to live is thus transmuted into the will to self-realization; and self-realization involves self-giving in relations to others. When this desire for self-realization is fully explored it becomes apparent that it is subject to the paradox that the highest form of self-realization is the consequence of self-giving, but that it cannot be the intended consequence without being prematurely limited. Thus the will to live is finally transmuted into its opposite in the sense that only in self-giving can the self be fulfilled, for: "He that findeth his life shall lose it: and he that loseth his life for my sake shall find it."

On the other hand the will-to-live is also spiritually transmuted into the will-to-power or into the desire for "power and glory." Man, being more than a natural creature, is not interested merely in physical survival but in prestige and social approval. Having the intelligence to anticipate the perils in which he stands in nature and history, he invariably seeks to gain security against these perils by enhancing his power, individually and collectively. Possessing a darkly unconscious sense of his insignificance in the total scheme of things, he seeks to compensate for his insignificance by pretensions of pride. The conflicts between men are thus never simple conflicts between competing survival impulses. They are conflicts in which each man or group seeks to guard its power and prestige against the peril of competing expressions of power and pride. Since the very possession of power and prestige always involves some encroachment upon the prestige and power of others, this conflict is by its very nature a more stubborn and difficult one than the mere competition between various survival impulses in nature. It remains to be added that this conflict expresses itself even more cruelly in collective than in individual terms. Human behaviour being less individualistic than secular liberalism assumed, the struggle between classes, races and other groups in human society is not as easily resolved by the expedient of dissolving the groups as liberal democratic idealists assumed.

Since the survival impulse in nature is transmuted into two different and contradictory spiritualized forms, which we may briefly designate as the will-to-live-truly and the will-to-power, man is at variance with himself. The power of the second impulse places him more fundamentally in conflict with his fellowman than democratic liberalism realizes. The fact he cannot realize himself, except in organic relation with his fellows, makes the community more important than bourgeois individualism understands. The fact that the two impulses, though standing in contradiction to each other, are also mixed and compounded with each other on every level of human life, makes the simple distinctions between good and evil, between selfishness and altruism, with which liberal idealism has tried to estimate moral and political facts, invalid. The fact that the will-to-power inevitably justifies itself in terms of the morally more acceptable will to realize man's true nature means that the egoistic corruption of universal ideals is a much more persistent fact in human conduct than any moralistic creed is inclined to admit.

If we survey any period of history, and not merely the present tragic era of world catastrophe, it becomes quite apparent that human ambitions, lusts and desires, are more inevitably inordinate, that both human creativity and human evil reach greater heights, and that conflicts in the community between varying conceptions of the good and between competing expressions of vitality are of more tragic proportions than was anticipated in the basic philosophy which underlies democratic civilization....

The general confidence of an identity between self-interest and the commonweal, which underlies liberal democratic political theory, is succinctly expressed in Thomas Paine's simple creed: "Public good is not a term opposed to the good of the individual; on the contrary it is the good of every individual collected. It is the good of all, because it is the good of every one; for as the public body is every individual collected, so the public good is the collected good of those individuals."...

Perhaps the most remarkable proof of the power of this optimistic creed, which underlies democratic thought, is that Marxism, which is ostensibly a revolt against it, manages to express the same optimism in another form. While liberal democrats dreamed of a simple social harmony, to be achieved by a cool prudence and a calculating egotism, the actual facts of social history revealed that the static class struggle of agrarian societies had been fanned into the flames of a dynamic struggle. Marxism was the social creed and the social cry of those classes who knew by their miseries that the creed of the liberal optimists was a snare and a delusion. Marxism insisted that the increasingly overt social conflict in democratic society would have to become even more overt, and would finally be fought to a bitter conclusion. But Marxism was also convinced that after the triumph of the lower classes of society, a new society would emerge in which exactly that kind of harmony between all social forces would be established, which Adam Smith had regarded as a possibility for any kind of society. The similarities between classical laissez-faire theory and the vision of an anarchistic millennium in Marxism are significant, whatever may be the superficial differences. Thus the provisionally cynical Lenin, who can trace all the complexities of social conflict in contemporary society with penetrating shrewdness, can also express the utopian hope that the revolution will usher in a period of history which will culminate in the Marxist millennium of anarchism. "All need for force will vanish," declared Lenin, "since people will grow accustomed to observing the elementary conditions of social existence without force and without subjection." ...

The Marxists, too, are children of light. Their provisional cynicism does not even save them from the usual stupidity, nor from the fate, of other stupid children of light. That fate is to have their creed become the vehicle and instrument of the children of darkness. A new oligarchy is arising in Russia, the spiritual characteristics of which can hardly be distinguished from those of the American "go-getters" of the latter nineteenth and early twentieth centuries. And in the light of history Stalin will probably have the same relation to the early dreamers of the Marxist dreams which Napoleon has to the liberal dreamers of the eighteenth century.

Democratic theory, whether in its liberal or in its more radical form, is just as stupid in analyzing the relation between the national and the international community as in seeking a too simple harmony between the individual and the national community. Here, too, modern liberal culture exhibits few traces of moral cynicism. The morally autonomous modern national state does indeed arise; and it acknowledges no law beyond its interests. The actual behaviour of the nations is cynical. But the creed of liberal civilization is sentimental. This is true not only of the theorists whose creed was used by the architects of economic imperialism and of the more covert forms of national egotism in the international community, but also of those whose theories were appropriated by the proponents of an explicit national egotism. A straight line runs from Mazzini to Mussolini in the history of Italian nationalism. Yet there was not a touch of moral cynicism in the thought of Mazzini. He was, on the contrary, a pure universalist.

Even the philosophy of German romanticism, which has been accused with some justification of making specific contributions to the creed of German Nazism, reveals the stupidity of the children of light much more than the malice of the children of darkness. There is of course a strong note of moral nihilism in the final fruit of this romantic movement as we have it in Nietzsche; though even Nietzsche was no nationalist. But the earlier romantics usually express the same combination of individualism and universalism which characterizes the theory of the more naturalistic and rationalistic democrats of the western countries. Fichte resolved the conflict between the individual and the community through the instrumentality of the "just law" almost as easily as the utilitarians resolved it by the calculations of the prudent egotist and as easily as Rousseau resolved it by his conception of a "general will," which would fulfill the best purposes of each individual will. This was no creed of a community, making itself the idolatrous end of human existence. The theory was actually truer than the more individualistic and naturalistic forms of the democratic creed; for romanticism understood that the individual requires the community for his fulfillment. Thus even Hegel, who is sometimes regarded as the father of state absolutism in modern culture, thought of the national state as providing "for the reasonable will, insofar as it is in the individual only implicitly the universal will coming to a consciousness and an understanding of itself and being found."

This was not the creed of a collective egotism which negated the right of the individual. Rather it was a theory which, unlike the more purely democratic creed, understood the necessity of social fulfillment for the individual, and which, in common with the more liberal theories, regarded this as a much too simple process.

If the theory was not directed toward the annihilation of the individual, as is the creed of modern religious nationalism, to what degree was it directed against the universal community? Was it an expression of the national community's defiance of any interest or law above and beyond itself? This also is not the case. Herder believed that "fatherlands" might "lie peaceably side by side and aid each other as families. It is the grossest barbarity of human speech to speak of fatherlands in bloody battle with each other." Unfortunately this is something more than a barbarity of speech. Herder was a universalist, who thought a nice harmony between various communities could be achieved if only the right would be granted to each to express itself according to its unique and peculiar genius. He thought the false universalism of imperialism, according to which one community makes itself the standard and the governor of others, was merely the consequence of a false philosophy, whereas it is in fact one of the perennial corruptions of man's collective life.

Fichte, too, was a universalist who was fully conscious of moral obligations which transcend the national community. His difficulty, like that of all the children of light, was that he had a too easy resolution of the conflict between the nation and the community of nations. He thought that philosophy, particularly German philosophy, could achieve a synthesis between national and universal interest. "The patriot," he declared, "wishes the purpose of mankind to be reached first of all in that nation of which he is a member.... This purpose is the only possible patriotic goal.... Cosmopolitanism is the will that the purpose of life and of man be attained in all mankind, Patriotism is the will that this purpose be attained first of all in that nation of which we are members." It is absurd to regard such doctrine as the dogma of national egotism, though Fichte could not express it without insinuating a certain degree of national pride into it. The pride took the form of the complacent assumption that German philosophy enabled the German nation to achieve a more perfect relation to the community of mankind than any other nation. He was, in other words, one of the many stupid children of light, who failed to understand the difficulty of the problem which he was considering; and his blindness included failure to see the significance of the implicit denial of an ideal in the thought and action of the very idealist who propounds it....

The preservation of a democratic civilization requires the wisdom of the serpent and the harmlessness of the dove. The children of light must be armed with the wisdom of the children of darkness but remain free from their malice. They must know the power of self-interest in human society without giving it moral justification. They must have this wisdom in order that they may beguile, deflect, harness and restrain self-interest, individual and collective, for the sake of the community.

ERIK H. ERIKSON

Selection from *Childhood and Society*
(1950)

Never was psychoanalysis more popular among educated Americans than in the twenty years after World War II, and no psychoanalyst won a greater following during that era than Erik H. Erikson (1902–94). Although he worked within the broad Freudian tradition, Erikson differed from many of Freud's orthodox followers, who stressed the largely determining power of instinctual drives and early childhood experiences in shaping the human personality. Erikson instead posited a more holistic and voluntaristic model in which individuals strived, in the face of enfolding biological and cultural pressures, to become aware of and interact with an ever-widening radius of the human world over the entire course of the life cycle. This revisionary schema is displayed in the selection that follows, in which Erikson sets forth his "Eight Ages of Man," the title of this chapter of the 1950 book that established his reputation, *Childhood and Society*. This book also included a chapter ("Reflections on the American Identity") that won widespread attention as a critique of the cultural conditions under which people experienced adolescence in the United States. Erikson later developed his ideas about identity formation in relation to major historical figures in many times and places. In *Young Man Luther* (New York, 1958) Erikson sought to explain Martin Luther's break with the Catholic Church in terms of Luther's youthful "identity crisis." In *Gandhi's Truth* (1969) Erikson offered a psychohistorical interpretation of the leader of the Indian independence movement, Mohandas Gandhi.

Erikson immigrated to the United States from Hitler's Europe in 1933, under the name he was given at birth, Erik Homberger. At the end of the 1930s, he changed his last name to Erikson, and forty years later was criticized for ignoring his Jewish ancestry and thus to some extent falsifying his "identity." He was in fact the son of a German Jewish woman. The man now thought to be his biological father, whom Erikson never knew, was a Dane. Erikson's biological ancestry and the cultural identity he created for himself in the relatively fluid United States, along with the controversy about his relation to his Jewishness, render Erikson's life all the more striking an episode in the history of his generation of American intellectuals. What was Erikson's "real" identity? Who decides, and on what basis? Late in his career Erikson criticized the dividing up of human beings into narrower categories than Erikson thought their circumstances warranted. See, for example, his "Pseudospeciation in the Nuclear Age," *Political Psychology*, 6 (1985), 213–17.

The definitive study of all aspects of Erikson's life and work is Lawrence J. Friedman, *Identity's Architect: A Biography of Erik H. Erikson* (New York, 1999). For a helpful analysis of the environment in which Erikson's ideas became important, see Ellen Herman, *The Romance of American Psychology: Political Culture in the Age of Experts* (New York, 1995). See also Eli Zaretsky, "Charisma or Rationalization? Domesticity and Psychoanalysis in the United States in the 1950s," *Critical Inquiry* (Winter 2000), 328–54. The standard study of the psychoanalytic movement in the United States during Erikson's generation is Nathan

G. Hale, Jr., *The Rise and Crisis of Psychoanalysis in the United States: Freud and the Americans, 1917–1985* (New York, 1995). A concise interpretation of *Childhood and Society* in its historical context is Steven Weiland, "Erik Erikson in America: *Childhood and Society* and National Identity," *American Studies*, 23 (Fall 1982), 5–23. An incisive, brief overview of Erikson's life and ideas by a former student is Howard Gardner, "The Enigma of Erik Erikson," *New York Review of Books,* June 14, 1999.

The first demonstration of social trust in the baby is the ease of his feeding, the depth of his sleep, the relaxation of his bowels. The experience of a mutual regulation of his increasingly receptive capacities with the maternal techniques of provision gradually helps him to balance the discomfort caused by the immaturity of homeostasis with which he was born. In his gradually increasing waking hours he finds that more and more adventures of the senses arouse a feeling of familiarity, of having coincided with a feeling of inner goodness. Forms of comfort, and people associated with them, become as familiar as the gnawing discomfort of the bowels. The infant's first social achievement, then, is his willingness to let the mother out of sight without undue anxiety or rage, because she has become an inner certainty as well as an outer predictability. Such consistency, continuity, and sameness of experience provide a rudimentary sense of ego identity which depends, I think, on the recognition that there is an inner population of remembered and anticipated sensations and images which are firmly correlated with the outer population of familiar and predictable things and people.

What we here call trust coincides with what Therese Benedek has called confidence. If I prefer the word "trust," it is because there is more naïveté and more mutuality in it: an infant can be said to be trusting where it would go too far to say that he has confidence. The general state of trust, furthermore, implies not only that one has learned to rely on the sameness and continuity of the outer providers, but also that one may trust oneself and the capacity of one's own organs to cope with urges; and that one is able to consider oneself trustworthy enough so that the providers will not need to be on guard lest they be nipped.

The constant tasting and testing of the relationship between inside and outside meets its crucial test during the rages of the biting stage, when the teeth cause pain from within and when outer friends either prove of no avail or withdraw from the only action which promises relief: biting. Not that teething itself seems to cause all the dire consequences sometimes ascribed to it. As outlined earlier, the infant now is driven to "grasp" more, but he is apt to find desired presences elusive: nipple and breast, and the mother's focused attention and care. Teething seems to have a prototypal significance and may well be the model for the masochistic tendency to assure cruel comfort by enjoying one's hurt whenever one is unable to prevent a significant loss.

In psychopathology the absence of basic trust can best be studied in infantile schizophrenia, while lifelong underlying weakness of such trust is apparent in adult personalities in whom withdrawal into schizoid and depressive states is habitual. The re-establishment of a state of trust has been found to be the basic requirement for therapy in these cases. For no matter what conditions may have caused a psychotic break, the bizarreness and withdrawal in the behavior of many very sick individuals hides an attempt to recover social mutuality by a testing of the borderlines between senses and physical reality, between words and social meanings.

Psychoanalysis assumes the early process of differentiation between inside and outside to be the origin of projection and introjection which remain some of our deepest and most dangerous defense mechanisms. In introjection we feel and act as if an outer goodness had become an inner certainty. In projection, we experience an inner harm as an outer one: we endow significant people with the evil which actually is in us. These two mechanisms, then, projection and introjection, are assumed to be modeled after whatever

Source: Erik H. Erikson, *Childhood and Society* (New York: Norton, 1950), 247–59.

goes on in infants when they would like to externalize pain and internalize pleasure, an intent which must yield to the testimony of the maturing senses and ultimately of reason. These mechanisms are, more or less normally, reinstated in acute crises of love, trust, and faith in adulthood and can characterize irrational attitudes toward adversaries and enemies in masses of "mature" individuals.

The firm establishment of enduring patterns for the solution of the nuclear conflict of basic trust versus basic mistrust in mere existence is the first task of the ego, and thus first of all a task for maternal care. But let it be said here that the amount of trust derived from earliest infantile experience does not seem to depend on absolute quantities of food or demonstrations of love, but rather on the quality of the maternal relationship. Mothers create a sense of trust in their children by that kind of administration which in its quality combines sensitive care of the baby's individual needs and a firm sense of personal trustworthiness within the trusted framework of their culture's life style. This forms the basis in the child for a sense of identity which will later combine a sense of being "all right," of being oneself, and of becoming what other people trust one will become. There are, therefore (within certain limits previously defined as the "musts" of child care), few frustrations in either this or the following stages which the growing child cannot endure if the frustration leads to the ever-renewed experience of greater sameness and stronger continuity of development, toward a final integration of the individual life cycle with some meaningful wider belongingness. Parents must not only have certain ways of guiding by prohibition and permission; they must also be able to represent to the child a deep, an almost somatic conviction that there is a meaning to what they are doing. Ultimately, children become neurotic not from frustrations, but from the lack or loss of societal meaning in these frustrations.

But even under the most favorable circumstances, this stage seems to introduce into psychic life (and become prototypical for) a sense of inner division and universal nostalgia for a paradise forfeited. It is against this powerful combination of a sense of having been deprived, of having been divided, and of having been abandoned—that basic trust must maintain itself throughout life.

Each successive stage and crisis has a special relation to one of the basic elements of society, and this for the simple reason that the human life cycle and man's institutions have evolved together. In this chapter we can do little more than mention, after the description of each stage, what basic element of social organization is related to it. This relation is twofold: man brings to these institutions the remnants of his infantile mentality and his youthful fervor, and he receives from them—as long as they manage to maintain their actuality—a reinforcement of his infantile gains.

The parental faith which supports the trust emerging in the newborn, has throughout history sought its institutional safe-guard (and, on occasion, found its greatest enemy) in organized religion. Trust born of care is, in fact, the touchstone of the *actuality* of a given religion. All religions have in common the periodical childlike surrender to a Provider or providers who dispense earthly fortune as well as spiritual health; some demonstration of man's smallness by way of reduced posture and humble gesture; the admission in prayer and song of misdeeds, of misthoughts, and of evil intentions; fervent appeal for inner unification by divine guidance; and finally, the insight that individual trust must become a common faith, individual mistrust a commonly formulated evil, while the individual's restoration must become part of the ritual practice of many, and must become a sign of trustworthiness in the community. We have illustrated how tribes dealing with one segment of nature develop a collective magic which seems to treat the Supernatural Providers of food and fortune as if they were angry and must be appeased by prayer and self-torture. Primitive religions, the most primitive layer in all religions, and the religious layer in each individual, abound with efforts at atonement which try to make up for vague deeds against a maternal matrix and try to restore faith in the goodness of one's strivings and in the kindness of the powers of the universe.

Each society and each age must find the institutionalized form of reverence which derives vitality from its world-image—from predestination to indeterminacy. The clinician can only observe that many are proud to be without religion whose children cannot afford their being without it. On the other hand, there are many who seem to derive a vital faith from social action or scientific pursuit. And again, there are many who profess faith, yet in practice breathe mistrust both of life and man.

In describing the growth and the crises of the human person as a series of alternative basic attitudes such as trust vs. mistrust, we take recourse to the term a "sense of," although, like a "sense of health," or a "sense of being unwell," such "senses" pervade surface and depth, consciousness and the unconscious. They are, then, at the same time, ways of *experiencing* accessible to introspection; ways of *behaving,* observable by others; and unconscious *inner states* determinable by test and analysis. It is important to keep these three dimensions in mind, as we proceed.

Muscular maturation sets the stage for experimentation with two simultaneous sets of social modalities: holding on and letting go. As is the case with all of these modalities, their basic conflicts can lead in the end to either hostile or benign expectations and attitudes. Thus, to hold can become a destructive and cruel retaining or restraining, and it can become a pattern of care: to have and to hold. To let go, too, can turn into an inimical letting loose of destructive forces, or it can become a relaxed "to let-pass" and "to let be."

Outer control at this stage, therefore, must be firmly reassuring. The infant must come to feel that the basic faith in existence, which is the lasting treasure saved from the rages of the oral stage, will not be jeopardized by this about-face of his, this sudden violent wish to have a choice, to appropriate demandingly, and to eliminate stubbornly. Firmness must protect him against the potential anarchy of his as yet untrained sense of discrimination, his inability to hold on and to let go with discretion. As his environment encourages him to "stand on his own feet," it must protect him against meaningless and arbitrary experiences of shame and of early doubt.

The latter danger is the one best known to us. For if denied the gradual and well-guided experience of the autonomy of free choice (or if, indeed, weakened by an initial loss of trust) the child will turn against himself all his urge to discriminate and to manipulate. He will overmanipulate himself, he will develop a precocious conscience. Instead of taking possession of things in order to test them by purposeful repetition, he will become obsessed by his own repetitiveness. By such obsessiveness, of course, he then learns to repossess the environment and to gain power by stubborn and minute control, where he could not find large-scale mutual regulation. Such hollow victory is the infantile model for a compulsion neurosis. It is also the infantile source of later attempts in adult life to govern by the letter, rather than by the spirit.

Shame is an emotion insufficiently studied, because in our civilization it is so early and easily absorbed by guilt. Shame supposes that one is completely exposed and conscious of being looked at: in one word, self-conscious. One is visible and not ready to be visible; which is why we dream of shame as a situation in which we are stared at in a condition of incomplete dress, in night attire, "with one's pants down." Shame is early expressed in an impulse to bury one's face, or to sink, right then and there, into the ground. But this, I think, is essentially rage turned against the self. He who is ashamed would like to force the world not to look at him, not to notice his exposure. He would like to destroy the eyes of the world. Instead he must wish for his own invisibility. This potentiality is abundantly used in the educational method of "shaming" used so exclusively by some primitive peoples. Visual shame precedes auditory guilt, which is a sense of badness to be had all by oneself when nobody watches and when everything is quiet—except the voice of the superego. Such shaming exploits an increasing sense of being small, which can develop only as the child stands up and as his awareness permits him to note the relative measures of size and power.

Too much shaming does not lead to genuine propriety but to a secret determination to try to get away with things, unseen—if, indeed, it does not result in defiant shamelessness. There is an impressive American ballad in which a murderer to be hanged on the gallows before the eyes of the community, instead of feeling duly chastened, begins to berate the onlookers, ending every salvo of defiance with the words, "God damn your eyes." Many a small child, shamed beyond endurance, may be in a chronic mood (although not in possession of either the courage or the words) to express defiance in similar terms. What I mean by this sinister reference is that there is a limit to a child's and an adult's endurance in the face of demands to consider himself, his body, and his wishes as evil and dirty, and to his belief in the infallibility of those who pass such judgment. He may be apt to turn things around, and to consider as evil only the fact that they exist: his chance will come when they are gone, or when he will go from them.

Doubt is the brother of shame. Where shame is dependent on the consciousness of being upright and exposed, doubt, so clinical observation leads me to believe, has much to do with a consciousness of having a front and a back—and especially a "behind." For this reverse area of the body, with its aggressive and libidinal focus in the sphincters and in the buttocks, cannot be seen by the child, and yet it can be dominated by the will of others. The "behind" is the small being's dark continent, an area of the body which can be magically dominated and effectively invaded by those who would attack one's power of autonomy and who would designate as evil those products of the bowels which were felt to be all right when they were being passed. This basic sense of doubt in whatever one has left behind forms a substratum for later and more verbal forms of compulsive doubting; this finds its adult expression in paranoiac fears concerning hidden persecutor's and secret persecutions threatening from behind (and from within the behind).

This stage, therefore, becomes decisive for the ratio of love and hate, cooperation and willfulness, freedom of self-expression and its suppression. From a sense of self-control without loss of self-esteem comes a lasting sense of good will and pride; from a sense of loss of selfcontrol and of foreign overcontrol comes a lasting propensity for doubt and shame.

If, to some reader, the "negative" potentialities of our stages seem overstated throughout, we must remind him that this is not only the result of a preoccupation with clinical data. Adults, and seemingly mature and unneurotic ones, display a sensitivity concerning a possible shameful "loss of face" and fear of being attacked "from behind" which is not only highly irrational and in contrast to the knowledge available to them, but can be of fateful import if related sentiments influence, for example, interracial and international policies.

We have related basic trust to the institution of religion. The lasting need of the individual to have his will reaffirmed and delineated within an adult order of things which at the same time reaffirms and delineates the will of others has an institutional safeguard in the *principle of law and order.* In daily life as well as in the high courts of law—domestic and international—this principle apportions to each his privileges and his limitations, his obligations and his rights. A sense of rightful dignity and lawful independence on the part of adults around him gives to the child of good will the confident expectation that the kind of autonomy fostered in childhood will not lead to undue doubt or shame in later life. Thus the sense of autonomy fostered in the child and modified as life progresses, serves (and is served by) the preservation in economic and political life of a sense of justice.

There is in every child at every stage a new miracle of vigorous unfolding, which constitutes a new hope and a new responsibility for all. Such is the sense and the pervading quality of initiative. The criteria for all these senses and qualities are the same: a crisis, more or less beset with fumbling and fear, is resolved, in that the child suddenly seems to "grow together" both in his person and in his body. He appears "more himself," more loving, relaxed and brighter in his judgment, more activated and activating. He is in free possession of a surplus of energy which permits him to forget failures quickly and to approach what seems desirable (even if it also seems uncertain and even dangerous) with undiminished and more accurate direction. Initiative adds to autonomy the quality of undertaking, planning and "attacking" a task for the sake of being active and on the move, where before self-will, more often than not, inspired acts of defiance or, at any rate, protested independence.

I know that the very word "initiative" to many, has an American, and industrial connotation. Yet, initiative is a necessary part of every act, and man needs a sense of initiative for whatever he learns and does, from fruit-gathering to a system of enterprise.

The ambulatory stage and that of infantile genitality add to the inventory of basic social modalities that of "making," first in the sense of "being on the make." There is no simpler, stronger word for it; it suggests pleasure in attack and conquest. In the boy, the emphasis remains on phallic-intrusive modes; in the girl it turns to modes of "catching" in more aggressive forms of snatching or in the milder form of making oneself attractive and endearing.

The danger of this stage is a sense of guilt over the goals contemplated and the acts initiated in one's exuberant enjoyment of new locomotor and mental power: acts of aggressive manipulation and coercion which soon go far beyond the executive capacity of organism and mind and therefore call for an energetic halt on one's contemplated initiative. While autonomy concentrates on keeping potential rivals out, and therefore can lead to jealous rage most often directed against encroachments by younger siblings, initiative brings with it anticipatory rivalry with those who have been there first and may, therefore, occupy with their superior equipment the field toward which one's initiative is directed. Infantile jealousy and rivalry, those often embittered and yet essentially futile attempts at demarcating a sphere of unquestioned privilege, now come to a climax in a final contest for a favored position with the mother; the usual failure leads to resignation, guilt, and anxiety. The child indulges in fantasies of being a giant and a tiger, but in his dreams he runs in terror for dear life. This, then, is the stage of the "castration complex," the intensified fear of finding the (now energetically erotized) genitals harmed as a punishment for the fantasies attached to their excitement.

Infantile sexuality and incest taboo, castration complex and superego all unite here to bring about that specifically human crisis during which the child must turn from an exclusive, pregenital attachment to his parents to the slow process of becoming a parent, a carrier of tradition. Here the most fateful split and transformation in the emotional powerhouse occurs, a split between potential human glory and potential total destruction. For here the child becomes forever divided in himself. The instinct fragments which before had enhanced the growth of his infantile body and mind now become divided into an infantile set which perpetuates the exuberance of growth potentials, and a parental set which supports and increases self-observation, self-guidance, and self-punishment.

The problem, again, is one of mutual regulation. Where the child, now so ready to over-manipulate himself, can gradually develop a sense of moral responsibility, where he can gain some insight into the institutions, functions, and roles which permit his responsible participation, he will find pleasurable accomplishment in wielding tools and weapons, in manipulating meaningful toys—and in caring for younger children.

Naturally, the parental set is at first infantile in nature: the fact that human conscience remains partially infantile throughout life is the core of human *tragedy*. For the superego of the child can be primitive, cruel, and uncompromising, as may be observed in instances where children overcontrol and overconstrict themselves to the point of self-obliteration; where they develop an over-obedience more literal than the one the parent has wished to exact; or where they develop deep regressions and lasting resentments because the parents themselves do not seem to live up to the new conscience. One of the deepest conflicts in life is the hate for a parent who served as the model and the executor of the superego, but who (in some form) was found trying to get away with the very transgressions which the child can no longer tolerate in himself. The suspiciousness and evasiveness which is thus mixed in with the all-or-nothing quality of the superego, this organ of moral tradition, makes moral (in the sense of moralistic) man a great potential danger to his own ego—and to that of his fellow men.

In adult pathology, the residual conflict over initiative is expressed either in hysterical denial, which causes the repression of the wish or the abrogation of its executive organ by paralysis, inhibition, or impotence; or in overcompensatory showing off, in which the scared individual, so eager to "duck," instead "sticks his neck out." Then also a plunge into psychosomatic disease is now common. It is as if the culture had made a man over-advertise himself and so identify with his own advertisement that only disease can offer him escape.

But here, again, we must not think only of individual psychopathology, but of the inner powerhouse of rage which must be submerged at this stage, as some of the fondest hopes and the wildest phantasies are repressed and inhibited. The resulting self-righteousness—often the principal reward for goodness—can later be most intolerantly turned against others in the form of persistent moralistic surveillance, so that the prohibition rather than the guidance of initiative becomes the dominant endeavor. On the other hand, even moral man's initiative is apt to burst the boundaries of self-restriction, permitting him to do to others, in his or in other lands, what he would neither do nor tolerate being done in his own home.

In view of the dangerous potentials of man's long childhood, it is well to look back at the blueprint of the life-stages and to the possibilities of guiding the young of the race while they are young. And here we note that according to the wisdom of the ground plan the child is at no time more ready to learn quickly and avidly, to become bigger in the sense of sharing obligation and performance than during this period of his development. He is eager and able to make things cooperatively, to combine with other children for the purpose of constructing and planning, and he is willing to profit from teachers and to emulate ideal prototypes. He remains, of course, identified with the parent of the same sex, but for the present he looks for opportunities where work-identification seems to promise a field of initiative without too much infantile conflict or oedipal guilt and a more realistic identification based on a spirit of equality experienced in doing things together. At any rate, the "oedipal" stage results not only in the oppressive establishment of a moral sense restricting the horizon of the permissible; it also sets the direction toward the possible and the tangible which permits the dreams of early childhood to be attached to the goals of an active adult life. Social institutions, therefore, offer children of this age an *economic ethos,* in the form of ideal adults recognizable by their uniform and their functions, and fascinating enough to replace, the heroes of picture book and fairy tale.

Thus the inner stage seems all set for "entrance into life," except that life must first be school life, whether school is field or jungle or classroom. The child must forget past hopes and wishes, while his exuberant imagination is tamed and harnessed to the laws of impersonal things—even the three R's. For before the child, psychologically already a rudimentary parent, can become a biological parent, he must begin to be a worker and potential provider. With the oncoming latency period, the normally advanced child forgets, or rather sublimates, the necessity to "make" people by direct attack or to become papa and mama in a hurry: he now learns to win recognition by producing things. He has mastered the ambulatory field and the organ modes. He has experienced a sense of finality regarding the fact that there is no workable future within the womb of his family, and thus becomes ready to apply himself to given skills and tasks, which go far beyond the mere playful expression of his organ modes or the pleasure in the function of his limbs. He develops a sense of industry—i.e., he adjusts himself to the inorganic laws of the tool world. He can become an eager and absorbed unit of a productive situation. To bring a productive situation to completion is an aim which gradually supersedes the whims and wishes of play. His ego boundaries include his tools and skills: the work principle (Ives Hendrick) teaches him the pleasure of work completion by steady attention and persevering diligence. In all cultures, at this stage, children receive some *systematic instruction,* although, as we saw in the chapter on American Indians, it is by no means always in the kind of school which literate people must organize around special teachers who have learned how to teach literacy. In preliterate people and in nonliterate pursuits much is learned from adults who become teachers by dint of gift and inclination rather than by appointment, and perhaps the greatest amount is learned from older children. Thus the *fundamentals of technology* are developed, as the child becomes ready to handle the utensils, the tools, and the weapons used by the big people. Literate people, with more specialized careers, must prepare the child by teaching him things which first of all make him literate, the widest possible basic education for the greatest number of possible careers. The more confusing specialization becomes, however, the more indistinct are the eventual goals of initiative; and the more complicated social reality, the vaguer are the father's and mother's role in it. School seems to be a culture all by itself, with its own goals and limits, its achievements and disappointment.

The child's danger, at this stage, lies in a sense of inadequacy and inferiority. If he despairs of his tools and skills or of his status among his tool partners, he may be discouraged from identification with them and with a section of the tool world. To lose the hope of such "industrial" association may pull him back to the more isolated, less tool-conscious familial rivalry of the oedipal time. The child despairs of his equipment in the tool world and in anatomy, and considers himself doomed to mediocrity or inadequacy. It is at this point that wider society becomes significant in its ways of admitting the child to an understanding of meaningful roles in its technology and economy. Many a child's development is disrupted when family life has failed to prepare him for school life, or when school life fails to sustain the promises of earlier stages.

Regarding the period of a developing sense of industry, I have referred to *outer and inner hindrances* in the use of new capacities but not to aggravations of new human drives, nor to submerged rages resulting from their frustration. This stage differs from the earlier ones in that it is not a swing from an inner upheaval to a new mastery. Freud calls it the latency stage because violent drives are normally dormant. But it is only a lull before the storm of puberty, when all the earlier drives reemerge in a new combination, to be brought under the dominance of genitality.

On the other hand, this is socially a most decisive stage: since industry involves doing things beside and with others, a first sense of division of labor and of differential opportunity, that is, a sense of the *technological ethos* of a culture, develops at this time. We have pointed in the last section to the danger threatening individual and society where the schoolchild begins to feel that the color of his skin, the background of his parents, or the fashion of his clothes rather than his wish and his will to learn will decide his worth as an apprentice, and thus his sense of *identity*—to which we must now turn. But there is another, more fundamental danger, namely man's restriction of himself and constriction of his horizons to include only his work to which, so the Book says, he has been sentenced after his expulsion from paradise. If he accepts work as his only obligation, and "what works" as his only criterion of worthwhileness, he may become the conformist and thoughtless slave of his technology and of those who are in a position to exploit it.

With the establishment of a good initial relationship to the world of skills and tools, and with the advent of puberty, childhood proper comes to an end. Youth begins. But in puberty and adolescence all samenesses and continuities relied on earlier are more or less questioned again, because of a rapidity of body growth which equals that of early childhood and because of the new addition of genital maturity. The growing and developing youths, faced with this physiological revolution within them, and with tangible adult tasks ahead of them are now primarily concerned with what they appear to be in the eyes of others as compared with what they feel they are, and with the question of how to connect the roles and skills cultivated earlier with the occupational prototypes of the day. In their search for a new sense of continuity and sameness, adolescents have to refight many of the battles of earlier years, even though to do so they must artificially appoint perfectly well-meaning people to play the roles of adversaries; and they are ever ready to install lasting idols and ideals as guardians of a final identity.

The integration now taking place in the form of ego identity is, as pointed out, more than the sum of the childhood identifications. It is the accrued experience of the ego's ability to integrate all identifications with the vicissitudes of the libido, with the aptitudes developed out of endowment, and with the opportunities offered in social roles. The sense of ego identity, then, is the accrued confidence that the inner sameness and continuity prepared in the past are matched by the sameness and continuity of one's meaning for others, as evidenced in the tangible promise of a "career."

The danger of this stage is role confusion. Where this is based on a strong previous doubt as to one's sexual identity, delinquent and outright psychotic episodes are not uncommon. If diagnosed and treated correctly, these incidents do not have the same fatal significance which they have at other ages. In most instances, however, it is the inability to settle on an occupational identity which disturbs individual young people. To keep themselves together they temporarily overidentify, to the point of apparent complete loss of identity, with the heroes of cliques and crowds. This initiates the stage of "falling in love," which is by no means entirely, or even primarily, a sexual matter—except where the mores demand it. To a considerable extent adolescent love is an attempt to arrive at a definition of one's identity by projecting one's diffused ego image on another and by seeing it thus reflected and gradually clarified. This is why so much of young love is conversation.

Young people can also be remarkably clannish, and cruel in their exclusion of all those who are "different," in skin color or cultural background, in tastes and gifts, and often in such petty aspects of dress and gesture as have been temporarily selected as the signs of an in-grouper or out-grouper. It is important to understand (which does not mean condone or participate in) such intolerance as a defense against a sense of identity confusion. For adolescents not only help one another temporarily through much discomfort by forming cliques and by stereotyping themselves, their ideals, and their enemies; they also perversely test each other's capacity to pledge fidelity. The readiness for such testing also explains the appeal which simple and cruel totalitarian doctrines have on the minds of the youth of such countries and classes as have lost or are losing their group identities (feudal, agrarian, tribal, national) and face world-wide industrialization, emancipation, and wider communication.

The adolescent mind is essentially a mind of the *moratorium,* a psychosocial stage between childhood and adulthood, and between the morality learned by the child, and the ethics to be developed by the adult. It is an ideological mind—and, indeed, it is the ideological outlook of a society that speaks most clearly to the adolescent who is eager to be affirmed by his peers, and is ready to be confirmed by rituals, creeds, and programs which at the same time define what is evil, uncanny, and inimical. In searching for the social values which guide identity, one therefore confronts the problems of *ideology* and *aristocracy,* both in their widest possible sense which connotes that within a defined world image and a predestined course of history, the best people will come to rule and rule develops the best in people. In order not to become cynically or apathetically lost, young people must somehow be able to convince themselves that those who succeed in their anticipated adult world thereby shoulder the obligation of being the best. We will discuss later the dangers which emanate from human ideals harnessed to the management of super-machines, be they guided by nationalistic or international, communist or capitalist ideologies. In the last part of this book we shall discuss the way in which the revolutions of our day attempt to solve and also to exploit the deep need of youth to redefine its identity in an industrialized world.

The strength acquired at any stage is tested by the necessity to transcend it in such a way that the individual can take chances in the next stage with what was most vulnerably precious in the previous one. Thus, the young adult, emerging from the search for and the insistence on identity, is eager and willing to fuse his identity with that of others. He is ready for intimacy, that is, the capacity to commit himself to concrete affiliations and partnerships and to develop the ethical strength to abide by such commitments, even though they may call for significant sacrifices and compromises. Body and ego must now be masters of the organ modes and of the nuclear conflicts, in order to be able to face the fear of ego loss in situations which call for self-abandon: in the solidarity of close affiliations, in orgasms and sexual unions, in close friendships and in physical combat, in experiences of inspiration by teachers and of intuition from the recesses of the self. The avoidance of such experiences because of a fear of ego loss may lead to a deep sense of isolation and consequent self-absorption.

The counterpart of intimacy is distantiation: the readiness to isolate and, if necessary, to destroy those forces and people whose essence seems dangerous to one's own, and whose "territory" seems to encroach on the extent of one's intimate relations. Prejudices thus developed (and utilized and exploited in politics and in war) are a more mature outgrowth of the blinder repudiations which during the struggle for identity differentiate sharply and cruelly between the familiar and the foreign. The danger of this stage is that intimate, competitive, and combative relations are experienced with and against the self-same people. But as the areas of adult duty are delineated, and as the competitive encounter, and the sexual embrace, are differentiated, they eventually become subject to that *ethical sense* which is the mark of the adult.

Strictly speaking, it is only now that *true genitality* can fully develop; for much of the sex life preceding these commitments is of the identity-searching kind, or is dominated by phallic or vaginal strivings which make of sex-life a kind of genital combat. On the other hand, genitality is all too often described as a permanent state of reciprocal sexual bliss. This then, may be the place to complete our discussion of genitality.

For a basic orientation in the matter I shall quote what has come to me as Freud's shortest saying. It has often been claimed, and bad habits of conversation seem to sustain the claim, that psychoanalysis as a treatment attempts to convince the patient that before God and man he has only one obligation: to have good orgasms, with a fitting "object," and that regularly. This, of course, is not true. Freud was once asked what he thought a normal person should be able to do well. The questioner probably expected a complicated answer. But Freud, in the curt way of his old days, is reported to have said: "Lieben und arbeiten" (to love and to work). It pays to ponder on this simple formula; it gets deeper as you think about it. For when Freud said "love" he meant *genital* love, and genital *love;* when he said love *and* work, he meant a general work-productiveness which would not preoccupy the individual to the extent that he loses his right or capacity to be a genital and a loving being. Thus we may ponder, but we cannot improve on "the professor's" formula.

Genitality, then, consists in the unobstructed capacity to develop an orgastic potency so free of pregenital interferences that genital libido (not just the sex products discharged in Kinsey's "outlets") is expressed in heterosexual mutuality, with full sensitivity of both penis and vagina, and with a convulsion-like discharge of tension from the whole body. This is a rather concrete way of saying something about a process which we really do not understand. To put it more situationally: the total fact of finding, via the climactic turmoil of the orgasm, a supreme experience of the mutual regulation of two beings in some way takes the edge off the hostilities and potential rages caused by the oppositeness of male and female, of fact and fancy, of love and hate. Satisfactory sex relations thus make sex less obsessive, overcompensation less necessary, sadistic controls superfluous.

Preoccupied as it was with curative aspects, psychoanalysis often failed to formulate the matter of genitality in a way significant for the processes of society in all classes, nations, and levels of culture. The kind of mutuality in orgasm which psychoanalysis has in mind is apparently easily obtained in classes and cultures which happen to make a leisurely institution of it. In more complex societies this mutuality is interfered with by so many factors of health, of tradition, of opportunity, and of temperament, that the proper formulation of sexual health would be rather this: A human being should be potentially able to accomplish mutuality of genital orgasm, but he should also be so constituted as to bear a certain amount of frustration in the matter without undue regression wherever emotional preference or considerations of duty and loyalty call for it.

While psychoanalysis has on occasion gone too far in its emphasis on genitality as a universal cure for society and has thus provided a new addiction and a new commodity for many who wished to so interpret its teachings, it has not always indicated all the goals that genitality actually should and must imply. In order to be of lasting social significance, the utopia of genitality should include:

1. mutuality of orgasm
2. with a loved partner
3. of the other sex
4. with whom one is able and willing to share a mutual trust
5. and with whom one is able and willing to regulate the cycles of
   a. work
   b. procreation
   c. recreation
6. so as to secure to the offspring, too, all the stages of a satisfactory development.

It is apparent that such utopian accomplishment on a large scale cannot be an individual or, indeed, a therapeutic task. Nor is it a purely sexual matter by any means. It is integral to a culture's style of sexual selection, cooperation, and competition.

The danger of this stage is isolation, that is the avoidance of contacts which commit to intimacy. In psychopathology, this disturbance can lead to severe "character-problems." On the other hand, there are partnerships which amount to an isolation à deux, protecting both partners from the necessity to face the next critical development—that of generativity.

In this book the emphasis is on the childhood stages, otherwise the section on generativity would of necessity be the central one, for this term encompasses the evolutionary development which has made man the teaching and instituting as well as the learning animal. The fashionable insistence on dramatizing the dependence of children on adults often blinds us to the dependence of the older generation on the younger one. Mature man needs to be needed, and maturity needs guidance a well as encouragement from what has been produced and must be taken care of.

Generativity, then, is primarily the concern in establishing and guiding the next generation, although there are individuals who, through misfortune or because of special and genuine gifts in other directions, do not apply this drive to their own offspring. And indeed, the concept generativity is meant to include such more popular synonyms as *productivity* and *creativity,* which, however, cannot replace it.

It has taken psychoanalysis some time to realize that the ability to lose oneself in the meeting of bodies and minds leads to a gradual expansion of ego-interests and to a libidinal investment in that which is being generated. Generativity thus is an essential stage on the psychosexual as well as on the psychosocial schedule. Where such enrichment fails altogether, regression to an obsessive need for pseudo-intimacy takes place, often with a pervading sense of stagnation and personal impoverishment. Individuals, then, often begin to indulge themselves as if they were their own—or one another's—one and only child; and where conditions favor it, early invalidism, physical or psychological, becomes the vehicle of self-concern. The mere fact of having or even wanting children, however, does not "achieve" generativity. In fact, some young parents suffer, it seems, from the retardation of the ability to develop this stage. The reasons are often to be found in early childhood impressions; in excessive self-love based on a too strenuously self-made personality; and finally (and here we return to the beginnings) in the lack of some faith, some "belief in the species," which would make a child appear to be a welcome trust of the community.

As to the institutions which safeguard and reinforce generativity, one can only say that all institutions codify the ethics of generative succession. Even where philosophical and spiritual tradition suggests the renunciation of the right to procreate or to produce, such early turn to "ultimate concerns," wherever instituted in monastic movements, strives to settle at the same time the matter of its relationship to the Care for the creatures of this world and to the Charity which is felt to transcend it.

If this were a book on adulthood, it would be indispensable and profitable at this point to compare economic and psychological theories (beginning with the strange convergencies and divergencies of Marx and Freud) and to proceed to a discussion of man's relationship to his production as well as to his progeny.

Only in him who in some way has taken care of things and people and has adapted himself to the triumphs and disappointments adherent to being, the originator of others or the generator of products and ideas—only in him may gradually ripen the fruit of these seven stages. I know no better word for it than ego integrity. Lacking a clear definition, I shall point to a few constituents of this state of mind. It is the ego's accrued assurance of its proclivity for order and meaning. It is a post-narcissistic love of the human ego—not of the self—as an experience which conveys some world order and spiritual sense, no matter how dearly paid for. It is the acceptance of one's one and only life cycle as something that had to be and that, by necessity, permitted of no substitutions: it thus means a new, a different love of one's parents. It is a comradeship with the ordering ways of distant times and different pursuits, as expressed in the simple products and sayings of such times and pursuits. Although aware of the relativity of all the various life styles which have given meaning to human striving, the possessor of integrity is ready to defend the dignity of his own life style against all physical and economic threats. For he knows that an individual life is the accidental coincidence of but one life cycle with but one segment of history; and that for him all human integrity stands or falls with the one style of integrity of which he partakes. The style of integrity developed by his culture or civilization thus becomes the "patrimony of his soul," the seal of his moral paternity of himself ("...pero el honor/Es patrimonio del alma": Calderón). In such final consolidation, death loses its sting.

The lack or loss of this accrued ego integration is signified by fear of death: the one and only life cycle is not accepted as the ultimate of life. Despair expresses the feeling that the time is now short, too short for the attempt to start another life and to try out alternate roads to integrity. Disgust hides despair, if often only in the form of "a thousand little disgusts" which do not add up to one big remorse: "*mille petits dégoûts de soi, dont le total ne fait pas un remords, mais un gêne obscure.*" (Rostand)

Each individual, to become a mature adult, must to a sufficient degree develop all the ego qualities mentioned, so that a wise Indian, a true gentleman, and a mature peasant share and recognize in one another the final stage of integrity. But each cultural entity, to develop the particular style of integrity suggested by its historical place, utilizes a particular combination of these conflicts, along with specific provocations and prohibitions of infantile sexuality. Infantile conflicts become creative only if sustained by the firm support of cultural institutions and of the special leader classes representing them. In order to approach or experience integrity, the individual must know how to be a follower of image bearers in religion and in politics, in the economic order and in technology, in aristocratic living and in the arts and sciences. Ego integrity, therefore, implies an emotional integration which permits participation by followership as well as acceptance of the responsibility of leadership.

Webster's Dictionary is kind enough to help us complete this outline in a circular fashion. Trust (the first of our ego values) is here defined as "the assured reliance on another's integrity," the last of our values. I suspect that Webster had business in mind rather than babies, credit rather than faith. But the formulation stands. And it seems possible to further paraphrase the relation of adult integrity and infantile trust by saying that healthy children will not fear life if their elders have integrity enough not to fear death.

In this book the emphasis is on the childhood stages. The foregoing conception of the life cycle, however, awaits systematic treatment. To prepare this, I shall conclude this chapter with a diagram. In this, as in the diagram of pregenital zones and modes, the diagonal represents the normative sequence of psychosocial gains made as at each stage one more nuclear conflict adds a new ego quality, a new criterion of accruing human strength. Below the diagonal there is space for the precursors of each of these solutions, all of which begin with the beginning; above the diagonal there is space for the designation of the derivatives of these gains and their transformations in the maturing and the mature personality.

The underlying assumptions for such charting are (1) that the human personality in principle develops according to steps predetermined in the growing person's readiness to be driven toward, to be aware of, and to interact with, a widening social radius; and (2) that society, in principle, tends to be so constituted as to meet and invite this succession of potentialities for interaction and attempts to safeguard and to encourage the proper rate and the proper sequence of their enfolding. This is the "maintenance of the human world."

But a chart is only a tool to think with, and cannot aspire to be a prescription to abide by, whether in the practice of child-training, in psychotherapy, or in the methodology of child study. In the presentation of the psychosocial stages in the form of an *epigenetic chart* analogous to the one employed in Chapter 2 for an analysis of Freud's psychosexual stages, we have definite and delimited methodological steps in mind. It is one purpose

		1	2	3
III	LOCOMOTOR-GENITAL			INITIATIVE VS. GUILT
II	MUSCULAR-ANAL		AUTONOMY VS. SHAME, DOUBT	
I	ORAL SENSORY	BASIC TRUST VS. MISTRUST		

of this work to facilitate the comparison of the stages first discerned by Freud as sexual to other schedules of development (physical, cognitive). But any one chart delimits one schedule only, and it must not be imputed that our outline of the psychosocial schedule is intended to imply obscure generalities concerning other aspects of development—or, indeed, of existence. If the chart, for example, lists a series of conflicts or crises, we do not consider all development a series of crises: we claim only that psychosocial development proceeds by critical steps—"critical" being a characteristic of turning points, of moments of decision between progress and regression, integration and retardation.

It may be useful at this point to spell out the methodological implications of an epi-genetic matrix. The more heavily-lined squares of the diagonal signify both a sequence of stages and a gradual development of component parts: in other words, the chart for-malizes a progression through time of a differentiation of parts. This indicates (1) that each critical item of psychosocial strength discussed here is systematically related to all others, and that they all depend on the proper development in the proper sequence of each item; and (2) that each item exists in some form before its critical time normally arrives.

If I say, for example, that a favorable ratio of basic trust over basic mistrust is the first step in psychosocial adaptation, a favorable ratio of autonomous will over shame and doubt, the second, the corresponding diagrammatic statement expresses a number of fundamental relations that exist between the two steps, as well as some facts fundamen-tal to each. Each comes to its ascendance, meets its crisis, and finds its lasting solution during the stage indicated. But they all must exist from the beginning in some form, for every act calls for an integration of all. Also, an infant may show something like "auton-omy" from the beginning in the particular way in which he angrily tries to wriggle him-self free when tightly held. However, under normal conditions, it is not until the second year that he begins to experience the whole *critical opposition of being an autonomous creature and being a dependent one;* and it is not until then that he is ready for a decisive encounter with his environment, an environment which, in turn, feels called upon to convey to him its particular ideas and concepts of autonomy and coercion in ways deci-sively contributing to the character and the health of his personality in his culture. It is this encounter, together with the resulting crisis, that we have tentatively described for each stage. As to the progression from one stage to the next, the diagonal indicates the sequence to be followed. However, it also makes room for variations in tempo and inten-sity. An individual, or a culture, may linger excessively over trust and proceed from I 1 over I 2 to II 2, or an accelerated progression may move from I 1 over II 1 to II 2. Each such acceleration or (relative) retardation, however, is assumed to have a modifying influ-ence on all later stages.

An epigenetic diagram thus lists a system of stages dependent on each other; and while individual stages may have been explored more or less thoroughly or named more or less fittingly, the diagram suggests that their study be pursued always with the total configuration of stages in mind. The diagram invites, then, a thinking through of all its empty boxes: if we have entered Basic Trust in I 1 and Integrity in VIII 8, we leave the question open, as to what trust might have become in a stage dominated by the need for integrity even as we have left open what it may look like and, indeed, be called in the stage dominated by a striving for autonomy (II 1). All we mean to emphasize is that trust must have developed in its own right, before it becomes something more in the critical encounter in which autonomy develops—and so on, up the vertical. If, in the last stage

(VIII 1), we would expect trust to have developed into the most mature *faith* that an aging person can muster in his cultural setting and historical period, the chart permits the consideration not only of what old age can be, but also what its preparatory stages must have been. All of this should make it clear that a chart of epigenesis suggests a global form of thinking and rethinking which leaves details of methodology and terminology to further study.

		1	2	3	4	5	6	7	8
VIII	MATURITY								EGO INTEGRITY VS. DESPAIR
VII	ADULTHOOD							GENERA-TIVITY VS. STAGNATION	
VI	YOUNG ADULTHOOD						INTIMACY VS. ISOLATION		
V	PUBERTY AND ADOLESCENCE					IDENTITY VS. ROLE CONFUSION			
IV	LATENCY				INDUSTRY VS. INFERIORITY				
III	LOCOMOTOR-GENITAL			INITIATIVE VS. GUILT					
II	MUSCULAR-ANAL		AUTONOMY VS. SHAME, DOUBT						
I	ORAL SENSORY	BASIC TRUST VS. MISTRUST							

JAMES BALDWIN

"Many Thousands Gone"
(1951)

Harlem-born James Baldwin (1924–87) fled the antiblack racism of the United States in 1948 to make his life in Paris, where he discovered to his great surprise that he was "as American as any Texas GI." While abroad Baldwin engaged in things American with relentless intensity and with a trenchant analytic style. In Paris and in Switzerland, Baldwin found a voice that made him one of the most admired writers of his generation. In the critical essay of 1951 reprinted here, Baldwin complained that black Americans were too often presented as merely a bundle of consequences of white prejudice, rather than as products of a dense and particular history. But this dense and particular history, Baldwin also argued, was indissoluably bound up with America itself. Black people were not a thing apart. "Negroes are Americans and their destiny is the country's destiny," he insisted, and went on to explain that liberation from racism required the acceptance of the fact that black and white people were entangled with one another.

Baldwin spoke in the name of a national "we" rather than a racial one, addressing an audience across the color line, asking Americans in general to achieve, through a more sound and realistic grasp of the life of black people, to come to a better "understanding of ourselves and of all men." Baldwin developed this line of thought in an extended critique of *Native Son*, the great novel of African-American life published by Richard Wright in 1941. Baldwin's account of how Wright constructs and narrates the life of his major character, Bigger Thomas, seems at first to require a knowledge of *Native Son*, but soon it becomes clear to the reader that Baldwin has his own agenda and that Wright is a convenient springboard for Baldwin's own message.

This essay gained a wide audience when reprinted alongside several others of the same viewpoint in Baldwin's *Notes of a Native Son* (1955). Baldwin later published two other collections of essays, *Nobody Knows My Name* (1961) and *The Fire Next Time* (1963). He also wrote a number of novels, but even the most widely appreciated of these—*Go Tell It on the Mountain* (1954) and *Another Country* (1962)—were never as influential as his critical essays. Although Baldwin ended his expatriation in 1957, he continued to live abroad much of the time during the remaining thirty years of his life and was a major figure in Europe as well as the United States. His funeral was held in New York's Cathedral of St. John the Divine, a short distance from the Harlem ghetto in which he spent his childhood.

For a perspicacious analysis of Baldwin's writings on race and nationality, see Ross Posnock, *Color and Culture: Black Writers and the Making of the Modern Intellectual* (Cambridge, Mass., 1998), 220–59. Among the many biographical studies are James Campbell, *Talking at the Gates: A Life of James Baldwin* (New York, 1991); and Herb Boyd, *Baldwin's Harlem: A Biography of James Baldwin* (New York, 2008). Baldwin's perspective on black life in the United States can be instructively studied in relation to that of his contemporary, Ralph Ellison, whose novel, *Invisible Man* (1952), and critical essays (especially those collected in *Shadow and Act* [1964]) address some of the same themes.

It is only in his music, which Americans are able to admire because a protective sentimentality limits their understanding of it, that the Negro in America has been able to tell his story. It is a story which otherwise has yet to be told and which no American is prepared to hear. As is the inevitable result of things unsaid, we find ourselves until today oppressed with a dangerous and reverberating silence; and the story is told, compulsively, in symbols and signs, in hieroglyphics; it is revealed in Negro speech and in that of the white majority and in their different frames of reference. The ways in which the Negro has affected the American psychology are betrayed in our popular culture and in our morality; in our estrangement from him is the depth of our estrangement from ourselves. We cannot ask: what do we *really* feel about him—such a question merely opens the gates on chaos. What we really feel about him is involved with all that we feel about everything, about everyone, about ourselves.

The story of the Negro in America is the story of America—or, more precisely, it is the story of Americans. It is not a very pretty story: the story of a people is never very pretty. The Negro in America, gloomily referred to as that shadow which lies athwart our national life, is far more than that. He is a series of shadows, self-created, intertwining, which now we helplessly battle. One may say that the Negro in America does not really exist except in the darkness of our minds.

This is why his history and his progress, his relationship to all other Americans, has been kept in the social arena. He is a social and not a personal or a human problem; to think of him is to think of statistics, slums, rapes, injustices, remote violence; it is to be confronted with an endless cataloguing of losses, gains, skirmishes; it is to feel virtuous, outraged, helpless, as though his continuing status among us were somehow analogous to disease—cancer, perhaps, or tuberculosis—which must be checked, even though it cannot be cured. In this arena the black man acquires quite another aspect from that which he has in life. We do not know what to do with him in life; if he breaks our sociological and sentimental image of him we are panic-stricken and we feel ourselves betrayed. When he violates this image, therefore, he stands in the greatest danger (sensing which, we uneasily suspect that he is very often playing a part for our benefit); and, what is not always so apparent but is equally true, we are then in some danger ourselves—hence our retreat or our blind and immediate retaliation.

Our dehumanization of the Negro then is indivisible from our dehumanization of ourselves: the loss of our own identity is the price we pay for our annulment of his. Time and our own force act as our allies, creating an impossible, a fruitless tension between the traditional master and slave. Impossible and fruitless because, literal and visible as this tension has become, it has nothing to do with reality.

Time has made some changes in the Negro face. Nothing has succeeded in making it exactly like our own, though the general desire seems to be to make it blank if one cannot make it white. When it has become blank, the past as thoroughly washed from the black face as it has been from ours, our guilt will be finished—at least it will have ceased to be visible, which we imagine to be much the same thing. But, paradoxically, it is we who prevent this from happening; since it is we, who, every hour that we live, reinvest the black face with our guilt; and we do this—by a further paradox, no less ferocious—helplessly, passionately, out of an unrealized need to suffer absolution.

Source: James Baldwin, *Partisan Review* (November–December 1951), 665–80.

Today, to be sure, we know that the Negro is not biologically or mentally inferior; there is no truth in those rumors of his body odor or his incorrigible sexuality; or no more truth than can be easily explained or even defended by the social sciences. Yet, in our most recent war, his blood was segregated as was, for the most part, his person. Up to today we are set at a division, so that he may not marry our daughters or our sisters, nor may he—for the most part—eat at our tables or live in our houses. Moreover, those who do, do so at the grave expense of a double alienation: from their own people, whose fabled attributes they must either deny or, worse, cheapen and bring to market; from us, for we require of them, when we accept them, that they at once cease to be Negroes and yet not fail to remember what being a Negro means—to remember, that is, what it means to us. The threshold of insult is higher or lower, according to the people involved, from the bootblack in Atlanta to the celebrity in New York. One must travel very far, among saints with nothing to gain or outcasts with nothing to lose, to find a place where it does not matter—and perhaps a word or a gesture or simply a silence will testify that it matters even there.

For it means something to be a Negro, after all, as it means something to have been born in Ireland or in China, to live where one sees space and sky or to live where one sees nothing but rubble or nothing but high buildings. We cannot escape our origins, however hard we try, those origins which contain the key—could we but find it—to all that we later become. What it means to be a Negro is a good deal more than this essay can discover; what it means to be a Negro in America can perhaps be suggested by an examination of the myths we perpetuate about him.

Aunt Jemima and Uncle Tom are dead, their places taken by a group of amazingly well-adjusted young men and women, almost as dark, but ferociously literate, well-dressed and scrubbed, who are never laughed at, who are not likely ever to set foot in a cotton or tobacco field or in any but the most modern of kitchens. There are others who remain, in our odd idiom, "underprivileged"; some are bitter and these come to grief; some are unhappy, but, continually presented with the evidence of a better day soon to come, are speedily becoming less so. Most of them care nothing whatever about race. They want only their proper place in the sun and the right to be left alone, like any other citizen of the republic. We may all breathe more easily. Before, however, our joy at the demise of Aunt Jemima and Uncle Tom approaches the indecent, we had better ask whence they sprang, how they lived? Into what limbo have they vanished?

However inaccurate our portraits of them were, these portraits do suggest, not only the conditions, but the quality of their lives and the impact of this spectacle on our consciences. There was no one more forbearing than Aunt Jemima, no one stronger or more pious or more loyal or more wise; there was, at the same time, no one weaker or more faithless or more vicious and certainly no one more immoral. Uncle Tom, trustworthy and sexless, needed only to drop the title "Uncle" to become violent, crafty, and sullen, a menace to any white woman who passed by. They prepared our feast tables and our burial clothes; and, if we could boast that we understood them, it was far more to the point and far more true that they understood us. They were, moreover, the only people in the world who did; and not only did they know us better than we knew ourselves, but they knew us better than we knew them. This was the piquant flavoring to the national joke, it lay behind our uneasiness as it lay behind our benevolence: Aunt Jemima and Uncle Tom, our creations, at the last evaded us; they had a life—their own, perhaps a better life than ours—and they would never tell us what it was. At the point where we were driven most privately and painfully to conjecture what depths of contempt, what heights of indifference, what prodigies of resilience, what untamable superiority allowed them so vividly to endure, neither perishing nor rising up in a body to wipe us from the earth, the image perpetually shattered and the word failed. The black man in our midst carried murder in his heart, he wanted vengeance. We carried murder too, we wanted peace.

In our image of the Negro breathes the past we deny, not dead but living yet and powerful, the beast in our jungle of statistics. It is this which defeats us, which continues to defeat us, which lends to interracial cocktail parties their rattling, genteel, nervously smiling air: in any drawing room at such a gathering the beast may spring, filling the air with flying things and an unenlightened wailing. Wherever the problem touches there is confusion, there is danger. Wherever the Negro face appears a tension is created, the tension of a silence filled with things unutterable. It is a sentimental error, therefore, to believe that the past is dead; it means nothing to say that it is all forgotten, that the Negro himself has forgotten it. It is not a question of memory. Oedipus did not remember the thongs that bound his feet; nevertheless the marks they left testified to that doom toward which his feet were leading him. The man does not remember the hand that struck him, the darkness that frightened him, as a child; nevertheless, the hand and the darkness remain with him, indivisible from himself forever, part of the passion that drives him wherever he thinks to take flight.

The making of an American begins at that point where he himself rejects all other ties, any other history, and himself adopts the vesture of his adopted land. This problem has been faced by all Americans throughout our history—in a way it *is* our history—and it baffles the immigrant and sets on edge the second generation until today. In the case of the Negro the past was taken from him whether he would or no; yet to forswear it was meaningless and availed him nothing, since his shameful history was carried, quite literally, on his brow. Shameful; for he was heathen as well as black and would never have discovered the healing blood of Christ had not we braved the jungles to bring him these glad tidings. Shameful; for, since our role as missionary had not been wholly disinterested, it was necessary to recall the shame from which we had delivered him in order more easily to escape our own. As he accepted the alabaster Christ and the bloody cross—in the bearing of which he would find his redemption, as, indeed, to our outraged astonishment, he sometimes did—he must, henceforth, accept that image we then gave him of himself: having no other and standing, moreover, in danger of death should he fail to accept the dazzling light thus brought into such darkness. It is this quite simple dilemma that must be borne in mind if we wish to comprehend his psychology.

However we shift the light which beats so fiercely on his head, or *prove*, by victorious social analysis, how his lot has changed, how we have both improved, our uneasiness refuses to be exorcised. And nowhere is this more apparent than in our literature on the subject—"problem" literature when written by whites, "protest" literature when written by Negroes—and nothing is more striking than the tremendous disparity of tone between the two creations. *Kingsblood Royal* bears, for example, almost no kinship to *If He Hollers Let Him Go,* though the same reviewers praised them both for what were, at bottom, very much the same reasons. These reasons may be suggested, far too briefly but not at all unjustly, by observing that the presupposition is in both novels exactly the same: black is a terrible color with which to be born into the world.

Now the most powerful and celebrated statement we have yet had of what it means to be a Negro in America is unquestionably Richard Wright's *Native Son.* The feeling which prevailed at the time of its publication was that such a novel, bitter, uncompromising, shocking, gave proof, by its very existence, of what strides might be taken in a free democracy; and its indisputable success, proof that Americans were now able to look full in the face without flinching the dreadful facts. Americans, unhappily, have the most remarkable ability to alchemize all bitter truths into an innocuous but piquant confection and to transform their moral contradictions, or public discussion of such contradictions, into a proud decoration, such as are given for heroism on the field of battle. Such a book, we felt with pride, could never have been written before—which was true. Nor could it be written today. It bears already the aspect of a landmark; for Bigger and his brothers have undergone yet another metamorphosis; they have been accepted in baseball leagues and by colleges hitherto exclusive; and they have made a most favorable appearance on the national screen. We have yet to encounter, nevertheless, a report so indisputably authentic, or one that can begin to challenge this most significant novel.

It is, in a certain American tradition, the story of an unremarkable youth in battle with the force of circumstance; that force of circumstance which plays and which has played so important a part in the national fables of success or failure. In this case the force of circumstance is not poverty merely but color, a circumstance which cannot be overcome, against which the protagonist battles for his life and loses. It is, on the surface, remarkable that this book should have enjoyed among Americans the favor it did enjoy; no more remarkable, however, than that it should have been compared, exuberantly, to Dostoevsky, though placed a shade below Dos Passos, Dreiser, and Steinbeck; and when the book is examined, its impact does not seem remarkable at all, but becomes, on the contrary, perfectly logical and inevitable.

We cannot, to begin with, divorce this book from the specific social climate of that time: it was one of the last of those angry productions, encountered in the late twenties and all through the thirties, dealing with the inequities of the social structure of America. It was published one year before our entry into the last world war—which is to say, very few years after the dissolution of the WPA and the end of the New Deal and at a time when bread lines and soup kitchens and bloody industrial battles were bright in everyone's memory. The rigors of that unexpected time filled us not only with a genuinely bewildered and despairing idealism—so that, because there at least was *something* to fight for, young men went off to die in Spain—but also with a genuinely bewildered self-consciousness. The Negro, who had been during the magnificent twenties a passionate and delightful primitive, now became, as one of the things we were most self-conscious about, our most oppressed minority. In the thirties, swallowing Marx whole, we discovered the Worker and realized—I should think with some relief—that the aims of the Worker and the aims of the Negro were one. This theorem—to which we shall return—seems now to leave rather too much out of account; it became, nevertheless, one of the slogans of the "class struggle" and the gospel of the New Negro.

As for this New Negro, it was Wright who became his most eloquent spokesman; and his work, from its beginning, is most clearly committed to the social struggle. Leaving aside the considerable question of what relationship precisely the artist bears to the revolutionary, the reality of man as a social being is not his only reality and that artist is strangled who is forced to deal with human beings solely in social terms; and who has, moreover, as Wright had, the necessity thrust on him of being the representative of some thirteen million people. It is a false responsibility (since writers are not congressmen) and impossible, by its nature, of fulfillment. The unlucky shepherd soon finds that, so far from being able to feed the hungry sheep, he has lost the wherewithal for his own nourishment: having not been allowed—so fearful was his burden, so present his audience!—to recreate his own experience. Further, the militant men and women of the thirties were not, upon examination, significantly emancipated from their antecedents, however bitterly they might consider themselves estranged or however gallantly they struggled to build a better world. However they might extol Russia, their concept of a better world was quite helplessly American and betrayed a certain thinness of imagination, a suspect reliance on suspect and badly digested formulae, and a positively fretful romantic haste. Finally, the relationship of the Negro to the Worker cannot be summed up, nor even greatly illuminated, by saying that their aims are one. It is true only insofar as they both desire better working conditions and useful only insofar as they unite their strength as workers to achieve these ends. Further than this we cannot in honesty go.

In this climate Wright's voice first was heard and the struggle which promised for a time to shape his work and give it purpose also fixed it in an ever more unrewarding rage. Recording his days of anger he has also nevertheless recorded, as no Negro before him had ever done, that fantasy Americans hold in their minds when they speak of the Negro: that fantastic and fearful image which we have lived with since the first slave fell beneath the lash. This is the significance of *Native Son* and also, unhappily, its overwhelming limitation.

Native Son begins with the *Brring!* of an alarm clock in the squalid Chicago tenement where Bigger and his family live. Rats live there too, feeding off the garbage, and we first encounter Bigger in the act of killing one. One may consider that the entire book, from that harsh *Brring!* to Bigger's weak "Good-by" as the lawyer, Max, leaves him in the death cell, is an extension, with the roles inverted, of this chilling metaphor. Bigger's situation and Bigger himself exert on the mind the same sort of fascination. The premise of the book is, as I take it, clearly conveyed in these first pages: we are confronting a monster created by the American republic and we are, through being made to share his experience, to receive illumination as regards the manner of his life and to feel both pity and horror at his awful and inevitable doom. This is an arresting and potentially rich idea and we would be discussing a very different novel if Wright's execution had been more perceptive and if he had not attempted to redeem a symbolical monster in social terms.

One may object that it was precisely Wright's intention to create in Bigger a social symbol, revelatory of social disease and prophetic of disaster. I think, however, that it is this assumption which we ought to examine more carefully. Bigger has no discernible relationship to himself, to his own life, to his own people, nor to any other people—in this respect, perhaps, he is most American—and his force comes, not from his significance as a social (or anti-social) unit, but from his significance as the incarnation of a myth. It is remarkable that, though we follow him step by step from the tenement room to the death cell, we know as little about him when this journey is ended as we did when it began; and, what is even more remarkable, we know almost as little about the social dynamic which we are to believe created him. Despite the details of slum life which we are given, I doubt that anyone who has thought about it, disengaging himself from sentimentality, can accept this most essential premise of the novel for a moment. Those Negroes who surround him, on the other hand, his hard-working mother, his ambitious sister, his poolroom cronies, Bessie, might be considered as far richer and far more subtle and accurate illustrations of the ways in which Negroes are controlled in our society and the complex techniques they have evolved for their survival. We are limited, however, to Bigger's view of them, part of a deliberate plan which might not have been disastrous if we were not also limited to Bigger's perceptions. What this means for the novel is that a necessary dimension has been cut away; this dimension being the relationship that Negroes bear to one another, that depth of involvement and unspoken recognition of shared experience which creates a way of life. What the novel reflects—and at no point interprets—is the isolation of the Negro within his own group and the resulting fury of impatient scorn. It is this which creates its climate of anarchy and unmotivated and unapprehended disaster; and it is this climate, common to most Negro protest novels, which has led us all to believe that in Negro life there exists no tradition, no field of manners, no possibility of ritual or intercourse, such as may, for example, sustain the Jew even after he has left his father's house. But the fact is not that the Negro has no tradition but that there has as yet arrived no sensibility sufficiently profound and tough to make this tradition articulate. For a tradition expresses, after all, nothing more than the long and painful experience of a people; it comes out of the battle waged to maintain their integrity or, to put it more simply, out of their struggle to survive. When we speak of the Jewish tradition we are speaking of centuries of exile and persecution, of the strength which endured and the sensibility which discovered in it the high possibility of the moral victory.

This sense of how Negroes live and how they have so long endured is hidden from us in part by the very speed of the Negro's public progress, a progress so heavy with complexity, so bewildering and kaleidoscopic, that he dare not pause to conjecture on the darkness which lies behind him; and by the nature of the American psychology which, in order to apprehend or be made able to accept it, must undergo a metamorphosis so profound as to be literally unthinkable and which there is no doubt we will resist until we are compelled to achieve our own identity by the rigors of a time that has yet to come. Bigger, in the meanwhile, and all his furious kin, serve only to whet the notorious national taste for the sensational and to reinforce all that we now find it necessary to believe. It is not Bigger whom we fear, since his appearance among us makes our victory certain. It is the others, who smile, who go to church, who give no cause for complaint, whom we sometimes consider with amusement, with pity, even with affection—and in whose faces we sometimes surprise the merest arrogant hint of hatred, the faintest, withdrawn, speculative shadow of contempt—who make us uneasy; whom we cajole, threaten, flatter, fear; who to us remain unknown, though we are not (we feel with both relief and hostility and with bottomless confusion) unknown to them. It is out of our reaction to these hewers of wood and drawers of water that our image of Bigger was created.

It is this image, living yet, which we perpetually seek to evade with good works; and this image which makes of all our good works an intolerable mockery. The "nigger," black, benighted, brutal, consumed with hatred as we are consumed with guilt, cannot be thus blotted out. He stands at our shoulders when we give our maid her wages, it is his hand which we fear we are taking when struggling to communicate with the current "intelligent" Negro, his stench, as it were, which fills our mouths with salt as the monument is unveiled in honor of the latest Negro leader. Each generation has shouted behind him, *Nigger!* as he walked our streets; it is he whom we would rather our sisters did not marry; he is banished into the vast and wailing outer darkness whenever we speak of the "purity" of our women, of the "sanctity" of our homes, of "American" ideals. What is more, he knows it. He is indeed the "native son": he is the "nigger." Let us refrain from inquiring at the moment whether or not he actually exists; for we *believe* that he exists. Whenever we encounter him amongst us in the flesh, our faith is made perfect and his necessary and bloody end is executed with a mystical ferocity of joy.

But there is a complementary faith among the damned which involves their gathering of the stones with which those who walk in the light shall stone them; or there exists among the intolerably degraded the perverse and powerful desire to force into the arena of the actual those fantastic crimes of which they have been accused, achieving their vengeance and their own destruction through making the nightmare real. The American image of the Negro lives also in the Negro's heart; and when he has surrendered to this image life has no other possible reality. Then he, like the white enemy with whom he will be locked one day in mortal struggle, has no means save this of asserting his identity. This is why Bigger's murder of Mary can be referred to as an "act of creation" and why, once this murder has been committed, he can feel for the first time that he is living fully and deeply as a man was meant to live. And there is, I should think, no Negro living in America who has not felt, briefly or for long periods, with anguish sharp or dull, in varying degrees and to varying effect, simple, naked and unanswerable hatred; who has not wanted to smash any white face he may encounter in a day, to violate, out of motives of the cruelest vengeance, their women, to break the bodies of all white people and bring them low, as low as that dust into which he himself has been and is being trampled; no Negro, finally, who has not had to make his own precarious adjustment to the "nigger" who surrounds him and to the "nigger" in himself.

Yet the adjustment must be made—rather, it must be attempted, the tension perpetually sustained—for without this he has surrendered his birthright as a man no less than his birthright as a black man. The entire universe is then peopled only with his enemies, who are not only white men armed with rope and rifle, but his own far-flung and contemptible kinsmen. Their blackness is his degradation and it is their stupid and passive endurance which makes his end inevitable.

Bigger dreams of some black man who will weld all blacks together into a mighty fist, and feels, in relation to his family, that perhaps they had to live as they did precisely because none of them had ever done anything, right or wrong, which mattered very much. It is only he who, by an act of murder, has burst the dungeon cell. He has made it manifest that *he* lives and that his despised blood nourishes the passions of a man. He has forced his oppressors to see the fruit of that oppression: and he feels, when his family and his friends come to visit him in the death cell, that they should not be weeping or frightened, that they should be happy, *proud* that he has dared, through murder and now through his own imminent destruction, to redeem their anger and humiliation, that he has hurled into the spiritless obscurity of their lives the lamp of his passionate life and death. Henceforth, they may remember Bigger—who has died, as we may conclude, for them. But they do not feel this; they only know that he has murdered two women and precipitated a reign of terror; and that now he is to die in the electric chair. They therefore weep and are honestly frightened—for which Bigger despises them and wishes to "blot" them out. What is missing in his situation and in the representation of his psychology—which makes his situation false and his psychology incapable of development—is any revelatory apprehension of Bigger as one of the Negro's realities or as one of the Negro's roles. This failure is part of the previously noted failure to convey any sense of Negro life as a continuing and complex group reality. Bigger, who cannot function therefore as a reflection of the social illness, having, as it were, no society to reflect, likewise refuses to function on the loftier level of the Christ-symbol. His kinsmen are quite right to weep and be frightened, even to be appalled: for it is not his love for them or for himself which causes him to die, but his hatred and his self-hatred; he does not redeem the pains of a despised people, but reveals, on the contrary, nothing more than his own fierce bitterness at having been born one of them. In this also he is the "native son," his progress determinable by the speed with which the distance increases between himself and the auction-block and all that the auction-block implies. To have penetrated this phenomenon, this inward contention of love and hatred, blackness and whiteness, would have given him a stature more nearly human and an end more nearly tragic; and would have given us a document more profoundly and genuinely bitter and less harsh with an anger which is, on the one hand, exhibited and, on the other hand, denied.

Native Son finds itself at length so trapped by the American image of Negro life and by the American necessity to find the ray of hope that it cannot pursue its own implications. This is why Bigger must be at the last redeemed, to be received, if only by rhetoric, into that community of phantoms which is our tenaciously held ideal of the happy social life. It is the socially conscious whites who receive him—the Negroes being capable of no such objectivity—and we have, by way of illustration, that lamentable scene in which Jan, Mary's lover, forgives him for her murder; and, carrying the explicit burden of the novel, Max's long speech to the jury. This speech, which really ends the book, is one of the most desperate performances in American fiction. It is the question of Bigger's humanity which is at stake, the relationship in which he stands to all other Americans—and, by implication, to all people—and it is precisely this question which it cannot clarify, with which it cannot, in fact, come to any coherent terms. He is the monster created by the American republic, the present awful sum of generations of oppression; but to say that he is a monster is to fall into the trap of making him subhuman and he must, therefore, be made representative of a way of life which is real and human in precise ratio to the degree to which it seems to us monstrous and strange. It seems to me that this idea carries, implicitly, a most remarkable confession: that is, that Negro life is in fact as debased and impoverished as our theology claims; and, further, that the use to which Wright puts this idea can only proceed from the assumption—not entirely unsound—that Americans, who evade, so far as possible, all genuine experience, have therefore no way of assessing the experience of others and no way of establishing themselves in relation to any way of life which is not their own. The privacy or obscurity of Negro life makes that life capable, in our imaginations, of producing anything at all; and thus the idea of Bigger's monstrosity can be presented without fear of contradiction, since no American has the knowledge or authority to contest it and no Negro has the voice. It is an idea, which, in the framework of the novel, is dignified by the possibility it promptly affords of presenting Bigger as the herald of disaster, the danger signal of a more bitter time to come when not Bigger alone but all his kindred will rise, in the name of the many thousands who have perished in fire and flood and by rope and torture, to demand their rightful vengeance.

But it is not quite fair, it seems to me, to exploit the national innocence in this way. The idea of Bigger as a warning boomerangs not only because it is quite beyond the limit of probability that Negroes in America will ever achieve the means of wreaking vengeance upon the state but also because it cannot be said that they have any desire to do so. *Native Son* does not convey the altogether savage paradox of the American Negro's situation, of which the social reality which we prefer with such hopeful superficiality to study is but, as it were, the shadow. It is not simply the relationship of oppressed to oppressor, of master to slave, nor is it motivated merely by hatred; it is also, literally and morally, a *blood* relationship, perhaps the most profound reality of the American experience, and we cannot begin to unlock it until we accept how very much it contains of the force and anguish and terror of love.

Negroes are Americans and their destiny is the country's destiny. They have no other experience besides their experience on this continent and it is an experience which cannot be rejected, which yet remains to be embraced. If, as I believe, no American Negro exists who does not have his private Bigger Thomas living in the skull, then what most significantly fails to be illuminated here is the paradoxical adjustment which is perpetually made, the Negro being compelled to accept the fact that this dark and dangerous and unloved stranger is part of himself forever. Only this recognition sets him in any wise free and it is this, this necessary ability to contain and even, in the most honorable sense of the word, to *exploit* the "nigger," which lends to Negro life its high element of the ironic and which causes the most well-meaning of their American critics to make such exhilarating errors when attempting to understand them. To present Bigger as a warning is simply to reinforce the American guilt and fear concerning him, it is most forcefully to limit him to that previously mentioned social arena in which he has no human validity, it is simply to condemn him to death. For he has always been a warning, he represents the evil, the sin and suffering which we are compelled to reject. It is useless to say to the courtroom in which this heathen sits on trial that he is their responsibility, their creation, and his crimes are theirs; and that they ought, therefore, to allow him to live, to make articulate to himself behind the walls of prison the meaning of his existence. The meaning of his existence has already been most adequately expressed, nor does anyone wish, particularly not in the name of democracy, to think of it any more; as for the possibility of articulation, it is this possibility which above all others we most dread. Moreover, the courtroom, judge, jury, witnesses and spectators, recognize immediately that Bigger is their creation and they recognize this not only with hatred and fear and guilt and the resulting fury of self-righteousness but also with that morbid fullness of pride mixed with horror with which one regards the extent and power of one's wickedness. They know that death is his portion, that he runs to death; coming from darkness and dwelling in darkness, he must be, as often as he rises, banished, lest the entire planet be engulfed. And they know, finally, that they do not wish to forgive him and that he does not wish to be forgiven; that he dies, hating them, scorning that appeal which they cannot make to that irrecoverable humanity of his which cannot hear it; and that he *wants* to die because he glories in his hatred and prefers, like Lucifer, rather to rule in hell than serve in heaven.

For, bearing in mind the premise on which the life of such a man is based, i.e., that black is the color of damnation, this is his only possible end. It is the only death which will allow him a kind of dignity or even, however horribly, a kind of beauty. To tell this story, no more than a single aspect of the story of the "nigger," is inevitably and richly to become involved with the force of life and legend, how each perpetually assumes the guise of the other, creating that dense, many-sided and shifting reality which is the world we live in and the world we make. To tell his story is to begin to liberate us from his image and it is, for the first time, to clothe this phantom with flesh and blood, to deepen, by our understanding of him and his relationship to us, our understanding of ourselves and of all men.

But this is not the story which *Native Son* tells, for we find here merely, repeated in anger, the story which we have told in pride. Nor, since the implications of this anger are evaded, are we ever confronted with the actual or potential significance of our pride; which is why we fall, with such a positive glow of recognition, upon Max's long and bitter summing up. It is addressed to those among us of good will and it seems to say that, though there are whites and blacks among us who hate each other, we will not; there are those who are betrayed by greed, by guilt, by blood lust, but not we; we will set our faces against them and join hands and walk together into that dazzling future when there will be no white or black. This is the dream of all liberal men, a dream not at all dishonorable, but, nevertheless, a dream. For, let us join hands on this mountain as we may, the battle is elsewhere. It proceeds far from us in the heat and horror and pain of life itself where all men are betrayed by greed and guilt and blood-lust and where no one's hands are clean. Our good will, from which we yet expect such power to transform us, is thin, passionless, strident: its roots, examined, lead us back to our forebears, whose assumption it was that the black man, to become truly human and acceptable, must first become like us. This assumption once accepted, the Negro in America can only acquiesce in the obliteration of his own personality, the distortion and debasement of his own experience, surrendering to those forces which reduce the person to anonymity and which make themselves manifest daily all over the darkening world.

GEORGE F. KENNAN

Selection from *American Diplomacy, 1900–1950* (1951)

No theorist of American foreign policy had more influence among intellectuals of the mid-century decades than George Kennan (1904–2005). As a relatively junior foreign service officer in 1947 Kennan wrote a then-anonymous article (the author was listed as "X") urging a policy of "containment" toward the Soviet Union, and criticizing as naive those who believed cooperation between the United States and the Soviet Union was possible in the wake of the defeat of a common enemy, the Axis powers of World War II. Kennan's identity was soon known, and he became a prominent voice in the Department of State, eventually serving as ambassador to the Soviet Union and later to Yugoslavia. Yet Kennan's diplomatic career was punctuated by disagreements with his superiors, many of whom Kennan believed were pursuing the containment policy in too narrowly military a fashion. Kennan left the government, and his diplomatic career was eventually dwarfed by his written work as a historian and as a critic of the conduct of the United States in foreign affairs. In what proved to be his most famous book, *American Diplomacy, 1900–1950*, from which our selection is taken, Kennan sketched the "realist," interest-driven approach that he and others contrasted to more "idealist," principle-driven styles of foreign policy.

From the 1950s Kennan was a professor at the Institute for Advanced Study in Princeton, New Jersey, where he turned out a series of important volumes on American–Soviet relations and a steady stream of books and articles commenting on international politics. He remained an active voice in the public discussion even as late as the Iraq war of President George W. Bush, of which he was highly critical. Kennan also wrote several autobiographical volumes, including *Memoirs, 1925–1950* (1967), a vivid account of his experiences in American embassies in Europe during a quarter-century of dramatic events surrounding World War II.

Two of the most comprehensive studies of Kennan are David Mayers, *George Kennan and the Dilemmas of US Foreign Policy* (New York, 1988), and Richard L. Russel, *George F. Kennan's Strategic Thought* (New York, 1990). When Kennan reached his one hundredth birthday there appeared a number of reflections on his remarkable career. One of the most thoughtful of these was Ronald Steel, "George Kennan at 100," *New York Review of Books*, April 29, 2004. Kennan's career as an advisor to government officials is treated at length in Bruce Kuklick, *Blind Oracles: Intellectuals and War from Kennan to Kissinger* (Princeton, 2006).

...I see the most serious fault of our past policy formulation to lie in something that I might call the legalistic-moralistic approach to international problems. This approach runs like a red skein through our foreign policy of the last fifty years. It has in it something of the old emphasis on arbitration treaties, something of the Hague Conferences and schemes for universal disarmament, something of the more ambitious American concepts of the role of international law, something of the League of Nations and the United Nations, something of the Kellogg Pact, something of the idea of a universal "Article 51" past, something of the belief in World Law and World Government. But it is none of these, entirely. Let me try to describe it.

It is the belief that it should be possible to suppress the chaotic and dangerous aspirations of governments in the international field by the acceptance of some system of legal rules and restraints. This belief undoubtedly represents in part an attempt to transpose the Anglo-Saxon concept of individual law into the international field and to make it applicable to governments as it is applicable here at home to individuals. It must also stem in part from the memory of the origin of our own political system—from the recollection that we were able, through acceptance of a common institutional and juridical framework, to reduce to harmless dimensions the conflicts of interest and aspiration among the original thirteen colonies and to bring them all into an ordered and peaceful relationship with one another. Remembering this, people are unable to understand that what might have been possible for the thirteen colonies in a given set of circumstances might not be possible in the wider international field.

It is the essence of this belief that, instead of taking the awkward conflicts of national interest and dealing with them on their merits with a view to finding the solutions least unsettling to the stability of international life, it would be better to find some formal criteria of a juridical nature by which the permissible behavior of states could be defined. There would then be judicial entities competent to measure the actions of governments against these criteria and to decide when their behavior was acceptable and when unacceptable. Behind all this, of course, lies the American assumption that the things for which other peoples in this world are apt to contend are for the most part neither creditable nor important and might justly be expected to take second place behind the desirability of an orderly world, untroubled by international violence. To the American mind, it is implausible that people should have positive aspirations, and ones that they regard as legitimate, more important to them than the peacefulness and orderliness of international life. From this standpoint, it is not apparent why other people should not join us in accepting the rules of the game in international politics, just as we accept such rules in the competition of sport in order that the game may not become too cruel and too destructive and may not assume an importance we did not mean it to have.

If they were to do this, the reasoning runs, then the troublesome and chaotic manifestations of the national ego could be contained and rendered either unsubstantial or subject to easy disposal by some method familiar and comprehensible to our American usage. Departing from this background, the mind of American statesmanship, stemming as it does in so large a part from the legal profession in our country, gropes with unfailing persistence for some institutional framework which would be capable of fulfilling this function.

I cannot undertake in this short lecture to deal exhaustively with this thesis or to point out all the elements of unsoundness which I feel it contains. But some of its more outstanding weaknesses are worthy of mention.

Source: George F. Kennan, *American Diplomacy* (Chicago: University of Chicago Press, 1951). Reprinted by permission of the University of Chicago Press.

In the first place, the idea of the subordination of a large number of states to an international juridical regime, limiting their possibilities for aggression and injury to other states, implies that these are all states like our own, reasonably content with their international borders and status, at least to the extent that they would be willing to refrain from pressing for change without international agreement. Actually, this has generally been true only of a portion of international society. We tend to underestimate the violence of national maladjustments and discontents elsewhere in the world if we think that they would always appear to other people as less important than the preservation of the juridical tidiness of international life.

Second, while this concept is often associated with a revolt against nationalism, it is a curious thing that it actually tends to confer upon the concept of nationality and national sovereignty an absolute value it did not have before. The very principle of "one government, one vote," regardless of physical or political differences between states, glorifies the concept of national sovereignty and makes it the exclusive form of participation in international life. It envisages a world composed exclusively of sovereign national states with a full equality of status. In doing this, it ignores the tremendous variations in the firmness and soundness of national divisions: the fact that the origins of state borders and national personalities were in many instances fortuitous or at least poorly related to realities. It also ignores the law of change. The national state pattern is not, should not be, and cannot be a fixed and static thing. By nature, it is an unstable phenomenon in a constant state of change and flux. History has shown that the will and the capacity of individual peoples to contribute to their world environment is constantly changing. It is only logical that the organizational forms (and what else are such things as borders and governments?) should change with them. The function of a system of international relationships is not to inhibit this process of change by imposing a legal strait jacket upon it but rather to facilitate it; to ease its transitions, to temper the asperities to which it often leads, to isolate and moderate the conflicts to which it gives rise, and to see that these conflicts do not assume forms too unsettling for international life in general. But this is a task for diplomacy, in the most old-fashioned sense of the term. For this, law is too abstract, too inflexible, too hard to adjust to the demands of the unpredictable and the unexpected.

By the same token, the American concept of world law ignores those means of international offense—those means of the projection of power and coercion over other peoples—which by-pass institutional forms entirely or even exploit them against themselves: such things as ideological attack, intimidation, penetration, and disguised seizure of the institutional paraphernalia of national sovereignty. It ignores, in other words, the device of the puppet state and the set of techniques by which states can be converted into puppets with no formal violation of, or challenge to, the outward attributes of their sovereignty and their independence.

This is one of the things that have caused the peoples of the satellite countries of eastern Europe to look with a certain tinge of bitterness on the United Nations. The organization failed so completely to save them from domination by a great neighboring country, a domination no less invidious by virtue of the fact that it came into being by processes we could not call "aggression." And there is indeed some justification for their feeling, because the legalistic approach to international affairs ignores in general the international significance of political problems and the deeper sources of international instability. It assumes that civil wars will remain civil and not grow into international wars. It assumes the ability of each people to solve its own internal political problems in a manner not provocative of its international environment. It assumes that each nation will always be able to construct a government qualified to speak for it and cast its vote in the international arena and that this government will be acceptable to the rest of the international community in this capacity. It assumes, in other words, that domestic issues will not become international issues and that the world community will not be put in the position of having to make choices between rival claimants for power within the confines of the individual state.

Finally, this legalistic approach to international relations is faulty in its assumptions concerning the possibility of sanctions against offenses and violations. In general, it looks to collective action to provide such sanction against the bad behavior of states. In doing so, it forgets the limitations on the effectiveness of military coalition. It forgets that, as a circle of military associates widens in any conceivable political-military venture, the theoretical total of available military strength may increase, but only at the cost of compactness and ease of control. And the wider a coalition becomes, the more difficult it becomes to retain political unity and general agreement on the purposes and effects of what is being done. As we are seeing in the case of Korea, joint military operations against an aggressor have a different meaning for each participant and raise specific political issues for each one which are extraneous to the action in question and affect many other facets of international life. The wider the circle of military associates, the more cumbersome the problem of political control over their actions, and the more circumscribed the least common denominator of agreement. This law of diminishing returns lies so heavily on the possibilities for multilateral military action that it makes it doubtful whether the participation of smaller states can really add very much to the ability of the great powers to assure stability of international life. And this is tremendously important, for it brings us back to the realization that even under a system of world law the sanction against destructive international behavior might continue to rest basically, as it has in the past, on the alliances and relationships among the great powers themselves. There might be a state, or perhaps more than one state, which all the rest of the world community together could not successfully coerce into following a line of action to which it was violently averse. And if this is true, where are we? It seems to me that we are right back in the realm of the forgotten art of diplomacy from which we have spent fifty years trying to escape.

These, then, are some of the theoretical deficiencies that appear to me to be inherent in the legalistic approach to international affairs. But there is a greater deficiency still that I should like to mention before I close. That is the inevitable association of legalistic ideas with moralistic ones: the carrying-over into the affairs of states of the concepts of right and wrong, the assumption that state behavior is a fit subject for moral judgment. Whoever says there is a law must of course be indignant against the law-breaker and feel a moral superiority to him. And when such indignation spills over into military contest, it knows no bounds short of the reduction of the law-breaker to the point of complete submissiveness—namely, unconditional surrender. It is a curious thing, but it is true, that the legalistic approach to world affairs, rooted as it unquestionably is in a desire to do away with war and violence, makes violence more enduring, more terrible, and more destructive to political stability than did the older motives of national interest. A war fought in the name of high moral principle finds no early end short of some form of total domination.

In this way, we see that the legalistic approach to international problems is closely identified with the concept of total war and total victory, and the manifestations of the one spill over only too easily into the manifestations of the other. And the concept of total war is something we would all do well to think about a little in these troubled times. This is a relatively new concept, in Western civilization at any rate. It did not really appear on the scene until World War I. It characterized both of these great world wars, and both of them—as I have pointed out—were followed by great instability and disillusionment. But it is not only a question now of the desirability of this concept; it is a question of its feasibility. Actually, I wonder whether even in the past total victory was not really an illusion from the standpoint of the victors. In a sense, there is no total victory short of genocide, unless it be a victory over the minds of men. But the total military victories are rarely victories over the minds of men. And we now face the fact that it is very questionable whether in a new global conflict there could ever be any such thing as total *military* victory. I personally do not believe that there could. There might be a great weakening of the armed forces of one side or another, but I think it out of the question that there should be such a thing as a general and formal submission of the national will on either side. The attempt to achieve this unattainable goal, however, could wreak upon civilization another set of injuries fully as serious as those caused by World War I or World War II, and I leave it to you to answer the question as to how civilization could survive them.

It was asserted not long ago by a prominent American that "war's very object is victory" and that "in war there can be no substitute for victory." Perhaps the confusion here lies in what is meant by the term "victory." Perhaps the term is actually misplaced. Perhaps there can be such a thing as "victory" in a battle, whereas in war there can be only the achievement or nonachievement of your objectives. In the old days, wartime objectives were generally limited and practical ones, and it was common to measure the success of your military operations by the extent to which they brought you closer to your objectives. But where your objectives are moral and ideological ones and run to changing the attitudes and traditions of an entire people or the personality of a regime, then victory is probably something not to be achieved entirely by military means or indeed in any short space of time at all; and perhaps that is the source of our confusion.

In any case, I am frank to say that I think there is no more dangerous delusion, none that has done us a greater disservice in the past or that threatens to do us a greater disservice in the future, than the concept of total victory. And I fear that it springs in large measure from the basic faults in the approach to international affairs which I have been discussing here. If we are to get away from it, this will not mean that we shall have to abandon our respect for international law, or our hopes for its future usefulness as the gentle civilizer of events which I mentioned in one of the earlier lectures. Nor will it mean that we have to go in for anything that can properly be termed "appeasement"—if one may use a word so cheapened and deflated by the abuse to which it has been recently subjected. But it will mean the emergence of a new attitude among us toward many things outside our borders that are irritating and unpleasant today—an attitude more like that of the doctor toward those physical phenomena in the human body that are neither pleasing nor fortunate—an attitude of detachment and soberness and readiness to reserve judgment. It will mean that we will have the modesty to admit that our own national interest is all that we are really capable of knowing and understanding—and the courage to recognize that if our purposes and undertakings here at home are decent ones, unsullied by arrogance or hostility toward other people or delusions of superiority, then the pursuit of our national interest can never fail to be conducive to a better world. This concept is less ambitious and less inviting in its immediate prospects than those to which we have so often inclined, and less pleasing to our image of ourselves. To many it may seem to smack of cynicism and reaction. I cannot share these doubts. Whatever is realistic in concept, and founded in an endeavor to see both ourselves and others as we really are, cannot be illiberal. . . .

WHITTAKER CHAMBERS

Selection from *Witness* (1952)

Whittaker Chambers (1904–61) became a national figure in 1948 when he accused a former official of the State Department, Alger Hiss, of having passed classified documents to Chambers while Chambers had been a Soviet agent during the 1930s. A series of dramatic congressional hearings and trials brought the confessed ex-Communist Chambers into sustained public conflict with the all-denying Hiss. Hiss's second trial for perjury ended in conviction early in 1950 when a jury found that Hiss had lied under oath while denying having known and aided Chambers. Immediately after Hiss's conviction, Senator Joseph McCarthy began his reckless campaign against subversion that added the word *McCarthyism* to the American political vocabulary. Chambers himself was not an uncritical supporter of McCarthy's methods, but his own style of anti-Communism was also very sweeping. Chambers believed that secular liberalism was a dangerous step toward Stalin's terror, and he defended simple patriotism and traditional religious faith with a passion that many found eloquent. No one expressed the extreme anti-Communist sensibility of the period with more telling effect than Chambers did in his best-selling autobiography, *Witness* (New York, 1952), the prologue to which is reprinted here. By addressing the American public through the medium of a letter to his own children, Chambers established the persona of the man of experience instructing innocents. By leading them to Golgotha, Chambers invited his readers to see him as a Christ-like martyr, sacrificing himself to save them.

For a sensitive reading of *Witness,* with attention to Chambers's use of Shakespearean and other literary tropes to construct his own narrative of himself, see Eric J. Sundquist, "Witness Recalled," *Commentary* (December 1988), 57–63. The best single work on the Hiss-Chambers case itself is Allen Weinstein, *Perjury* (New York, 1978; 2nd ed., 1997), which argues that Hiss did pass classified documents to Chambers and that Chambers, for all his melodramatic exaggerations, told in *Witness* a much more accurate story about his own experience as a Communist than had been generally believed. Although most historians now believe that Hiss lied, he continued to profess his innocence until his death in 1996. The critical discussion that the Hiss-Chambers case generated at the time constitutes in itself a formidable and fascinating body of literature, represented by Alastair Cooke in *A Generation on Trial* (New York, 1950), and by Murray Kempton, "A Sheltered Life," in Kempton's *Part of Our Time: Some Monuments and Ruins of the Thirties* (New York, 1955), 13–35. For a fine biographical study, see Sam Tanenhaus, *Whitaker Chambers: A Biography* (New York, 1997).

Beloved Children,

I am sitting in the kitchen of the little house at Medfield, our second farm which is cut off by the ridge and a quarter-mile across the fields from our home place, where you are. I am writing a book. In it I am speaking to you. But I am also speaking to the world. To both I owe an accounting.

It is a terrible book. It is terrible in what it tells about men. If anything, it is more terrible in what it tells about the world in which you live. It is about what the world calls the Hiss-Chambers Case, or even more simply, the Hiss Case. It is about a spy case. All the props of an espionage case are there—foreign agents, household traitors, stolen documents, microfilm, furtive meetings, secret hideaways, phony names, an informer, investigations, trials, official justice.

But if the Hiss Case were only this, it would not be worth my writing about or your reading about. It would be another fat folder in the sad files of the police, another crime drama in which the props would be mistaken for the play (as many people have consistently mistaken them). It would not be what alone gave it meaning, what the mass of men and women instinctively sensed it to be, often without quite knowing why. It would not be what, at the very beginning, I was moved to call it: "a tragedy of history."

For it was more than human tragedy. Much more than Alger Hiss or Whittaker Chambers was on trial in the trials of Alger Hiss. Two faiths were on trial. Human societies, like human beings, live by faith and die when faith dies. At issue in the Hiss Case was the question whether this sick society, which we call Western civilization, could in its extremity still cast up a man whose faith in it was so great that he would voluntarily abandon those things which men hold good, including life, to defend it. At issue was the question whether this man's faith could prevail against a man whose equal faith it was that this society is sick beyond saving, and that mercy itself pleads for its swift extinction and replacement by another. At issue was the question whether, in the desperately divided society, there still remained the will to recognize the issues in time to offset the immense rally of public power to distort and pervert the facts.

At heart, the Great Case was this critical conflict of faiths; that is why it was a great case. On a scale personal enough to be felt by all, but big enough to be symbolic, the two irreconcilable faiths of our time—Communism and Freedom—came to grips in the persons of two conscious and resolute men. Indeed, it would have been hard, in a world still only dimly aware of what the conflict is about, to find two other men who knew so clearly. Both had been schooled in the same view of history (the Marxist view). Both were trained by the same party in the same selfless, semisoldierly discipline. Neither would nor could yield without betraying, not himself, but his faith; and the different character of these faiths was shown by the different conduct of the two men toward each other throughout the struggle. For, with dark certitude, both knew, almost from the beginning, that the Great Case could end only in the destruction of one or both of the contending figures, just as the history of our times (both men had been taught) can end only in the destruction of one or both of the contending forces.

But this destruction is not the tragedy. The nature of tragedy is itself misunderstood. Part of the world supposes that the tragedy in the Hiss Case lies in the acts of disloyalty revealed. Part believes that the tragedy lies in the fact that an able, intelligent man, Alger

Source: Whittaker Chambers, *Witness* (Washington, D.C.: Regnery-Gateway, 1952), 3–22. Reprinted by permission of Regnery-Gateway Publishers.

Hiss, was cut short in the course of a brilliant public career. Some find it tragic that Whittaker Chambers, of his own will, gave up a $30,000-a-year job and a secure future to haunt for the rest of his days the ruins of his life. These are shocking facts, criminal facts, disturbing facts: they are not tragic.

Crime, violence, infamy are not tragedy. Tragedy occurs when a human soul awakes and seeks, in suffering and pain, to free itself from crime, violence, infamy, even at the cost of life. The struggle is the tragedy—not defeat or death. That is why the spectacle of tragedy has always filled men, not with despair, but with a sense of hope and exaltation. That is why this terrible book is also a book of hope. For it is about the struggle of the human soul—of more than one human soul. It is in this sense that the Hiss Case is a tragedy. This is its meaning beyond the headlines, the revelations, the shame and suffering of the people involved. But this tragedy will have been for nothing unless men understand it rightly, and from it the world takes hope and heart to begin its own tragic struggle with the evil that besets it from within and from without, unless it faces the fact that the world, the whole world, is sick unto death and that, among other things, this Case has turned a finger of fierce light into the suddenly opened and reeking body of our time.

My children, as long as you live, the shadow of the Hiss Case will brush you. In every pair of eyes that rests on you, you will see pass, like a cloud passing behind a woods in winter, the memory of your father—dissembled in friendly eyes, lurking in unfriendly eyes. Sometimes you will wonder which is harder to bear: friendly forgiveness or forthright hate. In time, therefore, when the sum of your experience of life gives you authority, you will ask yourselves the question: What was my father?

I will give you an answer. I was a witness. I do not mean a witness for the Government or against Alger Hiss and the others. Nor do I mean the short, squat, solitary figure, trudging through the impersonal halls of public buildings to testify before Congressional committees, grand juries, loyalty boards, courts of law. A man is not primarily a witness *against* something. That is only incidental to the fact that he is a witness *for* something. A witness, in the sense that I am using the word, is a man whose life and faith are so completely one that when the challenge comes to step out and testify for his faith, he does so, disregarding all risks, accepting all consequences.

One day in the great jury room of the Grand Jury of the Southern District of New York, a juror leaned forward slightly and asked me: "Mr. Chambers, what does it mean to be a Communist?" I hesitated for a moment, trying to find the simplest, most direct way to convey the heart of this complex experience to men and women to whom the very fact of the experience was all but incomprehensible. Then I said:

"When I was a Communist, I had three heroes. One was a Russian. One was a Pole. One was a German Jew.

"The Pole was Felix Djerjinsky. He was ascetic, highly sensitive, intelligent. He was a Communist. After the Russian Revolution, he became head of the Tcheka and organizer of the Red Terror. As a young man, Djerjinsky had been a political prisoner in the Paviak Prison in Warsaw. There he insisted on being given the task of cleaning the latrines of the other prisoners. For he held that the most developed member of any community must take upon himself the lowliest tasks as an example to those who are less developed. That is one thing that it meant to be a Communist.

"The German Jew was Eugen Leviné. He was a Communist. During the Bavarian Soviet Republic in 1919, Leviné was the organizer of the Workers and Soldiers Soviets. When the Bavarian Soviet Republic was crushed, Leviné was captured and court-martialed. The court-martial told him: 'You are under sentence of death.' Leviné answered: 'We Communists are always under sentence of death.' That is another thing that it meant to be a Communist.

"The Russian was not a Communist. He was a pre-Communist revolutionist named Kalyaev. (I should have said Sazonov.) He was arrested for a minor part in the assassination of the Tsarist prime minister, von Plehve. He was sent into Siberian exile to one of the worst prison camps, where the political prisoners were flogged. Kalyaev sought some way to protest this outrage to the world. The means were few, but at last he found a way. In protest against the flogging of other men, Kalyaev drenched himself in kerosene, set himself on fire and burned himself to death. That also is what it meant to be a Communist."

That also is what it means to be a witness.

But a man may also be an involuntary witness. I do not know any way to explain why God's grace touches a man who seems unworthy of it. But neither do I know any other way to explain how a man like myself—tarnished by life, unprepossessing, not brave—could prevail so far against the powers of the world arrayed almost solidly against him, to destroy him and defeat his truth. In this sense, I am an involuntary witness to God's grace and to the fortifying power of faith.

It was my fate to be in turn a witness to each of the two great faiths of our time. And so we come to the terrible word, Communism. My very dear children, nothing in all these pages will be written so much for you, though it is so unlike anything you would want to read. In nothing shall I be so much a witness, in no way am I so much called upon to fulfill my task, as in trying to make clear to you (and to the world) the true nature of Communism and the source of its power, which was the cause of my ordeal as a man, and remains the historic ordeal of the world in the 20th century. For in this century, within the next decades, will be decided for generations whether all mankind is to become Communist, whether the whole world is to become free, or whether, in the struggle, civilization as we know it is to be completely destroyed or completely changed. It is our fate to live upon that turning point in history.

The world has reached that turning point by the steep stages of a crisis mounting for generations. The turning point is the next to the last step. It was reached in blood, sweat, tears, havoc and death in World War II. The chief fruit of the First World War was the Russian Revolution and the rise of Communism as a national power. The chief fruit of the Second World War was our arrival at the next to the last step of the crisis with the rise of Communism as a world power. History is likely to say that these were the only decisive results of the world wars.

The last war simplified the balance of political forces in the world by reducing them to two. For the first time, it made the power of the Communist sector of mankind (embodied in the Soviet Union) roughly equal to the power of the free sector of mankind (embodied in the United States). It made the collision of these powers all but inevitable. For the world wars did not end the crisis. They raised its tensions to a new pitch. They raised the crisis to a new stage. All the politics of our time, including the politics of war, will be the politics of this crisis.

Few men are so dull that they do not know that the crisis exists and that it threatens their lives at every point. It is popular to call it a social crisis. It is in fact a total crisis—religious, moral, intellectual, social, political, economic. It is popular to call it a crisis of the Western world. It is in fact a crisis of the whole world. Communism, which claims to be a solution of the crisis, is itself a symptom and an irritant of the crisis.

In part, the crisis results from the impact of science and technology upon mankind which, neither socially nor morally, has caught up with the problems posed by that impact. In part, it is caused by men's efforts to solve those problems. World wars are the military expression of the crisis. World-wide depressions are its economic expression. Universal desperation is its spiritual climate. This is the climate of Communism. Communism in our time can no more be considered apart from the crisis than a fever can be acted upon apart from an infected body.

I see in Communism the focus of the concentrated evil of our time. You will ask: Why, then, do men become Communists? How did it happen that you, our gentle and loved father, were once a Communist? Were you simply stupid? No, I was not stupid. Were you morally depraved? No, I was not morally depraved. Indeed, educated men become Communists chiefly for moral reasons. Did you not know that the crimes and horrors of Communism are inherent in Communism? Yes, I knew that fact. Then why did you become a Communist? It would help more to ask: How did it happen that this movement, once a mere muttering of political outcasts, became this immense force that now contests the mastery of mankind? Even when all the chances and mistakes of history are allowed for, the answer must be: Communism makes some profound appeal to the human mind. You will not find out what it is by calling Communism names. That will not help much to explain why Communism whose horrors, on a scale unparalleled in history, are now public knowledge, still recruits its thousands and holds its millions—among them some of the best minds alive. Look at Klaus Fuchs, standing in the London dock, quiet, doomed, destroyed, and say whether it is possible to answer in that way the simple question: Why?

First, let me try to say what Communism is not. It is not simply a vicious plot hatched by wicked men in a sub-cellar. It is not just the writings of Marx and Lenin, dialectical materialism, the Politburo, the labor theory of value, the theory of the general strike, the Red Army, secret police, labor camps, underground conspiracy, the dictatorship of the proletariat, the technique of the coup d'état. It is not even those chanting, bannered millions that stream periodically, like disorganized armies, through the heart of the world's capitals: Moscow, New York, Tokyo, Paris, Rome. These are expressions of Communism, but they are not what Communism is about.

In the Hiss trials, where Communism was a haunting specter, but which did little or nothing to explain Communism, Communists were assumed to be criminals, pariahs, clandestine men who lead double lives under false names, travel on false passports, deny traditional religion, morality, the sanctity of oaths, preach violence and practice treason. These things are true about Communists, but they are not what Communism is about.

The revolutionary heart of Communism is not the theatrical appeal: "Workers of the world, unite. You have nothing to lose but your chains. You have a world to gain." It is a simple statement of Karl Marx, further simplified for handy use: "Philosophers have explained the world; it is necessary to change the world." Communists are bound together by no secret oath. The tie that binds them across the frontiers of nations, across barriers of language and differences of class and education, in defiance of religion, morality, truth, law, honor, the weaknesses of the body and the irresolutions of the mind, even unto death, is a simple conviction: It is necessary to change the world. Their power, whose nature baffles the rest of the world, because in a large measure the rest of the world has lost that power, is the power to hold convictions and to act on them. It is the same power that moves mountains; it is also an unfailing power to move men. Communists are that part of mankind which has recovered the power to live or die—to bear witness—for its faith. And it is a simple, rational faith that inspires men to live or die for it.

It is not new. It is, in fact, man's second oldest faith. Its promise was whispered in the first days of the Creation under the Tree of the Knowledge of Good and Evil: "Ye shall be as gods." It is the great alternative faith of mankind. Like all great faiths, its force derives from a simple vision. Other ages have had great visions. They have always been different versions of the same vision: the vision of God and man's relationship to God. The Communist vision is the vision of Man without God.

It is the vision of man's mind displacing God as the creative intelligence of the world. It is the vision of man's liberated mind, by the sole force of its rational intelligence, redirecting man's destiny and reorganizing man's life and the world. It is the vision of man, once more the central figure of the Creation, not because God made man in His image, but because man's mind makes him the most intelligent of the animals. Copernicus and his successors displaced man as the central fact of the universe by proving that the earth was not the central star of the universe. Communism restores man to his sovereignty by the simple method of denying God.

The vision is a challenge and implies a threat. It challenges man to prove by his acts that he is the masterwork of the Creation—by making thought and act one. It challenges him to prove it by using the force of his rational mind to end the bloody meaninglessness of man's history—by giving it purpose and a plan. It challenges him to prove it by reducing the meaningless chaos of nature, by imposing on it his rational will to order, abundance, security, peace. It is the vision of materialism. But it threatens, if man's mind is unequal to the problems of man's progress, that he will sink back into savagery (the A and the H bombs have raised the issue in explosive forms), until nature replaced him with a more intelligent form of life.

It is an intensely practical vision. The tools to turn it into reality are at hand—science and technology, whose traditional method, the rigorous exclusion of all supernatural factors in solving problems, has contributed to the intellectual climate in which the vision flourishes, just as they have contributed to the crisis in which Communism thrives. For the vision is shared by millions who are not Communists (they are part of Communism's secret strength). Its first commandment is found, not in the *Communist Manifesto,* but in the first sentence of the physics primer: "All of the progress of mankind to date results from the making of careful measurements." But Communism, for the first time in history, has made this vision the faith of a great modern political movement.

Hence the Communist Party is quite justified in calling itself the most revolutionary party in history. It has posed in practical form the most revolutionary question in history: God or Man? It has taken the logical next step which three hundred years of rationalism hesitated to take, and said what millions of modern minds think, but do not dare or care to say: If man's mind is the decisive force in the world, what need is there for God? Henceforth man's mind is man's fate.

This vision is the Communist revolution, which, like all great revolutions, occurs in man's mind before it takes form in man's acts. Insurrection and conspiracy are merely methods of realizing the vision; they are merely part of the politics of Communism. Without its vision, they, like Communism, would have no meaning and could not rally a parcel of pickpockets. Communism does not summon men to crime or to utopia, as its easy critics like to think. On the plane of faith, it summons mankind to turn its vision into practical reality. On the plane of action, it summons men to struggle against the inertia of the past which, embodied in social, political and economic forms, Communism claims, is blocking the will of mankind to make its next great forward stride. It summons men to overcome the crisis, which, Communism claims, is in effect a crisis of rending frustration, with the world, unable to stand still, but unwilling to go forward along the road that the logic of a technological civilization points out—Communism.

This is Communism's moral sanction, which is twofold. Its vision points the way to the future; its faith labors to turn the future into present reality. It says to every man who joins it: the vision is a practical problem of history; the way to achieve it is a practical problem of politics, which is the present tense of history. Have you the moral strength to take upon yourself the crimes of history so that man at last may close his chronicle of age-old, senseless suffering, and replace it with purpose and a plan? The answer a man makes to this question is the difference between the Communist and those miscellaneous socialists, liberals, fellow travelers, unclassified progressives and men of good will, all of whom share a similar vision, but do not share the faith because they will not take upon themselves the penalties of the faith. The answer is the root of that sense of moral superiority which makes Communists, though caught in crime, berate their opponents with withering self-righteousness.

The Communist vision has a mighty agitator and a mighty propagandist. They are the crisis. The agitator needs no soap box. It speaks insistently to the human mind at the point where desperation lurks. The propagandist writes no Communist gibberish. It speaks insistently to the human mind at the point where man's hope and man's energy fuse to fierceness.

The vision inspires. The crisis impels. The workingman is chiefly moved by the crisis. The educated man is chiefly moved by the vision. The workingman, living upon a mean margin of life, can afford few visions—even practical visions. An educated man, peering from the Harvard Yard, or any college campus, upon a world in chaos, finds in the vision the two certainties for which the mind of man tirelessly seeks: a reason to live and a reason to die. No other faith of our time presents them with the same practical intensity. That is why Communism is the central experience of the first half of the 20th century, and may be its final experience—will be, unless the free world, in the agony of its struggle with Communism, overcomes its crisis by discovering, in suffering and pain, a power of faith which will provide man's mind, at the same intensity, with the same two certainties: a reason to live and a reason to die. If it fails, this will be the century of the great social wars. If it succeeds, this will be the century of the great wars of faith.

You will ask: Why, then, do men cease to be Communists? One answer is: Very few do. Thirty years after the Russian Revolution, after the known atrocities, the purges, the revelations, the jolting zigzags of Communist politics, there is only a handful of ex-Communists in the whole world. By ex-Communists I do not mean those who break with Communism over differences of strategy and tactics (like Trotsky) or organization (like Tito). Those are merely quarrels over a road map by people all of whom are in a hurry to get to the same place.

Nor, by ex-Communists, do I mean those thousands who continually drift into the Communist Party and out again. The turnover is vast. These are the spiritual vagrants of our time whose traditional faith has been leached out in the bland climate of rationalism. They are looking for an intellectual night's lodging. They lack the character for Communist faith because they lack the character for any faith. So they drop away, though Communism keeps its hold on them.

By an ex-Communist, I mean a man who knew clearly why he became a Communist, who served Communism devotedly and knew why he served it, who broke with Communism unconditionally and knew why he broke with it. Of these there are very few—an index to the power of the vision and the power of the crisis.

History very largely fixes the patterns of force that make men Communists. Hence one Communist conversion sounds much like another—rather impersonal and repetitious, awesome and tiresome, like long lines of similar people all stolidly waiting to get in to see the same movie. A man's break with Communism is intensely personal. Hence the account of no two breaks is likely to be the same. The reasons that made one Communist break may seem without force to another ex-Communist.

It is a fact that a man can join the Communist Party, can be very active in it for years, without completely understanding the nature of Communism or the political methods that follow inevitably from its vision. One day such incomplete Communists discover that the Communist Party is not what they thought it was. They break with it and turn on it with the rage of an honest dupe, a dupe who has given a part of his life to a swindle. Often they forget that it takes two to make a swindle.

Others remain Communists for years, warmed by the light of its vision, firmly closing their eyes to the crimes and horrors inseparable from its practical politics. One day they have to face the facts. They are appalled at what they have abetted. They spend the rest of their days trying to explain, usually without great success, the dark clue to their complicity. As their understanding of Communism was incomplete and led them to a dead end, their understanding of breaking with it is incomplete and leads them to a dead end. It leads to less than Communism, which was a vision and a faith. The world outside Communism, the world in crisis, lacks a vision and a faith. There is before these ex-Communists absolutely nothing. Behind them is a threat. For they have, in fact, broken not with the vision, but with the politics of the vision. In the name of reason and intelligence, the vision keeps them firmly in its grip—self-divided, paralyzed, powerless to act against it.

Hence the most secret fold of their minds is haunted by a terrifying thought: What if we were wrong? What if our inconstancy is our guilt? That is the fate of those who break without knowing clearly that Communism is wrong because something else is right, because to the challenge: *God or Man?*, they continue to give the answer: *Man*. Their pathos is that not even the Communist ordeal could teach them that man without God is just what Communism said he was: the most intelligent of the animals, that man without God is a beast, never more beastly than when he is most intelligent about his beastliness. *"Er nennt's Vernunft,"* says the Devil in Goethe's *Faust, "und braucht's allein, nur tierischer als jedes Tier zu sein"*—Man calls it reason and uses it simply to be more beastly than any beast. Not grasping the source of the evil they sincerely hate, such ex-Communists in general make ineffectual witnesses against it. They are witnesses against something; they have ceased to be witnesses for anything.

Yet there is one experience which most sincere ex-Communists share, whether or not they go only part way to the end of the question it poses. The daughter of a former German diplomat in Moscow was trying to explain to me why her father, who, as an enlightened modern man, had been extremely pro-Communist, had become an implacable anti-Communist. It was hard for her because, as an enlightened modern girl, she shared the Communist vision without being a Communist. But she loved her father and the irrationality of his defection embarrassed her. "He was immensely pro-Soviet," she said, "and then—you will laugh at me—but you must not laugh at my father—and then—one night—in Moscow—he heard screams. That's all. Simply one night he heard screams."

A child of Reason and the 20th century, she knew that there is a logic of the mind. She did not know that the soul has a logic that may be more compelling than the mind's. She did not know at all that she had swept away the logic of the mind, the logic of history, the logic of politics, the myth of the 20th century, with five annihilating words: one night he heard screams.

What Communist has not heard those screams? They come from husbands torn forever from their wives in midnight arrests. They come, muffled, from the execution cellars of the secret police, from the torture chambers of the Lubianka, from all the citadels of terror now stretching from Berlin to Canton. They come from those freight cars loaded with men, women and children, the enemies of the Communist State, locked in, packed in, left on remote sidings to freeze to death at night in the Russian winter. They come from minds driven mad by the horrors of mass starvation ordered and enforced as a policy of the Communist State. They come from the starved skeletons, worked to death, or flogged to death (as an example to others) in the freezing filth of sub-arctic labor camps. They come from children whose parents are suddenly, inexplicably, taken away from them—parents they will never see again.

What Communist has not heard those screams? Execution, says the Communist code, is the highest measure of social protection. What man can call himself a Communist who has not accepted the fact that Terror is an instrument of policy, right if the vision is right, justified by history, enjoined by the balance of forces in the social wars of this century? Those screams have reached every Communist's mind. Usually they stop there. What judge willingly dwells upon the man the laws compel him to condemn to death—the laws of nations or the laws of history?

But one day the Communist really hears those screams. He is going about his routine party tasks. He is lifting a dripping reel of microfilm from a developing tank. He is justifying to a Communist fraction in a trade union an extremely unwelcome directive of the Central Committee. He is receiving from a trusted superior an order to go to another country and, in a designated hotel, at a designated hour, meet a man whose name he will never know, but who will give him a package whose contents he will never learn. Suddenly, there closes around that Communist a separating silence, and in that silence he hears screams. He hears them for the first time. For they do not merely reach his mind. They pierce beyond. They pierce to his soul. He says to himself. "Those are not the screams of man in agony. Those are the screams of a soul in agony." He hears them for the first time because a soul in extremity has communicated with that which alone can hear it—another human soul.

Why does the Communist ever hear them? Because in the end there persists in every man, however he may deny it, a scrap of soul. The Communist who suffers this singular experience then says to himself: "What is happening to me? I must be sick." If he does not instantly stifle that scrap of soul, he is lost. If he admits it for a moment, he has admitted that there is something greater than Reason, greater than the logic of mind, of politics, of history, of economics, which alone justifies the vision. If the party senses his weakness, and the party is peculiarly cunning at sensing such weakness, it will humiliate him, degrade him, condemn him, expel him. If it can, it will destroy him. And the party will be right. For he has betrayed that which alone justifies its faith—the vision of Almighty Man. He has brushed the only vision that has force against the vision of Almighty Mind. He stands before the fact of God.

The Communist Party is familiar with this experience to which its members are sometimes liable in prison, in illness, in indecision. It is recognized frankly as a sickness. There are ways of treating it—if it is confessed. It is when it is not confessed that the party, sensing a subtle crisis, turns upon it savagely. What ex-Communist has not suffered this experience in one form or another, to one degree or another? What he does about it depends on the individual man. That is why no ex-Communist dare answer for his sad fraternity the question: Why do men break with Communism? He can only answer the question: How did you break with Communism? My answer is: Slowly, reluctantly, in agony.

Yet my break began long before I heard those screams. Perhaps it does for everyone. I do not know how far back it began. Avalanches gather force and crash, unheard, in men as in the mountains. But I date my break from a very casual happening. I was sitting in our apartment on St. Paul Street in Baltimore. It was shortly before we moved to Alger Hiss's apartment in Washington. My daughter was in her high chair. I was watching her eat. She was the most miraculous thing that had ever happened in my life. I liked to watch her even when she smeared porridge on her face or dropped it meditatively on the floor. My eye came to rest on the delicate convolutions of her ear—those intricate, perfect ears. The thought passed through my mind: "No, those ears were not created by any chance coming together of atoms in nature (the Communist view). They could have been created only by immense design." The thought was involuntary and unwanted. I crowded it out of my mind. But I never wholly forgot it or the occasion. I had to crowd it out of my mind. If I had completed it, I should have had to say: Design presupposes God. I did not then know that, at that moment, the finger of God was first laid upon my forehead.

One thing most ex-Communists could agree upon: they broke because they wanted to be free. They do not all mean the same thing by "free." Freedom is a need of the soul, and nothing else. It is in striving toward God that the soul strives continually after a condition of freedom. God alone is the inciter and guarantor of freedom. He is the only guarantor. External freedom is only an aspect of interior freedom. Political freedom, as the Western world has known it, is only a political reading of the Bible. Religion and freedom are indivisible. Without freedom the soul dies. Without the soul there is no justification for freedom. Necessity is the only ultimate justification known to the mind. Hence every sincere break with Communism is a religious experience, though the Communist fail to identify its true nature, though he fail to go to the end of the experience. His break is the political expression of the perpetual need of the soul whose first faint stirring he has felt within him, years, months or days before he breaks. A Communist breaks because he must choose at last between irreconcilable opposites—God or Man, Soul or Mind, Freedom or Communism.

Communism is what happens when, in the name of Mind, men free themselves from God. But its view of God, its knowledge of God, its experience of God, is what alone gives character to a society or a nation, and meaning to its destiny. Its culture, the voice of this character, is merely that view, knowledge, experience, of God, fixed by its most intense spirits in terms intelligible to the mass of men. There has never been a society or a nation without God. But history is cluttered with the wreckage of nations that became indifferent to God, and died.

The crisis of Communism exists to the degree in which it has failed to free the peoples that it rules from God. Nobody knows this better than the Communist Party of the Soviet Union. The crisis of the Western world exists to the degree in which it is indifferent to God. It exists to the degree in which the Western world actually shares Communism's materialist vision, is so dazzled by the logic of the materialist interpretation of history, politics and economics, that it fails to grasp that, for it, the only possible answer to the Communist challenge: Faith in God or Faith in Man? is the challenge: Faith in God.

Economics is not the central problem of this century. It is a relative problem which can be solved in relative ways. Faith is the central problem of this age. The Western world does not know it, but it already possesses the answer to this problem—but only provided that its faith in God and the freedom He enjoins is as great as Communism's faith in Man.

My dear children, before I close this foreword, I want to recall to you briefly the life that we led in the ten years between the time when I broke with Communism and the time when I began to testify—the things we did, worked for, loved, believed in. For it was that happy life, which, on the human side, in part made it possible for me to do later on the things I had to do, or endure the things that happened to me.

Those were the days of the happy little worries, which then seemed so big. We know now that they were the golden days. They will not come again. In those days, our greatest worry was how to meet the payments on the mortgage, how to get the ploughing done in time, how to get health accreditation for our herd, how to get the hay in before the rain. I sometimes took my vacation in hay harvest so that I could help work the load. You two little children used to trample the load, drive the hay truck in the fields when you could barely reach the foot pedals, or drive the tractor that pulled up the loaded harpoons to the mow. At evening, you would break off to help Mother milk while I went on haying. For we came of age on the farm when we decided not to hire barn help, but to run the herd ourselves as a family.

Often the ovenlike heat in the comb of the barn and the sweet smell of alfalfa made us sick. Sometimes we fell asleep at the supper table from fatigue. But the hard work was good for us; and you knew only the peace of a home governed by a father and mother whose marriage the years (and an earlier suffering which you could not remember) had deepened into the perfect love that enveloped you.

Mother was a slight, overalled figure forever working for you in the house or beside you in the barns and gardens. Papa was a squat, overalled figure, fat but forceful, who taught John, at nine, the man-size glory of driving the tractor; or sat beside Ellen, at the wheel of the truck, an embodiment of security and power, as we drove loads of cattle through the night. On summer Sundays, you sat between Papa and Mama in the Quaker meeting house. Through the open doors, as you tried not to twist and turn in the long silence, you could see the far, blue Maryland hills and hear the redbirds and ground robins in the graveyard behind.

Only Ellen had a vague, troubled recollection of another time and another image of Papa. Then (it was during the years 1938 and 1939), if for any reason she pattered down the hall at night, she would find Papa, with the light on, writing, with a revolver on the table or a gun against the chair. She knew that there were people who wanted to kill Papa and who might try to kidnap her. But a wide sea of sunlight and of time lay between that puzzling recollection and the farm.

The farm was your kingdom, and the world lay far beyond the protecting walls thrown up by work and love. It is true that comic strips were not encouraged, comic books were banned, the radio could be turned on only by permission which was seldom given (or asked), and you saw few movies. But you grew in the presence of eternal wonders. There was the birth of lambs and calves. You remember how once, when I was away and the veterinarian could not come, you saw Mother reach in and turn the calf inside the cow so that it could be born. There was also the death of animals, sometimes violent, sometimes slow and painful—nothing is more constant on a farm than death.

Sometimes, of a spring evening, Papa would hear that distant honking that always makes his scalp tingle, and we would all rush out to see the wild geese, in lines of hundreds, steer up from the southwest, turn over the barn as over a landmark, and head into the north. Or on autumn nights of sudden cold that set the ewes breeding in the orchard, Papa would call you out of the house to stand with him in the now celebrated pumpkin patch and watch the northern lights flicker in electric clouds on the horizon, mount, die down, fade and mount again till they filled the whole northern sky with ghostly light in motion.

Thus, as children, you experienced two of the most important things men ever know—the wonder of life and the wonder of the universe, the wonder of life within the wonder of the universe. More important, you knew them not from books, not from lectures, but simply from living among them. Most important, you knew them with reverence and awe—that reverence and awe that has died out of the modern world and been replaced by man's monkeylike amazement at the cleverness of his own inventive brain.

I have watched greatness touch you in another way. I have seen you sit, uninvited and unforced, listening in complete silence to the third movement of the Ninth Symphony. I thought you understood, as much as children can, when I told you that that music was the moment at which Beethoven finally passed beyond the suffering of his life on earth and reached for the hand of God, as God reaches for the hand of Adam in Michelangelo's vision of the Creation.

And once, in place of a bedtime story, I was reading Shakespeare to John—at his own request, for I never forced such things on you. I came to that passage in which Macbeth, having murdered Duncan, realizes what he has done to his own soul, and asks if all the water in the world can ever wash the blood from his hand, or will it not rather

The multitudinous seas incarnadine?

At that line, John's whole body twitched. I gave great silent thanks to God. For I knew that if, as children, you could thus feel in your souls the reverence and awe for life and the world, which is the ultimate meaning of Beethoven and Shakespeare, as man and woman you could never be satisfied with less. I felt a great faith that sooner or later you would understand what I once told you, not because I expected you to understand it then, but because I hoped that you would remember it later: "True wisdom comes from the overcoming of suffering and sin. All true wisdom is therefore touched with sadness."

If all this sounds unduly solemn, you know that our lives were not; that all of us suffer from an incurable itch to puncture false solemnity. In our daily lives, we were fun-loving and gay. For those who have solemnity in their souls generally have enough of it there, and do not need to force it into their faces.

Then, on August 3, 1948, you learned for the first time that your father had once been a Communist, that he had worked in something called "the underground," that it was shameful, and that for some reason he was in Washington telling the world about it. While he was in the underground, he testified, he had worked with a number of other Communists. One of them was a man with the odd name of Alger Hiss. Later, Alger Hiss denied the allegation. Thus the Great Case began, and with it our lives were changed forever.

Dear children, one autumn twilight, when you were much smaller, I slipped away from you in play and stood for a moment alone in the apple orchard near the barn. Then I heard your two voices, piping together anxiously, calling to me: "Papa! Papa!" from the harvested cornfield. In the years when I was away five days a week in New York, working to pay for the farm, I used to think of you both before I fell asleep at night. And that is how you almost always came to me—voices of beloved children, calling to me from the gathered fields at dusk.

You called to me once again at night in the same orchard. That was a good many years later. A shadow deeper and more chilling than the autumn evening had closed upon us—I mean the Hiss Case. It was the first year of the Case. We had been doing the evening milking together. For us, one of the few happy results of the Case was that at last I could be home with you most of the time (in life these good things usually come too little or too late). I was washing and disinfecting the cows, and putting on and taking off the milkers. You were stripping after me.

In the quiet, there suddenly swept over my mind a clear realization of our true position—obscure, all but friendless people (some of my great friends had already taken refuge in aloofness; the others I had withdrawn from so as not to involve them in my affairs). Against me was an almost solid line-up of the most powerful groups and men in the country, the bitterly hostile reaction of much of the press, the smiling skepticism of much of the public, the venomous calumnies of the Hiss forces, the all but universal failure to understand the real meaning of the Case or my real purpose. A sense of the enormous futility of my effort, and my own inadequacy, drowned me. I felt a physical cold creep through me, settle around my heart and freeze any pulse of hope. The sight of you children, guiltless and defenseless, was more than I could bear. I was alone against the world; my longing was to be left completely alone, or not to be at all. It was that death of the will which Communism, with great cunning, always tries to induce in its victims.

I waited until the last cow was stripped and the last can lifted into the cooler. Then I stole into the upper barn and out into the apple orchard. It was a very dark night. The stars were large and cold. This cold was one with the coldness in myself. The lights of the barn, the house and the neighbors' houses were warm in the windows and on the ground; they were not for me. Then I heard Ellen call me in the barn and John called: "Papa!" Still calling, Ellen went down to the house to see if I were there. I heard John opening gates as he went to the calf barn, and he called me there. With all the longing of my love for you, I wanted to answer. But if I answered, I must come back to the living world. I could not do that.

John began to call me in the cow stable, in the milk house. He went into the dark side of the barn (I heard him slide the door back), into the upper barn, where at night he used to be afraid. He stepped outside in the dark, calling: "Papa! Papa!"—then, frantically, on the verge of tears: "Papa!" I walked over to him. I felt that I was making the most terrible surrender I should have to make on earth. "Papa," he cried and threw his arms around me, "don't ever go away." "No," I said, "no, I won't ever go away." Both of us knew that the words "go away" stood for something else, and that I had given him my promise not to kill myself. Later on, as you will see, I was tempted, in my wretchedness, to break that promise.

My children, when you were little, we used sometimes to go for walks in our pine woods. In the open fields, you would run along by yourselves. But you used instinctively to give me your hands as we entered those woods, where it was darker, lonelier, and in the stillness our voices sounded loud and frightening. In this book I am again giving you my hands. I am leading you, not through cool pine woods, but up and up a narrow defile between bare and steep rocks from which in shadow things uncoil and slither away. It will be dark. But, in the end, if I have led you aright, you will make out three crosses, from two of which hang thieves. I will have brought you to Golgotha—the place of skulls. This is the meaning of the journey. Before you understand, I may not be there, my hands may have slipped from yours. It will not matter. For when you understand what you see, you will no longer be children. You will know that life is pain, that each of us hangs always upon the cross of himself. And when you know that this is true of every man, woman and child on earth, you will be wise.

Your Father

HANNAH ARENDT

"Ideology and Terror"
(1953)

In *The Origins of Totalitarianism* (New York, 1951), émigré political theorist Hannah Arendt (1906–71) identified as central to the regimes of both Hitler and Stalin a distinctive state of mind induced by a tightly controlled environment of terror. Two years later she published our selection here as a free-standing essay, but this sharply formulated version of the main argument of her book was incorporated into later editions of *Origins of Totalitarianism*.

Born of highly assimilated Jewish parents in Kant's city of Konigsberg, Arendt arrived in the United States in 1941 a refugee from Hitler's Europe. She is one of forty-eight refugee intellectuals whose careers are surveyed in a book that can serve as an introduction to the study of the intellectual migration from Central Europe: Lewis A. Coser, *Refugee Scholars in America: Their Impact and Their Experiences* (New Haven, 1984). As a student in the 1920s Arendt had been involved with her mentor, Martin Heidegger, who later became rector of his university under the authority of the Nazi regime. This intimacy between the most eminent of the German philosophers to side with the Nazis and his Jewish, democracy-affirming student became a matter of renewed discussion twenty years after Arendt's death when it was learned that Arendt had renewed this relationship after World War II.

Arendt's influence has increased with time. Today she is one of the most respected and widely studied American intellectuals of the generation that flourished in the third quarter of the twentieth century. Her analysis of totalitarianism, long resisted by thinkers eager to drive a conceptual wedge between the "rightist" Nazis and the "leftist" Stalinists, gained renewed credibility after the collapse of communism in Europe in 1989. Arendt wrote many books after *Origins of Totalitarianism,* including *The Human Condition* (New York, 1958), *Eichmann and Jerusalem: A Report on the Banality of Evil* (New York, 1963), and *On Revolution* (New York, 1963). Prominent among the many books devoted to Arendt's thought are Margaret Canovan, *Hannah Arendt: A Reinterpretation of Her Political Thought* (New York, 1992); and Hannah Fenichel Pitkin, *The Attack on the Blob: Hannah Arendt's Concept of the Social* (Chicago, 1999). An excellent starting point in the study of Arendt is Dana Villa, ed., *The Cambridge Companion to Hannah Arendt* (New York, 2000). Two forthright discussions of Arendt's contemporary relevance are Elisabeth Young-Bruhl, *Why Arendt Matters* (New Haven, 2006); and Samantha Power's introduction to the Schocken Books edition of *The Origins of Totalitarianism* (New York, 2004).

The following considerations have grown out of a study of the origins, the elements and the functioning of that novel form of government and domination which we have come to call totalitarian. Wherever it rose to power, it developed entirely new political institutions and destroyed all social, legal and political traditions of the country. No matter what the specifically national tradition or the particular spiritual source of its ideology, totalitarian government always transformed classes into masses, supplanted the party system, not by one-party dictatorships, but by a mass movement, shifted the center of power from the army to the police, and established a foreign policy openly directed toward world domination. Present totalitarian governments have developed from one-party systems; whenever these became truly totalitarian, they started to operate according to a system of values so radically different from all others, that none of our traditional legal, moral, or common sense utilitarian categories could any longer help us to come to terms with, or judge, or predict its course of action....

Total terror, the essence of totalitarian government, exists neither for nor against men. It is supposed to provide the forces of Nature or History with an incomparable instrument to accelerate their movement. This movement, proceeding according to its own law, cannot in the long run be hindered; eventually its force will always prove more powerful than the most powerful forces engendered by the actions and the will of men. But it can be slowed down and is slowed down almost inevitably by the freedom of man, which even totalitarian rulers cannot deny, for this freedom—irrelevant and arbitrary as they may deem it—is identical with the fact that men are being born and that therefore each of them *is* a new beginning, begins, in a sense, the world anew. From the totalitarian point of view, the fact that men are born and die can be only regarded as an annoying interference with higher forces. Terror, therefore, as the obedient servant of natural or historical movement has to eliminate from the process not only freedom in any specific sense, but the very source of freedom which is given with the fact of the birth of man and resides in his capacity to make a new beginning. In the iron band of terror, which destroys the plurality of men and makes out of many the One who unfailingly will act as though he himself were part of the course of History or Nature, a device has been found not only to liberate the historical and natural forces, but to accelerate them to a speed they never would reach if left to themselves. Practically speaking, this means that terror executes on the spot the death sentences which Nature is supposed to have pronounced on races or individuals who are "unfit to live," or History on "dying classes," without waiting for the slower and less efficient processes of Nature or History themselves.

In this concept, where the essence of government itself has become motion, a very old problem of political thought seems to have found a solution similar to the one already noted for the discrepancy between legality and justice. If the essence of government is defined as lawfulness, and if it is understood that laws are the stabilizing forces in the public affairs of men (as indeed it always has been since Plato invoked Zeus, the God of the boundaries, in his *Laws*) then the problem of movement of the body politic and the actions of its citizens arises. Lawfulness sets limitations to actions, but does not inspire them; the greatness, but also the perplexity of laws in free societies is that they only tell what one should not, but never what one should do. The necessary movement of a body politic can

Source: Hannah Arendt, "Ideology and Terror: A Novel Form of Government." Reprinted by permission of Harcourt, Inc. Copyright © 1953 and renewed 1981 by Hannah Arendt.

never be found in its essence if only because this essence—again since Plato—has always been defined with a view to its permanence. Duration seemed one of the surest yardsticks for the goodness of a government. It is still, for Montesquieu, the supreme proof for the badness of tyranny that only tyrannies are liable to be destroyed from within, to decline by themselves, whereas all other governments are destroyed through exterior circumstances. Therefore what the definition of governments always needed was what Montesquieu called a "principle of action" which, different in each form of government, would inspire government and citizens alike in their public activity and serve as a criterion beyond the merely negative yardstick of lawfulness, for judging all action in public affairs. Such guiding principles and criteria of action are, according to Montesquieu, honor in a monarchy, virtue in a republic and fear in a tyranny.

In a perfect totalitarian government, where all men have become One Man, where all action aims at the acceleration of the movement of Nature or History, where every single act is the execution of a death sentence which Nature or History has already pronounced, that is, under conditions where terror can be completely relied upon to keep the movement in constant motion, no principle of action separate from its essence would be needed at all. Yet as long as totalitarian rule has not conquered the earth and with the iron band of terror made each single man a part of one mankind, terror in its double function as essence of government and principle, not of action, but of motion cannot be fully realized. Just as lawfulness in constitutional government is insufficient to inspire and guide men's actions, so terror in totalitarian government is not sufficient to inspire and guide human behavior.

While under present conditions totalitarian domination still shares with other forms of government the need for a guide for the behavior of its citizens in public affairs, it does not need and could not even use a principle of action strictly speaking, since it will eliminate precisely the capacity of man to act. Under conditions of total terror not even fear can any longer serve as an advisor of how to behave, because terror chooses its victims without reference to individual actions or thoughts, exclusively in accordance with the objective necessity of the natural or historical process. Under totalitarian conditions, fear probably is more widespread than ever before; but fear has lost its practical usefulness when actions guided by it can no longer help to avoid the dangers man fears. The same is true for sympathy or support of the regime; for total terror not only selects its victims according to objective standards; it chooses its executioners with as complete a disregard as possible for the candidate's conviction and sympathies. The consistent elimination of conviction as a motive for action has become a matter of record since the great purges in Soviet Russia and the satellite countries. The aim of totalitarian education has never been to instill convictions but to destroy the capacity to form any. The introduction of purely objective criteria into the selective system of the SS troops was Himmler's great organizational invention; he selected the candidates from photographs according to purely racial criteria. Nature itself decided, not only who was to be eliminated, but also who was to be trained as an executioner.

No guiding principle of behavior, taken itself from the realm of human action, such as virtue, honor, fear, is necessary or can be useful to set into motion a body politic which no longer uses terror as a means of intimidation, but whose essence *is* terror. In its stead, it has introduced an entirely new principle into public affairs that dispenses with human will to action altogether and appeals to the craving need for some insight into the law of movement according to which the terror functions and upon which, therefore, all private destinies depend.

The inhabitants of a totalitarian country are thrown into and caught in the process of Nature or History for the sake of accelerating its movement; as such, they can only be executioners or victims of its inherent law. The process may decide that those who today eliminate races and individuals or the members of dying classes and decadent peoples are tomorrow those who must be sacrificed. What totalitarian rule needs to guide the behavior of its subjects is a *preparation* to fit each of them equally well for the role of executioner and the role of victim. This two-sided preparation, the substitute for a principle of action, is the ideology.

Ideologies—isms which to the satisfaction of their adherents can explain everything and every occurrence by deducing it from a single premise—are a very recent phenomenon and, for many decades, this played a negligible role in political life. Only with the wisdom of hindsight can we discover in them certain elements which have made them so disturbingly useful for totalitarian rule. Not before Hitler and Stalin were the great political potentialities of the ideologies discovered.

Ideologies are known for their scientific character: they combine the scientific approach with results of philosophical relevance and pretend to be scientific philosophy. The word "ideology" seems to imply that an idea can become the subject matter of a science just as animals are the subject matter of zoology, and that the suffix *-logy* in ideology, as in zoology, indicates nothing but the *logoi,* the scientific statements made on it. If this were true, an ideology would indeed be a pseudo-science and a pseudo-philosophy, transgressing at the same time the limitations of science and the limitations of philosophy. Deism, for example, would then be the ideology which treats the *idea* of God, with which philosophy is concerned, in the scientific manner of theology for which God is a revealed reality. (A theology which is not based on revelation as a given reality but treats God as an idea would be as mad as a zoology which is no longer sure of the physical, tangible existence of animals.) Yet we know that this is only part of the truth. Deism, though it denies divine revelation, does not simply make "scientific" statements on a God which is only an "idea," but uses the idea of God in order to explain the course of the world. The "ideas" of isms—race in racism, God in deism, etc.—never form the subject matter of the ideologies and the suffix *-logy* never indicates simply a body of "scientific" statements.

An ideology is quite literally what its name indicates: it is the *logic of an idea.* Its subject matter is history to which the "idea" is applied; the result of this application is not a body of statements about something that *is,* but the unfolding of a process which is in constant change. The ideology treats the course of events as though it followed the same "law" as the logical exposition of its "idea." Ideologies pretend to know the mysteries of the whole historical process—the secrets of the past, the intricacies of the present, the uncertainties of the future—because of the logic inherent in their respective ideas.

Ideologies are never interested in the miracle of being. They are historical, concerned with becoming and perishing, with the rise and fall of cultures, even if they try to explain history by some "law of nature." The word "race" in racism does not signify any genuine curiosity about the human races as a field for scientific exploration, but is the "idea" by which the movement of history is explained as one consistent process.

The "idea" of an ideology is neither the eternal essence grasped by the eyes of the mind nor the regulator of reason—as it was from Plato to Kant—but has become an instrument of explanation. To an ideology, history does not appear in the *light* of an idea (which would imply that history is seen sub specie of some ideal eternity which itself is beyond historical motion) but as something which can be *calculated* by it. What fits the "idea" into this new role is its own "logic," that is a movement which is the consequence of the "idea" itself and needs no outside factor to set it into motion. Racism is the belief that there is a motion inherent in the very "idea" of race, just as deism is the belief that a motion is inherent in the very notion of God.

The movement of history and the logical process of this notion are supposed to correspond to each other, so that whatever happens, happens according to the logic of one "idea." However, the only possible movement in the realm of logic is the process of deduction from a premise. Dialectical logic, with its process from thesis through antithesis to synthesis which in turn becomes the thesis of the next dialectical movement is not different in principle, once an ideology gets hold of it; the first thesis becomes the premise and its advantage for ideological explanation is that this dialectical device can explain away factual contradictions as stages of one identical, consistent movement.

As soon as logic as a *movement* of thought—and not as a necessary control of thinking—is applied to an idea, this idea is transformed into a *premise*. Ideological world explanations performed this operation long before it became so eminently fruitful for totalitarian reasoning. The purely negative coercion of logic, the prohibition of contradictions, became "productive" so that a whole line of thought could be initiated, and forced upon the mind, by drawing conclusions in the manner of mere argumentation. This argumentative process could be interrupted neither by a new idea (which would have been another premise with a different set of consequences) nor by a new experience. Ideologies always assume that one idea is sufficient to explain everything in the development from the premise, and that no experience can teach anything because everything is comprehended in this consistent process of logical deduction. The danger in exchanging the necessary insecurity of philosophical thought for the total explanation of an ideology and its Weltanschauung, is not even so much the risk of falling for some usually vulgar, always uncritical assumption as of exchanging the freedom inherent in man's capacity to think for the straightjacket of logic with which man can force himself almost as violently as he is forced by some outside power.

The transformation of an idea into a premise and the use of the logic of deduction as only demonstration for truth, is certainly only one of the totalitarian elements in ideologies. Another is obviously the claim of all Weltanschauungen to offer total explanations of everything, mainly, of course, of past, present and future. And the emancipation from reality this method always implies, since it pretends to know beforehand everything that experience may still have in store, might, psychologically speaking, be even more important. Yet, we insisted on this peculiar logicality of ideologies because the true totalitarian rulers (Hitler and Stalin, not their forerunners) used it more than any other element when they converted ideologies—racism and the premise of the law of nature, or dialectical materialism and the premise of the law of history—into foundation stones for the new totalitarian body politic.

The device both totalitarian rulers used to transform their respective ideologies into weapons with which each of their subjects would force himself into step with the terror movement was deceptively simple and inconspicuous: they took them dead seriously, took pride the one in his supreme gift for "ice cold reasoning" (Hitler) and the other in the "mercilessness of his dialectics," and proceeded to drive ideological implications into extremes of logical consistency which, to the onlooker, looked preposterously "primitive" and absurd: a "dying class" consisted of people condemned to death; races that are "unfit to live" were to be exterminated. Whoever agreed that there are such things as "dying classes" and did not draw the consequence of killing their members, or that the right to live had something to do with race and did not draw the consequence of killing "unfit races," was plainly either stupid or a coward. This stringent logicality as a guide to action permeates the whole structure of totalitarian movements and governments. It is exclusively the work of Hitler and Stalin who, although they did not add a single new thought to the ideas and propaganda slogans of their movements, for this reason alone must be considered ideologists of the greatest importance.

What distinguished these new totalitarian ideologists from their predecessors was that it was no longer primarily the "idea" of the ideology—the struggle of classes and the exploitation of the workers or the struggle of races and the care for Germanic peoples—which appealed to them, but the logical process which could be developed from it. According to Stalin, neither the idea nor the oratory but "the irresistible force of logic thoroughly overpowered (Lenin's) audience." The power, which Marx thought was born when the idea seized the masses, was discovered to reside, not in the idea itself, but in its logical process which "like a mighty tentacle seizes you on all sides as in a vise and from whose grip you are powerless to tear yourself away; you must either surrender or make up your mind to utter defeat." (Stalin's speech of January 28, 1924; quoted from Lenin, *Selected Works*, vol. I, p. 33, Moscow, 1947.) Only when the realization of the ideological aims, the classless society or the master race, were at stake, could this force show itself. In the process of realization, the original substance upon which the ideologies based themselves as long as they had to appeal to the masses—the exploitation of the workers or the national aspirations of Germany—is gradually lost, devoured as it were by the process itself: in perfect accordance with "ice cold reasoning" and the "irresistible force of logic," the workers lost under Bolshevik rule even those rights they had been granted under Tsarist oppression and the German people suffered a kind of warfare which did not pay the slightest regard to the minimum requirements for survival of the German nation. It is in the nature of ideological politics—and is not simply a betrayal committed for the sake of self-interest or lust for power—that the real content of the ideology (the working class or the Germanic peoples), which originally had brought about the "idea" (the struggle of classes as the law of history or the struggle of races as the law of nature), is devoured by the logic with which the "idea" is carried out.

The preparation of victims and executioners which totalitarianism requires in place of Montesquieu's principle of action is not the ideology itself—racism or dialectical materialism—but its inherent logicality. The most persuasive argument in this respect, an argument of which Hitler like Stalin was very fond, is: You can't say A without saying B and C and so on, down to the end of the murderous alphabet. Here, the coercive force of logicality seems to have its source; it springs from our fear of contradicting ourselves. To the extent that the Bolshevik purge succeeds in making its victims confess to crimes they never committed it relies chiefly on this basic fear and argues as follows: We are all agreed on the premise that history is a struggle of classes and on the role of the Party in its conduct. You know therefore that, historically speaking, the Party is always right (in the words of Trotsky: "We can only be right with and by the Party, for history has provided no other way of being in the right."). At this historical moment, that is in accordance with the law of History, certain crimes are due to be committed which the Party, knowing the law of History, must punish. For these crimes, the Party needs criminals; it may be that the Party, though knowing the crimes, does not quite know the criminals; more important than to be sure about the criminals is to punish the crimes, because without such punishment, History will not be advanced but may even be hindered in its course. You, therefore, either have committed the crimes or have been called by the Party to play the role of the criminal—in either case, you have objectively become an enemy of the Party. If you don't confess, you cease to help History through the Party, and have become a real enemy.—The coercive force of the argument is: if you refuse, you contradict yourself and, through this contradiction, render your whole life meaningless; the A which you said dominates your whole life through the consequences of B and C which it logically engenders.

Totalitarian rulers rely on the compulsion with which we can compel ourselves, for the limited mobilization of people which even they still need; this inner compulsion is the tyranny of logicality against which nothing stands but the great capacity of men to start something new. The tyranny of logicality begins with the mind's submission to logic as a never-ending process, on which man relies in order to engender his thoughts. By this submission, he surrenders his inner freedom as he surrenders his freedom of movement when he bows down to an outward tyranny. Freedom as an inner capacity of man is identical with the capacity to begin, just as freedom as a political reality is identical with a space of movement between men. Over the beginning, no logic, no cogent deduction can have any power, because its chain presupposes, in the form of a premise, the beginning. As terror is needed lest with the birth of each new human being a new beginning arise and raise its voice in the world, so the self-coercive force of logicality is mobilized lest anybody ever start thinking—which as the freest and purest of all human activities is the very opposite of the compulsory process of deduction. Totalitarian government can be safe only to the extent that it can mobilize man's own will power in order to force him into that gigantic movement of History or Nature which supposedly uses mankind as its material and knows neither birth nor death.

The compulsion of total terror on one side, which, with its iron band, presses masses of isolated men together *and* supports them in a world which has become a wilderness for them, and the self-coercive force of logical deduction on the other, which prepares each individual in his lonely isolation against all others, correspond to each other and need each other in order to set the terror-ruled movement into motion and keep it moving. Just as terror, even in its pre-total, merely tyrannical form ruins all relationships between men, so the self-compulsion of ideological thinking ruins all relationships with reality. The preparation has succeeded when people have lost contact with their fellow men as well as the reality around them; for together with these contacts, men lose the capacity of both experience and thought. The ideal subject of totalitarian rule is not the convinced Nazi or the convinced Communist, but people for whom the distinction between fact and fiction (i.e., the reality of experience) and the distinction between true and false (i.e., the standards of thought) no longer exist.

The question we raised at the start of these considerations and to which we now return is what kind of basic experience in the living-together of men permeates a form of government whose essence is terror and whose principle of action is the logicality of ideological thinking. That such a combination was never used before in the varied forms of political domination is obvious. Still, the basic experience on which it rests must be human and known to men, insofar as even this most "original" of all political bodies has been devised by, and is somehow answering the needs of, men.

It has frequently been observed that terror can rule absolutely only over men who are isolated against each other and that, therefore, one of the primary concerns of all tyrannical government is to bring this isolation about. Isolation may be the beginning of terror; it certainly is its most fertile ground; it always is its result. This isolation is, as it were, pretotalitarian; its hallmark is impotence insofar as power always comes from men acting together, "acting in concert" (Burke); isolated men are powerless by definition.

Isolation and impotence, that is the fundamental inability to act at all, have always been characteristic of tyrannies. Political contacts between men are severed in tyrannical government and the human capacities for action and power are frustrated. But not all contacts between men are broken and not all human capacities destroyed. The whole sphere of private life with the capacities for experience, fabrication and thought are left intact. We know that the iron band of total terror leaves no space for such private life and that the self-coercion of totalitarian logic destroys man's capacity for experience and thought just as certainly as his capacity for action.

What we call isolation in the political sphere, is called loneliness in the sphere of social intercourse. Isolation and loneliness are not the same. I can be isolated—that is in a situation in which I cannot act, because there is nobody who will act with me—without being lonely; and I can be lonely—that is in a situation in which I as a person feel myself deserted by all human companionship—without being isolated. Isolation is that impasse into which men are driven when the political sphere of their lives, where they act together in the pursuit of a common concern, is destroyed. Yet isolation, though destructive of power and the capacity for action, not only leaves intact but is required for all so-called productive activities of men. Man insofar as he is *homo faber* tends to isolate himself with his work, that is to leave temporarily the realm of politics. Fabrication (*poiesis*, the making of things), as distinguished from action (*praxis*) on one hand and sheer labor on the other, is always performed in a certain isolation from common concerns, no matter whether the result is a piece of craftsmanship or of art. In isolation, man remains in contact with the world as the human artifice; only when the most elementary forms of human creativity, which is the capacity to add something of one's own to the common world, are destroyed, isolation becomes altogether unbearable. This can happen in a world whose chief values are dictated by labor, that is where all human activities have been transformed into laboring. Under such conditions, only the sheer effort of labor which is the effort to keep alive is left and the relationship with the world as a human artifice is broken. Isolated man who lost his place in the political realm of action is deserted by the world of things as well, if he is no longer recognized as *homo faber* but treated as an *animal laborans* whose necessary "metabolism with nature" is of concern to no one. Isolation then becomes loneliness. Tyranny based on isolation generally leaves the productive capacities of man intact; a tyranny over "laborers," however, as for instance the rule over slaves in antiquity, would automatically be a rule over lonely, not only isolated, men and tend to be totalitarian.

While isolation concerns only the political realm of life, loneliness concerns human life as a whole. Totalitarian government, like all tyrannies, certainly could not exist without destroying the public realm of life, that is, without destroying, by isolating men, their political capacities. But totalitarian domination as a form of government is new in that it is not content with this isolation and destroys private life as well. It bases itself on loneliness, on the experience of not belonging to the world at all, which is among the most radical and desperate experiences of man.

Loneliness, the common ground for terror, the essence of totalitarian government, and for ideology or logicality, the preparation of its executioners and victims, is closely connected with uprootedness and superfluousness which have been the curse of modern masses since the beginning of the industrial revolution and have become acute with the rise of imperialism at the end of the last century and the break-down of political institutions and social traditions in our own time. To be uprooted means to have no place in the world, recognized and guaranteed by others; to be superfluous means not to belong to the world at all. Uprootedness can be the preliminary condition for superfluousness, just as isolation can (but must not) be the preliminary condition for loneliness. Taken in itself, without consideration of its recent historical causes and its new role in politics, loneliness is at the same time contrary to the basic requirements of the human condition *and* one of the fundamental experiences of every human life. Even the experience of the materially and sensually given world depends upon my being in contact with other men, upon our *common* sense which regulates and controls all other senses and without which each of us would be enclosed in his own particularity of sense data which in themselves are unreliable and treacherous. Only because we have common sense, that is only because not one man, but men in the plural inhabit the earth can we trust our immediate sensual experience. Yet, we have only to remind ourselves that one day we shall have to leave this common world which will go on as before and for whose continuity we are superfluous in order to realize loneliness, the experience of being abandoned by everything and everybody.

Loneliness is not solitude. Solitude requires being alone whereas loneliness shows itself most sharply in company with others. Apart from a few stray remarks—usually framed in a paradoxical mood like Cato's statement (reported by Cicero, *De Re Publica*, I, 17): *numquam minus solum esse quam cum solus esset*, "never was he less alone than when he was alone," or never was he less lonely than when he was in solitude—it seems that Epictetus, the emancipated slave philosopher of Greek origin, was the first to distinguish between loneliness and solitude. His discovery, in a way, was accidental, his chief interest being neither solitude nor loneliness, but being alone (*monos*) in the sense of absolute independence. As Epictetus sees it (*Dissertationes*, Book 3, ch. 13) the lonely man (*eremos*) finds himself surrounded by others with whom he cannot establish contact or to whose hostility he is exposed. The solitary man, on the contrary, is alone and therefore "can be together with himself" since men have the capacity of "talking with themselves." In solitude, in other words, I am "by myself," together with my self, and therefore two-in-one, whereas in loneliness I am actually one, deserted by all others. All thinking, strictly speaking, is done in solitude and is a dialogue between me and myself; but this dialogue of the two-in-one does not lose contact with the world of my fellow-men because they are represented in the self with whom I lead the dialogue of thought. The problem of solitude is that this two-in-one needs the others in order to become one again: one unchangeable individual whose identity can never be mistaken for that of any other. For the confirmation of my identity I depend entirely upon other people; and it is the great saving grace of companionship for solitary men that it makes them "whole" again, saves them from the dialogue of thought in which one remains always equivocal, restores the identity which makes them speak with the single voice of one unexchangeable person.

Solitude can become loneliness; this happens when all by myself I am deserted by my own self. Solitary men have always been in danger of loneliness, when they can no longer find the redeeming grace of companionship to save them from duality and equivocality and doubt. Historically, it seems as though this danger became sufficiently great to be noticed by others and recorded by history only in the nineteenth century. It showed itself clearly when philosophers, for whom alone solitude is a way of life and a condition of work, were no longer content with the fact that "philosophy is only for the few" and began to insist that nobody "understands" them. Characteristic in this respect is the anecdote reported from Hegel's deathbed which hardly could have been told of any great philosopher before him: "Nobody has understood me except one; and he also misunderstood." Conversely, there is always the chance that a lonely man finds himself and starts the thinking dialogue of solitude. This seems to have happened to Nietzsche in Sils Maria when he conceived of *Zarathustra*. In two poems ("Sils Maria" and "Aus hohen Bergen") he tells of the empty expectation and the yearning waiting of the lonely until suddenly *"um Mittag wars, da wurde Eins zu Zwei… Nun feiern wir, vereinten Siegs gewiss,/ das Fest der Feste;/ Freund Zarathustra kam, der Gast der Gäste!"* ("Noon was, when One became Two…Certain of united victory we celebrate the feast of feasts; friend Zarathustra came, the guest of guests.")

What makes loneliness so unbearable is the loss of one's own self which can be realized in solitude, but confirmed in its identity only by the trusting and trustworthy company of my equals. In this situation, man loses trust in himself as the partner of his thoughts and that elementary confidence in the world which is necessary to make experiences at all. Self and world, capacity for thought and experience are lost at the same time.

The only capacity of the human mind which needs neither the self nor the other nor the world in order to function safely and which is as independent of experience as it is of thinking is the ability of logical reasoning whose premise is the self-evident. The elementary rules of cogent evidence, the truism that two and two equals four cannot be perverted even under the conditions of absolute loneliness. It is the only reliable "truth" human beings can fall back upon once they have lost the mutual guarantee, the common sense, men need in order to experience and live and know their way in a common world. But this "truth" is empty or rather no truth at all, because it does not reveal anything. (To define consistency as truth as some modern logicians do means to deny the existence of truth.) Under the conditions of loneliness, therefore, the self-evident is no longer just a means of the intellect and begins to be productive, to develop its own lines of "thought." That thought processes characterized by strict self-evident logicality, from which apparently there is no escape, have some connection with loneliness was once noticed by Luther (whose experiences in the phenomena of solitude and loneliness probably were second to no one's and who once dared to say that "there must be a God because man needs one being whom he can trust") in a little-known remark on the Bible text "it is not good that man should be alone": A lonely man, says Luther, "always deduces one thing from the other and thinks everything to the worst." (*"Ein solcher (sc. einsamer) Mensch folgert immer eins aus dem andern und denkt alles zum Argsten."* In: *Erbauliche Schriften*, "Warum die Einsamkeit zu fliehen?") The famous extremism of totalitarian movements, far from having anything to do with true radicalism, consists indeed in this "thinking everything to the worst," in this deducing process which always arrives at the worst possible conclusions.

What prepares men for totalitarian domination in the nontotalitarian world is the fact that loneliness, once a borderline experience usually suffered in certain marginal social conditions like old age, has become an everyday experience of the ever-growing masses of our century. The merciless process into which totalitarianism drives and organizes the masses looks like a suicidal escape from this reality. The "ice-cold reasoning" and the "mighty tentacle" of dialectics which "seizes you as in a vise" appears like a last support in a world where nobody is reliable and nothing can be relied upon. It is the inner coercion whose only content is the strict avoidance of contradictions that seems to confirm a man's identity outside all relationships with others. It fits him into the iron band of terror even when he is alone, and totalitarian domination tries never to leave him alone except in the extreme situation of solitary confinement. By destroying all space between men and pressing men against each other, even the productive potentialities of isolation are annihilated; by teaching and glorifying the logical reasoning of loneliness where man knows that he will be utterly lost if ever he lets go of the first premise from which the whole process is being started, even the slim chances that loneliness may be transformed into solitude and logic into thought are obliterated.

If it is true that tyranny bears the germs of its own destruction because it is based upon powerlessness which is the negation of man's political condition, then, one is tempted to predict the downfall of totalitarian domination without outside interference, because it rests on the one human experience which is the negation of man's social condition. Yet, even if this analogy were valid—and there are reasons to doubt it—it would operate only after the full realization of totalitarian government which is possible only after the conquest of the earth.

Apart from such considerations—which as predictions are of little avail and less consolation—there remains the fact that the crisis of our time and its central experience have brought forth an entirely new form of government which as a potentiality and an ever-present danger is only too likely to stay with us from now on, just as other forms of government which came about at different historical moments and rested on different fundamental experiences have stayed with mankind regardless of temporary defeats—monarchies, and republics, tyrannies, dictatorships and despotism.

But there remains also the truth that every end in history necessarily contains a new beginning; this beginning is the promise, the only "message" which the end can ever produce. Beginning, before it becomes a historical event, is the supreme capacity of man; politically, it is identical with man's freedom. *Initium ut esset homo creatus est*—"that a beginning be made man was created" said Augustine. (*Civitas Dei, Book* 12, ch. 20) This beginning is guaranteed by each new birth; it is indeed every man.

J. ROBERT OPPENHEIMER

"The Sciences and Man's Community" (1954)

The explosion of two atomic bombs over Japan in August 1945 suddenly made J. Robert Oppenheimer (1903–67) the most famous scientist in the world, with the exception only of Albert Einstein. Oppenheimer was dubbed by the press as "the Father of the Atomic Bomb" for having led the team of scientists and engineers that created the new weapon. Oppenheimer's standing as an icon and as a source of wisdom in an apparently science-defined era was sustained during the postwar years when, while serving as the chief science advisor to the government of the United States, he proved to be a compelling voice in public debates about the meaning of the scientific enterprise. The essay reprinted here exemplifies his vindication of science's potential to contribute to a more humane and democratic future. Oppenheimer's other writings in this genre are collected in a posthumous volume edited by Freeman Dyson, *Atom and Void: Essays on Science and Community* (Princeton, 1980).

In 1954 Oppenheimer was purged on the basis of extravagantly manipulated accounts of his communist connections prior to his entry into government service. The purge took the form of a withdrawal of a "security clearance" which was required for anyone advising the government on the science and technology of weapons. Oppenheimer's mistreatment soon became one of the most discussed examples of the zealotry and recklessness of the McCarthy Era. In truth, Oppenheimer had been very close to the communist movement, but the many scholarly studies of his life and career establish that he cut off his communist connections when he joined the bomb project in 1942. Oppenheimer was not among the several participants in that project who passed classified information to the Soviet Union. The historical record shows that Oppenheimer, while often imperious and incautious, was indeed an American patriot.

The best of the many biographies of Oppenheimer is Kai Bird and Martin J. Sherwin, *American Prometheus: The Triumph and Tragedy of J. Robert Oppenheimer* (New York, 2005). Detailed studies of many aspects of Oppenheimer's career, written on the occasion of the centennial of his birth, are collected in Cathryn Carson and David A. Hollinger, eds., *Reappraising Oppenheimer: Centennial Studies and Reflections* (Berkeley, 2005). A valuable account of Oppenheimer's role as a public commentator on issues in science's relation to culture is Charles Thorpe, *Oppenheimer: The Tragic Intellect* (New York, 2006). An excellent study of Oppenheimer's complicated political and personal relationships with fellow physicists Edward Teller and Ernest O. Lawrence is Greg Herken, *Brotherhood of the Bomb* (New York, 2002).

Oppenheimer spent the first half of his career at the University of California at Berkeley, where he, along with Teller and Lawrence, led in the development of the premier physics department in the world. In 1947 Oppenheimer left Berkeley for Princeton, New Jersey, where he served as director of the Institute for Advanced Study until his death twenty years later. A man of broad interests in the arts and humanities as well as science, Oppenheimer became an emblem for his generation's hope that the sciences and the arts could function harmoniously. He was known for the frequency with which he quoted the poetry of John Donne, and for his ability to offer his own translations from Sanskrit, the classical literature of which he studied while a professor of physics at Berkeley. Oppenheimer's humanistic as well as his scientific and political engagements are themes of *Dr. Atomic,* the opera about his life written by composer John Adams in 2005.

The house called "science"...is a vast house indeed. It does not appear to have been built upon any plan but to have grown as a great city grows. There is no central chamber, no one corridor from which all others debouch. All about the periphery men are at work studying the vast reaches of space and the state of affairs billions of years ago; studying the intricate and subtle but wonderfully meet mechanisms by which life proliferates, alters, and endures; studying the reach of the mind and its ways of learning; digging deep into the atoms and the atoms within atoms and their unfathomed order. It is a house so vast that none of us know it, and even the most fortunate have seen most rooms only from the outside or by a fleeting passage, as in a king's palace open to visitors. It is a house so vast that there is not and need not be complete concurrence on where its chambers stop and those of the neighboring mansions begin.

It is not arranged in a line nor a square nor a circle nor a pyramid, but with a wonderful randomness suggestive of unending growth and improvisation. Not many people live in the house, relatively speaking—perhaps if we count all its chambers and take residence requirements quite lightly, one tenth of one per cent, of all the people in this world—probably, by any reasonable definition, far fewer. And even those who live here live elsewhere also, live in houses where the rooms are not labelled atomic theory or genetics or the internal constitution of the stars, but quite different names like power and production and evil and beauty and history and children and the word of God.

We go in and out; even the most assiduous of us is not bound to this vast structure. One thing we find throughout the house: there are no locks; there are no shut doors; wherever we go there are the signs and usually the words of welcome. It is an open house, open to all comers.

The discoveries of science, the new rooms in this great house, have changed the way men think of things outside its walls. We have some glimmering now of the depth in time and the vastness in space of the physical world we live in. An awareness of how long our history and how immense our cosmos touches us even in simple earthly deliberations. We have learned from the natural history of the earth and from the story of evolution to have a sense of history, of time and change. We learn to talk of ourselves, and of the nature of the world and its reality as not wholly fixed in a silent quiet moment, but as unfolding with novelty and alteration, decay and new growth. We have understood something of the inner harmony and beauty of strange primitive cultures, and through this see the qualities of our own life in an altered perspective, and recognize its accidents as well as its inherent necessities. We are, I should think, not patriots less but patriots very differently for loving what is ours and understanding a little of the love of others for their lands and ways. We have begun to understand that it is not only in his rational life that man's psyche is intelligible, that even in what may appear to be his least rational actions and sentiments we may discover a new order. We have the beginnings of an understanding of what it is in man, and more in simple organisms, that is truly heritable, and rudimentary clues as to how the inheritance occurs....

We have seen that in the atomic world we have been led by experience to use descriptions and ideas that apply to the large-scale world of matter, to the familiar world of our schoolday physics; ideas like the position of a body and its acceleration and its impulse and the forces acting on it; ideas like wave and interference; ideas like cause and probability. But what is new, what was not anticipated a half-century ago, is that, though to an

Source: J. Robert Oppenheimer, *Atoms and Void* (Princeton: Princeton University Press, 1989), 64–75.

atomic system there is a potential applicability of one or another of these ideas, in any real situation only some of these ways of description can be actual. This is because we need to take into account not merely the atomic system we are studying, but the means we use in observing it, and the fitness of these experimental means for defining and measuring selected properties of the system. All such ways of observing are needed for the whole experience of the atomic world; all but one are excluded in any actual experience. In the specific instance, there is a proper and consistent way to describe what the experience is; what it implies; what it predicts and thus how to deal with its consequences. But any such specific instance excludes by its existence the application of other ideas, other modes of prediction, other consequences. They are, we say, complementary to one another; atomic theory is in part an account of these descriptions and in part an understanding of the circumstances to which one applies, or another or another.

And so it is with man's life. He may be any of a number of things; he will not be all of them. He may be well versed, he may be a poet, he may be a creator in one or more than one science; he will not be all kinds of man or all kinds of scientist; and he will be lucky if he has a bit of familiarity outside the room in which he works.

So it is with the great antinomies that through the ages have organized and yet dis-united man's experience: the antinomy between the ceaseless change and wonderful novelty and the perishing of all earthly things, and the eternity which inheres in every happening; in the antinomy between growth and order, between the spontaneous and changing and irregular and the symmetrical and balanced; in the related antinomy between freedom and necessity; between action, the life of the will, and observation and analysis and the life of reason; between the question "how?" and the questions "why?" and "to what end?"; between the causes that derive from natural law, from unvarying regularities in the natural world, and those other causes that express purposes and define goals and ends.

So it is in the antinomy between the individual and the community; man who is an end in himself and man whose tradition, whose culture, whose works, whose words have meaning in terms of other men and his relations to them. All our experience has shown that we can neither think, nor in any true sense live, without reference to these antinomic modes. We cannot in any sense be both the observers and the actors in any specific instance, or we shall fail properly to be either one or the other; yet we know that our life is built of these two modes, is part free and part inevitable, is part creation and part discipline, is part acceptance and part effort. We have no written rules that assign us to these ways; but we know that only folly and death of the spirit results when we deny one or the other, when we erect one as total and absolute and make the others derivative and secondary. We recognize this when we live as men. We talk to one another; we philosophize; we admire great men and their moments of greatness; we read; we study; we recognize and love in a particular act that happy union of the generally incompatible. With all of this we learn to use some reasonable part of the full register of man's resources.

We are, of course, an ignorant lot; even the best of us knows how to do only a very few things well; and of what is available in knowledge of fact, whether of science or of history, only the smallest part is in any one man's knowing.

The greatest of the changes that science has brought is the acuity of change; the greatest novelty the extent of novelty. Short of rare times of great disaster, civilizations have not known such rapid alteration in the conditions of their life, such rapid flowering of many varied sciences, such rapid changes in the ideas we have about the world and one another. What has been true in the days of a great disaster or great military defeat for one people at one time is true for all of us now, in the sense that our ends have little in common with our beginnings. Within a lifetime what we learned at school has been rendered inadequate by new discoveries and new inventions; the ways that we learn in childhood are only very meagerly adequate to the issues that we must meet in maturity.

In fact, of course, the notion of universal knowledge has always been an illusion; but it is an illusion fostered by the monistic view of the world in which a few great central truths determine in all its wonderful and amazing proliferation everything else that is true. We are not today tempted to search for these keys that unlock the whole of human knowledge and of man's experience. We know that we are ignorant; we are well taught it, and the more surely and deeply we know our own job the better able we are to appreciate the full measure of our pervasive ignorance. We know that these are inherent limits, compounded, no doubt, and exaggerated by that sloth and that complacency without which we would not be men at all.

But knowledge rests on knowledge; what is new is meaningful because it departs slightly from what was known before; this is a world of frontiers, where even the liveliest of actors or observers will be absent most of the time from most of them. Perhaps this sense was not so sharp in the village—that village which we have learned a little about but probably do not understand too well—the village of slow change and isolation and fixed culture which evokes our nostalgia even if not our full comprehension. Perhaps in the villages men were not so lonely; perhaps they found in each other a fixed community, a fixed and only slowly growing store of knowledge—a single world. Even that we may doubt, for there seem to be always in the culture of such times and places vast domains of mystery, if not unknowable, then imperfectly known, endless and open.

As for ourselves in these times of change, of ever-increasing knowledge, of collective power and individual impotence, of heroism and of drudgery, of progress and of tragedy, we too are brothers. And if we, who are the inheritors of two millennia of Christian tradition, understand that for us we have come to be brothers second by being children first, we know that in vast parts of the world where there has been no Christian tradition, and with men who never have been and never may be Christian in faith there is nevertheless a bond of brotherhood. We know this not only because of the almost universal ideal of human brotherhood and human community; we know it at first hand from the more modest, more diverse, more fleeting associations which are the substance of our life. The ideal of brotherhood, the ideal of fraternity in which all men, wicked and virtuous, wretched and fortunate, are banded together has its counterpart in the experience of communities, not ideal, not universal, imperfect, impermanent, as different from the ideal and as reminiscent of it as are the ramified branches of science from the ideal of a unitary, all-encompassing science of the eighteenth century.

Each of us knows from his own life how much even a casual and limited association of men goes beyond him in knowledge, in understanding, in humanity, and in power. Each of us, from a friend or a book or by concerting of the little we know with what others know, has broken the iron circle of his frustration. Each of us has asked help and been given it, and within our measure each of us has offered it. Each of us knows the great new freedom sensed almost as a miracle, that men banded together for some finite purpose experience from the power of their common effort. We are likely to remember the times of the last war, where the common danger brought forth in soldier, in worker, in scientist, and engineer a host of new experiences of the power and the comfort in even bleak undertakings, of common, concerted, co-operative life. Each of us knows how much he has been transcended by the group of which he has been or is a part; each of us has felt the solace of other men's knowledge to stay his own ignorance, of other men's wisdom to stay his folly, of other men's courage to answer his doubts or his weakness.

These are the fluid communities, some of long duration when circumstances favored—like the political party or many a trade union—some fleeting and vivid, encompassing in the time of their duration a moment only of the member's life; and in our world at least they are ramified and improvised, living and dying, growing and falling off almost as a form of life itself. This may be more true of the United States than of any other country. Certainly the bizarre and comical aspects impressed de Tocqueville more than a century ago when he visited our land and commented on the readiness with which men would band together: to improve the planting of a town, or for political reform, or for the pursuit or inter-exchange of knowledge, or just for the sake of banding together, because they liked one another or disliked someone else. Circumstances may have exaggerated the role of the societies, of the fluid and yet intense communities in the United States; yet these form a common pattern for our civilization. It brought men together in the Royal Society and in the French Academy and in the Philosophical Society that Franklin founded, in family, in platoon, on a ship, in the laboratory, in almost everything but a really proper club.

If we err today—and I think we do—it is in expecting too much of knowledge from the individual and too much of synthesis from the community. We tend to think of these communities, no less than of the larger brotherhood of man, as made up of individuals, as composed of them as an atom is of its ingredients. We think similarly of general laws and broad ideas as made up of the instances which illustrate them, and from an observation of which we may have learned them.

Yet this is not the whole. The individual event, the act, goes far beyond the general law. It is a sort of intersection of many generalities, harmonizing them in one instance as they cannot be harmonized in general. And we as men are not only the ingredients of our communities; we are their intersection, making a harmony which does not exist between the communities except as we, the individual men, may create it and reveal it. So much of what we think, our acts, our judgments of beauty and of right and wrong, come to us from our fellow men that what would be left were we to take all this away would be neither recognizable nor human. We are men because we are part of, but not because only part of, communities; and the attempt to understand man's brotherhood in terms only of the individual man is as little likely to describe our world as is the attempt to describe general laws as the summary of their instances. These are indeed two complementary views, neither reducible to the other, no more reducible than is the electron as wave to the electron as particle.

And this is the mitigant of our ignorance. It is true that none of us will know very much; and most of us will see the end of our days without understanding in all its detail and beauty the wonders uncovered even in a single branch of a single science. Most of us will not even know, as a member of any intimate circle, anyone who has such knowledge; but it is also true that, although we are sure not to know everything and rather likely not to know very much, we can know anything that is known to man, and may, with luck and sweat, even find out some things that have not before been known to him. This possibility, which, as a universal condition of man's life is new, represents today a high and determined hope, not yet a reality; it is for us in England and in the United States not wholly remote or unfamiliar. It is one of the manifestations of our belief in equality, that belief which could perhaps better be described as a commitment to unparalleled diversity and unevenness in the distribution of attainments, knowledge, talent, and power.

This open access to knowledge, these unlocked doors and signs of welcome, are a mark of a freedom as fundamental as any. They give a freedom to resolve difference by converse, and, where converse does not unite, to let tolerance compose diversity. This would appear to be a freedom barely compatible with modern political tyranny. The multitude of communities, the free association for converse or for common purpose, are acts of creation. It is not merely that without them the individual is the poorer; without them a part of human life, not more nor less fundamental than the individual, is foreclosed. It is a cruel and humorless sort of pun that so powerful a present form of modern tyranny should call itself by the very name of a belief in community, by a word "communism" which in other times evoked memories of villages and village inns and of artisans concerting their skills, and of men of learning content with anonymity. But perhaps only a malignant end can follow the systematic belief that all communities are one community; that all truth is one truth; that all experience is compatible with all other; that total knowledge is possible; that all that is potential can exist as actual. This is not man's fate; this is not his path; to force him on it makes him resemble not that divine image of the all-knowing and all-powerful but the helpless, iron-bound prisoner of a dying world. The open society, the unrestricted access to knowledge, the unplanned and uninhibited association of men for its furtherance—these are what may make a vast, complex, ever-growing, ever-changing, ever more specialized and expert technological world nevertheless a world of human community.

So it is with the unity of science—that unity that is far more a unity of comparable dedication than a unity of common total understanding. This heartening phrase, "the unity of science," often tends to evoke a wholly false picture, a picture of a few basic truths, a few critical techniques, methods, and ideas, from which all discoveries and understanding of science derive; a sort of central exchange, access to which will illuminate the atoms and the galaxies, the genes and the sense organs. The unity of science is based rather on just such a community as I have described. All parts of it are open to all of us, and this is no merely formal invitation. The history of science is rich in example of the fruitfulness of bringing two sets of techniques, two sets of ideas, developed in separate contexts for the pursuit of new truth, into touch with one another. The sciences fertilize each other; they grow by contact and by common enterprise. Once again, this means that the scientist may profit from learning about any other science; it does not mean that he must learn about them all. It means that the unity is a potential unity, the unity of the things that might be brought together and might throw light one on the other. It is not global or total or hierarchical.

Even in science, and even without visiting the room in its house called atomic theory, we are again and again reminded of the complementary traits in our own life, even in our own professional life. We are nothing without the work of others our predecessors, others our teachers, others our contemporaries. Even when, in the measure of our adequacy and our fullness, new insight and new order are created, we are still nothing without others. Yet we are more.

There is a similar duality in our relations to wider society. For society our work means many things: pleasure, we hope, for those who follow it; instruction for those who perhaps need it; but also and far more widely, it means a common power, a power to achieve that which could not be achieved without knowledge. It means the cure of illness and the alleviation of suffering; it means the easing of labor and the widening of the readily accessible frontiers of experience, of communication, and of instruction. It means, in an earthy way, the power of betterment—that riddled word. We are today anxiously aware that the power to change is not always necessarily good.

As new instruments of war, of newly massive terror, add to the ferocity and totality of warfare, we understand that it is a special mark and problem of our age that man's ever-present preoccupation with improving his lot, with alleviating hunger and poverty and exploitation, must be brought into harmony with the over-riding need to limit and largely to eliminate resort to organized violence between nation and nation. The increasingly expert destruction of man's spirit by the power of police, more wicked if not more awful than the ravages of nature's own hand, is another such power, good only if never to be used.

We regard it as proper and just that the patronage of science by society is in large measure based on the increased power which knowledge gives. If we are anxious that the power so given and so obtained be used with wisdom and with love of humanity, that is an anxiety we share with almost everyone. But we also know how little of the deep new knowledge which has altered the face of the world, which has changed—and increasingly and ever more profoundly must change—man's views of the world, resulted from a quest for practical ends or an interest in exercising the power that knowledge gives. For most of us, in most of those moments when we were most free of corruption, it has been the beauty of the world of nature and the strange and compelling harmony of its order, that has sustained, inspirited, and led us. That also is as it should be. And if the forms in which society provides and exercises its patronage leave these incentives strong and secure, new knowledge will never stop as long as there are men.

We know that our work is rightly both an instrument and an end. A great discovery is a thing of beauty; and our faith—our binding, quiet faith—is that knowledge is good and good in itself. It is also an instrument; it is an instrument for our successors, who will use it to probe elsewhere and more deeply; it is an instrument for technology, for the practical arts, and for man's affairs. So it is with us as scientists; so it is with us as men. We are at once instrument and end, discoverers and teachers, actors and observers. We understand, as we hope others understand, that in this there is a harmony between knowledge in the sense of science, that specialized and general knowledge which it is our purpose to uncover, and the community of man. We, like all men, are among those who bring a little light to the vast unending darkness of man's life and world. For us as for all men, change and eternity, specialization and unity, instrument and final purpose, community and individual man alone, complementary each to the other, both require and define our bonds and our freedom.

PETER F. DRUCKER

"Innovation—The New Conservatism?"
(1959)

Although most widely known as a guru of business management, Peter F. Drucker (1909–2005) was an ambitious theorist of the human condition and of the circumstances of modernity. While many conservatives of his generation focused on the virtues of the market, Drucker concentrated instead on the corporation and on the virtues of economic planning. Drucker saw the corporation as an institution basic to society, and capable of harmonizing the interests of management and workers. Drucker accepted much of the liberal left's critique of the industrial order, but rejected most social democratic programs for reforming it. He was critical of the New Deal but supported some of its measures, including the Tennessee Valley Authority, excoriated by more market-oriented conservatives. Drucker looked to enlightened corporate management to recognize the needs of workers for a meaningful life and for a substantial share of responsibility for running a business. Indeed, Drucker believed that corporations could take over many functions performed by the state. In the essay reprinted here, Drucker distinguishes between the sorts of planning (usually done by governments) that stifle innovation by excessively detailed regulation, and the planning that divides authority among a variety of agents in different economic locales. Drucker invokes a pantheon of great conservative theorists at the end of this selection, but his style of conservatism was grounded in a social vision quite different from the more rigidly individualist orientation of most prominent American conservatives of his generation, including Milton Friedman and Ayn Rand, whose writings are also found in *The American Intellectual Tradition*.

Drucker was born in Vienna of Protestant parents, was educated in Germany, and then moved to the United States in 1934. Already a prominent theorist of business management by the time of World War II, Drucker made his most distinctive and enduring contribution in 1946 with *Concept of the Corporation* (New York, 1946). A prolific writer, Drucker eventually published thirty-nine books, several of which have been translated into more than thirty languages. Among the most popular of his later works was *The Age of Discontinuity: Guidelines to Our Changing Society* (New York, 1968). Drucker spent most of his career as a professor of management at New York University and the Claremont Graduate University in California. A great coiner of phrases, Drucker is generally credited with contributing the terms "privatization" and "knowledge workers" to our vocabulary. He was also one of the first thinkers to employ the term "postmodern."

The most discerning and informative analysis of Drucker's ideas and their place in intellectual history is Nils Gilman, "The Prophet of Post-Fordism: Peter Drucker and the Legitimation of the Corporation," in Nelson Lichtenstein, ed., *American Capitalism: Social Thought and Political Economy in the 20th Century* (Philadelphia, 2006), 109–33. See also Daniel Immerwahr, "Polanyi in the United States: Peter Drucker, Karl Polanyi, and the Midcentury Critique of Economic Society," *Journal of the History of Ideas,* 70 (July 2009), 445–66. Drucker tells his own life story in an autobiography, *Adventures of a Bystander* (New York, 1980).

Innovation is risk. Present resources are committed to future, highly uncertain results. Present action and behavior are subordinated to the potential of an as yet unknown and uncomprehended future reality.

Innovation can best be defined as man's attempt to create order, in his own mind and in the universe around him, by taking risk and creating risk. It can be defined as the organized, indeed deliberate, seeking of risk to replace both the blind chance of premodern times (as symbolized in the Renaissance belief in *Fortuna* as the presiding genius of human destiny) and the certainty of the more recent but still outdated belief in inevitable progress, both chanceless and riskless.

This is bold, very bold. It entails not just one heavy risk, but three: the risk of being overtaken by innovation, which one might call the risk of exposure; the risk of failure of the innovating attempt; and, heaviest of all, the risk of innovation's success.

Innovation can change, almost overnight, the established order, render obsolete what only yesterday seemed impregnable, make dominant what only yesterday was negligible.

Economists tell us that the large business enterprise of today has a built-in momentum that may give it an advantage way beyond anything deserved by efficiency or managerial excellence, and may keep it strong, powerful and big long after it has ceased to be aggressive and competitive. There is something in this. Yet, of the hundred largest manufacturing companies in the United States only thirty years ago, more than half have disappeared from the list today. Some have vanished altogether, others have fallen way behind. Their places have largely been taken by companies which, thirty years ago, either did not exist at all or were insignificant. The newcomers owe their present position not to financial manipulation but to new technology, new processes or new products—that is, to innovation.

The risk of exposure in innovation changes the nature of international politics and international economics. There is always present the possibility of a sudden landslide that can completely alter the international landscape and the position and balance of forces. This might be a change in the international economy, in international resource-geography or transportation-geography. It might be a change in political constellation, in military or industrial balance of power, or national policy—all capable of changing, almost overnight, the international position of a whole country, even of the biggest and mightiest.

Such dramatic changes have of course occurred throughout history—but they came fairly infrequently. The cause may have been that mysterious historical event, one nation's decline in vigor or another nation's sudden outburst of creative energy. It may have been foreign invasion or a sudden shift in trade routes. Once in a long while it was the result of new technology, especially military technology. But what was rare "turning point" in the past has now become ever-present danger. What happened as by-product is now capable of being purposeful goal. What was *Fortuna,* in other words, is now risk.

This not only applies to a country internationally. It applies fully as much to institutions, groups and forces within a country, within an economy. Each technology, each industry, each business lives under the risk of being made obsolete without warning, of being destroyed or damaged by innovation, technological or social.

This risk cannot be avoided. On the contrary, any attempt to prevent innovation, even any attempt to ignore it, can only make the risk greater. Nor can the risk be shrugged off as "all in the day's work." It must be accepted and provided for.

Source: Peter F. Drucker, *Landmarks of Tomorrow* (New York: Harper, 1959), 46–59.

Little needs to be said about the second risk in innovation, that of failure.

Innovation must anticipate the future and must commit resources, efforts and destinies to this anticipation. But no human being can possibly predict the future, let alone control it. Innovation must therefore have a high failure rate. It may fail because the innovation was faulty in vision, insufficient in design or premature in timing. It may fail because of inability to produce the planned results or to produce them in the available time. Or—perhaps the cruelest but also the most common risk—the innovating attempt may succeed brilliantly, only to be obsolete by the time it is completed, overtaken by events, by the growth of knowledge, or simply no longer appropriate. Thus very few of the main lines of medical research that would have appeared to a well-informed man as most important and most promising thirty years ago have contributed much to the great medical advances since.

These two risks lead to a paradoxical conclusion. More and speeded-up innovation alone can protect against the risk of being overtaken by the innovation of others. But this necessity only commits even more resources to a gamble in which failure is more probable than success.

Yet, both the risk of exposure and the risk of failure are minor compared to the third risk: that of the success of innovation.

Innovation does not create new laws of nature. It is not even primarily concerned with finding such laws. It aims, however, at directing and channeling the forces of nature according to human needs and human vision. It aims furthermore at directing and channeling the values, beliefs, institutions and human resources of society according to those needs and that vision.

What impact beyond the desired one will a successful innovation have? What new and unexpected changes will it produce? What will it do to the fabric of society, its beliefs, its bonds of community?

A minor example: The development of effective insecticides such as DDT was rightly considered a great achievement. It made possible the truly innovating vision of control of disease-bearing and destructive pests. But unexpectedly, the new insecticides killed beneficial insects as effectively as destructive ones, bees as well as malaria-bearing mosquitoes. This unforeseen result not only threatens bird life deprived of its food; it threatens all the trees and flowers—among them our major fruit trees—dependent on insects for pollination.

Innovation is thus not only opportunity. It is not only risk. It is first and foremost responsibility. No one is responsible for chance; no one can do anything about it. One can only welcome inevitable progress or bemoan it; at most one can attempt to delay it. But innovation is deliberate choice; and we are responsible for its consequences.

The essential choices are between values, in respect both to aim and to means. Precisely because it makes technology and social structure open-ended, innovation poses the continuous question what its values are. Should we aim at strengthening our traditions or at weakening them? Should we aim high or be expedient?

There may be areas where the values are given and outside the innovating decisions. Industrialists in a free economy might claim that they must and do operate under an objective rule of profitability. Industrialists in a socialist economy might similarly claim that production determines their decisions. Neither is a clear and unambiguous measure. Profitability over the long run is, for instance, something quite different from profits this year or next; the difference is one of basic values. Similarly production may be measured by units, value, quality or cost—and all Soviet sources indicate that there is as much disagreement over the concrete meaning of production in that country as there is in a free economy over profitability.

But inevitable to all social innovation is a value decision in respect to the objective, the specifications selected, the institution built and the methods chosen. Every social innovation—whether by government or school district, business or labor union—expresses a view of what man and society are and what they ought to be.

Innovation is therefore always ethics—as much as it is intellectual process and aesthetic perception. It needs ethics...as much to decide what value considerations are relevant as to decide which are right. Traditional ethics, regardless of school, looked for the right response to a given situation. We need ethics today that concern themselves with the problems of creating the right situation. Ethics, most philosophers would agree, have been rather arid since Spinoza, though hardly for want of books written on the subject. The climate of "inevitable progress" could not have been congenial to a discipline that assumes choice to be both relevant and rational. Now, perhaps, we can expect new fundamental and fruitful work in ethics—we certainly need it.

The risks and responsibilities of innovation require themselves major innovations. The first risk, that of exposure to innovation, makes planning necessary. The second risk, that of failure in innovation, prohibits, however, any *central* planning and demands a competing multiplicity of local plans. The third risk, that of the impact of successful innovation, demands a new attitude to change, a new politics of change in society. It demands essentially a new conservatism.... The alternative to planning by centralized fiat is not "no plan." It is *planning by self-control.*

Wherever we look today, we see planning. Long-range planning is the central theme of today's businessman. Every day my mail contains yet another speech or article on the long-range planning of a well-known company—in English, in German, in French, in Italian, in Dutch, in Spanish or Portuguese or in Japanese. Company after company is setting up a long-range planning department. And so is city after city.

Most universities work on a long-range plan. So do hospitals and school districts, research laboratories, professional societies, newspapers and magazines, international bodies, the military, political parties, government departments and law firms. Indeed long-range planning threatens to become something of a fad. There is more than a grain of truth in the Washington gibe: "We don't want to do the job so let's set up another long-range planning study."

In many cases planning is still weak in its understanding of the job and of the methods used. There is the tendency to confuse planning with the futile attempt to outguess the fluctuations of the business cycle. There is the tendency to try to do planning by projecting the trends of the past into the future whereas the starting point of planning must always be the recognition that the future will be different. There is the all-too-common belief that planning eliminates risk—the most dangerous delusion of all, since planning is actually risk-creating and risk-taking.

But there is also a growing understanding of the nature and function of planning, and growing knowledge of the proper tools and methods. We are learning the difference between planning and prediction or forecast, and between what we would like to see happen and what we can try to make happen. We are learning the difference between blind gambling and rational choice among risks based on informed judgment. We are learning that the aim of planning is not to perpetuate the present but to anticipate and force the new. The purpose is innovation.

Above all we are learning that the only protection against the risk of exposure in innovation is to innovate. We can defend ourselves against the constant threat of being overtaken by innovation only by taking the offensive. The best statement of this new attitude comes perhaps from the world of business: The time to change the theory of the business on which a company operates, and to innovate in respect to its character, function, objectives, product, market and organization, is when the company is most successful and most profitable. For every theory of the business eventually becomes obsolete. If a company waits until it starts to go downhill, it has usually waited too long.

This process requires an attitude that has been far from common. It requires that rarest of human insights: the willingness to question one's own success. But it is the only attitude that can make productive—can indeed make bearable—the risk of innovation. It is easy, for instance, to think through a country's foreign policy when it has failed—any editorial writer can do that. It is much more difficult to innovate a new concept of the country's foreign policy when the present one is highly successful. Yet this is the only way to prevent failure. And the aim of long-range planning is to make effective this attitude in an organized, systematic, continuous effort of innovation.

Because of the risk of innovation our choice is not between centralized plan and no plan but between centralized plan and localized plan. But the risk of failure in innovation converts this into a choice between local plan (which alone can work) and no plan, into which central planning degenerates.

The risk of failure in innovation makes centralized planning impossible, indeed converts it into chaos and tyranny, and makes its certain outcome collapse. The odds are simply too heavy against the success of any one plan. We have to commit present resources to highly uncertain future results, stake ourselves on our ability to perceive the as yet unknown and to do the as yet impossible. Therefore we have to plan. But to expect any one such plan to come out right is folly, and so is the expectation that any one group of planners will come out right no matter how many alternative plans they develop. Elementary mathematics shows that the outcome of such a gamble must be worse than to have no plan at all and to play random chance.

At the same time the very stake in his planning forces the centralized planner to try to control everything; anything uncontrolled becomes a danger. Centralized planners would probably tend to become tyrants anyhow; absolute power always hungers for more power. But even if the planners did not want to tyrannize, centralized planning for the entire economy or for the entire society propels them inevitably toward it. The more the central plan embraces, the riskier the venture, the greater the odds against its success.

The inability to foresee, thirty years ago, the recent breakthrough areas in medicine may, at first glance, sound like an argument against organized systematic innovation. But the major breakthroughs that did occur were all the result of genuine innovation rather than of chance. The breakthroughs would not have been made if one man, or one group of men, no matter how knowledgeable, responsible or wise, had been the central planners of medical research. They were achieved only because the planning was multiple, pluralistic, autonomous, local. The example is thus both a cogent argument *against* centralized planning and a cogent argument *for* local planning.

We are concerned here with control, not with ownership, with centralized planning rather than with nationalization (though the two may tend to go together). Centralized planning by nation-wide industrial cartel—such as Roosevelt's NRA attempted—would be just as bad as centralized planning by the dictatorship of the proletariat....

Centralized planning is also possible where the objective is sharply defined, the planning period very short and the costs not very important. The best example is war. It is no accident that the very idea of planning came out of the experience of World War I, especially out of the work of the American and German War Industries Boards. Even for war, however, experience argues against centralized planning for innovation; what can be planned centrally is the use of resources available, in existence and known. One of Churchill's strengths as a wartime leader was to understand this. He centralized decisions, even on details, in his own hand. He set up complete controls over existing resources. But he encouraged, initiated, pushed and fought for decentralized, autonomous, competing planning for all innovations, technological, strategic and social.

The argument against central planning is not an argument against planning by the central organ—whether the government of a country, the general staff of an army or the top management of a business. On the contrary, without effective planning by the central organ, planning altogether is impossible. The central organ must plan in respect to its own jobs: foreign policy and defense in the case of a government for instance, or basic objectives, financial policy and organization structure in the case of a large business—for it too faces both the risk of exposure and the risk of failure in innovation. In addition the central organ must represent the common interest in respect to local, autonomous planning. It must co-ordinate, balance and guide. It must make the final risk-taking decisions. It must set standards of conduct and of performance. Above all it must stimulate the local organs to plan rather than to drift. But it must not be *the* planner, must not even insist on conformity in the local planning efforts, but rather encourage diversity, competition and independence.

There is plenty of room to disagree where the line should be drawn between the sphere and authority of the center in planning, and the sphere and authority of local planning. We find this disagreement in international and national affairs. It is a live issue in a university between the central administration and the faculties, departments and individual scholars, and in a large business between top management and divisions, functional staffs and individual managers or professionals. There is also plenty of room for argument over the best pattern of co-operation, competition and autonomy between the pluralist innovating efforts of a society, a government, an army, a university or a business. But the principle is simple and clear: The risk in innovation is too great to allow uniformity and centralization; it requires different, autonomous, alternative, competing, local efforts.

Despite all the ink spilled over it, central planning is no longer the real issue. More real and much more difficult is the question: how "local" should local planning be? If too small or too narrow, a local organ will have neither the vision nor the resources to plan for innovation. If too large or too diverse, it will in itself become a central planner...

What makes the question of the best unit of local planning so difficult—but also so important—is that different purposes require different definitions of what "local" means and different organs for the job. There is no formula; and there should be no uniformity.

This concept of local planning may seem disorderly, wasteful, illogical. But the greatest planner of all knows otherwise. Nature provides against the risks of life by multiplicity and competition. It would be so much more orderly if there were only one plant and one animal. But when the mighty dinosaurs succumbed to a change in environment, there were available some obscure, wretched creatures, ancestors of the present mammals, to take their place—for they had produced an apparently useless innovation: self-control of their body temperature. It would be much less wasteful if the female frog laid only two or three eggs, or if there were just one sperm cell in the human semen to fertilize the female

ovum. But rather than eliminate the overwhelming odds against the embryo frog's surviving to maturity or against the sperm's reaching the ovum, nature provides millions of
both. And it is this multiplicity, this purposeful duplication, this result-focused logic, this
cooperative competition, that is the true order.

Centralized planning was a first reaction to the new power of innovation and its new
risks. But it attempted to organize a manifestation of the post-Cartesian world-view by
Cartesian means: Centralized planning sees the world as a machine. Planning we need;
but the risk in innovation alone forbids centralized planning and demands autonomous,
competing, local innovation. Centralized planning attempts to order our search for new
vision and a new capacity of achievement on the model of mechanical order, the measure
of which is efficiency. But productive planning has to be modeled after a higher order—
that of life, the measure of which is creativity. The aim of innovation is not a static conversion of input into output but a dynamic transmutation of ignorance into knowledge and of
impotence into power. Its operational problem is not efficiency but risk.

Perhaps the most important— though the least tangible—consequence of innovation
is the new responsibility it requires. It is above all a political responsibility.

If value choice is both inevitable and meaningful, a genuine, constructive conservatism
becomes both possible and necessary. For then it becomes essential to take responsibility
for the strengthening of basic values and the observance of fundamental principles; to
demand respect for the historical roots of a society but to despise its self-glorification; to
respect one's fellow man but to know one's own weaknesses, limitations and fallibility;
to demand a high goal and to take the long view. These are traditionally the qualities of the
conservative temperament.

Conservatism found its profoundest spokesmen in the age of "inevitable progress":
Burke and Acton, John Adams, Marshall and Calhoun, Stahl and De Tocqueville. It
was the creed of great statesmen: Washington, Hamilton and Lincoln; Castlereagh and
Disraeli; Metternich. But it could not be fully effective as a political force—not even in
the countries of the Anglo-American tradition—because it either became pure reaction
or it resigned itself to the role of retarder and brake, rather than creative force. Individual
conservatives—George Washington is the great example in this country, Disraeli in
England—could rise above this by becoming great and yet truly conservative innovators.
But conservatism as such could only be an antibody (though a badly needed one). The age
belonged to the liberal, the radical, the progressive, if not to the revolutionary.

Today both liberalism and conservatism in their traditional meaning are moribund.
Indeed ideological parties are probably obsolete and certainly meaningless. And any
revival of traditional conservatism is most unlikely.

We need something new: the conservative innovator, who accepts innovation and
with it accepts, indeed asserts, responsibility for its risks and results. Precisely because
an age of innovation can no longer ask whether there should be change or even how fast,
but only argue over what it should be, aim for and do, this may well be the age of those
who believe that responsibility rather than success is the measure of man: the age of the
conservatives.

JOHN COURTNEY MURRAY

Selection from *We Hold These Truths* (1960)

No single person did more than the Jesuit priest John Courtney Murray (1904–67) to provide a theoretical basis for the more complete involvement of Catholics in the intellectual life of the United States. Murray first gained fame as a vigorous opponent of Paul Blanshard, whose *American Freedom and Catholic Power* (Boston, 1949) charged that the political culture of Catholic leadership was too authoritarian to be consistent with democratic institutions. In 1960, the year of the successful presidential campaign of the Catholic John F. Kennedy, Murray published a book constructing American democratic ideology in terms that made it seem closer to medieval Catholic doctrines than to the secular philosophers of the Enlightenment. "The American Bill of Rights," Murray insisted in the chapter of *We Hold These Truths: Catholic Reflections on the American Proposition* reprinted here, is "far more the product of Christian history" than of "eighteenth-century rationalist theory." Elsewhere, Murray elaborated an argument that carried great resonance with liberals within and beyond the Catholic community. The Spanish regime of the fascist Francisco Franco, so often defended by American Catholic thinkers of the 1940s and 1950s to the chagrin of their Protestant, Jewish, and agnostic contemporaries, was exactly opposite to true Catholic teaching; this teaching, according to Murray, was more fully expressed in the religious pluralism and sharp separation of church and state found in the United States. Murray's effort to vindicate American democracy on Christian terms bears comparison to the writings of Protestant theologian Reinhold Niebuhr.

Murray's ideas were considered subversive of Catholic authority when he first developed them in writings of the 1950s, some of which were stopped from initial publication by his superiors. But Murray's basic conception of the compatibility of Catholic faith with democratic political culture of the American variety was later to be accepted by more and more lay and clerical voices within the Catholic community of the United States. This was especially true after Vatican II, the liberalizing initiative of Pope John XXIII on which Murray himself was a formidable influence behind the scenes in Rome.

Murray's use of history was highly selective and has often been criticized as tendentious. But he brought to the study of Catholic history one genuinely historical insight that many Catholic scholars had resisted: the insight that Catholic doctrine, like other ideas and practices of human beings, changed over time. For an excellent account of Murray's historic role and of his most egregious manipulations of the historical record, see Patrick Allitt, "The Significance of John Courtney Murray," in Mary Segers, ed., *Catholic Polity and American Politics* (New Haven, 1990), 53–67. Murray is also a major character in Allitt's *Catholic Intellectuals and Conservative Politics in America, 1950–1985* (Ithaca, 1993). For probing and informative studies of Catholic intellectual life before and after Murray, see Philip Gleason, *Keeping the Faith: American Catholicism Past and Present* (Notre Dame, 1987). See also John T. McGreevy, "Thinking on One's Own: Catholicism in the American Intellectual Imagination, 1928–1960," *Journal of American History*, 84 (1997), 97–131.

As it arose in America, the problem of pluralism was unique in the modern world, chiefly because pluralism was the native condition of American society. It was not, as in Europe and in England, the result of a disruption or decay of a previously existent religious unity. This fact created the possibility of a new solution; indeed, it created a demand for a new solution. The possibility was exploited and the demand was met by the American Constitution.

The question here concerns the position of the Catholic conscience in the face of the new American solution to a problem that for centuries has troubled, and still continues to trouble, various nations and societies. A new problem has been put to the universal Church by the fact of America—by the uniqueness of our social situation, by the genius of our newly conceived constitutional system, by the lessons of our singular national history, which has molded in a special way the consciousness and temper of the American people, within whose midst the Catholic stands, sharing with his fellow citizens the same national heritage. The Catholic community faces the task of making itself intellectually aware of the conditions of its own coexistence within the American pluralistic scene. We have behind us a lengthy historical tradition of acceptance of the special situation of the Church in America, in all its differences from the situations in which the Church elsewhere finds herself. But it is a question here of pursuing the subject, not in the horizontal dimension of history but in the vertical dimension of theory....

The first truth to which the American Proposition makes appeal is stated in that landmark of Western political theory, the Declaration of Independence. It is a truth that lies beyond politics; it imparts to politics a fundamental human meaning. I mean the sovereignty of God over nations as well as over individual men. This is the principle that radically distinguishes the conservative Christian tradition of America from the Jacobin laicist tradition of Continental Europe. The Jacobin tradition proclaimed the autonomous reason of man to be the first and the sole principle of political organization. In contrast, the first article of the American political faith is that the political community, as a form of free and ordered human life, looks to the sovereignty of God as to the first principle of its organization. In the Jacobin tradition religion is at best a purely private concern, a matter of personal devotion, quite irrelevant to public affairs. Society as such, and the state which gives it legal form, and the government which is its organ of action are by definition agnostic or atheist. The statesman as such cannot be a believer, and his actions as a statesman are immune from any imperative or judgment higher than the will of the people, in whom resides ultimate and total sovereignty (one must remember that in the Jacobin tradition "the people" means "the party"). This whole manner of thought is altogether alien to the authentic American tradition.

From the point of view of the problem of pluralism this radical distinction between the American and the Jacobin traditions is of cardinal importance. The United States has had, and still has, its share of agnostics and unbelievers. But it has never known organized militant atheism on the Jacobin, doctrinaire Socialist, or Communist model; it has rejected parties and theories which erect atheism into a political principle. In 1799, the year of the Napoleonic coup d'état which overthrew the Directory and established a dictatorship in France, President John Adams stated the first of all American first principles in his remarkable proclamation of March 6:

Source: John Courtney Murray, *We Hold These Truths* (New York, 1960), 27–39, 42–43. Reprinted by permission of Rowman & Littlefield Publishing Group.

...it is also most reasonable in itself that men who are capable of social arts and relations, who owe their improvements to the social state, and who derive their enjoyments from it, should, as a society, make acknowledgements of dependence and obligation to Him who hath endowed them with these capacities and elevated them in the scale of existence by these distinctions....

President Lincoln on May 30, 1863, echoed the tradition in another proclamation:

Whereas the Senate of the United States, devoutly recognizing the supreme authority and just government of Almighty God in all the affairs of men and nations, has by a resolution requested the President to designate and set apart a day for national prayer and humiliation; And whereas it is the duty of nations as well as of men to own their dependence upon the overruling power of God, to confess their sins and trespasses in humble sorrow, yet with the assured hope that genuine repentance will lead to mercy and pardon....

The authentic voice of America speaks in these words. And it is a testimony to the enduring vitality of this first principle—the sovereignty of God over society as well as over individual men—that President Eisenhower in June, 1952, quoted these words of Lincoln in a proclamation of similar intent. There is, of course, dissent from this principle, uttered by American secularism (which, at that, is a force far different in content and purpose from Continental laicism). But the secularist dissent is clearly a dissent; it illustrates the existence of the American affirmation. And it is continually challenged. For instance, as late as 1952 an opinion of the United States Supreme Court challenged it by asserting: "We are a religious people whose institutions presuppose a Supreme Being." Three times before in its history—in 1815, 1892, and 1931—the Court had formally espoused this same principle.

The affirmation in Lincoln's famous phrase, "this nation under God," sets the American proposition in fundamental continuity with the central political tradition of the West. But this continuity is more broadly and importantly visible in another, and related, respect. In 1884 the Third Plenary Council of Baltimore made this statement: "We consider the establishment of our country's independence, the shaping of its liberties and laws, as a work of special Providence, its framers 'building better than they knew,' the Almighty's hand guiding them." The providential aspect of the matter, and the reason for the better building, can be found in the fact that the American political community was organized in an era when the tradition of natural law and natural rights was still vigorous. Claiming no sanction other than its appeal to free minds, it still commanded universal acceptance. And it furnished the basic materials for the American consensus.

The evidence for this fact has been convincingly presented by Clinton Rossiter in his book, *Seedtime of the Republic*, a scholarly account of the "noble aggregate of 'self-evident truths' that vindicated the campaign of resistance (1765–1775), the resolution for independence (1776), and the establishment of the new state governments (1776–1780)." These truths, he adds, "had been no less self-evident to the preachers, merchants, planters, and lawyers who were the mind of colonial America." It might be further added that these truths firmly presided over the great time of study, discussion, and decision which produced the Federal Constitution. "The great political philosophy of the Western world," Rossiter says, "enjoyed one of its proudest seasons in this time of resistance and revolution." By reason of this fact the American Revolution, quite unlike its French counterpart, was less a revolution than a conservation. It conserved, by giving newly vital form to, the liberal tradition of politics, whose ruin in Continental Europe was about to be consummated by the first great modern essay in totalitarianism.

The force for unity inherent in this tradition was of decisive importance in what concerns the problem of pluralism. Because it was conceived in the tradition of natural law the American Republic was rescued from the fate, still not overcome, that fell upon the European nations in which Continental Liberalism, a deformation of the liberal tradition, lodged itself, not least by the aid of the Lodges. There have never been "two Americas," in the sense in which there have been, and still are, "two Frances," "two Italys," "two Spains." Politically speaking, America has always been one. The reason is that a consensus was once established, and it still substantially endures, even in the quarters where its origins have been forgotten.

Formally and in the first instance this consensus was political, that is, it embraced a whole constellation of principles bearing upon the origin and nature of society, the function of the state as the legal order of society, and the scope and limitations of government. "Free government"—perhaps this typically American shorthand phrase sums up the consensus. "A free people under a limited government" puts the matter more exactly. It is a phrase that would have satisfied the first Whig, St. Thomas Aquinas.

To the early Americans government was not a phenomenon of force, as the later legal positivists would have it. Nor was it a "historical category," as Marx and his followers were to assert. Government did not mean simply the power to coerce, though this power was taken as integral to government. Government, properly speaking, was the right to command. It was authority. And its authority derived from law. By the same token its authority was limited by law. In his own way Tom Paine put the matter when he said, "In America Law is the King." But the matter had been better put by Henry of Bracton (d. 1268) when he said, "The king ought not to be under a man, but under God and under the law, because the law makes the king." This was the message of Magna Charta; this became the first structural rib of American constitutionalism.

Constitutionalism, the rule of law, the notion of sovereignty as purely political and therefore limited by law, the concept of government as an empire of laws and not of men—these were ancient ideas, deeply implanted in the British tradition at its origin in medieval times. The major American contribution to the tradition—a contribution that imposed itself on all subsequent political history in the Western world—was the written constitution. However, the American document was not the *constitution octroyée* of the nineteenth-century Restorations—a constitution graciously granted by the King or Prince-President. Through the American techniques of the constitutional convention and of popular ratification, the American Constitution is explicitly the act of the people. It embodies their consensus as to the purposes of government, its structure, the extent of its powers and the limitations on them, etc. By the Constitution the people define the areas where authority is legitimate and the areas where liberty is lawful. The Constitution is therefore at once a charter of freedom and a plan for political order....

Americans agreed to make government constitutional and therefore limited in a new sense, because it is representative, republican, responsible government. It is limited not only by law but by the will of the people it represents. Not only do the people adopt the Constitution; through the techniques of representation, free elections, and frequent rotation of administrations they also have a share in the enactment of all subsequent statutory legislation. The people are really governed; American political theorists did not pursue the Rousseauist will-o'-the-wisp: how shall the individual in society come to obey only himself? Nevertheless, the people are governed because they consent to be governed; and they consent to be governed because in a true sense they govern themselves.

The American consensus therefore includes a great act of faith in the capacity of the people to govern themselves. The faith was not unrealistic. It was not supposed that every-body could master the technical aspects of government, even in a day when these aspects were far less complex than they now are. The supposition was that the people could under-stand the general objectives of governmental policy, the broad issues put to the decision of government, especially as these issues raised moral problems. The American consensus accepted the premise of medieval society, that there is a sense of justice inherent in the people, in virtue of which they are empowered, as the medieval phrase had it, to "judge, direct, and correct" the processes of government.

It was this political faith that compelled early American agreement to the institutions of a free speech and a free press. In the American concept of them, these institutions do not rest on the thin theory proper to eighteenth-century individualistic rationalism, that a man has a right to say what he thinks merely because he thinks it. The American agree-ment was to reject political censorship of opinion as unrightful, because unwise, impru-dent, not to say impossible. However, the proper premise of these freedoms lay in the fact that they were social necessities. "Colonial thinking about each of these rights had a strong social rather than individualistic bias," Rossiter says. They were regarded as conditions essential to the conduct of free, representative, and responsible government. People who are called upon to obey have the right first to be heard. People who are to bear burdens and make sacrifices have the right first to pronounce on the purposes which their sacrifices serve. People who are summoned to contribute to the common good have the right first to pass their own judgment on the question, whether the good proposed be truly a good, the people's good, the common good. Through the technique of majority opinion this popular judgment becomes binding on government.

A second principle underlay these free institutions—the principle that the state is dis-tinct from society and limited in its offices toward society. This principle too was inherent in the Great Tradition. Before it was cancelled out by the rise of the modern omicompetent society-state, it had found expression in the distinction between the order of politics and the order of culture, or, in the language of the time, the distinction between *studium* and *imperium*. The whole order of ideas in general was autonomous in the face of government; it was immune from political discipline, which could only fall upon actions, not ideas. Even the medieval Inquisition respected this distinction of orders; it never recognized a crime of opinion, *crimen opinionis*; its competence extended only to the repression of organized conspiracy against public order and the common good. It was, if you will, a Committee on un-Christian Activities; it regarded activities, not ideas, as justiciable.

The American Proposition, in reviving the distinction between society and state, which had perished under the advance of absolutism, likewise renewed the principle of the incompetence of government in the field of opinion. Government submits itself to judgment by the truth of society; it is not itself a judge of the truth in society. Freedom of the means of communication whereby ideas are circulated and criticized, and the freedom of the academy (understanding by the term the range of institutions organized for the pur-suit of truth and the perpetuation of the intellectual heritage of society) are immune from legal inhibition or government control. This immunity is a civil right of the first order, essential to the American concept of a free people under a limited government.

"A free people": this term too has a special sense in the American Proposition. America has passionately pursued the ideal of freedom, expressed in a whole system of political and civil rights, to new lengths; but it has not pursued this ideal so madly as to rush over the edge of the abyss, into sheer libertarianism, into the chaos created by the nineteenth-century theory of the "outlaw conscience," *conscientia exlex*, the conscience that knows no law higher than its own subjective imperatives. Part of the inner architecture of the American ideal of freedom has been the profound conviction that only a virtuous people can be free. It is not an American belief that free government is inevitable, only that it is possible, and that its possibility can be realized only when the people as a whole are inwardly governed by the recognized imperatives of the universal moral law.

The American experiment reposes on Acton's postulate, that freedom is the highest phase of civil society. But it also reposes on Acton's further postulate, that the elevation of a people to this highest phase of social life supposes, as its condition, that they understand the ethical nature of political freedom. They must understand, in Acton's phrase, that freedom is "not the power of doing what we like, but the right of being able to do what we ought." The people claim this right, in all its articulated forms, in the face of government; in the name of this right, multiple limitations are put upon the power of government. But the claim can be made with the full resonance of moral authority only to the extent that it issues from an inner sense of responsibility to a higher law. In any phase civil society demands order. In its highest phase of freedom it demands that order should not be imposed from the top down, as it were, but should spontaneously flower outward from the free obedience to the restraints and imperatives that stem from inwardly possessed moral principle. In this sense democracy is more than a political experiment; it is a spiritual and moral enterprise. And its success depends upon the virtue of the people who undertake it. Men who would be politically free must discipline themselves. Likewise institutions which would pretend to be free with a human freedom must in their workings be governed from within and made to serve the ends of virtue. Political freedom is endangered in its foundations as soon as the universal moral values, upon whose shared possession the self-discipline of a free society depends, are no longer vigorous enough to restrain the passions and shatter the selfish inertia of men. The American ideal of freedom as ordered freedom, and therefore an ethical ideal, has traditionally reckoned with these truths, these truisms.

This brings us to the threshold of religion, and therefore to the other aspect of the problem of pluralism, the plurality of religions in America. However, before crossing this threshold one more characteristic of the American Proposition, as implying a consensus, needs mention, namely, the Bill of Rights. The philosophy of the Bill of Rights was also tributary to the tradition of natural law, to the idea that man has certain original responsibilities precisely as man, antecedent to his status as citizen. These responsibilities are creative of rights which inhere in man antecedent to any act of government; therefore they are not granted by government and they cannot be surrendered to government. They are as inalienable as they are inherent. Their proximate source is in nature, and in history insofar as history bears witness to the nature of man; their ultimate source, as the Declaration of Independence states, is in God, the Creator of nature and the Master of history. The power of this doctrine, as it inspired both the Revolution and the form of the Republic, lay in the fact that it drew an effective line of demarcation around the exercise of political or social authority. When government ventures over this line, it collides with the duty and right of resistance. Its authority becomes arbitrary and therefore nil; its act incurs the ultimate anathema, "unconstitutional."

One characteristic of the American Bill of Rights is important for the subject here, namely, the differences that separate it from the Declaration of the Rights of Man in the France of '89. In considerable part the latter was a parchment-child of the Enlightenment, a top-of-the-brain concoction of a set of men who did not understand that a political com-munity, like man himself, has roots in history and in nature. They believed that a state could be simply a work of art, a sort of absolute beginning, an artifact of which abstract human reason could be the sole artisan. Moreover, their exaggerated individualism had shut them off from a view of the organic nature of the human community; their social atomism would permit no institutions or associations intermediate between the individ-ual and the state.

In contrast, the men who framed the American Bill of Rights understood history and tradition, and they understood nature in the light of both. They too were individualists, but not to the point of ignoring the social nature of man. They did their thinking within the tradition of freedom that was their heritage from England. Its roots were not in the top of anyone's brain but in history. Importantly, its roots were in the medieval notion of the *homo liber et legalis*, the man whose freedom rests on law, whose law was the age-old custom in which the nature of man expressed itself, and whose lawful freedoms were pos-sessed in association with his fellows. The rights for which the colonists contended against the English Crown were basically the rights of Englishmen. And these were substantially the rights written into the Bill of Rights.

Of freedom of religion there will be question later. For the rest, freedom of speech, assembly, association, and petition for the redress of grievances, security of person, home, and property—these were great historical as well as civil and natural rights. So too was the right to trial by jury, and all the procedural rights implied in the Fifth- and later in the Fourteenth- Amendment provision for "due process of law." The guarantee of these and other rights was new in that it was written, in that it envisioned these rights with an amplitude, and gave them a priority, that had not been known before in history. But the Bill of Rights was an effective instrument for the delimitation of government authority and social power, not because it was written on paper in 1789 or 1791, but because the rights it proclaims had already been engraved by history on the conscience of a people. The American Bill of Rights is not a piece of eighteenth-century rationalist theory; it is far more the product of Christian history. Behind it one can see, not the philosophy of the Enlightenment but the older philosophy that had been the matrix of the common law. The "man" whose rights are guaranteed in the face of law and government is, whether he knows it or not, the Christian man, who had learned to know his own personal dignity in the school of Christian faith.

Perhaps one day the noble many-storeyed mansion of democracy will be dismantled, levelled to the dimensions of a flat majoritarianism, which is no mansion but a barn, per-haps even a tool shed in which the weapons of tyranny may be forged. Perhaps there will one day be wide dissent even from the political principles which emerge from natural law, as well as dissent from the constellation of ideas that have historically undergirded these principles—the idea that government has a moral basis; that the universal moral law is the foundation of society; that the legal order of society—that is, the state—is subject to judgment by a law that is not statistical but inherent in the nature of man; that the eternal reason of God is the ultimate origin of all law; that this nation in all its aspects—as a soci-ety, a state, an ordered and free relationship between governors and governed—is under God. The possibility that widespread dissent from these principles should develop is not foreclosed. If that evil day should come, the results would introduce one more paradox into history. The Catholic community would still be speaking in the ethical and political idiom familiar to them as it was familiar to their fathers, both the Fathers of the Church and the Fathers of the American Republic. The guardianship of the original American consensus, based on the Western heritage, would have passed to the Catholic community, within which the heritage was elaborated long before America was. And it would be for others, not Catholics, to ask themselves whether they still shared the consensus which first fashioned the American people into a body politic and determined the structure of its fundamental law.

What has been said may suffice to show the grounds on which Catholics participate in the American consensus. These grounds are drawn from the materials of the consensus itself. It has been a greatly providential blessing that the American Republic never put to the Catholic conscience the questions raised, for instance, by the Third Republic. There has never been a schism within the American Catholic community, as there was among French Catholics, over the right attitude to adopt toward the established polity. There has never been the necessity for nice distinctions between the regime and the legislation; nor has there ever been the need to proclaim a policy of *ralliement*. In America the *ralliement* has been original, spontaneous, universal. It has been a matter of conscience and conviction, because its motive was not expediency in the narrow sense—the need to accept what one is powerless to change. Its motive was the evident coincidence of the principles which inspired the American Republic with the principles that are structural to the Western Christian political tradition.

DANIEL BELL

"The End of Ideology in the West"
(1960)

In the wake of the violent excesses associated with Hitler and Stalin—two bona fide ideologues—political ideologies came under sharp suspicion during the 1950s. The sociologist Daniel Bell (1919–) was among a host of American intellectuals who gave voice to this suspicion, who believed that the problems of industrial society defied the solutions offered by the traditional right and left, and who placed their political hopes on a nondoctrinaire pluralistic consensus of enlightened democratic capitalists. Although the catchphrase for this anti-ideological impulse was contributed by Bell's book, *The End of Ideology: On the Exhaustion of Political Ideas in the Fifties* (New York, 1960), Bell's actual formulation of this impulse was ambivalent. He was troubled by the widespread turning away from systematic political argument that accompanied the rejection of the "terrible simplifiers," the ideologues. The animated discussion stimulated by Bell is represented in the anthology *The End of Ideology Debate* (New York, 1968), edited by Chaim I. Waxman.

Bell's thought and career during the years leading up to the "end of ideology debate" is the subject of an excellent historical study: Howard Brick, *Daniel Bell and the Decline of Intellectual Radicalism: Social Theory and Political Reconciliation in the 1940s* (Madison, Wis., 1986). For Bell's work as a whole, see Malcolm Waters, *Daniel Bell* (New York, 1995). Bell's later work includes *The Coming of Postindustrial Society* (New York, 1973) and *The Cultural Contradictions of Capitalism* (New York, 1976). The debate in which his ideas were caught up included voices less guarded than Bell's about the prospects for a world in which perpetual economic growth made social conflict less likely and in which "politics" would gradually be replaced by "knowledge" and "information" as the basis for decisions made in the public interest. For an example, see Robert E. Lane, "The Decline of Politics and Ideology in a Knowledgeable Society," *American Sociological Review*, 31 (1966), 649–62.

Men commit the error of not knowing when to limit their hopes.
—Machiavelli

There have been few periods in history when man felt his world to be durable, suspended surely, as in Christian allegory, between chaos and heaven. In an Egyptian papyrus of more than four thousand years ago, one finds: "...impudence is rife...the country is spinning round and round like a potter's wheel...the masses are like timid sheep without a shepherd...one who yesterday was indigent is now wealthy and the sometime rich overwhelm him with adulation." The Hellenistic period as described by Gilbert Murray was one of a "failure of nerve"; there was "the rise of pessimism, a loss of self-confidence, of hope in this life and of faith in normal human effort." And the old scoundrel Talleyrand claimed that only those who lived before 1789 could have tasted life in all its sweetness.

This age, too, can add appropriate citations made all the more wry and bitter by the long period of bright hope that preceded it—for the two decades between 1930 and 1950 have an intensity peculiar in written history: world-wide economic depression and sharp class struggles; the rise of fascism and racial imperialism in a country that had stood at an advanced stage of human culture; the tragic self-immolation of a revolutionary generation that had proclaimed the finer ideals of man; destructive war of a breadth and scale hitherto unknown; the bureaucratized murder of millions in concentration camps and death chambers.

For the radical intellectual who had articulated the revolutionary impulses of the past century and a half, all this has meant an end to chiliastic hopes, to millenarianism, to apocalyptic thinking—and to ideology. For ideology, which once was a road to action, has come to be a dead end.

Whatever its origins among the French *philosophes*, ideology as a way of translating ideas into action was given its sharpest phrasing by the left Hegelians, by Feuerbach and by Marx. For them, the function of philosophy was to be critical, to rid the present of the past. ("The tradition of all the dead generations weighs like a nightmare on the brain of the living," wrote Marx.) Feuerbach, the most radical of all the left Hegelians, called himself Luther II. Man would be free, he said, if we could demythologize religion. The history of all thought was a history of progressive disenchantment, and if finally, in Christianity, God had been transformed from a parochial deity to a universal abstraction, the function of criticism—using the radical tool of alienation, or self-estrangement—was to replace theology by anthropology, to substitute Man for God. Philosophy was to be directed at life, man was to be liberated from the "specter of abstractions" and extricated from the bind of the supernatural. Religion was capable only of creating "false consciousness." Philosophy would reveal "true consciousness." And by placing Man, rather than God, at the center of consciousness, Feuerbach sought to bring the "infinite into the finite."

If Feuerbach "descended into the world," Marx sought to transform it. And where Feuerbach proclaimed anthropology, Marx, reclaiming a root insight of Hegel, emphasized History and historical contexts. The world was not generic Man, but men; and of men, classes of men. Men differed because of their class position. And truths were class truths.

Source: Daniel Bell, *The End of Ideology: On the Exhaustion of Political Ideas in the Fifties* (New York: Crowell Collier & Macmillan, 1961), 393–402 (Collier edition, 1961). Reprinted by permission of Daniel Bell. Copyright © by Daniel Bell. Footnotes omitted.

All truths, thus, were masks, or partial truths, but the real truth was the revolutionary truth. And this real truth was rational.

Thus a dynamic was introduced into the analysis of ideology, and into the creation of a new ideology. By demythologizing religion, one recovered (from God and sin) the potential in man. By the unfolding of history, rationality was revealed. In the struggle of classes, true consciousness, rather than false consciousness, could be achieved. But if truth lay in action, one must act. The left Hegelians, said Marx, were only *littérateurs*. (For them a magazine was "practice.") For Marx, the only real action was in politics. But action, revolutionary action as Marx conceived it, was not mere social change. It was, in its way, the resumption of all the old millenarian, chiliastic ideas of the Anabaptists. It was, in its new vision, a new ideology.

Ideology is the conversion of ideas into social levers. Without irony, Max Lerner once entitled a book "Ideas Are Weapons." This is the language of ideology. It is more. It is the commitment to the consequences of ideas. When Vissarion Belinsky, the father of Russian criticism, first read Hegel and became convinced of the philosophical correctness of the formula "what is, is what ought to be," he became a supporter of the Russian autocracy. But when it was shown to him that Hegel's thought contained the contrary tendency, that dialectically the "is" evolves into a different form, he became a revolutionary overnight. "Belinsky's conversion," comments Rufus W. Mathewson, Jr., "illustrates an attitude toward ideas which is both passionate and myopic, which responds to them on the basis of their immediate relevances alone, and inevitably reduces them to tools."

What gives ideology its force is its passion. Abstract philosophical inquiry has always sought to eliminate passion, and the person, to rationalize all ideas. For the ideologue, truth arises in action, and meaning is given to experience by the "transforming moment." He comes alive not in contemplation, but in "the deed." One might say, in fact, that the most important, latent, function of ideology is to tap emotion. Other than religion (and war and nationalism), there have been few forms of channelizing emotional energy. Religion symbolized, drained away, dispersed emotional energy from the world onto the litany, the liturgy, the sacraments, the edifices, the arts. Ideology fuses these energies and channels them into politics.

But religion, at its most effective, was more. It was a way for people to cope with the problem of death. The fear of death—forceful and inevitable—and more, the fear of violent death, shatters the glittering, imposing, momentary dream of man's power. The fear of death, as Hobbes pointed out, is the source of conscience; the effort to avoid violent death is the source of law. When it was possible to believe, really believe, in heaven and hell, then some of the fear of death could be tempered or controlled; without such belief, there is only the total annihilation of the self.

It may well be that with the decline in religious *faith* in the last century and more, this fear of death as total annihilation, unconsciously expressed, has probably increased. One may hypothesize, in fact, that here is a cause of the breakthrough of the irrational, which is such a marked feature of the changed moral temper of our time. Fanaticism, violence, and cruelty are not, of course, unique in human history. But there was a time when such frenzies and mass emotions could be displaced, symbolized, drained away, and dispersed through religious devotion and practice. Now there is only this life, and the assertion of self becomes possible—for some even necessary—in the domination over others. One can challenge death by emphasizing the omnipotence of a movement (as in the "inevitable" victory of communism), or overcome death (as did the "immortality" of Captain Ahab) by bending others to one's will. Both paths are taken, but politics, because it can institutionalize power, in the way that religion once did, becomes the ready avenue for domination. The modern effort to transform the world chiefly or solely through politics (as contrasted with the religious transformation of the self) has meant that all other institutional ways of mobilizing emotional energy would necessarily atrophy. In effect, sect and church became party and social movement.

A social movement can rouse people when it can do three things: simplify ideas, establish a claim to truth, and, in the union of the two, demand a commitment to action. Thus, not only does ideology transform ideas, it transforms people as well. The nineteenth-century ideologies, by emphasizing inevitability and by infusing passion into their followers, could compete with religion. By identifying inevitability with progress, they linked up with the positive values of science. But more important, these ideologies were linked, too, with the rising class of intellectuals, which was seeking to assert a place in society.

The differences between the intellectual and the scholar, without being invidious, are important to understand. The scholar has a bounded field of knowledge, a tradition, and seeks to find his place in it, adding to the accumulated, tested knowledge of the past as to a mosaic. The scholar, qua scholar, is less involved with his "self." The intellectual begins with *his* experience, *his* individual perceptions of the world, *his* privileges and deprivations, and judges the world by these sensibilities. Since his own status is of high value, his judgments of the society reflect the treatment accorded him. In a business civilization, the intellectual felt that the wrong values were being honored, and rejected the society. Thus there was a "built-in" compulsion for the free-floating intellectual to become political. The ideologies, therefore, which emerged from the nineteenth century had the force of the intellectuals behind them. They embarked upon what William James called "the faith ladder," which in its vision of the future cannot distinguish possibilities from probabilities, and converts the latter into certainties.

Today, these ideologies are exhausted. The events behind this important sociological change are complex and varied. Such calamities as the Moscow Trials, the Nazi-Soviet pact, the concentration camps, the suppression of the Hungarian workers, form one chain; such social changes as the modification of capitalism, the rise of the Welfare State, another. In philosophy, one can trace the decline of simplistic, rationalistic beliefs and the emergence of new stoic-theological images of man, e.g., Freud, Tillich, Jaspers, etc. This is not to say that such ideologies as communism in France and Italy do not have a political weight, or a driving momentum from other sources. But out of all this history, one simple fact emerges: for the radical intelligentsia, the old ideologies have lost their "truth" and their power to persuade.

Few serious minds believe any longer that one can set down "blueprints" and through "social engineering" bring about a new utopia of social harmony. At the same time, the older "counter-beliefs" have lost their intellectual force as well. Few "classic" liberals insist that the State should play no role in the economy, and few serious conservatives, at least in England and on the Continent, believe that the Welfare State is "the road to serfdom." In the Western world, therefore, there is today a rough consensus among intellectuals on political issues: the acceptance of a Welfare State; the desirability of decentralized power; a system of mixed economy and of political pluralism. In that sense, too, the ideological age has ended.

And yet, the extraordinary fact is that while the old nineteenth-century ideologies and intellectual debates have become exhausted, the rising states of Asia and Africa are fashioning new ideologies with a different appeal for their own people. These are the ideologies of industrialization, modernization, Pan-Arabism, color, and nationalism. In the distinctive difference between the two kinds of ideologies lies the great political and social problems of the second half of the twentieth century. The ideologies of the nineteenth century were universalistic, humanistic, and fashioned by intellectuals. The mass ideologies of Asia and Africa are parochial, instrumental, and created by political leaders. The driving forces of the old ideologies were social equality and, in the largest sense, freedom. The impulsions of the new ideologies are economic development and national power.

And in this appeal, Russia and China have become models. The fascination these countries exert is no longer the old idea of the free society, but the new one of economic growth. And if this involves the wholesale coercion of the population and the rise of new elites to drive the people, the new repressions are justified on the ground that without such coercions economic advance cannot take place rapidly enough. And even for some of the liberals of the West, "economic development" has become a new ideology that washes away the memory of old disillusionments.

It is hard to quarrel with an appeal for rapid economic growth and modernization, and few can dispute the goal, as few could ever dispute an appeal for equality and freedom. But in this powerful surge—and its swiftness is amazing—any movement that instates such goals risks the sacrifice of the present generation for a future that may see only a new exploitation by a new elite. For the newly risen countries, the debate is not over the merits of communism—the content of that doctrine has long been forgotten by friends and foes alike. The question is an older one: whether new societies can grow by building democratic institutions and allowing people to make choices—and sacrifices—voluntarily, or whether the new elites, heady with power, will impose totalitarian means to transform their countries. Certainly in these traditional and old colonial societies where the masses are apathetic and easily manipulated, the answer lies with the intellectual classes and their conceptions of the future.

Thus one finds, at the end of the fifties, a disconcerting caesura. In the West, among the intellectuals, the old passions are spent. The new generation, with no meaningful memory of these old debates, and no secure tradition to build upon, finds itself seeking new purposes within a framework of political society that has rejected, intellectually speaking, the old apocalyptic and chiliastic visions. In the search for a "cause," there is a deep, desperate, almost pathetic anger. The theme runs through a remarkable book, *Convictions,* by a dozen of the sharpest young Left Wing intellectuals in Britain. They can-not define the content of the "cause" they seek, but the yearning is clear. In the U.S. too there is a restless search for a new intellectual radicalism. Richard Chase, in his thoughtful assessment of American society, *The Democratic Vista,* insists that the greatness of nineteenth-century America for the rest of the world consisted in its radical vision of man (such a vision as Whitman's), and calls for a new radical criticism today. But the problem is that the old politico-economic radicalism (pre-occupied with such matters as the socialization of industry) has lost its meaning while the stultifying aspects of contemporary culture (e.g., television) cannot be redressed in political terms. At the same time, American culture has almost completely accepted the avant-garde, particularly in art, and the older academic styles have been driven out completely. The irony, further, for those who seek "causes" is that the workers, whose grievances were once the driving energy for social change, are more satisfied with the society than the intellectuals. The workers have not achieved utopia, but their expectations were less than those of the intellectuals, and the gains correspondingly larger.

The young intellectual is unhappy because the "middle way" is for the middle-aged, not for him; it is without passion and is deadening. Ideology, which by its nature is an all-or-none affair, and temperamentally the thing he wants, is intellectually devitalized, and few issues can be formulated any more, intellectually, in ideological terms. The emotional energies—and needs—exist, and the question of how one mobilizes these energies is a difficult one. Politics offers little excitement. Some of the younger intellectuals have found an outlet in science or university pursuits, but often at the expense of narrowing their talent into mere technique; others have sought self-expression in the arts, but in the wasteland the lack of content has meant, too, the lack of the necessary tension that creates new forms and styles.

Whether the intellectuals in the West can find passions outside of politics is moot. Unfortunately, social reform does not have any unifying appeal, nor does it give a younger generation the outlet for "self-expression" and "self-definition" that it wants. The trajectory of enthusiasm has curved East, where, in the new ecstasies for economic utopia, the "future" is all that counts.

The end of ideology is not—should not be—the end of utopia as well. If anything, one can begin anew the discussion of utopia only by being aware of the trap of ideology. The point is that ideologists are "terrible simplifiers." Ideology makes it unnecessary for people to confront individual issues on their individual merits. One simply turns to the ideological vending machine, and out comes the prepared formulae. And when these beliefs are suffused by apocalyptic fervor, ideas become weapons, and with dreadful results.

There is now, more than ever, some need for utopia, in the sense that men need—as they have always needed—some vision of their potential, some manner of fusing passion with intelligence. Yet the ladder to the City of Heaven can no longer be a "faith ladder," but an empirical one: a utopia has to specify *where* one wants to go, *how* to get there, the costs of the enterprise, and some realization of, and justification for the determination of *who* is to pay.

The end of ideology closes the book, intellectually speaking, on an era, the one of easy "left" formulae for social change. But to close the book is not to turn one's back upon it. This is all the more important now when a "new Left," with few memories of the past, is emerging. This "new Left" has passion and energy, but little definition of the future. Its outriders exult that it is "on the move." But where it is going, what it means by Socialism, how to guard against bureaucratization, what one means by democratic planning or workers' control—any of the questions that require hard thought, are only answered by bravura phrases.

It is in attitudes towards Cuba and the new States in Africa that the meaning of intellectual maturity, and of the end of ideology, will be tested. For among the "new Left," there is an alarming readiness to create a tabula rasa, to accept the word "Revolution" as an absolution for outrages, to justify the suppression of civil rights and opposition—in short, to erase the lessons of the last forty years with an emotional alacrity that is astounding. The fact that many of these emerging social movements are justified in their demands for freedom, for the right to control their own political and economic destinies, does not mean they have a right to a blank check for everything they choose to do in the name of their emancipation. Nor does the fact that such movements take power in the name of freedom guarantee that they will not turn out to be as imperialist, as grandeur-concerned (in the name of Pan-Africanism or some other ideology), as demanding their turn on the stage of History, as the States they have displaced.

If the end of ideology has any meaning, it is to ask for the end of rhetoric, and rhetoricians, of "revolution" of the day when the young French anarchist Vaillant tossed a bomb into the Chamber of Deputies, and the literary critic Laurent Tailhade declared in his defense: "What do a few human lives matter; it was a beau geste." (A beau geste that ended, one might say, in a mirthless jest: two years later, Tailhade lost an eye when a bomb was thrown into a restaurant.) Today, in Cuba, as George Sherman, reporting for the *London Observer* summed it up: "The Revolution is law today although nobody has said clearly what that law is. You are expected to be simply for or against it and judge and be judged accordingly. Hatred and intolerance are wiping out whatever middle ground may have existed."

The problems which confront us at home and in the world are resistant to the old terms of ideological debate betweeen "left" and "right," and if "ideology" by now, and with good reason, is an irretrievably fallen word, it is not necessary that "utopia" suffer the same fate. But it will if those who now call loudest for new utopias begin to justify degrading *means* in the name of some Utopian or revolutionary *end,* and forget the simple lessons that if the old debates are meaningless, some old verities are not—the verities of free speech, free press, the right of opposition and of free inquiry.

And if the intellectual history of the past hundred years has any meaning—and lesson—it is to reassert Jefferson's wisdom (aimed at removing the dead hand of the past, but which can serve as a warning against the heavy hand of the future as well), that "the present belongs to the living." This is the wisdom that revolutionists, old and new, who are sensitive to the fate of their fellow men, rediscover in every generation. "I will never believe," says a protagonist in a poignant dialogue written by the gallant Polish philosopher Leszek Kolakowski, "that the moral and intellectual life of mankind follows the law of economics, that is by saving today we can have more tomorrow; that we should use lives now so that truth will triumph or that we should profit by crime to pave the way for nobility."

And these words, written during the Polish "thaw," when the intellectuals had asserted, from their experience with the "future," the claims of humanism, echo the protest of the Russian writer Alexander Herzen, who, in a dialogue a hundred years ago, reproached an earlier revolutionist who would sacrifice the present mankind for a promised tomorrow: "Do you truly wish to condemn all human beings alive today to the sad role of caryatids...supporting a floor for others some day to dance on?...This alone should serve as a warning to people: an end that is infinitely remote is not an end, but, if you like, a trap; an end must be nearer—it ought to be, at the very least, the labourer's wage or pleasure in the work done. Each age, each generation, each life has its own fullness...."

W. W. ROSTOW

Selection from *The Stages of Economic Growth* (1960)

W. W. Rostow (1916–2003) was the boldest and most widely quoted of the "modernization theorists" of the 1950s and 1960s. A host of social scientists, historians, and policy makers confronted a rapidly changing world scene after World War II, in which the old colonial empires run from Europe were being replaced by new regimes, for influence over which the United States competed with its great Cold War rival, the Soviet Union. The notion took hold that most of the societies of Asia, Africa, and Latin America were "traditional" in character, and on their way to joining the more highly developed, industrialized, technology-intensive, largely democratic societies of the North Atlantic West in "modernity." Hence the transition from one kind of society to another was "modernization." In 1960, the economic historian Rostow published an unusually confident and sweeping version of this perspective on the direction of world history. *The Stages of Economic Growth* analyzed the modernization process in terms of a series of specific steps that brought a society to the point of an economic "take-off," which would launch it on its way toward achieving the "high mass-consumption" order best exemplified by the United States. Rostow articulated this vision within the context of the Cold War and of the Marxist economic theory espoused by the Soviet Union; he subtitled his book *A Non-Communist Manifesto*, invoking Marx's own *Communist Manifesto* of more than a century before.

Rostow became one of the most important academic advisors to the presidential administrations of both John F. Kennedy and Lyndon Johnson. He was an energetic "hawk" in arguments over the escalation of the American military presence in Vietnam, and thus became the target of sustained attacks by opponents of the Vietnam War. The selection in this sourcebook by Noam Chomsky exemplifies the controversy surrounding Rostow's defense of the Vietnam War. A valuable collection of documents and scholarly writings on social scientific intellectuals and government during Rostow's generation is Christopher Simpson, ed., *Universities and Empire: Money and Politics in the Social Sciences During the Cold War* (New York, 1998), to which Rostow contributed and was also the subject of study by several other contributors.

Although modernization theory was sharply criticized in the 1970s, 1980s, and 1990s, Rostow continued to defend and update the arguments put forth in *The Stages of Economic Growth*. In a second edition of 1971 and a third edition of 1990, Rostow offered extensive and detailed responses to his critics. Modified, much chastened versions of modernization theory became popular again in the 1990s, after the collapse of the Soviet Union and the greater integration of the world capitalist economy.

A helpful analysis of the role of modernization theory in the early 1960s is Michael E. Latham, *Modernization as Ideology: American Social Science and "Nation-Building" in the Kennedy Era* (Chapel Hill, 2000). See also David Engerman et al., *Modernization, Development, and the Globalization of the Cold War* (Amherst, Mass., 2000). The best and most comprehensive study is Nils Gilman, *Mandarins of the Future* (Baltimore, 2004).

It is possible to identify all societies, in their economic dimensions, as lying within one of five categories: the traditional society, the preconditions for take-off, the take-off, the drive to maturity, and the age of high mass-consumption.

First, the traditional society. A traditional society is one whose structure is developed within limited production functions, based on pre-Newtonian science and technology, and on pre-Newtonian attitudes towards the physical world. Newton is here used as a symbol for that watershed in history when men came widely to believe that the external world was subject to a few knowable laws, and was systematically capable of productive manipulation.

The conception of the traditional society is, however, in no sense static; and it would not exclude increases in output. Acreage could be expanded; some ad hoc technical innovations, often highly productive innovations, could be introduced in trade, industry and agriculture; productivity could rise with, for example, the improvement of irrigation works or the discovery and diffusion of a new crop. But the central fact about the traditional society was that a ceiling existed on the level of attainable output per head. This ceiling resulted from the fact that the potentialities which flow from modern science and technology were either not available or not regularly and systematically applied.

Both in the longer past and in recent times the story of traditional societies was thus a story of endless change. The area and volume of trade within them and between them fluctuated, for example, with the degree of political and social turbulence, the efficiency of central rule, the upkeep of the roads. Population—and, within limits, the level of life—rose and fell not only with the sequence of the harvests, but with the incidence of war and of plague. Varying degrees of manufacture developed; but, as in agriculture, the level of productivity was limited by the inaccessibility of modern science, its applications, and its frame of mind.

Generally speaking, these societies, because of the limitation on productivity, had to devote a very high proportion of their resources to agriculture; and flowing from the agricultural system there was an hierarchical social structure, with relatively narrow scope—but some scope—for vertical mobility. Family and clan connexions played a large role in social organization. The value system of these societies was generally geared to what might be called a long-run fatalism; that is, the assumption that the range of possibilities open to one's grandchildren would be just about what it had been for one's grandparents. But this long-run fatalism by no means excluded the short-run option that, within a considerable range, it was possible and legitimate for the individual to strive to improve his lot, within his lifetime. In Chinese villages, for example, there was an endless struggle to acquire or to avoid losing land, yielding a situation where land rarely remained within the same family for a century.

Although central political rule—in one form or another—often existed in traditional societies, transcending the relatively self-sufficient regions, the centre of gravity of political power generally lay in the regions, in the hands of those who owned or controlled the land. The landowner maintained fluctuating but usually profound influence over such central political power as existed, backed by its entourage of civil servants and soldiers, imbued with attitudes and controlled by interests transcending the regions.

In terms of history then, with the phrase "traditional society" we are grouping the whole pre-Newtonian world: the dynasties in China; the civilization of the Middle East

Source: W. W. Rostow, The Stages of Economic Growth (New York: Cambridge University Press, 1960), 4–16.

and the Mediterranean; the world of medieval Europe. And to them we add the post-Newtonian societies which, for a time, remained untouched or unmoved by man's new capability for regularly manipulating his environment to his economic advantage.

To place these infinitely various, changing societies in a single category, on the ground that they all shared a ceiling on the productivity of their economic techniques, is to say very little indeed. But we are, after all, merely clearing the way in order to get at the subject of this book; that is, the post-traditional societies, in which each of the major characteristics of the traditional society was altered in such ways as to permit regular growth: its politics, social structure, and (to a degree) its values, as well as its economy.

The second stage of growth embraces societies in the process of transition; that is, the period when the preconditions for take-off are developed; for it takes time to transform a traditional society in the ways necessary for it to exploit the fruits of modern science, to fend off diminishing returns, and thus to enjoy the blessings and choices opened up by the march of compound interest.

The preconditions for take-off were initially developed, in a clearly marked way, in Western Europe of the late seventeenth and early eighteenth centuries as the insights of modern science began to be translated into new production functions in both agriculture and industry, in a setting given dynamism by the lateral expansion of world markets and the international competition for them. But all that lies behind the break-up of the Middle Ages is relevant to the creation of the preconditions for take-off in Western Europe. Among the Western European states, Britain, favoured by geography, natural resources, trading possibilities, social and political structure, was the first to develop fully the preconditions for take-off.

The more general case in modern history, however, saw the stage of preconditions arise not endogenously but from some external intrusion by more advanced societies. These invasions—literal or figurative—shocked the traditional society and began or hastened its undoing; but they also set in motion ideas and sentiments which initiated the process by which a modern alternative to the traditional society was constructed out of the old culture.

The idea spreads not merely that economic progress is possible, but that economic progress is a necessary condition for some other purpose, judged to be good: be it national dignity, private profit, the general welfare, or a better life for the children. Education, for some at least, broadens and changes to suit the needs of modern economic activity. New types of enterprising men come forward—in the private economy, in government, or both—willing to mobilize savings and to take risks in pursuit of profit or modernization. Banks and other institutions for mobilizing capital appear. Investment increases, notably in transport, communications, and in raw materials in which other nations may have an economic interest. The scope of commerce, internal and external, widens. And, here and there, modern manufacturing enterprise appears, using the new methods. But all this activity proceeds at a limited pace within an economy and a society still mainly characterized by traditional low-productivity methods, by the old social structure and values, and by the regionally based political institutions that developed in conjunction with them.

In many recent cases, for example, the traditional society persisted side by side with modern economic activities, conducted for limited economic purposes by a colonial or quasi-colonial power.

Although the period of transition—between the traditional society and the take-off—saw major changes in both the economy itself and in the balance of social values, a decisive feature was often political. Politically, the building of an effective centralized national state—on the basis of coalitions touched with a new nationalism, in opposition to the traditional landed regional interests, the colonial power, or both, was a decisive aspect of the preconditions period; and it was, almost universally, a necessary condition for take-off...

We come now to the great watershed in the life of modern societies: the third stage in this sequence, the take-off. The take-off is the interval when the old blocks and resistances to steady growth are finally overcome. The forces making for economic progress, which yielded limited bursts and enclaves of modern activity, expand and come to dominate the society. Growth becomes its normal condition. Compound interest becomes built, as it were, into its habits and institutional structure.

In Britain and the well-endowed parts of the world populated substantially from Britain (the United States, Canada etc.) the proximate stimulus for take-off was mainly (but not wholly) technological. In the more general case, the take-off awaited not only the buildup of social overhead capital and a surge of technological development in industry and agriculture, but also the emergence to political power of a group prepared to regard the modernization of the economy as serious, high-order political business.

During the take-off, the rate of effective investment and savings may rise from, say, 5% of the national income to 10% or more; although where heavy social overhead capital investment was required to create the technical preconditions for take-off the investment rate in the preconditions period could be higher than 5%, as, for example, in Canada before the 1890's and Argentina before 1914. In such cases capital imports usually formed a high proportion of total investment in the preconditions period and sometimes even during the take-off itself, as in Russia and Canada during their pre-1914 railway booms.

During the take-off new industries expand rapidly, yielding profits a large proportion of which are reinvested in new plant; and these new industries, in turn, stimulate, through their rapidly expanding requirement for factory workers, the services to support them, and for other manufactured goods, a further expansion in urban areas and in other modern industrial plants. The whole process of expansion in the modern sector yields an increase of income in the hands of those who not only save at high rates but place their savings at the disposal of those engaged in modern sector activities. The new class of entrepreneurs expands; and it directs the enlarging flows of investment in the private sector. The economy exploits hitherto unused natural resources and methods of production.

New techniques spread in agriculture as well as industry, as agriculture is commercialized, and increasing numbers of farmers are prepared to accept the new methods and the deep changes they bring to ways of life. The revolutionary changes in agricultural productivity are an essential condition for successful take-off; for modernization of a society increases radically its bill for agricultural products. In a decade or two both the basic structure of the economy and the social and political structure of the society are transformed in such a way that a steady rate of growth can be, thereafter, regularly sustained.

One can approximately allocate the take-off of Britain to the two decades after 1783; France and the United States to the several decades preceding 1860; Germany, the third quarter of the nineteenth century; Japan, the fourth quarter of the nineteenth century; Russia and Canada the quarter-century or so preceding 1914; while during the 1950's India and China have, in quite different ways, launched their respective take-offs.

After take-off there follows a long interval of sustained if fluctuating progress, as the now regularly growing economy drives to extend modern technology over the whole front of its economic activity. Some 10–20% of the national income is steadily invested, permitting output regularly to outstrip the increase in population. The make-up of the economy changes unceasingly as technique improves, new industries accelerate, older industries level off. The economy finds its place in the international economy: goods formerly imported are produced at home; new import requirements develop, and new export commodities to match them. The society makes such terms as it will with the requirements of modern efficient production, balancing off the new against the older values and institutions, or revising the latter in such ways as to support rather than to retard the growth process.

Some sixty years after take-off begins (say, forty years after the end of take-off) what may be called maturity is generally attained. The economy, focused during the take-off around a relatively narrow complex of industry and technology, has extended its range into more refined and technologically often more complex processes; for example, there may be a shift in focus from the coal, iron, and heavy engineering industries of the railway phase to machine-tools, chemicals, and electrical equipment. This, for example, was the transition through which Germany, Britain, France, and the United States had passed by the end of the nineteenth century or shortly thereafter. But there are other sectoral patterns which have been followed in the sequence from take-off to maturity.

Formally, we can define maturity as the stage in which an economy demonstrates the capacity to move beyond the original industries which powered its take-off and to absorb and to apply efficiently over a very wide range of its resources—if not the whole range—the most advanced fruits of (then) modern technology. This is the stage in which an economy demonstrates that it has the technological and entrepreneurial skills to produce not everything, but anything that it chooses to produce. It may lack (like contemporary Sweden and Switzerland, for example) the raw materials or other supply conditions required to produce a given type of output economically; but its dependence is a matter of economic choice or political priority rather than a technological or institutional necessity.

Historically, it would appear that something like sixty years was required to move a society from the beginning of take-off to maturity. Analytically the explanation for some such interval may lie in the powerful arithmetic of compound interest applied to the capital stock, combined with the broader consequences for a society's ability to absorb modern technology of three successive generations living under a regime where growth is the normal condition. But, clearly, no dogmatism is justified about the exact length of the interval from take-off to maturity.

We come now to the age of high mass-consumption, where, in time, the leading sectors shift towards durable consumers' goods and services: a phase from which Americans are beginning to emerge; whose not unequivocal joys Western Europe and Japan are beginning energetically to probe; and with which Soviet society is engaged in an uneasy flirtation.

As societies achieved maturity in the twentieth century two things happened: real income per head rose to a point where a large number of persons gained a command over consumption which transcended basic food, shelter, and clothing; and the structure of the working force changed in ways which increased not only the proportion of urban to total population, but also the proportion of the population working in offices or in skilled factory jobs—aware of and anxious to acquire the consumption fruits of a mature economy.

In addition to these economic changes, the society ceased to accept the further extension of modern technology as an overriding objective. It is in this post-maturity stage, for example, that, through the political process, Western societies have chosen to allocate increased resources to social welfare and security. The emergence of the welfare state is one manifestation of a society's moving beyond technical maturity; but it is also at this stage that resources tend increasingly to be directed to the production of consumers' durables and to the diffusion of services on a mass basis, if consumers' sovereignty reigns. The sewing machine, the bicycle, and then the various electric-powered household gadgets were gradually diffused. Historically, however, the decisive element has been the cheap mass automobile with its quite revolutionary effects—social as well as economic—on the life and expectations of society.

For the United States, the turning point was, perhaps, Henry Ford's moving assembly line of 1913–14; but it was in the 1920's, and again in the post-war decade, 1946–56, that this stage of growth was pressed to, virtually, its logical conclusion. In the 1950's Western Europe and Japan appear to have fully entered this phase, accounting substantially for a momentum in their economies quite unexpected in the immediate post-war years. The Soviet Union is technically ready for this stage, and, by every sign, its citizens hunger for it; but Communist leaders face difficult political and social problems of adjustment if this stage is launched.

Beyond, it is impossible to predict, except perhaps to observe that Americans, at least, have behaved in the past decade as if diminishing relative marginal utility sets in, after a point, for durable consumers' goods; and they have chosen, at the margin, larger families—behaviour in the pattern of Buddenbrooks dynamics. Americans have behaved as if, having been born into a system that provided economic security and high mass-consumption, they placed a lower valuation on acquiring additional increments of real income in the conventional form as opposed to the advantages and values of an enlarged family. But even in this adventure in generalization it is a shade too soon to create—on the basis of one case—a new stage-of-growth, based on babies, in succession to the age of consumers' durables: as economists might say, the income-elasticity of demand for babies may well vary from society to society. But it is true that the implications of the baby boom along with the not wholly unrelated deficit in social overhead capital are likely to dominate the American economy over the next decade rather than the further diffusion of consumers' durables....

These stages are not merely descriptive. They are not merely a way of generalizing certain factual observations about the sequence of development of modern societies. They have an inner logic and continuity. They have an analytic bone-structure, rooted in a dynamic theory of production.

The classical theory of production is formulated under essentially static assumptions which freeze—or permit only once-over change—in the variables most relevant to the process of economic growth. As modern economists have sought to merge classical production theory with Keynesian income analysis they have introduced the dynamic variables: population, technology, entrepreneurship etc. But they have tended to do so in forms so rigid and general that their models cannot grip the essential phenomena of growth, as they appear to an economic historian. We require a dynamic theory of production which isolates not only the distribution of income between consumption, saving, and investment (and the balance of production between consumers and capital goods) but which focuses directly and in some detail on the composition of investment and on developments within particular sectors of the economy. The argument that follows is based on such a flexible, disaggregated theory of production.

When the conventional limits on the theory of production are widened, it is possible to define theoretical equilibrium positions not only for output, investment, and consumption as a whole, but for each sector of the economy.

Within the framework set by forces determining the total level of output, sectoral optimum positions are determined on the side of demand, by the levels of income and of population, and by the character of tastes; on the side of supply, by the state of technology and the quality of entrepreneurship, as the latter determines the proportion of technically available and potentially profitable innovations actually incorporated in the capital stock.

In addition, one must introduce an extremely significant empirical hypothesis: namely, that deceleration is the normal optimum path of a sector, due to a variety of factors operating on it, from the side of both supply and demand.

The equilibria which emerge from the application of these criteria are a set of sectoral paths, from which flows, as first derivatives, a sequence of optimum patterns of investment.

Historical patterns of investment did not, of course, exactly follow these optimum patterns. They were distorted by imperfections in the private investment process, by the policies of governments, and by the impact of wars. Wars temporarily altered the profitable directions of investment by setting up arbitrary demands and by changing the conditions of supply; they destroyed capital; and, occasionally, they accelerated the development of new technology relevant to the peacetime economy and shifted the political, and social framework in ways conducive to peacetime growth. The historical sequence of business cycles and trend-periods results from these deviations of actual from optimal patterns; and such fluctuations, along with the impact of wars, yield historical paths of growth which differ from those which the optima, calculated before the event, would have yielded.

Nevertheless, the economic history of growing societies takes a part of its rude shape from the effort of societies to approximate the optimum sectoral paths.

At any period of time, the rate of growth in the sectors will vary greatly; and it is possible to isolate empirically certain leading sectors, at early stages of their evolution, whose rapid rate of expansion plays an essential direct and indirect role in maintaining the overall momentum of the economy. For some purposes it is useful to characterize an economy in terms of its leading sectors; and a part of the technical basis for the stages of growth lies in the changing sequence of leading sectors. In essence it is the fact that sectors tend to have a rapid growth-phase, early in their life, that makes it possible and useful to regard economic history as a sequence of stages rather than merely as a continuum, within which nature never makes a jump.

The stages-of-growth also require, however, that elasticities of demand be taken into account, and that this familiar concept be widened; for these rapid growth phases in the sectors derive not merely from the discontinuity of production functions but also from high price- or income-elasticities of demand. Leading sectors are determined not merely by the changing flow of technology and the changing willingness of entrepreneurs to accept available innovations: they are also partially determined by those types of demand which have exhibited high elasticity with respect to price, income, or both.

The demand for resources has resulted, however, not merely from demands set up by private taste and choice, but also from social decisions and from the policies of governments—whether democratically responsive or not. It is necessary, therefore, to look at the choices made by societies in the disposition of their resources in terms which transcend conventional market processes. It is necessary to look at their welfare functions, in the widest sense, including the non-economic processes which determined them.

The course of birth-rates, for example, represents one form of welfare choice made by societies, as income has changed; and population curves reflect (in addition to changing death-rates) how the calculus about family size was made in the various stages; from the usual (but not universal) decline in birth-rates, during or soon after the take-off, as urbanization took hold and progress became a palpable possibility, to the recent rise, as Americans (and others in societies marked by high mass-consumption) have appeared to seek in larger families values beyond those afforded by economic security and by an ample supply of durable consumers' goods and services.

And there are other decisions as well that societies have made as the choices open to them have been altered by the unfolding process of economic growth; and these broad collective decisions, determined by many factors—deep in history, culture, and the active political process—outside the market-place, have interplayed with the dynamics of market demand, risk-taking, technology and entrepreneurship, to determine the specific content of the stages of growth for each society.

How, for example, should the traditional society react to the intrusion of a more advanced power: with cohesion, promptness, and vigour, like the Japanese; by making a virtue of fecklessness, like the oppressed Irish of the eighteenth century; by slowly and reluctantly altering the traditional society, like the Chinese?

When independent modern nationhood is achieved, how should the national energies be disposed: in external aggression, to right old wrongs or to exploit newly created or perceived possibilities for enlarged national power; in completing and refining the political victory of the new national government over old regional interests; or in modernizing the economy?

Once growth is under way, with the take-off, to what extent should the requirements of diffusing modern technology and maximizing the rate of growth be moderated by the desire to increase consumption per capita and to increase welfare?

When technological maturity is reached, and the nation has at its command a modernized and differentiated industrial machine, to what ends should it be put, and in what proportions: to increase social security, through the welfare state; to expand mass consumption into the range of durable consumers' goods and services; to increase the nation's stature and power on the world scene; or to increase leisure?

And then the question beyond, where history offers us only fragments: what to do when the increase in real income itself loses its charm? Babies, boredom, three-day weekends, the moon, or the creation of new inner, human frontiers in substitution for the imperatives of scarcity?

In surveying now the broad contours of each stage-of-growth, we are examining, then, not merely the sectoral structure of economies, as they transformed themselves for growth, and grew; we are also examining a succession of strategic choices made by various societies concerning the disposition of their resources, which include but transcend the income- and price-elasticities of demand.

LIONEL TRILLING

"On the Teaching of Modern Literature" (1961)

Modernism is often identified as the twentieth century's most commanding movement in literature and the arts. Not everyone who has so identified modernism has agreed upon just what defines it, but most celebrants of this multitudinous movement have at least emphasized its self-consciousness, its determination to face the worst as well as the best in the human prospect, and its penchant for aesthetic and moral complexity. The literary critic Lionel Trilling (1905-75) was among the most probing and influential commentators on modernist literature during the midcentury, when the prestige of this distinctive body of writing was at its height. In the essay of 1961 reprinted herein, Trilling reacts to many of the classics of modernism in the specific personal, moral, and professional context of college teaching. Although he expresses his admiration, and even his awe, for the great modernists, he betrays also a dual ambivalence: Is the impact of this literature on students altogether healthy? And is this literature trivialized when one is obliged to address it at the level of a midterm essay?

Trilling's career is ably analyzed in William Chace, *Lionel Trilling: Criticism and Politics* (Stanford, 1980). The special standing accorded to modernist literature by Trilling and his contemporaries is addressed in David A. Hollinger, "The Canon and Its Keepers," in Hollinger's *In the American Province: Studies in the History and Historiography of Ideas* (Bloomington, 1985), 74-91. For a discussion of Trilling in the setting of a comprehensive, critical history of academic literary scholarship, see Gerald Graff, *Professing Literature: An Institutional History* (Chicago, 1987). Cornel West, in *The American Evasion of Philosophy* (Madison, Wis., 1989), juxtaposes Trilling with Ralph Waldo Emerson, William James, W. E. B. Du Bois, W. V. O. Quine, C. Wright Mills, and other diverse American intellectuals who West believes practiced a distinctive type of cultural criticism. See also the essay by Thomas Bender, "Lionel Trilling and American Culture," *American Quarterly*, 42 (1990), 324-47. The perspective, tone, and technique that Trilling displayed in "On the Teaching of Modern Literature" can be compared with features of Paul De Man, "Literary History and Literary Modernity," in De Man's *Blindness and Insight* (New Haven, 1971), perhaps the most influential discussion of literary modernism by any of the "poststructuralist" critics prominent in the generation immediately following Trilling's. Many insights into Trilling's life and work can be gleaned from Diana Trilling, *The Beginning of the Journey: The Marriage of Diana and Lionel Trilling* (New York, 1993). A convenient compendium of responses to Trilling is Morris Dickstein, ed., *Trilling and the Critics* (New York, 1999).

I propose to consider here a particular theme of modern literature which appears so frequently and with so much authority that it may be said to constitute one of the shaping and controlling ideas of our epoch. I can identify it by calling it the disenchantment of our culture with culture itself—it seems to me that the characteristic element of modern literature, or at least of the most highly developed modern literature, is the bitter line of hostility to civilization which runs through it. It happens that my present awareness of this theme is involved in a personal experience, and I am impelled to speak of it not abstractly but with the husks of the experience clinging untidily to it. I shall go so far in doing this as to describe the actual circumstances in which the experience took place. These circumstances are pedagogic—they consist of some problems in teaching modern literature to undergraduates and my attempt to solve these problems. I know that pedagogy is a depressing subject to all persons of sensibility, and yet I shall not apologize for touching upon it because the emphasis upon the teaching of literature and especially of modern literature is in itself one of the most salient and significant manifestations of the culture of our time. Indeed, if, having in mind Matthew Arnold's lecture, "On the Modern Element in Literature," we are on the hunt for *the* modern element in modern literature, we might want to find it in the susceptibility of modern literature to being made into an academic subject.

For some years I have taught the course in modern literature in Columbia College. I did not undertake it without misgiving and I have never taught it with an undivided mind. My doubts do not refer to the value of the literature itself, only to the educational propriety of its being studied in college. These doubts persist even though I wholly understand that the relation of our collegiate education to modernity is no longer an open question. The unargued assumption of most curriculums is that the real subject of all study is the modern world; that the justification of all study is its immediate and presumably practical relevance to modernity; that the true purpose of all study is to lead the young person to be at home in, and in control of, the modern world. There is really no way of quarreling with the assumption or with what follows upon it, the instituting of courses of which the substance is chiefly contemporary or at least makes ultimate reference to what is contemporary.

It might be asked why anyone should *want* to quarrel with the assumption. To that question I can return only a defensive, eccentric, self-depreciatory answer. It is this: that to some of us who teach and who think of our students as the creators of the intellectual life of the future, there comes a kind of despair. It does not come because our students fail to respond to ideas, rather because they respond to ideas with a happy vagueness, a delighted glibness, a joyous sense of power in the use of received or receivable generalizations, a grateful wonder at how easy it is to formulate and judge, at how little resistance language offers to their intentions. When that despair strikes us, we are tempted to give up the usual and accredited ways of evaluating education, and instead of prizing responsiveness and aptitude, to set store by some sign of personal character in our students, some token of individual will. We think of this as taking the form of resistance and imperviousness, of personal density or gravity, of some power of supposing that ideas are real, a power which will lead a young man to say what Goethe thought was the modern thing to say, "But is this really true—is it true for *me?*" And to say this not in the facile way, not following the progressive educational prescription to "think for yourself," which means to think in the

Source: Lionel Trilling, *Beyond Culture* (New York: Harcourt Brace Jovanovich, 1961), 3–27. Reprinted by permission of the Wylie Agency, Inc. Copyright © 1961 by Lionel Trilling.

progressive pieties rather than in the conservative pieties (if any of the latter do still exist), but to say it from his sense of himself as a person rather than as a bundle of attitudes and responses which are all alert to please the teacher and the progressive community.

We can't do anything about the quality of personal being of our students, but we are led to think about the cultural analogue of a personal character that is grave, dense, and resistant—we are led to think about the past. Perhaps the protagonist of Thomas Mann's story, "Disorder and Early Sorrow" comes to mind, that sad Professor Cornelius with his intense and ambivalent sense of history. For Professor Cornelius, who is a historian, the past is dead, is death itself, but for that very reason it is the source of order, value, piety, and even love. If we think about education in the dark light of the despair I have described, we wonder if perhaps there is not to be found in the past that quiet place at which a young man might stand for a few years, at least a little beyond the competing attitudes and generalizations of the present, at least a little beyond the contemporary problems which he is told he can master only by means of attitudes and generalizations, that quiet place in which he can be silent, in which he can *know* something—in what year the Parthenon was begun, the order of battle at Trafalgar, how Linear B was deciphered; almost anything at all that has nothing to do with the talkative and attitudinizing present, anything at all but variations on the accepted formulations about *anxiety,* and *urban society,* and *alienation,* and *Gemeinschaft* and *Gesellschaft,* all the matter of the academic disciplines which are founded upon the modern self-consciousness and the modern self-pity. The modern self-pity is certainly not without its justification; but, if the circumstances that engender it are ever to be overcome, we must sometimes wonder whether this work can be done by minds which are taught in youth to accept these sad conditions of ours as the only right objects of contemplation. And quite apart from any practical consequences, one thinks of the simple aesthetic personal pleasure of having to do with young minds, and maturing minds, which are free of cant, which are, to quote an old poet, "fierce, moody, patient, venturous, modest, shy."

This line of argument I have called eccentric and maybe it ought to be called obscurantist and reactionary. Whatever it is called, it is not likely to impress a Committee on the Curriculum. It was, I think, more or less the line of argument of my department in Columbia College, when, up to a few years ago, it would decide, whenever the question came up, not to carry its courses beyond the late nineteenth century. But our rationale could not stand against the representations which a group of students made to our Dean and which he communicated to us. The students wanted a course in modern literature—very likely, in the way of students, they said that it was a scandal that no such course was being offered in the College. There was no argument that could stand against this expressed desire: we could only capitulate and then with pretty good grace, muster the arguments that justified our doing so. Was not the twentieth century more than half over? Was it not nearly fifty years since Eliot wrote "Portrait of a Lady"? George Meredith had not died until 1909, and even the oldest among us had read one of his novels in a college course—many American universities had been quick to bring into their purview the literature of the later nineteenth century, and even the early twentieth century; there was a strong supporting tradition for our capitulation. Had not Yeats been Matthew Arnold's contemporary for twenty-three years?

Our resistance to the idea of the course had never been based on an adverse judgment of the literature itself. We are a department not only of English but of comparative literature, and if the whole of modern literature is surveyed, it could be said—and we were willing to say it—that no literature of the past surpassed the literature of our time in power and magnificence. Then too, it is a difficult literature, and it is difficult not merely as defenders of modern poetry say that all literature is difficult. We nowadays believe that Keats is a very difficult poet, but his earlier readers did not. We now see the depths and subtleties of Dickens, but his contemporary readers found him as simply available as a plate of oysters on the half shell. Modern literature, however, shows its difficulties at first blush; they are literal as well as doctrinal difficulties—if our students were to know their modern literary heritage, surely they needed all the help that a teacher can give?

These made cogent reasons for our decision to establish, at long last, the course in modern literature. They also made a ground for our display of a certain mean-spirited, last-ditch vindictiveness. I recall that we said something like, "Very well, if they want the modern, let them have it—let them have it, as Henry James says, full in the face. We shall give the course, but we shall give it on the highest level, and if they think, as students do, that the modern will naturally meet them in a genial way, let them have their gay and easy time with Yeats and Eliot, with Joyce and Proust and Kafka, with Lawrence, Mann, and Gide."

Eventually the course fell to me to give. I approached it with an uneasiness which has not diminished with the passage of time—it has, I think, even increased. It arises, this uneasiness, from my personal relation with the works that form the substance of the course. Almost all of them have been involved with me for a long time—I invert the natural order not out of lack of modesty but taking the cue of W. H. Auden's remark that a real book reads us. I have been read by Eliot's poems and by *Ulysses* and by *Remembrance of Things Past* and by *The Castle* for a good many years now, since early youth. Some of these books at first rejected me; I bored them. But as I grew older and they knew me better, they came to have more sympathy with me and to understand my hidden meanings. Their nature is such that our relationship has been very intimate. No literature has ever been so shockingly personal as that of our time—it asks every question that is forbidden in polite society. It asks us if we are content with our marriages, with our family lives, with our professional lives, with our friends. It is all very well for me to describe my course in the College catalogue as "paying particular attention to the role of the writer as a critic of his culture"—this is sheer evasion: the questions asked by our literature are not about our culture but about ourselves. It asks us if we are content with ourselves, if we are saved or damned—more than with anything else, our literature is concerned with salvation. No literature has ever been so intensely spiritual as ours. I do not venture to call it actually religious, but certainly it has the special intensity of concern with the spiritual life which Hegel noted when he spoke of the great modern phenomenon of the secularization of spirituality.

I do not know how other teachers deal with this extravagant personal force of modern literature, but for me it makes difficulty. Nowadays the teaching of literature inclines to a considerable technicality, but when the teacher has said all that can be said about formal matters; about verse-patterns, metrics, prose conventions, irony, tension, etc., he must confront the necessity of bearing personal testimony. He must use whatever authority he may possess to say whether or not a work is true; and if not, why not; and if so, why so. He can do this only at considerable cost to His privacy. How does one say that Lawrence is right in his great rage against the modern emotions, against the modern sense of life and ways of being, unless one speaks from the intimacies of one's own feelings, and one's own sense of life, and one's own wished-for way of being? How, except with the implication of personal judgment, does one say to students that Gide is perfectly accurate in his representation of the awful boredom and slow corruption of respectable life? Then probably one rushes in to say that this doesn't of itself justify homosexuality and the desertion of one's dying wife, certainly not. But then again, having paid one's *devoirs* to morality, how does one rescue from morality Gide's essential point about the supreme rights of the individual person, and without making it merely historical, academic?

My first response to the necessity of dealing with matters of this kind was resentment of the personal discomfort it caused me. These are subjects we usually deal with either quite unconsciously or in the privacy of our own conscious minds, and if we now and then disclose our thoughts about them, it is to friends of equal age and especial closeness. Or if we touch upon them publicly, we do so in the relative abstractness and anonymity of print. To stand up in one's own person and to speak of them in one's own voice to an audience which each year grows younger as one grows older—that is not easy, and probably it is not decent.

And then, leaving aside the personal considerations, or taking them merely as an indication of something wrong with the situation, can we not say that, when modern literature is brought into the classroom, the subject being taught is betrayed by the pedagogy of the subject? We have to ask ourselves whether in our day too much does not come within the purview of the academy. More and more, as the universities liberalize themselves, and turn their beneficent imperialistic gaze upon what is called Life Itself, the feeling grows among our educated classes that little can be experienced unless it is validated by some established intellectual discipline, with the result that experience loses much of its personal immediacy for us and becomes part of an accredited societal activity. This is not entirely true and I don't want to play the boring academic game of pretending that it is entirely true, that the university mind wilts and withers whatever it touches. I must believe and I do believe, that the university study of art is capable of confronting the power of a work of art fully and courageously. I even believe that it can discover and disclose power where it has not been felt before. But the university study of art achieves this end chiefly with works of art of an older period. Time has the effect of seeming to quiet the work of art, domesticating it and making it into a classic, which is often another way of saying that it is an object of merely habitual regard. University study of the right sort can reverse this process and restore to the old work its freshness and force—can, indeed, disclose unguessed-at power. But with the works of art of our own present age, university study tends to accelerate the process by which the radical and subversive work becomes the classic work, and university study does this in the degree that it is vivacious and responsive and what is called non-academic. In one of his poems Yeats mocks the literary scholars, "the bald heads forgetful of their sins," "the old, learned, respectable bald heads," who edit the poems of the fierce and passionate young men.

> Lord, what would they say
> Did their Catullus walk this way?

Yeats, of course, is thinking of his own future fate, and no doubt there is all the radical and comical discrepancy that he sees between the poet's passions and the scholars' close-eyed concentration on the text. Yet for my part, when I think of Catullus, I am moved to praise the tact of all those old heads, from Heinsius and Bentley to Munro and Postgate, who worked on Codex G and Codex O and drew conclusions from them about the lost Codex V—for doing only this and for not trying to realize and demonstrate the true intensity and the true quality and the true cultural meaning of Catullus's passion and managing to bring it somehow into eventual accord with their respectability and baldness. Nowadays we who deal with books in universities live in fear that the World, which we imagine to be a vital, palpitating, passionate, reality-loving World, will think of us as old, respectable, and bald, and we see to it that in our dealings with Yeats (to take him as the example) his wild cry of rage and sexuality is heard by our students and quite thoroughly understood by them as—what is it that we eventually call it?—*a significant expression of our culture.* The exasperation of Lawrence and the subversiveness of Gide, by the time we have dealt with them boldly and straightforwardly, are notable instances of the *alienation of modern man as exemplified by the artist.* "Compare Yeats, Gide, Lawrence, and Eliot in the use which they make of the theme of sexuality to criticize the deficiencies of modern culture. Support your statement by specific references to the work of each author. [Time: one hour.]" And the distressing thing about our examination questions is that they are not ridiculous, they make perfectly good sense—such good sense that the young person who answers them can never again know the force and terror of what has been communicated to him by the works he is being examined on.

Very likely it was with the thought of saving myself from the necessity of speaking personally and my students from having to betray the full harsh meaning of a great literature that I first taught my course in as *literary* a way as possible. A couple of decades ago the discovery was made that a literary work is a structure of words: this doesn't seem a surprising thing to have learned except for its polemical tendency, which is to urge us to minimize the amount of attention we give to the poet's social and personal will, to what he wants to happen outside the poem as a result of the poem; it urges us to fix our minds on what is going on inside the poem. For me this polemical tendency has been of the greatest usefulness, for it has corrected my inclination to pay attention chiefly to what the poet *wants.* For two or three years I directed my efforts toward dealing with the matter of the course chiefly as structures of words, in a formal way, with due attention paid to the literal difficulty which marked so many of the works. But it went against the grain. It went against my personal grain. It went against the grain of the classroom situation, for formal analysis is best carried on by question-and-answer, which needs small groups, and the registration for the course in modern literature in any college is sure to be large. And it went against the grain of the authors themselves—structures of words they may indeed have created, but these structures were not pyramids or triumphal arches, they were manifestly contrived to be not static and commemorative but mobile and aggressive, and one does not describe a quinquereme or a howitzer or a tank without estimating how much *damage* it can do.

Eventually I had to decide that there was only one way to give the course, which was to give it without strategies and without conscious caution. It was not honorable, either to the students or to the authors, to conceal or disguise my relation to the literature, my commitment to it, my fear of it, my ambivalence toward it. The literature had to be dealt with in the terms it announced for itself. As for the students, I have never given assent to the modern saw about "teaching students, not subjects"—I have always thought it right to teach subjects, believing that if one give his first loyalty to the subject, the student is best instructed. So I resolved to give the course with no considerations in mind except my own interests. And since my own interests lead me to see literary situations as cultural situations, and cultural situations as great elaborate fights about moral issues, and moral issues as having something to do with gratuitously chosen images of personal being, and images of personal being as having something to do with literary style, I felt free to begin with what for me was a first concern, the animus of the author, the objects of his will, the things he wants or wants to have happen.

My cultural and non-literary method led me to decide that I would begin the course with a statement of certain themes or issues that might especially engage our attention. I even went so far in non-literariness as to think that my purposes would best be served if I could contrive a "background" for the works we would read—I wanted to propose a history for the themes or issues that I hoped to discover. I did not intend that this history should be either very extensive or very precise. I wanted merely to encourage a *sense* of a history, some general intuition of a past, in students who, as it seems to me, have not been provided with any such thing by their education and who are on the whole glad to be without it. And because there is as yet no adequate general work of history of the culture of the last two hundred years, I asked myself what books of the age just preceding ours had most influenced our literature, or, since I was far less concerned with showing influence than with discerning a tendency, what older books might seem to fall into a line the direction of which pointed to our own literature and thus might serve as a prolegomenon to the course.

It was virtually inevitable that the first work that should have sprung to mind was Sir James Frazer's *The Golden Bough*, not, of course, the whole of it, but certain chapters, those that deal with Osiris, Attis, and Adonis. Anyone who thinks about modern literature in a systematic way takes for granted the great part played in it by myth, and especially by those examples of myth which tell about gods dying and being reborn—the imagination of death and rebirth, reiterated in the ancient world in innumerable variations that are yet always the same, captivated the literary mind at the very moment when, as all accounts of the modern age agree, the most massive and compelling of all the stories of resurrection had lost much of its hold upon the world.

Perhaps no book has had so decisive an effect upon modern literature as Frazer's. It was beautifully to my purpose that it had first been published ten years before the twentieth century began. Yet forty-three years later, in 1933, Frazer delivered a lecture, very eloquent, in which he bade the world be of good hope in the face of the threat to the human mind that was being offered by the Nazi power. He was still alive in 1941. Yet he had been born in 1854, three years before Matthew Arnold gave the lecture "On the Modern Element in literature." Here, surely, was history, here was the past I wanted, beautifully connected with our present. Frazer was wholly a man of the nineteenth century, and the more so because the eighteenth century was so congenial to him—the lecture of 1933 in which he predicted the Nazi defeat had as its subject Condorcet's *Progress of the Human Mind;* when he took time from his anthropological studies to deal with literature, he prepared editions of Addison's essays and Cowper's letters. He had the old lost belief in the virtue and power of rationality. He loved and counted on order, decorum, and good sense. This great historian of the primitive imagination was in the dominant intellectual tradition of the West which, since the days of the pre-Socratics, has condemned the ways of thought that we call primitive.

It can be said of Frazer that in his conscious intention he was a perfect representative of what Arnold meant when he spoke of a modern age. And perhaps nothing could make clearer how the conditions of life and literature have changed in a hundred years than to note the difference between the way in which Arnold defines the modern element in literature and the way in which we must define it.

Arnold used the word *modern* in a wholly honorific sense. So much so that he seems to dismiss all temporal idea from the word and makes it signify certain timeless intellectual and civic virtues—his lecture, indeed, was about the modern element in the ancient literatures. A society, he said, is a modern society when it maintains a condition of repose, confidence, free activity of the mind, and the tolerance of divergent views. A society is modern when it affords sufficient material well-being for the conveniences of life and the development of taste. And, finally, a society is modern when its members are intellectually mature, by which Arnold means that they are willing to judge by reason, to observe facts in a critical spirit, and to search for the law of things. By this definition Periclean Athens is for Arnold a modern age, Elizabethan England is not; Thucydides is a modern historian, Sir Walter Raleigh is not.

I shall not go into further details of Arnold's definition or description of the modern. I have said enough, I think, to suggest what Arnold was up to, what he wanted to see realized as the desideratum of his own society, what ideal he wanted the works of intellect and imagination of his own time to advance. And at what a distance his ideal of the modern puts him from our present sense of modernity, from our modern literature! To anyone conditioned by our modern literature, Arnold's ideal of order, convenience, decorum, and rationality might well seem to reduce itself to the small advantages and excessive limitations of the middle-class life of a few prosperous nations of the nineteenth century. Arnold's historic sense presented to his mind the long, bitter, bloody past of Europe, and he seized passionately upon the hope of true civilization at last achieved. But the historic sense of our literature has in mind a long excess of civilization to which may be ascribed the bitterness and bloodiness both of the past and of the present and of which the peaceful aspects are to be thought of as mainly contemptible—its order achieved at the cost of extravagant personal repression, either that of coercion or that of acquiescence; its repose otiose; its tolerance either flaccid or capricious; its material comfort corrupt and corrupting; its taste a manifestation either of timidity or of pride; its rationality attained only at the price of energy and passion.

For the understanding of this radical change of opinion nothing is more illuminating than to be aware of the doubleness of mind of the author of *The Golden Bough*. I have said that Frazer in his conscious mind and in his first intention exemplifies all that Arnold means by the modern. He often speaks quite harshly of the irrationality and the orgiastic excesses of the primitive religions he describes, and even Christianity comes under his criticism both because it stands in the way of rational thought and because it can draw men away from intelligent participation in the life of society. But Frazer had more than one intention, and he had an unconscious as well as a conscious mind. If he deplores the primitive imagination, he also does not fail to show it as wonderful and beautiful. It is the rare reader of *The Golden Bough* who finds the ancient beliefs and rituals wholly alien to him. It is to be expected that Frazer's adduction of the many pagan analogues to the Christian mythos will be thought by Christian readers to have an adverse effect on faith, it was undoubtedly Frazer's purpose that it should, yet many readers will feel that Frazer makes all faith and ritual indigenous to humanity, virtually biological; they feel, as De Quincey put it, that not to be at least a *little* superstitious is to lack generosity of mind. Scientific though his purpose was, Frazer had the effect of validating those old modes of experiencing the world which modern men, beginning with the Romantics, have sought to revive in order to escape from positivism and common sense.

The direction of the imagination upon great and mysterious objects of worship is not the only means men use to liberate themselves from the bondage of quotidian fact, and although Frazer can scarcely be held accountable for the ever-growing modern attraction to the extreme mental states—to rapture, ecstasy, and transcendence, which are achieved by drugs, trance, music and dance, orgy, and the derangement of personality—yet he did provide a bridge to the understanding and acceptance of these states, he proposed to us the idea that the desire for them and the use of them for heuristic purposes is a common and acceptable manifestation of human nature.

This one element of Frazer's masterpiece could scarcely fail to suggest the next of my prolegomenal works. It is worth remarking that its author was in his own way as great a classical scholar as Frazer himself—Nietzsche was Professor of Classical Philology at the University of Basel when, at the age of twenty-seven, he published his essay *The Birth of Tragedy*. After the appearance of this stunningly brilliant account of Greek civilization, of which Socrates is not the hero but the villain, what can possibly be left to us of that rational and ordered Greece, that modern, that eighteenth-century, Athens that Arnold so entirely relied on as the standard for judging all civilizations? Professor Kaufmann is right when he warns us against supposing that Nietzsche exalts Dionysus over Apollo and tells us that Nietzsche "emphasizes the Dionysiac only because he feels that the Apollonian genius of the Greeks cannot be fully understood apart from it." But no one reading Nietzsche's essay for the first time is likely to heed this warning. What will reach him before due caution intervenes, before he becomes aware of the portentous dialectic between Dionysus and Apollo, is the excitement of suddenly being liberated from Aristotle, the joy of finding himself acceding to the author's statement that "art rather than ethics constitutes the essential metaphysical activity of man," that tragedy has its source in the Dionysiac rapture, "whose closest analogy is furnished by physical intoxication," and that this rapture, in which "the individual forgets himself completely," was in itself no metaphysical state but an orgiastic display of lust and cruelty, "of sexual promiscuity overriding every form of tribal law." This sadic and masochistic frenzy, Nietzsche is at pains to insist, needs the taming hand of Apollo before it can become tragedy, but it is the primal stuff of the great art, and to the modern experience of tragedy this explanation seems far more pertinent than Aristotle's, with its eagerness to forget its origin in its achievement of a state of noble imperturbability.

Of supreme importance in itself, Nietzsche's essay had for me the added pedagogic advantage of allowing me to establish a historical line back to William Blake. Nothing is more characteristic of modern literature than its discovery and canonization of the primal, non-ethical energies, and the historical point could be made the better by remarking the correspondence of thought of two men of different nations and separated from each other by a good many decades, for Nietzsche's Dionysian orgy and Blake's Hell are much the same thing.

Whether or not Joseph Conrad read either Blake or Nietzsche I do not know, but his *Heart of Darkness* follows in their line. This very great work has never lacked for the admiration it deserves, and it has been given a kind of canonical place in the legend of modern literature by Eliot's having it so clearly in mind when he wrote *The Waste Land* and his having taken from it the epigraph to "The Hollow Men." But no one, to my knowledge, has ever confronted in an explicit way its strange and terrible message of ambivalence toward the life of civilization. Consider that its protagonist, Kurtz, is a progressive and a liberal and that he is the highly respected representative of a society which would have us believe it is benign, although in fact it is vicious. Consider too that he is a practitioner of several arts, a painter, a writer, a musician, and into the bargain a political orator. He is at once the most idealistic and the most practically successful of all the agents of the Belgian exploitation of the Congo. Everybody knows the truth about him which Marlow discovers—that Kurtz's success is the result of a terrible ascendancy he has gained over the natives of his distant station, an ascendancy which is derived from his presumed magical or divine powers, that he has exercised his rule with an extreme of cruelty, that he has given himself to unnamable acts of lust. This is the world of the darker pages of *The Golden Bough*. It is one of the great points of Conrad's story that Marlow speaks of the primitive life of the jungle not as being noble or charming or even free but as being base and sordid—and for *that* reason compelling: he himself feels quite overtly its dreadful attraction. It is to this devilish baseness that Kurtz has yielded himself, and yet Marlow, although he does indeed treat him with hostile irony, does not find it possible to suppose that Kurtz is anything but a hero of the spirit. For me it is still ambiguous whether Kurtz's famous deathbed cry, "The horror! The horror!" refers to the approach of death or to his experience of savage life. Whichever it is, to Marlow the fact that Kurtz could utter this cry at the point of death, while Marlow himself, when death threatens him, can know it only as a weary grayness, marks the difference between the ordinary man and a hero of the spirit. Is this not the essence of the modern belief about the nature of the artist, the man who goes down into that hell which is the historical beginning of the human soul, a beginning not outgrown but established in humanity as we know it now, preferring the reality of this hell to the bland lies of the civilization that has overlaid it?

This idea is proposed again in the somewhat less powerful but still very moving work with which I followed *Heart of Darkness*, Thomas Mann's *Death in Venice*. I wanted this story not so much for its account of an extravagantly Apollonian personality surrendering to forces that, in his Apollonian character, he thought shameful—although this was certainly to my purpose—but rather for Aschenbach's fevered dreams of the erotic past, and in particular that dream of the goat-orgy which Mann, being the kind of writer he is, having the kind of relation to Nietzsche he had, might well have written to serve as an illustration of what *The Birth of Tragedy* means by religious frenzy, the more so, of course, because Mann chooses that particular orgiastic ritual, the killing and eating of the goat, from which tragedy is traditionally said to have been derived.

A notable element of this story in which the birth of tragedy plays an important part is that the degradation and downfall of the protagonist is not represented as tragic in the usual sense of the word—that is, it is not represented as a great deplorable event. It is a commonplace of modern literary thought that the tragic mode is not available even to the gravest and noblest or our writers. I am not sure that this is the deprivation that some people think it to be and a mark of our spiritual inferiority. But if we ask why it has come about, one reason may be that we have learned to think our way back through tragedy to the primal stuff out of which tragedy arose. If we consider the primitive forbidden ways of conduct which traditionally in tragedy lead to punishment by death, we think of them as being the path to reality and truth, to an ultimate self-realization. We have always wondered if tragedy itself may not have been saying just this in a deeply hidden way, drawing us to think of the hero's sin and death as somehow conferring justification, even salvation of a sort—no doubt this is what Nietzsche had in mind when he said that "tragedy denies ethics." What tragedy once seemed to hint, our literature now is willing to say quite explicitly. If Mann's Aschenbach dies at the height of his intellectual and artistic powers, overcome by a passion that his ethical reason condemns, we do not take this to be a defeat, rather a kind of terrible rebirth: at his latter end the artist knows a reality that he had until now refused to admit to consciousness.

Thoughts like these suggested that another of Nietzsche's works, *The Genealogy of Morals*, might be in point. It proposes a view of society which is consonant with the belief that art and not ethics constitutes the essential metaphysical activity of man and with the validation and ratification of the primitive energies. Nietzsche's theory of the social order dismisses all ethical impulse from its origins—the basis of society is to be found in

the rationalization of cruelty: as simple as that. Nietzsche has no ultimate Utopian intention in saying this, no hope of revising the essence of the social order, although he does
believe that its pain can be mitigated. He represents cruelty as a social necessity, for only
by its exercise could men ever have been induced to develop a continuity of will: nothing else than cruel pain could have created in mankind that memory of intention which
makes society possible. The method of cynicism which Nietzsche pursued—let us be clear
that it is a method and not an attitude—goes so far as to describe punishment in terms
of the pleasure derived from the exercise of cruelty: "Compensation," he says, "consists in
a legal warrant entitling one man to exercise his cruelty on another." There follows that
most remarkable passage in which Nietzsche describes the process whereby the individual
turns the cruelty of punishment against himself and creates the bad conscience and the
consciousness of guilt which manifests itself as a pervasive anxiety. Nietzsche's complexity
of mind is beyond all comparison, for in this book which is dedicated to the liberation of
the conscience, Nietzsche makes his defense of the bad conscience as a decisive force in
the interests of culture. It is much the same line of argument that he takes when, having
attacked the Jewish morality and the priestly existence in the name of the health of the
spirit, he reminds us that only by his sickness does man become interesting.

From *The Genealogy of Morals* to Freud's *Civilization and Its Discontents* is but a step,
and some might think that, for pedagogic purposes, the step is so small as to make the
second book supererogatory. But although Freud's view of society and culture has indeed
a very close affinity to Nietzsche's, Freud does add certain considerations which are essential to our sense of the modern disposition.

For one thing, he puts to us the question of whether or not we want to *accept* civilization. It is not the first time that the paradox of civilization has been present to the
mind of civilized people, the sense that civilization makes men behave worse and suffer
more than does some less developed state of human existence. But hitherto all such ideas
were formulated in a moralizing way—civilization was represented as being "corrupt," a
divagation from a state of innocence. Freud had no illusions about a primitive innocence,
he conceived no practicable alternative to civilization. In consequence, there was a unique
force to the question he asked: whether we wished to accept civilization, with all its contradictions, with all its pains—pains, for "discontents" does not accurately describe what
Freud has in mind. He had his own answer to the question—his tragic, or stoic, sense of
life dictated it: we do well to accept it, although we also do well to cast a cold eye on the
fate that makes it our better part to accept it. Like Nietzsche, Freud thought that life was
justified by our heroic response to its challenge.

But the question Freud posed has not been set aside or closed up by the answer that
he himself gave to it. His answer, like Nietzsche's, is essentially in the line of traditional
humanism—we can see this in the sternness with which he charges women not to interfere with men in the discharge of their cultural duty, not to claim men for love and the
family to the detriment of their free activity in the world. But just here lies the matter of
Freud's question that the world more and more believes Freud himself did not answer.
The pain that civilization inflicts is that of the instinctual renunciation that civilization
demands, and it would seem that fewer and fewer people wish to say with Freud that the
loss of instinctual gratification, emotional freedom, or love, is compensated for either by
the security of civilized life or by the stern pleasures of the masculine moral character.

With Freud's essay I brought to a close my list of prolegomenal books for the first
term of the course. I shall not do much more than mention the books with which I introduced the second term, but I should like to do at least that. I began with *Rameau's Nephew,*

thinking that the peculiar moral authority which Diderot assigns to the envious, untalented, unregenerate protagonist was peculiarly relevant to the line taken by the ethical explorations of modern literature. Nothing is more characteristic of the literature of our time than the replacement of the hero by what has come to be called the anti-hero, in whose indifference to or hatred of ethical nobility there is presumed to lie a special authenticity. Diderot is quite overt about this—he himself in his public character is the deuteragonist, the "honest consciousness," as Hegel calls him, and he takes delight in the discomfiture of the decent, dull person he is by the Nephew's nihilistic mind.

It seemed to me too that there was a particular usefulness in the circumstance that this anti-hero should avow so openly his *envy,* which Tocqueville has called the ruling emotion of democracy, and that, although he envied anyone at all who had access to the creature comforts and the social status which he lacked, what chiefly animated him was envy of men of genius. Ours is the first cultural epoch in which many men aspire to high achievement in the arts and, in their frustration, form a dispossessed class which cuts across the conventional class lines, making a proletariat of the spirit.

Although *Rameau's Nephew* was not published until fairly late in the century, it was known in manuscript by Goethe and Hegel; it suited the temper and won the admiration of Marx and Freud for reasons that are obvious. And there is ground for supposing that it was known to Dostoevski, whose *Notes from Underground* is a restatement of the essential idea of Diderot's dialogue in terms both more extreme and less genial. The Nephew is still on the defensive—he is naughtily telling secrets about the nature of man and society. But Dostoevski's underground man shouts aloud his envy and hatred and carries the ark of his self hatred and alienation into a remorseless battle with what he calls "the good and the beautiful," mounting an attack upon every belief not merely of bourgeois society but of the whole humanist tradition. The inclusion of *Notes from Underground* among my prolegomenal books constituted something of a pedagogic risk, for if I wished to emphasize the subversive tendency of modern literature, here was a work which made all subsequent subversion seem like affirmation, so radical and so brilliant was its negation of our traditional pieties and its affirmation of our new pieties.

I hesitated in compunction before following *Notes from Underground* with Tolstoi's *Death of Ivan Ilyitch,* which so ruthlessly and with such dreadful force destroys the citadel of the commonplace life in which we all believe we can take refuge from ourselves and our fate. But I did assign it and then two of Pirandello's plays which, in the atmosphere of the sordidness of the commonplace life, undermine all certitudes of the commonplace, common-sense mind.

From time to time I have raised with myself the question of whether my choice of these prolegomenal works was not extravagant, quite excessively tendentious. I have never been able to believe that it is. And if these works do indeed serve to indicate in an accurate way the nature of modern literature, a teacher might find it worth asking how his students respond to the strong dose.

One response I have already described—the readiness of the students to engage in the process that we might call the socialization of the anti-social, or the acculturation of the anti-cultural, or the legitimization of the subversive. When the term-essays come in, it is plain to me that almost none of the students have been taken aback by what they have read: they have wholly contained the attack. The chief exceptions are the few who simply do not comprehend, although they may be awed by, the categories of our discourse. In their papers, like poor hunted creatures in a Kafka story, they take refuge first in misunderstood large phrases, then in bad grammar, then in general incoherence. After my pedagogical exasperation has run its course, I find that I am sometimes moved to give them a queer respect, as if they had stood up and said what in fact they don't have the wit to stand up and say: "Why do you harry us? Leave us alone. We are not Modern Man. We are the Old People. Ours is the Old Faith. We serve the little Old Gods, the gods of the copybook maxims, the small, dark, somewhat powerful deities of lawyers, doctors, engineers, accountants. With them is neither sensibility nor angst. With them is no disgust—it is they, indeed, who make ready the way for 'the good and the beautiful' about which low-minded doubts have been raised in this course, that 'good and beautiful' which we do not possess and don't want to possess but which we know justifies our lives. Leave us alone and let us worship our gods in the way they approve, in peace and unawareness." Crass, but—to use that interesting modern word which we have learned from the curators of museums—authentic. The rest, the minds that give me the A papers and the B papers and even the C+ papers, move through the terrors and mysteries of modern literature like so many Parsifals, asking no questions at the behest of wonder and fear. Or like so many seminarists who have been systematically instructed in the constitution of Hell and the ways to damnation. Or like so many *readers*, entertained by moral horror stories. I asked them to look into the Abyss, and, both dutifully and gladly, they have looked into the Abyss, and the Abyss has greeted them with the grave courtesy of all objects of serious study, saying: "Interesting, am I not? And *exciting*, if you consider how deep I am and what dread beasts lie at my bottom. Have it well in mind that a knowledge of me contributes materially to your being whole, or well-rounded, men."

In my distress over the outrage I have conspired to perpetrate upon a great literature, I wonder if perhaps I have not been reading these papers too literally. After all, a term-essay is not a diary of the soul, it is not an occasion for telling the truth. What my students might reveal of their true feelings to a younger teacher they will not reveal to me; they will give me what they conceive to be the proper response to the official version of terror I have given them. I bring to mind their faces, which are not necessarily the faces of the authors of these unperturbed papers, nor are they, not yet, the faces of fathers of families, or of theatergoers, or of buyers of modern paintings: not yet. I must think it possible that in ways and to a degree which they keep secret they have responded directly and personally to what they have read.

And if they have? And if they have, am I the more content?

What form would I want their response to take? It is a teacher's question that I am asking, not a critic's. We have decided in recent years to think of the critic and the teacher of literature as one and the same, and no doubt it is both possible and useful to do so. But there are some points at which the functions of the two do not coincide, or can be made to coincide only with great difficulty. Of criticism we have been told, by Arnold, that "it must be apt to study and praise elements that for fulness of spiritual perfection are wanted, even though they belong to a power which in the practical sphere may be maleficent." But teaching, or at least undergraduate teaching, is not given the same licensed mandate—cannot be given it because the teacher's audience, which stands before his very eyes, as the critic's audience does not, asks questions about "the practical sphere," as the critic's audience does not. For instance, on the very day that I write this, when I had said to my class all I could think of to say about *The Magic Mountain* and invited questions and comments, one student asked, "How would you generalize the idea of the educative value of illness, so that it would be applicable not only to a particular individual, Hans Castorp, but to young people at large?" It makes us smile, but it was asked in all seriousness, and it is serious in its substance, and it had to be answered seriously, in part by the reflection that this idea, like so many ideas encountered in the books of the course, had to be thought of as having reference only to the private life; that it touched the public life only in some indirect or tangential way; that it really ought to be encountered in solitude, even in secrecy, since to talk about it in public and in our academic setting was to seem to propose for it a public practicality and thus to distort its meaning. To this another student replied; he said that, despite the public ritual of the classroom, each student inevitably experienced the books in privacy and found their meaning in reference to his own life. True enough, but the teacher sees the several privacies coming together to make a group, and they propose—no doubt the more because they come together every Monday, Wednesday, and Friday at a particular hour—the idea of a community, that is to say, "the practical sphere."

This being so, the teacher cannot escape the awareness of certain circumstances which the critic, who writes for an ideal, uncircumstanced reader, has no need to take into account. The teacher considers, for example, the social situation of his students—they are not of patrician origin, they do not come from homes in which stubbornness, pride, and conscious habit prevail, nor are they born into a culture marked by these traits, a culture in which other interesting and valuable things compete with and resist ideas; they come, mostly, from "good homes" in which authority and valuation are weak or at least not very salient and bold, so that ideas have for them, at their present stage of development, a peculiar power and preciousness. And in this connection the teacher will have in mind the special prestige that our culture, in its upper reaches, gives to art, and to the ideas that art proposes—the agreement, ever growing in assertiveness, that art yields more truth than any other intellectual activity. In this culture what a shock it is to encounter Santayana's acerb skepticism about art, or Keat's remark, which the critics and scholars never take notice of, presumably because they suppose it to be an aberration, that poetry is "not so fine a thing as philosophy—For the same reason that an eagle is not so fine a thing as a truth." For many students no ideas that they will encounter in any college discipline will equal in force and sanction the ideas conveyed to them by modern literature.

The author of *The Magic Mountain* once said that all his work could be understood as an effort to free himself from the middle class, and this, of course, will serve to describe the chief intention of all modern literature. And the means of freedom which Mann prescribes (the characteristic irony notwithstanding) is the means of freedom which in effect all of modern literature prescribes. It is, in the words of Claudia Chauchat, "*se perdre et même...se laisser dépérir*," and thus to name the means is to make plain that the end is not merely freedom from the middle class but freedom from society itself. I venture to say that the idea of losing oneself up to the point of self-destruction, of surrendering oneself to experience without regard to self-interest or conventional morality, of escaping wholly from the societal bonds, is an "element" somewhere in the mind of every modern person who dares to think of what Arnold in his unaffected Victorian way called "the fulness of spiritual perfection." But the teacher who undertakes to present modern literature to his students may not allow that idea to remain in the *somewhere* of his mind; he must take it from the place where it exists habitual and unrealized and put it in the conscious forefront of his thought. And if he is committed to an admiration of modern literature, he must also be committed to this chief idea of modern literature. I press the logic of the situation not in order to question the legitimacy of the commitment, or even the propriety of expressing the commitment in the college classroom (although it does seem odd!), but to confront those of us who do teach modern literature with the striking actuality of our enterprise.

MILTON FRIEDMAN

Selection from *Capitalism and Freedom* (1962)

One of the most effective twentieth-century American champions of the free market was Milton Friedman (1912–2006), longtime leader of the "Chicago School" of economics that built upon the classical economic theories of Adam Smith and John Stuart Mill. The selection that follows is the introduction to *Capitalism and Freedom*, Friedman's most accessible and popular book. Published during the high tide of liberal politics in the United States, in the era of Presidents Kennedy and Johnson, this book was for many years a favorite text of dissenters. Yet its standing increased in the later part of the century. Friedman himself was a prominent advisor to Republican presidents Richard Nixon and Ronald Reagan. When the fall of the Soviet Empire stimulated greater interest in free markets in many parts of the world, Friedman's ideas became more influential abroad. By the time of its fortieth anniversary edition in 2002, *Capitalism and Freedom* had become one of the most widely discussed works of political economy in the world. Friedman has been known as a "conservative" because of the widespread association of that word with free market ideologies as opposed to those favoring a more managed economy, so it is important to note that when Friedman refers to himself as a "liberal," he is speaking in an older idiom in which liberalism was understood to embrace "free markets" rather than to regulate them.

Friedman was unusual among economists for combining technical, disciplinary work of the highest quality (he was awarded the Nobel Prize in 1976) with popular writings, including a column in *Newsweek* and a series of television programs that became the basis for a book he coauthored with his wife, Rose D. Friedman, *Free to Choose* (New York, 1980). Friedman taught at the University of Chicago for thirty years before taking up residence at the Hoover Institution on the campus of Stanford University.

Friedman's ideas can be instructively studied in relation to the work of economists more skeptical of free markets. Two of the most influential and accessible of these have been John Kenneth Galbraith, most easily approached through his *The Essential Galbraith* (New York, 2001); and Paul Krugman, especially his *Peddling Prosperity* (New York, 1994). Krugman wrote a discerning commentary on Friedman's ideas immediately after Friedman's death: Paul Krugman, "Who was Milton Friedman?" *New York Review of Books* (February 15, 2007).

It is widely believed that politics and economics are separate and largely unconnected; that individual freedom is a political problem and material welfare an economic problem; and that any kind of political arrangements can be combined with any kind of economic arrangements. The chief contemporary manifestation of this idea is the advocacy of "democratic socialism" by many who condemn out of hand the restrictions on individual freedom imposed by "totalitarian socialism" in Russia, and who are persuaded that it is possible for a country to adopt the essential features of Russian economic arrangements and yet to ensure individual freedom through political arrangements. The thesis of this chapter is that such a view is a delusion, that there is an intimate connection between economics and politics, that only certain combinations of political and economic arrangements are possible, and that in particular, a society which is socialist cannot also be democratic, in the sense of guaranteeing individual freedom.

Economic arrangements play a dual role in the promotion of a free society. On the one hand, freedom in economic arrangements is itself a component of freedom broadly understood, so economic freedom is an end in itself. In the second place, economic freedom is also an indispensable means toward the achievement of political freedom.

The first of these roles of economic freedom needs special emphasis because intellectuals in particular have a strong bias against regarding this aspect of freedom as important. They tend to express contempt for what they regard as material aspects of life, and to regard their own pursuit of allegedly higher values as on a different plane of significance and as deserving of special attention. For most citizens of the country, however, if not for the intellectual, the direct importance of economic freedom is at least comparable in significance to the indirect importance of economic freedom as a means to political freedom.

The citizen of Great Britain, who after World War II was not permitted to spend his vacation in the United States because of exchange control, was being deprived of an essential freedom no less than the citizen of the United States, who was denied the opportunity to spend his vacation in Russia because of his political views. The one was ostensibly an economic limitation on freedom and the other a political limitation, yet there is no essential difference between the two.

The citizen of the United States who is compelled by law to devote something like 10 per cent of his income to the purchase of a particular kind of retirement contract, administered by the government, is being deprived of a corresponding part of his personal freedom. How strongly this deprivation may be felt and its closeness to the deprivation of religious freedom, which all would regard as "civil" or "political" rather than "economic," were dramatized by an episode involving a group of farmers of the Amish sect. On grounds of principle, this group regarded compulsory federal old age programs as an infringement of their personal individual freedom and refused to pay taxes or accept benefits. As a result, some of their livestock were sold by auction in order to satisfy claims for social security levies. True, the number of citizens who regard compulsory old age insurance as a deprivation of freedom may be few, but the believer in freedom has never counted noses.

A citizen of the United States who under the laws of various states is not free to follow the occupation of his own choosing unless he can get a license for it, is likewise being

Source: Milton Friedman, *Capitalism and Freedom* (Chicago: University of Chicago Press, 1962), 7–21. Reprinted by permission of the University of Chicago Press.

deprived of an essential part of his freedom. So is the man who would like to exchange some of his goods with, say, a Swiss for a watch but is prevented from doing so by a quota. So also is the Californian who was thrown into jail for selling Alka Seltzer at a price below that set by the manufacturer under so-called "fair trade" laws. So also is the farmer who cannot grow the amount of wheat he wants. And so on. Clearly, economic freedom, in and of itself, is an extremely important part of total freedom.

Viewed as a means to the end of political freedom, economic arrangements are important because of their effect on the concentration or dispersion of power. The kind of economic organization that provides economic freedom directly, namely, competitive capitalism, also promotes political freedom because it separates economic power from political power and in this way enables the one to offset the other.

Historical evidence speaks with a single voice on the relation between political freedom and a free market. I know of no example in time or place of a society that has been marked by a large measure of political freedom, and that has not also used something comparable to a free market to organize the bulk of economic activity.

Because we live in a largely free society, we tend to forget how limited is the span of time and the part of the globe for which there has ever been anything like political freedom: the typical state of mankind is tyranny, servitude, and misery. The nineteenth century and early twentieth century in the Western world stand out as striking exceptions to the general trend of historical development. Political freedom in this instance clearly came along with the free market and the development of capitalist institutions. So also did political freedom in the golden age of Greece and in the early days of the Roman era.

History suggests only that capitalism is a necessary condition for political freedom. Clearly it is not a sufficient condition. Fascist Italy and Fascist Spain, Germany at various times in the last seventy years, Japan before World Wars I and II, tzarist Russia in the decades before World War I—are all societies that cannot conceivably be described as politically free. Yet, in each, private enterprise was the dominant form of economic organization. It is therefore clearly possible to have economic arrangements that are fundamentally capitalist and political arrangements that are not free.

Even in those societies, the citizenry had a good deal more freedom than citizens of a modern totalitarian state like Russia or Nazi Germany, in which economic totalitarianism is combined with political totalitarianism. Even in Russia under the Tzars, it was possible for some citizens, under some circumstances, to change their jobs without getting permission from political authority because capitalism and the existence of private property provided some check to the centralized power of the state.

The relation between political and economic freedom is complex and by no means unilateral. In the early nineteenth century, Bentham and the Philosophical Radicals were inclined to regard political freedom as a means to economic freedom. They believed that the masses were being hampered by the restrictions that were being imposed upon them, and that if political reform gave the bulk of the people the vote, they would do what was good for them, which was to vote for laissez faire. In retrospect, one cannot say that they were wrong. There was a large measure of political reform that was accompanied by economic reform in the direction of a great deal of laissez faire. An enormous increase in the well-being of the masses followed this change in economic arrangements.

The triumph of Benthamite liberalism in nineteenth-century England was followed by a reaction toward increasing intervention by government in economic affairs. This tendency to collectivism was greatly accelerated, both in England and elsewhere, by the two World Wars. Welfare rather than freedom became the dominant note in democratic countries. Recognizing the implicit threat to individualism, the intellectual descendants of the Philosophical Radicals—Dicey, Mises, Hayek, and Simons, to mention only a few—feared that a continued movement toward centralized control of economic activity would prove *The Road to Serfdom,* as Hayek entitled his penetrating analysis of the process. Their emphasis was on economic freedom as a means toward political freedom.

Events since the end of World War II display still a different relation between economic and political freedom. Collectivist economic planning has indeed interfered with individual freedom. At least in some countries, however, the result has not been the suppression of freedom, but the reversal of economic policy. England again provides the most striking example. The turning point was perhaps the "control of engagements" order which, despite great misgivings, the Labour party found it necessary to impose in order to carry out its economic policy. Fully enforced and carried through, the law would have involved centralized allocation of individuals to occupations. This conflicted so sharply with personal liberty that it was enforced in a negligible number of cases, and then repealed after the law had been in effect for only a short period. Its repeal ushered in a decided shift in economic policy, marked by reduced reliance on centralized "plans" and "programs," by the dismantling of many controls, and by increased emphasis on the private market. A similar shift in policy occurred in most other democratic countries.

The proximate explanation of these shifts in policy is the limited success of central planning or its outright failure to achieve stated objectives. However, this failure is itself to be attributed, at least in some measure, to the political implications of central planning and to an unwillingness to follow out its logic when doing so requires trampling rough-shod on treasured private rights. It may well be that the shift is only a temporary interruption in the collectivist trend of this century. Even so, it illustrates the close relation between political freedom and economic arrangements.

Historical evidence by itself can never be convincing. Perhaps it was sheer coincidence that the expansion of freedom occurred at the same time as the development of capitalist and market institutions. Why should there be a connection? What are the logical links between economic and political freedom? In discussing these questions we shall consider first the market as a direct component of freedom, and then the indirect relation between market arrangements and political freedom. A by-product will be an outline of the ideal economic arrangements for a free society.

As liberals, we take freedom of the individual, or perhaps the family, as our ultimate goal in judging social arrangements. Freedom as a value in this sense has to do with the interrelations among people; it has no meaning whatsoever to a Robinson Crusoe on an isolated island (without his Man Friday). Robinson Crusoe on his island is subject to "constraint," he has limited "power," and he has only a limited number of alternatives, but there is no problem of freedom in the sense that is relevant to our discussion. Similarly, in a society freedom has nothing to say about what an individual does with his freedom; it is not an all-embracing ethic. Indeed, a major aim of the liberal is to leave the ethical problem for the individual to wrestle with. The "really" important ethical problems are those that face an individual in a free society—what he should do with his freedom. There are thus two sets of values that a liberal will emphasize—the values that are relevant to relations among people, which is the context in which he assigns first priority to freedom; and the values that are relevant to the individual in the exercise of his freedom, which is the realm of individual ethics and philosophy.

The liberal conceives of men as imperfect beings. He regards the problem of social organization to be as much a negative problem of preventing "bad" people from doing harm as of enabling "good" people to do good; and, of course, "bad" and "good" people may be the same people, depending on who is judging them.

The basic problem of social organization is how to co-ordinate the economic activities of large numbers of people. Even in relatively backward societies, extensive division of labor and specialization of function is required to make effective use of available resources. In advanced societies, the scale on which co-ordination is needed, to take full advantage of the opportunities offered by modern science and technology, is enormously greater. Literally millions of people are involved in providing one another with their daily bread, let alone with their yearly automobiles. The challenge to the believer in liberty is to reconcile this widespread interdependence with individual freedom.

Fundamentally, there are only two ways of co-ordinating the economic activities of millions. One is central direction involving the use of coercion—the technique of the army and of the modern totalitarian state. The other is voluntary co-operation of individuals— the technique of the market place.

The possibility of co-ordination through voluntary co-operation rests on the elementary—yet frequently denied—proposition that both parties to an economic transaction benefit from it, *provided the transaction is bi-laterally voluntary and informed.*

Exchange can therefore bring about co-ordination without coercion. A working model of a society organized through voluntary exchange is a *free private enterprise exchange economy*—what we have been calling competitive capitalism.

In its simplest form, such a society consists of a number of independent households—a collection of Robinson Crusoes, as it were. Each household uses the resources it controls to produce goods and services that it exchanges for goods and services produced by other households, on terms mutually acceptable to the two parties to the bargain. It is thereby enabled to satisfy its wants indirectly by producing goods and services for others, rather than directly by producing goods for its own immediate use. The incentive for adopting this indirect route is, of course, the increased product made possible by division of labor and specialization of function. Since the household always has the alternative of producing directly for itself, it need not enter into any exchange unless it benefits from it. Hence, no exchange will take place unless both parties do benefit from it. Co-operation is thereby achieved without coercion.

Specialization of function and division of labor would not go far if the ultimate productive unit were the household. In a modern society, we have gone much farther. We have introduced enterprises which are intermediaries between individuals in their capacities as suppliers of service and as purchasers of goods. And similarly, specialization of function and division of labor could not go very far if we had to continue to rely on the barter of product for product. In consequence, money has been introduced as a means of facilitating exchange, and of enabling the acts of purchase and of sale to be separated into two parts.

Despite the important role of enterprises and of money in our actual economy, and despite the numerous and complex problems they raise, the central characteristic of the market technique of achieving co-ordination is fully displayed in the simple exchange economy that contains neither enterprises nor money. As in that simple model, so in the complex enterprise and money-exchange economy, co-operation is strictly individual and voluntary *provided:* (*a*) that enterprises are private, so that the ultimate contracting parties are individuals and (*b*) that individuals are effectively free to enter or not to enter into any particular exchange, so that every transaction is strictly voluntary.

It is far easier to state these provisos in general terms than to spell them out in detail, or to specify precisely the institutional arrangements most conducive to their maintenance. Indeed, much of technical economic literature is concerned with precisely these questions. The basic requisite is the maintenance of law and order to prevent physical coercion of one individual by another and to enforce contracts voluntarily entered into, thus giving substance to "private." Aside from this, perhaps the most difficult problems arise from monopoly—which inhibits effective freedom by denying individuals alternatives to the particular exchange—and from "neighborhood effects"—effects on third parties for which it is not feasible to charge or recompense them...

So long as effective freedom of exchange is maintained, the central feature of the market organization of economic activity is that it prevents one person from interfering with another in respect of most of his activities. The consumer is protected from coercion by the seller because of the presence of other sellers with whom he can deal. The seller is protected from coercion by the consumer because of other consumers to whom he can sell. The employee is protected from coercion by the employer because of other employers for whom he can work, and so on. And the market does this impersonally and without centralized authority.

Indeed, a major source of objection to a free economy is precisely that it does this task so well. It gives people what they want instead of what a particular group thinks they ought to want. Underlying most arguments against the free market is a lack of belief in freedom itself.

The existence of a free market does not of course eliminate the need for government. On the contrary, government is essential both as a forum for determining the "rules of the game" and as an umpire to interpret and enforce the rules decided on. What the market does is to reduce greatly the range of issues that must be decided through political means, and thereby to minimize the extent to which government need participate directly in the game. The characteristic feature of action through political channels is that it tends to require or enforce substantial conformity. The great advantage of the market, on the other hand, is that it permits wide diversity. It is, in political terms, a system of proportional representation. Each man can vote, as it were, for the color of tie he wants and get it; he does not have to see what color the majority wants and then, if he is in the minority, submit.

It is this feature of the market that we refer to when we say that the market provides economic freedom. But this characteristic also has implications that go far beyond the narrowly economic. Political freedom means the absence of coercion of a man by his fellow men. The fundamental threat to freedom is power to coerce, be it in the hands of a monarch, a dictator, an oligarchy, or a momentary majority. The preservation of freedom requires the elimination of such concentration of power to the fullest possible extent and the dispersal and distribution of whatever power cannot be eliminated—a system of checks and balances. By removing the organization of economic activity from the control of political authority, the market eliminates this source of coercive power. It enables economic strength to be a check to political power rather than a reinforcement.

Economic power can be widely dispersed. There is no law of conservation which forces the growth of new centers of economic strength to be at the expense of existing centers. Political power, on the other hand, is more difficult to decentralize. There can be numerous small independent governments. But it is far more difficult to maintain numerous equipotent small centers of political power in a single large government than it is to have numerous centers of economic strength in a single large economy. There can be many millionaires in one large economy. But can there be more than one really outstanding leader, one person on whom the energies and enthusiasms of his country-men are centered? If the central government gains power, it is likely to be at the expense of local governments. There seems to be something like a fixed total of political power to be distributed. Consequently, if economic power is joined to political power, concentra-tion seems almost inevitable. On the other hand, if economic power is kept in separate hands from political power, it can serve as a check and a counter to political power.

The force of this abstract argument can perhaps best be demonstrated by example. Let us consider first, a hypothetical example that may help to bring out the principles involved, and then some actual examples from recent experience that illustrate the way in which the market works to preserve political freedom.

One feature of a free society is surely the freedom of individuals to advocate and propagandize openly for a radical change in the structure of the society—so long as the advocacy is restricted to persuasion and does not include force or other forms of coercion. It is a mark of the political freedom of a capitalist society that men can openly advocate and work for socialism. Equally, political freedom in a socialist society would require that men be free to advocate the introduction of capitalism. How could the freedom to advo-cate capitalism be preserved and protected in a socialist society?

In order for men to advocate anything, they must in the first place be able to earn a living. This already raises a problem in a socialist society, since all jobs are under the direct control of political authorities. It would take an act of self-denial whose difficulty is under-lined by experience in the United States after World War II with the problem of "security" among Federal employees, for a socialist government to permit its employees to advocate policies directly contrary to official doctrine.

But let us suppose this act of self-denial to be achieved. For advocacy of capitalism to mean anything, the proponents must be able to finance their cause—to hold public meet-ings, publish pamphlets, buy radio time, issue newspapers and magazines, and so on. How could they raise the funds? There might and probably would be men in the socialist society with large incomes, perhaps even large capital sums in the form of government bonds and the like, but these would of necessity be high public officials. It is possible to conceive of a minor socialist official retaining his job although openly advocating capitalism. It strains credulity to imagine the socialist top brass financing such "subversive" activities.

The only recourse for funds would be to raise small amounts from a large number of minor officials. But this is no real answer. To tap these sources, many people would already have to be persuaded, and our whole problem is how to initiate and finance a cam-paign to do so. Radical movements in capitalist societies have never been financed this way. They have typically been supported by a few wealthy individuals who have become persuaded—by a Frederick Vanderbilt Field, or an Anita McCormick Blaine, or a Corliss Lamont, to mention a few names recently prominent, or by a Friedrich Engels, to go far-ther back. This is a role of inequality of wealth in preserving political freedom that is sel-dom noted—the role of the patron.

In a capitalist society, it is only necessary to convince a few wealthy people to get funds to launch any idea, however strange, and there are many such persons, many inde-pendent foci of support. And, indeed, it is not even necessary to persuade people or finan-cial institutions with available funds of the soundness of the ideas to be propagated. It is only necessary to persuade them that the propagation can be financially successful; that the newspaper or magazine or book or other venture will be profitable. The competitive publisher, for example, cannot afford to publish only writing with which he personally agrees; his touchstone must be the likelihood that the market will be large enough to yield a satisfactory return on his investment.

In this way, the market breaks the vicious circle and makes it possible ultimately to finance such ventures by small amounts from many people without first persuading them. There are no such possibilities in the socialist society; there is only the all-powerful state.

Let us stretch our imagination and suppose that a socialist government is aware of this problem and is composed of people anxious to preserve freedom. Could it provide the funds? Perhaps, but it is difficult to see how. It could establish a bureau for subsidizing subversive propaganda. But how could it choose whom to support? If it gave to all who asked, it would shortly find itself out of funds, for socialism cannot repeal the elementary economic law that a sufficiently high price will call forth a large supply. Make the advocacy of radical causes sufficiently remunerative, and the supply of advocates will be unlimited.

Moreover, freedom to advocate unpopular causes does not require that such advocacy be without cost. On the contrary, no society could be stable if advocacy of radical change were costless, much less subsidized. It is entirely appropriate that men make sacrifices to advocate causes in which they deeply believe. Indeed, it is important to preserve freedom only for people who are willing to practice self-denial, for otherwise freedom degenerates into license and irresponsibility. What is essential is that the cost of advocating unpopular causes be tolerable and not prohibitive.

But we are not yet through. In a free market society, it is enough to have the funds. The suppliers of paper are as willing to sell it to the *Daily Worker* as to the *Wall Street Journal*. In a socialist society, it would not be enough to have the funds. The hypothetical supporter of capitalism would have to persuade a government factory making paper to sell to him, the government printing press to print his pamphlets, a government post office to distribute them among the people, a government agency to rent him a hall in which to talk, and so on.

Perhaps there is some way in which one could overcome these difficulties and preserve freedom in a socialist society. One cannot say it is utterly impossible. What is clear, however, is that there are very real difficulties in establishing institutions that will effectively preserve the possibility of dissent. So far as I know, none of the people who have been in favor of socialism and also in favor of freedom have really faced up to this issue, or made even a respectable start at developing the institutional arrangements that would permit freedom under socialism. By contrast, it is clear how a free market capitalist society fosters freedom.

A striking practical example of these abstract principles is the experience of Winston Churchill. From 1933 to the outbreak of World War II, Churchill was not permitted to talk over the British radio, which was, of course, a government monopoly administered by the British Broadcasting Corporation. Here was a leading citizen of his country, a Member of Parliament, a former cabinet minister, a man who was desperately trying by every device possible to persuade his countrymen to take steps to ward off the menace of Hitler's Germany. He was not permitted to talk over the radio to the British people because the BBC was a government monopoly and his position was too "controversial."

Another striking example, reported in the January 26, 1959 issue of *Time*, has to do with the "Blacklist Fadeout." Says the *Time* story,

> The Oscar-awarding ritual is Hollywood's biggest pitch for dignity, but two years ago dignity suffered. When one Robert Rich was announced as top writer for the *The Brave One*, he never stepped forward. Robert Rich was a pseudonym,

masking one of about 150 writers...blacklisted by the industry since 1947 as suspected Communists or fellow travelers. The case was particularly embarrassing because the Motion Picture Academy had barred any Communist or Fifth Amendment pleader from Oscar competition. Last week both the Communist rule and the mystery of Rich's identity were suddenly rescripted.

Rich turned out to be Dalton (*Johnny Got His Gun*) Trumbo, one of the original "Hollywood Ten" writers who refused to testify at the 1947 hearings on Communism in the movie industry. Said producer Frank King, who had stoutly insisted that Robert Rich was "a young guy in Spain with a beard": "We have an obligation to our stockholders to buy the best script we can. Trumbo brought us *The Brave One* and we bought it."...

In effect it was the formal end of the Hollywood black list. For barred writers, the informal end came long ago. At least 15% of current Hollywood films are reportedly written by blacklist members. Said Producer King, "There are more ghosts in Hollywood than in Forest Lawn. Every company in town has used the work of blacklisted people. We're just the first to confirm what everybody knows."

One may believe, as I do, that communism would destroy all of our freedoms, one may be opposed to it as firmly and as strongly as possible, and yet, at the same time, also believe that in a free society it is intolerable for a man to be prevented from making voluntary arrangements with others that are mutually attractive because he believes in or is trying to promote communism. His freedom includes his freedom to promote communism. Freedom also, of course, includes the freedom of others not to deal with him under those circumstances. The Hollywood blacklist was an unfree act that destroys freedom because it was a collusive arrangement that used coercive means to prevent voluntary exchanges. It didn't work precisely because the market made it costly for people to preserve the blacklist. The commercial emphasis, the fact that people who are running enterprises have an incentive to make as much money as they can, protected the freedom of the individuals who were blacklisted by providing them with an alternative form of employment, and by giving people an incentive to employ them.

If Hollywood and the movie industry had been government enterprises or if in England it had been a question of employment by the British Broadcasting Corporation it is difficult to believe that the "Hollywood Ten" or their equivalent would have found employment. Equally, it is difficult to believe that under those circumstances, strong proponents of individualism and private enterprise—or indeed strong proponents of any view other than the status quo—would be able to get employment.

Another example of the role of the market in preserving political freedom, was revealed in our experience with McCarthyism. Entirely aside from the substantive issues involved, and the merits of the charges made, what protection did individuals, and in particular government employees, have against irresponsible accusations and probings into matters that it went against their conscience to reveal? Their appeal to the Fifth Amendment would have been a hollow mockery without an alternative to government employment.

Their fundamental protection was the existence of a private-market economy in which they could earn a living. Here again, the protection was not absolute. Many potential private employers were, rightly or wrongly, averse to hiring those pilloried. It may well be that there was far less justification for the costs imposed on many of the people involved than for the costs generally imposed on people who advocate unpopular causes. But the important point is that the costs were limited and not prohibitive, as they would have been if government employment had been the only possibility.

It is of interest to note that a disproportionately large fraction of the people involved apparently went into the most competitive sectors of the economy—small business, trade, farming—where the market approaches most closely the ideal free market. No one who buys bread knows whether the wheat from which it is made was grown by a Communist or a Republican, by a constitutionalist or a Fascist, or, for that matter, by a Negro or a white. This illustrates how an impersonal market separates economic activities from political views and protects men from being discriminated against in their economic activities for reasons that are irrelevant to their productivity—whether these reasons are associated with their views or their color.

As this example suggests, the groups in our society that have the most at stake in the preservation and strengthening of competitive capitalism are those minority groups which can most easily become the object of the distrust and enmity of the majority—the Negroes, the Jews, the foreign-born, to mention only the most obvious. Yet, paradoxically enough, the enemies of the free market—the Socialists and Communists—have been recruited in disproportionate measure from these groups. Instead of recognizing that the existence of the market has protected them from the attitudes of their fellow countrymen, they mistakenly attribute the residual discrimination to the market.

AYN RAND

"Man's Rights"
(1963)

One of the most persistently popular of all American authors, the conservative novelist and essayist Ayn Rand (1905–82) has provoked angry dismissals as well as cultlike adulation for many generations. The essay of 1963 reprinted here is one of the most succinct statements of her basic defense of the rights of individuals and her antagonism toward state regulation of economic life. The most important of her theoretical works are collected in *The Virtue of Selfishness* (New York, 1965). But it was through her fiction that Rand won her greatest audience. In *The Fountainhead* (New York, 1943) and *Atlas Shrugged* (New York, 1957), Rand presented a series of heroic individuals surrounded by persons lacking in talent and enterprise. In her fiction, the population was divided between producers and looters: Her admirable characters possess the intelligence and spunk to create things of value, despite the pressures and distractions of those who accomplish little and try to profit from the creativity of others.

The quality of her art as a novelist was consistently judged mediocre by literary critics and her grasp of philosophy was often ridiculed—"Nietzsche for dummies," was a common dismissal—but Rand was unmatched in her ability to convey basic libertarian ideas to millions of Americans. In the calendar year 2008 alone, more than a quarter-century after her death, her various works sold more than 800,000 copies. Her atheism and notoriously unconventional personal life—she had a publicly recognized affair with her married disciple, Nathaniel Branden—made her an annoyance and an embarrassment to many of her fellow conservatives, including Whittaker Chambers and William F. Buckley, Jr., but she won and retained a popular following greater than that of any of her critics.

Rand was born Alisa Rosenbaum in St. Petersburg, Russia, and immigrated to the United States in 1926. She was, in fact, a "New York Jewish intellectual," like Hannah Arendt, Clement Greenberg, Lionel Trilling, and several other authors found in *The American Intellectual Tradition*, but she is rarely recognized as such because most of the Jewish intellectuals of her generation were on the political left and would have nothing to do with her. Deeply affected by the Bolshevik Revolution and its negative effect on her own family, Rand spent her life attacking collectivism of all sorts. She worked for several years as a screenwriter in Hollywood, and generated controversy in 1947 when she testified before the House Un-American Activities Committee against what she insisted was the influence of communism in the motion picture industry.

By far the best study of Rand's ideas and career is Jennifer Burns, *Goddess of the Market: Ayn Rand and the American Right* (New York, 2009).

If one wishes to advocate a free society—that is, capitalism—one must realize that its indispensable foundation is the principle of individual rights. If one wishes to uphold individual rights, one must realize that capitalism is the only system that can uphold and protect them. And if one wishes to gauge the relationship of freedom to the goals of today's intellectuals, one may gauge it by the fact that the concept of individual rights, is evaded, distorted, perverted and seldom discussed, most conspicuously seldom by the so-called "conservatives."

"Rights" are a moral concept—the concept that provides a logical transition from the principles guiding an individual's actions to the principles guiding his relationship with others—the concept that preserves and protects individual morality in a social context— the link between the moral code of a man and the legal code of a society, between ethics and politics. *Individual rights are the means of subordinating society to moral law.*

Every political system is based on some code of ethics. The dominant ethics of mankind's history were variants of the altruist-collectivist doctrine which subordinated the individual to some higher authority, either mystical or social. Consequently, most political systems were variants of the same statist tyranny, differing only in degree, not in basic principle, limited only by the accidents of tradition, of chaos, of bloody strife and periodic collapse. Under all such systems, morality was a code applicable to the individual, but not to society. Society was placed *outside* the moral law, as its embodiment or source or exclusive interpreter—and the inculcation of self-sacrificial devotion to social duty was regarded as the main purpose of ethics in man's earthly existence.

Since there is no such entity as "society," since society is only a number of individual men, this meant, in practice, that the rulers of society were exempt from moral law; subject only to traditional rituals, they held total power and exacted blind obedience—on the implicit principle of: "The good is that which is good for society (or for the tribe, the race, the nation), and the ruler's edicts are its voice on earth."

This was true under all statist systems and under all variants of the altruist-collectivist ethics, mystical or social. "The Divine Right of Kings" summarizes the political theory of the first—"*Vox populi, vox dei*" of the second. As witness: the theocracy of Egypt, with the Pharaoh as an embodied god—the unlimited majority-rule or *democracy* of Athens—the welfare-state run by the Emperors of Rome—the Inquisition of the late Middle Ages—the absolute monarchy of France—the welfare-state of Bismarck's Prussia—the gas-chambers of Nazi Germany—the slaughterhouse of the Soviet Union.

All these political systems were expressions of the altruist-collectivist ethics—and their common characteristic is the fact that society stood above the moral law, as an omnipotent, sovereign whim-worshiper. Thus, politically, all these systems were variants of an *amoral* society.

The most profoundly revolutionary achievement of the United States of America was *the subordination of society to moral law.*

The principle of man's individual rights represented the extension of morality into the social system—as a limitation on the power of the state, as man's protection against the brute force of the collective, as the subordination of *might* to *right*. The United States was the first *moral* society in history.

All previous systems had regarded man as a sacrificial means to the ends of others, and society as an end in itself. The United States regarded man as an end in himself, and

Source: Ayn Rand, *The Virtue of Selfishness* (New York: New American Library, 1964), 12–16.

society as a means to the peaceful, orderly, *voluntary* co-existence of individuals. All previous systems had held that man's life belongs to society, that society can dispose of him in any way it pleases, and that any freedom he enjoys is his only by favor, by the *permission* of society, which may be revoked at any time. The United States held that man's life is his by *right* (which means: by moral principle and by his nature), that a right is the property of an individual, that society as such has no rights, and that the only moral purpose of a government is the protection of individual rights.

A "right" is a moral principle defining and sanctioning a man's freedom of action in a social context. There is only *one* fundamental right (all the others are its consequences or corollaries): a man's right to his own life. Life is a process of self-sustaining and self-generated action: the right to life means the right to engage in self-sustaining and self-generated action—which means: the freedom to take all the actions required by the nature of a rational being for the support, the furtherance, the fulfillment and the enjoyment of his own life. (Such is the meaning of the right to life, liberty and the pursuit of happiness.)

The concept of a "right" pertains only to action—specifically, to freedom of action. It means freedom from physical compulsion, coercion or interference by other men.

Thus, for every individual, a right is the moral sanction of a *positive*—of his freedom to act on his own judgment, for his own goals, by his own *voluntary, uncoerced* choice. As to his neighbors, his rights impose no obligations on them except of a *negative* kind: to abstain from violating his rights.

The right to life is the source of all rights—and the right to property is their only implementation. Without property rights, no other rights are possible. Since man has to sustain his life by his own effort, the man who has no right to the product of his effort has no means to sustain his life. The man who produces while others dispose of his product, is a slave.

Bear in mind that the right to property is a right to action, like all the others: it is not the right *to an object,* but to the action and the consequences of producing or earning that object. It is not a guarantee that a man *will* earn any property, but only a guarantee that he will own it if he earns it. It is the right to gain, to keep, to use and to dispose of material values.

The concept of individual rights is so new in human history that most men have not grasped it fully to this day. In accordance with the two theories of ethics, the mystical or the social, some men assert that rights are a gift of God—others, that rights are a gift of society. But, in fact, the source of rights is man's nature.

The Declaration of Independence stated that men "are endowed by their Creator with certain inalienable rights." Whether one believes that man is the product of a Creator or of nature, the issue of man's origin does not alter the fact that he is an entity of a specific kind—a rational being—that he cannot function successfully under coercion, and that rights are a necessary condition of his particular mode of survival.

"The source of man's rights is not divine law or congressional law, but the law of identity. A is A—and Man is Man. *Rights* are conditions of existence required by man's nature for his proper survival. If man is to live on earth, it is *right* for him to use his mind, it is *right* to act on his own free judgment, it is *right* to work for his values and to keep the product of his work. If life on earth is his purpose, he has a *right* to live as a rational being: nature forbids him the irrational." *(Atlas Shrugged)*

To violate man's rights means, to compel him to act against his own judgment, or to expropriate his values. Basically, there is only one way to do it: by the use of physical force. There are two potential violators of man's rights: the criminals and the government. The great achievement of the United States was to draw a distinction between these two—by forbidding to the second the legalized version of the activities of the first.

The Declaration of Independence laid down the principle that "to secure these rights; governments are instituted among men." This provided the only valid justification of a government and defined its only proper purpose: to protect man's rights by protecting him from physical violence.

Thus the government's function was changed from the role of ruler to the role of servant. The government was set to protect man from criminals—and the Constitution was written to protect man from the government. The Bill of Rights was not directed against private citizens, but against the government—as an explicit declaration that individual rights supersede any public or social power.

The result was the pattern of a civilized society which—for the brief span of some hundred and fifty years—America came close to achieving. A civilized society is one in which physical force is banned from human relationships—in which the government, acting as a policeman, may use force *only* in retaliation and *only* against those who initiate its use.

This was the essential meaning and intent of America's political philosophy, implicit in the principle of individual rights. But it was not formulated explicitly, nor fully accepted nor consistently practiced.

America's inner contradiction was the altruist-collectivist ethics. Altruism is incompatible with freedom, with capitalism and with individual rights. One cannot combine the pursuit of happiness with the moral status of a sacrificial animal.

It was the concept of individual rights that had given birth to a free society. It was with the destruction of individual rights that the destruction of freedom had to begin.

A collectivist tyranny dare not enslave a country by an outright confiscation of its values, material or moral. It has to be done by a process of internal corruption. Just as in the material realm the plundering of a country's wealth is accomplished by inflating the currency—so today one may witness the process of inflation being applied to the realm of rights. The process entails such a growth of newly-promulgated "rights" that people do not notice the fact that the meaning of the concept is being reversed. Just as bad money drives out good money, so these "printing-press rights" negate authentic rights.

Consider the curious fact that never has there been such a proliferation, all over the world, of two contradictory phenomena: of alleged new "rights" and of slave-labor camps.

The "gimmick" was the switch of the concept of rights from the political to the economic realm.

The Democratic Party platform of 1960 summarizes the switch boldly and explicitly. It declares that a Democratic Administration "will reaffirm the economic bill of rights which Franklin Roosevelt wrote into our national conscience sixteen years ago."

Bear clearly in mind the meaning of the concept of *"rights"* when you read the list which that platform offers:

"1. The right to a useful and remunerative job in the industries or shops or farms or mines of the nation.

"2. The right to earn enough to provide adequate food and clothing and recreation.

"3. The right of every farmer to raise and sell his products at a return which will give him and his family a decent living.

"4. The right of every businessman, large and small, to trade in an atmosphere of freedom from unfair competition and domination by monopolies at home and abroad.

"5. The right of every family to a decent home.

"6. The right to adequate medical care and the opportunity to achieve and enjoy good health.

"7. The right to adequate protection from the economic fears of old age, sickness, accidents and unemployment.

"8. The right to a good education."

A single question added to each of the above eight clauses would make the issue clear: *At whose expense?*

Jobs, food, clothing, recreation (!), homes, medical care, education, etc., do not grow in nature. These are man-made values—goods and services produced by men. *Who* is to provide them?

If some men are entitled *by right* to the products of the work of others, it means that those others are deprived of rights and condemned to slave-labor.

Any alleged "right" of one man, which necessitates the violation of the rights of another, is not and cannot be a right.

No man can have a right to impose an unchosen obligation, an unrewarded duty or an involuntary servitude on another man. There can be no such thing as *"the right to enslave."*

A right does not include the material implementation of that right by other men: it includes only the freedom to earn that implementation by one's own effort.

Observe, in this context, the intellectual precision of the Founding Fathers: they spoke of the right to *the pursuit* of happiness—not of the right to happiness. It means that a man has the right to take the actions he deems necessary to achieve his happiness; it does *not* mean that others must make him happy.

The right to life means that a man has the right to support his life by his own work (on any economic level, as high as his ability will carry him); it does *not* mean that others must provide him with food, clothing and shelter.

The right to property means that a man has the right to take the economic actions necessary to earn property, to use it and to dispose of it; it does *not* mean that others must provide him with property.

The right of free speech means that a man has the right to express his ideas without danger of suppression, interference or punitive action by the government. It does *not* mean that others must provide him with a lecture hall, a radio station or a printing press through which to express his ideas.

Any undertaking that involves more than one man, requires the *voluntary* consent of every participant. Every one of them has the *right* to make his own decision, but none has the right to force his decision on the others.

There is no such thing as "a right to a job"—there is only the right of free trade, that is: a man's right to take a job if another man chooses to hire him. There is no "right to a home," only the right of free trade: the right to build a home or to buy it. There are no "rights to a 'fair' wage or a 'fair' price" if no one chooses to pay it, to hire a man or to buy his product. There are no "rights of consumers" to milk, shoes, movies or champagne if no producers choose to manufacture such items (there is only the right to manufacture them oneself). There are no "rights" of special groups, there are no "rights of farmers, of workers, of businessmen, of employees, of employers, of the old, of the young, of the unborn." There are only *the Rights of Man*—rights possessed by every individual man and by *all* men as individuals.

Property rights and the right of free trade are man's only "economic rights" (they are in fact, *political* rights)—and there can be no such thing as "an *economic* bill of rights." But observe that the advocates of the latter have all but destroyed the former.

Remember that rights are moral principles which define and protect a man's freedom of action, but impose no obligations on other men. Private citizens are not a threat to one another's rights or freedom. A private citizen who resorts to physical force and violates the rights of others is a criminal—and men have legal protection against him.

Criminals are a small minority in any age or country. And the harm they have done to mankind is infinitesimal when compared to the horrors—the bloodshed, the wars, the persecutions, the confiscations, the famines, the enslavements, the wholesale destructions—perpetrated by mankind's governments. A government is the most dangerous threat to man's rights: it holds a legal monopoly on the use of physical force against legally disarmed victims. When unlimited and unrestricted by individual rights, a government is men's deadliest enemy. It is not as protection against *private* actions, but against governmental actions that the Bill of Rights was written.

Such is the state of one of today's most crucial issues: *political* rights versus "*economic* rights." It's either-or. One destroys the other. But there are, in fact, no "economic rights," no "collective rights,'" no "public-interest rights." The term "individual rights" is a redundancy: there is no other kind of rights and no one else to possess them.

Those who advocate laissez-faire capitalism are the only advocates of man's rights.

Part Four

Reassessing Identities and Solidarities

Introduction

With just what kinds of people should an individual try to identify, and to work with, and for what purposes? The question sounds like a simple one, but from the early 1960s to the present, it has been a challenging one for many people in the United States. The era was marked by increased immigration from parts of the world outside Europe, by a maturation of a long-term struggle on the part of black-skinned descendants of slaves to attain basic civil rights, by sustained interaction between the American government and new nations in Asia and Africa, by the emergence of a new feminist movement, and by an expansion of the professional apparatus of the sciences. These conditions stimulated many reassessments of the significance of the lines dividing people by race, ethnicity, religion, gender, occupation, geographic location, economic position, generation, and basic worldview. Not all twenty selections in Part Four illustrate these uncertainties in identity and solidarity, but most of them do.

The Protestant leaders Wilfred Cantwell Smith and Harold John Ockenga illustrate the sharply contrasting impulses to expand one's solidarities and to consolidate them. Smith and Ockenga speak in relation to religious identity—as does Sam Harris, who calls for a new secular solidarity—but similarly conflicting impulses are found in many domains. Harold Cruse, Martin Luther King., Jr., and Henry Louis Gates, Jr., explore in strikingly different ways the question of just how blackness affects the choices people make about with whom to identify, and with whom to make common cause. Feminist theorists Betty Friedan, Nancy Chodorow, and Catharine MacKinnon address the significance of the male–female distinction and the political implications of how society has constructed it. Thomas Kuhn's analysis of the dynamics of scientific communities generated an extensive controversy about how knowledge-based communities are constituted and altered, leading to Richard Rorty's reflections on how science itself can be seen as a kind of solidarity, if not a model for other solidarities. C. Wright Mills, Herbert Marcuse, Noam Chomsky, John Rawls, and Samuel Huntington all explore challenges in the achieving of viable political solidarities, taking into account a variety of different, specific contexts for political action and its theoretical justification. Edward Said calls attention to the tendency of thinkers in the North Atlantic West to misunderstand the world beyond, sometimes as a result of racial and religious prejudice. Environmentalists during this period developed the slogan "One earth, one humanity, one destiny," but Stewart Brand reviews an extensive panorama of environmentalist issues and finds that unification around scientific knowledge is the best foundation for action in defense of the environment. Susan Sontag's call for an "erotics of art" and Joan Scott's poststructuralist analysis of "experience" remind us that not everything of interest to intellectuals in the last fifty years can be classified in terms of "identity" and "solidarity." Indeed, those who confront questions of identity and solidarity almost always have multiple engagements. For an overview of how issues in identity and solidarity looked at the end of this remarkable epoch, see David A. Hollinger, "From Identity to Solidarity," *Daedalus* (Fall 2006), 23–31.

Recommendations for Further Reading

Harold R. Isaacs, *Idols of the Tribe: Group Identity and Political Change* (New York, 1975); Howard Brick, *The Age of Contradiction: American Thought and Culture in the 1960s* (New York, 1998); David Harvey, *The Condition of Postmodernity* (New York, 1989); Fredric Jameson, *Postmodernism, or, The Cultural Logic of Late Capitalism* (Durham, N.H., 1991); Judith Butler and Joan W. Scott, *Feminists Theorize the Political* (New York, 1992); Giles Gunn, *Thinking Across the Grain: Ideology, Intellect, and the New Pragmatism* (Chicago, 1992); James Davison Hunter, *Culture Wars: The Struggle to Define America* (New York, 1992); Linda S. Kauffman, ed., *American Feminist Thought at Century's End* (Cambridge, Mass., 1993); John Guillory, *Cultural Capital: The Problem of Literary Canon Formation* (Chicago, 1993); Giovanna Borradon, *The American Philosopher: Conversations with Quine, Davidson, Putnam, Nozick, Danto, Rorty, Cavell, MacIntyre, and Kuhn* (Chicago, 1994); David Farber, *The Age of Great Dreams: America in the 1960s* (New York, 1994); David Farber, ed., *The Sixties: From Memory to History* (Chapel Hill, 1994); Tom Engelhardt, *The End of Victory Culture: Cold War America and the Disillusioning of a Generation* (New York, 1995); Dan Danielsen and Karen Engle, eds., *After Identity: A Reader in Law and Culture* (New York, 1995); Louis Menand, ed., *The Future of Academic Freedom* (Chicago, 1996); Daniel J. Kevles, *The Baltimore Case: A Trial of Politics, Science, and Character* (New York, 1998); Thomas Bender and Carl E. Schorske, eds., *American Academic Culture in Transformation: Fifty Years, Four Disciplines* (Princeton, 1997); Peter Novick, *The Holocaust in American Life* (Boston, 1999); David Hoeveler, *The Postmodernist Turn: American Thought and Culture in the 1970s* (New York, 1996); Andrea Sterk, ed. *Religion, Scholarship and Higher Education* (Notre Dame, 2002); Tamar Jacoby, ed., *Reinventing the Melting Pot: New Immigrants and What It Means to Be an American* (New York, 2004); Stanley A. Renshon, ed., *One America? Political Leadership, National Identity, and the Dilemmas of Diversity* (Washington, D.C., 2001); Jonathan Rieder, ed., *The Fractious Nation? Unity and Division in Contemporary American Life* (Berkeley, 2003); Peter Shuck, *Diversity in America* (Cambridge, Mass., 2003); Thomas Bender, ed., *Rethinking American History in a Global Age* (Berkeley, 2002); Paula M. L. Moya and Michael R. Hames-Garcia, eds., *Reclaiming Identity: Realist Theory and the Predicament of Postmodernism* (Berkeley, 2000); Carrie Tirado Bramen, *The Uses of Variety* (Cambridge. Mass., 2000); Samuel Scheffler, *Boundaries and Allegiances* (New York, 2001); Mary C. Waters and Reed Ueda, eds., *The New Americans: A Guide to Immigration Since 1965* (Cambridge, Mass., 2007); C. Loring Brace, *"Race" Is a Four-Letter Word* (New York, 2005); Kwame Anthony Appiah, *The Ethics of Identity* (Princeton, 2005); John Lie, *Modern Peoplehood* (Cambridge, Mass., 2004); Jeffrey Stout, *Democracy and Tradition* (Princeton, 2004); Stephen Steinberg, *Race Relations: A Critique* (Stanford, 2007); Werner Sollors, *Ethnic Modernism* (Cambridge, Mass., 2008); Derek Rubin and Jaap Verheul, eds., *American Multiculturalism after 9/11* (Amsterdam, 2009); David A. Hollinger, *Cosmopolitanism and Solidarity* (Madison, Wis., 2006); David A. Hollinger, ed., *The Humanities and the Dynamics of Inclusion Since World War II* (Baltimore, 2006); Jonathan Zimmerman, *Innocents Abroad: American Teachers in the American Century* (Cambridge, Mass., 2006); Sarah Song, *Justice, Gender, and the Politics of Multiculturalism* (New York, 2007); James T. Kloppenberg, *Reading Obama: Dreams, Hope, and the American Political Tradition* (Princeton, 2010).

WILFRED CANTWELL SMITH

"Christianity's Third Great Challenge" (1960)

The liberal, ecumenical leadership of American Protestantism subjected itself, during the middle decades of the twentieth century, to a vigorous self-interrogation well exemplified by this essay by the scholar of comparative religions, Wilfred Cantwell Smith (1916-2000). Deeply affected by their exposure to non-Western cultures through academic study and through foreign missionary engagements, ecumenical leaders grew increasingly critical of what they saw as the parochial, narrow constructions of Christianity common among the average American churchgoer. In this essay of 1960, Smith insisted that modern life was irreversibly "multicultural," and that Christians of all persuasions needed to cultivate a less arrogant attitude toward people with ideas and practices different from their own. Smith characterized the challenge of engaging non-Christian religious orientations as the third epochal challenge in the entire history of Christianity, comparable only to the challenge of Greek philosophy in ancient times and the challenge of Darwinian science in the nineteenth century. Smith's perspective on Christianity can be contrasted to that of the evangelical leader Harold John Ockenga, a selection from whom follows Smith in *The American Intellectual Tradition*.

Smith himself was a Canadian by birth, but spent a major portion of his career based at the Harvard Divinity School. He taught at a missionary college in India during the 1940s, and was shaken by the conflict between Hindus and Muslims during the struggle for Indian independence. Although Smith studied many religions, his work focused on Islam, about which he wrote several books. His most enduring legacy was as a theorist of religion, especially through the influence of his major work, *The Meaning and End of Religion* (New York, 1962), which argued that the very concept of religion was distinctly European. This theme in Smith's work continues to animate recent thinking in religious studies, as illustrated by the respectful but critical treatise by Talal Asad, "Reading a Modern Classic: W. C. Smith's *The Meaning and End of Religion*," *History of Religion*, 40 (2001), 205-22. Smith's most important writings have been collected in Kenneth Cracknell, ed., *Wilfred Cantwell Smith: A Reader* (New York, 2002). An appreciative study of Smith is Edward H. Hughes, *Wilfred Cantwell Smith: A Theology for the World* (New York, 1986).

The most valuable single volume on ecumenical Protestantism during Smith's generation is William R. Hutchison, ed., *Between the Times: The Travail of the Protestant Establishment in America, 1900-1960* (New York, 1989). A helpful overview of American Protestant history during the twenty years prior to 1960, including an account of the sharpening polarization between ecumenists and evangelicals, is Martin E. Marty, *Modern American Religion: Under God, Indivisible, 1941-1960* (Chicago, 1996). For a long-term analysis of the growth of religious pluralism that culminates in ideas like Smith's, see William R. Hutchison, *Religious Pluralism in America: The Contentious History of a*

Founding Ideal (New Haven, 2003). For explorations of the historic role of ecumenical Protestants in twentieth-century America, see two essays by David A. Hollinger, "Jesus Matters in the USA," *Modern Intellectual History*, 1 (2004), 135–49, and "The Realist-Pacifist Summit Meeting of 1942 and the Political Reorientation of Ecumenical Protestantism in the United States," *Church History*, 69 (September 2010), 1–24.

The religious aspect of the general question of the West's relations with the rest of the world is our topic. However, to avoid the danger of subordinating religious to temporal considerations it is better to look at it the other way around: to start from within the Christian tradition, and to recognize that one of its newest and most challenging tasks is to discover and proclaim its message for man in the cosmopolitan world of today. Whichever way we look at it, the matter is an important one.

For many years I lived in the city of Lahore, in what was then India (and is now a part of Pakistan), I was teaching history in a missionary college—a college that was Christian in name and strove to be so in spirit, though a slight majority of the staff and virtually all but a few dozens of our thousand and more students were members of other communities: Muslims, Hindus, Sikhs. The college community therefore constituted a living personal instance of religious diversity. In this way it was representative of the city in which it stood, of India at large, and indeed of the world in which we live. Man's life today is cast in a multicultural context. We live in a pluralistic world. The religious man too lives in a world of many traditions, of variegated spiritual life. One's faith is at best partial unless it is a faith that is alive and powerful in a society in which other men of faith—intelligent, devout and upright—are heirs to many different heritages.

In fact, we have emerged into an age of minorities. The art of living as a minority group is far from easy, and often far from pleasant. But it is one that all men will now have to learn. Many of us come out of a background which taught us that minorities are other people—and some of us are slow to recognize that in the world of today and tomorrow all men are minorities within this new total society of mankind. Christians have tended to think of themselves as secure in a position of authority. In the narrow societies from which most of us come, our English-language group has been supreme. White men have assumed that they are dominant and Negroes, for instance, a minority to be dealt with in one way or another. The West has built up a diplomatic and economic world order of its own pattern into which other groups have, with more or less success, gradually come to play a role; but the west remains Western. These kinds of situations, in which a "we" could look out with some superiority over a subordinate or tolerated or perhaps patronized or even equal "they," is in process of giving way to the new reality in which every community on earth is becoming a minority in a complexity of diverse groups. Every "we" to which men belong is taking its place in an environment in which it is no longer a virtue to recognize outsiders even as equals—every "we," except the "we" of humanity itself which few of us have as yet learned to pronounce, lives in a world in which it is subordinate; all the "theys" taken together are already numerically superior, and will soon doubtless be more powerful.

Communists are a minority, and the world will have no peace until they abandon their explosive unwillingness to remain so. Yet so are capitalists. White men are a minority of mankind and the sooner they recognize it, the better. Westerners are a minority, but they seem almost incapable of adjusting themselves to the new world in which this is so. Religiously, unbelievers are a minority, Buddhists are a minority, Muslims are a minority, Christians are a minority.

All of us must take our stand in a society that far transcends us and our group. This does not mean that we should give up our values or our convictions. That is far too facile and destructive a solution. That way lies relativistic chaos. Rather, we must learn to hold

Source: The Christian Century (April 27, 1960), 505–8.

them and to honor them in a way that will not make us either disruptive or absurd. We must learn, in our new situation, what has always been our primary task: to love both God and our neighbor. Fortunately we know before we start that these two can never be in conflict; on the contrary, each becomes truer the more fully we can apprehend both at once.

To return to the situation in Lahore. Within the college I could see two things which the local population, including the Hindus and Muslims within the community, confirmed: first, that by and large the missionaries were motivated by a good will and dedication to service that were of real importance and consequence; second, that theologically, ideologically, they simply did not understand the religious traditions that they were confronting and did not make themselves understood. At the conceptual level the two groups were talking past each other, not with each other. No one doubted that the community and good will created by the college were of outstanding value, as was the educational service provided. On the other hand, there apparently had not been a conversion within this missionary college at any time during the present century, and none seemed likely. Today, with the resurgence of the Hindu and Islamic faiths in India and Pakistan, the function and future of this and similar colleges is quite problematic, as is true in the rest of Asia. The missionary is unsure of his role in the new situation that is arising.

Furthermore, during those years in Lahore which led up to the partition of India in 1947, the ideological gulf between the Christian group on the one hand, and the religious communities of Asia on the other, was by no means the only instance of religious diversity. In the town as in the country at large I had the opportunity of watching the situation developing from the divergencies between the Muslim group on the one hand and the Hindu and Sikh groups on the other—divergencies that eventually led to the splitting of the country and the setting up of two dominions, India and Pakistan, which came to birth in holocaust. I could see what began as separation between the communities gradually being transformed into tension, and that into misunderstanding, then mistrust, alienation, antagonism, bitterness, hatred, and finally violence and massacre. In the end much of the Old City was burned and one half of the population of Lahore was driven out, as part of the total cataclysm of loot and arson and fury in which perhaps a million persons were raped or killed and ten million refugees permanently driven from their homes.

The clash of religious difference is a serious matter. And let no Christian disdainfully imagine that it is something in which chiefly other people are involved. Christian history is disfigured by its aggressive crusades and inquisitions, its St. Bartholemew massacres and Protestant persecutions and a long bleak tale of bitterness. It is perhaps true that on the whole no other major religious community on earth has shown more fierce intolerance than has the Christian, in the less lovely pages of our history. Nor is it a thing of the past. Christian treatment of Jews has at times been mean and ugly, culminating in the brutality of the nazis in our own day—and it can still be shameful.

It will at once be countered that these things are not really Christian; and, of course, with as much vigor as anyone I would hold this to be essentially true. But let us nonetheless remember that Christians have in fact done these things, sometimes in the very name of Christianity.

Indeed, I would make the indictment that the fundamental defect of our Western, partly Christian society in the view of outsiders is arrogance. The political and economic aspects of imperialism have had more than their share of attention, but in the end they are no more important than the human relations between Christendom and the non-Western world—relations which have had too much arrogance, sometimes overt and contemptuous, often subtle and unconscious but still disastrous. If the number one problem today in international affairs is communist expansionism, the number two problem is the depth and bitterness and increase of anti-Westernism throughout much of the world; and the basic clue to this antagonism is Western arrogance. The treatment of Jews and Negroes shows that at home also we have not yet learned to practice Christian love, nor even fully to believe in it. For it is not merely a question of practice falling short of ideals. It is the distorted ideal itself—the basic doctrine that we are saved, outsiders are damned.

Once again, when one speaks of inquisitions of arrogance, of South African apartheid, the modern sensitive Christian conscience feels that all this is wrong. Therein lies our salvation. It *is* wrong. And we know that it is wrong because we are Christian—though other people too, for other reasons, know that it is wrong. If Christian doctrine taught that in the eyes of God Christians held a special place more favored than other people's, and nothing within the Christian scheme made us feel that this view is wrong; then there would be little hope for us. Nonetheless, the Christian church does teach that in faith in Christ there is ultimate and final truth; through it, ultimate and final salvation. These are serious proclamations, not to be treated lightly or casually compromised. Convictions of this kind are not to be set aside cavalierly for the sake of friendly relations with other groups. Nor are they to be thought of as nice but not quite true—something that one accepts but does not believe. Disaster has already taken place when one has to choose between giving up one's faith and giving up one's human relations!

The problem is serious. So far, no theological answer to it has been given. The official doctrine of the church has been that non-Christians are going to hell. Not many modern Christians really believe this anymore, but no clear alternative has been formulated by the church. In other words, the Christian community is at the moment theologically unequipped for living in the 20th century, with its pluralistic mankind; I am here less concerned to develop or push one particular theological position than I am to urge theologians to join in taking up the challenge, and in the meantime to urge all Christians to love and respect the faith of Hindus, Buddhists, Muslims and the others—if necessary, without waiting for the theologians. Man's first duty is to love, as it is his greatest joy and privilege.

Our thinking on this matter has to be clarified; our doctrines must be improved; otherwise we shall not love enough. The past theological position has stood in the way of our seeing our neighbor outside Christendom in the full truth and worth of his person and faith. And the present lack of theological position continues this situation. It is the function of theology to express and nourish the Christian faith in this instance that faith in its now cosmopolitan situation is not yet adequately served, and the remedy for that situation is not finding proper expression or nourishment. Hence the failure of Christendom to meet the rest of today's world adequately.

Although this failure is a very serious matter, it need not be too discouraging, since no one else has succeeded any better—far from it. In fact, that the whole of mankind with its radically different civilizations, religious traditions and value systems, its radically different economic and political statuses, should become one community, so that we should be loyal to each other across cultural and creedal as well as political frontiers, both in theory and in practice—this is quite a new challenge. And it is one we must face. Conceivably we could face it successfully, provided we do so with the warmth and power of our religious faith, together with a readiness to revise our misconceptions. And if man can rise to this occasion, it will be a mighty and wonderful achievement.

Unlike many, I would urge strongly that the world of which man dreams cannot be established if the religious quality of its integration be ignored. But we cannot meet the challenge on this level easily. Its proportions can be grasped more truly if we see the situation in its long-range historical context. I suggest that ours is the third massive challenge with which Christian thought has been confronted in the course of its long development. First, there was the challenge of Greek philosophy, which the church met in its earlier days, almost as soon as the Christian movement was launched in the Mediterranean world. To this challenge many of the best minds of the church applied themselves for centuries, and from the encounter Christian theology emerged modified and, most of us would say, enriched. The second great challenge of this kind was that of science in the 19th century. Again a great many of the church's finest minds were devoted to the matter, and from the encounter Christian thought emerged profoundly modified, having a different and, most of us would say, a truer, deeper, intellectual understanding of the faith. In this second half of the 20th century the church now faces the challenge of man's other religions. This challenge also deserves the creative attention of first-class minds (more attention than the church is apparently giving it), both because of the vitality and weight of the issues and because of the rich rewards in human cooperation and fellowship that will flow from a solution.

The positive quality of our task must be stressed. It is not simply a negative concern to get rid of obstacles to worldwide brotherhood. Rather, it is the positive matter of providing the only constructive basis possible for that fellowship. If a hundred years ago the standard Western approach to Asia was that its religions are wrong, more recently the standard secular attitude has been that its religions do not matter—that progress consists in leaving behind "the shackles of the past," including its value structures. This outlook, so prevalent today, with its almost total disinterest in the Asian classics, is every whit as arrogant as the dogmatic religious one, and a good deal more useless. The task of constructing a worldwide human harmony is far too monumental to be undertaken it except with religious faith. The necessary energy, perseverance, creative imagination, good will and sustaining vision are available to us from no other source. Economics, politics and technology are presenting man with a global society. It is the task of men of faith to turn that world society into a world community.

Of the main aspects of this whole matter that deserve consideration, I would call attention to two. First, I suggest that we drop the phrase "non-Christian." It is misleading and essentially false. Fundamentally, there are no non-Christians in Asia. There are Muslims, Hindus, Buddhists and so on. But there is perhaps no more effective way of misunderstanding the faith of these men than by thinking of them negatively, stressing what they are not, instead of acknowledging what they are. It is perhaps legitimate to speak of non-Christians in New York City or Toronto, if one is thinking of those who have lost their faith, or have none. But for the devout of Asia, the term is surely out of place. It is almost as if one were to introduce the archbishop of Canterbury by saying, "May I present a non-Baptist?" or to describe the Roman Catholic Church as non-Presbyterian. More seriously, it is important to realize that God neither today nor on the Day of Judgment will think of a Hindu or a Muslim as being a non-Christian. Of this surely one can feel very confident.

Second, I suggest that we abandon as utterly unworthy the traditional notion that if Christianity is true, then it must follow that other faiths are false or, at the least, inadequate. This entire formulation seems to me inept; the ideas juxtaposed just do not cohere. It would take a book to analyze the point of view that this implies, and to put forward a persuasive alternative. For the moment let me simply point out some ways in which such a position gets one tied up in un-Christian knots. For example, there is the danger of the converse proposition: that if anyone else's faith turns out to be valid or adequate, then it would follow that Christianity must be false—a form of logic that has in fact driven many from their own faith, and indeed from any faith at all. If one's chances of getting to heaven—or, to use a metaphor currently more acceptable, of coming into God's presence—are dependent on other people's not getting there, then one becomes walled up within the quite intolerable position which says that the Christian has a vested interest in other men's damnation. It is shocking to admit it, but this actually takes place. When an observer comes back from Asia or from a study of Asian religious traditions and reports that, contrary to accepted theory, some Hindus and Buddhists and some Muslims lead a pious and moral life and seem very near to God by any possible standard, so that so far as one can see in these particular cases at least faith is as "adequate" as Christian faith, then presumably a Christian should be overjoyed, enthusiastically hopeful that this be true, even though he might be permitted a fear lest it not be so. Instead, I have sometimes witnessed just the opposite: an emotional resistance to the news, one hoping firmly that it is not so though perhaps with a covert fear that it might be. Whatever the rights and wrongs of the situation theoretically, I submit that practically this is just not Christian, and indeed is not tolerable. It will not do to have a faith that can be undermined by God's saving one's neighbor, or to be afraid lest other men turn out to be closer to God than one had been led to suppose.

The question used to be asked: how is it possible to take the Christian faith seriously and at the same time believe other ways to be valid? I predict that the day is coming—indeed is perhaps already here for those of us fortunate enough to have Jewish, Muslim or Hindu friends—when the contrary question will press more cogently: how is it possible to hold a firm, deep, vibrant Christian faith, wholehearted and committed, without knowing that God meets other men in other ways? This is not to hold that all religions are essentially the same, which seems to me glib and obviously untrue. It is rather to hold that God loves all men equally, reaches out after them wherever they may be, and loves them within whatever situation he may find them. If *this* is not true, then the Christian faith is false.

If we take seriously the revelation of God in Christ—if we really mean what we say when we affirm that his life, his death on the cross, and his final triumph out of the very midst of self-sacrifice embody the ultimate truth and power and glory of the universe—then two orders of inference follow. For one, there is the order of ideas, of theological concepts, of doctrine. Here the doctrines that Christians have derived have tended to affirm a Christian exclusivism, a separation between those who believe and those who do not, a division of mankind into a "we" and a "they," a gulf between Christendom and the rest of the world—a gulf profound, ultimate and cosmic. On the moral level, on the other hand, what follows is of quite a different kind. In this order of consideration, if the Christian revelation be true, then there follows a moral imperative toward reconciliation, community, harmony and brotherhood. At this level all men are included: we strive to break down barriers, to close up gulfs; we recognize the members of the religions of Asia as one with Christians, as sons of the universal Father, seeking him and finding him, being sought by him and being found by him. At this level we do not begin to be truly Christian until we have reached out toward a community that turns all mankind into one total "we."

Of course, as I suggested earlier, there can be no final conflict between the two orders, between intellectual truth and moral value. But if for the moment there seems to be a conflict between doctrine and moral imperative, I for one have but little hesitation in holding that doctrine as formulated in the past must be expanded so as to be enabled to include the moral truth that now presses hard upon us. We shall not go far wrong if we insist that loyalty to Christ impels us to love our new neighbors of other faiths as we do ourselves.

HAROLD JOHN OCKENGA

"Resurgent Evangelical Leadership" (1960)

The more aggressive presence of evangelical Protestantism in American public life was a prominent development in the second half of the twentieth century. This development was centered in three institutions: the National Association of Evangelicals (founded in 1942), Fuller Theological Seminary (founded in 1947), and the magazine *Christianity Today* (founded in 1956). A key figure in the establishing and sustaining of all three of these institutions was the Boston preacher and theologian Harold John Ockenga (1905–85). Although the most famous, popular figure in this evangelical movement was the revivalist preacher Billy Graham, who became a close friend of Presidents Richard Nixon, George Herbert Walker Bush, and George W. Bush, no one sketched the vision of evangelical leadership more vividly and indefatigably than Ockenga. In the essay of 1960 reprinted here, Ockenga emphasizes his movement's determination to hold fast to orthodox doctrine and to resist liberalization. Ockenga also explains his understanding of how the evangelicalism of his generation differed from the fundamentalism of an earlier time even as Ockenga and his contemporaries remained committed to the central assertions of the fundamentalists.

Ockenga's ideas can be instructively studied in relation to those of Wilfred Cantwell Smith, a selection from whom precedes Ockenga in the pages of *The American Intellectual Tradition*. Smith represented the ecumenical, liberal wing of American Protestantism against which the evangelicals defined themselves, and in specific opposition to which the National Association of Evangelicals, Fuller Theological Seminary, and *Christianity Today* had all been designed. While the ecumenists pushed for more commodious constructions of Christianity and called for new alliances with persons and groups of a great range of spiritual orientations, the evangelicals sought to bring people together around a clearly defined, more strictly constructed version of the Christian faith.

A convenient summary of the differences between the evangelical and ecumenical divisions of American Protestantism during the midcentury decades, as registered in the major periodicals of each side of the split, can be found in two articles by Mark Toulouse, "*Christianity Today* and American Public Life: A Case Study," *Journal of Church and State*, 25 (1993), 241–84, and "*The Christian Century* and American Public Life: The Crucial Years, 1956–1968," in Jay P. Dolan and James P. Wind, eds., *New Dimensions in American Religious History* (Grand Rapids, Mich., 1993), 44–82. An emblem for the divergent orientations of the two magazines is the fact that in the early 1960s, *Christianity Today* was largely silent about the Civil Rights Movement and published a number of articles by J. Edgar Hoover warning Christians against the communist infiltration of American life, while the *Christian Century* was a vocal supporter of Martin Luther King, Jr.'s, civil rights activities.

An excellent account of Ockenga's career and ideas can be found in George Marsden, *Reforming Fundamentalism: Fuller Seminary and the New Evangelicalism* (Grand Rapids,

Mich., 1987; 2nd ed., rev., 1995), a book much broader in scope than its title suggests. See also Joel Carpenter, ed., *Two Reformers of Fundamentalism: Harold John Ockenga and Carl F. H. Henry* (New York, 1988). The most recent and ambitious scholarly study of Ockenga's popular hero, Billy Graham, is Grant Wacker, "Billy Graham's America," *Church History*, 78 (2009), 489–511.

What the Communist party is in the vanguard of the world revolution, the evangelical movement must be in the world revival.

What is an evangelical? An evangelical is a Christian "holding or conformed to what the majority of Protestants regard as the fundamental doctrines of the Gospel, such as the Trinity, the fallen condition of man, Christ's atonement for sin, salvation by faith, not works, and regeneration by the Holy Ghost." A subsidiary definition is "in a special sense, spiritually minded and zealous for practical Christian living, distinguished from merely orthodox." Another secondary definition is "seeking the conversion of sinners, as evangelical labors or preaching."

The doctrinal position of an evangelical is that of orthodox or creedal Christianity. This doctrinal basis is stated in the incorporation papers of the Church, namely the New Testament, and in the great creeds and confessions of Christendom. It is the Chalcedonian Creed and the later reformed confessions such as those of Heidelberg, Augsburg, and Westminster. Only those who embrace these objective truths have the right to the name evangelical.

Evangelical Christianity should be differentiated from other movements. First, it must be differentiated from Roman Catholicism, or sacerdotal Christianity, which emphasizes a salvation mediated by sacraments and erected on tradition rather than on the Word of God. Second, it must be distinguished from liberal or modernist Christianity. Many modernists appropriate the name evangelical merely because they are non-Roman Catholic, but do not embrace the basic truths of historic orthodoxy. It is a misnomer to call a modernist an evangelical. Third, an evangelical must be distinguished from a fundamentalist in areas of intellectual and ecclesiastical attitude. This distinction was made by Dr. J. Gresham Machen who was often called a fundamentalist. Said he, "The term fundamentalism is distasteful to the present writer and to many persons who hold views similar to his. It seems to suggest that we are adherents of some strange new sect, whereas in point of fact we are conscious simply of maintaining historic Christian faith and moving in the great central current of Christian life" (cf. *Valiant for Truth*, by Ned B. Stonehouse, pp. 40, 337, 343, 405, 428).

The evangelical depends upon the Bible as the authoritative Word of God and the norm of judgment in faith and practice. This brings him into tension with Romanism which, while giving lip service to the Bible, exalts tradition and papal infallibility above the Bible; with modernism which exalts the autonomy of the human mind; and with neo-orthodoxy which identifies the Word of God with something above and beyond the Bible but witnessed to in the Bible.

Has evangelicalism fallen into eclipse? The history of the last five decades has been largely under the aegis of a triumphant modernism. Basically, modernism is evolutionary naturalism applied to the Bible and to Christianity. By it the supernatural in the origins and nature of Christianity was sacrificed by the accommodation of Christian theology to the data of the scientific method and the dicta of the scientific mind. Hence, by presupposition, there could be no Virgin Birth, no miracles, and no Resurrection as the Bible taught. Modernism was based on higher criticism's view of the Bible. The books are redated in accordance with evolutionary naturalism; ethical monotheism is tolerated only later than polytheism, and the writing of the prophetic sections is placed after the events. Modernism developed a new theology concerning Christ, man, sin, salvation, the Church,

Source: Christianity Today (October 10, 1960), 14–16.

and the Church's mission. To say the least, the content of modernism was not the content of biblical theology. The departure from biblical concepts was radical.

Against this came the fundamentalist reaction. The name fundamentalist was derived from a series of treatises written by leading orthodox scholars on various biblical doctrines and published in 1917 by the Bible Institute of Los Angeles with the aid of Lyman Stuart Foundation. The contributors to *The Fundamentals* were men like Melvin Grove Kyle, James Orr, George Robinson, W. H. Griffith Thomas, F. Bettex, George Frederick Wright and others, all recognized biblical scholars of their day. The resistance to modernist attack upon biblical Christianity precipitated the modernist-fundamentalist controversy which raged for several decades following publication of *The Fundamentals*. This reached its height in the successful effort of the Presbyterians, led by Clarence Edward Macartney, to oust Harry Emerson Fosdick from the pulpit of a Presbyterian church in New York City. In the controversy there arose the emphasis upon the essentials or fundamentals of the Christian faith, such as, the inspiration of the Scriptures, the Virgin Birth, the miracles of Christ, the vicarious atonement of Christ, and the bodily resurrection of Christ.

Time revealed certain weaknesses in the fundamentalist cause. First was the diversion of strength from the great offensive work of missions, evangelism, and Christian education to the defense of the faith. The fundamentalists were maneuvered into the position of holding the line against the constant and unremitting attacks of the modernists or liberals. Gradually the liberals took over the control of the denominations and began a series of acts of discrimination, ostracism, and persecution of the evangelicals. Many evangelicals suffered at the hands of ecclesiastical modernism. This reduced fundamentalism to a holding tactic, impotent in denominational machinery and indifferent to societal problems rising in the secular world. The Christian Reformed Church was a notable exception to this trend.

The cause of the fundamentalist defeat in the ecclesiastical scene lay partially in fundamentalism's erroneous doctrine of the Church which identified the Church with believers who were orthodox in doctrine and separatist in ethics. Purity of the Church was emphasized above the peace of the Church. Second Corinthians 6:14–17 was used to justify the continuous process of fragmentation, contrary to the meaning of the passage itself. Emphasis was upon contention for the faith rather than the commission of missions, evangelism, education, and worship. The number of competent scholars declined in evangelical ranks as the decades passed.

Then came the rise of neo-orthodoxy under the influence of Karl Barth and Emil Brunner in which theology professed a return to biblical concepts without the acceptance of biblical authority. Neo-orthodoxy accepted the Word of God as revelation but differentiated this from the written Word. It spoke about the creation of man but repudiated the historical Adam. It believed in immortality but not in the physical resurrection of Jesus. Due to the aridity of modernism and a nostalgia of people for biblical ideas concerning God, man, sin, and redemption, the influence of neo-orthodoxy grew rapidly. Nevertheless, its attitude toward evangelical Christianity is essentially hostile because of its refusal to accept the biblical authority as the ground of its theology. The watershed of modern theology remains one's attitude toward the Bible as the ultimate and final authority for faith and action.

Is evangelicalism reviving? Is it emerging to challenge the theological world today? A new respect for the evangelical position is evidenced by the emergence of scholars whose works must be recognized. Westminster Press recently published a trilogy on *The Case for Liberalism*, *The Case for Neo-Orthodoxy*, and *The Case for Orthodoxy*. Here Protestant orthodoxy was again recognized as a live option. Great publishing houses today are not only willing to publish books by evangelical scholars, but several are actively seeking such books.

This may be due to a change in the intellectual climate of orthodoxy. The younger orthodox scholars are repudiating the separatist position, have repented of the attitude of solipsism, have expressed a willingness to re-examine the problems facing the theological world, have sought a return to the theological dialogue and have recognized the honesty and Christianity of some who hold views different from their own in some particulars.

Simultaneously, all branches of theological thought have felt the impact of mass evangelism under Billy Graham. In him we have seen the phenomenon of an evangelical who crossed all theological lines in his work while maintaining a strictly orthodox position. His work has not been disregarded by those of other theological convictions and has compelled them to rethink the basis of their approach.

Evangelical theology is synonymous with fundamentalism or orthodoxy. In doctrine the evangelicals and the fundamentalists are one. The evangelical must acknowledge his debt to the older fundamentalist leaders. It is a mistake for an evangelical to divorce himself from historic fundamentalism as some have sought to do. These older leaders of the orthodox cause paid a great price in persecution, discrimination, obloquy, and scorn which they suffered at the hands of those who under the name of modernism repudiated biblical Christianity. For decades these fundamentalists were steadfast to Christ and to biblical truth regardless of the cost. They maintained the knowledge of orthodox Christianity through Bible schools, radio programs, Christian conferences, and Bible conferences. In the true New Testament sense, they were witnesses, or martyrs.

The evangelical defense of the faith theologically is identical with that of the older fundamentalists. The evangelical believes in creedal Christianity, in the apologetic expression of Christianity, in the revelational content and framework of Christianity. Therefore, he stands by the side of these fundamentalist leaders. He differentiates his position from theirs in ecclesiology. These men were driven by controversy and discrimination to various shades of separatism. Some were compelled to leave their denominations, some operated as autonomous units within their denominations. Through controversy, in suffering, they sired a breed of fundamentalists who, in following them, confused courtesy in contending for the faith with compromise of the faith; academic respectability with theological apostasy; and common grace with special grace. They developed the theory that any contact, conversation, or communication with modernism was compromise and should be condemned.

Let it be repeated that there is a solidarity of doctrine between fundamentalism and evangelicalism. They are one in creed. They accept the inspiration and dependability of the Bible, the Trinity, the deity of Christ, the creation and fall of man, the vicarious atonement by Christ on Calvary, justification by faith and not by works, regeneration and sanctification by the Spirit, the spiritual unity of the Church, the evangelical, educational, and societal mission of the Church, and the kingdom of Christ experiential, ethical, and eschatalogical. The evangelical and the fundamentalist could sign the same creed.

Moreover, they have a common source of life, for they belong to one family. Christian life comes from the Christian faith and cannot be divorced from it. The repudiation of Christian truth cannot eventuate in a Christian life. In this the evangelical stands with the fundamentalist. But the evangelical goes a bit further and condemns doctrinal orthodoxy which does not result in a life of love and service. The test which Jesus gave to his disciples was that of brotherly love but it was given in the framework of an acceptance of his Deity, his miracles, his messiahship, and his imminent death as Saviour. If, therefore, the fundamentalist criticizes the evangelical or vice versa, that criticism should be within the family relationship and demonstrate the spirit and attitude of love which is a test of true discipleship.

The evangelical has general objectives he wishes to see achieved. One of them is a revival of Christianity in the midst of a secular world. The world is helpless in the presence of its problems. Its attempt at solutions totally disregards the orthodox message and answer. The evangelical wishes to retrieve Christianity from a mere eddy of the main stream into the full current of modem life. He desires to win a new respectability for orthodoxy in the academic circles by producing scholars who can defend the faith on intellectual ground. He hopes to recapture denominational leadership from within the denominations rather than abandoning those denominations to modernism. He intends to restate his position carefully and cogently so that it must be considered in the theological dialogue. He intends that Christianity will be the mainspring in many of the reforms of the societal order. It is wrong to abdicate responsibility for society under the impetus of a theology which overemphasizes the eschatalogical.

The National Association of Evangelicals summoned together a fellowship in action of many of those denominations not in the Federal Council, and for the first time it gave them a sense of unity and strength. Many individual congregations whose denominations were in the Federal Council of Churches were received into the NAE in order to articulate their convictions and give them an opportunity of cooperative action on an evangelical and orthodox base. The influence of this movement was great. While the parent organization of the National Association of Evangelicals has not reached a numerical strength which some had expected for it, it nevertheless has stimulated many subsidiary movements which originated as commissions within the National Association or were bound together with the National Association. Many of these are powerful organizations and movements in their own right, such as the National Sunday School Association, the National Radio Broadcasters, the Evangelical Foreign Missions Association, Youth for Christ, World Evangelical Fellowship and other related movements such as Child Evangelism Fellowship, the Christian Business Men's Committee, Inter-Varsity Christian Fellowship, and so on. It was, in fact, the parallel organizations to the NAE in England, India, and other areas that sparked the great Billy Graham campaigns in other parts of the world. Thus, the influence of the NAE has been far greater than its numerical strength.

Another objective was the training and feeding of evangelical ministers into the churches. Since the seminaries determine the course of the Church, it was felt necessary to fortify existing evangelical seminaries with additional professors and funds. As a result, several new evangelical seminaries were established. Here was adopted a positive attitude in inquiry, teaching, and proclamation of biblical Christianity. The students who passed through this training came forth with a certainty and knowledge expressed by "Thus saith the Lord" and with a practical program joined with a passion. In addition, there was inculcated an understanding of the connection of Christian principles with political and economic freedom.

It was the intention of evangelical strategy to reach evangelical churches who were pastored by ministers uncertain in their theological conviction. There are many ministers who have been trained in liberal theological seminaries who want to believe biblical Christianity but cannot because they lack theological education which supports the position. To reach these ministers with the rationale of biblical Christianity is the objective of *Christianity Today*.

An up-to-date strategy for the evangelical cause must be based upon the principle of infiltration. We have learned from modern militarism that the frontal attack has come to an end with certain notable exceptions. The French Maginot line was circumvented and thus antedated. The Communists in their battles in Korea, Indochina, and Tibet used the principle of infiltration. Once the line was infiltrated, defenses crumbled and a new line had to be established. We evangelicals need to realize that the liberals, or modernists, have been using this strategy for years. They have infiltrated our evangelical denominations, institutions, and movements and then have taken over the control of them. It is time for firm evangelicals to seize their opportunity to minister in and influence modernist groups. Why is it incredible that the evangelicals should be able to infiltrate the denominations and strengthen the things that remain, and possibly resume control of such denominations? Certainly they have a responsibility to do so unless they are expelled from denominations. We do not repudiate the reformation principle, but we believe that a man has a responsibility within his denomination unless that denomination has officially and overtly repudiated biblical Christianity.

Evangelicals need a plan of action. The pressing demand is for an over-all strategy instead of piecemeal action by fragmentized groups. The younger evangelicals are determined to join hands with evangelicals everywhere in testimony and in action. They want to defend and maintain the institutions, endowments, and organizations which remain within the evangelical theological position.

It demands that each one of us make a personal commitment. We should examine our activities to make sure that we are engaged in intelligent service. Let us ask ourselves what is this organization accomplishing? Does this organization fit in with God's plan? Is this movement advancing God's cause? We must not dissipate our energy and money by serving on and supporting every work which is called to our attention. We must take an inventory of our investment of money. We should ask, is this institution or movement contributing to the ends which I seek? Should I continue my support of this movement? It is folly for businessmen and foundations to support institutions, movement, and individuals which subvert that for which the businessmen and foundations stand. This is paramountly true in Christian organizations. It is our responsibility to implement the strategy of evangelicalism by personal commitment.

An evangelical makes no apology in asking the help of convinced and committed Christians. This commitment is essential in developing evangelical leadership. Every evangelical should find his place in the implementation of the modern evangelical resurgence in Christianity.

C. WRIGHT MILLS

"Letter to the New Left"
(1960)

The radical sociologist C. Wright Mills (1916–62) is remembered as a great sixties voice, but he did almost all of his work in the 1950s. Indeed, he died at the age of forty-six just as the New Left—which he addressed in a spirit of hope in the essay reprinted here—was getting started. But Mills attained a stature in death far greater than that which he enjoyed in life, and not only in the eyes of participants in the New Left. His skeptical view of American society, and of the varieties of social science that confirmed its public self-conception as a successful democracy, played much better amid the contentions of the Vietnam Era than in the 1950s.

In *The Power Elite* (New York, 1956), his most famous work, Mills insisted that the crucial decisions about the United States were being made not through a democratic give-and-take of competing interests groups but, rather, through the concerted will of a single group of rich men who had gone to the same schools and now served on the same inter-locking boards directing major business, military, and political institutions. This thesis was strongly disputed by a number of leading social scientists—most notably by Robert A. Dahl in *Who Governs?* (New Haven, 1960)—but *The Power Elite* stimulated a vigorous debate over the character of American "pluralism." An earlier book, *White Collar* (New York, 1951), is remembered along with David Riesman's *The Lonely Crowd* (New York, 1950) and William H. Whyte's *The Organization Man* (New York, 1956) for making the social psychology and politics of middle-class professionals a major preoccupation of a generation of critics, novelists, and researchers. Prominent among Mills's other books was *The Sociological Imagination* (New York, 1959), a defense of classical Enlightenment virtues against what Mills saw as the tendency of his disciplinary community of sociology to accommodate a status quo dominated by business values. In recent years, the work of Mills that has attracted the most attention is found in essays that were brought out in a posthumous volume, *Power, Politics, and People* (New York, 1963), which includes "Letter to the New Left," which first appeared in the journal *Studies on the Left*. The "you" addressed in this piece is at once the particular author of a book Mills appreciated and the general movement he believed was beginning to take form.

Mills grew up in Texas in a Catholic family, and was thus unusual among the "New York intellectuals" of the period (Mills spent most of his career at Columbia University in New York City, where he was a colleague of Daniel Bell and Lionel Trilling), most of whom were of either immigrant-Jewish or Anglo-Protestant background. Sound insights into Mills's work are found in the scattered articles of Richard Gillam, including "White Collar from Start to Finish," *Theory and Society*, 10 (1981), 1–30. The best book on Mills is Daniel Geary, *Radical Ambition* (Berkeley, 2009).

It is no exaggeration to say that since the end of World War II in Britain and the United States smug conservatives, tired liberals and disillusioned radicals have carried on a weary discourse in which issues are blurred and potential debate muted; the sickness of complacency has prevailed, the bi-partisan banality flourished. There is no need—after your book—to explain again why all this has come about among "people in general" in the NATO countries; but it may be worthwhile to examine one style of cultural work that is in effect an intellectual celebration of apathy.

Many intellectual fashions, of course, do just that; they stand in the way of a release of the imagination—about the cold war, the Soviet bloc, the politics of peace, about any new beginnings at home and abroad. But the fashion I have in mind is the weariness of many NATO intellectuals with what they call "ideology," and their proclamation of "the end of ideology." So far as I know, this began in the mid-fifties, mainly in intellectual circles more or less associated with the Congress for Cultural Freedom and the magazine *Encounter*. Reports on the Milan Conference of 1955 heralded it; since then, many cultural gossips have taken it up as a posture and an unexamined slogan. Does it amount to anything?

Its common denominator is not liberalism as a political philosophy, but the liberal rhetoric, become formal and sophisticated and used as an uncriticised weapon with which to attack Marxism. In the approved style, various of the elements of this rhetoric appear simply as snobbish assumptions. Its sophistication is one of tone rather than of ideas: in it, the *New Yorker* style of reportage has become politically triumphant. The disclosure of fact—set forth in a bright-faced or in a dead-pan manner—is the rule. The facts are duly weighed, carefully balanced, always hedged. Their power to outrage, their power truly to enlighten in a political way, their power to aid decision, even their power to clarify some situation—all that is blunted or destroyed.

So reasoning collapses into reasonableness. By the more naive and snobbish celebrants of complacency, arguments and facts of a displeasing kind are simply ignored; by the more knowing they are duly recognized, but they are neither connected with one another nor related to any general view. Acknowledged in a scattered way, they are never put together: to do so is to risk being called, curiously enough, "one-sided."

This refusal to relate isolated facts and fragmentary comment with the changing institutions of society makes it impossible to understand the structural realities which these facts might reveal; the longer-run trends of which they might be tokens. In brief, fact and idea are isolated, so the real questions are not even raised, analysis of the meanings of fact not even begun.

Practitioners of the no-more-ideology school do of course smuggle in general ideas under the guise of reportage, by intellectual gossip, and by their selection of the notions they handle. Ultimately, the end-of-ideology is based upon a disillusionment with any real commitment to socialism in any recognizable form. *That* is the only "ideology" that has really ended for these writers. But with its ending, *all* ideology, they think, has ended. *That* ideology they talk about; their own ideological assumptions, they do not.

Underneath this style of observation and comment there is the assumption that in the West there are no more real issues or even problems of great seriousness. The mixed economy plus the welfare state plus prosperity—that is the formula. US capitalism will continue to be workable; the welfare state will continue along the road to ever greater

Source: C. Wright Mills, *Power, Politics, and People* (New York: Oxford, 1963), 247–59.

justice. In the meantime, things everywhere are very complex, let us not be careless, there are great risks....

This posture—one of "false consciousness" if there ever was one—stands in the way, I think, of considering with any chances of success what may be happening in the world.

First and above all, it does rest upon a simple provincialism. If the phrase "the end of ideology" has any meaning at all, it pertains to self-selected circles of intellectuals in the richer countries. It is in fact merely their own self-image. The total population of these countries is a fraction of mankind; the period during which such a posture has been assumed is very short indeed. To speak in such terms of much of Latin America, Africa, Asia, the Soviet bloc is merely ludicrous. Anyone who stands in front of audiences—intellectual or mass—in any of these places and talks in such terms will merely be shrugged off (if the audience is polite) or laughed at out loud (if the audience is more candid and knowledgeable). The end-of-ideology is a slogan of complacency, circulating among the prematurely middle-aged, centred in the present, and in the rich Western societies. In the final analysis, it also rests upon a disbelief in the shaping by men of their own futures- -as history and as biography. It is a consensus of a few provincials about their own immediate and provincial position.

Second, the end-of-ideology is of course itself an ideology—a fragmentary one, to be sure, and perhaps more a mood. The end-of-ideology is in reality the ideology of an ending: the ending of political reflection itself as a public fact. It is a weary know-it-all justification—by tone of voice rather than by explicit argument—of the cultural and political default of the NATO intellectuals.

All this is just the sort of thing that I at least have always objected to, and do object to, in the "socialist realism" of the Soviet Union.

There too, criticism of milieux are of course permitted—but they are not to be connected with criticism of the structure itself: one may not question "the system." There are no "antagonistic contradictions."

There too, in novels and plays, criticisms of characters, even of party members, are permitted—but they must be displayed as "shocking exceptions": they must be seen as survivals from the old order, not as systematic products of the new.

There too, pessimism is permitted—but only episodically and only within the context of the big optimism: the tendency is to confuse any systematic or structural criticism with pessimism itself. So they admit criticisms, first of this and then of that: but engulf them all by the long-run historical optimism about the system as a whole and the goals proclaimed by its leaders.

I neither want nor need to overstress the parallel, yet in a recent series of interviews in the Soviet Union concerning socialist realism I was very much struck by it. In Uzbekistan and Georgia as well as in Russia, I kept writing notes to myself, at the end of recorded interviews: "This man talks in a style just like Arthur Schlesinger Jr." "Surely this fellow's the counterpart of Daniel Bell, except not so—what shall I say?—so gossipy: and certainly neither so petty nor so vulgar as the more envious status-climbers. Perhaps this is because here they are not thrown into such a competitive status-panic about the ancient and obfuscating British models of prestige." The would-be enders of ideology, I kept thinking, "Are they not the self-coordinated, or better the fashion-coordinated, socialist realists of the NATO world?" And: "Check this carefully with the files of *Encounter* and *The Reporter.*" I have now done so; it's the same kind of...thing.

Certainly there are many differences—above all, the fact that socialist realism is part of an official line; the end of ideology is self-managed. But the differences one knows. It is more useful to stress the parallels—and the generic fact that both of these postures stand opposed to radical criticisms of their respective societies.

In the Soviet Union, only political authorities at the top—or securely on their way up there—can seriously tamper with structural questions and ideological lines. These authorities, of course, are much more likely to be intellectuals (in one or another sense of the word—say a man who actually writes his own speeches) than are American politicians (about the British, you would know better than I). Moreover, such Soviet authorities, since the death of Stalin, *have* begun to tamper quite seriously with structural questions and basic ideology—although for reasons peculiar to the tight and official joining of culture and politics in their set-up, they must try to disguise this fact.

The end-of-ideology is very largely a mechanical reaction—*not* a creative response—*to* the ideology of Stalinism. As such it takes from its opponent something of its inner quality. What does it all mean? That these people have become aware of the uselessness of Vulgar Marxism, but not yet aware of the uselessness of the liberal rhetoric.

But the most immediately important thing about the "end of ideology" is that it is merely a fashion, and fashions change. Already this one is on its way out. Even a few Diehard Anti-Stalinists are showing signs of a reappraisal of their own past views; some are even beginning to recognise publicly that Stalin himself no longer runs the Soviet party and state. They begin to see the poverty of their comfortable ideas as they come to confront Khrushchev's Russia.

We who have been consistently radical in the moral terms of our work throughout the postwar period are often amused nowadays that various writers—sensing another shift in fashion—begin to call upon intellectuals to work once more in ways that are politically explicit. But we shouldn't be merely amused—we ought to try to make their shift more than a fashion change.

The end-of-ideology is on the way out because it stands for the refusal to work out an explicit political philosophy. And alert men everywhere today do feel the need of such a philosophy. What we should do is to continue directly to confront this need. In doing so, it may be useful to keep in mind that to have a working political philosophy means to have a philosophy that enables you to work. And for that, at least four kinds of work are needed, each of them at once intellectual and political.

In these terms, think—for a moment longer—of the end-of-ideology:

(1) It is a kindergarten fact that any political reflection that is of possible public significance is *ideological*: in its terms, policies, institutions, men of power are criticized or approved. In this respect, the end-of-ideology stands, negatively, for the attempt to withdraw oneself and one's work from political relevance; positively, it is an ideology of political complacency which seems the only way now open for many writers to acquiesce in or to justify the status quo.

(2) So far as orienting *theories* of society and of history are concerned, the end-of-ideology stands for, and presumably stands upon, a fetishism of empiricism: more academically, upon a pretentious methodology used to state trivialities about unimportant social areas; more essayistically, upon a naive journalistic empiricism—which I have already characterized above—and upon a cultural gossip in which "answers" to the vital and pivotal issues are merely assumed. Thus political bias masquerades as epistemological excellence, and there are no orienting theories.

(3) So far as the *historic agency of change* is concerned, the end-of-ideology stands upon the identification of such agencies with going institutions; perhaps upon their

piecemeal reform, but never upon the search for agencies that might be used or that might themselves make for a structural change of society. The problem of agency is never posed as a problem to solve, as our problem. Instead there is talk of the need to be pragmatic, flexible, open. Surely all this has already been adequately dealt with: such a view makes sense politically only if the blind drift of human affairs is in general beneficent.

(4) So far as political and human *ideals* are concerned, the end-of-ideology stands for a denial of their relevance—except as abstract ikons. Merely to hold such ideals seriously is in this view "utopian."

But enough. Where do *we* stand on each of these four aspects of political philosophy? Various of us are of course at work on each of them, and all of us are generally aware of our needs in regard to each. As for the articulation of ideals: there I think your magazines have done their best work so far. That is *your* meaning—is it not?—the emphasis upon cultural affairs. As for ideological analysis, and the rhetoric with which to carry it out: I don't think any of us are nearly good enough, but that will come with further advance on the two fronts where we are weakest: theories of society, history, human nature; and the major problem—ideas about the historical agencies of structural change.

We have frequently been told by an assorted variety of dead-end people that the meanings of Left and of Right are now liquidated, by history and by reason. I think we should answer them in some such way as this:

The Right, among other things, means—what you are doing, celebrating society as it is, a going concern. Left means, or ought to mean, just the opposite. It means: structural criticism and reportage and theories of society, which at some point or another are focussed politically as demands and programmes. These criticisms, demands, theories, programmes are guided morally by the humanist and secular ideals of Western civilizations—above all, reason and freedom and justice. To be "Left" means to connect up cultural with political criticism, and both with demands and programmes. And it means all this inside *every* country of the world.

Only one more point of definition: absence of public issues there may well be, but this is not due to any absence of problems or of contradictions, antagonistic and otherwise. Impersonal and structural changes have not eliminated problems or issues. Their absence from many discussions—that is an ideological condition, regulated in the first place by whether or not intellectuals detect and state problems as potential *issues* for probable publics, and as *troubles* for a variety of individuals. One indispensable means of such work on these central tasks is what can only be described as ideological analysis. To be actively Left, among other things, is to carry on just such analysis.

To take seriously the problem of the need for a political orientation is not of course to seek for A Fanatical and Apocalyptic Vision, for An Infallible and Monolithic Lever of Change, for Dogmatic Ideology, for A Startling New Rhetoric, for Treacherous Abstractions—and all the other bogeymen of the dead-enders. These are of course "the extremes," the straw men, the red herrings, used by our political enemies as the polar opposite of where they think they stand.

They tell us, for example, that ordinary men can't always be political "heroes." Who said they could? But keep looking around you; and why not search out the conditions of such heroism as men do and might display? They tell us we are too "impatient," that our "pretentious" theories are not well enough grounded. That is true, but neither are they trivial; why don't they get to work, refuting or grounding them? They tell us we "don't really understand" Russia—and China—today. That is true; we don't; neither do they; we are studying it. They tell us we are "ominous" in our formulations. That is true: we do have enough imagination to be frightened—and we don't have to hide it: we are not afraid we'll panic. They tell us we "are grinding axes." Of course we are: we do have, among other points of view, morally grounded ones; and we are aware of them. They tell us, in their wisdom, we don't understand that The Struggle is Without End. True: we want to change its form, its focus, its object.

We are frequently accused of being "utopian"—in our criticisms and in our proposals; and along with this, of basing our hopes for a New Left *politics* "merely on reason," or more concretely, upon the intelligentsia in its broadest sense.

There is truth in these charges. But must we not ask: what now is really meant by utopian? And: Is not our utopianism a major source of our strength? "Utopian" nowadays I think refers to any criticism or proposal that transcends the up-close milieux of a scatter of individuals: the milieux which men and women can understand directly and which they can reasonably hope directly to change. In this exact sense, our theoretical work is indeed utopian—in my own case, at least, deliberately so. What needs to be understood, and what needs to be changed, is not merely first this and then that detail of some institution or policy. If there is to be a politics of a New Left, what needs to be analysed is the *structure* of institutions, the *foundation* of policies. In this sense, both in its criticisms and in its proposals, our work is necessarily structural—and so, *for us,* just now—utopian.

Which brings us face to face with the most important issue of political reflection—and of political action—in our time: the problem of the historical agency of change, of the social and institutional means of structural change. There are several points about this problem I would like to put to you.

First, the historic agencies of change for liberals of the capitalist societies have been an array of voluntary associations, coming to a political climax in a parliamentary or congressional system. For socialists of almost all varieties, the historic agency has been the working class—and later the peasantry; also parties and unions variously composed of members of the working class or (to blur, for now, a great problem) of political parties acting in its name—"representing its interests."

I cannot avoid the view that in both cases, the historic agency (in the advanced capitalist countries) has either collapsed or become most ambiguous: so far as structural change is concerned, *these* don't seem to be at once available and effective as *our* agency any more. I know this is a debatable point among us, and among many others as well; I am by no means certain about it. But surely the fact of it—if it be that—ought not to be taken as an excuse for moaning and withdrawal (as it is by some of those who have become involved with the end-of-ideology); it ought not to be bypassed (as it is by many Soviet scholars and publicists, who in their reflections upon the course of advanced capitalist societies simply refuse to admit the political condition and attitudes of the working class).

Is anything more certain than that in 1970—indeed this time next year—our situation will be quite different, and—the chances are high—decisively so? But of course, that isn't saying much. The seeming collapse of our historic agencies of change ought to be taken as a problem, an issue, a trouble—in fact, as *the* political problem which *we* must turn into issue and trouble.

Second, is it not obvious that when we talk about the collapse of agencies of change, we cannot seriously mean that such agencies do not exist. On the contrary, the means of history-making—of decision and of the enforcement of decision—have never in world history been so enlarged and so available to such small circles of men on both sides of The Curtains as they now are. My own conception of the shape of power—the theory of the power elite—I feel no need to argue here. This theory has been fortunate in its critics, from the most diverse points of political view, and I have learned from several of these critics. But I have not seen, as of this date, any analysis of the idea that causes me to modify any of its essential features.

The point that is immediately relevant does seem obvious: what is utopian for us is not at all utopian for the presidium of the Central Committee in Moscow, or the higher circles of the Presidency in Washington, or—recent events make evident—for the men of Strategic Air Command and CIA. The historic agencies of change that have collapsed are those which were at least thought to be open to *the left* inside the advanced Western nations: those who have wished for structural changes of these societies. Many things follow from this obvious fact; of many of them, I am sure, we are not yet adequately aware.

Third, what I do not quite understand about some New Left writers is why they cling so mightily to "the working class" of the advanced capitalist societies as *the* historic agency, or even as the most important agency, in the face of the really impressive historical evidence that now stands against this expectation.

Such a labor metaphysic, I think, is a legacy from Victorian Marxism that is now quite unrealistic.

It is an historically specific idea that has been turned into an a-historical and unspecific hope.

The social and historical conditions under which industrial workers tend to become a-class-for-themselves, and a decisive political force, must be fully and precisely elaborated. There have been, there are, there will be such conditions; of course these conditions vary according to national social structure and the exact phase of their economic and political development. Of course we can't "write off the working class." But we must *study* all that, and freshly. Where labor exists as an agency, of course we must work with it, but we must not retreat it as The Necessary Lever—as nice old Labor Gentlemen in your country and elsewhere tend to do.

Although I have not yet completed my own comparative studies of working classes, generally it would seem that only at certain (earlier) stages of industrialization, and in a political context of autocracy, etc., do wage-workers tend to become a class-for-themselves, etc. The "etcs." mean that I can here merely raise the question.

It is with this problem of agency in mind that I have been studying, for several years now, the cultural apparatus, the intellectuals—as a possible, immediate, radical agency of change. For a long time, I was not much happier with this idea than were many of you; but it turns out now, in the spring of 1960, that it may be a very relevant idea indeed.

In the first place, is it not clear that if we try to be realistic in our utopianism—and that is no fruitless contradiction—a writer in our countries on the Left today *must* begin there? For that is what we are, that is where we stand.

In the second place, the problem of the intelligentsia is an extremely complicated set of problems on which rather little factual work has been done. In doing this work, we must—above all—not confuse the problems of the intellectuals of West Europe and North America with those of the Soviet Bloc or with those of the underdeveloped worlds. In each of the three major components of the world's social structure today, the character and the role of the intelligentsia is distinct and historically specific. Only by detailed comparative studies of them in all their human variety can we hope to understand any one of them.

In the third place, who is it that is getting fed up? Who is it that is getting disgusted with what Marx called "all the old crap"? Who is it that is thinking and acting in radical ways? All over the world—in the bloc, outside the bloc and in between—the answer's the same: it is the young intelligentsia.

I cannot resist copying out for you, with a few changes, some materials I've just prepared for a 1960 paperback edition of a book of mine on war:

"In the spring and early summer of 1960—more of the returns from the American decision and default are coming in. In Turkey, after student riots, a military junta takes over the state, of late run by Communist-Container Menderes. In South Korea too, students and others knock over the corrupt American-puppet regime of Syngman Rhee. In Cuba, a genuinely left-wing revolution begins full-scale economic reorganization—without the domination of US corporations. Average age of its leaders: about 30—and certainly a revolution without any Labor As Agency. On Taiwan, the eight million Taiwanese under the American-imposed dictatorship of Chiang Kai-shek, with his two million Chinese grow increasingly restive. On Okinawa—a US military base—the people get their first chance since World War II ended to demonstrate against US seizure of their island: and some students take that chance, snake-dancing and chanting angrily to the visiting President: "Go home, go home—take away your missiles." (Don't worry, 12,000 US troops easily handled the generally grateful crowds; also the President was "spirited out the rear end of the United States compound"—and so by helicopter to the airport). In Great Britain, from Aldermaston to London, young—but you were there. In Japan, weeks of student rioting succeed in rejecting the President's visit, jeopardize a new treaty with the USA, displace the big-business, pro-American Prime Minister, Kishi. And even in our own pleasant Southland, Negro and white students are—but let us keep that quiet: it really is disgraceful.

"That is by no means the complete list; that was yesterday; see today's newspaper. Tomorrow, in varying degree, the returns will be more evident. Will they be evident enough? They will have to be very obvious to attract real American attention: sweet complaints and the voice of reason—these are not enough. In the slum countries of the world today, what are they saying? The rich Americans, they pay attention only to violence—and to money. You don't care what they say, American? Good for you. Still, they may insist; things are no longer under the old control; you're not getting it straight, American: your country—it would seem—may well become the target of a world hatred of the like of which the easy-going Americans have never dreamed. Neutralists and Pacifists and Unilateralists and that confusing variety of Leftists around the world—all those tens of millions of people, of course they are misguided, absolutely controlled by small conspiratorial groups of trouble-makers, under direct orders straight from Moscow and Peking. Diabolically omnipotent, it is *they* who create all this messy unrest. It is *they* who have given the tens of millions the absurd idea that they shouldn't want to remain, or to become, the seat of American nuclear bases—those gay little outposts of American civilization. So now they don't want U-2's on their territory; so now they want to contract out of the American military machine; they want to be neutral among the crazy big antagonists. And they don't want their own societies to be militarized.

"But take heart, American: you won't have time to get really bored with your friends abroad: they won't be your friends much longer. You don't need *them;* it will all go away; don't let them confuse you."

Add to that: In the Soviet bloc, who is it that has been breaking out of apathy? It has been students and young professors and writers; it has been the young intelligentsia of Poland and Hungary, and of Russia too. Never mind that they've not won; never mind that there are other social and moral types among them. First of all, it has been these types. But the point is clear—isn't it?

That's why we've got to study these new generations of intellectuals around the world as real live agencies of historic change. Forget Victorian Marxism except whenever you need it; and read Lenin again (be careful)—Rosa Luxemburg, too.

"But it's just some kind of moral upsurge, isn't it?" Correct. But under it: no apathy. Much of it is direct non-violent action, and it seems to be working, here and there. Now we must learn from their practice and work out with them new forms of action.

"But it's all so ambiguous. Turkey, for instance. Cuba, for instance." Of course it is; history-making is always ambiguous; wait a bit; in the meantime, *help* them to focus their moral upsurge in less ambiguous political ways; work out with them the ideologies, the strategies, the theories that will help them consolidate their efforts: new theories of structural changes of and by human societies in our epoch.

"But it's utopian, after all, isn't it?" No—not in the sense you mean. Whatever else it may be, it's not that: tell it to the students of Japan.

Isn't all this, isn't it something of what we are trying to mean by the phrase, "The New Left?" Let the old men ask sourly, "Out of Apathy—into what?" The Age of Complacency is ending. Let the old women complain wisely about "the end of ideology." We are beginning to move again.

HAROLD CRUSE

"Revolutionary Nationalism and the Afro-American" (1962)

One of the most creative and independent of black nationalist thinkers of any period, Harold Cruse (1916–2005) was more ambitious, theoretically, than his more famous contemporary, Malcolm X. Cruse engaged the varieties of Marxist, liberal, and separatist thought, arguing consistently against integrationist strategies and in favor of black autonomy. He criticized black intellectual leadership for failing to provide what he considered a coherent and historically grounded program. He blamed much of this failure on the willingness of too many black radicals of the past to be guided by the Communist Party of the United States, of which Cruse himself had been a member in the late 1940s. In the essay of 1962 reprinted here, Cruse addressed the communist revolution in Cuba and outlined the most important of the ideas that he later developed in his most famous and substantial work, *The Crisis of the Negro Intellectual* (New York, 1967).

When that book was published, Cruse, unhappy with what he regarded as the shallow sloganeering done in the name of "Black Power" and impatient with the integrationist thrust of the mainstream Civil Rights Movement, had given up on the United States. He had purchased tickets for a move to Paris, where he had expected, in the tradition of earlier black expatriates, to make a new future. But shortly before he was scheduled to depart, Christopher Lasch, an influential white historian, published a laudatory review of Cruse's book in the *New York Review of Books* (February 29, 1968). Cruse changed his plans and decided to stay in the United State and participate in the debates about race and politics to the center of which Lasch's review had catapulted him. Later that year the largely self-taught Cruse, who was not a college graduate, found himself a professor of history at the University of Michigan, where he taught until his retirement twenty years later. The ideal of the "organic intellectual," arising from disadvantaged social strata and making a distinctive intellectual mark without the benefit of established institutions, is often celebrated but rarely enacted. Cruse was the real thing.

Cruse later wrote *Plural but Equal: Blacks and Minorities in America's Plural Society* (New York, 1988). A compendium of his work, with commentaries, is William Jelani Cobb, ed., *The Essential Harold Cruse: A Reader* (New York, 2002). Cruse's ideas and career are analyzed skillfully in Cedric Johnson, *Revolutionaries to Race Leaders: Black Power and the Making of African American Politics* (Minneapolis, 2007), 3–41. For another interpretation, less forgiving of what are often seen as blind spots and inconsistencies in Cruse's thought, see Richard King, *Race, Culture, and the Intellectuals: 1940–1970* (Washington, D.C., 2004), esp. 268–77. Cruse's ideas are instructively considered in relation to those of Malcolm X and

Martin Luther King, Jr. Malcolm X's speech of 1964, "The Ballot or the Bullet," is widely available. King's "Letter from a Birmingham Jail" of 1963 is included within *The American Intellectual Tradition*.

Cruse wrote "Revolutionary Nationalism and the Afro-American" during an early 1960s period when African-American leaders were involved in searching inquiries about the situation of blacks in the United States and throughout the world. An invaluable but underutilized source for understanding this historical moment in African-American discourse is Harold Isaacs, *The New World of Negro Americans* (New York, 1963).

Many of Western Marxism's fundamental theoretical formulations concerning revolution and nationalism are seriously challenged by the Cuban Revolution. American Marxism, which, since World War II, has undergone a progressive loss of influence and prestige, is challenged most profoundly. For, while most American Marxists assert that the Cuban Revolution substantiates their theories of nationalism, national liberation and revolution, in fact, the Cuban success is more nearly a *succes de circonstance*. Orthodox Marxists were unable to foresee it, and, indeed, they opposed Castro until the last minute. One would hope that such a development might cause American radicals to re-evaluate their habitual methods of perceiving social realities, but in the spate of written analyses of the Cuban Revolution one looks in vain for a new idea or a fleeting spark of creative theoretical inspiration apropos of the situation in the United States.

The failure of American Marxists to work out a meaningful approach to revolutionary nationalism has special significance to the American Negro. For the Negro has a relationship to the dominant culture of the United States similar to that of colonies and semi-dependents to their particular foreign overseers: the Negro is the American problem of underdevelopment. The failure of American Marxists to understand the bond between the Negro and the colonial peoples of the world has led to their failure to develop theories that would be of value to Negroes in the United States.

As far as American Marxists are concerned, it appears that thirty-odd years of failure on the North American mainland are now being offered compensatory vindication "90 miles from home." With all due respect to the Marxists, however, the hard facts remain. Revolutionary nationalism has not waited for western Marxist thought to catch up with the realities of the "underdeveloped" world. From underdevelopment itself have come the indigenous schools of theory and practice for achieving independence. The liberation of the colonies before the socialist revolution in the west is not orthodox Marxism (although it might be called Maoism or Castroism). As long as American Marxists cannot deal with the implications of revolutionary nationalism, both abroad and at home, they will continue to play the role of revolutionaries by proxy.

The revolutionary initiative has passed to the colonial world, and in the United States is passing to the Negro, while western Marxists theorize, temporize and debate. The success of the colonial and semi-colonial revolutions is not now, if it ever was, dependent upon the prior success of the western proletariat. Indeed, the reverse may now be true; namely, that the success of the latter is aided by the weakening of the imperial outposts of western capitalism. What is true of the colonial world is also true of the Negro in the United States. Here, the Negro is the leading revolutionary force, independent and ahead of the Marxists in the development of a movement towards social change.

The American Negro shares with colonial peoples many of the socio-economic factors which form the material basis for present day revolutionary nationalism. Like the peoples of the underdeveloped countries, the Negro suffers in varying degree from hunger, illiteracy, disease, ties to the land, urban and semi-urban slums, cultural starvation, and the psychological reactions to being ruled over by others not of his kind. He experiences the tyranny imposed upon the lives of those who inhabit underdeveloped countries. In the words of a Mexican writer, Enrique Gonzales Pedrero, underdevelopment creates a situation where that which exists "only half exists," where "countries are almost countries, only fifty percent nations, and a man who inhabits these countries is a dependent being, a

Source: *Studies on the Left*, 2 (1962), 12–25.

sub-man." Such a man depends "not on himself but on other men and other outside worlds that order him around, counsel and guide him like a newly born infant."

From the beginning, the American Negro has existed as a colonial being. His enslavement coincided with the colonial expansion of European powers and was nothing more or less than a condition of domestic colonialism. Instead of the United States establishing a colonial empire in Africa, it brought the colonial system home and installed it in the Southern states. When the Civil War broke up the slave system and the Negro was emancipated, he gained only partial freedom. Emancipation elevated him only to the position of a semi-dependent man, not to that of an equal or independent being.

The immense wealth and democratic pretensions of the American way of life have often served to obscure the real conditions under which the 18 to 20 million Negroes in the United States live. As a wage laborer or tenant farmer, the Negro is discriminated against and exploited. Those in the educated, professional, and intellectual classes suffer a similar fate. Except for a very small percentage of the Negro intelligentsia, the Negro functions in a sub-cultural world made up, usually of necessity, only of his own racial kind. This is much more than a problem of racial discrimination: it is a problem of political, economic, cultural, and administrative underdevelopment.

American Marxists, however, have never been able to understand the implications of the Negro's position in the social structure of the United States. They have no more been able to see the Negro as having revolutionary potentialities in his own right, than European Marxists could see the revolutionary aspirations of their colonials as being independent of and not subordinate to, their own. If western Marxism had no adequate revolutionary theory for the colonies, it is likewise true that American Marxists have no adequate theory for the Negro. The belief of some American Marxists in a political alliance of Negroes and whites is based on a superficial assessment of the Negro's social status: the notion that the Negro is an integral part of the American nation in the same way as is the white working class. Although this idea of Negro and white "unity" is convenient in describing the American multi-national and multi-racial makeup, it can not withstand a deeper analysis of the components which make American society what it is.

Negroes have never been equal to whites of any class in economic, social, cultural, or political status, and very few whites of any class have ever regarded them as such. The Negro is not really an integral part of the American nation beyond the convenient formal recognition that he lived within the borders of the United States. From the white's point of view, the Negro is not related to the "we," the Negro is the "they." This attitude assumes its most extreme expression in the Southern states and spreads out over the nation in varying modes of racial mores. The only factor which differentiates the Negro's status from that of a pure *colonial status* is that his position is maintained in the "home" country in close proximity to the dominant racial group.

It is not at all remarkable then, that the semi-colonial status of the Negro has given rise to nationalist movements. It would be surprising if it had not. Although Negro Nationalism today is a reflection of the revolutionary nationalism that is changing the world, the present nationalist movement stems from a tradition dating back to the period of the first World War.

Negro Nationalism came into its own at that time with the appearance of Marcus Garvey and his "Back to Africa" movement. Garvey mobilized large sections of the discontented urban petit-bourgeois and working class elements from the West Indies and the South into the greatest mass movement yet achieved in Negro history. The Garvey movement was *revolutionary nationalism* being expressed in the very heart of western capitalism. Despite the obvious parallels to colonial revolutions, however, Marxists of all parties not only rejected Garvey, but have traditionally ostracized Negro Nationalism.

American Marxism has neither understood the nature of Negro Nationalism, nor dealt with its roots in American society. When the Communists first promulgated the Negro question as a "national question" in 1928, they wanted a national question without nationalism. They posed the question mechanically because they did not really understand it. They relegated the "national" aspects of the Negro question to the "black belt" of the South, despite the fact that Garvey's "national movement" had been organized in 1916 in a northern urban center where the Negro was, according to the communists, a "national minority," but not a "nation," as he was in the Southern states. Of course, the national character of the Negro has little to do with what part of the country he lives in. Wherever he lives, he is restricted. His "national boundaries" are the color of his skin, his racial characteristics, and the social conditions within his sub-cultural world.

The ramifications of the national and colonial question are clear only if the initial bourgeois character of national movements is understood. However, according to American Marxism, Negro movements do not have "bourgeois nationalist" beginnings. American Marxists have fabricated the term "Negro Liberation Movement"—an "all-class" affair united around a program of civil and political equality, the beginnings of which they approximately date back to the founding of the National Association for the Advancement of Colored People in 1909. True, the NAACP was, from its inception, and is still, a bourgeois movement. However, it is a distortion to characterize this particular organization as the sole repository of the beginnings of the Negro bourgeois movement. For, such a narrow analysis cannot explain how or why there are two divergent trends in Negro life today: pro-integration and anti-integration. That is to say, it does not explain the origins of the Nationalist wing, composed of black Nationalists, Black Muslims, and other minor Negro Nationalist groupings, as an outgrowth of basic conflicts within the early bourgeois movements (circa 1900), from which also developed the present day NAACP-Martin Luther King-Student coalition.

Furthermore, the Marxian version of the NAACP's origins does not explain why the Nationalist wing and the NAACP wing oppose each other, or why the overwhelming majority of Negroes are "uncommitted" to either one. There is widespread dissatisfaction among various classes of Negroes with the NAACP's approach to racial problems. On the other hand, in recent years, the Nationalists have been gaining support and prestige among "uncommitted" Negroes. This is especially true of the Muslims, the newest Negro Nationalist phenomenon.

The rise of free African nations and the Cuban Revolution have, without a doubt, stirred up the latent nationalism of many Negroes. The popular acclaim given Fidel Castro by the working class Negroes of Harlem during his visit in the fall of 1960 demonstrated that the effects of the colonial revolutions are reaching the American Negro and arousing his nationalist impulses. Many Negroes, who are neither Nationalists nor supporters of the NAACP, are becoming impatient with the NAACP-Martin Luther King-Student legalistic and "passive resistance" tactics. They suspect that the long drawn out battle of attrition with which the NAACP integration movement is faced may very well end in no more than pyrrhic victories. They feel that racial integration, as a goal, lacks the tangible objectives needed to bring about genuine equality. After all, "social" and "racial" equality remain intangible goals unless they are related to the seizure and retention of objectives which can be used as levers to exert political, social, economic and administrative power in society. Power cannot be wielded from integrated lunch counters, waiting rooms, schools, housing, baseball teams, or love affairs, even though these are social advances.

There emerges from this dilemma a recognizable third trend, personified in the case of Robert F. Williams. Williams was forced to take an anti-NAACP position, but he was not a Nationalist and was critical of the "Marxists." As a rebel, Williams' objectives were the same as those of the NAACP; he differed only in his *approach*. However, his seeming "revolutionary" stance is thwarted by the same lack of substance that makes a program of "racial integration" unsatisfactory to many Negroes. Williams resorted to arms for *defense* purposes—but arms are superfluous in terms of the objectives of racial integration. Arms symbolize a step beyond mere "racial integration," to the seizure of actual centers of social power. The adherents of this third trend—young social rebels who are followers of Williams' Monroe Movement—are faced with this predicament. They are neither avowed Nationalists nor NAACPers. They consider themselves "revolutionary," but are shy of having revolutionary objectives.

However, they are not a force as yet, and their future importance will rest, no doubt, upon how much influence the Nationalist wing will exert in the Negro community. In short, the main trends in Negro life are becoming more and more polarized around the issues of pro and anti-integration.

Negro historiography does not offer a very clear explanation of how the Negro has become what he is today. As written, Negro history appears as a parade of lesser and greater personalities against a clamor of many contending anonymous voices and a welter of spasmodic trends all negating each other. Through the pages of Negro history the Negro marches, always arriving but never getting anywhere. His "national goals" are always receding.

Integration vs. separation have become polarized around two main wings of racial ideology, with fateful implications for the Negro movement and the country at large. Yet we are faced with a problem in racial ideology without any means of properly understanding how to deal with it. The dilemma arises from a lack of comprehension of the historical origins of the conflict.

Furthermore, the problem is complicated by a lack of recognition even that it exists. The fundamental economic and cultural issues at stake in this conflict cannot be dealt with by American sociologists for the simple reason that sociologists never admit that such issues should exist at all in American society. They talk of "Americanizing" all the varied racial elements in the United States; however, when it is clear that certain racial elements are *not* being "Americanized," socially, economically, or culturally, the sociologists proffer nothing but total evasion, or more studies on the "nature of prejudice." Hence the problems remain with us in a neglected state of suspension until they break out in what are considered to be "negative," "anti-social," "anti-white," "anti-democratic" reactions.

One of the few attempts to bring a semblance of order to the dominant trends in the chaos of Negro history was made by Marxist historians in the 1930's and 1940's. However, it proved to be a one-sided analysis which failed to examine the class structure of the Negro people. Viewing Negro history as a parade from slavery to socialism, the Marxist historians favor certain Negro personalities uncritically while ignoring others who played vital roles. Major figures, such as Booker T. Washington and Marcus Garvey, who do not fit into the Communist stereotype of Negro heroes are ignored or downgraded. In the process, Marxist historians have further obscured the roots of the current conflict in racial ideology.

Under the aegis of other slogans, issues and rivalries, the pro-integration vs. anti-integration controversy first appeared at the turn of the century in the famous Booker T. Washington-W. E. B. DuBois debate. Washington's position was that the Negro had to achieve economic self-sufficiency before demanding his political rights. This position led Washington to take a less "militant" stand on civil rights than did other Negro leaders, such as DuBois, who accused Washington of compromising with the racists on the Negro's political position in the South.

It is not sufficient, however, to judge Washington purely on the political policies he advocated for the Negro in the South. For Washington gave voice to an important trend in Negro life, one that made him the most popular leader American Negroes have had. The Washington-DuBois controversy was not a debate between representatives of reaction and progress, as Communist historians have asserted, but over the correct tactics for the emerging Negro bourgeoisie.

From the Reconstruction era on, the would-be Negro bourgeoisie in the United States confronted unique difficulties quite unlike those experienced by the young bourgeoisie in colonial areas. As a class, the Negro bourgeoisie wanted liberty and equality, but *also* money, prestige, and political power. How to achieve all this within the American framework was a difficult problem, since the whites had a monopoly on these benefits of western civilization, and looked upon the new aspirants as interlopers and upstarts. The Negro bourgeoisie was trapped and stymied by the entrenched and expanding power of American capitalism. Unlike the situation in the colonial areas, the Negro could not seize the power he wanted or oust "foreigners." Hence, he turned inward toward organizations of fraternal, religious, nationalistic, educational and political natures. There was much frustrated bickering and internal conflict within this new class over strategy and tactics. Finally the issues boiled down to that of *politics vs. economics,* and emerged in the Washington-DuBois controversy.

In this context, it is clear that Washington's program for a "separate" Negro economy was not compatible with the idea of integration into the dominant white economy. In 1907 DuBois complained of Washington that:

> He is striving nobly to make Negro artisans business men and property owners; but it is impossible, under modern competitive methods, for workingmen and property-owners to defend their rights and exist without the right of suffrage.

Yet, Washington could not logically seek participation in "white" politics in so far as such politics were a reflection of the mastery of whites in the surrounding economy. He reasoned that since Negroes had no chance to take part in the white world as producers and proprietors, what value was there in seeking political rights *immediately*? Herbert Aptheker, the leading Marxist authority on Negro history, quotes Washington as saying.

> Brains, property, and character for the Negro will settle the question of civil rights. The best course to pursue in regard to a civil rights bill in the South is to let it alone; let alone and it will settle itself. Good school teachers and plenty of money to pay them will be more potent in settling the race question than many civil rights bills and investigation committees.

This was the typical Washington attitude—a bourgeois attitude, practical and pragmatic, based on the expediencies of the situation. Washington sought to train and develop a new class. He had a longer range view than most of his contemporaries, and for his plans he wanted racial peace at any cost.

Few of the implications of this can be found in Marxist interpretations of Negro history. By taking a partisan position in favor of DuBois, Marxists dismiss the economic aspects of the question in favor of the purely political. However, this is the same as saying that the Negro bourgeoisie had no right to try to become capitalists—an idea that makes no historical sense whatsoever. If a small proprietor, native to an underdeveloped country, should want to oust foreign capitalists and take over his internal markets, why should not the Negro proprietor have the same desire? Of course, a substantial Negro bourgeoisie never developed in the United States. Although this fact obscured and complicated the problems of Negro Nationalism, it does not change the principles involved. Washington sought to develop a Negro bourgeoisie. He failed. But his failure was no greater than that of those who sought equality through politics.

Washington's role in developing an economic program to counteract the Negro's position is central to the emergence of Negro Nationalism, and accounts for much of his popularity among Negroes. Yet Aptheker makes the error of assessing Washington purely on political grounds. On this basis, of course, Aptheker finds him not "revolutionary" or "militant" in the fashion that befits a Negro leader, past or present. He rejects the historico-economic-class basis of Washington's philosophy, although these are essential in analyzing social movements, personalities, or historical situations. Aptheker has not seen Washington in the light of what he was: the leading spokesman and theoretician of the new Negro capitalists, whom he was trying to mold into existence. All that Aptheker has to say about Washington is summed up by him as follows:

> Mr. Washington's policy amounted objectively to an acceptance by the Negro of second class citizenship. His appearance on the historical stage and the growth of his influence coincided with and reflected the propertied interests' resistance to the farmers and workers' great protest movements in the generations spanning the close of the nineteenth and the opening of the twentieth centuries. American imperialism conquers the South during these years and Mr. Washington's program of industrial education, ultra-gradualism and opposition to independent political activity and trade unionism assisted in this conquest.

Thus is the Marxian schema about the "Negro people" projected back into history—a people without classes or differing class interests. It is naive to believe that any aspiring member of the bourgeoisie would have been interested in trade-unionism and the political action of farmers. But American Marxists cannot "see" the Negro at all unless he is storming the barricades, either in the present or in history. Does it make any sense to look back into history and expect to find Negroes involved in trade unionism and political action in the most lynch-ridden decade the South has ever known? Anyone reading about the South at the turn of the century must wonder how Negroes managed to survive at all, let alone become involved in political activity when such politics was dominated by the Ku Klux Klan. According to Aptheker, however, the Negroes who supported Washington were wrong. It was the handful of Negro militants from above the Mason-Dixon line who had never known slavery, who had never known Southern poverty and illiteracy, the whip of the lynch-mad KKK, or the peasant's agony of landlessness, who were correct in their high-sounding idealistic criticism of Washington. These were, Aptheker tells us, within a politically revolutionary tradition—a tradition which had not even emerged when Washington died!

After the Washington-DuBois debate, DuBois went on to help form the NAACP in 1909. Washington died in 1915. The controversy continued, however, in the conflict between the NAACP and the Garvey movement.

In 1916, Marcus Garvey, the West Indian-born Nationalist, organized his "Back to Africa" movement in the United States. Garvey had, from his earliest years, been deeply influenced by the racial and economic philosophies of Booker T. Washington. Adopting what he wanted from Washington's ideas, Garvey carried them further—advocating Negro self-sufficiency in the United States linked, this time, with the idea of regaining access to the African homeland, as a basis for constructing a viable black economy. Whereas Washington had earlier chosen an accommodationist position in the South to achieve his objectives, Garvey added the racial ingredient of Black Nationalism to Washington's ideas with potent effect. This development paralleled the bourgeois origins of the colonial revolutions then in their initial stages in Africa and Asia. Coming from a British colony, Garvey had the psychology of a colonial revolutionary and acted as such.

With the rise of Nationalism, DuBois and the NAACP took a strong stand against the Garvey Movement and against revolutionary nationalism. The issues were much deeper than mere rivalry between different factions for the leadership of Negro politics. The rise of Garvey Nationalism meant that the NAACP became the accommodationists and the Nationalists became the militants. From its very inception, the Negro bourgeois movement found itself deeply split over aims, ideology and tactics, growing out of its unique position of contending for its aims in the very heart of western capitalism.

Neither the nationalist side of the bourgeois movement nor the reformist NAACP wing, however, were able to vanquish the social barriers facing Negroes in the United States. The Garvey Movement found its answer in seeking a way out—"Back to Africa!" where the nationalist revolution had elbow room, where there was land, resources, sovereignty—all that the black man had been denied in the United States.

The Garvey era manifested the most self-conscious expression of nationality in the entire history of the Negro in the United States. To refrain from pointing this out, as Aptheker does in his essays on Negro history, is inexcusable. In his essay, "The Negro in World War I," Aptheker says: "What was the position of the Negro People during the years of Wilson's 'New Freedom'?" He then mentions the activities of the NAACP, the National Race Congress of 1915, and the formation in 1915 of the Association for the Study of Negro Life and History. But in discussing the racial unrest of the time, Aptheker fails to mention the Garvey Movement, despite the fact that it had organized more Negroes than any other organization in the three years following its establishment in 1916. The causes for these omissions are, of course, apparent: orthodox western Marxism cannot incorporate nationalism into its schema.

With the NAACP and the Garvey Movement growing apace, the "Negro People" had two "Negro Liberation Movements" to contend with. Never was an oppressed people so richly endowed with leadership; the only difficulty was that these two movements were at bitter odds with one another. Furthermore, within the Negro community, prejudice about lighter and darker skin coloring also served as a basis for class stratification. Thus when retaliating against DuBois' criticisms of his movement, Garvey attacked him on the basis of his skin color, and assailed the assimilation values of the upper class Negro leadership. In addition, the Garvey "blacks" and the NAACP "coloreds" disagreed as to which was the true "motherland"—black Africa or white America.

During the period when the Communists looked upon the Negro question as a national question, some Communist writers perceived the positive, as well as the negative, aspects of Garvey's appeal. Harry Haywood, for example, wrote that the Garvey Movement "reflected the widening rift between the policies of the Negro bourgeois reformism and the life needs of the sorely pressed people." He sees in Garvey's "renunciation of the whole program of interracialism" a belief that the upper class Negro leadership was "motivated solely by their desire for cultural assimilation," and that they "banked their hopes for Negro equality on support from the white enemy." Haywood sympathized with this position, seeing in the "huge movement led by Garvey" a "deep feeling for the intrinsic national character of the Negro problem."

In 1959, the Communists withdrew the concept of "self-determination" in the black belt, and sidestepped the question of the Negro's "national character." Instead, they adopted a position essentially the same as the NAACP. Their present goal is to secure "with all speed" the "fullest realization of genuinely equal economic, political and social status with all other nationalities and individual citizens of the United States"—this to be accompanied by "genuinely representative government, with proportionate representation in the areas of Negro majority population in the South." This position is essentially no different from that supported by the NAACP.

Thus, it is not surprising that it is difficult to understand the present conflict within the Negro movement; the roots of the conflict have been obliterated. While most historians do not attempt at all to bring order to the chaos of Negro history, those that have— the Marxists—find it convenient from a theoretical standpoint to see Negroes in history as black proletarian "prototypes" and forerunners of the "black workers" who will participate in the proletarian revolution. This Aptheker-Communist Party mythology, created around a patronizing deification of Negro slave heroes (Denmark Vesey, Nat Turner, Sojourner Truth, Frederick Douglass, etc.), results in abstracting them from their proper historical context and making it appear that they are relevant to modern reality. Of course, there will be those Marxists who will argue that their inability to come to terms in theory with Negro Nationalism does not arise from an error in their interpretations of the role of the Negro bourgeoisie, of Washington, or of DuBois. They will defend all the historical romanticism and the sentimental slave hero worship of the Aptheker Cult. They will say that all this is "past history" and has no bearing on the "new situation." But if one takes this position, then of what value is history of any kind, and particularly, of what value is the Marxist historical method? The inability to view Negro history in a theoretical perspective leads to the inability to cope with the implications of Negro Nationalism.

To the extent that the myth of a uniform "Negro People" has endured, a clear understanding of the causes of Negro Nationalism has been prevented. In reality, no such uniformity exists. There *are* class divisions among Negroes, and it is misleading to maintain that the interests of the Negro working and middle classes are identical. To be sure, a middle class NAACP leader and an illiterate farmhand in Mississippi or a porter who lives in Harlem, all want civil rights. However, it would be far more enlightening to examine why the NAACP is not composed of Negro porters and farmhands, but only of Negroes of a certain "type."

What we must ask is why these classes are not all striving in the same directions and to the same degree of intensity. Why are some lagging behind the integration movement, and still others in conflict with it? Where is the integration movement going? Into what is the integration movement integrating? Is the Negro middle class integrating into the white middle class? Are integrated lunch counters and waiting stations commensurate with integration into the "mainstream of American life"? And what exactly *is* the "mainstream of American life"? Will the Negro ten percent of the population get ten percent representation in the local, state, and national legislatures?—or ten percent representation in the exclusive club of the "Power Elite"?

Why are some Negroes anti-integration, others pro-integration, and still others "uncommitted"? Why is there such a lack of real unity among different Negro classes towards one objective? Why are there only some 400,000 members in the NAACP out of a total Negro population of some 18 to 20 million? Why does this membership constantly fluctuate? Why is the NAACP called a "Negro" organization when it is an *interracial* organization? Why are the Negro Nationalist organizations "all Negro"? Why do Nationalist organizations have a far greater proportion of working class Negro membership than the NAACP? Finally, why is it that the Marxists, of all groups, are at this late date tail-ending organizations such as the NAACP (King, CORE, etc.), which do not have the broad support of Negro workers and farmers? We must consider why the interests of the Negro bourgeoisie have become separated from those of the Negro working classes.

Tracing the origins of the Negro bourgeoisie back to the Booker T. Washington period (circa 1900), E. Franklin Frazier, a Negro sociologist and non-Marxist scholar, came to the enlightening conclusion that "the black bourgeois lacks the economic basis that would give it roots in the world of reality." Frazier shows that *the failure of the Negro to establish an economic base in American society served to sever the Negro bourgeoisie, in its "slow and difficult occupational differentiation," from any economic, and therefore cultural and organizational ties with the Negro working class.* Since the Negro bourgeoisie does not, in the main, control the Negro "market" in the United States economy, and since it derives its income from whatever "integrated" occupational advantages it has achieved, it has neither developed a sense of association of its status with that of the Negro working class, nor a "community" of economic, political, or cultural interests conducive for cultivating "nationalistic sentiments." Today, except for the issue of "civil rights," no unity of interests exists between the Negro middle class and the Negro working class.

Furthermore, large segments of the modern Negro bourgeoisie have played a continually regressive "non-national" role in Negro affairs. Thriving off the crumbs of integration, these bourgeois elements have become de-racialized and de-cultured, leaving the Negro working class without voice or leadership, while serving the negative role of class buffer between the deprived working class and the white ruling elites. In this respect, such groups have become a social millstone around the necks of the Negro working class—a point which none of the militant phrases that accompany the racial integration movement down the road to "racial attrition" should be allowed to obscure.

The dilemma of the Negro intellectual in the United States results from the duality of his position. Detached from the Negro working class, he tries to "integrate" and to gain full membership in a stagnating and declining western society. At the same time, failing to gain entry to the status quo he resorts to talking like a "revolutionary," championing revolutionary nationalism and its social dynamism in the underdeveloped world. But this gesture of flirting with the revolutionary nationalism of the non-west does not mask the fact that the American Negro intellectual is floating in ideological space. He is caught up in the world contradiction. Forced to face up to the colonial revolution and to make shallow propaganda out of it for himself, the American Negro intellectual is unable to cement his ties with the more racial-minded sections of the Negro working class. For, this would require him to take a nationalistic stand in American politics—which he is loath to do. Nevertheless, the impact of revolutionary nationalism in the non-western world is forcing certain Negro intellectuals to take a "nationalist" position in regard to their American situation.

Although Frazier does not delve into the nature of Nationalism or connect the rise of Nationalism with the failure of the Negro bourgeoisie to establish the "economic basis" of which he writes, it can be seen that the sense of a need for "economic self-sufficiency" is one of the causes for the persistence of nationalist groupings in Negro life. The attempt to organize and agitate for Negro ascendency in and control of the Negro market is expressed in such racial slogans as "Buy Black." The Negro Nationalist ideology regards all the social ills from which Negroes suffer as being caused by the lack of economic control over the segregated Negro community. Since the Nationalists do not envision a time when whites will voluntarily end segregation, they feel that it is necessary to gain control of the economic welfare of the segregated Negro community. Moreover, many Negro Nationalists, such as the Black Muslims, actually believe that "racial separation" is in the best interests of both races. Others maintain this separatist position because of the fact of the persistence of segregation.

Thus, when Communists and other Marxists imply that "racial integration" represents an all class movement for liberation, it indicates that they have lost touch with the realities of Negro life. They fail to concern themselves with the mind of the working class Negro in the depths of the ghetto, or the nationalistic yearnings of those hundreds of thousands of ghetto Negroes whose every aspiration has been negated by white society. Instead, the Marxists gear their position to Negro middle class aspirations and ideology. Such Marxists support the position of the Negro bourgeoisie in denying, condemning, or ignoring the existence of Negro Nationalism in the United States—while regarding the reality of Nationalism in the colonial world as something peculiar to "exotic" peoples. The measure of the lack of appeal to the working classes of the Marxist movement is indicated by the fact that Negro Nationalist movements are basically working class in character while the new Negroes attracted to the Marxist movement are of bourgeois outlook and sympathies.

Ironically, even within Marxist organizations Negroes have had to function as a numerical minority, and were subordinated to the will of a white majority on all crucial matters of racial policy. What the Marxists called "Negro-white unity" within their organizations was, in reality, white domination. Thus, the Marxist movement took a position of favoring a "racial equality" that did not even exist within the organization of the movement itself.

Today, the Marxist organizations which advocate "racial integration" do not have a single objective for the Negro that is not advocated by the NAACP or some other reform organization. It is only by virtue of asserting the "necessity of socialism" that the Marxist movement is not altogether superfluous. It could not be otherwise. For Marxism has stripped the Negro question of every theoretical concern for the class, color, ethnic, economic, cultural, psychological, and "national" complexities. They have no program apart from uttering the visionary call for "integration plus socialism" or "socialism plus integration."

However, when Marxists speak of socialism to the Negro, they leave many young Negro social rebels unimpressed. Many concrete questions remain unanswered. What guarantee do Negroes have that socialism means racial equality any more than does "capitalist democracy"? Would socialism mean the assimilation of the Negro into the dominant racial group? Although this would be "racial democracy" of a kind, the Negro would wield no political power as a minority. If he desired to exert political power as a racial minority, he might, even under socialism, be accused of being "nationalistic." In other words, the failure of American capitalist abundance to help solve the crying problems of the Negro's existence cannot be fobbed off on some future socialist heaven.

We have learned that the *means* to the *end* are just as important as the end itself. In this regard, Marxists have always been very naive about the psychology of the Negro. It was always an easy matter for Marxists to find Negro careerists, social climbers, and parlor radicals to agree with the Marxist position on the Negro masses. However, it rarely occurred to Marxists that, to the average Negro, the *means* used by Marxists were as significant as the ends. Thus, except in times of national catastrophe (such as in the depression of the 30's), Marxist means, suitable only for bourgeois form, seldom approximated the aspirations of the majority of Negroes. Lacking a working class character, Marxism in the United States cannot objectively analyze the role of the bourgeoisie or take a political position in Negro affairs that would be more in keeping with the aspirations of the masses.

The failure to deal adequately with the Negro question is the chief cause of American Marxism's ultimate alienation from the vital stream of American life. This political and theoretical deficiency poses a serious and vexing problem for the younger generation who today have become involved in political activity centered around the defense of Cuba. Some accept Marxism; other voice criticisms of Marxist parties as being "conservative," or otherwise limited in their grasp of present realities. All of these young people are more or less part of what is loosely called the "New Left" (a trend not limited to the United States).

It is now the responsibility of these new forces to find the new thinking and new approaches needed to cope with the old problems. Open-minded whites of the "New Left" must understand that Negro consciousness in the United States will be plagued with the conflict between the compulsions toward "integration" and the compulsions toward "separation." It is the inescapable result of semi-dependence.

The Negro in the United States can no more look to American Marxist schema than the colonials and semi-dependents could conform to the western Marxist timetable for revolutionary advances. Those on the American left who support revolutionary nationalism in Asia, Africa, and Latin America, must also accept the validity of Negro Nationalism in the United States. Is it not just as valid for Negro Nationalists to want to separate from American whites as it is for Cuban Nationalists to want to separate economically and politically from the United States? The answer cannot hinge merely on pragmatic practicalities. *It is a political question which involves the inherent right accruing to individuals, groups, nations and national minorities, i.e., the right of political separation from another political entity when joint existence is incompatible, coercive, unequal, or otherwise injurious to the rights of one or both.* This is a principle that must be upheld, all expedient prejudices to the contrary.

It is up to the Negro to take the organizational, political and economic steps necessary to raise and defend his status. The present situation in racial affairs will inevitably force nationalist movements to make demands which should be supported by people who are not Negro Nationalists. The Nationalists may be forced to demand the right of political separation. This too must be upheld because it is the surest means of achieving Federal action on all Negro demands of an economic or political nature. It will be the most direct means of publicizing the fact that the American government's policy on "underdeveloped" areas must be complemented by the same approach to Negro underdevelopment in the United States.

It is pointless to argue, as many do, that Negro Nationalism is an invalid ideology for Negroes to have in American life, or that the Nationalist ideas of "economic self-sufficiency" or the "separate Negro economy" are unrealistic or Utopian. Perhaps they are, but it must be clearly understood that as long as racial segregation remains a built-in characteristic of American society, Nationalist ideology will continue to grow and spread. If allowed to spread unchecked and unameliorated, the end result can only be racial wars in the United States. This is no idle prophecy, for there are many convinced Negro Nationalists who maintain that the idea of the eventual acceptance of the Negro as a full-fledged American without regard to race, creed, or color, is also Utopian and will never be realized. These Nationalists are acting on their assumptions.

Can it be said, in all truth, that Nationalist groups such as the Black Muslims are being unrealistic when they reject white society as a lost cause in terms of fulfilling any humanistic promises for the Negro? For whites to react subjectively to this attitude solves nothing. It must be understood. It must be seen that this rejection of white society has valid reasons. White society, the Muslims feel, is sick, immoral, dishonest, and filled with hate for non-whites. Their rejection of white society is analogous to the colonial people's rejection of imperialist rule. The difference is only that people in colonies can succeed and Negro Nationalists cannot. The peculiar position of Negro Nationalists in the United States requires them to set themselves against the dominance of whites and still manage to live in the same country.

It has to be admitted that it is impossible for American society as it is now constituted to integrate or assimilate the Negro. Jim Crow is a built-in component of the American social structure. There is no getting around it. Moreover, there is no organized force in the United States at present, capable of altering the structural form of American society.

Due to his semi-dependent status in society, the American Negro is the only potentially revolutionary force in the United States today. From the Negro, himself, must come the revolutionary social theories of an economic, cultural and political nature that will be his guides for social action—the new philosophies of social change. If the white working class is ever to move in the direction of demanding structural changes in society, it will be the Negro who will furnish the initial force.

The more the system frustrates the integration efforts of the Negro, the more he will be forced to resolve in his own consciousness the contradiction and conflict inherent in the pro and anti-integration trends in his racial and historical background. Out of this process, new organizational forms will emerge in Negro life to cope with new demands and new situations. To be sure, much of this will be empirical, out of necessity, and no one can say how much time this process will take to work itself towards its own logical ends. But it will be revolutionary pioneering by that segment of our society most suitable to and most amenable to pioneering—the have-nots, the victims of the American brand of social underdevelopment.

The coming coalition of Negro organizations will contain Nationalist elements in roles of conspicuous leadership. It cannot and will not be subordinate to any white groups with which it is "allied." There is no longer room for the "revolutionary paternalism" that has been the hallmark of organizations such as the Communist Party. This is what the "New Left" must clearly understand in its future relations with Negro movements that are indigenous to the Negro community.

THOMAS S. KUHN

Selection from *The Structure of Scientific Revolutions* (1962)

The extraordinary discussion surrounding *The Structure of Scientific Revolutions* is an indicator not only of the insight of its author, the historian of science Thomas S. Kuhn (1922–96), but also of the significance assigned by twentieth-century intellectuals to issues in the theoretical basis of science. This book of 1962 quickly became one of the most widely quoted and earnestly assessed academic works of the past generation. Much of the controversy centers on arguments made by Kuhn in our selection, the penultimate chapter of *Structure*. Here Kuhn places the logical aspect of scientific "proof" in a larger social and psychological context. New theories become accepted as true by communities of scientists not because these theories satisfy some absolute criteria of validity, according to Kuhn, but rather because these new theories seem more capable than competing theories of satisfying certain special needs of these communities. Nothing is more needed by such communities than a framework to guide future scientific work directed at explaining the particular problems upon which the community happens to have focused its immediate attention. When Kuhn speaks in these pages of competing "paradigms," he refers to these general theoretical frameworks that serve to guide specialized scientific work. When the relevant scientific community replaces an old paradigm with another, a "revolution" is constituted, as in several of the historical episodes to which Kuhn alludes: the intellectual innovations we associate with the names of Copernicus, Newton, and Darwin.

 An overview of Kuhn's major arguments can be found in Barry Barnes, "Thomas Kuhn," in Quentin Skinner, ed., *The Return of Grand Theory in the Human Sciences* (New York, 1985), 83–100. An accessible book-length exposition of his thought is Alexander Bird, *Thomas Kuhn* (Princeton, 2000). For a discussion of *The Structure of Scientific Revolutions* from the viewpoint of the discipline of history, see David A. Hollinger, "T. S. Kuhn's Theory of Science and Its Implications for History," in Hollinger's *In the American Province: Studies in the History and Historiography of Ideas* (Bloomington, 1985), 105–29. The most important of Kuhn's post-1962 writings are collected in his *The Road Since Structure* (Chicago, 2000), a volume edited by James Conant and James Haugeland. The most discerning of the many memorial essays to appear after Kuhn's death is J. L. Heilbron, "Thomas Samuel Kuhn," *Isis*, 89 (1998), 505–15.

... What is the process by which a new candidate for paradigm replaces its predecessor? Any new interpretation of nature, whether a discovery or a theory, emerges first in the mind of one or a few individuals. It is they who first learn to see science and the world differently, and their ability to make the transition is facilitated by two circumstances that are not common to most other members of their profession. Invariably their attention has been intensely concentrated upon the crisis-provoking problems; usually, in addition, they are men so young or so new to the crisis-ridden field that practice has committed them less deeply than most of their contemporaries to the world view and rules determined by the old paradigm. How are they able, what must they do, to convert the entire profession or the relevant professional subgroup to their way of seeing science and the world? What causes the group to abandon one tradition of normal research in favor of another?

To see the urgency of those questions, remember that they are the only reconstructions the historian can supply for the philosopher's inquiry about the testing, verification, or falsification of established scientific theories. In so far as he is engaged in normal science, the research worker is a solver of puzzles, not a tester of paradigms. Though he may, during the search for a particular puzzle's solution, try out a number of alternative approaches, rejecting those that fail to yield the desired result, he is not testing the *paradigm* when he does so. Instead he is like the chess player who, with a problem stated and the board physically or mentally before him, tries out various alternative moves in the search for a solution. These trial attempts, whether by the chess player or by the scientist, are trials only of themselves, not of the rules of the game. They are possible only so long as the paradigm itself is taken for granted. Therefore, paradigm testing occurs only after persistent failure to solve a note-worthy puzzle has given rise to crisis. And even then it occurs only after the sense of crisis has evoked an alternate candidate for paradigm. In the sciences the testing situation never consists, as puzzle solving does, simply in the comparison of a single paradigm with nature. Instead, testing occurs as part of the competition between two rival paradigms for the allegiance of the scientific community.

Closely examined, this formulation displays unexpected and probably significant parallels to two of the most popular contemporary philosophical theories about verification. Few philosophers of science still seek absolute criteria for the verification of scientific theories. Noting that no theory can ever be exposed to all possible relevant tests, they ask not whether a theory has been verified but rather about its probability in the light of the evidence that actually exists. And to answer that question one important school is driven to compare the ability of different theories to explain the evidence at hand. That insistence on comparing theories also characterizes the historical situation in which a new theory is accepted. Very probably it points one of the directions in which future discussions of verification should go.

In their most usual forms, however, probabilistic verification theories all have recourse to one or another of the pure or neutral observation-languages discussed in Section X. One probabilistic theory asks that we compare the given scientific theory with all others that might be imagined to fit the same collection of observed data. Another demands the construction in imagination of all the tests that the given scientific theory might conceivably

Source: Thomas S. Kuhn, *The Structure of Scientific Revolutions* (Chicago: University of Chicago Press, 1962), 143–59. Reprinted by permission of Thomas S. Kuhn and the University of Chicago Press. Copyright © 1962 by the University of Chicago Press.

be asked to pass. Apparently some such construction is necessary for the computation of specific probabilities, absolute or relative, and it is hard to see how such a construction can possibly be achieved. If, as I have already urged, there can be no scientifically or empirically neutral system of language or concepts, then the proposed construction of alternate tests and theories must proceed from within one or another paradigm-based tradition. Thus restricted it would have no access to all possible experiences or to all possible theories. As a result, probabilistic theories disguise the verification situation as much as they illuminate it. Though that situation does, as they insist, depend upon the comparison of theories and much widespread evidence, the theories and observations at issue are always closely related to ones already in existence. Verification is like natural selection: it picks out the most viable among the actual alternatives in a particularly historical situation. Whether that choice is the best that could have been made if still other alternatives had been available or if the data had been of another sort is not a question that can usefully be asked. There are no tools to employ in seeking answers to it.

A very different approach to this whole network of problems has been developed by Karl R. Popper who denies the existence of any verificiation procedures at all. Instead, he emphasizes the importance of falsification, i.e., of the test that, because its outcome is negative, necessitates the rejection of an established theory. Clearly, the role thus attributed to falsification is much like the one this essay assigns to anomalous experiences, i.e., to experiences that, by evoking crisis, prepare the way for a new theory. Nevertheless, anomalous experiences may not be identified with falsifying ones. Indeed, I doubt that the latter exist. As has repeatedly been emphasized before, no theory ever solves all the puzzles with which it is confronted at a given time; nor are the solutions already achieved often perfect. On the contrary, it is just the incompleteness and imperfection of the existing data-theory fit that, at any time, define many of the puzzles that characterize normal science. If any and every failure to fit were ground for theory rejection, all theories ought to be rejected at all times. On the other hand, if only severe failure to fit justifies theory rejection, then the Popperians will require some criterion of "improbability" or of "degree of falsification." In developing one they will almost certainly encounter the same network of difficulties that has haunted the advocates of the various probabilistic verification theories.

Many of the preceding difficulties can be avoided by recognizing that both of these prevalent and opposed views about the underlying logic of scientific inquiry have tried to compress two largely separate processes into one. Popper's anomalous experience is important to science because it evokes competitors for an existing paradigm. But falsification, though it surely occurs, does not happen with, or simply because of, the emergence of an anomaly or falsifying instance. Instead, it is a subsequent and separate process that might equally well be called verification since it consists in the triumph of a new paradigm over the old one. Furthermore, it is in that joint verification-falsification process that the probabilist's comparison of theories plays a central role. Such a two-stage formulation has, I think, the virtue of great verisimilitude, and it may also enable us to begin explicating the role of agreement (or disagreement) between fact and theory in the verification process. To the historian, at least, it makes little sense to suggest that verification is establishing the agreement of fact with theory. All historically significant theories have agreed with the facts, but only more or less. There is no more precise answer to the question whether or how well an individual theory fits the facts. But questions much like that can be asked when theories are taken collectively or even in pairs. It makes a great deal of sense to ask which of two actual and competing theories fits the facts *better*. Though neither Priestley's nor Lavoisier's theory, for example, agreed precisely with existing observations, few contemporaries hesitated more than a decade in concluding that Lavoisier's theory provided the better fit of the two.

This formulation, however, makes the task of choosing between paradigms look both easier and more familiar than it is. If there were but one set of scientific problems, one world within which to work on them, and one set of standards for their solution, paradigm competition might be settled more or less routinely by some process like counting the number of problems solved by each. But, in fact, these conditions are never met completely. The proponents of competing paradigms are always at least slightly at cross-purposes. Neither side will grant all the non-empirical assumptions that the other needs in order to make its case. Like Proust and Berthollet arguing about the composition of chemical compounds, they are bound partly to talk through each other. Though each may hope to convert the other to his way of seeing his science and its problems, neither may hope to prove his case. The competition between paradigms is not the sort of battle that can be resolved by proofs.

We have already seen several reasons why the proponents of competing paradigms must fail to make complete contact with each other's viewpoints. Collectively these reasons have been described as the incommensurability of the pre- and postrevolutionary normal-scientific traditions, and we need only recapitulate them briefly here. In the first place, the proponents of competing paradigms will often disagree about the list of problems that any candididate for paradigm must resolve. Their standards or their definitions of science are not the same. Must a theory of motion explain the cause of the attractive forces between particles of matter or may it simply note the existence of such forces? Newton's dynamics was widely rejected because, unlike both Aristotle's and Descartes's theories, it implied the latter answer to the question. When Newton's theory had been accepted, a question was therefore banished from science. That question, however, was one that general relativity may proudly claim to have solved. Or again, as disseminated in the nineteenth century, Lavoisier's chemical theory inhibited chemists from asking why the metals were so much alike, a question that phlogistic chemistry had both asked and answered. The transition to Lavoisier's paradigm had, like the transition to Newton's, meant a loss not only of a permissible question but of an achieved solution. That loss was not, however, permanent either. In the twentieth century questions about the qualities of chemical substances have entered science again, together with some answers to them.

More is involved, however, than the incommensurability of standards. Since new paradigms are born from old ones, they ordinarily incorporate much of the vocabulary and apparatus, both conceptual and manipulative, that the traditional paradigm had previously employed. But they seldom employ these borrowed elements in quite the traditional way. Within the new paradigm, old terms, concepts, and experiments fall into new relationships one with the other. The inevitable result is what we must call, though the term is not quite right, a misunderstanding between the two competing schools. The laymen who scoffed at Einstein's general theory of relativity because space could not be "curved"—it was not that sort of thing—were not simply wrong or mistaken. Nor were the mathematicians, physicists, and philosophers who tried to develop a Euclidean version of Einstein's theory. What had previously been meant by space was necessarily flat, homogeneous, isotropic, and unaffected by the presence of matter. If it had not been, Newtonian physics would not have worked. To make the transition to Einstein's universe, the whole conceptual web whose strands are space, time, matter, force, and so on, had to be shifted and laid down again on nature whole. Only men who had together undergone or failed to undergo that transformation would be able to discover precisely what they agreed or disagreed about. Communication across the revolutionary divide is inevitably partial. Consider, for another example, the men who called Copernicus mad because he proclaimed that the earth moved. They were not either just wrong or quite wrong. Part of what they meant by "earth" was fixed position. Their earth, at least could not be moved. Correspondingly, Copernicus' innovation was not simply to move the earth. Rather, it was a whole new way of regarding the problems of physics and astronomy, one that necessarily changed the meaning of both "earth" and "motion." Without those changes the concept of a moving earth was mad. On the other hand, once they had been made and understood, both Descartes and Huyghens could realize that the earth's motion was a question with no content for science.

These examples point to the third and most fundamental aspect of the incommensurability of competing paradigms. In a sense that I am unable to explicate further, the proponents of competing paradigms practice their trades in different worlds. One contains constrained bodies that fall slowly, the other pendulums that repeat their motions again and again. In one, solutions are compounds, in the other mixtures. One is embedded in a flat, the other in a curved, matrix of space. Practicing in different worlds, the two groups of scientists see different things when they look from the same point in the same direction. Again, that is not to say that they can see anything they please. Both are looking at the world, and what they look at has not changed. But in some areas they see different things, and they see them in different relations one to the other. That is why a law that cannot even be demonstrated to one group of scientists may occasionally seem intuitively obvious to another. Equally, it is why before they can hope to communicate fully, one group or the other must experience the conversion that we have been calling a paradigm shift. Just because it is a transition between incommensurables, the transition between competing paradigms cannot be made a step at a time, forced by logic and neutral experience. Like the gestalt switch, it must occur all at once (though not necessarily in an instant) or not at all.

How, then, are scientists brought to make this transposition? Part of the answer is that they are very often not. Copernicanism made few converts for almost a century after Copernicus' death. Newton's work was not generally accepted, particularly on the Continent, for more than half a century after the *Principia* appeared. Priestley never accepted the oxygen theory, nor Lord Kelvin the electromagnetic theory, and so on. The difficulties of conversion have often been noted by scientists themselves. Darwin, in a particularly perceptive passage at the end of his *Origin of Species,* wrote: "Although I am fully convinced of the truth of the views given in this volume…, I by no means expect to convince experienced naturalists whose minds are stocked with a multitude of facts all viewed, during a long course of years, from a point of view directly opposite to mine…. [B]ut I look with confidence to the future,—to young and rising naturalists, who will be able to view both sides of the question with impartiality." And Max Planck, surveying his own career in his *Scientific Autobiography,* sadly remarked that "a new scientific truth does not triumph by convincing its opponents and making them see the light, but rather because its opponents eventually die, and a new generation grows up that is familiar with it."

These facts and others like them are too commonly known to need further emphasis. But they do need re-evaluation. In the past they have most often been taken to indicate that scientists, being only human, cannot always admit their errors, even when confronted with strict proof. I would argue, rather, that in these matters neither proof nor error is at issue. The transfer of allegiance from paradigm to paradigm is a conversion experience that can-not be forced. Lifelong resistance, particularly from those whose productive careers have committed them to an older tradition of normal science, is not a violation of scientific standards but an index to the nature of scientific research itself. The source of resistance is the assurance that the older paradigm will ultimately solve all its problems, that nature can be shoved into the box the paradigm provides. Inevitably, at time of revolution, that assurance seems stubborn and pigheaded as indeed it sometimes becomes. But it is also something more. That same assurance is what makes normal or puzzle-solving science possible. And it is only through normal science that the professional community of scientists succeeds, first, in exploiting the potential scope and precision of the older paradigm and, then, in isolating the difficulty through the study of which a new paradigm may emerge.

Still, to say that resistance is inevitable and legitimate, that paradigm change cannot be justified by proof, is not to say that no arguments are relevant or that scientists cannot be persuaded to change their minds. Though a generation is sometimes required to effect the change, scientific communities have again and again been converted to new paradigms. Furthermore, these conversions occur not despite the fact that scientists are human but because they are. Though some scientists, particularly the older and more experienced ones, may resist indefinitely, most of them can be reached in one way or another. Conversions will occur a few at a time until, after the last holdouts have died, the whole profession will again be practicing under a single, but now a different, paradigm. We must therefore ask how conversion is induced and how resisted.

What sort of answer to that question may we expect? Just because it is asked about techniques of persuasion, or about argument and counterargument in a situation in which there can be no proof, our question is a new one, demanding a sort of study that has not previously been undertaken. We shall have to settle for a very partial and impressionistic survey. In addition, what has already been said combines with the result of the survey to suggest that, when asked about persuasion rather than proof, the question of the nature of scientific argument has no single or uniform answer. Individual scientists embrace a new paradigm for all sorts of reasons and usually for several at once. Some of these reasons— for example, the sun worship that helped make Kepler a Copernican—lie outside the apparent sphere of science entirely. Others must depend upon idiosyncrasies of autobiography and personality. Even the nationality or the prior reputation of the innovator and his teachers can sometimes play a significant role. Ultimately, therefore, we must learn to ask this question differently. Our concern will not then be with the arguments that in fact convert one or another individual, but rather with the sort of community that always sooner or later re-forms as a single group....

Probably the single most prevalent claim advanced by the proponents of a new paradigm is that they can solve the problems that have led the old one to a crisis. When it can legitimately be made, this claim is often the most effective one possible. In the area for which it is advanced the paradigm is known to be in trouble. That trouble has repeatedly been explored, and attempts to remove it have again and again proved vain. "Crucial experiments"—those able to discriminate particularly sharply between the two paradigms—have been recognized and attested before the new paradigm was even invented. Copernicus thus claimed that he had solved the long-vexing problem of the length of the calendar year, Newton that he had reconciled terrestrial and celestial mechanics, Lavoisier that he had solved the problems of gas-identity and of weight relations, and Einstein that he had made electrodynamics compatible with a revised science of motion.

Claims of this sort are particularly likely to succeed if the new paradigm displays a quantitative precision strikingly better than its older competitor. The quantitative superiority of Kepler's Rudolphine tables to all those computed from the Ptolemaic theory was a major factor in the conversion of astronomers to Copernicanism. Newton's success in predicting quantitative astronomical observations was probably the single most important reason for his theory's triumph over its more reasonable but uniformly qualitative competitors. And in this century the striking quantitative success of both Planck's radiation law and the Bohr atom quickly persuaded many physicists to adopt them even though, viewing physical science as a whole, both these contributions created many more problems than they solved.

The claim to have solved the crisis-provoking problem is, however, rarely sufficient by itself. Nor can it always legitimately be made. In fact, Copernicus' theory was not more accurate than Ptolemy's and did not lead directly to any improvement in the calendar. Or again, the wave theory of light was not, for some years after it was first announced, even as successful as its corpuscular rival in resolving the polarization effects that were a principal cause of the optical crisis. Sometimes the looser practice that characterizes extraordinary research will produce a candidate for paradigm that initially helps not at all with the problems that have evoked crisis. When that occurs, evidence must be drawn from other parts of the field as it often is anyway. In those other areas particularly persuasive arguments can be developed if the new paradigm permits the prediction of phenomena that had been entirely unsuspected while the old one prevailed.

Copernicus' theory, for example, suggested that planets should be like the earth, that Venus should show phases, and that the universe must be vastly larger than had previously been supposed. As a result, when sixty years after his death the telescope suddenly displayed mountains on the moon, the phases of Venus, and an immense number of previously unsuspected stars, those observations brought the new theory a great many converts, particularly among non-astronomers. In the case of the wave theory, one main source of professional conversions was even more dramatic. French resistance collapsed suddenly and relatively completely when Fresnel was able to demonstrate the existence of a white spot at the center of the shadow of a circular disk. That was an effect that not even he had anticipated but that Poisson, initially one of his opponents, had shown to be a necessary if absurd consequence of Fresnel's theory. Because of their shock value and because they have so obviously not been "built into" the new theory from the start, arguments like these prove especially persuasive. And sometimes that extra strength can be exploited even though the phenomenon in question had been observed long before the theory that accounts for it was first introduced. Einstein, for example, seems not to have anticipated that general relativity would account with precision for the well-known anomaly in the motion of Mercury's perihelion, and he experienced a corresponding triumph when it did so.

All the arguments for a new paradigm discussed so far have been based upon the competitors' comparative ability to solve problems. To scientists those arguments are ordinarily the most significant and persuasive. The preceding examples should leave no doubt about the source of their immense appeal. But, for reasons to which we shall shortly revert, they are neither individually nor collectively compelling. Fortunately, there is also another sort of consideration that can lead scientists to reject an old paradigm in favor of a new. These are the arguments, rarely made entirely explicit, that appeal to the individual's sense of the appropriate or the aesthetic—the new theory is said to be "neater," "more suitable," or "simpler" than the old. Probably such arguments are less effective in the sciences than in mathematics. The early versions of most new paradigms are crude. By the time their full aesthetic appeal can be developed, most of the community has been persuaded by other means. Nevertheless, the importance of aesthetic considerations can sometimes be decisive. Though they often attract only a few scientists to a new theory, it is upon those few that its ultimate triumph may depend. If they had not quickly taken it up for highly individual reasons, the new candidate for paradigm might never have been sufficiently developed to attract the allegiance of the scientific community as a whole.

To see the reason for the importance of these more subjective and aesthetic considerations, remember what a paradigm debate is about. When a new candidate for paradigm is first proposed, it has seldom solved more than a few of the problems that confront it, and most of those solutions are still far from perfect. Until Kepler, the Copernican theory scarcely improved upon the predictions of planetary position made by Ptolemy. When Lavoisier saw oxygen as "the air itself entire," his new theory could cope not at all with the problems presented by the proliferation of new gases, a point that Priestley made with great success in his counterattack. Cases like Fresnel's white spot are extremely rare. Ordinarily, it is only much later, after the new paradigm has been developed, accepted, and exploited that apparently decisive arguments—the Foucault pendulum to demonstrate the rotation of the earth or the Fizeau experiment to show that light moves faster in air than in water— are developed. Producing them is part of normal science, and their role is not in paradigm debate but in postrevolutionary texts.

Before those texts are written, while the debate goes on, the situation is very different. Usually the opponents of a new paradigm can legitimately claim that even in the area of crisis it is little superior to its traditional rival. Of course, it handles some problems better, has disclosed some new regularities. But the older paradigm can presumably be articulated to meet these challenges as it has met others before. Both Tycho Brahe's earth-centered astronomical system and the later versions of the phlogiston theory were responses to challenges posed by a new candidate for paradigm, and both were quite successful. In addition, the defenders of traditional theory and procedure can almost always point to problems that its new rival has not solved but that for their view are no problems at all. Until the discovery of the composition of water, the combustion of hydrogen was a strong argument for the phlogiston theory and against Lavoisier's. And after the oxygen theory had triumphed, it could still not explain the preparation of a combustible gas from carbon, a phenomenon to which the phlogistonists had pointed as strong support for their view. Even in the area of crisis, the balance of argument and counterargument can sometimes be very close indeed. And outside that area the balance will often decisively favor the tradition. Copernicus destroyed a time-honored explanation of terrestrial motion without replacing it; Newton did the same for an older explanation of gravity, Lavoisier for the common properties of metals, and so on. In short, if a new candidate for paradigm had to be judged from the start by hardheaded people who examined only relative problem solving ability, the sciences would experience very few major revolutions. Add the counterarguments generated by what we previously called the incommensurability of paradigms, and the sciences might experience no revolutions at all.

But paradigm debates are not really about relative problem-solving ability, though for good reasons they are usually couched in those terms. Instead, the issue is which paradigm should in the future guide research on problems many of which neither competitor can yet claim to resolve completely. A decision between alternate ways of practicing science is called for, and in the circumstances that decision must be based less on past achievement than on future promise. The man who embraces a new paradigm at an early stage must often do so in defiance of the evidence provided by problem solving. He must, that is, have faith that the new paradigm will succeed with the many large problems that confront it, knowing only that the older paradigm has failed with a few. A decision of that kind can only be made on faith.

That is one of the reasons why prior crisis proves so important. Scientists who have not experienced it will seldom renounce the hard evidence of problem solving to follow what may easily prove and will be widely regarded as a will-o'-the-wisp. But crisis alone is not enough. There must also be a basis, though it need be neither rational nor ultimately correct, for faith in the particular candidate chosen. Something must make at least a few scientists feel that the new proposal is on the right track, and sometimes it is only personal and inarticulate aesthetic considerations that can do that. Men have been converted by them at times when most of the articulable technical arguments pointed the other way. When first introduced, neither Copernicus' astronomical theory nor De Broglie's theory of matter had many other significant grounds of appeal. Even today Einstein's general theory attracts men principally on aesthetic grounds, an appeal that few people outside of mathematics have been able to feel.

This is not to suggest that new paradigms triumph ultimately through some mystical aesthetic. On the contrary, very few men desert a tradition for these reasons alone. Often those who do turn out to have been misled. But if a paradigm is ever to triumph it must gain some first supporters, men who will develop it to the point where hardheaded arguments can be produced and multiplied. And even those arguments, when they come, are not individually decisive. Because scientists are reasonable men, one or another argument will ultimately persuade many of them. But there is no single argument that can or should persuade them all. Rather than a single group conversion, what occurs is an increasing shift in the distribution of professional allegiances.

At the start a new candidate for paradigm may have few supporters, and on occasions the supporters' motives may be suspect. Nevertheless, if they are competent, they will improve it, explore its possibilities, and show what it would be like to belong to the community guided by it. And as that goes on, if the paradigm is one destined to win its fight, the number and strength of the persuasive arguments in its favor will increase. More scientists will then be converted, and the exploration of the new paradigm will go on. Gradually the number of experiments, instruments, articles, and books based upon the paradigm will multiply. Still more men, convinced of the new view's fruitfulness, will adopt the new mode of practicing normal science, until at last only a few elderly hold-outs remain. And even they, we cannot say, are wrong. Though the historian can always find men—Priestley, for instance—who were unreasonable to resist for as long as they did, he will not find a point at which resistance becomes illogical or unscientific. At most he may wish to say that the man who continues to resist after his whole profession has been converted has ipso facto ceased to be a scientist.

BETTY FRIEDAN

Selection from *The Feminine Mystique* (1963)

A journalist who had written primarily for popular women's magazines created one of the most influential works of social criticism of the entire era since World War II. Betty Friedan (1921–2006) accused the very magazines for which she wrote of conveying a destructively narrow image of what it meant to be a woman. These magazines shared with the advertising industry, many social scientists, and much of the educational establishment a tendency to mystify certain aspects of femininity, especially the ability to bear children and to stimulate men sexually. Friedan's *The Feminine Mystique* (New York, 1963) called on women to seek rewarding careers without renouncing family life. In the selection from this book reprinted here, Friedan complains audaciously that the writings of even the great Margaret Mead perpetuated—and endowed with quasi-scientific status—many of the same constraining ideas about femininity and masculinity that dominated the popular media. Throughout *The Feminine Mystique,* Friedan promotes an intellectual ideal of womanhood and urges women to seek fulfillment through serious endeavors in philosophy, the sciences, and the arts, as well as in business, politics, and public affairs.

Although most later feminists have praised Friedan for her pioneering accomplishments, the limitations of her analysis have been widely debated in relation to recent feminist theory. Friedan did not try to explain in social-theoretical terms women's subordination to men, nor did she speak to the specific problems of poor and black women. Her perspective, it is often observed, was largely confined to the needs and dilemmas of white middle-class women. Further, Friedan's emphasis on the human characteristics that women share with men contrasts with the emphasis of some later theorists on the differences between men and women.

The most important study of Friedan is Daniel Horowitz, *Betty Friedan and the Making of the Feminine Mystique* (Amherst, Mass., 1998). See also Joanne Boucher, "Betty Friedan and the Radical Past of Liberal Feminism," *New Politics*, 9 (Summer 2003), 1–16.

... Centering primarily on cultural anthropology and sociology and reaching its extremes in the applied field of family-life education, functionalism began as an attempt to make social science more "scientific" by borrowing from biology the idea of studying institutions as if they were muscles or bones, in terms of their "structure" and "function" in the social body. By studying an institution only in terms of its function within its own society, the social scientists intended to avert unscientific value judgments. In practice, functionalism was less a scientific movement than a scientific word-game. "The function is" was often translated "the function should be"; the social scientists did not recognize their own prejudices in functional disguise any more than the analysts recognized theirs in Freudian disguise. By giving an absolute meaning and a sanctimonious value to the generic term "woman's role," functionalism put American women into a kind of deep freeze—like Sleeping Beauties, waiting for a Prince Charming to waken them, while all around the magic circle the world moved on.

The social scientists, male and female, who, in the name of functionalism, drew this torturously tight circle around American women, also seemed to share a certain attitude which I will call "the feminine protest." If there is such a thing as a masculine protest—the psychoanalytic concept taken over by the functionalists to describe women who envied men and wanted to be men and therefore denied that they were women and became more manly than any man—its counterpart can be seen today in a feminine protest, made by men and women alike, who deny what women really are and make more of "being a woman" than it could ever be. The feminine protest, at its most straightforward, is simply a means of protecting women from the dangers inherent in assuming true equality with men. But why should any social scientist, with godlike manipulative superiority, take it upon himself—or herself—to protect women from the pains of growing up?

Protectiveness has often muffled the sound of doors closing against women; it has often cloaked a very real prejudice, even when it is offered in the name of science. If an old-fashioned grandfather frowned at Nora, who is studying calculus because she wants to be a physicist, and muttered, "Woman's place is in the home," Nora would laugh impatiently, "Grandpa, this is 1963." But she does not laugh at the urbane pipe-smoking professor of sociology, or the book by Margaret Mead, or the definitive two-volume reference on female sexuality, when they tell her the same thing. The complex, mysterious language of functionalism, Freudian psychology, and cultural anthropology hides from her the fact that they say this with not much more basis than grandpa.

So our Nora would smile at Queen Victoria's letter, written in 1870: "The Queen is most anxious to enlist everyone who can speak or write to join in checking this mad, wicked folly of 'Woman's Rights' with all its attendant horrors, on which her poor feeble sex is bent, forgetting every sense of womanly feeling and propriety. ... It is a subject which makes the Queen so furious that she cannot contain herself. God created men and women different—then let them remain each in their own position."

But she does not smile when she reads in *Marriage for Moderns*:

> The sexes are complementary. It is the works of my watch that move the hands and enable me to tell time. Are the works, therefore, more important than the

Source: Betty Friedan, *The Feminine Mystique* (New York: W. W. Norton, 1963), 127–31, 134–37, 145–46. Reprinted by permission of W. W. Norton & Co., Inc. Copyright © 1983, 1974, 1973, 1963 by Betty Friedan.

case?...Neither is superior, neither inferior. Each must be judged in terms of its own functions. Together they form a functioning unit. So it is with men and women—together they form a functioning unit. Either alone is in a sense incomplete. They are complementary.... When men and women engage in the same occupations or perform common functions, the complementary relationship may break down.

This book was published in 1942. Girls have studied it as a college text for the past twenty years. Under the guise of sociology, or "Marriage and Family Life," or "Life Adjustment," they are offered advice of this sort:

The fact remains, however, that we live in a world of reality, a world of the present and the immediate future, on which there rests the heavy hand of the past, a world in which tradition still holds sway and the mores exert a stronger influence than does the theorist...a world in which most men and women do marry and in which most married women are homemakers. To talk about what might be done if tradition and the mores were radically changed or what may come about by the year 2000 may be interesting mental gymnastics, but it does not help the young people of today to adjust to the inevitables of life or raise their marriages to a higher plane of satisfaction.

Of course, this "adjustment to the inevitables of life" denies the speed with which the conditions of life are now changing—and the fact that many girls who so adjust at twenty will still be alive in the year 2000. This functionalist specifically warns against any and all approaches to the "differences between men and women" except "adjustment" to those differences as they now stand. And if, like our Nora, a woman is contemplating a career, he shakes a warning finger.

For the first time in history, American young women in great numbers are being faced with these questions: Shall I voluntarily prepare myself for a lifelong celibate career? Or shall I prepare for a temporary vocation, which I shall give up when I marry and assume the responsibilities of homemaking and motherhood? Or should I attempt to combine homemaking and a career?... The great majority of married women are homemakers....

If a woman can find adequate self-expression through a career rather than through marriage, well and good. Many young women, however, overlook the fact that there are numerous careers that do not furnish any medium or offer any opportunity for self-expression. Besides they do not realize that only the minority of women, as the minority of men, have anything particularly worthwhile to express.

And so Nora is left with the cheerful impression that if she chooses a career, she is also choosing celibacy. If she has any illusions about combining marriage and career, the functionalist admonishes her:

How many individuals... can successfully pursue two careers simultaneously? Not many. The exceptional person can do it, but the ordinary person cannot. The problem of combining marriage and homemaking with another career is especially difficult, since it is likely that the two pursuits will demand qualities of different types. The former, to be successful, requires self-negation; the latter,

self-enhancement. The former demands cooperation; the latter competition....
There is greater opportunity for happiness if husband and wife supplement each
other than there is when there is duplication of function....

And just in case Nora has any doubts about giving up her career ambitions, she is offered
this comforting rationalization:

A woman who is an effective homemaker must know something about teaching,
interior decoration, cooking, dietetics, consumption, psychology, physiology,
social relations, community resources, clothing, household equipment, housing, hygiene and a host of other things.... She is a general practitioner rather
than a specialist....

The young woman who decides upon homemaking as her career need have
no feeling of inferiority.... One may say, as some do, "Men can have careers
because women make homes." One may say that women are released from the
necessity for wage earning and are free to devote their time to the extremely
important matter of homemaking because men specialize in breadwinning. Or
one may say that together the breadwinner and the homemaker form a complementary combination second to none.

This marriage textbook is not the most subtle of its school. It is almost too easy to
see that its functional argument is based on no real chain of scientific fact. (It is hardly
scientific to say "this is what is, therefore this is what should be.") But this is the essence of
functionalism as it came to pervade all of American sociology in this period, whether or
not the sociologist called himself a "functionalist." In colleges which would never stoop
to the "role-playing lessons" of the so-called functional family course, young women were
assigned Talcott Parsons' authoritative "analysis of sex-roles in the social structure of
the United States," which contemplates no alternative for a woman other than the role of
"housewife," patterned with varying emphasis on "domesticity," "glamour," and "good
companionship."

It is perhaps not too much to say that only in very exceptional cases can an
adult man be genuinely self-respecting and enjoy a respected status in the
eyes of others if he does not "earn a living" in an approved occupational
role....In the case of the feminine role the situation is radically different....
The woman's fundamental status is that of her husband's wife, the mother of
his children....

Parsons, a highly respected sociologist and the leading functional theoretician,
describes with insight and accuracy the sources of strain in this "segregation of sex roles."
He points out that the "domestic" aspect of the housewife role "has declined in importance to the point where it scarcely approaches a full-time occupation for a vigorous person": that the "glamour pattern" is "inevitably associated with a rather early age level" and
thus "serious strains result from the problem of adaptation to increasing age," that the
"good companion" pattern—which includes "humanistic" cultivation of the arts and community welfare—"suffers from a lack of fully institutionalized status....It is only those
with the strongest initiative and intelligence who achieve fully satisfying adaptations in
this direction." He states that "it is quite clear that in the adult feminine role there is quite
sufficient strain and insecurity so that widespread manifestations are to be expected in the
form of neurotic behavior." But Parsons warns:

It is, of course, possible for the adult woman to follow the masculine pattern and seek a career in fields of occupational achievement in direct competition with men of her own class. It is, however, notable that in spite of the very great progress of the emancipation of women from the traditional domestic pattern only a very small fraction have gone very far in this direction. It is also clear that its generalization would only be possible with profound alterations in the structure of the family.

True equality between men and women would not be "functional"; the status quo can be maintained only if the wife and mother is exclusively a homemaker or, at most, has a "job" rather than a "career" which might give her status equal to that of her husband. Thus Parsons finds sexual segregation "functional" in terms of keeping the social structure as it is, which seems to be the functionalist's primary concern....

Functionalism was an easy out for American sociologists. There can be no doubt that they were describing things "as they were," but in so doing, they were relieved of the responsibility of building theory from facts, of probing for deeper truth. They were also relieved of the need to formulate questions and answers that would be inevitably controversial (at a time in academic circles, as in America as a whole, when controversy was not welcome). They assumed an endless present, and based their reasoning on denying the possibility of a future different from the past. Of course, their reasoning would hold up only as long as the future did not change. As C. P. Snow has pointed out, science and scientists are future-minded. Social scientists under the functional banner were so rigidly present-minded that they denied the future; their theories enforced the prejudices of the past, and actually prevented change.

Sociologists themselves have recently come to the conclusion that functionalism was rather "embarrassing" because it really said nothing at all. As Kingsley Davis pointed out in his presidential address on "The Myth of Functional Analysis as a Special Method in Sociology and Anthropology" at the American Sociological Association in 1959:

> For more than thirty years now "functional analysis" has been debated among sociologists and anthropologists.... However strategic it may have been in the past, it has now become an impediment rather than a prop to scientific progress.... The claim that functionalism cannot handle social change because it posits an integrated static society is true by definition....

Unfortunately, the female objects of functional analysis were profoundly affected by it. At a time of great change for women, at a time when education, science, and social science should have helped women bridge the change, functionalism transformed "what is" for women, or "what was," to "what should be." Those who perpetrated the feminine protest, and made more of being a woman than it can ever be, in the name of functionalism or for whatever complex of personal or intellectual reasons, closed the door of the future on women. In all the concern for adjustment, one truth was forgotten: women were being adjusted to a state inferior to their full capabilities. The functionalists did not wholly accept the Freudian argument that "anatomy is destiny," but they accepted whole-heartedly an equally restrictive definition of woman: woman is what society says she is. And most of the functional anthropologists studied societies in which woman's destiny was defined by anatomy.

The most powerful influence on modern women, in terms both of functionalism and the feminine protest, was Margaret Mead. Her work on culture and personality—book after book, study after study—has had a profound effect on the women in my generation, the one before it, and the generation now growing up. She was, and still is, the symbol of the woman thinker in America. She has written millions of words in the thirty-odd years between *Coming of Age in Samoa* in 1928 and her latest article on American women in the *New York Times Magazine* or *Redbook*. She is studied in college classrooms by girls taking courses in anthropology, sociology, psychology, education, and marriage and family life; in graduate schools by those who will one day teach girls and counsel women; in medical schools by future pediatricians and psychiatrists; even in theological schools by progressive young ministers. And she is read in the women's magazines and the Sunday supplements, where she publishes as readily as in the learned journals, by girls and women of all ages. Margaret Mead is her own best popularizer—and her influence has been felt in almost every layer of American thought.

But her influence, for women, has been a paradox. A mystique takes what it needs from any thinker of the time. The feminine mystique might have taken from Margaret Mead her vision of the infinite variety of sexual patterns and the enormous plasticity of human nature, a vision based on the differences of sex and temperament she found in three primitive societies: the Arapesh, where both men and women were "feminine" and "maternal" in personality and passively sexual, because both were trained to be cooperative, unaggressive, responsive to the needs and demands of others; the Mundugumor, where both husband and wife were violent, aggressive, positively sexed, "masculine"; and the Tchambuli, where the woman was the dominant, impersonal managing partner, and the man the less responsible and emotionally dependent person.

> If those temperamental attitudes which we have traditionally regarded as feminine—such as passivity, responsiveness, and a willingness to cherish children—can so easily be set up as the masculine pattern in one tribe, and in another be outlawed for the majority of women as well as for the majority of men, we no longer have any basis for regarding such aspects of behavior as sex-linked.... The material suggests that we may say that many, if not all, of the personality traits which we have called masculine or feminine are as lightly linked to sex, as are the clothing, the manners, and the form of headdress that a society at a given period assigns to either sex.

From such anthropological observations, she might have passed on to the popular culture a truly revolutionary vision of women finally free to realize their full capabilities in a society which replaced arbitrary sexual definitions with a recognition of genuine individual gifts as they occur in either sex. She had such a vision, more than once:

> Where writing is accepted as a profession that may be pursued by either sex with perfect suitability, individuals who have the ability to write need not be debarred from it by their sex, nor need they, if they do write, doubt their essential masculinity or femininity... and it is here that we can find a ground-plan for building a society that would substitute real differences for arbitrary ones. We must recognize that beneath the superficial classifications of sex and race the same potentialities exist, recurring generation after generation, only to perish because society has no place for them.
>
> Just as society now permits the practice of an art to members of either sex, so it might also permit the development of many contrasting temperamental gifts in each sex. It would abandon its various attempts to make boys fight and

to make girls remain passive, or to make all children fight.... No child would be relentlessly shaped to one pattern of behavior, but instead there should be many patterns, in a world that had learned to allow to each individual the pattern which was most congenial to his gifts.

But this is not the vision the mystique took from Margaret Mead; nor is it the vision that she continues to offer. Increasingly, in her own pages, her interpretation blurs, is subtly transformed, into a glorification of women in the female role—as defined by their sexual biological function. At times she seems to lose her own anthropological awareness of the malleability of human personality, and to look at anthropological data from the Freudian point of view—sexual biology determines all, anatomy is destiny....

As a matter of fact, the lens of "anatomy is destiny" seemed to be peculiarly right for viewing the cultures and personalities of Samoa, Manus, Arapesh, Mundugumor, Tchambuli, Iatmul and Bali; right as perhaps it never was right, in that formulation, for Vienna at the end of the nineteenth century or America in the twentieth.

In the primitive civilizations of the South Sea islands, anatomy was still destiny when Margaret Mead first visited them. Freud's theory that the primitive instincts of the body determined adult personality could find convincing demonstration. The complex goals of more advanced civilizations, in which instinct and environment are increasingly controlled and transformed by the human mind, did not then form the irreversible matrix of every human life. It must have been much easier to see biological differences between men and women as the basic force in life in those unclothed primitive peoples. But only if you go to such an island with the Freudian lens in your eye, accepting before you start what certain irreverent anthropologists call the toilet-paper theory of history, will you draw from observations in primitive civilizations of the role of the unclothed body, male or female, a lesson for modern women which assumes that the unclothed body can determine in the same way the course of human life and personality in a complex modern civilization.

Anthropologists today are less inclined to see in primitive civilization a laboratory for the observation of our own civilization, a scale model with all the irrelevancies blotted out; civilization is just not that irrelevant.

Because the human body is the same in primitive South Sea tribes and modern cities, an anthropologist, who starts with a psychological theory that reduces human personality and civilization to bodily analogies, can end up advising modern women to live through their bodies in the same way as the women of the South Seas. The trouble is that Margaret Mead could not recreate a South Sea world for us to live in: a world where having a baby is the pinnacle of human achievement....

The role of Margaret Mead as the professional spokesman of femininity would have been less important if American women had taken the example of her own life, instead of listening to what she said in her books. Margaret Mead has lived a life of open challenge, and lived it proudly, if sometimes self-consciously, as a woman. She has moved on the frontiers of thought and added to the superstructure of our knowledge. She has demonstrated feminine capabilities that go far beyond childbirth; she made her way in what was still very much a "man's world" without denying that she was a woman; in fact, she proclaimed in her work a unique woman's knowledge with which no male anthropologist could compete. After so many centuries of unquestioned masculine authority, how natural for someone to proclaim a feminine authority. But the great human visions of stopping wars, curing sickness, teaching races to live together, building new and beautiful structures for people to live in, are more than "other ways of having children."

It is not easy to combat age-old prejudices. As a social scientist, and as a woman, she struck certain blows against the prejudicial image of woman that may long outlast her own life. In her insistence that women are human beings—unique human beings, not men with something missing—she went a step beyond Freud. And yet, because her observations were based on Freud's bodily analogies, she cut down her own vision of women by glorifying the mysterious miracle of femininity, which a woman realizes simply by being female, letting the breasts grow and the menstrual blood flow and the baby suck from the swollen breast. In her warning that women who seek fulfillment beyond their biological role are in danger of becoming desexed witches, she spelled out again an unnecessary choice. She persuaded younger women to give up part of their dearly won humanity rather than lose their femininity. In the end she did the very thing that she warned against, re-creating in her work the vicious circle that she broke in her own life....

MARTIN LUTHER KING, JR.

Selection from "Letter from a Birmingham Jail" (1963)

When the civil rights leader Martin Luther King, Jr. (1929–68), was jailed in Birmingham, Alabama, along with twenty-four hundred other antisegregationist demonstrators, a group of local white clergy published an attack on King. The black preacher from Atlanta had broken laws prohibiting blacks from using certain public accommodations and had otherwise promoted "unwise and untimely" demonstrations, according to their statement. King responded from his jail cell. His "Letter from a Birmingham Jail" began as a local document of a local dispute, but when published in the *Christian Century* on June 12, 1963, it quickly became the central text in the nationwide discussion of the theory of civil disobedience. King began his letter with a detailed account of Birmingham city politics and of the process by which the Southern Christian Leadership Conference—of which King was president—had become involved in the struggle to desegregate Birmingham. The following selection begins at the point in the letter when King turns to the issue of just versus unjust laws. Although King's distinctly religious and strictly nonviolent approach was not to the tastes of everyone concerned with civil rights, the argument made in the letter won wide acclaim. The following year, King was awarded the Nobel Peace Prize. King's most important books were *Stride Toward Freedom: The Montgomery Story* (New York, 1958) and *Why We Can't Wait* (New York, 1964).

A comprehensive edition of King's papers is being published by the University of California Press under the editorship of Clayborne Carson. Six volumes have now been published. Among the finest of the numerous books on King, two are of special merit: Jonathan Rieder, *The Word of the Lord Is Upon Me* (Cambridge, Mass., 2008); and Eric Sundquist, *King's Dream* (New York, 2009).

… You express a great deal of anxiety over our willingness to break laws. This is certainly a legitimate concern. Since we so diligently urge people to obey the Supreme Court's decision of 1954 outlawing segregation in the public schools, at first glance it may seem rather paradoxical for us consciously to break laws. One may well ask, "How can you advocate breaking some laws and obeying others?" The answer lies in the fact that there are two types of laws: just and unjust. I agree with St. Augustine that "an unjust law is no law at all."

Now what is the difference between the two? How does one determine whether a law is just or unjust? A just law is a man-made code that squares with the moral law or the law of God. An unjust law is a code that is out of harmony with the moral law. To put it in the terms of St. Thomas Aquinas, an unjust law is a human law that is not rooted in eternal law and natural law. Any law that uplifts human personality is just. Any law that degrades human personality is unjust. All segregation statutes are unjust because segregation distorts the soul and damages the personality. It gives the segregator a false sense of superiority and the segregated a false sense of inferiority. Segregation, to use the terminology of the Jewish philosopher Martin Buber, substitutes an "I-it" relationship for an "I-thou" relationship and ends up relegating persons to the status of things. Hence segregation is not only politically, economically and sociologically unsound, it is sinful. Paul Tillich has said that sin is separation. Is not segregation an existential expression of man's tragic separation, his awful estrangement, his terrible sinfulness? Thus it is that I can urge men to disobey segregation ordinances, for such ordinances are morally wrong.

Let us consider some of the ways in which a law can be unjust. A law is unjust, for example, if the majority group compels a minority group to obey the statute but does not make it binding on itself. By the same token a law in all probability is just if the majority is itself willing to obey it. Also, a law is unjust if it is inflicted on a minority that, as a result of being denied the right to vote, had no part in enacting or devising the law. Who can say that the legislature of Alabama which set up that state's segregation laws was democratically elected? Throughout Alabama all sorts of devious methods are used to prevent Negroes from becoming registered voters, and there are some counties in which, even though Negroes constitute a majority of the population, not a single Negro is registered. Can any law enacted under such circumstances be considered democratically structured?

Sometimes a law is just on its face and unjust in its application. For instance, I have been arrested on a charge of parading without a permit. Now there is nothing wrong in having an ordinance which requires a permit for a parade. But such an ordinance becomes unjust when it is used to maintain segregation and to deny citizens the First-amendment privilege of peaceful assembly and protest.

I hope you are able to see the distinction I am trying to point out. In no sense do I advocate evading the law, as would the rabid segregationist. That would lead to anarchy. One who breaks an unjust law must do so *openly, lovingly,* and with a willingness to accept the penalty. I submit that an individual who breaks a law that conscience tells him is unjust and who willingly accepts the penalty of imprisonment in order to arouse the conscience of the community over its injustice is in reality expressing the highest respect for law.

Source: The Christian Century (June 12, 1963), 769–75. Reprinted by arrangement with the Estate of Martin Luther King, Jr., c/o Writers House as agent for the proprietor New York, N.Y. Copyright © 1963 by Martin Luther King, Jr., copyright renewed 1991 Coretta Scott King.

Of course, there is nothing new about this kind of civil disobedience. It was evidenced sublimely in the refusal of Shadrach, Meshach and Abednego to obey the laws of Nebuchadnezzar, on the ground that a higher moral law was at stake. It was practiced superbly by the early Christians who were willing to face hungry lions rather than submit to certain unjust laws of the Roman empire. To a degree, academic freedom is a reality today because Socrates practiced civil disobedience. We should never forget that everything Adolf Hitler did in Germany was "legal" and everything the Hungarian freedom fighters did in Hungary was "illegal." It was "illegal" to aid and comfort a Jew in Hitler's Germany. Even so, I am sure that had I lived in Germany at the time I would have aided and comforted my Jewish brothers. If today I lived in a communist country where certain principles dear to the Christian faith are suppressed, I would openly advocate disobeying that country's antireligious laws.

I must make two honest confessions to you, my Christian and Jewish brothers. First, I must confess that over the past few years I have been gravely disappointed with the white moderate. I have almost reached the regrettable conclusion that the Negro's great stumbling block in his stride toward freedom is not the White Citizen's Counciler or the Ku Klux Klanner but the white moderate who is more devoted to "order" than to justice; who prefers a negative peace which is the absence of tension to a positive peace which is the presence of justice; who constantly says "I agree with you in the goal you seek, but I cannot agree with your methods"; who paternalistically believes he can set the timetable for another man's freedom; who lives by a mythical concept of time and who constantly advises the Negro to wait for a "more convenient season." Shallow understanding from people of good will is more frustrating than absolute misunderstanding from people of ill will. Lukewarm acceptance is much more bewildering than outright rejection.

I had hoped that the white moderate would understand that law and order exist for the purpose of establishing justice and that when they fail in this purpose they block social progress. I had hoped that the white moderate would understand that the present tension in the south is a necessary phase of the transition from an obnoxious negative peace, in which the Negro passively accepted his unjust plight, to a substantive and positive peace, in which all men will respect the dignity and worth of human personality. Actually, we who engage in nonviolent direct action are not the creators of tension. We merely bring to the surface the hidden tension that is already alive. We bring it out in the open where it can be seen and dealt with. Like a boil that can never be cured so long as it is covered up but must be opened with all its pus-flowing ugliness to the natural medicines of air and light, injustice must be exposed, with all the tension its exposure creates, to the light of human conscience and the air of national opinion before it can be cured.

In your statement you assert that our actions, even though peaceful, must be condemned because they precipitate violence. But is this a logical assertion? Isn't this like condemning a robbed man because his possession of money precipitated an act of robbery? Isn't this like condemning Socrates because his unswerving commitment to truth and his philosophical inquiries precipitated the act by the misguided populace in which they made him drink hemlock? Isn't this like condemning Jesus because his unique God-consciousness and never-ceasing devotion to God's will precipitated the evil act of crucifixion? We must come to see that, as the federal courts have consistently affirmed, it is wrong to urge an individual to cease his efforts to gain his basic constitutional rights because the quest may precipitate violence. Society must protect the robbed and punish the robber.

I had also hoped that the white moderate would reject the myth concerning time in relation to the struggle for freedom. I have just received a letter from a white brother in Texas. He writes: "All Christians know that the colored people will receive equal rights eventually, but it is possible that you are in too great a religious hurry. It has taken Christianity almost 2,000 years to accomplish what it has. The teachings of Christ take time to come to earth." Such an attitude stems from a tragic misconception of time, from the strangely irrational notion that there is something in the very flow of time that will inevitably cure all ills. Actually, time itself is neutral; it can be used either destructively or constructively. More and more I feel that the people of ill will have used time much more effectively than have the people of good will. We will have to repent in this generation not merely for the hateful words and actions of the bad people but for the appalling silence of the good people. Human progress never rolls in on wheels of inevitability; it comes through the tireless efforts of men willing to be co-workers with God, and without this hard work time itself becomes an ally of the forces of social stagnation. We must use time creatively, in the knowledge that the time is always ripe to do right. Now is the time to make real the promise of democracy and transform our pending national elegy into a creative psalm of brotherhood. Now is the time to lift our national policy from the quicksand of racial injustice to the solid rock of human dignity.

You speak of our activity in Birmingham as extreme. At first I was rather disappointed that fellow clergymen would see my nonviolent efforts as those of an extremist. I began thinking about the fact that I stand in the middle of two opposing forces in the Negro community. One is a force of complacency made up of Negroes who, as a result of long years of oppression, are so completely drained of self-respect and a sense of "somebodiness" that they have adjusted to segregation, and of a few middle class Negroes who, because of a degree of academic and economic security and because in some ways they profit by segregation, have unconsciously become insensitive to the problems of the masses. The other force is one of bitterness and hatred, and it comes perilously close to advocating violence. It is expressed in the various black nationalist groups that are springing up across the nation, the largest and best-known being Elijah Muhammad's Muslim movement. Nourished by the Negro's frustration over the continued existence of racial discrimination, this movement is made up of people who have lost faith in America, who have absolutely repudiated Christianity, and who have concluded that the white man is an incorrigible "devil."

I have tried to stand between these two forces, saying that we need emulate neither the "do-nothingism" of the complacent nor the hatred of the black nationalist. For there is the more excellent way of love and nonviolent protest. I am grateful to God that, through the influence of the Negro church, the way of nonviolence became an integral part of our struggle.

If this philosophy had not emerged, by now many streets of the south would, I am convinced, be flowing with blood. And I am further convinced that if our white brothers dismiss as "rabble-rousers" and "outside agitators" those of us who employ nonviolent direct action and if they refuse to support our nonviolent efforts, millions of Negroes will, out of frustration and despair, seek solace and security in black nationalist ideologies—a development that would inevitably lead to a frightening racial nightmare.

Oppressed people cannot remain oppressed forever. The yearning for freedom eventually manifests itself, and that is what has happened to the American Negro. Something within has reminded him of his birthright of freedom, and something without has reminded him that it can be gained. Consciously or unconsciously, he has been caught up by the Zeitgeist, and with his black brothers of Africa and his brown and yellow brothers of Asia, South America and the Caribbean, the U.S. Negro is moving with a sense of great urgency toward the promised land of racial justice. If one recognizes this vital urge that has engulfed the Negro community, he should readily understand why public demonstrations are taking place. The Negro has many pent-up resentments and latent frustrations, and he must release them. So let him march; let him make prayer pilgrimages to the city hall; let him go on freedom rides—and try to understand why he must do so. If his repressed emotions are not released in nonviolent ways, they will seek expression through violence; this is not a threat but a fact of history. I have not said to my people, "Get rid of your discontent." Rather, I have tried to say that this normal and healthy discontent can be channeled into the creative outlet of nonviolent direct action. And now this approach is being termed extremist.

But though I was initially disappointed at being categorized as an extremist, as I continued to think about the matter I gradually gained a measure of satisfaction from the label. Was not Jesus an extremist for love: "Love your enemies, bless them that curse you, do good to them that hate you, and pray for them which despitefully use you, and persecute you." Was not Amos an extremist for justice: "Let justice roll down like waters and righteousness like an everflowing stream." Was not Paul an extremist for the Christian gospel: "I bear in my body the marks of the Lord Jesus." Was not Martin Luther an extremist: "Here I stand; I can do no other so help me God." And John Bunyan: "I will stay in jail to the end of my days before I make a butchery of my conscience." And Abraham Lincoln: "This nation can-not survive half slave and half free." And Thomas Jefferson: "We hold these truths to be self-evident, that all men are created equal... ." So the question is not whether we will be extremists but what kind of extremists we will be. Will we be extremists for hate or for love? Will we be extremists for the preservation of injustice or for the extension of justice? Perhaps the south, the nation and the world are in dire need of creative extremists.

I had hoped that the white moderate would see this need. Perhaps I was too optimistic; perhaps I expected too much. I suppose I should have realized that few members of the oppressor race can understand the deep groans and passionate yearnings of the oppressed race, and still fewer have the vision to see that injustice must be rooted out by strong, persistent and determined action. I am thankful, however, that some of our white brothers have grasped the meaning of this social revolution and committed themselves to it. They are still all too few in quantity, but they are big in quality. Some—such as Ralph McGill, Lillian Smith, Harry Golden and James McBride-Dabbs—have written about our struggle in eloquent and prophetic terms. Others have marched with us down nameless streets of the south. They have languished in filthy, roach-infested jails, suffering the abuse and brutality of policemen who view them as "dirty nigger lovers." Unlike so many of their moderate brothers and sisters, they have recognized the urgency of the moment and sensed the need for powerful "action" antidotes to combat the disease of segregation.

Let me take note of my other major disappointment. Though there are some notable exceptions, I have also been disappointed with the white church and its leadership. I do not say this as one of those negative critics who can always find something wrong with the church. I say this as a minister of the gospel, who loves the church; who was nurtured in its bosom; who has been sustained by its spiritual blessings and who will remain true to it as long as the cord of life shall lengthen.

When I was suddenly catapulted into the leadership of the bus protest in Montgomery, Alabama, a few years ago I felt we would be supported by the white church. I felt that the white ministers, priests and rabbis of the South would be among our strongest allies. Instead, some have been outright opponents, refusing to understand the freedom movement and misrepresenting its leaders; all too many others have been more cautious than courageous and have remained silent and secure behind stained-glass windows.

In spite of my shattered dreams I came to Birmingham with the hope that the white religious leadership of this community would see the justice of our cause and with deep moral concern would serve as the channel through which our just grievances could reach the power structure. But again I have been disappointed.

I have heard numerous southern religious leaders admonish their worshipers to comply with a desegregation decision because it is the *law,* but I have longed to hear white ministers declare, "Follow this decree because integration is morally *right* and because the Negro is your brother." In the midst of blatant injustices inflicted upon the Negro I have watched white churchmen stand on the sideline and mouth pious irrelevancies and sanctimonious trivialities. In the midst of a mighty struggle to rid our nation of racial and economic injustice I have heard many ministers say, "Those are social issues with which the gospel has no real concern," and I have watched many churches commit themselves to a completely otherworldly religion which makes a strange, unbiblical distinction between body and soul, between the sacred and the secular.

We are moving toward the close of the 20th century with a religious community largely adjusted to the status quo—a taillight behind other community agencies rather than a headlight leading men to higher levels of justice.

I have traveled the length and breadth of Alabama, Mississippi and all the other southern states. On sweltering summer days and crisp autumn mornings I have looked at the south's beautiful churches with their lofty spires pointing heavenward, and at her impressive religious education buildings. Over and over I have found myself asking: "What kind of people worship here? Who is their God? Where were their voices when the lips of Governor Barnett dripped with words of interposition and nullification? Where were they when Governor Wallace gave a clarion call for defiance and hatred? Where were their voices of sup-port when bruised and weary Negro men and women decided to rise from the dark dungeons of complacency to the bright hills of creative protest?"

Yes, these questions are still in my mind. In deep disappointment I have wept over the laxity of the church. But be assured that my tears have been tears of love. There can be no deep disappointment where there is not deep love. Yes, I love the church. How could I do otherwise? I am in the rather unique position of being the son, the grandson and the great-grandson of preachers. Yes, I see the church as the body of Christ. But, oh! How we have blemished and scarred that body through social neglect and through fear of being nonconformists.

There was a time when the church was very powerful—in the time when the early Christians rejoiced at being deemed worthy to suffer for what they believed. In those days the church was not merely a thermometer that recorded the ideas and principles of popular opinion; it was a thermostat that transformed the mores of society. Whenever the early Christians entered a town the power structure immediately sought to convict them for being "disturbers of the peace" and "outside agitators." But the Christians pressed on, in the conviction that they were "a colony of heaven," called to obey God rather than man.

Small in number, they were big in commitment. By their effort and example they brought an end to such ancient evils as infanticide and gladiatorial contest.

Things are different now. So often the contemporary church is a weak, ineffectual voice with an uncertain sound. So often it is an archdefender of the status quo. Far from being disturbed by the presence of the church, the power structure of the average community is consoled by the church's silent—and often even vocal—sanction of things as they are.

But the judgment of God is upon the church as never before. If today's church does not recapture the sacrificial spirit of the early church, it will lose its authenticity, forfeit the loyalty of millions, and be dismissed as an irrelevant social club with no meaning for the 20th century. Every day I meet young people whose disappointment with the church has turned into outright disgust.

Perhaps I have once again been too optimistic. Is organized religion too inextricably bound to the status quo to save our nation and the world? Perhaps I must turn my faith to the inner spiritual church, the church within the church, as the true *ecclesia* and the hope of the world. But again I am thankful to God that some noble souls from the ranks of organized religion have broken loose from the paralyzing chains of conformity and joined us as active partners in the struggle for freedom. They have left their secure congregations and walked the streets of Albany, Georgia, with us. They have gone down the highways of the south on torturous rides for freedom. Yes, they have gone to jail with us. Some have been kicked out of their churches, have lost the support of their bishops and fellow ministers. But they have acted in the faith that right defeated is stronger than evil triumphant. Their witness has been the spiritual salt that has preserved the true meaning of the gospel in these troubled times. They have carved a tunnel of hope through the dark mountain of disappointment.

I hope the church as a whole will meet the challenge of this decisive hour. But even if the church does not come to the aid of justice, I have no despair about the future. I have no fear about the outcome of our struggle in Birmingham, even if our motives are at present misunderstood. We will reach the goal of freedom in Birmingham and all over the nation, because the goal of America is freedom. Abused and scorned though we may be, our destiny is tied up with America's destiny. Before the pilgrims landed at Plymouth we were here. Before the pen of Jefferson etched across the pages of history the mighty words of the Declaration of Independence, we were here. For more than two centuries our forebears labored in this country without wages; they made cotton king; they built the homes of their masters while suffering gross injustice and shameful humiliation—and yet out of a bottomless vitality they continued to thrive and develop. If the inexpressible cruelties of slavery could not stop us, the opposition we now face will surely fail. We will win our freedom because the sacred heritage of our nation and the eternal will of God are embodied in our echoing demands.

Before closing I feel impelled to mention one other point in your statement that has troubled me profoundly. You warmly commended the Birmingham police force for keeping "order" and "preventing violence." I doubt that you would have so warmly commended the police force if you had seen its angry dogs sinking their teeth into six unarmed, nonviolent Negroes. I doubt that you would so quickly commend the policemen if you were to observe their ugly and inhuman treatment of Negroes here in the city jail; if you were to watch them push and curse old Negro women and young Negro girls; if you were to see them slap and kick old Negro men and young boys; if you were to observe them, as they did on two occasions, refuse to give us food because we wanted to sing our grace together. I cannot join you in your praise of the Birmingham police department.

It is true that the police have exercised discipline in handling the demonstrators. In this sense they have conducted themselves rather "nonviolently" in public. But for what purpose? To preserve the evil system of segregation. Over the past few years I have consistently preached that nonviolence demands that the means we use must be as pure as the ends we seek. I have tried to make clear that it is wrong to use immoral means to attain moral ends. But now I must affirm that it is just as wrong, or perhaps even more so, to use moral means to preserve immoral ends. Perhaps Mr. Connor and his policemen have been rather nonviolent in public, as was Chief Pritchett in Albany, Georgia, but they have used the moral means of nonviolence to maintain the immoral end of racial injustice. As T. S. Eliot has said, there is no greater treason than to do the right deed for the wrong reason.

I wish you had commended the Negro sit-inners and demonstrators of Birmingham for their sublime courage, their willingness to suffer and their amazing discipline in the midst of great provocation. One day the south will recognize its real heroes. They will be the James Merediths, with a noble sense of purpose facing jeering and hostile mobs and the agonizing loneliness that characterizes the life of the pioneer. They will be old, oppressed, battered Negro women, symbolized in a 72-year-old woman in Montgomery, Alabama, who rose up with a sense of dignity and with her people decided not to ride segregated buses, and who responded with ungrammatical profundity to one who inquired about her: "My feet is tired, but my soul is rested." They will be the young high school and college students, the young ministers of the gospel and a host of their elders courageously and nonviolently sitting in at lunch counters and willingly going to jail for conscience' sake. One day the South will know that when these disinherited children of God sat down at lunch counters they were in reality standing up for what is best in the American dream and for the most sacred values in our Judeo-Christian heritage, thereby bringing our nation back to those great wells of democracy which were dug deep by the founding fathers in their formulation of the Constitution and the Declaration of Independence.

Never before have I written so long a letter. I can assure you that it would have been much shorter if I had been writing from a comfortable desk, but what else can one do when he is alone for days in a narrow jail cell, other than write long letters, think long thoughts and pray long prayers?

If I have said anything in this letter that overstates the truth and indicates an unreasonable impatience, I beg you to forgive me. If I have said anything that *understates* the truth and indicates my having a patience that allows me to settle for anything less than brotherhood, I beg God to forgive me.

I hope this letter finds you strong in the faith. I also hope that circumstances will soon make it possible for me to meet each of you, not as an integrationist or a civil rights leader but as a fellow clergyman and a Christian brother. Let us all hope that the dark clouds of racial prejudice will soon pass away and the deep fog of misunderstanding will be lifted from our fear-drenched communities and in some not too distant tomorrow the radiant stars of love and brotherhood will shine over our great nation with all their scintillating beauty.

SUSAN SONTAG

"Against Interpretation"
(1964)

Explorers of the uncertain cultural terrain that separates the "postmodern" from the "modern" have turned increasingly to the early work of Susan Sontag (1933–2004). In a series of essays written in the mid-1960s, Sontag criticized as a stagnant, academicized establishment a tradition of "modernist" thought about the arts that had long seen itself as a bold, iconoclastic avant-garde. Drawing upon an older, romantic tradition, Sontag insisted that criticism should not try to tell us what art "means," but should show us "the sensuous surface" of art. She endorsed "erotic" rather than "hermeneutic" priorities, and championed style over content. The arts now the most alive, Sontag insisted, were popular arts like film, often eschewed as beneath serious scrutiny by the critics of Clement Greenberg's generation.

Although Sontag wrote well before currency of the term *postmodernism,* this label came eventually to stand for the blurring of "high" and "low" art, the liberation of art from political and moral purposes, the focusing on the surfaces instead of the allegedly deep structures of art, and the separation of art objects from large-scale interpretive schemes—all themes of "Against Interpretation," the essay of 1964 reprinted here. Sontag's ideas can be profitably contrasted to those set forth in two "modernist" classics found in this sourcebook, Greenberg's "Avant-Garde and Kitsch" and Lionel Trilling's "On the Teaching of Modern Literature."

Sontag also distinguished herself as a writer of fiction—her best known novel is *Death Kit* (1967)—but her stature as a critical essayist of exceptionally wide range has been sustained not only by *Against Interpretation* (1966), in which our selection was first reprinted, but also by *On Photography* (1977), *Illness as Metaphor* (1979), and *AIDS and Its Metaphors* (1988). Sontag was among the most appreciated of the nation's "celebrity intellectuals," and her name was often invoked in popular films and comic strips.

Two studies of her work are Sohnya Sayers, *Susan Sontag: Elegiac Modernist* (New York, 1990); and Liam Kennedy, *Susan Sontag: Mind as Passion* (Manchester, U.K., 1995). Her obituary in the *New York Times* (December 28, 2004) offered a cogent and informative account of her life and work. Sontag's son, David Rieff, has edited her private journals in *Reborn: Journals and Notebooks, 1947–1963* (New York, 2008).

The earliest *experience* of art must have been that it was incantatory, magical; art was an instrument of ritual. (Cf. the paintings in the caves at Lascaux, Altamira, Niaux, La Pasiega, etc.) The earliest *theory* of art, that of the Greek philosophers, proposed that art was mimesis, imitation of reality.

It is at this point that the peculiar question of the *value* of art arose. For the mimetic theory, by its very terms, challenges art to justify itself.

Plato, who proposed the theory, seems to have done so in order to rule that the value of art is dubious. Since he considered ordinary material things as themselves mimetic objects, imitations of transcendent forms or structures, even the best painting of a bed would be only an "imitation of an imitation." For Plato, art is neither particularly useful (the painting of a bed is no good to sleep on), nor, in the strict sense, true. And Aristotle's arguments in defense of art do not really challenge Plato's view that all art is an elaborate trompe l'oeil, and therefore a lie. But he does dispute Plato's idea that art is useless. Lie or no, art has a certain value according to Aristotle because it is a form of therapy. Art is useful, after all, Aristotle counters, medicinally useful in that it arouses and purges dangerous emotions.

In Plato and Aristotle, the mimetic theory of art goes hand in hand with the assumption that art is always figurative. But advocates of the mimetic theory need not close their eyes to decorative and abstract art. The fallacy that art is necessarily a "realism" can be modified or scrapped without ever moving outside the problems delimited by the mimetic theory.

The fact is, all Western consciousness of and reflection upon art have remained within the confines staked out by the Greek theory of art as mimesis or representation. It is through this theory that art as such—above and beyond given works of art—becomes problematic, in need of defense. And it is the defense of art which gives birth to the odd vision by which something we have learned to call "form" is separated off from something we have learned to call "content," and to the well-intentioned move which makes content essential and form accessory.

Even in modern times, when most artists and critics have discarded the theory of art as representation of an outer reality in favor of the theory of art as subjective expression, the main feature of the mimetic theory persists. Whether we conceive of the work of art on the model of a picture (art as a picture of reality) or on the model of a statement (art as the statement of the artist), content still comes first. The content may have changed. It may now be less figurative, less lucidly realistic. But it is still assumed that a work of art is its content. Or, as it's usually put today, that a work of art by definition *says* something. ("What X is saying is...," "What X is trying to say is...," "What X said is.. ." etc., etc.)

None of us can ever retrieve that innocence before all theory when art knew no need to justify itself, when one did not ask of a work of art what it said because one knew (or thought one knew) what it *did*. From now to the end of consciousness, we are stuck with the task of defending art. We can only quarrel with one or another means of defense. Indeed, we have an obligation to overthrow any means of defending and justifying art which becomes particularly obtuse or onerous or insensitive to contemporary needs and practice.

This is the case, today, with the very idea of content itself. Whatever it may have been in the past, the idea of content is today mainly a hindrance, a nuisance, a subtle or not so subtle philistinism.

Source: Susan Sontag, "Against Interpretation" from *Against Interpretation* (New York, 1966). Reprinted by permission of Farrar, Straus and Giroux, LLC. Copyright © 1964, 1966, renewed 1994 by Susan Sontag.

Though the actual developments in many arts may seem to be leading us away from the idea that a work of art is primarily its content, the idea still exerts an extraordinary hegemony. I want to suggest that this is because the idea is now perpetuated in the guise of a certain way of encountering works of art thoroughly ingrained among most people who take any of the arts seriously. What the overemphasis on the idea of content entails is the perennial, never consummated project of *interpretation*. And, conversely, it is the habit of approaching works of art in order to *interpret* them that sustains the fancy that there really is such a thing as the content of a work of art.

Of course, I don't mean interpretation in the broadest sense, the sense in which Nietzsche (rightly) says, "There are no facts, only interpretations." By interpretation, I mean here a conscious act of the mind which illustrates a certain code, certain "rules" of interpretation.

Directed to art, interpretation means plucking a set of elements (the X, the Y, the Z, and so forth) from the whole work. The task of interpretation is virtually one of translation. The interpreter says, Look, don't you see that X is really—or, really means—A? That Y is really B? That Z is really C?

What situation could prompt this curious project for transforming a text? History gives us the materials for an answer. Interpretation first appears in the culture of late classical antiquity, when the power and credibility of myth had been broken by the "realistic" view of the world introduced by scientific enlightenment. Once the question that haunts post-mythic consciousness—that of the *seemliness* of religious symbols—had been asked, the ancient texts were, in their pristine form, no longer acceptable. Then interpretation was summoned, to reconcile the ancient texts to "modern" demands. Thus, the Stoics, to accord with their view that the gods had to be moral, allegorized away the rude features of Zeus and his boisterous clan in Homer's epics. What Homer really designated by the adultery of Zeus with Leto, they explained, was the union between power and wisdom. In the same vein, Philo of Alexandria interpreted the literal historical narratives of the Hebrew Bible as spiritual paradigms. The story of the exodus from Egypt, the wandering in the desert for forty years, and the entry into the promised land, said Philo, was really an allegory of the individual soul's emancipation, tribulations, and final deliverance. Interpretation thus presupposes a discrepancy between the clear meaning of the text and the demands of (later) readers. It seeks to resolve that discrepancy. The situation is that for some reason a text has become unacceptable; yet it cannot be discarded. Interpretation is a radical strategy for conserving an old text, which is thought too precious to repudiate, by revamping it. The interpreter, without actually erasing or rewriting the text, is altering it. But he can't admit to doing this. He claims to be only making it intelligible, by disclosing its true meaning. However far the interpreters alter the text (another notorious example is the Rabbinic and Christian "spiritual" interpretations of the clearly erotic Song of Songs), they must claim to be reading off a sense that is already there.

Interpretation in our own time, however, is even more complex. For the contemporary zeal for the project of interpretation is often prompted not by piety toward the troublesome text (which may conceal an aggression), but by an open aggressiveness, an overt contempt for appearances. The old style of interpretation was insistent, but respectful; it erected another meaning on top of the literal one. The modern style of interpretation excavates, and as it excavates, destroys; it digs "behind" the text, to find a sub-text which is the true one. The most celebrated and influential modern doctrines, those of Marx and Freud, actually amount to elaborate systems of hermeneutics, aggressive and impious theories of interpretation. All observable phenomena are bracketed, in Freud's phrase, as *manifest content.* This manifest content must be probed and pushed aside to find the true meaning—the *latent content*—beneath. For Marx, social events like revolutions and wars; for Freud, the events of individual lives (like neurotic symptoms and slips of the tongue) as well as texts (like a dream or a work of art)—all are treated as occasions for interpretation. According to Marx and Freud, these events only seem to be intelligible. Actually, they have no meaning without interpretation. To understand is to interpret. And to interpret is to restate the phenomenon, in effect to find an equivalent for it.

Thus, interpretation is not (as most people assume) an absolute value, a gesture of mind situated in some timeless realm of capabilities. Interpretation must itself be evaluated, within a historical view of human consciousness. In some cultural contexts, interpretation is a liberating act. It is a means of revising, of transvaluing, of escaping the dead past. In other cultural contexts, it is reactionary, impertinent, cowardly, stifling.

Today is such a time, when the project of interpretation is largely reactionary, stifling. Like the fumes of the automobile and of heavy industry which befoul the urban atmosphere, the effusion of interpretations of art today poisons our sensibilities. In a culture whose already classical dilemma is the hypertrophy of the intellect at the expense of energy and sensual capability, interpretation is the revenge of the intellect upon art.

Even more. It is the revenge of the intellect upon the world. To interpret is to impoverish, to deplete the world—in order to set up a shadow world of "meanings." It is to turn *the* world into *this* world. ("This world"! As if there were any other.)

The world, our world, is depleted, impoverished enough. Away with all duplicates of it, until we again experience more immediately what we have.

In most modern instances, interpretation amounts to the philistine refusal to leave the work of art alone. Real art has the capacity to make us nervous. By reducing the work of art to its content and then interpreting *that,* one tames the work of art. Interpretation makes art manageable, conformable.

This philistinism of interpretation is more rife in literature than in any other art. For decades now, literary critics have understood it to be their task to translate the elements of the poem or play or novel or story into something else. Sometimes a writer will be so uneasy before the naked power of his art that he will install within the work itself—albeit with a little shyness, a touch of the good taste of irony—the clear and explicit interpretation of it. Thomas Mann is an example of such an overcooperative author. In the case of more stubborn authors, the critic is only too happy to perform the job.

The work of Kafka, for example, has been subjected to a mass ravishment by no less than three armies of interpreters. Those who read Kafka as a social allegory see case studies of the frustrations and insanity of modern bureaucracy and its ultimate issuance in the totalitarian state. Those who read Kafka as a psychoanalytic allegory see desperate revelations of Kafka's fear of his father, his castration anxieties, his sense of his own impotence, his thralldom to his dreams. Those who read Kafka as a religious allegory explain that K. in *The Castle* is trying to gain access to heaven, that Joseph K. in *The Trial* is being judged by the inexorable and mysterious justice of God.... Another oeuvre that has attracted interpreters like leeches is that of Samuel Beckett. Beckett's delicate dramas of the withdrawn consciousness—pared down to essentials, cut off, often represented as physically immobilized—are read as a statement about modern man's alienation from meaning or from God, or as an allegory of psychopathology.

Proust, Joyce, Faulkner, Rilke, Lawrence, Gide... one could go on citing author after author; the list is endless of those around whom thick encrustations of interpretation have taken hold. But it should be noted that interpretation is not simply the compliment that mediocrity pays to genius. It is, indeed, the modern way of understanding something, and is applied to works of every quality. Thus, in the notes that Elia Kazan published on his production of *A Streetcar Named Desire,* it becomes clear that, in order to direct the play, Kazan had to discover that Stanley Kowalski represented the sensual and vengeful barbarism that was engulfing our culture, while Blanche Du Bois was Western civilization, poetry, delicate apparel, dim lighting, refined feelings and all, though a little the worse for wear to be sure. Tennessee Williams' forceful psychological melodrama now became intelligible: it was *about* something, about the decline of Western civilization. Apparently, were it to go on being a play about a handsome brute named Stanley Kowalski and a faded mangy belle named Blanche Du Bois, it would not be manageable.

It doesn't matter whether artists intend, or don't intend, for their works to be interpreted. Perhaps Tennessee Williams thinks *Streetcar* is about what Kazan thinks it to be about. It may be that Cocteau in *The Blood of a Poet* and in *Orpheus* wanted the elaborate readings which have been given these films, in terms of Freudian symbolism and social critique. But the merit of these works certainly lies elsewhere than in their "meanings." Indeed, it is precisely to the extent that Williams' plays and Cocteau's films do suggest these portentous meanings that they are defective, false, contrived, lacking in conviction.

From interviews, it appears that Resnais and Robbe-Grillet consciously designed *Last Year at Marienbad* to accommodate a multiplicity of equally plausible interpretations. But the temptation to interpret *Marienbad* should be resisted. What matters in Marienbad is the pure, untranslatable, sensuous immediacy of some of its images, and its rigorous if narrow solutions to certain problems of cinematic form.

Again, Ingmar Bergman may have meant the tank rumbling down the empty night street in *The Silence* as a phallic symbol. But if he did, it was a foolish thought. ("Never trust the teller, trust the tale," said Lawrence.) Taken as a brute object, as an immediate sensory equivalent for the mysterious abrupt armored happenings going on inside the hotel, that sequence with the tank is the most striking moment in the film. Those who reach for a Freudian interpretation of the tank are only expressing their lack of response to what is there on the screen.

It is always the case that interpretation of this type indicates a dissatisfaction (conscious or unconscious) with the work, a wish to replace it by something else.

Interpretation, based on the highly dubious theory that a work of art is composed of items of content, violates art. It makes art into an article for use, for arrangement into a mental scheme of categories.

Interpretation does not, of course, always prevail. In fact, a great deal of today's art may be understood as motivated by a flight from interpretation. To avoid interpretation, art may become parody. Or it may become abstract. Or it may become ("merely") decorative. Or it may become non-art.

The flight from interpretation seems particularly a feature of modern painting. Abstract painting is the attempt to have, in the ordinary sense, no content; since there is no content, there can be no interpretation. Pop Art works by the opposite means to the same result; using a content so blatant, so "what it is," it, too, ends by being uninterpretable.

A great deal of modern poetry as well, starting from the great experiments of French poetry (including the movement that is misleadingly called Symbolism) to put silence into poems and to reinstate the *magic* of the word, has escaped from the rough grip of interpretation. The most recent revolution in contemporary taste in poetry—the revolution that has deposed Eliot and elevated Pound—represents a turning away from content in poetry in the old sense, an impatience with what made modern poetry prey to the zeal of interpreters.

I am speaking mainly of the situation in America, of course. Interpretation runs rampant here in those arts with a feeble and negligible avant-garde: fiction and the drama. Most American novelists and playwrights are really either journalists or gentlemen sociologists and psychologists. They are writing the literary equivalent of program music. And so rudimentary, uninspired, and stagnant has been the sense of what might be done with form in fiction and drama that even when the content isn't simply information, news, it is still peculiarly visible, handier, more exposed. To the extent that novels and plays (in America), unlike poetry and painting and music, don't reflect any interesting concern with changes in their *form,* these arts remain prone to assault by interpretation.

But programmatic avant-gardism—which has meant, mostly, experiments with form at the expense of content—is not the only defense against the infestation of art by interpretations. At least, I hope not. For this would be to commit art to being perpetually on the run. (It also perpetuates the very distinction between form and content which is, ultimately, an illusion.) Ideally, it is possible to elude the interpreters in another way, by making works of art whose surface is so unified and clean, whose momentum is so rapid, whose address is so direct that the work can be... just what it is. Is this possible now? It does happen in films, I believe. This is why cinema is the most alive, the most exciting, the most important of all art forms right now. Perhaps the way one tells how alive a particular art form is, is by the latitude it gives for making mistakes in it, and still being good. For example, a few of the films of Bergman—though crammed with lame messages about the modern spirit, thereby inviting interpretations—still triumph over the pretentious intentions of their director. In *Winter Light* and *The Silence,* the beauty and visual sophistication of the images subvert before our eyes the callow pseudo-intellectuality of the story and some of the dialogue. (The most remarkable instance of this sort of discrepancy is the work of D. W. Griffith.) In good films, there is always a directness that entirely frees us from the itch to interpret. Many old Hollywood films, like those of Cukor, Walsh, Hawks, and countless other directors, have this liberating anti-symbolic quality, no less than the best work of the new European directors, like Truffaut's *Shoot the Piano Player* and *Jules and Jim,* Godard's *Breathless* and *Vivre Sa Vie,* Antonioni's *L'Avventura,* and Olmi's *The Fiancés.*

The fact that films have not been overrun by interpreters is in part due simply to the newness of cinema as an art. It also owes to the happy accident that films for such a long time were just movies; in other words, that they understood to be part of mass, as opposed to high, culture, and were left alone by most people with minds. Then, too, there is always something other than content in the cinema to grab hold of, for those who want to analyze. For the cinema, unlike the novel, possesses a vocabulary of forms—the explicit, complex, and discussable technology of camera movements, cutting, and composition of the frame that goes into the making of a film.

What kind of criticism, of commentary on the arts, is desirable today? For I am not saying that works of art are ineffable, that they cannot be described or paraphrased. They can be. The question is how. What would criticism look like that would serve the work of art, not usurp its place?

What is needed, first, is more attention to form in art. If excessive stress on *content* provokes the arrogance of interpretation, more extended and more thorough descriptions of *form* would silence. What is needed is a vocabulary—a descriptive, rather than prescriptive, vocabulary—for forms.[1] The best criticism, and it is uncommon, is of this sort

---

1.   One of the difficulties is that our idea of form is spatial (the Greek metaphors for form are all derived

that dissolves considerations of content into those of form. On film, drama, and painting respectively, I can think of Erwin Panofsky's essay, "Style and Medium in the Motion Pictures," Northrop Frye's essay "A Conspectus of Dramatic Genres," Pierre Francastel's essay "The Destruction of a Plastic Space." Roland Barthes' book *On Racine* and his two essays on Robbe-Grillet are examples of formal analysis applied to the work of a single author. (The best essays in Erich Auerbach's *Mimesis*, like "The Scar of Odysseus," are also of this type.) An example of formal analysis applied simultaneously to genre and author is Walter Benjamin's essay, "The Story Teller: Reflections on the Works of Nicolai Leskov."

Equally valuable would be acts of criticism which would supply a really accurate, sharp, loving description of the appearance of a work of art. This seems even harder to do than formal analysis. Some of Manny Farber's film criticism, Dorothy Van Ghent's essay "The Dickens World: A View from Todgers'," Randall Jarrell's essay on Walt Whitman are among the rare examples of what I mean. These are essays which reveal the sensuous surface of art without mucking about in it.

Transparence is the highest, most liberating value in art—and in criticism—today. Transparence means experiencing the luminousness of the thing in itself, of things being what they are. This is the greatness of, for example, the films of Bresson and Ozu and Renoir's *The Rules of the Game*.

Once upon a time (say, for Dante), it must have been a revolutionary and creative move to design works of art so that they might be experienced on several levels. Now it is not. It reinforces the principle of redundancy that is the principal affliction of modern life.

Once upon a time (a time when high art was scarce), it must have been a revolutionary and creative move to interpret works of art. Now it is not. What we decidedly do not need now is further to assimilate Art into Thought, or (worse yet) Art into Culture.

Interpretation takes the sensory experience of the work of art for granted, and proceeds from there. This cannot be taken for granted, now. Think of the sheer multiplication of works of art available to every one of us, superadded to the conflicting tastes and odors and sights of the urban environment that bombard our senses. Ours is a culture based on excess, on overproduction; the result is a steady loss of sharpness in our sensory experience. All the conditions of modern life—its material plenitude, its sheer crowdedness—conjoin to dull our sensory faculties. And it is in the light of the condition of our senses, our capacities (rather than those of another age), that the task of the critic must be assessed.

What is important now is to recover our senses. We must learn to see more, to *hear* more, to *feel* more.

Our task is not to find the maximum amount of content in a work of art, much less to squeeze more content out of the work than is already there. Our task is to cut back content so that we can see the thing at all.

The aim of all commentary on art now should be to make works of art—and, by analogy, our own experience—more, rather than less, real to us. The function of criticism should be to show *how it is what it is*, even *that it is what it is*, rather than to show *what it means*.

In place of a hermeneutics we need an erotics of art.

---

from notions of space). This is why we have a more ready vocabulary of forms for the spatial than for the temporal arts. The exception among the temporal arts, of course, is the drama; perhaps this is because the drama is a narrative (i.e., temporal) form that extends itself visually and pictorially, upon a stage.... What we don't have yet is a poetics of the novel, any clear notion of the forms of narration. Perhaps film criticism will be the occasion of a breakthrough here, since films are primarily a visual form, yet they are also a subdivision of literature.

HERBERT MARCUSE

Selection from *One-Dimensional Man* (1964)

Herbert Marcuse (1898–1979) did not like being called "the father of the New Left," but journalists insisted on repeating the appellation because of the appeal of Marcuse's writings to student radicals of the late 1960s and 1970s. A persistent critic of contemporary liberalism, Marcuse complained that the liberal ideal of "tolerance" served to protect the inequalities of power that only a more radical assault could effectively challenge. This notion of "Repressive Tolerance," which Marcuse developed in an essay of that name contributed to *A Critique of Pure Tolerance*, a book of 1965 coauthored with Barrington Moore and Robert Paul Wolfe, had great appeal to a constituency certain of its analysis of what was wrong with society, and impatient with political processes designed to promote compromises among a variety of different interests. In the most popular of his books, *One-Dimensional Man*, the introduction to which is reprinted here, Marcuse argued that the consumer-oriented capitalism of highly advanced industrial societies discouraged critical thought, rendered established power elusive, and made it extremely difficult to organize oppositional movements.

Marcuse had been a well-established social philosopher in Germany when, as a Jew, he fled Hitler in 1934 to take up residence in the United States. He was a central figure in the "Frankfurt School," a group of émigré thinkers including Theodor Adorno, Leo Lowenthal, and Franz Neuman. Before and after Marcuse's immigration he wrote extensively on the philosophies of Hegel and Marx. He rose to prominence in the intellectual life of his new country in 1955, with the publication of *Eros and Civilization*, an ambitious accommodation of Marx with the Freudianism then at its peak of popularity in the United States.

Marcuse's role in the Frankfurt School is clarified in Martin Jay, *The Dialectical Imagination: A History of the Frankfurt School and the Institute of Social Research, 1923–1950* (Boston, 1973). An accessible biography is Barry Katz, *Herbert Marcuse and the Art of Liberation: An Intellectual Biography* (London, 1982). A recent work that interprets Marcuse's work in relation to that of several other German and émigré intellectuals of his time is Richard Wolin, *Heidegger's Children: Hannah Arendt, Karl Lowith, Hans Jonas, and Herbert Marcuse* (Princeton, 2001). An excellent sampling of the latest work on Marcuse is John Abromeit and W. Mark Cobb, eds., *Herbert Marcuse: A Critical Reader* (New York, 2004).

A comfortable, smooth, reasonable, democratic unfreedom prevails in advanced industrial civilization, a token of technical progress. Indeed, what could be more rational than the suppression of individuality in the mechanization of socially necessary but painful performances; the concentration of individual enterprises in more effective, more productive corporations; the regulation of free competition among unequally equipped economic subjects; the curtailment of prerogatives and national sovereignties which impede the international organization of resources. That this technological order also involves a political and intellectual coordination may be a regrettable and yet promising development.

The rights and liberties which were such vital factors in the origins and earlier stages of industrial society yield to a higher stage of this society: they are losing their traditional rationale and content. Freedom of thought, speech, and conscience were—just as free enterprise, which they served to promote and protect—essentially *critical* ideas, designed to replace an obsolescent material and intellectual culture by a more productive and rational one. Once institutionalized, these rights and liberties shared the fate of the society of which they had become an integral part. The achievement cancels the premises.

To the degree to which freedom from want, the concrete substance of all freedom, is becoming a real possibility, the liberties which pertain to a state of lower productivity are losing their former content. Independence of thought, autonomy, and the right to political opposition are being deprived of their basic critical function in a society which seems increasingly capable of satisfying the needs of the individuals through the way in which it is organized. Such a society may justly demand acceptance of its principles and institutions, and reduce the opposition to the discussion and promotion of alternative policies *within* the status quo. In this respect, it seems to make little difference whether the increasing satisfaction of needs is accomplished by an authoritarian or a non-authoritarian system. Under the conditions of a rising standard of living, non-conformity with the system itself appears to be socially useless, and the more so when it entails tangible economic and political disadvantages and threatens the smooth operation of the whole. Indeed, at least in so far as the necessities of life are involved, there seems to be no reason why the production and distribution of goods and services should proceed through the competitive concurrence of individual liberties.

Freedom of enterprise was from the beginning not altogether a blessing. As the liberty to work or to starve, it spelled toil, insecurity, and fear for the vast majority of the population. If the individual were no longer compelled to prove himself on the market, as a free economic subject, the disappearance of this kind of freedom would be one of the greatest achievements of civilization. The technological processes of mechanization and standardization might release individual energy into a yet uncharted realm of freedom beyond necessity. The very structure of human existence would be altered; the individual would be liberated from the work world's imposing upon him alien needs and alien possibilities. The individual would be free to exert autonomy over a life that would be his own. If the productive apparatus could be organized and directed toward the satisfaction of the vital needs, its control might well be centralized; such control would not prevent individual autonomy, but render it possible.

This is a goal within the capabilities of advanced industrial civilization, the "end" of technological rationality. In actual fact, however, the contrary trend operates: the

Source: Herbert Marcuse, *One-Dimensional Man* (Boston, 1964), 1–18.

apparatus imposes its economic and political requirements for defense and expansion on labor time and free time, on the material and intellectual culture. By virtue of the way it has organized its technological base, contemporary industrial society tends to be totalitarian. For "totalitarian" is not only a terroristic political coordination of society, but also a non-terroristic economic-technical coordination which operates through the manipulation of needs by vested interests. It thus precludes the emergence of an effective opposition against the whole. Not only a specific form of government or party rule makes for totalitarianism, but also a specific system of production and distribution which may well be compatible with a "pluralism" of parties, newspapers, "countervailing powers," etc.

Today political power asserts itself through its power over the machine process and over the technical organization of the apparatus. The government of advanced and advancing industrial societies can maintain and secure itself only when it succeeds in mobilizing, organizing, and exploiting the technical, scientific, and mechanical productivity available to industrial civilization. And this productivity mobilizes society as a whole, above and beyond any particular individual or group interests. The brute fact that the machine's physical (only physical?) power surpasses that of the individual, and of any particular group of individuals, makes the machine the most effective political instrument in any society whose basic organization is that of the machine process. But the political trend may be reversed; essentially the power of the machine is only the stored-up and projected power of man. To the extent to which the work world is conceived of as a machine and mechanized accordingly, it becomes the *potential* basis of a new freedom for man.

Contemporary industrial civilization demonstrates that it has reached the stage at which "the free society" can no longer be adequately defined in the traditional terms of economic, political, and intellectual liberties, not because these liberties have become insignificant, but because they are too significant to be confined within the traditional forms. New modes of realization are needed, corresponding to the new capabilities of society.

Such new modes can be indicated only in negative terms because they would amount to the negation of the prevailing modes. Thus economic freedom would mean freedom *from* the economy—from being controlled by economic forces and relationships; freedom from the daily struggle for existence, from earning a living. Political freedom would mean liberation of the individuals *from* politics over which they have no effective control. Similarly, intellectual freedom would mean the restoration of individual thought now absorbed by mass communication and indoctrination, abolition of "public opinion" together with its makers. The unrealistic sound of these propositions is indicative, not of their utopian character, but of the strength of the forces which prevent their realization. The most effective and enduring form of warfare against liberation is the implanting of material and intellectual needs that perpetuate obsolete forms of the struggle for existence.

The intensity, the satisfaction and even the character of human needs, beyond the biological level, have always been preconditioned. Whether or not the possibility of doing or leaving, enjoying or destroying, possessing or rejecting something is seized as a *need* depends on whether or not it can be seen as desirable and necessary for the prevailing societal institutions and interests. In this sense, human needs are historical needs and, to the extent to which the society demands the repressive development of the individual, his needs themselves and their claim for satisfaction are subject to overriding critical standards.

We may distinguish both true and false needs. "False" are those which are super-imposed upon the individual by particular social interests in his repression: the needs which perpetuate toil, aggressiveness, misery, and injustice. Their satisfaction might be most gratifying to the individual, but this happiness is not a condition which has to be maintained and protected if it serves to arrest the development of the ability (his own and others) to recognize the disease of the whole and grasp the chances of curing the disease. The result then is euphoria in unhappiness. Most of the prevailing needs to relax, to have fun, to behave and consume in accordance with the advertisements, to love and hate what others love and hate, belong to this category of false needs.

Such needs have a societal content and function which are determined by external powers over which the individual has no control; the development and satisfaction of these needs is heteronomous. No matter how much such needs may have become the indi-vidual's own, reproduced and fortified by the conditions of his existence; no matter how much he identifies himself with them and finds himself in their satisfaction, they continue to be what they were from the beginning—products of a society whose dominant interest demands repression.

The prevalence of repressive needs is an accomplished fact, accepted in ignorance and defeat, but a fact that must be undone in the interest of the happy individual as well as all those whose misery is the price of his satisfaction. The only needs that have an unqualified claim for satisfaction are the vital ones—nourishment, clothing, lodging at the attainable level of culture. The satisfaction of these needs is the prerequisite for the realization of *all* needs, of the unsublimated as well as the sublimated ones.

For any consciousness and conscience, for any experience which does not accept the prevailing societal interest as the supreme law of thought and behavior, the established universe of needs and satisfactions is a fact to be questioned—questioned in terms of truth and falsehood. These terms are historical throughout, and their objectivity is historical. The judgment of needs and their satisfaction, under the given conditions, involves stan-dards of *priority*—standards which refer to the optimal development of the individual, of all individuals, under the optimal utilization of the material and intellectual resources available to man. The resources are calculable. "Truth" and "falsehood" of needs designate objective conditions to the extent to which the universal satisfaction of vital needs and, beyond it, the progressive alleviation of toil and poverty, are universally valid standards. But as historical standards, they do not only vary according to area and stage of develop-ment, they also can be defined only in (greater or lesser) *contradiction* to the prevailing ones. What tribunal can possibly claim the authority of decision?

In the last analysis, the question of what are true and false needs must be answered by the individuals themselves, but only in the last analysis; that is, if and when they are free to give their own answer. As long as they are kept incapable of being autonomous, as long as they are indoctrinated and manipulated (down to their very instincts), their answer to this question cannot be taken as their own. By the same token, however, no tribunal can justly arrogate to itself the right to decide which needs should be developed and satisfied. Any such tribunal is reprehensible, although our revulsion does not do away with the question: how can the people who have been the object of effective and productive domination by themselves create the conditions of freedom.

The more rational, productive, technical, and total the repressive administration of society becomes, the more unimaginable the means and ways by which the administered individuals might break their servitude and seize their own liberation. To be sure, to impose Reason upon an entire society is a paradoxical and scandalous idea—although one might dispute the righteousness of a society which ridicules this idea while making its own population into objects of total administration. All liberation depends on the consciousness of servitude, and the emergence of this consciousness is always hampered by the predominance of needs and satisfactions which, to a great extent, have become the individual's own. The process always replaces one system of preconditioning by another; the optimal goal is the replacement of false needs by true ones, the abandonment of repressive satisfaction.

The distinguishing feature of advanced industrial society is its effective suffocation of those needs which demand liberation—liberation also from that which is tolerable and rewarding and comfortable—while it sustains and absolves the destructive power and repressive function of the affluent society. Here, the social controls exact the overwhelming need for the production and consumption of waste; the need for stupefying work where it is no longer a real necessity; the need for modes of relaxation which soothe and prolong this stupefication; the need for maintaining such deceptive liberties as free competition at administered prices, a free press which censors itself, free choice between brands and gadgets.

Under the rule of a repressive whole, liberty can be made into a powerful instrument of domination. The range of choice open to the individual is not the decisive factor in determining the degree of human freedom, but *what* can be chosen and what *is* chosen by the individual. The criterion for free choice can never be an absolute one, but neither is it entirely relative. Free election of masters does not abolish the masters or the slaves. Free choice among a wide variety of goods and services does not signify freedom if these goods and services sustain social controls over a life of toil and fear—that is, if they sustain alienation. And the spontaneous reproduction of superimposed needs by the individual does not establish autonomy; it only testifies to the efficacy of the controls.

Our insistence on the depth and efficacy of these controls is open to the objection that we overrate greatly the indoctrinating power of the "media," and that by themselves the people would feel and satisfy the needs which are now imposed upon them. The objection misses the point. The preconditioning does not start with the mass production of radio and television and with the centralization of their control. The people enter this stage as pre-conditioned receptacles of long standing; the decisive difference is in the flattening out of the contrast (or conflict) between the given and the possible, between the satisfied and the unsatisfied needs. Here, the so-called equalization of class distinctions reveals its ideological function. If the worker and his boss enjoy the same television program and visit the same resort places, if the typist is as attractively made up as the daughter of her employer, if the Negro owns a Cadillac, if they all read the same newspaper, then this assimilation indicates not the disappearance of classes, but the extent to which the needs and satisfactions that serve the preservation of the Establishment are shared by the underlying population.

Indeed, in the most highly developed areas of contemporary society, the transplantation of social into individual needs is so effective that the difference between them seems to be purely theoretical. Can one really distinguish between the mass media as instruments of information and entertainment, and as agents of manipulation and indoctrination? Between the automobile as nuisance and as convenience? Between the horrors and the comforts of functional architecture? Between the work for national defense and the work for corporate gain? Between the private pleasure and the commercial and political utility involved in increasing the birth rate?

We are again confronted with one of the most vexing aspects of advanced industrial civilization: the rational character of its irrationality. Its productivity and efficiency, its capacity to increase and spread comforts, to turn waste into need, and destruction into construction, the extent to which this civilization transforms the object world into an extension of man's mind and body makes the very notion of alienation questionable. The people recognize themselves in their commodities; they find their soul in their automobile, hi-fi set, split-level home, kitchen equipment. The very mechanism which ties the individual to his society has changed, and social control is anchored in the new needs which it has produced.

The prevailing forms of social control are technological in a new sense. To be sure, the technical structure and efficacy of the productive and destructive apparatus has been a major instrumentality for subjecting the population to the established social division of labor throughout the modern period. Moreover, such integration has always been accompanied by more obvious forms of compulsion: loss of livelihood, the administration of justice, the police, the armed forces. It still is. But in the contemporary period, the technological controls appear to be the very embodiment of Reason for the benefit of all social groups and interests—to such an extent that all contradiction seems irrational and all counteraction impossible.

No wonder then that, in the most advanced areas of this civilization, the social controls have been introjected to the point where even individual protest is affected at its roots. The intellectual and emotional refusal "to go along" appears neurotic and impotent. This is the socio-psychological aspect of the political event that marks the contemporary period: the passing of the historical forces which, at the preceding stage of industrial society, seemed to represent the possibility of new forms of existence.

But the term "introjection" perhaps no longer describes the way in which the individual by himself reproduces and perpetuates the external controls exercised by his society. Introjection suggests a variety of relatively spontaneous processes by which a Self (Ego) transposes the "outer" into the "inner." Thus introjection implies the existence of an inner dimension distinguished from and even antagonistic to the external exigencies—an individual consciousness and an individual unconscious *apart from* public opinion and behavior. The idea of "inner freedom" here has its reality: it designates the private space in which man may become and remain "himself."

Today this private space has been invaded and whittled down by technological reality. Mass production and mass distribution claim the *entire* individual, and industrial psychology has long since ceased to be confined to the factory. The manifold processes of introjection seem to be ossified in almost mechanical reactions. The result is, not adjustment but *mimesis:* an immediate identification of the individual with *his* society and, through it, with the society as a whole.

This immediate, automatic identification (which may have been characteristic of primitive forms of association) reappears in high industrial civilization; its new "immediacy," however, is the product of a sophisticated, scientific management and organization. In this process, the "inner" dimension of the mind in which opposition to the status quo can take root is whittled down. The loss of this dimension, in which the power of negative thinking—the critical power of Reason—is at home, is the ideological counterpart to the very material process in which advanced industrial society silences and reconciles the opposition. The impact of progress turns Reason into submission to the facts of life, and to the dynamic capability of producing more and bigger facts of the same sort of life. The efficiency of the system blunts the individuals' recognition that it contains no facts which do not communicate the repressive power of the whole. If the individuals find themselves in the things which shape their life, they do so, not by giving, but by accepting the law of things—not the law of physics but the law of their society.

I have just suggested that the concept of alienation seems to become questionable when the individuals identify themselves with the existence which is imposed upon them and have in it their own development and satisfaction. This identification is not illusion but reality. However, the reality constitutes a more progressive stage of alienation. The latter has become entirely objective; the subject which is alienated is swallowed up by its alienated existence. There is only one dimension, and it is everywhere and in all forms. The achievements of progress defy ideological indictment as well as justification; before their tribunal, the "false consciousness" of their rationality becomes the true consciousness.

This absorption of ideology into reality does not, however, signify the "end of ideology." On the contrary, in a specific sense advanced industrial culture is *more* ideological than its predecessor, inasmuch as today the ideology is in the process of production itself. In a provocative form, this proposition reveals the political aspects of the prevailing technological rationality. The productive apparatus and the goods and services which it produces "sell" or impose the social system as a whole. The means of mass transportation and communication, the commodities of lodging, food, and clothing, the irresistible output of the entertainment and information industry carry with them prescribed attitudes and habits, certain intellectual and emotional reactions which bind the consumers more or less pleasantly to the producers and, through the latter, to the whole. The products indoctrinate and manipulate; they promote a false consciousness which is immune against its falsehood. And as these beneficial products become available to more individuals in more social classes, the indoctrination they carry ceases to be publicity; it becomes a way of life. It is a good way of life—much better than before—and as a good way of life, it militates against qualitative change. Thus emerges a pattern of *one-dimensional thought and behavior* in which ideas, aspirations, and objectives that, by their content, transcend the established universe of discourse and action are either repelled or reduced to terms of this universe. They are redefined by the rationality of the given system and of its quantitative extension.

The trend may be related to a development in scientific method: operationalism in the physical, behaviorism in the social sciences. The common feature is a total empiricism in the treatment of concepts; their meaning is restricted to the representation of particular operations and behavior. The operational point of view is well illustrated by P. W. Bridgman's analysis of the concept of length.

> We evidently know what we mean by length if we can tell what the length of any and every object is, and for the physicist nothing more is required. To find the length of an object, we have to perform certain physical operations. The concept of length is therefore fixed when the operations by which length is measured are fixed: that is, the concept of length involves as much and nothing more than the set of operations by which length is determined. In general, we mean by any

concept nothing more than a set of operations; the concept is synonymous with the corresponding set of operations.

Bridgman has seen the wide implications of this mode of thought for the society at large:

> To adopt the operational point of view involves much more than a mere restriction of the sense in which we understand "concept," but means a far-reaching change in all our habits of thought, in that we shall no longer permit ourselves to use as tools in our thinking concepts of which we cannot give an adequate account in terms of operations.

Bridgman's prediction has come true. The new mode of thought is today the predominant tendency in philosophy, psychology, sociology, and other fields. Many of the most seriously troublesome concepts are being "eliminated" by showing that no adequate account of them in terms of operations or behavior can be given. The radical empiricist onslaught...thus provides the methodological justification for the debunking of the mind by the intellectuals—a positivism which, in its denial of the transcending elements of Reason, forms the academic counterpart of the socially required behavior.

Outside the academic establishment, the "far-reaching change in all our habits of thought" is more serious. It serves to coordinate ideas and goals with those exacted by the prevailing system, to enclose them in the system, and to repel those which are irreconcilable with the system. The reign of such a one-dimensional reality does not mean that materialism rules, and that the spiritual, metaphysical, and bohemian occupations are petering out. On the contrary, there is a great deal of "Worship together this week," "Why not try God," Zen, existentialism, and beat ways of life, etc. But such modes of protest and transcendence are no longer contradictory to the status quo and no longer negative. They are rather the ceremonial part of practical behaviorism, its harmless negation, and are quickly digested by the status quo as part of its healthy diet.

One-dimensional thought is systematically promoted by the makers of politics and their purveyors of mass information. Their universe of discourse is populated by self-validating hypotheses which, incessantly and monopolistically repeated, become hypnotic definitions or dictations. For example, "free" are the institutions which operate (and are operated on) in the countries of the Free World; other transcending modes of freedom are by definition either anarchism, communism, or propaganda. "Socialistic" are all encroachments on private enterprises not undertaken by private enterprise itself (or by government contracts), such as universal and comprehensive health insurance, or the protection of nature from all too sweeping commercialization, or the establishment of public services which may hurt private profit. This totalitarian logic of accomplished facts has its Eastern counterpart. There, freedom is the way of life instituted by a communist regime, and all other transcending modes of freedom are either capitalistic, or revisionist, or leftist sectarianism. In both camps, non-operational ideas are non-behavioral and subversive. The movement of thought is stopped at barriers which appear as the limits of Reason itself.

Such limitation of thought is certainly not new. Ascending modern rationalism, in its speculative as well as empirical form, shows a striking contrast between extreme critical radicalism in scientific and philosophic method on the one hand, and an uncritical quietism in the attitude toward established and functioning social institutions. Thus Descartes' *ego cogitans* was to leave the "great public bodies" untouched, and Hobbes held that "the present ought always to be preferred, maintained, and accounted best." Kant agreed with Locke in justifying revolution *if and when* it has succeeded in organizing the whole and in preventing subversion.

However, these accommodating concepts of Reason were always contradicted by the evident misery and injustice of the "great public bodies" and the effective, more or less conscious rebellion against them. Societal conditions existed which provoked and permitted real dissociation from the established state of affairs; a private as well as political dimension was present in which dissociation could develop into effective opposition, testing its strength and the validity of its objectives.

With the gradual closing of this dimension by the society, the self-limitation of thought assumes a larger significance. The interrelation between scientific-philosophical and societal processes, between theoretical and practical Reason, asserts itself "behind the back" of the scientists and philosophers. The society bars a whole type of oppositional operations and behavior; consequently, the concepts pertaining to them are rendered illusory or meaningless. Historical transcendence appears as metaphysical transcendence, not acceptable to science and scientific thought. The operational and behavioral point of view, practiced as a "habit of thought" at large, becomes the view of the established universe of discourse and action, needs and aspirations. The "cunning of Reason" works, as it so often did, in the interest of the powers that be. The insistence on operational and behavioral concepts turns against the efforts to free thought and behavior *from* the given reality and *for* the suppressed alternatives. Theoretical and practical Reason, academic and social behaviorism meet on common ground: that of an advanced society which makes scientific and technical progress into an instrument of domination.

"Progress" is not a neutral term; it moves toward specific ends, and these ends are defined by the possibilities of ameliorating the human condition. Advanced industrial society is approaching the stage where continued progress would demand the radical subversion of the prevailing direction and organization of progress. This stage would be reached when material production (including the necessary services) becomes automated to the extent that all vital needs can be satisfied while necessary labor time is reduced to marginal time. From this point on, technical progress would transcend the realm of necessity, where it served as the instrument of domination and exploitation which thereby limited its rationality; technology would become subject to the free play of faculties in the struggle for the pacification of nature and of society.

Such a state is envisioned in Marx's notion of the "abolition of labor." The term "pacification of existence" seems better suited to designate the historical alternative of a world which—through an international conflict which transforms and suspends the contradictions within the established societies—advances on the brink of a global war. "Pacification of existence" means the development of man's struggle with man and with nature, under conditions where the competing needs, desires, and aspirations are no longer organized by vested interests in domination and scarcity—an organization which perpetuates the destructive forms of this struggle.

Today's fight against this historical alternative finds a firm mass basis in the underlying population, and finds its ideology in the rigid orientation of thought and behavior to the given universe of facts. Validated by the accomplishments of science and technology, justified by its growing productivity, the status quo defies all transcendence. Faced with the possibility of pacification on the grounds of its technical and intellectual achievements, the mature industrial society closes itself against this alternative. Operationalism, in theory and practice, becomes the theory and practice of *containment*. Underneath its obvious dynamics, this society is a thoroughly static system of life: self-propelling in its oppressive productivity and in its beneficial coordination. Containment of technical progress goes hand in hand with its growth in the established direction. In spite of the political fetters imposed by the status quo, the more technology appears capable of creating the conditions for pacification, the more are the minds and bodies of man organized against this alternative.

The most advanced areas of industrial society exhibit throughout these two features: a trend toward consummation of technological rationality, and intensive efforts to contain this trend within the established institutions. Here is the internal contradiction of this civilization: the irrational element in its rationality. It is the token of its achievements. The industrial society which makes technology and science its own is organized for the ever-more-effective domination of man and nature, for the ever-more-effective utilization of its resources. It becomes irrational when the success of these efforts opens new dimensions of human realization. Organization for peace is different from organization for war; the institutions which served the struggle for existence cannot serve the pacification of existence. Life as an end is qualitatively different from life as a means.

Such a qualitatively new mode of existence can never be envisaged as the mere by-product of economic and political changes, as the more or less spontaneous effect of the new institutions which constitute the necessary prerequisite. Qualitative change also involves a change in the *technical* basis on which this society rests—one which sustains the economic and political institutions through which the "second nature" of man as an aggressive object of administration is stabilized. The techniques of industrialization are political techniques; as such, they prejudge the possibilities of Reason and Freedom.

To be sure, labor must precede the reduction of labor, and industrialization must precede the development of human needs and satisfactions. But as all freedom depends on the conquest of alien necessity, the realization of freedom depends on the *techniques* of this conquest. The highest productivity of labor can be used for the perpetuation of labor, and the most efficient industrialization can serve the restriction and manipulation of needs.

When this point is reached, domination—in the guise of affluence and liberty—extends to all spheres of private and public existence, integrates all authentic opposition, absorbs all alternatives. Technological rationality reveals its political character as it becomes the great vehicle of better domination, creating a truly totalitarian universe in which society and nature, mind and body are kept in a state of permanent mobilization for the defense of this universe.

NOAM CHOMSKY

"The Responsibility of Intellectuals" (1967)

Noam Chomsky (1928–) came to prominence in the late 1950s and early 1960s as a theorist of language and of the human mind. But he won a large constituency well beyond the discipline of linguistics during the Vietnam War, when he emerged as one of academia's most vociferous critics of the war policies of the administration of President Lyndon Johnson. In "The Responsibility of Intellectuals," reprinted here, Chomsky depicted the Johnson administration as a pack of liars, and called upon intellectuals to reclaim the classic role of "speaking truth to power." This and other essays in the same voice were collected in Chomsky's *American Power and the New Mandarins* (New York, 1969).

Chomsky's emphasis on intellectual independence and high principle was felt by many observers to stand parallel to an emphasis found in his technical work as a linguist. In *Cartesian Linguistics* (New York, 1966), *Language and Mind* (New York, 1968), and a series of other works, Chomsky argued that the human mind contained innate linguistic capabilities that could not be explained by environmental conditioning. B. F. Skinner and other "behaviorists" had represented the mind as too passive, as too much the product of the history of stimuli, insisted Chomsky. Critics replied that Chomsky was willfully blind to the ways in which social and cultural experience shaped the mind's capabilities. The controversy over Chomsky's ideas divided linguists the world over from the early 1960s through the end of the twentieth century.

Chomsky has remained active in debates about the relation of intellect to political power. He and a number of his contemporaries discuss this relationship in *The Cold War and The University: Toward an Intellectual History of the Postwar Years* (New York, 1997). Some of the contributors to that volume (especially the biologist R. C. Lewontin and the historian David Montgomery) present a view of this relationship somewhat different from Chomsky's.

Two studies of Chomsky's work attend carefully to both his political writings and his technical work in linguistics: Neil Smith, *Chomsky: Ideas and Ideals* (New York, 1999); and James A. McGilvray, *Chomsky* (New York, 1999). McGilvray is also the editor of the *Cambridge Companion to Chomsky* (New York, 2005). An excellent survey of the intellectual history of the 1960s that deals with Chomsky and his contemporaries both as political figures and as practitioners of various academic callings is Howard Brick, *Age of Contradiction: American Thought and Culture in the 1960s* (New York, 1998). Chomsky's discomfort with postmodernist notions of truth and power is apparent in his responses to the French philosopher Michel Foucault in a debate of 1974, the transcript of which is published in *The Chomsky-Foucault Debate: On Human Nature* (New York, 2006).

Twenty years ago, Dwight Macdonald published a series of articles in *Politics* on the responsibilities of peoples, and specifically, the responsibility of intellectuals. I read them as an undergraduate, in the years just after the war, and had occasion to read them again a few months ago. They seem to me to have lost none of their power or persuasiveness. Macdonald is concerned with the question of war guilt. He asks the question: To what extent were the German or Japanese people responsible for the atrocities committed by their governments? And, quite properly, he turns the question back to us: To what extent are the British or American people responsible for the vicious terror bombings of civilians, perfected as a technique of warfare by the Western democracies and reaching their culmination in Hiroshima and Nagasaki, surely among the most unspeakable crimes in history? To an undergraduate in 1945–1946—to anyone whose political and moral consciousness had been formed by the horrors of the 1930s, by the war in Ethiopia, the Russian purge, the "China incident," the Spanish Civil War, the Nazi atrocities, the Western reaction to these events and, in part, complicity in them—these questions had particular significance and poignancy.

With respect to the responsibility of intellectuals, there are still other, equally disturbing questions. Intellectuals are in a position to expose the lies of governments, to analyze actions according to their causes and motives and often hidden intentions. In the Western world at least, they have the power that comes from political liberty, from access to information and freedom of expression. For a privileged minority, Western democracy provides the leisure, the facilities, and the training to seek the truth lying hidden behind the veil of distortion and misrepresentation, ideology, and class interest through which the events of current history are presented to us. The responsibilities of intellectuals, then, are much deeper than what Macdonald calls the "responsibility of peoples," given the unique privileges that intellectuals enjoy.

The issues that Macdonald raised are as pertinent today as they were twenty years ago. We can hardly avoid asking ourselves to what extent the American people bear responsibility for the savage American assault on a largely helpless rural population in Vietnam, still another atrocity in what Asians see as the "Vasco da Gama era" of world history. As for those of us who stood by in silence and apathy as this catastrophe slowly took shape over the past dozen years, on what page of history do we find our proper place? Only the most insensible can escape these questions. I want to return to them, later on, after a few scattered remarks about the responsibility of intellectuals and how, in practice, they go about meeting this responsibility in the mid-1960s.

It is the responsibility of intellectuals to speak the truth and to expose lies. This, at least, may seem enough of a truism to pass without comment. Not so, however. For the modern intellectual, it is not at all obvious. Thus we have Martin Heidegger writing, in a pro-Hitler declaration of 1933, that "truth is the revelation of that which makes a people certain, clear, and strong in its action and knowledge"; it is only this kind of "truth" that one has a responsibility to speak. Americans tend to be more forthright. When Arthur Schlesinger was asked by the *New York Times*, in November 1965, to explain the contradiction between his published account of the Bay of Pigs incident and the story he had given the press at the time of the attack, he simply remarked that he had lied; and a few

Source: Noam Chomsky, *American Power and the New Mandarins* (New York: Pantheon, 1967), 323–32, 347–53, 356–59.

days later, he went on to compliment the *Times* for also having suppressed information on the planned invasion, in "the national interest," as this was defined by the group of arrogant and deluded men of whom Schlesinger gives such a flattering portrait in his recent account of the Kennedy administration. It is of no particular interest that one man is quite happy to lie in behalf of a cause which he knows to be unjust; but it is significant that such events provoke so little response in the intellectual community—no feeling, for example, that there is something strange in the offer of a major chair in humanities to a historian who feels it to be his duty to persuade the world that an American-sponsored invasion of a nearby country is nothing of the sort. And what of the incredible sequence of lies on the part of our government and its spokesmen concerning such matters as negotiations in Vietnam? The facts are known to all who care to know. The press, foreign and domestic, has presented documentation to refute each falsehood as it appears. But the power of the government propaganda apparatus is such that the citizen who does not undertake a research project on the subject can hardly hope to confront government pronouncements with fact.

The deceit and distortion surrounding the American invasion of Vietnam are by now so familiar that they have lost their power to shock. It is therefore well to recall that although new levels of cynicism are constantly being reached, their clear antecedents were accepted at home with quiet toleration. It is a useful exercise to compare government statements at the time of the invasion of Guatemala in 1954 with Eisenhower's admission—to be more accurate, his boast—a decade later that American planes were sent "to help the invaders." Nor is it only in moments of crisis that duplicity is considered perfectly in order. "New Frontiersmen," for example, have scarcely distinguished themselves by a passionate concern for historical accuracy, even when they are not being called upon to provide a "propaganda cover" for ongoing actions. For example, Arthur Schlesinger describes the bombing of North Vietnam and the massive escalation of military commitment in early 1965 as based on a "perfectly rational argument": "...so long as the Vietcong thought they were going to win the war, they obviously would not be interested in any kind of negotiated settlement." The date is important. Had the statement been made six months earlier, one could attribute it to ignorance. But this statement appeared after months of front-page news reports detailing the United Nations, North Vietnamese, and Soviet initiatives that preceded the February 1965 escalation and that, in fact, continued for several weeks after the bombing began, after months of soul-searching by Washington correspondents who were trying desperately to find some mitigating circumstances for the startling deception that had been revealed. (Chalmers Roberts, for example, wrote with unconscious irony that late February 1965 "hardly seemed to Washington to be a propitious moment for negotiations [since] Mr. Johnson ... had just ordered the first bombing of North Vietnam in an effort to bring Hanoi to a conference table where bargaining chips on both sides would be more closely matched.") Coming at this moment, Schlesinger's statement is less an example of deceit than of contempt—contempt for an audience that can be expected to tolerate such behavior with silence, if not approval.

To turn to someone closer to the actual formation and implementation of policy, consider some of the reflections of Walt Rostow, a man who, according to Schlesinger, brought a "spacious historical view" to the conduct of foreign affairs in the Kennedy administration. According to his analysis, the guerrilla warfare in Indochina in 1946 was launched by Stalin, and Hanoi initiated the guerrilla war against South Vietnam in 1958 (*The View from the Seventh Floor*, pp. 39 and 152). Similarly, the Communist planners probed the "free world spectrum of defense" in Northern Azerbaijan and Greece (where

Stalin "supported substantial guerrilla warfare"—ibid., pp. 36 and 148), operating from plans carefully laid in 1945. And in Central Europe, the Soviet Union was not "prepared to accept a solution which would remove the dangerous tensions from Central Europe at the risk of even slowly staged corrosion of communism in East Germany" (ibid., p. 156).

It is interesting to compare these observations with studies by scholars actually concerned with historical events. The remark about Stalin's initiating the first Vietnamese war in 1946 does not even merit refutation. As to Hanoi's purported initiative of 1958, the situation is more clouded. But even government sources concede that in 1959 Hanoi received the first direct reports of what Diem referred to as his own Algerian war, and that only after this did they lay their plans to involve themselves in this struggle. In fact, in December 1958 Hanoi made another of its many attempts—rebuffed once again by Saigon and the United States —to establish diplomatic and commercial relations with the Saigon government on the basis of the status quo. Rostow offers no evidence of Stalin's support for the Greek guerrillas: in fact, though the historical record is far from clear, it seems that Stalin was by no means pleased with the adventurism of the Greek guerrillas, who, from his point of view, were upsetting the satisfactory postwar imperialist settlement.

Rostow's remarks about Germany are more interesting still. He does not see fit to mention, for example, the Russian notes of March–April 1952, which proposed unification of Germany under internationally supervised elections, with withdrawal of all troops within a year, *if* there was a guarantee that a reunified Germany would not be permitted to join a Western military alliance. And he has also momentarily forgotten his own characterization of the strategy of the Truman and Eisenhower administrations: "to avoid any serious negotiation with the Soviet Union until the West could confront Moscow with German rearmament within an organized European framework, as a fait accompli"—to be sure, in defiance of the Potsdam agreements.

But most interesting of all is Rostow's reference to Iran. The facts are that there was a Russian attempt to impose by force a pro-Soviet government in Northern Azerbaijan that would grant the Soviet Union access to Iranian oil. This was rebuffed by superior Anglo-American force in 1946, at which point the more powerful imperialism obtained full rights to Iranian oil for itself, with the installation of a pro-Western government. We recall what happened when, for a brief period in the early 1950s, the only Iranian government with something of a popular base experimented with the curious idea that Iranian oil should belong to the Iranians. What is interesting, however, is the description of Northern Azerbaijan as part of "the free world spectrum of defense." It is pointless, by now, to comment on the debasement of the phrase "free world." But by what law of nature does Iran, with its resources, fall within Western dominion? The bland assumption that it does is most revealing of deep-seated attitudes towards the conduct of foreign affairs.

In addition to this growing lack of concern for truth, we find, in recent statements, a real or feigned naiveté with regard to American actions that reaches startling proportions. For example, Arthur Schlesinger has recently characterized our Vietnamese policies of 1954 as "part of our general program of international goodwill." Unless intended as irony, this remark shows either a colossal cynicism or an inability, on a scale that defies comment, to comprehend elementary phenomena of contemporary history. Similarly, what is one to make of the testimony of Thomas Schelling before the House Foreign Affairs Committee, January 27, 1966, in which he discusses the two great dangers if all Asia "goes Communist"? First, this would exclude "the United States and what we call Western civilization from a large part of the world that is poor and colored and potentially hostile." Second, "a country like the United States probably cannot maintain self-confidence if just

about the greatest thing it ever attempted, namely to create the basis for decency and prosperity and democratic government in the underdeveloped world, had to be acknowledged
as a failure or as an attempt that we wouldn't try again." It surpasses belief that a person
with even minimal acquaintance with the record of American foreign policy could produce such statements.

It surpasses belief, that is, unless we look at the matter from a more historical point
of view, and place such statements in the context of the hypocritical moralism of the past;
for example, of Woodrow Wilson, who was going to teach the Latin Americans the art of
good government, and who wrote (1902) that it is "our peculiar duty" to teach colonial
peoples "order and self-control... [and]...the drill and habit of law and obedience." Or
of the missionaries of the 1840s, who described the hideous and degrading opium wars
as "the result of a great design of Providence to make the wickedness of men subserve his
purposes of mercy toward China, in breaking through her wall of exclusion, and bringing the empire into more immediate contact with western and Christian nations." Or, to
approach the present, of A. A. Berle, who, in commenting on the Dominican intervention,
has the impertinence to attribute the problems of the Caribbean countries to imperialism—*Russian* imperialism.

As a final example of this failure of skepticism, consider the remarks of Henry
Kissinger in concluding his presentation in a Harvard-Oxford television debate on
American Vietnam policies. He observed, rather sadly, that what disturbs him most is
that others question not our judgment but our motives—a remarkable comment on the
part of one whose professional concern is political analysis, that is, analysis of the actions
of governments in terms of motives that are unexpressed in official propaganda and perhaps only dimly perceived by those whose acts they govern. No one would be disturbed
by an analysis of the political behavior of Russians, French, or Tanzanians, questioning
their motives and interpreting their actions in terms of long-range interests, perhaps well
concealed behind official rhetoric. But it is an article of faith that American motives are
pure and not subject to analysis...Although it is nothing new in American intellectual
history—or, for that matter, in the general history of imperialist apologia—this innocence
becomes increasingly distasteful as the power it serves grows more dominant in world
affairs and more capable, therefore, of the unconstrained viciousness that the mass media
present to us each day. We are hardly the first power in history to combine material interests, great technological capacity, and an utter disregard for the suffering and misery of the
lower orders. The long tradition of naiveté and self-righteousness that disfigures our intellectual history, however, must serve as a warning to the Third World, if such a warning is
needed, as to how our protestations of sincerity and benign intent are to be interpreted.

The basic assumptions of the "New Frontiersmen" should be pondered carefully by
those who look forward to the involvement of academic intellectuals in politics. For example, I have referred to Arthur Schlesinger's objections to the Bay of Pigs invasion, but the
reference was imprecise. True, he felt that it was a "terrible idea," but "not because the
notion of sponsoring an exile attempt to overthrow Castro seemed intolerable in itself."
Such a reaction would be the merest sentimentality, unthinkable to a tough-minded realist. The difficulty, rather, was that it seemed unlikely that the deception could succeed.
The operation, in his view, was ill-conceived but not otherwise objectionable. In a similar vein, Schlesinger quotes with approval Kennedy's "realistic" assessment of the situation resulting from Trujillo's assassination: "There are three possibilities in descending
order of preference: a decent democratic regime, a continuation of the Trujillo regime or a
Castro regime. We ought to aim at the first, but we really can't renounce the second until

we are sure that we can avoid the third." The reason why the third possibility is so intolerable is explained a few pages later: "Communist success in Latin America would deal a much harder blow to the power and influence of the United States." Of course, we can never really be sure of avoiding the third possibility; therefore, in practice, we will always settle for the second, as we are now doing in Brazil and Argentina, for example...

The backward countries have incredible, perhaps insurmountable problems, and few available options; the United States has a wide range of options, and has the economic and technological resources, though evidently neither the intellectual nor the moral resources, to confront at least some of these problems. It is easy for an American intellectual to deliver homilies on the virtues of freedom and liberty, but if he is really concerned about, say, Chinese totalitarianism or the burdens imposed on the Chinese peasantry in forced industrialization, then he should face a task that is infinitely more significant and challenging—the task of creating, in the United States, the intellectual and moral climate, as well as the social and economic conditions, that would permit this country to participate in modernization and development in a way commensurate with its material wealth and technical capacity. Massive capital gifts to Cuba and China might not succeed in alleviating the authoritarian-ism and terror that tend to accompany early stages of capital accumulation, but they are far more likely to have this effect than lectures on democratic values. It is possible that even without "capitalist encirclement" in its varying manifestations, the truly democratic elements in revolutionary movements—in some instances soviets and collectives, for example—might be undermined by an "elite" of bureaucrats and technical intelligentsia; but it is a near certainty that the fact of capitalist encirclement, which all revolutionary movements now have to face, will guarantee this result. The lesson, for those who are concerned to strengthen the democratic, spontaneous, and popular elements in developing societies, is quite clear. Lectures on the two-party system, or even the really substantial democratic values that have been in part realized in Western society, are a monstrous irrelevance in the face of the effort that is required to raise the level of culture in Western society to the point where it can provide a "social lever" for both economic development and the development of true democratic institutions in the Third World—and for that matter, at home as well.

A good case can be made for the conclusion that there is indeed something of a consensus among intellectuals who have already achieved power and affluence, or who sense that they can achieve them by "accepting society" as it is and promoting the values that are "being honored" in this society. And it is also true that this consensus is most noticeable among the scholar-experts who are replacing the free-floating intellectuals of the past. In the university, these scholar-experts construct a "value-free technology" for the solution of technical problems that arise in contemporary society, taking a "responsible stance" towards these problems, in the sense noted earlier. This consensus among the responsible scholar-experts is the domestic analogue to that proposed, in the international arena, by those who justify the application of American power in Asia, whatever the human cost, on the grounds that it is necessary to contain the "expansion of China" (an "expansion" which is, to be sure, hypothetical for the time being)—to translate from State Department Newspeak, on the grounds that it is essential to reverse the Asian nationalist revolutions, or at least to prevent them from spreading. The analogy becomes clear when we look carefully at the ways in which this proposal is formulated. With his usual lucidity, Churchill outlined the general position in a remark to his colleague of the moment, Joseph Stalin, at Teheran in 1943: "... the government of the world must be entrusted to satisfied nations, who wished nothing more for themselves than what they had. If the world-government were in the hand of hungry nations, there would always be danger. But none of us had any reason to seek for anything more. The peace would be kept by peoples who lived in their own way and were not ambitious. Our power placed us above the rest. We were like rich men dwelling at peace within their habitations."

For a translation of Churchill's biblical rhetoric into the jargon of contemporary social science, one may turn to the testimony of Charles Wolf, senior economist of the RAND Corporation, at the congressional committee hearings cited earlier:

> I am dubious that China's fears of encirclement are going to be abated, eased, relaxed in the long-term future. But I would hope that what we do in Southeast Asia would help to develop within the Chinese body politic more of a realism and willingness to live with this fear than to indulge it by support for liberation movements, which admittedly depend on a great deal more than external support... the operational question for American foreign policy is not whether that fear can be eliminated or substantially alleviated, but whether China can be faced with a structure of incentives, of penalties and rewards, of inducements that will make it willing to live with this fear.

The point is further clarified by Thomas Schelling: "There is growing experience which the Chinese can profit from, that although the United States may be interested in encircling them, may be interested in defending nearby areas from them, it is, nevertheless, prepared to behave peaceably if they are."

In short, we are prepared to live peaceably within our—to be sure, rather extensive—habitations. And quite naturally, we are offended by the undignified noises from the servants' quarters. If, let us say, a peasant-based revolutionary movement tries to achieve independence from foreign domination or to overthrow semifeudal structures supported by foreign powers, or if the Chinese irrationally refuse to respond properly to the schedule of reinforcement that we have prepared for them, if they object to being encircled by the benign and peace-loving "rich men" who control the territories on their borders as a natural right, then, evidently, we must respond to this belligerence with appropriate force.

It is this mentality that explains the frankness with which the United States government and its academic apologists defend the American refusal to permit a political settlement in Vietnam at a local level, a settlement based on the actual distribution of political forces. Even government experts freely admit that the National Liberation Front is the only "truly mass-based political party in South Vietnam"; that the NLF had "made a conscious and massive effort to extend political participation, even if it was manipulated, on the local level so as to involve the people in a self-contained, self-supporting revolution" (p. 374); and that this effort had been so successful that no political groups, "with the possible exception of the Buddhists, thought themselves equal in size and power to risk entering into a coalition, fearing that if they did the whale would swallow the minnow" (p. 362). Moreover, they concede that until the introduction of overwhelming American force, the NLF had insisted that the struggle "should be fought out at the political level and that the use of massed military might was in itself illegitimate.... The battleground was to be the minds and loyalties of the rural Vietnamese, the weapons were to be ideas" (pp. 91–92; cf. also pp. 93, 99–108, 155 f.); and correspondingly, that until mid-1964, aid from Hanoi "was largely confined to two areas—doctrinal know-how and leadership personnel" (p. 321). Captured NLF documents contrast the enemy's "military superiority" with their own "political superiority" (p. 106), thus fully confirming the analysis of American military spokesmen who define our problem as how, "with considerable armed force but little political power, [to] contain an adversary who has enormous political force but only modest military power."

Similarly, the most striking outcome of both the Honolulu conference in February and the Manila conference in October was the frank admission by high officials of the Saigon government that "they could not survive a 'peaceful settlement' that left the Vietcong *political* structure in place even if the Vietcong guerrilla units were disbanded," that "they are not able to compete *politically* with the Vietnamese Communists." Thus, Mohr continues, the Vietnamese demand a "pacification program" which will have as "its core … the destruction of the clandestine Vietcong political structure and the creation of an iron-like system of government political control over the population." And from Manila, the same correspondent, on October 23, quotes a high South Vietnamese official as saying: "Frankly, we are not strong enough now to compete with the Communists on a purely political basis. They are organized and disciplined. The non-Communist nationalists are not—we do not have any large, well-organized political parties and we do not yet have unity. We cannot leave the Vietcong in existence." Officials in Washington understand the situation very well. Thus Secretary Rusk has pointed out that "if the Vietcong come to the conference table as full partners they will, in a sense, have been victorious in the very aims that South Vietnam and the United States are pledged to prevent" (January 28, 1966). Similarly, Max Frankel reported from Washington: "Compromise has had no appeal here because the Administration concluded long ago that the non-Communist forces of South Vietnam could not long survive in a Saigon coalition with Communists. It is for that reason—and not because of an excessively rigid sense of protocol—that Washington has steadfastly refused to deal with the Vietcong or recognize them as an independent political force."

In short, we will—magnanimously—permit Vietcong representatives to attend negotiations, but only if they will agree to identify themselves as agents of a foreign power and thus forfeit the right to participate in a coalition government, a right which they have now been demanding for a half-dozen years We know well that in any representative coalition, our chosen delegates could not last a day without the support of American arms. Therefore, we must increase American force and resist meaningful negotiations, until the day when a client government can exert both military and political control over its own population—a day which may never dawn, for as William Bundy has pointed out, we could never be sure of the security of a Southeast Asia "from which the Western presence was effectively withdrawn." Thus if we were to "negotiate in the direction of solutions that are put under the label of neutralization," this would amount to capitulation to the Communists. According to this reasoning, then, South Vietnam must remain, permanently, an American military base.

All of this is of course reasonable, so long as we accept the fundamental political axiom that the United States, with its traditional concern for the rights of the weak and downtrodden, and with its unique insight into the proper mode of development for backward countries, must have the courage and the persistence to impose its will by force until such time as other nations are prepared to accept these truths—or simply to abandon hope.

If it is the responsibility of the intellectual to insist upon the truth, it is also his duty to see events in their historical perspective. Thus one must applaud the insistence of the Secretary of State on the importance of historical analogies, the Munich analogy, for example. As Munich showed, a powerful and aggressive nation with a fanatic belief in its manifest destiny will regard each victory, each extension of its power and authority, as a prelude to the next step. The matter was very well put by Adlai Stevenson, when he spoke of "the old, old route whereby expansive powers push at more and more doors, believing they will open, until, at the ultimate door, resistance is unavoidable and major war breaks out." Herein lies the danger of appeasement, as the Chinese tirelessly point out to the Soviet Union, which they claim is playing Chamberlain to our Hitler in Vietnam. Of course, the aggressiveness of liberal imperialism is not that of Nazi Germany, though the distinction may seem rather academic to a Vietnamese peasant who is being gassed or incinerated. We do not want to occupy Asia; we merely wish, to return to Mr. Wolf, "to help the Asian countries progress toward economic modernization, as relatively 'open' and stable societies, to which our access, as a country and as individual citizens, is free and comfortable." The formulation is appropriate. Recent history shows that it makes little difference to us what form of government a country has as long as it remains an "open society," in our peculiar sense of this term—a society, that is, which remains open to American economic penetration or political control. If it is necessary to approach genocide in Vietnam to achieve this objective, then this is the price we must pay in defense of freedom and the rights of man....

In pursuing the aim of helping other countries to progress towards open societies, with no thought of territorial aggrandizement, we are breaking no new ground. Hans Morgenthau has aptly described our traditional policy towards China as one of favoring "what you might call freedom of competition with regard to the exploitation of China." In fact, few imperialist powers have had explicit territorial ambitions. Thus in 1784, the British Parliament announced that "to pursue schemes of conquest and extension of dominion in India are measures repugnant to the wish, honor, and policy of this nation." Shortly after, the conquest of India was in full swing. A century later, Britain announced its intentions in Egypt under the slogan "Intervention, Reform, Withdrawal." It is unnecessary to comment on which parts of this promise were fulfilled, within the next half century. In 1936, on the eve of hostilities in North China, the Japanese stated their Basic Principles of National Policy. These included the use of moderate and peaceful means to extend her strength, to promote social and economic development, to eradicate the menace of Communism, to correct the aggressive policies of the great powers, and to secure her position as the stabilizing power in East Asia. Even in 1937, the Japanese government had "no territorial designs upon China." In short, we follow a well-trodden path.

It is useful to remember, incidentally, that the United States was apparently quite willing, as late as 1939, to negotiate a commercial treaty with Japan and arrive at a modus vivendi if Japan would "change her attitude and practice towards our rights and interests in China," as Secretary Hull put it. The bombing of Chungking and the rape of Nanking were rather unpleasant, it is true, but what was really important was our rights and interests in China, as the responsible, unhysterical men of the day saw quite clearly. It was the closing of the Open Door by Japan that led inevitably to the Pacific war, just as it is the closing of the Open Door by "Communist" China itself that may very well lead to the next, and no doubt last, Pacific war.

Quite often, the statements of sincere and devoted technical experts give surprising insight into the intellectual attitudes that lie in the background of the latest savagery. Consider, for example, the following comment by economist Richard Lindholm, in 1959, expressing his frustration over the failure of economic development in "free Vietnam": " ... the use of American aid is determined by how the Vietnamese use their incomes and their savings. The fact that a large portion of the Vietnamese imports financed with American aid are either consumer goods or raw materials used rather directly to meet consumer demands is an indication that the Vietnamese people desire these goods, for they have shown their desire by their willingness to use their piasters to purchase them."

In short, the Vietnamese *people* desire Buicks and air conditioners, rather than sugar-refining equipment or road-building machinery, as they have shown by their behavior in a free market. And however much we may deplore their free choice, we must allow the people to have their way. Of course, there are also those two-legged beasts of burden that one stumbles on in the countryside, but as any graduate student of political science can explain, they are not part of a responsible modernizing elite, and therefore have only a superficial biological resemblance to the human race.

In no small measure, it is attitudes like this that lie behind the butchery in Vietnam, and we had better face up to them with candor, or we will find our government leading us towards a "final solution" in Vietnam, and in the many Vietnams that inevitably lie ahead.

Let me finally return to Macdonald and the responsibility of intellectuals. Macdonald quotes an interview with a death-camp paymaster who bursts into tears when told that the Russians would hang him. "Why should they? What have I done?" he asked. Macdonald concludes: "Only those who are willing to resist authority themselves when it conflicts too intolerably with their personal moral code, only they have the right to condemn the death-camp paymaster." The question "What have I done?" is one that we may well ask ourselves, as we read, each day, of fresh atrocities in Vietnam—as we create, or mouth, or tolerate the deceptions that will be used to justify the next defense of freedom.

EDWARD W. SAID

Selection from *Orientalism*
(1978)

That Western knowledge about "the East" (especially the parts often called "the Middle East" and heavily inflected with the Islamic religion) had been badly distorted by the imperialist matrix of its creation was a key argument in a book of 1978 destined to become one of the most actively debated books of literary scholarship written in the twentieth century. In *Orientalism* Edward Said (1935–2003) founded what came to be called "post-colonial theory," and inspired countless studies of non-Western societies from a perspective proudly emancipated from the colonial setting in which so many Europeans and Americans had formed their understanding of vast segments of the globe. In the introduction to *Orientalism*, reprinted here, Said outlines his central points and explains his approach. For all its heuristic value, Said's analysis of "Orientalism" has been subject to strong empirical critiques, exemplified by Suzanne Marchand, *German Orientalism in the Age of Empire* (New York, 2009).

Ethnically Palestinian, Said spent his childhood in Egypt before immigrating with his parents to the United States. Unlike many Palestinians, he was not a Muslim. His family had been Protestant, but in his adult career Said was a resolute secularist. A leading participant in the controversies over Israel that intensified throughout his life, Said was the most visible defender of the Palestinian cause in the United States. Quarrels—sometimes bitter and vituperative—about his role in the Arab-Israeli debates often overlapped with disputes over *Orientalism*.

Although known for his insistence that knowledge often reflected the concentrations of power that surrounded the practice of scholarship, Said was a persistent and often eloquent defender of an independent role for scholars. He vigorously resisted efforts to reduce scholarship to special pleading. This theme became more prominent in his later career, and was developed forcefully in his contribution to Louis Menand, ed., *The Future of Academic Freedom* (Chicago, 1996), 214–28, and in lectures delivered shortly before his death and published posthumously as *Humanism and Democratic Criticism* (New York, 2004).

Said was a professor of comparative literature at Columbia University for forty years, during which time he published numerous works of literary criticism, including *The World, the Text, and the Critic* (New York, 1983). He also published a brief autobiography, *Out of Place: A Memoir* (New York, 1999). Although he lived only until the age of sixty-seven, Said completed more than twenty books. His works have been translated into thirty-six languages. The best starting place for a study of his work is the symposium "Edward Said: Continuing the Conversation," *Critical Inquiry* (Winter 2005), 365–529.

... The Orient is not only adjacent to Europe; it is also the place of Europe's greatest and richest and oldest colonies, the source of its civilizations and languages, its cultural contestant, and one of its deepest and most recurring images of the Other. In addition, the Orient has helped to define Europe (or the West) as its contrasting image, idea, personality, experience. Yet none of this Orient is merely imaginative. The Orient is an integral part of European *material* civilization and culture. Orientalism expresses and represents that part culturally and even ideologically as a mode of discourse with supporting institutions, vocabulary, scholarship, imagery, doctrines, even colonial bureaucracies and colonial styles. In contrast, the American understanding of the Orient will seem considerably less dense, although our recent Japanese, Korean, and Indochinese adventures ought now to be creating a more sober, more realistic "Oriental" awareness. Moreover, the vastly expanded American political and economic role in the Near East (the Middle East) makes great claims on our understanding of that Orient.

It will be clear to the reader (and will become clearer still throughout the many pages that follow) that by Orientalism I mean several things, all of them, in my opinion, interdependent. The most readily accepted designation for Orientalism is an academic one, and indeed the label still serves in a number of academic institutions. Anyone who teaches, writes about, or researches the Orient—and this applies whether the person is an anthropologist, sociologist, historian, or philologist—either in its specific or its general aspects, is an Orientalist, and what he or she does is Orientalism. Compared with *Oriental studies* or *area studies*, it is true that the term *Orientalism* is less preferred by specialists today, both because it is too vague and general and because it connotes the high-handed executive attitude of nineteenth-century and early-twentieth-century European colonialism. Nevertheless books are written and congresses held with "the Orient" as their main focus, with the Orientalist in his new or old guise as their main authority. The point is that even if it does not survive as it once did, Orientalism lives on academically through its doctrines and theses about the Orient and the Oriental.

Related to this academic tradition, whose fortunes, transmigrations, specializations, and transmissions are in part the subject of this study, is a more general meaning for Orientalism. Orientalism is a style of thought based upon an ontological and epistemological distinction made between "the Orient" and (most of the time) "the Occident." Thus a very large mass of writers, among whom are poets, novelists, philosophers, political theorists, economists, and imperial administrators, have accepted the basic distinction between East and West as the starting point for elaborate theories, epics, novels, social descriptions, and political accounts concerning the Orient, its people, customs, "mind," destiny, and so on. *This* Orientalism can accommodate Aeschylus, say, and Victor Hugo, Dante and Karl Marx....

The interchange between the academic and the more or less imaginative meanings of Orientalism is a constant one, and since the late eighteenth century there has been a considerable, quite disciplined—perhaps even regulated—traffic between the two. Here I come to the third meaning of Orientalism, which is something more historically and materially defined than either of the other two. Taking the late eighteenth century as a very roughly defined starting point Orientalism can be discussed and analyzed as the corporate institution for dealing with the Orient—dealing with it by making statements about

Source: Edward W. Said, *Orientalism* (New York: Random House, 1978). 1–15, 19–20, 22–23, 25–28. Reprinted with the permission of the Wylie Agency, Inc. Copyright © 1978 by Edward Said.

it, authorizing views of it, describing it, by teaching it, settling it, ruling over it: in short, Orientalism as a Western style for dominating, restructuring, and having authority over the Orient. I have found it useful here to employ Michel Foucault's notion of a discourse, as described by him in *The Archaeology of Knowledge* and in *Discipline and Punish*, to identify Orientalism. My contention is that without examining Orientalism as a discourse one cannot possibly understand the enormously systematic discipline by which European culture was able to manage—and even produce—the Orient politically, sociologically, militarily, ideologically, scientifically, and imaginatively during the post-Enlightenment period. Moreover, so authoritative a position did Orientalism have that I believe no one writing, thinking, or acting on the Orient could do so without taking account of the limitations on thought and action imposed by Orientalism. In brief, because of Orientalism the Orient was not (and is not) a free subject of thought or action. This is not to say that Orientalism unilaterally determines what can be said about the Orient, but that it is the whole network of interests inevitably brought to bear on (and therefore always involved in) any occasion when that peculiar entity "the Orient" is in question. How this happens is what this book tries to demonstrate. It also tries to show that European culture gained in strength and identity by setting itself off against the Orient as a sort of surrogate and even underground self....

I have begun with the assumption that the Orient is not an inert fact of nature. It is not merely *there*, just as the Occident itself is not just *there* either. We must take seriously Vico's great observation that men make their own history, that what they can know is what they have made, and extend it to geography: as both geographical and cultural entities—to say nothing of historical entities—such locales, regions, geographical sectors as "Orient" and "Occident" are man-made. Therefore as much as the West itself, the Orient is an idea that has a history and a tradition of thought, imagery, and vocabulary that have given it reality and presence in and for the West. The two geographical entities thus support and to an extent reflect each other.

Having said that, one must go on to state a number of reasonable qualifications. In the first place, it would be wrong to conclude that the Orient was *essentially* an idea, or a creation with no corresponding reality. When Disraeli said in his novel *Tancred* that the East was a career, he meant that to be interested in the East was something bright young Westerners would find to be an all-consuming passion; he should not be interpreted as saying that the East was *only* a career for Westerners. There were—and are—cultures and nations whose location is in the East, and their lives, histories, and customs have a brute reality obviously greater than anything that could be said about them in the West. About that fact this study of Orientalism has very little to contribute, except to acknowledge it tacitly. But the phenomenon of Orientalism as I study it here deals principally, not with a correspondence between Orientalism and Orient, but with the internal consistency of Orientalism and its ideas about the Orient (the East as career) despite or beyond any correspondence, or lack thereof, with a "real" Orient. My point is that Disraeli's statement about the East refers mainly to that created consistency, that regular constellation of ideas as the pre-eminent thing about the Orient, and not to its mere being, as Wallace Stevens's phrase has it.

A second qualification is that ideas, cultures, and histories cannot seriously be understood or studied without their force, or more precisely their configurations of power, also being studied. To believe that the Orient was created—or, as I call it, "Orientalized"—and to believe that such things happen simply as a necessity of the imagination, is to be disingenuous. The relationship between Occident and Orient is a relationship of power,

of domination, of varying degrees of a complex hegemony, and is quite accurately indicated in the title of K. M. Panikkar's classic *Asia and Western Dominance*. The Orient was
Orientalized not only because it was discovered to be "Oriental" in all those ways considered commonplace by an average nineteenth-century European, but also because it *could
be*—that is, submitted to being—*made* Oriental. There is very little consent to be found,
for example, in the fact that Flaubert's encounter with an Egyptian courtesan produced
a widely influential model of the Oriental woman; she never spoke of herself, she never
represented her emotions, presence, or history. *He* spoke for and represented her. He was
foreign, comparatively wealthy, male, and these were historical facts of domination that
allowed him not only to possess Kuchuk Hanem physically but to speak for her and tell his
readers in what way she was "typically Oriental." My argument is that Flaubert's situation
of strength in relation to Kuchuk Hanem was not an isolated instance. It fairly stands for
the pattern of relative strength between East and West, and the discourse about the Orient
that it enabled.

This brings us to a third qualification. One ought never to assume that the structure of Orientalism is nothing more than a structure of lies or of myths which, were the
truth about them to be told, would simply blow away. I myself believe that Orientalism
is more particularly valuable as a sign of European-Atlantic power over the Orient than
it is as a veridic discourse about the Orient (which is what, in its academic or scholarly
form, it claims to be). Nevertheless, what we must respect and try to grasp is the sheer
knitted-together strength of Orientalist discourse, its very close ties to the enabling socio-
economic and political institutions, and its redoubtable durability. After all, any system of
ideas that can remain unchanged as teachable wisdom (in academies, books, congresses,
universities, foreign-service institutes) from the period of Ernest Renan in the late 1840s
until the present in the United States must be something more formidable than a mere
collection of lies. Orientalism, therefore, is not an airy European fantasy about the Orient,
but a created body of theory and practice in which, for many generations, there has been
a considerable material investment. Continued investment made Orientalism, as a system of knowledge about the Orient, an accepted grid for filtering through the Orient into
Western consciousness, just as that same investment multiplied—indeed, made truly
productive—the statements proliferating out from Orientalism into the general culture.

Gramsci has made the useful analytic distinction between civil and political society in
which the former is made up of voluntary (or at least rational and noncoercive) affiliations
like schools, families, and unions, the latter of state institutions (the army, the police, the
central bureaucracy) whose role in the polity is direct domination. Culture, of course, is to
be found operating within civil society, where the influence of ideas, of institutions, and
of other persons works not through domination but by what Gramsci calls consent. In
any society not totalitarian, then, certain cultural forms predominate over others, just as
certain ideas are more influential than others; the form of this cultural leadership is what
Gramsci has identified as *hegemony*, an indispensable concept for any understanding of
cultural life in the industrial West. It is hegemony, or rather the result of cultural hegemony at work, that gives Orientalism the durability and the strength I have been speaking
about so far. Orientalism is never far from what Denys Hay has called the idea of Europe,
a collective notion identifying "us" Europeans as against all "those" non-Europeans, and
indeed it can be argued that the major component in European culture is precisely what
made that culture hegemonic both in and outside Europe: the idea of European identity
as a superior one in comparison with all the non-European peoples and cultures. There
is in addition the hegemony of European ideas about the Orient, themselves reiterating

European superiority over Oriental backwardness, usually overriding the possibility that a more independent, or more skeptical, thinker might have had different views on the matter.

In a quite constant way, Orientalism depends for its strategy on this flexible *positional* superiority, which puts the Westerner in a whole series of possible relationships with the Orient without ever losing him the relative upper hand. And why should it have been otherwise, especially during the period of extraordinary European ascendancy from the late Renaissance to the present? The scientist, the scholar, the missionary, the trader, or the soldier was in, or thought about, the Orient because he *could be there,* or could think about it, with very little resistance on the Orient's part. Under the general heading of knowledge of the Orient, and within the umbrella of Western hegemony over the Orient during the period from the end of the eighteenth century, there emerged a complex Orient suitable for study in the academy, for display in the museum, for reconstruction in the colonial office, for theoretical illustration in anthropological, biological, linguistic, racial, and historical theses about mankind and the universe, for instances of economic and sociological theories of development, revolution, cultural personality, national or religious character....

And yet, one must repeatedly ask oneself whether what matters in Orientalism is the general group of ideas overriding the mass of material—about which who could deny that they were shot through with doctrines of European superiority, various kinds of racism, imperialism, and the like, dogmatic views of "the Oriental" as a kind of ideal and unchanging abstraction?—or the much more varied work produced by almost uncountable individual writers, whom one would take up as individual instances of authors dealing with the Orient. In a sense the two alternatives, general and particular, are really two perspectives on the same material: in both instances one would have to deal with pioneers in the field like William Jones, with great artists like Nerval or Flaubert. And why would it not be possible to employ both perspectives together, or one after the other? Isn't there an obvious danger of distortion (of precisely the kind that academic Orientalism has always been prone to) if either too general or too specific a level of description is maintained systematically?

My two fears are distortion and inaccuracy, or rather the kind of inaccuracy produced by too dogmatic a generality and too positivistic a localized focus. In trying to deal with these problems I have tried to deal with three main aspects of my own contemporary reality that seem to me to point the way out of the methodological or perspectival difficulties I have been discussing, difficulties that might force one, in the first instance, into writing a coarse polemic on so unacceptably general a level of description as not to be worth the effort, or in the second instance, into writing so detailed and atomistic a series of analyses as to lose all track of the general lines of force informing the field, giving it its special cogency. How then to recognize individuality and to reconcile it with its intelligent, and by no means passive or merely dictatorial, general and hegemonic context?

I mentioned three aspects of my contemporary reality: I must explain and briefly discuss them now, so that it can be seen how I was led to a particular course of research and writing.

1. *The distinction between pure and political knowledge.* It is very easy to argue that knowledge about Shakespeare or Wordsworth is not political whereas knowledge about contemporary China or the Soviet Union is. My own formal and professional designation is that of "humanist," a title which indicates the humanities as my field and therefore the unlikely eventuality that there might be anything political about what I do in that field. Of course, all these labels and terms are quite unnuanced as I use them here, but the general

truth of what I am pointing to is, I think, widely held. One reason for saying that a humanist who writes about Wordsworth, or an editor whose specialty is Keats, is not involved in anything political is that what he does seems to have no direct political effect upon reality in the everyday sense. A scholar whose field is Soviet economics works in a highly charged area where there is much government interest, and what he might produce in the way of studies or proposals will be taken up by policymakers, government officials, institutional economists, intelligence experts. The distinction between "humanists" and persons whose work has policy implications, or political significance, can be broadened further by saying that the former's ideological color is a matter of incidental importance to politics (although possibly of great moment to his colleagues in the field, who may object to his Stalinism or fascism or too easy liberalism), whereas the ideology of the latter is woven directly into his material—indeed, economics, politics, and sociology in the modern academy are ideological sciences—and therefore taken for granted as being "political."

Nevertheless the determining impingement on most knowledge produced in the contemporary West (and here I speak mainly about the United States) is that it be nonpolitical, that is, scholarly, academic, impartial, above partisan or small-minded doctrinal belief. One can have no quarrel with such an ambition in theory, perhaps, but in practice the reality is much more problematic. No one has ever devised a method for detaching the scholar from the circumstances of life, from the fact of his involvement (conscious or unconscious) with a class, a set of beliefs, a social position, or from the mere activity of being a member of a society. These continue to bear on what he does professionally, even though naturally enough his research and its fruits do attempt to reach a level of relative freedom from the inhibitions and the restrictions of brute, everyday reality. For there is such a thing as knowledge that is less, rather than more, partial than the individual (with his entangling and distracting life circumstances) who produces it. Yet this knowledge is not therefore automatically nonpolitical.

Whether discussions of literature or of classical philology are fraught with—or have unmediated—political significance is a very large question that I have tried to treat in some detail elsewhere. What I am interested in doing now is suggesting how the general liberal consensus that "true" knowledge is fundamentally non-political (and conversely, that overtly political knowledge is not "true" knowledge) obscures the highly if obscurely organized political circumstances obtaining when knowledge is produced. No one is helped in understanding this today when the adjective "political" is used as a label to discredit any work for daring to violate the protocol of pretended suprapolitical objectivity. We may say, first, that civil society recognizes a gradation of political importance in the various fields of knowledge. To some extent the political importance given a field comes from the possibility of its direct translation into economic terms; but to a greater extent political importance comes from the closeness of a field to ascertainable sources of power in political society. Thus an economic study of long-term Soviet energy potential and its effect on military capability is likely to be commissioned by the Defense Department, and thereafter to acquire a kind of political status impossible for a study of Tolstoi's early fiction financed in part by a foundation. Yet both works belong in what civil society acknowledges to be a similar field, Russian studies, even though one work may be done by a very conservative economist, the other by a radical literary historian. My point here is that "Russia" as a general subject matter has political priority over nicer distinctions such as "economics" and "literary history," because political society in Gramsci's sense reaches into such realms of civil society as the academy and saturates them with significance of direct concern to it....

Orientalism is not a mere political subject matter or field that is reflected passively by culture, scholarship, or institutions; nor is it a large and diffuse collection of texts about the Orient; nor is it representative and expressive of some nefarious "Western" imperialist plot to hold down the "Oriental" world. It is rather a *distribution* of geopolitical awareness into aesthetic, scholarly, economic, sociological, historical, and philological texts; it is an *elaboration* not only of a basic geographical distinction (the world is made up of two unequal halves, Orient and Occident) but also of a whole series of "interests" which, by such means as scholarly discovery, philological reconstruction, psychological analysis, landscape and sociological description, it not only creates but also maintains; it *is*, rather than expresses, a certain *will* or *intention* to understand, in some cases to control, manipulate, even to incorporate, what is a manifestly different (or alternative and novel) world; it is, above all, a discourse that is by no means in direct, corresponding relationship with political power in the raw, but rather is produced and exists in an uneven exchange with various kinds of power, shaped to a degree by the exchange with power political (as with a colonial or imperial establishment), power intellectual (as with reigning sciences like comparative linguistics or anatomy, or any of the modern policy sciences), power cultural (as with orthodoxies and canons of taste, texts, values), power moral (as with ideas about what "we" do and what "they" cannot do or understand as "we" do). Indeed, my real argument is that Orientalism is—and does not simply represent—a considerable dimension of modern political-intellectual culture, and as such has less to do with the Orient than it does with "our" world.

Because Orientalism is a cultural and a political fact, then, it does not exist in some archival vacuum; quite the contrary, I think it can be shown that what is thought, said, or even done about the Orient follows (perhaps occurs within) certain distinct and intellectually knowable lines. Here too a considerable degree of nuance and elaboration can be seen working as between the broad superstructural pressures and the details of composition, the facts of textuality. Most humanistic scholars are, I think, perfectly happy with the notion that texts exist in contexts, that there is such a thing as intertextuality, that the pressures of conventions, predecessors, and rhetorical styles limit what Walter Benjamin once called the "overtaxing of the productive person in the name of…the principle of 'creativity,' " in which the poet is believed on his own, and out of his pure mind, to have brought forth his work. Yet there is a reluctance to allow that political, institutional, and ideological constraints act in the same manner on the individual author…

Perhaps it is true that most attempts to rub culture's nose in the mud of politics have been crudely iconoclastic; perhaps also the social interpretation of literature in my own field has simply not kept up with the enormous technical advances in detailed textual analysis. But there is no getting away from the fact that literary studies in general, and American Marxist theorists in particular, have avoided the effort of seriously bridging the gap between the superstructural and the base levels in textual, historical scholarship; on another occasion I have gone so far as to say that the literary-cultural establishment as a whole has declared the serious study of imperialism and culture off limits. For Orientalism brings one up directly against that question—that is, to realizing that political imperialism governs an entire field of study, imagination, and scholarly institutions—in such a way as to make its avoidance an intellectual and historical impossibility. Yet there will always remain the perennial escape mechanism of saying that a literary scholar and a philosopher, for example, are trained in literature and philosophy respectively, not in politics or ideological analysis. In other words, the specialist argument can work quite effectively to block the larger and, in my opinion, the more intellectually serious perspective.

Here it seems to me there is a simple two-part answer to be given, at least so far as the study of imperialism and culture (or Orientalism) is concerned. In the first place, nearly every nineteenth-century writer (and the same is true enough of writers in earlier periods) was extraordinarily well aware of the fact of empire: this is a subject not very well studied, but it will not take a modern Victorian specialist long to admit that liberal cultural heroes like John Stuart Mill, Arnold, Carlyle, Newman, Macaulay, Ruskin, George Eliot, and even Dickens had definite views on race and imperialism, which are quite easily to be found at work in their writing. So even a specialist must deal with the knowledge that Mill, for example, made it clear in *On Liberty* and *Representative Government* that his views there could not be applied to India (he was an India Office functionary for a good deal of his life, after all) because the Indians were civilizationally, if not racially, inferior. The same kind of paradox is to be found in Marx, as I try to show in this book. In the second place, to believe that politics in the form of imperialism bears upon the production of literature, scholarship, social theory, and history writing is by no means equivalent to saying that culture is therefore a demeaned or denigrated thing. Quite the contrary: my whole point is to say that we can better understand the persistence and the durability of saturating hegemonic systems like culture when we realize that their internal constraints upon writers and thinkers were *productive,* not unilaterally inhibiting....

The kind of political questions raised by Orientalism, then, are as follows: What other sorts of intellectual, aesthetic, scholarly, and cultural energies went into the making of an imperialist tradition like the Orientalist one? How did philology, lexicography, history, biology, political and economic theory, novel-writing, and lyric poetry come to the service of Orientalism's broadly imperialist view of the world? What changes, modulations, refinements, even revolutions take place within Orientalism? What is the meaning of originality, of continuity, of individuality, in this context? How does Orientalism transmit or reproduce itself from one epoch to another? In fine, how can we treat the cultural, historical phenomenon of Orientalism as a kind of *willed human work*—not of mere unconditioned ratiocination—in all its historical complexity, detail, and worth without at the same time losing sight of the alliance between cultural work, political tendencies, the state, and the specific realities of domination? Governed by such concerns a humanistic study can responsibly address itself to politics *and* culture. But this is not to say that such a study establishes a hard-and-fast rule about the relationship between knowledge and politics. My argument is that each humanistic investigation must formulate the nature of that connection in the specific context of the study, the subject matter, and its historical circumstances.

2. *The methodological question....*

There is nothing mysterious or natural about authority. It is formed, irradiated, disseminated; it is instrumental, it is persuasive; it has status, it establishes canons of taste and value; it is virtually indistinguishable from certain ideas it dignifies as true, and from traditions, perceptions, and judgments it forms, transmits, reproduces. Above all, authority can, indeed must, be analyzed. All these attributes of authority apply to Orientalism, and much of what I do in this study is to describe both the historical authority in and the personal authorities of Orientalism.

My principal methodological devices for studying authority here are what can be called *strategic location,* which is a way of describing the author's position in a text with regard to the Oriental material he writes about, and *strategic formation,* which is a way of analyzing the relationship between texts and the way in which groups of texts, types of texts, even textual genres, acquire mass, density, and referential power among themselves and thereafter in the culture at large. I use the notion of strategy simply to identify the problem every writer on the Orient has faced: how to get hold of it, how to approach it, how not to be defeated or overwhelmed by its sublimity, its scope, its awful dimensions. Everyone who writes about the Orient must locate himself vis-à-vis the Orient; translated into his text, this location includes the kind of narrative voice he adopts, the type of structure he builds, the kinds of images, themes, motifs that circulate in his text—all of which add up to deliberate ways of addressing the reader, containing the Orient, and finally, representing it or speaking in its behalf. None of this takes place in the abstract, however. Every writer on the Orient (and this is true even of Homer) assumes some Oriental precedent, some previous knowledge of the Orient, to which he refers and on which he relies. Additionally, each work on the Orient *affiliates* itself with other works, with audiences, with institutions, with the Orient itself. The ensemble of relationships between works, audiences, and some particular aspects of the Orient therefore constitutes an analyzable formation—for example, that of philological studies, of anthologies of extracts from Oriental literature, of travel books, of Oriental fantasies—whose presence in time, in discourse, in institutions (schools, libraries, foreign services) gives it strength and authority...

Orientalism responded more to the culture that produced it than to its putative object, which was also produced by the West. Thus the history of Orientalism has both an internal consistency and a highly articulated set of relationships to the dominant culture surrounding it. My analyses consequently try to show the field's shape and internal organization, its pioneers, patriarchal authorities, canonical texts, doxological ideas, exemplary figures, its followers, elaborators, and new authorities; I try also to explain how Orientalism borrowed and was frequently informed by "strong" ideas, doctrines, and trends ruling the culture. Thus there was (and is) a linguistic Orient, a Freudian Orient, a Spenglerian Orient, a Darwinian Orient, a racist Orient—and so on. Yet never has there been such a thing as a pure, or unconditional, Orient; similarly, never has there been a nonmaterial form of Orientalism, much less something so innocent as an "idea" of the Orient. In this underlying conviction and in its ensuing methodological consequences do I differ from scholars who study the history of ideas. For the emphases and the executive form, above all the material effectiveness, of statements made by Orientalist discourse are possible in ways that any hermetic history of ideas tends completely to scant. Without those emphases and that material effectiveness Orientalism would be just another idea, whereas it is and was much more than that. Therefore I set out to examine not only scholarly works but also works of literature, political tracts, journalistic texts, travel books, religious and philological studies. In other words, my hybrid perspective is broadly historical and "anthropological," given that I believe all texts to be worldly and circumstantial in (of course) ways that vary from genre to genre, and from historical period to historical period...

3. *The personal dimension.* In the *Prison Notebooks* Gramsci says: "The starting-point of critical elaboration is the consciousness of what one really is, and is 'knowing thyself' as a product of the historical process to date, which has deposited in you an infinity of traces, without leaving an inventory." The only available English translation inexplicably leaves Gramsci's comment at that, whereas in fact Gramsci's Italian text concludes by adding, "therefore it is imperative at the outset to compile such an inventory."

Much of the personal investment in this study derives from my awareness of being an "Oriental" as a child growing up in two British colonies. All of my education, in those colonies (Palestine and Egypt) and in the United States, has been Western, and yet that deep early awareness has persisted. In many ways my study of Orientalism has been an attempt to inventory the traces upon me, the Oriental subject, of the culture whose domination has been so powerful a factor in the life of all Orientals. This is why for me the Islamic Orient has had to be the center of attention. Whether what I have achieved is the inventory prescribed by Gramsci is not for me to judge, although I have felt it important to be conscious of trying to produce one. Along the way, as severely and as rationally as I have been able, I have tried to maintain a critical consciousness, as well as employing those instruments of historical, humanistic, and cultural research of which my education has made me the fortunate beneficiary. In none of that, however, have I ever lost hold of the cultural reality of, the personal involvement in having been constituted as, "an Oriental."

The historical circumstances making such a study possible are fairly complex, and I can only list them schematically here. Anyone resident in the West since the 1950s, particularly in the United States, will have lived through an era of extraordinary turbulence in the relations of East and West. No one will have failed to note how "East" has always signified danger and threat during this period, even as it has meant the traditional Orient as well as Russia. In the universities a growing establishment of area-studies programs and institutes has made the scholarly study of the Orient a branch of national policy. Public affairs in this country include a healthy interest in the Orient, as much for its strategic and economic importance as for its traditional exoticism. If the world has become immediately accessible to a Western citizen living in the electronic age, the Orient too has drawn nearer to him, and is now less a myth perhaps than a place crisscrossed by Western, especially American, interests.

One aspect of the electronic, postmodern world is that there has been a reinforcement of the stereotypes by which the Orient is viewed. Television, the films, and all the media's resources have forced information into more and more standardized molds. So far as the Orient is concerned, standardization and cultural stereotyping have intensified the hold of the nineteenth-century academic and imaginative demonology of "the mysterious Orient." This is nowhere more true than in the ways by which the Near East is grasped. Three things have contributed to making even the simplest perception of the Arabs and Islam into a highly politicized, almost raucous matter: one, the history of popular anti-Arab and anti-Islamic prejudice in the West, which is immediately reflected in the history of Orientalism; two, the struggle between the Arabs and Israeli Zionism, and its effects upon American Jews as well as upon both the liberal culture and the population at large; three, the almost total absence of any cultural position making it possible either to identify with or dispassionately to discuss the Arabs or Islam. Furthermore, it hardly needs saying that because the Middle East is now so identified with Great Power politics, oil economics, and the simple-minded dichotomy of freedom-loving, democratic Israel and evil, totalitarian, and terroristic Arabs, the chances of anything like a clear view of what one talks about in talking about the Near East are depressingly small.

My own experiences of these matters are in part what made me write this book. The life of an Arab Palestinian in the West, particularly in America, is disheartening. There exists here an almost unanimous consensus that politically he does not exist, and when it is allowed that he does, it is either as a nuisance or as an Oriental. The web of racism, cultural stereotypes, political imperialism, dehumanizing ideology holding in the Arab or the Muslim is very strong indeed, and it is this web which every Palestinian has come to feel as his uniquely punishing destiny. It has made matters worse for him to remark that no person academically involved with the Near East—no Orientalist, that is—has ever in the United States culturally and politically identified himself wholeheartedly with the Arabs; certainly there have been identifications on some level, but they have never taken an "acceptable" form as has liberal American identification with Zionism, and all too frequently they have been radically flawed by their association either with discredited political and economic interests (oil-company and State Department Arabists, for example) or with religion.

The nexus of knowledge and power creating "the Oriental" and in a sense obliterating him as a human being is therefore not for me an exclusively academic matter. Yet it is an *intellectual* matter of some very obvious importance. I have been able to put to use my humanistic and political concerns for the analysis and description of a very worldly matter, the rise, development, and consolidation of Orientalism. Too often literature and culture are presumed to be politically, even historically innocent; it has regularly seemed otherwise to me, and certainly my study of Orientalism has convinced me (and I hope will convince my literary colleagues) that society and literary culture can only be understood and studied together. In addition, and by an almost inescapable logic, I have found myself writing the history of a strange, secret sharer of Western anti-Semitism. That anti-Semitism and, as I have discussed it in its Islamic branch, Orientalism resemble each other very closely is a historical, cultural, and political truth that needs only to be mentioned to an Arab Palestinian for its irony to be perfectly understood. But what I should like also to have contributed here is a better understanding of the way cultural domination has operated. If this stimulates a new kind of dealing with the Orient, indeed if it eliminates the "Orient" and "Occident" altogether, then we shall have advanced a little in the process of what Raymond Williams has called the "unlearning" of "the inherent dominative mode."

NANCY J. CHODOROW

"Gender, Relation, and Difference in Psychoanalytic Perspective"
(1979)

One of the most historically significant intellectual events of the 1970s in the United States was the rapid and diverse development of feminist theory. One theme in this feminist intellectual flourishing was the demonstration that certain aspects of the psychoanalytic tradition could be separated from Freud's alleged sexism. In the essay of 1979 reprinted here, California psychoanalyst Nancy Chodorow (1944–) offers an account of the development of male and female identity that, while resonating with Erikson and other "ego"-centered pschoanalysts' notions of identity formation, was strikingly at odds with most Freudian and post-Freudian perspectives on gender identity. But it was as an intervention in contemporary discussions of gender that Chodorow's ideas gained their greatest significance. Chodorow argued that "gender difference" involves no "essence of gender," but is "socially and psychologically created and situated." Chodorow's attack on "essentialist" notions of gender contrasted with the emphasis of several other feminist theorists of the same generation, especially Carol Gilligan, whose most widely discussed work was *In a Different Voice: Psychological Theory and Women's Development* (Cambridge, Mass., 1982). Chodorow's understanding of identity and gender invites comparison with that displayed in several other selections within this sourcebook, especially those of Charlotte Perkins Gilman, Erik H. Erikson, Betty Friedan, Catharine MacKinnon, and Joan Scott.

This essay of Chodorow's states briefly some of the ideas she elaborated at greater length in *The Reproduction of Mothering* (Berkeley, 1978). In the introduction to a second edition of that book (Berkeley, 1999), Chodorow describes some of the controversies surrounding the book, and indicates how some of her emphases changed in later years. Her writings of the 1970s, she explains in that introduction, were written "from the daughter's point of view more than that of the mother." Chodorow is also the author of *Feminism and Psychoanalytic Theory* (New Haven, 1989) and *The Power of Feelings: Personal Meaning in Psychoanalysis, Gender, and Culture* (New Haven, 1999).

Chodorow's early work bears study in relation to other feminist classics of the 1970s, including Kate Millet, *Sexual Politics* (New York, 1970); Shulamith Firestone, *The Dialectic of Sex* (New York, 1970); and Adrienne Rich, *Of Woman Born* (New York, 1976).

I would go so far as to say that even before slavery or class domination existed, men built an approach to women that would serve one day to introduce differences among us all.

—Claude Lévi-Strauss

In both the nineteenth- and twentieth-century women's movements, many feminists have argued that the degendering of society, so that gender and sex no longer determined social existence, would eliminate male dominance. This view assumes that gender differentiating characteristics are acquired. An alternate sexual politics and analysis of sexual inequality has tended toward an essentialist position, posing male–female difference as innate. Not the degendering of society, but its appropriation by women, with women's virtues, is seen as the solution to male dominance. These virtues are uniquely feminine, and usually thought to emerge from women's biology, which is then seen as intrinsically connected to or entailing a particular psyche, a particular social role (such as mothering), a particular body image (more diffuse, holistic, non-phallocentric), or a particular sexuality (not centered on a particular organ; at times, lesbianism). In this view, women are intrinsically better than men and their virtues are not available to men. Proponents of the degendering model have sometimes also held that "female" virtues or qualities—nurturance, for instance—should be spread throughout society and replace aggression and competitiveness; but these virtues are nevertheless seen as acquired, a product of women's development or social location, and acquirable by men, given appropriate development, experience and social reorganization. (Others who argue for degendering have at times held that women need to acquire certain "male" characteristics and modes of action—autonomy, independence, assertiveness—again, assuming that such characteristics are acquired.)

This essay evaluates the essentialist view of difference and examines the contribution that psychoanalytic theory can make to understanding the question of sex or gender difference. It asks whether gender is best understood by focussing on differences between men and women and on the uniqueness of each and whether gender difference should be a central organizing concept for feminism. The concept of difference to which I refer here is abstract and irreducible. It assumes the existence of an essence of gender, so that differences between men and women are seen to establish and define each gender as a unique and absolute category.

I will not discuss differences among women. I think we have something else in mind when we speak of differences in this connection. Differences among women—of class, race, sexual preference, nationality, and ethnicity, between mothers and non-mothers—are all significant for feminist theory and practice, but these remain concrete differences, analyzable in terms of specific categories and modes of understanding. We can see how they are socially situated and how they grow from particular social relations and organization; how they may contain physiological elements (race and sexual preference, for example) yet only gain a specific meaning in particular historical contexts and social formations.

I suggest that gender difference is not absolute, abstract, or irreducible; it does not involve an essence of gender. Gender differences, and the experience of difference, like differences among women, are socially and psychologically created and situated. In addition,

Source: Nancy Chodorow, *Feminism and Psychoanalytic Theory* (New Haven: Yale University Press, 1979), 99–113. Reprinted by permission of Nancy J. Chodorow.

I want to suggest a relational notion of difference. Difference and gender difference do not exist as things in themselves; they are created relationally, that is, in relationship. We cannot understand difference apart from this relational construction.

The issues I consider here are relevant both to feminist theory and to particular strands of feminist politics. In contrast to the beginning of the contemporary women's movement, there is now a widespread view that gender differences are essential, that women are fundamentally different from men, and that these differences must be recognized, theorized, and maintained. This finds some political counterpart in notions that women's special nature guarantees the emergence of a good society after the feminist revolution and legitimates female dominance, if not an exclusively female society. My conclusions lead me to reject those currents of contemporary feminism that would found a politics on essentialist conceptions of the feminine.

There is also a preoccupation among some women with psychological separateness and autonomy, with individuality as a necessary women's goal. This preoccupation grows out of many women's feelings of not having distinct autonomy as separate selves, in comparison, say, to men. This finds some political counterpart in equal rights arguments, ultimately based on notions of women exclusively as individuals rather than as part of a collectivity or social group. I suggest that we need to situate such a goal in an understanding of psychological development and to indicate the relationship between our culture's individualism and gender differentiation.

Psychoanalysis clarifies for us many of the issues involved in questions of difference by providing a developmental history of the emergence of separateness, differentiation, and the perception of difference in early childhood. Thus it provides a particularly useful arena in which to see the relational and situated construction of difference, and of gender difference. Moreover, psychoanalysis gives an account of these issues from a general psychological perspective, as well as with specific relation to the question of gender. In this context, I will discuss two aspects of the general subject of separateness, differentiation, and perceptions of difference and their emergence. First, I will consider how separation–individuation occurs relationally in the first "me"–"not-me" division, in the development of the "I," or self. I will suggest that we have to understand this separation–individuation in relation to other aspects of development, that it has particular implications for women, and that differentiation is not synonymous with difference or separateness. Second, I will talk about the ways that difference and gender difference are created distinctly, in different relational contexts, for girls and boys, and, hence, for women and men. The argument here advances a reading of psychoanalysis that stresses the relational ego. It contrasts with certain prevalent (Lacan-influenced) feminist readings of psychoanalysis, in particular with the views advanced by French theorists of difference like Luce Irigaray and with the Freudian orthodoxy of Juliet Mitchell.

I do not deal in this essay with the male and female body. We clearly live an embodied life; we live with those genital and reproductive organs and capacities, those hormones and chromosomes, that locate us physiologically as male or female. But, as psychoanalysis has shown us, there is nothing self-evident about this biology. How anyone experiences, fantasizes about, or internally represents her or his embodiment grows from experience, learning, and self-definition in the family and in the culture. Such self-definitions may be shaped by completely non-biological considerations, which may also shape perceptions of anatomical "sex differences" and the psychological development of these differences into forms of sexual object choice, mode, or aim; into femininity or masculinity; into activity or passivity; into one's choice of the organ of erotic pleasure; and so forth. We cannot know what people would make of their bodies in a non-gender or non-sexually organized world, what kind of sexual structuration or gender identities would develop. We do know that the cultural, social, and psychological significance of biological sex differences, gender difference, and different sexualities is not obvious. There might be a multiplicity of sexual organizations, identities, and practices, and perhaps even of genders themselves. Bodies would be bodies (we do not want to deny people their bodily experience). But particular bodily attributes would not necessarily be so determining of who we are, what we do, how we are perceived, and who are our sexual partners.

Psychoanalysis talks of the process of "differentiation" or "separation-individuation." A child of either gender is born originally with what is called a "narcissistic relation to reality": cognitively and libidinally it experiences itself as merged and continuous with the world in general, and with its mother or caretaker in particular. Differentiation, or separation-individuation, means coming to perceive a demarcation between the self and the object world, coming to perceive the subject/self as distinct, or separate from, the object/other. An essential early task of infantile development, it involves the development of ego boundaries (a sense of personal psychological division from the rest of the world) and of a body ego (a sense of the permanence of one's physical separateness and the predictable boundedness of one's own body, of a distinction between inside and outside).

This differentiation requires physiological maturation (for instance, the ability to perceive object constancy), but such maturation is not enough. Differentiation happens *in relation to* the mother, or to the child's primary caretaker. It develops through experiences of the mother's departure and return, and through frustration, which emphasizes the child's separateness and the fact that it doesn't control all its own experiences and gratifications. Some of these experiences and gratifications come from within, some from without. If it were not for these frustrations, these disruptions of the experience of primary oneness, total holding, and gratification, the child would not need to begin to perceive the other, the "outer world," as separate, rather than as an extension of itself. Developing separateness thus involves, in particular, perceiving the mother or primary caretaker as separate and "not-me," where once these were an undifferentiated symbiotic unity.

Separateness, then, is not simply given from birth, nor does it emerge from the individual alone. Rather, separateness is defined relationally; differentiation occurs in relationship: "*I*" am "*not-you*." Moreover, "*you*," or the other, is also distinguished. The child learns to see the particularity of the mother or primary caretaker in contrast to the rest of the world. Thus, as the self is differentiated from the object world, the object world is itself differentiated into its component parts.

Now, from a psychoanalytic perspective, learning to distinguish me and not-me is necessary for a person to grow into a functioning human being. It is also inevitable, since experiences of departure, of discontinuity in handling, feeding, where one sleeps, how one is picked up and by whom, of less than total relational and physical gratification, are unavoidable. But for our understanding of "difference" in this connection, the concept of differentiation and the processes that characterize it need elaboration.

First, in most psychoanalytic formulations, and in prevalent understandings of development, the mother, or the outside world, is depicted simply as the other, not-me, one who does or does not fulfill an expectation. This perception arises originally from the infant's cognitive inability to differentiate self and world; the infant does not distinguish between its desires for love and satisfaction and those of its primary love-object and object of identification. The self here is the infant or growing child, and psychoanalytic accounts take the viewpoint of this child.

However, adequate separation, or differentiation, involves not merely perceiving the separateness, or otherness, of the other. It involves perceiving the person's subjectivity and selfhood as well. Differentiation, separation, and disruption of the narcissistic relation to reality are developed through learning that the mother is a separate being with separate interests and activities that do not always coincide with just what the infant wants at the time. They involve the ability to experience and perceive the object/other (the mother) in aspects apart from its sole relation to the ability to gratify the infant's/subject's needs and wants; they involve seeing the object as separate from the self and from the self's needs. The infant must change here from a "relationship to a subjectively conceived object to a relationship to an object objectively perceived."

In infantile development this change requires cognitive sophistication, the growing ability to integrate various images and experiences of the mother that comes with the development of ego capacities. But these capacities are not enough. The ability to perceive the other as a self, finally, requires an emotional shift and a form of emotional growth. The adult self not only experiences the other as distinct and separate. It also does not experience the other solely in terms of its own needs for gratification and its own desires.

This interpretation implies that true differentiation, true separateness, cannot be simply a perception and experience of self–other, of presence–absence. It must precisely involve two selves, two presences, two subjects. Recognizing the other as a subject is possible only to the extent that one is not dominated by felt need and one's own exclusive subjectivity. Such recognition permits appreciation and perception of many aspects of the other person, of her or his existence apart from the child's/the self's. Thus, how we understand differentiation—only from the viewpoint of the infant as a self, or from the viewpoint of two interacting selves—has consequences for what we think of as a mature self. If the mature self grows only out of the infant as a self, the other need never be accorded her or his own selfhood.

The view that adequate separation–individuation, or differentiation, involves not simply perceiving the otherness of the other, but her or his selfhood/subjectivity as well, has important consequences, not only for an understanding of the development of selfhood, but also for perceptions of women. Hence, it seems to me absolutely essential to a feminist appropriation of psychoanalytic conceptions of differentiation. Since women, as mothers, are the primary caretakers of infants, if the child (or the psychoanalytic account) only takes the viewpoint of the infant as a (developing) self, then the mother will be perceived (or depicted) only as an object. But, from a feminist perspective, perceiving the particularity of the mother must involve according the mother her own selfhood. This is a necessary part of the developmental process, though it is also often resisted and experienced only conflictually and partially. Throughout life, perceptions of the mother fluctuate between perceiving her particularity and selfhood and perceiving her as a narcissistic extension, a not-separate other whose sole reason for existence is to gratify one's own wants and needs.

Few accounts recognize the import of this particular stance toward the mother. Alice Balint's marvelous protofeminist account is the best I know of the infantile origins of adult perceptions of mother as object:

> Most men (and women)—even when otherwise quite normal and capable of an
> "adult," altruistic form of love which acknowledges the interests of the partner—
> retain towards their own mothers this naive egoistic attitude throughout their
> lives. For all of us it remains self-evident that the interests of mother and child

are identical, and it is the generally acknowledged measure of the goodness or badness of the mother how far she really feels this identity of interests.

Now, these perceptions, as a product of infantile development, are somewhat inevitable as long as women have nearly exclusive maternal responsibilities, and they are one major reason why I advocate equal parenting as a necessary basis of sexual equality. But I think that, even within the ongoing context of women's mothering, as women we can and must liberate ourselves from such perceptions in our personal emotional lives as much as possible, and certainly in our theorizing and politics.

A second elaboration of psychoanalytic accounts of differentiation concerns the affective or emotional distinction between differentiation or separation–individuation, and *difference*. Difference and differentiation are, of course, related to and feed into one another; it is in some sense true that cognitive or linguistic distinction, or division, must imply difference. However, it is possible to be separate, to be differentiated, without caring about or emphasizing difference, without turning the cognitive fact into an emotional, moral, or political one. In fact, assimilating difference to differentiation is defensive and reactive, a reaction to not feeling separate enough. Such assimilation involves arbitrary boundary creation and an assertion of hyper-separateness to reinforce a lack of security in a person's sense of self as a separate person. But one can be separate from and similar to someone at the same time. For example, one can recognize another's subjectivity and humanity as one recognizes one's own, seeing the commonality of both as active subjects. Or a woman can recognize her similarity, commonality, even continuity, with her mother, because she has developed enough of an unproblematic sense of separate self. At the same time, the other side of being able to experience separateness and commonality, of recognizing the other's subjectivity, is the ability to recognize differences with a small "d," differences that are produced and situated historically—for instance, the kinds of meaningful differences among women that I mentioned earlier.

The distinction between differentiation/separateness and difference relates to a third consideration, even more significant to our assessment of difference and gender difference. Following Mahler, much psychoanalytic theory has centered its account of early infant development on separation–individuation, on the creation of the separate self, on the "me"–"not-me" distinction. Yet there are other ways of looking at the development of self, other important and fundamental aspects to the self: "me"–"not-me" is not all there is to "me." Separation, the "me"–"not-me" division, looms larger, both in our psychological life and theoretically, to the extent that these other aspects of the self are not developed either in individual lives or in theoretical accounts.

Object-relations theory shows that in the development of self the primary task is not the development of ego boundaries and a body ego. Along with the earliest development of its sense of separateness, the infant constructs an internal set of unconscious, affectively loaded representations of others in relation to its self, and an internal sense of self in relationship emerges. Images of felt good and bad aspects of the mother or primary care-taker, caretaking experiences, and the mothering relationship become part of the self, of a relational ego structure, through unconscious mental processes that appropriate and incorporate these images. With maturation, these early images and fragments of perceived experience become put together into a self. As externality and internality are established, there-fore, what comes to be internal includes what originally were aspects of the other and the relation to the other. (Similarly, what is experienced as external may include what was originally part of the developing self's experience.) Externality and internality, then, do not follow easily observable physiological boundaries but are constituted by psychological and emotional processes as well.

These unconscious early internalizations that affect and constitute the internal quality of selfhood may remain more or less fragmented, or they may develop a quality of wholeness. A sense of continuity of experience and the opportunity to integrate a complex of (at least somewhat) complementary and consistent images enables the "I" to emerge as a continuous being with an identity. This more internal sense of self, or of "I," is not dependent on separateness or difference from an other. A "true self," or "central self," emerges through the experience of continuity that the mother or caretaker helps to provide, by protecting the infant from having continually to react to and ward off environmental intrusions and from being continually in need.

The integration of a "true self" that feels alive and whole involves a particular set of internalized feelings about others in relation to the self. These include developing a sense that one is able to affect others and one's environment (a sense that one has not been inhibited by over-anticipation of all one's needs), a sense that one has been accorded one's own feelings and a spontaneity about these feelings (a sense that one's feelings or needs have not been projected onto one), and a sense that there is a fit between one's feelings and needs and those of the mother or caretaker. These feelings all give the self a sense of agency and authenticity.

This sense of agency, then, is fostered by caretakers who do not project experiences or feelings onto the child and who do not let the environment impinge indiscriminately. It is evoked by empathic caretakers who understand and validate the infant as a self in its own right, and the infant's experience as real. Thus, the sense of agency, which is one basis of the inner sense of continuity and wholeness, grows out of the nature of the parent infant relationship.

Another important aspect of internalized feelings about others in relation to the self concerns a certain wholeness that develops through an internal sense of relationship with another. The "thereness" of the primary parenting person grows into an internal sense of the presence of another who is caring and affirming. The self comes into being here first through feeling confidently alone in the presence of its mother, and then through this presence's becoming internalized. Part of its self becomes a good internal mother. This suggests that the central core of self is, internally, a relational ego, a sense of self-in-good-relationship. The presence or absence of others, their sameness or difference, does not then become an issue touching the infant's very existence. A "capacity to be alone," a relational rather than a reactive autonomy, develops because of a sense of the ongoing presence of another.

These several senses of agency, of a true self that does not develop reactively, of a relational self or ego core, and of an internal continuity of being, are fundamental to an unproblematic sense of self, and provide the basis of both autonomy and spontaneity. The strength, or wholeness, of the self, in this view, does not depend only or even centrally on its degree of separateness, although the extent of confident distinctness certainly affects and is part of the sense of self. The more secure the central self, or ego core, the less one has to define one's self through separateness from others. Separateness becomes, then, a more rigid, defensive, rather fragile, secondary criterion of the strength of the self and of the "success" of individuation.

This view suggests that no one has a separateness consisting only of "me"–"not-me" distinctions. Part of myself is always that which I have taken in; we are all to some degree incorporations and extensions of others. Separateness from the mother, defining oneself as apart from her (and from other women), is not the only or final goal for women's ego strength and autonomy, even if many women must also attain some sense of reliable separateness. In the process of differentiation, leading to a genuine autonomy, people maintain contact with those with whom they had their earliest relationships: indeed this contact is part of who we are. "I am" is not definition through negation, is not "who I am not." Developing a sense of confident separateness must be a part of all children's development. But once this confident separateness is established, one's relational self can become more central to one's life. Differentiation is not distinctness and separateness, but a particular way of being, connected to others. This connection to others, based on early incorporations, in turn enables us to feel that empathy and confidence that are basic to the recognition of the other as a self.

What does all this have to do with male–female difference and male dominance? Before turning to the question of gender difference, I want to reiterate what we as feminists learn from the general inquiry into "differentiation." First, we learn that we can only think of differentiation and the emergence of the self relationally. Differentiation occurs, and separation emerges, in relationship; they are not givens. Second, we learn that to single out separation as the core of a notion of self and of the process of differentiation may well be inadequate; it is certainly not the only way to discuss the emergence of self or what constitutes a strong self. Differentiation includes the internalization of aspects of the primary caretaker and of the caretaking relationship.

Finally, we learn that essential, important attitudes toward mothers and expectations of mothers—attitudes and expectations that enter into experiences of women more generally—emerge in the earliest differentiation of self. These attitudes and expectations arise during the emergence of separateness. Given that differentiation and separation are developmentally problematic, and given that women are primary caretakers, the mother, who is a woman, becomes and remains for children of both genders the other, or object. She is not accorded autonomy or selfness on her side. Such attitudes arise also from the gender-specific character of the early, emotionally charged self and object images that affect the development of self and the sense of autonomy and spontaneity. They are internalizations of feelings about the self in relation to the mother, who is then often experienced as either overwhelming or over-denying. These attitudes are often unconscious and always have a basis in unconscious, emotionally charged feelings and conflicts. A precipitate of the early relationship to the mother and of an unconscious sense of self, they may be more fundamental and determining of psychic life than more conscious and explicit attitudes to "sex differences" or "gender differences" themselves.

This inquiry suggests a psychoanalytic grounding for goals of emotional psychic life other than autonomy and separateness. It suggests, instead, an individuality that emphasizes our connectedness with, rather than our separation from, one another. Feelings of inadequate separateness, the fear of merger, are indeed issues for women, because of the ongoing sense of oneness and primary identification with our mothers (and children). A transformed organization of parenting would help women to resolve these issues. However, autonomy, spontaneity, and a sense of agency need not be based on self-other distinctions, on the individual as individual. They can be based on the fundamental interconnectedness, not synonymous with merger, that grows out of our earliest unconscious developmental experience, and that enables the creation of a non-reactive separateness. I turn now to the question of gender differences. We are not born with perceptions of gender differences; these emerge developmentally. In the traditional psychoanalytic view, however, when sexual difference is first seen it has self-evident value. A girl perceives her lack of a penis, knows instantly that she wants one, and subsequently defines herself and her mother as lacking, inadequate, castrated; a boy instantly knows having a penis is better, and fears the loss of his own. This traditional account violates a fundamental rule of psychoanalytic interpretation. When the analyst finds trauma, shock, strong fears, or conflict, it is a signal to look for the roots of such feelings. Because of his inability to focus on the pre-Oedipal years and the relationship of mother to child, Freud could not follow his own rule here.

Clinical and theoretical writings since Freud suggest another interpretation of the emergence of perceptions of gender difference. This view reverses the perception of which gender experiences greater trauma, and retains only the claim that gender identity and the sense of masculinity and femininity develop differently for men and women. These accounts suggest that core gender identity and masculinity are conflictual for men, and are bound up with the masculine sense of self in a way that core gender identity and femininity are not for women. "Core gender identity" here refers to a cognitive sense of gendered self, the sense that one is male or female. It is established in the first two years concomitantly with the development of the sense of self. Later evaluations of the desirability of one's gender and of the activities and modes of behavior associated with it, or of one's own sense of adequacy at fulfilling gender role expectations, are built upon this fundamental gender identity. They do not create or change it.

Most people develop an unambiguous core gender identity, a sense that they are female or male. But because women mother, the sense of maleness in men differs from the sense of femaleness in women. Maleness is more conflictual and more problematic. Underlying, or built into, core male gender identity is an early, non-verbal, unconscious, almost somatic sense of primary oneness with the mother, an underlying sense of femaleness that continually, usually unnoticeably, but sometimes insistently, challenges and undermines the sense of maleness. Thus, because of a primary oneness and identification with his mother, a primary femaleness, a boy's and a man's core gender identity itself—the seemingly unproblematic cognitive sense of being male— is an issue. A boy must learn his gender identity as being not-female, or not-mother. Subsequently, again because of the primacy of the mother in early life and because of the absence of concrete, real, available male figures of identification and love who are as salient for him as female figures, learning what it is to be masculine comes to mean learning to be not-feminine, or not-womanly.

Because of early developed, conflictual core gender identity problems, and later problems of adequate masculinity, it becomes important to men to have a clear sense of gender difference, of what is masculine and what is feminine, and to maintain rigid boundaries between these. Researchers find, for example, that fathers sex-type children more than mothers. They treat sons and daughters more differently and enforce gender role expectations more vigorously than mothers do. Boys and men come to deny the feminine identification within themselves and those feelings they experience as feminine: feelings of dependence, relational needs, emotions generally. They come to emphasize differences, not commonalities or continuities, between themselves and women, especially in situations that evoke anxiety, because these commonalities and continuities threaten to challenge gender difference or to remind boys and men consciously of their potentially feminine attributes.

These conflicts concerning core gender identity interact with and build upon particular ways that boys experience the processes of differentiation and the formation of the self. Both sexes establish separateness in relation to their mother, and internalizations in the development of self take in aspects of the mother as well. But because the mother is a woman, these experiences differ by gender. Though children of both sexes are originally part of herself, a mother unconsciously and often consciously experiences her son as more of an "other" than her daughter. Reciprocally, a son's male core gender identity develops away from his mother. The male's self, as a result, becomes based on a more fixed "me"–"not-me" distinction. Separateness and difference as a component of differentiation become more salient. By contrast, the female's self is less separate and involves a less fixed "me"–"not-me" distinction, creating the difficulties with a sense of separateness and autonomy that I mentioned above.

At the same time, core gender identity for a girl is not problematic in the sense that it is for boys. It is built upon, and does not contradict, her primary sense of oneness and identification with her mother and is assumed easily along with her developing sense of self. Girls grow up with a sense of continuity and similarity to their mother, a relational connection to the world. For them, difference is not originally problematic or fundamental to their psychological being or identity. They do not define themselves as "not-men," or "not-male," but as "I, who am female." Girls and women may have problems with their sense of continuity and similarity, if it is too strong and they have no sense of a separate self. However, these problems are not the inevitable products of having a sense of continuity and similarity, since, as I argue here, selfhood does not depend only on the strength and impermeability of ego boundaries. Nor are these problems bound up with questions of gender; rather, they are bound up with questions of self.

In the development of gender identification for girls it is not the existence of core gender identity, the unquestioned knowledge that one is female, that is problematic. Rather, it is the later-developed conflicts concerning this identity, and the identifications, learning, and cognitive choices that it implies. The difficulties that girls have in establishing a "feminine" identity do not stem from the inaccessibility and negative definition of this identity, or its assumption by denial (as in the case of boys). They arise from identification with a negatively valued gender category, and an ambivalently experienced maternal figure, whose mothering and femininity, often conflictual for the mother herself, are accessible, but devalued. Conflicts here arise from questions of relative power, and social and cultural value. I would argue that these conflicts come later in development, and are less pervasively determining of psychological life for women than are masculine conflicts around core gender identity and gender difference.

Men's and women's understanding of difference, and gender difference, must thus be understood in the relational context in which these are created. They stem from the respective relation of boys and girls to their mother, who is their primary caretaker, love-object, and object of identification, and who is a woman in a sexually and gender-organized world. This relational context contrasts profoundly for girls and boys in a way that makes difference, and gender difference, central for males—one of the earliest, most basic male developmental issues—and not central for females. It gives men a psychological investment in difference that women do not have.

According to psychoanalytic accounts since Freud, it is very clear that males are "not females" in earliest development. Core gender identity and the sense of masculinity are defined more negatively, in terms of that which is not female or not-mother, than positively. By contrast, females do not develop as "not-males." Female core gender identity and the sense of femininity are defined positively, as that which is female, or like mother.

Difference from males is not so salient. An alternative way to put this is to suggest that, developmentally, the maternal identification represents and is experienced as generically human for children of both genders.

But, because men have power and cultural hegemony in our society, a notable thing happens. Men use and have used this hegemony to appropriate and transform these experiences. Both in everyday life and in theoretical and intellectual formulations, men have come to define maleness as that which is basically human, and to define women as not-men. This transformation is first learned in, and helps to constitute, the Oedipal transition—the cultural, affective, and sexual learnings of the meaning and valuation of sex differences. Because Freud was not attentive to pre-Oedipal development (and because of his sexism), he took this meaning and valuation as a self-evident given, rather than a developmental and cultural product.

We must remember that this transformed interpretation of difference, an interpretation learned in the Oedipal transition, is produced by means of male cultural hegemony and power. Men have the means to institutionalize their unconscious defenses against repressed yet strongly experienced developmental conflicts. This interpretation of difference is imposed on earlier developmental processes; it is not the deepest, unconscious root of either the female or the male sense of gendered self. In fact, the primary sense of gendered self that emerges in earliest development constantly challenges and threatens men, and gives a certain potential psychological security, even liberation, to women. The transformed interpretation of difference is not inevitable, given other parenting arrangements and other arrangements of power between the sexes. It is especially insofar as women's lives and self-definition become oriented to men that difference becomes more salient for us, as does differential evaluation of the sexes. Insofar as women's lives and self-definition become more oriented toward themselves, differences from men become less salient.

What are the implications of this inquiry into psychoanalytic understandings of differentiation and gender difference for our understanding of difference, and for our evaluation of the view that difference is central to feminist theory? My investigation suggests that our own sense of differentiation, of separateness from others, as well as our psychological and cultural experience and interpretation of gender or sexual difference, are created through psychological, social, and cultural processes, and through relational experiences. We can only understand gender difference, and human distinctness and separation, relationally and situationally. They are part of a system of asymmetrical social relationships embedded in inequalities of power, in which we grow up as selves, and as women and men. Our experience and perception of gender are processual; they are produced developmentally and in our daily social and cultural lives.

Difference is psychologically salient for men in a way that it is not for women, because of gender differences in early formative developmental processes and the particular unconscious conflicts and defenses these produce. This salience, in turn, has been transmuted into a conscious cultural preoccupation with gender difference. It has also become intertwined with and has helped to produce more general cultural notions, particularly, that individualism, separateness, and distance from others are desirable and requisite to autonomy and human fulfillment. Throughout these processes, it is women, as mothers, who become the objects apart from which separateness, difference, and autonomy are defined.

It is crucial for us as feminists to recognize that the ideologies of difference which define us as women and as men, as well as inequality itself, are produced, socially, psychologically, and culturally, by people living in and creating their social, psychological, and cultural worlds. Women participate in the creation of these worlds and ideologies, even if our ultimate power and access to cultural hegemony are less than those of men. To speak of difference as a final, irreducible concept and to focus on gender differences as central is to reify them and to deny the reality of those processes which create the meaning and significance of gender. To see men and women as qualitatively different kinds of people, rather than seeing gender as processual, reflexive, and constructed, is to reify and deny relations of gender, to see gender differences as permanent rather than as created and situated.

We certainly need to understand how difference comes to be important, how it is produced as salient, and how it reproduces sexual inequality. But we should not appropriate differentiation and separation, or difference, for ourselves and take it as a given. Feminist theories and feminist inquiry based on the notion of essential difference, or focused on demonstrating difference, are doing feminism a disservice. They ultimately rely on the defensively constructed masculine models of gender that are presented to us as our cultural heritage, rather than creating feminist understandings of gender and difference that grow from our own politics, theorizing, and experience.

RICHARD RORTY

"Science as Solidarity" (1986)

After a distinguished career as an analytic philosopher of the sort often accused of speaking only to a coterie of professional colleagues, Richard Rorty (1931–2007) became, in the 1980s, a cultural critic and public intellectual. In *Philosophy and the Mirror of Nature* (Princeton, 1979), Rorty complained that philosophers' traditional epistemological preoccupations had proved to be dead ends. It was time to admit that the long-sought "foundation" for knowledge simply did not exist. Philosophers should acknowledge that all discourses, including those of the natural sciences, were culture bound, and they should use their intellect and learning to help people understand one another and to build sustaining communities. In later books and articles, including "Science as Solidarity" (1986), which follows, Rorty developed both his ideal of "social solidarity" and his "antifoundational" perspective on scientific knowledge. In this essay, Rorty drew some conclusions from the work of Thomas Kuhn that were more radical than Kuhn and most of Kuhn's followers were willing to accept. Rorty's most popular and accessible work, *Contingency, Irony and Solidarity* (New York, 1988), also addressed literary and political issues. His *Achieving Our Country* (Cambridge, Mass., 1998) offers an interpretation of the history of the political left in the United States in the twentieth century.

Although Rorty became the most widely appreciated American philosopher since Dewey, his ideas were often, and even vociferously, contested, especially by the philosophers whose work Rorty believed was a waste of time. An important collection of essays interpreting Rorty in relation to the intellectual history of the United States is John Pettigrew, ed., *A Pragmatist's Progress?* (New York, 2000). For the arguments between Rorty and other philosophers, see Robert Brandom, ed., *Rorty and His Critics* (Cambridge, Mass., 2000). Rorty was the son of James Rorty, a political journalist of the 1930s and 1940s, and was the grandson of the chief leader of the American "social gospel," Walter Rauschenbusch. A detailed study of his life to about 1980 is Neil Gross, *Richard Rorty: The Making of an American Philosopher* (Chicago, 2008).

In our culture, the notions of "science," "rationality," "objectivity," and "truth" are bound up with one another. Science is thought of as offering "hard," "objective" truth: truth as correspondence to reality, the only sort of truth worthy of the name. Humanists like philosophers, theologians, historians, and literary critics have to worry about whether they are being "scientific"—whether they are entitled to think of their conclusions, no matter how carefully argued, as worthy of the term "true." We tend to identify seeking "objective truth" with "using reason," and so we think of the natural sciences as paradigms of rationality. We also think of rationality as a matter of following procedures laid down in advance, of being "methodical." So we tend to use "methodical," "rational," "scientific," and "objective" as synonyms.

Worries about "cognitive status" and "objectivity" are characteristic of a secularized culture in which the scientist replaces the priest. The scientist is now seen as the person who keeps humanity in touch with something beyond itself. As the universe was depersonalized, beauty (and, in time, even moral goodness) came to be thought of as "subjective." So truth is now thought of as the only point at which human beings are responsible to something nonhuman. A commitment to "rationality" and to "method" is thought to be a recognition of this responsibility. The scientist becomes a moral exemplar, one who selflessly exposes himself again and again to the hardness of fact.

One result of this way of thinking is that any academic discipline which wants a place at the trough, but is unable to offer the predictions and the technology provided by the natural sciences, must either pretend to imitate science or find some way of obtaining "cognitive status" without the necessity of discovering facts. Practitioners of these disciplines must either affiliate themselves with this quasi-priestly order by using terms like "behavioral sciences" or else find something other than "fact" to be concerned with. People in the humanities typically choose the latter strategy. They either describe themselves as concerned with "value" as opposed to facts, or as developing and inculcating habits of "critical reflection."

Neither sort of rhetoric is very satisfactory. No matter how much humanists talk about "objective values," the phrase always sounds vaguely confused. It gives with one hand what it takes back with the other. The distinction between the objective and the subjective was designed to parallel that between fact and value, so an objective value sounds as vaguely mythological as a winged horse. Talk about the humanists' special skill at critical reflection fares no better. Nobody really believes that philosophers or literary critics are better at critical thinking, or at taking big broad views of things, than theoretical physicists or microbiologists. So society tends to ignore both these kinds of rhetoric. It treats humanities as on a par with the arts, and thinks of both as providing pleasure rather than truth. Both are, to be sure, thought of as providing "high" rather than "low" pleasures. But an elevated and spiritual sort of pleasure is still a long way from the grasp of a truth.

These distinctions between hard facts and soft values, truth and pleasure, and objectivity and subjectivity are awkward and clumsy instruments. They are not suited to dividing up culture; they create more difficulties than they resolve. It would be best to find another vocabulary, to start afresh. But in order to do so, we first have to find a new way of describing the natural sciences. It is not a question of debunking or downgrading

Source: John Nelson, Allan Megill, and Donald McCloskey, eds., The Rhetoric of the Human Sciences (Madison, Wis.: University of Wisconsin Press, 1986), 38–52. Reprinted by permission of the University of Wisconsin Press. Copyright © 1987.

the natural scientist, but simply of ceasing to see him as a priest. We need to stop think-ing of science as the place where the human mind confronts the world, and of the sci-entist as exhibiting proper humility in the face of superhuman forces. We need a way of explaining why scientists are, and deserve to be, moral exemplars which does not depend on a distinction between objective fact and something softer, squishier, and more dubious.

To get such a way of thinking, we can start by distinguishing two senses of the term "rationality." In one sense, the one I have already discussed, to be rational is to be methodical: that is, to have criteria for success laid down in advance. We think of poets and painters as using some faculty other than "reason" in their work because, by their own confession, they are not sure of what they want to do before they have done it. They make up new standards of achievement as they go along. By contrast, we think of judges as knowing in advance what criteria a brief will have to satisfy in order to invoke a favor-able decision, and of business people as setting well-defined goals and being judged by their success in achieving them. Law and business are good examples of rationality, but the scientist, knowing in advance what would count as disconfirming his hypothesis and prepared to abandon that hypothesis as a result of the unfavorable outcome of a single experiment, seems a truly heroic example. Further, we seem to have a clear criterion for the success of a scientific theory—namely, its ability to predict, and thereby to enable us to control some portion of the world. If to be rational means to be able to lay down criteria in advance, then it is plausible to take natural science as the paradigm of rationality.

The trouble is that in this sense of "rational" the humanities are never going to qual-ify as rational activities. If the humanities are concerned with ends rather than means, then there is no way to evaluate their success in terms of antecedently specified criteria. If we already knew what criteria we wanted to satisfy, we would not worry about whether we were pursuing the right ends. If we thought we knew the goals of culture and society in advance, we would have no use for the humanities—as totalitarian societies in fact do not. It is characteristic of democratic and pluralistic societies to continually redefine their goals. But if to be rational means to satisfy criteria, then this process of redefinition is bound to be nonrational. So if the humanities are to be reviewed as rational activities, rationality will have to be thought of as something other than the satisfaction of criteria which are statable in advance.

Another meaning for "rational" is, in fact, available. In this sense, the word means something like "sane" or "reasonable" rather than "methodical." It names a set of moral virtues: tolerance, respect for the opinions of those around one, willingness to listen, reli-ance on persuasion rather than force. These are the virtues which members of a civilized society must possess if the society is to endure. In this sense of "rational," the word means something more like "civilized" than like "methodical." When so construed, the distinc-tion between the rational and the irrational has nothing in particular to do with the dif-ference between the arts and the sciences. On this construction, to be rational is simply to discuss any topic—religious, literary, or scientific—in a way which eschews dogmatism, defensiveness, and righteous indignation.

There is no problem about whether, in this latter, weaker, sense, the humanities are "rational disciplines." Usually humanists display the moral virtues in question. Sometimes they don't, but then sometimes scientists don't either. Yet these moral virtues are felt to be not enough. Both humanists and the public hanker after rationality in the first, stronger sense of the term: a sense which is associated with objective truth, correspondence to real-ity, and method, and criteria.

We should not try to satisfy this hankering, but rather try to eradicate it. No matter what one's opinion of the secularization of culture, it was a mistake to try to make the natural scientist into a new sort of priest, a link between the human and the nonhuman. So was the idea that some sorts of truths are "objective" whereas others are merely "subjective" or "relative"—the attempt to divide up the set of true sentences into "genuine knowledge" and "mere opinion," or into the "factual" and "judgmental." So was the idea that the scientist has a special method which, if only the humanists would apply it to ultimate values, would give us the same kind of self-confidence about the moral ends as we now have about technological means. I think that we should content ourselves with the second, "weaker" conception of rationality, and avoid the first, "stronger" conception. We should avoid the idea that there is some special virtue in knowing in advance what criteria you are going to satisfy, in having standards by which to measure progress.

One can make these issues somewhat more concrete by taking up the current controversy among philosophers about the "rationality of science." For some twenty years, ever since the publication of Thomas Kuhn's book *The Structure of Scientific Revolutions,* philosophers have been debating whether science is rational. Attacks on Kuhn for being an "irrationalist" are now as frequent and as urgent as were, in the thirties and forties, attacks on the logical positivists for saying that moral judgments were "meaningless." We are constantly being warned of the danger of "relativism," which will beset us if we give up our attachment to objectivity, and to the idea of rationality as obedience to criteria.

Whereas Kuhn's enemies routinely accuse him of reducing science to "mob psychology," and pride themselves on having (by a new theory of meaning, or reference, or verisimilitude) vindicated the "rationality of science," his pragmatist friends (such as myself) routinely congratulate him on having softened the distinction between science and nonscience. It is fairly easy for Kuhn to show that the enemies are attacking a straw man. But it is harder for him to save himself from his friends. For he has said that "there is no theory-independent way to reconstruct phrases like 'really there.'" He has asked whether it really helps "to imagine that there is some one full, objective, true account of nature and that the proper measure of scientific achievement is the extent to which it brings us closer to that ultimate goal." We pragmatists quote these passages incessantly in the course of our effort to enlist Kuhn in our campaign to drop the objective-subjective distinction altogether.

What I am calling "pragmatism" might also be called "left-wing Kuhnianism." It has been also rather endearingly called (by one of its critics, Clark Glymour) the "new fuzziness," because it is an attempt to blur just those distinctions between the objective and the subjective and between fact and value which the criterial conception of rationality has developed. We fuzzies would like to substitute the idea of "unforced agreement" for that of "objectivity." We should like to put all of culture on an epistemological level—or, to put it another way, we would like to get rid of the idea of "epistemological level" or "cognitive status." We would like to disabuse social scientists and humanists of the idea that there is something called "scientific status" which is a desirable goal. In our view, "truth" is a univocal term. It applies equally to the judgments of lawyers, anthropologists, physicists, philologists, and literary critics. There is no point in assigning degrees of "objectivity" or "hardness" to such disciplines. For the presence of unforced agreement in all of them gives us everything in the way of "objective truth" which one could possibly want: namely, intersubjective agreement.

As soon as one says that objectivity is intersubjectivity, one is likely to be accused of being a relativist. That is the epithet traditionally applied to pragmatists. But this epithet is ambiguous. It can name any of three different views. The first is the silly and self-refuting view that every belief is as good as every other. The second is the wrong-headed view that "true" is an equivocal term, having as many meanings as there are contexts of justification. The third is the ethnocentric view that there is nothing to be said about either truth or rationality apart from descriptions of the familiar procedures of justification which a given society—*ours*—uses in one or another area of inquiry. The pragmatist does hold this third, ethnocentric, view. But he does not hold the first or the second.

But "relativism" is not an appropriate term to describe this sort of ethnocentrism. For we pragmatists are not holding a positive theory which says that something is relative to something else. Instead, we are making the purely *negative* point that we would be better off without the traditional distinctions between knowledge and opinion, construed as the distinction between truth as correspondence to reality and truth as a commendatory term for well-justified belief. Our opponents call this negative claim "relativistic" because they cannot imagine that anybody would seriously deny that truth has an intrinsic nature. So when we say that there is nothing to be said about truth save that each of us will commend as true those beliefs which he or she finds good to believe, the realist is inclined to interpret this as one more positive theory about the nature of truth: a theory according to which truth is simply the contemporary opinion of a chosen individual or group. Such a theory would, of course, be self-refuting. But we pragmatists do not have a theory of truth, much less a relativistic one. As partisans of solidarity, our account of the value of cooperative human inquiry has only an ethical base, not an epistemological or metaphysical one.

To say that we must be ethnocentric may sound suspicious, but this will only happen if we identify ethnocentrism with pig-headed refusal to talk to representatives of other communities. In my sense of ethnocentrism, to be ethnocentric is simply to work by our own lights. The defense of ethnocentrism is simply that there are no other lights to work by. Beliefs suggested by another individual or another culture must be tested by trying to weave them together with beliefs which we already have. We *can* so test them, because everything which we can identify as a human being or as a culture will be something which shares an enormous number of beliefs with us. (If it did not, we would simply not be able to recognize that it was speaking a language, and thus that it had any beliefs at all.)

This way of thinking runs counter to the attempt, familiar since the eighteenth century, to think of political liberalism as based on a conception of the nature of man. To most thinkers of the Enlightenment, it seemed clear that the access to Nature which physical science had provided should now be followed by the establishment of social, political, and economic institutions which were "in accordance with Nature." Ever since, liberal social thought has centered on social reform as made possible by objective knowledge of what human beings are like—not knowledge of what Greeks or Frenchmen or Chinese are like, but of humanity as such. This tradition dreams of a universal human community which will exhibit a nonparochial solidarity because it is the expression of an ahistorical human nature.

Philosophers who belong to this tradition, who wish to ground solidarity in objectivity, have to construe truth as correspondence to reality. So they must construct an epistemology which had room for a kind of justification which is not merely social but natural, springing from human nature itself, and made possible by a link between that part of nature and the rest of nature. By contrast, we pragmatists, who wish to reduce objectivity to solidarity, do not require either a metaphysics or an epistemology. We do not need an account of a relation between beliefs and objects called "correspondence," nor an account of human cognitive abilities which ensures that our species is capable of entering into that relation. We see the gap between truth and justification not as something to be bridged by isolating a natural and transcultural sort of rationality which can be used to criticize certain cultures and praise others, but simply as the gap between the actual good and the possible better. From a pragmatist point of view, to say that what is rational for us now to believe may not be *true* is simply to say that somebody may come up with a better idea.

On this pragmatist view of rationality as civility, inquiry is a matter of continually reweaving a web of beliefs rather than the application of criteria to cases. Criteria change in just the way other beliefs change, and there is no touchstone which can preserve any criterion from possible revision. That is why the pragmatist is not frightened by the specter of "cultural relativism." Our interchange with other communities and cultures is not to be thought of as a clash between irreconcilable systems of thought, deductively inferred from incompatible first premises. Alternative cultures should not be thought of on the model of alternative geometries—as irreconcilable because they have axiomatic structures and contradictory axioms. Such geometries are *designed* to be irreconcilable. Individual and cultural webs of belief are not so designed, and do not have axiomatic structures.

Cultures can, indeed, protect themselves by institutionalizing knowledge-claims and making people suffer who do not hold certain beliefs. But such institutional backups take the form of bureaucrats and policemen, not of "rules of language" or "criteria of rationality." The criterial conception of rationality has suggested that every distinct culture comes equipped with certain unchallengeable axioms, "necessary truths," and that these form barriers to communication between cultures. So it has seemed as if there could be no conversation between cultures but only subjugation by force. On the pragmatic conception of rationality, there are no such barriers. The distinction between different cultures differs only in degree from the distinction between theories held by members of a single culture. The Tasmanian aborigines and the British colonies, for example, had trouble in communicating, but this trouble was different only in extent from the difficulties in communication experienced by Gladstone and Disraeli. The trouble in all such cases is just the difficulty of explaining why other people disagree with us, and of reweaving our beliefs so as to fit the fact of disagreement together with the other beliefs we hold. The same pragmatist (and, more specifically, Quinean) arguments which dispose of the positivist's distinction between analytic and synthetic truths dispose of the anthropologists' distinction between the intercultural and the intracultural.

Another reason for describing us as "relativistic" is that we pragmatists drop the idea that inquiry is destined to converge to a single point—that Truth is "out there" waiting for human beings to arrive at it. This idea seems to us an unfortunate attempt to carry a religious conception over into a culture. All that is worth preserving of the claim that rational inquiry will converge to a single point is the claim that we must be able to explain why past false views were held in the past, and thus explain how we go about reeducating our benighted ancestors. To say that we think we are heading in the right direction is just to say, with Kuhn, that we can, by hindsight, tell the story of the past as a story of progress.

But the fact that we can trace such a direction and tell such a story does not mean that we have gotten closer to a goal which is out there waiting for us. We cannot, I think, imagine a moment at which the human race could settle back and say, "Well, now that we've finally arrived at the Truth we can relax." Paul Feyerabend is right in suggesting that we should discard the metaphor of inquiry, and human activity generally, as converging rather than proliferating, becoming more unified rather than more diverse. On the contrary, we should relish the thought that the sciences as well as the arts will *always* provide a spectacle of fierce competition between alternative theories, movements, and schools. The end of human activity is not rest, but rather richer and better human activity. We should think of human progress as making it possible for human beings to do more interesting things and be more interesting people, not as heading toward a place which has somehow been prepared for us in advance. To drop the criterial conception of rationality in favor of the pragmatist conception would be to give up the idea of Truth as something to which we were responsible. Instead we should think of "true" as a word which applies to those beliefs upon which we are able to agree, as roughly synonymous with "justified." To say that beliefs can be agreed upon without being true is, once again, merely to say that somebody might come up with a better idea.

Another way of characterizing this line of thought is to say that pragmatists would like to drop the idea that human beings are responsible to a nonhuman power. We hope for a culture in which questions about the "objectivity of value" or the "rationality of science" would seem equally unintelligible. Pragmatists would like to replace the desire for objectivity—the desire to be in touch with a reality which is more than some community with which we identify ourselves—with the desire for solidarity with that community. They think that the habits of relying on persuasion rather than force, of respect for the opinions of colleagues, of curiosity and eagerness for new data and ideas, are the *only* virtues which scientists have. They do not think that there is an intellectual virtue called "rationality" over and above these moral virtues.

On this view there is no reason to praise scientists for being more "objective" or "logical" or "methodical" or "devoted to truth" than other people. But there is plenty of reason to praise the institutions they have developed and within which they work, and to use these as models for the rest of culture. For these institutions give concreteness and detail to the idea of "unforced agreement." Reference to such institutions fleshes out the idea of "a free and open encounter"—the sort of encounter in which truth cannot fail to win. On this view, to say that truth will win in such an encounter is not to make a metaphysical claim about the connection between human reason and the nature of things. It is merely to say that the best way to find out what to believe is to listen to as many suggestions and arguments as you can.

My rejection of traditional notions of rationality can be summed up by saying that the only sense in which science is exemplary is that it is a model of human solidarity. We should think of the institutions and practices which make up various scientific communities as providing suggestions about the way in which the rest of culture might organize itself. When we say that our legislatures are "unrepresentative" or "dominated by special interests," or that the art world is dominated by "fashion," we are contrasting these areas of culture with areas which seem to be in better order. The natural sciences strike us as being such areas. But, on this view, we shall not explain this better order by thinking of the scientists as having a "method" which the rest of us would do well to imitate, nor as benefiting from the desirable hardness of their subjects compared with the undesirable softness of other subjects. If we say that sociology or literary criticism "is not a science," we shall mean merely that the amount of agreement among sociologists or literary critics on what counts as significant work, work which needs following up, is less than among, say, microbiologists.

Pragmatists will not attempt to explain this latter phenomenon by saying that societies or literary texts are squishier than molecules, or that the human sciences cannot be as "value-free" as the natural sciences, or that the sociologists and critics have not yet found their paradigms. Nor will they assume that "a science" is necessarily something which we want sociology to be. One consequence of their view is the suggestion that perhaps "the human sciences" *should* look quite different from the natural sciences. This suggestion is not based on epistemological or metaphysical considerations which show that inquiry into societies must be different from inquiry into things. Instead, it is based on the observation that natural scientists are interested primarily in predicting and controlling the behavior of things, and that prediction and control may not be what we want from our sociologists and our literary critics.

Despite the encouragement he has given it, however, Kuhn draws back from this pragmatist position. He does so when he asks for an explanation of "why science works." The request for such an explanation binds him together with his opponents and separates him from his left-wing friends. Anti-Kuhnians tend to unite in support of the claim that "merely psychological or sociological reasons" will not explain why natural science is so good at predicting. Kuhn joins them when he says that he shares "Hume's itch"—the desire for "an explanation of the viability of the whole language game that involves 'induction' and underpins the form of life we live."

Pragmatists think that one will suffer from Hume's itch only if one has been scratching oneself with what has sometimes been called "Hume's fork"—the distinction between "relations of ideas" and "matters of fact." This distinction survives in contemporary philosophy as the distinction between "questions of language" and "questions of fact." We pragmatists think that philosophers of language such as Wittgenstein, Quine, Goodman, Davidson, and others have shown us how to get along without these distinctions. Once one has lived without them for a while, one learns to live without those between knowledge and opinion, or between subjective and objective, as well. The purposes served by the latter distinctions come to be served by the unproblematic sociological distinction between areas in which unforced agreement is relatively infrequent and areas in which it is relatively frequent. So we do not itch for an explanation of the success of recent Western science any more than for the success of recent Western politics. That is why we fuzzies applaud Kuhn when he says that "one does not know what a person who denies the rationality of learning from experience is trying to say," but are aghast when he goes on to ask *why* "we have no rational alternatives to learning from experience."

On the pragmatist view, the contrast between "relations of ideas" and "matters of fact" is a special case of the bad seventeenth-century contrasts between being "in us" and being "out there," between subject and object, between our beliefs and what those beliefs (moral, scientific, theological, etc.) are trying to get right. Pragmatists avoid this latter contrast by instead contrasting our beliefs with proposed alternative beliefs. They recommend that we worry only about the choice between two hypotheses, rather than about whether there is something which "makes" either true. To take this stance would rid us of questions about the objectivity of value, the rationality of science, and the causes of the viability of our language games. All such theoretical questions would be replaced with practical questions about whether we ought to keep our present values, theories, and practices or try to replace them with others. Given such a replacement, there would be nothing to be responsible to except ourselves.

This may sound like solipsistic fantasy, but the pragmatist regards it as an alternative account of the nature of intellectual and moral responsibility. He is suggesting that instead of invoking anything like the idea-fact, or language-fact, or mind-world, or subject-object distinctions to explicate our intuition that there is something out there to be responsible to, we just drop that intuition. We should drop it in favor of the thought that we might be better than we presently are—in the sense of being better scientific theorists, or citizens, or friends. The backup for this intuition would be the actual or imagined existence of other human beings who were already better (utopian fantasies, or actual experience, of superior individuals or societies). On this account, to be responsible is a matter of what Peirce called "contrite fallibilism" rather than of respect for something beyond. The desire for "objectivity" boils down to a desire to acquire beliefs which will eventually receive unforced agreement in the course of a free and open encounter with people holding other beliefs.

Pragmatists interpret the goal of inquiry (in any sphere of culture) as the attainment of an appropriate mixture of unforced agreement with tolerant disagreement (where what counts as appropriate is determined, within that sphere, by trial and error). Such a reinterpretation of our sense of responsibility would, if carried through, gradually make unintelligible the subject-object model of inquiry, the child-parent model of moral obligation, and the correspondence theory of truth. A world in which those models, and that theory, no longer had any intuitive appeal would be a pragmatist's paradise.

When Dewey urged that we try to create such a paradise, he was said to be irresponsible. For, it was said, he left us bereft of weapons to use against our enemies; he gave us nothing with which to "answer the Nazis." When we new fuzzies try to revive Dewey's repudiation of criteriology, we are said to be "relativistic." We must, people say, believe that every coherent view is as good as every other, since we have no "outside" touchstone for choice among such views. We are said to leave the general public defenseless against the witch doctor, the defender of creationism, or anyone else who is clever and patient enough to deduce a consistent and wide-ranging set of theorems from his "alternative first principles."

Nobody is convinced when we fuzzies say that we can be just as morally indignant as the next philosopher. We are suspected of being contritely fallibilist when righteous fury is called for. Even when we actually display appropriate emotions we get nowhere, for we are told that we have no *right* to these emotions. When we suggest that one of the few things we know (or need to know) about truth is that it is what wins in a free and open encounter, we are told that we have defined "true" as "satisfies the standards of our community." But we pragmatists do not hold this relativist view. We do not infer from "there is no way to step outside communities to a neutral standpoint" that "there is no rational way to justify liberal communities over totalitarian communities." For that inference involves just the notion of "rationality" as a set of ahistorical principles which pragmatists abjure. What we in fact infer is that there is no way to beat totalitarians in argument by appealing to shared common premises, and no point in pretending that a common human nature makes the totalitarians unconsciously hold such premises.

The claim that we fuzzies have no right to be furious at moral evil, no right to commend our views as true unless we simultaneously refute ourselves by claiming that there are objects out there which *make* those views true, begs all the theoretical questions. But it gets to the practical and moral heart of the matter. This is the question of whether notions like "unforced agreement" and "free and open encounter"—descriptions of social situations—can take the place in our moral lives of notions like "the world," "the will of God," "the moral law," "what our beliefs are trying to represent accurately," and "what makes our beliefs true." All the philosophical presuppositions which make Hume's fork seem inevitable are ways of suggesting that human communities must justify their existence by striving to attain a nonhuman goal. To suggest that we can forget about Hume's fork, forget about being responsible to what is "out there," is to suggest that human communities can only justify their existence by comparisons with other actual and possible human communities.

I can make this contrast a bit more concrete by asking whether free and open encounters, and the kind of community which permits and encourages such encounters, are for the sake of truth and goodness, or whether "the quest for truth and goodness" is simply the quest for that kind of community. Is the sort of community which is exemplified by groups of scientific inquirers and by democratic political institutions a means to an end, or is the formation of such communities the only goal we need? Dewey thought that it was the only goal we needed, and I think he was right. But whether he was or not, this question is the one to which the debates about Kuhn's "irrationalism" and the new fuzzies' "relativism" will eventually boil down.

Dewey was accused of blowing up the optimism and flexibility of a parochial and jejune way of life (the American) into a philosophical system. So he did, but his reply was that any philosophical system is going to be an attempt to express the ideals of *some* community's way of life. He was quite ready to admit that the virtue of his philosophy was, indeed, nothing more than the virtue of the way of life which it commended. On his view, philosophy does not justify affiliation with a community in the light of something ahistorical called "reason" or "transcultural principles." It simply expatiates on the special advantages of that community over other communities. Dewey's best argument for doing philosophy this way is also the best argument we partisans of solidarity have against partisans of objectivity: it is Nietzsche's argument that the traditional Western metaphysico-epistemological way of firming up our habits is not working anymore.

What would it be like to be less fuzzy and parochial than this? I suggest that it would be to become less genial, tolerant, open-minded, and fallibilist than we are now. In the nontrivial, pejorative, sense of "ethnocentric," the sense in which we congratulate ourselves on being less ethnocentric now than our ancestors were three hundred years ago, the way to avoid ethnocentrism is precisely to abandon the sort of thing we fuzzies are blamed for abandoning. It is to have only the most tenuous and cursory formulations of criteria for changing our beliefs, only the loosest and most flexible standards. Suppose that for the last three hundred years we had been using an explicit algorithm for determining how just a society was, and how good a physical theory was. Would we have developed either parliamentary democracy or relativity physics? Suppose that we had the sort of "weapons" against the fascists of which Dewey was said to deprive us—firm, unrevisable, moral principles which were not merely "ours" but "universal" and "objective." How could we avoid having these weapons turn in our hands and bash all the genial tolerance out of our own heads?

Imagine, to use another example, that a few years from now you open your copy of the *New York Times* and read that the philosophers, in convention assembled, have unanimously agreed that values are objective, science rational, truth a matter of correspondence to reality, and so on. Recent breakthroughs in semantics and meta-ethics, the report goes on, have caused the last remaining noncognitivists in ethics to recant. Similar breakthroughs in philosophy of science have led Kuhn formally to abjure his claim that there is no theory-independent way to reconstruct statements about what is "really there." All the new fuzzies have repudiated all their former views. By way of making amends for the intellectual confusion which the philosophical profession has recently caused, the philosophers have adopted a short, crisp, set of standards of rationality and morality. Next year the convention is expected to adopt the report of the committee charged with formulating a standard of aesthetic taste.

Surely the public reaction to this would not be "Saved!" but rather "Who on earth do these philosophers think they *are*?" It is one of the best things about the form of intellectual life we Western liberals lead that this *would* be our reaction. No matter how much we moan about the disorder and confusion of the current philosophical scene, about the treason of the clerks, we do not really want things any other way. What prevents us from relaxing and enjoying the new fuzziness is perhaps no more than cultural lag, the fact that the rhetoric of the Enlightenment praised the emerging natural sciences in a vocabulary which was left over from a less liberal and tolerant era. This rhetoric enshrined all the old philosophical oppositions between mind and world, appearance and reality, subject and object, truth and pleasure. Dewey thought that it was the continued prevalence of such oppositions which prevented us from seeing that modern science was a new and promising invention, a way of life which had not existed before and which ought to be encouraged and imitated, something which required a new rhetoric rather than justification by an old one.

Suppose that Dewey was right about this, and that eventually we learn to find the fuzziness which results from breaking down such oppositions spiritually comforting rather than morally offensive. What would the rhetoric of the culture, and in particular of the humanities, sound like? Presumably it would be more Kuhnian, in the sense that it would mention particular concrete achievements—paradigms—more, and "method" less. There would be less talk about rigor and more about originality. The image of the great scientist would not be of somebody who got it right but of somebody who made it new. The new rhetoric would draw more on the vocabulary of Romantic poetry and social-ist politics, and less on that of Greek metaphysics, religious morality, or Enlightenment scientism. A scientist would rely on a sense of solidarity with the rest of her profession, rather than a picture of herself as battling through the veils of illusion, guided by the light of reason.

If all this happened, the term "science," and thus the oppositions between the human-ities, the arts, and the sciences, might gradually fade away. Once "science" was deprived of an honorific sense, we might not need it for taxonomy. We might feel no more need for a term which groups together paleontology, physics, anthropology, and psychology than we do for one which groups together engineering, law, social work, and medicine. The people now called "scientists" would no longer think of themselves as a member of a quasi-priestly order, nor would the public think of themselves as in the care of such an order.

In this situation, "the humanities" would no longer think of themselves as such, nor would they share a common rhetoric. Each of the disciplines which now fall under that rubric would worry as little about its method or cognitive status as do mathematics, civil engineering, and sculpture. It would worry as little about its philosophical foundations. For terms which denoted disciplines would not be thought to divide "subject-matters," chunks of the world which had "interfaces" with each other. Rather, they would be thought to denote communities whose boundaries were as fluid as the interests of their members. In this heyday of the fuzzy, there would be as little reason to be self-conscious about the nature and status of one's discipline as, in the ideal democratic community, about the nature and status of one's race or sex. For one's ultimate loyalty would be to the larger community which permitted and encouraged this kind of freedom and insouciance. This community would serve no higher end than its own preservation and self-improvement, the preservation and enhancement of civilization. It would identify rationality with that effort, rather than with the desire for objectivity. So it would feel no need for a foundation more solid than reciprocal loyalty.

JOHN RAWLS

"The Idea of an Overlapping Consensus" (1987)

Although most American intellectuals of the middle decades of the twentieth century assumed that politics and ethics were subjects for philosophical analysis, the discipline of philosophy itself was then turning its attention instead toward problems of language and of the character of scientific knowledge. "The only philosophy we need," one extreme slogan of the period ran, "is philosophy of science." In this disciplinary context, the Harvard philosopher John Rawls (1921–2002) was unusual in his effort to apply the rigorous analytic techniques of modern philosophy to the question of "justice," a classical topic for political and ethical theory. After publishing a series of essays in professional journals during the 1950s and 1960s, Rawls in 1971 produced his huge book, *A Theory of Justice* (Cambridge, Mass., 1971), which succeeded not only in winning the respectful attention of legal theorists, political scientists, and academics of a variety of other disciplines, but also in restoring ethical and political philosophy to the agenda of academic philosophers.

But the specific theory of justice Rawls elaborated in this pivotal volume generated extensive controversy. In an effort to advance the cause of equal justice, regardless of the historical circumstances of individuals and groups, Rawls centered his theory on the highly abstract, imagined "original position" in which all persons were equal, and not defined by whatever property and position and other particular characteristics that came to them in actual social life. As Rawls considered the complaints of his critics, he gradually moved in a more historical direction, seeking to advance his democratic, egalitarian goals while coming to grips with the actual situations in which human beings find themselves.

Our selection, the 1987 essay "The Idea of an Overlapping Consensus," was a key step in Rawls's gradual development of a more historically grounded method for deciding what a just society would look like. Here, Rawls emphasizes the need—and indeed the capacity—that human beings have for reaching agreements on certain issues even though they are divided among themselves in a variety of respects. The lived diversity of social life, Rawls insisted, need not be an insuperable barrier to discovering fair principles and practices. This direction in Rawls's philosophy culminated in another influential book, *Political Liberalism* (New York, 1993). In that volume and in other works of the 1990s, he advanced the idea of "public reason," encouraging societies to accept common, rational principles for governing civil affairs, eschewing religious and other particularistic claims on the commonweal.

Although Rawls's ideas can be contrasted to the more radically historicist philosopher Richard Rorty, from whom a selection also appears in *The American Intellectual Tradition*, Rawls was more systematically engaged by the libertarian Robert Nozick and by the communitarians Michael Walzer and Michael Sandel. Rawls was a persistently secular thinker, but began in a liberal Protestant milieu vividly expressed in his Princeton undergraduate thesis that stimulated extensive discussion when discovered recently. For a cogent analysis of Rawls's early religious sensibility and his later secularity, see Joshua Cohen and Thomas Nagel, "John Rawls: On My Religion," *Times Literary Supplement* (March 18, 2009). The best starting point for the study of Rawls is Thomas Pogge, *John Rawls: His Life and Theory of Justice* (New York, 2007).

The aims of political philosophy depend on the society it addresses. In a constitutional democracy one of its most important aims is presenting a political conception of justice that can not only provide a shared public basis for the justification of political and social institutions but also helps ensure stability from one generation to the next. Now a basis of justification that rests on self- or group-interests alone cannot be stable; such a basis must be, I think, even when moderated by skilful constitutional design, a mere modus vivendi, dependent on a fortuitous conjunction of contingencies. What is needed is a regulative political conception of justice that can articulate and order in a principled way the political ideals and values of a democratic regime, thereby specifying the aims the constitution is to achieve and the limits it must respect. In addition, this political conception needs to be such that there is some hope of its gaining the support of an overlapping consensus, that is, a consensus in which it is affirmed by the opposing religious, philosophical and moral doctrines likely to thrive over generations in a more or less just constitutional democracy, where the criterion of justice is that political conception itself.

In the first part of my discussion (Secs I–II) I review three features of a political conception of justice and note why a conception with these features is appropriate given the historical and social conditions of a modern democratic society, and in particular, the condition I shall refer to as the fact of pluralism. The second part (Secs III–VII) takes up four illustrative—but I think misplaced—objections we are likely to have to the idea of an overlapping consensus, and to its corollary that social unity in a democracy cannot rest on a shared conception of the meaning, value and purpose of human life. This corollary does not imply, as one might think, that therefore social unity must rest solely on a convergence of self- and group-interests, or on the fortunate outcome of political bargaining. It allows for the possibility of stable social unity secured by an overlapping consensus on a reasonable political conception of justice. It is this conception of social unity for a democratic society I want to explain and defend.

By way of background, several comments. When Hobbes addressed the contentious divisions of his day between religious sects, and between the Crown, aristocracy and middle-classes, the basis of his appeal was self-interest: men's fear of death and their desire for the means of a commodious life. On this basis he sought to justify obedience to an existing effective (even if need be absolute) sovereign. Hobbes did not think this form of psychological egoism was true; but he thought it was accurate enough for his purposes. The assumption was a political one, adopted to give his views practical effect. In a society fragmented by sectarian divisions and warring interests, he saw no other common foothold for political argument.

How far Hobbes's perception of the situation was accurate we need not consider, for in our case matters are different. We are the beneficiaries of three centuries of democratic thought and developing constitutional practice; and we can presume not only some public understanding of, but also some allegiance to, democratic ideals and values as realized in existing political institutions. This opens the way to elaborate the idea of an overlapping consensus on a political conception of justice: such a consensus, as we shall see, is moral both in its object and grounds, and so is distinct from a consensus, inevitably fragile, founded solely on self- or group-interest, even when ordered by a well-framed constitution. The idea of an overlapping consensus enables us to understand how a constitutional

Source: *Oxford Journal of Legal Studies*, 7 (1987), 1–25.

regime characterized by the fact of pluralism might, despite its deep divisions, achieve stability and social unity by the public recognition of a reasonable political conception of justice.

I

The thesis of the first part of my discussion is that the historical and social conditions of a modern democratic society require us to regard a conception of justice for its political institutions in a certain way. Or rather, they require us to do so, if such a conception is to be both practicable and consistent with the limits of democratic politics. What these conditions are, and how they affect the features of a practicable conception, I note in connection with three features of a political conception of justice, two of which I now describe, leaving the third for the next section.

The first feature of a political conception of justice is that, while such a conception is, of course, a moral conception, it is a moral conception worked out for a specific kind of subject, namely, for political, social and economic institutions. In particular, it is worked out to apply to what we may call the "basic structure" of a modern constitutional democracy. (I shall use "constitutional democracy," and "democratic regime" and similar phrases interchangeably.) By this structure I mean a society's main political, social and economic institutions, and how they fit together into one unified scheme of social cooperation. The focus of a political conception of justice is the framework of basic institutions and the principles, standards and precepts that apply to them, as well as how those norms are expressed in the character and attitudes of the members of society who realize its ideals. One might suppose that this first feature is already implied by the meaning of a political conception of justice: for if a conception does not apply to the basic structure of society, it would not be a political conception at all. But I mean more than this, for I think of a political conception of justice as a conception framed in the first instance solely for the special case of the basic structure.

The second feature complements the first: a political conception is not to be understood as a general and comprehensive moral conception that applies to the political order, as if this order was only another subject, another kind of case, falling under that conception. Thus, a political conception of justice is different from many familiar moral doctrines, for these are widely understood as general and comprehensive views. Perfectionism and utilitarianism are clear examples, since the principles of perfection and utility are thought to apply to all kinds of subjects ranging from the conduct of individuals and personal relations to the organization of society as a whole, and even to the law of nations. Their content as political doctrines is specified by their application to political institutions and questions of social policy. Idealism and Marxism in their various forms are also general and comprehensive. By contrast, a political conception of justice involves, so far as possible, no prior commitment to any wider doctrine. It looks initially to the basic structure and tries to elaborate a reasonable conception for that structure alone.

Now one reason for focusing directly on a political conception for the basic structure is that, as a practical political matter, no general and comprehensive view can provide a publicly acceptable basis for a political conception of justice. The social and historical conditions of modern democratic regimes have their origins in the Wars of Religion following the Reformation and the subsequent development of the principle of toleration, and in the growth of constitutional government and of large industrial market economies. These conditions profoundly affect the requirements of a workable conception of justice: among other things, such a conception must allow for a diversity of general and comprehensive doctrines, and for the plurality of conflicting, and indeed incommensurable, conceptions of the meaning, value and purpose of human life (or what I shall call for short "conceptions of the good") affirmed by the citizens of democratic societies.

This diversity of doctrines—the fact of pluralism—is not a mere historical condition that will soon pass away; it is, I believe, a permanent feature of the public culture of modern democracies. Under the political and social conditions secured by the basic rights and liberties historically associated with these regimes, the diversity of views will persist and may increase. A public and workable agreement on a single general and comprehensive conception could be maintained only by the oppressive use of state power. Since we are concerned with securing the stability of a constitutional regime, and wish to achieve free and willing agreement on a political conception of justice that establishes at least the constitutional essentials, we must find another basis of agreement than that of a general and comprehensive doctrine. And so, as this alternative basis, we look for a political conception of justice that might be supported by an overlapping consensus.

We do not, of course, assume that an overlapping consensus is always possible, given the doctrines currently existing in any democratic society. It is often obvious that it is not, not at least until firmly held beliefs change in fundamental ways. But the point of the idea of an overlapping consensus on a political conception is to show how, despite a diversity of doctrines, convergence on a political conception of justice may be achieved and social unity sustained in long-run equilibrium, that is, over time from one generation to the next.

II

So far I have noted two features of a political conception of justice: first, that it is expressly framed to apply to the basic structure of society: and second, that it is not to be seen as derived from any general and comprehensive doctrine.

Perhaps the consequences of these features are clear. Yet it may be useful to survey them. For while no one any longer supposes that a practicable political conception for a constitutional regime can rest on a shared devotion to the Catholic or the Protestant Faith, or to any other religious view, it may still be thought that general and comprehensive philosophical and moral doctrines might serve in this role. The second feature denies this not only for Hegel's idealism and Marxism, and for teleological moral views, as I have said, but also for many forms of liberalism as well. While I believe that in fact any workable conception of political justice for a democratic regime must indeed be in an appropriate sense liberal—I come back to this question later—its liberalism will not be the liberalism of Kant or of J. S. Mill, to take two prominent examples.

Consider why: the public role of a mutually recognized political conception of justice is to specify a point of view from which all citizens can examine before one another whether or not their political institutions are just. It enables them to do this by citing what are recognized among them as valid and sufficient reasons singled out by that conception itself. Questions of political justice can be discussed on the same basis by all citizens, whatever their social position, or more particular aims and interests, or their religious, philosophical or moral views. Justification in matters of political justice is addressed to others who disagree with us, and therefore it proceeds from some consensus: from premises that we and others recognize as true, or as reasonable for the purpose of reaching a working agreement on the fundamentals of political justice. Given the fact of pluralism, and given that justification begins from some consensus, no general and comprehensive doctrine can assume the role of a publicly acceptable basis of political justice.

From this conclusion it is clear what is problematic with the liberalisms of Kant and Mill. They are both general and comprehensive moral doctrines: general in that they apply to a wide range of subjects, and comprehensive in that they include conceptions of what is of value in human life, ideals of personal virtue and character that are to inform our thought and conduct as a whole. Here I have in mind Kant's ideal of autonomy and his connecting it with the values of the Enlightenment, and Mill's ideal of individuality and his connecting it with the values of modernity. These two liberalisms both comprehend far more than the political. Their doctrines of free institutions rest in large part on ideals and values that are not generally, or perhaps even widely, shared in a democratic society. They are not a practicable public basis of a political conception of justice, and I suspect the same is true of many liberalisms besides those of Kant and Mill.

Thus we come to a third feature of a political conception of justice, namely, it is not formulated in terms of a general and comprehensive religious, philosophical or moral doctrine but rather in terms of certain fundamental intuitive ideas viewed as latent in the public political culture of a democratic society. These ideas are used to articulate and order in a principled way its basic political values. We assume that in any such society there exists a tradition of democratic thought, the content of which is at least intuitively familiar to citizens generally. Society's main institutions, together with the accepted forms of their interpretation, are seen as a fund of implicitly shared fundamental ideas and principles. We suppose that these ideas and principles can be elaborated into a political conception of justice, which we hope can gain the support of an overlapping consensus. Of course, that this can be done can be verified only by actually elaborating a political conception of justice and exhibiting the way in which it could be thus supported. It's also likely that more than one political conception may be worked up from the fund of shared political ideas; indeed, this is desirable, as these rival conceptions will then compete for citizens' allegiance and be gradually modified and deepened by the contest between them.

Here I cannot, of course, even sketch the development of a political conception. But in order to convey what is meant, I might say that the conception I have elsewhere called "justice as fairness" is a political conception of this kind. It can be seen as starting with the fundamental intuitive idea of political society as a fair system of social cooperation between citizens regarded as free and equal persons, and as born into the society in which they are assumed to lead a complete life. Citizens are further described as having certain moral powers that would enable them to take part in social cooperation. The problem of justice is then understood as that of specifying the fair terms of social cooperation between citizens so conceived. The conjecture is that by working out such ideas, which I view as implicit in the public political culture, we can in due course arrive at widely acceptable principles of political justice.

The details are not important here. What is important is that, so far as possible, these fundamental intuitive ideas are not taken for religious, philosophical or metaphysical ideas. For example, when it is said that citizens are regarded as free and equal persons, their freedom and equality are to be understood in ways congenial to the public political culture and explicable in terms of the design and requirements of its basic institutions. The conception of citizens as free and equal is, therefore, a political conception, the content of which is specified in connection with such things as the basic rights and liberties of democratic citizens. The hope is that the conception of justice to which this conception of citizens belongs will be acceptable to a wide range of comprehensive doctrines and hence supported by an overlapping consensus.

But, as I have indicated and should emphasize, success in achieving consensus requires that political philosophy try to be, so far as possible, independent and autonomous from other parts of philosophy, especially from philosophy's long-standing problems and controversies. For given the aim of consensus, to proceed otherwise would be self-defeating. But as we shall see (in Sec IV) we may not be able to do this entirely when we attempt to answer the objection that claims that aiming for consensus implies scepticism or indifference to religious, philosophical or moral truth. Nevertheless, the reason for avoiding deeper questions remains. For as I have said above, we can present a political view either by starting explicitly from within a general and comprehensive doctrine, or we can start from fundamental intuitive ideas regarded as latent in the public political culture. These two ways of proceeding are very different, and this difference is significant even though we may sometimes be forced to assert certain aspects of our own comprehensive doctrine. So while we may not be able to avoid comprehensive doctrines entirely, we do what we can to reduce relying on their more specific details, or their more disputed features. The question is: what is the least that must be asserted; and if it must be asserted, what is its least controversial form ?

Finally, connected with a political conception of justice is an essential companion conception of free public reason. This conception involves various elements. A crucial one is this: just as a political conception of justice needs certain principles of justice for the basic structure to specify its content, it also needs certain guidelines of enquiry and publicly recognized rules of assessing evidence to govern its application. Otherwise, there is no agreed way for determining whether those principles are satisfied, and for settling what they require of particular institutions, or in particular situations. Agreement on a conception of justice is worthless—not an effective agreement at all—without agreement on these further matters. And given the fact of pluralism, there is, I think, no better practicable alternative than to limit ourselves to the shared methods of, and the public knowledge available to, common sense, and the procedures and conclusions of science when these are not controversial. It is these shared methods and this common knowledge that allows us to speak of *public* reason. As I shall stress later on, the acceptance of this limit is not motivated by scepticism or indifference to the claims of comprehensive doctrines; rather, it springs from the fact of pluralism, for this fact means that in a pluralist society free public reason can be effectively established in no other way.

III

I now turn to the second part of my discussion (Secs III–VII) and take up four objections likely to be raised against the idea of social unity founded on an overlapping consensus on a political conception of justice. These objections I want to rebut, for they can prevent our accepting what I believe is the most reasonable basis of social unity available to us. I begin with perhaps the most obvious objection, namely, that an overlapping consensus is a mere modus vivendi. But first several explanatory comments.

Earlier I noted what it means to say that a conception of justice is supported by an overlapping consensus. It means that it is supported by a consensus including the opposing religious, philosophical and moral doctrines likely to thrive over generations in the society effectively regulated by that conception of justice. These opposing doctrines we assume to involve conflicting and indeed incommensurable comprehensive conceptions of the meaning, value and purpose of human life (or conceptions of the good), and there are no resources within the political view to judge those conflicting conceptions. They are equally permissible provided they respect the limits imposed by the principles of political justice. Yet despite the fact that there are opposing comprehensive conceptions affirmed in society, there is no difficulty as to how an overlapping consensus may exist. Since different premises may lead to the same conclusions, we simply suppose that the essential elements of the political conception, its principles, standards and ideals, are theorems, as it were, at which the comprehensive doctrines in the consensus intersect or converge.

To fix ideas I shall use a model case of an overlapping consensus to indicate what is meant; and I shall return to this example from time to time. It contains three views: one view affirms the political conception because its religious doctrine and account of faith lead to a principle of toleration and underwrite the fundamental liberties of a constitutional regime; the second view affirms the political conception on the basis of a comprehensive liberal moral doctrine such as those of Kant and Mill; while the third supports the political conception not as founded on any wider doctrine but rather as in itself sufficient to express political values that, under the reasonably favourable conditions that make a more or less just constitutional democracy possible, normally outweigh whatever other values may oppose them. Observe about this example that only the first two views—the religious doctrine and the liberalism of Kant or Mill—are general and comprehensive. The political conception of justice itself is not; although it does hold that under reasonably favourable conditions, it is normally adequate for questions of political justice. Observe also that the example assumes that the two comprehensive views agree with the judgments of the political conception in this respect.

To begin with the objection: some will think that even if an overlapping consensus should be sufficiently stable, the idea of political unity founded on an overlapping consensus must still be rejected, since it abandons the hope of political community and settles instead for a public understanding that is at bottom a mere modus vivendi. To this objection, we say that the hope of political community must indeed be abandoned, if by such a community we mean a political society united in affirming a general and comprehensive doctrine. This possibility is excluded by the fact of pluralism together with the rejection of the oppressive use of state power to overcome it. I believe there is no practicable alternative superior to the stable political unity secured by an overlapping consensus on a reasonable political conception of justice. Hence the substantive question concerns the significant features of such a consensus and how these features affect social concord and the moral quality of public life. I turn to why an overlapping consensus is not a mere modus vivendi.

A typical use of the phrase "modus vivendi" is to characterize a treaty between two states whose national aims and interests put them at odds. In negotiating a treaty each state would be wise and prudent to make sure that the agreement proposed represents an equilibrium point: that is, that the terms and conditions of the treaty are drawn up in such a way that it is public knowledge that it is not advantageous for either state to violate it. The treaty will then be adhered to because doing so is regarded by each as in its national interest, including its interest in its reputation as a state that honours treaties. But in general both states are ready to pursue their goals at the expense of the other, and should conditions change they may do so. This background highlights the way in which a treaty is a mere modus vivendi. A similar background is present when we think of social consensus founded on self- or group-interests, or on the outcome of political bargaining: social unity is only apparent as its stability is contingent on circumstances remaining such as not to upset the fortunate convergence of interests.

Now, that an overlapping consensus is quite different from a modus vivendi is clear from our model case. In that example, note two aspects: first, the object of consensus, the political conception of justice, is itself a moral conception. And second, it is affirmed on moral grounds, that is, it includes conceptions of society and of citizens as persons, as well as principles of justice, and an account of the cooperative virtues through which those principles are embodied in human character and expressed in public life. An overlapping consensus, therefore, is not merely a consensus on accepting certain authorities, or on complying with certain institutional arrangements, founded on a convergence of self- or group-interests. All three views in the example affirm the political conception: as I have said, each recognizes its concepts, principles and virtues as the shared content at which their several views coincide. The fact that those who affirm the political conception start from within their own comprehensive view, and hence begin from different premises and grounds, does not make their affirmation any less religious, philosophical or moral, as the case may be.

The preceding two aspects (moral object and moral grounds) of an overlapping consensus connect with a third aspect, that of stability: that is, those who affirm the various views supporting the political conception will not withdraw their support of it should the relative strength of their view in society increase and eventually become dominant. So long as the three views are affirmed and not revised, the political conception will still be supported regardless of shifts in the distribution of political power. We might say: each view supports the political conception for its own sake, or on its own merits; and the test for this is whether the consensus is stable with respect to changes in the distribution of power among views. This feature of stability highlights a basic contrast between an overlapping consensus and a modus vivendi, the stability of which does depend on happenstance and a balance of relative forces.

This becomes clear once we change our example and include the views of Catholics and Protestants in the sixteenth century. We no longer have an overlapping consensus on the principle of toleration. At that time both faiths held that it was the duty of the ruler to uphold the true religion and to repress the spread of heresy and false doctrine. In this case the acceptance of the principle of toleration would indeed be a mere modus vivendi, because if either faith becomes dominant, the principle of toleration will no longer be followed. Stability with respect to the distribution of power no longer holds. So long as views held by Catholics and Protestants in the sixteenth century are very much in the minority, and are likely to remain so, they do not significantly affect the moral quality of public life and the basis of social concord. For the vast majority in society are confident that the distribution of power will range over and be widely shared by views in the consensus that affirm the political conception of justice for its own sake. But should this situation change, the moral quality of political life will also change in ways I assume to be obvious and to require no comment.

The preceding remarks prompt us to ask which familiar conceptions of justice can belong to a consensus stable with respect to the distribution of power. It seems that while some teleological conceptions can so belong, others quite possibly cannot, for example, utilitarianism. Or at least this seems to be the case unless certain assumptions are made limiting the content of citizens' desires, preferences, or interests. Otherwise there appears to be no assurance that restricting or suppressing the basic liberties of some may not be the best way to maximize the total (or average) social welfare. Since utilitarianism in its various forms is a historically prominent and continuing part of the tradition of democratic thought, we may hope there are ways of construing or revising utilitarian doctrine so that it can support a conception of justice appropriate for a constitutional regime, even if it can do so only indirectly as a means to the greatest welfare. Insofar as utilitarianism is likely to persist in a well-ordered society, the overlapping consensus is in that case all the more stable and secure.

IV

I turn to the second objection to the idea of an overlapping consensus on a political conception of justice: namely, that the avoidance of general and comprehensive doctrines implies indifference or scepticism as to whether a political conception of justice is true. This avoidance may appear to suggest that such a conception might be the most reasonable one for us even when it is known not to be true, as if truth were simply beside the point. In reply, it would be fatal to the point of a political conception to see it as sceptical about, or indifferent to, truth, much less as in conflict with it. Such scepticism or indifference would put political philosophy in conflict with numerous comprehensive doctrines, and thus defeat from the outset its aim of achieving an overlapping consensus. In following the method of avoidance, as we may call it, we try, so far as we can, neither to assert nor to deny any religious, philosophical or moral views, or their associated philosophical accounts of truth and the status of values. Since we assume each citizen to affirm some such view or other, we hope to make it possible for all to accept the political conception as true, or as reasonable, from the standpoint of their own comprehensive view, whatever it may be.

Properly understood, then, a political conception of justice need be no more indifferent, say, to truth in morals than the principle of toleration, suitably understood, need be indifferent to truth in religion. We simply apply the principle of toleration to philosophy itself. In this way we hope to avoid philosophy's long-standing controversies, among them controversies about the nature of truth and the status of values as expressed by realism and subjectivism. Since we seek an agreed basis of public justification in matters of justice, and since no political agreement on those disputed questions can reasonably be expected, we turn instead to the fundamental intuitive ideas we seem to share through the public political culture. We try to develop from these ideas a political conception of justice congruent with our considered convictions on due reflection. Just as with religion, citizens situated in thought and belief within their comprehensive doctrines, regard the political conception of justice as true, or as reasonable, whatever the case may be.

Some may not be satisfied with this: they may reply that, despite these protests, a political conception of justice must express indifference or scepticism. Otherwise it could not lay aside fundamental religious, philosophical and moral questions because they are politically difficult to settle, or may prove intractable. Certain truths, it may be said, concern things so important that differences about them have to be fought out, even should this mean civil war. To this we say first, that questions are not removed from the political agenda, so to speak, solely because they are a source of conflict. Rather, we appeal to a political conception of justice to distinguish between those questions that can be reasonably removed from the political agenda and those that cannot, all the while aiming for an overlapping consensus. Some questions still on the agenda will be controversial, at least to some degree; this is normal with political issues.

To illustrate: from within a political conception of justice let's suppose we can account both for equal liberty of conscience, which takes the truths of religion off the political agenda, and the equal political and civil liberties, which by ruling out serfdom and slavery takes the possibility of those institutions off the agenda. But controversial issues inevitably remain: for example, how more exactly to draw the boundaries of the basic liberties when they conflict (where to set "the wall between church and state"); how to interpret the requirements of distributive justice even when there is considerable agreement on general principles for the basic structure; and finally, questions of policy such as the use of nuclear weapons. These cannot be removed from politics. But by avoiding comprehensive doctrines we try to bypass religion and philosophy's profoundest controversies so as to have some hope of uncovering a basis of a stable overlapping consensus.

Nevertheless in affirming a political conception of justice we may eventually have to assert at least certain aspects of our own comprehensive (by no means necessarily fully comprehensive) religious or philosophical doctrine. This happens whenever someone insists, for example, that certain questions are so fundamental, that to ensure their being rightly settled justifies civil strife. The religious salvation of those holding a particular religion, or indeed the salvation of a whole people, may be said to depend on it. At this point we may have no alternative but to deny this, and to assert the kind of thing we had hoped to avoid. But the aspects of our view that we assert should not go beyond what is necessary for the political aim of consensus. Thus, for example, we may assert in some form the doctrine of free religious faith that supports equal liberty of conscience; and given the existence of a just constitutional regime, we deny that the concern for salvation requires anything incompatible with that liberty. We do not state more of our comprehensive view than we think would advance the quest for consensus.

The reason for this restraint is to respect, as best we can, the limits of free public reason (mentioned earlier at the end of Sec II). Let's suppose that by respecting these limits we succeed in reaching an overlapping consensus on a conception of political justice. Some might say that reaching this reflective agreement is itself sufficient grounds for regarding that conception as true, or at any rate highly probable. But we refrain from this further step: it is unnecessary and may interfere with the practical aim of finding an agreed public basis of justification. The idea of an overlapping consensus leaves this step to be taken by citizens individually in accordance with their own general and comprehensive views.

In doing this a political conception of justice completes and extends the movement of thought that began three centuries ago with the gradual acceptance of the principle of toleration and led to the non-confessional state and equal liberty of conscience. This extension is required for an agreement on a political conception of justice given the historical and social circumstances of a democratic society. In this way the full autonomy of democratic citizens connects with a conception of political philosophy as itself autonomous and independent of general and comprehensive doctrines. In applying the principles of toleration to philosophy itself it is left to citizens individually to resolve for themselves the questions of religion, philosophy and morals in accordance with the views they freely affirm.

V

A third objection is the following: even if we grant that an overlapping consensus is not a modus vivendi, it may be said that a workable political conception must be general and comprehensive. Without such a doctrine on hand, there is no way to order the many conflicts of justice that arise in public life. The idea is that the deeper the conceptual and philosophical bases of those conflicts, the more general and comprehensive the level of

philosophical reflection must be if their roots are to be laid bare and an appropriate ordering found. It is useless, the objection concludes, to try to work out a political conception of
justice expressly for the basic structure apart from any comprehensive doctrine. And as we
have just seen, we may be forced to refer, at least in some way, to such a view.

This objection is perfectly natural: we are indeed tempted to ask how else could these
conflicting claims be adjudicated. Yet part of the answer is found in the third view in our
model case: namely, a political conception of justice regarded not as a consequence of a
comprehensive doctrine but as in itself sufficient to express values that normally outweigh
whatever other values oppose them, at least under the reasonably favourable conditions
that make a constitutional democracy possible. Here the criterion of a just regime is specified by that political conception; and the values in question are seen from its principles
and standards, and from its account of the cooperative virtues of political justice, and
the like. Those who hold this conception have, of course, other views as well, views that
specify values and virtues belonging to other parts of life; they differ from citizens holding the two other views in our example of an overlapping consensus in having no fully
(as opposed to partially) comprehensive doctrine within which they see all values and
virtues as being ordered. They don't say such a doctrine is impossible, but rather practically speaking unnecessary. Their conviction is that, within the scope allowed by the basic
liberties and the other provisions of a just constitution, all citizens can pursue their way
of life on fair terms and properly respect its (non-public) values. So long as those constitutional guarantees are secure, they think no conflict of values is likely to arise that would
justify their opposing the political conception as a whole, or on such fundamental matters
as liberty of conscience, or equal political liberties, or basic civil rights, and the like.

Those holding this partially comprehensive view might explain it as follows. We
should not assume that there exist reasonable and generally acceptable answers for all
or even for many questions of political justice that might be asked. Rather, we must be
prepared to accept the fact that only a few such questions can be satisfactorily resolved.
Political wisdom consists in identifying those few, and among them the most urgent. That
done, we must frame the institutions of the basic structure so that intractable conflicts are
unlikely to arise; we must also accept the need for clear and simple principles, the general
form and content of which we hope can be publicly understood. A political conception is at
best but a guiding framework of deliberation and reflection which helps us reach political
agreement on at least the constitutional essentials. If it seems to have cleared our view and
made our considered convictions more coherent; if it has narrowed the gap between the
conscientious convictions of those who accept the basic ideas of a constitutional regime,
then it has served its practical political purpose. And this remains true even though we
can't fully explain our agreement: we know only that citizens who affirm the political
conception, and who have been raised in and are familiar with the fundamental ideas
of the public political culture, find that, when they adopt its framework of deliberation,
their judgments converge sufficiently so that political cooperation on the basis of mutual
respect can be maintained. They view the political conception as itself normally sufficient
and may not expect, or think they need, greater political understanding than that.

But here we are bound to ask: how can a political conception of justice express values
that, under the reasonably favourable conditions that make democracy possible, normally
outweigh whatever other values conflict with them? One way is this. As I have said, the
most reasonable political conception of justice for a democratic regime will be, broadly
speaking, liberal. But this means, as I will explain in the next section, that it protects
the familiar basic rights and assigns them a special priority; it also includes measures to

ensure that all persons in society have sufficient material means to make effective use of those basic rights. Faced with the fact of pluralism, a liberal view removes from the political agenda the most divisive issues, pervasive uncertainty and serious contention about which must undermine the bases of social cooperation.

The virtues of political cooperation that make a constitutional regime possible are, then, *very great* virtues. I mean, for example, the virtues of tolerance and being ready to meet others halfway, and the virtue of reasonableness and the sense of fairness. When these virtues (together with the modes of thought and sentiments they involve) are widespread in society and sustain its political conception of justice, they constitute a very great public good, part of society's political capital. Thus, the values that conflict with the political conception of justice and its sustaining virtues may be normally outweighed because they come into conflict with the very conditions that make fair social cooperation possible on a footing of mutual respect.

Moreover, conflicts with political values are much reduced when the political conception is supported by an overlapping consensus, the more so the more inclusive the consensus. For in this case the political conception is not viewed as incompatible with basic religious, philosophical and moral values. We avoid having to consider the claims of the political conception of justice against those of this or that comprehensive view; nor need we say that political values are intrinsically more important than other values and that's why the latter are overridden. Indeed, saying that is the kind of thing we hope to avoid, and achieving an overlapping consensus enables us to avoid it.

To conclude: given the fact of pluralism, what does the work of reconciliation by free public reason, and thus enables us to avoid reliance on general and comprehensive doctrines, is two things: first, identifying the fundamental role of political values in expressing the terms of fair social cooperation consistent with mutual respect between citizens regarded as free and equal; and second, uncovering a sufficiently inclusive concordant fit among political and other values as displayed in an overlapping consensus.

VI

The last difficulty I shall consider is that the idea of an overlapping consensus is Utopian; that is, there are not sufficient political, social, or psychological forces either to bring about an overlapping consensus (when one does not exist), or to render one stable (should one exist). Here I can only touch on this intricate question and I merely outline one way in which such a consensus might come about and its stability made secure. For this purpose I use the idea of a liberal conception of political justice, the content of which I stipulate to have three main elements (noted previously): first, a specification of certain basic rights, liberties and opportunities (of the kind familiar from constitutional democratic regimes); second, an assignment of a special priority to those rights, liberties and opportunities, especially with respect to the claims of the general good and of perfectionist values; and third, measures assuring to all citizens adequate all-purpose means to make effective use of their basic liberties and opportunities.

Now let's suppose that at a certain time, as a result of various historical events and contingencies, the principles of a liberal conception have come to be accepted as a mere modus vivendi, and that existing political institutions meet their requirements. This acceptance has come about, we may assume, in much the same way as the acceptance of the principle of toleration as a modus vivendi came about following the Reformation: at first reluctantly, but nevertheless as providing the only alternative to endless and destructive civil strife. Our question, then, is this: how might it happen that over generations the initial acquiescence in a liberal conception of justice as a modus vivendi develops into a stable and enduring overlapping consensus? In this connection I think a certain looseness in our comprehensive views, as well as their not being fully comprehensive, may be particularly significant. To see this, let's return to our model case.

One way in which that example is atypical is that two of the three doctrines were described as fully general and comprehensive, a religious doctrine of free faith and the comprehensive liberalism of Kant or Mill. In these cases the acceptance of the political conception was said to be derived from and to depend solely on the comprehensive doctrine. But how far in practice does the allegiance to a political conception actually depend on its derivation from a comprehensive view? There are several possibilities. For simplicity distinguish three cases: the political conception is derived from the comprehensive doctrine; it is not derived from but is compatible with that doctrine; and last, the political conception is incompatible with it. In everyday life we have not usually decided, or even thought much about, which of these cases hold. To decide among them would raise highly complicated issues; and it is not clear that we need to decide among them. Most people's religious, philosophical and moral doctrines are not seen by them as fully general and comprehensive, and these aspects admit of variations of degree. There is lots of slippage, so to speak, many ways for the political conception to cohere loosely with those (partially) comprehensive views, and many ways within the limits of a political conception of justice to allow for the pursuit of different (partially) comprehensive doctrines. This suggests that many if not most citizens come to affirm their common political conception without seeing any particular connection, one way or the other, between it and their other views. Hence it is possible for them first to affirm the political conception and to appreciate the public good it accomplishes in a democratic society. Should an incompatibility later be recognized between the political conception and their wider doctrines, then they might very well adjust or revise these doctrines rather than reject the political conception.

At this point we ask: in virtue of what political values might a liberal conception of justice gain an allegiance to itself? An allegiance to institutions and to the conception that regulates them may, of course, be based in part on long-term self- and group-interests, custom and traditional attitudes, or simply on the desire to conform to what is expected and normally done. Widespread allegiance may also be encouraged by institutions securing for all citizens the political values included under what Hart calls the minimum content of natural law. But here we are concerned with the further bases of allegiance generated by a liberal conception of justice.

Now when a liberal conception effectively regulates basic political institutions, it meets three essential requirements of a stable constitutional regime. First, given the fact of pluralism—the fact that necessitates a liberal regime as a modus vivendi in the first place—a liberal conception meets the urgent political requirement to fix, once and for all, the content of basic rights and liberties, and to assign them special priority. Doing this takes those guarantees off the political agenda and puts them beyond the calculus of social interests, thereby establishing clearly and firmly the terms of social cooperation on a footing of mutual respect. To regard that calculus as relevant in these matters leaves the status and content of those rights and liberties still unsettled; it subjects them to the shifting circumstances of time and place, and by greatly raising the stakes of political controversy, dangerously increases the insecurity and hostility of public life. Thus, the unwillingness to take these matters off the agenda perpetuates the deep divisions latent in society; it betrays a readiness to revive those antagonisms in the hope of gaining a more favourable position should later circumstances prove propitious. So, by contrast, securing the basic liberties and recognizing their priority achieves the work of reconciliation and seals mutual acceptance on a footing of equality.

The second requirement is connected with a liberal conception's idea of free public reason. It is highly desirable that the form of reasoning a conception specifies should be, and can publicly be seen to be, correct and reasonably reliable in its own terms. A liberal conception tries to meet these desiderata in several ways. As we have seen, in working out a political conception of justice it starts from fundamental intuitive ideas latent in the shared public culture; it detaches political values from any particular comprehensive and sectarian (non-public) doctrine; and it tries to limit that conception's scope to matters of political justice (the basic structure and its social policies). Further, (as we saw in Sec II) it recognizes that an agreement on a political conception of justice is to no effect without a companion agreement on guidelines of public enquiry and rules for assessing evidence. Given the fact of pluralism, these guidelines and rules must be specified by reference to the forms of reasoning available to common sense, and by the procedures and conclusions of science when not controversial. The role of these shared methods and this common knowledge in applying the political conception makes reason *public,* the protection given to freedom of speech and thought makes it *free.* The claims of religion and philosophy (as previously emphasized) are not excluded out of scepticism or indifference, but as a condition of establishing a shared basis for free public reason.

A liberal conception's idea of public reason also has a certain simplicity. To illustrate: even if general and comprehensive teleological conceptions were acceptable as political conceptions of justice, the form of public reasoning they specify would be politically unworkable. For if the elaborate theoretical calculations involved in applying their principles are publicly admitted in questions of political justice (consider, for example, what is involved in applying the principle of utility to the basic structure), the highly speculative nature and enormous complexity of these calculations are bound to make citizens with conflicting interests highly suspicious of one another's arguments. The information they presuppose is very hard if not impossible to obtain, and often there are insuperable problems in reaching an objective and agreed assessment. Moreover, even though we think our arguments sincere and not self-serving when we present them, we must consider what it is reasonable to expect others to think who stand to lose when our reasoning prevails. Arguments supporting political judgments should, if possible, not only be sound but such that they can be publicly seen to be sound. The maxim that justice must not only be done, but be seen to be done, holds good not only in law but in free public reason.

The third requirement met by a liberal conception is related to the preceding ones. The basic institutions enjoined by such a conception, and its conception of free public reason—when effectively working over time—encourage the cooperative virtues of political life: the virtue of reasonableness and a sense of fairness, a spirit of compromise and a readiness to meet others halfway, all of which are connected with the willingness if not the desire to cooperate with others on political terms that everyone can publicly accept consistent with mutual respect. Political liberalism tests principles and orders institutions with an eye to their influence on the moral quality of public life, on the civic virtues and habits of mind their public recognition tends to foster, and which are needed to sustain a stable constitutional regime. This requirement is related to the preceding two in this way. When the terms of social cooperation are settled on a footing of mutual respect by fixing once and for all the basic liberties and opportunities with their priority, and when this fact itself is publicly recognized, there is a tendency for the essential cooperative virtues to develop.

And this tendency is further strengthened by successful conduct of free public reason in arriving at what are regarded as just policies and fair understandings.

The three requirements met by a liberal conception are evident in the fundamental structural features of the public world it realizes, and in its effects on citizens' political character, a character that takes the basic rights and liberties for granted and disciplines its deliberations in accordance with the guidelines of free public reason. A political conception of justice (liberal or otherwise) specifies the form of a social world—a background framework within which the life of associations, groups and individual citizens proceeds. Inside that framework a working consensus may often be secured by a convergence of self- or group-interests; but to secure stability that framework must be honoured and seen as fixed by the political conception, itself affirmed on moral grounds.

The conjecture, then, is that as citizens come to appreciate what a liberal conception does, they acquire an allegiance to it, an allegiance that becomes stronger over time. They come to think it both reasonable and wise for them to confirm their allegiance to its principles of justice as expressing values that, under the reasonably favourable conditions that make democracy possible, normally counterbalance whatever values may oppose them. With this an overlapping consensus is achieved.

VII

I have just outlined how it may happen that an initial acquiescence in a liberal conception of justice as a mere modus vivendi changes over time into a stable overlapping consensus. Thus the conclusion just reached is all we need to say in reply to the objection that the idea of such a consensus is utopian. Yet to make this conclusion more plausible, I shall indicate, necessarily only briefly, some of the main assumptions underlying the preceding account of how political allegiance is generated.

First, there are the assumptions contained in what I shall call a reasonable moral psychology, that is, a psychology of human beings as capable of being reasonable and engaging in fair social cooperation. Here I include the following: (1) besides a capacity for a conception of the good, people have a capacity to acquire conceptions of justice and fairness (which specify fair terms of cooperation) and to act as these conceptions require; (2) when they believe that institutions or social practices are just, or fair (as these conceptions specify), they are ready and willing to do their part in those arrangements provided they have reasonable assurance that others will also do their part; (3) if other persons with evident intention strive to do their part in just or fair arrangements, people tend to develop trust and confidence in them; (4) this trust and confidence becomes stronger and more complete as the success of shared cooperative arrangements is sustained over a longer time; and also (5) as the basic institutions framed to secure our fundamental interests (the basic rights and liberties) are more firmly and willingly recognized.

We may also suppose that everyone recognizes what I have called the historical and social conditions of modern democratic societies: (i) the fact of pluralism and (ii) the fact of its permanence, as well as (iii) the fact that this pluralism can be overcome only by the oppressive use of state power (which presupposes a control of the state no group possesses). These conditions constitute a common predicament. But also seen as part of this common predicament is (iv) the fact of moderate scarcity and (v) the fact of there being numerous possibilities of gains from well-organized social cooperation, if only cooperation can be established on fair terms. All these conditions and assumptions characterize the circumstances of political justice.

Now we are ready to draw on the preceding assumptions to answer once again the question: how might an overlapping consensus on a liberal conception of justice develop from its acceptance as a mere modus vivendi? Recall our assumption that the comprehensive doctrines of most people are not fully comprehensive, and how this allows scope for the development of an independent allegiance to a liberal conception once how it works is appreciated. This independent allegiance in turn leads people to act with evident intention in accordance with liberal arrangements, since they have reasonable assurance (founded on past experience) that others will also comply with them. So gradually over time, as the success of political cooperation continues, citizens come to have increasing trust and confidence in one another.

Note also that the success of liberal institutions may come as a discovery of a new social possibility: the possibility of a reasonably harmonious and stable pluralist society. Before the successful and peaceful practice of toleration in societies with liberal political institutions there was no way of knowing of that possibility. It can easily seem more natural to believe, as the centuries' long practice of intolerance appeared to confirm, that social unity and concord requires agreement on a general and comprehensive religious, philosophical or moral doctrine. Intolerance was accepted as a condition of social order and stability. The weakening of that belief helps to clear the way for liberal institutions. And if we ask how the doctrine of free faith might develop, perhaps it is connected with the fact that it is difficult, if not impossible, to believe in the damnation of those with whom we have long cooperated on fair terms with trust and confidence.

To conclude: the third view of our model case, seen as a liberal conception of justice, may encourage a mere modus vivendi to develop eventually into an overlapping consensus precisely because it is not general and comprehensive. The conception's limited scope together with the looseness of our comprehensive doctrines allows leeway for it to gain an initial allegiance to itself and thereby to shape those doctrines accordingly as conflicts arise, a process that takes place gradually over generations (assuming a reasonable moral psychology). Religions that once rejected toleration may come to accept it and to affirm a doctrine of free faith; the comprehensive liberalisms of Kant and Mill, while viewed as suitable for non-public life and as possible bases for affirming a constitutional regime, are no longer proposed as political conceptions of justice. On this account an overlapping consensus is not a happy coincidence, even if aided as it no doubt must be by historical good fortune, but is rather in part the work of society's public tradition of political thought.

VIII

I conclude by commenting briefly on what I have called political liberalism. We have seen that this view steers a course between the Hobbesian strand in liberalism—liberalism as a modus vivendi secured by a convergence of self- and group-interests as coordinated and balanced by well-designed constitutional arrangements—and a liberalism founded on a comprehensive moral doctrine such as that of Kant or Mill. By itself, the former cannot secure an enduring social unity, the latter cannot gain sufficient agreement. Political liberalism is represented in our model case of an overlapping consensus by the third view once we take the political conception in question as liberal. So understood political liberalism is the view that under the reasonably favourable conditions that make constitutional democracy possible, political institutions satisfying the principles of a liberal conception of justice realize political values and ideals that normally outweigh whatever other values oppose them.

Political liberalism must deal with two basic objections: one is the charge of scepticism and indifference, the other that it cannot gain sufficient support to assure compliance with its principles of justice. Both of these objections are answered by finding a reasonable liberal conception of justice that can be supported by an overlapping consensus. For such a consensus achieves compliance by a concordant fit between the political conception and general and comprehensive doctrines together with the public recognition of the very great value of the political virtues. But as we saw, success in finding an overlapping consensus forces political philosophy to be, so far as possible, independent of and autonomous from other parts of philosophy, especially from philosophy's long-standing problems and controversies. And this in turn gives rise to the objection that political liberalism is sceptical of religious and philosophical truth, or indifferent to their values. But if we relate the nature of a political conception to the fact of pluralism and with what is essential for a shared basis of free public reason, this objection is seen to be mistaken. We can also note (see the end of Sec IV) how political philosophy's independence and autonomy from other parts of philosophy connects with the freedom and autonomy of democratic citizenship.

Some may think that to secure stable social unity in a constitutional regime by looking for an overlapping consensus detaches political philosophy from philosophy and makes it into politics. Yes and no: the politician, we say, looks to the next election, the statesman to the next generation, and philosophy to the indefinite future. Philosophy sees the political world as an on-going system of cooperation over time, in perpetuity practically speaking. Political philosophy is related to politics because it must be concerned, as moral philosophy need not be, with practical political possibilities. This has led us to out line, for example, how it is possible for the deep divisions present in a pluralistic society to be reconciled through a political conception of justice that gradually over generations becomes the focus of an overlapping consensus. Moreover, this concern with practical possibility compels political philosophy to consider fundamental institutional questions and the assumptions of a reasonable moral psychology.

Thus political philosophy is not mere politics: in addressing the public culture it takes the longest view, looks to society's permanent historical and social conditions, and tries to mediate society's deepest conflicts. It hopes to uncover and to help to articulate, a shared basis of consensus on a political conception of justice drawing upon citizens' fundamental intuitive ideas about their society and their place in it. In exhibiting the possibility of an overlapping consensus in a society with a democratic tradition confronted by the fact of pluralism, political philosophy assumes the role Kant gave to philosophy generally: the defence of reasonable faith. In our case this becomes the defence of reasonable faith in the real possibility of a just constitutional regime.

CATHARINE MacKINNON

Selection from *Feminism Unmodified: Discourses on Life and Law* (1987)

In the explosion of feminist theory in the 1980s, one of the most provocative and influential voices was the legal academic Catharine MacKinnon (1946–). In the selection reprinted here from her book of 1987, *Feminism Unmodified* (Cambridge, Mass., 1987), MacKinnon argued that the cause of genuine equality for women was impeded by the ways in which the law—and popular thinking about gender—focused on the matter of how different women were from men, or similar to them. Directing attention away from the classic "sameness/difference" question, MacKinnon addressed hierarchies of power and the ways in which these hierarchies themselves create and reinforce the very differences between men and women that are most at issue in cases of sex discrimination. MacKinnon pointed out that most jobs are designed from the start with the assumption that the person employed will not have child care responsibilities.

MacKinnon's ideas are profitably studied in relation to other feminist theorists of the same historical moment, including Carol Gilligan, whose *In a Different Voice: Psychological Theory and Women's Development* (Cambridge, Mass., 1982) attributed to women of a different style of moral reasoning. Gilligan was one of MacKinnon's most explicit targets. Of equal importance was Judith Butler's *Gender Trouble: Feminism and the Subversion of Identity* (New York, 1990), which argued that male and female were performative rather that existential categories. Gloria Anzaldua's *Borderlands/La Frontera* (San Francisco, 1987) was a distinctive variation on feminist theory in relation to the situation of Latino women. Other leading feminist theorists of the same generation include Nancy Chodorow and Joan Scott, whose work is also included in *The American Intellectual Tradition*.

MacKinnon grew up as the daughter of a Minnesota congressman and judge. She has spent most of her career as a professor of law at the University of Michigan, and has served as a consultant to municipal, state, and federal government agencies in the fashioning of laws designed to protect women. She has produced a steady stream of essays and books and commentaries on specific legal cases. The most widely noted of MacKinnon's books are *Toward a Feminist Theory of the State* (Cambridge, Mass., 1989) and *Only Words* (Cambridge, Mass., 1993). She gained the greatest popular attention as a critic of pornography and as an advocate of the use of state power to curtail it. MacKinnon's adamant opposition to pornography was not shared by all feminists. For an example of one who thought MacKinnon's approach was needlessly "puritanical" and insufficiently respectful of free-speech rights, see Ellen Willis's *No More Nice Girls* (Middletown, Conn., 1992).

What is a gender question a question of? What is an inequality question a question of? These two questions underlie applications of the equality principle to issues of gender, but they are seldom explicitly asked. I think it speaks to the way gender has structured thought and perception that mainstream legal and moral theory tacitly gives the same answer to them both: these are questions of sameness and difference. The mainstream doctrine of the law of sex discrimination that results is, in my view, largely responsible for the fact that sex equality law has been so utterly ineffective at getting women what we need and are socially prevented from having on the basis of a condition of birth: a chance at productive lives of reasonable physical security, self-expression, individuation, and minimal respect and dignity. Here I expose the sameness/difference theory of sex equality, briefly show how it dominates sex discrimination law and policy and underlies its discontents, and propose an alternative that might do something.

According to the approach to sex equality that has dominated politics, law, and social perception, equality is an equivalence, not a distinction, and sex is a distinction. The legal mandate of equal treatment—which is both a systemic norm and a specific legal doctrine—becomes a matter of treating likes alike and unlikes unlike; and the sexes are defined as such by their mutual unlikeness. Put another way, gender is socially constructed as difference epistemologically; sex discrimination law bounds gender equality by difference doctrinally. A built-in tension exists between this concept of equality, which presupposes sameness, and this concept of sex, which presupposes difference. Sex equality thus becomes a contradiction in terms, something of an oxymoron, which may suggest why we are having such a difficult time getting it.

Upon further scrutiny, two alternate paths to equality for women emerge within this dominant approach, paths that roughly follow the lines of this tension. The leading one is: be the same as men. This path is termed gender neutrality doctrinally and the single standard philosophically. It is testimony to how substance gets itself up as form in law that this rule is considered formal equality. Because this approach mirrors the ideology of the social world, it is considered abstract, meaning transparent of substance; also for this reason it is considered not only to be *the* standard, but *a* standard at all. It is so far the leading rule that the words "equal to" are code for, equivalent to, the words "the same as"—referent for both unspecified.

To women who want equality yet find that you are different, the doctrine provides an alternate route: be different from men. This equal recognition of difference is termed the special benefit rule or special protection rule legally, the double standard philosophically. It is in rather bad odor. Like pregnancy, which always calls it up, it is something of a doctrinal embarrassment. Considered an exception to true equality and not really a rule of law at all, this is the one place where the law of sex discrimination admits it is recognizing something substantive. Together with the Bona Fide Occupational Qualification (BFOQ), the unique physical characteristic exception under ERA policy, compensatory legislation, and sex-conscious relief in particular litigation, affirmative action is thought to live here.

The philosophy underlying the difference approach is that sex *is* a difference, a division, a distinction, beneath which lies a stratum of human commonality, sameness. The moral thrust of the sameness branch of the doctrine is to make normative rules conform

Source: Catharine MacKinnon, *Feminism Unmodified: Discourses on Life and Law* (Cambridge, Mass.: Harvard University Press, 1987), 32–45.

to this empirical reality by granting women access to what men have access to: to the extent that women are no different from men, we deserve what they have. The differences branch, which is generally seen as patronizing but necessary to avoid absurdity, exists to value or compensate women for what we are or have become distinctively as women (by which is meant, unlike men) under existing conditions.

My concern is not with which of these paths to sex equality is preferable in the long run or more appropriate to any particular issue, although most discourse on sex discrimination revolves about these questions as if that were all there is. My point is logically prior: to treat issues of sex equality as issues of sameness and difference *is to take a particular approach.* I call this the difference approach because it is obsessed with the sex difference. The main theme in the fugue is "we're the same, we're the same, we're the same." The counterpoint theme (in a higher register) is "but we're different, but we're different, but we're different." Its underlying story is: on the first day, difference was; on the second day, a division was created upon it; on the third day, irrational instances of dominance arose. Division may be rational or irrational. Dominance either seems or is justified. Difference *is.*

There is a politics to this. Concealed is the substantive way in which man has become the measure of all things. Under the sameness standard, women are measured according to our correspondence with man, our equality judged by our proximity to his measure. Under the difference standard, we are measured according to our lack of correspondence with him, our womanhood judged by our distance from his measure. Gender neutrality is thus simply the male standard, and the special protection rule is simply the female standard, but do not be deceived: masculinity, or maleness, is the referent for both. Think about it like those anatomy models in medical school. A male body is the human body; all those extra things women have are studied in ob/gyn. It truly is a situation in which more is less. Approaching sex discrimination in this way—as if sex questions are difference questions and equality questions are sameness questions—provides two ways for the law to hold women to a male standard and call that sex equality.

Having been very hard on the difference answer to sex equality questions, I should say that it takes up a very important problem: how to get women access to everything we have been excluded from, while also valuing everything that women are or have been allowed to become or have developed as a consequence of our struggle either not to be excluded from most of life's pursuits or to be taken seriously under the terms that have been permitted to be our terms. It negotiates what we have managed in relation to men. Legally articulated as the need to conform normative standards to existing reality, the strongest doctrinal expression of its sameness idea would prohibit taking gender into account in any way.

Its guiding impulse is: we're as good as you. Anything you can do, we can do. Just get out of the way. I have to confess a sincere affection for this approach. It has gotten women some access to employment and education, the public pursuits, including academic, professional, and blue-collar work; the military; and more than nominal access to athletics. It has moved to change the dead ends that were all we were seen as good for and has altered what passed for women's lack of physical training, which was really serious training in passivity and enforced weakness. It makes you want to cry sometimes to know that it has had to be a mission for many women just to be permitted to do the work of this society, to have the dignity of doing jobs a lot of other people don't even want to do.

The issue of including women in the military draft has presented the sameness answer to the sex equality question in all its simple dignity and complex equivocality. As a citizen,

I should have to risk being killed just like you. The consequences of my resistance to this risk should count like yours. The undercurrent is: what's the matter, don't you want me to learn to kill ... just like you? Sometimes I see this as a dialogue between women in the afterlife. The feminist says to the soldier, "we fought for your equality." The soldier says to the feminist, "oh, no, *we* fought for *your* equality."

Feminists have this nasty habit of counting bodies and refusing not to notice their gender. As applied, the sameness standard has mostly gotten men the benefit of those few things women have historically had—for all the good they did us. Almost every sex discrimination case that has been won at the Supreme Court level has been brought by a man. Under the rule of gender neutrality, the law of custody and divorce has been transformed, giving men an equal chance at custody of children and at alimony. Men often look like better "parents" under gender-neutral rules like level of income and presence of nuclear family, because men make more money and (as they say) initiate the building of family units. In effect, they get preferred because society advantages them before they get into court, and law is prohibited from taking that preference into account because that would mean taking gender into account. The group realities that make women more in need of alimony are not permitted to matter, because only individual factors, gender-neutrally considered, may matter. So the fact that women will live their lives, as individuals, as members of the group women, with women's chances in a sex-discriminatory society, may not count, or else it is sex discrimination. The equality principle in this guise mobilizes the idea that the way to get things for women is to get them for men. Men have gotten them. Have women? We still have not got equal pay, or equal work, far less equal pay for equal work, and we are close to losing separate enclaves like women's schools through this approach.

Here is why. In reality, which this approach is not long on because it is liberal idealism talking to itself, virtually every quality that distinguishes men from women is already affirmatively compensated in this society. Men's physiology defines most sports, their needs define auto and health insurance coverage, their socially designed biographies define workplace expectations and successful career patterns, their perspectives and concerns define quality in scholarship, their experiences and obsessions define merit, their objectification of life defines art, their military service defines citizenship, their presence defines family, their inability to get along with each other—their wars and rulerships— defines history, their image defines god, and their genitals define sex. For each of their differences from women, what amounts to an affirmative action plan is in effect, otherwise known as the structure and values of American society. But whenever women are, by this standard, "different" from men and insist on not having it held against us, whenever a difference is used to keep us second class and we refuse to smile about it, equality law has a paradigm trauma and it's crisis time for the doctrine.

What this doctrine has apparently meant by sex inequality is not what happens to us. The law of sex discrimination that has resulted seems to be looking only for those ways women are kept down that have *not* wrapped themselves up as a difference—whether original, imposed, or imagined. Start with original: what to do about the fact that women actually have an ability men still lack, gestating children in utero. Pregnancy therefore is a difference. Difference doctrine says it is sex discrimination to give women what we need, because only women need it. It is not sex discrimination not to give women what we need because then only women will not get what we need. Move into imposed: what to do about the fact that most women are segregated into low-paying jobs where there are no men. Suspecting that the structure of the marketplace will be entirely subverted if comparable worth is put into effect, difference doctrine says that because there is no man to set a standard from which women's treatment is a deviation, there is no sex discrimination here, only sex difference. Never mind that there is no man to compare with because no man would do that job if he had a choice, and of course he has because he is a man, so he won't.

Now move into the so-called subtle reaches of the imposed category, the de facto area. Most jobs in fact require that the person, gender neutral, who is qualified for them will be someone who is not the primary caretaker of a preschool child. Pointing out that this raises a concern of sex in a society in which women are expected to care for the children is taken as day one of taking gender into account in the structuring of jobs. To do that would violate the rule against not noticing situated differences based on gender, so it never emerges that day one of taking gender into account was the day the job was structured with the expectation that its occupant would have no child care responsibilities. Imaginary sex differences—such as between male and female applicants to administer estates or between males aging and dying and females aging and dying—I will concede, the doctrine can handle.

I will also concede that there are many differences between women and men. I mean, can you imagine elevating one half of a population and denigrating the other half and producing a population in which everyone is the same? What the sameness standard fails to notice is that men's differences from women are equal to women's differences from men. There is an *equality* there. Yet the sexes are not socially equal. The difference approach misses the fact that hierarchy of power produces real as well as fantasized differences, differences that are also inequalities. What is missing in the difference approach is what Aristotle missed in his empiricist notion that equality means treating likes alike and unlikes unlike, and nobody has questioned it since. Why should you have to be the same as a man to get what a man gets simply because he is one? Why does maleness provide an original entitlement, not questioned on the basis of *its* gender, so that it is women—women who want to make a case of unequal treatment in a world men have made in their image (this is really the part Aristotle missed)—who have to show in effect that they are men in every relevant respect, unfortunately mistaken for women on the basis of an accident of birth?

The women that gender neutrality benefits, and there are some, show the suppositions of this approach in highest relief. They are mostly women who have been able to construct a biography that somewhat approximates the male norm, at least on paper. They are the qualified, the least of sex discrimination's victims. When they are denied a man's chance, it looks the most like sex bias. The more unequal society gets, the fewer such women are permitted to exist. Therefore, the more unequal society gets, the *less* likely the difference doctrine is to be able to do anything about it, because unequal power creates both the appearance and the reality of sex differences along the same lines as it creates its sex inequalities.

The special benefits side of the difference approach has not compensated for the differential of being second class. The special benefits rule is the only place in mainstream equality doctrine where you get to identify as a woman and not have that mean giving up all claim to equal treatment—but it comes close. Under its double standard, women who stand to inherit something when their husbands die have gotten the exclusion of a small percentage of the inheritance tax, to the tune of Justice Douglas waxing eloquent about the difficulties of all women's economic situation. If we're going to be stigmatized as different, it would be nice if the compensation would fit the disparity. Women have also gotten three more years than men get before we have to be advanced or kicked out of the military hierarchy, as compensation for being precluded from combat, the usual way to advance. Women have also gotten excluded from contact jobs in male-only prisons because we might get raped, the Court taking the viewpoint of the reasonable rapist on women's employment opportunities. We also get protected out of jobs because of our fertility. The reason is that the job has health hazards, and somebody who might be a real person some day and therefore could sue—that is, a fetus—might be hurt if women, who apparently are not real persons and therefore can't sue either for the hazard to our health or for the lost employment opportunity, are given jobs that subject our bodies to possible harm. Excluding women is always an option if equality feels in tension with the pursuit itself. They never seem to think of excluding men. Take combat. Somehow it takes the glory out of the foxhole, the buddiness out of the trenches, to imagine us out there. You get the feeling they might rather end the draft, they might even rather not fight wars at all than have to do it with us.

The double standard of these rules doesn't give women the dignity of the single standard; it also does not (as the differences standard does) suppress the gender of its referent, which is, of course, the female gender. I must also confess some affection for this standard. The work of Carol Gilligan on gender differences in moral reasoning gives it a lot of dignity, more than it has ever had, more, frankly, than I thought it ever could have. But she achieves for moral reasoning what the special protection rule achieves in law: the affirmative rather than the negative valuation of that which has accurately distinguished women from men, by making it seem as though those attributes, with their consequences, really are somehow ours, rather than what male supremacy has attributed to us for its own use. For women to affirm difference, when difference means dominance, as it does with gender, means to affirm the qualities and characteristics of powerlessness.

Women have done good things, and it is a good thing to affirm them. I think quilts are art. I think women have a history. I think we create culture. I also know that we have not only been excluded from making what has been considered art; our artifacts have been excluded from setting the standards by which art is art. Women have a history all right, but it is a history both of what was and of what was not allowed to be. So I am critical of affirming what we have been, which necessarily is what we have been permitted, as if it is women's, ours, possessive. As if equality, in spite of everything, already ineluctably exists.

I am getting hard on this and am about to get harder on it. I do not think that the way women reason morally is morality "in a different voice." I think it is morality in a higher register, in the feminine voice. Women value care because men have valued us according to the care we give them, and we could probably use some. Women think in relational terms because our existence is defined in relation to men. Further, when you are powerless, you don't just speak differently. A lot, you don't speak. Your speech is not just differently articulated, it is silenced. Eliminated, gone. You aren't just deprived of a language with which to articulate your distinctiveness, although you are; you are deprived of a life out of which articulation might come. Not being heard is not just a function of lack of recognition, not just that no one knows how to listen to you, although it is that; it is also silence of the deep kind, the silence of being prevented from having anything to say. Sometimes it is permanent. All I am saying is that the damage of sexism is real, and reifying that into differences is an insult to our possibilities.

So long as these issues are framed this way, demands for equality will always appear to be asking to have it both ways: the same when we are the same, different when we are different. But this is the way men have it: equal and different too. They have it the same as women when they are the same and want it, and different from women when they are different and want to be, which usually they do. Equal and different too would only be parity. But under male supremacy, while being told we get it both ways, both the specialness of the pedestal and an even chance at the race, the ability to be a woman and a person, too, few women get much benefit of either.

There is an alternative approach, one that threads its way through existing law and expresses, I think, the reason equality law exists in the first place. It provides a second answer, a dissident answer in law and philosophy, to both the equality question and the gender question. In this approach, an equality question is a question of the distribution of power. Gender is also a question of power, specifically of male supremacy and female subordination. The question of equality, from the standpoint of what it is going to take to get it, is at root a question of hierarchy, which—as power succeeds in constructing social perception and social reality—derivatively becomes a categorical distinction, a difference. Here, on the first day that matters, dominance was achieved, probably by force. By the second day, division along the same lines had to be relatively firmly in place. On the third day, if not sooner, differences were demarcated, together with social systems to exaggerate them in perception and in fact, *because* the systematically differential delivery of benefits and deprivations required making no mistake about who was who. Comparatively speaking, man has been resting ever since. Gender might not even code as difference, might not mean distinction epistemologically, were it not for its consequences for social power.

I call this the dominance approach, and it is the ground I have been standing on in criticizing mainstream law. The goal of this dissident approach is not to make legal categories trace and trap the way things are. It is not to make rules that fit reality. It is critical of reality. Its task is not to formulate abstract standards that will produce determinate outcomes in particular cases. Its project is more substantive, more jurisprudential than formulaic, which is why it is difficult for the mainstream discourse to dignify it as an approach to doctrine or to imagine it as a rule of law at all. It proposes to expose that which women have had little choice but to be confined to, in order to change it.

The dominance approach centers on the most sex-differential abuses of women as a gender, abuses that sex equality law in its difference garb could not confront. It is based on a reality about which little of a systematic nature was known before 1970, a reality that calls for a new conception of the problem of sex inequality. This new information includes not only the extent and intractability of sex segregation into poverty, which has been known before, but the range of issues termed violence against women, which has not been. It combines women's material desperation, through being relegated to categories of jobs that pay nil, with the massive amount of rape and attempted rape—44 percent of all women—about which virtually nothing is done, the sexual assault of children—38 percent of girls and 10 percent of boys—which is apparently endemic to the patriarchal family, the battery of women that is systematic in one quarter to one third of our homes; prostitution, women's fundamental economic condition, what we do when all else fails, and for many women in this country, all else fails often, and pornography, an industry that traffics in female flesh, making sex inequality into sex to the tune of eight billion dollars a year in profits largely to organized crime.

These experiences have been silenced out of the difference definition of sex equality largely because they happen almost exclusively to women. Understand: for this reason, they are considered *not* to raise sex equality issues. Because this treatment is done almost uniquely to women, it is implicitly treated as a difference, the sex difference, when in fact it is the socially situated subjection of women. The whole point of women's social relegation to inferiority as a gender is that for the most part these things aren't done to men. Men are not paid half of what women are paid for doing the same work on the basis of their equal difference. Everything they touch does not turn valueless because they touched it. When they are hit, a person has been assaulted. When they are sexually violated, it is not simply tolerated or found entertaining or defended as the necessary structure of the family, the price of civilization, or a constitutional right.

Does this differential describe the sex difference? Maybe so. It does describe the systematic relegation of an entire group of people to a condition of inferiority and attribute it to their nature. If this differential were biological, maybe biological intervention would have to be considered. If it were evolutionary, perhaps men would have to evolve differently. Because I think it is political, I think its politics construct the deep structure of society. Men who do not rape women have nothing wrong with their hormones. Men who are made sick by pornography and do not eroticize their revulsion are not underevolved. This social status in which we can be used and abused and trivialized and humiliated and bought and sold and passed around and patted on the head and put in place and told to smile so that we look as though we're enjoying it all is not what some of us have in mind as sex equality

This second approach—which is not abstract, which is at odds with socially imposed reality and therefore does not look like a standard according to the standard for standards—became the implicit model for racial justice applied by the courts during the sixties. It has since eroded with the erosion of judicial commitment to racial equality. It was based on the realization that the condition of Blacks in particular was not fundamentally a matter of rational or irrational differentiation on the basis of race but was fundamentally a matter of white supremacy, under which racial differences became invidious as a consequence. To consider gender in this way, observe again that men are as different from women as women are from men, but socially the sexes are not equally powerful. To be on the top of a hierarchy is certainly different from being on the bottom, but that is an obfuscatingly neutralized way of putting it, as a hierarchy is a great deal more than that. If gender were merely a question of difference, sex inequality would be a problem of mere sexism, of mistaken differentiation, of inaccurate categorization of individuals. This is what the difference approach thinks it is and is therefore sensitive to. But if gender is an inequality first, constructed as a socially relevant differentiation in order to keep that inequality in place, then sex inequality questions are questions of systematic dominance, of male supremacy, which is not at all abstract and is anything but a mistake.

If differentiation into classifications, in itself, is discrimination, as it is in difference doctrine, the use of law to change group-based social inequalities becomes problematic, even contradictory. This is because the group whose situation is to be changed must necessarily be legally identified and delineated, yet to do so is considered in fundamental tension with the guarantee against legally sanctioned inequality. If differentiation is discrimination, affirmative action, and any legal change in social inequality, is discrimination—but the existing social differentiations which constitute the inequality are not? This is only to say that, in the view that equates differentiation with discrimination, changing an unequal status quo is discrimination, but allowing it to exist is not.

Looking at the difference approach and the dominance approach from each other's point of view clarifies some otherwise confusing tensions in sex equality debates. From the point of view of the dominance approach, it becomes clear that the difference approach adopts the point of view of male supremacy on the status of the sexes. Simply by treating the status quo as "the standard," it invisibly and uncritically accepts the arrangements under male supremacy. In this sense, the difference approach is masculinist, although it can be expressed in a female voice. The dominance approach, in that it sees the inequalities of the social world from the standpoint of the subordination of women to men, is feminist.

If you look through the lens of the difference approach at the world as the dominance approach imagines it—that is, if you try to see real inequality through a lens that has difficulty seeing an inequality as an inequality if it also appears as a difference—you see demands for change in the distribution of power as demands for special protection. This is because the only tools that the difference paradigm offers to comprehend disparity equate the recognition of a gender line with an admission of lack of entitlement to equality under law. Since equality questions are primarily confronted in this approach as matters of empirical fit—that is, as matters of accurately shaping legal rules (implicitly modeled on the standard men set) to the way the world is (also implicitly modeled on the standard men set)—any existing differences must be negated to merit equal treatment. For ethnicity as well as for gender, it is basic to mainstream discrimination doctrine to preclude any true diversity among equals or true equality within diversity.

To the difference approach, it further follows that any attempt to change the way the world actually is looks like a moral question requiring a separate judgment of how things ought to be. This approach imagines asking the following disinterested question that can be answered neutrally as to groups: against the weight of empirical difference, should we treat some as the equals of others, even when they may not be entitled to it because they are not up to standard? Because this construction of the problem is part of what the dominance approach unmasks, it does not arise with the dominance approach, which therefore does not see its own foundations as moral. If sex inequalities are approached as matters of imposed status, which are in need of change if a legal mandate of equality means anything at all, the question whether women should be treated unequally means simply whether women should be treated as less. When it is exposed as a naked power question, there is no separable question of what ought to be. The only real question is what is and is not a gender question. Once no amount of difference justifies treating women as subhuman, eliminating that is what equality law is for. In this shift of paradigms, equality propositions become no longer propositions of good and evil, but of power and powerlessness, no more disinterested in their origins or neutral in their arrival at conclusions than are the problems they address.

There came a time in Black people's movement for equality in this country when slavery stopped being a question of how it could be justified and became a question of how it could be ended. Racial disparities surely existed, or racism would have been harmless, but at that point—a point not yet reached for issues of sex—no amount of group difference mattered anymore. This is the same point at which a group's characteristics, including empirical attributes, become constitutive of the fully human, rather than being defined as exceptions to or as distinct from the fully human. To one-sidedly measure one group's differences against a standard set by the other incarnates partial standards. The moment when one's particular qualities become part of the standard by which humanity is measured is a millennial moment.

To summarize the argument: seeing sex equality questions as matters of reasonable or unreasonable classification is part of the way male dominance is expressed in law. If you follow my shift in perspective from gender as difference to gender as dominance, gender changes from a distinction that is presumptively valid to a detriment that is presumptively suspect. The difference approach tries to map reality; the dominance approach tries to challenge and change it. In the dominance approach, sex discrimination stops being a question of morality and starts being a question of politics.

You can tell if sameness is your standard for equality if my critique of hierarchy looks like a request for special protection in disguise. It's not. It envisions a change that would make possible a simple equal chance for the first time. To define the reality of sex as difference and the warrant of equality as sameness is wrong on both counts. Sex, in nature, is not a bipolarity; it is a continuum. In society it is made into a bipolarity. Once this is done, to require that one be the same as those who set the standard—those which one is already socially defined as different from—simply means that sex equality is conceptually designed never to be achieved. Those who most need equal treatment will be the least similar, socially, to those whose situation sets the standard as against which one's entitlement to be equally treated is measured. Doctrinally speaking, the deepest problems of sex inequality will not find women "similarly situated" to men. Far less will practices of sex inequality require that acts be intentionally discriminatory. All that is required is that the status quo be maintained. As a strategy for maintaining social power first structure reality unequally, then require that entitlement to alter it be grounded on a lack of distinction in situation; first structure perception so that different equals inferior, then require that discrimination be activated by evil minds who *know* they are treating equals as less.

I say, give women equal power in social life. Let what we say matter, then we will discourse on questions of morality. Take your foot off our necks, then we will hear in what tongue women speak. So long as sex equality is limited by sex difference, whether you like it or don't like it, whether you value it or seek to negate it, whether you stake it out as a grounds for feminism or occupy it as the terrain of misogyny, women will be born, degraded, and die. We would settle for that equal protection of the laws under which one would be born, live, and die, in a country where protection is not a dirty word and equality is not a special privilege.

HENRY LOUIS GATES, JR.

Selection from *Loose Canons: Notes on the Culture Wars* (1990)

One of the most formidable debaters in the "culture wars" of the 1990s was Henry Louis Gates, Jr. (1950–). Reprinted here is his most pointed discussion of just how the literature produced by persons of different communities of descent does and does not constitute a distinctive ethnoracial canon. This essay of 1990, "The Master's Pieces," analyzed the challenges Gates was then facing as the coeditor of an anthology of African-American literature. Were the poems, essays, and novels written by black Americans "black literature," or just literature written by blacks? Gates addresses this question head-on, while criticizing the white intellectuals who failed to recognize the vitality of black writing in America and while criticizing, simultaneously, black colleagues who reduced the tradition of black writing to a simple, race-specific essence. Along the way, Gates offers an extended commentary on the whole notion of a "canon" and the roles that collections of received texts can play in a culture. The references to Allan Bloom refer to Bloom's best-selling attack on multiculturalist educational programs, *The Closing of the American Mind: How Higher Education Has Failed Democracy and Impoverished the Souls of Today's Students* (New York, 1987).

The project around which this essay revolves, *The Norton Anthology of African-American Literature* (New York, 1997), did appear a few years later, coedited by Gates and Nellie Y. McKay. For an earlier meditation by a leading African-American writer on some of the same issues that engaged Gates in 1990, see Ralph Ellison, "The Little Man in Chehaw Station," first published in 1977 but most easily available in Ellison's *Going to the Territory* (New York, 1986), 3–38.

Gates has been a prominent public figure as well as an academic literary critic. His television programs and frequent columns for the *New Yorker* have made him one of his generation's most visible intellectuals. He is also the author of a memoir of his West Virginia childhood in the 1950s, *Colored People* (New York, 1994).

Gates has consistently argued against two dangers he has seen displayed in the multicultural debates, one the confining of people to a narrow ethnoracial box, and the other the wholesale denial that ethnoracial identities matter at all. When serving as the Jefferson Lecturer for the National Endowment for the Humanities in 2002, Gates summed up his ideas in phrases that have been widely quoted. "I rebel at the notion that I can't be part of other groups, that I can't construct identities through elective affinity, that race must be the most important thing about me. Is that what I want on my gravestone: Here lies an African American? So I'm divided. I want to be black, to know black, to luxuriate in whatever I might be calling blackness at any particular time—but to do so in order to come out the other side, to experience a humanity that is neither colorless nor reducible to color."

Two critical overviews of the multicultural debates are Nathan Glazer, *We Are All Multiculturalists Now* (New York, 1997), and David A. Hollinger, *Postethnic America: Beyond Multiculturalism* (3rd ed., expanded, New York, 2006). For a comprehensive and policy-engaged study by a legal scholar, see Peter Schuck, *Diversity in America* (Cambridge, Mass., 2004).

As writers, teachers, or intellectuals, most of us would like to claim greater efficacy for our labors than we're entitled to. These days, literary criticism likes to think of itself as "war by other means." But it should start to wonder: Have its victories come too easily? The recent move toward politics and history in literary studies has turned the analysis of texts into a marionette theater of the political, to which we bring all the passions of our real-world commitments. And that's why it is sometimes necessary to remind ourselves of the distance from the classroom to the streets. Academic critics write essays, "readings" of literature, where the bad guys (for example, racism or patriarchy) lose, where the forces of oppression are subverted by the boundless powers of irony and allegory that no prison can contain, and we glow with hard-won triumph. We pay homage to the marginalized and demonized, and it feels almost as if we've righted a real-world injustice. I always think of the folktale about the fellow who killed seven with one blow.

Ours was the generation that took over buildings in the late sixties and demanded the creation of black and women's studies programs, and now, like the return of the repressed, has come back to challenge the traditional curriculum. And some of us are even attempting to redefine the canon by editing anthologies. Yet it sometimes seems that blacks are doing better in the college curriculum than they are in the streets.

This is not a defeatist moan. Just an acknowledgment that the relation between our critical postures and the social struggles they reflect upon is far from transparent. That doesn't mean there's no relation, of course, only that it's a highly mediated one. In any event, I do think we should be clear about when we've swatted a fly and when we've toppled a giant...

But the question I want to turn to now is this: How does the debate over canon formation affect the development of African-American literature as a subject of instruction in the American academy?

Curiously enough, the first use of the word *canon* in relation to the African-American literary tradition occurs in 1846, in a speech delivered by Theodore Parker. Parker was a theologian, a Unitarian clergyman, and a publicist for ideas, whom Perry Miller described eloquently as "the man who next only to Emerson ... was to give shape and meaning to the Transcendental movement in America." In a speech on "The Mercantile Classes" delivered in 1846, Parker laments the sad state of "American" letters:

> Literature, science, and art are mainly in [poor men's] hands, yet are controlled by the prevalent spirit of the nation...In England, the national literature favors the church, the crown, the nobility, the prevailing class. Another literature is rising, but is not yet national, *still less canonized*. We have no American literature which is permanent. Our scholarly books are only an imitation of a foreign type; they do not reflect our morals, manners, politics, or religion, not even our rivers, mountains, sky. They have not the smell of our ground in their breath.

Parker, to say the least, was not especially pleased with American letters and their identity with the English tradition. Did Parker find any evidence of a truly American literature?

> The American literature is found only in newspapers and speeches, perhaps in some novel, hot, passionate, but poor and extemporaneous. That is our national

Source: Henry Louis Gates, Jr., "The Master's Pieces: On Canon Formation and the African-American Tradition," in *Loose Canons: Notes on the Culture Wars*, 19–42. Used by permission of Oxford University Press, Inc. Copyright © 1992 by Henry Louis Gates, Jr.

literature. Does that favor man—represent man? Certainly not. All is the reflection of this most powerful class. The truths that are told are for them, and the lies. Therein the prevailing sentiment is getting into the form of thoughts.

Parker's analysis, we see plainly, turns upon an implicit reflection theory of base and super-structure. It is the occasional literature, "poor and extemporaneous," wherein "American" literature dwells, but a literature, like English literature, which reflects the interests and ideologies of the upper classes.

Three years later, in his major oration on "The American Scholar," Parker had at last found an entirely original genre of American literature:

> Yet, there is one portion of our permanent literature, if literature it may be called, which is wholly indigenous and original… [W]e have one series of lit-erary productions that could be written by none but Americans, and only here; I mean the Lives of Fugitive Slaves. But as these are not the work of the men of superior culture they hardly help to pay the scholar's debt. Yet all the original romance of Americans is in them, not in the white man's novel.

Parker was right about the originality, the peculiarly *American* quality, of the slave narra-tives. But he was wrong about their inherent inability to "pay the scholar's debt"; scholars had only to learn to *read* the narratives for their debt to be paid in full. Parker was put off by the language of the slaves' narratives. He would have done well to heed the admo-nition that Emerson had made in his 1844 speech, "Emancipation in the British West Indies": "Language," Emerson wrote, "must be raked, the secrets of slaughter-houses and infamous holes that cannot front the day, must be ransacked, to tell what negro slavery has been." The narratives, for Parker, were not instances of great literature, but they were a prime site of America's "original romance." As Charles Sumner said in 1852, the fugi-tive slaves and their narratives "are among the heroes of our age. Romance has no storms of more thrilling interest than theirs. Classical antiquity has preserved no examples of adventurous trial more worthy of renown." Parker's and Sumner's divergent views reveal that the popularity of the narratives in antebellum America most certainly did not reflect any sort of common critical agreement about their nature and status as art. Still, the impli-cations of these observations upon black canon formation would not be lost upon those who would soon seek to free the black slave, or to elevate the ex-slave, through the agency of literary production.

Johann Herder's ideas of the "living spirit of a language" were brought to bear with a vengeance upon eighteenth- and nineteenth-century considerations of the place in nature of the black. Indeed the relationship between the social and political subjectivity of the Negro and the production of art had been discussed by a host of commentators, including Hume, Hegel, and Kant, since Morgan Godwyn wondered aloud about it in 1684. But it was probably Emerson's comments that generated our earliest efforts at canon formation. As Emerson said, again in his speech on "Emancipation in the West Indies":

> If [racial groups] are rude and foolish, down they must go. When at last in a race a new principle appears, an idea—*that* conserves it; ideas only save races. If the black man is feeble and not important to the existing races, not on a parity with the best race, the black man must serve, and be exterminated. But if the black man carries in his bosom an indispensable element of a new and coming civi-lization; for the sake of that element, no wrong nor strength nor circumstance

can hurt him; he will survive and play his part... [N]ow let [the blacks] emerge, clothed and in their own form.

The forms in which they would be clothed would be registered in anthologies that established the canon of black American literature.

The first attempt to define a black canon that I have found is that by Armand Lanusse, who edited *Les Cenelles,* an anthology of black French verse published at New Orleans in 1845—the first black anthology, I believe, ever published. Lanusse's introduction is a defense of poetry as an enterprise for black people, in their larger efforts to defend the race against "the spiteful and calumnious arrows shot at us," at a target defined as the collective black intellect. Despite this stated political intention, these poems imitate the styles and themes of the French Romantics, and never engage directly the social and political experiences of black Creoles in New Orleans in the 1840s. *Les Cenelles* argues for a political effect—that is, the end of racism—by publishing apolitical poems, poems which share as silent second texts the poetry written by Frenchmen three thousand miles away. We are just like the French—so, treat us like Frenchmen, not like blacks. An apolitical art being put to uses most political.

Four years later, in 1849, William G. Allen published an anthology in which he canonized Phillis Wheatley and George Moses Horton. Like Lanusse, Allen sought to refute intellectual racism by the act of canon formation. "The African's called inferior," he wrote. "But what race has ever displayed intellect more exaltedly, or character more sublime?" Pointing to the achievements of Pushkin, Placido, and Augustine, as the great "African" tradition to which African-Americans were heir, Allen claimed Wheatley and Horton as the exemplars of this tradition, Horton being "decidedly the superior genius," no doubt because of his explicitly racial themes, a judgment quite unlike that which propelled Armand Lanusse into canon formation. As Allen put it, with the publication of their anthology:

> Who will now say that the African is incapable of attaining to intellectual or moral greatness? What he now is, degrading circumstances have made him. What he is capable of becoming, the past clearly evinces. The African is strong, tough and hardy. Hundreds of years of oppression have not subdued his spirit, and though Church and State have combined to enslave and degrade him, in spite of them all, he is increasing in strength and power, and in the respect of the entire world.

Here, then, we see the poles of black canon formation, established firmly by 1849: Is "black" poetry racial in theme, or is "black" poetry any sort of poetry written by black people? This quandary has been at play in the tradition ever since.

I won't trace in detail the history of this tension over definitions of the African-American canon, and the direct relation between the production of black poetry and the end of white racism. Suffice it to point to such seminal attempts at canon formation in the 1920s as James Weldon Johnson's *The Book of American Negro Poetry* (1922), Alain Locke's *The New Negro* (1925), and V. F. Calverton's *An Anthology of American Negro Literature* (1929), each of which defined as its goal the demonstration of the existence of the black tradition as a political defense of the racial self against racism...

Johnson's and Calverton's anthologies "frame" the [Harlem] Renaissance period, making a comparison between their ideological concerns useful. Calverton's anthology made two significant departures from Johnson's model, both of which are worth considering, if only briefly. Calverton's was the first attempt at black canon formation to provide for the influence and presence of black vernacular literature in a major way. "Spirituals," "Blues," and "Labor Songs" each comprised a genre of black literature for him. We all understand the importance of this gesture and the influence it had upon Sterling Brown, Arthur Davis, and Ulysses Lee, the editors of *The Negro Caravan* (1941). Calverton, whose real name was George Goetz, announced in his introductory essay, "The Growth of Negro Literature," that his selection principles had been determined by his sense of the history of black literary *forms,* leading him to make selections because of their formal "representative value," as he put it. These forms, he continued, were *Negro* forms, virtually self-contained in a hermetic black tradition, especially in the vernacular tradition, where artistic American originality was to be found:

> ... [I]t is no exaggeration whatsoever to contend that [the Negro's contributions to American art and literature] are more striking and singular in substance and structure than any contributions that have been made by the white man to American culture. In fact, they constitute America's chief claim to originality in its cultural history....The white man in America has continued, and in an inferior manner, a culture of European origin. He has not developed a culture that is definitely and unequivocally American. In respect of originality, then, the Negro is more important in the growth of American culture than the white man...While the white man has gone to Europe for his models, and is seeking still a European approval of his artistic endeavors, the Negro in his art forms has never sought the acclaim of any culture other than his own. This is particularly true of those forms of Negro art that come directly from the people.

And note that Calverton couched his argument in just that rhetoric of nationalism, of American exceptionalism, that had long been used to exclude, or anyway occlude, the contribution of the Negro. In an audacious reversal, it turns out that *only* the Negro is really American, the white man being a pale imitation of his European forebears.

If Calverton's stress upon the black vernacular heavily influenced the shaping of *The Negro Caravan*—certainly one of the most important anthologies in the tradition—his sense of the black canon as a formal self-contained entry most certainly did not. As the editors put it in the introduction to the volume:

> [We]...do not believe that the expression "Negro literature" is an accurate one, and...have avoided using it. "Negro literature" has no application if it means structural peculiarity, or a Negro school of writing. The Negro writes in the forms evolved in English and American literature... The editors consider Negro writers to be American writers, and literature by American Negroes to be a segment of American literature...
>
> The chief cause for objection to the term is that "Negro literature" is too easily placed by certain critics, white and Negro, in an alcove apart. The next step is a double standard of judgment, which is dangerous for the future of Negro writers. "A Negro novel," thought of as a separate form, is too often condoned as "good enough for a Negro." That Negroes in America have had a hard time, and that inside stories of Negro life often present unusual and attractive reading matter are incontrovertible facts; but when they enter literary criticism these facts do damage to both the critics and artists.

Yet immediately following this stern admonition, we're told the editors haven't been too concerned to maintain "an even level of literary excellence," because the tradition is defined by both form and content:

> Literature by Negro authors about Negro experience...must be considered as significant, not only because of a body of established masterpieces, but also because of the illumination it sheds upon a social reality.

...The black canon, for these editors, was that literature which most eloquently refuted white racist stereotypes and which embodied the shared "theme of struggle that is present in so much Negro expression." Theirs, in other words, was a canon that was unified thematically by self-defense against racist literary conventions, and by the expression of what the editors called "strokes of freedom." The formal bond that Calverton had claimed was of no academic or political use to these editors, precisely because they wished to project an integrated canon of American literature...

Form, then, or the community of structure and sensibility, was called upon to reveal the sheer arbitrariness of American "racial" classifications, and their irrelevance to American canon formation. Above all else, these editors sought to expose the essentialism at the center of racialized subdivisions of the American literary tradition. If we recall that this anthology appeared just thirteen years before *Brown v. Board,* we should not be surprised by the "integrationist" thrust of the poetics espoused here. Ideological desire and artistic premise were one. African-American literature, then, was a misnomer; "American literature" written by Negroes more aptly designated this body of writing. So much for a definition of the African-American tradition based on formal relationships of revision, text to text.

At the opposite extreme in black canon formation is the canon defined by Amiri Baraka and Larry Neal in *Black Fire,* published in 1968, an anthology so very familiar to us all. This canon, the blackest canon of all, was defined both by formal innovations and by themes: formally, individual selections tend to aspire to the vernacular or to black music, or to performance; theoretically, each selection reinforces the urge toward black liberation, toward "freedom now" with an up-against-the-wall subtext. The hero, the valorized presence in this volume, is the black vernacular: no longer summoned or invoked through familiar and comfortable rubrics such as "The Spirituals" and "The Blues," but *embodied, assumed, presupposed* in a marvelous act of formal bonding often obscured by the stridency of the political message the anthology meant to announce. Absent completely was a desire to "prove" our common humanity with white people, by demonstrating our power of intellect. One mode of essentialism—"African" essentialism—was used to critique the essentialism implicit in notions of a common or universal American heritage. No, in *Black Fire,* art and act were one.

I have been thinking about these strains in black canon formation because a group of us will be editing still another anthology, which will constitute still another attempt at canon formation: W. W. Norton will be publishing the *Norton Anthology of African-American Literature.* The editing of this anthology has been a great dream of mine for a long time. After a year of readers' reports, market surveys, and draft proposals, Norton has enthusiastically embarked upon the publishing of our anthology.

I think that I am most excited about the fact that we will have at our disposal the means to edit an anthology that will define a canon of African-American literature for instructors and students at any institution which desires to teach a course in

African-American literature. Once our anthology is published, no one will ever again be able to use the unavailability of black texts as an excuse not to teach our literature. A well-marked anthology functions in the academy to *create* a tradition, as well as to define and preserve it. A Norton anthology opens up a literary tradition as simply as opening the cover of a carefully edited and ample book.

I am not unaware of the politics and ironies of canon formation. The canon that we define will be "our" canon, one possible set of selections among several possible sets of selections. In part to be as eclectic and as democratically "representative" as possible, most other editors of black anthologies have tried to include as many authors and selections (especially excerpts) as possible, in order to preserve and "resurrect" the tradition. I call this the Sears and Roebuck approach, the "dream book" of black literature.

We have all benefited from this approach to collection. Indeed, many of our authors have managed to survive only because an enterprising editor was determined to marshal as much evidence as she or he could to show that the black literary tradition existed. While we must be deeply appreciative of that approach and its results, our task will be a different one.

Our task will be to bring together the "essential" texts of the canon, the "crucially central" authors, those whom we feel to be indispensable to an understanding of the shape, and shaping, of the tradition. A canon is often represented as the "essence" of the tradition, indeed, as the marrow of tradition: the connection between the texts of the canon is meant to reveal the tradition's inherent, or veiled, logic, its internal rationale.

None of us is naive enough to believe that "the canonical" is self-evident, absolute, or neutral. It is a commonplace of contemporary criticism to say that scholars make canons. But, just as often, writers make canons, too, both by critical revaluation and by reclamation through revision. Keenly aware of this—and, quite frankly, aware of my own biases—I have attempted to bring together a group of scholar-critics whose notions of the black canon might not necessarily agree with my own, or with each others'. I have tried to bring together a diverse array of ideological, methodological, and theoretical perspectives, so that we together might produce an anthology that most fully represents the various definitions of what it means to speak of an African-American literary tradition, and what it means to *teach* that tradition. And while we are at the earliest stages of organization, I can say that my own biases toward canon formation are to stress the formal relationships that obtain among texts in the black tradition—relations of revision, echo, call and response, antiphony, what have you—and to stress the vernacular roots of the tradition. For the vernacular, or oral literature, in our tradition, has a canon of its own.

But my pursuit of this project has required me to negotiate a position between, on the one hand, William Bennett, who claims that black people can have no canon, no masterpieces, and, on the other hand, those on the critical left who wonder why we want to establish the existence of a canon, any canon, in the first place. On the right hand, we face the outraged reactions of those custodians of Western culture who protest that the canon, that transparent decanter of Western values, may become—breathe the word—*politicized*. But the only way to answer the charge of "politics" is with an emphatic *tu quoque*. That people can maintain a straight face while they protest the irruption of politics into something that has always been political from the beginning—well, it says something about how remarkably successful official literary histories have been in presenting themselves as natural and neutral objects, untainted by worldly interests.

I agree with those conservatives who have raised the alarm about our students' ignorance of history. But part of the history we need to teach has to be the history of the idea of the "canon," which involves (though it's hardly exhausted by) the history of literary pedagogy and of the institution of the school. Once we understand how they arose, we no longer see literary canons as objets trouvés washed up on the beach of history. And we can begin to appreciate their ever-changing configuration in relation to a distinctive institutional history.

Universal education in this country was justified by the argument that schooling made good citizens, good American citizens; and when American literature started to be taught in our schools, part of the aim was to show what it was to be an American. As Richard Brodhead, a leading scholar of American literature, has observed, "no past lives without cultural mediation. The past, however worthy, does not survive by its own intrinsic power." One function of "literary history" is, then, to disguise that mediation, to conceal all connections between institutionalized interests and the literature we remember. Pay no attention to the man behind the curtain, booms the Great Oz of literary history.

Cynthia Ozick once chastised feminists by warning that *strategies become institutions.* But isn't that really another way of warning that their strategies, heaven forfend, may *succeed?* Here we approach the scruples of those on the cultural left, who worry about, well, the price of success. "Who's co-opting whom?" might be their slogan. To them, the very idea of the canon is hierarchical, patriarchal, and otherwise politically suspect. They'd like us to disavow it altogether.

But history and its institutions are not just something we study, they're also something we live, and live through. And how effective and how durable our interventions in contemporary cultural politics will be depends upon our ability to mobilize the institutions that buttress and reproduce that culture. The choice isn't between institutions and no institutions. The choice is always: What kind of institutions shall there be? Fearing that our strategies will become institutions, we could seclude ourselves from the real world and keep our hands clean, free from the taint of history. But that is to pay obeisance to the status quo, to the entrenched arsenal of sexual and racial authority, to say that they shouldn't change, become something other, and, let's hope, better than they are now.

Indeed, this is one case where we've got to borrow a leaf from the right, which is exemplarily aware of the role of education in the reproduction of values. We must engage in this sort of canon deformation precisely because Mr. Bennett is correct: the teaching of literature *is* the teaching of values; not inherently, no, but contingently, yes; it is—it has become—the teaching of an aesthetic and political order, in which no women or people of color were ever able to discover the reflection or representation of their images, or hear the resonances of their cultural voices. The return of "the" canon, the high canon of Western masterpieces, represents the return of an order in which my people were the subjugated, the voiceless, the invisible, the unrepresented, and the unrepresentable. Who would return us to that medieval never-never land?

The classic critique of our attempts to reconstitute our own subjectivity, as women, as blacks, etc., is that of Jacques Derrida: "This is the risk. The effect of Law is to build a structure of the subject, and as soon as you say, 'well, the woman is a subject and this subject deserves equal rights,' and so on—then you are caught in the logic of phallocentricism and you have rebuilt the empire of Law." To expressions such as this, made by a critic whose stands on sexism and racism have been exemplary, we must respond that the Western male subject has long been constituted historically for himself and in himself. And, while we readily accept, acknowledge, and partake of the critique of *this* subject as transcendent, to deny us the process of exploring and reclaiming our subjectivity before we critique it is the critical version of the grandfather clause, the double privileging of categories that happen to be *preconstituted.* Such a position leaves us nowhere, invisible and voiceless in the republic of Western letters. Consider the irony: precisely when we (and other Third World peoples) obtain the complex wherewithal to define our black subjectivity in the republic of Western letters, our theoretical colleagues declare that there ain't no such thing as a subject, so why should we be bothered with that? In this way, those of us in feminist criticism or African-American criticism who are engaged in the necessary work of canon deformation and reformation confront the skepticism even of those who are allies on other fronts, over this matter of the death of the subject and our own discursive subjectivity.

So far I've been talking about social identity and political agency as if they were logically connected. I think they are. And that has a lot to do with what I think the task of the critic today must be.

Simone de Beauvoir wrote that one is not born a woman; no, and one is not born a Negro; but then, as Donna Haraway has pointed out, one isn't even born an organism. Lord knows that black art has been attacked for well over a century as being "not universal," though no one ever says quite what this might mean. If this means an attack against *self-identification,* then I must confess that I am opposed to "universality." This line of argument is an echo from the political right. As Allan Bloom wrote:

> ... [T]he substantial human contact, indifferent to race, soul to soul, that prevails in all other aspects of student life simply does not usually exist between the two races. There are exceptions, perfectly integrated black students, but they are rare and in a difficult position. I do not believe this somber situation is the fault of the white students who are rather straightforward in such matters and frequently embarrassingly eager to prove their liberal credentials in the one area where Americans are especially sensitive to a history of past injustice... Thus, just at the moment when everyone else has become "a person," blacks have become blacks... "They stick together" was a phrase once used by the prejudiced, by this or that distinctive group, but it has become true by and large of the black students.

Self-identification proves a condition for agency, for social change. And to benefit from such collective agency, we need to construct ourselves, just as the nation was constructed, just as the class was, just as *all* the furniture in the social universe was. It's utopian to think we can now disavow our social identities; there's not another one to take its place. You can't opt out of a Form of Life. We can't become one of those bodiless vapor trails of sentience portrayed on that "Star Trek" episode, though often it seems as if the universalists want us to be just that. You can't opt out of history. History may be a nightmare, as Joyce suggested, but it's time to stop pinching ourselves.

But there's a treacherous non sequitur here, from "socially constructed" to essentially unreal. I suppose there's a lurking positivism in the sentiment, in which social facts are unreal compared to putatively biological ones. We go from "constructed" to "unstable," which is one non sequitur; or to "changeable by will," which is a bigger problem still, since the "will" is yet another construction.

And theory is conducive to these slippages, however illegitimate, because of the real ascendancy of the paradigm of dismantlement. Reversals don't work, we're told; dismantle the scheme of difference altogether. And I don't deny the importance, on the level of theory, of the project; it's important to remember that "race" is *only* a sociopolitical category, nothing more. At the same time—in terms of its practical performative force—that doesn't help me when I'm trying to get a taxi on the corner of 125th and Lenox Avenue. ("Please sir, it's only a metaphor.")

Maybe the most important thing here is the tension between the imperatives of agency and the rhetoric of dismantlement. An example: Foucault says, and let's take him at his word, that the "homosexual" as life form was invented sometime in the mid-nineteenth century. Now, if there's no such thing as a homosexual, then homophobia, at least as directed toward people rather than acts, loses its rationale. But you can't respond to the discrimination against gay people by saying, "I'm sorry, I don't exist; you've got the wrong guy." The simple historical fact is, Stonewall was necessary, concerted action was necessary to take action against the very structures that, as it were, called the homosexual into being, that subjected certain people to this imaginary identity. To reverse Audre Lorde, *only* the master's tools will ever dismantle the master's house.

Let me be specific. Those of us working in my own tradition confront the hegemony of the Western tradition, generally, and of the larger American tradition, specifically, as we set about theorizing about our tradition, and engaging in attempts at canon formation. Long after white American literature has been anthologized and canonized, and recanonized, our attempts to define a black American canon, foregrounded on its own against a white backdrop, are often decried as racist, separatist, nationalist, or "essentialist." Attempts to derive theories about our literary tradition from the black tradition—a tradition, I might add, that must include black vernacular forms as well as written literary forms—are often greeted by our colleagues in traditional literature departments as misguided attempts to secede from a union which only recently, and with considerable kicking and screaming, has been forged. What is *wrong* with you people, our friends ask us in genuine passion and concern; after all, aren't we all just citizens of literature here?

Well, yes and no. It is clear that every black American text must confess to a complex ancestry, one high and low (literary and vernacular), but also one white and black. There can be no doubt that white texts inform and influence black texts (and vice versa), so that a thoroughly integrated canon of American literature is not only politically sound, it is *intellectually* sound as well. But the attempts of scholars such as Arnold Rampersad, Houston Baker, M. H. Washington, Nellie McKay, and others to define a black American canon, and to pursue literary interpretation from within this canon, are not meant to refute the soundness of these gestures of integration. Rather, it is a question of perspective, a question of emphasis. Just as we can and must cite a black text within the larger American tradition, we can and must cite it within its own tradition, a tradition not defined by a pseudoscience of racial biology, or a mystically shared essence called blackness, but by the repetition and revision of shared themes, topoi, and tropes, a process that binds the signal texts of the black tradition into a canon just as surely as separate links bind together into a chain. It is no more, or less, essentialist to make this claim than it is to claim the existence of French, English, German, Russian, or American literature—as long as we proceed inductively, from the texts to the theory. For nationalism has always been the dwarf in the critical, canonical chess machine. For anyone to deny us the right to engage in attempts to constitute ourselves as discursive subjects is for them to engage in the double privileging of categories that happen to be preconstituted.

In our attempts at canon formation we are demanding a return to history in a manner scarcely conceived of by the new historicists. Nor can we opt out of our own private histories, which Houston Baker calls the African-American autobiographical moment, and which I call the autocritography. Let me end, as I began, with an anecdote, one that I had forgotten for so long until just the other day.

Recently at Cornell, I was listening to Hortense Spillers, the great black feminist critic, read her important essay, "Mama's Baby, Papa's Maybe." Her delivery, as usual, was flawless, compelling, inimitable. And although I had read this essay as a manuscript, I had never before felt—or heard—the following lines:

> The African-American male has been touched, therefore, by the *mother,* handled by her in ways that he cannot escape, and in ways that the white American male is allowed to temporize by a fatherly reprieve. This human and historic development—the text that has been inscribed on the benighted heart of the continent—takes us to the center of an inexorable difference in the depths of American women's community: the African-American woman, the mother, the daughter, becomes historically the powerful and shadowy evocation of a cultural synthesis long evaporated—the law of the Mother—only and precisely because legal enslavement removed the African-American male not so much from sight as from *mimetic* view as a partner in the prevailing social fiction of the Father's name, the Father's law,
>
> Therefore, the female, in this order of things, breaks in upon the imagination with a forcefulness that marks both a denial and an "illegitimacy." Because of this peculiar American denial, the black American male embodies the *only* American community of males which has had the specific occasion to learn *who* the female is within itself, the infant child who bears the life against the could-be fateful gamble, against the odds of pulverization and murder, including her own. It is the heritage of the *mother* that the African-American male must regain as an aspect of his own personhood—the power of "yes" to the "female" within.

How curious a figure—men, black men, gaining their voices through the black mother. Precisely when some committed feminists or some committed black nationalists would essentialize all "others" out of their critical endeavor, Hortense Spillers rejects that glib and easy solution, calling for a revoicing of the "master's" discourse in the cadences and timbres of the Black Mother's voice.

As I sat there before her, I recalled, to my own astonishment, my own first public performance, when I was a child of four years. My mom attended a small black Methodist Church in Piedmont, West Virginia, just as her mom had done for the past fifty years. I was a fat little kid, a condition that my mom defended as "plump." I remember that I had just been given a brand new gray suit for the occasion, and a black stringy-brim Dobbs hat, so it must have been Easter, because my brother and I always got new hats for Easter, just as my dad and mom did.

At any rate, the day came to deliver my Piece. What is a Piece? A Piece is what people in our church called a religious recitation. I don't know what the folk etymology might be, but I think it reflects the belief that each of the fragments of our praise songs, taken together, amounts to a Master Text. And each of us, during a religious program, was called upon to say our Piece. Mine, if you can believe it, was "Jesus was a boy like me, and like Him I want to be." That was it—I was only four. So, after weeks of practice in elocution, hair pressed and greased down, shirt starched and pants pressed, I was ready to give my Piece.

I remember skipping along to the church with all the other kids, driving everyone crazy, saying over and over, "Jesus was a boy like me, and like Him I want to be." "Will you shut up!" my friends demanded. Just jealous, I thought. They probably don't even know their Pieces.

Finally, we made it to the church, and it was packed—bulging and glistening with black people, eager to hear Pieces, despite the fact that they heard all of the Pieces already, year after year, bits and fragments of a repeated Master Text.

Because I was the youngest child on the program, I was the first to go. Miss Sarah Russell (whom we called Sister Holy Ghost—behind her back, of course) started the program with a prayer, then asked if little Skippy Gates would step forward. I did so.

And then the worst happened: I completely forgot the words of my Piece. Standing there, pressed and starched, just as clean as I could be, in front of just about everybody in our part of town, I could not for the life of me remember one word of that Piece.

After standing there I don't know how long, struck dumb and captivated by all of those staring eyes, I heard a voice from near the back of the church proclaim, "Jesus was a boy like me, and like Him I want to be."

And my mother, having arisen to find my voice, smoothed her dress and sat down again. The congregation's applause lasted as long as its laughter as I crawled back to my seat.

For me, I realized as Hortense Spillers spoke, much of my scholarly and critical work has been an attempt to learn how to speak in the strong, compelling cadences of my mother's voice. To reform core curricula, to account for the comparable eloquence of the African, the Asian, and the Middle Eastern traditions, is to begin to prepare our students for their roles as citizens of a world culture, educated through a truly human notion of "the humanities," rather than—as Bennett and Bloom would have it—as guardians at the last frontier outpost of white male Western culture, the Keepers of the Master's Pieces. And for us as scholar-critics, learning to speak in the voice of the black female is perhaps the ultimate challenge of producing a discourse of the critical Other.

JOAN W. SCOTT

Selection from "The Evidence of Experience" (1991)

"Deconstruction" and "poststructuralism" were among the buzzwords of the 1980s and 1990s for many literary scholars, philosophers, and historians. What these terms most consistently flagged was a series of efforts to explain how the basic categories of discourse—including the distinctions between genders, races, and classes—had been historically and ideologically produced. Rather than accepting uncritically such categories and tools of thought, one should understand that these very distinctions were products of particular circumstances determined by specific power relations in the human societies in which these concepts had gained their credibility.

Among the clearest of the academic theorists who wrote in this vein was the historian and feminist theorist Joan W. Scott (1941-). Her *Gender and the Politics of History* (New York, 1988) did more than any other work to move the historical profession from the study of "women" to the study of "gender." Twenty years later a symposium assessed the influence of this book: *American Historical Review* (December 2008), 1344–1430. Scott followed this book with the essay of 1991 reprinted here in a slightly abbreviated version. "The Evidence of Experience" warns against the uncritical reliance upon what human subjects offered as their own "experience." Scott argues that the representations people routinely offer as testimony to be believed because they are based, after all, on experience, are actually the aggregate result of a complex process of mediation in which life as lived is comprehended and described only through prior structures. Writing in a mode consistent with that of Thomas Kuhn and Richard Rorty, who are also represented in this volume, but inspired more directly by the French philosopher Michel Foucault, Scott distinguished herself though her critical examination of leading works of historical scholarship, such as E. P. Thompson's *Making of the English Working Class* and through her vigorous critiques of contemporary theorists of historical knowledge such as John Toews.

For a lucid account of the role of "The Evidence of Experience" in the larger "linguistic turn," and for an especially fair-minded summary of the debates the essay generated among historians, see Martin Jay, *Songs of Experience: Modern American and European Variations on a Universal Theme* (Berkeley, 2004), 349–55. Scott's theoretical work can be read profitably in relation to the leading works of two other feminist scholars, Judith Butler, *Gender Trouble: Feminism and the Subversion of Identity* (New York, 1990); and Seyla Benhabib, *Situating the Self: Gender, Community, and Postmodernism in Contemporary Ethics* (New York, 1992).

Documenting the experience of others... has been at once a highly successful and limiting strategy for historians of difference. It has been successful because it remains so comfortably within the disciplinary framework of history, working according to rules that permit calling old narratives into question when new evidence is discovered. The status of evidence is, of course, ambiguous for historians. On the one hand, they acknowledge that "evidence only counts as evidence and is only recognized as such in relation to a potential narrative, so that the narrative can be said to determine the evidence as much as the evidence determines the narrative." On the other hand, historians' rhetorical treatment of evidence and their use of it to falsify prevailing interpretations, depends on a referential notion of evidence which denies that it is anything but a reflection of the real. Michel de Certeau's description is apt. Historical discourse, he writes,

> gives itself credibility in the name of the reality which it is supposed to represent, but this authorized appearance of the "real" serves precisely to camouflage the practice which in fact determines it. Representation thus disguises the praxis that organizes it.

When the evidence offered is the evidence of "experience," the claim for referentiality is further buttressed—what could be truer, after all, than a subject's own account of what he or she has lived through? It is precisely this kind of appeal to experience as uncontestable evidence and as an originary point of explanation—as a foundation on which analysis is based—that weakens the critical thrust of histories of difference. By remaining within the epistemological frame of orthodox history, these studies lose the possibility of examining those assumptions and practices that excluded considerations of difference in the first place. They take as self-evident the identities of those whose experience is being documented and thus naturalize their difference. They locate resistance outside its discursive construction and reify agency as an inherent attribute of individuals, thus decontextualizing it. When experience is taken as the origin of knowledge, the vision of the individual subject (the person who had the experience or the historian who recounts it) becomes the bedrock of evidence on which explanation is built. Questions about the constructed nature of experience, about how subjects are constituted as different in the first place, about how one's vision is structured—about language (or discourse) and history—are left aside. The evidence of experience then becomes evidence for the fact of difference, rather than a way of exploring how difference is established, how it operates, how and in what ways it constitutes subjects who see and act in the world.

To put it another way, the evidence of experience, whether conceived through a metaphor of visibility or in any other way that takes meaning as transparent, reproduces rather than contests given ideological systems—those that assume that the facts of history speak for themselves and those that rest on notions of a natural or established opposition between, say, sexual practices and social conventions, or between homosexuality and heterosexuality. Histories that document the "hidden" world of homosexuality, for example, show the impact of silence and repression on the lives of those affected by it and bring to light the history of their suppression and exploitation. But the project of making experience visible precludes critical examination of the workings of the ideological system itself, its categories of representation (homosexual/heterosexual, man/woman, black/white as

Source: Joan W. Scott, "The Evidence of Experience," *Critical Inquiry*, 17, 773–97 (Chicago: University of Chicago Press, 1991). Reprinted by permission of the University of Chicago Press.

fixed immutable identities), its premises about what these categories mean and how they operate, and of its notions of subjects, origin, and cause. Homosexual practices are seen as the result of desire, conceived as a natural force operating outside or in opposition to social regulation. In these stories homosexuality is presented as a repressed desire (experience denied), made to seem invisible, abnormal, and silenced by a "society" that legislates heterosexuality as the only normal practice. Because this kind of (homosexual) desire cannot ultimately be repressed—because experience is there—it invents institutions to accommodate itself. These institutions are unacknowledged but not invisible; indeed, it is the possibility that they can be seen that threatens order and ultimately overcomes repression. Resistance and agency are presented as driven by uncontainable desire; emancipation is a teleological story in which desire ultimately overcomes social control and becomes visible. History is a chronology that makes experience visible, but in which categories appear as nonetheless ahistorical: desire, homosexuality, heterosexuality, femininity, masculinity, sex, and even sexual practices become so many fixed entities being played out over time, but not themselves historicized. Presenting the story in this way excludes, or at least understates, the historically variable interrelationship between the meanings "homosexual" and "heterosexual," the constitutive force each has for the other, and the contested and changing nature of the terrain that they simultaneously occupy...

Not only does homosexuality define heterosexuality by specifying its negative limits, and not only is the boundary between the two a shifting one, but both operate within the structures of the same "phallic economy"—an economy whose workings are not taken into account by studies that seek simply to make homosexual experience visible. One way to describe this economy is to say that desire is defined through the pursuit of the phallus— that veiled and evasive signifier which is at once fully present but unattainable, and which gains its power through the promise it holds out but never entirely fulfills. Theorized this way, homosexuality and heterosexuality work according to the same economy, their social institutions mirroring one another. The social institutions through which gay sex is practiced may invert those associated with dominant heterosexual behavior (promiscuous versus restrained, public versus private, anonymous versus known, and so on), but they both operate within a system structured according to presence and lack. To the extent that this system constructs desiring subjects (those who are legitimate as well as those who are not), it simultaneously establishes them and itself as given and outside of time, as the way things work, the way they inevitably are.

The project of making experience visible precludes analysis of the workings of this system and of its historicity; instead, it reproduces its terms. We come to appreciate the consequences of the closeting of homosexuals and we understand repression as an interested act of power or domination; alternative behaviors and institutions also become available to us. What we don't have is a way of placing those alternatives within the framework of (historically contingent) dominant patterns of sexuality and the ideology that supports them. We know they exist, but not how they have been constructed; we know their existence offers a critique of normative practices, but not the extent of the critique. Making visible the experience of a different group exposes the existence of repressive mechanisms, but not their inner workings or logics; we know that difference exists, but we don't understand it as relationally constituted. For that we need to attend to the historical processes that, through discourse, position subjects and produce their experiences. It is not individuals who have experience, but subjects who are constituted through experience. Experience in this definition then becomes not the origin of our explanation, not the authoritative (because seen or felt) evidence that grounds what is known, but rather that which we seek to explain, that about which knowledge is produced. To think about experience in this way is to historicize it as well as to historicize the identities it produces. This kind of historicizing represents a reply to the many contemporary historians who have argued that an unproblematized "experience" is the foundation of their practice; it is a historicizing that implies critical scrutiny of all explanatory categories usually taken for granted, including the category of "experience."

History has been largely a foundationalist discourse. By this I mean that its explanations seem to be unthinkable if they do not take for granted some primary premises, categories, or presumptions. These foundations (however varied, whatever they are at a particular moment) are unquestioned and unquestionable; they are considered permanent and transcendent. As such they create a common ground for historians and their objects of study in the past and so authorize and legitimize analysis; indeed, analysis seems not to be able to proceed without them. In the minds of some foundationalists, in fact, nihilism, anarchy, and moral confusion are the sure alternatives to these givens, which have the status (if not the philosophical definition) of eternal truths.

Historians have had recourse to many kinds of foundations, some more obviously empiricist than others. What is most striking these days is the determined embrace, the strident defense, of some reified, transcendent category of explanation by historians who have used insights drawn from the sociology of knowledge, structural linguistics, feminist theory, or cultural anthropology to develop sharp critiques of empiricism. This turn to foundations even by antifoundationalists appears, in Fredric Jameson's characterization, as "some extreme form of the return of the repressed."

"Experience" is one of the foundations that has been reintroduced into historical writing in the wake of the critique of empiricism; unlike "brute fact" or "simple reality," its connotations are more varied and elusive. It has recently emerged as a critical term in debates among historians about the limits of interpretation and especially about the uses and limits of post-structuralist theory for history. In these debates those most open to interpretive innovation—those who have insisted on the study of collective mentalities, of economic, social, or cultural determinations of individual behavior, and even of the influences of unconscious motives on thought and action—are among the most ardent defenders of the need to attend to "experience." Feminist historians critical of biases in "male-stream" histories and seeking to install women as viable subjects, social historians insisting on the materialist basis of the discipline on the one hand and on the "agency" of individuals or groups on the other, and cultural historians who have brought symbolic analysis to the study of behavior, have joined political historians whose stories privilege the purposive actions of rational actors and intellectual historians who maintain that thought originates in the minds of individuals. All seem to have converged on the argument that experience is an "irreducible" ground for history.

The evolution of "experience" appears to solve a problem of explanation for professed anti-empiricists even as it reinstates a foundational ground. For this reason it is interesting to examine the uses of "experience" by historians. Such an examination allows us to ask whether history can exist without foundations and what it might look like if it did...

An example of the way "experience" establishes the authority of an historian can be found in R. G. Collingwood's *Idea of History*, the 1946 classic that has been required reading in historiography courses for several generations. For Collingwood, the ability of the historian to reenact past experience is tied to his autonomy, "where by autonomy I mean the condition of being one's own authority, making statements or taking action on one's own initiative and not because those statements or actions are authorized or prescribed by anyone else." The question of where the historian is situated—who he is, how he is defined in relation to others, what the political effects of his history may be—never enters the discussion. Indeed, being free of these matters seems to be tied to Collingwood's definition of autonomy, an issue so critical for him that he launches into an uncharacteristic tirade about it. In his quest for certainty, the historian must not let others make up his mind for him, Collingwood insists, because to do that means

> giving up his autonomy as an historian and allowing someone else to do for him what, if he is a scientific thinker, he can only do for himself. There is no need for me to offer the reader any proof of this statement. If he knows anything of historical work, he already knows of his own experience that it is true. If he does not already know that it is true, he does not know enough about history to read this essay with any profit, and the best thing he can do is to stop here and now.

For Collingwood it is axiomatic that experience is a reliable source of knowledge because it rests on direct contact between the historian's perception and reality (even if the passage of time makes it necessary for the historian to imaginatively reenact events of the past). Thinking on his own means owning his own thoughts, and this proprietary relationship guarantees an individual's independence, his ability to read the past correctly, and the authority of the knowledge he produces. The claim is not only for the historian's autonomy, but also for his originality. Here "experience" grounds the identity of the researcher as an historian.

Another, very different use of "experience" can be found in E. P. Thompson's *Making of the English Working Class*, the book that revolutionized social and labor history. Thompson specifically set out to free the concept of "class" from the ossified categories of Marxist structuralism. For this project "experience" was a key concept. "We explored," Thompson writes of himself and his fellow New Left historians, "both in theory and in practice, those junction-concepts (such as 'need,' 'class,' and 'determine') by which, through the missing term, 'experience,' structure is transmuted into process, and the subject re-enters into history."

Thompson's notion of experience joined ideas of external influence and subjective feeling, the structural and the psychological. This gave him a mediating influence between social structure and social consciousness. For him experience meant "social being"—the lived realities of social life, especially the affective domains of family and religion and the symbolic dimensions of expression. This definition separated the affective and the symbolic from the economic and the rational. "People do not only experience their own experience as ideas, within thought and its procedures," he maintained, "they also experience their own experience as *feeling*." This statement grants importance to the psychological dimension of experience, and it allows Thompson to account for agency. Feeling, Thompson insists, is "handled" culturally as "norms, familial and kinship obligations and reciprocities, as values or (through more elaborated forms) within art and religious beliefs." At the same time it somehow precedes these forms of expression and so provides an escape from a strong structural determination: "For any living generation, in any 'now,'" Thompson asserts, "the ways in which they 'handle' experience defies prediction and escapes from any narrow definition of determination."

And yet in his use of it, experience, because it is ultimately shaped by relations of production, is a unifying phenomenon, overriding other kinds of diversity. Since these relations of production are common to workers of different ethnicities, religions, regions, and trades they necessarily provide a common denominator and emerge as a more salient determinant of "experience" than anything else. In Thompson's use of the term, experience is the start of a process that culminates in the realization and articulation of social consciousness, in this case a common identity of class. It serves an integrating function, joining the individual and the structural, and bringing together diverse people into that coherent (totalizing) whole which is a distinctive sense of class. "'Experience' (we have found) has, in the last instance, been generated in 'material life,' has been structured in class ways, and hence 'social being' has determined 'social consciousness.'" In this way unequivocal and uniform identity is produced through objective circumstances and there is no reason to ask how this identity achieved predominance—it had to.

The unifying aspect of experience excludes whole realms of human activity by simply not counting them as experience, at least not with any consequences for social organization or politics. When class becomes an overriding identity, other subject-positions are subsumed by it, those of gender, for example (or, in other instances of this kind, of history, race, ethnicity, and sexuality). The positions of men and women and their different relationships to politics are taken as reflections of material and social arrangements rather than as products of class politics itself; they are part of the "experience" of capitalism. Instead of asking how some experiences become more salient than others, how what matters to Thompson is defined as experience, and how differences are dissolved, experience becomes itself cumulative and homogenizing, providing the common denominator on which class consciousness is built.

Thompson's own role in determining the salience of certain things and not others is never addressed. Although his author's voice intervenes powerfully with moral and ethical judgments about the situations he is recounting, the presentation of the experiences themselves is meant to secure their objective status. We forget that Thompson's history, like the accounts offered by political organizers in the nineteenth century of what mattered in workers' lives, is an interpretation, a selective ordering of information that through its use of originary categories and teleological accounts legitimizes a particular kind of politics (it becomes the only possible politics) and a particular way of doing history (as a reflection of what happened, the description of which is little influenced by the historian if, in this case, he only has the requisite moral vision that permits identification with the experiences of workers in the past).

In Thompson's account class is finally an identity rooted in structural relations that preexist politics. What this obscures is the contradictory and contested process by which class itself was conceptualized and by which diverse kinds of subject-positions were assigned, felt, contested, or embraced. As a result, Thompson's brilliant history of the English working class, which set out to historicize the category of class, ends up essentializing it. The ground may seem to be displaced from structure to agency by insisting on the subjectively felt nature of experience, but the problem Thompson sought to address isn't really solved. Working-class "experience" is now the ontological foundation of working-class identity, politics, and history.

This kind of use of experience has the same foundational status if we substitute "women's" or "black" or "lesbian" or "homosexual" for "working-class" in the previous sentence. Among feminist historians, for example, "experience" has helped to legitimize a critique of the false claims to objectivity of traditional historical accounts. Part of the project of some feminist history has been to unmask all claims to objectivity as an ideological cover for masculine bias by pointing out the shortcomings, incompleteness, and exclusiveness of mainstream history. This has been achieved by providing documentation about women in the past that calls into question existing interpretations made without consideration of gender. But how do we authorize the new knowledge if the possibility of all historical objectivity has been questioned? By appealing to experience, which in this usage connotes both reality and its subjective apprehension—the experience of women in the past and of women historians who can recognize something of themselves in their foremothers...

"Because of its drive towards a political massing together of women," writes Denise Riley, "feminism can never wholeheartedly dismantle 'women's experience,' however much this category conflates the attributed, the imposed, and the lived, and then sanctifies the resulting mélange." The kind of argument for a women's history (and for a feminist politics) that Riley criticizes closes down inquiry into the ways in which female subjectivity is produced, the ways in which agency is made possible, the ways in which race and sexuality intersect with gender, the ways in which politics organize and interpret experience—in sum, the ways in which identity is a contested terrain, the site of multiple and conflicting claims. In Riley's words, "it masks the likelihood that ... [experiences] have accrued to women not by virtue of their womanhood alone, but as traces of domination, whether natural or political." I would add that it masks the necessarily discursive character of these experiences as well.

But it is precisely the discursive character of experience that is at issue for some historians because attributing experience to discourse seems somehow to deny its status as an unquestionable ground of explanation. This seems to be the case for John Toews, who wrote a long article in the *American Historical Review* in 1987 called "Intellectual History after the Linguistic Turn: The Autonomy of Meaning and the Irreducibility of Experience." The term *linguistic turn* is a comprehensive one used by Toews to refer to approaches to the study of meaning that draw on a number of disciplines, but especially on theories of language "since the primary medium of meaning was obviously language." The question for Toews is how far linguistic analysis has gone and should go, especially in view of the poststructuralist challenge to foundationalism. Reviewing a number of books that take on questions of meaning and its analysis, Toews concludes that

> the predominant tendency [among intellectual historians] is to adapt traditional historical concerns for extralinguistic origins and reference to the semiological challenge, to reaffirm in new ways that, in spite of the relative autonomy of cultural meanings, human subjects still make and remake the worlds of meaning in which they are suspended, and to insist that these worlds are not creations ex nihilo but responses to, and shapings of, changing worlds of experience ultimately irreducible to the linguistic forms in which they appear.

By definition, he argues, history is concerned with explanation; it is not a radical hermeneutics, but an attempt to account for the origin, persistence, and disappearance of certain meanings "at particular times and in specific sociocultural situations." For him explanation requires a separation of experience and meaning: experience is that reality which demands meaningful response. "Experience," in Toews's usage, is taken to be so self-evident that he never defines the term. This is telling in an article that insists on establishing the importance and independence, the irreducibility of "experience." The absence of definition allows experience to resonate in many ways, but it also allows it to function as a universally understood category—the undefined word creates a sense of consensus by attributing to it an assumed, stable, and shared meaning.

Experience, for Toews, is a foundational concept. While recognizing that meanings differ and that the historian's task is to analyze the different meanings produced in societies and over time, Toews protects "experience" from this kind of relativism. In doing so he establishes the possibility for objective knowledge and for communication among historians, however diverse their positions and views. This has the effect (among others) of removing historians from critical scrutiny as active producers of knowledge.

The insistence on the separation of meaning and experience is crucial for Toews, not only because it seems the only way to account for change, but also because it protects the world from "the hubris of wordmakers who claim to be makers of reality." Even if Toews here uses "wordmakers" metaphorically to refer to those who produce texts, those who engage in signification, his opposition between "words" and "reality" echoes the distinction he makes earlier in the article between language (or meaning) and experience. This opposition guarantees both an independent status for human agents and the common ground on which they can communicate and act. It produces a possibility for "intersubjective communication" among individuals despite differences between them, and also reaffirms their existence as thinking beings outside the discursive practices they devise and employ.

Toews is critical of J. G. A. Pocock's vision of "intersubjective communication" based on rational consensus in a community of free individuals, all of whom are equally masters of their own wills. "Pocock's theories," he writes, "often seem like theoretical reflections of familiar practices because the world they assume is also the world in which many contemporary Anglo-American historians live or think they live." Yet the separation of meaning and experience that Toews offers does not really provide an alternative. A more diverse community can be posited, of course, with different meanings given to experience. Since the phenomenon of experience itself can be analyzed outside the meanings given to it, the subjective position of historians then can seem to have nothing to do with the knowledge they produce. In this way experience authorizes historians and it enables them to counter the radical historicist stance that, Toews says, "undermines the traditional historians' quest for unity, continuity, and purpose by robbing them of any standpoint from which a relationship between past, present, and future could be objectively reconstructed." Here he establishes as self-evident (and unproblematic) the reflective nature of historical representation, and he assumes that it will override whatever diversity there is in the background, culture, and outlook of historians. Attention to experience, he concludes, "is essential for our self-understanding, and thus also for fulfilling the historian's task of connecting memory with hope."

Toews's "experience" thus provides an object for historians that can be known apart from their own role as meaning makers and it then guarantees not only the objectivity of their knowledge, but their ability to persuade others of its importance. Whatever diversity and conflict may exist among them, Toews's community of historians is rendered homogeneous by its shared object (experience). But as Ellen Rooney has so effectively pointed out, using the field of literary theory as her example, this kind of homogeneity can exist only because of the exclusion of the possibility that "historically irreducible interests divide and define reading communities." Inclusiveness is achieved by denying that exclusion is inevitable, that difference is established through exclusion, and that the fundamental differences that accompany inequalities of power and position cannot be overcome by persuasion. In Toews's article no disagreement about the meaning of the term *experience* can be entertained, since experience itself lies somehow outside its signification. For that reason, perhaps, Toews never defines it.

Even among those historians who do not share all of Toews's ideas about the objectivity or continuous quality of history writing, the defense of "experience" works in much the same way: it establishes a realm of reality outside of discourse and it authorizes the historian who has access to it. The evidence of experience works as a foundation providing both a starting point and a conclusive kind of explanation, beyond which few questions can or need to be asked. And yet it is precisely the questions precluded—questions about discourse, difference, and subjectivity, as well as about what counts as experience and who gets to make that determination—that would enable us to historicize experience, and to reflect critically on the history we write about it, rather than to premise our history on it.

Gayatri Chakravorty Spivak begins an essay addressed to the Subaltern Studies collective with a contrast between the work of historians and literary scholars:

> A historian confronts a text of counterinsurgency or gendering where the subaltern has been represented. He unravels the text to assign a new subject-position to the subaltern, gendered or otherwise.
>
> A teacher of literature confronts a sympathetic text where the gendered subaltern has been represented. She unravels the text to make visible the assignment of subject-positions...
>
> The performance of these tasks, of the historian and the teacher of literature, must critically "interrupt" each other, bring each other to crisis, in order to serve their constituencies; especially when each seems to claim all for its own.

Spivak's argument here seems to be that there is a difference between history and literature that is both methodological and political. History provides categories that enable us to understand the social and structural positions of people (as workers, subalterns, and so on) in new terms, and these terms define a collective identity with potential political (maybe even revolutionary, but certainly subversive) effects. Literature relativizes the categories history assigns, and exposes the processes that construct and position subjects. In Spivak's discussion, both are critical operations, although she clearly favors the deconstructive task of literature. Although her essay has to be read in the context of a specific debate within Indian historiography, its general points must also be considered. In effect, her statements raise the question of whether historians can do other than construct subjects by describing their experience in terms of an essentialized identity.

Spivak's characterization of the Subaltern Studies historians' reliance on a notion of consciousness as a "*strategic* use of positivist essentialism" doesn't really solve the problem of writing history either, since whether it's strategic or not, essentialism appeals to the idea that there are fixed identities, visible to us as social or natural facts. A refusal of essentialism seems particularly important once again these days within the field of history, as disciplinary pressure builds to defend the unitary subject in the name of his or her "experience." Neither does Spivak's invocation of the special political status of the subaltern justify a history aimed at producing subjects without interrogating and relativizing the means of their production. In the case of colonial and postcolonial peoples, but also of various others in the West, it has been precisely the imposition of a categorical (and universal) subject-status (*the* worker, *the* peasant, *the* woman, *the* black) that has masked the operations of difference in the organization of social life. Each category taken as fixed works to solidify the ideological process of subject-construction, making the process less rather than more apparent, naturalizing rather than analyzing it.

It ought to be possible for historians (as for the teachers of literature Spivak so dazzlingly exemplifies) to "make visible the assignment of subject-positions," not in the sense of capturing the reality of the objects seen, but of trying to understand the operations of the complex and changing discursive processes by which identities are ascribed, resisted, or embraced, and which processes themselves are unremarked and indeed achieve their effect because they are not noticed. To do this a change of object seems to be required, one that takes the emergence of concepts and identities as historical events in need of explanation.

This does not mean that one dismisses the *effects* of such concepts and identities, nor that one does not explain behavior in terms of their operations. It does mean assuming that the appearance of a new identity is not inevitable or determined, not something that was always there simply waiting to be expressed, not something that will always exist in the form it was given in a particular political movement or at a particular historical moment. Stuart Hall writes:

> The fact is "black" has never been just there either. It has always been an unstable identity, psychically, culturally and politically. It, too, is a narrative, a story, a history. Something constructed, told, spoken, not simply found. People now speak of the society I come from in totally unrecognizable ways. Of course Jamaica is a black society, they say. In reality it is a society of black and brown people who lived for three or four hundred years without ever being able to speak of themselves as "black." Black is an identity which had to be learned and could only be learned in a certain moment. In Jamaica that moment is the 1970s.

To take the history of Jamaican black identity as an object of inquiry in these terms is necessarily to analyze subject-positioning, at least in part, as the effect of discourses that placed Jamaica in a late twentieth-century international racist political economy; it is to historicize the "experience" of blackness.

Treating the emergence of a new identity as a discursive event is not to introduce a new form of linguistic determinism, nor to deprive subjects of agency. It is to refuse a separation between "experience" and language and to insist instead on the productive quality of discourse. Subjects are constituted discursively, but there are conflicts among discursive systems, contradictions within any one of them, multiple meanings possible for the concepts they deploy. And subjects do have agency. They are not unified, autonomous individuals exercising free will, but rather subjects whose agency is created through situations and statuses conferred on them. Being a subject means being "subject to definite conditions of existence, conditions of endowment of agents and conditions of exercise." These conditions enable choices, although they are not unlimited. Subjects are constituted discursively and experience is a linguistic event (it doesn't happen outside established meanings), but neither is it confined to a fixed order of meaning. Since discourse is by definition shared, experience is collective as well as individual. Experience can both confirm what is already known (we see what we have learned to see) and upset what has been taken for granted (when different meanings are in conflict we readjust our vision to take account of the conflict or to resolve it—that is what is meant by "learning from experience," though not everyone learns the same lesson or learns it at the same time or in the same way). Experience is a subject's history. Language is the site of history's enactment. Historical explanation cannot, therefore, separate the two.

The question then becomes how to analyze language, and here historians often (though not always and not necessarily) confront the limits of a discipline that has typically constructed itself in opposition to literature. (These are not the same limits Spivak points to; her contrast is about the different kinds of knowledge produced by history and literature, mine is about different ways of reading and the different understandings of the relationship between words and things implicit in those readings. In neither case are the limits obligatory for historians; indeed, recognition of them makes it possible for us to get beyond them.) The kind of reading I have in mind would not assume a direct correspondence between words and things, nor confine itself to single meanings, nor aim for the resolution of contradiction. It would not render process as linear, nor rest explanation on simple correlations or single variables. Rather it would grant to "the literary" an integral, even irreducible, status of its own. To grant such status is not to make "the literary" foundational, but to open new possibilities for analyzing discursive productions of social and political reality as complex, contradictory processes...

It is finally by tracking "the appropriation of language...in both directions, over the gap," and by situating and contextualizing that language that one historicizes the terms by which experience is represented, and so historicizes "experience" itself.

Reading for "the literary" does not seem at all inappropriate for those whose discipline is devoted to the study of change. It is not the only kind of reading I am advocating, although more documents than those written by literary figures are susceptible to such readings. Rather it is a way of changing the focus and the philosophy of our history, from one bent on naturalizing "experience" through a belief in the unmediated relationship between words and things, to one that takes all categories of analysis as contextual, contested, and contingent. How have categories of representation and analysis—such as class, race, gender, relations of production, biology, identity, subjectivity, agency, experience, even culture—achieved their foundational status? What have been the effects of their articulations? What does it mean for historians to study the past in terms of these categories and for individuals to think of themselves in these terms? What is the relationship between the salience of such categories in our own time and their existence in the past? Questions such as these open consideration of what Dominick LaCapra has referred to as the "transferential" relationship between the historian and the past, that is, of the relationship between the power of the historian's analytic frame and the events that are the object of his or her study. And they historicize both sides of that relationship by denying the fixity and transcendence of anything that appears to operate as a foundation, turning attention instead to the history of foundationalist concepts themselves. The history of these concepts (understood to be contested and contradictory) then becomes the evidence by which "experience" can be grasped and by which the historian's relationship to the past he or she writes about can be articulated. This is what Foucault meant by genealogy:

> If interpretation were the slow exposure of the meaning hidden in an origin, then only metaphysics could interpret the development of humanity. But if interpretation is the violent or surreptitious appropriation of a system of rules, which in itself has no essential meaning, in order to impose a direction, to bend it to a new will, to force its participation in a different game, and to subject it to secondary rules, then the development of humanity is a series of interpretations. The role of genealogy is to record its history: the history of morals, ideals, and metaphysical concepts, the history of the concept of liberty or of the ascetic life; as they stand for the emergence of different interpretations, they must be made to appear as events on the stage of historical process.

Experience is not a word we can do without, although, given its usage to essentialize identity and reify the subject, it is tempting to abandon it altogether. But *experience* is so much a part of everyday language, so imbricated in our narratives that it seems futile to argue for its expulsion. It serves as a way of talking about what happened, of establishing difference and similarity, of claiming knowledge that is "unassailable." Given the ubiquity of the term, it seems to me more useful to work with it, to analyze its operations and to redefine its meaning. This entails focussing on processes of identity production, insisting on the discursive nature of "experience" and on the politics of its construction. Experience is at once always already an interpretation *and* something that needs to be interpreted. What counts as experience is neither self-evident nor straightforward; it is always contested, and always therefore political. The study of experience, therefore, must call into question its originary status in historical explanation. This will happen when historians take as their project *not* the reproduction and transmission of knowledge said to be arrived at through experience, but the analysis of the production of that knowledge itself. Such an analysis would constitute a genuinely nonfoundational history, one which retains its explanatory power and its interest in change but does not stand on or reproduce naturalized categories. It also cannot guarantee the historian's neutrality, for deciding which categories to historicize is inevitably political, necessarily tied to the historian's recognition of his or her stake in the production of knowledge. Experience is, in this approach, not the origin of our explanation, but that which we want to explain. This kind of approach does not undercut politics by denying the existence of subjects; it instead interrogates the processes of their creation and, in so doing, refigures history and the role of the historian and opens new ways for thinking about change.

SAMUEL P. HUNTINGTON

"The Clash of Civilizations"
(1993)

The end of the Soviet Union in the early 1990s generated a host of sweeping, sometimes speculative analyses of the direction of world history. None received more attention than the contribution of Samuel P. Huntington (1927–2008), a Harvard-based political scientist long known for his bold and pungent hypotheses on world affairs. Huntington's notion that cultures rather than economic interests or political ideologies would define the future was first outlined in an essay of 1993, "The Clash of Civilizations," the bulk of which is reprinted here. Shortly thereafter, in *The Clash of Civilizations and the Remaking of World Order* (New York, 1996), Huntington developed his ideas in the form of a best-selling book. Huntington's basic terms were sometimes contested. An example of the critical discussion surrounding his analysis is Stephen Holmes, "In Search of New Enemies," *London Review of Books* (April 24, 1997), 3–10.

Huntington first gained attention as a young theorist of the modernization process, especially with his first book, *The Soldier and the State: The Theory and Politics of Civil-Military Relations* (New York, 1957). Later Huntingon published a series of controversial books that often challenged ideas prevailing among his academic colleagues. Prominent among these later works was a skeptical study of American democracy, *American Politics: The Promise of Disharmony* (New York, 1981). Early in the twenty-first century, he entered the debates over American national identity and cultural diversity with *Who Are We? The Challenges to America's National Identity* (New York, 2004), a work that consolidated his reputation as one of the nation's most articulate and influential "neoconservatives." For a perspicacious analysis of Huntington's role in the controveries over "modernization," see Nils Gilman, *Mandarins of the Future* (Baltimore, 2003), 228–34.

World politics is entering a new phase, and intellectuals have not hesitated to proliferate visions of what it will be—the end of history, the return of traditional rivalries between nation states, and the decline of the nation state from the conflicting pulls of tribalism and globalism, among others. Each of these visions catches aspects of the emerging reality. Yet they all miss a crucial, indeed a central, aspect of what global politics is likely to be in the coming years.

It is my hypothesis that the fundamental source of conflict in this new world will not be primarily ideological or primarily economic. The great divisions among humankind and the dominating source of conflict will be cultural. Nation states will remain the most powerful actors in world affairs, but the principal conflicts of global politics will occur between nations and groups of different civilizations. The clash of civilizations will dominate global politics. The fault lines between civilizations will be the battle lines of the future.

Conflict between civilizations will be the latest phase in the evolution of conflict in the modern world. For a century and a half after the emergence of the modern international system with the Peace of Westphalia, the conflicts of the Western world were largely among princes—emperors, absolute monarchs and constitutional monarchs attempting to expand their bureaucracies, their armies, their mercantilist economic strength and, most important, the territory they ruled. In the process they created nation states, and beginning with the French Revolution the principal lines of conflict were between nations rather than princes. In 1793, as R. R. Palmer put it, "The wars of kings were over; the wars of peoples had begun." This nineteenth-century pattern lasted until the end of World War 1. Then, as a result of the Russian Revolution and the reaction against it, the conflict of nations yielded to the conflict of ideologies, first among communism, fascism-Nazism and liberal democracy, and then between communism and liberal democracy. During the Cold War, this latter conflict became embodied in the struggle between the two superpowers, neither of which was a nation state in the classical European sense and each of which defined its identity in terms of its ideology.

These conflicts between princes, nation states and ideologies were primarily conflicts within Western civilization, "Western civil wars," as William Lind has labeled them. This was as true of the Cold War as it was of the world wars and the earlier wars of the seventeenth, eighteenth and nineteenth centuries. With the end of the Cold War, international politics moves out of its Western phase, and its center-piece becomes the interaction between the West and non-Western civilizations and among non-Western civilizations. In the politics of civilizations, the peoples and governments of non-Western civilizations no longer remain the objects of history as targets of Western colonialism but join the West as movers and shapers of history.

During the cold war the world was divided into the First, Second and Third Worlds. Those divisions are no longer relevant. It is far more meaningful now to group countries not in terms of their political or economic systems or in terms of their level of economic development but rather in terms of their culture and civilization.

What do we mean when we talk of a civilization? A civilization is a cultural entity. Villages, regions, ethnic groups, nationalities, religious groups, all have distinct cultures at different levels of cultural heterogeneity. The culture of a village in southern Italy may

Source: Foreign Affairs, 72, no. 3 (Summer 1993), 22–49. Reprinted by permission of *Foreign Affairs*. Copyright © 2005 by the Council on Foreign Relations, Inc.

be different from that of a village in northern Italy, but both will share in a common Italian culture that distinguishes them from German villages. European communities, in turn, will share cultural features that distinguish them from Arab or Chinese communities. Arabs, Chinese and Westerners, however, are not part of any broader cultural entity. They constitute civilizations. A civilization is thus the highest cultural grouping of people and the broadest level of cultural identity people have short of that which distinguishes humans from other species. It is defined both by common objective elements, such as language, history, religion, customs, institutions, and by the subjective self-identification of people. People have levels of identity: a resident of Rome may define himself with varying degrees of intensity as a Roman, an Italian, a Catholic, a Christian, a European, a Westerner. The civilization to which he belongs is the broadest level of identification with which he intensely identifies. People can and do redefine their identities and, as a result, the composition and boundaries of civilizations change.

Civilizations may involve a large number of people, as with China ("a civilization pretending to be a state," as Lucian Pye put it), or a very small number of people, such as the Anglophone Caribbean. A civilization may include several nation states, as is the case with Western, Latin American and Arab civilizations, or only one, as is the case with Japanese civilization. Civilizations obviously blend and overlap, and may include subcivilizations. Western civilization has two major variants, European and North American, and Islam has its Arab, Turkic and Malay subdivisions. Civilizations are nonetheless meaningful entities, and while the lines between them are seldom sharp, they are real. Civilizations are dynamic; they rise and fall; they divide and merge. And, as any student of history knows, civilizations disappear and are buried in the sands of time.

Westerners tend to think of nation states as the principal actors in global affairs. They have been that, however, for only a few centuries. The broader reaches of human history have been the history of civilizations. In *A Study of History*, Arnold Toynbee identified 21 major civilizations; only six of them exist in the contemporary world.

Civilization identity will be increasingly important in the future, and the world will be shaped in large measure by the interactions among seven or eight major civilizations. These include Western, Confucian, Japanese, Islamic, Hindu, Slavic-Orthodox, Latin American and possibly African civilization. The most important conflicts of the future will occur along the cultural fault lines separating these civilizations from one another.

Why will this be the case?

First, differences among civilizations are not only real; they are basic. Civilizations are differentiated from each other by history, language, culture, tradition and, most important, religion. The people of different civilizations have different views on the relations between God and man, the individual and the group, the citizen and the state, parents and children, husband and wife, as well as differing views of the relative importance of rights and responsibilities, liberty and authority, equality and hierarchy. These differences are the product of centuries. They will not soon disappear. They are far more fundamental than differences among political ideologies and political regimes. Differences do not necessarily mean conflict, and conflict does not necessarily, mean violence. Over the centuries, however, differences among civilizations have generated the most prolonged and the most violent conflicts.

Second, the world is becoming a smaller place. The interactions between peoples of different civilizations are increasing; these increasing interactions intensify civilization consciousness and awareness of differences between civilizations and commonalities within civilizations. North African immigration to France generates hostility among

Frenchmen and at the same time increased receptivity to immigration by "good" European Catholic Poles. Americans react far more negatively to Japanese investment than to larger investments from Canada and European countries. Similarly, as Donald Horowitz has pointed out, "An Ibo may be...an Owerri Ibo or an Onitsha Ibo in what was the Eastern region of Nigeria. In Lagos, he is simply an Ibo. In London, he is a Nigerian. In New York, he is an African." The interactions among peoples of different civilizations enhance the civilization-consciousness of people that, in turn, invigorates differences and animosities stretching or thought to stretch back deep into history.

Third, the processes of economic modernization and social change throughout the world are separating people from longstanding local identities. They also weaken the nation state as a source of identity. In much of the world religion has moved in to fill this gap, often in the form of movements that are labeled "fundamentalist." Such movements are found in Western Christianity, Judaism, Buddhism and Hinduism, as well as in Islam. In most countries and most religions the people active in fundamentalist movements are young, college-educated, middle-class technicians, professionals and business persons. The "unsecularization of the world," George Weigel has remarked, "is one of the dominant social facts of life in the late twentieth century." The revival of religion, "la revanche de Dieu," as Gilles Kepel labeled it, provides a basis for identity and commitment that transcends national boundaries and unites civilizations.

Fourth, the growth of civilization-consciousness is enhanced by the dual role of the West. On the one hand, the West is at a peak of power. At the same time, however, and per-haps as a result, a return to the roots phenomenon is occurring among non-Western civilizations. Increasingly one hears references to trends toward a turning inward and "Asianization" in Japan, the end of the Nehru legacy and the "Hinduization" of India, the failure of Western ideas of socialism and nationalism and hence "re-Islamization" of the Middle East, and now a debate over Westernization versus Russianization in Boris Yeltsin's country. A West at the peak of its power confronts non-Wests that increasingly have the desire, the will and the resources to shape the world in non-Western ways.

In the past, the elites of non-Western societies were usually the people who were most involved with the West, had been educated at Oxford, the Sorbonne or Sandhurst, and had absorbed Western attitudes and values. At the same time, the populace in non-Western countries often remained deeply imbued with the indigenous culture. Now, however, these relationships are being reversed. A de-Westernization and indigenization of elites is occurring in many non-Western countries at the same time that Western, usually American, cultures, styles and habits become more popular among the mass of the people.

Fifth, cultural characteristics and differences are less mutable and hence less easily compromised and resolved than political and economic ones. In the former Soviet Union, communists can become democrats, the rich can become poor and the poor rich, but Russians cannot become Estonians and Azeris cannot become Armenians. In class and ideological conflicts, the key question was "Which side are you on?" and people could and did choose sides and change sides. In conflicts between civilizations, the question is "What are you?" That is a given that cannot be changed. And as we know, from Bosnia to the Caucasus to the Sudan, the wrong answer to that question can mean a bullet in the head. Even more than ethnicity, religion discriminates sharply and exclusively among people. A person can be half-French and half-Arab and simultaneously even a citizen of two countries. It is more difficult to be half-Catholic and half-Muslim.

Finally, economic regionalism is increasing. The proportions of total trade that were intraregional rose between 1980 and 1989 from 51 percent to 59 percent in Europe, 33 percent to 37 percent in East Asia, and 32 percent to 36 percent in North America. The importance of regional economic blocs is likely to continue to increase in the future. On the one hand, successful economic regionalism will reinforce civilization-consciousness. On the other hand, economic regionalism may succeed only when it is rooted in a common civilization. The European Community rests on the shared foundation of European culture and Western Christianity. The success of the North American Free Trade Area depends on the convergence now underway of Mexican, Canadian and American cultures. Japan, in contrast, faces difficulties in creating a comparable economic entity in East Asia because Japan is a society and civilization unique to itself. However strong the trade and investment links Japan may develop with other East Asian countries, its cultural differences with those countries inhibit and perhaps preclude its promoting regional economic integration like that in Europe and North America.

Common culture, in contrast, is clearly facilitating the rapid expansion of the economic relations between the People's Republic of China and Hong Kong, Taiwan, Singapore and the overseas Chinese communities in other Asian countries. With the Cold War over, cultural commonalities increasingly overcome ideological differences, and mainland China and Taiwan move closer together. If cultural commonality is a prerequisite for economic integration, the principal East Asian economic bloc of the future is likely to be centered on China...

Culture and religion also form the basis of the Economic Cooperation Organization, which brings together ten non-Arab Muslim countries: Iran, Pakistan, Turkey, Azerbaijan, Kazakhstan, Kyrgyzstan, Turkmenistan, Tadjikistan, Uzbekistan and Afghanistan. One impetus to the revival and expansion of this organization, founded originally in the 1960 by Turkey, Pakistan and Iran, is the realization by the leaders of several of these countries that they had no chance of admission to the European Community. Similarly, Caricom, the Central American Common Market and Mercosur rest on common cultural foundations. Efforts to build a broader Caribbean-Central American economic entity bridging the Anglo-Latin divide, however, have to date failed.

As people define their identity in ethnic and religious terms, they are likely to see an "us" versus "them" relation existing between themselves and people of different ethnicity or religion. The end of ideologically defined states in Eastern Europe and the former Soviet Union permits traditional ethnic identities and animosities to come to the fore. Differences in culture and religion create differences over policy issues, ranging from human rights to immigration to trade and commerce to the environment. Geographical propinquity gives rise to conflicting territorial claims from Bosnia to Mindanao. Most important, the efforts of the West to promote its values of democracy and liberalism as universal values, to maintain its military predominance and to advance its economic interests engender countering responses from other civilizations. Decreasingly able to mobilize support and form coalitions on the basis of ideology, governments and groups will increasingly attempt to mobilize support by appealing to common religion and civilization identity...

The west is now at an extraordinary peak of power in relation to other civilizations. Its superpower opponent has disappeared from the map. Military conflict among Western states is unthinkable, and Western military power is unrivaled. Apart from Japan, the West faces no economic challenge. It dominates international political and security institutions and with Japan international economic institutions. Global political and security issues are effectively settled by a directorate of the United States, Britain and France, world economic issues by a directorate of the United States, Germany and Japan, all of which maintain extraordinarily close relations with each other to the exclusion of lesser and largely non-Western countries. Decisions made at the U.N. Security Council or in the International Monetary Fund that reflect the interests of the West are presented to the world as reflecting the desires of the world community. The very phrase "the world community" has become the euphemistic collective noun (replacing "the Free World") to give global legitimacy to actions reflecting the interests of the United States and other Western powers. Through the IMF and other international economic institutions, the West promotes its economic interests and imposes on other nations the economic policies it thinks appropriate...

That at least is the way in which non-Westerners see the new world, and there is a significant element of truth in their view. Differences in power and struggles for military, economic and institutional power are thus one source of conflict between the West and other civilizations. Differences in culture, that is basic values and beliefs, are a second source of conflict. V. S. Naipaul has argued that Western civilization is the "universal civilization" that "fits all men." At a superficial level much of Western culture has indeed permeated the rest of the world. At a more basic level, however, Western concepts differ fundamentally from those prevalent in other civilizations. Western ideas of individualism, liberalism, constitutionalism, human rights, equality, liberty, the rule of law, democracy, free markets, the separation of church and state, often have little resonance in Islamic, Confucian, Japanese, Hindu, Buddhist or Orthodox cultures. Western efforts to propagate such ideas produce instead a reaction against "human rights imperialism" and a reaffirmation of indigenous values, as can be seen in the support for religious fundamentalism by the younger generation in non-Western cultures. The very notion that there could be a "universal civilization" is a Western idea, directly at odds with the particularism of most Asian societies and their emphasis on what distinguishes one people from another. Indeed, the author of a review of 100 comparative studies of values in different societies concluded that "the values that are most important in the West are least important worldwide." In the political realm, of course, these differences are most manifest in the efforts of the United States and other Western powers to induce other peoples to adopt Western ideas concerning democracy and human rights. Modern democratic government originated in the West. When it has developed in non-Western societies it has usually been the product of Western colonialism or imposition.

The central axis of world politics in the future is likely to be, in Kishore Mahbubani's phrase, the conflict between "the West and the Rest" and the responses of non-Western civilizations to Western power and values. Those responses generally take one or a combination of three forms. At one extreme, non-Western states can, like Burma and North Korea, attempt to pursue a course of isolation, to insulate their societies from penetration or "corruption" by the West, and, in effect, to opt out of participation in the Western-dominated global community. The costs of this course, however, are high, and few states have pursued it exclusively. A second alternative, the equivalent of "band-wagoning" in international relations theory, is to attempt to join the West and accept its values and institutions. The third alternative is to attempt to "balance" the West by developing economic and military power and cooperating with other non-Western societies against the West, while preserving indigenous values and institutions; in short, to modernize but not to Westernize...

This article does not argue that civilization identities will replace all other identities, that nation states will disappear, that each civilization will become a single coherent political entity, that groups within a civilization will not conflict with and even fight each other. This paper does set forth the hypotheses that differences between civilizations are real and important; civilization-consciousness is increasing; conflict between civilizations will supplant ideological and other forms of conflict as the dominant global form of conflict; international relations, historically a game played out within Western civilization, will increasingly be de-Westernized and become a game in which non-Western civilizations are actors and not simply objects; successful political, security and economic international institutions are more likely to develop within civilizations than across civilizations; conflicts between groups in different civilizations will be more frequent, more sustained and more violent than conflicts between groups in the same civilization; violent conflicts between groups in different civilizations are the most likely and most dangerous source of escalation that could lead to global wars; the paramount axis of world politics will be the relations between "the West and the Rest"; the elites in some torn non-Western countries will try to make their countries part of the West, but in most cases face major obstacles to accomplishing this; a central focus of conflict for the immediate future will be between the West and several Islamic-Confucian states.

This is not to advocate the desirability of conflicts between civilizations. It is to set forth descriptive hypotheses as to what the future may be like. If these are plausible hypotheses, however, it is necessary to consider their implications for Western policy. These implications should be divided between short-term advantage and long-term accommodation. In the short term it is clearly in the interest of the West to promote greater cooperation and unity within its own civilization, particularly between its European and North American components; to incorporate into the West societies in Eastern Europe and Latin America whose cultures are close to those of the West; to promote and maintain cooperative relations with Russia and Japan; to prevent escalation of local inter-civilization conflicts into major inter-civilization wars; to limit the expansion of the military strength of Confucian and Islamic states; to moderate the reduction of Western military capabilities and maintain military superiority in East and Southwest Asia; to exploit differences and conflicts among Confucian and Islamic states; to support in other civilizations groups sympathetic to Western values and interests; to strengthen international institutions that reflect and legitimate Western interests and values and to promote the involvement of non-Western states in those institutions.

In the longer term other measures would be called for. Western civilization is both Western and modern. Non-Western civilizations have attempted to become modern without becoming Western. To date only Japan has fully succeeded in this quest. Non-Western civilizations will continue to attempt to acquire the wealth, technology, skills, machines and weapons that are part of being modern. They will also attempt to reconcile this modernity with their traditional culture and values. Their economic and military strength relative to the West will increase. Hence the West will increasingly have to accommodate these non-Western modern civilizations whose power approaches that of the West but whose values and interests differ significantly from those of the West. This will require the West to maintain the economic and military power necessary to protect its interests in relation to these civilizations. It will also, however, require the West to develop a more profound under-standing of the basic religious and philosophical assumptions underlying other civilizations and the ways in which people in those civilizations see their interests. It will require an effort to identify elements of commonality between Western and other civilizations. For the relevant future, there will be no universal civilization, but instead a world of different civilizations, each of which will have to learn to coexist with the others.

SAM HARRIS

Selection from *The End of Faith*
(2004)

A group of strident, iconoclastic writers dubbed by the press as "the new atheists" commanded extensive attention in the early years of the twenty-first century. Stimulated in part by the apparent role of religious belief in inspiring the terrorist attacks of September 11, 2001, but responding also to the greater public religiosity brought into American political life by the conservative President George W. Bush, these writers blamed anachronistic religious ideas for a great range of injustices and barbarities. Among the most vigorous of the new atheists was neuroscientist Sam Harris (1967–), the first chapter of whose *The End of Faith: Religion, Terror, and the Future of Reason* (New York, 2004) is reprinted here. Harris followed this book with another, *Letter to a Christian Nation* (New York, 2006), responding to critics.

Study of the varieties of nonbelief—including agnosticism and mere indifference, in addition to avowed atheism—has intensified in recent years in relation to surveys showing the gradual diminution of religious identity in the United States, which remains the most religiously affirming society in the industrialized North Atlantic West. Credible surveys of the early twenty-first century showed a steady decline in religious identity, especially in the population under the age of thirty, in the Pacific and northeastern sections of the country, and among scientists.

A distinguishing theme in the writings of the new atheists—a group that included Tufts University philosopher Daniel Dennett, the British journalist Christopher Hitchens, and the Oxford University biologist Richard Dawkins—was an impatience with liberalized, ostensibly sophisticated versions of religious faith. Harris insists that religious "moderates" are really the core of the problem: They stop short of repudiating the irrational nonsense that enables obscurantists and fanatics to do their damage. Yet many thinkers who see themselves as opposed to obscurantism and fanaticism quickly argued that the new atheists were throwing the baby out with the bathwater, and that the religious moderates excoriated by Harris actually help to move society in more rational directions. The new atheists have also been criticized for exaggerating the certainty with which existing scientific knowledge renders untenable some of the more general forms of religious belief. Helpful examples of this line of criticism from a scientist who has no brief for religion are H. Allen Orr, "A Mission to Convert," *New York Review of Books* (January 11, 2007), and "A Religion for Darwinians?" *New York Review of Books* (August 16, 2007). Orr calls attention to the work of the freethinking philosopher, Philip Kitcher, *Living with Darwin: Evolution, Design, and the Future of Faith* (New York, 2007), which displays a more humble and cautious style of secular rationalism.

A helpful guide to the study of atheism is Michael Martin, ed., *The Cambridge Companion to Atheism* (New York, 2007). A collection of essays by nonbelievers displaying a great range of sensibilities—few as strident as Harris's—is Louise M. Antony, ed., *Philosophers without Gods: Meditations on Atheism and the Secular Life* (New York, 2007). A popular, readable account of the controversy over the new atheism is Anthony Gottlieb, "Atheists with Attitude," *New Yorker* (May 21, 2007). For a discussion of the relevance of religious belief to public policy that addresses Harris, see David A. Hollinger, "Religious Ideas: Should They Be Critically Engaged or Given a Pass?" *Representations*, 101 (2008), 144–54.

The young man boards the bus as it leaves the terminal. He wears an overcoat. Beneath his overcoat, he is wearing a bomb. His pockets are filled with nails, ball bearings, and rat poison.

The bus is crowded and headed for the heart of the city. The young man takes his seat beside a middle-aged couple. He will wait for the bus to reach its next stop. The couple at his side appears to be shopping for a new refrigerator. The woman has decided on a model, but her husband worries that it will be too expensive. He indicates another one in a brochure that lies open on her lap. The next stop comes into view. The bus doors swing. The woman observes that the model her husband has selected will not fit in the space underneath their cabinets. New passengers have taken the last remaining seats and begun gathering in the aisle. The bus is now full. The young man smiles. With the press of a button he destroys himself, the couple at his side, and twenty others on the bus. The nails, ball bearings, and rat poison ensure further casualties on the street and in the surrounding cars. All has gone according to plan.

The young man's parents soon learn of his fate. Although saddened to have lost a son, they feel tremendous pride at his accomplishment. They know that he has gone to heaven and prepared the way for them to follow. He has also sent his victims to hell for eternity. It is a double victory. The neighbors find the event a great cause for celebration and honor the young man's parents by giving them gifts of food and money.

These are the facts. This is all we know for certain about the young man. Is there anything else that we can infer about him on the basis of his behavior? Was he popular in school? Was he rich or was he poor? Was he of low or high intelligence? His actions leave no clue at all. Did he have a college education? Did he have a bright future as a mechanical engineer? His behavior is simply mute on questions of this sort, and hundreds like them. Why is it so easy, then, so trivially easy—you-could-almost-bet-your-life-on it easy—to guess the young man's religion?

A belief is a lever that, once pulled, moves almost everything else in a person's life. Are you a scientist? A liberal? A racist? These are merely species of belief in action. Your beliefs define your vision of the world; they dictate your behavior; they determine your emotional responses to other human beings. If you doubt this, consider how your experience would suddenly change if you came to believe one of the following propositions: 1. You have only two weeks to live. 2. You've just won a lottery prize of one hundred million dollars. 3. Aliens have implanted a receiver in your skull and are manipulating your thoughts.

These are mere words—until you believe them. Once believed, they become part of the very apparatus of your mind, determining your desires, fears, expectations, and subsequent behavior.

There seems, however, to be a problem with some of our most cherished beliefs about the world: they are leading us, inexorably, to kill one another. A glance at history, or at the pages of any newspaper, reveals that ideas which divide one group of human beings from another, only to unite them in slaughter, generally have their roots in religion. It seems that if our species ever eradicates itself through war, it will not be because it was written in the stars but because it was written in our books; it is what we do with words like "God" and "paradise" and "sin" in the present that will determine our future.

Source: Sam Harris, *The End of Faith* (New York, 2005), 11–48.

Our situation is this: most of the people in this world believe that the Creator of the universe has written a book. We have the misfortune of having many such books on hand, each making an exclusive claim as to its infallibility. People tend to organize themselves into factions according to which of these incompatible claims they accept—rather than on the basis of language, skin color, location of birth, or any other criterion of tribalism. Each of these texts urges its readers to adopt a variety of beliefs and practices, some of which are benign, many of which are not. All are in perverse agreement on one point of fundamental importance, however: "respect" for other faiths, or for the views of unbelievers, is not an attitude that God endorses. While all faiths have been touched, here and there, by the spirit of ecumenicalism, the central tenet of every religious tradition is that all others are mere repositories of error or, at best, dangerously incomplete. Intolerance is thus intrinsic to every creed. Once a person believes—*really* believes—that certain ideas can lead to eternal happiness, or to its antithesis, he cannot tolerate the possibility that the people he loves might be led astray by the blandishments of unbelievers. Certainty about the next life is simply incompatible with tolerance in this one.

Observations of this sort pose an immediate problem for us, however, because criticizing a person's faith is currently taboo in every corner of our culture. On this subject, liberals and conservatives have reached a rare consensus: religious beliefs are simply beyond the scope of rational discourse. Criticizing a person's ideas about God and the afterlife is thought to be impolitic in a way that criticizing his ideas about physics or history is not. And so it is that when a Muslim suicide bomber obliterates himself along with a score of innocents on a Jerusalem street, the role that faith played in his actions is invariably discounted. His motives must have been political, economic, or entirely personal. Without faith, desperate people would still do terrible things. Faith itself is always, and everywhere, exonerated.

But technology has a way of creating fresh moral imperatives. Our technical advances in the art of war have finally rendered our religious differences—and hence our religious *beliefs*—antithetical to our survival. We can no longer ignore the fact that billions of our neighbors believe in the metaphysics of martyrdom, or in the literal truth of the book of Revelation, or any of the other fantastical notions that have lurked in the minds of the faithful for millennia—because our neighbors are now armed with chemical, biological, and nuclear weapons. There is no doubt that these developments mark the terminal phase of our credulity. Words like "God" and "Allah" must go the way of "Apollo" and "Baal," or they will unmake our world.

A few minutes spent wandering the graveyard of bad ideas suggests that such conceptual revolutions are possible. Consider the case of alchemy: it fascinated human beings for over a thousand years, and yet anyone who seriously claims to be a practicing alchemist today will have disqualified himself for most positions of responsibility in our society. Faith-based religion must suffer the same slide into obsolescence.

What is the alternative to religion as we know it? As it turns out, this is the wrong question to ask. Chemistry was not an "alternative" to alchemy; it was a wholesale exchange of ignorance at its most rococo for genuine knowledge. We will find that, as with alchemy, to speak of "alternatives" to religious faith is to miss the point.

Of course, people of faith fall on a continuum: some draw solace and inspiration from a specific spiritual tradition, and yet remain fully committed to tolerance and diversity, while others would burn the earth to cinders if it would put an end to heresy. There are, in other words, religious *moderates* and religious *extremists*, and their various passions and projects should not be confused. One of the central themes of this book, however, is that religious moderates are themselves the bearers of a terrible dogma: they imagine that the path to peace will be paved once each of us has learned to respect the unjustified beliefs of others. I hope to show that the very ideal of religious tolerance—born of the notion that every human being should be free to believe whatever he wants about God—is one of the principal forces driving us toward the abyss.

We have been slow to recognize the degree to which religious faith perpetuates man's inhumanity to man. This is not surprising, since many of us still believe that faith is an essential component of human life. Two myths now keep faith beyond the fray of rational criticism, and they seem to foster religious extremism and religious moderation equally: (1) most of us believe that there are good things that people get from religious faith (e.g., strong communities, ethical behavior, spiritual experience) that cannot be had elsewhere; (2) many of us also believe that the terrible things that are sometimes done in the name of religion are the products not of *faith* per se but of our baser natures—forces like greed, hatred, and fear—for which religious beliefs are themselves the best (or even the only) remedy. Taken together, these myths seem to have granted us perfect immunity to outbreaks of reasonableness in our public discourse.

Many religious moderates have taken the apparent high road of pluralism, asserting the equal validity of all faiths, but in doing so they neglect to notice the irredeemably sectarian truth claims of each. As long as a Christian believes that only his baptized brethren will be saved on the Day of Judgment, he cannot possibly "respect" the beliefs of others, for he knows that the flames of hell have been stoked by these very ideas and await their adherents even now. Muslims and Jews generally take the same arrogant view of their own enterprises and have spent millennia passionately reiterating the errors of other faiths. It should go without saying that these rival belief systems are all equally uncontaminated by evidence.

And yet, intellectuals as diverse as H. G. Wells, Albert Einstein, Carl Jung, Max Planck, Freeman Dyson, and Stephen Jay Gould have declared the war between reason and faith to be long over. On this view, there is no need to have all of our beliefs about the universe cohere. A person can be a God-fearing Christian on Sunday and a working scientist come Monday morning, without ever having to account for the partition that seems to have erected itself in his head while he slept. He can, as it were, have his reason and eat it too . . . It is only because the church has been politically hobbled in the West that anyone can afford to think this way. In places where scholars can still be stoned to death for doubting the veracity of the Koran, Gould's notion of a "loving concordat" between faith and reason would be perfectly delusional.

This is not to say that the deepest concerns of the faithful, whether moderate or extreme, are trivial or even misguided. There is no denying that most of us have emotional and spiritual needs that are now addressed—however obliquely and at a terrible price—by mainstream religion. And these are needs that a mere *understanding* of our world, scientific or otherwise, will never fulfill. There is clearly a sacred dimension to our existence, and coming to terms with it could well be the highest purpose of human life. But we will find that it requires no faith in untestable propositions—Jesus was born of a virgin; the Koran is the word of God—for us to do this.

The idea that any one of our religions represents the infallible word of the One True God requires an encyclopedic ignorance of history, mythology, and art even to be entertained—as the beliefs, rituals, and iconography of each of our religions attest to centuries of cross-pollination among them. Whatever their imagined source, the doctrines of modern religions are no more tenable than those which, for lack of adherents, were cast upon the scrap heap of mythology millennia ago; for there is no more evidence to justify a belief in the literal existence of Yahweh and Satan than there was to keep Zeus perched upon his mountain throne or Poseidon churning the seas.

According to Gallup, 35 percent of Americans believe that the Bible is the literal and inerrant word of the Creator of the universe. Another 48 percent believe that it is the "inspired" word of the same—still inerrant, though certain of its passages must be interpreted symbolically before their truth can be brought to light. Only 17 percent of us remain to doubt that a personal God, in his infinite wisdom, is likely to have authored this text—or, for that matter, to have created the earth with its 250,000 species of beetles. Some 46 percent of Americans take a literalist view of creation (40 percent believe that God has guided creation over the course of millions of years). This means that 120 million of us place the big bang 2,500 years *after* the Babylonians and Sumerians learned to brew beer. If our polls are to be trusted, nearly 230 million Americans believe that a book showing neither unity of style nor internal consistency was authored by an omniscient, omnipotent, and omnipresent deity. A survey of Hindus, Muslims, and Jews around the world would surely yield similar results, revealing that we, as a species, have grown almost perfectly intoxicated by our myths. How is it that, in this one area of our lives, we have convinced ourselves that our beliefs about the world can float entirely free of reason and evidence?

It is with respect to this rather surprising cognitive scenery that we must decide what it means to be a religious "moderate" in the twenty-first century. Moderates in every faith are obliged to loosely interpret (or simply ignore) much of their canons in the interests of living in the modern world. No doubt an obscure truth of economics is at work here: societies appear to become considerably less productive whenever large numbers of people stop making widgets and begin killing their customers and creditors for heresy. The first thing to observe about the moderate's retreat from scriptural literalism is that it draws its inspiration not from scripture but from cultural developments that have rendered many of God's utterances difficult to accept as written. In America, religious moderation is further enforced by the fact that most Christians and Jews do not read the Bible in its entirety and consequently have no idea just how vigorously the God of Abraham wants heresy expunged. One look at the book of Deuteronomy reveals that he has something very specific in mind should your son or daughter return from yoga class advocating the worship of Krishna:

> If your brother, the son of your father or of your mother, or your son or daughter, or the spouse whom you embrace, or your most intimate friend, tries to secretly seduce you, saying, "Let us go and serve other gods," unknown to you or your ancestors before you, gods of the peoples surrounding you, whether near you or far away, anywhere throughout the world, you must not consent, you must not listen to him; you must show him no pity, you must not spare him or conceal his guilt. No, you must kill him, your hand must strike the first blow in putting him to death and the hands of the rest of the people following. You must stone him to death, since he has tried to divert you from Yahweh your God.... (Deuteronomy 13:7–11)

While the stoning of children for heresy has fallen out of fashion in our country, you will not hear a moderate Christian or Jew arguing for a "symbolic" reading of passages of this sort. (In fact, one seems to be explicitly blocked by God himself in Deuteronomy 13:1—"Whatever I am now commanding you, you must keep and observe, adding nothing to it, taking nothing away.") The above passage is as canonical as any in the Bible, and it is only by ignoring such barbarisms that the Good Book can be reconciled with life in the modern world. This is a problem for "moderation" in religion: it has nothing underwriting it other than the unacknowledged neglect of the letter of the divine law.

The only reason anyone is "moderate" in matters of faith these days is that he has assimilated some of the fruits of the last two thousand years of human thought (democratic politics, scientific advancement on every front, concern for human rights, an end to cultural and geographic isolation, etc.). The doors leading out of scriptural literalism do not open from the *inside*. The moderation we see among nonfundamentalists is not some sign that faith itself has evolved; it is, rather, the product of the many hammer blows of modernity that have exposed certain tenets of faith to doubt. Not the least among these developments has been the emergence of our tendency to value evidence and to be convinced by a proposition to the degree that there is evidence for it. Even most fundamentalists live by the lights of reason in this regard; it is just that their minds seem to have been partitioned to accommodate the profligate truth claims of their faith. Tell a devout Christian that his wife is cheating on him, or that frozen yogurt can make a man invisible, and he is likely to require as much evidence as anyone else, and to be persuaded only to the extent that you give it. Tell him that the book he keeps by his bed was written by an invisible deity who will punish him with fire for eternity if he fails to accept its every incredible claim about the universe, and he seems to require no evidence whatsoever.

Religious moderation springs from the fact that even the least educated person among us simply *knows* more about certain matters than anyone did two thousand years ago— and much of this knowledge is incompatible with scripture. Having heard something about the medical discoveries of the last hundred years, most of us no longer equate disease processes with sin or demonic possession. Having learned about the known distances between objects in our universe, most of us (about half of us, actually) find the idea that the whole works was created six thousand years ago (with light from distant stars already in transit toward the earth) impossible to take seriously. Such concessions to modernity do not in the least suggest that faith is compatible with reason, or that our religious traditions are in principle open to new learning: it is just that the utility of ignoring (or "reinterpreting") certain articles of faith is now overwhelming. Anyone being flown to a distant city for heart-bypass surgery has conceded, tacitly at least, that we have learned a few things about physics, geography, engineering, and medicine since the time of Moses.

So it is not that these texts have maintained their integrity over time (they haven't); it is just that they have been effectively edited by our neglect of certain of their passages. Most of what remains—the "good parts"—has been spared the same winnowing because we do not yet have a truly modern understanding of our ethical intuitions and our capacity for spiritual experience. If we better understood the workings of the human brain, we would undoubtedly discover lawful connections between our states of consciousness, our modes of conduct, and the various ways we use our attention. What makes one person happier than another? Why is love more conducive to happiness than hate? Why do we generally prefer beauty to ugliness and order to chaos? Why does it feel so good to smile and laugh, and why do these shared experiences generally bring people closer together? Is the ego an illusion, and, if so, what implications does this have for human life? Is there life after death? These are ultimately questions for a mature science of the mind. If we ever develop such a science, most of our religious texts will be no more useful to mystics than they now are to astronomers.

While moderation in religion may seem a reasonable position to stake out, in light of all that we have (and have not) learned about the universe, it offers no bulwark against religious extremism and religious violence. From the perspective of those seeking to live by the letter of the texts, the religious moderate is nothing more than a failed fundamentalist. He is, in all likelihood, going to wind up in hell with the rest of the unbelievers. The problem that religious moderation poses for all of us is that it does not permit anything very critical to be said about religious literalism. We cannot say that fundamentalists are crazy, because they are merely practicing their freedom of belief; we cannot even say that they are mistaken in *religious* terms, because their knowledge of scripture is generally unrivaled. All we can say, as religious moderates, is that we don't like the personal and social costs that a full embrace of scripture imposes on us. This is not a new form of faith, or even a new species of scriptural exegesis; it is simply a capitulation to a variety of all-too-human interests that have nothing, in principle, to do with God. Religious moderation is the product of *secular* knowledge and scriptural *ignorance*—and it has no bona fides, in religious terms, to put it on a par with fundamentalism. The texts themselves are unequivocal: they are perfect in all their parts. By their light, religious moderation appears to be nothing more than an unwillingness to fully submit to God's law. By failing to live by the letter of the texts, while tolerating the irrationality of those who do, religious moderates betray faith and reason equally. Unless the core dogmas of faith are called into question— i.e., that we know there is a God, and that we know what he wants from us—religious moderation will do nothing to lead us out of the wilderness.

The benignity of most religious moderates does not suggest that religious faith is anything more sublime than a desperate marriage of hope and ignorance, nor does it guarantee that there is not a terrible price to be paid for limiting the scope of reason in our dealings with other human beings. Religious moderation, insofar as it represents an attempt to hold on to what is still serviceable in orthodox religion, closes the door to more sophisticated approaches to spirituality, ethics, and the building of strong communities. Religious moderates seem to believe that what we need is not radical insight and innovation in these areas but a mere dilution of Iron Age philosophy. Rather than bring the full force of our creativity and rationality to bear on the problems of ethics, social cohesion, and even spiritual experience, moderates merely ask that we relax our standards of adherence to ancient superstitions and taboos, while otherwise maintaining a belief system that was passed down to us from men and women whose lives were simply ravaged by their basic ignorance about the world. In what other sphere of life is such subservience to tradition acceptable? Medicine? Engineering? Not even politics suffers the anachronism that still dominates our thinking about ethical values and spiritual experience.

Imagine that we could revive a well-educated Christian of the fourteenth century. The man would prove to be a total ignoramus, except on matters of faith. His beliefs about geography, astronomy, and medicine would embarrass even a child, but he would know more or less everything there is to know about God. Though he would be considered a fool to think that the earth is flat, or that trepanning constitutes a wise medical intervention, his religious ideas would still be beyond reproach. There are two explanations for this: either we perfected our religious understanding of the world a millennium ago—while our knowledge on all other fronts was still hopelessly inchoate—or religion, being the mere maintenance of dogma, is one area of discourse that does not admit of progress. We will see that there is much to recommend the latter view.

With each passing year, do our religious beliefs conserve more and more of the data of human experience? If religion addresses a genuine sphere of understanding and human necessity, then it should be susceptible to *progress*; its doctrines should become more useful, rather than less. Progress in religion, as in other fields, would have to be a matter of *present* inquiry, not the mere reiteration of past doctrine. Whatever is true now should be *discoverable* now, and describable in terms that are not an outright affront to the rest of what we know about the world. By this measure, the entire project of religion seems perfectly backward. It cannot survive the changes that have come over us—culturally, technologically, and even ethically. Otherwise, there are few reasons to believe that we will survive *it*.

Moderates do not want to kill anyone in the name of God, but they want us to keep using the word "God" as though we knew what we were talking about. And they do not want anything too critical said about people who *really* believe in the God of their fathers, because tolerance, perhaps above all else, is sacred. To speak plainly and truthfully about the state of our world—to say for instance, that the Bible and the Koran both contain mountains of life-destroying gibberish—is antithetical to tolerance as moderates currently conceive it. But we can no longer afford the luxury of such political correctness. We must finally recognize the price we are paying to maintain the iconography of our ignorance.

Finding ourselves in a universe that seems bent upon destroying us, we quickly discover, both as individuals and as societies, that it is a good thing to understand the forces arrayed against us. And so it is that every human being comes to desire genuine knowledge about the world. This has always posed a special problem for religion, because every religion preaches the truth of propositions for which it has no evidence. In fact, every religion preaches the truth of propositions for which no evidence is even *conceivable*. This put the "leap" in Kierkegaard's leap of faith.

What if all our knowledge about the world were suddenly to disappear? Imagine that six billion of us wake up tomorrow morning in a state of utter ignorance and confusion. Our books and computers are still here, but we can't make heads or tails of their contents. We have even forgotten how to drive our cars and brush our teeth. What knowledge would we want to reclaim first? Well, there's that business about growing food and building shelter that we would want to get reacquainted with. We would want to relearn how to use and repair many of our machines. Learning to understand spoken and written language would also be a top priority, given that these skills are necessary for acquiring most others. When in this process of reclaiming our humanity will it be important to know that Jesus was born of a virgin? Or that he was resurrected? And how would we relearn these truths, if they are indeed *true*? By reading the Bible? Our tour of the shelves will deliver similar pearls from antiquity—like the "fact" that Isis, the goddess of fertility, sports an impressive pair of cow horns. Reading further, we will learn that Thor carries a hammer and that Marduk's sacred animals are horses, dogs, and a dragon with a forked tongue. Whom shall we give top billing in our resurrected world? Yaweh or Shiva? And when will we want to relearn that premarital sex is a sin? Or that adulteresses should be stoned to death? Or that the soul enters the zygote at the moment of conception? And what will we think of those curious people who begin proclaiming that one of our books is distinct from all others in that it was actually written by the Creator of the universe?

There are undoubtedly spiritual truths that we would want to relearn—once we manage to feed and clothe ourselves—and these are truths that we have learned imperfectly in our present state. How is it possible, for instance, to overcome one's fear and inwardness and simply love other human beings? Assume, for the moment, that such a process of personal transformation exists and that there is something worth knowing about it; there is, in other words, some skill, or discipline, or conceptual understanding, or dietary supplement that allows for the reliable transformation of fearful, hateful, or indifferent persons into loving ones. If so, we should be positively desperate to know about it. There may even be a few biblical passages that would be useful in this regard—but as for whole rafts of untestable doctrines, clearly there would be no reasonable basis to take them up again. The Bible and Koran, it seems certain, would find themselves respectfully shelved next to Ovid's *Metamorphoses* and the *Egyptian Book of the Dead.*

The point is that most of what we currently hold sacred is not sacred for any reason other than that it was thought sacred *yesterday*. Surely, if we could create the world anew, the practice of organizing our lives around untestable propositions found in ancient literature—to say nothing of killing and dying for them—would be impossible to justify. What stops us from finding it impossible *now*?

Many have observed that religion, by lending meaning to human life, permits communities (at least those united under a single faith) to cohere. Historically this is true, and on this score religion is to be credited as much for wars of conquest as for feast days and brotherly love. But in its effect upon the *modern* world—a world already united, at least potentially, by economic, environmental, political, and epidemiological necessity—religious ideology is dangerously retrograde. Our past is not sacred for being *past*, and there is much that is behind us that we are struggling to *keep* behind us, and to which, it is to be hoped, we could never return with a clear conscience: the divine right of kings, feudalism, the caste system, slavery, political executions, forced castration, vivisection, bearbaiting, honorable duels, chastity belts, trial by ordeal, child labor, human and animal sacrifice, the stoning of heretics, cannibalism, sodomy laws, taboos against contraception, human radiation experiments—the list is nearly endless, and if it were extended indefinitely, the proportion of abuses for which religion could be found directly responsible is likely to remain undiminished. In fact, almost every indignity just mentioned can be attributed to an insufficient taste for evidence, to an uncritical faith in one dogma or another. The idea, therefore, that religious faith is somehow a *sacred* human convention—distinguished, as it is, both by the extravagance of its claims and by the paucity of its evidence—is really too great a monstrosity to be appreciated in all its glory. Religious faith represents so uncompromising a misuse of the power of our minds that it forms a kind of perverse, cultural singularity—vanishing point beyond which rational discourse proves impossible. When foisted upon each generation anew, it renders us incapable of realizing just how much of our world has been unnecessarily ceded to a dark and barbarous past.

Our world is fast succumbing to the activities of men and women who would stake the future of our species on beliefs that should not survive an elementary school education. That so many of us are still dying on account of ancient myths is as bewildering as it is horrible, and our own attachment to these myths, whether moderate or extreme, has kept us silent in the face of developments that could ultimately destroy us. Indeed, religion is as much a living spring of violence today as it was at any time in the past. The recent conflicts in Palestine (Jews v. Muslims), the Balkans (Orthodox Serbians v. Catholic Croatians; Orthodox Serbians v. Bosnian and Albanian Muslims), Northern Ireland (Protestants v. Catholics), Kashmir (Muslims v. Hindus), Sudan (Muslims v. Christians and animists), Nigeria (Muslims v. Christians), Ethiopia and Eritrea (Muslims v. Christians), Sri Lanka (Sinhalese Buddhists v. Tamil Hindus), Indonesia (Muslims v. Timorese Christians), and the Caucasus (Orthodox Russians v. Chechen Muslims; Muslim Azerbaijanis v. Catholic and Orthodox Armenians) are merely a few cases in point. In these places religion has been the *explicit* cause of literally millions of deaths in the last ten years. These events should strike us like psychological experiments run amok, for that is what they are. Give people divergent, irreconcilable, and untestable notions about what happens after death, and then oblige them to live together with limited resources. The result is just what we see: an unending cycle of murder and cease-fire. If history reveals any categorical truth, it is that an insufficient taste for evidence regularly brings out the worst in us. Add weapons of mass destruction to this diabolical clockwork, and you have found a recipe for the fall of civilization.

What can be said of the nuclear brinkmanship between India and Pakistan if their divergent religious beliefs are to be "respected"? There is nothing for religious pluralists to criticize but each country's poor diplomacy—while, in truth, the entire conflict is born of an irrational embrace of myth. Over one million people died in the orgy of religious killing that attended the partitioning of India and Pakistan. The two countries have since fought three official wars, suffered a continuous bloodletting at their shared border, and are now poised to exterminate one another with nuclear weapons simply because they disagree about "facts" that are every bit as fanciful as the names of Santa's reindeer. And their discourse is such that they are capable of mustering a suicidal level of enthusiasm for these subjects *without* evidence. Their conflict is only nominally about land, because their incompatible claims upon the territory of Kashmir are a direct consequence of their religious differences. Indeed, the only reason India and Pakistan are different countries is that the beliefs of Islam cannot be reconciled with those of Hinduism. From the point of view of Islam, it would be scarcely possible to conceive a way of scandalizing Allah that is not perpetrated, each morning, by some observant Hindu. The "land" these people are actually fighting over is not to be found in this world. When will we realize that the concessions we have made to faith in our political discourse have prevented us from even speaking about, much less uprooting, the most prolific source of violence in our history?

> Mothers were skewered on swords as their children watched. Young women were stripped and raped in broad daylight, then...set on fire. A pregnant woman's belly was slit open, her fetus raised skyward on the tip of sword and then tossed onto one of the fires that blazed across the city.

This is not an account of the Middle Ages, nor is it a tale from Middle Earth. This is *our* world. The cause of this behavior was not economic, it was not racial, and it was not political. The above passage describes the violence that erupted between Hindus and Muslims in India in the winter of 2002. The only difference between these groups consists in what they believe about God. Over one thousand people died in this monthlong series of riots— nearly half as many as have died in the Israeli-Palestinian conflict in more than a decade. And these are tiny numbers, considering the possibilities. A nuclear war between India and Pakistan seems almost inevitable, given what most Indians and Pakistanis believe about the afterlife. Arundhati Roy has said that Western concern over this situation is just a matter of white imperialists believing that "blacks cannot be trusted with the Bomb." This is a grotesque charge. One might argue that no group of people can quite be "trusted" with the bomb, but to ignore the destabilizing role that religion plays on the subcontinent is both reckless and disingenuous. We can only hope that the forces of secularism and rationality will keep the missiles in their silos for a while yet, until the deeper reasons for this conflict can be finally addressed.

While I do not mean to single out the doctrine of Islam for special abuse, there is no question that, at this point in history, it represents a unique danger to all of us, Muslim and non-Muslim alike. Needless to say, many Muslims are basically rational and tolerant of others. As we will see, however, these modern virtues are not likely to be products of their faith.... Indeed, it has grown rather obvious that the liabilities of the Muslim faith are by no means confined to the beliefs of Muslim "extremists." The response of the Muslim world to the events of September 11, 2001, leaves no doubt that a significant number of human beings in the twenty-first century believe in the possibility of martyrdom. We have, in response to this improbable fact, declared a war on "terrorism." This is rather like declaring war on "murder"; it is a category error that obscures the true cause of our troubles. Terrorism is not a *source* of human violence, but merely one of its inflections. If Osama bin Laden were the leader of a nation, and the World Trade Center had been brought down with missiles, the atrocities of September 11 would have been acts of war. It should go without saying that we would have resisted the temptation to declare a war on "war" in response.

To see that our problem is with Islam itself, and not merely with "terrorism," we need only ask ourselves *why* Muslim terrorists do what they do. Why would someone as conspicuously devoid of personal grievances or psychological dysfunction as Osama bin Laden—who is neither poor, uneducated, delusional, nor a prior victim of Western aggression—devote himself to cave-dwelling machinations with the intention of killing innumerable men, women, and children he has never met? The answer to this question is obvious—if only because it has been patiently articulated ad nauseam by bin Laden himself. The answer is that men like bin Laden *actually* believe what they say they believe. They believe in the literal truth of the Koran. Why did nineteen well-educated, middle-class men trade their lives in this world for the privilege of killing thousands of our neighbors? Because they believed that they would go straight to paradise for doing so. It is rare to find the behavior of human beings so fully and satisfactorily explained. Why have we been reluctant to accept this explanation?

As we have seen, there is something that most Americans share with Osama bin Laden, the nineteen hijackers, and much of the Muslim world. We, too, cherish the idea that certain fantastic propositions can be believed without evidence. Such heroic acts of credulity are thought not only acceptable but redeeming—even *necessary*. This is a problem that is considerably deeper and more troubling than the problem of anthrax in the mail. The concessions we have made to religious faith—to the idea that belief can be sanctified by something other than *evidence*—have rendered us unable to name, much less address, one of the most pervasive causes of conflict in our world.

It is important to specify the dimension in which Muslim "extremists" are actually extreme. They are extreme in their *faith*. They are extreme in their devotion to the literal word of the Koran and the hadith (the literature recounting the sayings and actions of the Prophet), and *this* leads them to be extreme in the degree to which they believe that modernity and secular culture are incompatible with moral and spiritual health. Muslim extremists are certain that the exports of Western culture are leading their wives and children away from God. They also consider our unbelief to be a sin so grave that it merits death whenever it becomes an impediment to the spread of Islam. These sundry passions are not reducible to "hatred" in any ordinary sense. Most Muslim extremists have never been to America or even met an American. And they have far fewer grievances with Western imperialism than is the norm around the globe. Above all, they appear to be suffering from a fear of contamination. As has been widely noted, they are also consumed by feelings of "humiliation"—humiliation over the fact that while their civilization has foundered, they have watched a godless, sin-loving people become the masters of everything they touch. This feeling is also a product of their faith. Muslims do not merely feel the outrage of the poor who are deprived of the necessities of life. They feel the outrage of a chosen people who have been subjugated by barbarians. Osama bin Laden wants for nothing. What, then, does he want? He has not called for the equal distribution of wealth around the globe. Even his demand for Palestinian statehood seems an afterthought, stemming as much from his anti-Semitism as from any solidarity he feels with the Palestinians (needless to say, such anti-Semitism and solidarity are also products of his faith). He seems most exercised over the presence of unbelievers (American troops and Jews) in the Muslim holy land and over what he imagines to be the territorial ambitions of Zionists. These are purely theological grievances. It would be much better, for all concerned, if he merely hated us.

To be sure, hatred is an eminently human emotion, and it is obvious that many Muslim extremists feel it. But faith is still the mother of hatred here, as it is wherever people define their moral identities in religious terms. The only salient difference between Muslims and non-Muslims is that the latter have not proclaimed their faith in Allah, and in Mohammed as his prophet. Islam is a missionary religion: there is not likely to be an underlying doctrine of racism, or even nationalism, animating the militant Muslim world. Muslims can be both racist and nationalistic, of course, but it seems all but certain that if the West underwent a massive conversion to Islam—and, perforce, repudiated all Jewish interests in the Holy Land—the basis for Muslim "hatred" would simply disappear.

Most Muslims who commit atrocities are explicit about their desire to get to paradise. One failed Palestinian suicide bomber described being "pushed" to attack Israelis by "the love of martyrdom." He added, "I didn't want revenge for anything. I just wanted to be a martyr." Mr. Zaydan, the would-be martyr, conceded that his Jewish captors were "better than many, many Arabs." With regard to the suffering that his death would have inflicted upon his family, he reminded his interviewer that a martyr gets to pick seventy people to join him in paradise. He would have been sure to invite his family along.

As I have said, people of faith tend to argue that it is not faith itself but man's baser nature that inspires such violence. But I take it to be self-evident that ordinary people cannot be moved to burn genial old scholars alive for blaspheming the Koran, or celebrate the violent deaths of their children, unless they believe some improbable things about the nature of the universe. Because most religions offer no valid mechanism by which their core beliefs can be tested and revised, each new generation of believers is condemned to inherit the superstitions and tribal hatreds of its predecessors. If we would speak of the baseness of our natures, our willingness to live, kill, and die on account of propositions for which we have no evidence should be among the first topics of discussion.

Most people in positions of leadership in our country will say that there is no direct link between the Muslim faith and "terrorism." It is clear, however, that Muslims hate the West in the very terms of their faith and that the Koran mandates such hatred. It is widely claimed by "moderate" Muslims that the Koran mandates nothing of the kind and that Islam is a "religion of peace." But one need only read the Koran itself to see that this is untrue:

> Prophet, make war on the unbelievers and the hypocrites and deal rigorously with them. Hell shall be their home: an evil fate. (Koran 9:73)
>
> Believers, make war on the infidels who dwell around you. Deal firmly with them. Know that God is with the righteous. (Koran 9:123)

Religious Muslims cannot help but disdain a culture that, to the degree that it is secular, is a culture of infidels; to the degree that it is religious, our culture is the product of a partial revelation (that of Christians and Jews), inferior in every respect to the revelation of Islam. The reality that the West currently enjoys far more wealth and temporal power than any nation under Islam is viewed by devout Muslims as a diabolical perversity, and this situation will always stand as an open invitation for jihad. Insofar as a person is Muslim—that is, insofar as he believes that Islam constitutes the only viable path to God and that the Koran enunciates it perfectly—he will feel contempt for any man or woman who doubts the truth of his beliefs. What is more, he will feel that the eternal happiness of his children is put in peril by the mere presence of such unbelievers in the world. If such people happen to be making the policies under which he and his children must live, the potential for violence imposed by his beliefs seems unlikely to dissipate. This is why economic advantages and education, in and of themselves, are insufficient remedies for the causes of religious violence. There is no doubt that many well-educated, middle-class fundamentalists are ready to kill and die for God. As Samuel Huntington and others have observed, religious fundamentalism in the developing world is not, principally, a movement of the poor and uneducated.

To see the role that faith plays in propagating Muslim violence, we need only ask why so many Muslims are eager to turn themselves into bombs these days. The answer: because the Koran makes this activity seem like a career opportunity. Nothing in the history of Western colonialism explains this behavior (though we can certainly concede that this history offers us much to atone for). Subtract the Muslim belief in martyrdom and jihad, and the actions of suicide bombers become completely unintelligible, as does the spectacle of public jubilation that invariably follows their deaths; insert these peculiar beliefs, and one can only marvel that suicide bombing is not more widespread. Anyone who says that the doctrines of Islam have "nothing to do with terrorism"—and our airways have been filled with apologists for Islam making this claim—is just playing a game with words.

> The believers who stay at home—apart from those that suffer from a grave impediment—are not the equal of those who fight for the cause of God with their goods and their persons. God has given those that fight with their goods and their persons a higher rank than those who stay at home. God has promised all a good reward; but far richer is the recompense of those who fight for Him.... He that leaves his dwelling to fight for God and His apostle and is then overtaken by death, shall be rewarded by God.... The unbelievers are your inveterate enemies. (Koran 4:95–101)

Outright prestidigitation with the articles of faith regularly produces utterances of this sort: "Islam is a religion of peace. The very word 'Islam,' after all, means 'peace.' And suicide is forbidden in the Koran. So there is no scriptural basis whatsoever for the actions of these terrorists." To such magician's patter, we might add that the phrase "dirty bomb" does not appear anywhere in the text of the Koran. Yes, the Koran seems to say something that can be construed as a prohibition against suicide—"Do not destroy yourselves" (4:29)—but it leaves many loopholes large enough to fly a 767 through:

> Let those who would exchange the life of this world for the hereafter, fight for the cause of God; whoever fights for the cause of God, whether he dies or triumphs, We shall richly reward him.... The true believers fight for the cause of God, but the infidels fight for the devil. Fight then against the friends of Satan.... Say: "Trifling are the pleasures of this life. The hereafter is better for those who would keep from evil...." (Koran 4:74–78)

When the above invitations to martyrdom are considered in light of the fact that Islam does not distinguish between religious and civil authority, the twin terrors of

Koranic literalism spring into view: on the level of the state, a Muslim aspiration for world domination is explicitly enjoined by God; on the level of the individual, the metaphysics of martyrdom provides a rationale for ultimate self-sacrifice toward this end. As Bernard Lewis observes, since the time of the Prophet, Islam has been "associated in the minds and memories of Muslims with the exercise of political and military power." The metaphysics of Islam are particularly inauspicious where tolerance and religious diversity are concerned, for martyrdom is the only way that a Muslim can bypass the painful litigation that awaits us all on the Day of Judgment and proceed directly to paradise. Rather than spend centuries moldering in the earth in anticipation of being resurrected and subsequently interrogated by wrathful angels, the martyr is immediately transported to Allah's Garden, where a flock of "dark-eyed" virgins awaits him.

Because they are believed to be nothing less than verbatim transcripts of God's utterances, texts like the Koran and the Bible must be appreciated, and criticized, for any *possible* interpretations to which they are susceptible—and to which they will be subjected, with varying emphases and elisions, throughout the religious world. The problem is not that some Muslims neglect to notice the few references to nonaggression that can be found in the Koran, and that this leads them to do terrible things to innocent unbelievers; the problem is that most Muslims believe that the Koran is the *literal word of God*. The corrective to the worldview of Osama bin Laden is not to point out the single line in the Koran that condemns suicide, because this ambiguous statement is set in a thicket of other passages that can be read only as direct summons to war against the "friends of Satan." The appropriate response to the bin Ladens of the world is to correct everyone's reading of these texts by making the same evidentiary demands in religious matters that we make in all others. If we cannot find our way to a time when most of us are willing to admit that, at the very least, *we are not sure* whether or not God wrote some of our books, then we need only count the days to Armageddon—because God has given us far many more reasons to kill one another than to turn the other cheek.

We live in an age in which most people believe that mere words—"Jesus," "Allah," "Ram"—can mean the difference between eternal torment and bliss everlasting. Considering the stakes here, it is not surprising that many of us occasionally find it necessary to murder other human beings for using the wrong magic words, or the right ones for the wrong reasons. How can any person presume to know that this is the way the universe works? Because it says so in our holy books. How do we know that our holy books are free from error? Because the books *themselves* say so. Epistemological black holes of this sort are fast draining the light from our world.

There is, of course, much that is wise and consoling and beautiful in our religious books. But words of wisdom and consolation and beauty abound in the pages of Shakespeare, Virgil, and Homer as well, and no one ever murdered strangers by the thousands because of the inspiration he found there. The belief that certain books were written by God (who, for reasons difficult to fathom, made Shakespeare a far better writer than himself) leaves us powerless to address the most potent source of human conflict, past and present. How is it that the absurdity of this idea does not bring us, hourly, to our knees? It is safe to say that few of us would have thought so many people could believe such a thing, if they did not *actually* believe it. Imagine a world in which generations of human beings come to believe that certain *films* were made by God or that specific software was coded by him. Imagine a future in which millions of our descendants murder each other over rival interpretations of *Star Wars* or Windows 98. Could anything—*anything*—be more ridiculous? And yet, this would be no more ridiculous than the world we are living in....

It is time we recognized that belief is not a private matter; it has never been merely private. In fact, beliefs are scarcely more private than actions are, for every belief is a fount of action *in potentia*. The belief that it will rain puts an umbrella in the hand of every man or woman who owns one. It should be easy enough to see that belief in the full efficacy of prayer, for instance, becomes an emphatically *public* concern the moment it is actually put into practice: the moment a surgeon lays aside his worldly instruments and attempts to suture his patients with prayer, or a pilot tries to land a passenger jet with nothing but repetitions of the word "Hallelujah" applied to the controls, we are swiftly delivered from the provinces of private faith to those of a criminal court.

As a man believes, so he will act. Believe that you are the member of a chosen people, awash in the salacious exports of an evil culture that is turning your children away from God, believe that you will be rewarded with an eternity of unimaginable delights by dealing death to these infidels—and flying a plane into a building is scarcely more than a matter of being asked to do it. It follows, then, that certain beliefs are *intrinsically* dangerous. We all know that human beings are capable of incredible brutality, but we would do well to ask, What sort of ideology will make us *most* capable of it? And how can we place these beliefs beyond the fray of normal discourse, so that they might endure for thousands of years, unperturbed by the course of history or the conquests of reason? These are problems of both cultural and psychological engineering. It has long been obvious that the dogma of faith—particularly in a scheme in which the faithful are promised eternal salvation and doubters are damned—is nothing less than their perfect solution.

It is time we admitted, from kings and presidents on down, that there is no evidence that any of our books was authored by the Creator of the universe. The Bible, it seems certain, was the work of sand-strewn men and women who thought the earth was flat and for whom a wheelbarrow would have been a breathtaking example of emerging technology. To rely on such a document as the basis for our worldview—however heroic the efforts of redactors—is to repudiate two thousand years of civilizing insights that the human mind has only just begun to inscribe upon itself through secular politics and scientific culture. We will see that the greatest problem confronting civilization is not merely religious extremism: rather, it is the larger set of cultural and intellectual accommodations we have made to faith itself. Religious moderates are, in large part, responsible for the religious conflict in our world, because their beliefs provide the context in which scriptural literalism and religious violence can never be adequately opposed.

Every sphere of genuine discourse must, at a minimum, admit of *discourse*—and hence the possibility that those standing on its fringe can come to understand the truths that it strives to articulate. This is why any sustained exercise of reason must necessarily transcend national, religious, and ethnic boundaries. There is, after all, no such thing as an inherently American (or Christian, or Caucasian) *physics*. Even spirituality and ethics meet this criterion of universality because human beings, whatever their background, seem to converge on similar spiritual experiences and ethical insights when given the same methods of inquiry. Such is not the case with the "truths" of religion, however. Nothing that a Christian and a Muslim can say to each other will render their beliefs mutually vulnerable to discourse, because the very tenets of their faith have immunized them against the power of conversation. Believing strongly, without evidence, they have kicked themselves loose of the world. It is therefore in the very nature of faith to serve as an impediment to further inquiry. And yet, the fact that we are no longer killing people for heresy in the West suggests that bad ideas, however sacred, cannot survive the company of good ones forever.

Given the link between belief and action, it is clear that we can no more tolerate a diversity of religious beliefs than a diversity of beliefs about epidemiology and basic hygiene. There are still a number of cultures in which the germ theory of disease has yet to put in an appearance, where people suffer from a debilitating ignorance on most matters relevant to their physical health. Do we "tolerate" these beliefs? Not if they put our own health in jeopardy.

Even apparently innocuous beliefs, when unjustified, can lead to intolerable consequences. Many Muslims, for instance, are convinced that God takes an active interest in women's clothing. While it may seem harmless enough, the amount of suffering that this incredible idea has caused is astonishing. The rioting in Nigeria over the 2002 Miss World Pageant claimed over two hundred lives; innocent men and women were butchered with machetes or burned alive simply to keep that troubled place free of women in bikinis. Earlier in the year, the religious police in Mecca prevented paramedics and firefighters from rescuing scores of teenage girls trapped in a burning building. Why? Because the girls were not wearing the traditional head covering that Koranic law requires. Fourteen girls died in the fire; fifty were injured. Should Muslims really be free to believe that the Creator of the universe is concerned about hemlines?...

It is time we recognized that the only thing that permits human beings to collaborate with one another in a truly open-ended way is their willingness to have their beliefs modified by new facts. Only openness to evidence and argument will secure a common world for us. Nothing guarantees that reasonable people will agree about everything, of course, but the unreasonable are certain to be divided by their dogmas. This spirit of mutual inquiry is the very antithesis of religious faith.

While we may never achieve closure in our view of the world, it seems extraordinarily likely that our descendants will look upon many of our beliefs as both impossibly quaint and suicidally stupid. Our primary task in our discourse with one another should be to identify those beliefs that seem least likely to survive another thousand years of human inquiry, or most likely to prevent it, and subject them to sustained criticism. Which of our present practices will appear most ridiculous from the point of view of those future generations that might yet survive the folly of the present? It is hard to imagine that our religious preoccupations will not top the list. It is natural to hope that our descendants will look upon us with gratitude. But we should also hope that they look upon us with pity and disgust, just as we view the slaveholders of our all-too-recent past. Rather than congratulate ourselves for the state of our civilization, we should consider how, in the fullness of time, we will seem hopelessly backward, and work to lay a foundation for such refinements in the present. We must find our way to a time when faith, without evidence, disgraces anyone who would claim it. Given the present state of our world, there appears to be no other future worth wanting....

STEWART BRAND

Selection from *Whole Earth Discipline: An Ecopragmatist Manifesto* (2009)

Stewart Brand (1938–) is best known for the ecologically pioneering *Whole Earth Catalog*, which helped to create the modern environmentalist movement and popularized the idea of "alternative energy." Brand published the *Catalog* regularly between 1968 and 1972 and periodically thereafter. One of the most capacious of environmental thinkers, Brand tries in his most recent book, *Whole Earth Discipline* (New York, 2009), to engage the entire panorama of ecological issues and to critically review the earlier history of their discussion. In the chapter from that book reprinted here, Brand defends a science-centered approach but explains the productive function often played by more romantic environmentalists in mobilizing political action. Conversational in style but attending closely to technicalities, Brand has proved able to reach a wide popular audience even while engaging the scientific and engineering constituencies of the environmental movement.

Brand has been a pioneer also in thinking about digitalization. His *Two Cybernetic Frontiers* (New York, 1974) is credited with the first use of the term "personal computer" in print. He was the chief founder in 1984 of the "hacker's conference," which has since been an annual event for explorers of the computer frontiers. Often called a "futurologist," Brand is the cofounder of the Long Now Foundation and of the consulting firm Global Business Network. His other books include *The Media Lab: Inventing the Future at M.I.T.* (New York, 1987) and *The Clock of the Long Now: Time and Responsibility* (New York, 1999).

Brand grew up in Illinois. Along with novelist Ken Kesey, Brand was part of the late 1960s counterculture group known as "The Merry Pranksters" and is described in that role by Tom Wolfe in *The Electric Kool-Aid Acid Test* (New York, 1968). Brand was among those featured in the popular book by television journalist Tom Brokaw, *Boom: Voices of the 60s* (New York, 2007). He has lived for nearly thirty years in a tugboat anchored in San Francisco Bay.

Brand's career is now the subject of several scholarly studies, including Fred Turner, *From Counterculture to Cyberculture: Stewart Brand, the Whole Earth Network, and the Rise of Digital Utopianism* (Chicago, 2006), and Andrew J. Kirk, *Counterculture Green: The Whole Earth Catalog and American Environmentalism* (Lawrence, Kans., 2007).

Environmentalists own the color green. That's extraordinary, an astonishing accomplishment. No movement has owned a color globally since the Communists took over red. Red means nothing now. How long will Green mean something?

"What is the environmental movement?" It was the editor of a Green magazine asking. I heard myself say, "The environmental movement is a body of science, technology, and emotion engaged in directing public discourse, public policy, and private behavior toward ensuring the health of natural systems."

My theory is that the success of the environmental movement is driven by two powerful forces—romanticism and science—that are often in opposition, with a third force emerging. The romantics identify with natural systems; the scientists study natural systems. The romantics are moralistic, rebellious against the perceived dominant power, and dismissive of any who appear to stray from the true path. They hate to admit mistakes or change direction. The scientists are ethical rather than moralistic, rebellious against any perceived dominant paradigm, and combative against one another. For them, identifying mistakes is what science *is,* and direction change is the goal.

It's fortunate that there are so many romantics in the movement, because they are the ones who inspire the majority in most developed societies to see themselves as environmentalists. But that also means that scientists and their perceptions are always in the minority; they are easily ignored, suppressed, or demonized when their views don't fit the consensus story line.

A new set of environmental players is shifting the balance. Engineers are arriving who see any environmental problem neither as a romantic tragedy nor as a scientific puzzle but simply as something to fix. They look to the scientists for data to fix the problem with, and the scientists appreciate the engineers because new technology is what makes science go forward. The romantics distrust engineers—sometimes correctly—for their hubris and are uncomfortable with the prospect of fixing things because the essence of tragedy is that it can't be fixed.

Romantics love problems; scientists discover and analyze problems; engineers solve problems.

That is a gross oversimplification. Stereotypes were not responsible for the burst of U.S. environmental legislation passed in the 1970s—the Clean Air, Clean Water, and Endangered Species acts, and the creation of the Environmental Protection Agency. What would I call the dedicated lawyers who got those bills written, passed, and signed— "political engineers"?

Where in my character set are the duck hunters who pioneered the conservation movement in the 1930s by protecting wetlands and who are still at it seventy years later? Some 24 million acres of North American waterfowl habitat are being preserved, protected, and restored by the 775,000 well-armed members of Ducks Unlimited.

Real people, not paper cutouts, made recycling happen, cleaned the air in Los Angeles and the Thames in London, and elevated ecology to a philosophy; made ecotourism an industry, wildlife films an entertainment genre, and *watershed* a term of art for planners; planted countless urban trees and slowed the destruction of the Amazon rain forest; stopped acid rain and ozone depletion, saved condors and whooping cranes, built global Green organizations, created wildland parks at every governmental level

Source: Stewart Brand, *The Whole Earth Discipline: An Ecopragmatist Manifesto* (New York, Viking, 2010), 207–33.

from county to World Heritage Sites.... The list could fill the rest of this book. It does fill Paul Hawken's broadside on the proliferation of environmental activist groups, *Blessed Unrest: How the Largest Movement in the World Came into Being and Why No One Saw It Coming* (2007).

I'm going to stick with my stock characters, though, because they offer a way to think about some important changes that are going on. When concern about climate change went mainstream all over the world in 2007, Greens everywhere felt vindicated. "Today's torrent of environmental progress," declared the head of Sierra Club that summer, "rivals that in the heady years around the first Earth Day in 1970." The world was finally coming around to the Green point of view, and all environmentalists had to do was to seize the opportunity and bear down on their agenda to win final victory.

Wrong. The long-evolved Green agenda is suddenly outdated—too negative, too tradition-bound, too specialized, too politically one-sided for the scale of the climate problem. Far from taking a new dominant role, environmentalists risk being marginalized more than ever, with many of their deep goals and well-honed strategies irrelevant to the new tasks. Accustomed to saving natural systems from civilization, Greens now have the unfamiliar task of saving civilization from a natural system—climate dynamics.

It may seem hardest to change course when you think you're triumphant, but it's actually an opportune time. Resources abound; new people with new ideas show up. With the old guard swamped by events, Young Turks can strike out in divergent directions. An unsentimental review of the past can toss out entrenched ideas that are no longer useful and poke around in long-taboo areas for potential new value. That's the mode I'll try to frame here, not just for my fellow mossback environmentalists but also for the new climate-driven environmentalists—the Green bio-hackers, Green technophiles, Green urbanists, and Green infrastructure rebuilders.

It was romantics—charismatic figures such as Henry Thoreau, John Muir, David Brower, Ed Abbey, Dave Foreman, and Julia Butterfly Hill—who taught us to be rings of bone, open to all of it, ready to redirect our lives based on our deepest connection to nature. The year I graduated from Stanford, Brower launched the Sierra Club's Exhibit Format series of nature photography books. His first one, *This is the American Earth* (1960), made with photographer Ansel Adams, set me on a path I'm still on. Desert writer Ed Abbey introduced the further romance of protest, and role models like Earth-Firster Dave Foreman and mythic tree sitter Julia Butterfly Hill played it out.

Certain knowledge of what to fight for, and what to fight against, gives meaning to life and provides its own version of discipline: *never* give up. That kind of meaning is illusory, I now believe, and blinkered. Fealty to a mystical absolute is a formula for disaster, especially in transformative times.

California was a great place to get over mysticism in the 1960s and 1970s. Such an endless parade of gurus and mystics came through, peddling their wares, that they canceled each other out. They couldn't compete with the drugs, and the drugs canceled each other out as well. Fervent visions, shared to excess, became clanking clichés. All that was left was daily reality, with its endless negotiation, devoid of absolutes, but alive with surprises.

In 1997 my growing distrust of romanticism in all its forms was crystallized by a book: *The Idea of Decline in Western History*, by Arthur Herman, which explores one question: What is behind the ever-popular narrative of decline? Decade after decade, leading intellectuals in Europe and America explain that the world is going to hell, progress is a lie, and bad people, bad ideas, and bad institutions are to blame for the irreversible degradation of all that is true and good.

Overwhelming real-world evidence to the contrary matters not at all to the calamitists.

Herman distinguishes two forms of the lament: historical pessimism (Jacob Burckhardt, Oswald Spengler, Henry Adams, Arnold Toynbee, Paul Kennedy) and a much more frightening cultural pessimism (Arthur Schopenhauer, Friedrich Nietzsche, Martin Heidegger, Jean-Paul Sartre, Frantz Fanon, Michel Foucault, Herbert Marcuse, Noam Chomsky, and many contemporary Greens). Herman writes:

> The historical pessimist sees civilization's virtues under attack from malign and destructive forces that it cannot overcome; cultural pessimism claims that those forces form the civilizing process from the start. The historical pessimist worries that his own society is about to destroy itself, the cultural pessimist concludes that it needs to be destroyed.

Thus spake Nietzsche: "There is an element of decay in everything that characterizes modern man." And: "Are we not straying as through an infinite nothing? Do we not feel the breath of empty space? Has it not become colder? Is not night continually closing in on us?"

A standard eco-pessimist could announce almost triumphantly in 1992:

> Modern humanity is rapidly destroying the natural world on which it depends for its survival. Everywhere on our planet, the picture is the same. Forests are being cut down, wetlands drained, coral reefs grubbed up, agricultural lands eroded, salinized, desertified, or simply paved over. Pollution is now generalized—our groundwater, streams, rivers, estuaries, seas and oceans, the air we breathe, the food we eat, are all affected. Just about every living creature on earth now contains in its body traces of agricultural and industrial chemicals— many of which are known or suspected carcinogens or mutagens.
>
> As a result of our activities, it is probable that thousands of species are being made extinct every day. Only a fraction of these are known to science.... By destroying the natural world in this way we are making our planet progressively less habitable. If current trends persist, in no more than a few decades it will cease to be capable of supporting complex forms of life.

(That was Edward Goldsmith's opening salvo in *The Way: An Ecological World-view.* His worries are accurate individually, but they are selective, one-sided, and overaggregated into a paralyzing spasm of angst.)

Arthur Herman traces the origin of romanticism and its decay narrative to one man and one event—Jean-Jacques Rousseau and the French Revolution of 1789. Rousseau embraced an imaginary primitivism and declared, "Everything degenerates in the hands of men." His vision of a return to innocence and freedom seemed to be at hand with the overthrow of the French monarchy. The intelligentsia of Europe thrilled to the coming of a new dawn in 1789, and then watched it turn into blood and terror by 1793. With that trauma, the romantic stance became one of despair and defiance, and it has remained so ever since.

Following the deep seam of romanticism through successive centuries, Herman finds it leading through Oswald Spengler's *Decline of the West* (1918) directly to Nazi Germany. "Hitler's generation was the first European generation raised on cultural pessimism."

There is a troubling Green thread in the Nazi movement. I first came across it in 1977 with an article I ran in *CoEvolution* on the German *wandervögel* (wanderbirds)— young hippielike back-to-the-land romantic strivers of the late nineteenth century who were all too easily co-opted into the Hitler Youth. I learned from Herman's book that biologist Ernst Haeckel, coiner of the word *ecology (oekologie*, 1866), championed eugenics and selective euthanasia to purge an imperiled Europe of "degenerates such as Jews and Negroes." According to Peter Coates in *Nature: Western Attitudes Since Ancient Times* (2004), "Nazi Germany led Europe in the creation of nature reserves and the implementation of progressive forestry sensitive to what we would now call biodiversity."

Summarizing the ongoing debate about "the Green face of Nazism," Nils Gilman at Global Business Network wrote me that,

> The key and I think undebated points are these: (1) the Nazis used their green credentials to win and widen their popular support, (2) virtually no one at the time, inside or outside Germany, saw any contradiction between the Nazis' environmentalism and the rest of their political program. In sum: while there's obviously no necessary connection between eco-friendliness and fascism/nativism, there are lots of ways in which the two movements can and have connected historically, and may again in the future.

How times change. Germany is once again the Greenest country in Europe, but this time the political framework is so leftist that the powerful Green party members, *Die Grünen*, are commonly called watermelons: green on the outside, red on the inside. That flip is common in the world. In the old days, conservation was conservative, the proper activity of duck hunters and Teddy Roosevelts. And progress used to belong to progressives; but then it frightened them, and they turned on it. They came to oppose what they viewed as the technological threats of progress, the despoliation of nature by progress, and the capitalist engine of progress. That in turn offended the conservatives, who were fond of capitalism, and opposing the newly antiprogress progressives meant opposing their environmental programs as well. The flip was complete.

It has become a problem. Worldwide, the political stereotype these days is that Green equals left, left equals Green, and right equals anti-Green. That may be helpful for liberals, grounding them in the science and practice of natural systems, but it blinds conservatives and badly hampers Green perspective. Becoming politically narrow limits Greens' thinking and marginalizes their effectiveness, because whatever they say is automatically dismissed by anyone who has doubts about liberals. Countless conservatives refused to take climate change seriously because they couldn't abide the idea of Al Gore being right.

I saw a version of this narrowness played out after 1966, when I was inspired by a rooftop LSD trip to distribute buttons that read, "Why haven't we seen a photograph of the whole Earth yet?" Everyone in the New Left opposed Kennedy's space program, seeing it (correctly) as a cold war episode that they thought (incorrectly) was being carried out to no good purpose by crew-cut military squares. (Only Abbie Hoffman disagreed with his compatriots: "Are you kidding? We're going to the fucking MOON!") Environmentalists joined the leftist opposition to the space program: "We have to clean up the Earth before we can leave it."

The exception was Jacques Cousteau, the pioneer of underwater exploration. In a 1976 interview for *CoEvolution*, he told me that in the 1960s his fellow ocean specialists were scandalized by the expense and irrelevance of the U.S. space program, but he supported it for philosophical reasons that quickly became practical. Cousteau realized that satellites were the only way to monitor the health of the oceans.

Despite their best efforts to shut it down or ignore it, environmentalists gained more from the space program than anyone else, and sooner. Directly inspired by the 1969 photos of Earth from space, the first Earth Day in 1970 attracted 20 million Americans to the rallies, and the environmental movement took off, with a planetary icon and a coherence it has maintained ever since. Robert Poole wrote in *Earthrise* (2008): "As soon as the Earth became visible…it began to acquire friends, starting in 1969 with Friends of the Earth. The years 1969–72 saw no fewer than seven major national environmental organizations come into being."

What made Cousteau prescient about what the perspective from space would bring? He had no allergy to new technology: He was the inventor of the scuba gear that made underwater exploration possible. His explorer's heart saw space as the next ocean, and his scientific perspective made him ask what satellites could do for him. Being apolitical, he was free of loyalties to any narrow agenda. To disagree with his scientific peers was not a violation of solidarity but part of his job as a scientist.

Solidarity is a leftover idea of the left—"Which Side Are You On?" was a union song—that has no place in the environmental movement. It led Friends of the Earth in Britain to throw away their trustee Hugh Montefiore over nuclear power. (He supported nuclear to head off climate change.) The man who fired Montefiore, FOE director Tony Juniper, said that debate was welcome within the organization but not in public. That strikes me as a self-defeating practice. It is more important for an organization or a movement to be right than to be consistent, and figuring out what is right takes debate, as open as possible, because what is right keeps on changing as circumstances change.

A romantic stance, or a political agenda, is fine for giving people a sense of identity and motivating their efforts; but it's poor at solving problems. "One of the points of pragmatism is that there is no escape from the need to wrestle seriously with the particulars of a given problem," writes Daniel Farber in his law book *Eco-pragmatism* (2000).

Paul Hawken has one of the great business-card stories:

> I have given nearly one thousand talks about the environment in the past fifteen years, and after every speech a smaller crowd gathered to talk, ask questions, and exchange business cards. The people offering their cards were working on the most salient issues of our day: climate change, poverty, deforestation, peace, water, hunger, conservation, human rights, and more. They were from the nonprofit and nongovernmental world, also known as civil society. They looked after rivers and bays, educated consumers about sustainable agriculture, retrofitted houses with solar panels, lobbied state legislatures about pollution, fought against corporate-weighted trade policies, worked to green inner cities, or taught children about the environment. Quite simply, they were trying to safeguard nature and ensure justice.

Hawken kept the growing pile of cards until they provoked him into action. As he researched his book *Blessed Unrest* and set about building an online database of such organizations, he began to realize that there are over a million of them loose in the world. They are flourishing because of their specificity, because they wrestle with particulars. They are invisible for the same reason, and effective for the same reason. As Hawken notes, "Feedback loops are short, learning is accelerated." Unfettered by ideology, slogans, fame, or even an aggregate name, the organizations live by improvisation and focus on results. Their story is about improvement, not decline.

Science is the only news. When you scan a news portal or magazine, all the human interest stuff is the same old he-said-she-said, the politics and economics the same sorry cyclical dramas, the fashions a pathetic illusion of newness; even the technology is predictable if you know the science. Human nature doesn't change much; science does, and the change accrues, altering the world irreversibly.

In stark contrast to romantic cultural pessimism, science is imbued with a double optimism. One part is the scientific process itself, driven by accelerating capability: science makes science go faster and better. The other part is the content—much of what is discovered is either good news or news that can be made good, thanks to ever-deepening knowledge, tools, and techniques. Because the findings of science are not just matters of opinion, they sweep past systems of thought based only on opinion. The swarming edges of science pose ever more and better questions, better put. They're phrased to elicit hard answers, the answers get found, and the questioners move on.

No wonder static, self-obsessed romanticism acts so threatened by science. It is. A romantic loves the tree, not its genome. A scientist loves both.

Literary agent John Brockman points out another angle on the news from science:

Through science we create technology and in using our new tools we recreate ourselves. But until very recently in our history, no democratic populace, no legislative body, ever indicated by choice, by vote, how this process should play out. Nobody ever voted for printing. Nobody ever voted for electricity. Nobody ever voted for radio, the telephone, the automobile, the airplane, television. Nobody ever voted for space travel. Nobody ever voted for nuclear power, the personal computer, the Internet, email, the Web, Google, cloning, the sequencing of the entire human genome.

Science proposes, society disposes.

Environmentalists do best when they follow where science leads, as they did with climate change. They do worst when they get nervous about where science leads, as they did with genetic engineering. You can see the romantic affliction at work right there. Climate change fit in with the romantic idea of decline and disaster. Genetic engineering looked like Dr. Frankenstein's sin against nature in Mary Shelley's classic romantic story.

I would like to see the environmental movement—and indeed everybody—become fearless about following science. Part of that process lies in learning which scientists and which research to track most closely.

Our first duty is to be wary of confirmation bias—the inclination to notice and believe whatever supports our current theory, and ignore or disbelieve everything that doesn't support our views. It takes harsh self-discipline to overcome. "Darwin writes in his autobiography," reports Bell Labs researcher Richard Hamming, "that he found it necessary to write down every piece of evidence which appeared to contradict his beliefs because otherwise they would disappear from his mind."

Another hard task is to beware of the plausible little stories we tell ourselves. In 1998 I was sure that the Y2K bug would be a major problem, and said so in public and to clients of Global Business Network. My wrong prediction was based on a neat little story I told myself. My own PC was pathetically vulnerable to bugs in the software, which could lead to a cascade of problems ending in the blue screen of death. Surely, I presumed, the huge old mainframes of the world and their ancient software would be even more vulnerable to a bug as deeply embedded as I thought Y2K must be. The world was facing the blue screen of death! I should have listened to Danny Hillis, who has designed whole computer platforms. He predicted that Y2K would lead, at worst, to some dog licenses not being renewed on time. I should have listened at a dinner in 1998 with senior Amazon.com engineers. One of them responded to my rant about Y2K by sweetly inquiring, "Do you also believe in fairies?"

Lesson: Question convenient fables; listen most closely to the scientists who know the facts best, have studied them longest, and aren't biased by an agenda or an employer with an agenda.

Following the publication of his *Plows, Plagues and Petroleum,* climatologist William Ruddiman found he was suddenly the target of a barrage of propaganda:

> These newsletters opened a window on a different side of science, a parallel universe of which I had been only partly aware. The content of these newsletters purports to be scientific but actually has more in common with hardball politics.
>
> Most of these articles come from contrarian web sites that receive large amounts of financial support from industry sources. In many cases, the authors are paid directly by industry for the articles they write....
>
> This alternative universe is really quite amazing. In it, you can "learn" that CO_2 does not cause any climatic warming at all. You can find out that the world has not become warmer in the last century, or that any warming that has occurred results from the Sun having grown stronger, and not from rising levels of greenhouse gases. One way or another, most of the basic findings of mainstream science are rejected or ignored.

Quasi-scientific propaganda against climate change is no different from quasi-scientific propaganda against genetic engineering. Both try to harness science to a political agenda.

Eliminating "bought" scientists still leaves plenty of legitimate scientists who disagree, sometimes fiercely, on any particular issue. "In science," John Brockman reminds those confused by the combat, "debate is the way people work together, the way they advance their ideas." Geneticist Pamela Ronald, in *Tomorrow's Table,* offers a short course on how to distinguish science from rumor and how to weigh a scientific debate. Her major points:

> Examine the primary source of information.... Ask if the work was published in a peer-reviewed journal.... Check if the journal has a good reputation for scientific research.... Determine if there is an independent confirmation by another published study.... Assess whether a potential conflict of interest exists....

I would add to that: Watch for trends. Over time, what does the growing preponderance of evidence indicate? Is a consensus among scientists emerging?

Environmentalists were right to be inspired by marine biologist Rachel Carson's book on pesticides, *Silent Spring,* but wrong to place DDT in the category of Absolute Evil (which she did not). Most of her scientific assessments proved right, some didn't—such as her view that DDT causes cancer. In an excess of zeal that Carson did not live to moderate, DDT was banned worldwide, and malaria took off in Africa. Quoted in a 2007 *National Geographic* article, Robert Gwadz of the National Institutes of Health said, "The ban on DDT may have killed 20 million children." These days, environmental organizations such as World Wildlife Fund support the judicious antimalaria use of DDT on household walls as one element of "integrated vector management," along with bed nets, larvicides in standing water, and other measures that could lead to totally eradicating the disease from the world. When malaria disappears, so can DDT.

Science too often gets perverted by politics. You can see it in two exemplary case studies: *Lament for an Ocean: The Collapse of the Atlantic Cod Fishery: A True Crime Story* (1998), by Michael Harris, and *Degrees of Disaster: Prince William Sound: How Nature Reels and Rebounds* (1994), by Jeff Wheelwright. In the cod story, you learn that while independent scientists were predicting the collapse of the declining fishery in the 1980s, Canadian politicians and government scientists pretended all was well, in part because they felt a responsibility to protect the jobs of the fishing communities of Newfoundland. The collapse came in 1989. Fishing for cod was totally banned in 1992, but the cod fishery still has not recovered, and it may never; tens of thousands of jobs were lost permanently in Newfoundland and other Maritime Provinces.

A similar sequence is playing out in one fishery after another—haddock, tuna, salmon, rockfish. Three fishery-preserving strategies that show promise are: ocean reserves that ban all fishing in designated areas and allow stocks to recover; a system of catch shares called "individual transferable quotas," which has already saved the halibut fishery in Alaska; and carefully managed mariculture. As Jacques Cousteau told me in 1976, "Fishing is hunting....It must be eliminated completely and replaced by farming if we are to be civilized. What we call civilization originated in farming. We are still barbarians in the sea."

Degrees of Disaster, the close-up story of the *Exxon Valdez* oil spill, is replete with awkward truths that didn't make it into the warring scientific reports so sumptuously funded by both sides of the controversy. The massive cleanup efforts did more environmental harm than the spill itself, though they did provide an economic boom for the Prince William Sound region. The biologically richest ocean habitat in the area was *inside* the emptied cargo holds of the grounded ship: an entire food chain from bacteria up to herring and salmon was feeding on the oil. People were worried about aromatic hydrocarbons in wild salmon after the spill, but it turned out that the highest level reached was one ten-thousandth of what was normally found in the local traditionally smoked salmon. The real lesson of the oil spill at Prince William Sound is how resilient many natural systems are and how rapidly they bounce back when human pressure backs off even a little.

Environmentalists do a public service when they help to depoliticize science. In 2008, Britain's Labour government was poised to ban plastic grocery bags because they were thought to get into the sea and entangle marine birds and mammals. A marine biologist at Greenpeace, David Santillo, spoke up: "It's very unlikely that many animals are killed by plastic bags. On a global basis, plastic bags aren't an issue." The government action, it turned out, was based on a misreading of a Canadian report that 100,000 marine animals were killed by entanglement in discarded fishing gear and nets in a period of four years. Grocery bags had nothing to do with the problem.

Scientists freely criticize each other and lambaste anti-Darwinians, but they are weirdly polite with environmentalists. It smells of condescension. Every biologist I know is dismayed by the Green campaign against genetic engineering, but the only one who speaks out is Peter Raven. Climatologists see the need for nuclear power, but the only ones who publicly criticize environmentalists for their opposition are Jim Lovelock and James Hansen. It's time to stop coddling environmentalists. Their motivation is not fragile. Their effectiveness will increase to the degree that they are armed with scientific sophistication and discipline. If they are treated as peers by scientists—which means harshly—they might become peers.

Years ago, environmentalists hated cars and always tried to ban them. Then Amory Lovins came along. He decided that the automobile was the perfect leverage point for large-scale energy conservation, and he set about designing and promoting radically more efficient cars. Lovins single-handedly converted the environmental movement from loathing the auto industry to fruitfully engaging with it. That's the engineering approach. Instead of yelling "Stop!" engineers figure out what the problem is, and then make it go away. They don't have to argue about what is wrong; they show what is right.

Another Green issue that responded well to an engineering approach is the design of buildings. Paul Hawken describes how the LEED rating system came into existence:

> Buildings...use 40 percent of all material and 48 percent of the energy in the United States alone. In 1993 David Gottfried, a successful but disillusioned developer, and Rick Fedrizzi, an executive at the Carrier corporation, gathered a small group of architects, suppliers, builders, and designers in order to create a rigorous set of green building standards. Today, the US Green Building Council (USGBC) comprises 6,200 institutional members and 85,000 active participants, and green building councils exist in Japan, Spain, Canada, India, and Mexico. No one has done the metrics, but in its short life USGBC may have had a greater impact than any other single organization in the world on materials saved, toxins eliminated, greenhouse gases avoided, and human health enhanced. It collaborates with designers, architects, and businesses—not always easy, because their movement means the company's products must change—in order to define and incrementally raise the environmental standards of green buildings by means of a rating system called Leadership in Energy and Environmental Design (LEED).

Now developers and city planners compete to earn the highest LEED ratings—Silver, Gold, or Platinum. The bragging rights are worth the extra money they spend.

For many environmentalists, the entry to an engineer's way of thinking came with a book by Janine Benyus, *Biomimicry: Innovation Inspired by Nature* (1997). The book is meant to inspire engineers to study nature for design ideas, but along the way, it teaches nonengineers to respect engineering. "Unlike the Industrial Revolution," Benyus writes, "the Biomimicry Revolution introduces an era based not on what we can *extract* from nature, but on what we can *learn* from her." Among the examples she explores are

> solar cells copied from leaves, steely fibers woven spider-style, shatterproof ceramics drawn from mother-of-pearl, cancer cures compliments of chimpanzees, perennial grains inspired by tallgrass, computers that signal like cells, and a closed-loop economy that takes its lessons from redwoods, coral reefs, and oak-hickory forests.

And she extracts nine basic principles:

> Nature runs on sunlight. Nature uses only the energy it needs. Nature fits form to function. Nature recycles everything. Nature rewards cooperation. Nature banks on diversity. Nature demands local expertise. Nature curbs excesses from within. Nature taps the power of limits.

In this formulation, Nature looks suspiciously like a liberal Democrat. Since Benyus got her degree in forestry, she could probably compile a fine Devil's Dictionary version of her list. Here's mine:

> Nature rewards efficiency: The most efficient way of life is that of a parasite. Nature is merciless: The best way to control your niche is to annihilate competitors. Nature honors property: Stake out your turf and defend it with your life, or starve. Nature favors opportunistic invaders, such as kudzu and humans. Nature is parsimonious: Eat excess children.

Through the success of the book and a campaign of lectures and workshops by Benyus and coworkers, biomimicry established itself firmly and effectively. A 2008 book from the National Academy of Sciences noted:

> In the last decade, there has been an explosion of information about unusual natural structures that are superstrong, superadhesive, superhydrophobic, superhydrophilic, superefficient, self-cleaning, self-healing, and self-replicating, with superior designs and intricate shapes. Biological materials are also often multifunctional, a characteristic highly desirable in artificial materials and processes.

Along the way, researchers discovered that nature is extremely difficult to mimic in detail. You can fruitfully steal ideas and mechanisms, but natural processes defy simple imitation because they are the irrational product of timeless evolution rather than design. A 2008 article in *National Geographic* spelled out the problem:

> The main reason biomimetics hasn't yet come of age is that from an engineering standpoint, nature is famously, fabulously, wantonly complex.... To make the abalone's shell so hard, 15 different proteins perform a carefully choreographed dance that several teams of top scientists have yet to comprehend. The power of spider silk lies not just in the cocktail of proteins that it is composed of, but in the mysteries of the creature's spinnerets, where 600 spinning nozzles weave seven different kinds of silk into highly resilient configurations.

Birds showed us that heavier-than-air flight is possible, and their structure suggested two wings at the front of a flying machine and a stabilizer in back. But the bird's wing flap was too hard to imitate, so for propulsion humans devised rotating wings (the propeller)—something new to nature. (The idea presumably came from the previous invention of windmills. Instead of taking energy out, put energy in; run the vanes backward, and make wind.)

As the designers and builders of our fabricated infrastructure, engineers are comfortable with taking on natural infrastructure, nudging nature's processes where needed with human ingenuity. Got a flood-prone river? Moderate it with dams and collect some electricity, free of greenhouse gases, at the same time.

Greens interested in engineering solutions for environmental problems but nervous about their hubris will watch with fascination and horror what happens over the coming decades in China, a nation run by engineers rather than lawyers. *New Scientist* reported in 2007:

> Until this year's 17th National Congress of the Communist Party of China... every member of the central bastion of power—the Standing Committee of

the Politburo—was an engineer by training. President Hu Jintao is a graduate of Beijing's Tsinghua University, often referred to as China's MIT, while the premier, Wen Jiabao, trained as a geologist.

When China goes Green, it goes Green big. "The Chinese have purchased 35 million solar water heaters, more than the rest of the world combined," said a 2007 article in *Seed* magazine, and

> China currently ranks sixth in the world in total wind power production,...but by 2020 it aims to increase its share by 1,200 percent, to 30,000 megawatts of power....In 2000, [Beijing] took 26,000 heavily polluting minibuses off the road in a week....Across China, the government is constructing massive solar-and biofuel-powered eco-cities 30 times the size of the largest green communities elsewhere in the world.

When Kevin Kelly was traveling in China in 2006, he found that every elementary school in every village had a sign over the door in Mandarin with the following guidance:

> LOOK UP TO SCIENCE.
> CARE FOR YOUR FAMILY.
> RESPECT LIFE.
> RESIST CULTY RELIGION.

(That raises the question of whether environmentalism is a culty religion. It clearly won't be in China.)

Meanwhile, in North America and Europe, environmental problems are treated as commercial opportunities, and Green entrepreneurs lead the way. Engineers are being hired in droves. They don't know or care much about environmental traditions, causes, or romantic attitudes. Because they are interested in solving problems, not in changing behavior, technology is the first thing they reach for when looking for a solution. A leading Green venture capitalist in Silicon Valley, Vinod Khosla, told *New Scientist* that improvements in energy efficiency or changes in the laws produce only small, incremental gains. "A new technology, on the other hand, can make a 200 per cent or a 400 per cent or a 1000 per cent difference."

A notable example of rethinking a whole industrial domain in environmental terms is the discipline of "Green chemistry," named and defined by Paul Anastas in 1991, when he was head of industrial chemistry at the Environmental Protection Agency. His now-canonical "Twelve Principles of Green Chemistry" are not known to most environmentalists; but they should be, because they outline exactly how to head off the worst form of pollution after greenhouse gases, namely toxic chemicals. ("Minimize waste by using catalytic reactions," advises one principle. "Maximize atom economy," says another.)

When environmentalists are wrong, it is frequently technology that they are wrong about, and they wind up supporting parochial Green goals at the cost of comprehensive ones. That happened with space technology, nuclear technology, and genetic engineering. If your default position on a new technology is suspicion, you forfeit the ability to deploy it for your own purposes. "The environmental movement has so far concentrated its attention upon the evils that technology has done rather than upon the good that technology has failed to do," says Freeman Dyson. But focusing on Green technological opportunity requires a shift in attitude toward novelty.

What a joy it would be to see a new generation of hardcore environmentalists as intrigued by new infrastructure-scale technologies as they are (and as I am) by new ultralight hiking gear made of titanium and Pertex. Their seriousness would be driven not by the romantic love of decline but by a desire to grab progress and direct it toward Green goals. Their potential tools would range from the molecular (genes and atoms) to the cosmic (solar winds and dark energy). They would follow their cellphones into the core of life.

"How you think matters more than what you think," says political scientist Philip Tetlock. The most important distinction in quality of judgment, he declares, was first expressed by the ancient Greek poet Archilochus: "The fox knows many things; the hedgehog one great thing." Hedgehogs have a grand theory they are happy to extend into many domains, relishing its parsimony, expressing their views with great confidence. Foxes, on the other hand, are skeptical about grand theories, diffident in their forecasts, and ready to adjust their ideas based on actual events. Hedgehogs don't notice or care when they're wrong. Foxes learn. Hedgehogs are great proponents, but foxes are invariably better forecasters and policy makers.

The authoritative book on this subject is Tetlock's *Expert Political Judgment* (2005). From his perspective as a psychology researcher, Tetlock watched political advisers on the left and the right make bizarre rationalizations about their wrong predictions at the time of the rise of Gorbachev in the 1980s and the eventual collapse of the Soviet Union. (Liberals were sure that Reagan was a dangerous idiot; conservatives were sure that the USSR was permanent.) The whole exercise struck Tetlock as what used to be called an "outcome-irrelevant learning structure." No feedback, no correction.

So Tetlock took advantage of getting tenure at the University of California–Berkeley to start a long-term research project, now twenty years old, to examine in detail the outcomes of expert political forecasts about international affairs. He studied the aggregate accuracy of 284 experts making 28,000 forecasts, looking for pattern in their comparative success rates. Most of his findings were negative—conservatives did no better or worse than liberals; optimists did no better or worse than pessimists. Only one pattern emerged consistently.

Tetlock borrowed the hedgehog-fox distinction from essayist Isaiah Berlin, who gave as examples of single-minded hedgehogs Plato, Dante, Hegel, and Proust; as open-minded foxes, Aristotle, Shakespeare, Voltaire, and Joyce. The aggregate prediction success rate of foxes is significantly greater, Tetlock found, especially in short-term forecasts. Hedgehog experts are not only worse prognosticators than fox experts (especially in long-term forecasts); *they even fare worse than normal attention-paying dilettantes* like you and me— apparently blinded by their extensive expertise and beautiful theory. Furthermore, foxes win not only in the accuracy of their predictions but also the accuracy of the likelihood they assign to their predictions; in this they exhibit something close to the admirable discipline of weather forecasters.

The value of hedgehogs is that they occasionally get right the farthest-out predictions, but that comes at the cost of a great many wrong far-out predictions. The charismatic expert who exudes confidence and has a great story to tell is probably wrong about what's going to happen. The boring expert who afflicts you with a cloud of howevers is probably right. "There is an inverse relationship between what makes people attractive as public presenters and what makes them accurate in these forecasting exercises," Tetlock told a San Francisco audience. He added that hedgehogs annoy only their political opposition, while foxes annoy across the political spectrum.

As with political experts, so with environmental experts. Two celebrated commentators worth analyzing are Bjørn Lomborg, author of *The Skeptical Environmentalist* (2001), and Amory Lovins. I once heard a Lomborg fan ask Jared Diamond what he thought of Lomborg's book. Diamond's answer, as I recall it, was: "The problem is, Lomborg argues from details. He says the ecological collapse of Easter Island offers no general lessons because it was due to the fragility of one kind of palm tree. Arguing with that kind of reasoning is like arguing with a Creationist about some inverted geology they've found in Texas that they say disproves Darwin. If you take the time to research their example and disprove their interpretation, you find out it doesn't matter. They don't care. They've found some other detail they think supports their theory." (Diamond went on to praise Lomborg for his efforts to focus the world's attention on eradicating malaria in Africa.)

Lomborg's constant message, delivered with sweet reasonableness, is that environmentalists mean well, but they always exaggerate dangers. With his background in statistics, he drills happily into data, making his case with a profusion of details. That kind of expertise can make hedgehogs overconfident, Tetlock writes:

> They have so much case-specific knowledge at their fingertips, and they are so skilled at marshalling that knowledge to construct compelling cause-effect scenarios, that they talk themselves into assigning extreme probabilities that stray further from the objective base-rate probabilities. As expertise rises, we should therefore expect confidence in forecasts to rise faster, far faster, than forecast accuracy.

One scientist who has taken the trouble to refute Lomborg in his own mode is water conservationist Peter Gleick in a lengthy 2001 review of *The Skeptical Environmentalist* for the Union of Concerned Scientists. Gleick meticulously dissects the book's "selective use of data, misuse of data, misinterpretations, inappropriate precision, errors of fact."

As for Amory Lovins, he doesn't just argue from details, he backs up a truck full of numbers and citations and dumps them on you, saying that if you won't master them, you can't possibly argue with him. Events have proven him profoundly right about energy efficiency and conservation and wrong in his forecasts about nuclear power. I predict that he will maintain a hedgehog stance on that subject and never have a good word to say about nuclear (nor, I expect, will Lomborg ever have a good word to say about environmentalists). If I have the pleasure of being wrong about Lovins, I'll bet his change of opinion develops around microreactors, which fit in with his views about distributed micropower.

Tetlock writes that hedgehogs deploy a routine set of excuses when proven wrong: "I was almost right"; "I was just off on timing"; "I made the right mistake" (right policy, wrong prediction); "Happenstance went against me." Each excuse provides an opportunity to explain one more time the deep rightness of the original theory.

Scientists are trained to be foxes. One outspoken voice on climate is Stanford climatologist Stephen Schneider. In 1971 he wrote an influential paper that predicted global *cooling,* based on the previous three decades of cold weather and his model of how the increase of dust and particles in the air (called aerosols) from human activity might trigger an eventual ice age. In 1974 he publicly retracted the paper, having become convinced that his model overestimated aerosol effects and underestimated carbon dioxide effects. With better data and a better model, he reversed his position to extreme concern about global warming, which he maintains to this day.

Naturally, climate denialists mocked him about being so flexible (for political reasons, they assumed), just as an English legislator once chided John Maynard Keynes for reversing his position on money policy during the Great Depression. Keynes replied, "When the facts change, I change my mind. What do you do, sir?"

"Whenever I start to feel certain I am right...a little voice inside tells me to start worrying," one of Phil Tetlock's respondents told him—a statement he considers "a defining marker of the fox temperament." Another comes from the French fox Voltaire: "Doubt is not a pleasant condition, but certainty is absurd."

Every interview with a public figure should include the question "What have you been wrong about, and how did that change your views?" The answer will tell us if the person is intellectually honest or a tale spinner with delusions of infallibility. Let me quickly furnish a partial list of things I've been wrong about in public. In the 1960s, I pushed communes as a path to the future, Buckminster Fuller domes as habitable, and cocaine as harmless. In the 1970s, I was sure the 1973 oil crisis would lead to police in the streets of the United States, that nuclear power was bad, and that small was always beautiful, villages especially. I was totally wrong about the Y2K bug in 2000. In 2003 I was so sure that a Democrat would win the 2004 presidential election that I made a public bet about it. Hey, I was just off on timing.

Fessing up aids learning. From these mistakes and others, I have learned to suspect my excesses of optimism and pessimism. Apparently I often think that societies catch on faster than they do, and that large complex systems are more brittle than they are. Bear in mind I might be wrong that way about climate. And many of my faulty opinions turn out to be based on ignorance; dismissing nuclear was one of those.

One source of confusion for people is that the views of hedgehogs are strongly stated and strongly held, while the views of foxes are modestly stated and loosely held. Guess who gets audience share. What we need is more brazen foxes who don't mind strongly stating their loosely held views (this book tries to be an example), and audiences that honor honest opinion change. When some pontificator begins, "As I've always said,..." the right response is "Uh oh."

Failure to acknowledge a mistake is paralyzing. During the Iraq War, a friend who consulted for the George W. Bush White House told me, "The Neoconservatives don't even try to say they were right about Iraq anymore. They spend all their effort trying to prove they weren't wrong. That means you never change policy because you can never have the discussion that begins, 'Well, Plan A didn't work. What have we got for Plan B?'" It's a bad idea to appoint or elect hedgehogs to power positions.

The most powerful fox I've known personally was California governor Jerry Brown. He had a remarkable technique with protesters, based on sheer curiosity. Whenever he saw a lineup of demonstrators, he would walk over and engage them: "Tell me what you're concerned about." Someone would launch into their rant, and Brown would listen. After a bit he would interrupt, "Let me see if I got it. You're saying that..." And he would state their position, often with greater clarity and eloquence than theirs. They would just melt. They'd been heard! He got it! They knew he probably wouldn't change his position on the issue they were protesting, but, who knows, he might, because Governor Brown was famous for occasionally reversing his opinion and his policy, in response to events.

I used a variant of Brown's approach in designing the debate format for the Seminars About Long-term Thinking I run for Long Now in San Francisco. We had one such debate on the Greening of nuclear power and another on synthetic biology. Whichever debater goes first holds forth for fifteen minutes and then is interviewed for ten minutes by the second debater, who has to conclude by summarizing the first debater's argument *to the first debater's satisfaction*: "You got it." Then they reverse roles.

Audiences love it. They relish watching public figures struggle to state an opposing opinion right out loud, without sarcasm. Better still, the shared probe for depth of understanding of the issue replaces the usual win-lose mutual deafness of public debates. As a result, audience members find that the hard edges of their own opinions start to soften.

There is nowhere a good venue for honest debate about environmental issues. News media like loud fights between glib hedgehogs, not polite debate that reaches for depth. Environmentalist organizations don't have enough money to host big conferences. Maybe some Green philanthropists could help with that. The most direct solution might be for scientific conferences, which are well funded, to invite more environmentalists to come and debate formally in their venue.

If Greens don't embrace science and technology and jump ahead to a leading role in both, they may follow the Reds into oblivion. They need to become early adopters of new tools and adventurous explorers of new situations. Instead of always saying "No" and "Stop," their strategy can be to affirm and redirect. They could give a new technology the benefit of the doubt—but never throw away their doubt—using it to shape the technology in gentler ways to better ends.

Rather than cherishing the role of romantic rebels and avoiding government, Green activists should leap into government, seeking to emulate the all-embracing government-run Green plans of New Zealand and the Netherlands. They can take inspiration from governmental foxes like Franklin Roosevelt, described thus by his contemporary Isaiah Berlin:

> Roosevelt stands out principally by his astonishing appetite for life and by his apparently complete freedom from fear of the future; as a man who welcomed the future eagerly as such, and conveyed the feeling that whatever the times might bring, all would be grist to his mill, nothing would be too formidable or crushing to be subdued and used and moulded into the pattern of the new and unpredictable forms of life into the building of which he, Roosevelt, and his allies and devoted subordinates would throw themselves with unheard-of energy and gusto.

It wasn't just attitude. He made it work.

Chronologies

The documents listed in the first column are texts often mentioned in studies of the intellectual history of the United States. The second column shows European works frequently discussed in America. The third column lists some of the significant social, cultural, and political events that took place simultaneously with the publication or production of the works listed in columns 1 and 2.

Year	American Documents	European Documents	Political, Social, and Cultural Events
1865	Lincoln's "Second Inaugural"	J. S. Mill, *Examination of Sir William Hamilton's Philosophy*	Union victory
1866	John Greenleaf Whittier, "Snowbound"	T. H. Huxley, "On the Improving of Natural Knowledge"	
1867	Horatio Alger, *Ragged Dick*	Karl Marx, *Capital* (vol. 1)	
1868	Elizabeth Stuart Phelps, *Gates Ajar*		
1869	Harriet Beecher Stowe, *Oldtown Folks* Louisa May Alcott, *Little Women*	Matthew Arnold *Culture and Anarchy* J. S. Mill, *On the Subjugation of Women*	Transcontinental railway completed
1870	Thomas Wentworth Higginson, *Army Life in a Black Regiment*		

Note: The date assigned to a document is generally the year of its first regular publication or, in the case of a single address, play, or opera, of its initial delivery or performance. Variations are noted in parentheses. Except for texts generally known by their original titles, foreign documents are in English.

Year	American Documents	European Documents	Political, Social, and Cultural Events
1871	Walt Whitman, *Democratic Vistas* Lewis Henry Morgan, *Systems of Consanguinity and Affinity*	Charles Darwin, *Descent of Man*	Paris Commune
1872	Charles Hodge, *Systematic Theology*		
1873	Mark Twain and C. D. Warner, *The Gilded Age* [Chauncey] Wright, "The Evolution of Self-Consciousness" Octavius B. Frothingham, *Religion of Humanity* Whitelaw Reid, "The Scholar in Politics"	Herbert Spencer, *Sociology*	
1874	John Fiske, *Outlines of the Cosmic Philosophy* Charles Hodge, *What Is Darwinism?* John William Draper, *History of the Conflict Between Religion and Science*	John Tyndall, "Belfast Address"	
1875	Mary Baker Eddy, *Science and Health*		

Year	American Documents	European Documents	Political, Social, and Cultural Events
1876	Mark Twain, *Tom Sawyer*		American centennial Telephone invented
	Asa Gray, *Darwiniana*		Battle of the Little Big Horn
1877	Henry James, *The American*	W. K. Clifford, "Ethics of Belief"	Great Railway Strike End of Reconstruction
	Charles S. Peirce, "Fixation of Belief"	Leo Tolstoy, *Anna Karenina*	
1878	Lewis Henry Morgan, *Ancient Society*		
	Charles S. Peirce, "How to Make Our Ideas Clear"		
1879	Henry George, *Progress and Poverty*		
	Newman Smyth, *Old Faiths in New Light*		
	Albion Tourgee, *A Fool's Errand*		
1880	Lew Wallace, *Ben-Hur*	Fyodor Dostoevsky, *The Brothers Karamazov*	
1881	Oliver Wendell Holmes, Jr., *The Common Law*		Massive immigration from eastern and southern Europe begins
	Joel Chandler Harris, *Uncle Remus*		
	Henry James, *Portrait of a Lady*		
	Helen Hunt Jackson, *Century of Dishonor*		

Year	American Documents	European Documents	Political, Social, and Cultural Events
1882		Friedrich Nietzsche, *The Gay Science*	Edison's electric light becomes widely available
1883	Lester Frank Ward, *Dynamic Sociology* Henry A. Rowland, "A Plea for Pure Science" Charles Augustus Briggs, *Biblical Study* William Graham Sumner, *What Social Classes Owe to Each Other*		
1884	William Dean Howells, *The Rise of Silas Lapham* Francis Parkman, *Montcalm and Wolfe*		
1885	Mark Twain, *Adventures of Huckleberry Finn* Josiah Royce, *Religious Aspect of Philosophy* John Fiske, *The Idea of God as Affected by Modern Knowledge*		
1886	Henry James, *Bostonians* Henry James, *The Princess Cassimassima*	Friedrich Nietzsche, *Beyond Good and Evil*	Haymarket riot

Year	American Documents	European Documents	Political, Social, and Cultural Events
	Josiah Strong, *Our Country*		
1887	John Dewey, *Psychology*	Friedrich Nietzsche, *Genealogy of Morals*	
	William Dean Howells, "Pernicious Fiction"	Tönnies, *Gemeinschaft und Gesellschaft*	
1888	Edward Bellamy, *Looking Backward, 2000–1887*		
	Russell Conwell, "Acres of Diamonds"		
1889	Robert Ingersoll, "Why I Am an Agnostic"	Ernst Haeckel, *Riddles of the Universe*	
	Andrew Carnegie, "Gospel of Wealth"		
	Mark Twain, *A Connecticut Yankee in King Arthur's Court*		
	Ignatius Donnelly, *Caesar's Column*		
	W. C. Brownell, *French Traits*		
1890	William James, *Principles of Psychology*	James Frazer, *Golden Bough*	Massacre at Wounded Knee
	William Dean Howells, *Hazard of New Fortunes*	Villers de l'Isle Adam, *Axel*	

Year	American Documents	European Documents	Political, Social, and Cultural Events
	Jacob Riis, *How the Other Half Lives*	Gabriel de Tarde, *Laws of Imitation*	
	Emily Dickinson, *Poems* (posthumous)		
	Alfred Thayer Mahan, *Influence of Sea Power on History*		
1891	Hamlin Garland, *Main-Travelled Roads*		
	Joseph LeConte, *Evolution and Its Relation to Religious Thought*		
1892	Charlotte Perkins Gilman, *The Yellow Wallpaper*	Karl Pearson, *The Grammar of Science*	Populist Omaha convention
	Elizabeth Cady Stanton, "Solitude of Self "		
1893	Frederick Jackson Turner, "Significance of the Frontier in American History"	T. H. Huxley, *Evolution and Ethics*	Chicago World's Fair
	Clarence Darrow, "Realism in Literature and Art"	Emile Durkheim, *Division of Labor in Society*	
	Charles S. Peirce, "Evolutionary Love"		
1894	Henry Demarest Lloyd, *Wealth Against Commonwealth*		Pullman strike

Year	American Documents	European Documents	Political, Social, and Cultural Events
	Mark Twain, *The Tragedy of Pudd'nhead Wilson*		
1895	Stephen Crane, *Red Badge of Courage*		
	Elizabeth Cady Stanton, *The Woman's Bible*		
	Booker T. Washington, "Atlanta Address"		
	Oliver Wendell Holmes, Jr., "The Soldier's Faith"		
1896	Andrew Dickson White, *The Warfare of Science with Theology in Christendom*		McKinley defeats Bryan
			Plessy v. Ferguson
	Harold Frederic, *The Damnation of Theron Ware*		
1897	William James, *The Will to Believe*		
	Charles Sheldon, *In His Steps*		
	Oliver Wendell Holmes, Jr., "Path of the Law"		
1898	Josiah Royce, "The Problem of Job"	Rudyard Kipling, "The White Man's Burden"	Spanish-American War
	Charlotte Perkins Gilman, *Women and Economics*		

Year	American Documents	European Documents	Political, Social, and Cultural Events
1899	Thorstein Veblen, *Theory of the Leisure Class* Elbert Hubbard, "Message to Garcia" Kate Chopin, *The Awakening* Edwin Markham, "The Man with the Hoe" John Bates Clark, *Distribution of Wealth*		Dreyfus affair in France
1900	Josiah Royce, *World and Individual* Clarence Stedman, *An American Anthology* Theodore Dreiser, *Sister Carrie*	Rediscovery of Mendel's genetics Sigmund Freud, *The Interpretation of Dreams*	
1901	Frank Norris, *The Octopus* E. A. Ross, *Social Control* Booker T. Washington, *Up from Slavery*	George Bernard Shaw, *Man and Superman*	
1902	William James, *Varieties of Religious Experience* Jane Addams, *Democracy and Social Ethics*	Joseph Conrad, *Heart of Darkness* Vladimir Lenin, *What Is to Be Done?* André Gide, *The Immoralist*	

Year	American Documents	European Documents	Political, Social, and Cultural Events
	Owen Wister, *The Virginian*		
	Charles Horton Cooley, *Human Nature and Social Order*		
1903	W. E. B. Du Bois, *Souls of Black Folk*	Bertrand Russell, *Principles of Mathematics*	Wright brothers' first flight
	John Dewey, *Studies in Logical Theory*	G. E. Moore, *Principia Ethica*	
	Jack London, *Call of the Wild*		
	Henry James, *The Ambassadors*		
	Helen Thompson Wooley, *Mental Traits of Sex*		
1904	Henry James, *The Golden Bowl*	Max Weber, *The Protestant Ethic and the Spirit of Capitalism*	
	Henry Adams, *Mont-Saint-Michel and Chartres*		
	Thorstein Veblen, *Theory of Business Enterprise*		
1905	Lincoln Steffens, *Shame of the Cities*	Einstein's special theory of relativity	
	Thomas Dixon, *The Clansman*		
	Edith Wharton, *House of Mirth*		
	Mary Chesnut, *A Diary from Dixie*		

Year	American Documents	European Documents	Political, Social, and Cultural Events
1906	Upton Sinclair, *The Jungle*		
	William Graham Sumner, *Folkways*		
	Thorstein Veblen, "The Place of Science in Civilization"		
	George Santayana, *The Life of Reason*		
1907	William James, *Pragmatism*	Henri Bergson, *Creative Evolution*	
	Henry James, *The American Scene*		
	Simon Patten, *New Basis for Civilization*		
	Henry Adams, *The Education of Henry Adams*		
1908	Arthur F. Bentley, *Process of Government*	Vladimir Lenin, *Materialism and Empirico-Criticism*	
	Walter Rauschenbusch, *Christianity and the Social Crisis*	Graham Wallas, *Human Nature and Politics*	
1909	Herbert Croly, *Promise of American Life*		
	William James, *A Pluralistic Universe*		
	W. C. Brownell, *American Prose Masters*		

Year	American Documents	European Documents	Political, Social, and Cultural Events
1910	Jane Addams, *Twenty Years at Hull-House*	Sigmund Freud, *Origins and Development of Psychoanalysis*	
	William James, "Moral Equivalent of War"		
1911	Fredcrick Winslow Taylor, *Principles of Scientific Management*		Triangle Shirtwaist Factory fire
	Franz Boas, *Mind of Primitive Man*		Nationalist Revolution in China
1912	James Harvey Robinson, *The New History*	Emile Durkheim, *Elementary Forms of Religious Life*	
	Mary Antin, *The Promised Land*		
	Ezra Pound, *Ripostes*		
	James Weldon Johnson, *The Autobiography of an Ex-Colored Man*		
1913	Charles Beard, *An Economic Interpretation of the Constitution of the United States*	Marcel Proust, *Swann's Way*	Wilson takes office
		Sigmund Freud, *Totem and Taboo*	Armory show
	Eleanor Hodgeman Porter, *Pollyanna*		
	Walter Lippmann, *A Preface to Politics*		
	Josiah Royce, *Problem of Christianity*		

Year	American Documents	European Documents	Political, Social, and Cultural Events
	Willa Cather, *O Pioneers*		
1914	Walter Lippmann, *Drift and Mastery*		World War I begins in Europe
	Louis Brandeis, *Other People's Money*		
	John D. Watson, *Behaviorism*		
1915	Van Wyck Brooks, *America's Coming-of-Age*	Einstein's general theory of relativity	Armenian genocide attracts world attention
	Horace Kallen, "Democracy vs. the Melting Pot"		
	Charlotte Perkins Gilman, *Herland*		
1916	John Dewey, *Democracy and Education*	James Joyce, *Portrait of the Artist as a Young Man*	
	Randolph Bourne, "Trans-National America"		
	Madison Grant, *The Passing of the Great Race*		
1917	Walter Rauschenbusch, *A Theology for the Social Gospel*	Vladimir Lenin, *Imperialism*	U.S. enters World War I
			Bolshevik Revolution
	H. L. Mencken, *A Book of Prefaces*		
	Randolph Bourne, "Twilight of Idols"		

Year	American Documents	European Documents	Political, Social, and Cultural Events
	Elsie Clews Parsons, *Social Rule*		
	T. S. Eliot, *Prufrock*		
1918	Willa Cather, *My Antonia*	Lytton Strachey, *Eminent Victorians*	Armistice in Europe
	W. I. Thomas and F. Znanicki, *The Polish Peasant in Europe and America*	Oswald Spengler, *Decline of the West* (vol. 1)	
1919	Sherwood Anderson, *Winesburg, Ohio*	J. M. Keynes, *Economic Consequences of the Peace*	Versailles Treaty
	John Reed, *Ten Days That Shook the World*	Max Weber, "Vocation of Science"	
	Irving Babbitt, *Rousseau and Romanticism*	Karl Barth, *Commentary on Romans*	
	T. S. Eliot, "Tradition and the Individual Talent"	H. G. Wells, *Outline of History*	
1920	Sinclair Lewis, *Main Street*		U.S. women obtain right to vote
	Edith Wharton, *Age of Innocence*		
	Oliver Wendell Holmes, Jr., *Collected Legal Papers*		
	John Dewey, *Reconstruction in Philosophy*		
	F. Scott Fitzgerald, *This Side of Paradise*		
	Ezra Pound, "Hugh Selwyn Mauberley"		

Year	American Documents	European Documents	Political, Social, and Cultural Events
1921	James Harvey Robinson, *Mind in the Making* Thorstein Veblen, *Engineers and the Price System*		Radio developed
1922	T. S. Eliot, "The Waste Land" Sinclair Lewis, *Babbitt* John Dewey, *Human Nature and Conduct* Walter Lippmann, *Public Opinion* e. e. cummings, "Enormous Room" W. F. Ogburn, *Social Change* Harold Stearns, ed., *Civilization in the United States*	James Joyce, *Ulysses* Ludwig Wittgenstein, *Tractatus Logico-Philosophicus* Oswald Spengler, *Decline of the West* (vol. 2) W. B. Yeats, *Later Poems*	Mussolini seizes power
1923	Robert Frost, *New Hampshire* Thorstein Veblen, *Absentee Ownership* Jean Toomer, *Cane*	D. H. Lawrence, *Studies in Classic American Literature*	
1924	Emma Goldman, *My Disillusionment with Russia* Herman Melville, *Billy Budd* (posthumous) Shailer Mathews, *Faith of Modernism*	Thomas Mann, *Magic Mountain*	Immigration drastically reduced

Year	American Documents	European Documents	Political, Social, and Cultural Events
1925	F. Scott Fitzgerald, *The Great Gatsby*	Franz Kafka, *The Trial*	Scopes trial
	Sinclair Lewis, *Arrowsmith*	W. B. Yeats, *A Vision*	
	Alfred North Whitehead, *Science and the Modern World*	Adolf Hitler, *Mein Kampf*	
	John Dewey, *Experience and Nature*		
	E. Stanley Jones, *The Christ of the Indian Road*		
	Alain Locke, ed., *The New Negro*		
	Charles Merriam, *New Aspects of Politics*		
	William Carlos Williams, *In the American Grain*		
	Bruce Barton, *The Man Nobody Knows*		
1926	Ernest Hemingway, *The Sun Also Rises*	Franz Kafka, *The Castle*	
	H. L. Mencken, *Notes on Democracy*	I. A. Richards, *Science and Poetry*	
	Lewis Mumford, *The Golden Day*	Pavlov, *Conditioned Reflexes*	
1927	Sinclair Lewis, *Elmer Gantry*	Virginia Woolf, *To the Lighthouse*	Lindberg's flight to Europe
	Morris R. Cohen, "Property and Sovereignty"		

Year	American Documents	European Documents	Political, Social, and Cultural Events
	Percy C. Bridgman, *The Logic of Modern Physics*	Martin Heidegger, *Being and Time*	
	V. L. Parrington, *Main Currents in American Thought*	Heisenberg's principle of uncertainty	
	Charles and Mary Beard, *The Rise of American Civilization*		
	John Dewey, *The Public and Its Problems*		
1928	Margaret Mead, *Coming of Age in Samoa*	Arthur Eddington, *Nature of the Physical World*	
	Eugene O'Neill, *Strange Interlude*	D. H. Lawrence, *Lady Chatterley's Lover*	
1929	Joseph Wood Krutch, *Modern Temper*	Karl Mannheim, *Ideology and Utopia*	Wall Street crash
	William Faulkner, *The Sound and the Fury*		
	Ernest Hemingway, *A Farewell to Arms*		
	Robert and Helen Lynd, *Middletown*		
	Walter Lippmann, *Preface to Morals*		
	John Dewey, *Quest for Certainty*		
	Thomas Wolfe, *Look Homeward, Angel*		
1930	Twelve Southerners, *I'll Take My Stand*	Sigmund Freud, *Civilization and Its Discontents*	

Year	American Documents	European Documents	Political, Social, and Cultural Events
	Jerome Frank, *Law and the Modern Mind*		
	Edith Hamilton, *The Greek Way*		
	Norman Forster, *Humanism in America*		
1931	Edmund Wilson, *Axel's Castle*	Kurt Gödel's proof of the impossibility of a complete mathematical system	Japanese invade Manchuria
	Pearl Buck, *The Good Earth*		Empire State Building completed
	Lincoln Steffens, *Autobiography*		
	Morris R. Cohen, *Reason and Nature*		
	Constance Rourke, *American Humor*		
1932	Reinhold Niebuhr, *Moral Man and Immoral Society*	Aldous Huxley, *Brave New World*	
	Adolph Berle and Gardiner Means, *Modern Corporation and Private Property*		
	William Faulkner, *Light in August*		
	Carl Becker, "Everyman His Own Historian"		
	William Ernest Hocking et al., *Rethinking Missions*		

Year	American Documents	European Documents	Political, Social, and Cultural Events
	James T. Farrell, *Young Lonigan*		
	John Chamberlain, *Farewell to Reform*		
1933	Wesley Mitchell et al., *Recent Social Trends*	John Strachey, *Coming Struggle for Power*	Franklin D. Roosevelt takes office
	Sidney Hook, *Toward an Understanding of Karl Marx*	André Malraux, *Man's Fate*	Hitler comes to power
1934	Ruth Benedict, *Patterns of Culture*		
	Malcolm Cowley, *Exile's Return*		
	Lewis Mumford, *Technics and Civilization*		
	Henry Roth, *Call It Sleep*		
	John Dewey, *A Common Faith*		
	John Dewey, *Art as Experience*		
	T. S. Eliot, *After Strange Gods*		
	Matthew Josephson, *The Robber Barons*		
	Charles Beard, "History Written as an Act of Faith"		
	George Herbert Mead, *Mind, Self and Society* (posthumous)		

Year	American Documents	European Documents	Political, Social, and Cultural Events
1935	John Dewey, *Liberalism and Social Action* Kenneth Burke, *Permanence and Change* Thurman Arnold, *Symbols of Government* Reinhold Niebuhr, *An Interpretation of Christian Ethics*	Karl Popper, *Logic of Scientific Discovery* Rudolf Carnap, *Philosophy and Logical Syntax*	Mussolini invades Ethiopia Soviets call for "Popular Front" Congress of Industrial Organizations founded
1936	John Dos Passos, *USA* William Faulkner, *Absalom! Absalom!* H. D. Lasswell, *Politics: Who Gets What, When, How?* Arthur O. Lovejoy, *The Great Chain of Being* John Steinbeck, *In Dubious Battle*	A. J. Ayer, *Language, Truth, and Logic* J. M. Keynes, *General Theory of Employment Interest, and Money*	Spanish Civil War begins Moscow trials begin Hoover Dam completed
1937	Thurman Arnold, *Folklore of Capitalism* John Dewey et al., *Not Guilty* Zora Neale Hurston, *Their Eyes Were Watching God*		Japanese massacre of Chinese in Nanking

Year	American Documents	European Documents	Political, Social, and Cultural Events
	Robert and Helen Lynd, *Middletown in Transition*		
	Talcott Parsons, *The Structure of Social Action*		
	Karen Horney, *The Neurotic Personality of Our Time*		
1938	Lewis Mumford, *The Culture of Cities*	George Orwell, *Homage to Catalonia*	Munich pact
	John Dewey, *Logic*	Jean-Paul Sartre, *Nausea*	
	B. F. Skinner, *Behavior of Organisms*		
	Thornton Wilder, *Our Town*		
1939	John Steinbeck, *Grapes of Wrath*	W. H. Auden, "September, 1939"	Nazi–Soviet pact opens World War II in Europe
	John Dewey, *Freedom and Culture*	W. H. Auden, "In Memory of W. B. Yeats"	
	Carey McWilliams, *Factories in the Field*		
	Cleanth Brooks, *Modern Poetry and the Tradition*		
1940	Edmund Wilson, *To the Finland Station*		France falls to Nazi Germany
	Erich Fromm, *Escape from Freedom*		
	Richard Wright, *Native Son*		

Year	American Documents	European Documents	Political, Social, and Cultural Events
	Ernest Hemingway, *For Whom the Bell Tolls*		
	Eugene O'Neill, *Long Day's Journey into Night*		
1941	James Burnham, *The Managerial Revolution*	Arthur Koestler, *Darkness at Noon*	Hitler attacks Soviet Union
	Henry Luce, "The American Century"		Japanese bomb Pearl Harbor, bringing U.S. into World War II
	Joseph Davies, *Mission to Moscow*		
	James Agee and Walker Evans, *Let Us Now Praise Famous Men*		
	F. O. Matthiessen, *American Renaissance*		
	W. J. Cash, *The Mind of the South*		
1942	Henry Wallace, "The Century of the Common Man"	Albert Camus, *The Stranger*	
	Suzanne K. Langer, *Philosophy in a New Key*		
	Alfred Kazin, *On Native Grounds*		
	Joseph Schumpeter, *Capitalism, Socialism, and Democracy*		
	Margaret Mead, *And Keep Your Powder Dry*		

Year	American Documents	European Documents	Political, Social, and Cultural Events
	Carl Hempel, "The Function of General Laws in History"		
	Mary McCarthy, *The Company She Keeps*		
1943	Reinhold Niebuhr, *Nature and Destiny of Man*		
	Carey McWilliams, *Brothers Under the Skin*		
	Wendell Willkie, *One World*		
	C. L. Hull, *Principles of Behavior*		
	Ayn Rand, *The Fountainhead*		
1944	Gunnar Myrdal, *An American Dilemma*	F. A. Hayek, *Road to Serfdom*	Mass murder of European Jews in process
	David Lilienthal, *TVA: Democracy on the March*	Max Horkheimer and Theodor Adorno, *Dialectic of Enlightenment*	G.I. Bill
	Reinhold Niebuhr, *The Children of Light and the Children of Darkness*		Bretton Woods conference on World Financial System
	C. L. Stevenson, *Ethics and Language*		
	Helene Deutsch, *Psychology of Women*		

Year	American Documents	European Documents	Political, Social, and Cultural Events
1945	Dwight Macdonald, "The Responsibility of Peoples" Vannevar Bush, *Science—The Endless Frontier*	Karl Popper, *Open Society and Its Enemies*	World War II ends U.S. drops atomic bombs on Japan United Nations founded
1946	Robert Penn Warren, *All the King's Men* Peter Drucker, *Concept of the Corporation* Hans Morgenthau, *Scientific Man vs. Power Politics* John Hersey, *Hiroshima* James B. Conant, *Understanding Science*	Jean-Paul Sartre, *Existentialism and Humanism* R. G. Collingwood, *Idea of History* (posthumous)	
1947	Lionel Trilling, *Middle of the Journey* Paul Samuelson, *Foundations of Economic Analysis*	Michael Oakeshott, "Rationalism in Politics"	Truman Doctrine India declares independent from British Empire
1948	Norman Mailer, *The Naked and the Dead* B. F. Skinner, *Walden Two* Norbert Wiener, *Control and Connection*	George Orwell, *Nineteen Eighty-Four*	Alger Hiss accused of spying Universal Declaration of Human Rights Indonesia declares independence from Dutch Empire

Year	American Documents	European Documents	Political, Social, and Cultural Events
	James Gould Cozzens, *Guard of Honor*		
	Alfred Kinsey, *Sexual Behavior in the Human Male*		
1949	Robert K. Merton, *Social Theory and Social Structure*	Simone de Beauvoir, *The Second Sex*	NATO pact
	Paul Blanshard, *American Freedom and Catholic Power*	Fernand Braudel, *Mediterranean in the Age of Philip II*	Communist revolution in China
	Morton White, *Social Thought in America*	Gilbert Ryle, *Concept of Mind*	
	Lillian Smith, *Killers of the Dream*		
	Arthur Miller, *Death of a Salesman*		
	Aldo Leopold, *Sand County Almanac*		
	Joseph Campbell, *The Hero with a Thousand Faces*		
1950	Lionel Trilling, *The Liberal Imagination*		Korean War begins
	Henry Steele Commager, *The American Mind*		McCarthy claims government is influenced by Communists
	T. W. Adorno et al., *The Authoritarian Personality*		
	David Riesman et al., *The Lonely Crowd*		

Year	American Documents	European Documents	Political, Social, and Cultural Events
	Erik Erikson, *Childhood and Society*		Television becomes widely available
1951	C. Wright Mills, *White Collar*	Albert Camus, *The Rebel*	
	Talcott Parsons, *The Social System*		
	Hannah Arendt, *Origins of Totalitarianism*		
	Isaac Asimov, *Foundation*		
	W. V. O. Quine, "Two Dogmas of Empiricism"		
	J. D. Salinger, *Catcher in the Rye*		
	George Kennan, *American Diplomacy, 1900–1950*		
	Hans Reichenbach, *The Rise of Scientific Philosophy*		
	Kenneth Arrow, *Social Choice and Individual Values*		
	C. Vann Woodward, *Origins of the New South*		
1952	Ralph Ellison, *Invisible Man*		
	Whittaker Chambers, *Witness*		
	Reinhold Niebuhr, *The Irony of American History*		

Year	American Documents	European Documents	Political, Social, and Cultural Events
	Paul Tillich, *The Courage to Be* Herman Wouk, *The Caine Mutiny*		
1953	Daniel J. Boorstin, *The Genius of American Politics* Saul Bellow, *The Adventures of Augie March* Leo Strauss, *Natural Right and History* Alfred Kinsey, *Sexual Behavior in the Human Female*	Ludwig Wittgenstein, *Philosophical Investigations* (posthumous) Watson–Crick model for DNA C. Milosz, *The Captive Mind* Roland Barthes, *Writing Degree Zero*	Cease-fire in Korea
1954	David Potter, *People of Plenty* Wallace Stevens, *Collected Poems*	Jacques Ellul, *Technological Society* William Golding, *Lord of the Flies* Graham Greene, *The Quiet American*	Oppenheimer hearings Army–McCarthy hearings *Brown v. School Board of Topeka*
1955	Walter Lippmann, *The Public Philosophy* Louis Hartz, *The Liberal Tradition in America* James Baldwin, *Notes of a Native Son* Herbert Marcuse, *Eros and Civilization*	Claude Levi-Strauss, *Tristes Tropiques*	Bandung Conference of non-aligned nations of Asia and Africa

Year	American Documents	European Documents	Political, Social, and Cultural Events
	C. Vann Woodward, *The Strange Career of Jim Crow*		
	Will Herberg, *Protestant–Catholic–Jew*		
	Edward Steichen, *The Family of Man*		
	Richard Hofstadter, *Age of Reform*		
	Vladimir Nabokov, *Lolita*		
1956	C. Wright Mills, *Power Elite*		Khrushchev's "secret speech"
	Allen Ginsberg, *Howl*		Soviets crush rebellion in Hungary
	William H. Whyte, *The Organization Man*		
	Walter Kaufmann, ed., *Existentialism from Dostoevsky to Sartre*		
1957	James Gould Cozzens, *By Love Possessed*	Milovan Djilas, *New Class*	*Sputnik*
	Dwight Macdonald, *Memoirs of a Revolutionist*	Roland Barthes, *Mythologies*	
	Ayn Rand, *Atlas Shrugged*		
	Mary McCarthy, *Memories of a Catholic Girlhood*		
	Leon Festinger, *A Theory of Cognitive Dissonance*		

Year	American Documents	European Documents	Political, Social, and Cultural Events
	Jack Kerouac, *On the Road*		
1958	Daniel Lerner, *The Passing of Traditional Society*	Boris Pasternak, *Doctor Zhivago*	
	John Kenneth Galbraith, *The Affluent Society*		
	Martin Luther King, Jr., *Stride Toward Freedom*		
	William Lederer and Eugene Burdick, *The Ugly American*		
1959	Harold Rosenberg, *Tradition of the New*	C. P. Snow, *The Two Cultures*	Dalai Lama flees Tibet amid tightening of Chinese control
	Norman O. Brown, *Life Against Death*		
	William A. Williams, *The Tragedy of American Diplomacy*		
	C. Wright Mills, *The Sociological Imagination*		
1960	W. W. Rostow, *Stages of Economic Growth*	E. H. Gombrich, *Art and Illusion*	FDA approves oral contraception
	Paul Goodman, *Growing Up Absurd*	Hans Gadamer, *Truth and Method*	Proliferation of independent nations in Africa and Asia accelerates
	Daniel Bell, *The End of Ideology*	Gunter Grass, *The Tin Drum*	

Year	American Documents	European Documents	Political, Social, and Cultural Events
	Bruno Bettelheim, *The Informed Heart*		
	Angus Campbell et al., *The American Voter*		
	Harper Lee, *To Kill a Mockingbird*		
	S. M. Lipset, *Political Man*		
	John Courtney Murray, *We Hold These Truths*		
1961	Ernest Nagel, *The Structure of Science*	Michel Foucault, *Madness and Civilization*	
	Robert A. Dahl, *Who Governs?*	Frantz Fanon, *Wretched of the Earth*	
	Joseph Heller, *Catch-22*		
	Erving Goffman, *Asylums*		
1962	Thomas S. Kuhn, *The Structure of Scientific Revolutions*		Vatican II begins
	Michael Harrington, *The Other America*		Cuban missile crisis
	Ken Kesey, *One Flew Over the Cuckoo's Nest*		
	Milton Friedman, *Capitalism and Freedom*		

Year	American Documents	European Documents	Political, Social, and Cultural Events
	Marshall McLuhan, *Gutenberg Galaxy*		
	Rachel Carson, *Silent Spring*		
	SDS, *Port Huron Statement*		
1963	Betty Friedan, *The Feminine Mystique*	John A. T. Robinson, *Honest to God*	John F. Kennedy assassinated
	Mary McCarthy, *The Group*		
	Sylvia Plath, *The Bell Jar*		
	Nathan Glazer and Daniel Moynihan, *Beyond the Melting Pot*		
	Martin Luther King, Jr., "Letter from a Birmingham Jail"		
1964	Saul Bellow, *Herzog*		Civil Rights Act
	Hannah Arendt, *Eichmann in Jerusalem*		Chaney, Goodman, and Schwerner murdered in Mississippi
	Clifford Geertz, "Ideology as a Cultural System"		
	Ralph Ellison, *Shadow and Act*		
	Clark Kerr, *The Uses of the University*		
	Ken Kesey, *Sometimes a Great Notion*		

Year	American Documents	European Documents	Political, Social, and Cultural Events
	Herbert Marcuse, *One-Dimensional Man* Richard Hofstadter, *The Paranoid Style in American Politics*		
1965	Herbert Marcuse, "Repressive Tolerance" Lionel Trilling, *Beyond Culture* Malcolm X, *Autobiography* Harvey Cox, *The Secular City*	Louis Althusser, *For Marx*	Johnson commits troops to Vietnam Watts riot Restrictions on immigration sharply reduced Voting Rights Act
1966	Peter Berger and Thomas Luckerman, *The Social Construction of Reality* Philip Rieff, *The Triumph of the Therapeutic*	Michel Foucault, *The Order of Things* Jacques Lacan, *Écrits* Hans Blumenberg, *Legitimacy of the Modern Age*	National Organization for Women founded Cultural Revolution begins in China
1967	Harold Cruse, *The Crisis of the Negro Intellectual* John Kenneth Galbraith, *The New Industrial State*	Jacques Derrida, *Of Grammatology* Jacques Derrida, *Writing and Difference*	*Loving v. Virginia*
1968	James D. Watson, *The Double Helix* John Updike, *Couples* Richard Herr, *Dispatches*	Jürgen Habermas, *Knowledge and Human Interests* Jean Piaget, *Structuralism*	Martin Luther King, Jr., assassinated Abortive revolution in France

Year	American Documents	European Documents	Political, Social, and Cultural Events
1969	Kurt Vonnegut, *Slaughterhouse Five* Theodore Roszak, *Making of a Counter-Culture* *Whole Earth Catolog* begins publication	Michel Foucault, *Archaeology of Knowledge*	Stonewall riot Humans walk on moon
1970	Robin Morgan, ed., *Sisterhood Is Powerful* Kate Millett, *Sexual Politics* Richard Macksey and Eugenio Donato, eds., *The Structuralist Controversy* Shulamith Firestone, *Dialectic of Sex*		Killings at Kent State University Incursion into Cambodia
1971	John Rawls, *Theory of Justice* B. F. Skinner, *Beyond Freedom and Dignity* E. O. Wilson, *Insect Societies* Paul de Man, *Blindness and Insight*	Antonio Gramsci, *Prison Notebooks* (posthumous)	Pentagon Papers released by Daniel Ellsberg
1972	Lionel Trilling, *Sincerity and Authenticity*		Watergate break-in
1973	Thomas Pynchon, *Gravity's Rainbow*	Jürgen Habermas, *Legitimation Crisis*	*Roe v. Wade* Vietnam War ends

Year	American Documents	European Documents	Political, Social, and Cultural Events
	Daniel Bell, *The Coming of Postindustrial Society*		OPEC-related oil crisis
	Hayden White, *Metahistory*		
	Clifford Geertz, *Interpretation of Cultures*		
1974	Robert Nozick, *Anarchy, State, and Utopia*		Nixon resigns
1975	E. O. Wilson *Sociobiology*	Michel Foucault, *Discipline and Punish*	
	Peter Singer, *Animal Liberation*		
1976	Alex Haley, *Roots*	Michel Foucault, *History of Sexuality*	
	Daniel Bell, *The Cultural Contradictions of Capitalism*		
1977	Toni Morrison, *Song of Solomon*		
	Carl Sagan, *Dragons of Eden*		
1978	Nancy Chodorow, *The Reproduction of Mothering*		*Regents v. Bakke*
	Edward Said, *Orientalism*		
1979	Richard Rorty, *Philosophy and the Mirror of Nature*	Jean-François Lyotard, *The Postmodern Condition*	Islamic Revolution in Iran
	Christopher Lasch, *The Culture of Narcissism*		

Year	American Documents	European Documents	Political, Social, and Cultural Events
1980	Carl Sagan, *Cosmos*	Umberto Eco, *The Name of the Rose*	Personal computers become widely available
1981	Stephen Jay Gould, *The Mismeasure of Man* Alasdair MacIntyre, *After Virtue* Richard Rodriguez, *Hunger of Memory*	Bernard Williams, *Moral Luck*	
1982	Peter Singer, *The Expanding Circle* Richard Rorty, *Consequences of Pragmatism* Alice Walker, *The Color Purple* Michael Sandel, *Liberalism and the Limits of Justice* Carol Gilligan, *In a Different Voice*		
1983	Clifford Geertz, *Local Knowledge* Benedict Anderson, *Imagined Communities* Michael Walzer, *Spheres of Justice*		U.S. invades Grenada
1984	Richard John Neuhaus, *The Naked Public Square*	Milan Kundera, *The Unbearable Lightness of Being*	
1985	Don DeLillo, *White Noise*	Bernand Williams, *Ethics and the Limits of Philosophy*	Chernobyl meltdown

Year	American Documents	European Documents	Political, Social, and Cultural Events
	Margaret Atwood, *The Handmaid's Tale*		
1986	Marc Reisner, *Cadillac Desert*		
1987	Allan Bloom, *The Closing of the American Mind*		
	Catharine MacKinnon, *Feminism Unmodified*		
	Tony Morrison, *Beloved*		
	Gloria Anzaldúa, *Borderlands/La Frontera*		
1988	Joan Scott, *Gender and the Politics of History*	Salman Rushdie, *Satanic Verses*	
1989	Richard Rorty, *Irony, Contingency and Solidarity*	David Harvey, *The Condition of Postmodernity*	Berlin wall falls
1990	Judith Butler, *Gender Trouble*		
	Mike Davis, *City of Quartz*		
1991	Arthur M. Schlesinger, Jr., *The Disuniting of America*		Soviet Union dissolved
1992	Cormac McCarthy, *All the Pretty Horses*		European Union founded